NEW COMPLETE DO-IT-YOURSELF MANUAL

Reader's Digest

NEW COMPLETE DO-IT-YOURSELF MANUAL

The Reader's Digest Association, Inc., Pleasantville, New York • Montreal

The acknowledgments and credits that appear on the facing page
and on page 528 are hereby made a part of this copyright page.

Library of Congress Cataloging in Publication Data
New complete do-it-yourself manual   /   Reader's Digest.

       p.   cm.
     Rev. ed. of: Reader's digest complete do-it-yourself manual. 1973.
     Includes index.
     ISBN 0-89577-378-3
     1. Dwellings — Maintenance and repair — Amateurs' manuals.
I. Reader's Digest Association.   II. Reader's digest complete
do-it-yourself manual.
TH4817.3.N48 1991
643'.7 — dc20   90-46830

Warning
All do-it-yourself activities involve a degree of risk. Skills, materials,
tools, and site conditions vary widely. Although the editors have made
every effort to ensure accuracy, the reader remains responsible for the
selection and use of tools, materials, and methods. Always obey local
codes and laws, follow manufacturers' operating instructions, and
observe safety precautions.

New Complete Do-it-yourself Manual

Staff

Senior Staff Editor
Sally French

Senior Art Editor
Kenneth Chaya

Senior Editors
Joseph Gonzalez
Robert V. Huber

Senior Associate Editors
Don Earnest
Melanie Hulse

Associate Editors
Theresa Lane
Gerald Williams

Art Associates
Morris Karol
Carol Nehring
Angel Weyant

Research Editor
Mary Jane Hodges

Contributors

Editors/Writers
Gerry Schremp
Nancy Shuker

Designer
Virginia Wells Blaker

Production Coordinator
Jessica Mitchell

Copy Editor
Katherine G. Ness

Indexer
Sydney Wolfe Cohen

Writers
Stephen Andrews
Beverly Bremer
Mark Bremer
Therese Hoehlein Cerbie
Laura Dearborn
Merle Henkenius
Jay Stein
Laura Tringali
John Warde

Researcher
Nathalie Laguerre

Artists
Ron Bertuzzi
Sylvia Bokor
Gordon Chapman
Chris Duerk
Mario Ferro
John Gist
Karin Kretschmann
Victor Lazzaro
Lieu & Silks
Ed Lipinski
Mari Maléter

Max Menikoff
Ken Rice
Gerhard Richter
Ray Skibinski
Allyson Smith
Robert Steimle
Victoria Vebell
Robert Villani

Photographers
Gene and Katie Hamilton
Morris Karol

Consultants

Henri de Marne, Chief
David Alford
Michael Byrne
Daniel J. Decker
Phil Englander
Allan E. Fitchett
George Frechter

Clark Garner
Eugene Goeb
Walter A. Grub, Jr.
Higgins & Higgins, Inc.
Carolyn Klass
Joseph Laquatra, Ph.D.

Scott Lewis
James Lotto
Jim McCann
Americo Napolitano
Norman Oehlke
Gerald Persico
Henry Printz

John Schmidt
Emil Shikh
Stanley H. Smith, Ph.D.
Leonard Urso
John Vogestad
Linda Wagenet

Reader's Digest General Books

Editor in Chief
John A. Pope, Jr.

Managing Editor
Jane Polley

Executive Editor
Susan J. Wernert

Art Director
David Trooper

Group Editors
Will Bradbury
Norman B. Mack
Kaari Ward

Group Art Editors
Evelyn Bauer
Robert M. Grant
Joel Musler

Chief of Research
Monica Borrowman

Copy Chief
Edward W. Atkinson

Picture Editor
Richard Pasqual

Rights and Permissions
Pat Colomban

Head Librarian
Jo Manning

Acknowledgments

The editors are grateful to the following individuals and organizations for the assistance they provided:

Salvatore Alfano
American Lighting Association
American Olean Tile Company
American Plywood Association
American Standard Inc.
Asphalt Institute
Association of Home Appliance Manufacturers
Barry Supply Company
Rudolf Bass, Inc.
The Belden Brick Company
Bemis Manufacturing Company
Bentley Brothers
Berner Air Products, Inc.

Betco Block & Products, Inc.
James Billado
Bionaire Corporation
Black & Decker, Inc.
Robert Bosch Power Tool Corporation
Brick Institute of America
The Budd Company
The Carpet and Rug Institute
Columbia Home Decor, Inc.
Albert Constantine & Son Inc.
CreteCore Corp.
Crown Corporation, NA
Defender Industries
Delta Faucet
Delta International Machinery Corp.
Design Directions Inc.
Dow Chemical Company

Cy Drake Locksmiths, Inc.
Elgar Products, Inc.
Emco Specialties, Inc.
Emerson Quiet Cool
The Family Handyman
Federal Emergency Management Agency
Fire Glow Distributors, Inc.
Fluidmaster, Inc.
Formica Corporation
Friedrich Air Conditioning Co.
Garrett Wade
Goldblatt Tool Co.
Hadley Products Division
Hardwood Plywood Manufacturers Association
Hasko Utilities Co., Inc.
A. C. Hathorne, Inc., Roofers
Honeywell Inc.

The Hydronics Institute, Inc.
Ideal Industries, Inc.
Lennox International Inc.
Lomanco Inc.
Makita U.S.A., Inc.
Mannington Mills, Inc.
Milwaukee Electric Tool Corp.
National Concrete Masonry Association
National Electrical Manufacturers Association
National Fire Protection Association
National Kitchen and Bath Association
National Wood Window & Door Association
Nordic Woodstove & Fireplace Shop

Orco Block Co., Inc.
Padco Inc.
Peoples Westchester Savings Bank
Pittsburgh Corning Corporation
Porter-Cable
Portland Cement Association
P.V.C. Supply Co., Inc.
Quaker City Manufacturing Company
Radio Shack
Resources Conservation Inc.
Reynolds Metals Company
Rosetta Electric Co., Inc.
Ryobi America Corporation
Sancar Wallcoverings Inc.
George Sbriglia
Schlage Lock Company
F. Schumacher & Co.

Shopsmith, Inc.
Skil Corporation
Small Homes Council— Building Research Council
The Stanley Works
Noris J. Stone & Sons, Inc.
Harold Switzgable, Jr.
Thermal Form, Inc.
3M Do-It-Yourself Division
Trenwyth Industries, Inc.
USG Interiors, Inc.
Vermont Castings Inc.
Wagner Spray Tech Corp.
Wallcovering Information Bureau
Western Wood Products Association
Wetzler Clamp Co., Inc.

Contents

Contents

Emergency repairs
in your home

  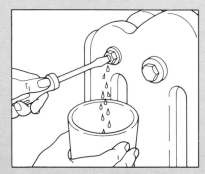

When a natural disaster or a household emergency occurs, you need to know quickly how to keep matters from getting worse. This section is a kind of fast-action guide, placed at the front of the manual to make it easy to find in a hurry. The following pages tell you how to handle yourself and protect your family during a natural disaster or fire and how to make superficial repairs or clean up in the aftermath of such disasters. The section also outlines steps to take when faced with a household emergency, such as a power failure or a clogged drain. In some cases, only temporary measures are given here; for more permanent repairs, look in the sections pertaining to the subject in question—such as the sections on plumbing (p.197) and electricity (p.235).

Emergency repairs / Natural disasters

Protecting your home

TORNADO

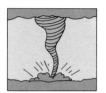

Before tornado season find a low, windowless, structurally strong place where you can take shelter—in the basement, under stairs, or in an inside hall or closet on the lowest floor.

After a tornado, enter a building only when you are sure that it is sound. Check the foundation for shifting or cracking. Look for walls and ceilings that appear to be ready to collapse.

If you smell gas, shut off the main gas valve immediately. Turn off the water if there is a leak.

Shut off the electricity. Check for short circuits.

HURRICANE

Take in lawn furniture and any other loose items. Tie down objects too large to move. Take in awnings.

Shutter windows or cover them with plywood or boards nailed into studs. At the very least, tape them (see *Broken window,* facing page).

Store candles or oil lamps and flashlights in case of power failure.

Cut dead branches from trees on your property and any branches that are dangerously close to the house.

Lock all doors and windows to reduce vibration. Close draperies and blinds to contain flying glass. Put folded towels along inside sills to keep rain from blowing in.

FLOOD

If time permits, move valued belongings to the highest spot in the house—or to a neighbor's house, if it is on higher land.

Raise heavy appliances and furniture by putting concrete blocks, bricks, or layers of boards under the corners.

Open basement windows to allow water in and avoid a cave-in due to unequal pressure between the inside and the outside.

Listen to a portable radio; if you are told to evacuate, turn off the gas, electricity, and water, lock the house, and leave immediately.

When you return, clean up, following directions on facing page.

WINTER STORM

Cover the water pipes with insulating jackets. Or, if none are readily available, tie thick layers of newspaper around the pipes and let water trickle from faucets.

Clean out gutters and downspouts to prevent ice blockage and aid runoff.

Make sure windows and storm windows are shut tightly and locked.

Plug window drafts with rope caulk, wide tape, or folded newspaper.

Be prepared for a power failure and loss of heat (see p.12).

Store enough food and water to last several days or a week. Buy extra fuel for fireplace or stove. Keep flashlights, candles, and a battery-powered radio at hand.

EARTHQUAKE

If you live in an earthquake zone, add extra bracing and foundation bolts to an older house and have the chimney and hot-water tank strapped in place.

During an earthquake the safest place is under a strong doorway, against an inside wall, or under heavy furniture, such as a desk or bed.

After an earthquake be wary of flooding and tidal waves. If you're in a low-lying area near a large body of water, head for high ground quickly.

Enter a damaged building carefully, as described for *Tornado,* above, and shut off the utilities.

Shutting off electrical power

CAUTION: If the floor is damp or the wiring has gotten wet, it is dangerous to touch the main switch box. Have the electricity turned off by your power company.

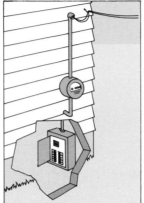

Main electrical shutoff is fuse or circuit breaker box. The four box types are shown at right.

On a fuse box lower or pull lever to the *Off* position to shut off all electrical power.

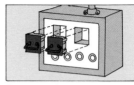

On a cartridge-type box pull out plastic boxes holding cartridge fuses to shut off power.

If a circuit breaker box has one or two main switches, flip them to shut off power.

On other circuit breaker boxes flip all switches to *Off* to shut off power completely.

Shutting off the gas

CAUTION: If you smell gas, open the windows and shut off the main valve. Do not light a flame or turn any electrical switch on or off. Do not use your phone. Leave at once and report the leak from a neighbor's phone. If your home uses LP gas, stay out of the basement; LP gas is heavier than air and sinks to a lower level.

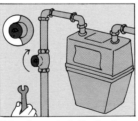

Natural-gas shutoff valve is on meter intake pipe. Turn it to a horizontal position with wrench.

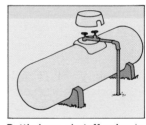

Bottled-gas shutoff valve is generally a knob or lever on top of tank. Turn it clockwise.

Shutting off the water

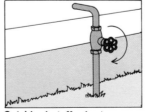

Outside shutoff valve in warm-climate home is often at point where water pipe enters house.

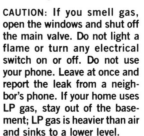

Basement shutoff valve is common in colder areas. It may be on a pipe or set into wall.

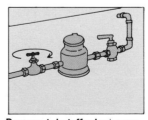

Fixture shutoff valve is under or next to fixture. It lets you turn off broken or overflowing fixture.

Leaky roof

If your house has an open, unfinished attic, you can often temporarily patch a leak from inside as shown in the first two pictures at right. After a storm, a roof area with damaged or missing shingles can be protected by covering it as shown in the two pictures at far right. Let the roof dry before making permanent repairs (p.384).

Broken window

If you can't shutter or board over windows during a storm, tape any large panes to reinforce them a bit and to prevent shattering. Use cloth-backed tape and make an X on the inside of the glass. If a window does break, wear heavy gloves to avoid cuts, and use a sturdy container to dispose of the pieces. To replace glass, see p.421.

Flood damage

Enter a house only if you're sure that it is structurally sound and the gas and electricity are off. Shovel and hose out mud and silt before they dry, scrub and disinfect the floors and woodwork, and follow the directions at right. Before replacing wallcoverings and insulation, let the house dry thoroughly. This often takes months.

Frozen and burst pipes

The fastest way to thaw a metal pipe is with a propane torch, but take care not to let the pipe get so hot you can't touch it with a bare hand. Never use a torch on plastic pipe, near a gas line or flammable material, or without a flameproof back sheet; use a hair dryer or heat lamp instead. Temporary fixes for leaking pipes are at far right.

From inside attic fill small (dry) hole with roof cement or a caulking compound; coat surrounding area.

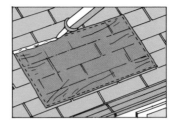

Cut a board to fit snugly between rafters. Position it over patch and drive nails at an angle into rafters.

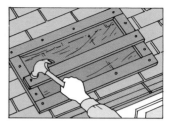

Cover a large damaged roof area with plastic sheeting. Double edges; staple to roof. Caulk around edges.

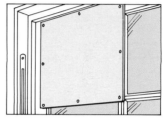

If high winds may return, tack wood strips along edges of plastic and at intervals in between.

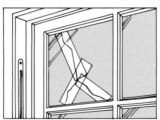

If a window cracks, put duct tape over crack to prevent it from spreading and producing a larger break.

With a broken window, first remove all loose pieces. Wear heavy gloves and work from top down.

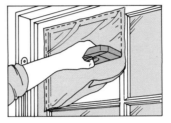

Staple or tape plastic over window, doubling edges. Use polyethylene sheeting or a heavy-duty trash bag.

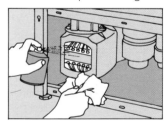

If it's windy, back up plastic. Tack a sheet of cardboard or a couple of boards over stapled sheeting.

After flood, open windows to speed drying. If stuck, remove inside stop and push in sash from outside.

Rid basement of water with a gasoline-driven pump. To prevent cave-ins, lower water by only 2 ft. a day.

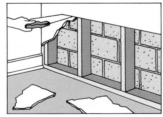

If wall is waterlogged, remove covering and insulation to well above waterline; trim edges with handsaw.

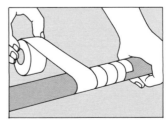

Unplug appliances; dry. Spray with moisture-displacing lubricant. Have repairman check before using.

Heat frozen pipe with constantly moving propane torch. Work from an open faucet toward frozen area.

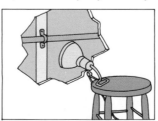

Thaw walled-in pipe slowly with heat lamp clamped to chair or ladder and set a few inches from wall.

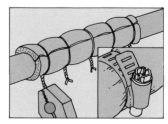

Fix a small leak by tightly wrapping plastic or duct tape around it. Shut off water and dry pipe first.

For stronger repair, secure slit rubber hose around pipe with worm-drive clamps or tightly twisted wire.

If the lights suddenly go out and appliances stop running, you may have a blown fuse or a tripped circuit breaker. If neighboring houses are also blacked out, the problem probably lies with your electric power company.

Partial blackout. A power failure in one or two rooms is often caused by an overloaded circuit (p.241). Turn off a few of the lights and appliances on that circuit; replace the fuse or reset the circuit breaker. If the fuse blows or the circuit breaker trips again, there is a short circuit. Examine all electrical cords for loose connections, frayed sections, or defective plugs. If you find nothing, turn off and disconnect all appliances and lights and replace the fuse or reset the breaker again. If the fuse blows or the circuit trips, there is a short in the house wiring; call an electrician. If the house wiring is OK, plug in one appliance at a time until you find the one causing the short. Repair or replace it.

Full blackout. In case of a full power failure, turn off all lights and appliances in the house to avoid overloading the circuits when power is restored, but leave one light or radio on to alert you when service resumes. Open the refrigerator and freezer as little as possible during the blackout; food should stay frozen for up to 48 hours in a closed, fully loaded freezer locker. After power is restored, wait about 10 minutes and then turn on one switch at a time.

If a blackout occurs in freezing weather, close off all but the most essential and best-insulated rooms and build a slow-burning fire in a fireplace or stove. If you have municipal water, open all the faucets and let the water run slowly to keep the pipes from freezing. If the power may be off for 36 hours or more, bottle a supply of drinking water and drain the main water system of the house. Generally, if you want the system drained (before going on a long winter trip, for instance), you should have a plumber do it for you; with his special equipment, he can blow water from the pipes far more efficiently than you can. But in an emergency you can do the job yourself, as shown at right.

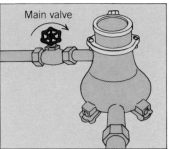
Main valve

Water inlet valve

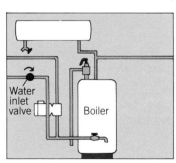
Water inlet valve · Boiler

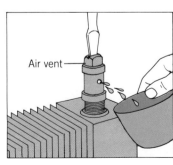
Air vent

Draining the system.
If power may be out at least 36 hours in freezing weather, have the house water system drained. If no plumber is available, you can do it yourself (but not as well as a plumber) by following these steps:
1. Turn off the main water supply valve.

2. Stop the water supply to the water heater by closing valve on pipe leading into heater. If you have a gas heater, turn off the gas cock. If you have an electric water heater, switch off its circuit breaker or remove the fuse that controls heater's circuit.

3. If your heating system utilizes a boiler, shut off the water inlet valve to the boiler (the valve should be near the boiler on pipe leading into it). Then flush all the toilets in the house and open all faucets.

4. If house is heated by a hot-water system, open the valves on all radiators (if they have individual valves). Then open the air vents on one or more radiators (baseboard or other type) on highest floor of house. Hold cup under vent and catch water as it spurts out.

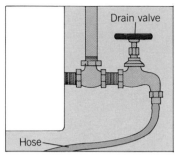
Drain valve · Hose

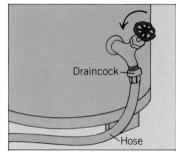
Draincock · Hose

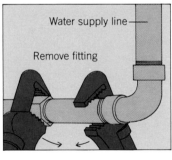
Water supply line · Remove fitting

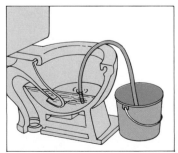

5. Let the water in the boiler cool (check the temperature indicator on the unit). Attach a hose to the drain valve near the base of the boiler and lead it outdoors or to a drain lower than the boiler. Open the outlet and let the water flow out.

6. Attach a hose to the draincock of the water heater and direct the hose into a drain, to a place lower than the heater's draincock, or outdoors and away from the house. Open the drain valve and let the water run out.
CAUTION: The water will be very hot.

7. Open draincock on main water supply line. If no such spigot exists, disconnect a fitting at lowest point in system to allow rest of water to run out. If your water comes from a well, switch pump circuit off; drain above-ground pump lines and the storage tank.

8. Empty toilet bowls and tanks by siphoning or bailing and sponging. Pour a mixture of half antifreeze and half water into toilet bowls and into every sink, basin, tub, and shower. Pour 1 qt. antifreeze into all washers. (When power returns, put washers through cycle.)

Drains and toilets

Among the most inconvenient emergencies is a plumbing failure, such as a clogged sink or toilet. Usually these problems can be fixed with a plunger. If a drain is badly clogged, you may have to clean out the drainpipe.

Chemical drain cleaner. You may be able to clear a partially clogged sink with a liquid drain cleaner. If you try this, exercise extreme caution; drain cleaners contain chemicals that can burn your skin. Follow the directions on the container to the letter. If you splash cleaner on your skin, flood it immediately with cold water. If the drain is still clogged after adding drain cleaner and some of the liquid remains in the sink, do not try to clear the drain by other means; the leftover cleaner may splatter you. Call a plumber.

Actually, the best use of a drain cleaner is for maintenance. Use it once a month or so to prevent clogging. Or, safer still (especially if you have a septic system), treat your drains monthly with 2 teaspoons of baking soda washed down with a tea-kettle full of boiling water.

Items lost down the drain. A valuable ring or other item dropped down a sink drain is not necessarily lost; it may lodge in the U-shaped trap beneath the sink. You can retrieve it by opening the plug on the trap or by removing the entire trap, emptying it into a bucket, and fishing out the item. Do this as you would in cleaning a clogged drain. (For help with other plumbing problems, see p. 197.)

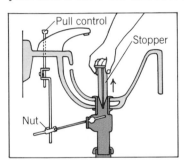

Remove sink stopper or strainer before trying to unclog drain. In most washbasins, simply pull stopper up and out. On some, you must first reach under sink and remove a nut that connects pull control to stopper mechanism.

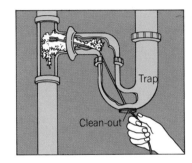

If plunger doesn't work after several tries, place a bucket beneath the U-shaped trap under sink. Use wrench to unscrew clean-out plug on trap. Let water run out, then clear blockage by hand or with stiff wire, such as a straightened coat hanger. Replace clean-out plug.

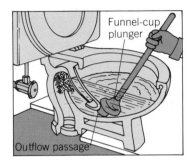

To unclog toilet, add or bail out water until bowl is half full. Use a funnel-cup plunger that fits snugly into toilet's outflow passage. Pump plunger vigorously down and up 10 times, then remove it abruptly. Pour water into toilet bowl. If water level rises, repeat process.

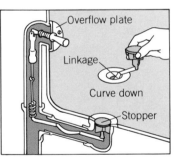

Remove stopper on most bathtubs by unscrewing screws on overflow plate and pulling out assembly. Ease stopper out. (After unclogging drain, hold stopper with curved part of linkage facing down, and work stopper gently back and forth to fit it into place.)

Remove entire trap and clean it if trap has no clean-out plug. Trap is held by two coupling nuts. Open top nut with a pipe wrench (tape its jaws to protect chrome nuts). Then support trap and remove lower nut. When replacing nuts, do not overtighten them, or joint may leak.

If plunger doesn't work after several attempts, try a toilet auger. Insert its curved end into outflow passage and crank handle until tip of auger bites into clog. Slowly pull out clog or break it up by moving auger handle back and forth. If this doesn't work, call a plumber.

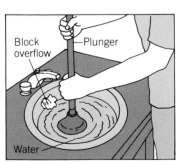

Position plunger over drain and cover its cup with water. Block overflow drain, if any, with a wet cloth to create a vacuum. Tilt cup to get rid of trapped air. Pump plunger vigorously down and up 10 times, then remove it abruptly; let water drain out. Repeat as often as necessary.

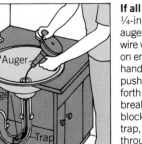

If all else fails, use a ¼-in. flexible-bulb auger, or snake—a thin wire with coiled spring on end. Crank auger handle clockwise while pushing wire back and forth in drain until it breaks up blockage. If blockage is beyond the trap, work the auger through clean-out hole.

If toilet won't flush fully, stopper ball may be falling too quickly. Open tank; loosen thumb-screw on guide arm; raise arm ½ in.; refasten. Or shorten lift wire by unhooking it from lift arm, bending it slightly, and rehooking it. Or hook lift wire into another hole on lift arm.

Keeping your family warm on an icy winter day or night is a high priority—it affects both comfort and health, especially in those who are elderly. If the heat goes out in the dead of winter, do all you can to keep the warm air inside and the cold air out. But before going to extreme lengths, make a few simple checks. Sometimes the heat goes off merely because a switch has been accidentally flipped off, the thermostat needs adjustment, or a circuit breaker has tripped or a fuse has blown.

First check the thermostat temperature and time settings. Push the temperature setting 8 to 10 degrees above room temperature; the heat should come on within 5 minutes. Check the circuit breaker and fuse box. If a breaker has tripped, reset it. If a fuse has blown, replace it with one of the same amperage. If the breaker trips or the fuse burns out again, the system may have a short circuit; call a repairman. Follow the other checks described below. If the heat doesn't come on, call a repairman.

While waiting for repairs, make sure that all doors, windows, and storm windows are closed tightly. Seal cracks around doors and windows with rope caulk or newspaper. Close draperies or shutters. Go to a neighbor's if you can. Otherwise, gather everyone into one or two rooms and close off the rest of the house. If you have a fireplace, stove, or portable kerosene heater, use it, but leave a window open a crack for ventilation. If the heat will be off a long time, have the water system drained (p.12).

 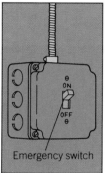

If there is no heat: 1. Adjust thermostat. Make sure emergency switch on heating system or by cellar door is on. Check fuse or circuit breaker box; reset tripped breaker or replace blown fuse.

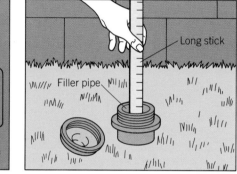

2. If heating system burns oil, check oil level. If tank has no gauge, dip a long clean stick into filler pipe, if possible; remove stick, and look for oil mark on it to check level of oil.

3. Press safety relay button on oil burner once. If burner doesn't respond, press burner motor reset button once. If this fails, call repairman and tell him what buttons have been pushed.

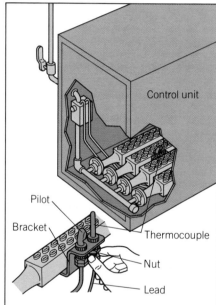

If pilot light on gas burner goes out, turn off gas and wait for combustion chamber to air out. Clean pilot (see facing page) and relight, following directions on burner. If problem persists, change thermocouple (device that cuts off gas flow if pilot light blows out). With unit shut off and cooled down, unscrew thermocouple lead from control unit and unscrew nut holding thermocouple to pilot-light bracket. Remove thermocouple and lead and install new ones.

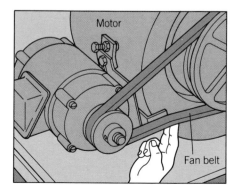

4. If you have a warm-air system, turn off power and check fan belt. Reseat belt if it has slipped off shaft; replace it, if broken. If motor runs noisily, bearings may be worn; call a repairman.

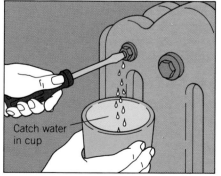

5. Hot-water system may contain too much air. With pump running, open vent on each radiator or convector (some systems have single purge valve on boiler). When water spurts, close vent.

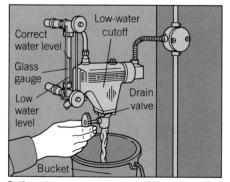

6. If you have steam heat, let boiler cool, then check water level. If it is not halfway up glass gauge, add water. If level is OK, drain low-water cutoff in case sediment is blocking it, then refill.

No air conditioning   No hot water

On most central air-conditioning systems, you must turn the power on 24 hours before using it. To start any air conditioner, set the thermostat to 8 to 10 degrees cooler than room temperature and turn the switch to *Cool*. If the unit fails to come on, turn the thermostat all the way down and try again.

If the unit switches on but does not cool sufficiently, the filter may be dirty. Clean it or replace it. On most room air conditioners, the front grille can be snapped off to gain access to the filter.

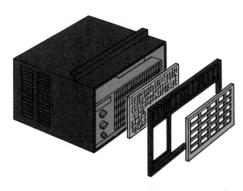

If your air conditioning will not go on, the circuit breaker may have tripped or the fuse may have blown. If so, turn off the unit and reset the breaker or replace the fuse with one of the same amperage rating (p.237). Turn the unit back on. If the circuit trips or the fuse blows again, the area may be experiencing a power brownout; if so, keep the unit off until full power is restored. If there is no brownout, the circuit may be overloaded. Unplug everything on the circuit except the air conditioner and try again. If the problem persists, the circuit may be shorted or the unit may need repair; call for service.

To keep cool until your air conditioner is repaired, securely fix a large box fan into a window, facing so that it blows air to the outside. Seal any openings between window frame and fan with plywood or heavy cardboard. Close all other windows and doors in the room except one at the opposite (preferably shady) side of the room. Turn on the fan; it will pull air in through the open window or door.

Checking a water heater

On electric heater, if top thermostat shuts off power, push reset button once. If cutoff recurs, upper or lower thermostat or heating element is defective. Have it replaced.

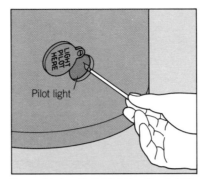

On gas heater, if pilot light is off, relight it following detailed instructions printed on metal plate on heater. If you are unsure of how to proceed, call the gas company.

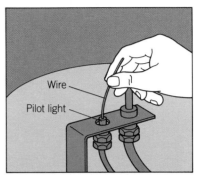

If pilot light still goes out, clean openings with a thin copper wire, and brush out air inlets at base of heater. If problem persists, replace thermocouple (see facing page).

Cold water from a hot-water faucet may simply mean that the power or gas is off. Check for a tripped circuit breaker or burned-out fuse (p.237), a pilot light that's out, or a valve that's not on at the gas meter or the heater. Also make sure that the heater is level; a tipped water heater won't function properly. If the heater still fails to do its job, try the remedies shown above.

If the hot water is discolored, turn off the power or gas supply, then drain the tank (p.12) and refill it. If an electric heater leaks, turn off the power and tighten the mounting bolts for both the upper and lower heating elements. Replace any worn gaskets. Check all pipe connections and the draincock for leaks; tighten the connections if needed, but do not overtighten them. If water is coming from the pressure-relief valve, the valve is probably defective. Have it replaced. Never let even a "little" leak go; have it fixed immediately.

Whether your water heater is electric or gas, if it still leaks after all connections have been tightened, replace it immediately or it may cause a major flood in your house. To help detect leaks, you can put a small battery-operated water alarm next to the heater. This gadget will sound a loud electronic alarm if its sensor gets wet.

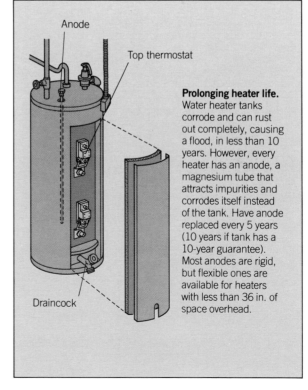

Prolonging heater life. Water heater tanks corrode and can rust out completely, causing a flood, in less than 10 years. However, every heater has an anode, a magnesium tube that attracts impurities and corrodes itself instead of the tank. Have anode replaced every 5 years (10 years if tank has a 10-year guarantee). Most anodes are rigid, but flexible ones are available for heaters with less than 36 in. of space overhead.

Emergency repairs/Fires

Take every precaution to prevent a fire in your home (don't forget to check the batteries in your smoke alarms regularly), but be prepared for a fire in the event that you are faced with one. Make a family fire plan so that everyone will know what to do. If a fire breaks out, stay between the fire and the exit and leave quickly, closing doors as you go to keep the fire from spreading. If you have to open a door, feel it first; if it is hot, find another way out. If the room is smoky, keep low (smoke rises).

Putting out a fire. If the fire is small, put it out with an all-purpose fire extinguisher (rated ABC), aiming at the base of the fire and spraying with sweeping motions. If you have no extinguisher, use water to put out burning wood, paper, cloth, or plas-tics. Put out a grease fire by smothering it or by dous-ing it with baking soda or salt (but not sugar or flour). If you are faced with an electrical fire, cut off the power and use an extinguisher with a C in its rating.

After a fire. Take steps quickly to prevent fur-ther damage, which your insurance company won't pay for. This means boarding up damaged doors and windows, arranging for emergency services to repair a damaged roof, removing debris, and tak-ing salvaged items to a safe place until the insur-ance inspector can see them. In cold weather have the main water system drained (p.12), or at least heat the house with a portable stove and put anti-freeze into all drains and toilets. Have the electrical system and all electronic equipment certified safe before using it. Because cleaning up fire damage differs from regular cleaning, you would do best to hire a fire restoration contractor. (To locate one, check the Yellow Pages.)

Send garments and draperies to a dry cleaner with an ozone chamber; improper cleaning can set odors permanently in fabrics. Wipe leather goods with a damp cloth, then a dry one. Stuff purses and shoes with newspaper so that they will retain their shape. Dry leather goods away from the sun or heat, then clean them with saddle soap.

Put art, books, papers, and other porous materi-als into a freezer until a specialist can be retained. Use a vacuum freezer, if possible; a local frozen food company might help you.

Cleaning up after a fire

1. Drill small holes in a slightly sagging ceiling to let out trapped water. Catch water in buckets. Wear a face mask for protection against dirty water and debris. Make and fully drain one small hole at a time. **CAUTION:** Don't use an electric drill. If the sag in the ceiling is severe, stay out of the room and call a professional.

2. Remove soot from walls, ceilings, and floors with warm water; to each gallon add 1 cup chlorine bleach and 5 tablespoons trisodium phosphate or other heavy-duty cleaner (available in paint or hardware stores). Rinse with clear warm water. **CAUTION:** Wear gloves and safety glasses, and keep cleaning agents away from children.

3. Move rugs outdoors to dry. Take up any water-soaked carpeting and the padding underneath. If carpet and padding are salvageable, move them outdoors and spread them out as much as possible to dry. If the electrical system has been checked, use fans or blowers to dry floors. Otherwise, ventilate as well as possible.

4. If water got under resilient floor covering or tiles, it may warp the wood underneath and cause odors. Take up the tiles or remove all the floor covering, carefully rolling it up so that it can be reused. If material is brittle, use a heat lamp to soften it so that you can roll it up with-out cracking it.

5. To fix small blisters in linoleum or soft vinyl flooring, puncture them with a nail, and pump epoxy through nail hole, using a glue gun (p.90) with a syringe, or hypodermic, nozzle. Or shoot diluted linoleum paste through hole with a glue syringe. Weight down floor covering with bricks or boards until adhesive dries.

6. To scrub mud or dirt from furniture, use brush dipped in a cleaning solution with a pine-oil base. Let dry thoroughly in a well-ventilated shady place. (If dried in sun, wood might warp.) Dry drawers separately to prevent sticking. If mildew forms, remove it with solution of 1 cup chlorine bleach and 1 quart warm water; rinse.

Hand tools and how to use them

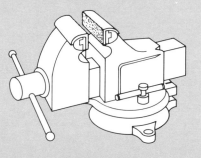
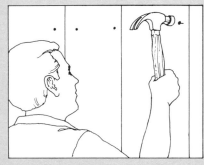
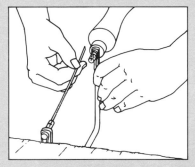

Contents

Even with the advent of power tools, hand tools remain indispensable for most household repairs and woodworking projects. This chapter guides you through the bewildering array of common and specialty hand tools. It provides a clear understanding of how they are used and what to look for when buying them. A tool that is carefully chosen, prepared, and maintained can last a lifetime. For this reason—and for satisfaction in using the tool—look for the best quality at the best price.

Most general-purpose hand tools are covered in this section. However, tools that are used mainly for a particular type of job, such as painting, plumbing, or masonry, are covered in the appropriate chapters. If you cannot find the tool you are looking for here, check the individual chapter or the index.

Hand tools/A homeowner's tool kit

The first group of tools on this page includes those that are generally recognized as essential. The ones in the second group speed or simplify the tasks performed by the basic ones.

Buy tools as you need them, rather than in prepackaged sets, and get the best quality you can afford. Good tools not only inspire good craftsmanship, they are safer and easier to use and maintain.

Supplies and other equipment. In addition to your tools, it is helpful to have these items on hand: candle, machine oil, penetrating lubricant, pencils, fasteners (pp.80–87), tapes (p.90), adhesives (pp.88–90), sandpaper and steel wool (p.50), sharpening stone (pp.44–45), wire brush, paintbrushes, dustpan and brush, lint-free rags or cheesecloth, clip-on light, grounded extension cord, single-edge razor blades with holder, scissors, toolbox, and a stepladder.

Safety and safety gear. A 40-tooth circular saw blade turning at 5,800 rpm can send some 1,300 teeth through your hand before you can react and jerk it away. Avoid accidents by using appropriate safety gear whenever you work. It will protect your body—

Safety goggles   Respirator

and may save your life—but only if you use it. Follow the safety practices described on the next page, and heed the warnings in the literature accompanying your tools.

The essentials

Butt chisel
Putty knife
Adjustable wrench
Slip-joint pliers
Needle-nose pliers
Multipurpose tool
Block plane
Four-in-one rasp
Hacksaw
Crosscut saw
Drain auger
Retractable steel ruler
Nail set
Curved-claw hammer
Push drill and drill point
3 Standard screwdrivers
2 Phillips screwdrivers
Combination square
Level
Utility knife
C-clamp
Toilet plunger

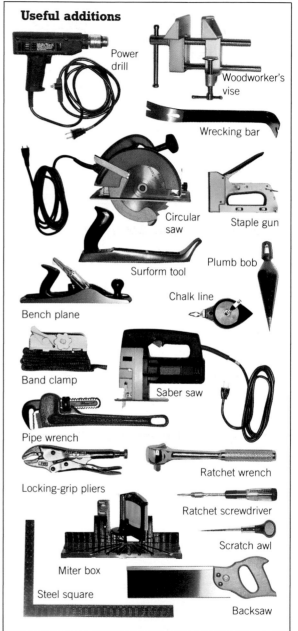

Useful additions

Power drill
Woodworker's vise
Wrecking bar
Circular saw
Staple gun
Plumb bob
Surform tool
Chalk line
Bench plane
Band clamp
Saber saw
Pipe wrench
Ratchet wrench
Locking-grip pliers
Ratchet screwdriver
Scratch awl
Miter box
Steel square
Backsaw

Organizing a workshop

With imagination and planning, almost any spot in a home can become a workshop. Think of the tasks you perform most often and organize the shop around those tasks.

Arrange your tools so that they are out of the way but easy to reach. Pegboard offers handy, easily rearranged storage, but a hanging cabinet with locking doors better protects tools and prevents their unauthorized use.

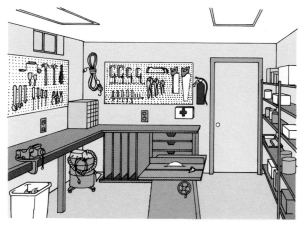

The workbench is the heart of the shop. A free-standing bench is best because it is accessible from all sides and very stable. Allow sufficient room to move easily around the bench and to accommodate large projects bristling with clamps. If space is limited, a sturdy drop-leaf bench or a commercially made folding bench is sufficient for many projects. You can mount a drop-leaf bench on any vertical surface, even on the inside of a closet door. A door-mounted bench is suitable only for light projects; put a board under the door to avoid straining the hinges.

Lighting. For general light, overhead fluorescent tubes are inexpensive and provide steady, even illumination. For task lighting, droplights or shaded clip-on work lights are portable and help dissipate shadows.

Minimize clutter. Because of the danger inherent in all tools, observe the rule "A place for every-thing and everything in its place." Provide storage for every item near its point of use. Develop the habit of putting tools down where they will be out of the way when not immediately in use, and store them safely when no longer needed.

Stationary power tools should be surrounded by enough space so that the work can be maneuvered freely and nearby objects won't obstruct—or fall on—the tool. Each tool should be plugged into an appropriate circuit. Standard outlets can be replaced with outlets that have built-in fuses to protect power tool motors from overload.

Provide dust control for all power tools. Sawdust and hot filings from a power grinder are serious fire hazards. Chemical fumes are also a danger. To reduce these hazards, be sure your shop is properly cleaned and ventilated. A wet-dry vacuum (p.76) can be used to collect dust and cool filings. Open doors and windows; use a fan to move dangerous fumes

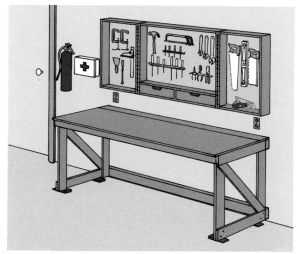

away from you. Store flammable substances in a fire-resistant area where they will stay cool and dry and be out of the reach of children.

▶ **CAUTION:** Extinguish gas pilot lights before using flammable substances indoors; do not smoke. The fumes, as well as the liquid, can ignite.

Hand tools/Constructing a workbench

A workbench is a shop's spine. Full-size benches can be purchased, but they are expensive and may not meet your needs. You can buy corner braces and cut 2 x 4 legs and rails and a plywood top that will allow you to assemble a bench when you need it and disassemble it quickly for storage. Or you can build a permanent bench, tailored to your work, your shop dimensions, and your height and arm span.

The bench shown here is inexpensive to build with construction-grade lumber (p.94). Before cutting, adjust leg measurements so that the bench will be tall enough; the top should be as high as your hip. If you intend to mount a vise (p.33), get it before building the bench. Check the installation instructions; some vises require modifications in the bench top. After assembly, seal the top with several coats of polyurethane varnish.

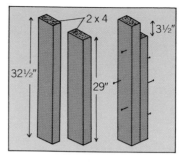

1. Measure and cut legs. Subtract thickness of plywood layers (step 6) from final height to determine length of long leg pieces. Cut other pieces 3½ in. shorter than long pieces. Glue and nail one long and one short piece to form a unit. Install nails in zigzag pattern.

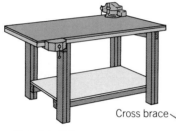

Bench shown was constructed with nails and bolts. Drywall or flathead wood screws (1¼-in., No. 8) can be used instead of nails.

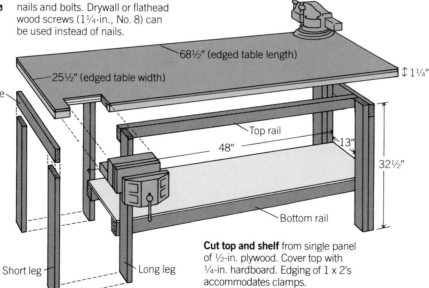

68½" (edged table length)

25½" (edged table width)

1¼"

Cross brace

Top rail

48"

13"

32½"

Bottom rail

Short leg   Long leg

Materials list:
1 4' x 8' sheet ½-in. plywood
1 4' x 8' sheet ¼-in. hardboard
5 8-ft. lengths 2 x 4
3 6-ft. lengths 1 x 2

8 ¼ x 3½-in. carriage bolts, flat washers, lock washers, nuts
16 ⁵⁄₁₆ x 3½-in. lag screws, flat washers

8d common nails
(or 1¼-in. No. 8 wood screws)
4d ringed nails
¼-in. twist bit
³⁄₁₆-in. twist bit
Carpenter's glue
C-clamps

Cut top and shelf from single panel of ½-in. plywood. Cover top with ¼-in. hardboard. Edging of 1 x 2's accommodates clamps.

2. Cut two cross braces 20 in. long. Set them in place across short leg pieces. Drill ¼-in.-diameter holes through braces and legs, two holes per leg. Do not fasten. Label braces and legs for reassembly, and set the braces aside.

Leg   Cross brace

3. Cut two top rails 45 in. long and two bottom rails 48 in. long. Align top rails with long leg pieces; bottom rails 8 in. from floor. Be sure labeled legs match and rails are inside them. Drill two ³⁄₁₆-in. holes through each connection. Fasten with lag screws and flat washers.

Rail   Flat washer

Leg   Lag screw

Rail

4. Assemble base. Put cross braces in place on legs. Fasten with carriage bolts, flat washers, lock washers, and nuts. Cut shelf, 13 x 48 in., from end of plywood panel. Put shelf in place on lower rails, and secure it with 8d nails or 1¼-in. wood screws.

Nut   Carriage bolt

Flat washer

Lock washer

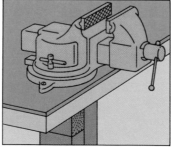

Woodworking vise may need a recess cut in the bench top to accommodate the fixed jaw. If you cover this jaw with hardboard when assembling bench, make liner plates (p.33) that are flush with bench top. Follow installation instructions included with vise.

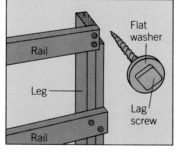

Machinist's vise is bolted through all layers of finished bench top. Position vise directly over a leg, near bench edge. Be sure handle can move freely. Use roundhead bolts, lock washers, and nuts (p.84) so that vise can be removed, if necessary.

Building a sawhorse

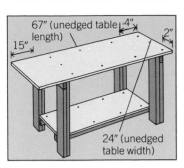

67" (unedged table length)
4"
15"
2"
24" (unedged table width)

5. Cut remaining plywood panel in half lengthwise; then trim panels to length. If mounting a woodworking vise, allow a 15-in. overhang at vise end, 4 in. at other end, and 2 in. at sides. Attach one panel to base with 4d ringed nails or countersunk screws.

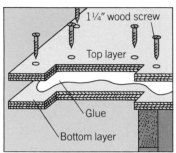

1¼" wood screw
Top layer
Glue
Bottom layer

6. Glue panels together with white or yellow glue. Clamp around perimeter, and weight the center to ensure proper bonding. For extra strength, install countersunk ringed nails or screws around perimeter at 1-ft. intervals. Cut notch for vise.

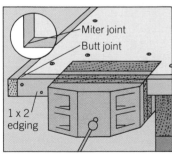

Miter joint
Butt joint
1 x 2 edging

7. Cut 1 x 2's for edging. Tack them around top rim, flush with bench top, with small ringed nails. Butt-join (p.100) or miter (p.108) corners. Fit vise to workbench, following manufacturer's instructions.

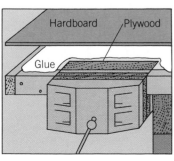

Hardboard
Plywood
Glue

8. Cut hardboard to same size as edged bench top. Apply glue to hardboard and to bench. Align all edges; then apply clamps and weights to maintain position until glue dries. Finish with at least three coats of polyurethane varnish (p.121).

Sawhorses are an essential component of any shop. The horse shown here is strong and sturdy and can be easily disassembled for storage. Metal or plastic sawhorse brackets and 2 x 4's also make a quickly assembled horse, but it may lack stability.

Mark and cut the angles carefully (p.48). The legs are splayed to grip the saddle and lean back between the stop blocks. The bottoms must be cut on two angles so that they will rest flat on the floor. The horse should be 24 to 30 inches tall.

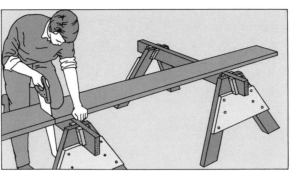

Side view

38"
6¼"
6¼"
75° Saddle 75°
Stop block
Cleat 8"–10"
Leg
75°
75°

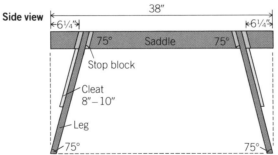

Cleat
Leg

Sawhorse height can be customized to accommodate your height. A longer leg will also have a wider splay at the base. Be sure to mark all angles accurately and cut carefully. If horse doesn't sit flat, trim ends with a rasp (p.43) or block plane (p.40).

1¼"
6¼"
Stop block (1 x 1)
75°
75°
38"

1. The saddle. Cut a length of 2 x 4 lumber 38 in. long. Make eight stop blocks 5½ in. long from 1 x 1 lumber. Set blocks on saddle at a 75° angle, with top of outside blocks 6¼ in. from each end and 1¼ in. from other block. Secure stop blocks with glue and 6d nails.

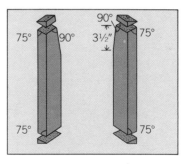

75°
3½"
90°
C
B
A
75°
75°
90°
75°

2. The legs. Using 2 x 4 stock, cut four legs to proper length. Saw angled lines in alphabetical order as shown. These cuts determine the splay of the legs seen when sawhorse is viewed from the end.

90°
75°
90°
3½"
75°
75°
75°

3. Turn legs to their narrow edge. Mark tops and bottoms as shown so that legs will be level with saddle and rest flat on floor. Two leg pieces rise to the right; and two to the left. Saw carefully. Use a rasp to smooth irregularities.

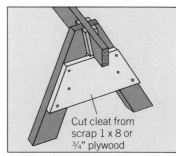

Cut cleat from scrap 1 x 8 or ¾" plywood

4. Assemble legs in pairs. Cut cleats. Use saddle thickness and depth to determine position of cleat; fasten to leg pairs with glue and nails. Assemble horse by sliding legs into channels formed by saddle's stop blocks.

Hammers come in a variety of head weights and shapes for different driving tasks; choose the style that best suits the job. The head weight (usually stated in ounces) determines the hammer weight, which may range from 7 ounces to several pounds. A bell-faced 16-ounce curved-claw hammer is a good all-purpose tool for nailing and nail-pulling.

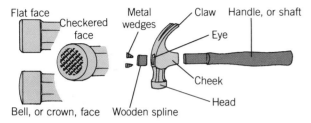

Flat face
Checkered face
Metal wedges
Claw
Handle, or shaft
Eye
Cheek
Head
Bell, or crown, face
Wooden spline

Look for a cleanly finished head of drop-forged steel; cast iron is brittle and may shatter or chip. The striking surface may be flat or slightly crowned or have a raised checkered pattern. Flat faces drive nailheads just to the wood's surface (head protrudes slightly above surface); bells drive them flush (top of nailhead aligns with wood's surface), in a dimple formed by the bell; and checkereds compensate for the slightly off-center blows that occur if you're doing a lot of rapid nailing.

The handle should be long enough to drive nails with the momentum of the swing—rather than pounding with your arm—but not so long that you can't control the arc. Handles are made from hardwood (usually hickory), fiberglass, or steel; these materials have slightly different shock-absorbing abilities. Try different weights, handle lengths, and composition until you find the tool that balances well and feels right for your hand and swing.

Hollow tubular handles may not withstand the leverage force in nail-pulling, which can reach several thousand pounds per square inch. Use these hammers only for light work.

If the head on a wooden handle becomes loose, try driving additional wedges through the eye of the head. If it's still loose or if the handle shrinks, cracks, or breaks, follow the instructions at right.

Driving and prying tools

Curved-claw. The hammer for pulling and driving nails

Straight-claw (or ripping). For dismantling or demolition

Short-handled sledge. For heavy-duty work

Mallet. With wooden or rubber head is used to drive wood chisels

Tack hammer. For upholstery nails, tacks, and brads

Pry bar. Gives leverage for removing nails or dismantling

Ball peen. For metalworking

Bricklayer's. Cuts and aligns bricks; chips mortar

Staple gun. Attachments increase its usefulness

Replacing a hammer handle

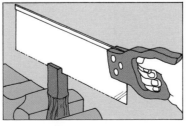
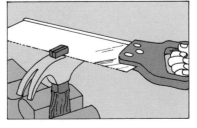
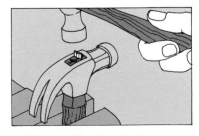

1. Clamp handle in a vise. Test-fit the hammer head; trim handle to fit snugly. If there isn't a slot for a spline, cut one.

2. Insert the handle through the eye and push head down until it seats tightly. Trim the top flush with the head.

3. Drive a spline into slot; drive wedges across the spline. This splays the wood in all directions, anchoring the head.

To drive a nail, hold it upright and tap it gently with the hammer, then take your hand away. Holding the hammer near the end of the handle, simply lift it, swinging your forearm from the elbow and let the weight of the head drop the hammer. For rough work, drive nails flush with surface; for finish work set nails below the surface with a nail set.

Keep the striking face clean and clear of oil or grease. If the hammer has a wooden handle, protect it from extremes of dampness and drying. Too much dampness will cause the wood to swell and eventually to crack; too much dryness will cause shrinking and a loose head. Either situation may result in having to replace the handle.

Staple gun
These handy tools make quick work of tacking jobs (such as fastening screening or fabric). Look for a gun that loads and operates easily. Some have two handle-pressure settings to accommodate staples of different sizes and to reduce recoil and jamming. Adapters can be added, enabling a stapler to drive other fasteners. If you need to do a lot of tacking, you may want to rent an electric stapler.

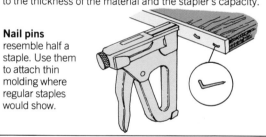

Rivet

Expanding fasteners

An attachment allows staple guns to drive small rivets and expanding fasteners. Match the size of the fastener to the thickness of the material and the stapler's capacity.

Grasp the handle lightly but firmly near the end. Allow the handle to form an extension of your arm and the swing's momentum to accomplish the work. The impact power may reach 300 pounds per square inch.

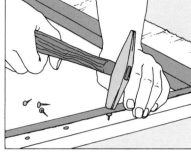

Tack hammers are designed specifically for tacking. The double-headed hammer has a slotted, magnetized head that holds tacks point-out to start them in wood and a plain head to drive them flush.

Nail pins
resemble half a staple. Use them to attach thin molding where regular staples would show.

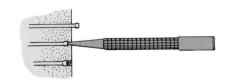

Clinching nails. Drive nails slightly longer than wood's thickness through wood. Hold a short-handled sledge against the nailhead. Clinch the points on the underside of the wood by bending them over with a claw hammer.

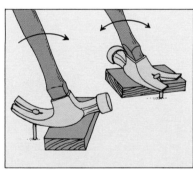

When pulling nails, use a wood block for better leverage and to protect the wood's surface. Pull handle toward the driving head when using a curved-claw. With a ripping hammer, a side-to-side rocking motion is more efficient.

Nail set
For a smooth surface when woodworking, use finishing nails and a nail set to conceal nailheads. Nail sets come in $\frac{1}{32}$-in. increments to match standard finishing nail sizes.

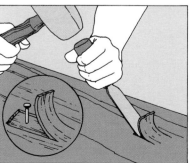

To hide a nailhead (called blind nailing), use a mallet and a sharp, narrow chisel to raise a sliver of wood. Drive the nail under the flap. Glue the sliver down and clamp until set.

Pry bars are made to slide between layers of wood. The claws are angled from the bar for leverage and split for nail-pulling. Use wedges to help hold the work away from the supporting material.

1. Stop hammering when nail is slightly above surface.
2. With nail set, drive head slightly below surface.
3. Fill hole with putty or wood filler. Sand smooth.

Hand tools/Saws

Types of handsaws

Crosscut saws and ripsaws look alike; only the set, or bend, and shape of their teeth differ. On some saws, the upper edge can serve as a straightedge for marking lines.

The backsaw is a short saw with a rigid blade. The handle, shaped like that of a crosscut saw, is attached at a higher angle so that the teeth can be kept almost flat to the work.

A coping saw is used in fine woodworking to make small-diameter curves and filigree or other decorative cuts. The blade can be rotated to cut in any direction relative to the frame.

The compass saw—and the similar but smaller keyhole saw—have tapered blades that allow you to cut gentle curves or to start plunge cuts through predrilled holes.

Hacksaws are used to cut metal. The detachable blades come in several teeth-per-inch ratios to suit the thickness of the metal to be cut. The blade can be turned to cut in four directions.

Handsaw blades come with teeth (or points) in two styles: crosscut for cutting across the grain and rip for cutting with the grain. Both types vary in the number of teeth per inch and in blade length. Alternate teeth bend outward from the center line, making a cut (called the kerf) slightly wider than the blade. In high-quality saws the blades are taper-ground: thinner along the top and thicker at the teeth, and thinner at the toe than near the handle. This helps keep the saw from binding in the kerf. Saws made of tempered or stainless steel are durable and easy to maintain.

A saw should feel comfortable in your hand. Buy one with the longest blade you can manage easily; the longer the blade, the fewer strokes needed to accomplish a cut. Most of the work of sawing is done on the push stroke; so be sure you can align the shoulder of your sawing arm over the work and use your body's weight for maximum leverage.

In starting a cut, always align the saw on the waste side of the marked line, otherwise the kerf width will make the board too short. Sight along the top of the saw. For a square edge, practice by holding a try square against the blade to maintain the saw 90° to the work. Extending your forefinger along the blade helps steady and guide the saw. If the saw wanders off the line despite all your concentration, the teeth of the saw may need sharpening or resetting.

The saw should glide through the wood with a minimum of effort. If the blade flexes, you may be pushing faster than the blade can cut, or the teeth may have dulled. Have saws professionally sharpened as soon as they begin to be difficult to use. A properly sharpened handsaw is more accurate, safer, and easier to use.

Keep some paraffin, paste wax, or plain bar soap handy to lubricate the sides—not the teeth—of the blade.

Hang saws up to avoid damaging the teeth. For long-term storage, coat the blades lightly with machine oil to prevent rust. Clean them periodically with steel wool and mineral spirits.

Crosscut saws

These saws vary from 10 to 16 teeth per inch; a greater number of teeth gives a smoother cut. Crosscut teeth are beveled to slice cleanly through boards from edge to edge.

Profile shows beveled teeth (enlarged for clarity)   Teeth in kerf

Before buying a crosscut saw, make two tests. Tap the blade; it should give a clear, ringing sound. Next, flex it. The blade should bend easily into a half circle and spring back into line when released.

Crosscut saws cut on the push stroke. Lean gently into the stroke. Avoid pushing faster than the blade can cut, you may bend the saw or damage the teeth.

Always use a crosscut saw for plywood, regardless of the wood's surface grain.

Sawing technique

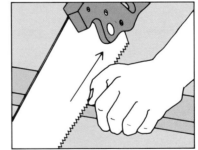

Starting a cut. Place the heel of a crosscut saw on the waste side of line. Support blade with the thumb of your free hand and carefully draw the saw backward with a few short pulls.

Finishing a cut. To avoid splintering, support the waste side of the work with your free hand and lighten the pressure of your strokes. If you find this awkward, flip the board over and finish the cut on the opposite side.

Ripsaws

Designed to trim lumber into different widths, ripsaws are inefficient for crosscutting. The chisel-shaped teeth, 5 to 12 per inch, chip through the long fibers of boards, parallel to the milled edges.

Coarser rip teeth may be measured in half points

Teeth in kerf

These saws cut only on the push stroke. To start a cut, place the saw's teeth almost flat against the work and carefully push forward, nicking the edge. Keep doing this until you have established a good kerf, then raise the saw to a comfortable cutting angle (usually somewhere between 45 and 60 degrees) and begin cutting with long, rhythmic strokes. The pull stroke will clear sawdust from the gullets (the spaces between the teeth) and the kerf.

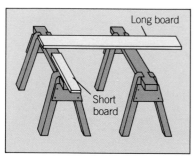

Support the work. A pair of sawhorses provides a secure base for sawing. You can build sawhorses to create a steady and portable work surface that matches your height (p.21).

Long board

Short board

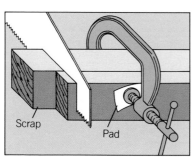

To trim a thin slice from the end of a piece of wood, clamp it to a scrap of similar size and saw through both pieces together. Protect the work with thick cardboard or thin wood under the jaws of the clamp.

Scrap

Pad

A Japanese handsaw

Browsing in a hardware store or tool catalog can turn up some handy, unusual, and beautiful tools. The *ryoba,* a double-edged Japanese saw, has rip teeth on one side and crosscut on the other, eliminating the need for two saws.

The teeth are set and shaped to cut only on the pull stroke. Pulling puts less stress on the saw, so these blades can be thinner than those of conventional saws and cut a narrower kerf. The oval handle is easy to grip and, after a little practice, affords greater control with less fatigue.

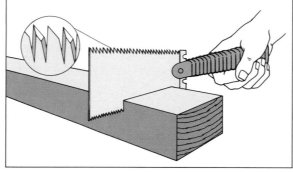

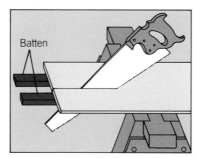

Making long cuts. To prevent a saw from binding in a long cut, put a wedge in the kerf to hold it open. A straight piece of scrap wood clamped along line serves as a guide.

Guide

Wedge

Kerf

Cutting hardboard. Support flexible material with long battens placed underneath. Shift the work as you cut so that the saw stays clear of the sawhorses.

Batten

Backsaws

Choose a backsaw for smooth, precise cuts. Its rectangular blade has fine teeth (either crosscut or rip) on one edge and a metal strip on the other edge to keep the blade rigid. Backsaw cuts are often made in a miter box. With patience and practice, a backsaw will produce cuts requiring little further trimming.

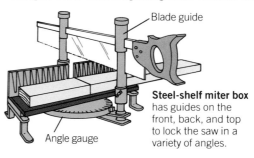

Blade guide

Steel-shelf miter box has guides on the front, back, and top to lock the saw in a variety of angles.

Angle gauge

Wooden miter boxes have one 90° and two 45° angle guides. Not truly accurate; use for rough work.

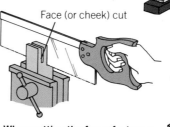

Face (or cheek) cut

When cutting the face of a tenon, use a backsaw with rip teeth. (A tenon forms part of a joint in woodworking.) When cutting the shoulder, use a backsaw with crosscut teeth.

Shoulder cut

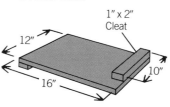 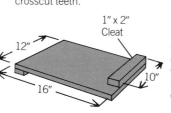

1" x 2" Cleat

12"

16"

10"

Use a bench hook in place of clamps or a vise. Hold work against the top cleat, hook bottom cleat over edge of table or bench.

Hand tools/Special-purpose saws

Coping saws

The coping saw's thin, replaceable blade is held taut in a flexible C-shaped frame. A hardwood handle controls the tension on the frame and the blade. Releasing the frame tension loosens the blade, allowing the cutting edge to be rotated 360° without

 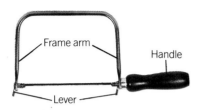

Cross pin

Frame arm

Handle

Slotted holding pin

Lever

removing it from the frame. The frame depth, sometimes called the throat, is the distance from the blade to the back of the frame. This assembly lets you create delicate ornamental work.

Coping saw blades have tiny cross pins on each end. These pins fit into slotted holding pins on the frame arms and anchor the blade in place. Mount blades in the frame to cut on the pull stroke (teeth point toward handle); you will have more control over the saw. Levers attached to the slotted pins control the blade's orientation in the frame. Be sure the levers are aligned and the blade is not twisted between the frame arms.

The blades are 6 to 6½ inches long with up to 20 teeth per inch. Some blades cut wood; others are meant for plastic, metal, or ceramic. Flat blades can be as narrow as $7/100$ inch. Fine spiral blades, called rods, have a continuous cutting surface and don't need to be turned to follow design lines. Use a rod to cut out circles as small as the diameter of a pencil. Test the blade tension by cutting a piece of scrap wood; a slack blade will buckle in the kerf, a tight one may snap. Protect your eyes with goggles.

Compass and keyhole saws

Compass saws have 12- to 14-inch blades that taper from the handle to the tip. The blades have 8 to 10 teeth per inch set in a crosscut pattern (p.24). You can purchase a single saw or a handle and a set of blades. Saws with pistol-grip handles have

Compass saw

blades that cut on the push stroke; straight-handled saws have blades that cut on the pull stroke.

Keyhole saws are identically shaped but smaller, usually 10 or 12 inches long with 10 teeth per inch, and are more maneuverable. Either saw can be used for straight cuts through a bored hole, for cutting gentle curves, or in places where a crosscut saw won't fit.

Coping saw techniques

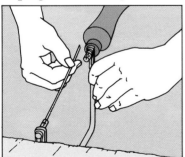

To install a blade, turn handle to loosen the frame's tension. Slip blade into slotted pin. Brace the frame against a firm surface and flex it gently. Attach the other end of blade. Release frame and tighten handle.

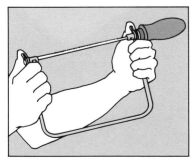

To reposition the frame or blade: turn handle to loosen frame. Move levers on slotted pins until you have the desired angle. Align levers so that blade is straight between frame arms.

For decorative cuts that can't be reached from the edge of the work: drill a hole, then pass the blade through and connect it to the frame. The depth of the frame may restrict access to some cuts.

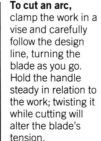

To cut an arc, clamp the work in a vise and carefully follow the design line, turning the blade as you go. Hold the handle steady in relation to the work; twisting it while cutting will alter the blade's tension.

Using other saws

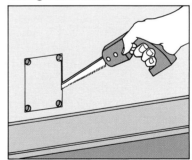

For straight cuts in tight places (making a hole for an electrical box, for instance), use a compass saw. To turn saw easily, drill holes at each corner. As the cut enlarges, bring the saw to a 45° angle.

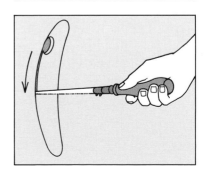

A keyhole saw cuts curves that are too tight for a compass saw and too far from an edge for a coping saw. Hold the saw at 90° to the work. Cut carefully; this saw's flexible blade tends to bind.

Hacksaws

With the proper blade, a hacksaw can cut through just about any thickness or kind of metal you have in your shop or home. The number of teeth per inch should relate to the thickness of the metal; in general, the thinner the metal, the finer the tooth.

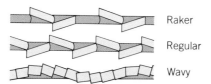

Raker

Regular

Wavy

Blades come with 14, 18, 24, or 32 teeth per inch set in one of three tooth patterns: raker, regular, or wavy. The large-toothed raker set is easy to control, cuts ferrous or nonferrous metals of various hardnesses, and is well suited for aggressive use on thicker materials. Regular-set blades are less expensive, but also less sturdy; use them for soft nonferrous metals such as aluminum. Wavy-set teeth are good for harder, thinner materials.

Hacksaw frames come in two styles, fixed or adjustable, and take blades from 8 to 16 inches long. The flat blades have a hole in each end that hooks on to posts on square-shanked pins in the frame arms. These pins can also be turned in 90° increments so that the blade can be positioned to cut in four directions. A wing nut loosens the pins.

Mount the blade to cut on the push stroke (teeth point away from the handle). Nick the cutting line with a file; this provides a shallow groove that starts the saw on line. Cut on the waste side of the line. Use both hands to guide the saw, applying even pressure. Hold the saw at a shallow angle; if cutting thin sheet metal or foil, choose a blade that allows at least two teeth to remain in contact with the material at all times. Saw in a steady rhythm. Working too fast creates friction, which can distort the blade. If the blade breaks during a cut, start the new blade at the opposite end of the line and work toward the starting cut. The new blade may be slightly thicker and bind in the old kerf.

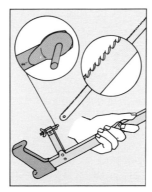

Blade can be mounted to cut on push or pull stroke. Holes in each end slip over posts on pins. Tighten with wing nut.

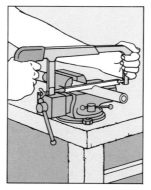

Grasp saw with both hands. Use the forward hand to help guide saw. Exert firm, even pressure throughout stroke.

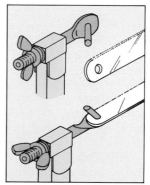

To change position of blade, remove it from frame. Turn the square-shanked pins 90°. Replace blade.

Keep frame clear of material by changing angle of blade. Oil the blade lightly to help speed the cutting.

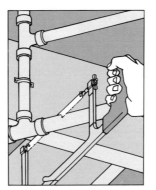

Invert the blade in tight places (for example, cutting pipe between ceiling joists). Saw with downward pressure.

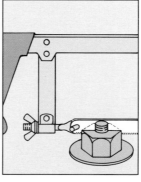

Frozen nuts can be removed by sawing them away from the bolt. A second cut may be necessary.

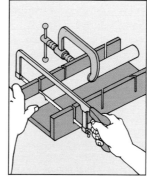

To ensure square ends when cutting plastic pipe, hold or clamp the pipe securely in a miter box.

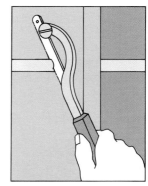

A mini-hacksaw uses standard (or broken) blades held by a clamp. Useful where a standard saw won't fit.

Utility knives

One of the handiest tools to have around the house, utility knives perform a variety of cutting, trimming, and scoring tasks with ease. Some styles have retractable blades; others have blades fixed in the handle with a screw. In some, extra blades can be stored in the handle.

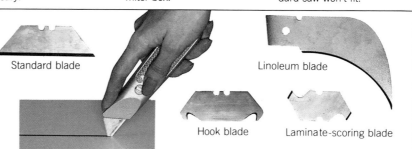

Standard blade

Linoleum blade

Hook blade

Laminate-scoring blade

Hand tools/Drills

Sharpening tools 44-45
Power drills 52-54

Unlike electric drills, hand-powered drills are completely portable, slim enough to fit awkward spaces, and they allow you to control the speed of cutting.

Most drills have three-jawed chucks that automatically center the bit. The jaws, contained by the chuck ring, open and close when you turn the chuck. Some drills will accept only bits with a particular *tang* (the nonpointed end of the bit). Whenever you use a drill, be certain the bit is properly centered and tightly in place before you begin work. A loose or improperly aligned bit is inaccurate and unsafe.

Use proper technique. Start the hole with an awl or a punch. Place the bit tip in the starter hole and align the drill at the desired angle. Keeping the tool aligned, begin drilling. The hand drill and the bit brace each have a grip to hold the drill steady and a handle to activate the mechanism. The push drill contains a spiral ratchet that drives the bit; the grip and the handle are the same piece. As with all cutting tools, lubricating the cutting edge speeds the cut and helps preserve the edge.

The push drill is the smallest of the hand drills. Its compact shape allows it to fit into tight corners, and its single handle leaves one hand free to steady the work or the tool. Use this drill as you would a spiral ratchet screwdriver: just push down repeatedly on the handle. The ratchet turns the bit, drilling on the push stroke, resetting when released.

Push drills accept only bits designed specifically to fit their chucks. These bits are called *drill points*. Drill points come in a range of sizes; they are not suitable for other drills or for a ratchet screwdriver.

Hand drills are also called eggbeater drills because of similar shape and drive mechanism. A side-mounted crank drives an interlocking gear and pinion; one turn of the crank turns the bit three or more times. Suitable for use on wood, soft metal, and plastics, the hand drill accepts twist or countersink bits with a shank size up to ¼ inch.

The bit brace is a woodworking tool used by craftsmen to bore precise large-diameter holes and to drive or remove screws. With care and an extra-long bit or an extension bit, a brace can also bore a deep hole. A reversible ratchet allows clockwise and counterclockwise turning. Bit braces are categorized by their length from head to jaws and by the sweep (the diameter of the circle traced as the handle turns). Their universal chuck jaws accommodate a wide variety of bits (see below). Additionally, the brace accepts a screwdriver bit to drive or remove screws.

Specialized bits for a bit brace bore particular kinds of holes. An expansion bit adjusts to several diameters; a Forstner bit cuts flat-bottomed holes; Jennings and solid-center bits cut deeply, cleanly, and precisely.

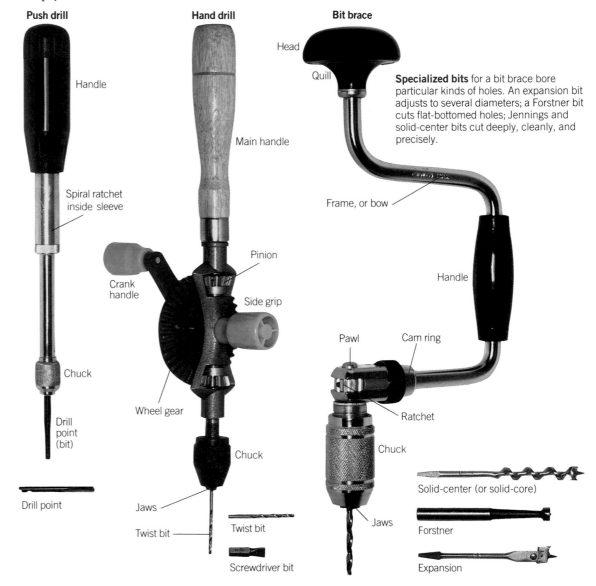

Push drill
- Handle
- Spiral ratchet inside sleeve
- Chuck
- Drill point (bit)
- Drill point

Hand drill
- Main handle
- Pinion
- Crank handle
- Side grip
- Wheel gear
- Chuck
- Jaws
- Twist bit
- Twist bit
- Screwdriver bit

Bit brace
- Head
- Quill
- Frame, or bow
- Handle
- Pawl
- Cam ring
- Ratchet
- Chuck
- Jaws
- Solid-center (or solid-core)
- Forstner
- Expansion

Screwdrivers

For safety and efficiency, it's best to have an assortment of screwdrivers of various types, widths, and lengths. Screwdrivers come with tips for square-drive and star-drive screws as well as for slotted and Phillips screws.

Screws are driven by torque (turning power); the thicker the shank, the more torque per turn. When driving screws, the screw and the screwdriver should always form a straight line.

For your own safety, never use any screwdriver for prying, punching, chiseling, or opening a can; use tools designed for those purposes.

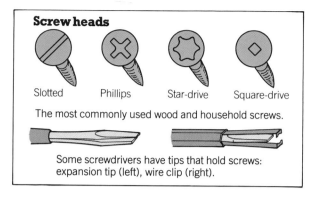

Choosing a screwdriver
A flared standard tip is adequate for flush screws, but for counter-bored screws use a straight-sided cabinet tip (far right) to avoid marring sides of the hole.

Blade must fit slot   Standard   Cabinet

Screw heads

Slotted   Phillips   Star-drive   Square-drive

The most commonly used wood and household screws.

Some screwdrivers have tips that hold screws: expansion tip (left), wire clip (right).

Screwdriver types

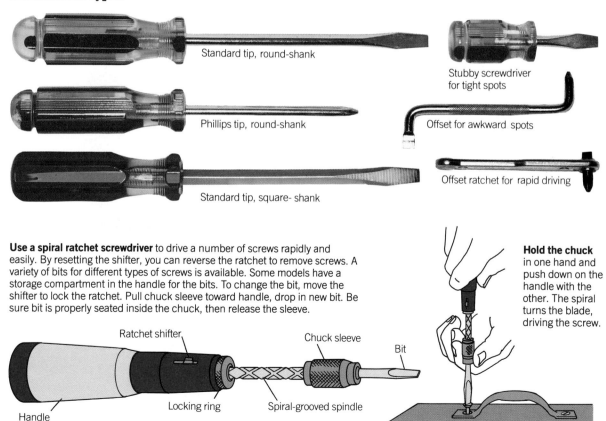

Standard tip, round-shank

Phillips tip, round-shank

Standard tip, square-shank

Stubby screwdriver for tight spots

Offset for awkward spots

Offset ratchet for rapid driving

Use a spiral ratchet screwdriver to drive a number of screws rapidly and easily. By resetting the shifter, you can reverse the ratchet to remove screws. A variety of bits for different types of screws is available. Some models have a storage compartment in the handle for the bits. To change the bit, move the shifter to lock the ratchet. Pull chuck sleeve toward handle, drop in new bit. Be sure bit is properly seated inside the chuck, then release the sleeve.

Ratchet shifter   Chuck sleeve

Bit

Handle

Locking ring   Spiral-grooved spindle

Hold the chuck in one hand and push down on the handle with the other. The spiral turns the blade, driving the screw.

Special techniques

Square-shanked screwdriver used with a wrench increases the torque. (Torque, not downward pressure, drives screws into wood.)

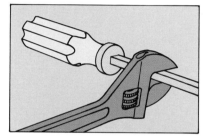

Tight places are easier to reach with an offset screwdriver. These have a driving tip at each end. Tips may be standard or Phillips or one of each.

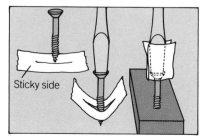

Sticky side

Taping the screw to the screwdriver helps to get it started in awkward places. Slit tape, push screw through, place driver in slot, and fold tape up.

Hand tools/Wrenches

For wrenches to grip tightly and operate smoothly, match the jaws' shape to that of the work. Some jaws seat against flat surfaces, such as square or hex nuts; others grip round surfaces, such as tubing or pipe; some are fixed and some adjustable. For general repairs or woodworking you need only two sizes of adjustable wrenches and a few open-end ones. Plumbing tasks and car repair require a wider variety. For jobs with lots of nuts and bolts, a battery-powered ratchet is ideal.

Match the wrench's size to the task. Adjustable wrenches are designated by their overall length; fixed-heads and ratchets by the capacity of their jaws (may be standard or metric). Handle length relates to jaw capacity for specific leverage; adding an "extension" by sliding a pipe over the handle can damage the tool, the bolt, or the work. Try a larger wrench or a penetrating lubricant.

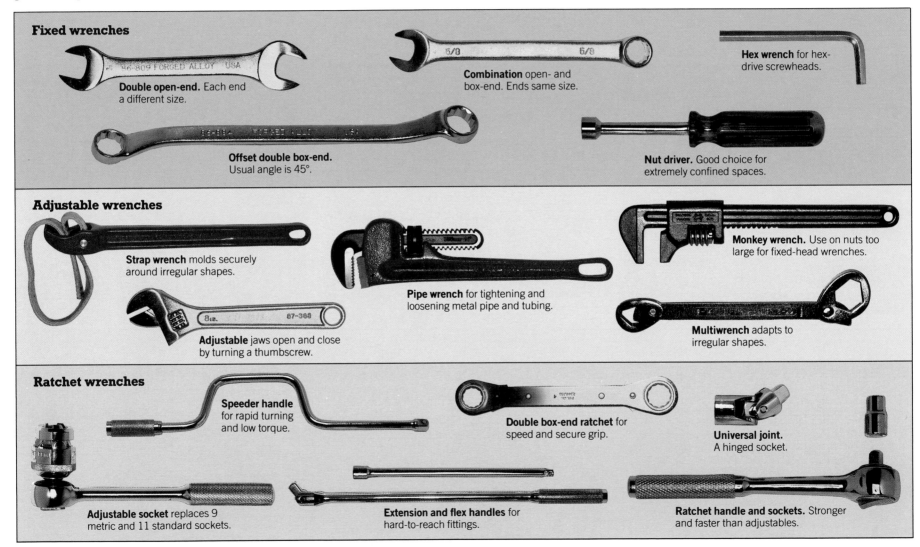

Fixed wrenches

Double open-end. Each end a different size.

Combination open- and box-end. Ends same size.

Hex wrench for hex-drive screwheads.

Offset double box-end. Usual angle is 45°.

Nut driver. Good choice for extremely confined spaces.

Adjustable wrenches

Strap wrench molds securely around irregular shapes.

Adjustable jaws open and close by turning a thumbscrew.

Pipe wrench for tightening and loosening metal pipe and tubing.

Monkey wrench. Use on nuts too large for fixed-head wrenches.

Multiwrench adapts to irregular shapes.

Ratchet wrenches

Speeder handle for rapid turning and low torque.

Double box-end ratchet for speed and secure grip.

Universal joint. A hinged socket.

Adjustable socket replaces 9 metric and 11 standard sockets.

Extension and flex handles for hard-to-reach fittings.

Ratchet handle and sockets. Stronger and faster than adjustables.

Fixed-wrench techniques

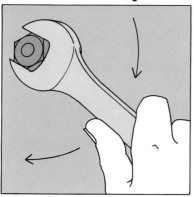

Open-end wrench is useful where the nut is accessible from only one side. Always pull a wrench toward you. Avoid overtightening, as this may damage the bolt.

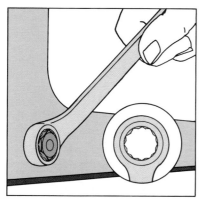

Box wrench can turn bolts where handle swing is as narrow as 30°; heads, called rings, are sometimes offset (bent) at 45°. Each ring has a different diameter. Inside the rings are 6 or 12 points that surround and grip the nut Most versatile are the 12-point rings.

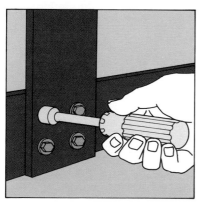

Nut driver is available in sizes to fit hex nuts from ³⁄₁₆ to ½ in.; some are self-adjusting from ¼ to ⁷⁄₁₆ in. Use the nut driver in the same way as you would a screwdriver. Some models have color-coded plastic handles that indicate size of the head.

Adjustable wrenches

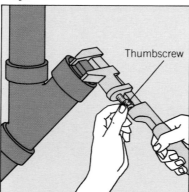

Thumbscrew

Monkey wrenches, often confused with pipe wrenches, are inefficient for round surfaces. Their flat, stable jaws need a straight surface to grip for turning. Adjust the jaw opening by turning the knurled nut in the handle. Monkey wrenches range in length from 9 to 18 in.

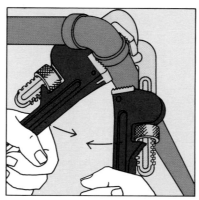

Use a pair of pipe wrenches to loosen frozen pipe joints. Put one wrench on the nut, the other on the pipe. Pull the handles toward each other. A pipe wrench is also useful for removing stripped (rounded-off) nuts.

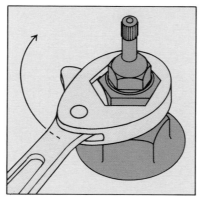

Multiwrench's handle has a crescent-shaped extension that slips into the split wrench head, forming part of the gripping mechanism. This unique design allows a single tool to accommodate various fittings with minimal adjusting.

Ratchet-wrench techniques

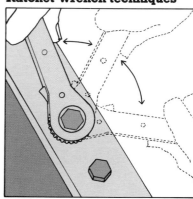

Ratchet box wrench combines the secure holding power of a standard box wrench with the efficiency of a ratchet. The ratchet grips when pulled, turning the bolt, and releases when pushed so you can reposition the handle without repositioning the head.

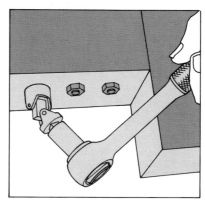

Universal joint, sometimes called a flex joint, is a socket attached to a hinge. Used with an extension handle, the depth of the socket permits access to nuts in recessed places. The hinge allows the handle to operate at a variety of angles.

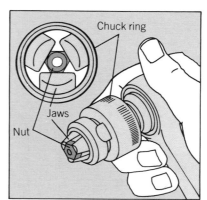

Chuck ring

Jaws

Nut

Adjustable socket takes the place of 20 or more individual sockets. To open the jaws, turn chuck ring. Center socket over nut and tighten ring. Jaws close tightly on nut, forming a nonslip grip. Socket fits ³⁄₈-in. ratchet handle.

31

Hand tools/Pliers

Gripping pliers

Some pliers grip, some cut, some do both; others adjust to grasp different-size objects. Those shown below are for gripping; they may have a cutter near the pivot point.

Bent-nose. Curved jaws reach into awkward spaces

Long-nose. For delicate tasks such as forming wire loops

Cutter

Lineman's. Broad-nosed gripping tool with a cutter near the pivot

Adjustable pliers

The jaws of adjustable pliers open to varying widths. To change their position, open the handles. Slide the pivot post along the slot to the proper width. Close handles to lock setting.

Groove-joint. Grip objects of any shape; jaws open to many widths

Slip-joint. Versatile, good for light gripping and turning

Cutting pliers

Taking their names from the position of their cutting edges (side, end), these pliers cut wire or small pieces of thin metal, strip casings from wire, cut tile, and cut or pull small nails and brads.

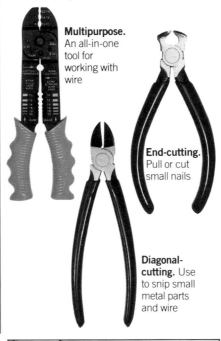

Multipurpose. An all-in-one tool for working with wire

End-cutting. Pull or cut small nails

Diagonal-cutting. Use to snip small metal parts and wire

Locking pliers

These pliers can substitute for clamps. Place jaws around object, turn the adjusting knob, and close the handles until they lock. Use release lever or pull handles open to unclamp.

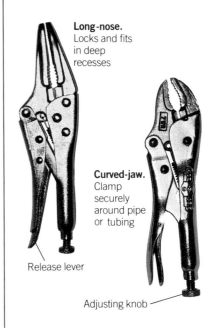

Long-nose. Locks and fits in deep recesses

Curved-jaw. Clamp securely around pipe or tubing

Release lever

Adjusting knob

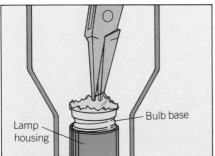

Lamp housing

Bulb base

Long-nose pliers hold small items for assembly, or reach into restricted areas. Needle-nose pliers, similar to but smaller than long-nose, are handy for eyeglass and jewelry repairs.

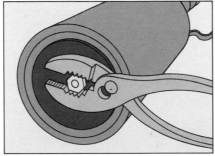

Slip-joint pliers are highly versatile. Their jaws have both flat and curved areas to grip objects of different shapes. The pivot can be adjusted (slipped) for narrow or wide jaw capacities.

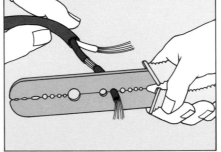

Multipurpose tool can be used to measure, cut, strip, and crimp wire. Be certain power is off before working with house wires (p.237); vinyl-coated handles do not insulate well against shock.

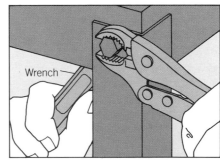

Wrench

Locking pliers provide a secure hold on damaged or frozen nuts or bolts. Hold bolt head with pliers; turn nut with a wrench. The jaws come in a variety of styles to suit different tasks.

Hand tools / Vises

Woodworking vises

Consisting of two large, flat jaws that adjust by turning a long screw, a vise is like a strong pair of hands that holds stock securely while you work on it. A half nut allows quick adjusting; the screw can skip over the nut's threads before locking into place.

These vises are usually mounted on the front edge of the workbench near a corner. Set the top of the jaws flush with the top of the bench. Use lag bolts and wood screws to secure the vise to the bench.

Line the jaws with thin wood plates to protect the work. You can attach the plates with countersunk screws or double-faced tape. Be sure to keep the plates sanded smooth and flat. Replace them when worn.

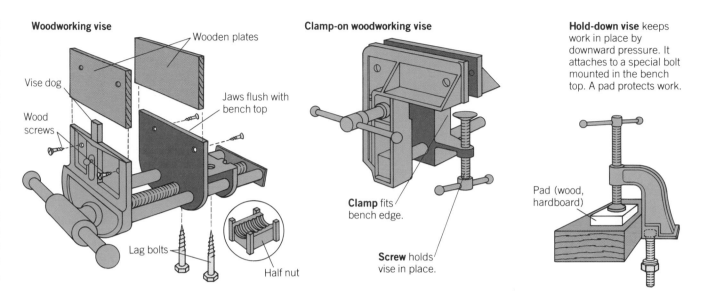

Woodworking vise
Wooden plates
Vise dog
Wood screws
Jaws flush with bench top
Lag bolts
Half nut

Clamp-on woodworking vise
Clamp fits bench edge.
Screw holds vise in place.

Hold-down vise keeps work in place by downward pressure. It attaches to a special bolt mounted in the bench top. A pad protects work.
Pad (wood, hardboard)

Machinist's vises

Also called bench vises, these tools sit on top of the bench and are primarily used for metalworking. Liners for the grooved jaws can be made by bending smooth metal (at least as wide as the vise's jaws) into right-angled plates that rest on the jaws.

There are three styles of machinist's vises. The most elaborate bolts to the bench and can be turned 360 degrees. Clamp-on vises, handy for light work, are less sturdy. They attach over the bench's edge with a threaded screw (like a C-clamp, p.34) and can be set up and taken down quickly. A drill press vise, also known as a general-purpose vise, bolts to a drill press's worktable (p.56). Its grooved jaws hold small or round work securely. Some models tilt or rotate for angled drilling.

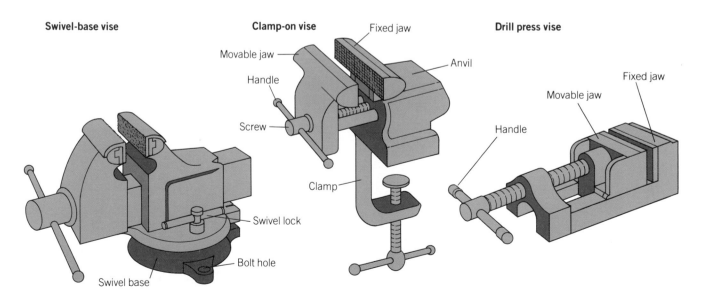

Swivel-base vise
Swivel lock
Bolt hole
Swivel base

Clamp-on vise
Fixed jaw
Movable jaw
Handle
Screw
Anvil
Clamp

Drill press vise
Movable jaw
Fixed jaw
Handle

Hand tools/Clamps

Indispensable accessories to almost any woodworking project from simple furniture repair to complex fitting and joinery, clamps come in a variety of sizes and styles. Buy clamps in pairs or sets of three. Use them to hold work while glue sets, to secure wood or metal in position while working on it, and for temporary assemblies.

Although both jaws are adjustable on some kinds of clamps, most have one fixed jaw and one movable jaw that opens and closes by turning a threaded bar. Most clamps can be used for a variety of purposes. Improvised clamping (facing page) often works but requires more care to set up. C-clamps, hand screws, and quick-action clamps are the most versatile. Light, easy-to-use spring clamps have many household applications. Acquire special-purpose clamps as needed.

Rehearse the clamping sequence before applying adhesive. Once the procedure is clear, begin applying clamps in the middle of the piece and work toward the ends. This forces trapped air out and coaxes the glue along the joint, aiding even bonding.

Put scrap wood between jaws and work to protect surfaces and distribute pressure evenly. Avoid overtightening the jaws; hand-tighten until a thin line of glue oozes from the joint.

Put plastic (similar to the kind used for sandwich bags) under the joints and the work to catch glue seeps and to prevent inadvertently bonding the work to the bench or the scrap. Be sure the work doesn't slide out of alignment during the clamping procedure. Clean excess glue from the surface with a damp rag, and allow to set.

C-clamps

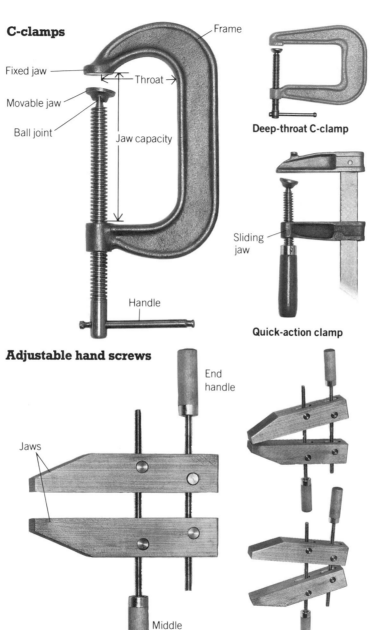

Frame
Fixed jaw
Throat
Movable jaw
Ball joint
Jaw capacity
Handle

Deep-throat C-clamp

Sliding jaw

Quick-action clamp

Adjustable hand screws

End handle

Jaws

Middle handle

Adjusts to many angles

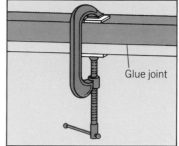

C-clamps are available in a range of sizes. Jaw capacities vary from 1 to 8 in., throat depths from 1 to 4 in. Turning the handle adjusts jaw opening. Some C-clamps have ball joints on the jaws that swivel to grip irregular shapes.

Glue joint

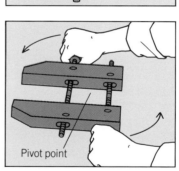

Deep-throat clamp can be improvised using a sturdy C-clamp and wood scraps. Be sure the block of scrap is higher than the wood joint. Put a long scrap over block and joint and clamp down. The long scrap will transfer pressure to the joint.

Scrap wood
Glue joint

Hand screw jaws can be parallel or angled. To open or close jaws in parallel, grasp a handle in each hand. Imagine a pivot point between the two handles; crank the handles around that point. To change angle, hold one handle steady, turn the other handle like a screwdriver.

Pivot point

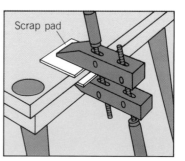

To clamp parallel but offset surfaces (for example, repairing a veneer bubble in a tabletop), adjust screws so that jaws are parallel but one jaw extends beyond the other. Clamp size is overall length of jaws. The most common sizes are 6, 8, 10, 12, and 14 in.

Scrap pad

Spring clamps

Band and web clamps

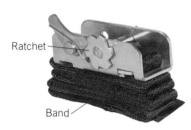

Ratchet

Band

Pipe and bar clamps

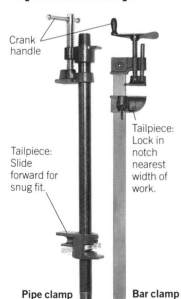

Crank handle

Tailpiece: Slide forward for snug fit.

Tailpiece: Lock in notch nearest width of work.

Pipe clamp **Bar clamp**

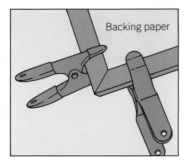

Backing paper

Open and close these clamps by squeezing the handles. Keep several on hand and use them whenever you need to hold something with light pressure. They can be repositioned quickly and easily. Some have vinyl-coated tips to prevent marring surfaces.

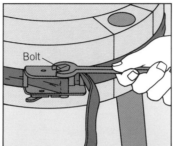

Bolt

Ideal for irregular or curved shapes, these clamps encircle the work, providing even pressure. Loosen or tighten the band by turning bolt on ratchet with a wrench. Be careful work doesn't slide out of position during tightening.

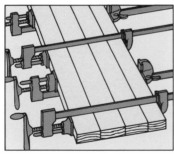

To adjust bar clamps, lock tailpiece in position on bar; turn handle on head to tighten jaws. For some glue-ups you may need several sizes and more than one pair in each size. For flat work alternate them above and below the work to prevent bowing.

Pipe clamp jaws come in two sizes, to fit either ½- or ¾-in. pipe. Have one end of pipe threaded; screw the head onto this section. Tailpiece locks into position with a lever. Space clamps 12 to 18 in. apart along work.

Special clamps

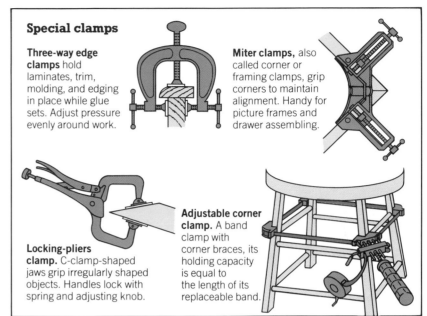

Three-way edge clamps hold laminates, trim, molding, and edging in place while glue sets. Adjust pressure evenly around work.

Miter clamps, also called corner or framing clamps, grip corners to maintain alignment. Handy for picture frames and drawer assembling.

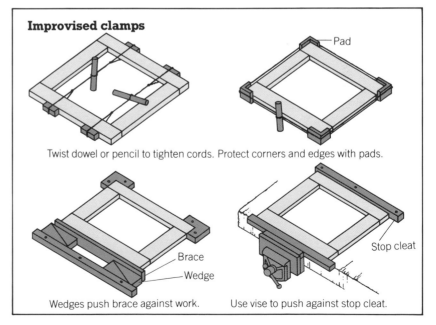

Locking-pliers clamp. C-clamp-shaped jaws grip irregularly shaped objects. Handles lock with spring and adjusting knob.

Adjustable corner clamp. A band clamp with corner braces, its holding capacity is equal to the length of its replaceable band.

Improvised clamps

Pad

Twist dowel or pencil to tighten cords. Protect corners and edges with pads.

Brace

Wedge

Stop cleat

Wedges push brace against work.   Use vise to push against stop cleat.

Hand tools / Chisels

Despite its simple appearance, a chisel is a precision tool with a razor-sharp cutting edge. Primarily a refining tool, its proper use requires careful attention and some delicacy. Concentrate on the edge; the tool's bevel and the wood's grain will draw the chisel in specific directions (below right).

Chisels come in a bewildering variety of shapes and sizes; some are designed for specific woodworking tasks, others are for cutting metal or stone. The cutting edge of a chisel is always beveled, but the sides of the blade may be either beveled or straight. Heavy, straight-sided chisels are called mortising chisels. Delicate, bevel-sided chisels are firmer or paring chisels. Mortising chisels are used with a mallet to remove waste; firmer and paring chisels are usually hand-driven to trim and shape.

Blade widths vary, as do the increments by which the widths increase. For example, blades between ⅛ inch and 1 inch wide increase by increments of ⅛ inch; blades between 1 inch and 1½ inches wide increase by ¼ inch. In general, narrow chisels are more useful than wide ones. A good starter set will include ¼-, ⅜-, ½-, and ¾-inch firmer chisels.

Chisels with high-impact plastic handles should have the steel tang all the way through the handle. These tools are adequate for most household chores, but are made of somewhat lower-grade steel and will need to be sharpened more frequently than those with high-quality blades. Specialty chisels have features that suit them to specific tasks; buy these tools as you need them.

When working with chisels, always secure the work with clamps, in a vise, or against a brace. Don't cut too deeply; it's better to pare thin shavings. Work with the grain (downhill) when cutting. If working against the grain (uphill) is unavoidable, be especially careful to avoid gouging. Whenever possible, use another tool to remove most of the waste (facing page). Protect the cutting edges; store chisels in tool rolls or a rack and don't drop them or knock them off the bench. Tip covers sometimes come with the tools or you can purchase them separately.

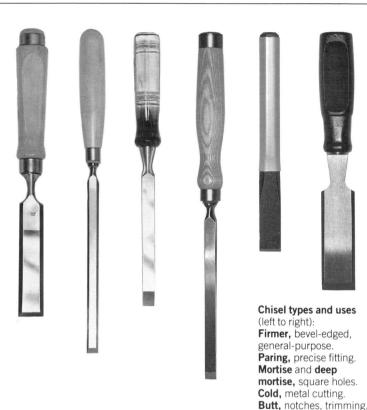

Chisel types and uses (left to right):
Firmer, bevel-edged, general-purpose.
Paring, precise fitting.
Mortise and **deep mortise,** square holes.
Cold, metal cutting.
Butt, notches, trimming.

Handles

Tang. Hand pressure, light mallet blows

Socket. Best for general-purpose use

Heavy-duty. Takes aggressive driving

Cutting bevels

15°
Paring. Narrow bevel for delicate work

20°
Firmer. Moderate bevel is most versatile

25°
Framing. Steep bevel for rough work

Positioning a chisel's bevel

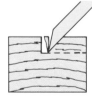
For deep cutting, bevel faces up. Drive chisel with hand pressure or light mallet blows.

For fine shaving, bevel faces down. Rock chisel on bevel to control depth of cut.

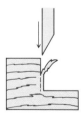
For square edges, bevel faces waste side of cut. Shavings will curl into recess.

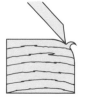
Convex curves. Bevel up for greater control. **Concave curves.** Bevel down acts as fulcrum to maneuver handle.

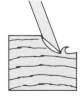
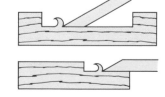
Bevel down fits into confined spaces. **Bevel up** is efficient in places where chisel can be almost level.

Removing waste

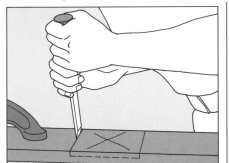

Align bevel to face waste side of cut. Grip chisel with both hands. Lean on chisel, using your body's weight to drive the edge into the wood.

Drive chisel with light mallet blows to remove waste quickly; work from both edges toward center. Hold chisel horizontally, bevel facing up.

Wide butt chisel is best for removing high point in center of joint; keep bevel facing up to ensure flat-bottomed cut. Guide chisel with both hands.

Mortising

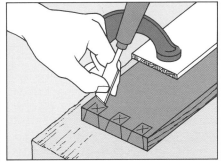

Score cut lines with utility knife to avoid splitting along grain. Remove waste by drilling overlapping holes. Tape on bit indicates cut depth.

Mortise chisel driven by mallet chops out waste at ends of cut. Hold chisel upright, 90° to work, for square ends. Do not cut too deeply.

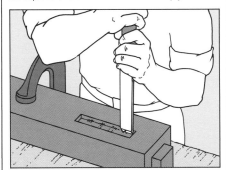

Grasp firmer chisel in both hands and push with body weight to cut sides of mortise. Do not use mallet; it may drive chisel past the cut depth.

Dovetailing

With work secured and flat on bench, scribe outline of cuts with corner of sharp chisel. Mark waste for removal. Cut outlines with small backsaw.

Drive a narrow firmer chisel with light mallet blows to chip out waste. Alternate vertical and horizontal cuts, removing small bits each time.

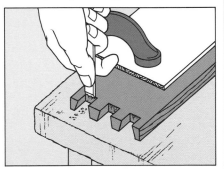

Clean any roughness or irregularity from sides and bottoms of the pins with a paring chisel. Be certain corners remain clean and square.

Rounding corners

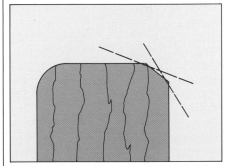

Clamp board to work top and protect work top with scrap wood. Use mallet to drive butt chisel straight down, cutting corner at about 45°.

With chisel's bevel facing waste side of cut line, start at outer edge and work toward layout line, gradually rounding off the corner.

To finish curve, clamp work upright. Pare fine shavings with bevel up. Hold the handle in one hand; guide the cutting edge with the other.

Planes are used primarily to trim and smooth wood, to straighten irregular edges, and to bevel (or *chamfer*) and round them. Special-purpose planes (pp.40–41) are designed to chisel out grooves for wood joints and to shave or trim wood into specific shapes.

The four types of bench planes are basically the same—a blade, called an *iron*, in a holder—except for their sizes. From the smallest to the largest they are called smooth, jack, fore, and jointer planes. Use a small plane to smooth or trim small stock; a larger one for broad surfaces and long stock.

Before buying a plane, consider how you will use it. A well-made plane of steel and plastic may work as well as one made of brass and exotic wood—and be a better investment when you consider cost and frequency of use. Note that planes may be cataloged by numbers that relate to their sizes.

Proper adjustment and a good quality iron are critical to the tool's performance. Be sure the depth-adjusting knob is accessible, easy to turn, and has minimal play. Check that the frog supports the iron completely. Try to scratch the plane iron with the tip of a pocketknife; if you can, it is too soft.

A plane may have a flat or grooved sole. Because of its larger surface area, a flat sole will create more drag than a grooved one. However, grooves can be troublesome when planing edges. Waxing either kind reduces drag.

The weight of the tool may be helpful for some tasks, tiring for others. A plane that has a plastic body will be lighter than a wooden one, and wood will be lighter than steel. Plastic may be the best choice; it is strong, light, and durable. Wood can shrink, swell, or crack if exposed to extremes of humidity and dryness. And steel planes may be too heavy for some work.

When working, use the shallowest blade depth that will produce uniform shavings. Plane with the grain of the wood, keeping the sole in contact with the surface. Remove chips and shavings from the throat. Lift the tool on the return stroke to prevent dulling the edge prematurely.

If the throat jams with shavings and chips, the blade cap is probably set too close to the iron's cutting edge. Scratches across the grain *(chatter marks)* indicate that the frog, the iron, and the blade cap are assembled improperly. Scratches along the grain mean a nicked or concave cutting edge, or uneven lateral adjustment. Check the adjustment before assuming that the iron needs honing.

If the plane skims the surface without cutting, a chip may be stuck on the edge, the cutter may be dull or too shallowly set, or the sole may have picked up so much resin from the wood that it floats. If necessary, clean the sole with a solvent such as mineral spirits. Waxing the sole will keep resin from accumulating and retard rust.

Protecting and maintaining the cutting edge of the iron (pp.44–45) is the single most important part of keeping a plane in working order. Lay the tool on its side each time you put it down; the iron projects beneath the sole and its razor-sharp edge will be damaged if thoughtlessly set down.

Store the plane on its side with the iron retracted. Check the iron's sharpness before using the plane again.

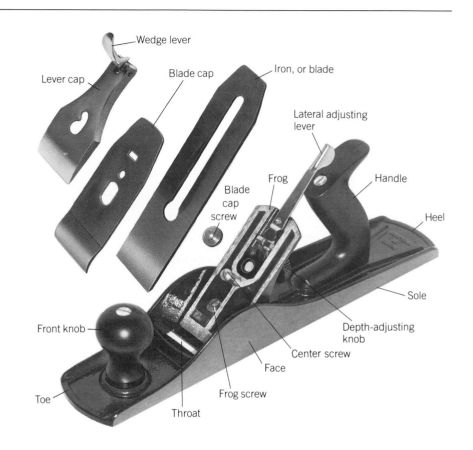

Bench planes

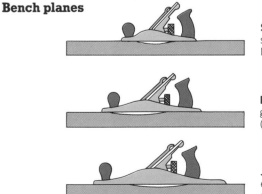

Smooth plane, No. 3 or 4, for finish smoothing, beveling, or small stock. Not good for flattening broad surfaces.

Fore plane, No. 6, an intermediate, general-purpose tool. No. 5 jack plane (not shown) is slightly smaller.

Jointer plane, No. 7, for trimming long edges, creating true flatness on broad surfaces or edge-joined boards (p.110).

Setting the plane

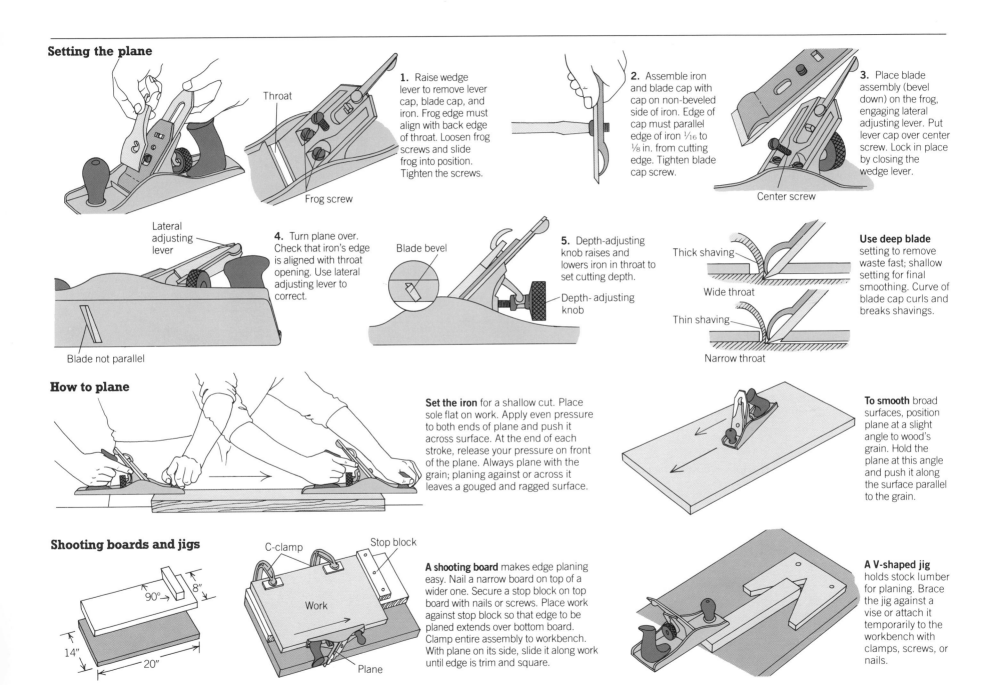

1. Raise wedge lever to remove lever cap, blade cap, and iron. Frog edge must align with back edge of throat. Loosen frog screws and slide frog into position. Tighten the screws.

Throat

Frog screw

2. Assemble iron and blade cap with cap on non-beveled side of iron. Edge of cap must parallel edge of iron $\frac{1}{16}$ to $\frac{1}{8}$ in. from cutting edge. Tighten blade cap screw.

3. Place blade assembly (bevel down) on the frog, engaging lateral adjusting lever. Put lever cap over center screw. Lock in place by closing the wedge lever.

Center screw

Lateral adjusting lever

4. Turn plane over. Check that iron's edge is aligned with throat opening. Use lateral adjusting lever to correct.

Blade not parallel

Blade bevel

5. Depth-adjusting knob raises and lowers iron in throat to set cutting depth.

Depth-adjusting knob

Thick shaving

Wide throat

Thin shaving

Narrow throat

Use deep blade setting to remove waste fast; shallow setting for final smoothing. Curve of blade cap curls and breaks shavings.

How to plane

Set the iron for a shallow cut. Place sole flat on work. Apply even pressure to both ends of plane and push it across surface. At the end of each stroke, release your pressure on front of the plane. Always plane with the grain; planing against or across it leaves a gouged and ragged surface.

To smooth broad surfaces, position plane at a slight angle to wood's grain. Hold the plane at this angle and push it along the surface parallel to the grain.

Shooting boards and jigs

C-clamp

Stop block

90°

8″

14″

20″

Work

Plane

A shooting board makes edge planing easy. Nail a narrow board on top of a wider one. Secure a stop block on top board with nails or screws. Place work against stop block so that edge to be planed extends over bottom board. Clamp entire assembly to workbench. With plane on its side, slide it along work until edge is trim and square.

A V-shaped jig holds stock lumber for planing. Brace the jig against a vise or attach it temporarily to the workbench with clamps, screws, or nails.

Although many of the tasks formerly done with specialty planes (for example, shaping moldings) are now done with power tools or in mills, a wide variety of special-purpose planes still exists. Some of these are single-purpose tools; others combine several cutting and trimming functions.

Among the single-purpose planes are the block plane (shown below) and the spokeshave (facing page). The bullnose plane (facing page) has an iron positioned at the front that cuts right up to an inside corner. Other types (not shown) include the trimming plane, a smaller version of the block plane. It averages around 3½ inches long and is used for small, delicate work. The scrub plane is similar to the smooth plane (p.38), but has a narrower iron. A hand router is used for cleaning waste from and smoothing three-sided, squared cuts such as dadoes and grooves (p.102). The multiple-purpose planes include rabbet and three-in-one planes (facing page).

Shop carefully with your specific needs in mind. A plane made of molded plastic, rather than exotic hardwood and brass, may be adequate. Choose a body that fits comfortably in your hand. Make sure that the tool adjusts easily and locks securely after it is adjusted. At home, keep the body clean of resin and shavings; maintain a sharp iron (pp.44–45).

Block plane

To bevel board edges, tilt tool 30° to 45° and move it in direction of grain. Bevel board ends first.

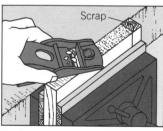

To plane end grain, clamp board between scrap wood; work from one end to the other.

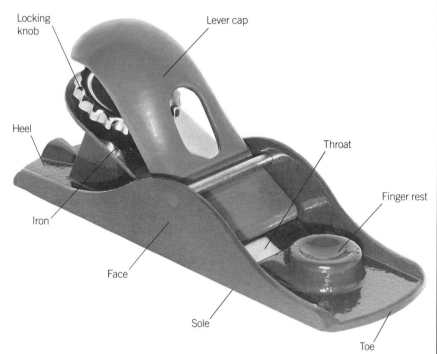

Locking knob

Lever cap

Heel

Iron

Throat

Finger rest

Face

Sole

Toe

Scrap

Adjusting a block plane

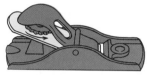

Blade   Throat

Turn locking knob counterclockwise to loosen lever cap. Make sure that blade is inserted with bevel up. Align cutting edge parallel to throat opening.

Adjust depth of cut by turning plane upside down and sliding the iron forward so that it protrudes from the throat a hair's breadth.

With plane upside down, check that iron edge is parallel to throat edge. Hold plane securely to maintain blade alignment, and tighten locking knob.

Resembling a bench plane, the block plane is smaller (about 6 inches long) and has its iron set at a lower angle, usually either 12½° or 25°. Unlike a bench plane, it cuts with the iron's bevel up. This makes it ideal for trimming end grain, although it will also bevel edges and smooth small milled areas. Because of its small size, the block plane is inefficient for smoothing broad surfaces; use a bench plane (pp.38–39) for such tasks.

Each time you use a block plane, check that the iron is razor-sharp (pp.44–45). To minimize splitting when working on end grain, first bevel the edges slightly; then, holding the tool at an oblique angle to the grain, move it straight across the work.

Rabbet planes

These planes create clean, square joints for woodworking and cabinetmaking. Although their shapes vary, they perform similar functions: both may be used to cut or trim rabbets and wide recesses, to trim and square inside corners, and to smooth edges and joints in moldings.

A duplex rabbet plane has different slots for positioning the iron. The forward position is for stopped cuts (cutting right up to the corner of a 90° angle), the second for straight planing and cutting. The three-in-one plane has only one blade position; the body disassembles as required for different cuts.

Duplex rabbet plane

Three-in-one plane

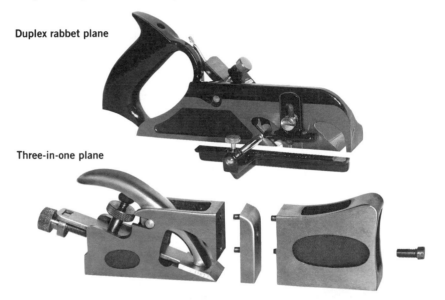

Rabbet plane cuts and trims rabbets and wide grooves. Set width of the cut by adjusting the fence.

Side rabbet plane is a compact tool that trims sides of grooves and rabbets for precise fit needed for square joints.

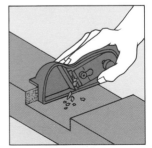

Bullnose plane iron extends to front of body; it's useful for trimming inside corners and rabbets in picture frames.

Spokeshave

The spokeshave was originally used to shape spokes for wagon wheels. Its wing-shaped body and small center-set blade smooth curved edges and do fine planing. Properly used, it can greatly reduce the need for sanding.

Buy a body with screws that govern blade depth. Blades and bodies come in straight, convex, or concave shapes to match different cutting tasks.

Work from the ends toward center, sliding downhill with the grain, for a smooth finish on curves. Planing uphill against the grain causes a ragged surface that requires further smoothing.

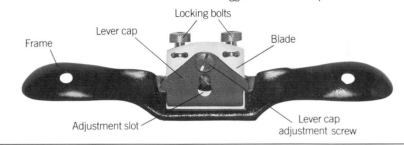

Scraper

This simple, inexpensive tool quickly becomes indispensable. Use it to trim fine shavings or to remove dried glue. A scraper will reduce time spent sanding by about 80 percent.

You can buy scrapers, or you can cut them from old saw blades or tempered sheet steel. Sharpen the edges as shown on pages 44–45.

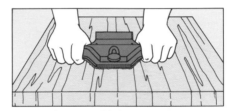

Rectangular scraper blades used in a spokeshave-like holder afford better control and protect hands from friction-caused heat. Curved blades smooth bowls and other round shapes.

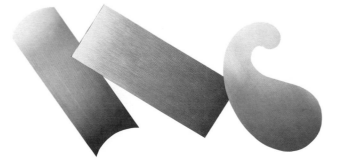

Hand scrapers are versatile smoothing tools that can be bought or made in various shapes (left). Properly sharpened edges have a rolled burr (above).

Files are used in metalworking to trim and smooth, as well as to shape and sharpen. They are classified by their shape, which often defines their use; their *cut,* which is the arrangement of the teeth; the overall length of the file; and the coarseness of its teeth. To confuse matters, sometimes the coarseness is also called the cut. Use large and coarse files for rough shaping and trimming, finer and

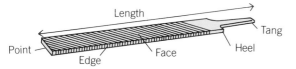

smaller ones for smoothing and sharpening. Never attempt to cut metal harder than the file's metal.

Shape. The most common profiles are flat, square, triangular, round, and half-round. The body may be *blunt* (the same shape from heel to point) or *tapered* (the body narrows from heel to point).

Cut. Teeth are arranged in ridgelike patterns referred to as single cut (*mill*), double cut (*bastard*), curved, and rasp (see right and facing page). Single-cut files have teeth in parallel diagonal rows. Double-cut teeth crisscross diagonally, forming a checkerboard. Curved teeth form parallel arcs. Rasp teeth are shaped into individual points. A standard file has teeth cut on the edges; if the edges are smooth and uncut, the file is called *safe.*

Length. Files are measured from *heel* to *point* (which may not actually be pointed), and the length affects the coarseness. On longer files the teeth and the spaces between them are proportionately larger. This means, for example, that a 12-inch bastard file is rougher than a 6-inch bastard file, even though they carry the same coarseness designation.

Coarseness, from roughest to smoothest, is rated as *bastard, second cut,* and *smooth cut. Coarse* and *dead smooth* ratings are not available in all types.
▶ **CAUTION:** Use handles with your files. The tangs are sharp enough to puncture your hand. And, despite the low profile of their teeth, files are cutting tools with multiple sharpened edges that can cut you as easily as they cut metal.

Types of files

Single cut is best for smoothing ferrous metals or for sharpening tools made of ferrous metal.

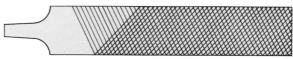

Double cut rapidly removes material from ferrous and nonferrous metals. Use it where a smooth finish isn't essential.

Curved teeth provide rapid material removal and a fairly smooth finish. Best for nonferrous metals, such as aluminum and brass.

Flat   Square   Triangular   Round   Half-round

Match file's shape to work's shape for greatest efficiency.

Care of files

Use a file card to brush accumulated debris from teeth. Thin sheet metal or stiff wire pushed between the ridges will also work. Rub teeth with chalk to reduce clogging.

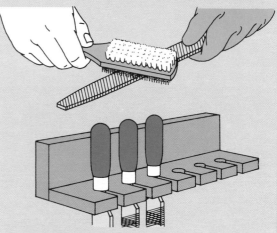

Store your files in slotted racks or protective sleeves. If scraped against each other, the teeth can be damaged — and they cannot be resharpened. Don't tap files against hard or metal surfaces to clean them.

Filing techniques

To shape or remove material, hold the file at both ends and at a slight angle to the work, and push it lengthwise, keeping file flat to avoid rounding edges. This is called *straight filing.*

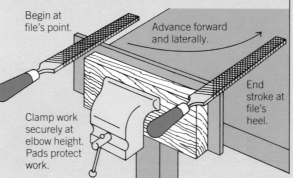

Begin at file's point.

Advance forward and laterally.

End stroke at file's heel.

Clamp work securely at elbow height. Pads protect work.

Draw filing produces a smoother finish. Hold file level and at a right angle to the stock. Push and pull it back and forth with steady pressure. Avoid rocking file over edges of stock.

Single cut bastard file

Rasps

Actually a file with quick-cutting, individually shaped teeth, a rasp is a good choice for trimming end grain, for rounding corners and edges, and for waste removal on wood, nonferrous metal, and plastic. The half-round style is the most versatile.

Rasps cut only on the push stroke. Match stroke pressure to hardness of material being worked: light for wood and plastic, heavier for metal. Because the high teeth leave a roughened surface, use rasps where appearance isn't critical. Or smooth surface with a double-cut file and an abrasive paper (p.50). Never try to cut metal harder than the rasp's metal.

Wood rasp

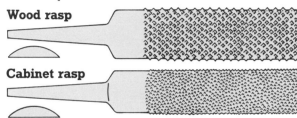

Cabinet rasp

Wood rasp's teeth are coarser than those of a cabinet rasp. Both come in a half-round shape that suits a wide variety of tasks.

Four-in-hand, or shoe, rasp is half rasp, half double-cut file.

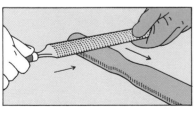

Flat side of half-round rasp trims flat planes and shapes outside curves. Apply even pressure through forward stroke; lift rasp for return.

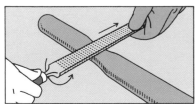

Round side shapes inside curves and enlarges holes. Ease pressure on rasp to cut less deeply as you near the final shape.

Surform

Somewhat resembling cheese graters, these variously shaped tools have open, edge-sharpened teeth. Shavings pass through the teeth without clogging them. Surforms can quickly shape or trim wood, soft metal, and plastic.

The most common frame shape, with handles front and rear, mimics the shape of a small bench plane. The frame may be steel or plastic. The blade hooks onto the back of the frame, and a screw secures it at the front. Although you cannot resharpen Surform blades, they are cheap and easy to replace.

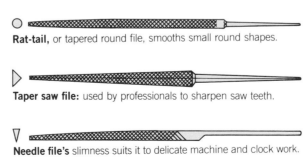

Straight-rasp plane

Block-type plane

Curved-rasp plane

Specialty files

Using the four basic variables of shape, length, cut, and coarseness, hundreds of special-purpose files have been created. For unusual jobs or for sharpening a particular tool, ask your supplier's advice; a file designed to accomplish that specific task may exist.

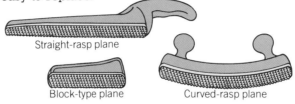

Rat-tail, or tapered round file, smooths small round shapes.

Taper saw file: used by professionals to sharpen saw teeth.

Needle file's slimness suits it to delicate machine and clock work.

Mower blade has integral handle and may be double or single cut.

Surform techniques

Change the angle of the tool to the work, and the Surform will produce different surface finishes.

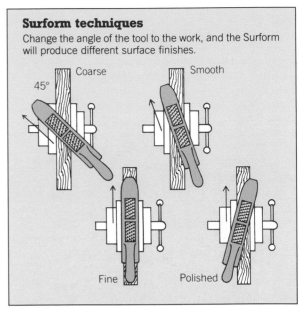

45°   Coarse   Smooth

Fine   Polished

Some specialty files are named for their function: chain-saw file, crosscut file. Other names describe the shape: rat-tail file, needle file. As with general-purpose files, the best technique is straight filing—cut on the push stroke, lift the tool on the return.

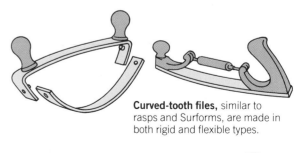

Curved-tooth files, similar to rasps and Surforms, are made in both rigid and flexible types.

Bent rifflers are available in triangular, half-round, round, and square styles for wood carving and metalworking.

In the sharpening process, you remove metal to create or restore a tool's cutting edge. Typically, this involves three steps: grinding, honing, and burr removal. Stropping, actually a form of polishing, puts a final razor-sharp edge on the blade.

Grinding is the shaping that turns a square-sided metal bar into a bevel-edged tool. The bevel's shape, its angle and length, is specific to each tool; honing refines this shape. A new tool may need to be honed—or reground—before its first use, but unless the tool is extremely dull or damaged, the original bevel will last a lifetime.

Honing, or whetting, is the main task of sharpening. Hone edges on an abrasive stone (see chart). Place the stone on a nonskid surface, such as a rubber pad, or clamp in a vise. Before you begin, spread a few drops of any non-food oil over the stone. When finished, pat the stone with a clean rag until the dirty oil (called *swarf*) is blotted up.

Follow the manual's cautions and instructions carefully when using a power grinder (p.73). Protect your eyes. Dip the tool in water to cool it; the wheel's friction can draw the *temper* (hardness) from it.

Test for sharpness by holding the blade to a light. A fully sharpened edge will not reflect light; incomplete sharpening glitters with bright spots.

Bevel grind

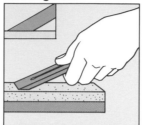

1. Honing. With bevel flat on coarse stone, pull blade across stone five or six times.

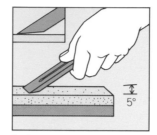

2. Secondary bevel. Raise blade 5°. Pull in one direction to refine cutting edge.

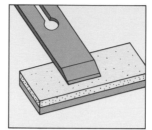

3. Removing burr. Turn blade over; rub flat on stone. Repeat steps 2 and 3 for razor edge.

4. Stropping. Drag bevel along smooth leather in one direction. Strop both sides of cutting edge.

Hollow grind

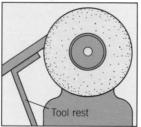

1. Grind on wheel with adjustable tool rest set to proper angle. Hone on flat stone.

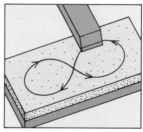

2. Clean burrs from both sides of bevel by lightly drawing figure 8's on a finishing stone.

Gouges

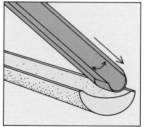

1. Slipstone's concave side hones bevel on convex side of gouge.

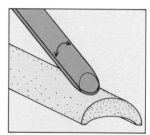

2. Reverse stone and gouge. Move gouge lightly back and forth to remove burr.

Kinds of grinds

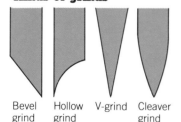

Bevel   Hollow   V-grind   Cleaver
grind   grind   grind

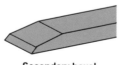

Secondary bevel strengthens edge.

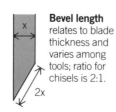

Bevel length relates to blade thickness and varies among tools; ratio for chisels is 2:1.

Bevel grind, found on chisels and plane irons, is also called *flat grind.* **Hollow grind** is sharper than **V-grind,** but more delicate. Both are used for cutlery. **Cleaver grind** combines sharpness and strength.

Cutlery or tool	Coarse honing	Fine honing	Finish honing	Sharpening stones
Plane irons, Chisels	Combination stone, coarse side	Combination stone, fine side	Hard Arkansas stone	
Axes, Hatchets	Combination ax stone, coarse side	Combination ax stone, fine side	Soft Arkansas stone	
Knives, carving	Combination stone, coarse side	Combination stone, fine side	Soft Arkansas stone	
Knives, kitchen, paring	Combination stone, coarse side	Sharpening steel		
Scissors, household	Combination stone, coarse side	Combination stone, fine side	Soft Arkansas stone	
Gouges	Slipstone, coarse side	Slipstone, fine side	Arkansas slip	

Household tools

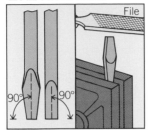

Restore screwdriver tips with file. If screwdriver's metal is too hard to file, repair with grinder.

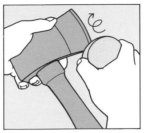

Sharpen ax by filing away nicks, then honing with ax stone (see chart). Use circular motion.

Stroke scissors forward diagonally from point to pivot. Use correct stone; keep bevel flat.

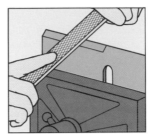

Mower blades can be touched up by hand with a specially designed file (pp.42–43).

Punches and awls

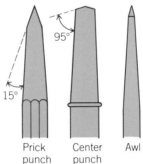

Prick punch   Center punch   Awl

Rotate handle to quickly hone needle-sharp points. Maintain proper angles (left).

Scrapers

1. File edges of scraper smooth and flat (p.42). Remove nicks to square edges.

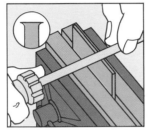

2. With firm pressure, draw round-shank screwdriver along edge, forming flat, even burr.

3. Curl burr back slightly by stroking length of scraper with shank at slight angle.

Twist bits

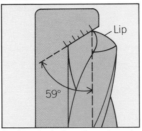

1. Check tip length and angle with special drill point gauge. Twist bits should measure 59°.

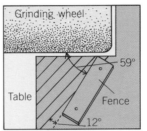

2. Set fence at 59° to face of grinding wheel. Mark parallel lines 12° from edge of fence.

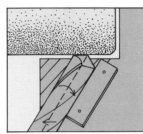

3. Start wheel. Hold bit against fence and wheel; roll it clockwise and swing it to 12° lines.

Knives

Draw edge across stone, maintaining bevel. Turn blade over, repeat. Finish edge by sliding it lightly along steel.

Auger bits

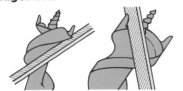

Use auger bit file for sharpening. File bevel only on lateral cutters; inside only of spurs. Don't try to sharpen lead screw.

Jigs

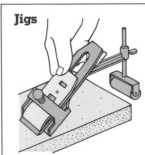

Rolling jig holds chisels and plane irons at proper angle (generally 30°) for honing. Roller aids movement.

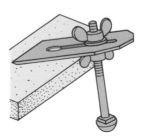

Carriage bolt and wing nuts are homemade substitute for rolling jig. Turn nuts to lock iron at proper angle.

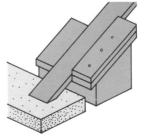

Wooden jig can be easily constructed. Cut block at proper angle; add brace to keep blade square.

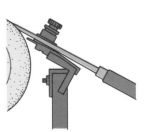

Grinding-wheel jig clamps blade in position; attaches to wheel's support rest. Use with hand-driven or power wheels.

Hand tools / Measuring and marking

Accurate measuring and marking is the most important aspect of any project. Properly measured parts fit together with ease; inaccurately measured ones result in a nightmare of adjusting and fitting—or starting over. There is wisdom and economy in the saying "Measure twice and cut once."

Learn proper technique and terminology. Lumber can be bought by the *linear,* or *running, foot* or by the *board foot* (a unit of volume, p.94). Pipe, however, requires at least three basic measurements, and possibly as many as six (p.216). Use the same set of tools throughout a project. The calibration of seemingly identical tools can differ by as much as ⅛ inch.

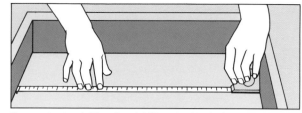

Compact retractable ruler. Add length of body (marked on case) to length of tape when taking inside measurements.

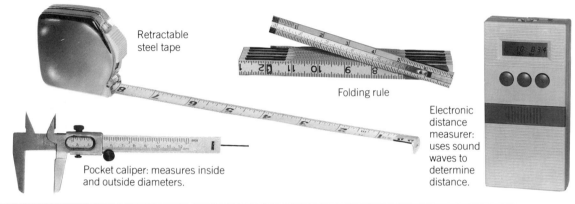

Retractable steel tape

Folding rule

Electronic distance measurer: uses sound waves to determine distance.

Pocket caliper: measures inside and outside diameters.

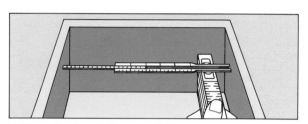

Folding rule, also called carpenter's (or zigzag) rule. Some models have a metal extension for measuring inside spans.

Marking and mortise gauges

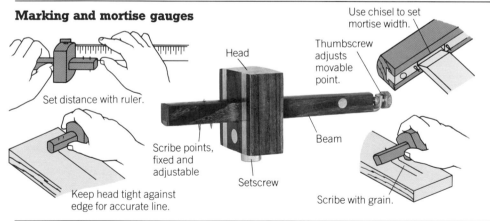

Set distance with ruler.

Keep head tight against edge for accurate line.

Head

Scribe points, fixed and adjustable

Setscrew

Beam

Use chisel to set mortise width.

Thumbscrew adjusts movable point.

Scribe with grain.

Mortise gauge has a pair of scribe points that mark two parallel lines at once. The head moves on the beam and can be set at a fixed distance from the board edge. Turn thumbscrew to adjust distance between scribe points. **Marking gauge** is similar to mortise gauge but has only one scribe point.

Scratch awl

Scribes lines, marks centers. Keep point sharp to ensure accuracy.

Chalk line

For long, straight lines, stretch chalk line taut between points. Snap center of line. Chalk dust traces line on surface.

Making a straightedge

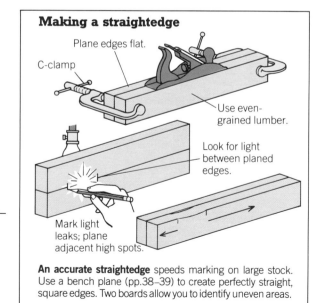

Plane edges flat.

C-clamp

Use even-grained lumber.

Look for light between planed edges.

Mark light leaks; plane adjacent high spots.

An accurate straightedge speeds marking on large stock. Use a bench plane (pp.38–39) to create perfectly straight, square edges. Two boards allow you to identify uneven areas.

Accurate angles

Properly measured, cut, and assembled angles are critical to strength and appearance. Protractor square locks in place for accurate marking. Try square is used to test, or *try,* squareness. The combination square's versatility is detailed at right. Rafter squares are printed with tables and formulas to calculate volume, lumber needs, and other information.

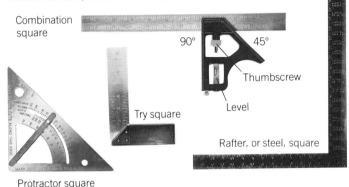

Combination square

90° 45°

Thumbscrew

Level

Try square

Rafter, or steel, square

Protractor square

Using a combination square

Use 90° angle to mark straight lines perpendicular to board edges.

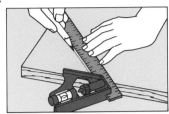

Mark miters by aligning the 45° angle on the board's edge.

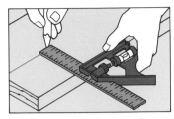

Improvised marking gauge. Set ruler; run 90° angle along board edge.

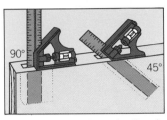

Measure depth by loosening thumbscrew and sliding ruler into hole.

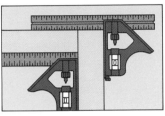

To test squareness of inside or outside corners, align frame as shown.

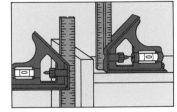

Level may be used horizontally and vertically to check level and plumb.

Ensuring level and plumb

Test surfaces for precise horizontals (*level*) or verticals (*plumb*) with a spirit level. Surfaces are level or plumb when the bubbles in the glass vials are centered in relation to marks on the vials. Test level for accuracy by turning it end over end; readings should be identical in both positions.

Levels come in lengths and shapes to suit various purposes. Shortest are the line level, small and light enough to hang on a string, and the torpedo level, which has level, plumb, and 45° vials along its 9-inch length; longest are mason's and carpenter's levels, which average 4 feet long. A circular level reads all horizontal directions at once; surface is level when bubble is centered in the round case. A multifunction level tests level and plumb and determines degrees of misalignment to within 0.5°.

Plumb bobs work simply by gravity. A weighted line attached to a fixed point will fall to a second point exactly beneath the first one.

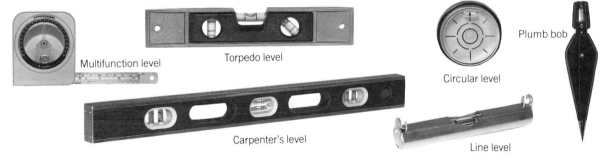

Multifunction level

Torpedo level

Circular level

Plumb bob

Carpenter's level

Line level

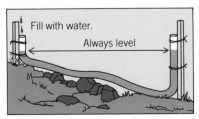

Clear tube partially filled with water finds level over uneven ground.

Line level centered on string (*line*). Adjust string until bubble centers.

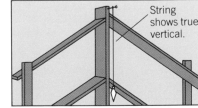

Plumb bob provides line for accurate uprights. Bob must fall unimpeded.

Hand tools/Marking angles and circles

Almost all do-it-yourself projects require a knowledge of simple geometry, so that angles can be measured and marked accurately, circles drawn, and tools set to cut at prescribed angles. The tools and techniques shown here will facilitate these tasks.

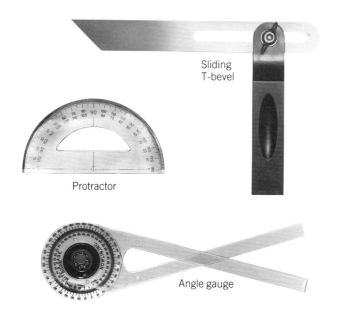

Protractor

Sliding T-bevel

Angle gauge

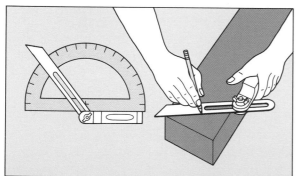

A sliding T-bevel is ideal for copying angles, drawing several lines at the same angle, and testing angles for accuracy. To set the blade at a specified angle, use a protractor.

Angles from a square

A rafter square can replace a protractor for laying out angles. Lay a straightedge from the 12-in. mark on the short arm to the indicated inch mark on the long arm's outer edge.

Long Blade	Angle
20¾"	60°
12"	45°
6⅞"	30°
3¼"	15°

12"

CAUTION: This technique is accurate enough for rough carpentry or outdoor projects. If precision is essential—say, in cabinetwork—use a protractor and a straightedge.

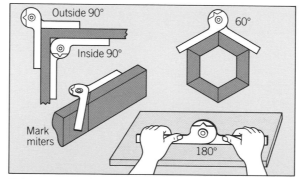

Outside 90°

Inside 90°

60°

Mark miters

180°

This versatile angle gauge sets and measures angles from 0° to 180°. Point arrow on head to angle needed, and legs automatically define it. Open legs to 180°, and gauge tells you if a surface is flat.

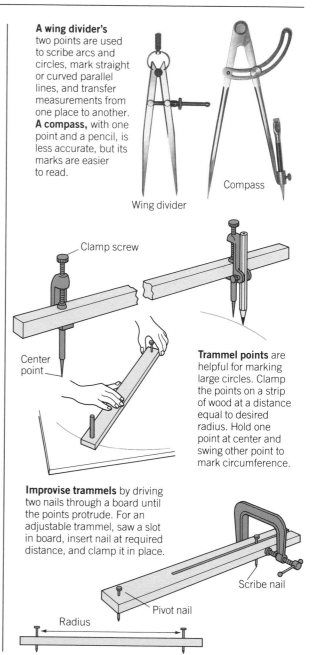

A wing divider's two points are used to scribe arcs and circles, mark straight or curved parallel lines, and transfer measurements from one place to another. **A compass,** with one point and a pencil, is less accurate, but its marks are easier to read.

Wing divider

Compass

Clamp screw

Center point

Trammel points are helpful for marking large circles. Clamp the points on a strip of wood at a distance equal to desired radius. Hold one point at center and swing other point to mark circumference.

Improvise trammels by driving two nails through a board until the points protrude. For an adjustable trammel, saw a slot in board, insert nail at required distance, and clamp it in place.

Scribe nail

Pivot nail

Radius

Workshop tricks

Professionals have developed a body of helpful lore that makes work go faster. The techniques given below will speed repetitive marking tasks, solve awkward measuring problems, and simplify the fitting and duplicating of contours.

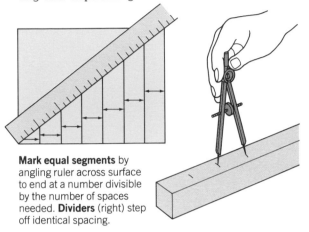

Mark equal segments by angling ruler across surface to end at a number divisible by the number of spaces needed. **Dividers** (right) step off identical spacing.

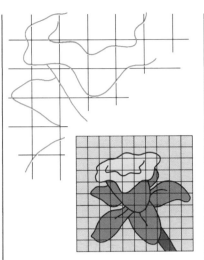

To reduce or enlarge patterns, place evenly spaced grid over design. Copy points where design crosses original grid onto a second grid at desired size.

Drawing a curve. Drive nail at top and ends of curve. Put stick against top nail parallel to base, another against top and an end nail. Tack sticks together. With pencil at juncture, push sticks along nails. Repeat on other side.

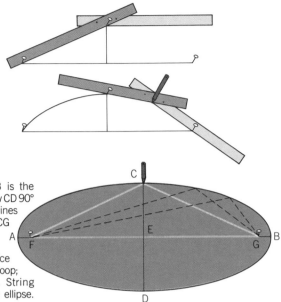

Drawing an ellipse. AB is the length, CD the width. Draw CD 90° to AB at center E so that lines halve each other. CF and CG are equal to half the length of AB. Put tacks at C, F, and G. Tie string (twice as long as FG) into a loop; place it around tacks. String guides pencil to draft an ellipse.

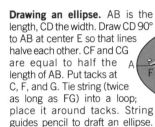

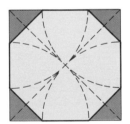

Hexagon. Draw a circle. With same radius, put compass point on perimeter. Strike six equally spaced arcs.

Octagon. Draw diagonals in square. Set compass to distance from corner to center, strike arcs from each corner. Draw eight lines connecting arcs.

Finding center of circle. With a square, draw a rectangle that touches circle. Center is point where diagonals of rectangle cross.

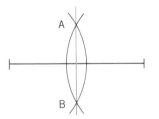

Halving line: From each end of line, draw intersecting arcs, then line AB.

Perpendicular line: Open compass to any distance. Place point on P, mark arcs at A and B. Open compass more than half the length of AB. With point on A, then B, draw arcs. Draw line from P to point where arcs intersect.

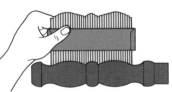

Contour gauge. Push the slim rods against a contour to duplicate its shape.

Trace irregular shapes with a compass. Follow contour with the point, transferring outline with pencil.

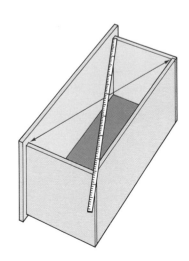

To test for squareness, measure diagonally. Adjust corners until measurements are identical.

Each abrasive—paper, metal wool, and powder—comes in various degrees of hardness and coarseness and is suitable for different tasks (see charts).

Papers. Traditionally called sandpaper, these are actually silicon carbide, aluminum oxide, emery, or garnet particles (*grit*) glued to a paper or cloth backing. Silicon carbide, which can be used wet or dry, is the hardest abrasive; garnet, the softest.

Abrasive papers are graded by number, which reflects the size of the grit particles. The higher the number, the finer the grit. Papers are either *closed coat* (grit spaced close together) or *open coat* (grit spaced widely and evenly). Use coarse open-coat papers for fast stock removal, fine closed-coat ones for soft substances—paint, aluminum, resinous wood—that would clog other papers.

Metal wools include steel, bronze, and copper. Steel, the most prevalent, is inexpensive, easy to work with, and comes in a variety of grades (see chart). Bronze wool (actually 97 percent copper) is used for tasks where the object will be exposed to, or submerged in, water. (Steel leaves behind tiny filaments, which rust and cause stains.) Copper wool, sold in supermarkets, is another corrosion-resistant substitute for steel.

Powders. Pumice, emery, and rottenstone are very soft abrasives. Mixed with a lubricant, they polish surfaces to varying degrees of gloss (p.123).

Abrasive papers

F = Fine (120-150) M = Medium (80-100) C = Coarse (50-60) EC = Extra coarse (30-40) SF = Super fine (360-400) EF = Extra fine (280-320) VF = Very fine (160-240)

	Uses	Aluminum oxide F	M	C	EC	Garnet (for wood) F	M	C	Emery cloth (for metal) F	M	C
Wood	Stripping; heavy sanding			●	●			●			
	Moderate sanding		●				●				
	Finish sanding	●				●					
Metal	Stripping; rust removal			●	●						●
	Light sanding			●	●						
	Deburring; cleaning	●	●						●		
	Finishing; polishing										●

	Uses	Aluminum oxide VF	F	M	C	EC	Silicon carbide (drywall) F	M	Silicon carbide SF	EF	VF
Plastic & fiberglass	Shaping				●	●					
	Light sanding			●				●			
	Finishing; scuffing	●	●					●			●
Drywall; plaster	Initial sanding							●			
	Finish sanding							●			
Varnish & paint	After sealer or primer	●								●	
	Between coats									●	

Steel wool

		Uses
4	Extra coarse	Cut, strip, clean metal, wood, tile
3	Coarse	Remove paint and other finishes
2	Medium coarse	Clean pipe threads, scrub floors
1	Medium	Remove rust, prepare surfaces
0	Fine	Clean nonferrous metals, tile
00	Very fine	Buff nonferrous metals, leather
000	Extra fine	Polish, buff furniture, chrome
0000	Super fine	Buff and smooth finishes

Powders

	Uses
Pumice	
Extra coarse	Buff and polish wood
Coarse	Smooth surfaces; remove dust and specks
Medium	Buff and polish final finish
Fine	Same as Medium
Extra fine	For highest luster on wood and metal
Emery	For buffing metal (also comes in stick form)
Rottenstone	For extremely high luster, glasslike finish

Using abrasives

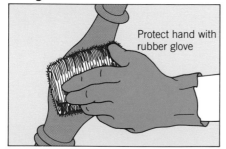

Coarse steel wool will quickly strip away dissolved finishes. Turn and fold the pad to expose fresh surfaces; discard when clogged.

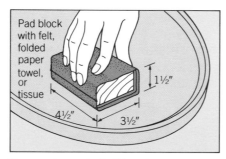

Tear sandpaper in half lengthwise and wrap around a padded block for ease of handling and to ensure flatness. Turn over when clogged.

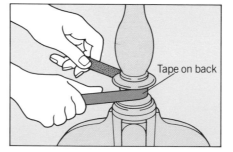

Cut sandpaper into strips or use abrasive cords to clean turned legs or chair rungs. Duct tape on back of paper will reduce tearing.

Pumice or rottenstone, mixed with oil, repairs light scratches and removes water marks or stains without damaging surrounding finish.

Power tools
and how to use them

Contents

Why not make life easier? For almost any do-it-yourself project there is a power tool that will perform faster, more efficiently, and with less effort than a hand tool. The following pages describe the major power tools, give some basic instructions for their use, and tell what to look for when buying them. Studying these pages should enable you to find the most appropriate tool for the work you want to do. You will probably want to purchase the tools you will be using most often, but you may find it more economical to rent tools you will use only for an occasional job.

Power tools/Electric drills

Its versatility makes the electric drill a wise choice for the homeowner's first power tool. Fitted with the proper bit or attachment, it can bore holes in almost any building material and perform many other operations, including driving screws, grinding, sanding, and polishing.

For best results, get a reversible model with variable-speed control. Reverse is useful in backing wood bits out of deep holes, in removing screws, and in reversing rotation on abrasive products to lengthen their life. The variable-speed control allows you to select the best drilling speed and to use a wider variety of special attachments.

Drill sizes. Electric drills come in various sizes, the most common of which are ¼, ⅜, and ½ inch. The size is determined by the largest bit shank that will fit into the chuck (the part of the drill that holds the bit). Drill power varies with size and model but typically ranges from ⅕ to ½ horsepower. Although speed usually decreases with increased size, torque (turning power) increases.

Because of its high speed, the ¼-inch drill is good for boring small holes and doing other lightweight jobs, but the ⅜-inch drill is a better choice for the homeowner, for it can handle most household jobs. With more power than smaller drills, the ½-inch drill can bore larger holes without overloading its motor. It turns at a lower speed, however, and is not so well suited for sanding and grinding, which require high speed.

Drill bits and attachments. You can use standard twist bits for drilling holes up to 1 inch in diameter in metal, wood, and most plastics. To drill into concrete, stone, brick, or plaster, however, you will need special carbide-tipped masonry bits.

A large variety of special bits and accessories is available for doing other jobs. Some of the most popular are described on the following three pages along with special-purpose drills. Although an accessory may do a job for which there is a specific tool, it may not do it as well or as easily as the specific tool. If you plan to use an accessory frequently, consider buying the proper tool instead.

Anatomy of a drill

Power/reversing switch

Twist bit

Holes for tightening bit with chuck key

Chuck

Trigger switch. In many models, the more you squeeze this trigger, the faster the drill spins.

Trigger lock

Masonry bits for drilling into concrete, stone, brick, plaster.

Chuck key clips onto cord to prevent loss or is stored in handle.

Electric drills come in a variety of models. The one shown here is a typical ⅜-in. reversible variable-speed drill. It will accept any of the bits and attachments shown on the following page.

Cordless drill

Rechargeable drills are convenient when working far from an outlet. A typical cordless drill will drive 50 ⅜-in. holes through 2-in.-thick pine before it needs recharging. Some models recharge in an hour or less.

With detachable battery pack, you can buy an extra power pack and recharge one while using other.

Recharging unit reenergizes the drill's batteries. Keep drill plugged in whenever it is not in use and it will always be ready.

Stops and guides

Detachable side handle provides added control. Adjustable depth gauge lets you drill to an exact depth. Drill guide keeps tool at correct angle. Vertical stand converts portable drill into a drill press for precise work. Drill stops do same job as depth gauge. Steel collar stop locks onto bit with a set-screw. Plastic stop is tightened with fingers.

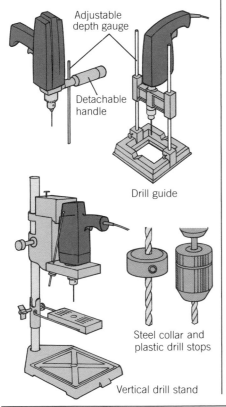

Adjustable depth gauge

Detachable handle

Drill guide

Steel collar and plastic drill stops

Vertical drill stand

Driving screws

To prepare wood for screws, drill holes for screw shanks, then pilot holes and, if desired, recesses for screwheads. Use two sizes of twist bit and a countersink bit or a single screw-pilot bit. Or use a tapered bit with adjustable countersink. To hide screwheads under wood plugs, use a plug cutter to cut plugs from scrap wood and a combination screw-pilot bit and counterbore to make the holes. Drive screws with a screwdriver bit.

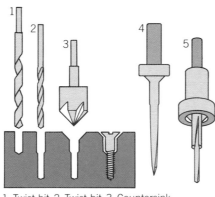

1. Twist bit 2. Twist bit 3. Countersink
4. Screw-pilot bit 5. Adjustable bit

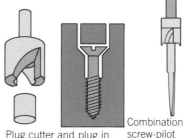

Plug cutter and plug in screw hole

Combination screw-pilot and counterbore

Special drill bits

Brad-point bits are ideal for woodworking; their center points give accurate starts. Hollow spiral bits are good for boring through walls to run electrical wires. Forstner bits cut flat-bottomed holes and are good for cutting overlapping or angled holes; use with drill guide only. Hole saws come in single cuplike shapes or in nests of rings. Step bits can be used to drill thin metal in place of several bits of increasing size. Spade bits bore wide holes.

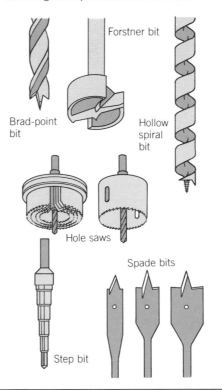

Forstner bit

Brad-point bit

Hollow spiral bit

Hole saws

Spade bits

Step bit

Hard-to-reach places

Flexible shaft attachment bends around obstacles and extends a drill's reach by 40 in. Drill bit extension can increase drilling depth by several feet. Right-angle attachment lets you drill in tight spots—for example, between joists.

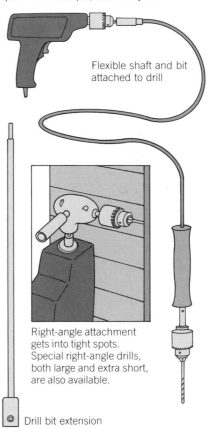

Flexible shaft and bit attached to drill

Right-angle attachment gets into tight spots. Special right-angle drills, both large and extra short, are also available.

Drill bit extension

Power tool maintenance. Most tools require little maintenance aside from using them properly and keeping them clean. Follow the manufacturer's recommendations. Use a tool only for its intended purpose and avoid forcing it beyond its capacity. Replace or sharpen any dull or damaged bits, blades, or other cutters. Never use the power cord to carry the tool or pull the plug. To clean a power tool, first unplug it, then wipe it with a damp cloth or sponge. Never submerge a tool in water or wipe it with solvents. If the tool's air vents become clogged, blow out the debris with compressed air.

Most modern tool motors are permanently lubricated and sealed and do not require oiling. On a few tools, however, you may need to oil certain parts, and you may be able to replace worn brushes or power cords or defective switches. Check your owner's manual.

Power tools/Drilling techniques

With proper use and a little care, your power drill—whether standard or cordless—can save you time and energy in drilling accurate holes. It can even pinch-hit for other tools you may need only occasionally. For basic drilling techniques, see the illustrated instructions at right. If you do your drilling on a workbench or table, clamp a piece of scrap wood under the work to keep from damaging the bench or tabletop. When drilling deep holes, occasionally withdraw the bit to clear it of debris.

Cordless tool maintenance. Many do-it-yourselfers invest in a cordless drill as either their only drill or as a second drill. To get the most out of your cordless drill or other rechargeable tools, take the following precautions: Use only the battery and charger that come with the tool; never attempt to switch batteries or chargers. Avoid dropping batteries, and never use a tool containing batteries as a hammer. To get longer battery life, turn the power off when you are not actually using the tool.

Recharging. When recharging a tool, make sure the outlet you plug it into has current; if the outlet works on a wall switch, make sure the switch is on. Don't charge—or store—a tool where the temperature is below 40°F or above 105°F. Batteries rely on chemical reactions that slow down in the cold and stop altogether below 32°F. In high temperatures, vapors are released from the battery pack and its storage capacity is diminished. Occasionally let the battery discharge completely before recharging, or in time it may resist taking a full charge.

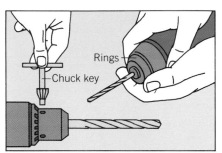

Basic drilling. 1. Insert a bit fully into the chuck. Unless your drill has a power-driven automatic chuck lock, turn the chuck key in all three holes so that all the jaws make contact with the bit. Or use a pair of chuck-locking rings.

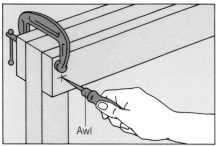

2. Make sure that the piece you are working on is firmly supported or clamped down. If possible, arrange the work so that you are drilling straight down or straight ahead. Make a starter hole with an awl or nail so that the drill bit won't wander.

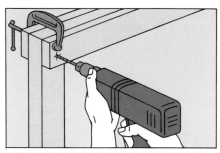

3. Place the bit in the starter hole and begin drilling at slow speed (if your drill is equipped with variable speed). Increase speed after the bit has penetrated the surface. Push firmly, but don't force the drill to cut too fast.

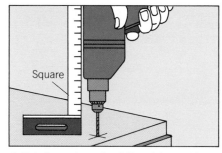

4. To help you keep the drill straight, position or clamp a try square or combination square near the drill and keep the drill parallel to the square. If you are drilling at other than a 90° angle, use a commercial drill guide or a T-bevel.

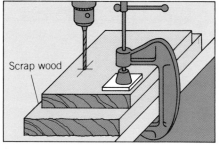

5. When drilling all the way through a piece of wood, clamp a piece of scrap wood behind it to prevent it from splintering. Or drill into the wood only until the point of the bit emerges, then complete the drilling from the other side.

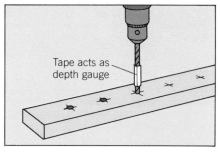

6. To make a hole of the depth you want, use a commercial drill stop or gauge, or wrap a piece of masking tape at the appropriate height on the bit. Then drill until the stop, gauge, or tape touches the surface of the material being drilled.

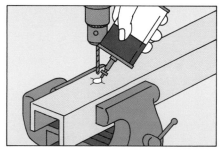

When drilling into iron or steel, start by marking spot with nail set and hammer. Put drop of light oil on mark; drill slowly, withdrawing bit and adding more oil from time to time. For ¼-in. to ½-in. holes, start with ¼-in. bit, then go to desired size.

To drill into stone, brick, or concrete, use a carbide-tipped masonry bit (preferably in a ½-in. drill) and drill slowly to prevent overheating. Occasionally withdraw bit partway from hole to clean off debris and cool with a sprinkle of water.

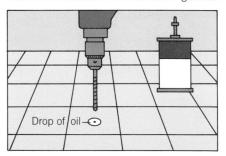

Before drilling into ceramic tile, break through glaze with punch or nail and apply drop of oil. Drill with special bit on slow speed. Before drilling glass, surround spot with circle of putty and fill with turpentine or kerosene. Use drill stand.

Special driving tools

Grinding, sanding, and polishing
In addition to drilling holes and driving screws, your drill will sharpen tool blades, sand wood, or polish metal. Simply attach one of the many accessories available for such jobs and use the drill freehand or in a stand.

In addition to the basic electric drill, there are many special drills, including the driver drill, which is specially designed to both drill holes and drive screws—with the change of a bit. If you drive a lot of screws, you may prefer to get a separate electric screwdriver, such as the handy cordless model shown below.

If you won't be driving many screws, you can simply use screwdriver bits in a variable-speed drill. Bits are available for driving standard slotted-head screws, Phillips-head screws, and others (p.82).

Possibly the most versatile hand power tool is a three-way combination tool that can be turned into a drill, screwdriver, or hammer drill with the twist of a collar. As a screwdriver, it regulates the torque to drive a screw with a special slip clutch. As a hammer drill, it bores easily into masonry, using a jackhammer action to drive the rotating bit into the work, breaking up any tough aggregate. The hammer drill (which you can also buy or rent as a separate tool) turns into a chisel or gouge when you insert the proper bit and set the drill for hammer action.

Finally, there is the brad nailer, which drives brads into most surfaces with the push of a button. It works best in softwoods and plywood; it may not be powerful enough to drive fasteners completely into some hardwoods and particleboards.

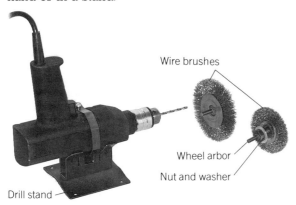

Wire brushes

Wheel arbor

Nut and washer

Drill stand

Bolt drill stand to workbench and clamp drill securely into it before using drill with grinding, polishing, or buffing wheels.

To use wheel on drill, fasten it to arbor with washer and nut, then lock it into place in drill chuck with chuck key.

Rotary file

Rotary rasp

Slotted screwdriver bit with spring-loaded, cup-like finder that covers screw head and keeps screwdriver blade in slot.

Phillips-head screwdriver bit

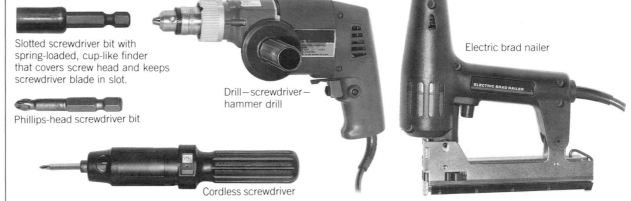

Drill—screwdriver— hammer drill

Electric brad nailer

Cordless screwdriver

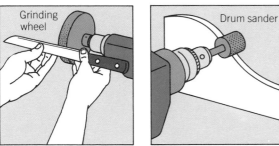

Use grinding, polishing, or buffing wheels as you would those on a full grinder (p.73). Wear a face shield.

Grinding wheel

Drum sander

Use rotary files or rasps, drum rasps, grinding stones, or any sanding devices either in a bolted-down drill or in a hand-held drill.

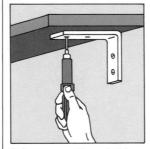

Drive screws with an electric screwdriver or use a drill, driver drill, or combination tool with a screwdriver bit on slow speed.

Concrete block

Use hammer drill for concrete. As you press against the drill, hammer action drives spinning bit into the masonry three times as fast as standard drill.

Chisel out recesses for hinges or remove plaster or tile with a hammer drill fitted with a chisel bit and set for hammer action.

Door

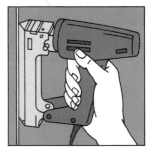

Brad nailer is handy for nailing in tight places or when doing a lot of nailing, as in reupholstering a chair or hanging insulation.

Power tools/Drill press

To keep a hand-held drill steady and at the correct angle is often difficult, but the drill press eliminates the problem. It holds the drill bit steady and allows you to drill to precise depths and at exact angles by simply adjusting the height or angle of the machine's table. The drill press consists of a variable-speed motor that turns a chuck along with its bit or other accessory. A feed lever lowers the chuck; when the lever is released, the chuck rises. Drill presses come in bench and floor models. Both must be bolted down for greater stability.

Bits and other accessories are available for a wide variety of jobs. Use only those designed for a drill press. Never exceed an accessory's maximum rpm rating; generally use low speeds for boring large holes or drilling in hardwoods or metals. Always wear safety glasses when using a drill press.

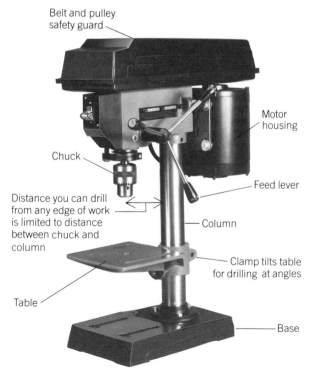

Belt and pulley safety guard

Chuck

Distance you can drill from any edge of work is limited to distance between chuck and column

Table

Motor housing

Feed lever

Column

Clamp tilts table for drilling at angles

Base

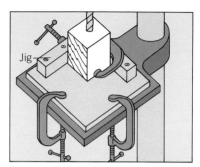

Jig

Clamp work securely to drill press table to avoid accidents and ensure accuracy. If needed, build a jig and secure it to table with clamps or other hardware.

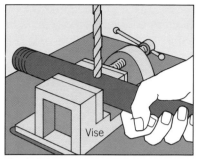

Vise

Use a vise to secure pipe or other hard-to-clamp work to the table of a drill press. A variety of special vises are available for drill press use.

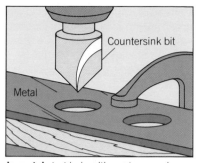

Countersink bit

Metal

In metal start hole with center punch. Drill with low speed and light pressure. When finished, remove burrs and sharp edges with a countersink bit.

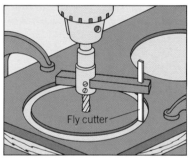

Fly cutter

Fly cutter makes large holes in wood, metal, or plastic. Clamp work. Position tip of bit, and lock cutter blade on arm. Use slow speed; keep hands away.

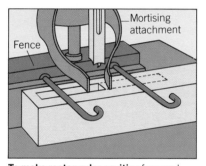

Mortising attachment

Fence

To make rectangular cavities for wood joints, slide the work along the fence of a mortising attachment and make a series of square holes in multiple passes.

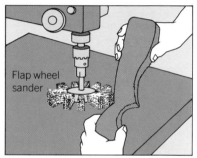

Flap wheel sander

For sanding curves, attach a flap wheel sander to drill press. Abrasive brushes radiating from hub will round and smooth any contours in work.

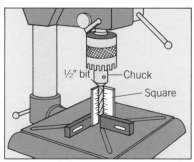

½" bit — Chuck

Square

Adjustments: 1. Put ½-in. bit into chuck. Place square in front of bit, then at side, to check that it is perpendicular to drill press table. Adjust, if needed.

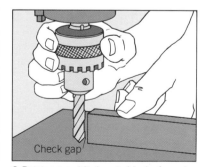

Check gap

2. Rotate same bit close to block of wood. If you see a wobble in gap between bit and wood, rechuck bit and test again. Replace chuck if wobble persists.

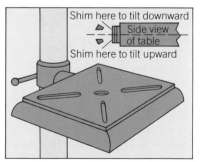

Shim here to tilt downward

Side view of table

Shim here to tilt upward

3. Check angle of table. If table tilts to front or back, have it squared at a machine shop. Adjust temporarily by inserting paper or foil shims, as shown.

Saber saw

Fitted with the appropriate blade, the saber saw can make straight or curved cuts in wood, metal, plastic, ceramic tile, leather, and other materials. It can rip a long piece of wood, crosscut a 2 x 4, or start a cut in the middle of a plywood panel. It can

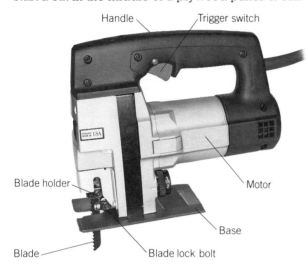

Handle
Trigger switch
Blade holder
Motor
Base
Blade
Blade lock bolt

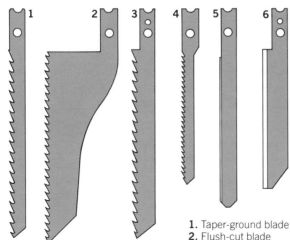

1. Taper-ground blade
2. Flush-cut blade
3. Rough-cut blade
4. Scrolling blade
5. Knife-edge blade
6. Carbide-grit blade

also be fitted with special rasps, files, and sanding accessories to smooth the edges you sawed with it.

The saw. Also called a bayonet saw or portable jigsaw, the saber saw consists of a motor-driven gear assembly that moves a shaft and its blade rapidly up and down. Generally, the blade moves in a straight up-and-down motion, cutting on the upstroke, but on some saws the blade can be adjusted to move in a small or large orbital pattern, cutting into the work at a slight angle on the upstroke and pushing away from the work on the downstroke. This results in faster cutting with less vibration and less wear on the blade. Some models also feature a scrolling mechanism that lets you turn the blade 360° while cutting without having to turn the entire saw. This gives greater control when cutting delicate scrollwork and allows you to work in confined areas. Still other models let you tilt the base to a 45° angle for making miter cuts.

A saber saw is rated according to its power (generally between 2 and 4½ amperes) and the length and speed of its blade stroke (the distance the blade travels up and down). The length of the blade stroke generally ranges from ½ to 1 inch. The longer the stroke, the more teeth are engaged in the cutting and the faster the cut. Blade speed is measured in strokes per minute (spm). A saw with adjustable speed lets you regulate blade speed to suit the job. Generally, use slower speeds for plastics and hard materials such as metal or thick stock. Some models have built-in sawdust blowers. Cordless saber saws are efficient and highly portable.

The blades. The more teeth per inch (tpi) in a saw blade, the more smoothly—and slowly—it cuts. Wood-cutting blades generally range from 3 to 14 tpi and metal-cutting blades from 14 to 32 tpi. Use a narrow scrolling blade to cut sharp curves and a taper-ground blade for ultra-smooth cuts. Carbide-grit blades are available for cutting masonry, ceramic tile, steel, fiberglass, and other materials; there are special knife-edge blades for rubber, leather, cork, vinyl, and cardboard. A flush-cutting blade will cut right up to a wall or other obstruction.

Score cut line with utility knife to prevent splintering. Or tape area to be cut, mark cut line on tape, and make cut with a fine-toothed blade at high speed.

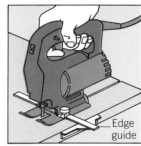

When cutting with grain, use edge guide or guide saw against a clamped-down board. If you hit a knot, feed blade slowly and let it do the cutting; don't force.

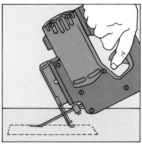

Begin an internal cut by tilting saw forward and resting front of its base on work. Start saw at medium speed and very slowly pivot blade into work.

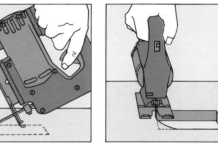

Continue cut at faster speed, if you wish. At each corner of cut, turn saw in a curve to cut next straight side. Later go back and trim off corner pieces.

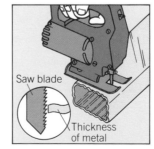

If you cut thin metal, use blade that will have at least two teeth in contact with edge of work at all times, or cut will be rough and blade may get damaged.

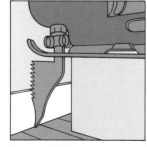

To cut molding on wall, use a flush-cutting blade. Prop the saw on a block of wood that is of a height that lets the blade reach just to the floor.

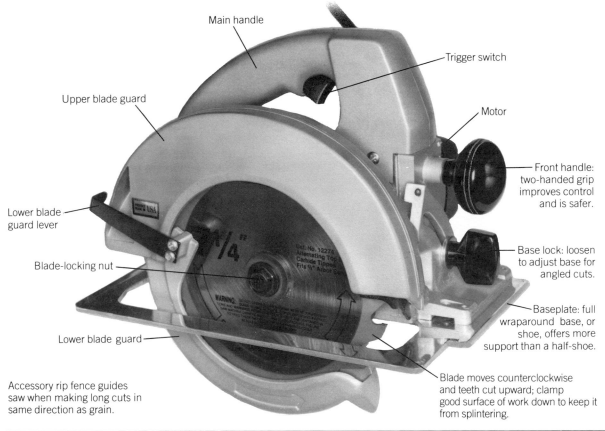

Main handle

Trigger switch

Upper blade guard

Motor

Front handle: two-handed grip improves control and is safer.

Lower blade guard lever

Base lock: loosen to adjust base for angled cuts.

Blade-locking nut

Baseplate: full wraparound base, or shoe, offers more support than a half-shoe.

Lower blade guard

Blade moves counterclockwise and teeth cut upward; clamp good surface of work down to keep it from splintering.

Accessory rip fence guides saw when making long cuts in same direction as grain.

The portable circular saw can make straight cuts in almost any material. It does most of the jobs otherwise done by cumbersome table saws or radial arm saws, but it can be carried to the job—the work need not be carried to the saw.

A motor enclosed in a case with handles drives a disc-shaped blade. Blade guards and locking devices make the saw safe—provided they are always used. Standard and cordless models are available.

The size of a circular saw is determined by the diameter of its blade—anywhere from $3\frac{3}{8}$ to $16\frac{5}{16}$ inches. The $7\frac{1}{4}$-inch models are the most popular and practical. You may find a small cordless version, called a trim saw, handy for such jobs as cutting thin plywood and moldings.

Blade speed is measured with no load (when not cutting). The more powerful the motor, the closer the saw comes to its no-load speed when cutting, and the smoother and faster it cuts. Generally, a 1-horsepower (or 11-ampere) motor drives a $7\frac{1}{4}$-inch saw efficiently. Weight also helps a saw cut smoother, but the saw should not be too heavy to handle easily.

A blade exists for every job. Generally, the more teeth per inch a blade has, the smoother it cuts. Blades are available with carbide-tipped teeth; these cost more, but they cut smoother and last longer between sharpenings. There are special abrasive blades for cutting masonry and metal.

Combination blade can be used for cutting across or with grain of wood. Large teeth cut fast, but produce rough edges. This blade is generally supplied with a new saw.

Rip blade is designed for fast cutting with the grain, has deep gullets, which clear waste efficiently and bind minimally. Not good for cutting plywood.

Crosscut blade for cutting across grain. Fine, alternately beveled teeth produce smooth cuts. Can also be used for plywood, wood veneers, and composition board when a plywood blade is not available.

Hollow-ground planer blade, good for crosscuts and miter (angled) cuts. Provides more clearance for cut because it is thinner between cutting edge and center of disc. Cuts slowly but smoothly.

Flooring blade for cutting rough lumber or flooring. Its tough carbide-tipped teeth are specially ground for added strength. It will even cut through an occasional nail.

Preparing the saw for cutting

Before using a circular saw, you must usually change and adjust the blade. Unplug the saw, pull back the lower blade guard, and push the teeth into a piece of scrap wood. Remove the blade-retaining fastener and carefully slide off the old blade; slide on the new one with its teeth facing forward and up. Replace the blade-retaining fastener and tighten it.

Set the depth of the cut so that the blade projects no more than ¼ inch below the stock being sawed. Use the scale on the baseplate as a rough guide to the proper blade setting.

If you want to make angled cuts for bevels or miter joints (p.108), you must also adjust the baseplate of the saw. Generally, this involves loosening a knob or wing nut and tilting the base so that when you use the saw, the blade

enters the work at the desired angle. Scales are provided near the adjusting knob or wing nut. They may be used as guides in setting the saw for cutting at a 45° angle, but these settings are only approximate. If you do use them, cut a piece of scrap and check the angle with a protractor before working on good stock. If you want an accurate angle, set it yourself, using a protractor and a sliding T-bevel (p.48).

To ensure smooth, accurate cutting with a circular saw, keep the bottom of the baseplate clean. Use lacquer thinner (if the base is metal) or mineral spirits (if it is plastic) to get rid of stubborn dirt, gum, and pitch. Give the bottom of the baseplate a coat of paste floor wax (not car wax) to help it glide smoothly along the work and make it easier to clean.

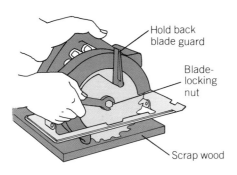
Hold back blade guard

Blade-locking nut

Scrap wood

Replace blade, using wrench supplied with saw, as described above. Always unplug saw before adjusting or changing blade.

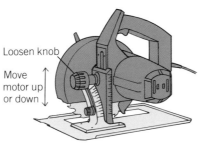
Loosen knob

Move motor up or down

Adjust depth of cut on this type of saw by releasing locking knob and sliding motor up or down a track, then tightening knob.

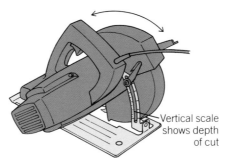
Vertical scale shows depth of cut

On other types of saws, adjust depth of cut by releasing a lever or loosening a knob or wing nut near rear of saw and moving motor in an arc.

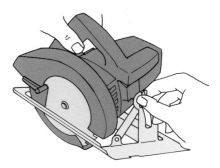

To saw at 45° angle, loosen tilt lock and adjust base to position indicated by notches or scale at bevel adjustment device. Test angle on scrap.

Circular saw safety

When used carelessly, a circular saw can be dangerous, but with a little care it will save you hours of hard work. Wear safety goggles, a dust mask, and earplugs when working, and observe all the general safety tips covered on page 19. In addition, make sure that the blade is securely attached. Remove the blade wrench. Also check that the lower blade guard, which retracts during a cut, is snapping back into place freely.

Always set the blade to the depth needed for the particular job; don't just set it to its full depth

and leave it there regardless of the depth of a cut. Although the latter practice seems convenient, it is dangerous; when a wide area of the blade moves against the work, it can create enough friction to cause kickback—a violent pushing back of the saw in the direction of the operator and a prime cause of circular saw accidents.

Other measures you should take to avoid kickback are: Make sure that the blade is sharp and clean; support the work adequately; clamp the work to a firm surface; don't saw wet wood; and

be especially deliberate when you are sawing warped or knotty wood.

Maintain a firm footing and never reach too far with the saw. Stand to the side so that you will be out of the way if the saw does kick back. Keep a firm grip on the saw; start it before the blade enters the work, and guide it straight along the cut line. Release the trigger immediately if the saw starts to bind. At the end of a cut, hold the tool firmly to keep it from dropping. Wait for the blade to stop before removing it from the work.

Power tools/Using a circular saw

Making simple cuts

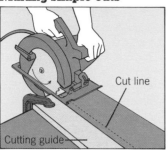
Cut line
Cutting guide

1. Mark cut line on back of work and clamp work face down over scrap wood. Set blade to cut through work and barely into scrap. Use rip fence, or else clamp or tack a straight board or other guide parallel to cut line at a distance equal to space between blade and edge of baseplate.

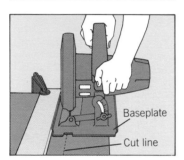
Baseplate
Cut line

2. With the saw turned off, rest its baseplate against the guide and touch the blade to the cut line to confirm exact placement. Back saw away a bit, turn it on, and when it reaches full speed, push it gently but firmly into cut line.

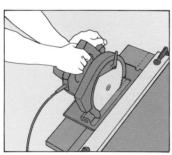

3. Whenever possible, hold the saw with both hands. Don't force cut; let the blade and the weight of the tool do the work. If the saw sticks, pull it back a bit and wait for the blade to return to full speed before continuing. If saw motor sounds strained, slow down.

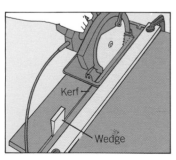
Kerf
Wedge

4. If wood is green or wet, the kerf (slot cut by blade) may close up and bind blade, possibly causing kickback. If kerf does close, stop saw and hammer a slim wedge into kerf behind saw to keep path open and avoid further binding.

Making other cuts

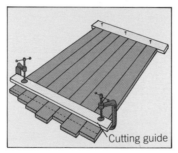
First cut

If stock is too thick for saw to cut through, make two passes. Cut one side of piece to slightly over half the thickness of the wood, then turn work over, align saw with first cut, and finish the job.

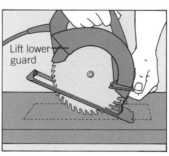
Cutting guide

To cut boards to same length, butt their squared ends against a straight strip of wood fastened to the work surface. Mark cut line across all boards; clamp or tack down a cutting guide, and saw all boards with one pass.

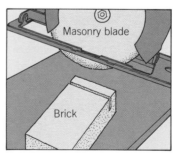
Lift lower guard

For interior cut, set blade depth. With saw in one hand, lift lower guard with other. Rest saw on rim of baseplate. Begin above work; lower blade slowly. Release guard when plate is flat; saw with both hands. Use handsaw in corners. **CAUTION:** Hand is near blade; use extreme care.

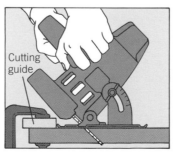
Cutting guide

On bevel cuts, long side of work is at top because blade tilts under the baseplate to keep saw safe. Mark cut line accordingly. Cut just beyond waste side of guideline. Use cutting guide for greater accuracy and safety.

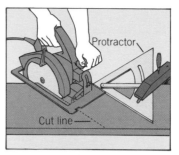
Protractor
Cut line

For diagonal cut, as in miter joints (p.108), use a protractor to set exact angle of cut, then mark cut line and clamp or tack down a guide fence (use protractor itself if it is a sturdy metal one). Make sure that the clamps are out of the way of the saw.

Two boards

Adjoining miters can be cut on two thin boards by overlapping the pieces face to face, clamping them firmly, and then cutting them together. This method ensures an exact fit. When working with molding, clamp the pieces back to back.

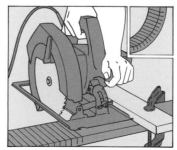
Masonry blade
Brick

To cut masonry, use a special masonry blade. Bricks can be sliced to fit any space. Cut concrete blocks, limestone, and ceramic tiles in several passes; start with shallow cut and increase depth on each subsequent pass.

To bend wood around a corner, make a series of parallel cuts as deep as wood is thick, less 1/8 in. Measure distance equal to radius of curve from end of stock and make first cut. Raise end of stock until kerf closes. Make other cuts as far apart as distance from raised end to table.

Miter saw

Cutting grooves

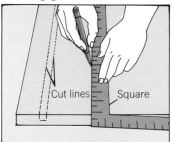

1. To use circular saw for cutting grooves and dadoes (p.102), mark the width and depth of the cut. Measure from edge of saw base to blade, mark distance on wood; clamp work to a solid surface, and fasten cutting guide to cut the line farthest from edge of work.

Cut lines   Square

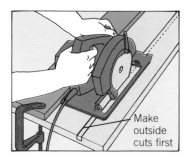

2. Set blade for exact depth of cut and make first cut. Then turn off saw and relocate cutting guide so that the blade will fall at the opposite side of the proposed cut. Make a cut along the guide.

Make outside cuts first

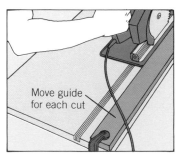

3. Make a series of parallel passes between the first two. Reset the cutting guide for each pass. Even though these inside cuts can be made freehand, cutting against a guide gives you more control and helps prevent accidents.

Move guide for each cut

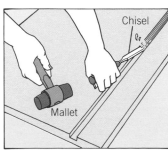

4. Saw should remove most of wood between outside cut lines. Use a chisel and a mallet to remove any remaining waste and to smooth bottom of groove.

Chisel

Mallet

If you will be making a large number of angled cuts for miter joints in doorframes, moldings, or picture frames, you will save time and materials by buying or renting a miter saw. Designed for cutting wood at various angles, this saw works quickly and precisely, but should generally not be used on metal.

Popularly called a chop saw or power miter box, the miter saw is basically a circular saw on a low metal stand. The round table on the stand turns to different angles along with the blade above it. The blade can be lowered by means of a handle to cut through wood clamped to the table. You can set the saw for any angle between 45° and 90° and make multiple cuts without resetting.

Miter saws come in various sizes. The most popular holds a 10-inch blade, which cuts a 2 x 4 at a 45° angle and a 2 x 6 at a 90° angle. Most saws come with a combination blade that cuts smoothly enough for most carpentry jobs. For an extra-smooth cut, try a carbide-tipped blade or a planer blade.

Before using your miter saw, bolt or clamp it down firmly. Also, follow the manufacturer's instructions to check the saw's 45° angle setting and the 90° angle between the blade and the fence.

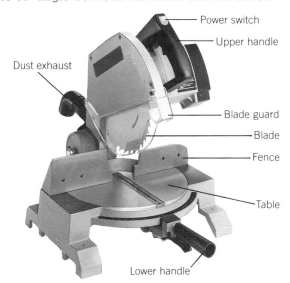

Power switch

Upper handle

Dust exhaust

Blade guard

Blade

Fence

Table

Lower handle

Cutting with a miter saw

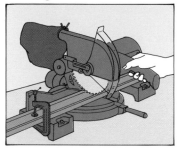

To set angle for cut, rotate saw table with lower handle and lock it in place. Mark work for cutting and clamp it firmly against saw fence. Turn saw on, let blade come to full speed, and move upper saw handle down to bring blade into work. Keep free hand away from blade area.

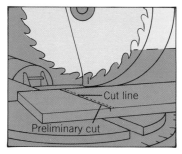

Because blade guard covers cut line, making it difficult to line up saw teeth, you should make a preliminary rough cut a fraction of an inch beyond cut line on the waste side. Lift handle and check location of cut, then shift work accordingly and make actual cut.

Cut line

Preliminary cut

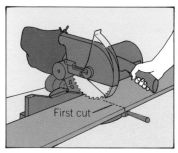

If a board is too wide to fit mouth of saw, cut it in two passes. Make first cut as deep as you can, then turn the board, carefully align it again, and make remaining cut along the same line.

First cut

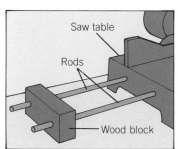

If work is too long to be supported on table, use an extension. If none is available for your saw model, make your own by passing two metal rods or pipes through a block of wood and into holes in base of saw.

Saw table

Rods

Wood block

An all-purpose, heavy-duty tool, the reciprocating saw is capable of cutting almost any material. It is ideal for rough-cutting lumber or firewood and for such construction jobs as sawing through walls to install windows, doors, air conditioners, or plumbing work. In the reciprocating saw, the blade is clamped to the end of a shaft that moves back and forth in line with the body of the tool.

Some reciprocating saws operate at only one speed—about 2,000 strokes per minute (spm)—or at either of two set speeds; others can be adjusted for a number of speeds. Variable speed is best. A few models can also be adjusted for reciprocal (back and forth) motion or orbital (moving slightly away from the work on the return stroke) motion. For best results, use low-speed reciprocal action for cutting metal, medium-speed reciprocal action for plastics and plastic laminates, and high-speed orbital action for wood and composition board.

Blades. Reciprocating saw blades range in length from 2½ to 12 inches and in purpose from cutting metal up to ¾ inch thick to cutting wood up to 12 inches thick. Use the shortest blade that will do the job, and be sure that the blade is suitable for cutting the material at hand.

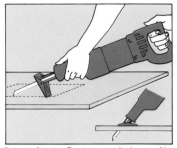

Basic cuts. Grasp saw handle with one hand and neck of saw with other. Hold base firmly against work with blade in air. Pull trigger switch and push blade into work.

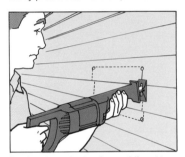

Internal cuts. Rest saw on its base with blade just above cut line. Some saws have tilting base; with others you must rest saw on edge of base. Start saw; slowly pivot blade into work; make cut.

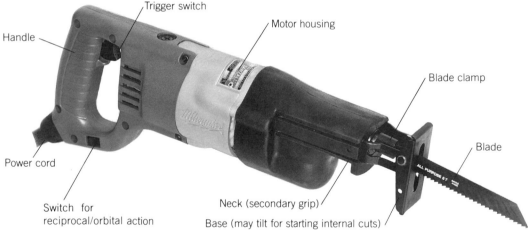

Trigger switch

Motor housing

Handle

Blade clamp

Blade

Power cord

Switch for reciprocal/orbital action

Neck (secondary grip)

Base (may tilt for starting internal cuts)

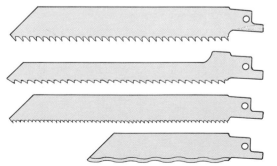

Coarse-toothed blade for rough cuts

Fine-toothed blade for smooth cuts in wood, plastic, and hard-board

Hacksaw blade for metal

Knife blade for cutting leather, rubber, cloth, and linoleum

Cutting through walls. Check that no wiring or plumbing is in area to be cut. Bore holes at corners of planned opening, insert saw blade into one of them, and cut through to other side.

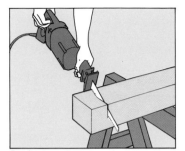

Cutting through aluminum siding. Use special blade at slow speed. Again, avoid pipes and wires. Keep hands off metal parts of saw while cutting in case you do hit an electrical wire.

Flush cuts. On some reciprocating saws, blade can be moved to outside of base with an offset blade adapter. This lets you cut flat against a wall or floor, as shown here.

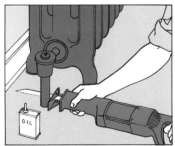

Cutting pipe. Before starting, add a few drops of light oil to cut line. With special fine-toothed blade, cut at low speed, stopping now and then to withdraw blade and add more oil.

Band saw

The fast-cutting band saw utilizes a flexible steel blade, in the form of a loop, that is driven clockwise around wheels inside the casing of the saw, thus providing a continuous cutting edge. Fitted with the proper blade, the band saw will make curved or straight cuts in wood, plastics, aluminum, copper, and sheet metal. It will square the end of a

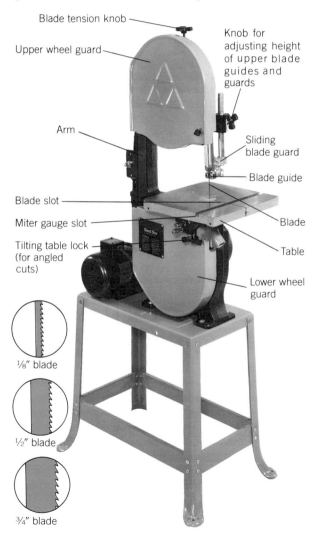

Blade tension knob

Upper wheel guard

Knob for adjusting height of upper blade guides and guards

Arm

Sliding blade guard

Blade guide

Blade slot

Miter gauge slot

Blade

Tilting table lock (for angled cuts)

Table

Lower wheel guard

⅛" blade

½" blade

¾" blade

heavy beam or slice through it lengthwise, or do intricate scrollwork. In order to cut metal, the saw must be equipped for multiple speed. Metal must be cut at low speed—about 300 feet per minute (fpm)—in contrast to about 3,000 fpm for wood.

The size of a band saw is determined by the diameter of its wheels, which is slightly less than the distance between the blade and the arm. Most band saws are large and cumbersome, but smaller homeowner models are available. These compact models can usually make cuts in stock up to 4 to 6 inches wide instead of 12 to 24 inches, as do the larger professional models.

Blades come in widths from ¹⁄₁₆ inch to 1 inch. For straight, fast cutting in thick stock, use a wide, coarse-toothed blade. For cutting curves, change to a narrower blade—the narrower the blade, the tighter the turn it can make.

When operating the saw, set the upper blade guide no more than ¼ inch above the work. The sliding blade guide and backup rollers support the blade as the work is pressed against it and helps guard against accidental hand contact with the blade. Only finger pressure is needed to feed 1- to 2-inch work into a sharp blade. Never use a dull blade. The extra pressure required to push the work into and past a dull blade increases the likelihood of accident.

The band saw can be equipped with a removable rip fence for making long cuts, a removable miter gauge for straight or angled crosscuts, and a tilting table (or head) for beveled cuts. The space between the blade and the upright arm often dictates the way work can be cut. You may have to turn the work upside down to make certain parts of the cut. If you have to make a long cut in one direction and a short one in another, do the short cut first, then back the work away from the blade, and reposition the work for the long cut.

Portable horizontal band saws are available for cutting metal. You can rent one if you need to cut a lot of pipe or bar metal or if you have many reinforcing bars (rebars) to cut for a concrete foundation.

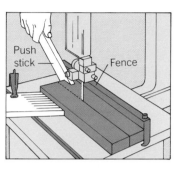

Push stick

Fence

Rip cuts. To cut along wood grain, position work against rip fence. Hold work in place with feather boards (p.65). Stand facing blade, but slightly to left (if blade breaks, it could fly off to the right). Move work into blade with push stick (p.65).

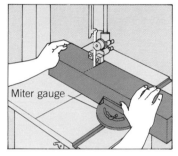

Miter gauge

Crosscuts. When you make cuts across the grain, hold the wood against miter gauge and adjust gauge to correct angle. Push stock into blade. Keep both hands at least 3 in. from blade at all times and pay attention. This saw cuts most materials fast.

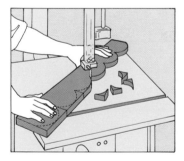

Curved cut. Holding work firmly with both hands, position it and move it against blade carefully. Stay just outside of cut line. Avoid backing out of a cut; when you must, turn saw off first and back out slowly and carefully, or you may pull blade off wheels.

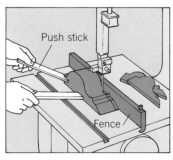

Push stick

Fence

Identical pieces. Saw thick piece of stock to desired shape. Then slice into thin pieces. To do so, slide shaped piece along rip fence and make as many cuts across thickness of piece as required. In this way, identical pieces can be made even of intricate curves.

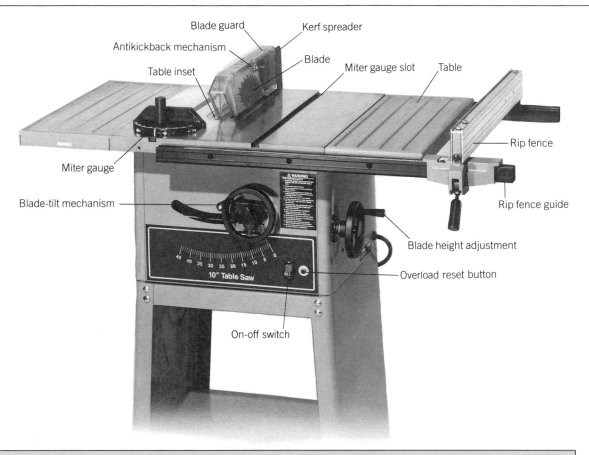

Blade guard · Kerf spreader · Antikickback mechanism · Blade · Miter gauge slot · Table · Table inset · Rip fence · Miter gauge · Rip fence guide · Blade-tilt mechanism · Blade height adjustment · Overload reset button · On-off switch

10" Table Saw

The most widely owned of all the large stationary tools, the table saw, or bench saw, contains a motor-driven circular blade mounted under a rigid table. The blade protrudes from a slot to cut work passed over it. A removable rip fence and miter gauge keep the work aligned. A table saw excels at precise, straight cuts. You can use it to rip long boards and to crosscut wide panels. You can raise or lower the blade to cut through thick or thin stock or to a precise depth, or tilt it for an angled cut.

For safety, a table saw has a blade guard, a splitter, and an antikickback mechanism. The guard shields the user's hands from the blade and face from flying chips. The splitter, or kerf spreader, prevents the kerf (the opening made by the blade) from closing and jamming the blade, causing the work to kick back toward the operator. The antikickback mechanism may be sharp fingerlike projections, spring-loaded pawls, rotating cams, or one-way wheels. The spreader and antikickback mechanism are part of the blade-guard assembly.

The size of a table saw is determined by the diameter of the largest blade it accepts—ranging from 8 to 16 inches and even larger. A popular size for the home workshop is 10 inches, which will cut through a board up to $3\frac{1}{2}$ inches thick.

Table saw blades are generally the same types as those used for portable circular saws (p.58). Also available are specialty blades, such as the dado head that can cut dadoes, grooves, and rabbets (pp.102–103) in a single pass.

Adjustments and use. Before using your saw, thoroughly familiarize yourself with how it works. Read the owner's manual carefully and follow the instructions for installing and adjusting the machine. Align the table, miter gauge, rip fence, and blade-tilt mechanism properly before making a cut. Use only sharp, clean blades to ensure safe, accurate work.

When operating a table saw, feed the work into the blade against the direction it is turning. Try to plan your work so that you are cutting from large, easy-to-control pieces instead of cutting small pieces into even smaller ones.

Table saw safety

Partly because of its popularity, the largest percentage of workshop accidents involves the table saw. Therefore, always use extreme caution when using one. In addition to the precautions noted on page 19, observe the following:

• Turn the saw off and unplug it before making adjustments or changing blades.
• Before restarting the saw, tighten all clamps and levers and remove any tools from the table.
• Stand to one side of the blade when sawing, not in front of it. Never reach across the blade.

• Use the blade guard for all through cuts.
• Never work freehand. Always hold the stock against the miter gauge or rip fence, and use push sticks, clamps, or jigs whenever your hands will come within 6 inches of the blade.
• Keep hands out of direct line of the blade.
• When you finish a cut, turn off the motor; don't touch the blade until it stops completely.
• Never clear away scraps with your fingers; do it with a stick that is at least 2 feet long.
• Avoid cutting warped or knotty wood.

Safety devices

Use pushers and hold-downs to handle stock on a table saw and to keep your hands away from the blade. You can cut pushers from solid wood or ¼-in. plywood. To make a feather board, saw one end of a 1 x 6 at a 60° angle; cut 8- to 10-in.-long slots ¼ in. apart in that end.

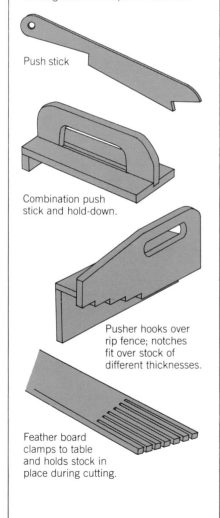

Push stick

Combination push stick and hold-down.

Pusher hooks over rip fence; notches fit over stock of different thicknesses.

Feather board clamps to table and holds stock in place during cutting.

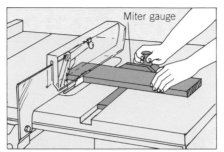

Crosscutting. Set miter gauge at 90°. Stand out of direct line of blade, hold work firmly against table and face of miter gauge with one hand; start saw and let it reach full speed, then push gauge and stock slowly forward with other hand.

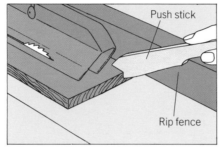

Ripping. Set fence for desired width and hold work against fence as you push it through saw blade with a push stick. Keep hands and body out of line of blade. Do not release work until all stock has completely cleared blade.

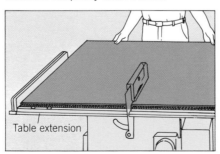

Large panels. Work must be fully supported. If panel extends beyond saw table, rig sawhorses to match the table's height and have someone hold panel as you cut. If you frequently cut large panels, consider buying a table extension.

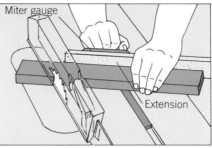

Miter cuts. Set miter gauge at desired angle, and proceed as for crosscut; hold work tightly against miter gauge—it may pivot or slide. To help control work, screw wood extension at least 1 in. wider than miter gauge to its face. Line with sandpaper.

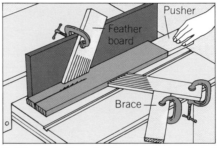

Holding work. If you don't have perfect control of work with your hands and push sticks, control stock by clamping braces and feather boards against it. Use scrap wood of same thickness to push work under feather board and past blade.

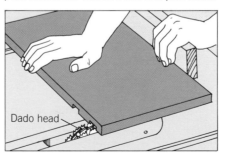

Grooves, dadoes, and rabbets. Cut in several passes or use dado head consisting of two outside blades and the necessary number of inside chippers. Install so that tips of chippers don't touch blades or each other; change the table insert.

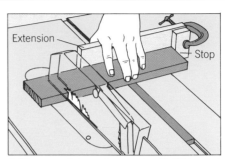

Cutting several pieces to same length. With wooden extension on miter gauge, clamp wood block to it at desired distance from blade to act as a stop. (Never use rip fence as stop.) Butt squared end of each piece in turn against stop; make cuts.

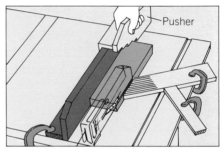

Bevel cuts. To make a bevel (angled) cut, tilt the saw blade to the desired angle, making sure that the blade guard will not hit the blade. Always position the fence or miter gauge on the side that the blade tilts away from.

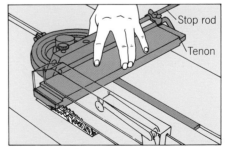

Tenons. Set dado head to height of tenon shoulder. Cut first side of tenon (p.104), then turn stock and cut opposite side. Adjust dado head if necessary, and cut two adjacent sides. To control length, use a stop rod on miter gauge.

Power tools/Radial arm saw

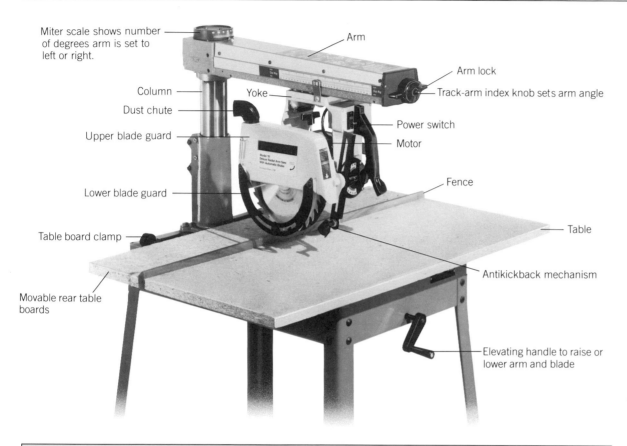

Miter scale shows number of degrees arm is set to left or right.

Arm

Column

Yoke

Arm lock

Track-arm index knob sets arm angle

Dust chute

Power switch

Upper blade guard

Motor

Lower blade guard

Fence

Table board clamp

Table

Movable rear table boards

Antikickback mechanism

Elevating handle to raise or lower arm and blade

Although it does much the same work as a table saw, the radial arm saw has distinct advantages. Most important, the blade enters the work from above; thus it is easy to watch the cut being made. In crosscutting, instead of pushing the work past the blade, you move the blade itself.

A radial arm saw is a circular saw suspended from a track on a metal arm over a wooden table. The motor and blade can be moved along the arm or locked in any position on it. The arm itself can be positioned at any angle for mitered cuts. The blade can be tilted to make bevel cuts or turned to a horizontal position to saw into the edges of stock. In this position, the saw can be fitted with other cutters for drilling, grinding, or sanding, or shaping moldings.

The size of the saw is determined by the largest blade it will accept. Blade types are similar to those used in portable circular saws. Professional models range up to 24 inches, but a good size for a home workshop is 10 or 12 inches. So-called portable models are available; although fairly heavy, they can be moved to the work site without too much difficulty.

Adjustments and use. Before operating a saw, familiarize yourself with the tool and make all adjustments called for by the owner's manual. Each time you use the saw, adjust the blade: lower it into the kerf (cut) so that the teeth are ⅛ inch below the saw table, then raise it ¹⁄₁₆ inch. When the blade is tilted for an angled cut, you'll have to make a new kerf in the saw table by lowering the moving blade. Afterward, adjust the blade for the actual cut in the same manner.

When making a crosscut, the blade of a radial arm saw cuts through the saw fence. Whenever a cut is made at a different angle, the blade will make a fresh cut in the fence. A slot will then be left for all similar cuts. The fence will eventually have to be replaced, but only infrequently. In making any kind of through cut, you also cut a fraction of an inch into the saw table. If the type of cutting you plan will leave cuts all over the surface of the table, tack down a temporary hardboard covering.

Radial arm saw safety

Like any power tool, a radial arm saw can cause accidents if operated carelessly. In addition to the precautions listed on page 19, always:
• Tighten all clamps, knobs, and nuts before starting the saw; remove tools from the table.
• Use only sharp blades, and keep the blades and the blade and arbor flanges clean.
• Use the fence to support or guide the work, and keep your hands out of the path of the saw blade.
• Avoid reaching around the blade or touching it before it comes to a full stop.

• Use the blade guard, splitter, and antikickback mechanism; use a push stick for narrow rips.
• When ripping, use the splitter and antikickback mechanism; feed the work into the blade against the direction of its rotation.
• When finished crosscutting, push the cutting head to rear of track; turn off and unplug saw before making adjustments or changing blades.
• Consider installing a *spring return,* a device that helps prevent the blade from continuing toward the operator after the cut is finished.

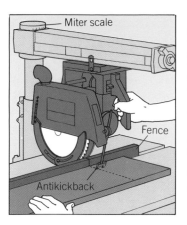

Basic crosscut. Lock arm at right angle to fence (0° on miter scale) and push blade to back of arm. Position work against saw fence with cut line at kerf (cut) in fence. Set the antikickback mechanism about ⅛ in. above work. Hold work against fence with one hand (four fingers on top of work and thumb against edge).

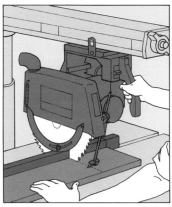

Turn on power and let blade reach full speed. Still holding work in place with one hand, grasp saw handle with free hand and pull blade slowly forward until it has just cut through the work. Then push blade to rear of arm; turn off power. Use the built-in brake to stop blade before removing the work or touching the blade.

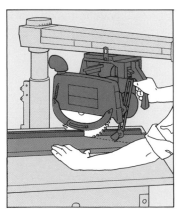

To cut diagonally, as in a miter joint (p.109), proceed as for crosscut, but move arm to desired angle and lock it into place. Position work and blade so that you are holding work on side away from direction of cut and so blade will move away from hand as it cuts through stock.

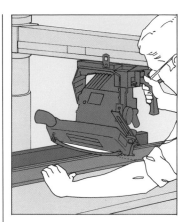

To make bevel cut, tilt motor and blade to desired angle and lock into place, and then make cut as usual. You can make a compound bevel cut, such as those used for crown molding (p.99), by both tilting the blade and resetting the angle of the arm, then making a crosscut, as shown here.

Rip cuts. For cuts up to 10 or 12 in. wide, lock arm at right angle to fence. Swivel motor and blade so that blade is between fence and motor, parallel to fence (in-rip position). Slide motor and blade along arm until blade is the desired distance from the fence. Lock into position. Using push stick, slide work along fence and into blade against blade rotation.

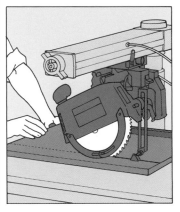

For wider rips, (up to 18 to 24 in., depending on saw), swivel motor and blade so that motor is between fence and blade, parallel to fence (out-rip position). Proceed as for in-rip cut, but feed work from opposite side of table so that it moves against rotation of blade. Because work is wide, you may feed it with hands, but keep them well out of blade's path.

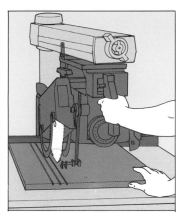

Grooves can be cut by raising blade to saw only partway into stock. (For large pieces, use the in-rip or out-rip position.) Cut a dado or rabbet (p.102–103) by making several passes with a single blade or one pass with a special dado head. In addition to dado-head assembly (p.65), there are other one-piece heads for making shaped cuts and decorative edges.

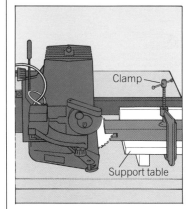

Horizontal cut across end grain is done by raising arm and swinging motor and blade 90° to horizontal position (with blade parallel to table). Build support table to hold work at least 1½ in. above saw table; secure it to saw table in place of rip fence. Clamp the work to the support table, adjust the blade height, and pull blade slowly into work.

Clamp

Support table

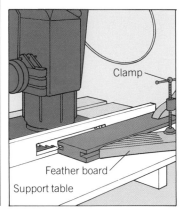

To rip horizontally, build a support table with fence slotted for blade. From in-rip position, turn motor so blade is horizontal at desired height. Move blade through slot far enough to get desired depth of cut, and lock it. Position work along fence, steadying it with feather board (p.65). Turn on saw and feed work into blade with push stick.

Clamp

Feather board

Support table

Power tools / Router

A motor turns a router's chuck at very high speeds, ranging from around 18,000 to 30,000 rpm. The chuck holds a *collet* that can be fitted with a variety of bits to cut grooves, trim edges, form recesses, shape moldings, and otherwise cut wood and plastic laminate. The bits are set for depth of cut by an adjustment on the router body. Routers come in two types: standard and plunge-cutting.

Router motor horsepower ranges from ½ hp for light woodworking to more than 2 hp in professional models. A low-powered router can do many jobs a high-powered router does, but it does them slower or in stages requiring several shallow passes.

What to look for when buying. Collets come in three sizes: ¼, ⅜, and ½ inch (the diameter of the bit shank the collet will hold). For light woodworking, ¼ inch should suffice; a collet that also takes larger shanks gives the tool more versatility.

Handles come in two styles, knob or D-shaped, and they may be mounted high or low on the router body. Test and decide which you prefer. Consider the placement of the on-off switch; it is best located where you can operate it without moving your hand. Also consider the ease of bit installation.

Practice on scrap wood to get the feel of the most efficient cutting speed. The motor's sound is a good guide; the bit should cut with only slight reduction in motor speed. Move the tool at a steady pace. Too slow movement may burn the wood and overheat the bit; too fast overloads the motor.

Safety. Wear goggles or a face shield and a dust mask. Or rig your wet-dry vacuum (p.76) to collect the dust. Protect ears with earplugs. Clamp the work and any jigs or guides securely. Watch for knots and nails; they can cause kickback, a sudden movement away from the intended path.

▶ **CAUTION:** The bit turns and cuts very fast; always keep fingers clear of it. Unplug the cord when changing bits or cutters. Make sure to lock the bit tightly in the collet.

Maintenance. Occasionally blow dust from the motor and the collet area with an air compressor, or extract it with a vacuum extension tool. Keep the collet area and bit shanks clean of dirt, pitch, and grease; wipe with mineral spirits (lacquer thinner if the dirt is stubborn). If you detect vibration or wobbling, check the ball bearings, collet, and bit shanks for wear. Take the tool to a repair shop.

Motor

Switch

Depth adjusting ring

Handle. Keep clean; grasp firmly.

MODEL 1001 ROUTER BASE

Collet. Keep free of dirt and chips

Depth stop scale

Depth stop lock knob

Base. Wax occasionally for friction-free movement.

Bit

Bit

Standard router bit always extends below base. To start an interior cut (plunge cut), tilt router, start motor, and lower whirling bit into work.

Plunge router bit remains above base, so tool can be positioned on work. When motor is turned on, router automatically lowers bit to depth set for cut.

Guiding and moving a router

To cut accurately, a router must be guided by an edge guide attached to the base, a bit with a pilot that moves against the edge being cut (opposite page), a straight piece of wood clamped to the work (below), or a template. Free-hand routing is for making signs or for other crafts.

In straight cut, move tool from left to right.

Straight piece of wood

Move router counterclockwise on outer edge, clockwise when cutting inside shape.

Making router cuts

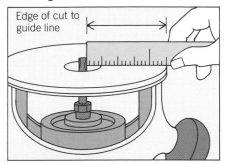

Positioning guide. Measure from edge of bit to edge of router base. On work, mark a line that distance from edge of cut; place straight-edged wood on line as guide (see next picture).

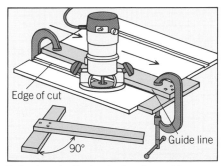

To begin cut with standard router, rest base on work with bit not quite touching. Turn on motor, move bit into work; continue bit into crosspiece of homemade guide to prevent splintering.

To cut groove in a narrow piece of wood, support the router base by clamping a block of scrap wood to either side of the work. A commercial edge guide is shown.

Routing a circle can be done with the same type of edge guide by keeping its two points touching the rim of work. Or use a circle guide, which requires drilling a hole in center of circle.

Router bits

When buying, consider how much you'll use a bit. For occasional use, a high-speed steel bit is fine; for frequent use, a costlier carbide-tipped bit stays sharp longer.

Bits are measured three ways: width of cut, depth of cut, and shank diameter.

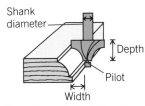

Care. Clean all-steel bits with mineral spirits. After first removing bearings, wipe off laminate glue with lacquer thinner. Store bits, working end up, in shank-size holes drilled in a block of wood. A dull bit will damage your router and your work; have it professionally sharpened.

Straight bits

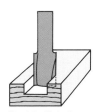

Double-flute for dadoes, grooves, and general stock removal

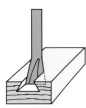

Stagger-tooth for plunge cutting dadoes, grooves, and slots

Grooving

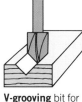

Dovetail creates strong joints for drawers, shelves, cabinets.

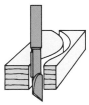

Hinge butt for dadoes, rabbets, hinge mortises, plunge cuts

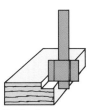

V-grooving bit for lettering, signs, picture frames

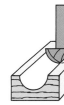

Core box for fluting and reeding surfaces; ornamentation

Piloted bits

Rabbeting cuts stepped edges for joints in drawers and cabinets.

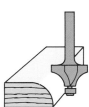

Beading for decorative edges on tables, frames, and moldings

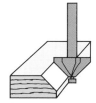

Cove makes decorative edges; with matching bit, drop-leaf joints.

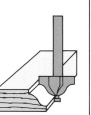

Corner-round or rounding-over bit for softening and decorating edges

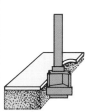

Chamfer cuts angle to make concealed joints, edges, moldings.

Roman ogee for decorative edges on furniture of different periods

Laminate bits

Four-flute single trims plastic laminate for countertops.

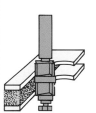

Four-flute double trims laminate on both sides of material.

Power tools/Sanders

Although hand sanding can produce beautiful results, it requires time and skill to get a smooth, straight surface. Electric sanders make the job quicker and easier.

Belt sander. A fast-working tool, the belt sander is ideal for smoothing a large surface, trimming off a bit of excess wood, or stripping old finish. It can also be used with a special belt on metal or plaster (but not wallboard).

The tool has two drumlike rollers that are fitted with abrasive belts. One of the drums is powered by a motor; the other is spring-loaded to provide correct belt tension.

The tool's size is expressed by its belt size. Generally, the longer and wider the belt, the heavier and more powerful the sander. The area of the belt that contacts the work is backed by a pad called a platen. A sander with a large platen is easier to control on flat surfaces but may be cumbersome when sanding edges.

Finishing sanders. These sanders are used to put a satinlike surface on a workpiece before finishing or to smooth it between coats of finish. The abrasive paper fits over a soft pad, and a motor moves the pad back and forth or in an orbital motion. Some models can be switched from one type of motion to the other. The orbital motion sands faster but may leave minor whorls. The slower back-and-forth motion leaves a smoother surface. Styles include large models used with two hands and small units that fit the palm of a hand.

Belt and disc sanders. You can buy or rent a combination belt and disc sander that bolts to a workbench or sits on the floor for sanding small workpieces or unassembled parts of larger units. This fast-cutting tool trims and shapes as well as smooths. The disc sander table can be tilted as much as 45°. It usually comes with a miter gauge for holding work against the sanding surface at the proper angle. Near the end of the belt sander is a backstop to keep the work from being thrown across the room if it slips from your grasp and to keep both the work and your fingers from getting trapped between the belt and the frame. The sanding belt itself can be raised or lowered to fit the job.

Heavy-duty, hand-held disc sanders are also available for automobile body work and for fast removal of excess wood or paint. You may want to buy or rent one for a special big job, such as removing old paint from the outside of your house.

Abrasives. Start a job with a coarse grade of abrasive and then go to a finer grain. Use a sanding belt, disc, or sheet designed to fit your sander. Finishing sanders usually take a quarter, third, or half sheet of abrasive paper; you have to cut it to fit. You can buy sheets to fit your sander exactly, but they will cost more.

Safety. Never set a sander down until it has stopped moving. Even if a sander is equipped with a dust bag, you should still wear a dust mask and protective glasses. Empty the dust bag frequently; an overfull bag will impair the sander's filtering efficiency. Whenever you change from sanding wood to sanding metal you should empty the bag; sparks from the metal could ignite the wood dust.

Belt sander

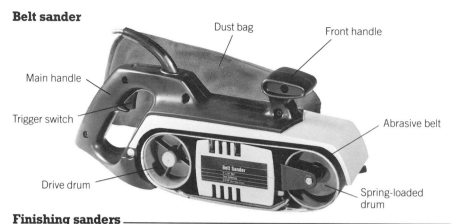

Dust bag — Front handle — Main handle — Trigger switch — Drive drum — Abrasive belt — Spring-loaded drum

Finishing sanders

Belt-disc sander

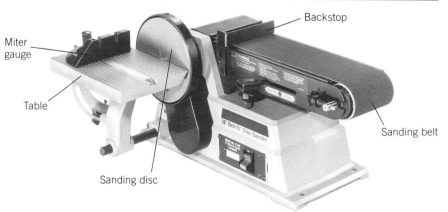

Miter gauge — Table — Sanding disc — Backstop — Sanding belt

Belt sander

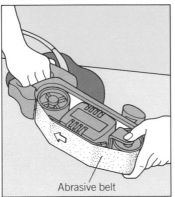

Abrasive belt

To change belt, turn off and unplug sander and pull front roller toward rear one to release belt tension. Lock into place. Slip off old belt and slip on new one, with arrow pointing in direction belt moves. Release front roller; it will spring forward and restore belt tension. Momentarily turn motor on to make sure that belt is tracking properly. Adjust if necessary.

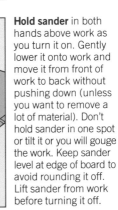

Hold sander in both hands above work as you turn it on. Gently lower it onto work and move it from front of work to back without pushing down (unless you want to remove a lot of material). Don't hold sander in one spot or tilt it or you will gouge the work. Keep sander level at edge of board to avoid rounding it off. Lift sander from work before turning it off.

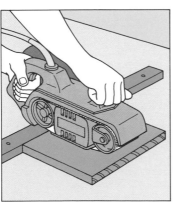

Brace small pieces of work securely before sanding them. One way of accomplishing this is to clamp or tack a strip of wood to the work surface and back the work against it. Another way is to build a jig, or simple frame, to hold the work in place while you sand it. Never try to hold a small piece of work in your hand while sanding.

Finishing sanders

Attach paper following instructions in owner's manual. Generally, you must secure one end of paper under a clamp or clip, then pull it over pad and attach other end as you did the first. Be sure paper is taut, or it will tear. Self-adhering abrasive sheets are also available; simply peel away protective backing and press them on without using clamp or clip.

Start sander before touching it to work. Use both hands for better control, but don't apply pressure. Sand with grain as much as possible and keep sander level; if you tip one edge or the other down, surface will be gouged. If you are sanding small pieces of work, clamp together several of same thickness to help keep sander level.

Use one-hand sander in tight spots or for overhead sanding. It is small enough to fit almost anywhere and light enough to let you use it in awkward positions or for long periods of time. You can also use it to sand flush up against walls or other obstructions. Cordless finishing sanders are available for working away from power source.

Belt-disc sander

When using belt in horizontal position, lock backstop no more than 1/16 in. from belt to avoid trapping work or your fingers in opening. Turn on power. Keep fingers away from belt; hold work firmly, with its end butted against backstop. Move work evenly across belt. Use extra caution when sanding thin pieces.

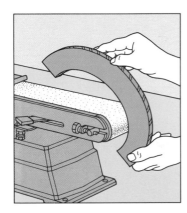

Sand curved pieces on idler drum of belt sander. Adjust the machine to the most comfortable angle for working and lock it in place. Turn sander on and let it come to full speed, then gently apply work to abrasive belt. Keep work moving at all times and remove it from belt before switching machine off.

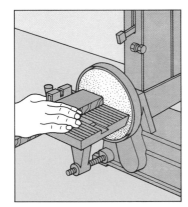

To use sanding disc, tilt table to angle needed and lock it in place with its inside edge no more than 1/16 in. from surface of the disc. Turn on motor and move work into left (downward-moving) side of disc. **CAUTION:** Never sand on right side of disc; work may fly up and injure you. Sanding on left side of disc pushes work down on table.

71

For smoothing the edges of wood and trimming doors to fit their frames, the portable power plane is a timesaver. You can use it to take off tissue-thin shavings or to remove stock up to 1/32 inch thick.

The plane's motor turns a cutter at high speed. To use the tool, turn it on, grip it in both hands, then place the front of the tool on the work, applying downward pressure on the front handle. As the cutter bites into the wood, apply equal pressure with both hands and keep the plane level. Near the end of the cut, slow down and shift the downward pressure to the main handle to minimize chipping, feathering, and rounding off the end of the cut.

The plane can be fitted with a fence that projects downward from the baseplate. When planing the edge of a board or door, hold this fence against the side of the work to produce a perfectly square-edged cut, or set it at an angle to cut a bevel.

Used to straighten, square, and flatten boards so that they align with other boards when joined to them, the jointer planes wood by means of a cylindrical cutter with two or more blades that revolve at high speed between the tool's two tables. The depth of cut is established by lowering or raising the infeed table. The work is pushed along a fence across the infeed table, into the cutter, and onto the outfeed table.

Bevels can be cut by locking the fence at the desired angle. Some jointers cut rabbets (p. 103). But even though the jointer can smooth and straighten surfaces, it cannot make both surfaces of a board parallel; that requires a thickness planer.

▶ **CAUTION:** Hands should never be over the cutter.

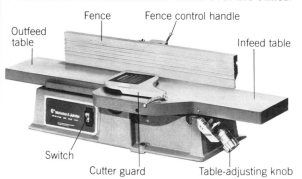

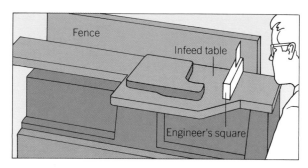

To ensure accurate cuts, occasionally check that fence is square with infeed table. Turn off and unplug machine; place an engineer's square against fence on infeed table. Look for a gap between fence and square. If you find one, adjust fence.

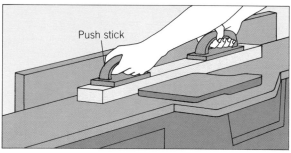

When surface joining, slowly slide edge along fence across cutter; use push sticks (p.65). If surface is warped, make light cuts until it is flat; hold work down against table; don't let it rock.

In planing end grain, prevent splintering by clamping scrap wood to side edge of work, flush with end to be planed.

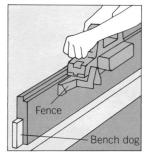

To cut a rabbet (p.103), adjust fence so that cutter is above area to be cut. Make several passes to get desired depth.

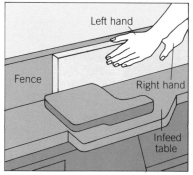

To square an edge, stand to left of infeed table with your feet turned slightly toward it. Hold stock against fence and table with left hand; push stock into cutter with right.

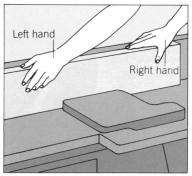

As work passes onto outfeed table, move left hand to hold work over outfeed table. Keep work pressed flat against fence; move work forward with right hand.

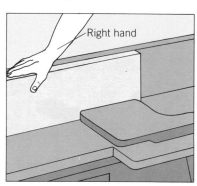

Before end of work reaches cutter, move right hand to outfeed table. Slide work forward as it clears cutter. Turn off machine and let it stop fully before removing work.

Thickness planer   Bench grinder

Although it may be the last major tool you want to buy, the thickness planer is a good tool to know about if you do a lot of woodworking—and particularly if you want to save money by buying rough lumber and planing it yourself. The thickness planer smooths rough lumber, cutting its second face perfectly parallel to the first. It also removes blemishes from wood and reduces a board's thickness. It will not straighten a warped board, however; warped stock should be flattened with a jointer.

Professional thickness planers are large, cumbersome machines, but small models are available for the home workshop. The machine is rated by the size wood it will accept. The model shown below will accept a 10-inch board.

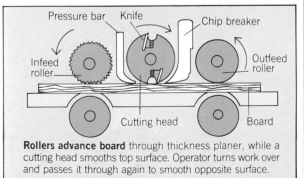

Rollers advance board through thickness planer, while a cutting head smooths top surface. Operator turns work over and passes it through again to smooth opposite surface.

Make your tools last longer by sharpening, cleaning, and polishing them on a bench grinder. Most bench grinders consist of a motor with two arbors for mounting wheels, a tool rest for each wheel, and spark and wheel guards and eye shields for safety. There are wheels for every job. A medium (150-grit) vitrified aluminum-oxide wheel is best for sharpening tools. You can remove rust from tools with a wire brush, and you can polish metal parts with a cloth buffing wheel and a buffing compound.

Before using a wheel, check it by rapping it with a screwdriver handle and listening for a ringing sound. If it makes a buzzing sound instead, it is chipped or cracked; replace it. Grinding wheels turn at about 3,450 rpm, so keep the metal wheel guards in place and wear a face shield—the machine's shields don't give enough protection. When turning on the power, stand to one side of the wheel in case it shatters. Always support the work on the tool rest, which should never be more than $\frac{1}{16}$ inch from the wheel. Hold the work firmly against the wheel. To prevent overheating, use light pressure; cool the work in water as needed. Some tools will require further sharpening on a honing stone (p.44).

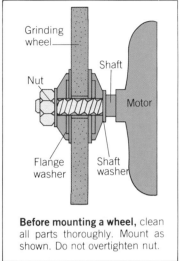

Before mounting a wheel, clean all parts thoroughly. Mount as shown. Do not overtighten nut.

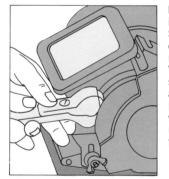

Dress wheel (resurface it) when dull or clogged. Start with a star-wheel dresser (available at most hardware stores). Wearing a face shield, support wheel dresser against tool rest and bring it into full contact with spinning wheel; using light force, sweep tool across wheel.

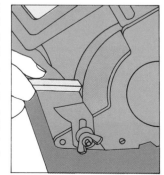

After two or three passes with star-wheel dresser, grinding wheel should run true, but it may be rougher than you wish. For finer grind, re-dress wheel with a boron-carbide stick or with a diamond dresser. Or you can dress a wheel in one step with a silicon-carbide stick, but it will take longer to get the same results.

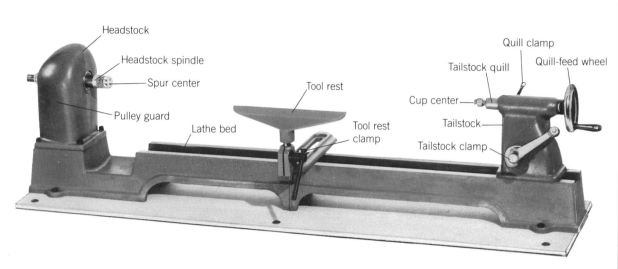

Headstock
Headstock spindle
Spur center
Pulley guard
Lathe bed
Tool rest
Tool rest clamp
Quill clamp
Tailstock quill
Quill-feed wheel
Cup center
Tailstock
Tailstock clamp

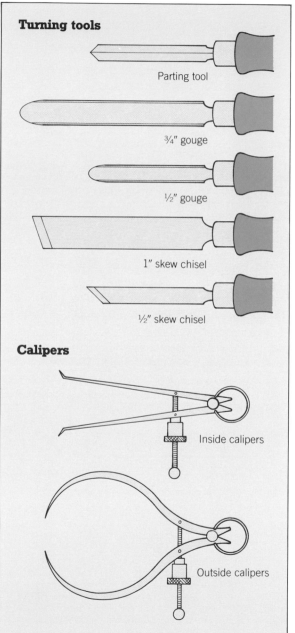

Turning tools

Parting tool

¾" gouge

½" gouge

1" skew chisel

½" skew chisel

Calipers

Inside calipers

Outside calipers

You can produce shapely cylindrical forms for newel posts and furniture legs by spinning a long block of solid or laminated wood on a lathe and cutting it with special chisels. The lathe turns the wood, which is supported on one end by the headstock and at the opposite end by the tailstock. The tool is mounted on a workbench or stand, and a motor is connected to the lathe with a belt. The speed is generally controlled by changing the belt from one pulley to another. Be sure to get a motor to suit your lathe, in both horsepower and rpms.

Turning techniques. There are two turning techniques: cutting and scraping. The preferred method for working on the spindle is cutting, in which the skin of the wood is sliced and shavings are peeled off. In scraping (not covered here), the tool is forced into the wood head-on and wood fibers are torn away. Scraping is ideal for shaping bowls from blocks of wood that are connected directly to a faceplate and mounted to the headstock spindle.

To cut wood on a lathe, start at low speed (400–700 rpm) and shape the work into a rough cylinder. Finish at high speed (1,200–2,000 rpm) if the stock is less than 3 inches in diameter, medium speed (700–1,200 rpm) if it is between 3 and 6 inches, or low speed if it is more than 6 inches in diameter.

Lathe chisels. Three types of chisels are used for cutting: gouges for rough cuts and coves (concave curves); skews for smooth, straight cuts and beads (convex curves); and parting tools for grooves, deep recesses, and sizing cuts (cutting a cylinder down to size). All three come in various sizes. Keep these tools clean and razor sharp for safe, precise cutting. Calipers are used to measure outside dimensions or inside cuts.

Safety. Before putting a block of wood on a lathe, check the wood for possible defects that could result in breaking or splintering. If you are turning a laminated block, make sure that the glue bonds are tight and firm (let them harden at least 24 hours) or it may come apart on the lathe and injure you. Tighten all adjusting levers and locks securely before turning on the machine; stand to one side as you switch on the power. Always use goggles or a full face mask and a dust mask when working at a lathe, and feed the cutting tools slowly into the spinning work.

Safety with tools 19
Power tool maintenance 53
Sharpening hand tools 44–45

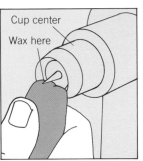

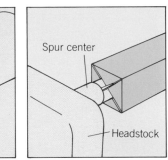

1. Square ends of stock and mark center of each end by drawing diagonal lines from corner to corner. With mallet, drive cup center at least ⅟₁₆ in. into stock where lines cross, then remove cup center and fit it into tailstock spindle.

2. Saw ⅛-in.-deep cuts along diagonal lines on opposite end of stock. Position spur center over these cuts, making sure that spurs will enter cuts. Use wooden mallet to seat spur center.

3. Remove tool rest from lathe. Lubricate cup center with candle wax or paraffin. (No lubrication is needed if you use a ball-bearing tailstock center.) Place spur center into headstock spindle and hold stock in position over lathe bed.

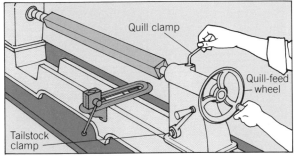

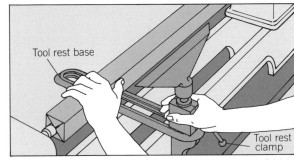

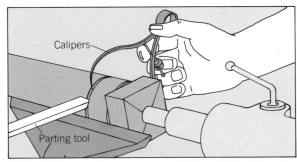

4. Move tailstock toward stock until cup center enters indentation made in Step 1. Lock tailstock clamp. Tighten cup center against stock with quill-feed wheel. Lock with quill clamp.

5. Replace tool rest and adjust it so that it is one-quarter of thickness of stock above center of stock and no more than ¼ in. from corner of stock—otherwise, it may pinch you or grab chisel. Rotate stock by hand to be sure stock clears rest.

6. Round off work using gouge, moving it back and forth, with cutting edge raised and rolled slightly in direction of travel. Set calipers ⅛ in. larger than desired diameter of work. Use parting tool to make series of cuts to size indicated by calipers; remove stock down to cuts.

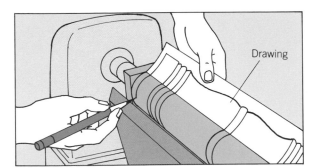

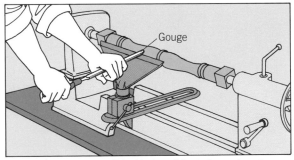

7. Make a drawing of planned cuts on heavy paper. Fold drawing in half lengthwise, and hold it against spindle. Following the drawing, pencil in cut lines on work. Continue to make cuts.

8. Rough-out cuts to within ⅟₁₆ in. of final size, using skew or gouge. Hold tool at proper angle to work and cut away waste stock. Stop occasionally to readjust position of tool rest and to check work.

9. Cut final shapes. Hold straightedge along work to check cylinders and straight tapers. Measure diameters of cuts with outside calipers. Remove tool rest and sand work. Make cut-out pattern for duplicating work, if needed.

Power tools/Wet-dry vacuum

Not only are wet-dry vacuums more powerful than household vacuums, they can pick up water from ruptured plumbing pipes and common home and shop spills. With their larger motors, tanks, hoses, and filters they are able to handle wood chips, paper scraps, wallboard dust, and other kinds of debris that spell trouble for ordinary vacuums.

Most wet-dry vacuums come with a 4- or 6-foot hose, a brush, wet- and dry-pickup floor nozzles, extension wands, and crevice wands. They are also generally equipped with casters for moving them around easily, and all have rust-free epoxy-coated or plastic tanks.

The real advantage in owning a wet-dry vacuum comes when you attach it to your power tools. For example, sawdust from a table saw can be drawn directly into the tank—a useful feature when working indoors, where dust might create health and cleanup problems. For light-duty work, or for use with hand-held power tools, a 5- to 8-gallon model with a 1-horsepower motor and a 1¼-inch hose will do. A 12- to 16-gallon tank (with a 2½-inch hose) powered by a 1½-horsepower motor will work best with stationary power tools. Cleaning filters often and replacing them when worn will make a wet-dry vacuum run better.

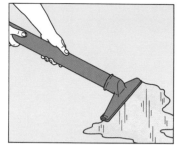

Wet-pickup floor nozzle contains a squeegee that leaves a wood or tile floor almost dry. Use a wide wet-pickup nozzle on carpeted floors.

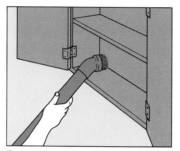

For small areas and the insides of cabinets and other closed spaces, use a brush attachment.

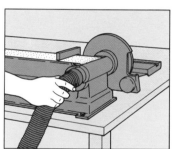

Hose fittings are molded into the castings of many shop tools, such as radial arm saws and sanders. For easy use, simply slide the hose of the vacuum onto these fittings.

Tools without hose fittings can still be connected by improvising hookups. For example, a hose taped inside the trough of a jointer catches most shavings.

Handle
Motor housing
Hose
Tank
Drain plug
Extension wand
Brush
Wide dry nozzle
Squeegee nozzles

WET DRY VAC
16 GALLON
1.5 H.P.
DOUBLE INSULATED

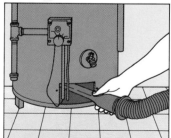

Use crevice wand to vacuum rust accumulation from burner of a gas water heater, but be sure to turn off unit first and let it cool. The heater will work better afterward.

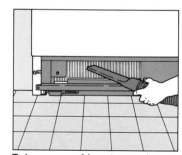

To keep your refrigerator running smoothly, regularly vacuum unit's condenser coil and fin tubes (located on bottom and rear of refrigerator).

Air compressor

Pressure gauge
On-off switch
Regulator
Hose connection
Towing handle
Motor/pulley guard
Air Compressor 2HP 12 GAL
Tank
Hose
Condensation drain
Wheel

A great many home projects can be made easier with a portable air compressor. This tool takes air and forces it at high pressure into a storage tank. The air is then released through a regulator and a hose to power small tools that do a wide variety of jobs, ranging from sanding and spray-painting to sawing, drilling, and nailing.

You can buy your own compressor and attachments or rent them for an occasional big job. Because most attachments need stored air to operate effectively, get a compressor that is mounted on a tank. Also, choose a unit that will handle the largest tool you are likely to use. To make using the attachments easier, choose lightweight hoses and quick-fit connections.

Air Pressure Requirements

Tool or accessory	cfm	psi
Air chuck	1–1.5	10–50
Circular saw (8 in.)	6–12	70–90
Drill (⅜ in.)	4–6	70–90
Laminate trimmer	6–8	70–90
Nailer	5–6	70–90
Polisher	2	70–90
Power washer	8.5	40–90
Saber saw	4.5–6	70–90
Sander	4–6	70–90
Spray gun	.75–5	10–70
Stapler	1.5–5	70–90

Get a compressor that has enough air volume, measured in cubic feet per minute (cfm), and enough air pressure, measured in pounds per square inch (psi), to run attachments you plan to use. Above chart gives average requirements.

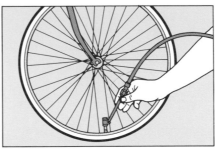

Air chucks are among the essential compressor attachments. When inflating tires, set the regulator to the recommended psi (pounds per square inch) to avoid overinflating.

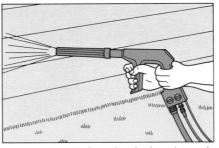

Power washer attachments mix air, water, and detergent for high-pressure cleaning. They are ideally suited to washing house siding and scrubbing masonry or cars, vans, and trucks.

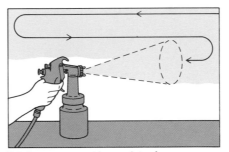

Paint sprayers provide a variety of spray patterns and pressure settings. Their interchangeable nozzles make them useful for painting wood, plastic, or metal, or adding clear finishes to wood.

Disc and finishing sanders are available as compressor attachments. Disc sanders can be used for removing large amounts of stock, while finishing sanders do an excellent job of smoothing and polishing.

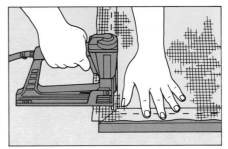

Labor-saving power staplers and nailers are available in a variety of sizes. Depending upon size and air requirements, these attachments can drive anything from tiny brads and staples to large framing nails.

Power rollers, coupled with a paint canister, allow you to apply work continuously without dealing with messy roller pans. Rollers are available with long, medium, or short nap.

Power tools/Multipurpose tool

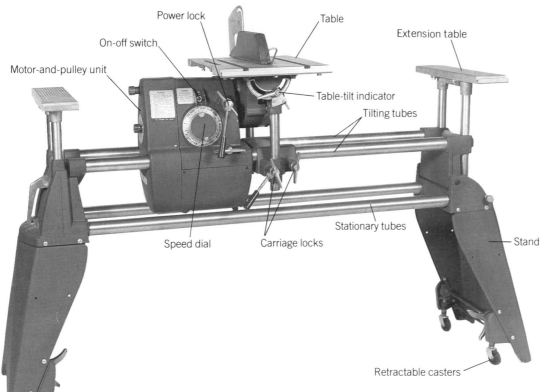

Power lock

On-off switch

Motor-and-pulley unit

Table

Extension table

Table-tilt indicator

Tilting tubes

Speed dial

Carriage locks

Stationary tubes

Stand

Retractable casters

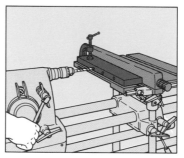

Table saw makes both rip cuts and crosscuts. The tool can also make compound miter cuts if the table and miter gauge are tilted to the desired angles.

Horizontal boring machine can be used for drilling dowel holes; do the work at a slow speed. Use the table to support the work and the fence to brace it.

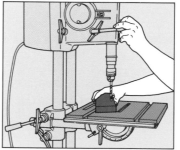

For vertical drill press, pivot the motor and drill into an upright position, and move the table into place under the drill chuck. To drill holes at an angle, tilt the table as needed.

A 12-in. disc sander mounted on the motor shaft makes the job of smoothing sawed edges easy. By tilting the table you can sand surfaces at precise angles.

For a homeowner working in a garage or a basement, a multipurpose tool solves a big problem: lack of space. The tool is so compact that it takes up less working and storage space than many an individual bench tool, but it can perform a wide variety of woodworking tasks, all powered by a single variable-speed motor-and-pulley system. The price of the multipurpose tool is roughly equivalent to the combined costs of the individual tools it replaces.

The basic machine typically includes a vertical drill press, horizontal boring machine, lathe, disc sander, and table saw, together with an extension table for holding long pieces of lumber, a rip fence, and a lumber-gripping miter gauge capable of multiple angles. On this base, other tools can be added, such as a planer, jointer, and various saws and sanders, as well as a wide range of accessories, including a router and dado cutters. With these attachments and a few handmade jigs, you'll be able to complete nearly any woodworking project, from a jigsaw puzzle to a grandfather clock.

Powering the multipurpose tool is a variable-speed pulley system powered by a motor, usually in excess of 1 horsepower. The machine's speed range should be broad enough to accommodate low-speed boring at 700 rpm as well as high-speed routing at 5,200 rpm. A 120-volt, 15-ampere standard house circuit will drive the motor. Plug the tool into a circuit all its own.

Chapter four

Fasteners and adhesives for joining materials

In home repair and improvement, the way in which one item is joined to another is critical. Your choice of nails, screws, wall anchors, or glue can make the difference between a project's success or failure. Equally important is how you attach a fastener or apply the glue. This section explains the factors you must consider in making a selection, the various alternatives, and the procedures you should follow to obtain an attractive, reliable result.

The fasteners presented here are those most readily available and most commonly used. Some specialized fasteners, such as screws for joining metal, are covered in more detail in the appropriate sections. The same is true of glues with specific applications.

79

Fasteners/Nails

Nail types

Common nail. For general-purpose use in heavy construction and rough work. Large head won't pull through.

Box nail. Lighter-gauge version of the common nail; use with thin wood that splits easily.

Wire nail. Smallest version of common nail. Sized in fractions of an inch and by wire gauge number.

Finishing nail. For trim and cabinetwork where nailheads must be concealed. Head is sunk and filled over (p.23).

Casing nail. Heavier version of finishing nail, with more holding power. Used for door and window casing or trim.

Wire brad. For small objects and molding. Usually sunk and filled. Comes in inch and gauge number sizes, like wire nails.

Drywall nail. Tightly secures wallboard panels with broad head and ringed or barbed shaft; often resin coated.

Ringed nail (also called annular-ring nail). Its sharp-edged ridges lock into wood, increasing its holding power.

Spiral nail. Turns like a screw when driven in; its tight grip eliminates squeaks in flooring.

Aluminum roofing nail. For corrugated metal and plastic roofing. Has plastic washer under head for watertight seal.

Roofing nail. Has extra-large head to hold asphalt shingles and similar roofings. Usually galvanized to resist moisture.

Masonry nail. Made of hardened steel. Used for fastening to concrete and other masonry walls and floors (p.86).

Double-headed nail. For temporary work; upper head projects for removal. Also called scaffold nail and duplex-head nail.

Cut nail. Stamped ("cut") from sheet steel, then hardened. This flat nail's blunt tip prevents splits when blind-nailing flooring.

Tacks. Made in cut or round form; used to fasten carpet or fabric to wood, and for similar light fastening jobs.

Staples. Made in many forms for varied uses, including holding fencing and, with insulated shoulders, electric wires.

Corrugated fastener. For light-duty miter and butt joints, such as on screens and picture frames. Drive it across joint.

Pointed fastener. For strengthening joints, its eight sharp prongs spread in wood to grip. Drive it straight in.

The two most useful nails are the common nail, for its strength, and the finishing nail, for the appearance it gives to the work. Other nails are either variants of these or special-purpose fasteners with enhanced holding or penetrating power.

Nail size. A common nail's length is designated by its penny size, a term that once indicated its price per hundred. Most nails come in a wide range of lengths and their diameters increase with length. Common nails are available in lengths from 1 inch, or 2 penny (abbreviated 2d), to 6 inches, or 60 penny (60d). The nail's diameter increases four times over that range. Some special-purpose nails, however, come in only one size or one diameter. For large jobs buy nails in pound quantities. The approximate number of common nails in a 1-pound box is given at left below; a box of finishing nails of equivalent size will yield about 75 percent more.

Small wire brads and wire nails are sized in inches and by wire gauge number. The higher the gauge number, the thinner the nail.

Driving nails. Drive common nails flush with the surface. Stop driving a finishing nail when it is almost flush; then use a nail set (p.23) to drive it flush or to sink it. To protect an irregular surface, such as molding, drive a finishing nail through a hole in a scrap of pegboard; then finish it with a nail set. To keep unsupported wood from bouncing, hold a block of wood (or better, steel) behind it.

▶ **CAUTION:** When driving cut, masonry, and other hardened nails, wear safety goggles and drive them with a hardened-steel hammer. They snap easily when misstruck and can chip a cheap cast-iron hammer, creating flying metal particles.

Penny nail gauge

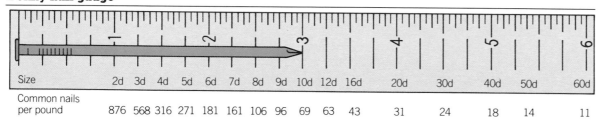

Size	2d	3d	4d	5d	6d	7d	8d	9d	10d	12d	16d	20d	30d	40d	50d	60d
Common nails per pound	876	568	316	271	181	161	106	96	69	63	43	31	24	18	14	11

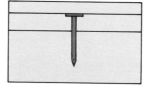

Nail a thinner piece to a thicker one with a nail three times the thickness of the thinner piece.

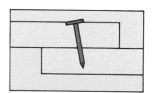

If thicknesses are the same, use a nail equal to both. Angle nail; it won't pierce other side.

Starting nails

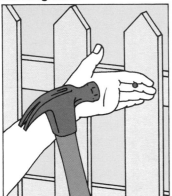

One way to hold a nail (instead of between your thumb and index finger) is to turn your palm up and put the nail between your outstretched fingers. This is especially useful for starting smaller nails; an accidental blow is likely to cause less harm on the fleshy part of the fingers.

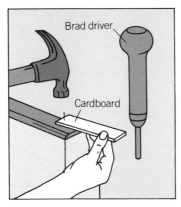

Push a small nail or a tack through a piece of thin cardboard to hold it while you drive the point in. Then rip away the cardboard. You can also hold a small nail or tack with long-nose pliers. When driving many small brads, a brad driver is helpful; insert a brad into the recess in the magnetic tip of the driver and push down on the handle to drive it in.

Brad driver

Cardboard

To start a nail in a hard-to-reach area or when only one hand is free, wedge it in the hammer's claw with its head against the neck of the hammer. Swing the hammer to drive the point in. Then disengage the claw and drive the nail in as usual. Wear safety goggles; the nail can fly out of the claw if you strike at an odd angle.

Angling nails

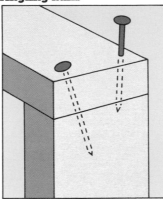

For greater holding power always drive nails at a slight angle. In most joints try to drive nails in opposite directions, such as toward each other, so that each will counter the tendency of others to pull out and the opposing nails will have a hook effect. If a joint will receive a large amount of stress, use nails with large heads and ringed shanks.

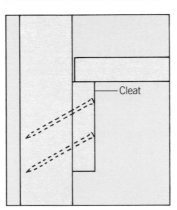

Cleat

When mounting a cleat for a shelf or other piece that may bear a heavy load, drive the nails at a downward angle; the load on the shelf will push the nails inward and strengthen the cleat. But don't angle masonry nails when putting them into a concrete or masonry wall; they must be driven straight (p.86).

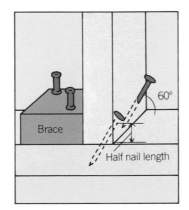

Brace

60°

Half nail length

To toenail one piece to another, tack or clamp a brace against one side (or firmly brace it with your foot). Hold the nail pointing slightly down and tap the point in about ⅛ in., then push the head up to a 60° angle and drive it in. Nail one side, then remove brace and do the other. Stagger the nails so that they don't hit each other.

Other nailing techniques

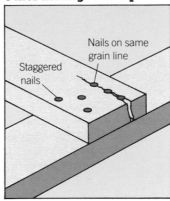

Nails on same grain line

Staggered nails

To avoid splitting wood, drive nails in a staggered pattern rather than along a grain line. Blunting the nail's point helps prevent splitting when you are nailing near the end of a piece. Another method is to cut the wood overlength, nail it in place, and then saw off the excess.

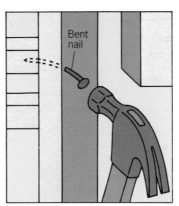

Bent nail

In a tight spot bend a nail slightly before driving it; this lets you hit the head squarely. In a corner or next to a wall, drive a nail with a nail set; hold the nail set on the nail with your thumb and two fingers. In a crevice that is hard to reach into, put the nail on the end of a steel rod that you have magnetized by rubbing with a strong magnet.

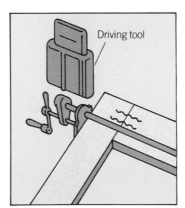

Driving tool

With a corrugated fastener, make sure both pieces are on a solid flat surface before driving in the fastener. Butt the pieces tightly together; preferably clamp them. To install many fasteners, buy a driving tool to hold them straight as you drive them. It also lets you sink the fasteners below the surface; then you can cover them with wood filler.

Fasteners / Screws

Drive heads

Slotted	Phillips	Square-drive (or Robinson)	Star-drive	One-way	Hex-head

Screw types

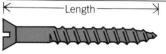 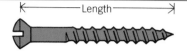 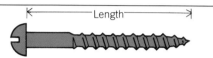

Flathead screw is a general-purpose wood screw driven flush with surface or countersunk below. Length encompasses entire screw.

Oval-head screw has a protruding head that has decorative appearance. The upper head is not counted when measuring length.

Roundhead screw is used for fastening thin board or metal to thicker wood. Head is excluded when measuring length.

Particleboard screw has wide threads that are deep, for extra holding power, and sharp, for cutting through tough glue in particleboard.

Drywall screw is thin, sharp, and hardened; has bugle-shaped head to dent wallboard surface and deep threads to cut into studs.

Sheet-metal screw is threaded its entire length. When driven in, it cuts threads and makes a hole. In metal, drill a starter hole (p.129).

Lag bolt (or screw) is a heavy-duty wood screw, up to 6 in. long. It is driven into a pilot hole by turning its hex-shaped head with a wrench.

Dowel screw joins leg to a tabletop. Screw it into top of leg, using locking pliers whose jaws you have padded. Then screw leg to top.

Hanger bolt has one end with wood-screw threads; other end has machine-screw threads that will accept a nut.

Screw hooks

Screw hook	Screw eye	L-hook

Washers for screws

Flush for flathead screw	Countersunk for oval-head screw	Flat for roundhead screw

Screw sizes

Gauge number	2	3	4	5	6	7	8	9	10	11	12	14	16
Shank hole	3/32″	3/32″	3/32″	1/8″	9/64″	5/32″	11/64″	11/64″	3/16″	13/64″	7/32″	15/64″	17/64″
Pilot hole	5/64″	5/64″	7/64″	7/64″	1/8″	9/64″	5/32″	5/32″	11/64″	3/16″	13/64″	7/32″	1/4″

Use screws when you need strong holding power and want to be able to take a joint apart without damaging it. Wood screws, which come in many sizes and head types, are traditional for joining wood. But special-purpose screws—for joining sheet metal, particleboard, and wallboard—can also create sturdy wood joints. Known as self-tapping or self-drilling screws, they have deep, sharp threads and seldom need a pilot hole when driven into softwood with a power drill or a screw gun.

Screw types. The Phillips, star, and square sockets prevent slippage when a power tool drives a screw. The hex head allows you to drive large lag bolts with a wrench. One-way screws, once driven in, are not easily removed.

Sizes. When purchasing screws, you'll need to specify the length in inches and the diameter by a gauge number. Lengths range up to 6 inches; gauge numbers 2 (about 3/32 inch) to 16 (about 1/4 inch) are most common.

Inserting screws. Use an awl or a nail to make a pilot hole for a No. 5 or smaller screw. For larger screws drill a pilot hole with a bit the same diameter as the screw minus the threads.

Two-thirds of a screw's length should go into the second piece of wood. For a tight joint, first drill a hole in the top piece to let the unthreaded shank pass without binding; this allows the screw to pull the pieces tightly together. To prevent splits, always drill a shank hole for large screws or when using hardwood.

Washers can provide bearing surface, protect wood, or be decorative.

Joining with wood screws

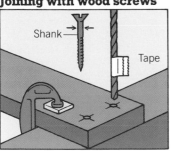

1. Clamp the pieces together. Mark the screw positions and select a drill bit equal to the diameter of the screw's shank (see chart, facing page). Mark the top piece's thickness on the bit with tape (or use a drill stop). Then drill a shank hole, stopping at tape.

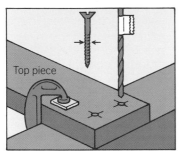

2. Select a drill bit equal to the screw's diameter minus the threads. With a piece of tape, mark the screw's length on the bit. Drill pilot hole, stopping at the tape.

3. If you are using flathead screws, drill a countersink hole of the same diameter as the screwhead. Check diameter by holding screwhead upside-down over hole.

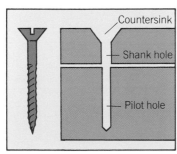

4. Rub wax on screw threads for easier installation. Insert screw in the hole and drive it in until screwhead is flush with surface of work.

Other techniques

To use drywall screws for joining wood, clamp the pieces together and put a Phillips-head bit on a variable-speed drill. Let the drill's weight sink the screw's point; then drive in screw on slow speed. Drill pilot hole first if top piece is more than ¾ in. thick or if working with hardwood.

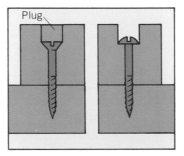

In weak end grain, drill a hole and insert a hardwood dowel. Then install the screw in usual way, driving it into the dowel to create a strong grip. Another method is to use a screw three times longer than normal. A dowel can be used when screwing into edge of plywood.

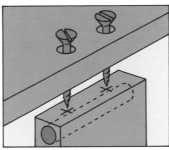

To fasten thick pieces with screws of normal length, drill a deep counterbore—a hole wide enough for the screwhead to pass through. Then install the screw, drilling a countersink for the head if you are using flathead screws.

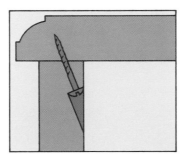

To attach a top on a table or cabinet, drill or chisel a long, angled pocket in the side of the frame or case. Before installing the screw, drill a pilot hole in the pocket at the same angle.

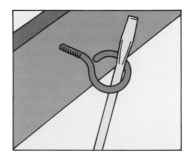

To install a screw eye that is too tight to turn by hand, first drill a pilot hole. Start screw eye in the hole by hand; then angle a screwdriver (or a metal rod or wooden dowel) through the eye to act as a lever. Finish turning it in.

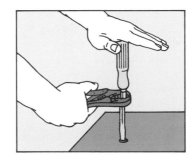

To install a hanger bolt, drill a pilot hole. Then turn two nuts most of the way onto the machine-threaded part of the bolt and tighten them so that they lock against each other. Then use a wrench on the nuts to drive in the wood-threaded half of the bolt.

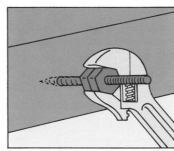

A stubborn screw can often be loosened by inserting a square-shanked screwdriver that fits snugly in slot. Then clamp locking pliers or an adjustable wrench onto the screwdriver's shank and push down hard, at the same time turning the screwdriver.

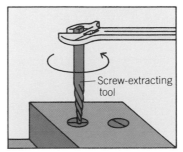

To remove a broken or unmovable screw, drill a small hole into top of the screw. Then insert screw-extracting tool and back out the screw, using a wrench to turn the tool. If you don't have such a tool, try using a square-tipped common nail gripped with locking pliers.

Fasteners/Bolts and nuts

To join materials in a way that's strong yet easy to take apart, use bolts and nuts. Select machine bolts or stove bolts (or machine screws) for metal and other thin materials. Select carriage bolts for wood pieces, such as a lawn chair, that you may dismantle.

Bolt sizes. Specify a bolt's size by its diameter, thread pitch, and length. The size is usually given in the form ¼″–20 × 1½″, where ¼″ is the diameter, 20 is the number of threads per inch, and 1½″ is the length. Diameter and thread-pitch combinations commonly range from ⅛″–40 to ½″–13; as a rule, the larger a bolt is, the fewer threads per inch it has. Lengths up to 6 inches are common; as with screws (p.82), the length excludes any protruding part of the head. A machine screw's diameter is given as a gauge number and can be as small as No. 1 gauge. (A machine screw is a stove bolt less than ½ inch in diameter.)

Bolts can have either coarse or fine threads. Some special-use machine bolts and screws have fine threads. Stove and carriage bolts have coarse.

Tighten a nut or hex-head bolt with a wrench; pliers can damage it.

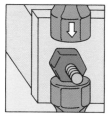
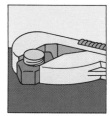

To loosen a frozen nut, soak it with penetrating oil for 10 or 15 min. If it still won't turn, hold a hammer against one side and hit the opposite side with another hammer. With a badly rusted nut, saw away two sides with a hacksaw; then twist with an adjustable wrench to break apart.

Types of bolts

Machine bolts come with hex heads or square heads and accept hex or square nuts.

Carriage bolts have an unslotted oval head; square shoulder sinks into wood to prevent turning.

Stove bolts are general utility bolts with slotted heads. Machine screws are same but smaller.

Stove bolt heads are flat to sink flush, oval for easy removal, or round to accept a washer.

Special threaded fasteners

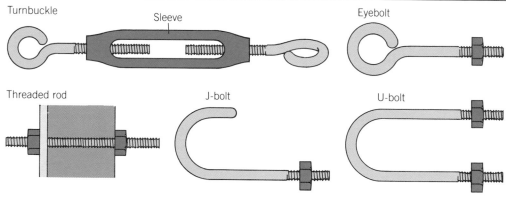

Turnbuckle · Sleeve · Eyebolt

Threaded rod · J-bolt · U-bolt

Other threaded fasteners include eyebolts and J-bolts, which accept ropes, wires, and hooks, and U-bolts, which fit onto pipes. A turnbuckle has threaded eyes or hooks that move in or out when you turn the sleeve, providing the diagonal pull that keeps a gate or screen door straight. Used with two or more nuts, a threaded rod (or an all thread) can join objects over a longer span than a bolt can.

Types of nuts

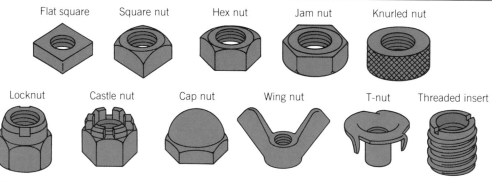

Flat square · Square nut · Hex nut · Jam nut · Knurled nut

Locknut · Castle nut · Cap nut · Wing nut · T-nut · Threaded insert

Common nuts include a jam nut, tightened against a square or hex nut to lock it. A locknut alone does the same job. A castle nut lets a wheel or other secured part move (a cotter pin put through a drilled hole in bolt's tip holds it in place). A cap nut is decorative and protective. Knurled nuts and wing nuts can be turned by hand. A T-nut goes into one side of a board to receive a bolt coming from the other side. A threaded insert screws into wood to accept a bolt.

Types of washers

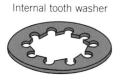

Flat washer · Split-ring lock washer · Internal tooth washer · External tooth washer

Common washers include a flat washer, which goes under a bolt head or a nut to spread the load and protect the surface. Split-ring and toothed lock washers prevent a nut from working loose.

Hollow-wall fasteners

Whenever possible, attach a load to the studs in a wall's framing. Always secure a large mirror, bookshelves, and other heavy loads to studs. Lag bolts and hanger bolts are ideal for this, but you can use any nails or screws long enough to go well into the studs; drill a pilot hole for a screw. For metal studs, use sheet-metal screws (p.82); drill up to the stud, dent it with a center punch, and drill a small pilot hole. To do it all in one step, install self-drilling metal-stud screws with an electric drill.

For a moderate load, use hollow-wall fasteners. Five common types are shown at right; new ones that work on the same principles are introduced regularly. To get the right-size fastener, you need

to know the wall's thickness. To find it, drill a ¼-inch hole at the spot where you plan to install the fastener, insert a 6d or smaller common nail headfirst into the hole, and pull the head tightly against the inside of the wall. Use your fingers or tape to mark the nail where it comes out of the wall. Remove it and measure distance.

For a light load, a plastic anchor is sufficient. Drill a hole slightly smaller in diameter than the anchor.

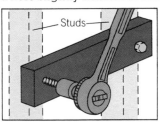

To hang a heavy object on a hollow wall, attach a board to the studs with lag bolts; then screw the object to the board. Locate studs with a stud finder or other device (p.191). Most studs are 16 or 24 in. apart, center to center.

Studs

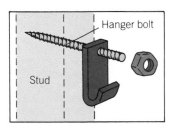

Another way to hang a heavy load is to drive a hanger bolt into a stud (p.83). Then use a nut on the machine-threaded end of the bolt to attach the load or a hook for it.

Hanger bolt
Stud

Fastener types and how to install them

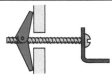

Winged toggle
Bolt

Toggle bolts have spring-loaded wings that open in the wall. A toggle bolt holds securely but needs a large hole, and toggle drops if bolt is removed. Select size to match wall thickness and weight of object.

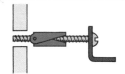
Put bolt through fixture into toggle. Drill hole. Fold toggle.

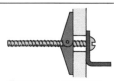
Push toggle through wall. Pull so that open toggle grips wall.

Tighten the bolt until the fixture is firmly attached to wall.

Hollow-wall anchors (Molly anchors) collapse as the bolt is turned, drawing metal shoulders against the inner wall. The anchor stays in place if bolt is removed. Select size that matches wall thickness.

Drill hole. Insert bolt in hole, pressing prongs on collar into surface.

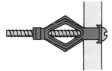
Tighten the bolt until you feel strong resistance.

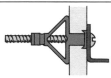
Remove bolt. Put it through fixture, then in anchor, and retighten.

Hollow-door anchors (jacknuts) are similar to hollow-wall anchors but are used for thinner materials, such as the wood or metal facing on a hollow-core door.

Drill hole. Insert bolt in the hole.

Tighten the bolt until you feel strong resistance.

Remove bolt. Put it through fixture, then in anchor, and tighten.

Plastic toggles have wings that spring open in the wall like a toggle bolt but do not require as large an entrance hole, and toggle is not lost if screw is removed. Select size that matches wall thickness.

Drill hole. Fold the toggle's wings together and insert it in hole.

Push a nail or supplied plastic pin in anchor to pop open wings.

Put screw through the fixture, then into anchor, and tighten.

Metal drive-in anchors have sharp pointed legs that stay tightly together as you hammer them in but then spread to hold securely when you put in the screw. One size fits wall thicknesses up to ¾ in.

Drill ⅛-in. hole in cinder block or plaster; hammer into wallboard.

Hold the anchor with legs horizontal and drive into the wall.

Put screw through fixture, then into anchor, and tighten.

Fasteners/Masonry and concrete

Use masonry nails to attach furring strips, window frames, and other wood pieces to masonry block or concrete. Drive the nails ⅞ to 1½ inches into masonry block or mortar joints and ¾ to 1 inch into concrete. (They can shatter tile, stone, and some brick.) Nail into the mortar between bricks if it's solid. Drill a pilot hole in hard cured concrete.

For safety and secure attachment, drive nails straight and hit them squarely; an off-blow can snap a nail. Use a hardened-steel hammer; the nail may chip a softer hammer. Always wear goggles.

If you're installing a large number of masonry nails—to mount furring strips for paneling, for example—consider a masonry fastening tool (shown below). It holds a nail (called a pin) straight and delivers a direct blow. For even faster production, get a similar driver (not shown) that uses a .22-caliber blank cartridge to drive the pin. Although it has built-in safety features, read the instructions and observe all recommended safety precautions; store the driver and cartridges in a locked cabinet.

Masonry nails and screws

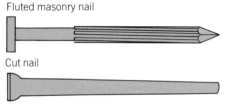

Fluted masonry nail

Cut nail

Masonry nails are made of steel hardened to withstand being driven into concrete and masonry. The flathead nail is usually fluted for more grip and can penetrate harder material than a cut nail. Drive both with a small sledge.
CAUTION: Masonry nails snap easily and can chip a cast-iron hammer. Always wear goggles and use a hardened-steel hammer.

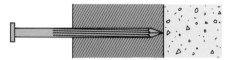

Drive the nail straight into the wood piece you are attaching until it reaches the concrete.

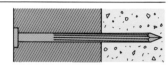

Then drive the nail into the concrete with heavy blows, hitting the nail squarely on the head.

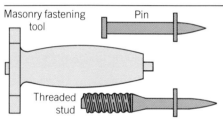

Masonry fastening tool

Pin

Threaded stud

Masonry pins are driven with a special tool to ensure that they are held and hit properly. Use a small sledgehammer to hit the tool. As the tool drives the pin, a washer near the end holds the pin in place in the tool's chamber; then the washer slides up the shank to provide extra bearing surface under the head. Threaded studs that accept nuts are also available.

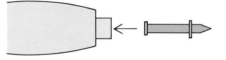

Insert the head of the pin into the chamber of the tool.

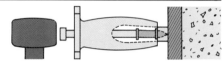

Place pin's point against piece you are attaching; tap tool's drive shaft until its other end touches pin. Drive in pin with heavy blows.

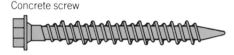

Concrete screw

Concrete screws are made of hardened steel and have sharp, wide threads that cut into concrete. They are installed the same way as a wood screw—by drilling pilot holes. If the piece you are attaching doesn't have holes for mounting, first drill holes large enough for the screws to pass through freely.

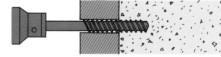

Holding the piece you are attaching in place, drill a hole in the wall equal to the diameter of the screw minus the threads.

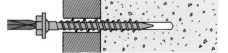

Put the screw through the mounting hole and drive it into wall, using a Phillips bit or hex driver on a variable-speed drill or screw gun.

Hand-drilling concrete and masonry

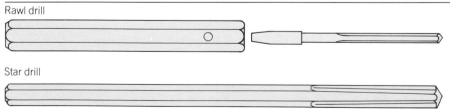

Rawl drill

Star drill

To hand-drill into concrete, brick, or stone, use a Rawl drill for holes smaller than ¼ in. For larger holes, up to 1 in. in diameter, use a star drill. Wearing gloves and goggles, grasp the drill near the center and hit it squarely with a small sledgehammer. After each blow, rotate the drill slightly. Every so often remove the drill and blow out the dust.

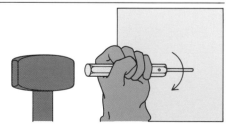

Plugs and anchors provide more security when hanging hooks, shelves, and other heavy fixtures on masonry and concrete walls. Most work by expanding against the sides of a hole when you insert a screw. Those below are typical; others work on similar principles. You can also use a plastic toggle (p.85); in a solid wall, its wings remain folded and press against the hole's sides. A plastic toggle is less likely to crack brick than are other anchors.

An alternative to anchors is the concrete screw (or masonry screw). You can drill a hole for it and install it with the fixture in place. (With an anchor you have to move the fixture after marking its position in order to drill a hole for the anchor.) Order concrete screws from a masonry supplier or a specialty hardware catalog.

Although it's easiest to drill into masonry or concrete with a carbide bit on an electric drill (p.54), you can drill by hand with a star drill or Rawl drill (bottom, facing page). To make a large hole, start with a small one and enlarge it progressively.

Masonry plugs and anchors

Wood dowel

Roundhead screw

Wood dowels provide a simple, inexpensive way to secure lightweight items to masonry. Use a ⅜- or ½-in. dowel for No. 10 and smaller screws; the dowel should be no more than ¼ in. larger in diameter than the screw.

Drill a hole wide enough for the dowel to fit snugly. Make it deep enough to accommodate the dowel.

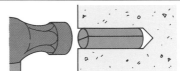
Split the dowel lengthwise, using a wood chisel. Then hold the pieces together and drive them flush.

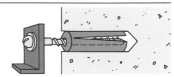
Slip a washer on a roundhead wood screw, put the screw through the fixture, and screw it into the dowel.

Lead anchor

Plastic plug

Plastic anchor

Lead anchors, plastic or fiber plugs, plastic anchors, and similar fasteners all expand inside a hole when you insert a sheet-metal or wood screw or a lag bolt. Select type and size according to the weight of the fixture. Lead holds better than plastic or fiber.

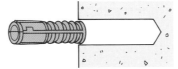
Drill a hole just wide enough for the lead anchor to fit snugly. Push the anchor shield into the hole.

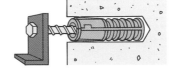
Slip a lag bolt through fixture and into anchor. If anchor turns in hole, wrap masking tape around it and reinsert.

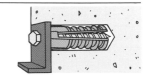
Drive the lag bolt in until the fixture is firmly against the wall. Be careful not to overtighten.

Machine-screw anchor

Setting tool

Machine-screw anchors hold very securely. A hard steel, wedge-shaped inner core causes the anchor's lead outer sleeve to spread when you put a special setting tool on the anchor and drive it all the way into its hole. The inner core has threads that accept a machine screw.

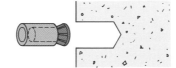
Drill a snug hole for anchor; make it slightly deeper than outer sleeve (not entire anchor length). Insert anchor.

Place setting tool on top of anchor. Use heavy blows from a small sledge to drive the anchor flush.

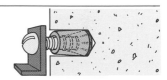
Slip a machine screw through the fixture. Then put it into the anchor and tighten until firmly attached.

Masonry bolt

Threaded end   Eyebolt

Masonry bolts are used to affix heavy objects, such as furniture and framing, to solid walls. A wedge in the bottom of the anchor causes the outer sleeve to spread when you thread a bolt into the anchor. These bolts come in a wide size range and with threaded ends, eyes, or hooks.

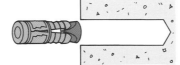
Drill a hole wide enough for anchor to fit snugly and deep enough to accommodate anchor. Insert anchor.

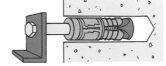
Slip the bolt through the fixture. Then put it into the anchor.

Tighten the bolt to expand the anchor in the hole and firmly secure the fixture.

Adhesives/General-purpose glues

Adhesive	Sample brand names	Typical uses	Components	Application	Characteristics	Solvent
Acrylic	3 Ton Adhesive Devcon Plastic Welder Duro Depend II	For fast, extra-strong bonding of wood, metal, glass, outdoor furniture.	Two parts, liquid and powder; mix parts just before using. Also liquid and paste; apply one to each surface.	Apply with brush, putty knife, or wood strip, depending on job.	Sets in as little as 5 min.; cures overnight. Waterproof; rigid; dries tan.	Acetone (nail polish remover)
Aliphatic (yellow, or carpenter's, glue)	Titebond Duro Professional Elmer's Carpenter's	General-purpose adhesive for furniture building and repair, cabinetwork.	One part, liquid; ready to use.	Apply from squeeze bottle; clamp for at least 45 min.	Sets within 1 hr.; cures overnight. Water-soluble, do not use on outdoor furniture; rigid; dries clear.	Warm water
Cellulose	Duco Cement (clear) Ambroid (amber)	For wood, china, glass, most fabrics, assembling models. Test plastics: if a drop etches the surface, it will probably bond that plastic.	One part, liquid; ready to use.	Apply directly from tube; use wood strip to apply from can. For strength, put two coats on both surfaces; let first get gummy before applying second.	Sets to 60% of strength in 2 hr.; cures to 90% in 2 days. Waterproof; moderately flexible; dries clear or amber.	Acetone (nail polish remover)
Cyanoacrylate (super, or instant, glue)	Krazy Glue Duro Quick Gel Hot Stuff	Liquid bonds most plastics, metals, vinyl, rubber, ceramics; gel bonds wood and other porous materials.	One part, liquid; or gel; ready to use.	Carefully apply one or several drops directly from tube. **CAUTION:** Do not get on skin or point at face.	Sets in 10 to 30 sec.; cures in 30 min. to 12 hr. Water-resistant; rigid to semirigid; extra-strong; dries clear.	Acetone (nail polish remover)
Epoxy	Dab Weldwood Crafter's Epoxy Devcon 2-Ton Epoxy Fiberglass Epoxy Super Glue Miracle Fast-Set Epoxy (5 min.)	For wood, metal, china, glass, most other materials. Especially good for bonding two dissimilar materials, such as metal to glass.	Two parts, both syrupy liquids; mix equal amounts just before using. Available in tubes, double-barrel syringes. Also comes as mixable putties.	Apply with wood strip, putty knife, brush, or matchstick, or from syringes. Knead putties together. Not easily removed; use expendable brushes.	Sets at room temperature in 5 min. to overnight, depending on type; cures in 3 hr. to several days. Waterproof; rigid to semirigid; extra-strong; dries clear or brownish.	Acetone (nail polish remover)
Polyvinyl acetate (PVA, or white, glue)	Duro Professional Wood Elmer's Glue-All Franklin's Home, Shop, and Craft	For general household repairs, furniture, interior woodwork, paper, ceramics.	One part, liquid; ready to use.	Use applicator on bottle for small jobs; for large jobs apply with brush.	Sets in about 8 hr. at 70°F; cures in 24 hr. Water-soluble, do not use on materials exposed to water; rigid; dries clear.	Soap, warm water
Polyvinyl chloride (PVC)	Sheer Magic	For quick repairs and craft work; china, marble, glass, wood, porcelain, metal, plastic.	One part, liquid; ready to use.	Apply directly from tube or use a wood paddle.	Sets in minutes; cures over a longer period; see label. Waterproof; semirigid; dries clear.	Acetone (nail polish remover)
Resorcinol	Elmer's Waterproof Glue National Casein Co. R-14 Weldwood Waterproof Glue	For extra-strong wood repairs; boatbuilding, outdoor furniture.	Two parts, liquid and powder; mix only amount needed just before using.	Apply with brush, roller, or wood strip, depending on job. Clean joint before glue sets; unremovable after hardening.	Sets and cures in 10 hr. at 70°F, in 6 hr. at 80°F, in 3½ hr. at 90°F. Waterproof; rigid; dries dark red.	Cool water before hardening
Styrene butadiene (rubber-base cement)	Black Magic (black) Brite Magic (white)	Versatile adhesive for temporary adhesion on metal, glass, many plastics; attaching sandpaper to sanding disc.	One part, thick paste; ready to use.	Use spatula, putty knife, or trowel for large jobs; apply directly from tube for small jobs.	Sets and cures in about 48 hr. Waterproof; rigid; dries black or white.	Mineral spirits, such as turpentine
Urea formaldehyde	Weldwood Plastic Resin Glue	For extra-strong furniture and cabinet repairs.	One part, powder; mix with water as directed just before using.	Apply with brush, roller, or spatula, depending on job.	Sets in 9 to 13 hr. at 70°F; cures in 24 hr. Water-resistant after curing; rigid; dries light brown.	Soap, warm water before hardening

Among the wide variety of adhesives available today, some can be applied to several materials. They are described on the facing page. The chart on this page lists ones that have more limited uses. In addition, many adhesives are formulated for specific applications, such as installing wallboard or ceiling tiles. Always buy the recommended adhesive for such jobs.

Water resistance. PVA and aliphatic adhesives (white glue and carpenter's glue) and water-base casein and hide glues are water-soluble. Do not use them on objects that will be exposed to weather or dampness. Choose a water-resistant adhesive for a piece that may have to withstand some dampness or brief water contact. Select a waterproof glue if a piece may be immersed or soaked regularly.

Preparing surfaces. Clean both surfaces thoroughly. Any oil or dirt—even a thin film—will prevent proper bonding. Strip the finish from wood (p.117) or sand it free of wax, paint, and varnish. Wipe metal, glass, and other nonporous materials with a degreasing agent, such as alcohol. Always follow label recommendations.

Clamping and curing. Most adhesives require clamping (pp.34–35) until they set. *Setting time* is the interval before the glue hardens. *Curing time* is the period it takes the bond to reach maximum strength. An object should not be used until the adhesive has cured. For glass, china, and other items that are difficult to clamp, instant and other fast-setting glues are ideal. If you must clamp an awkward object, consider such aids as masking tape, rubber bands, or small jigs.

Adhesive	Sample brand names	Typical uses	Application	Solvent
Bolt-locking compound (anaerobic resin)	Loctite 271 (permanent bond) Loctite 242 (breakable bond) Permatex Locksnuts (breakable bond)	For locking thread of bolts and screws; will harden in absence of air between closely fitted metal parts.	Squeeze from tube or bottle.	Soap, warm water before hardening
Casein glue	National Casein Co. No. 4420	Traditional furniture glue; good for oily woods such as teak and rosewood; good gap filler; stains softwoods.	Mix powder with water and apply with brush, roller, or wood strip, depending on job.	Warm water
Contact cement	Ashland Chemicals Contact Cement Weldwood Contact Cement	For permanently bonding laminated plastic to countertops; also for tasks where clamping is difficult, such as reattaching a wall tile.	Apply with brush or roller to both surfaces. Bonds instantly.	Acetone (nail polish remover)
Hide glue	Franklin Liquid Hide Glue Flake form usually carries retailer's name	Repairing furniture assembled with hide glue, which is incompatible with aliphatic and PVA glues; water-soluble, do not use on outdoor furniture.	Soak flakes in warm water until smooth and brushable; heat in double boiler to 130° F and apply hot; sets quickly. Apply liquid from bottle or brush on.	Warm water
Hot melt	Thermogrip Hot Melt Swingline Hot Melt	For quick repairs on leather and fabrics; gap filler for loose joints on furniture.	Apply with glue gun (p.90).	Acetone (nail polish remover)
Latex-base adhesive	Duralite Formula 55 Franklin Indoor-Outdoor Carpet Adhesive Miracle Floor/Carpet Adhesive	For fabrics, carpet, paper, cardboard.	Apply directly from tube or with wood paddle from can.	Lighter fluid
Liquid solder	Bondo Liquid Solder Liquid Steel	Bonds aluminum, tin, other metals and materials. Do not use to solder electrical connections.	Apply directly from tube or with brush or wood strip from can.	Acetone (nail polish remover)
Mastic	Franklin Construction Adhesive Ruscoe Pan-L-Bond Webtex 200 Acoustical Adhesive	For ceiling, wall, and floor tiles, plywood panels, concrete, asphalt, leather, textiles.	Apply directly from tube or with stick or notched trowel from can.	Usually mineral spirits; follow directions
Polyester	Fiberglass Resin Pettit Polyester Resin	For bonding fiberglass on boats; patching fiberglass sinks and porch roofs.	Add activator and brush on.	Acetone (nail polish remover)
Urethane	Dow Corning Urethane Bond Elmer's Stix-All	For strong, extra-flexible joint on wood or between wood and metal or glass.	Apply directly from tube.	Alcohol before hardening

CAUTION: Because most adhesives contain toxic solvents or resins that are flammable and release noxious fumes, work outdoors or in a well-ventilated area; don't smoke, eat, or drink. The adhesive itself can irritate skin and eyes and, if accidentally swallowed, cause poisoning. Never point an applicator at your face; lock glues out of children's reach.

Although it doesn't produce as strong a bond as most adhesives, hot-melt glue is a fast-setting adhesive that's handy for quick fixes on furniture, toys, shoes, carpeting, ceramic and floor tiles, and wood and leather crafts. The glue comes in solid sticks and is applied with an electric glue gun.

To use the glue, insert a stick in the gun. Wait 3 to 5 minutes for the gun to heat; then apply the glue by pulling the gun's trigger (or, on some guns, by pushing on the rear of the glue stick). Work quickly; some glue begins to set within 5 seconds; you have about 10 to 15 seconds from the time you start until you must press the pieces together. The glue sets to 90 percent of its strength within 1 minute.

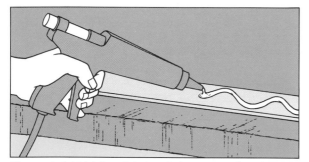

Along a straight joint apply hot-melt glue generously and quickly in a long wavy line on one surface; then, within 15 sec. of when you started, press the pieces together and hold them for 30 sec. Some excess should squeeze out; trim it with a knife.

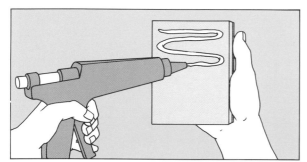

On a tile or other wide piece, quickly apply a thick ribbon of hot-melt glue in a wide zigzag pattern; then press the tile in place and hold it for 30 sec. until the glue sets. Use a knife to trim the excess that squeezes out.

Tape	Description	Use
Anti-slip tape	Heavy weatherproof plastic with rough-textured surface and strong adhesive.	For sure footing in tubs and showers, on steps, entrances, skateboards, and ladders.
Carpet tape	Plastic or cloth with moderately strong adhesive on two sides; also made in waterproof form for outdoor use.	Securing carpets and rugs to floor or patio. Apply tape to floor; then peel off backing and press carpet against top side. Many other uses include securing posters and other items to wall, sandpaper to block.
Cloth tape	Coated cloth with moderately strong adhesive; available in range of strong colors.	For repairs to books, albums, plastic upholstery, and other household items.
Duct tape	Strong, silver-colored, plastic-coated cloth with moderately strong adhesive; resistant to moisture and to heat and cold.	Sealing joints on ducts; a very versatile tape with many uses indoors and outdoors, often for temporary repairs as of cracked glass, ripped rug, or torn camping equipment.
Electrical tape	Thin, flame-retardant, stretchable vinyl with moderately strong adhesive; longer-lasting than older cloth friction tape.	Insulating temporary or emergency spliced electric joins in cords and other electrical components. Never use on household wiring.
Flue tape	Highly heat-resistant metal tape with strong adhesive.	For metal flue pipe joints on furnaces; stopping leaks on hot-air ducts.
Foam mounting tape	Flexible foam core with strong adhesive on both sides of core.	Mounting lightweight items on rough-textured surfaces, such as brick or concrete; apply like carpet tape (see above).
Masking tape	Beige crepe or white flat heavy paper with moderately strong adhesive.	Masking windows or defining lines when painting; for many other temporary jobs, including holding glued pieces together; highly versatile. Becomes difficult to remove if left on for a long period.
Mesh fiberglass tape	Strong, thin fiberglass mesh with tacky adhesive.	For repairs and joints on wallboard; used with wallboard joint compound.
Metal foil tape	Heavyweight aluminum foil with strong adhesive.	Sealing and repairing gutters, ducts, and aluminum siding.
Pipe-thread seal tape	Thin ribbon of Teflon with no adhesive.	For leakproof seal on threads of metal or plastic plumbing pipes.
Plastic tape	Thin, stretchable, waterproof vinyl with moderately strong adhesive; available in colors.	For light-duty repairs to plastic upholstery and similar materials; also used for color-coding items or areas.
Reflective tape	Weatherproof plastic tape with coating that shines when hit with light.	Marking edges of stairs, projecting corners, especially in basements, driveways, garages, entries; also for safety marking of bicycles, children's and runners' clothing.
Weather-sealing tape	Heavyweight weatherproof plastic tape with strong adhesive.	Sealing cracks around doors and windows, air-conditioners, cold-air ducts, and protective plastic enclosures.

Chapter five

Woodworking
Types of wood, techniques, and finishes

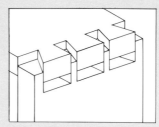

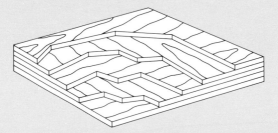

Wood is the material you will most often encounter when doing new projects and repair jobs. Durable, easily shaped, and available in an array of sizes, shapes, and colors, wood is satisfying to work with. From installing molding to building boxes, from cutting and fitting joints to putting the final polish on furniture, this chapter tells you what you need to know to work with wood.

Consult other chapters and the index for more information on tools and techniques, fasteners and adhesives, and the specific parts of your home that are made of wood.

91

Woodworking/Understanding the nature of wood

To work well with wood and wood products, it is essential to have a good understanding of their source—the tree, from its bark to its inner fibrous cells. Once you are familiar with the characteristics of different types of wood, you will be able to make the best choice for your specific purpose (see chart, facing page).

All trees are composed of roughly 60 percent cellulose and 25 percent lignin, which gives wood its hardness. The remaining 15 percent is made up of a variety of minerals, including ash and potassium; these in part determine a species' qualities, such as smell, color, and resistance to decay. The following elements are common to all trees: *outer bark,* a dead, corklike protective layer; *inner bark* (also called *bast*), which transports the nutrients that have developed in the leaves to the rest of the tree; *cambium,* a sheath of dividing cells that forms more wood and more inner bark; *sapwood,* the growing section that transports sap from the tree's roots to its leaves; *heartwood,* the dense, steellike, inactive center of the tree; *growth rings* marking the tree's age (one ring per year) and indicating its strength (the narrower the rings, the stronger the tree); *pith,* the tree's core; and *medullary rays,* bands of nutrient-bearing and -storing cells radiating from the pith to the outer bark.

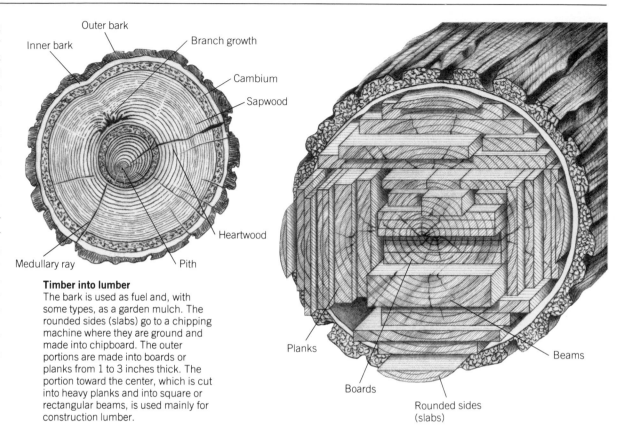

Timber into lumber
The bark is used as fuel and, with some types, as a garden mulch. The rounded sides (slabs) go to a chipping machine where they are ground and made into chipboard. The outer portions are made into boards or planks from 1 to 3 inches thick. The portion toward the center, which is cut into heavy planks and into square or rectangular beams, is used mainly for construction lumber.

Shrinking and warping

As the water in green (freshly cut) lumber evaporates, the lumber shrinks and hardens. Seasoning lumber in a kiln, or stacking it outdoors so that each piece gets aired (layers separated by 2 x 4's and loosely covered with a plastic sheet), will minimize the warpage that accompanies shrinking. Seasoning only reduces the water content; furthermore, seasoned wood, unless sealed, will absorb moisture from the atmosphere.

Avoid buying wood with defects (below). Correct warpage, such as checks, wanes, and some shakes, by cutting them away using a circular or table saw; cut cupped boards in half, straighten them on a joiner (p.110), reglue, and plane. Use twisted boards for shorter lengths; plane off twist.

Crook. Curved along its edge.

Bow. Curved along the length of its face.

Cup. Hollowed across its width.

Twist. Multiple lengthwise bends.

Sound knots. Firm but may split.

Checks. Cracks along growth rings.

Shakes. Hollows between growth rings.

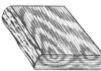
Wane. Corners off or untrimmed.

Types of wood

Hardwood and *softwood* are terms generally used to categorize wood, but they don't always accurately describe a particular species. In fact, some softwoods, such as Douglas fir, are harder than some hardwoods, such as Philippine mahogany.

Softwoods come from cone-bearing (coniferous) trees, such as pine, cedar, hemlock, redwood, and spruce. As a rule, softwoods are cheaper and easier to find than most hardwoods. Softwood is used mainly in structural framing, scaffolding, flooring, shingles (roofing and siding), decking, concrete forms, and other building uses. Some softwoods (sugar pine, for instance), are excellent for furniture and moldings. Lumberyards and many home centers carry softwoods in standard dimensions and lengths, called dimension lumber.

Hardwoods come from deciduous trees—those that seasonally shed their leaves, such as oak, ash, and birch. Hardwoods are usually stronger and longer-lasting than softwoods; they also cost more. They have better surface-finishing properties, and they can be cut, joined, and turned as successfully as softwoods provided your tools are kept razor-sharp. Not all hardwoods are available at lumberyards. You may have to locate a special dealer (check under *Lumber* in the Yellow Pages) or order from a woodworking supply catalog.

Pressure-treated wood

If your project will contact the soil in areas where there is a termite or moisture problem, build with pressure-treated lumber—softwood that has been treated with preservatives. Wood treated with creosote and pentachlorophenol is not readily available to homeowners; wood treated with water-borne preservatives containing inorganic arsenic is considered safer for home use.

▶ **CAUTION:** When working with treated wood, work outdoors; wear goggles, gloves, long sleeves and pants, and a dust mask; wash any areas of your skin that come in contact with sawdust; separately launder clothes that have been exposed to sawdust; and bury or bag wood scraps—never burn them.

Softwood

Species	Characteristics	Uses
Cedar, eastern red	Closed grain, fine texture, highly decay resistant, lightweight, fairly easy to work, finishes well	Chests and closets
Cedar, western red	Closed grain, coarse texture, highly decay resistant, lightweight, easy to work, finishes well	Shingles, moldings, doors, boatbuilding
Fir, Douglas	Closed grain, coarse texture, fairly heavy, medium workability, does not take paint readily	Piling, plywood veneer, residential framing
Hemlock, western	Closed grain, very fine texture, lightweight, machines well	Construction lumber, central layer of plywood panel
Pine, eastern white	Closed grain, medium texture, lightweight, easy to work, minimal shrinkage	Containers, knotty paneling
Pine, sugar	Closed grain, medium texture, lightweight, easy to work, minimal shrinkage	Doors, frames, window blinds
Redwood	Closed grain, medium texture, highly decay resistant, fairly heavy, finishes fairly well	Boards, joists, posts, outdoor furniture

Hardwood

Species	Characteristics	Uses
Birch, yellow	Closed grain, medium texture, heavy, difficult to work, finishes well	Cabinets, cupboards, plywood veneer, doors
Cherry, black	Closed grain, medium texture, fairly heavy, moderately easy to work	Furniture, caskets, fine veneer paneling
Mahogany (true)	Closed grain, fine texture, highly decay resistant, heavy, easy to work, finishes well	Furniture, fine veneers, paneling
Mahogany, Philippine (lauan)	Open grain, variable texture, highly decay resistant, lightweight, easy to work, finish may be blotchy	Heavy construction, industrial flooring, lower-quality furniture
Maple, sugar	Closed grain, medium texture, heavy, difficult to work, finishes well	Flooring (dance halls, bowling alleys), furniture
Oak, red	Open grain, coarse texture, decay resistant, heavy, fairly easy to work, finishes well	Fence posts, truck floors
Teak	Open grain, medium texture, highly decay resistant, very heavy, moderately easy to work, finishes well	Furniture, fine veneer paneling
Walnut, black	Open grain, fine texture, highly decay resistant, fairly heavy, easy to work, finishes well	Furniture, decorative paneling, cabinets

Woodworking/Buying wood

Before shopping for lumber, learn the common sizing and grading terms for your area; they differ slightly regionally. Comparison shop beforehand. Bring a list of what you need and a sketch of your project. Avoid defective wood (p.92). To allow for mistakes, buy 10 percent more than you need.

Shrinkage. Wood will shrink or swell while adjusting to your home's humidity, especially if it's not fully seasoned; let it rest for several weeks before cutting it. Wood is sold in *nominal* sizes—the size when cut at the mill. Shrinkage and planing make the true size smaller. The length, however, is the actual measurement. Some lumberyards will cut dimension lumber to lengths you specify.

Softwood is graded *stress* or *nonstress.* Dimension lumber (2 x 2's up to 4 x 16's), used for posts, studs, and beams, is stress graded; timber (thicknesses of 5 inches or more), used for timber-frame houses, is similarly graded. Board lumber (1 x 2's up to 1 x 12's), used in siding, flooring, and roof sheathing, is nonstress graded. Softwood may be bought planed on all four surfaces.

Hardwood's nominal sizes differ from those of softwood. Thickness is given in quarter-inch increments from 4/4 (1 inch thick) to 8/4 (2 inches thick); width is always the maximum that a log will yield. You buy by the board foot, and you must specify—and pay for it—if you want surfaces planed: S1S (surfaced one side), S2E (surfaced two edges), S1S2E (surfaced one side, two edges), S2S (surfaced two sides), and so on. Figure on further planing to get flat surfaces and squared edges.

Units of measure

Hardwood, dimension lumber, and timber are sold by the board foot: Multiply the nominal width by the nominal thickness (in inches) by the actual length (in feet); then divide by 12. Their lengths are in increments of 2 ft. Some suppliers sell 1-ft. increments.

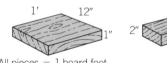

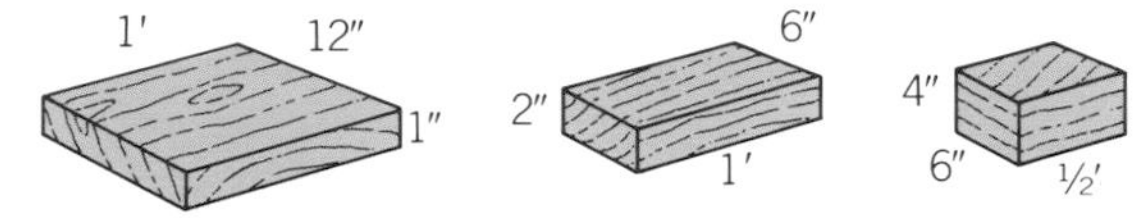

All pieces = 1 board foot

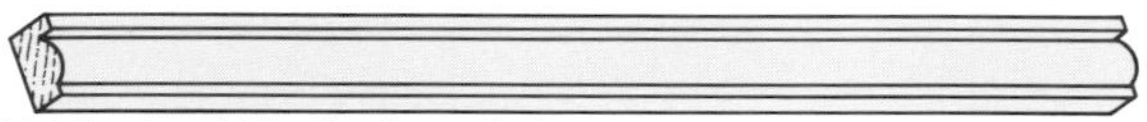

Molding is sold by the linear foot.

Nominal size	Actual size	Nominal size	Actual size
1 x 6	¾" x 5½"	2 x 8	1½" x 7¼"
1 x 8	¾" x 7¼"	2 x 10	1½" x 9¼"
1 x 10	¾" x 9¼"	2 x 12	1½" x 11¼"
1 x 12	¾" x 11¼"	3 x 4	2½" x 3½"
2 x 2	1½" x 1½"	4 x 4	3½" x 3½"
2 x 3	1½" x 2½"	4 x 6	3½" x 5½"
2 x 4	1½" x 3½"	6 x 6	5½" x 5½"
2 x 6	1½" x 5½"	8 x 8	7½" x 7½"

Reading softwood grade stamps

Softwood is graded by several trade groups. The example below is the stamp of a western agency.

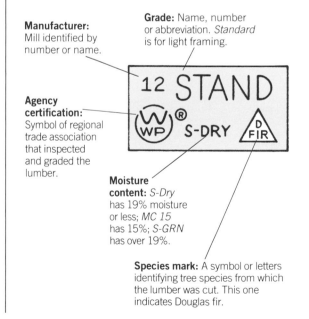

Manufacturer: Mill identified by number or name.

Grade: Name, number or abbreviation. *Standard* is for light framing.

Agency certification: Symbol of regional trade association that inspected and graded the lumber.

Moisture content: *S-Dry* has 19% moisture or less; *MC 15* has 15%; *S-GRN* has over 19%.

Species mark: A symbol or letters identifying tree species from which the lumber was cut. This one indicates Douglas fir.

Softwood grades

BOARDS are graded for appearance, not strength. These grading rules, set by a western agency, have been adopted in part by some of the five other regional rules-writing agencies. The grading scales listed below run from best to lowest in quality.

Select grades: B and better (top quality; few minor flaws), C (excellent; some natural flaws), D (more flaws allowed; some defects caused by manufacturing).

Finish grades: More manufacturing defects are allowed here. Superior (similiar to Select C), Prime (similar to Select D), and E (more flaws than in Superior or Prime).

Common Board grades: Quality ranges from 1 (best) through 4 (lowest). Some agencies provide a 5.

Siding grades: Available in Select, Common Boards, and Alternate Boards, depending on the species. Must be specially ordered by lumberyard.

Alternate Board grades: Less appearance-acceptable than Common Boards. Includes Select Merchantable, Construction, and Standard.

DIMENSION LUMBER is 2 in. to 4 in. thick and at least 2 in. wide. Its grades—uniform throughout the country—are listed here in decreasing order of strength.

Select Structural, No. 1, No. 2, and **No. 3:** Structural framing, roof trusses, concrete forms.

Stud: All stud uses, including load-bearing walls.

Construction, Standard, and **Utility:** Light framing.

Hardwood grades

The hardwood grades were established by a national agency and are uniform throughout the country. Grades aren't easy to identify; knowing minimum size boards helps: FAS and FAS1FACE are 6 in. wide x 8 ft. long ; Selects is 4 in. wide x 6 ft. long ; 1 and 2 Commons, 3 in. wide x 4 ft. long.

Firsts and Seconds (FAS): Cuttings are long, wide, and clear. The lumber is graded from the board's poor side. Used for superior-quality furniture and solid moldings.

FAS1FACE (FAS one face) or **Selects:** A combination of FAS and 1 Common (below); both sides are graded and the good side should be at least 83.3% clear. They can be used for the same purposes as FAS.

1 Common: Cuttings are of medium length and width. One side should be from 66.6% to 83.3% clear. It is graded from the poor side of the board. Good for furniture and cabinetry.

2 Common: Cuttings are short, narrow, and clear. One side should be 50% to 66.6% clear. It is graded from the poor side of the board. Used in combination with 1 Common for kitchen cabinets and bathroom vanities.

Plywood

Cheaper and lighter than most solid wood, plywood is strong and flexible and thus ideal for such applications as furniture and cabinetry, sheathing, paneling, and boatbuilding. Plywood is made of very thin layers of wood (called *plies*, or *veneers*) that are aligned and glued together. Generally, the middle layer, or core, is veneer, lumber, or manufactured wood. The outer plies (called *face* and *back*) are usually better appearance-quality wood than the interior ones. Face is better than back.

Veneer-core plywood, the strongest type, is made up of an odd (or occasionally even) number of plies; three, five, seven, and nine plies are common compositions. Veneer-core plywood is generally available in thicknesses up to 1⅛ inches. The plies are layered with the grain of each running at right angles to those of neighboring plies; this arrangement locks the grain, preventing the panel from shrinking widthwise. It also gives it strength in all directions and minimizes the distortion caused by warping and shrinkage. The plies are bonded with interior or exterior glue.

Although the grains of one ply are at right angles to those of another, the panel itself does have an overall grain running lengthwise. It is this grain direction that provides the panel with the greatest

Planning economical cuts
When planning to cut a plywood panel, it's important to keep in mind that each saw cut you make reduces the dimension by ⅛ in. You may find, as a result, that you'll have to alter your project's dimensions slightly in order to get all the pieces you need out of one panel. The example here illustrates a 4- x 8-ft. plywood panel sectioned for an eight-piece bookcase. Each piece is 9½ in. wide. A total of ½ in. is wasted by the four lengthwise cuts, and ⅛ in. is wasted by the fifth cut.

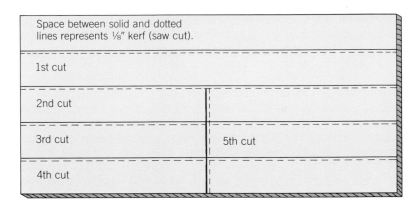

Space between solid and dotted lines represents ⅛″ kerf (saw cut).

1st cut

2nd cut

3rd cut — 5th cut

4th cut

strength. When installing a panel, run its grain horizontal to the joists or studs.

Lumber-core plywood is made in the same way as veneer-core except, of course, for the core, which is strips of solid lumber. It comes in thicknesses up to 1 inch. The edges of lumber-core plywood hold screws securely.

Plywood is further divided into two basic kinds: *construction* and *hardwood.* Construction plywood, which is primarily softwood, is available in 4- x 8-foot panels; its common thicknesses are ¼, ½, and ¾ inch. Hardwood plywood, used mainly for

decorative purposes, comes in panels 4 x 7, 4 x 8, or 4 x 10 feet; thicknesses range from ⅛ to ¾ inch.

Construction plywood is rated by the way it performs (span rating), regardless of thickness. Span rating refers to the maximum space (in inches) needed between supports to effectively support a panel. Most panels have one rating; sheathing has two (roof/floor). Plywood in lumberyards and home centers must meet the standards of the American Plywood Association (APA). You can special-order thicker panels and higher-grade face veneers if you must have them and are willing to pay more.

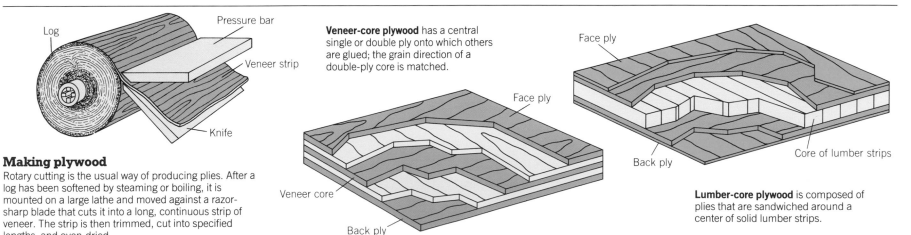

Making plywood
Rotary cutting is the usual way of producing plies. After a log has been softened by steaming or boiling, it is mounted on a large lathe and moved against a razor-sharp blade that cuts it into a long, continuous strip of veneer. The strip is then trimmed, cut into specified lengths, and oven-dried.

Log — Pressure bar — Veneer strip — Knife

Veneer-core plywood has a central single or double ply onto which others are glued; the grain direction of a double-ply core is matched.

Face ply — Veneer core — Back ply

Lumber-core plywood is composed of plies that are sandwiched around a center of solid lumber strips.

Face ply — Back ply — Core of lumber strips

Construction plywood is often used in place of wide lumber. Its plies, including its veneer core, may be softwood or hardwood or both. Construction plywood is bonded with phenol formaldehyde, an exterior adhesive.

This plywood may be manufactured from over 70 different species of trees; these are divided by the American Plywood Association (APA) into five groups, from the strongest and stiffest (Group 1) to the weakest and most flexible (Group 5). The rating on the panel's back or edge gives the group number of the face and back plies. When the face and back plies are different, the higher number is stamped. In sanded panels ⅜ inch thick or less, and in decorative panels (siding) of any thickness, only the face ply's group number is given.

Construction plywood is manufactured in *exterior* and *interior* types. Use interior plywood for indoor projects—never for exterior situations; weather will cause the plies to separate. There are also specialty grades of exterior plywood that have an overlay surface, such as *concrete-form ply* for making concrete forms (p.154). Construction plywood is further categorized into *engineered grades* and *appearance grades*. The former grades are used where strength is needed (sheathing), the latter where looks are important (cabinetry). Use *sanded plywood* for projects that will need a finish. Its panel stamp identifies the veneer of its face and back plies.

For construction that may be exposed to fungi and wood-destroying insects, use preservative-treated plywood and observe the same cautions as for pressure-treated wood (p. 93).

Hardwood plywood generally costs more than construction plywood. It can be identified by the species of its face ply; this is always a hardwood (ash, birch, or oak, for example) and thin (from ¼₂ inch up to ¹⁄₃₂ inch). Its other plies may be hardwood, softwood, or both; the core may be veneer, lumber, particleboard, or medium density fiberboard (MDF). It is bonded with urea-formaldehyde adhesive. Use only hardwood plywood that bears a stamp reading "Formaldehyde emissions 0.2 ppm conforms to HUD requirements." This ensures that it meets government standards.

Construction plywood grades

This plywood is available in various face-back veneer grade combinations. A-B is suitable when both face and back plies are to show; A-C or A-D is suitable if only A side will show.

Grade	Description
N	Smooth surface. Select; all heartwood or all sapwood. No open defects. No more than 6 repairs per panel. Not readily available.
A	Smooth; finishes well. No more than 18 repairs permitted. Synthetic repairs (filler or putty) permitted.
B	Solid surface. Shims, repair plugs, and tight knots permitted. Synthetic repairs permitted.
C Plugged	Improved C with minor splits, knotholes, and borer holes. Synthetic repairs and some broken grain permitted.
C	Small knots, knotholes, and splits within limits; synthetic or wood repairs, discoloration, sanding defects, and stitching of small veneer pieces to make a panel allowed.
D	Larger knots and knotholes within specified limits. Limited splits and stitching permitted.

Hardwood plywood grades

Hardwood plywood is identified by the species of its face ply and is graded by that ply. The grade is indicated by a letter or number stamped on the panel. The back ply is usually a lower grade.

Grade	Description
A	Top grade. Smooth, tight-cut veneers that are specially matched (spliced to make a face ply). Minor imperfections are permitted.
B	Less well matched face veneers. Inconspicuous flaws are permitted. Looks best stained.
2	No open defects (knotholes or splits). No matching for grain or color is done by manufacturer. Looks best painted.
3	Contains both natural and manufacturing defects (open joints, rough cuts); used mainly for inner plies.
4	Contains natural and manufacturing defects; used mainly for back plies.
SP	Includes random-matched wall paneling; may contain unusual features such as the patterns found in wormy chestnut, English brown oak, and bird's-eye maple.

Construction plywood panel marks

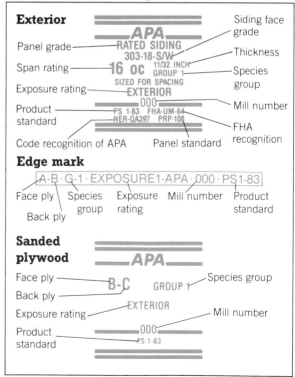

Working with plywood

Store plywood panels off the floor in a cool, dry place for several weeks. Lay them flat on 2 x 4's, or stack them on edge on 2 by 4's and brace them as they lean against a wall at a slight angle.

If you experience low tolerance to hardwood plywood's formaldehyde gas emissions, use sanded plywood instead, and give it a hardwood stain.

Sawing. Use a power saw with a carbide-tipped or special plywood blade; plywood's glue dulls a steel blade quickly. Avoid splintering the surface: Position the panel face up when sawing by hand or with a table saw. Adjust a table saw so that the blade clears the face ply by ¼ inch. When using a circular or a saber saw, have the panel face down and well supported. Wear a sanding respirator; work in a well-ventilated area.

Sanding. Be careful when using a power sander on hardwood plywood; you could easily sand right through the face ply. Never use a belt sander.

Fastening. Nails, brads, or screws won't hold in the edges of thin plywood, but you can center screws in edges ¾ inch or thicker if you first drill pilot holes. In face plies, space nails at 4-inch intervals for maximum panel strength. Remove nails by pulling them out straight—not at an angle; this could cause splintering.

Edge treatment. Fill gaps in panel edges with plaster spackling compound or wood putty; protect and improve their appearance with adhesive-backed veneer, wood strips, molding, or paint.

Grain direction. When using construction plywood for sheathing, make sure the panel grain runs horizontally, perpendicular to the studs; in flooring, perpendicular to the joists. In this way you will get the greatest strength from the panel. To further guarantee maximum strength in flooring, bridge the joists with 2 x 4's so that you can nail the panel on all four sides.

Finishing. Plywood's distinctive grain can be enhanced by applying a semitransparent oil-base stain; prior to staining, treat all edges with a sealant. If you want to paint plywood, first apply a primer and seal the edges.

Sawing plywood

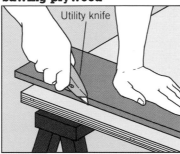

To hand-saw plywood, first score the face ply along the desired cut lines with a utility knife. Make lengthwise cuts first.

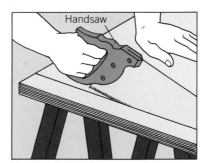

Holding the handsaw at a low angle, cut along the scored line. The entire panel should be well supported.

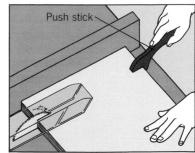

To cut on a table saw, use a push stick to advance the panel, face up, into the saw's guarded blade.

Edge treatments

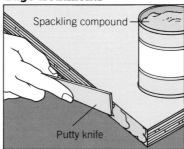

Before painting plywood, fill edge voids with plaster spackling compound or wood filler; when dry, sand smooth.

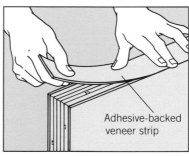

For a real-wood look, cut a peel-and-stick adhesive-backed veneer strip to size; press it down firmly as you apply.

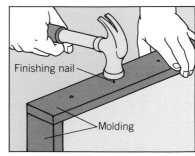

To protect edges from abrasions, apply adhesive and molding. Predrill holes in molding; nail with finishing nails.

Bending plywood

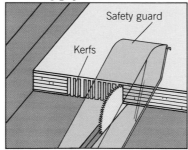

1. To bend thick plywood, make saw kerfs just below the face ply at ³⁄₁₆- to ¼-in. intervals. Cut only at curve.

2. To increase the panel's flexibility, soak the face ply with warm water. (On hardwood plywood this may raise grain.)

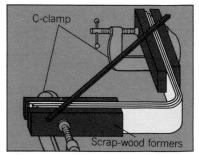

Thin plywood (¼ in. or less) in narrow strips will bend if dampened, then clamped and braced until dry.

Woodworking / Manufactured wood

Hardboard, waferboard, particleboard, and oriented strand board (OSB) are relatively cheap materials that, when used correctly, offer results as good as or better than plywood or lumber. These manufactured, or reconstituted, woods can be used for a variety of projects ranging from furniture to paneling. Parallel strand lumber, another kind of manufactured wood, comes in beams up to 66 feet long; it, too, is performance-competitive with lumber in light building framing.

Most manufactured woods are bonded with a phenol formaldehyde resin except particleboard and medium-density fiberboard (MDF), which are bonded with a urea formaldehyde resin. Buy only particleboard and MDF that is stamped HUD 24 CFR PART 3280; the stamp indicates that the federal standards concerning formaldehyde gas emissions have been observed.

▶ **CAUTION:** If you are sensitive to the gas emitted by urea formaldehyde (you experience dizziness, nausea, headache), choose a manufactured wood that has been bonded with safer phenol formaldehyde. When you work with manufactured woods, always wear a spray-paint respirator.

Hardboard, perhaps the most versatile of manufactured woods, is available in tempered and untempered panels. *Tempered* is strong and moisture-resistant; *untempered* absorbs paint readily. The principal kinds of hardboard are: standard, which has one smooth side; plastic-laminated, which has one side covered with easy-to-clean plastic laminate; prefinished, which has one painted surface; and perforated (pegboard), which is available in single and double thicknesses with a variety of hole arrangements.

Storage. Stack hardboard panels on at least four 4-foot 2 x 4's in a cool, dry, and well-aired space. Try not to mar the panel's smooth surface—it's difficult to restore. Other manufactured woods can be placed on edge, resting on blocks, in a similar environment. Manufactured woods can be worked immediately because their shrinking and swelling potential is minimal.

Gluing. Most manufactured woods take panel adhesives well; to apply, follow manufacturer's instructions. To glue a particleboard surface, first sand the area to be glued so that it will be roughened and better able to hold the adjoining section.

Fastening manufactured wood

Regular wood screws, nails, or brads will hold only when driven through to solid wood. For greater holding power, use adhesive.

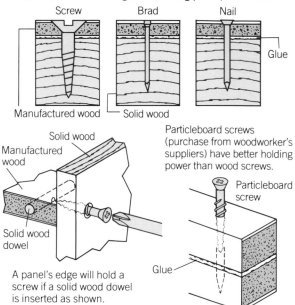

A panel's edge will hold a screw if a solid wood dowel is inserted as shown.

Particleboard screws (purchase from woodworker's suppliers) have better holding power than wood screws.

ALL PANELS 4' x 8'	WAFERBOARD (flakeboard) Thicknesses ¼″, ⅜″, ⁷⁄₁₆″, ½″, ⅝″, ¾″	ORIENTED STRAND BOARD (OSB) Thicknesses ¼″, ⅜″, ⁷⁄₁₆″, ½″, ⅝″, ¾″	PARTICLEBOARD (chipboard) Thicknesses ½″, ⅝″, ¾″	HARDBOARD (fiberboard) Thicknesses ⅛″, ¼″, ⁷⁄₁₆″, ½″
Composition	Wood chips randomly arranged; bonded with phenol formaldehyde.	Wood particles layered at right angles; bonded with phenol formaldehyde.	Wood chips, splinters, and sawdust bonded with urea formaldehyde.	Wood fibers and chips bonded with phenol formaldehyde or linseed oil.
Use	Wall and roof sheathing; wall paneling.	Subflooring; wall and roof sheathing.	Underlayment for countertops; core for furniture veneers.	Walls, doors, siding, drawer bottoms, tabletops.
Cutting	Regular woodworking tools.	Regular woodworking tools.	Tungsten carbide-tip tools.	Tungsten carbide-tip tools—panel face down; hand-held saw—panel face up.
Fastening	Fair nail- and screw-holding ability.	Fair nail- and screw-holding ability.	Poor nail- and screw-holding ability; must be fastened to solid wood.	Poor nail- and screw-holding ability; must be fastened to solid wood.
Finish	Test patch in hidden area for penetration Seal with oil-base primer; paint with acrylic latex paint.	Test patch in hidden area for penetration. Seal with oil-base primer; paint with acrylic latex paint.	Normally not finished because of its uses.	Sand with 120-grit paper before sealing with oil-base primer; apply two coats acrylic latex paint.

Moldings

Wood moldings are often used to hide construction seams in rooms; they are also used for embellishment. Softwood moldings are commonly available at retail lumberyards and home centers in lengths of 4, 6, 8, 10, and 12 feet; widths vary. Hardwood moldings are more expensive and are usually special-ordered. Buy picture-frame molding, which has a rabbet in which the picture rests, at a frame shop or lumberyard. Get slightly more molding than you need in case you err in cutting. Splice when needed; this extra work will help cut costs.

A type of molding called S4S (stands for *smooth 4 sides*) is rectangular in profile, comes in a variety of widths and thicknesses, and is useful when combining moldings to make a new profile.

Buying. To figure how much molding you will need for a ceiling or floor, jot down the width of each wall, round off the figures to the next higher foot, then add them. Save by buying cheap stock if you plan to paint moldings—paint will hide the flaws.

Installing. For a neat job, prime and paint before installing; apply a stain-blocking primer to knots. Attach moldings to walls with 6d or 8d finishing nails driven into studs (p.191). Sink the nails with a nail set; fill holes with wood putty or spackling compound, and when dry, sand putty flush. Touch up with paint. When combining moldings, first measure, cut, and miter each molding separately; if you make an error, only one section will be affected. Mitering (p.109) or coping (p.292) joints can be tricky. Practice first on scrap molding.

Common molding profiles

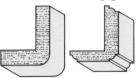

Corner guard protects corners, hides joints.

Stop prevents door from swinging through frame.

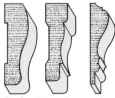

Casing trims door and window openings.

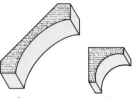

Cove covers wall-ceiling junctures.

Base cap is applied to the top of a base molding.

Crown makes ceiling-wall transition.

Batten hides the seam where wall panels meet.

Built-up molding profiles

Combination of several moldings can provide attractive trim for baseboards, ceilings, and walls.

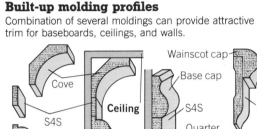 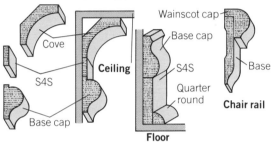

Cove — Wainscot cap — Base cap — S4S — Base — Ceiling — S4S — Quarter round — Chair rail — Base cap — Floor

Base hides seam where floor meets wall.

Chair rail prevents chair backs from marring walls.

Picture frame presents and protects artwork.

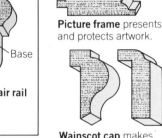

Wainscot cap makes paneling-wall transition.

Quarter round is often used in combined profiles.

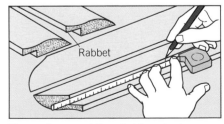

Picture-frame molding. 1. After mitering one end at a 45° angle, measure for length from the rabbet's inside edge at the mitered end.

Rabbet

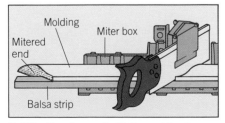

2. Miter the other end with the molding face up and the lip of its rabbet supported by a strip of balsa or basswood.

Molding — Miter box — Mitered end — Balsa strip

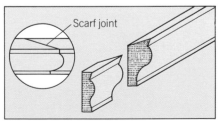

Splicing molding. 1. Mark the molding's end where it covers the stud. Miter both moldings at 45°. Splice is a version of a scarf joint (p.111).

Scarf joint

2. With the scarf joint directly over the stud, drive nail at an angle so that it fastens both the splice and the stud.

Scarf joint — Stud

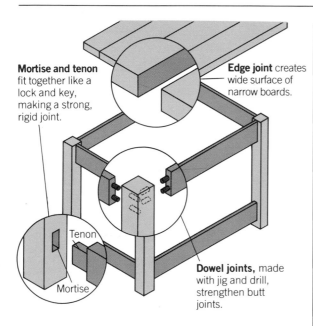

Mortise and tenon fit together like a lock and key, making a strong, rigid joint.

Edge joint creates wide surface of narrow boards.

Tenon

Mortise

Dowel joints, made with jig and drill, strengthen butt joints.

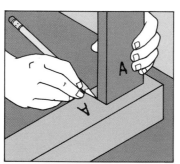

To mark joints for precise fit, align mating pieces. Mark their meeting points with an awl or a sharp pencil. This is more accurate than measuring with a ruler. Label matching components.

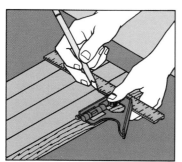

Mark and cut identical pieces, such as legs, simultaneously. By transferring markings to all pieces in one step, the possibility of errors is reduced.

There are many ways to join wood. Methods range from simply abutting or overlapping the pieces and nailing them together to cutting precise interlocking angles. Each joint has specific construction requirements and each may be suitable in several situations.

Think about the use—and abuse—that a finished piece will be subjected to, and choose the simplest joints that will serve. Joints such as miters (p.109) uniting end grain to end grain or butt joints (right) uniting end grain to long grain are weaker than those that join long grain to long grain (*edge,* p.110) or that interlock (*dovetail,* p.106).

Assess the required strength of the joints; they should be of nearly equal strength throughout the piece and be capable of withstanding the load and stress placed upon them. Then, visualize the finished work. Will the joints show? If so, choose those that will enhance the piece's appearance.

Next, ask these technical questions: how much shrinking or swelling are the joints likely to endure, and what is the fastener- or glue-holding ability of manufactured materials, if any (p.98)? Some joints require very precise execution; choose those that are within your ability to construct.

Having chosen suitable joints, draw them to scale on graph paper, and write down their measurements. Always measure from a common starting point. Use the same set of tools throughout. Measure twice and you'll cut only once. Scribe outlines accurately; mark waste areas with an X. Whenever possible, clamp duplicate pieces together, then mark and cut them as a single unit.

Butt joints: Nine ways to make corners

Also called L-joints, butt joints are quick to assemble and do not require precise fitting. They do, however, need strengthening with glue, metal plates and fasteners, special hardware, or dowels. Use fasteners of the correct size—oversize screws will split the joint materials; undersize ones won't adequately support the joint (pp.80–84). When gluing several joints simultaneously, practice the clamping procedure before applying the glue.

Triangular block, glued and screwed in place, stabilizes inside corner.

Square block can be attached from inside if you don't want screws to show.

Outside glue block supports joint without obstructing inside corner.

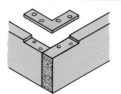

Flat metal corner plate set in recess provides smooth surface across joint.

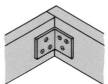

Inside corner brace pulls corner together; supports best if used on all corners.

Triangular gussets of ¼-in. plywood, glued and nailed in place, produce rigid joints.

Nails driven at angle grip better than nails driven straight.

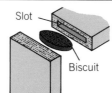

Slot

Biscuit

Wooden biscuits fit into slots, forming a strong joint (p.107).

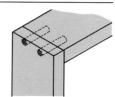

Dowels are strong but require precise fitting. Set invisibly or leave ends exposed.

Overlapping joints

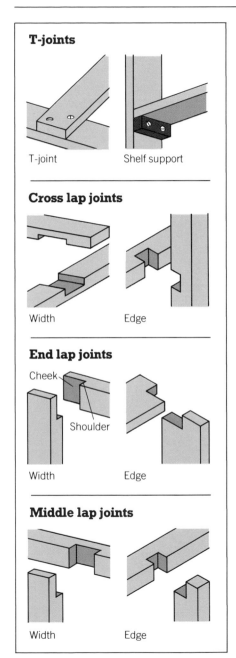

T-joints

T-joint | Shelf support

Cross lap joints

Width | Edge

End lap joints

Cheek | Shoulder

Width | Edge

Middle lap joints

Width | Edge

Among the easiest to construct, overlapping joints can be strengthened by adding glue and fasteners. Notching the pieces to form *full* or *half lap* joints that interlock as well as overlap provides stability and flush surfaces.

A T-joint—the simplest of the overlapping joints—requires no cutting. Place one piece across the other at the desired angle, and fasten the pieces together with glue and nails or other fasteners. Though strong, T-joints are somewhat crude. Use them for rough, temporary, or hidden construction.

Shelf supports, a form of T-joint, are easily assembled. Glue and screw small wooden blocks to the uprights; then simply rest the shelf in position on the blocks.

Full and half lap joints connect width-to-width, edge-to-edge, or edge-to-width. In a full lap, a thick piece is notched to receive the whole thickness of a thin piece. In a half lap, pieces of equal thickness are cut to half their thickness so that they interlock and are flush when joined. Cut them in the middle of each board (*cross lap*), at the ends (*end lap*), or one end to one middle (*middle lap*).

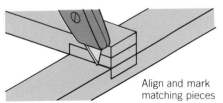

Align and mark matching pieces

For a precise fit, scribe the outline of each piece onto its partner as shown above. Remove the waste wood with a router or table saw (right) or a chisel (pp.36–37).

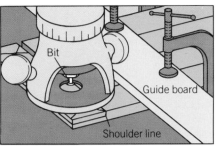

1. A router with a straight bit can cut several lap joints at the same time. Mark and align the pieces. Clamp a guide board across them, allowing for distance between bit and edge of base plate, so that bit is set for shoulder cut.

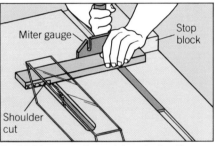

1. A table saw makes quick work of cutting end laps. Adjust saw blade height so that the teeth just touch the scribed cheek line. Using a miter gauge to guide work across saw table, make shoulder cut.

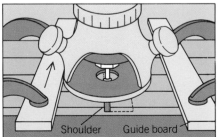

Use router to cut middle laps. Align and secure guide boards on both sides of joint. Cut both shoulders; then rout remaining waste by making several passes between the boards.

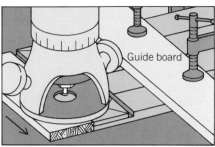

2. Rout the waste, beginning at the tips of the pieces and cutting progressively closer to guide board. If you are not experienced with a router, reposition the board to guide each cut.

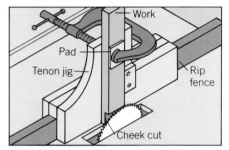

2. Cut joint face with a tenoning jig. Clamp work vertically in jig and remove waste in a single cut. If you don't have a jig, hold stock as for shoulder cut and remove waste in several passes. (A dado head requires fewer passes.)

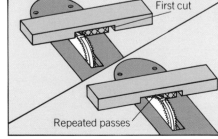

To cut middle laps on a table saw, set dado head as for shoulder cuts of end laps. Cut both shoulders; then remove waste between them.

Woodworking/Dado joints

A channel cut across the wood's grain is called a *dado*. (When the channel is cut with the grain, it is called a *groove*.) A dado joint is formed when a cross member is fitted into the channel. The cross member's end may be the full thickness of the board or a narrow tongue, called a *rabbet* (facing page). Dado joints always form right angles.

Because they completely enclose the ends of the crosspieces, dadoes resist twisting and warping. And when appearance counts—as in shelves, drawers, and cabinet furniture—dadoes conceal the unsightly end grain of the joined boards.

There are two basic types of dado: through and stopped. In a through dado the channel cuts completely across the board; in a stopped dado, it stops short of the board's edge. With stopped dadoes, one or both ends of the channel may be hidden.

Right-angled dadoes are easy to cut with a table saw or router. Dadoes may also be cut to other angles, as in the dovetail dado. These are particularly strong joints, but they require more care in their planning and execution for a clean, finished appearance.

The directions at right for cutting dadoes with a router assume that the bit is the same width as the dado. Dadoes wider than an available bit can be cut by making several passes with the router; clamp a guide board to the work and reset it each time slightly to one side of its previous position. Use a special bit for dovetail dadoes, cutting the channel in one pass, and shaping the tongue gradually in several passes to avoid making it too narrow.

Through dado

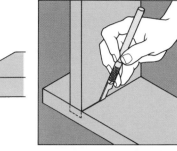

1. Scribe dado width onto board. Whenever possible, use mating piece of joint as a guide. Mark depth of dado; it should be no deeper than half the board's thickness.

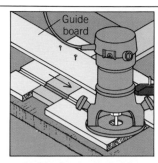

2. Sandwich workpiece between scrap boards to prevent splintering. Clamp guide board parallel to dado markings. Place it so that router's bit is centered and bit's edges just graze both marks. To cut ¾-in.-thick stock, set router depth to ⅜ in.

Stopped dado

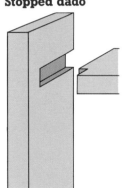

1. Mark width, depth, and outline dimensions. Clamp guide board parallel to width mark. Position stop block parallel to joint's end. Include the distance from bit to edge of router plate when setting the block.

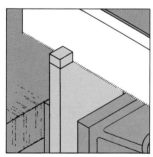

2. Turn router on. Place it against guide board at left end of marked dado. Lower bit into wood slowly to avoid burning out the motor. Move router from left to right, cutting channel.

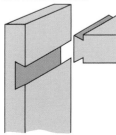

3. Clean all traces of debris from dado channel. If edges are rough, carefully make one more pass with router without resetting bit depth. Square dado's ends with a sharp chisel.

4. Mark and trim cross member to fit. Cut excess away with a backsaw. Saw carefully to create a notch with smooth, flat surfaces and square corners.

Dovetail dado

1. Dovetail dadoes must be cut to depth in a single pass. Mount a dovetailing bit in a router table. Set bit to full depth of dado. Clamp guide board to table. Pass board over bit, cutting channel.

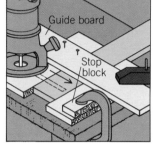

2. Shape each side of tongue individually. Mark board to show depth and greatest width of dado. Make successive alternating passes over dovetailing bit, removing equal amounts of waste from each side until proper size is achieved.

Rabbets

Often combined with dadoes or grooves to form interlocking joints, rabbets are L-shaped tongues cut across or parallel to the wood's grain. They support the joint members, increase the number of gluing surfaces, and conceal end grain.

Rabbet joints are used in furniture because they withstand pulling force from several directions. Although relatively easy to cut, rabbet-and-dado joints require careful measuring for a precise fit. If the rabbet will be paired with a stopped dado, trim the tongue so that the rabbet's board overlaps the uncut portion of the dado's board. For maximum strength, set dadoes away from the board's end. Cut them no wider or deeper than one-half the board's thickness.

Cut standard rabbets with a router, a radial arm saw, a table saw, or by hand with a special plane (pp.40–41). Use a piloted bit in your router or a dado head on your table saw to speed cutting and ensure accuracy. For multiple identical cuts, it is helpful to construct a jig to use as a guide.

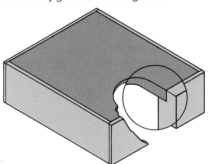

Rabbets in rear edges of cabinet top and sides receive back panel for flush fit.

Rabbet joint

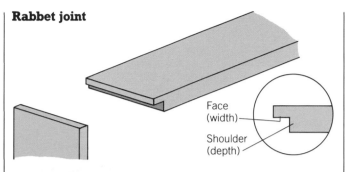

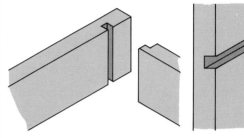

Face (width)
Shoulder (depth)

Cut rabbets up to ½ in. wide with router and rabbet bit. Mark joint outline. Set bit depth to equal rabbet depth. Secure guide board parallel to shoulder line, and make cut. If desired width is greater than ½ in., use a straight bit, resetting the guide board and making several passes to achieve correct dimensions, or use a table saw.

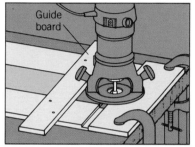

Guide board

1. When rabbeting with a table saw, cut shoulder first. Set blade height to equal rabbet depth; set fence, including blade thickness, to equal width. Align board against fence, and make cut. Position workpiece as shown. (A dado head can be set to cut wide or narrow rabbets in a single pass.)

Fence

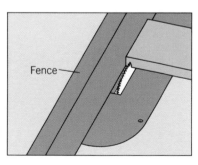

2. To make face cut, set blade height to equal rabbet width. Secure work on edge, so that waste will fall freely away from blade. Set distance between fence and blade for rabbet depth (include blade thickness in this measurement). Support work with a feather board for safety; make cut.

Fence
Feather board

Rabbet-and-dado joint

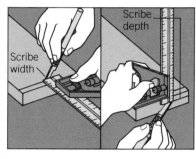

1. Mark rabbet dimensions with a combination square, as shown; transcribe corresponding measurements for dado. If using hand tools, planes and chisels cut well with the grain; saws are better for cutting across the grain.

Scribe depth
Scribe width

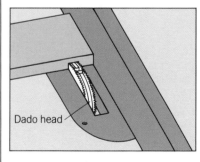

2. Cut dado first. Set the table saw's blade height to equal dado depth. Include blade thickness as part of adjustment, and set fence at the distance desired between far edge of dado and cut edge of board. Make the cut. With a single saw blade, make several passes to remove waste from channel; with a dado head, only one.

Dado head

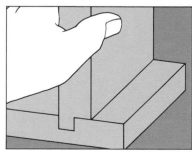

3. Adjust saw blade's height so that rabbet's tongue will be ¹⁄₁₆ in. shorter than dado's depth (allows for glue seepage). Cut face and shoulder of rabbet as described at left. But first practice: cut rabbet from scrap, then test-fit it in the dado. If it fits snugly, make identical cuts in the workpiece.

Woodworking / Mortise-and-tenon joints

These sturdy interlocking joints were once used in all types of carpentry. Today mortise-and-tenons are found mainly in furniture. And although they usually join two pieces at right angles, with careful planning they can unite boards at virtually any angle.

The mortise is the hole portion of the joint; it is cut in the upright, leg, or *stile,* of the work. The tenon is the *tongue* that is cut in the cross member, or *rail.* A tenon is described by its three dimensions. The *shoulder,* which defines its length; the *cheek,* or

width; and the *edge,* or thickness.

A mortise for leg-and-rail construction should be half as deep as the stock is wide. The tenon should be as close to one-third of the stock's thickness as possible and, if blind, about ⅛ inch shorter than the mortise is deep, to allow for glue seepage. When marking the cut lines, keep placing one part against the other to monitor the relationship of the dimensions.

You can cut this joint with hand or power (p.101) tools, but you will always need a chisel to finish the mortise.

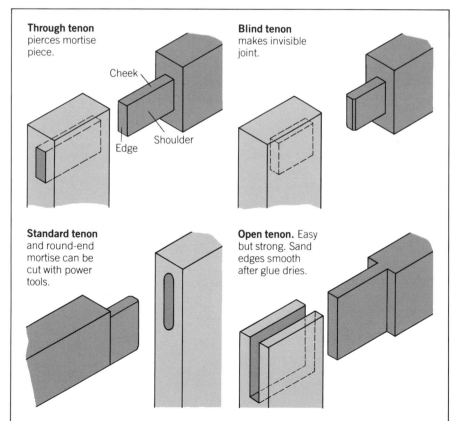

Through tenon pierces mortise piece.

Cheek / Edge / Shoulder

Blind tenon makes invisible joint.

Standard tenon and round-end mortise can be cut with power tools.

Open tenon. Easy but strong. Sand edges smooth after glue dries.

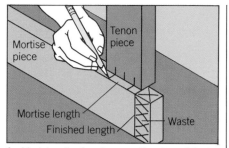

1. Mark length of work on mortise piece. (Waste at end ensures flush finish.) Divide wide side of tenon piece into quarters. Align end on cut line of mortise piece. Transcribe first and third marks to mortise piece, defining mortise's length.

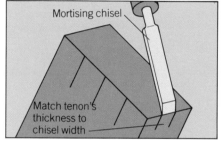

2. Turn tenon piece to narrow side; divide this side into thirds. Middle third equals mortise's width. To cut mortise, select a chisel ¹⁄₁₆ in. narrower than center portion. If necessary, adjust outline slightly to accommodate available tool.

3. Use chisel width to set distance between mortise gauge points. Align points on mortise line marked in step 1, and set gauge's head for correct placement of mortise outline. Scribe parallel lines, completing outline.

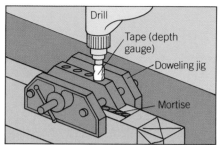

4. Drill out waste from within mortise outline. Choose a bit that makes holes that will just graze outline. Cut end holes first. A Forstner bit (p.28) will cut a flat-bottomed hole, but a twist bit will suffice. Doweling jig ensures straight holes.

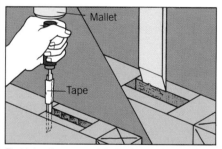

5. Using the same chisel selected in step 2, square ends and smooth bottom of mortise. Sides of long mortises can be trimmed quickly with a wide, razor-sharp chisel. Tape on chisel indicates depth of mortise.

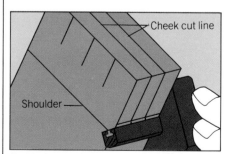

6. Mark tenon's shoulders (⅛ in. shorter than mortise's depth) on all four sides of tenon piece. Then, with mortise gauge at same setting as in step 3, scribe along both narrow edges and end, outlining the cheeks.

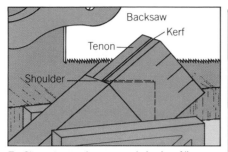

7. Clamp tenon piece on angle in vise. Align saw on waste side of cheek line. Hold saw teeth horizontal (as shown) and cut to shoulder line. Reverse piece in vise. Saw other side of same line, creating a V-shaped wedge in the saw kerf.

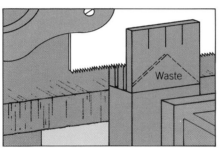

8. Clamp piece vertically. Keeping saw teeth horizontal, cut straight down to shoulder, removing waste and squaring the kerf. Don't saw past shoulder line, or cuts will show on finished joint.

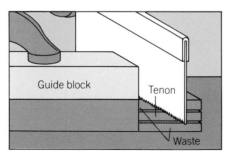

9. Clamp tenon piece flat on bench. Cut shoulders, freeing waste and exposing the cheeks. Use a guide block to ensure straight, square cuts. Be sure to place the saw on the waste side of each cut line.

10. Holding chisel at 45° angle, bevel the tenon's leading edges slightly to ease insertion into the mortise. If the cheek must be less than the full width of the stock, repeat steps 7, 8, and 9 on the edges, trimming them to size.

11. Test-fit the pieces; they should slide together easily. If they stick, rock tenon piece to remove. Adjust fit by trimming or shimming the tenon—not the mortise. Mark matching pieces for reassembling when gluing.

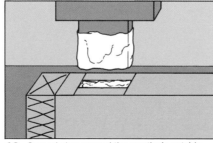

12. Spread glue around the mortise's outside edge and on the tenon's cheeks and edges. Assemble and clamp in position until glue sets. When glue is dry, trim waste from mortise piece so that it is even with the tenon piece.

Strengthening mortise-and-tenon joints

Wedges or dowels can be used to add strength, make repairs, or create decorative effects. Wedges can be added even if you can't disassemble the joint. Chip out a channel for the wedge with a razor-sharp chisel. Use a water-base glue in the channel and drive the wedge in with a mallet. Inserts made of a lighter or darker wood will create an inlaid effect.

Wedged tenon

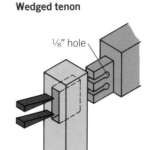

Doweled tenon

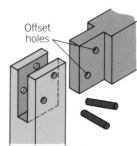

Wedging a through tenon

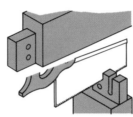

1. Drill small, evenly spaced holes two-thirds of the way down tenon. Saw slots. (Holes prevent splitting.)

2. Fashion finely tapered wedges from scrap wood with saw or chisel. Wedges should be slightly longer than slots.

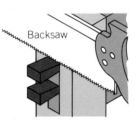

3. Glue and assemble joint. Apply glue to wedges, and tap them gently into place with rubber mallet. When glue dries, trim wedges.

Making a doweled tenon

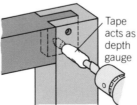

1. Drill through assembled (but unglued) joint until bit just touches tenon. Remove tenon, insert scrap wood, and finish drilling.

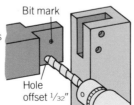

2. Find bit marks on tenon. Using same bit as in step 1, drill holes 1/32 in. closer to tenon's shoulder.

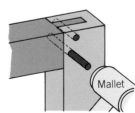

3. Glue and reassemble joint. Drive long wooden dowels through the holes. When glue is dry, trim ends with a backsaw.

Woodworking/Dovetail joints

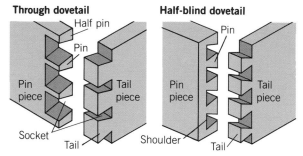

Through dovetail — Half pin, Pin, Pin piece, Tail piece, Socket, Tail

Half-blind dovetail — Pin, Pin piece, Tail piece, Shoulder, Tail

Decorative and durable, dovetail joints have flaring pins and tails that interlock securely. Because they resist being pulled apart, dovetails are ideal for parts of furniture that take a great deal of stress—drawers, for example. And their lines are so attractive that the joints are often left exposed.

The joint is composed of protrusions called *pins* on one piece and *tails* on the other. The spaces are always called *sockets*. Mark the pins first. Allow a half pin at each end, and space the remaining full pins evenly across the full width of the board. One pin per inch is sufficient for strength. They should be a bit narrower than the corresponding tails and 1/32 inch longer than the tail piece's thickness. A jig or template speeds marking and cutting.

Dovetails are commonly made in two styles. In *through* dovetails the tails pierce the pins completely. In *half-blind* dovetails, the pins are cut only partway through the wood's thickness and the tails' ends are hidden by the remaining wood.

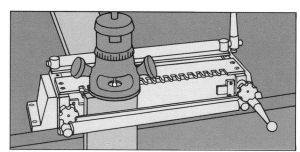

This jig is used with a router to simultaneously cut pins and tails for half-blind dovetails. A bit guide attached to router's base pilots the tool along the jig's outlines.

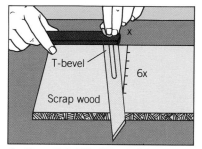

T-bevel, Scrap wood, 6x, x

1. Pin angle is 75°–80° or in 1:6 slope. Set T-bevel with a protractor. Another method is to draw on scrap wood a triangle whose base is one-sixth its height. Align tool against triangle's hypotenuse.

Mallet, BACK

4. Clamp board face up on bench. With chisel make alternate vertical and horizontal cuts halfway through board. Turn board over and complete cuts. Or cut across socket bottoms with thin-bladed coping saw (p.26).

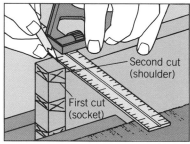

Second cut (shoulder), First cut (socket)

7. Mark and cut shoulders for the sockets that receive the half pins. Cut the socket first, then the shoulder; misfitting the half pins can distort the whole joint. Remove waste from remaining sockets as in steps 3 and 4.

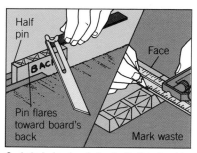

Half pin, BACK, Face, Pin flares toward board's back, Mark waste

2. Label pin piece's back. Scribe shoulder 1/32 in. wider than thickness of tail board. Clamp pin board upright; mark pins and half pins on end. With square, extend lines to shoulder on both sides of pin board.

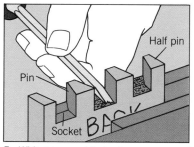

Half pin, Pin, Socket, BACK

5. With narrow chisel, clean corners of pins and sockets. They must be smooth and square in order to fit properly with tails. Undercut the socket bottoms, forming a very slight V-shape.

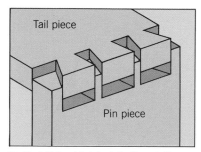

Tail piece, Pin piece

8. Test-fit the joint, but don't push it completely together. If too tight, trim. If perfect, apply glue and assemble. If loose, assemble and shim with veneer while glue is wet. When glue is dry, plane faces flush.

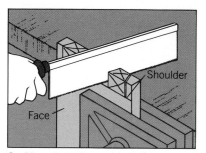

Shoulder, Face

3. Align dovetail saw (a small backsaw), on waste side of cut line. Begin cutting with saw at an angle so that you can see shoulder line. Hold saw horizontally by end of cut. Cut carefully; stop precisely at shoulder.

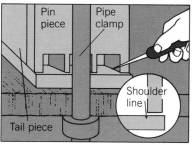

Pin piece, Pipe clamp, Shoulder line, Tail piece

6. To mark tails, first scribe shoulder line 1/32 in. wider than pin piece's thickness. Align pin piece on shoulder line. Trace pin's shape directly onto tail piece with a scratch awl. Label the matching pieces.

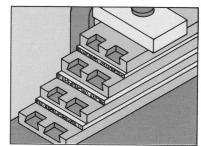

To cut multiple identical dovetails stack them as shown and cut them assembly-line fashion. Clamp securely, with scrap wood between the layers to prevent damaging the board faces.

Box joints

The right-angled fingers and slots of box joints slide together easily and, because of their large gluing area, form a very strong joint. They are also called finger joints.

The slots and fingers should be cubes as long and wide as the stock is thick. When marking the fingers, make them 1/32 inch longer than the stock's thickness to allow for fitting. One board should have a complete finger at each end; the other, slots. When using a table saw, adjust the measurements to accommodate your dado head. You must be able to assemble the head's blades and chippers to exactly equal the slot's dimensions.

A jig is essential for table sawing. All the jig elements must exactly equal the corresponding joint elements. Square the edges of a 1 x 6. Cut a piece 10

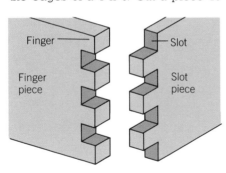

inches longer than the saw's miter gauge, and cut a slot in it the same size as the finished joint's slots. Make a small block of wood the same size as the joint's fingers. Glue it to the board precisely a finger's width from the dado head's cutting edge. Screw the jig to the saw's miter gauge. Slip each slot over the block as it is cut; the next cut is automatically aligned (see right).

Biscuit joints

Adhesives 88–90
Clamps 34–35

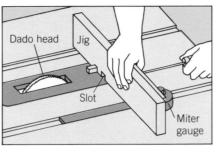

1. Screw jig to saw's miter gauge so that the distance between the saw blade's edge and the guide block's side exactly equals the thickness of one joint slot. Saw trial slots in scrap wood to test jig, and adjust before cutting joint.

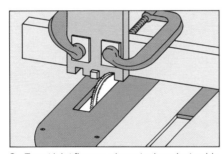

2. To cut joint fingers, place stock against guide block and carefully push entire assembly over turning dado head. Fit newly cut slot over block; saw next slot. Repeat. Place final slot over guide block and go on to next step.

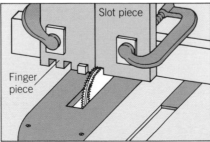

3. Put matching slot piece next to finished finger piece. Clamp both pieces securely to jig and cut first slot. Reverse slot piece and cut final slot. Remove finger piece and cut remaining slots as in step 2.

Fast, strong, invisible, and virtually foolproof, biscuit joints can replace box or dovetail joints, mortise-and-tenon joints, or doweled joints without sacrificing strength. And you can insert them into any joint to add strength.

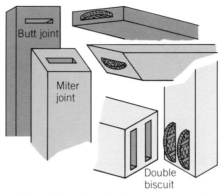

The biscuit, which comes ready-made in three sizes, is a beech-wood wafer shaped like a flat football. A tool called a *biscuit joiner* cuts slots in the adjoining pieces. Put white or yellow water-base glue in the slots, slip in the biscuit, and clamp the joint. The glue swells the biscuit, producing a tight fit even if the slots are slightly oversize. The elliptical shape allows some forgiveness in the lateral alignment.

The biscuit joiner is a small circular saw with a horizontally mounted plunge-cutting blade. A good joiner will have a conveniently located power switch and a fence that adjusts easily—and locks securely—for right-angled or mitered joints. The fence centers the slot and holds the blade parallel to the wood's edges. As with all power tools, observe proper safety precautions (p. 19) and maintenance procedures.

1. Align both pieces of joint. Mark center line for slot across both pieces with pencil. If cutting several joints, label mating pieces AA, BB, and so on. If using two or more biscuits in one joint, mark both sides of boards.

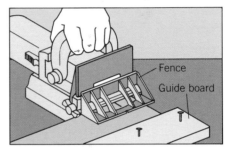

2. Secure piece against a guide board. Adjust joiner's fence height to half the wood's thickness. Align guide mark on joiner with center mark on wood. Hold tool firmly against joint and turn on motor. Push to cut slot.

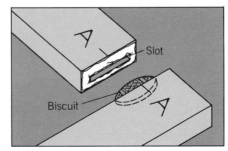

3. Repeat step 2 on mating piece. Blow sawdust from both slots. Apply white or yellow glue to slots and joint surfaces. Insert biscuit and align joint. Clamp until glue dries. Sand surface when glue is completely dry.

Properly made dowel joints are nearly as strong as mortise-and-tenon joints (pp.104–105). They require careful workmanship and some special equipment.

Use at least two dowels per joint. Their diameters should be one-third to one-half the thickness of the thinnest piece of wood being joined. Their lengths should be 1¼ times the thickness of the thinnest piece. You will be drilling complementary holes in each joint piece to accept the dowel pegs. Drill the holes ⅛ inch deeper than half the dowel's length. Dowels must be *fluted* (scored or grooved) so that air and excess glue can escape. A slight bevel on the ends eases insertion.

The tricky part of making dowel joints is aligning and drilling the holes precisely. A *dowel center,* a plug with a centered point, fits into the hole on one side of the joint and pricks the other piece to mark the opposite hole's center. Another method, using brads, is described below. A jig ensures that the holes are absolutely straight; self-centering doweling jigs are available for power drills.

Dowel joints

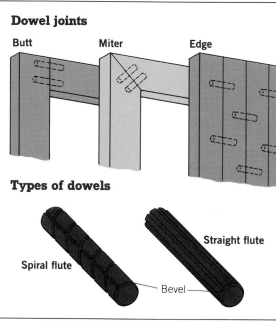

Butt   Miter   Edge

Types of dowels

Spiral flute   Straight flute   Bevel

Making dowels

 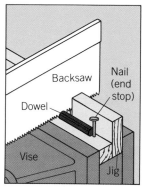

Backsaw   Dowel   Vise   Nail (end stop)   Jig

1. Make flutes first. Clamp hand saw in vise so that teeth extend ¼ in. above jaws. Hold dowel rod at right angle to blade. Press down and scrape dowel across teeth, scoring along the length of the rod. Rotate the dowel and repeat until the entire circumference is cut.

2. Cut fluted rod to required length. To speed sawing several dowels to the same length, make a jig. Drive a nail into a piece of scrap lumber to act as a stop, cut a blade slot in a taller piece, and clamp both pieces in vise. Bevel dowel ends with a rasp (or, if small enough, a pencil sharpener).

Marking and installing dowels

Edge

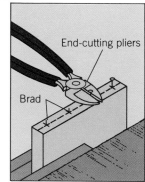

End-cutting pliers   Brad

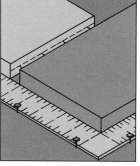

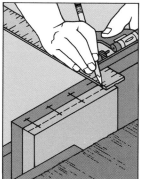

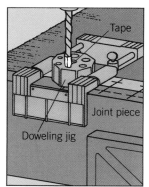

Tape   Joint piece   Doweling jig

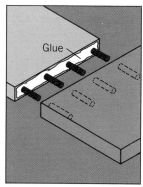

Glue

Position first mark so that the hole's outside edge will be two dowel diameters from edge of piece. Mark exact centers of remaining holes along one piece. Centers should be evenly spaced and surrounded by equal amounts of wood.

To transfer center marks to mating piece, hammer 1-in. wire brads partway into centers of marked piece. Be sure brads enter wood at a precise right angle. With side- or end-cutting pliers (p.32), clip off nailheads, allowing ¼ in. of brad to protrude.

To mark mating piece, place both joint pieces on a flat surface against the legs of a framing square. Make sure the correct faces are up. Push pieces together sharply so that protruding brads mark the mating piece. Remove brads. Drill holes in both pieces.

Another method is to use a doweling jig instead of brads. Clamp mating pieces of joint together with joint faces exposed. Square lines across joint faces to show locations of dowels. (Some jigs self-center: when set for stock thickness, the jig adjusts for correct dowel size and position.)

Attach jig to joint pieces following the manufacturer's instructions. Usually this means aligning a mark on the jig with the center marks inscribed on the stock. Drill all holes, using jig as a guide. Tape on drill bit acts as a depth gauge, if the jig doesn't have one.

Assemble the joint. Apply glue to surfaces of mating pieces and inside rim of each hole. Do not apply glue to dowels. Press or tap all dowels into one piece first, then fit mating piece over them. Tap joint together and draw it closed with clamps. Leave in place until glue dries.

Miter joints

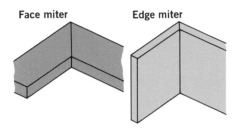

Face miter   Edge miter

Trimming the ends or the edges of lumber to an angle for joining is called mitering. Miters can be cut at any angle, but the most common is 45° so that the adjoining pieces form a right angle.

Miters occur in one of two orientations: either across the face of the stock to form a *face miter,* or along the edge of a board to form an *edge miter.* Face mitering is more common; it is used in picture frames, in door and window frames, and in frame-and-panel boxes. Molding can be face mitered to hide seams. Edge miters occur in fine furniture and cabinetmaking.

In a miter joint, both surfaces are end grain. Because end grain doesn't take glue or fasteners well, these joints are particularly weak. They can be strengthened with veneer feathers, splines (matching or contrasting wood set in grooves cut on the joint's faces), or glue blocks. You can also use dowels (facing page), biscuits (p. 107), or corrugated metal fasteners (p. 80).

Precise marking and cutting are crucial to a gapless fit. When hand-sawing, use a good-quality metal miter box. On a power saw, test the blade setting on scrap wood. Clamping a glued miter joint requires ingenuity. Test the arrangement before applying glue (p. 35).

Making a miter joint

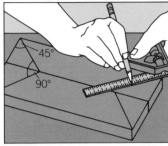

1. Mark joint by placing pieces side by side with ends flush. With a combination square, scribe a 45° angle on each piece. Check accuracy by laying the square against marked lines; they should form a 90° angle. Use a T-bevel (p. 48) for angles other than 45°.

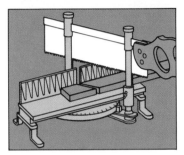

2. Cut marked pieces in a steel miter box, using a fine-tooth backsaw. Trimming a cut miter is difficult, so take care to make the cut properly the first time. Carefully align each piece in the box so that the saw teeth graze the waste side of the mark.

3. Check the accuracy of the saw cuts. Align joint pieces against inside edges of a steel square. There should be no visible gaps along seam or between the edges of the joint and the square.

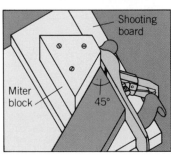

4. If trimming is necessary, carefully plane the pieces in a shooting board (p. 39) with a miter block. With a razor-sharp plane, shave slivers of wood with each pass. Test-fit the pieces frequently to avoid overcutting.

Strengthening miter joints

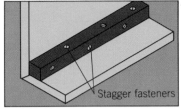

Stagger fasteners

Glue block, glued and fastened against the inside surfaces, strengthens edge-mitered pieces.

Veneer feather 1. After glue in joint is dry, use thin-bladed saw to cut angled slots across the corner.

2. Cut veneer chips oversize. Apply glue to chips and slip them into slots. Tap gently into place with rubber mallet.

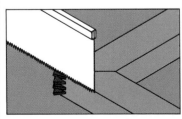

3. When glue is dry, saw off excess veneer. Smooth surfaces with razor-sharp chisel or block plane, then sand.

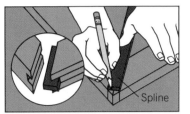

Spline

Spline.1. Align joint pieces. Center spline over joint. Draw lines down edges to mark depth of spline groove.

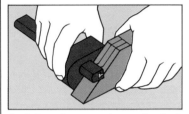

2. Set mortise gauge to equal spline's thickness (one-third of stock's thickness). Scribe groove outline.

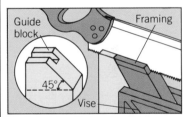

3. Cut slots with hand or power saw. Improvised guide block ensures identical, square-cut slots in both pieces.

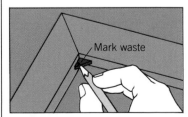

Mark waste

4. Test-fit spline in unglued joint; mark waste. Remove and trim spline; then assemble joint with glue.

Woodworking/Edge joints

When you want to extend the width of a board, as for a tabletop, edge-joining is the answer. Properly cut and glued edge joints form a bond stronger than solid wood—and several narrow boards resist warping better than a single wide one. The key is in creating square edges—a process called jointing—and using a good adhesive.

Before jointing, arrange the boards as they will be when joined. Notice how the tree's annual rings form arcs on each board's ends. Alternate these arcs to form an S-line across the end of the piece. This way, if the boards warp, the piece will merely become wavy and can be repaired by planing. Check also that the surface grain is arranged appealingly; then draw a large arrowhead across all the seams as a guide for reassembly.

Edges can be jointed with hand or power tools. A jointer (p.72) gives a smooth edge with the least effort, but a plane, a router, or a table saw will work too. Check that the cutters, blade, or bit is sharp and properly adjusted.

Whenever possible, joint abutting edges simultaneously. To hand-plane, clamp the boards back-to-back; for a router set them edge-to-edge. When assembled, each edge will compensate for irregularities in the other. If you use a jointer, you will have to work on one edge at a time.

Ideally, the finished edges will be slightly concave—so that the board is narrower in the middle than at the ends. You will need fewer clamps to close a concave joint (straightening the bow applies pressure on the ends). If planing the concavity proves difficult, joint the wood smooth and flat.

Assembling the pieces

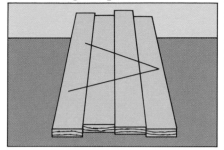

1. Check end grain and alternate arc patterns. Match surface grain (board ends need not be flush). Mark boards for reassembly.

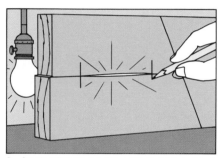

2. Stack adjacent boards edge-to-edge in front of a light. Mark gaps (where light shows through) for planing. A very slight concavity at seam's midpoint is acceptable.

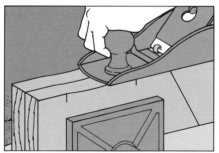

3. Arrange boards near vise or shooting board for planing. Work sequentially from one side of the panel to the other. Don't joint outside edges; they will be trimmed when panel is complete.

Jointing

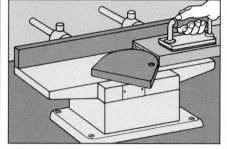

Jointer. Follow manufacturer's instructions to adjust cutters and set fence. Jointer will smooth edges perfectly flat. If concavity is desired, finish with hand plane. Work from each end to center.

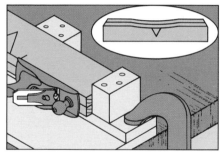

Hand plane and shooting board. Joint two edges at once. Stack boards back-to-back. Shave high spots from edges. Test against light or with straightedge. If desired, add concavity.

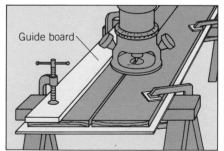

Router. If jointing wide boards, place them on boards with a gap between edges slightly smaller than the bit's diameter. Clamp securely and rout between boards in several passes.

Gluing

1. Collect enough pipe or bar clamps to have one per ft. along the panel. Rest boards on sawhorses. Spread a light coat of glue along each joint edge. Align mating pieces.

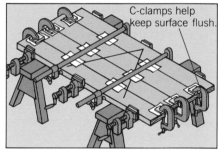

C-clamps help keep surface flush.

2. Alternate clamps above and below panel. Working from center to ends, tighten clamps. Tap boards with rubber mallet to align surfaces. When glue is dry, saw ends even.

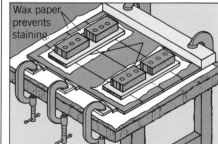

Wax paper prevents staining.

Join thin stock in homemade gluing jig, over a layer of wax paper. Use wedges to apply sideways clamping pressure. Place a weight on top of panel to prevent buckling.

Lengthening joints

Just as you can make surfaces wider by joining boards edge-to-edge (facing page), you can also lengthen wood by joining pieces end-to-end with cut-and-glued joints, mechanical fasteners, or a combination of both.

Lengthening joints are usually found in special situations—roof truss construction and boatbuilding, for example. They are often used to extend moldings (p.99) because their tapered overlap helps make splices invisible.

Much of the strength of these joints comes from the adhesive and the increased gluing surface. In addition to white or yellow glue, such adhesives as acrylic or resorcinol (a waterproof resin) will give good results. But even the best joint won't match the strength of uncut wood. If the boards are to be placed horizontally, the joint will need support posts below or struts from above to brace it against compression (vertical force, including gravity). Joints in boards that are oriented vertically will need bracing to resist horizontal force.

In general, the longer the seam, the stronger the joint. A slope of 1:8 for lumber is a good rule of thumb. However, calculating and constructing lengthening joints to withstand a great deal of stress is a job best left to a professional.

The scarf joint described at right will gracefully disguise seams when installing or repairing moldings and baseboards. If you have access to your roof or floor joists, and lengthening joints occur in them, check the joints periodically for cracking. If repair is needed, add bolts or plates as described at far right.

Simple scarf joint

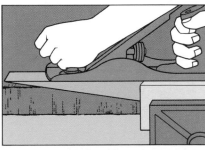

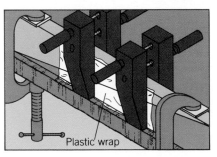

Plastic wrap

1. The scarf's *rise* should be at least 1:8; that is, the cut line should form a triangle whose hypotenuse is 8 times longer then its base. Different situations may demand different rise ratios. In general, the longer the scarf, the stronger the joint.

2. With saw blade on waste side of cutting line, carefully remove the waste. Use a fine-tooth crosscut saw (p.24) for stock larger than 1 x 4. Stock smaller than 1 x 4 can be cut with a backsaw. (On a power saw, use a finish-cut blade.)

3. Test-fit joint pieces. Both surfaces must touch completely; plane down any high spots. Shift board in vise so that joint face is closer to horizontal to speed planing. Sandwich joint between straight-edged boards (p.46) to guide and support plane.

4. Place joint on sturdy flat surface (or place a board under joint to hold its alignment). Apply glue and assemble joint. Secure with C-clamps and hand screws to keep joint from sliding. When glue is dry, clean seepage with chisel or scraper, and smooth edges with plane.

Other methods

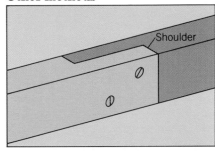

Shoulder

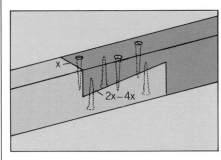

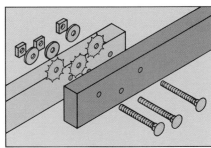

Width

Lap scarf. Easy to construct (p.101), each lap is half the thickness of the stock and 2 to 4 times as long. Shoulders must butt exactly against ends of laps. Fasten with glue and screws, bolts, or nails installed from each side in a staggered pattern.

Splayed lap scarf, also called dovetailed lap. Laps are 2 to 4 times longer than thickness of stock. Make thinnest part of lap at least one-third of stock thickness. Fasten with screws. Offset the fasteners to avoid splitting the stock. These joints must be supported from below.

Bolted joint requires no cutting. Overlap ends of lumber at a distance of at least twice the width of stock. Fasten with carriage bolts, flat or lock washers, and nuts. Toothed washers called *lumber connectors* placed between the pieces increase strength of joint.

Fish joint. Cut wood or metal plates 4 times longer than width of stock from material the same width as stock but half as thick. Sandwich butt-joined pieces between the plates. Fasten with glue and screws or nails, installed from each side.

111

Woodworking/Leg-and-rail joints

Corners for furniture and frame-and-panel construction (facing page) depend on support from leg-and-rail joints for stability. When planning a project, choose a joint style that is consistent with the quality and appearance of the item being built. Fine furniture calls for hidden mortise-and-tenon-style joints, but a workbench can employ one of the overlapping butt joints shown on this page.

Styles of leg-and-rail joints range from utilitarian to elaborate. As a rule, the simpler versions are butt joints (p.100) reinforced with wooden blocks or metal fasteners—screws, bolts, or special hardware. These are sturdy, easy to build, and appropriate for rough or temporary construction.

For furniture, dowels or metal corner braces are preferable. These are less conspicuous than overlapping butt joints, yet provide adequate strength. Metal corner braces permit tightening joints that loosen due to wear—and they are detachable, making it possible to disassemble and reassemble the piece as needed. Biscuit joints can replace dowel or mortise-and-tenon joints, but they must be cut with a special tool called a biscuit joiner.

Despite their strength, dowel and mortise-and-tenon joints may need further strengthening with fasteners or blocks. Think carefully before selecting mortise-and-tenon joints. Although they are stronger than dowels and biscuits, their extra strength might not be necessary—and they require precision in laying out and cutting.

A doweled leg-and-rail joint

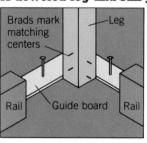

1. Assemble parts to set dowel positions (p.108). Mark leg piece, alternating dowels so that they don't collide. Tap wire brads into hole centers. Remove brad heads with pliers. Align pieces, then push together.

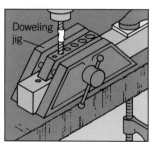

2. Be sure parts are clamped securely. With self-centering doweling jig (p.108) and drill, make holes in leg and rails. (Off-center holes can be made with same tool by shimming one side of jig.)

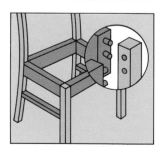

3. Assemble joints and establish clamping procedure before gluing. Determine how many and what kind of clamps (pp.34–35) you need. Apply a good-quality adhesive (pp.88–89); assemble and clamp joints.

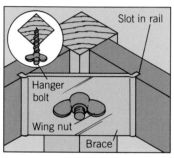

Metal corner brace can firm a wobbly chair or table leg. To install, saw slots perpendicular to inside face of rails. Slide brace into slots, drill pilot hole for hanger bolt, install bolt, and tighten wing nut.

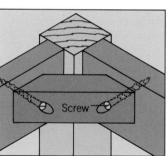

Wooden corner block, mitered to match assembled joints, adds stability. Block can replace metal corner brace if hanger bolt is added. Assemble joint first, then position block. Drill pilot holes for screws.

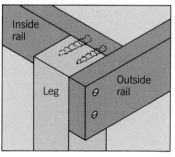

Dowels. Install two or more per rail for sturdy, permanent furniture joints. To keep dowels from colliding inside joint, stagger spacing on each side of leg. On narrow rails where this is not possible, install short dowels and reinforce joint with brace or block.

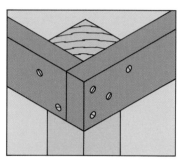

Overlapping butt joint (rails outside leg) is suitable for workbenches and other functional items. Assemble joint with adhesive and at least two fasteners per rail, staggered so they won't collide. Bolts (and no adhesive) allow easy disassembly or tightening of parts.

Overlapping butt joint with one rail inside leg is similar to above. Both joints rely solely on strength of adhesive and screws or bolts. When building this kind of joint, first install inside rail with screws. Then attach outside rail and fasten it with screws or bolts.

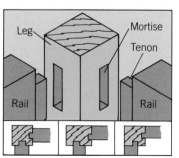

Mortise-and-tenon is the strongest and most intricate of leg-and-rail joints. Layouts vary according to the way rails join leg. Mortise-and-rabbet (bottom row: center and right) is slightly weaker; use it in case construction, where greater joint length adds strength.

Building boxes

Solid wood box

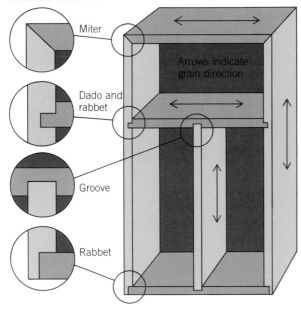

Miter

Dado and rabbet

Groove

Rabbet

Arrows indicate grain direction

Frame-and-panel box

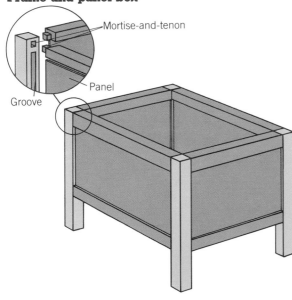

Mortise-and-tenon

Panel

Groove

The humble box is a building block for nearly all types of construction. Adding drawers (pp.114–115), shelves, and trim transforms a simple box into a distinctive piece of furniture; adding doors turns it into a cabinet.

There are two kinds of boxes: *solid wood,* also called case construction, and *frame-and-panel.* In solid wood boxes all the pieces are slabs of wood, plywood, or manufactured wood. In frame-and-panel, a skeleton of boards forms the box's shape. Thin panels—usually plywood, but sometimes glass or another material—are fastened onto the frame or enclosed in grooves cut in it.

Before cutting the pieces for a solid wood box, choose the corner joints. Although butt joints are a possibility, many stronger and more attractive joints are easily made with power tools. Add a back (usually plywood) for rigidity. Grain direction on each piece should parallel its long dimension so that the entire box will expand and contract evenly during temperature and humidity changes.

Because it is less likely to warp, frame-and-panel construction is often the choice in cabinets and chests. The relationship of frame to panel can inspire a wide variety of decorative effects. When building these boxes, cut the framing pieces first. If the panels will be on the outside of the frame, assemble the entire frame; then attach the panels. If the panels will be inside, follow the directions at right.

For either type of box, do all interior work, such as cutting shelf dadoes, before final assembly. Door hardware can be fitted before or after assembly.

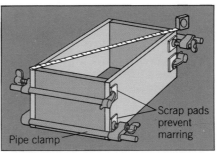
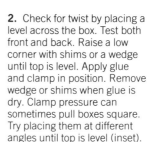

Pipe clamp

Scrap pads prevent marring

1. Test all corners for squareness with a steel square or by measuring diagonals (p.49). If the box isn't square or won't sit flat, check that all cuts are square. If the angle is close to 90°, a clamp attached so that one jaw makes less contact with the box surface than the other will help pull corners square. If very far off, box may need to be re-cut.

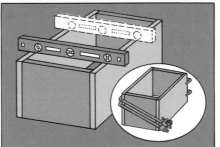

2. Check for twist by placing a level across the box. Test both front and back. Raise a low corner with shims or a wedge until top is level. Apply glue and clamp in position. Remove wedge or shims when glue is dry. Clamp pressure can sometimes pull boxes square. Try placing them at different angles until top is level (inset).

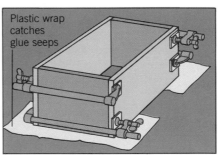

Plastic wrap catches glue seeps

3. When box is square and level, remove clamps, apply glue, and reassemble box. Replace clamps to hold box in alignment. Put plastic wrap under joints to catch glue seeps. If no glue will be used, nail or screw corners; then attach the back or bottom. Tighten clamps from opposite ends for even pressure. Scrap pads under clamp jaws prevent marring.

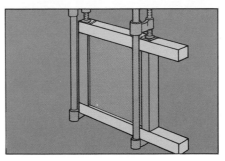

To build frame-and-panel boxes, first assemble two sides. If frame will enclose panel, test-fit with panel in place. If attached over frame, complete frame first. Align framing pieces. Check that corners are square; then apply glue and clamps. When glue is dry, fit rails and panels of other two sides to uprights of assembled units.

Woodworking/Making drawers

Essentially a box within a box, properly made drawers are a triumph of planning and layout. Build the cabinet and install the guides before building the drawers. This way, the drawer's dimensions can be taken from the cabinet's final dimensions for a precise fit. Regardless of the wood used, drawers are made with solid wood techniques (p.113).

A drawer is composed of two sides, a back, a bottom, and a front, which may be flush, false, or lipped. Flush drawer fronts fit within the interior dimensions of the cabinet opening. Their edges are usually rabbeted to enclose the sides and form smooth corners. These rabbets may be wider than the thickness of the sides to conceal interior fittings and slide hardware.

False and lipped fronts are also rabbeted. False fronts (facing page) are somewhat easier to make than the other two styles. Both false and lipped fronts overlap the edges of the cabinet opening and hide irregularities as well as fittings and hardware.

In either style of drawer, the front and sides are usually grooved to hold the bottom. Attach the bottom to the back with small nails or screws; don't use glue. Finish drawers inside and out with polyurethane or another varnish to reduce shrinking and swelling in response to humidity changes.

Light-duty drawers, such as those found in vanities, can be made by following the simple method outlined at right. Drawers to contain heavy items (facing page) or for better-quality furniture require skillfully constructed interlocking joints.

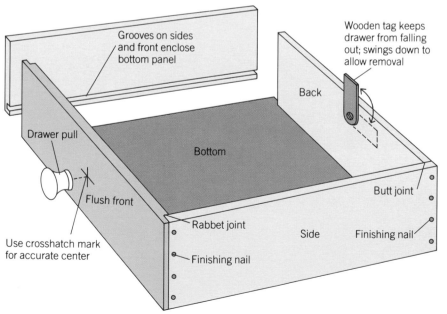

Grooves on sides and front enclose bottom panel

Wooden tag keeps drawer from falling out; swings down to allow removal

Back

Drawer pull

Bottom

Flush front

Use crosshatch mark for accurate center

Rabbet joint

Finishing nail

Side

Butt joint

Finishing nail

Assembling a drawer

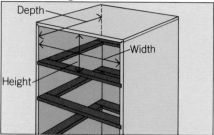

Depth

Width

Height

1. To determine sizes of drawer parts, measure height, width, and depth of opening. Allow space for hardware, for guides, glides, and kicker strips (right), and $\frac{1}{16}$ to $\frac{1}{8}$ in. for clearance. Double-check measurements before cutting drawer.

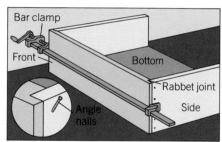

Bar clamp

Front

Bottom

Rabbet joint

Side

Angle nails

2. Cut rabbets on drawer front. Apply glue and clamp drawer front to sides and bottom. Using a bar clamp to hold sides, drive 4d finishing nails through sides into rabbet. Angling nails makes it harder for joint to separate under stress.

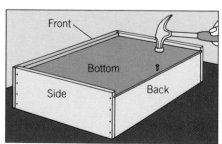

Front

Bottom

Side

Back

3. Secure back to partially assembled drawer with 4d finishing nails installed on an angle. Test drawer for squareness and twist (p.113). Attach bottom to back with small common nails or screws.

Guides and glides

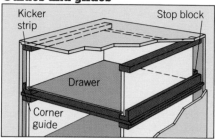

Kicker strip

Stop block

Drawer

Corner guide

Corner guides support drawer and act as bearing surfaces. **Stop blocks** prevent drawer from sliding too far back. **Kicker strips** on cabinet's sides prevent tilting, keep drawer from falling out.

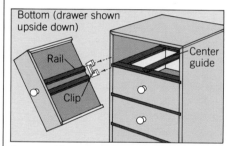

Bottom (drawer shown upside down)

Rail

Center guide

Clip

Center guide in cabinet flanked by rails on drawer bottom can be used on drawers that are supported at the sides. Plastic clip on drawer back slides over guide, fastens drawer to guide; keeps drawer from tilting when opened.

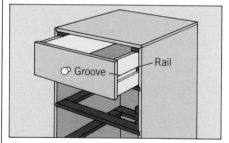

Groove

Rail

Glides for light-duty drawers can be made by attaching wooden rails to cabinet and cutting matching grooves in the drawers' sides. Cut grooves with a router (pp.68–69) or on a table saw (pp.64–65).

114

Extra-strength drawers

Choose materials for strength as well as appearance when building drawers for heavy-duty or frequent use, such as in kitchen cabinets. Use wood joints instead of fasteners to join drawer parts. Support drawers with metal sliding hardware that incorporates ball bearings or nylon rollers rather than with homemade wooden glides.

For drawers up to 24 inches wide, use ½-inch-thick plywood or solid stock for the sides and back, and ¼-inch-thick plywood for the bottom. If adding a false front, use ½-inch-thick stock. Make a flush or lipped front of solid lumber or ¾-inch-thick plywood. For wider drawers, use ¾-inch material for the sides, back, and front (whether or not a false front is planned) and ⅜-inch-thick plywood for the bottom.

The corner joints at the front of the drawer should be as strong as possible. Dovetails (p. 106) and dovetail dadoes (p. 102) are among the strongest joints. Box joints (p. 107) are as strong as dovetails and much easier to cut. Dado-and-rabbet joints (p. 103) are also a good choice; they can be cut easily with a table saw or a router. Attach the back to the sides with the same type of joint, or dado the sides and slide the back into the channels. Cut grooves in the front, sides, and back to support the bottom. Don't glue the bottom; attach it to the back with screws so that it can easily be replaced.

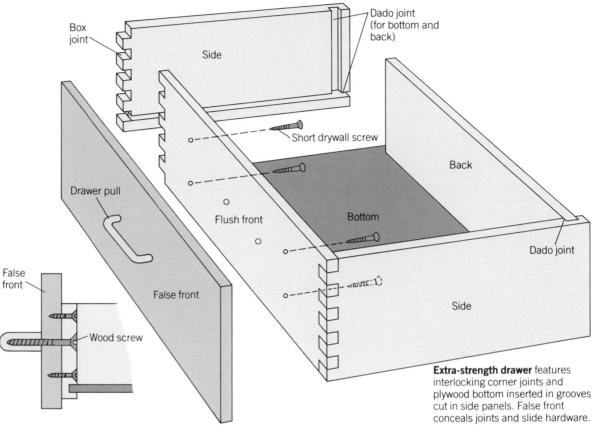

Extra-strength drawer features interlocking corner joints and plywood bottom inserted in grooves cut in side panels. False front conceals joints and slide hardware.

Drawer-hanging hardware

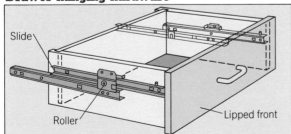

Side-mounted slides provide support and smooth operation even for heavy drawers. Clearance of ½ in. is usually required between drawer sides and cabinet (check manufacturer's instructions). Slides with full-extension design permit the drawers to be pulled entirely out of the cabinet. Lipped or false front conceals slides.

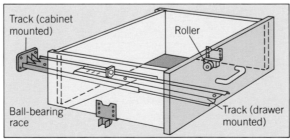

Center-mounted ball-bearing slides are easier to install than side-mounted type and take up less space (⅜ in. beneath drawer). They can replace conventional center guides (facing page) if cabinet and drawer parts are sturdy. Some slides have side-mounted rollers which provide additional support.

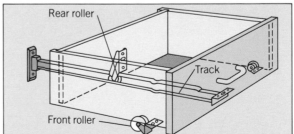

Center-mounted track slide with three rollers is economical and can be used on drawers with weak bottom panels. Install track from back to front in cabinet. Attach rollers to back and sides of drawer. Top of track is open so that drawer can be removed from cabinet by disengaging rear roller.

Woodworking / Cabinet fittings

Concealed hinges

Soss hinge

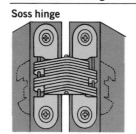

Pivot hinge

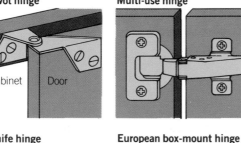

Cabinet   Door

Multi-use hinge

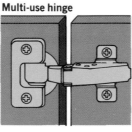

Cylinder hinge

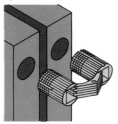

Knife hinge

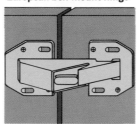

European box-mount hinge

Concealed hinges produce the look of a smooth surface across the front of cabinets. Soss, cylinder, and knife hinges are for fine furniture. Spring-loaded multi-use hinges suit kitchen and utility cabinets and can also be used on drop-leaf tables. Their design eliminates gaps when the leaf is folded down. Pivot and European box-mount hinges are mainstays of kitchen cabinet construction. Both allow flush-door cabinets to butt against each other with no gaps at the sides and to open at least 90°. Pivot hinges will show as a thin edge at the top when doors are closed. The knife hinge's knuckle protrudes in front of the cabinet.

Exposed hinges

Butt hinge

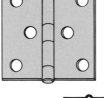

Overlay hinge

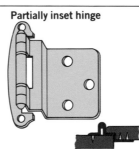

Partially inset hinge

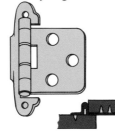

Exposed hinges are usually attached on the outside of cabinets. Butt hinges are the most versatile style. They can be recessed or surface-mounted, and attached so that they open to either 90° or 180°. Choose overlay hinges for cabinet doors that overlap the frame. Partially inset hinges are for lipped doors.

Latches

Push latch

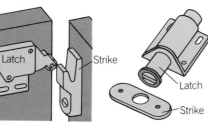

Latch   Strike

Touch latch

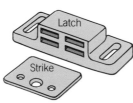

Latch

Strike

Magnetic latch

Latch

Strike

Spring-loaded push latch closes when roller hooks on strike plate. This latch and the cylindrical magnetic latch (touch latch) open and close with a light push on the door. Magnetic latch is inexpensive, easy to install. Gentle pulling opens door.

Glass-door latches and hinges

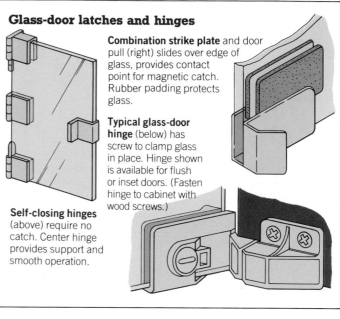

Combination strike plate and door pull (right) slides over edge of glass, provides contact point for magnetic catch. Rubber padding protects glass.

Typical glass-door hinge (below) has screw to clamp glass in place. Hinge shown is available for flush or inset doors. (Fasten hinge to cabinet with wood screws.)

Self-closing hinges (above) require no catch. Center hinge provides support and smooth operation.

Other cabinet fittings

Adjustable levelers eliminate shimming. Kick strip detaches for access beneath cabinet.

Desk clips secure top to sides; allow disassembly and response to humidity changes.

Chest lid support locks open, closes slowly, prevents lid from falling.

Keyhole fittings mortised into shelf supports enable shelves to hang from hidden screws. Tapered slot thickness holds fittings against screws.

Wall

Cabinet back

Wood finishes enhance grain, add or unify color, and create durable surfaces. A good finish also slows moisture loss and absorption, thus minimizing the shrinking and swelling of joints.

If the piece has a badly damaged or unattractive painted finish, stripping is the obvious choice. But don't just assume that complete stripping is necessary: treating a lightly distressed piece with a restorer may be enough to revive the finish. Before you do anything else, wash the piece thoroughly with an oil soap to remove surface grime. You can then assess the true condition of the finish.

First, repair damage and blemishes. Shallow dents and scratches can be raised by moistening the area with water. The wood absorbs the water and swells, restoring the original shape. When it is dry, sand the area lightly with 180-grit sandpaper. Burns and other large blemishes can be filled with burn-in sticks (stick shellac) or wood dough. Burn-in sticks come in a variety of colors to match common wood tones. They are melted into the blemish and scraped flush after hardening (p.502). Water-base filler and solvent-base wood dough are applied with a putty knife. Wood dough comes only in a dark or a light tone, and it won't absorb stain once it is dry. You can alter the original color of filler or wood dough by mixing in a Japan color (p.119) before applying it. Fillers and wood dough shrink; so mound them slightly, then sand flush when dry.

Sanding (p.118) is often given short shrift in the enthusiasm to wield a finishing brush, but it is the most important step to ensure a clear and smooth finish. Filling the wood's pores and sealing the wood create even finer surfaces for the stain. Filling and sealing (p.120) are essential for some finishes.

Safety. Wear rubber gloves, safety goggles, and a sanding or spray-paint respirator (p.354) around dust and fumes. Ventilate the work area and keep a fire extinguisher handy. Don't smoke. If you are working inside, extinguish pilot lights on gas appliances; the fumes from these substances can ignite or explode. Seal used rags in a metal container with a tight lid, and dispose of it properly (p.348).

A damaged finish can be removed mechanically by scraping or chemically by dissolving it with a stripper. Strippers come in two formulas. Those containing methylene chloride work in about 15 minutes and are available in cream or paste form. They dry quickly and are hazardous; so follow the safety recommendations on the container. Water-base strippers do as good a job but take much longer. They are nontoxic, nonflammable, and keep the dissolved finish soft for hours. The water does raise the grain; so plan to sand the raw wood. For either type, read and follow the directions on the label. Avoid the chemical baths used by dip-and-strip shops. They can discolor the wood and dissolve the glue that holds veneers and joints in place.

Some wood will retain deep blotches of old stain, water damage, or other discolorations. (The tannin in oak reacts with the iron in nails to form deep, dark spots.) Try sanding or bleaching (p.118). If you can't lighten the area sufficiently, your refinishing choices are limited to living with the blemish, restaining with a darker color, or painting.

1. Pour on a heavy coat of stripper and work it into the grain. Don't brush it out like paint. Keep surface horizontal as much as possible, turning the piece as necessary.

2. Scrape off softened finish with putty knife (round its corners to prevent gouging). Work with the grain. Catch drippings on a rag, layers of newspaper, or in a can.

A textured plastic pad, burlap, or coarse steel wool conforms to round or curved shapes to scour off softened finish. Turn pad frequently to expose clean surfaces.

Brass-bristle brush scrubs finish from turned and carved work without damaging detail. Twine or coarse string gets into narrow channels.

Wrap sandpaper around a block of wood to clean finish from right angles and corners. Wrapped dowels are handy for cleaning finish from moldings.

Heat gun will blister a difficult finish. Work carefully, keeping your hands well away from the muzzle of the gun. Do not use on veneered surfaces.

Woodworking/Sanding and bleaching

Sanding

A final finish enhances the wood's grain, but it also emphasizes any imperfections in the surface. Thorough sanding is essential for a clear finish. A power sander (p.70) will quickly level the surface; follow with hand sanding to smooth out scratches.

Sand with a series of papers, progressing from coarse to fine grit. Start with 80 grit for rough work, followed by 120 grit and then 180. Super-smooth surfaces require at least 240 grit. Clean the dust from the wood between grit changes, and keep checking that the sandpaper is free of debris that might gouge the surface. Sand with the grain.

A sanding block ensures even pressure on the wood and prevents gouging. The ideal block measures 4½ inches long by 3½ inches wide and is 1½ inches thick. This size accommodates half a standard sheet of sandpaper, reducing waste. A scrap of 2 x 4 wrapped with felt makes a good block. Scraper blades and cabinet scrapers (p.41) take practice to sharpen and use, but will reduce—and sometimes eliminate—sanding.

Sand all areas of a piece. Use both hands to apply firm, even pressure. In addition to smoothing the surface, you are removing any residue that may resist the finish. When working with small pieces, you can either clamp the work and move the sanding block or clamp the block and move the work. For concave surfaces, wrap the sandpaper around a dowel that fits the shape. You can use finger pressure to get into small areas, but be sure your pressure is even across the whole surface. The annoying tendency of end grain to overabsorb stain can be reduced by sanding diligently, then applying a sealer (p.120). Sand end grain in one direction, not back and forth.

Vacuum or brush off the sanding dust, then wipe down the piece with a tack cloth. Buy a cloth—or make one by kneading a little varnish into a piece of cheesecloth dampened with turpentine. Store in a jar with a tight lid.

Scraper is held at about an 80° angle to the wood and pulled at a slight bias to the grain for finish sanding. To smooth rough surfaces or to remove old finishes, push the blade, bowing it slightly in the center with your thumbs.

Pad sander quickly smooths flat surfaces. Guide the sander along the wood's grain. Don't lean on the tool; you could burn out the motor. The weight of the sander and the motion of the pad are sufficient to abrade the work.

Contour sander attaches to an electric drill. The spinning flaps, like the bristles of a brush, conform to intricate shapes and gently remove loosened debris. Pull fresh paper through the slots as needed.

Wrap a dowel or other curved sanding block with abrasive paper to smooth and clean curved shapes and moldings. Fold used 120-grit paper to clean delicate edges without blunting crisp detail.

Bleaching

When discolored areas won't sand off or you wish to lighten the wood's color in part or in total, reach for the bleach. Simple laundry bleach may be enough for oak, ash, mahogany, maple, walnut, and beech. Other species—chestnut, poplar, cedar, rosewood, and cherry, for example—resist bleaching. If laundry bleach doesn't do the job, try a commercial two-step wood bleach. If you use a two-step product, follow the directions on the label. With either type, protect your eyes and hands.

For best results, bleach only clean, finish-free surfaces. Allow the wood to fade to a shade slightly darker than the desired color—the wood will appear lighter after it dries. (You can repeat the bleaching if the color is still too dark when the wood is dry.) When the wood looks light enough, apply a neutralizing formula to stop the fading. Either bleach can be neutralized with a commercial solution or with a 50/50 mix of white vinegar and water. Rinse with warm water and let the wood dry.

Natural wood (left) bleached almost white (right). Bleaching raises the grain but doesn't penetrate deeply. Sand carefully. You can sand through to the original color.

Choosing and using stain

Stain enlivens the wood grain and unifies color on a single item or among several items. The color in the can varies according to each manufacturer's formula, and the final color depends on the wood—even two pieces of the same species can stain differently—and the finish. If you are trying to match a finish or do a spot repair, experimentation is critical. Test the color on a scrap of the wood used for the project or on an inconspicuous area of a finished piece. Err on the light side when using color: you can always go darker, but it is very difficult to remove or lighten stain. Apply two or three coats of your finish over the test to avoid surprises.

Water-soluble stains raise the grain; so the grain must be either deliberately raised and sanded before staining (see dent repair, p.117) or sanded after staining. Alcohol-soluble stains—fast drying and good for touch-ups—can be sprayed on. Oil-soluble stains are often used to tint varnish or lacquer for the final finish. *Note:* Oil-soluble varnish will dissolve oil-soluble stain. Seal the stained wood (p.120) before varnishing to prevent bleeding.

It isn't always necessary to stain. An attractive wood can simply be sealed with an appropriate finish (p.123). If you do decide to stain before applying finish, choose products from the same manufacturer throughout the project for best results.

Types of stain. *Penetrating stain* is absorbed into the fibers of the wood, resulting in a pure, clear color that accents the grain. *Pigmented stain* deposits a thin film of color on top of the wood, creating a semi-opaque finish that somewhat obscures the grain. Because it is absorbed so quickly, penetrating stain is harder to work with than the pigmented kind, but it is the best choice to highlight grain. Use pigmented stains on plainer wood. *Gel stains* combine the advantages of penetrating and pigmented stains: they are almost foolproof and allow the grain to remain visible.

Aniline dye stain is classed with the penetrating stains. It is a powder that must be dissolved in hot water or alcohol before use. The powder is available in a wide variety of colors. For better color control, start with a weak solution and build the intensity with repeated applications rather than one strong coat.

NGR (non-grain-raising) stain is a premixed penetrating stain made of water-soluble aniline dye dissolved in methanol alcohol. These stains result in clear, vibrant colors. Because they don't contain water, NGR's don't raise the grain. To decrease the color's intensity, use only NGR thinner.

Pigmented wiping stain is a finely ground pigment suspended in oil. Stir it often, or the particles will settle to the bottom of the can, resulting in uneven color. The colors of latex-base wiping stains are less intense than those of the oil-base ones. Although water soluble for easy cleanup, most won't raise the grain.

Gel stains combine dyes and pigments, offering both uniform staining and clear color. Because you rub in these jellylike stains, you have total control over the color. Rub hard for a light color; lightly for a darker one (or apply another coat). Gel stains are also handy for touch-ups.

Applying stain. Respect the fact that you are working with toxic and flammable chemicals. Protect yourself by following the safety precautions recommended by the manufacturer. Protect your project by refining your technique on scrap first. Each product has a preferred application method and recommended drying time between repeat coats, so follow the directions on the label.

Spraying on aniline dye stains reduces streaking, blotching, and lap marks. When brushing or wiping, follow the grain with long, smooth strokes. Don't overload the brush, or you'll get blotches. You can use the same methods for NGR stains, but use an NGR retarder to slow drying and to prevent lap marks.

Brush or wipe pigmented wiping stain first across the grain, then along it. Leave it on the wood the recommended amount of time; then wipe it off. Gel stains are simply wiped on along the grain with a lint-free cloth, then rubbed in until the color is even.

Japan color is a pure, concentrated pigment suspended in a varnish-like medium. Available in many colors, including black and white, it is used to tint fillers, to create custom stains, and to match an existing stain. When used in a strong enough concentration, Japan colors behave like paint, totally obscuring the grain. When mixed with varnish or lacquer, they color and finish in one step. But objects treated this way show damage easily—even a small scratch will reveal bare, uncolored wood.

Apply NGR stain with brush or foam pad.

NGR stain yields clear color, clean grain.

Rub on pigmented wiping stain with cloth.

Pigmented wiping stain is slightly opaque.

Filler

For an extremely smooth finish or to dramatically accent the grain pattern, fill the wood's pores with paste wood filler. Unlike the putty filler used to repair dents and damage, paste wood filler is made of crushed quartz (silex) and pigments mixed with a binder and driers. Open-grained species such as oak, walnut, rosewood, and mahogany usually require filler. If a natural look is desired, such as in Scandinavian-style furniture, or if you are using a wood with small pores, such as pine, maple, birch, or cherry, filling is not necessary.

Paste wood filler is available in a range of colors. Once dry it doesn't absorb stain; however, you can tint it with Japan colors (p.119) to produce any shade you desire. (In mixing a custom color, be sure to make enough to finish the entire job.) To accentuate the grain, apply a filler that contrasts with the wood's natural color: white or light-colored filler on dark wood, dark filler on light.

Filler is usually applied after staining, but it can be done beforehand. Alcohol-base stains (p.119) might dissolve filler, so they should be applied first. If you fill after staining, avoid damaging the stain when removing excess filler. Test the entire sequence—stain, filler, varnish—on a scrap of the same wood to be sure you can achieve the desired effect. Testing also shows if the filler changes the wood's color. Paste wood filler should be the consistency of thick cream. It can be thinned with turpentine, but check the label for the manufacturer's recommendations.

Sealer

Most finishes profit from the use of a sealer. Sealing before staining primes the wood, ensuring that the stain will be absorbed uniformly. Sealing after staining and filling but before final finishing decreases the number of finish coats needed. The sealer penetrates the wood, and keeps subsequent finish coats on top of the wood. Sealing end grain prevents overabsorption of stain. With oily woods such as rosewood, a sealer keeps the resins from bleeding through the finish. If left unsealed, these oils can contaminate the finish and prevent it from drying.

Thinned shellac is a good all-purpose sealer, except for polyurethane, under which any other sealer can be used. Use orange shellac for dark woods, white shellac for light woods.

Brush on filler heavily and evenly, forcing it into the wood's pores. Brush across, then with, the grain. Work in small sections: once filler hardens, it's almost impossible to remove. Stir filler thoroughly before using and often during use.

Another removal method is to scrape filler with a rigid, straight-edged, rounded-corner piece of metal, such as a scraper blade or stiff putty knife. Push tool along the grain, holding it at a slight bias. Clean filler from tool's edge after each pass.

Final finish	Sealer
All varnishes except polyurethane	1-lb.-cut shellac (facing page). Lacquer-base sealer. Varnish thinned 50% with recommended solvent
Polyurethane	Lacquer-base sealer. Polyurethane thinned 50% with mineral spirits
Lacquer	Lacquer-base sealer. 1-lb.-cut shellac
Shellac	1-lb.-cut shellac
Penetrating oil	None needed
Tung oil	None needed

As filler dries, in about 15 min., the surface sheen dulls. When this happens, vigorously scrub across the grain with a burlap rag. (Wiping too soon can pull filler out of pores.) Scrub until filler is removed completely from surface. Let dry overnight, then sand lightly—any residue will inhibit wood's absorption of stain.

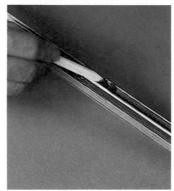

In corners and crevices remove filler with a pointed dowel. Wrap the dowel's tip with cloth to avoid gouging the wood. You can also scrub these areas with a soft brass-bristle brush. Change the cloth or clean the brush as it becomes clogged.

Softwoods (p.93) absorb stain unevenly, forming blotches and wild grain (left). Sealing before staining results in uniform color and prevents overabsorption on end grain (right).

Final finishes

There are two categories of wood finishes. *Surface finishes* harden on top of the wood, forming a protective film (polyurethane, lacquer, shellac, varnish). *Penetrating finishes* (oils) are absorbed into the wood and harden within the fibers. Subsequent layers of each finish adhere similarly: surface finishes bond mechanically to the "tooth" of a sanded surface; penetrating oils bond chemically, melting together and soaking into the wood. Each finish has specific characteristics of appearance and durability (p. 123).

When working with any final finish, treat all parts of a piece identically—backs as well as fronts, undersides as well as tops—so that it will react evenly to moisture changes and won't warp. Avoid working in cold or dampness—for example, an unheated basement. Allow the piece and the can of finish to acclimate to room temperature before working; otherwise bubbles may form in the final finish.

Polyurethane

Durable, fast-drying, and easy to apply, polyurethane comes in satin (matte) and high-gloss formulas. Generally it has an amber or yellowish cast that enhances the wood's natural color, but it can be tinted with Japan colors or an oil-base stain. Polyurethane can be thinned with turpentine or mineral spirits. Although it is sometimes called varnish, polyurethane is not a true varnish, which traditionally is made from distilled natural resins and oils. Spar varnish (urethane) is the best choice for marine or exterior work. Also a synthetic, it is highly resistant to abrasion, water seepage, and sun damage.

Brush polyurethane evenly over the surface, following the grain. Work from the center of the piece toward the ends. Several thin coats are better than one thick one. Allow each coat to dry (usually for 24 hours) before adding the next. The surface must be sanded (220 or 240 grit) between coats, or the subsequent coats won't adhere. Wipe the surface with a tack cloth (p. 118) before applying each coat of finish. Any dust will mar the finish with tiny bumps.

Padding lacquer and shellac

Valuable antiques often were finished by French polishing—a laborious technique of rubbing many coats of shellac and linseed oil into the wood. Today this finish can be approximated with padding lacquer and a special applicator pad. It is most practical for small projects, but it can be used on larger ones as well. Dab some lacquer on the pad and push it against your palm to work the lacquer through the pad. Apply the finish to the piece with light strokes. Keep the pad in constant motion, so that no imprint from the applicator mars the finish.

Shellac comes in two forms: flaked and liquid. Both are dissolved in denatured alcohol to the desired *cut*. Three pounds of shellac dissolved in 1 gallon of denatured alcohol—a 3-pound cut—is recommended for furniture. When mixed, all shellac has a short shelf life. Premixed shellac should be dated; use it within 6 months. Mix just enough flaked shellac for your immediate purpose. Apply shellac with long, even strokes, brushing it out quickly. Sand gently after 4 hours, and recoat as necessary.

Lacquer

Because it dries so quickly, lacquer is usually sprayed on rather than brushed on. As with any finish, several thin coats are better than a single thick coat. Whether spraying or brushing, apply each coat heavily enough to flow out and blend together, but not so heavily that you flood the surface. On large surfaces, work from the center toward the ends. If spraying, rehearse on scrap—aim for even coverage without lap marks or drips. If brushing, work along the grain with a good natural-bristle brush. Let the surface dry before recoating (about 4 hours if spraying, 24 if brushing). Light sanding between coats will remove any defects. After it has dried for 24 to 36 hours, polish the final coat as described on page 122. Don't use lacquer over painted or varnished surfaces; it acts like paint remover.

▶ **CAUTION:** Lacquer, and its spray, is flammable and toxic. Work outside if you can't construct a booth to contain the overspray. Always wear goggles and a spray-paint respirator (p.354). Use water-base lacquer (nonflammable and nontoxic) if possible.

On large surfaces, work from the center to both ends, using a natural-bristle brush. To avoid bubbles in finish, wipe brush against the can's side, not the rim, or in an empty coffee can.

Apply padding lacquer with the grain. Use a pendulum motion, beginning it before the pad touches the wood. Make applicator by wrapping cotton in cheesecloth to form an egg-shaped pad.

Holding gun 6–8 in. from the work and parallel to surface, spray lacquer lightly and evenly over surface. On flat surfaces, first spray across grain, then with it. Move gun continuously. Avoid spraying in humid conditions, or finish will "blush" (whiten). Thin lacquer according to label directions.

One-step finishes

To color and finish in a single step, use a penetrating oil (such as Danish or tung) or a commercial mixture of stain and polyurethane. Easy, fast application is the advantage, but the final result isn't as deep, clear, and rich as it is with finishes that are applied in stages.

Polyurethane one-step finishes are available in liquid brushing formulas or as gels that you wipe on with a rag. Wiping allows greater control over application and requires less cleanup. One-step stain and penetrating oil finishes should be wiped on. Because all these products differ, follow the manufacturer's instructions for application method, number of coats, and drying time between coats. Despite the name, more than one coat may be recommended.

Apply one-step finish with brush or clean lint-free cloth. Wipe off all excess with fresh cloths, turning them often to present clean surface to wood, until the color is uniform. Cotton swabs or a pointed dowel wrapped with cloth will clean excess finish from deep carvings.

Danish oil

Composed of penetrating oils and resins, Danish oil is easy to apply or repair. As the oil soaks into the wood, it reacts with oxygen in the air and hardens within the wood's fibers (a chemical reaction called *polymerization*). If the finish is damaged, invisible repairs can easily be made by sanding the area, reapplying some oil, and vigorously rubbing it in. Danish oil deepens the wood's color slightly; subsequent coats deepen it more.

Follow the manufacturer's directions for application methods and drying time between coats. The more coats you apply, the harder and more lustrous the finish will be. When you are done, seal the oil-soaked rags in a metal can with a tight lid; dispose of them properly (p.348).

Flood oil on wood, spread evenly with a clean rag, and allow to soak in. Remove excess after 15 to 30 min. For a self-filling finish, sand along the grain with 400-grit wet/dry paper while oil soaks in. The oily sanding dust packs into the pores, filling and finishing in one step.

Tung oil

This penetrating oil is derived from the seeds of tung trees. It is available in three forms: pure, polymerized, and in a varnish. Pure tung yields a durable surface with a matte finish. Polymerized tung, chemically altered by heating, leaves a glossier and even harder surface. Tung-oil varnish looks and acts more like a surface finish and is more prone to chipping. For optimum drying, apply tung oil when humidity is low and air temperature moderate.

Polymerized and pure tung oil are mixed commercially, creating products in a range of hardnesses and lusters. Each alters the wood's color slightly, but these finishes are the most natural-looking ones available.

Brush or wipe tung oil on in two fairly thin coats. Let the oil stand for the time specified; then rub vigorously along grain with a clean cloth or felt pad—the heat generated by rubbing helps oil penetrate the wood.

Polishes and waxing

Once dry, all finishes can be hand-polished to a lustrous sheen with abrasive powders (p.50) or a premixed polishing compound that imitates powder polishing. Pumice powder results in a satin sheen. For high gloss, use rottenstone instead of, or after, pumice.

Protect the finish with several thin coats of a high-quality furniture wax. Liquid wax is good for carved pieces and areas that receive light wear. Paste wax stands up better to hard use. Let the wax dry before buffing, otherwise you're just moving the wax around. Avoid silicone and lemon oil. If the piece ever needs refinishing, silicone can keep the new finish from adhering. So-called lemon oil is mostly kerosene, and can damage a finish.

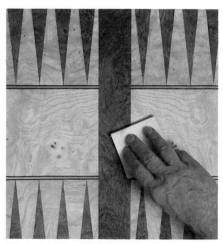

When polishing with abrasive powder, make a creamy paste of pumice and rubbing (paraffin) oil in small container. Pick up a little on felt or burlap pad and rub gently along grain. When done, clean surface with soft rags.

Characteristics of wood finishes

Type of finish	Appearance	Uses	Application	Comments
Varnish **Alkyd** **Natural resin** **Polyurethane** **Spar** **Tung-oil** **Water-base**	Hard built-up finish. Available in satin (flat, matte) and gloss forms. Colors range from clear to dark brown; all will darken wood somewhat.	**Alkyd.** General-purpose, good simulation of hand-rubbed finish. **Natural resin.** Restoration work. **Polyurethane.** Extremely durable; good for floors, table or desk tops, objects subjected to heavy wear. Thinned with mineral spirits or turpentine, can be used as a sealer. **Spar.** Exterior and marine use. **Tung-oil varnish.** Somewhat brittle; suitable for objects not heavily used. **Water-base.** Good for everyday utility objects.	**Liquid formula** is brushed on (can be sprayed on if sufficiently thinned). **Gel type** is wiped on with cloth pad, but needs more coats to achieve thickness of brushing varieties. Follow label directions for recommended number of coats and for drying time between coats.	Resists weather, water, heat, and alcohol. Difficult—if not impossible—to spot-repair. Long drying time makes finish vulnerable to marring by dust. Can be polished with abrasive powders to lustrous sheen. **Polyurethane** dries clear, but surface can look somewhat plastic. **Tung-oil varnish** looks more natural than polyurethane. **Spar varnish** yellows with age and exposure to sunlight. **Water-base** is environmentally safe (contains no volatile solvents), cleans up with water—but may raise wood grain. **CAUTION:** All forms except water-base are highly flammable. The fumes will ignite before the liquid. Use with adequate ventilation. Extinguish pilot lights; do not smoke or use near oil burner. Dispose of applicators in sealed containers (p.348).
Lacquer	Available in flat or glossy formulations and in a wide range of colors. Accents grain of wood; darkens it the least.	Furniture exposed to wear and household liquids. Picture frames, boxes, and other decorative objects.	Spraying—with professional equipment—is the best application method. Brushing is nearly impossible unless a retardant is added to slow the drying. Wear goggles and a spray-paint respirator to prevent injury from overspray.	Highly resistant to abrasion, damage, water, and alcohol. Can cloud if applied under humid conditions. Dries very quickly, so is less vulnerable to picking up dust than varnish. Most commercially made furniture is finished with lacquer. Brush formula is prone to lap marks. Offers less protection against shrinking and swelling in response to humidity changes than varnishes but more than oils. Synthetic-base lacquer is highly flammable. Water-base is nonflammable and nontoxic, but raises wood grain.
Padding lacquer **Shellac**	Deep, highly lustrous surface. **Padding lacquer** simulates antique hand-rubbed finish (French polishing). **Orange shellac** enhances the wood's color, resulting in deeper grain tones. **White shellac** dries clear, enhances wood grain slightly.	Most practical for small or medium-size decorative pieces.	Wipe on **padding lacquer** with an applicator pad or folded lint-free cloth (p.121). Brush or spray on **shellac.**	Both materials dry quickly, resist wear. Both can be damaged by alcohol or water. **Padding lacquer** can be tinted and applied over other finishes to change color or make spot repairs. **Shellac** turns cloudy when applied in damp conditions. Premixed shellac has a short shelf life. The can should be dated; do not buy if undated or more than 6 months old.
Danish oil	Natural-looking matte finish with enhanced grain. Available in natural (clear) or dark (walnut). Clear formula will darken the wood somewhat.	All interior objects. Especially suitable for carvings. Special formulations for exterior and marine use, and for oily woods such as teak and rosewood.	Wipe on, wipe off with clean lint-free rags. To fill pores and finish in one step, sand with fine sandpaper while wet. Apply three coats on objects that will receive heavy use.	Dust-free application. Magnifies defects, such as scratches, so wood must be sanded perfectly smooth before applying. Bonds with the wood; must be sanded off if another finish is desired. Easily spot-repaired.
Tung oil	Natural-looking finish; available in matte, medium-luster, and high-luster formulations. Degree of gloss increases with subsequent coats. Enhances grain, deepens wood's color.	Apply only to raw wood. All interior objects. Especially useful for carvings. Can be used on outdoor furniture and decks, but must be reapplied periodically (1–2 yr.).	Brush on or wipe on, rub in vigorously. Not subject to marring by dust. Can be sanded with fine sandpaper while wet to fill pores and finish in one step.	Hardens between wood's fibers for durable water- and alcohol-resistant finish. Seals and finishes in one step. Extremely difficult to remove if refinishing is ever needed. Easily spot-repaired. Congeals in can if stored in less-than-full container; decant into smaller container for storage.

Antiquing

Here's a quick way to turn wear and damage into an asset, or to give a fresh finish an aged look. By allowing dents and the less-used areas of an object to retain more color than highly used areas, you can create the effect of natural wear. Materials can be bought individually or in kits.

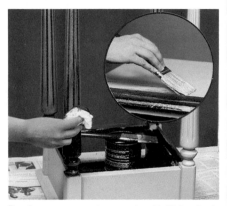

Brush on an opaque base coat and let it dry. Apply glaze. While it is wet, wipe it away, leaving color in recesses and at edges. On flat surfaces, drag a brush through glaze to simulate grain.

Sand glaze lightly with fine sandpaper. Finish with several thin coats of polyurethane or other varnish (p.121).

Ebonizing

You can create the look of ebony with brown paste wood filler and concentrated black stain. Raw or stripped oak can be ebonized with a homemade stain: Soak shredded steel wool in distilled vinegar for at least a week. The fluid that results reacts with the oak's tannic acid, turning the wood black.

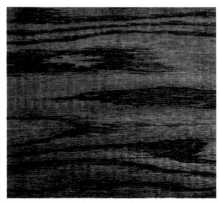

To simulate the dramatic black and brown grain of ebony, first fill the wood's pores with dark brown paste wood filler (p.120).

Apply commercial or homemade stain over filler. Repeat applications of stain until wood is a deep, rich black.

Graining

Wood grain can be simulated with a process similar to antiquing. The materials—a base coat, graining glaze, and brushes—can be purchased individually or in a kit. Natural wood tones give a traditional look; colors add a decorative accent. Practice on scrap to test colors and to perfect technique.

Apply base coat, brushing along the longest dimension. When dry, brush on glaze, then wipe with a brush, cloth, or textured pad to form grain patterns. Two or more glaze colors add richness.

When glaze is completely dry, coat with satin (matte) gloss polyurethane or lacquer to add depth and protect the finish.

Liming

Unlike bleaching, which literally removes the wood's color, liming is an effect created by filling the pores of open-grained woods (oak, chestnut, ash) with white paint or white paste wood filler (p.120). Always test the color and technique on a scrap of the same kind of wood as the final piece.

Cover surface with flat white paint or white paste wood filler. Scrub excess from surface with burlap or cloth, leaving paint in pores.

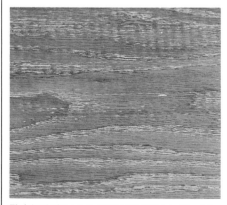

Finished piece has grain highlighted with white. Unusual effects can be created with pigmented filler or paint in colors other than white.

Chapter six

Metals and plastics
How to work with them

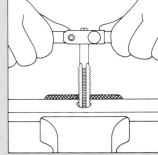

Contents

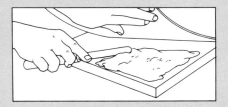
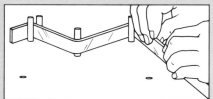

Home repairs often call for working with metals and plastics. Metals appear in many parts of a house, from roof flashing to tubular lawn chairs, from kitchen cabinets to window frames. Plastics are often used in place of glass (such as for windows and shower doors) or to provide waterproof counters in kitchens and bathrooms. Mastering the basic techniques shown in this section will enable you to handle a large number of household jobs involving metals and plastics—and even to be creative in using these materials.

Plastics are also widely used in floor coverings. Turn to the section on interior repairs and maintenance (p.271) for ways of working with these products. For working with plastic pipe, turn to the plumbing section (p.197).

Metals/Some metalworking basics

Although plastics have replaced metals in many applications around the home, metals still have a wide range of uses. A particular item can be made of either a pure metal, such as copper, or an alloy—a mixture of two or more metals, such as brass (an alloy of copper and zinc). Because different metals have different characteristics, they are often combined to produce certain desirable results. For example, chromium and nickel, which are highly resistant to corrosion, are added to steel to make stainless steel. The glossaries below describe some major characteristics of metals and explain some common metalworking techniques.

The metals most often used around the house are steel, aluminum alloys (pure aluminum is too soft), pewter, copper, and brass. Steel is a mixture of iron and carbon. The more carbon it contains, the harder it is. Most household jobs call for low-carbon, or *mild,* steel, which contains 0.1 to 0.3 percent carbon. There are also the harder medium-carbon steel (machine steel) and high-carbon steel (tool steel, used for blades and bits).

You can buy metal at metal supply houses, welding shops, and machine shops in a variety of forms. The most common are *sheet metal,* which comes in thicknesses up to ³⁄₁₆ inch, and *metal plate,* which is the same as sheet metal but thicker. Lengths of sheet metal that are no more than 12 inches wide are called *strips;* lengths of metal plate that are no more than 8 inches wide are called *flats.* Strips and flats are classified as bar metals, as are round, square, or hexagonal rods. T-shaped, U-shaped, and angled (L-shaped) lengths of metal are also available. Tubing and wire come in many shapes and sizes.

Measuring and marking metal

Plan metalworking projects in advance, carefully laying out and marking lines before cutting or shaping the metal. Inaccuracy leads to mistakes in bending, fitting, cutting, or drilling that cannot be corrected. The craftsman's motto "Measure twice, cut once" is especially true in metalworking, where mistakes cannot be covered over.

Plans and templates. Draw detailed plans of your project, showing every bend, cut, and connector. Test complicated designs by making paper or cardboard models. To help you cut accurately, make templates from sheet metal, cardboard, or heavy pa-

Using dividers

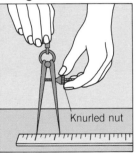

To set dividers, place one of the tool's legs on a rule, loosen knurled nut, and move other leg to desired distance; tighten nut.

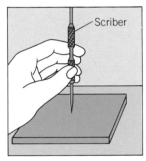

To secure leg of divider on the work, make a very small hole in the metal by pushing a scriber into it at the proper point.

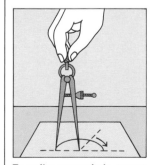

To scribe arc or circle, secure one leg of divider at center of circle and sweep other leg around, lightly scratching metal.

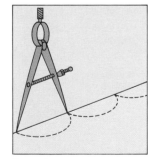

To mark equal spaces, secure one leg of tool on work and scribe with other. Swing first leg around to make second mark.

Descriptive terms

Brittle: Fragile or breakable; hardened steel and some cast irons are exceptionally brittle.

Conductive: Carries heat or electric current well.

Corrosion-resistant: Less likely to rust or otherwise corrode. Chromium, nickel, tin, and zinc are highly resistant to corrosion. They are used to plate metals that corrode quickly and are added to other metals to keep them from corroding.

Ductile: Can be drawn out to form a wire. Copper is both extremely ductile and highly conductive, making it ideal for use as electrical wiring.

Elastic: Returns to its original shape after being bent or twisted. Hard brass and stainless steel are highly elastic.

Ferrous: Containing iron. Iron and iron alloys are ferrous; all other metals and alloys are nonferrous.

Fusible: Can be joined with other metals after both metals have been melted. Brass and copper are fusible.

Hard: Resists denting or penetration. Cast iron and medium- and high-carbon steels are hard metals.

Malleable: Can be hammered, rolled, or bent without breaking or cracking; aluminum and copper are extremely malleable.

Tensile: Resistant to longitudinal pulling. Stainless steel and tool steel are highly tensile metals.

Tough: Resists forces that tend to break, bend, stretch, or crack metal; stainless steel is a tough metal.

Metalworking techniques

Annealing: Heating and then cooling metal to reduce the brittleness caused by too much bending and hammering.

Casting: Pouring molten metal into a mold of the desired shape so that the cooled metal will retain that shape.

Chasing: Ornamenting metal by indenting a design into it.

Coloring: Changing the color of metal with heat or chemicals.

Etching: Cutting a design into metal by covering it with an acid-resistant substance, scratching the design into the covering, and adding acid, which seeps through the scratches in the covering and eats into the metal.

Forging: Shaping metal by hammering or pressing it while hot.

Galvanizing: Depositing a coat of zinc on iron or steel.

Planishing: Hammering or rolling metal to make it smooth.

Plating: Coating one metal with another, usually to improve the appearance of the underlying metal or to make it corrosion-resistant. Chrome-plating—coating metal (or plastic) with a chromium alloy—serves both purposes.

Soldering: Joining two pieces of metal together by melting another metal (the solder) between them (pp. 134–135).

Sweating: Soldering one flat piece over another (p.135) or soldering a pipe inside a fitting (p.220).

Tempering: Heating and cooling steel to make it less brittle for use in making tools.

Welding: Joining pieces of metal by melting them together.

per, hold them against the metal or attach them with rubber cement, and scribe around them.

Tools and techniques. Before working with a piece of metal, be sure it is smooth and clean. File or grind away burrs, and scrub off any dirt or sediment with soapy water and steel wool. For most jobs, the metal's edges should be squared off before measuring or marking. (Whenever possible, use metal with factory-squared edges.) If one edge is angled slightly, it could throw off all your measurements. Check all edges with some type of square or spirit level.

When measuring with a steel rule, stand the rule on its edge and mark the beginning and end points of

a line with a scriber. (Enlarge the marks with a center punch if you are planning to drill holes at these points.) To scribe a line, lay the rule flat, as close to the marks as possible without covering them, press or clamp the rule down firmly to keep it from shifting, and draw the line along the edge of the rule.

Draw lines lightly with a scriber rather than penciling them. Pencil marks are hard to see, and they smudge easily. The scriber is a pencil-shaped metal tool with a sharp narrow point that draws fine incised lines into metal. A machinist's scriber has a second point at a right angle to the rest of the tool for marking hard-to-reach places.

Metal gauges. The thickness of metal is often measured in gauges. There are several incompatible systems of gauges, although in all of them the larger the gauge number, the thinner the metal. The two most widely used systems are the United States Standard for ferrous metals and the Brown and Sharpe for nonferrous metals. If you want to match a metal or a length of wire and don't know how thick it is, use a gauge for the appropriate system. This disc-shaped tool has slots of various sizes, marked with gauge numbers on one side and inches on the other. Simply slip the metal or wire into the slot it fits best and read the accompanying number.

Protractor head

Combination set is four tools in one. Add proper head to the basic steel rule to get a protractor, center guide, or square.

Centering head

Squaring head with spirit level

Tools used for measuring and marking include the versatile combination set, shown with its various units above and at right. If you prefer not to purchase this expensive tool, you can use the individual tools: a steel rule and square (p.47), and a protractor and T-bevel (p.48). Below are some essential marking tools and a metal gauge, used to find the thickness of metal. In addition to these tools, you may need a variety of files (p.42) for cleaning metal prior to marking it, trammel points (p.48) for marking off large circles and arcs, and calipers (p.46) for measuring inside and outside dimensions and gauging depths.

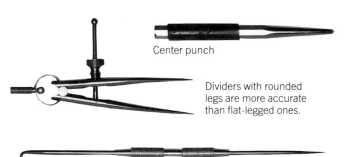

Center punch

Dividers with rounded legs are more accurate than flat-legged ones.

Scriber

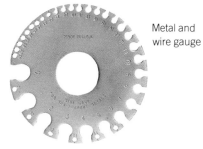

Metal and wire gauge

Locking nut

Use combination set with protractor head when scribing lines at angles. Loosen locking nut, set rule to correct angle, and tighten nut. Press flat face of head along edge of work and scribe line.

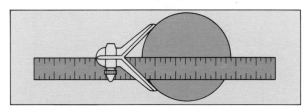

To find center of a circle, slide centering head onto rule, positioning it on circle with both jaws just touching perimeter. Rule will cut across center. Use inch marks on rule to estimate center point.

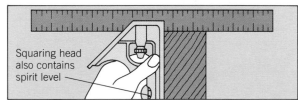

Squaring head also contains spirit level

To square off metal with squaring head, push straight part of head against one edge of work, with rule resting along adjoining edge. If rule lies flat along its entire length, work is squared.

Metals/Cutting

Although you can cut metal with a utility knife, a cold chisel, a table saw, or even a grinding wheel, the hacksaw and snips are the more usual metal-cutting tools. A hacksaw will cut almost any metal (p.26), but snips are useful only for sheet metal.

There are various types of snips. Simple tin snips are adequate for cutting straight lines in light-weight sheet metal, but snips with curved blades are needed for cutting arcs and circles. Aviation snips have a compound lever action that provides greater control and cutting power than tin snips. Those with yellow handles are used for cutting straight lines; those with red handles, for left-hand curves; and those with green handles, for right-hand curves.

If you are doing a lot of sheet-metal work, you can buy electric snips or shears. For extra ease in cutting either sheet metal or heavier metal, any power saw can be fitted with a metal-cutting blade, but use it cautiously. You can also equip your electric drill with a metal saw or a sheet-metal cutter.

Sheet-metal snips

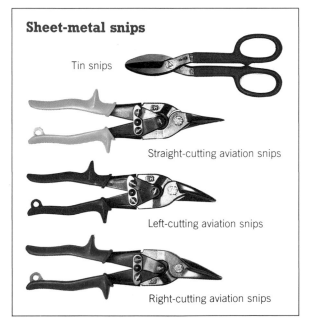

Tin snips

Straight-cutting aviation snips

Left-cutting aviation snips

Right-cutting aviation snips

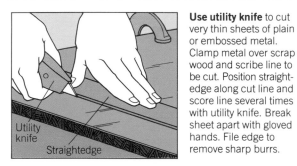

Use utility knife to cut very thin sheets of plain or embossed metal. Clamp metal over scrap wood and scribe line to be cut. Position straight-edge along cut line and score line several times with utility knife. Break sheet apart with gloved hands. File edge to remove sharp burrs.

Utility knife

Straightedge

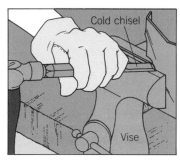

Use tin snips as you would scissors on heavy cardboard, but wear heavy work gloves to protect your hands. As you cut, open jaws of snips fully and make cuts as long as possible, but don't close the snips completely, or nicks will result. After cutting, file away sharp edges.

Tin snips

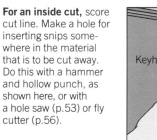

For an inside cut, score cut line. Make a hole for inserting snips some-where in the material that is to be cut away. Do this with a hammer and hollow punch, as shown here, or with a hole saw (p.53) or fly cutter (p.56).

Hollow punch

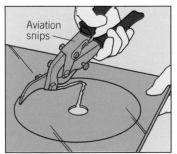

Work aviation snips into hole and make a rough cut, leaving about ¼ in. waste along cut line. Remove waste metal and make final cut. *Note:* Don't make first cut too close to cut line or the metal may bend during final cut instead of shearing off.

Aviation snips

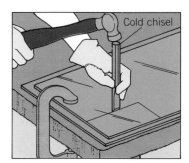

Cold chisel will cut metal. Clamp work over scrap wood or (for a sharper cut) metal and scribe cut line. Set chisel blade on cut line and strike it with a ball peen hammer. Move blade along line and strike again. Continue along entire line, then repeat until cut is complete.

Cold chisel

Another chisel method is to clamp work in a vise with cut line just above its jaws. Rest chisel blade on jaw of vise and tilt it to about a 30° angle so that its cutting edge is against cut line. Strike chisel with a ball peen hammer to make cut, as above.

Cold chisel

Vise

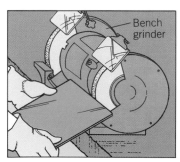

For tubing or thick stock, use a hacksaw (p.27). To cut very thin sheet metal with a hacksaw, clamp it between pieces of scrap wood and saw through both wood and metal. Use a coping saw with a metal-cutting blade for deep curves, a compass or keyhole saw for interior cuts.

Keyhole saw

After making a cut, beat out any crimps with a mallet on a flat surface. Remove burrs by filing (p.42). For extra-smooth finish, polish cut edge on a bench grinder (p.73). Grinder can also be used to cut bevels in edges of thick metal.

Bench grinder

Drilling

For drilling sheet metal, any type of drill will do, even a hand rotary drill. For heavier metal use a brace and bit or an electric drill. A drill press gives the greatest accuracy. Use regular twist bits (preferably with carbide tips) or high-speed steel bits. The high-speed bits last longer and drill through harder metals; their sizes may be given in fractions of an inch, millimeters, metal gauge sizes, letters, or numbers.

Clamp the work securely to keep it from shifting. If you are drilling all the way through the metal, back it up with scrap wood. Before drilling, make an indentation in the metal to keep the bit from wandering off-center. If you are drilling through thin sheet metal, sandwich it between pieces of scrap wood and drill through both wood and metal.

When drilling thick metal, lubricate the hole with a bit of light oil or turpentine before and during drilling to keep the bit from overheating. Back the bit out from time to time and brush away waste fragments; otherwise they may overheat and partially weld themselves to the bit.

Metalworking safety tips

Metal is relatively safe to work with, providing you take a little care. In addition to the safety precautions on page 19, always:
- Keep saw blades and drill bits sharp and clean; never force a tool.
- Clamp work securely. Never hold work with your hands while drilling, sawing, or soldering.
- Wear safety goggles when drilling, sawing, or grinding metal; tiny particles may fly into your eyes if they are left unprotected.
- Wear thick work gloves when sawing metal; sawed edges can be sharp enough to cause serious cuts, and tiny burrs can do painful damage to unprotected fingers.
- File or grind cut edges or newly drilled holes as soon as possible to prevent cuts.
- Make use of all available safety shields and devices your power tools are equipped with.

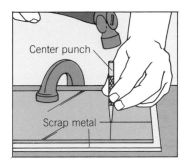

Clamp work down over hard surface (preferably scrap metal), and mark position of hole by scribing intersecting lines on metal. Position center punch where lines cross, and tap with hammer to indent the metal. This will keep bit from slipping out of position during drilling.

Add a few drops of oil to indentation. Drill at low speed if you are using a large drill or a drill press. (For best speed, check a chart for your drill.) Back drill out of hole now and then to brush away loose material and add a few drops of oil.

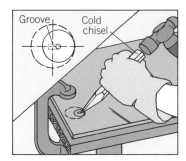

In thick metal, check that the hole being drilled is centered correctly. If it is slightly off-center, use a chisel to cut a groove between the drilled hole and the intended center. Guide drill bit along groove to the correct center. *Note:* This works with twist bits only.

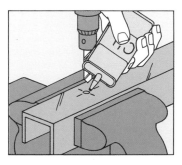

Drill larger holes (more than ¼ in. in diameter) in stages. First drill a ¼-in. hole, then drill with larger bit (up to ½ in.). Repeat with increasingly larger bits as needed. Or drill once with a step bit (p.53). For holes larger than 1 in., use a hole saw (p.53) or a fly cutter (p.56).

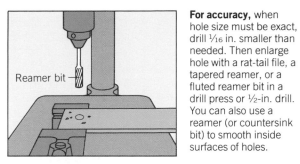

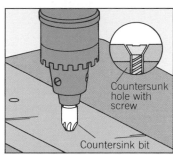

For accuracy, when hole size must be exact, drill ¹⁄₁₆ in. smaller than needed. Then enlarge hole with a rat-tail file, a tapered reamer, or a fluted reamer bit in a drill press or ½-in. drill. You can also use a reamer (or countersink bit) to smooth inside surfaces of holes.

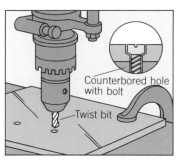

Make screwheads flush with surface of metal by enlarging and tapering top of pilot hole just enough to contain the screwhead. Drill pilot hole to needed size, then bore into it with countersink bit (p.53). Set drill at lowest speed, and lubricate the hole liberally as you proceed.

Sink bolt heads and nuts below surface of metal by counterboring. This process is same as countersinking, shown above, except that a straight twist bit is used instead of cone-shaped countersink bit. Once again, drill at slowest speed and lubricate work generously.

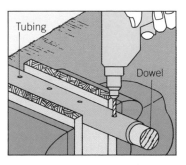

When drilling tubing, if hole is to be near end of a section, insert wooden dowel to reinforce it, then drill through tubing and into dowel. If hole is to go completely through tubing, drill through one side of tubing, entire thickness of dowel, and other side of tubing.

The cutter used to make threads inside a hole is called a *tap*. Taps are round bars of hardened tool steel, ground square on one end and threaded on the other; the ridges between the threaded channels have sharp cutting edges. A tap is fitted into a predrilled hole in the metal and turned with a spe-

Fully tapped hole

Blind hole

cial type of wrench. Taps can be used to cut threads completely through a piece of metal or partially through, creating a blind hole.

Selecting a tap. There are three major types of taps. On the *plug tap,* the first three to five threads are tapered; this makes starting easier but prevents threading close to the bottom of a blind hole. On the *tapered tap,* more threads are tapered for even easier starting, but less depth. The untapered *bottoming tap* cuts threads to the bottom of a blind hole, but the thread must be started with a plug or tapered tap. Taps and *dies* (for cutting exterior threads) are available in kits along with the tools needed for turning them. For best results, use taps made of high-speed steel (an extra-hard steel, usually stamped *HS*).

The size of a tap is stamped on its shank and is given in three parts: its diameter (in gauge numbers or inches), the number of threads per inch, and the type of threads. Different standards apply to the thread types, but the most common in the United States is the American National standard—NC for coarse and NF for fine. The tap should match in type and size the bolt for which it is cutting threads.

Starter holes. To accept a tap, a starter hole must be drilled. Use a table, like the one at right, to determine the size of the hole. Note that although the sizes of the most commonly used drill bits are given in fractions of inches, the sizes of some of the bits needed for tapping are expressed in numbers or letters.

Tapping tools

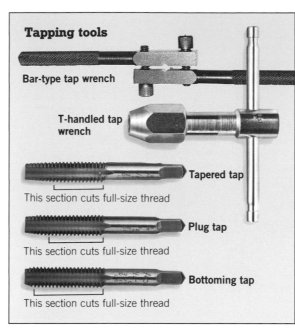

Bar-type tap wrench

T-handled tap wrench

Tapered tap

This section cuts full-size thread

Plug tap

This section cuts full-size thread

Bottoming tap

This section cuts full-size thread

Drill bit sizes for predrilling taps

Bolt and tap size	Drill bit size	Bit size in fractions
No. 8–32–NC	No. 29	9/64″
No. 10–24–NC	No. 25	5/32″
No. 12–24–NC	No. 16	11/64″
1/4″–20–NC	No. 7	13/64″
1/4″–28–NF	No. 3	7/32″
5/16″–24–NC	F	17/64″
3/8″–16–NC	5/16″	5/16″
3/8″–24–NF	21/64″	21/64″
1/2″–13–NC	27/64″	27/64″
1/2″–20–NF	29/64″	29/64″

This chart gives the bit size needed to drill a hole to accept a tap. The first column gives bolt and tap size. The other two columns give the drill bit size and its equivalent in fractions of an inch.

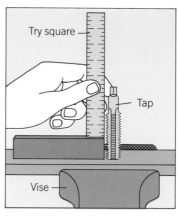

1. Clamp work securely in a vise, and drill a hole slightly smaller than the diameter of the tap. (Check table at left for size the hole should be.) Lubricate threads of tap with cutting fluid or (better still) swab them with semi-solid vegetable shortening. Insert the lubricated tap in hole, aligning it carefully. Check the tap against a square to make sure it is straight.

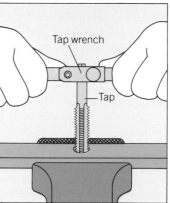

2. Use a tap wrench to turn tap clockwise. For first few turns, exert moderate downward pressure. Once first threads have been cut, pressure is no longer needed—threads will pull tap into hole as you proceed. After each turn or so, back tap out a bit, file burrs from edge of hole, brush away filings, and add more lubricant to the tap to keep it from breaking off in the hole.

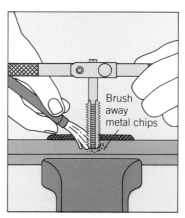

3. Continue the process of turning the tap, backing it out, brushing metal chips out of the threads, and adding lubricant. If you are threading a blind hole, as you near the bottom, remove tap completely after each turn or two, and use a piece of wire or a cotton swab to clean out metal chips.

Threading bolts

The method of cutting a thread around the outside of round metal stock is known as *die cutting.* It can be used to thread rods or pipes or other metal tubing or to rethread an old bolt. Die cutting is done by hand in a manner similar to the procedure followed when cutting an internal thread with a tap, but instead you use a die. A threading die is a piece of steel (preferably high-speed tool steel) in the shape of a disc or hexagon, with sharp internal threads. These threads are fitted over the metal rod or bolt; they cut into it as the die is turned by a wrench called a *diestock.* The threads in the die are ground away slightly on one side to make starting easier.

Bolt threads

Die sizes. Like taps, dies are sized the same as bolts (see facing page), and the size is marked on the die itself. If you want to make a bolt to match one you have on hand, measure the diameter of the bolt with calipers, and thread a rod of the same size. Determine the number of threads per inch with a thread gauge, as shown at right.

Adjusting a diestock. Unless you are using a hexagonal die with a standard wrench, you will have to turn the die with a diestock. Use one of the proper size. On some diestocks, the die is simply dropped in and secured by tightening a screw in the diestock. Other diestocks have guide plates. If yours does, clamp the rod you want threaded into a vise and fit the diestock over it, with the plate facing you. Rotate the plate until the guide fingers

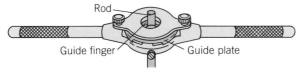

Rod · Guide finger · Guide plate

touch the rod lightly; then tighten the holding screws. Remove the diestock from the rod, and install the die with the tapered threads facing the guide plate. Return the tool to the rod with the guide plate facing down (or toward the vise), and cut the threads as shown at far right.

Die tools

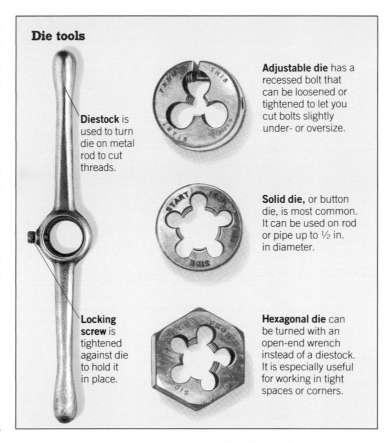

Diestock is used to turn die on metal rod to cut threads.

Locking screw is tightened against die to hold it in place.

Adjustable die has a recessed bolt that can be loosened or tightened to let you cut bolts slightly under- or oversize.

Solid die, or button die, is most common. It can be used on rod or pipe up to ½ in. in diameter.

Hexagonal die can be turned with an open-end wrench instead of a diestock. It is especially useful for working in tight spaces or corners.

Thread gauge

Find gauge blade that fits into threads of bolt you wish to match. Read number of threads on that blade, and use a die with same rating.

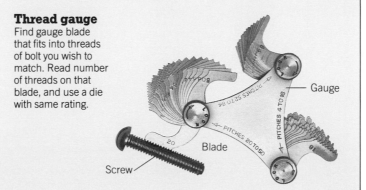

Gauge · Blade · Screw

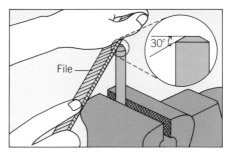

File · 30°

1. Clamp rod, tubing, or old bolt into a vise, and use a scriber to mark the place you want the threads to stop. With a file, cut a 30° angle around top of stock. This will help get the die started in cutting the threads.

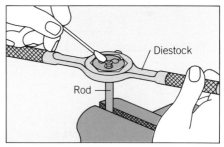

Diestock · Rod

2. Fit die into diestock. (If diestock has a guide plate, proceed as described in text.) Position die over rod, holding diestock at right angle to rod. Lubricate die by swabbing on semi-solid vegetable shortening or adding cutting fluid.

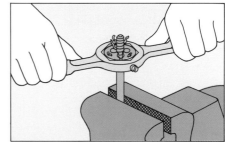

3. Applying downward pressure, turn diestock clockwise one or two turns. Back off, check threads, brush away chips, and add more lubricant. Repeat process as needed, but don't apply pressure after first threads are formed.

Metals/Bolts, screws, and adhesives

Once metal has been cut, you have a choice of several ways of joining the pieces or attaching them to other surfaces. Most obvious are bolting or screwing, but metals can also be joined with epoxy or other adhesives (see below), riveted (facing page), or soldered (pp.134–135). Yet another method is to fold the pieces in interlocking seams (pp.136–137).

Bolts are generally pushed completely through the pieces being joined and then capped with washers and nuts. In thick metal, however, holes are bored and threaded with taps (p.130) so that the bolts can be screwed directly into the work. Using a die (p.131), you can make new bolts from metal rods, or you can rethread worn bolts.

Self-tapping screws—sometimes called sheet metal screws—are used to fasten sheets of metal together or to fasten metal to another material. These screws cut their own threads as they are driven in. Generally, they pass through holes in the top piece of metal and into smaller pilot holes in the backup material.

Installing bolts

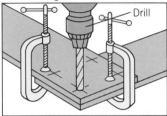

1. Clamp work together firmly and mark positions of all bolts. Drill first hole (holes should be just large enough to let bolt slip through).

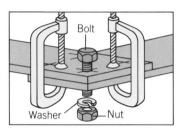

2. Slip bolt into hole, slide on a washer, and thread on a nut. Hold bolt head with a wrench (or a screwdriver if bolt head is slotted), and tighten nut with another wrench. Check alignment of work and reclamp.

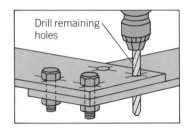

3. Drill second hole. Insert bolt, and add washer and nut to keep work from shifting. Then drill remaining holes, remove clamps, and add bolts, washers, and nuts.

Driving screws

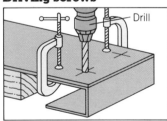

1. Clamp work securely, and mark positions of screws. Drill pilot holes slightly smaller than screw shanks through both pieces of metal or through metal and into backup material.

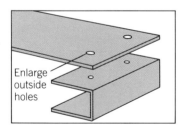

2. Unclamp work and enlarge holes in top piece of metal so that screw shank will pass through it easily. Then reclamp work, making sure all holes align.

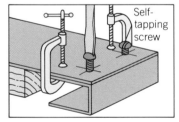

3. Drive in all screws most of the way; then go back and tighten one at a time. Screws will bite into walls of smaller holes in backup piece, drawing it up tightly against top piece.

Metal-bonding adhesives

Perhaps the strongest adhesive for bonding metal is epoxy. It comes in two parts, resin and hardener, which must be mixed just before using and applied as shown at right.

Other adhesives that bond metals include liquid solder, polyvinyl chloride (PVC), various instant glues, and two-part acrylic adhesives. Bolt-locking compound is good for cementing the threads of bolts into place, as it will harden in the absence of air.

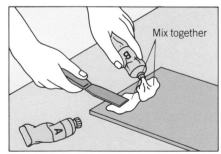

Working with epoxy: 1. Thoroughly clean surfaces to be bonded. Place equal parts of resin and hardener on one surface and mix them together (they may be in liquid or putty form).

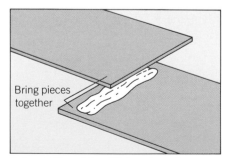

2. Spread the mixture thinly and evenly over both of the surfaces to be bonded. Carefully fit the pieces together and clamp them firmly. Wipe away any excess epoxy immediately.

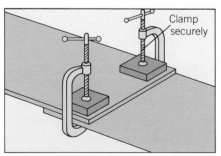

3. Let adhesive cure fully according to the manufacturer's instructions (anywhere from several hours to several days). Epoxy can be dissolved with acetone (nail polish remover).

Rivets

Sheets of metal can be fastened with rivets to provide maximum strength or decorative effects. Rivets pass through predrilled holes in the metals being joined. Installed, they function like bolts with heads on both sides. Rivets may be made of iron, brass, copper, aluminum, or some other metal. Get the ones that match the metal you are fastening. Rivet heads may be flat, rounded, or tapered for countersinking. (Countersink a rivet as you would a bolt, p. 129.)

There are two major types of rivets: solid and hollow. The hollow rivet is also called a blind rivet because it can be used when only one side of

the work is accessible. It is easily installed with a tool much like a stapler.

The solid rivet is installed with a rivet set, a length of hardened tool steel with a deep hole and a cupped depression in one end. The deep hole is positioned over the rivet before the rivet is flattened. The tool is hammered into the metals, flattening the pieces and drawing them together. The shallow cup is used to shape the rivet head. Rivet sets come in different sizes to fit rivets of different diameters.

To provide enough metal for shaping its end, the shank of the rivet should protrude beyond the pieces being joined for a distance between half and

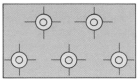

three-quarters its diameter. For greater strength, when using two rows of rivets, stagger the spacing between them, as shown; do not line them up side by side. When installing solid rivets, rest the work on a metal surface. If you are installing roundheaded rivets, make a resting surface by drilling into a block of metal a depression just large enough to accommodate a rivet head.

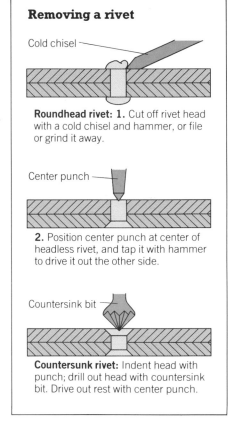

Removing a rivet

Cold chisel

Roundhead rivet: 1. Cut off rivet head with a cold chisel and hammer, or file or grind it away.

Center punch

2. Position center punch at center of headless rivet, and tap it with hammer to drive it out the other side.

Countersink bit

Countersunk rivet: Indent head with punch; drill out head with countersink bit. Drive out rest with center punch.

Blind rivets

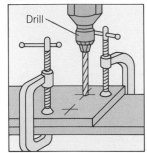

1. Mark locations of rivets. Select proper size rivets, and drill holes the same size as rivets through materials to be joined.

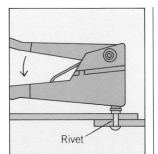

2. Open handles of riveter and push stem of rivet all the way into tool. Insert end of rivet in hole in metal.

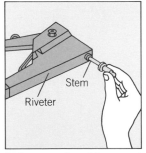

3. Squeeze riveter handles until rivet stem breaks off. If stem doesn't break, reseat rivet in tool and try again.

Rivet set

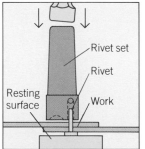

1. Slip rivet through predrilled holes from beneath. Fit deep hole of rivet set over rivet. Strike with flat end of ball peen hammer.

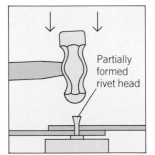

2. Remove rivet set, then hammer rivet stem until it spreads out and fits tightly. (Use rounded end of ball peen hammer.)

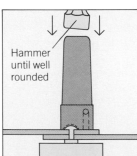

3. Place shallow cup-shaped depression over rivet. Strike set with flat end of hammer until rivet head is rounded off.

One of the oldest methods of joining metals is to heat them and use their heat to melt a softer metal, which then bonds them together. This process is called soldering; the bonding agent is the solder.

There are basically two types of solders. *Soft,* or *common, solders* have melting points under 800°F. Those that are *hard solders* have melting points above 1,100°F. Both common and hard solders come in bars, chips, sheets, or spools of wire. Special solder is required for bonding aluminum. Traditionally, soft solders were alloys of lead and tin, but since the federal Environmental Protection Agency banned the use of lead in plumbing, new types of solder have been developed for bonding pipes (p.220).

Hard solder, sometimes called silver solder, is an alloy of silver (or sometimes brass). Because of their higher melting points, hard solders create stronger bonds but cannot be used with metals that have low melting points. The high temperatures required for hard soldering call for special techniques that are best left to professionals.

Soldering tools. Soft solder can be applied with a soldering iron, gun, or pencil or with a torch. Generally, soldering guns and pencils are good only for small or delicate jobs, such as working with wires. For bonding metal of any weight, use a soldering iron. Irons range in size from 100 to 350 watts. For most household jobs, a 150- or 250-watt iron is best. Some gas-fueled models are available, but these are handy only if you plan to do a lot of soldering away from an electrical outlet. Buy a metal rest for your iron, or make one by securing a piece of bent metal to a block of wood.

Before using a soldering iron, clean its tip thoroughly and tin it (coat it with solder). In addition, while you are working, keep a damp cellulose sponge nearby and use it to wipe the tip of the iron clean from time to time. Never pick up an iron by its cord or its shaft; even if it is unplugged, a serious burn may result.

Torches. Although a gas-oxygen torch is ideal, a propane torch will suffice for most soft soldering jobs. A propane torch consists of a replaceable fuel cylinder and a screw-on top with a nozzle and a wheel for adjusting the flow of fuel. For heavy-duty jobs that require more heat, a cylinder of high-temperature fuel can be substituted for the propane.

When using a torch, work on a nonmetallic fireproof surface out of the way of anything flammable. A workbench topped with firebrick is a good choice. Although it is important to hold the pieces you are soldering steady, try not to use metal clamps or a vise, as the metal will draw heat away from where it is needed. If you do use clamps or a vise, slip scrap wood between the jaws of the tool and the work.

Cleaning the metal. Before joining any metal surfaces, make sure they are cleaned of all dirt, corrosion, or paint; otherwise, they won't bond. A scrubbing with soapy water and steel wool, followed by a thorough rinsing, may suffice. However, if the metal is painted or corroded, you will have to sand or file it or even use a grinding wheel on it.

Once the metal is clean, coat it with *flux,* a liquid

Using a soldering iron

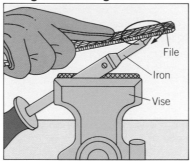

1. If tip of soldering iron is new or corroded, file it until it is smooth, rounded, and shiny. (Don't file tip made of iron unless it is corroded.) Use a bastard file and move it across and down tip with gentle circular motion.

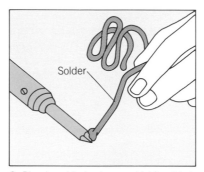

2. Plug in soldering iron and let it get hot. (This will take about 5 min.) Brush entire tip of iron with flux; then hold solder to tip of iron and turn iron slowly to tin it on all sides (coat it evenly with solder).

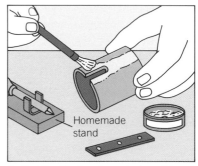

3. Test the fit of surfaces to be soldered, and remove any rough sections or corrosion by filing or scrubbing. Wash and dry work thoroughly. Brush the cleaned surfaces with liquid or paste flux; avoid touching them.

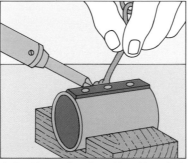

4. Position work to be soldered but don't touch fluxed areas. Apply iron to parts of work to be joined and heat them. Touch solder to work at tip of iron. If it doesn't melt, apply more heat and try again.

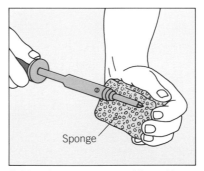

5. Move iron along seam, adding solder as needed. Solder will flow toward the heat. Wipe off iron from time to time with a damp sponge. If solder gets runny or if iron smokes, turn off iron until it cools a bit.

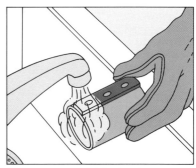

6. Let work cool slightly; then hold it under warm running water with pliers or tongs or in heavily gloved hands. When work is cool enough to handle, scrub it in soapy water to wash off excess flux before it stains.

or paste cleansing agent that prevents oxidation and helps the solder flow. Without flux, the solder will not bond properly. Apply it with a small paintbrush. Most fluxes are corrosive, and any excess must be cleaned off after soldering. Rosin and other noncorrosive fluxes can be used for electrical work, but they are generally inadequate for heavier jobs. Some wire solders come with rosin in the core; while these are adequate for electrical soldering, do not use them for other jobs.

Soldering procedures. The steps in soldering are: Clean the metal, flux it, heat it, apply solder to it, cool it, and clean it again. If you are joining flat surfaces, apply the solder separately to both surfaces, let them cool, then join them and apply heat to remelt the solder and make the bond. This process, called sweat soldering, is also used in plumbing.

Because of the electrical code requirement to use solderless connectors in house wiring, you probably won't do any electrical soldering, unless you are working with electronic equipment or appliances that have soldered connections. If you do solder electrical wires, however, use a soldering iron, gun, or pencil and a noncorrosive flux, such as rosin. Do not attempt to wash the soldered connection.

Welding. In addition to soldering, metals can be bonded by welding. In this process, metals are melted together to form a seamless joint that is as strong as the original metal. Welding requires high heat and special skills and is best left to professionals.

Soldering with a torch

1. Test the fit of surfaces to be joined; clean thoroughly, as described on facing page. Brush metal generously with liquid or paste flux. Without flux, metal will oxidize and the solder will not flow properly.

Flux

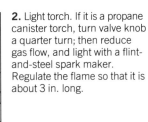

Spark maker — Torch

2. Light torch. If it is a propane canister torch, turn valve knob a quarter turn; then reduce gas flow, and light with a flint-and-steel spark maker. Regulate the flame so that it is about 3 in. long.

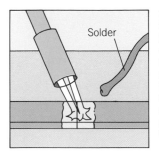

Solder

3. Move flame along the metal to heat it evenly. When flux begins to bubble and pop (after 7 to 10 sec.), touch the solder to work. If solder does not readily melt, remove it and heat metal a while longer; then try again. Let molten solder flow toward flame across entire joint. Clean to remove flux (facing page).

Hard-to-reach places

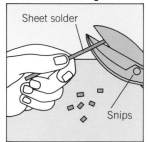

Sheet solder

Snips

1. Use a sharp knife or wire snips to cut solder into tiny pieces about the size of rice grains. Clean and flux the metal and fit it together for soldering as usual. Light torch, adjust its flame, and pass it back and forth over work until flux is dry (white and crystalline).

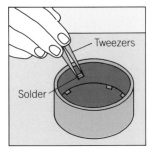

Tweezers

Solder

2. Use tweezers to position the cut-up bits of solder on the fluxed metal. Position them about ½ in. apart, all along the line to be soldered.

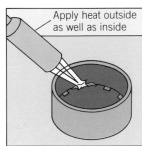

Apply heat outside as well as inside

3. Use the torch to apply heat until the solder flows and spreads evenly along the seam. Keep moving the torch flame in a figure 8 pattern to distribute the heat evenly. If the metal begins to glow red, move the torch away and let metal cool before resuming, or you may melt the work. Clean off flux, as on facing page.

Sweat soldering

Scriber

1. Before soldering one flat piece to another (sweat soldering), clean both pieces, then position top piece on bottom and mark position with a scriber. Remove top piece. Flux bottom piece and underside of top piece. Dry flux with torch, and scatter bits of solder ½ in. apart around fluxed areas on both pieces.

2. Heat solder until it flows over surfaces to form a film of uniform thickness. Move torch away from work occasionally to keep work from melting. If you need to turn the work, do it with a metal poker (you can use a scriber, an ice pick, or a piece of coat hanger wire with its end filed to a point). Let work cool.

Scrap wood

3. Position top piece of work on lower one and hold with poker. Clamp down if needed, but put scrap wood between clamp jaws and work. Move flame over work, heating all parts equally. Remove flame when a thin line of solder appears around edge of work. Fill in any gaps with extra solder. Cool and clean work.

Metals/Shaping sheet metal

Whether you are making or repairing heating and air-conditioning ducts, installing a hood over your kitchen range, replacing roof flashing or metal gutter pipes, or simply fashioning a shelf for a metal cabinet, you will have occasion to shape sheet metal to your needs. Any expanse of metal that is no more than ⅜ inch thick is classified as sheet metal. Anything thicker is regarded as metal plate.

Sheet metal can be shaped by bending, finished with hems, and joined together with locked seams. Few of the tools needed to shape sheet metal are specialized, and in most cases even these can be dispensed with. You can use homemade jigs and a mallet to do most shaping jobs.

Basic bends. Sheet metal is very malleable and can easily be bent into curves and angles. Sheets can

also be joined together. Straight or angled sheets can simply be overlapped and then fastened with screws, nuts and bolts, rivets, or solder, or their edges can be interlocked and reinforced with fasteners. Sharp or burred metal edges can be made safe by filing or by folding them into single or double hems. For extra strength, you can fold the edges over lengths of reinforcement wire.

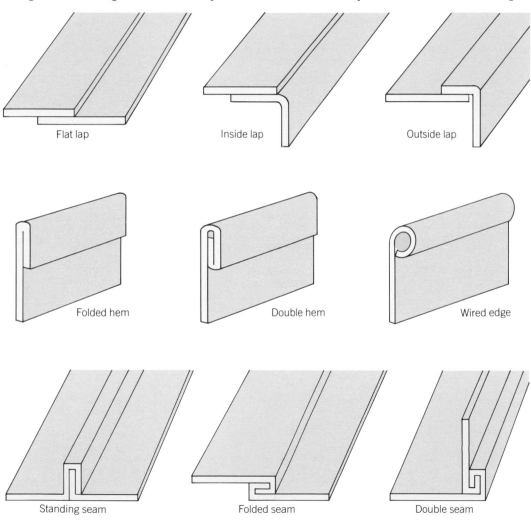

Flat lap   Inside lap   Outside lap

Folded hem   Double hem   Wired edge

Standing seam   Folded seam   Double seam

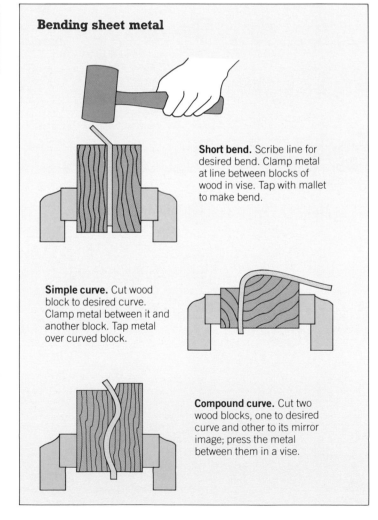

Bending sheet metal

Short bend. Scribe line for desired bend. Clamp metal at line between blocks of wood in vise. Tap with mallet to make bend.

Simple curve. Cut wood block to desired curve. Clamp metal between it and another block. Tap metal over curved block.

Compound curve. Cut two wood blocks, one to desired curve and other to its mirror image; press the metal between them in a vise.

Techniques. Measure and mark for the exact placement of bends before you even begin to cut the metal. When measuring, be sure to account for the folding of metal edges in seams and outside hems. When shaping sheet metal, clamp it securely so that it is supported solidly on both surfaces along its entire length. You can either secure the metal in a vise between two hardwood blocks or clamp it between the edge of your workbench and a straight hardwood board. Mold curves around hardwood forms shaped to the exact contours and sizes needed.

Use a mallet to do the shaping. Although a wooden mallet will suffice, less surface damage will result from a rubber, plastic, or rawhide mallet. Shape a bend with a series of tapping strikes. Don't try to do it with one blow. If you hammer too hard, the metal will buckle and distort.

▶ **CAUTION:** To avoid serious cuts, wear heavy leather work gloves when handling sheet metal.

Making a safe edge

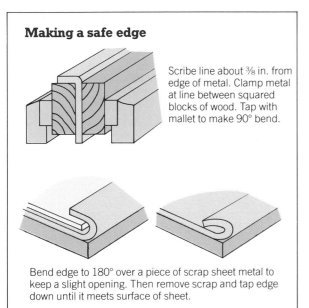

Scribe line about ⅜ in. from edge of metal. Clamp metal at line between squared blocks of wood. Tap with mallet to make 90° bend.

Bend edge to 180° over a piece of scrap sheet metal to keep a slight opening. Then remove scrap and tap edge down until it meets surface of sheet.

Folding a seam

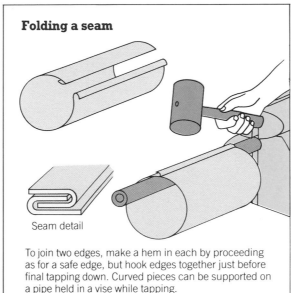

Seam detail

To join two edges, make a hem in each by proceeding as for a safe edge, but hook edges together just before final tapping down. Curved pieces can be supported on a pipe held in a vise while tapping.

Strengthening an edge

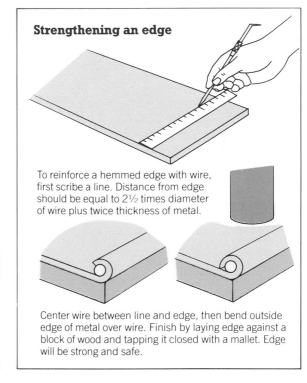

To reinforce a hemmed edge with wire, first scribe a line. Distance from edge should be equal to 2½ times diameter of wire plus twice thickness of metal.

Center wire between line and edge, then bend outside edge of metal over wire. Finish by laying edge against a block of wood and tapping it closed with a mallet. Edge will be strong and safe.

Special tools

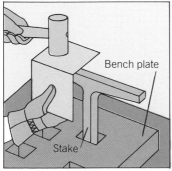

Bench plate

Stake

A sheet-metal stake of appropriate shape will facilitate bending. Either slip it into a special bench plate or clamp it in a vise. Position sheet metal with its bend line over the bending edge of the stake. Bend the metal with a series of light mallet blows.

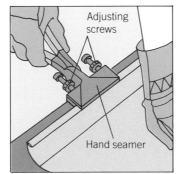

Adjusting screws

Hand seamer

Use a hand seamer to make preliminary bends for seams. Fit seamer over edge of metal at midpoint so that its jaws will close at fold line. Lock adjusting screws. Press down against work and bring handle of seamer over to make bend. Repeat every 3 to 4 in. along edge; then close seam.

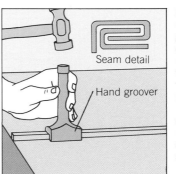

Seam detail

Hand groover

Hand groover helps make a flat locked, or grooved, seam. Fold edges of two sheets of metal and hook them together, as shown for folding seams, but only lightly tap together. Place channeled groove of appropriate-size hand groover over seam and tap with mallet along entire seam.

Soft bar metals, such as aluminum, copper, brass, wrought iron, and mild steel, can be bent cold without risking a fracture, but they will stretch on the outside of the bend and contract on the inside, causing some distortion in that area. To minimize the distortion, anneal the metal (see facing page) before working it. When bending steel, copper, or wrought iron (but not brass or aluminum), you can decrease the distortion by heating the metal with a torch, bending it red hot, placing it on an anvil, and while the metal is still hot, hammering away the distortion that does result.

Metal tubing. Because it is hollow, tubing tends to crimp when bent. To prevent crimping, work slowly and try to avoid sharp bends. Also, pack the tubing with wet sand before bending it; you can hose it clean later.

Tubing connectors. Sharp bends in tubing are best done with connectors. Standard elbows provide 90° turns, and adjustable elbows can be bent at any angle. There are also splicers for end-to-end connections, T-butts for right-angle connections, flanges for connecting tubing to walls or floors (useful for installing rails for the handicapped), and end plugs. Some connectors have an adjusting screw that pushes a clip against the walls of the tubing to make the connection tight.

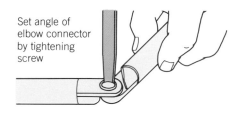

Set angle of elbow connector by tightening screw

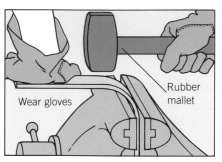

To make a sharp bend in bar metal, score it on underside at bending point and clamp it in vise. Push down on end of metal with gloved hand, and tap just above bending point with rubber mallet.

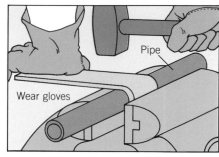

Curved bends can be made in same way. Simply clamp a length of pipe or rod of appropriate size in vise with metal. Push down on bar and tap it just beyond point where it contacts pipe or rod.

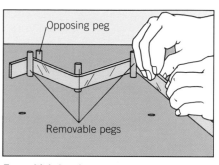

For multiple bends, make jig by boring peg holes in a board in desired pattern, with extra hole on opposing side of first bend. Insert pegs (dowels) as needed and bend metal between them.

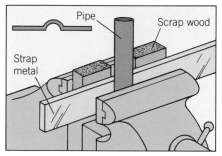

To make curved channel for pipe or wires, mark position of channel, and fasten metal in vise with two pieces of scrap wood straddling mark and pipe directly behind mark. Slowly tighten vise.

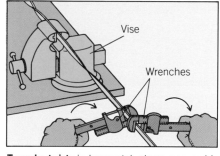

To make twists in bar metal, clamp one end in vise and grasp other end with two pipe wrenches facing in opposite directions. (Tape wrench jaws to protect metal.) Push wrenches in circular pattern.

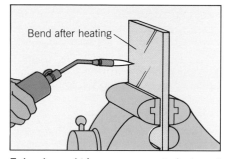

To bend wrought iron, copper, or steel, clamp it in a vise and use a torch (p.134) to heat it until it glows cherry red. Then, using tongs or wearing heavy gloves, grasp top of bar and push down.

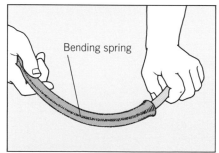

To bend thin-walled tubing, slip the tubing into a special bending spring; choose one that fits the tubing snugly. Make the bend by hand, or do it in a vise as you would bar metal.

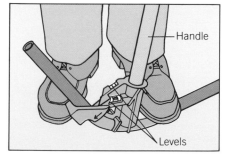

Use a tubing bender to make 45° or 90° bends. Slip tubing into bender with beginning of bending place at arrow. Step on tread and pull handle until spirit levels indicate desired degree of bend.

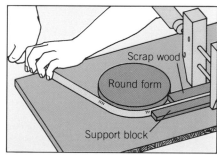

Make a jig by fastening a round wood form and a straight support block to plywood. Fill tubing with wet sand and clamp it against support block with scrap wood on other side. Bend it around form.

Repairing dents

Although metal is stronger than many other building materials, it is not indestructible. Sheet metal and plate are subject to dents, and many metals corrode easily, even to the extent of developing holes. But dents can often be straightened, and rust can be removed before it does irreversible damage.

Dealing with dents. If you have a dent in fairly thin metal and you can reach the opposite side of the damaged area, you can probably push it out with the heel of your hand or tap it out with a mallet, as shown at right.

If the opposite side of a dented metal is inaccessible, try pulling the dent out with a screw. To do so, drill a ⅛-inch hole in the dented area and insert a No. 8 screw into the hole, giving it two or three turns to anchor it in place. Grasp the head of the screw with locking pliers and pull straight out, firmly and smoothly—don't jerk or twist the screw, or you might pull it out of the metal. If the dent does not come out when you first pull, tap around the raised border of the dent with a hammer to release the pressure in the buckled metal, then pull again. Drill more holes and repeat the process, if necessary.

Fiberglass filler. Provided the metal is to be painted or otherwise covered, you can fill in dents or even holes made by repairs or rust. Use a fiberglass filler, sold in kits at most hardware stores and automotive supply outlets. Mix the filler, which is a type of epoxy, according to the directions; after applying it to the metal, let it cure for the full time recommended by the manufacturer (generally 1 to 2 hours) before sanding. (See also p.144.)

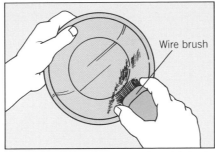
Remove rust with stiff wire brush (steel bristles for heavy rust; brass bristles for light). Or use brush attachment on a drill at high speed. (Wear safety goggles.) Sand smooth; apply paint or other finish.

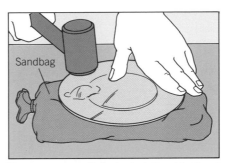
To remove a small dent, push it out by hand from opposite side. If that fails, hold dented area against a bag filled with sand; tap it gently from other side with a mallet until area smooths out.

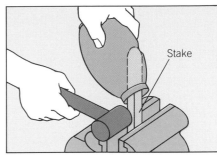
If only passage to opposite side of dent is narrow, clamp wooden or (preferably) steel stake in vise and press dent against it. Tap stake on side away from dent. Vibration will help push out dent.

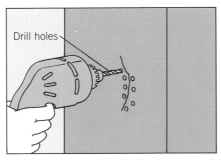
To repair a dent in thick metal or one you can't reach from the back, clean and sand the metal, then drill a series of small holes in the affected area to help anchor some fiberglass filler.

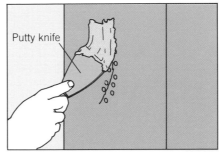
Prepare epoxy filler from a fiberglass repair kit. Use putty knife to fill dent with epoxy, pressing it into holes, mounding it a bit above surface, and overlapping edges of undented area.

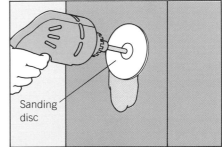
Let filler cure completely, then sand even with surrounding surface. Clean and paint the area. **CAUTION:** Wear a dust mask to filter out plastic dust when sanding.

Annealing

Repeated hammering and bending hardens many metals, making them susceptible to cracking and harder to work with. You can make metal malleable again by annealing it—that is, heating it to a red glow and letting it cool.

Work in a dimly lit area so that you can see the glow. Place the metal on firebricks or some other nonmetallic fireproof surface. Pass the flame of a torch back and forth over the metal, reaching all parts of the metal to heat it as evenly as possible. Watch closely. As soon as the metal turns the right color, turn off the torch and let the metal cool completely. Heat copper, brass, and bronze to a dull red; heat iron and steel to a cherry red. Do not try to anneal aluminum yourself.

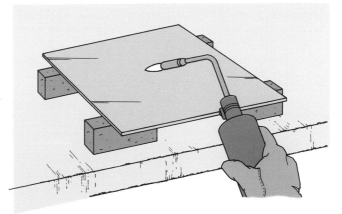

Plastics / Laminates

Plastic laminate, the durable countertop covering material, is made of layers of paper impregnated with resin at high temperature. A ¹⁄₁₆-inch thickness is standard. Sheets come in widths of 24, 30, 36, 48, and 60 inches and in lengths from 5 to 12 feet. Special laminates include adhesive-backed sheets that can be bonded to a surface with an iron and edging that bends around curves when heated.

Apply laminate to plywood, particleboard, or old laminate. Cover new unfinished material before installing it. When relaminating a piece, remove it to an open work area if possible.

If a piece won't be fastened in place—a detached tabletop or a door, for example—cover the reverse side with thin backing laminate to prevent warping. Apply backing laminate as you do regular laminate, but do it before the other sides. As a rule, cover the edges of a piece before the main surface (the top of a counter or the front of a door).

Cutting and trimming. The easiest way to cut laminate is by scoring and snapping it. For sawing, a saber saw is handiest. You can also use a circular or table saw, a hacksaw, a backsaw, or a crosscut saw. Always test a saw on a scrap to see if it causes chipping; clamp the laminate to a bench or other solid surface. Cut it about ⅛ inch oversize on all sides. For trimming, use a router with a carbide laminate bit. Or you can rent a routerlike laminate-trimming tool. If the laminate has a protective cover, don't remove it until after cutting and trimming.

Preparing surfaces. Laminate will not adhere properly unless surfaces are smooth, dry, and thoroughly clean. Fill holes with wood putty; sand rough spots. On old laminate, cement loose pieces; break bubbles and fill breaks with wood putty; sand well. Vacuum all dust before opening the adhesive.

Use a neoprene-base contact cement; a latex-base cement will not bond laminate permanently. Porous particleboard often requires two coats.

▶ **CAUTION:** Most neoprene-base contact cements are flammable and toxic. Work in a well-ventilated area away from pilot lights and motors. Wear goggles and a spray-paint respirator. Do not smoke.

Cutting techniques

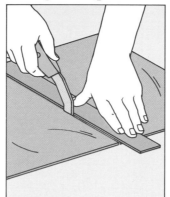

Use a utility knife with a laminate-scribing blade for most cuts. Place the laminate face up on floor or another solid surface, and score it several times along the same line, using a straightedge as a guide. Then turn the laminate over and mark the cut line on the back. Hold a piece of wood along the mark and bend up the waste to snap it off.

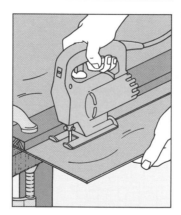

With a saber saw, place the laminate face down on a solid backing, with the waste extending beyond the edge. Clamp it in place with a straightedge to guide the saw. Use a fine-toothed metal-cutting blade at a slow speed. With a circular or table saw, use a hollow-ground or fine-toothed carbide-tipped blade set for a shallow cut. Place the laminate face up for a table saw.

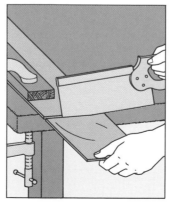

For short cuts, use a backsaw or a crosscut saw with a 12-point blade, or a hacksaw if the cut is short enough for the saw frame not to interfere. Clamp the laminate face up between a board and a solid backing. Hold the saw at a low angle, almost flat with the laminate, as you cut.

Laminating edges

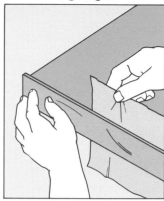

To cover an edge, brush contact cement on both surfaces; let dry (about 15 min.). Apply another coat to edge if it has dull spots. Then align laminate with edge, holding a kraft paper strip between them. Starting at one end, pull out paper and press laminate in place. Work carefully; surfaces will bond instantly. Roll with a rolling pin to remove air bubbles.

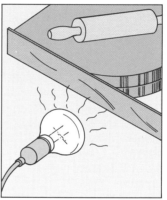

To round a corner, use bendable laminate edging and warm the strip with a heat lamp or gun until it's flexible. Then, wearing heavy, heat-resistant gloves, press the strip in place; roll with a rolling pin. A heating iron held just above the surface can also be used to warm the strip; it's faster, but you have to be extra-careful not to scorch the strip.

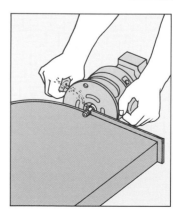

Trim the edges of the strip flush with adjoining surfaces, using a router with a straight carbide laminate-trimming bit. Let the cement set for 30 min. before trimming. **CAUTION:** Wear safety goggles and a particle mask to protect against flying pieces of laminate.

Laminating surfaces

Apply contact cement with a brush, roller, or notched applicator to the back of laminate and surface. Make sure to cover the entire area of both with even coats. Let the cement dry until kraft paper won't stick to either surface. Apply a second coat if the surface has dull spots.

To attach laminate, cover the surface with two overlapping pieces of kraft paper. Carefully align the laminate on top of the paper. Then start pulling out the paper at one end while pressing the laminate firmly in the center. Continue to press and pull until you've removed one piece of paper; then repeat with the other piece.

To remove air pockets and strengthen the glue bond, roll the surface with a rolling pin, applying as much pressure as possible. Roll the entire surface, starting in the center and working toward the edges. Let the adhesive set for 30 min. before doing any further work.

Finishing the job

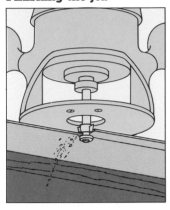

Before trimming, coat the laminate on the edges with petroleum jelly to protect them from scratches and scorching from the router bit. Using a carbide laminate-trimming bit that bevels, trim the laminate and angle its edges in one pass. **CAUTION:** Wear safety goggles and a particle mask to protect against flying pieces of laminate.

To make a sink cutout, mark the position of the sink on the countertop, following the directions and using the template supplied with sink. With a spade bit and power drill or a brace and bit, drill holes at corners of the sink outline. Then turn the top over; re-mark sink outline on bottom. Cut out area, using a saber saw with fine-toothed metal-cutting blade.

On a backsplash, laminate and trim the ends, front, and top, in that order. (Wait until you mount countertop to trim the top piece's back edge; you may need to shape it to the wall.) Put metal or plastic cove molding and a bead of silicone seal under the backsplash. Then clamp it in place, drill pilot holes, and attach it with wood screws from under the countertop.

Last
First
Backsplash
Second
Cove molding
Silicone seal

Repairing plastic laminate

Repeated cleanings with a mild liquid detergent and a soft brush will remove most stains. Stubborn stains, such as those from hair dye, ink, or price labels, can be lightened using a soft rag dampened with household chlorine bleach, liquid cleaner, or denatured alcohol; rinse immediately. Never scour. A burn from a hot pot usually requires relaminating the entire counter. Or you can cut out the area and inset a synthetic cutting surface; kits with a board and mounting hardware are available. Fix loose laminate as shown below.

To reattach loose laminate, spread contact cement under the laminate with a small putty knife. Press the laminate in place; then quickly pull the laminate away from the base. This will coat both surfaces evenly.

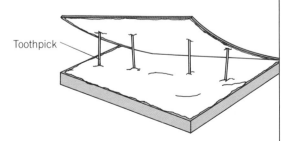

Toothpick

After pulling up the laminate, use toothpicks to prop it open until the cement is almost dry (5 min. less than the recommended drying time). Then press the laminate in place and roll it with a rolling pin.

Only synthetic marble made from acrylic, polyester, or a blend of the two can be handled by a nonprofessional. Unlike cultured marble, which contains marble chips, these materials have a uniform color and texture through the sheet and respond to cutting, shaping, and sanding much like an extra-dense hardwood—although special care should be taken because they are costly.

Sizes. Use a ¼-inch thickness for covering walls, ½-inch for countertops, and ¾-inch for unsupported expanses. Sheet sizes vary, but widths generally range from 22 to 36 inches and lengths from 5 to 12 feet. Kits (with directions) for enclosing tubs and showers are also available.

Cutting. Without removing the protective film, support the entire sheet, including the waste. Fit a circular saw with a 40-tooth carbide-tipped blade or a saber saw with a fine-tooth blade. Test it on scrap first and use a slow speed, for the material chips easily. Smooth sawn edges with a router. Wear a dust mask when sawing and routing.

Seaming. Done correctly, seams are invisible and as strong as the material itself. Before gluing, always dry-fit pieces. If necessary, shim adjoining pieces so that they are perfectly even. Peel the protective film away from the areas being joined. Clean edges with a cloth wetted with denatured or isopropyl alcohol; do not touch them afterward. Use only the adhesive made specifically for the material, and mix ingredients as directed. Be careful not to overtighten clamps; if all the glue is squeezed out, the seam will be weak.

The adhesive can also be used to fill nicks and gouges and to glue strips of the material under the edges of a countertop to make it look thicker. Before adding strips to edges, roughen both surfaces with 120-grit sandpaper. After applying glue, clamp the strips to the edges with spring clamps.

Support a countertop every 18 inches and at seams. Put supports within 3 inches of each side of an inset appliance; locate the cutout for an appliance at least 3 inches from the edge. Handle a top with a cutout carefully to avoid breaking it.

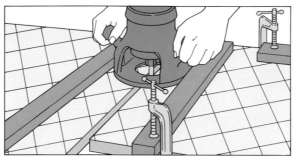

To prepare a seam, clamp both pieces with the edges to be joined slightly apart. Then trim both edges at once with a router. This smoothes the edges and ensures that they butt perfectly. Clean the edges with alcohol.

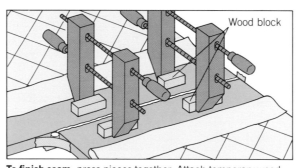

To finish seam, press pieces together. Attach temporary wood blocks on each side with hot-melt glue. Clamp the blocks together as shown; do not overtighten. After the adhesive dries, sand with 120-grit paper, then with 180-grit paper.

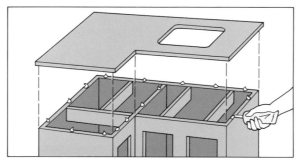

To install a top, first finish edges by routing to desired shape. Then apply dabs of silicone sealant at 10-in. intervals on cabinet frame, and lower the top into place. There is no need to clamp; the top's weight will apply enough pressure.

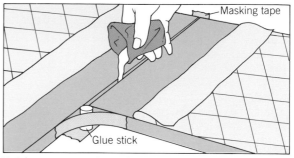

To join a seam, set pieces ⅛ in. apart with masking tape below and at ends to contain adhesive. If the seam is at a corner, dam the corner end with a hot-melt glue stick to round it. Mix adhesive as directed and fill seam one-third to half full.

To make a cutout, mark outline on material. Drill a starter hole in waste area, then cut, using a saber saw with a fine-tooth blade. Support waste area throughout to keep it from breaking off. Shift the supporting boards as needed to continue cutting along outline.

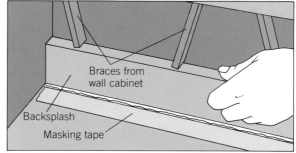

To add backsplash, put a protective strip of masking tape on countertop ¼ in. from seam area. Clean surfaces to be joined with alcohol. Apply adhesive to backsplash; brace in place. Wipe off excess with alcohol. Let dry; finish seam with fine sandpaper.

Acrylic sheets

Noted for its clarity, light weight, and break resistance, acrylic sheet often substitutes for glass in storm windows, shower doors, and household items. Thicknesses of ⅛, ¼, and ⅜ inch are common. Sheets are usually 8 feet long and 4 feet wide, although plastics suppliers and glaziers sell smaller pieces and will often cut to order.

Because it scratches easily, acrylic comes covered with protective paper. Mark on the paper (with a pencil), and leave the paper on until you have finished cutting, drilling, and finishing edges. When working on seams, remove only as much paper as needed. Mark bare plastic with a china marker.

To join acrylic, use the recommended solvent cement; it softens the plastic and welds the pieces together. When joining by the capillary-action method (bottom center), the pieces must fit together with no visible gap for a neat, clear seam. To test, put water drops on one edge; a smooth film should form when the pieces are pressed together.

You can join acrylic to wood with white glue and to metal with epoxy. But because acrylic responds to temperature changes more than wood or metal does, it's best to use bolts or screws, making large holes for the fasteners in the acrylic.

▶ **CAUTION:** When joining acrylic, work in a well-ventilated area and make sure you wear a spray-paint respirator—the solvent cement fumes are toxic. When bending acrylic, don't leave a strip heater unattended; the plastic is flammable.

Cutting and fabricating sheet acrylic

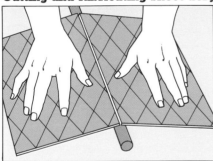

For straight cuts on ⅛-in. acrylic, score sheet several times along a straightedge, using a utility knife or a special acrylic scriber. Then snap apart over a wood dowel. For thicker pieces, use a saber saw with a special acrylic blade.

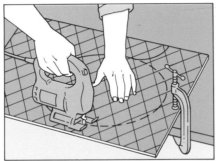

To cut a curve with a saber saw, start at an edge and cut inward. Move the saw slowly but run it at a high speed. Support the acrylic on the work surface, and turn it as needed while cutting.

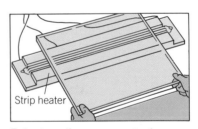

To drill acrylic, use a special acrylic bit, or round a twist bit's tip and blunt its two cutting edges with a file. Clamp the plastic in place with a scrap wood backing. For a perfectly straight hole, use a drill guide.

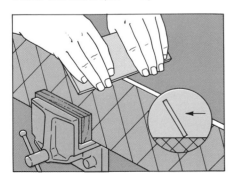

To finish edge, scrape away cut marks with metal straightedge (with a square edge). Sand with 100-grit wet-or-dry paper, then with finer paper. Buff with buffing wheel and metal polishing rouge until transparent; don't buff a seam edge.

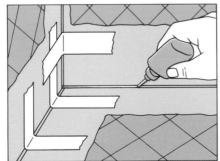

To join pieces, remove paper near edges and position pieces, using tape, jig, or other support. Pieces must fit together with no gaps. Carefully apply solvent cement, using a needle-nose applicator. Capillary action will draw in solvent.

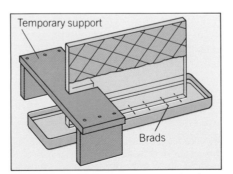

Temporary support

Brads

Another way to join is to place piece, edge down, in aluminum or glass tray; raise edge on brads. Pour in solvent cement to cover brads. Soak 6–8 min.; then blot and set on other piece. After 30 sec., clamp or weight for 1 hr.

Bending acrylic

To bend acrylic, you must heat it. For narrow pieces, a hot-air gun will do. Wider pieces require a strip heater, which you can buy or assemble from a kit.

Strip heater

To heat acrylic, remove protective paper and place plastic over a strip heater until it softens. Make sure that the plastic is at least ¼ in. from heating element.

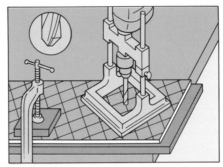

Bend heated sheet and hold 1–2 min. until it cools; wear heatproof gloves. Or use a jig and clamps to hold it at desired angle; protect plastic with soft flannel.

143

Plastics / Patching with fiberglass

Household objects made of fiberglass, wood, metal, and some plastics can be repaired or protected with a fiberglass patch. (Holes in gutters are one example.) You can buy fiberglass patching materials at paint, hardware, and auto and marine supply stores.

Fiberglass is indistinguishable from such plastics as ABS (used in shower stalls) and acrylic (used in bathtubs). Polyester resins won't bind to these surfaces and may remove the finish coating. Epoxy resin can be used on ABS and on some, but not all, acrylics. If in doubt, choose epoxy.

Patching involves filling in a damaged area with chemicals. If the area is large, apply chemicals to a reinforcing material; alternate layers of mat with cloth to fill a void or to build up a large area. When the chemicals harden, a solid, or "cured," fiberglass will form. Sand between layers; finish with a gel coat.

▶ **CAUTION:** Avoid skin contact. The chemicals are sticky, and fiberglass reinforcing materials cause itching. Make sure your arms, legs, and neck are protected. Safety goggles and polyethylene gloves or a barrier cream are a must. If resin or fiberglass reinforcing material gets on your skin or in your eyes, follow the manufacturer's recommendations. Don't inhale the chemicals' vapors; use a spray-paint respirator. Keep the workspace ventilated, and keep chemicals away from flames.

Product	Description	Uses
Fiberglass cloth	Woven from glass threads. Shiny; thinner than mat and woven roving but stronger. Sold by square yard up to 5' wide and in weights of 4 to 20 oz. Also in tape with selvaged edges.	Reinforcement before filling dents; covering large areas. To mold curved surface, make cuts. Layer with mat. Cover seams, edges, and corners.
Fiberglass mat	Pressed nonwoven glass fibers. Sold by square feet from 3' to 5' wide and in weights of ¾ to 3 oz.	Build up bulk when repairing holes; waterproofing.
Woven roving	Heavy woven fabric of untwisted strands of glass fiber. Sold by square yard from 3'2" to 5' wide and in weights of 16 to 45 oz.	Strong repair applications for large area buildups. Layer with fiberglass mat for adhesion strength.
Polyester laminating resin; finishing resin	Liquid thermosetting plastics that harden when catalyst is added. Available in regular or high viscosity and in various degrees of flexibility. Add catalyst to cure. Limited shelf life.	Laminating resin stays tacky; use for layering reinforcing materials. Finishing resin cures fully; use for final application. Use between 60°F and 90°F.
Gel coat	One of the polyester resins to which color pigments can be added.	Final protective, waterproof coat; touch-up of small areas.
Polyester filler and putty	Polyester resin compounds, some for special purposes (boats, cars); some can be tinted.	Fill cracks, dents, gouges, and scratches, with or without reinforcing materials.
Epoxy resin	Liquid thermosetting plastic of greater strength and binding power than polyester; more expensive. Skin contact can cause dermatitis; vapors can irritate. Add hardener to cure.	Coating, laminating, and repairing when strong adhesion required. (Laminate the base layer with polyester resin.)
Epoxy filler and putty	Epoxy resin compounds, some formulated for special purposes (such as under water).	Fill dents, scratches, gouges, small holes. Bond different materials.

To fill cracks or scratches, roughen the surface with coarse sandpaper to remove the old finish. Clean area with acetone or with soap and water. Dry thoroughly.

Cut fiberglass cloth about 2 in. larger than area. Mix resin and hardener following manufacturer's instructions. (Note limited pot life.) Apply a thin coat to the damaged area; then dip cloth in the resin.

Cover damaged area with cloth. Smooth out air bubbles and wrinkles with a spreader (purchase one when buying patching materials) or an inexpensive natural bristle paintbrush; let dry thoroughly.

Use fine sandpaper to feather the patch's edges so it blends with surrounding surface. Apply a second coat of resin. When it dries, sand again; finish with a tinted gel coat, or prime and paint.

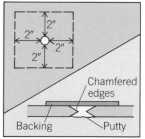

To fill a small hole, clean area with soap and water, wipe dry, and sand. Chamfer edges with a round file to form a V. Tape cardboard backing to one side of hole. Mix and apply putty; let dry, and sand.

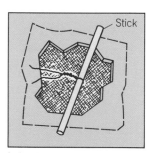

In hard-to-reach areas, thread wire through holes in backing; apply bead of contact cement. Force into hole, position, and twist wire around stick. Let glue dry; cut wire. For big holes, use resin-soaked mat with backing.

Chapter seven

Concrete and asphalt
Techniques and projects

Contents

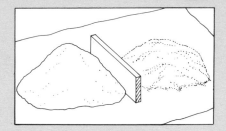

Strong, long-lasting, and economical, concrete can be surprisingly easy to work with. In the following pages, you'll learn all about this versatile, moldable stone: its properties and composition, how to mix your own or buy it ready-mixed, how to place, finish, and cure it. You'll find complete directions for laying walks, drives, and steps, as well as a guide to placing footings and foundations, repairing concrete surfaces, and making a blacktop drive look new. Even if you decide that a project such as building a house foundation is too big to tackle on your own, the information in this chapter will help you deal with contractors and evaluate their bids and their work more effectively.

Concrete/Ingredients

Concrete is one of the most durable, economical, and versatile of all building materials. It is a mixture of portland cement, fine aggregate (sand), coarse aggregate (gravel or crushed stone), and water. These ingredients are combined in varying proportions, depending on the desired strength and water resistance of the concrete. Mix-it-yourself concrete is most often described in terms of the cement-to-sand-to-gravel proportions. For example, a 1:2½:3 mix means that the concrete is made of 1 part cement, 2½ parts sand, and 3 parts gravel or crushed stone by volume.

Portland cement. This key ingredient of concrete is a mixture of minerals that are fired in a kiln, combined with gypsum, and then ground finer than flour. Manufactured according to strict standards set by the American Society for Testing and Materials (ASTM), portland cement is sold in 1-cubic-foot bags weighing 94 pounds.

When mixed with water, portland cement forms a paste that binds the aggregates together and solidifies into a very hard, rocklike mass. This paste makes up 25 to 40 percent of the total volume of the concrete.

Portland cement is available in gray, white, and in some areas, buff. You can also produce a desired color by adding a coloring agent to the concrete as it is being mixed.

Air-entraining portland cement, sold in specially marked bags, contains an agent that creates billions of microscopic air bubbles in the concrete. (This agent is also sold separately, to be added to concrete during the mixing process.) Air-entrainment not only makes concrete more workable, it also increases concrete's resistance to frost and reduces the scaling caused by deicing agents such as sodium chloride, or rock salt. In areas with harsh winters, building codes may require air-entrained concrete.

Aggregates. A combination of fine and coarse aggregates accounts for about 60 to 75 percent of a given volume of concrete. Aggregates are sold by the cubic foot or cubic yard.

Fine aggregate is sand that will pass through a ¼-inch screen. The sand should be clean and free of silt and debris, which can weaken the concrete. If you are purchasing sand from a noncommercial source, use the quart-jar test, shown at far right, to determine the material's silt content. If more than ⅛ inch of silt settles on top of the sand, it needs to be washed. Neither mortar sand nor beach sand is suitable for making concrete.

Sand is delivered wet to keep it from blowing away. How wet it is affects the amount of water you need to add to the concrete mix (p.149). To determine the water content of sand, squeeze a handful and compare it with the illustrations at right.

The most common types of coarse aggregate are gravel and crushed stone between ¼ and 1½ inches in diameter. Don't use aggregate larger than one-quarter the thickness of the concrete. Coarse aggregate should be hard, clean, and free of debris.

Water. Generally, water that is fit to drink is also suitable for making concrete. Avoid seawater or water containing oil, acid, organic matter, or other impurities.

Testing sand for moisture

Damp sand falls apart when you try to squeeze it into a ball. With damp sand, you will have to add more water to your concrete mix.

Sand of average wetness holds up as a ball or large clump when you squeeze it and leaves little moisture on the palm of your hand.

Very wet sand is dripping wet and will leave a lot of moisture on your hand. Such sand calls for less water in a concrete mix.

Grading aggregate

Coarse aggregate can be screened for uniform size (three sizes are shown here: ¼ to ⅜ in., ⅜ to ¾ in., ¾ to 1½ in.) or it can be "bank run," in which a variety of gravel sizes are combined.

Well-graded coarse aggregate, in which smaller particles fill in the voids between larger ones, increases the strength of the finished concrete and, by acting as filler, reduces its cost.

Testing sand for silt

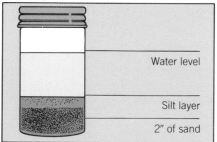

Put 2 in. of sand in a quart jar, fill the jar three-quarters full with water, shake well, and let stand for 1 hr. If more than ⅛ in. of silt settles on top of the sand layer, the sand needs washing.

Tools and storage

To work with concrete, you will need the following general-purpose equipment: a hammer and saw, for building the forms, or wooden retaining walls, into which concrete is generally poured (pp. 152–153); measuring and leveling tools, such as a 50-foot steel tape, a 4-foot spirit level, a steel square, and a mason's line; a wheelbarrow (preferably a contractor's wheelbarrow with wooden handles and a large pneumatic tire), for mixing and hauling small batches of concrete; two buckets, one for measuring cement, the other for aggregate; a third bucket, marked in gallons, for measuring water and adding it to the mix; and a square-ended shovel, for mixing and placing the concrete.

In addition, there are several concrete specialty tools that you can buy, rent, or make yourself:

Screed, or strike-off board, to remove excess concrete and bring the surface to grade. Use a straight 2 x 4 about 2 feet longer than the form's width.

Bull float, to smooth the surface of the concrete after screeding and before final finishing. You can make your own by attaching an old broom handle to a section of 1 x 8 as shown in the illustration at right. The bull float is generally used on large surfaces; for smaller jobs, use a *darby.*

Pointing trowel, to separate concrete from forms.

Edger, to round off the edges of concrete slabs.

Groover, or jointer, to cut grooves, or joints, at regular intervals in a slab.

Hand float, either of wood, to give a slab a rough surface, or of magnesium, for a smoother finish. Always use a magnesium float with air-entrained concrete; a wood float can tear the surface.

Steel trowel, for a hard, slick final finish.

Hard-bristled broom, for a rough final finish.

▶ **CAUTION:** Wet concrete is caustic; so wear waterproof gloves, a long-sleeved shirt, and long trousers when working with it. If you must stand in wet concrete, wear high rubber boots. Promptly wash splatters off your skin and rinse out clothing that becomes saturated from contact with concrete. Use a lanolin cream to relieve mild skin irritation; see a doctor if discomfort persists.

Measuring and leveling tools

4' spirit level

Steel square

Mason's line

50' steel tape

Placing and finishing tools

Screed

Bull float

Broom handle

1" x 8" x 48" board

Wedge

Pipe strap

Pointing trowel

Square-edged shovel

Darby

Magnesium float

Edger

Groover

Steel trowel

Hard-bristled broom

Storage

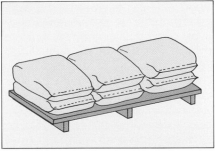

Always store cement in a dry place. To keep cement from absorbing moisture, stack the bags close together on a raised platform away from walls, and cover with a waterproof tarpaulin.

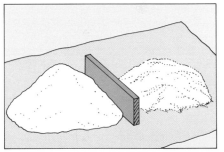

Store fine and coarse aggregates separately on a clean, hard surface. If you store them next to each other, place a wooden barrier between the piles. Outdoors, cover with plastic sheeting.

Close opened bags of cement tightly and store in sealed plastic bags. Cement must be kept dry and free-flowing. If it forms lumps that do not pulverize when squeezed, discard the cement.

147

Concrete / Estimating area and quantity

To determine how much concrete a project requires, first calculate its area in square feet. For a square or other rectangle, multiply length by width in feet. For circles, triangles, or irregular areas, follow the instructions at right. Next, multiply the square footage by the desired thickness in feet, not inches (for example, 4 inches is ⅓ foot). The result will be the total volume of concrete needed, expressed in cubic feet. To convert this number into cubic yards—the unit by which concrete is usually calculated and sold—divide it by 27, the number of cubic feet in a cubic yard. Thus to figure the amount of concrete needed for any square or rectangular slab, use the following formula:

$$\frac{\text{width (ft.)} \times \text{length (ft.)} \times \text{thickness (ft.)}}{27} = \text{cu. yd.}$$

For example, a concrete floor 15 feet wide, 25 feet long, and 4 inches (⅓ foot) thick would require:

$$\frac{15 \text{ ft.} \times 25 \text{ ft.} \times ⅓ \text{ ft.}}{27} = 4.63 \text{ cu. yd. of concrete.}$$

For a quick estimate of the amount of material needed for a concrete slab (say, for a driveway, patio, sidewalk, or foundation wall), use the chart at right. Locate the bar that corresponds to the thickness of the slab and its area in square feet. Then read down from the end of the bar to the scale at the bottom to get the number of cubic feet or cubic yards of concrete you will need.

Thicknesses and square footages not given on the chart can be calculated by addition. For example, to mix concrete for a 5-inch slab, add the amounts needed for 2-inch and 3-inch slabs; for 350 square feet, add the amounts required for 200 and 150 square feet at the thickness desired.

Whether you use the formula or the chart, the figure you obtain does not take into account waste or variations in concrete thickness caused by an uneven subgrade. To compensate, add an extra 5 to 10 percent to the amount of materials you order.

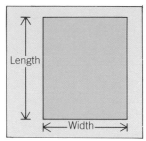

To calculate the area of a rectangle in square feet, multiply length by width in feet.

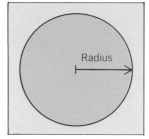

Figure the area of a circle by multiplying the square of its radius by 3.1416 (π).

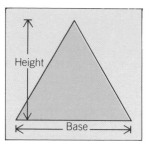

For the area of a triangle, multiply half the base length by the perpendicular height.

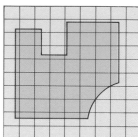

Draw irregular areas on graph paper (each square = 1 sq. ft.); add up whole squares and any that are more than ⅓ filled.

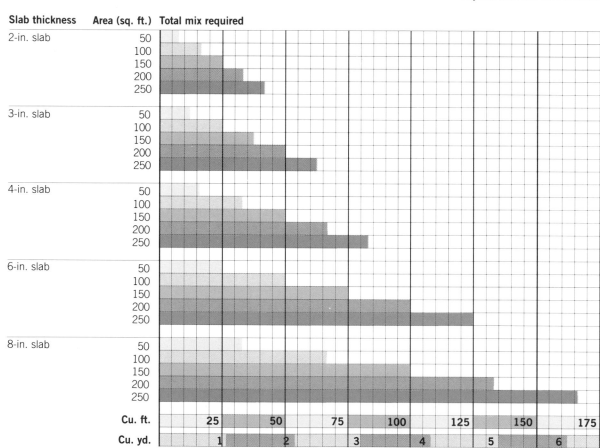

Slab thickness — **Area (sq. ft.)** — **Total mix required**

Slab thickness	Area (sq. ft.)
2-in. slab	50, 100, 150, 200, 250
3-in. slab	50, 100, 150, 200, 250
4-in. slab	50, 100, 150, 200, 250
6-in. slab	50, 100, 150, 200, 250
8-in. slab	50, 100, 150, 200, 250

Cu. ft.: 25 50 75 100 125 150 175
Cu. yd.: 1 2 3 4 5 6

The right mix

For concrete to be strong and durable, its components must be present in the proper proportions. The right mix depends on how the concrete will be used and what conditions it will be subjected to. For structures such as floors, drives, and walks exposed to moderate weather and wear, a mix of 1 part cement, 2½ parts sand, and 3 parts gravel or crushed stone is recommended. For projects not subject to wear and weather, you can use a 1:2¾:4 mix.

A critical factor in making concrete is the water-to-cement ratio, which must be kept constant. Too much water will weaken the concrete; too little will make it too stiff to be worked easily.

The top chart at right lists the amounts of dry ingredients and water needed to make 1 cubic yard of concrete according to two basic formulas. Note that water quantities are based on the sand's wetness. Because even a small amount of excess water can weaken concrete, test the sand for moisture (p.146) and add water accordingly.

Dry-mix and ready-mixed concrete. For jobs requiring a cubic yard or less of concrete, the least expensive way to make the concrete is to purchase the ingredients separately and mix them yourself (p.150). But for really small jobs, such as anchoring a post, consider using a prepackaged concrete mix that contains all the ingredients except water. Dry-mix costs more than the separate ingredients, but its convenience often outweighs the expense.

For jobs requiring more than a cubic yard of concrete, you can save effort and perhaps money by ordering it mixed and ready-to-place from a supplier. Before ordering ready-mix, estimate how much you need, then make sure the supplier will deliver that amount (there may be a minimum delivery requirement). Specify the concrete's intended use, the maximum aggregate size (it should not exceed one-quarter the slab's thickness), the minimum cement content (usually five or six bags per cubic yard), the concrete's compressive strength, or load-bearing capacity, at 28 days (at least 3,500 pounds per square inch for ordinary domestic use), and whether you want air-entraining or other additives.

Two basic recipes for making 1 cubic yard of non-air-entrained concrete[1]

Ingredients	1:2½:3 mix	1:2¾:4 mix
	Quantities needed	Quantities needed
Cement	6 bags	5 bags
Sand (fine aggregate)[2]	15 cu. ft.	14 cu. ft.
Gravel/crushed stone (coarse aggregate)[3]	18 cu. ft.	20 cu. ft.
Water (for damp sand)	33 gal. (5½ gal. per bag of cement)	33 gal. (6⅗ gal. per bag of cement)
Water (for wet sand)	30 gal. (5 gal. per bag of cement)	30 gal. (6 gal. per bag of cement)
Water (for very wet sand)	25½ gal. (4¼ gal. per bag of cement)	25½ gal. (5¹⁄₁₀ gal. per bag of cement)

[1]Use air-entrained concrete for structures subject to freezing, thawing, or deicing salts. For each cubic yard of air-entrained concrete, reduce the amount of water in the mix by 2 to 3 gallons and the amount of sand by 1 cubic foot.

[2]Determine wetness of sand (p.146) and choose appropriate quantity of water.

[3]Maximum aggregate size 1½ in.

Quantities of materials required for 100 square feet of concrete of various thicknesses[4]

Thickness of concrete slab	Amount of concrete	1:2½:3 mix			1:2¾:4 mix		
		Cement bags	Sand cu. ft.	Gravel cu. ft.	Cement bags	Sand cu. ft.	Gravel cu. ft.
2 in.	0.62 cu. yd.	3.7	9.3	11.2	3.1	8.7	12.4
3 in.	0.93 cu. yd.	5.6	14.0	16.7	4.7	13.0	18.8
4 in.	1.23 cu. yd.	7.4	18.5	22.1	6.2	17.2	24.8
5 in.	1.54 cu. yd.	9.2	23.0	27.7	7.7	21.6	30.8
6 in.	1.85 cu. yd.	11.1	27.8	33.3	9.3	25.9	37.2
8 in.	2.47 cu. yd.	14.8	37.0	44.5	12.4	34.6	49.6

[4]Add 5% to 10% to compensate for waste and uneven subgrade.

Concrete / Mixing

Small batches of concrete can be mixed by hand in a wheelbarrow or on a large flat surface such as a watertight wooden platform or a concrete driveway covered with heavy-duty plastic. If you need more than 2 cubic feet of concrete, save time and effort by renting a power mixer. When making more than a cubic yard of concrete or any amount of air-entrained concrete, always use a power mixer.

Using the proportions recommended for your project (p. 149), measure the dry ingredients by the shovelful or with buckets of known capacity; use different buckets for cement and aggregate. (For greater accuracy, make a bottomless wooden box with inside measurements of 12 inches square and 12 inches high. Placed on a flat surface, the box will hold 1 cubic foot of cement or aggregate.) Use a third bucket, marked in gallons, to measure the amount of water your concrete mix calls for. Follow the directions at right for mixing the concrete by hand and testing the consistency of a trial batch.

Power mixing. Position the mixer as close to the job site as possible. Add the coarse aggregate and about half the required amount of water. Turn the mixer on, then add the sand, cement, and the rest of the water. (Follow package instructions for adding air-entraining agents.) Continue mixing for 3 minutes, or longer if necessary, until the concrete is well mixed and uniform in color.

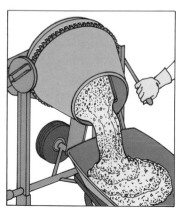

A power mixer's batch size, or mixing capacity, is usually 60 percent of its total volume; never exceed the batch size. Wash out the drum after each batch and scour it at the end of the day. To scour, add water and several shovelfuls of sand while drum is rotating. After a few minutes, empty the mixer and hose it out.

Mixing by hand

1. Using a square-ended shovel, spread the premeasured sand evenly on the mixing area, add the required amount of cement, and mix until you get a mass of uniform color without brown or gray streaks. Add coarse aggregate and turn the materials over at least three times or until all the aggregate is evenly distributed.

2. Form a shallow depression in the middle of the sand-cement-aggregate mixture; then slowly pour in some of the measured water and work it in well, making sure to reach all the way to the bottom of the mound.

3. Pour more water into the depression, pull dry ingredients from the sides of the ring into the water, and mix well. Continue adding water, a little at a time, and mixing the materials until they are thoroughly combined and evenly moist. When all the water has been absorbed, turn the batch three or four times to ensure a uniform mix.

Testing the mix

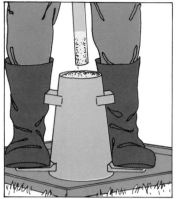

Wet concrete should not be soupy or too stiff. Make a trial batch and test its consistency using a slump cone, shown here, or a coffee can with both ends removed. Fill cone with concrete in three layers. Eliminate air pockets by tamping each layer about 25 times with a rounded rod before adding the next layer. Level the concrete, remove cone, and let concrete settle.

Measure the difference in height between the concrete and the cone. The height difference, or slump, should be 3 to 4 in. If it exceeds 4 in., concrete is too wet; add more aggregate. If slump is less than 3 in., the batch is too stiff; in this case, adding more water could alter the water-cement ratio and ruin the concrete. Make a new trial batch using less aggregate.

The ridge test is another way to gauge the consistency of concrete. Draw a shovel backward over the surface of the mix; as you go along, jab the shovel into the concrete to form a series of ridges. If the ridges remain clear-cut, the mix is correct. If they are indistinct, the concrete is too stiff. If they collapse or fill in, the concrete is too wet.

Placing, finishing, curing

Before mixing or taking delivery of concrete, prepare the job site, set up forms (pp. 152–158), and have tools—and helpers—at hand. Before placing the concrete, moisten the ground or subbase so that it won't absorb water from the mix. Never place concrete on frozen, muddy, or very wet ground. Concrete work is best done in warm weather.

After 45 minutes concrete may become too stiff to handle easily. Mix only as much as you can place in that time. If the concrete starts to stiffen, remix it *without adding water.* If it doesn't become workable again, throw it out. If you must transport concrete in a wheelbarrow from mixing site to forms, lay 2-foot-wide plywood strips to create a stable path.

Try to have ready-mix unloaded directly into the forms. With chutes and extensions most trucks can move concrete up to 24 feet. Beyond that, you'll have to use wheelbarrows or rent a pumper (p. 158). Make sure you have enough wheelbarrows and helpers to finish the job within the time allotted by the supplier.

Once placed, the concrete must be leveled and smoothed (steps 1, 2, and 3, at right). Compacting the concrete causes excess water to bleed to the top. When the water sheen appears, stop work and wait until the water evaporates and the concrete stiffens slightly. In cool or humid weather, this may take several hours; on hot, dry days, as little as 20 minutes. Only when the concrete loses its sheen is it ready to be finished (steps 4, 5, and 6). If you start too soon, the concrete may crumble later on.

Curing. To ensure its strength and durability, finished concrete has to be cured, or kept warm (above 50°F) and moist, for 5 days in warm weather (70°F or higher), 7 days in cooler weather (50°F–70°F). Cure concrete by any of these methods:

1. Spray the surface with water from a garden hose, then cover it with plastic sheeting or waterproof paper anchored at the edges with bricks.

2. Cover the concrete with burlap or canvas and keep the covering soaked during the curing period.

3. Use a lawn sprinkler or soaking hose to apply continuous moisture to the surface.

4. Spray a curing compound on the damp surface.

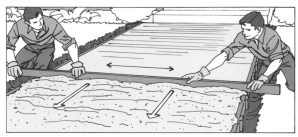

1. Start placing the concrete as far back in the form as possible and dump each succeeding load against the previous one. Use a shovel to spread the concrete and pack it into corners. Overfill the form by about ½ in. Without overdoing it, jab the shovel in and out of the concrete to eliminate air pockets.

2. Once a form is filled, compact and level the concrete with a strike-off board, or screed. Place the board on edge across one end of the form, then work it toward the other with a zigzag sawing motion. Fill in low spots and strike off again until the concrete is level with the top of the form.

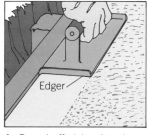
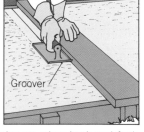

3. To smooth out any remaining ridges and voids, run a bull float back and forth over the concrete, slightly raising the float's leading edge to keep it from digging into the surface. For small jobs, sweep a darby (p. 147) in wide arcs over the concrete. Run a trowel between concrete and form to a depth of 1 in., then wait for the bleed water to evaporate before finishing the concrete.

4. Round off slab edges by running an edger back and forth between concrete and forms. Control joints cut to one-quarter the slab's depth prevent random cracking when the slab settles and shifts. Use a groover to cut these joints at regular intervals (spacing varies with job; see pp. 152–153, 154). Place a 2 x 8 across form and use it as a guide to run groover through slab.

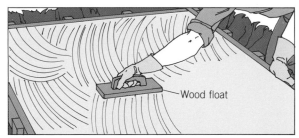

5. Floating the surface with a hand float helps to level and compact the concrete. Wood floats create a rough texture; for a smoother texture—and to avoid tearing the surface of air-entrained concrete—use a magnesium float. Hold the hand float flat on the concrete and move it back and forth in sweeping arcs. Edging and grooving may be repeated after floating.

6. For a smooth finish, run a steel trowel over the floated concrete. Hold blade flat against the surface and sweep it back and forth in arcs. Wait a few moments, then repeat once or twice depending on desired smoothness; lift leading edge of blade slightly higher with each troweling. For a rough finish, pull a stiff-bristled broom straight across the surface. For decorative finishes, see p. 158.

Concrete/Walkways

Before starting any concrete project, consult local building codes (p.193).

Dimensions. The width of a walk depends on its intended use: at least 5 feet for public sidewalks, 3 to 4 feet for the front walk of a house, and 2 to 3 feet for a service walk. A residential walk is usually 4 inches thick. If heavy trucks will be crossing the walkway, make it 6 inches thick.

Site preparation. The ground on which a concrete slab will be laid must be well drained, uniformly compacted, and free of sod, roots, and debris. If the ground is dry and firm and the winters in your area are mild, you can lay the concrete directly on bare soil. In this case, the excavation for a 4-inch-thick slab need be only 2 inches deep in order to bring the top of the walk the usual 2 inches above ground level.

If the soil is poorly drained or subject to frost-induced ground heave, you'll have to dig deeper in order to accommodate a gravel drainage bed. Where soil stability and drainage are especially poor, make the slab 1 or 2 inches thicker as well. For a 4-inch slab, dig 6 to 8 inches into the ground (steps 1 and 2, at right), assemble the forms (steps 3 and 4), then lay down a 4- to 6-inch base of gravel or crushed stone (step 6). In areas where drainage is not a problem but the soil (heavy clay, for example) may be difficult to grade, it's a good idea to lay concrete over a 2- to 3-inch gravel base.

Forms. Forms for a 4-inch-thick slab are usually made of 2 x 4's set on edge and braced every 3 to 4 feet by 18-inch stakes driven firmly into the ground. The forms should be of smooth, straight green lumber. Stakes can be steel or cut from 1 x 2's, 2 x 2's, or 2 x 4's.

Forms must be sturdy enough to resist the pressure exerted by concrete as it is being placed. Nail form boards to stakes securely (step 4). Use double-headed nails (p.80); they are easier to pull out when dismantling the form. To prevent sticking, apply motor oil or a commercial form-release agent to all form surfaces that

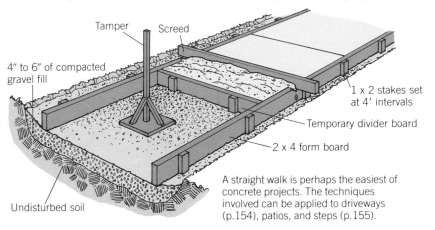

Tamper   Screed

4" to 6" of compacted gravel fill

1 x 2 stakes set at 4' intervals

Temporary divider board

2 x 4 form board

Undisturbed soil

A straight walk is perhaps the easiest of concrete projects. The techniques involved can be applied to driveways (p.154), patios, and steps (p.155).

will come in contact with concrete.

Lay long walks in 8- to 10-foot-long sections. To make these shorter work bays, install a temporary divider board between the side forms (step 8). Once the concrete in a section has been placed and smoothed (p.151), remove the divider, set it up farther down the walk, and lay the next section.

If you are building a walk right next to a wall, screeding becomes a problem. The solution is to divide the walk into sections and lay alternate sections. This way you and a helper can stand on either side of a filled bay and screed parallel to and away from the wall. When the concrete has stiffened enough to stand on, remove divider boards and fill the empty sections.

Pitch. To carry off surface water, a walk should slope about ¼ inch per foot away from the house toward the street. If you're laying a straight walk, say from a doorway to street level, on land that slopes gently away from the house, follow the natural grade when staking forms (step 3); the resulting lengthwise slope will ensure proper drainage. If the site is level, pitch the form across its width (step 5).

Joints. To control cracking, cut control joints (p.151) every 5 feet in a walk 3 to 5 feet wide; every 3 feet in a walk 2 to 3 feet wide; if you're laying the walk in sections, you can install ½-inch-thick semirigid fiber strips as control joints between sections (step 8). The same material should be placed as isolation joints wherever new concrete abuts an existing structure, such as steps, another slab, or a house foundation wall. The strip's top edge should be flush with or slightly lower than the slab top.

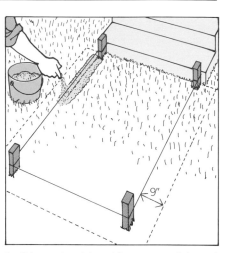

9"

1. Drive marker stakes at four corners of planned walk. Run string between stakes to outline the walk, then trickle sand over string to create an outline on the ground. Remove stakes and dig down to required depth. Extend excavation about 9 in. outside each sand line.

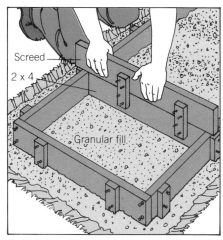

Screed

2 x 4

Granular fill

6. Install a bed of gravel or crushed stone up to the bottom edges of the form boards (push the fill under and beyond the form). Tamp this base well. To your screed, attach a length of 2 x 4 equal to the width of the slab and use it to level the granular fill.

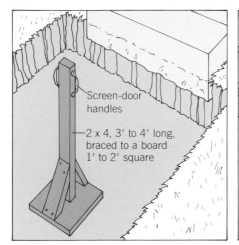

2. Save some of the dug-up turf to put back later along the edge of the finished slab. Clear the ground of all sod, roots, and debris. Dig out any soft, damp spots and fill them with gravel. Thoroughly compact the earth with a tamper, such as the homemade model shown here.

3. Restake walk's corners 1½ in. outside slab width. Run string between stakes and use as guide for driving intermediate stakes. Place a level on the ground next to a stake; draw a line where level's bottom edge crosses stake. Draw another line 2 in. above the first. Mark other stakes this way.

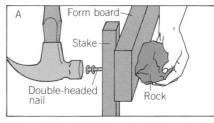
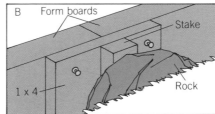

4. (A) Position form boards against inner faces of stakes, with top edge of boards 2 in. above ground level as marked on stakes. Drive double-headed nails through stakes into boards. (B) Where boards abut, nail a piece of 1 x 4 across joint, drive a stake, and brace with a rock.

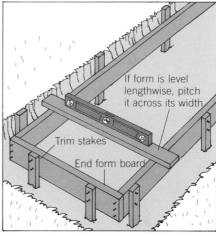

5. Measure between side forms to make sure they're parallel. Close off form; trim stakes flush with top of form. Place a level on a 2 x 4 as shown to check that form is level across its width. Then, if the site itself is level, lift one side of form as needed to create a side pitch of ¼ in. per ft.

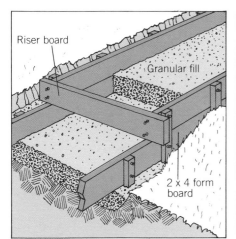

7. To create a shallow step in a gently sloped walk, build a two-tiered form as shown. Nail a riser board to the upper side forms. Lay a second level of gravel or crushed stone about 6 to 8 in. behind riser board. In this way, concrete will be doubly thick at step's edge.

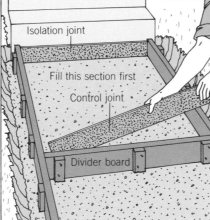

8. When a walk is laid in sections, ½-in.-thick semirigid fiber strips, cut the same length and width as divider board, can serve as control joints between sections. Prop a strip against the divider, then fill bay with concrete. When ready to lay next section, reset divider but leave joint in place.

9. Recheck form for level and pitch; run screed over gravel bed once more to ensure correct slab thickness and an even base. Oil the form boards to prevent sticking, dampen the granular base, then proceed to place, screed, bull-float, and finish the concrete as described on page 151.

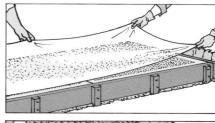

10. To cure the slab (p.151), sprinkle water on it, then cover with plastic sheets, waterproof paper, or wet burlap, laid flat and overlapped at joints. (Spray burlap often to keep it wet during entire curing period.) After curing, dismantle forms, but keep heavy traffic off walkway for a week.

Concrete/Driveways

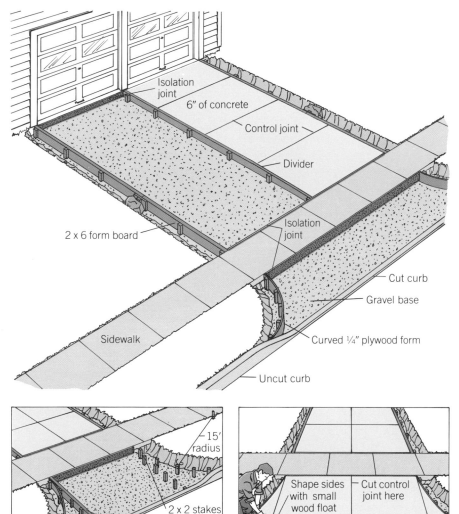

Labels on main illustration:
- Isolation joint
- 6" of concrete
- Control joint
- Divider
- 2 x 6 form board
- Isolation joint
- Cut curb
- Gravel base
- Curved ¼" plywood form
- Sidewalk
- Uncut curb

Labels on lower-left illustration:
- 15' radius
- 2 x 2 stakes
- Straight form
- Curved form

Labels on lower-right illustration:
- Shape sides with small wood float
- Cut control joint here

1. Stake and excavate drive's curved entryway as described in text. Grade excavation to slope down to street. Restake curves with 2 x 2's set 1 ft. apart. Nail ¼-in. plywood (p.96) to stakes. (Curved forms should slope up from uncut curb to sidewalk.) Build straight forms within curved ones from sidewalk down to cut curb.

2. Lay the gravel base, install isolation joints, then place and screed the concrete between the straight forms. Remove these forms, fill curved sections with concrete, and smooth with a darby or float. Use a small wood float to shape the concrete in the curved sections and blend it into the straight part of the entryway.

Building a concrete driveway involves the same basic steps as building a walk (pp.152–153). Drives, however, are usually subject to more and stricter building-code regulations. Consult your local building department and obtain the necessary permits (p.193).

Specifications. The driveway for a one-car garage should be at least 10 feet wide; for a two-car garage, about 16 to 24 feet, with a longitudinal control joint down the center. The slab's thickness depends on the vehicles that will be using it: 4 inches for cars; 6 inches for heavy trucks. Because trucks may back up onto the drive's street end, make this part 8 inches thick. Where soil stability or drainage is poor, make the main slab 1 or 2 inches thicker too. For a 6-inch slab, use 2 x 6's for the forms and dig at least 8 inches deep (to accommodate a 4-inch gravel bed and bring the slab 2 inches above grade).

To keep water from flowing into the garage, the drive's garage end should be about 1 inch below the garage floor. To keep water off the drive, its street end should be 1 or 2 inches above the road. (Check the local building code about breaking through curbs.)

Slope. Ideally, a driveway is built on land that slopes gently down from garage to street. To carry off rainwater, a slope of at least ¼ inch per running foot is necessary, but a rise greater than 1¾ inches per foot will cause a car entering the drive to scrape its rear bumper or underside. If the site slopes down from street to garage, you'll have to install a drain and drainage channel where the drive meets the garage. Check the local building code for drainage requirements.

On a level site you can provide a cross pitch to the entire slab by raising one side of the form (step 5, p.153), but for a 20-foot-wide drive this results in an awkward 5-inch (20 x ¼ inch) slant across the drive's width. Instead, make the drive higher at the center. This allows water to drain off both sides. After setting up the side form boards, install a divider running lengthwise down the center of the drive. Set the divider boards high enough on stakes to create the correct pitch (for a 20-foot-wide drive the divider must be 2½ inches higher than the side form boards). Start at the garage end. Lay and screed one side of the drive, replace the divider boards with strips of joint material (p.152), then lay the other side.

Controlling cracks. Set isolation joints where the drive meets the garage, walkways, and the street. Space control joints no more than 10 feet apart in either direction. Panels formed by control joints should be nearly square. Although often recommended for controlling cracks in slabs, wire mesh reinforcement is hard to work with and usually not needed—as long as control joints are properly spaced and cut to at least one-quarter the slab's depth.

Curved entryways. To create a curved apron from sidewalk to street, set stakes at the sidewalk's edge, 15 feet from either side of the driveway. Hammer a nail into the top of each stake, attach a 15-foot string to the nail, and use the string as a radius to stake the curves. Dig 10 inches deep between the curves; extend the excavation 9 inches beyond them. Build forms (step 1, at left); then place and finish the apron (step 2).

Steps

The dimensions of entryway steps are usually regulated by the local building code (p.193); consult your code before building any exterior steps.

Entryway steps should be at least as wide as or slightly wider than the door and walk they connect. A common width for exterior house steps is 48 inches.

A step consists of a *riser* (the vertical face) and a *tread* (the horizontal surface). For safety and comfort, the height of the riser and the depth of the tread should add up to 18 inches. The most common and practical arrangement combines risers 6 to 8 inches high with treads 12 to 10 inches deep. Riser height and tread depth must not vary within a flight of steps. To allow easy access to the doorway, make the landing at the top of the steps 3 feet deep.

Footings. In no-frost areas, build steps on a concrete base, or footing, at least 2 feet deep. Where frost is a problem, place the footing below the frost line. A convenient way to support a flight of up to three steps is to dig two or more postholes to the required depth beneath the bottom tread and fill them with concrete (step 2, at right). A flight of more than three steps should rest on walls or piers at least 6 inches thick (pp.156–158). To tie the steps to the house, drill two or more holes into the house foundation wall (pp.54, 86–87) below the location of the top landing, pack the holes with mortar (p.162), and insert tie rods. Place isolation joint material (p.152) between house wall and steps. If the steps will touch untreated wood, cover the wood with aluminum flashing before installing the isolation joint.

Formwork. Forms for concrete steps must be sturdy and well braced. Use wood that is straight, smooth, and free of blemishes. Cut and assemble the form, then brace and stake it as shown in step 3.

Starting at the bottom step, place concrete in the form, then screed and smooth treads and landing (step 5). When the bleed water has evaporated and the concrete has stiffened (20 minutes to a few hours; see p.151), remove the riser forms and finish the steps (step 6). Or finish just the landing and treads after the concrete has set; then leave all forms in place until the steps have cured for about a week.

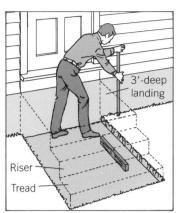

Riser

Tread

3'-deep landing

1. To determine the dimensions of a flight of entryway steps, clear and level an area extending 6 ft. in front of doorway and 2 in. wider than the planned steps. Measure distance from ground to bottom of doorsill and divide by desired number of steps. For a 21-in. rise, for example, build a flight of three steps with 7-in.-high risers and 11-in.-deep treads.

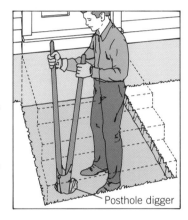

Posthole digger

2. Use a posthole digger to dig two or more 6- to 8-in.-diameter holes under planned location of bottom step. In areas subject to frost, holes should extend below frost line. (In a cold climate, where frost line may be 4 or more ft. deep, have a fencing company dig holes for the footings.) Tamp ground well.

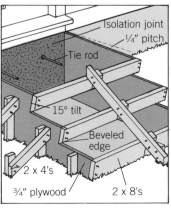

Isolation joint

1/4" pitch

Tie rod

15° tilt

Beveled edge

2 x 4's

3/4" plywood

2 x 8's

3. Install tie rods and isolation joint where shown. Construct side forms of 3/4-in. concrete-form ply; make risers tilt 15° forward. For drainage, give steps a downward pitch of 1/4 in. per ft. Build riser forms of 2 x 8's or 2 x 10's cut lengthwise to riser height. Bevel lower edges of riser boards. Use double-headed nails to build form; stake and brace it with 2 x 4's.

Rubble fill

4. Make sure form is flush against house wall. Risers should be level from left to right and the treads pitched downward. Use plastic sheets to keep concrete from splattering on door and siding. Oil interior of form before placing concrete. To save on concrete, partially fill form with brick, stone, or concrete rubble; keep fill at least 4 in. from form boards.

Plastic sheet

5. Place concrete in footing and lowest step first. Strike off excess concrete, then fill and strike off remaining steps. Jab shovel in and out of concrete to fill corners and eliminate air pockets. Starting at landing, strike off concrete a second time. Darby the landing, float the treads, and run an edger between the concrete and the top of riser forms (p.151).

Inside step tool

Kneeboard

Kneepad

6. When steps have set sufficiently to support their weight, you can remove riser forms, starting at top. Finish risers with a float, run an inside step tool along edge where riser and tread meet, and give treads a broomed slip-proof finish. Remove side forms when steps have cured; smooth any imperfections with concrete patching compound (p.159).

155

Concrete/Footings and foundations

A *footing* is the enlarged base of a foundation that helps distribute the structure's load. It is usually made of concrete. The footing for a foundation wall must rest on firm soil or on a gravel bed, with the base of the footing below the frost line or, in no-frost areas, at a minimum depth of 12 inches for a one-story house; such a footing should also contain two ½-inch reinforcing bars, or rebars. In general, a footing should be as thick as the width of the wall it supports and twice as wide.

Often used for house extensions and decks, *pier foundations* (facing page) are an economical way of supporting a building. In its simplest form, the *slab on grade* (facing page) is a thick-edged concrete slab placed at ground level; it also serves as the building's ground floor. A *perimeter foundation* (p.158) consists of foundation walls, which rest on a continuous footing and enclose a basement or crawl space.

▶ **CAUTION:** This section is meant as an overview of a job that, at least in parts, is probably best left to professionals. Building codes (p.193) strictly regulate foundation construction. Before starting a foundation, consult your local code, schedule inspections, and obtain all needed permits.

Staking the building site. With the plot plan as a guide, measure carefully from the property line or an existing structure to locate one corner of the planned building. Mark the corner by driving a stake (A on the illustration at center, right); drive a nail into the center of the stake's top. Measuring from this corner and the property line, locate and stake corner B. Drive a nail into stake B; run a taut line from

A to B. Measuring from these points, set stakes at the approximate location of corners C and D.

To create true right-angle corners, use the 3:4:5 method of triangulation. Set a stake (E) 3 feet from A, directly under line AB. Drive a nail into stake E. Attach the end of a 50-foot steel tape to the nail in stake A; have a helper run the tape to stake C. Place the tip of a folding rule against the nail in stake E; extend the rule to the steel tape at point F, 4 feet away from A. Have your helper move the tape sideways until the 4-foot mark on the tape coincides with the 5-foot mark on the rule. With sides of 3, 4, and 5 feet, triangle AEF contains a right angle at A. Adjust stake C as needed; run a taut line from A to C. To make sure that all corners are square, measure diagonals AD and BC, and move stake D until the diagonals are equal. Run lines between C and D and D and B; recheck all measurements.

Setting up batter boards. To preserve the building lines once excavation begins, construct batter boards at each corner of the site, at least 4 feet outside the corner stakes. These boards usually consist of two 1 x 6's, called ledgers, set at a right angle and nailed to three 2 x 4 stakes. The ledgers should be the same height as the top of a foundation wall or a few inches above the top of a slab. Level individual pairs of ledgers with a spirit level. On an uneven site, set up the first batter boards at the highest corner and use a water level (p.47) to ensure an equal height for all the ledgers. Transfer the building lines to the batter boards as shown at right.

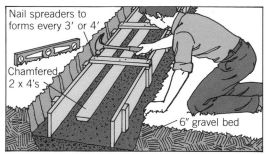
Nail spreaders to forms every 3' or 4'

Chamfered 2 x 4's

6" gravel bed

To build a footing for a garden wall, dig a trench 2 ft. wider than footing (see text for dimensions); base of footing should lie below frost line. Assemble and stake form (pp.152–153); level it in all directions. For a concrete wall, install chamfered and oiled 2 x 4's held by spreaders down center of form. The depression, or key, created in the footing will help secure the wall. In compact soil, a footing can be cast in a well-dug trench, without forms.

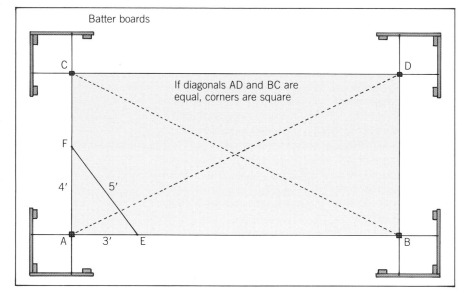

Batter boards

C

D

If diagonals AD and BC are equal, corners are square

F

4'   5'

A   3'   E   B

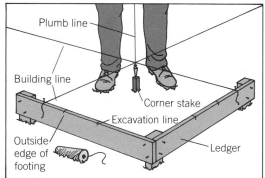

Plumb line

Building line

Corner stake

Excavation line

Outside edge of footing

Ledger

Extend building lines from corner stakes to batter boards. Drive small nails into tops of ledgers and attach strings to nails. Use a plumb line (p.47) to check that lines intersect directly over nail in each corner stake; adjust lines as needed. Saw notches, or *kerfs,* where building lines cross ledgers. The building line marks the outside face of the foundation wall; measuring from this line, cut kerfs for the outside edge of the footing and the excavation line. To mark any of these lines on the ground, run string between appropriate kerfs and dribble sand over string.

Pier foundations are vertical building supports that rest on individual footings. They are spaced around a building's perimeter and under the interior construction as local building codes specify. Rectangular piers are made of masonry or concrete with footings of concrete. Pier spacing and dimensions depend on the building's structural load and on the soil's load-bearing capacity. Typically, the piers for a one-story house on average soil are spaced 8 to 12 feet on center and measure at least 8 x 12 inches (solid masonry) or 10 x 10 inches (concrete).

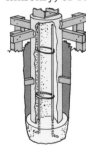

A pier's footing must lie beneath the frost line. It should be at least 8 inches thick and twice the dimensions of the pier.

Round concrete piers are often used to support wood decks. The piers resemble posthole footings (p.155), but they may rest on footings of their own and are usually placed in waxed cardboard forms called Sonotubes.

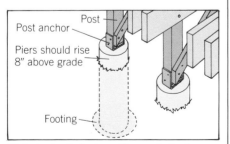

Dig holes for deck piers with a posthole digger or shovel. Place concrete for footing. Press two to four bent ½-in. rebars into concrete and hold in place with tie wire (see above). Install Sonotube. Fill tube with concrete; embed a post anchor in it.

Slab-on-grade foundations. The monolithic slab (center, right), in which a perimeter footing, or grade beam, is placed integrally with the slab, makes a good foundation for a house or outbuilding on a level site. Well suited to warm climates, such slabs are also used in colder areas with stable, well-drained subsoil. The slab should rest on a base consisting of tamped earth, 4 inches of gravel, a 6-mil polyethylene vapor (and radon) barrier, and 2 inches of sand. The grade beam should extend at least 1 foot below grade or below the frost line. Rigid insulation can be installed vertically against the slab's exterior edge.

In regions where frost penetration is a problem, the slab must include a concrete or concrete-block perimeter foundation wall whose footings extend below the frost line (bottom right). The perimeter wall and the slab are placed separately, with an isolation joint (p.152) between them. In this case, use rigid insulation as the joint material. Insulation can also be placed under the slab (between the gravel and the vapor barrier) or along either side of the foundation wall.

For a monolithic slab, the site is laid out and batter boards are built as described on the facing page. Forms should be assembled (p.152) so that the inner faces of the boards coincide with the building line and their tops are level. The slab must be at least 4 inches thick (thicker wherever it will support walls or columns); its top should be 6 to 8 inches above grade.

Standard equipment for digging the footing trench is a power shovel called a backhoe. Once the trench has been excavated to the required depth, two parallel rows of ½-inch rebars are placed in the bottom of the trench and lifted 3 inches off the ground by special wire stilts or pieces of rock. Placing a layer of 6-inch-square wire mesh in the center of the slab is recommended to control cracking (make sure the mesh extends through the grade beam). After the slab has been placed, screeded, and bull-floated (p.151), anchor bolts, spaced no more than 6 feet apart and 1 foot from any corner, are embedded along the perimeter to secure the house frame.

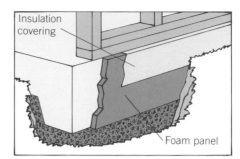

Forms for monolithic slab-and-grade-beam foundations are usually 2 x 8's braced with 2 x 4 stakes spaced no more than 3 ft. apart. An alternative is forming made of polystyrene foam panels. The easy-to-assemble forms stay in place after the concrete has cured, insulating the slab. Panel coverings provide a measure of protection against insects.

Monolithic slab foundation

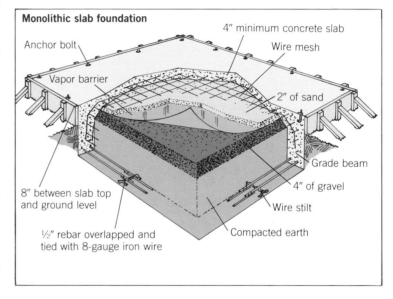

Slab-and-perimeter-wall foundation. Where frost penetration is a problem, a slab and its perimeter support are usually independent and the latter must reach below the frost line. The perimeter trench must be wide enough to accommodate the more complex formwork required by a concrete foundation wall (p.158) or to provide enough space to lay up a concrete-block wall (pp.178–179).

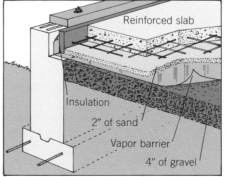

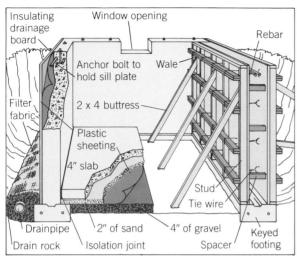

This cutaway drawing shows a basement at various stages of its construction. Reusable wall forms can be rented from masonry supply houses, or you can make your own forms of ¾-in. concrete-form plywood supported by 2 x 4 studs, which in turn are backed by pairs of 2 x 4 horizontal braces, called wales. Tie rods or wires hold the walls together; 1 x 2 spacers keep them the proper distance apart. The walls are further braced by buttresses.

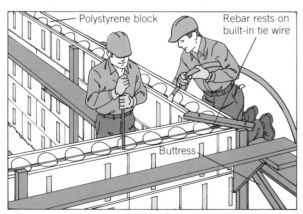

Stay-in-place concrete formwork assembled of hollow interlocking polystyrene blocks is a time- and money-saving alternative to the tedious jobs of building and stripping wooden forms for a basement foundation. Light and easy to install, the blocks also serve as insulation. Braced with 2 x 4 diagonal buttresses spaced at 8-ft. intervals, the polystyrene form shown here is being filled with concrete by means of a pump equipped with a 2-in. hose.

Perimeter foundation walls are costlier than slab foundations (p. 157) but have several advantages. Unlike slabs, they allow easy access to plumbing and wiring and can be built on sloping ground; they can also add valuable living space to a house.

Once building lines have been laid (p. 156) and the site excavated—a job best done by a professional excavator with a backhoe—a perimeter footing trench is dug with its base below the frost line, two No. 4 rebars are installed in the trench (p. 157), and the footing is placed. Local codes determine footing dimensions, but see p. 156 for a general rule of thumb. Footings for concrete walls should be keyed.

Concrete walls are usually 8 to 10 inches thick; concrete block walls (pp. 178–179), 8 to 12 inches. Basement walls should be at least 8 feet tall and rise no less than 8 inches above ground level.

Once the footing has set, the forms for a concrete wall are installed, leveled, and braced. Two No. 4 rebars running continuously 2 inches below the wall's top will minimize cracking. (The rebars can rest on the tie wires that hold the form walls together.) More reinforcement may be needed in areas with unstable soil or earthquake risk; consult local building officials and a structural engineer.

Forms are filled from the ready-mix truck's chute or by a pump and hose system at the chute's base. The concrete should be placed in 12-inch layers, with each layer well tamped to release air bubbles.

Moistureproof basement walls by covering their exterior with 6-mil polyethylene sheeting (overlap joints between sheets generously). Install a perimeter drain along the footing. Use 4-inch perforated drainpipe embedded in 12 to 18 inches of drain rock; cover the rock with filter fabric. Rigid insulating drainage boards placed against the moistureproofing insulate the basement while channeling water to the drainpipe. Start backfilling after the first-floor deck is in place; use coarse sand or bank-run gravel, topped with native soil. The topsoil should slope 1 to 2 inches per foot away from the foundation for 6 to 10 feet. Install isolation-joint material between the floor slab and the foundation wall (see above, left).

There are four ways to color concrete. You can add a coloring agent as the concrete is being mixed (p. 150). A cost-cutting alternative is to place uncolored concrete to within an inch of the form's top. When the surface sheen has evaporated, fill the form with a colored medium-consistency cement-sand mortar (pp. 162–163). Or you can dust a freshly floated slab with special colored powders. The least effective method is to apply concrete paint (p. 367) to a surface that's at least a year old.

A wide variety of textures can be worked into a concrete surface. Three are described below.

Score flagstone pattern onto a concrete walk with a bent piece of ½-in. copper pipe. Do this after bull-floating and repeat after hand-floating.

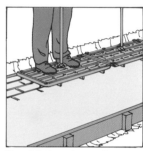

Special stamping pads can be used to create a brick, tile, or other pattern on a freshly floated or troweled concrete slab. You'll need at least two stamping pads for the job.

1. For an exposed-aggregate finish, screed the concrete; then cover it with a layer of rounded gravel. Embed gravel firmly, first with a 2 x 6 or a darby, then with a hand float.

2. After concrete has stiffened enough to hold gravel in place, brush and spray off excess concrete from around gravel. Keep brushing and spraying until gravel is evenly exposed.

Repairing damaged concrete

Improperly mixed, finished, or cured concrete can develop surface flaws. Here are the most common:

Dusting appears on a concrete surface as a fine powder that is easily rubbed off. To treat it, brush the surface; then apply a commercial concrete sealer (follow package directions). For severe cases, coat the concrete with a surface hardener before sealing it (magnesium-zinc fluosilicate hardeners are best).

To stop *scaling,* in which surface mortar peels off, apply two coats of a 1:1 solution of boiled linseed oil and turpentine. Keep off the surface until it has dried. For at least the next three years, repeat the treatment before winter starts.

Popouts are small fragments that break away from a concrete surface, leaving holes. To repair, brush dust and debris from the hole; then patch it with mortar or patching compound (see below).

Cracks in concrete. Before repairing cracked or broken concrete, make sure the damaged area is free of dirt and debris. To provide a good lock for the patch, undercut the sides of the crack.

Fix narrow cracks with masonry crack filler, which is sold in cartridges for use in a caulking gun. To fill wider vertical cracks in concrete, brick and concrete-block walls, see p.175. Techniques for repairing wide cracks and large holes in slabs are described at right.

Make your own patching mortar by mixing 1 part portland cement with 3 parts sand; then add enough water to form a stiff paste. Or buy a standard commercial patching mortar and follow package directions. To improve the bond, coat the damaged area with a commercial bonding agent or a 1:1 cement-sand grout (p.163) mixed with water to the consistency of thick paint; apply the patch material while the bonding agent or grout is still wet.

Epoxy or latex patching compounds cost more than patching mortars, but they form a stronger bond, do not require a bonding agent, and are self-curing. (Mortars, on the other hand, must be moist-cured for about a week; see p.151.)

▶ **CAUTION:** Wear gloves and safety goggles when chiseling, drilling, or sledgehammering concrete.

Filling cracks

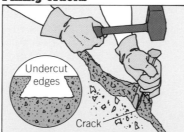

1. With hammer and cold chisel, chip away loose concrete. Holding chisel at an angle, undercut crack so that it's wider at base than at surface. Remove debris with an air compressor, shop vacuum, or hand bellows.

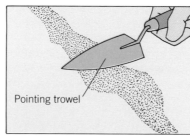

2. Dampen crack; coat it with a bonding agent if needed. With a trowel, pack patch material into crack and smooth it. When patch has set, brush or float it to match adjacent surface. Moist-cure a mortar patch.

Broken slabs

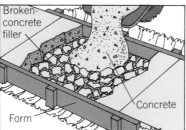

Break up a badly damaged slab with a sledgehammer. Remove loosened concrete and clean exposed surfaces. Set up forms; dampen repair area; then place, finish, and cure concrete (p.151) as for a new slab.

Mending step edges

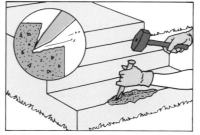

1. Chip away loose concrete from a crumbling step edge with a hammer and cold chisel. Holding chisel at an angle, undercut a V-shaped groove in step edge (see inset). Clean and moisten the repair area.

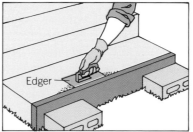

3. Prod patch with trowel tip several times to remove air bubbles. Use same trowel to smooth patch flush with rest of step. Run an edger between the step and the board to compact the patch.

Rebuilding step corners

1. Chisel away loose concrete, and brush off dust and debris from damaged area. Coat corner with a bonding agent if needed. With a pointed trowel, build up patch material in the shape of the original corner.

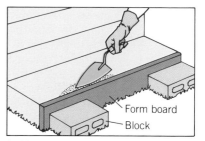

2. Make a riser-height form board; prop it against step with concrete blocks. Coat repair area with a bonding agent if needed; use a pointed trowel to apply patching mortar or an epoxy or latex patching compound.

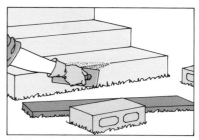

4. Allow about 1 hr. for patch to set up; then carefully remove the form board and touch up the repair with a trowel. Cure a mortar patch for up to 7 days. Keep traffic off new edge for a week after curing.

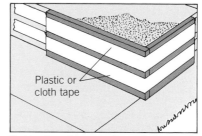

2. Use trowel to smooth patch flush with rest of step. Tape scrap lumber around corner. When patch has set, remove boards and float repaired area. Cure a mortar patch for up to 7 days; stay off corner for 3 weeks.

Asphalt/Sealing and patching a blacktop driveway

The asphalt, or blacktop, commonly used to pave roads, driveways, and walks is actually a type of concrete in which graded aggregates are held together by an extract of crude petroleum rather than by portland cement. Although more flexible than concrete, asphalt is also vulnerable to the effects of water seepage and frost, and needs periodic maintenance and repair.

To protect an asphalt drive from cracks and stains and to restore its appearance after repair work, treat it every few years as needed with an emulsified asphalt or coal-tar sealer. Ready-to-pour sealers are sold in 5-gallon pails—enough to cover up to 400 square feet of driveway. Some manufacturers recommend applying a second coat of sealer within 48 hours. But check package directions first—applying too much sealer can cause the drive to become overly slick.

Sealing a blacktop surface automatically takes care of hairline cracks. Wider cracks and depressions should be repaired as soon as they appear; otherwise, water can collect in them and later freeze, further damaging your drive. Seal cracks up to ½ inch wide with driveway crack filler sold in caulking-gun cartridges. Patch wider cracks with a sand and sealer mix. For potholes and very wide cracks, use a cold-mix asphalt patching compound.

Blacktop maintenance and repair jobs are best done in warm (over 60°F) weather, when asphalt materials are more malleable, set rapidly, and form a better bond. Always check manufacturer's directions before using patching materials and sealers. Have mineral spirits on hand for cleanup.

To seal an asphalt drive, remove dirt and debris. Pour enough sealer to coat 4 sq. ft.; spread it with a long-handled squeegee or broom. Repeat until entire drive is sealed. If suggested by manufacturer, apply another coat in 48 hr. Stay off drive at least a day.

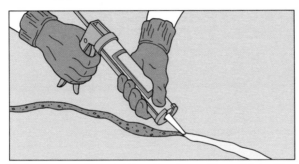

To fix narrow cracks up to ½ in. wide, clean out loose debris with a wire brush. If crack is deeper than ¼ in., partially fill it with sand, then apply crack filler from a caulking gun. Use a trowel or putty knife to smooth and level the patch. Do not overfill the crack.

Clean out wider cracks as described above. In an aluminum pie pan, mix sand and blacktop sealer to a putty-like consistency. Use a trowel to pack paste into crack and smooth it flush with driveway surface. If paste settles, add more as needed to level patch.

Mending potholes

While many cracks in a blacktop surface can be repaired with crack filler or a mixture of sand and sealer, large cracks and holes call for a cold-mix asphalt patching compound. If the damage is very extensive, have a professional repair it with a hot-mix asphalt patch. Unlike the latter, which must be heated and applied in molten form, cold mixes are sold ready-to-use in 60-pound bags. For proper application the material should be loose in the bag. If it is lumpy, store it in a warm place for several hours or overnight.

Clean and fill a pothole as described below. To protect the patch from water damage, coat it with blacktop sealer, or seal the entire drive to avoid a patchwork look.

1. Dig out loose paving; remove debris. Fill a deep hole with gravel to within 4 in. of surface. Tamp base with a 4 x 4. Lightly coat repair area with emulsified asphalt.

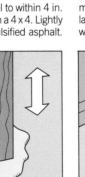

3. Use 4 x 4 to tamp down one layer of patching compound before placing the next. Build up patch until its top is about ½ in. above driveway surface.

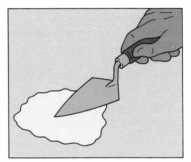

2. With a trowel or shovel, apply cold-mix asphalt patching compound in 1-in. layers. Pack each layer firmly and prod with trowel tip to remove air bubbles.

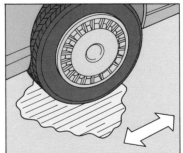

4. Tamp patch with 4 x 4 and sprinkle sand on it. Slowly drive a car back and forth over patch until it is level with driveway surface.

Chapter eight

Masonry
Building with brick, block, and stone

Contents

As old as civilization, the mason's art involves the laying of individual masonry units—bricks, concrete blocks, stones, or tiles—either dry or with the cementing agent known as mortar. Masonry construction offers strength and permanence. In addition, few building materials can match the beauty of stone and brick; even concrete blocks now come in attractive colors and finishes that disguise their utilitarian origin.

In this section you'll learn how to mix and throw mortar, build up new masonry structures course by course, and repair and clean old ones. (In the process, you'll also become conversant with the mason's special jargon.) Here, too, are projects to enhance your house and garden, from a simple brick walkway laid in sand to a flagstone patio, a glass block shower wall, a brick garden wall or barbecue, a simple dry stone wall, or a concrete block wall faced with stone veneer.

Masonry / Bricks and mortar

Made of fired clay, bricks come in thousands of combinations of shapes, types, colors, and textures. They are also available solid, cored, or with indentations (called *frogs*). Most bricks produced today are made to *face brick* specifications. Once reserved for facing walls exposed to weather, face bricks have largely replaced *common,* or *building, bricks* as the all-purpose brick. More uniform in color and size than building bricks, with sharper edges, squarer corners, and fewer flaws, face bricks are available in a wide range of colors and finishes. The term "building brick" is now usually applied to "seconds"—off-grade, slightly imperfect face bricks.

Yellow, heat-resistant *firebricks* are used to line fireplaces and hearths. They're bonded with a special fireclay mortar, sold in bags by firebrick dealers.

Driveways and patios are commonly made of *paving bricks* laid on a bed of sand, gravel, or concrete. Harder and more durable than regular bricks, pavers are sized for use with or without mortar.

Used bricks add a warm, rustic touch to a structure, but unless you haul and clean them yourself, they can be expensive. Often of poor or uncertain quality, used bricks are not recommended for exterior use. A good alternative is "new used" brick—a strong modern brick specially treated to look old.

Bricks are graded according to their resistance to the effects of freezing and thawing. Severe weathering (SW) bricks are highly resistant to frost action; they are used for foundations, retaining walls, and other structures in which bricks come in contact with the ground, as well as for above-ground con-

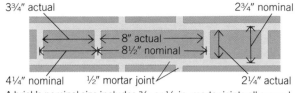

A brick's nominal size includes ⅜- or ½-in. mortar joints all around.

struction in regions with extremely cold winters. Moderate weathering (MW) bricks are used for above-ground exterior walls in areas with moderately cold or warm weather. No weathering (NW) bricks are meant mainly for interior projects.

Bricks are specified by their actual size (really an average, since bricks from the same run will vary somewhat from the specified dimensions) or by their nominal size, which includes the extra ⅜ or ½ inch all around taken up by the mortar joints between bricks. The actual dimensions of a standard brick are 3¾ inches wide x 2¼ inches high x 8 inches long; its nominal size, including ½-inch mortar joints, is 4¼ x 2¾ x 8½ inches. To facilitate fitting, many bricks are sized according to a modular system in which dimensions are based on 4- and 8-inch modules. The nominal dimensions of a standard modular brick, including ⅜-inch mortar joints all around, are 4 x 2⅔ x 8 inches.

Mortar is the bonding material that holds bricks and other masonry units together. A sound, well-mixed mortar is crucial to the integrity of a brick structure; it seals out wind and water, anchors metal ties and steel reinforcement, and compensates for variations in brick size and for flaws on brick surfaces. It can also can be tooled (p.168) and colored for decorative effect.

The components of mortar are portland cement (p.146), which gives the mix its bonding strength; hydrated lime, for workability; sand, for volume; and enough water to produce a plastic, workable consistency. Hydrated lime is sold in 50-pound bags, equaling 1 cubic foot. The sand should be clean, well-graded mortar, or masonry, sand, sold dry in 60-pound bags or damp in bulk. The water should be fit to drink. Never use beach sand or salt water.

Brick types and sizes

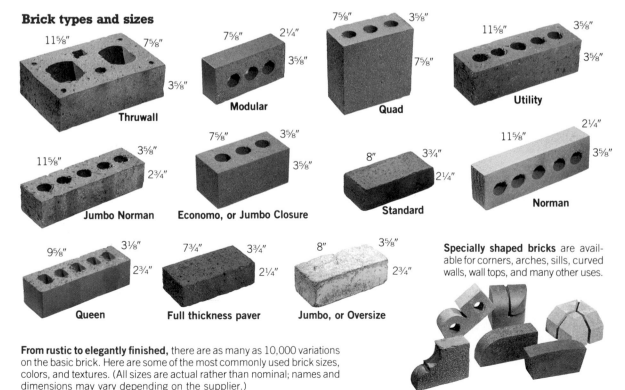

From rustic to elegantly finished, there are as many as 10,000 variations on the basic brick. Here are some of the most commonly used brick sizes, colors, and textures. (All sizes are actual rather than nominal; names and dimensions may vary depending on the supplier.)

Specially shaped bricks are available for corners, arches, sills, curved walls, wall tops, and many other uses.

You can also make mortar with masonry cement, a premixed combination of portland cement, lime, and additives that enhance workability. You need to add only sand and water. Masonry cement is sold in 70-pound bags, equaling 1 cubic foot.

Even easier to work with is ready-mix mortar, which contains all the necessary ingredients except water. Although more expensive than buying cement, lime, and sand separately, ready-mix will save you the time and effort of proportioning and mixing dry ingredients and is often the practical choice for small jobs around the home. Ready-mix is sold in 80-pound and smaller bags; one 80-pound bag yields ⅔ cubic foot of mortar.

Mortar strength depends on the proportion of cement to lime and sand: the less lime and sand per volume of cement, the stronger the mortar. The chart below, left, lists four mortar types, their applications, and the proportions of their dry ingredients by volume. Type N mortar—a 1:3 masonry cement–sand mix or a 1:1:6 portland cement–lime–sand

mix—is a good general-purpose mortar suitable for most above-ground outdoor projects.

Coloring mortar. Regular mortar is usually gray. White or colored mortar can be used to highlight or conceal joints. White mortar is made by mixing white masonry or portland cement with white sand. Masonry cement comes in a variety of colors. In addition, you can add a mineral oxide pigment to a white-cement mortar. Blend the pigment and the dry ingredients thoroughly (p. 165), add water, and stir well until no streaks are left. To check the final color, mix a sample batch and let it set. (You are likelier to achieve uniformity of color from batch to batch with colored masonry cement.)

Grout is a thin mixture of portland cement, sand, and water (some grouts include small proportions of lime; others contain crushed stone or gravel). It is used to fill cores in nonreinforced load-bearing masonry walls; to fill the space between wythes or tiers, of brick in multi-wythe walls; to anchor steel rods in reinforced walls; and in masonry repair jobs (p. 175).

Estimating quantities. To determine the number of bricks you'll need for a wall, first figure the wall's total square footage (p. 148); then subtract the area to be occupied by doors and windows. Count on 616 bricks per 100 square feet if you're using nonmodular standard bricks with ½-inch mortar joints; 675 bricks if you're using modular standard bricks with ⅜-inch joints; and double or triple those amounts if the wall is to be two or three bricks thick. Always increase your total brick order by at least 5 percent to cover breakage and waste.

For a 4-inch- (one-brick-) thick wall, plan to use about 8 cubic feet of mortar for each 100 square feet of standard bricks; about 20 cubic feet for the same area of an 8-inch wall. (These figures are for ½-inch mortar joints; with ⅜-inch joints you'll need about 25 percent less mortar.) Add 10 to 25 percent to your mortar estimates to allow for waste. See the chart below, center, for the quantities of masonry cement and sand needed to make enough Type N mortar to build 100 square feet of 4- and 8-inch-thick walls.

Selecting the right mortar

Application	Type	Portland cement	Hydrated lime	Masonry cement	Damp sand
		Proportions by volume			
Masonry structures on or below grade, such as foundations, retaining walls, and walks; load-bearing walls; general use.	M	1	¼		3
A high-adhesion mortar, good for reinforced walls, walls exposed to strong winds, and general use.	S	1	½		4½
A medium-strength, all-purpose mortar, good for most above-grade uses.	N			1	3
	N	1	1		6
Interior moderate- and non-load-bearing walls.	O	1	2		9

Brick and mortar quantities
(per 100 sq. ft. of wall)

Wall thickness	Number of bricks	Cu. ft. of mortar	Masonry cement bags	Cu. ft. of sand
			Mix by volume 1:3	
4"	616	8	2.7	8
8"	1,232	20	6.6	20

These figures are based on the use of standard bricks and ½-in. mortar joints; they do not allow for waste. Proportions are for a Type N masonry cement mortar. The sand is assumed to be loose damp sand, 1 cu. ft. (or roughly 6 shovelfuls) of which is equivalent to 80 lb. of dry sand.

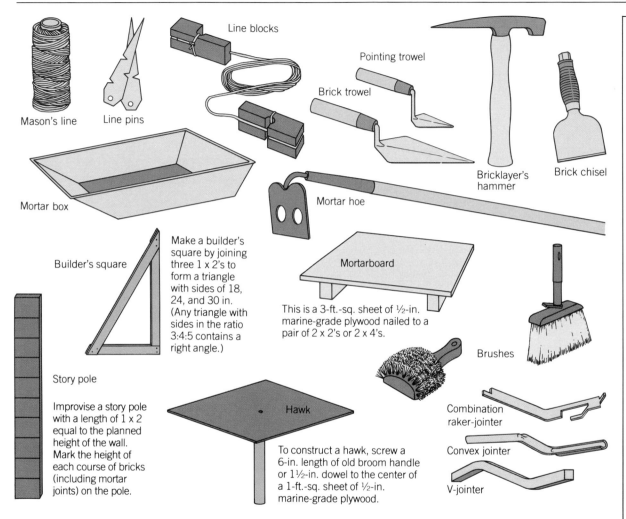

Mason's line

Line pins

Line blocks

Pointing trowel

Brick trowel

Bricklayer's hammer

Brick chisel

Mortar box

Mortar hoe

Builder's square

Make a builder's square by joining three 1 x 2's to form a triangle with sides of 18, 24, and 30 in. (Any triangle with sides in the ratio 3:4:5 contains a right angle.)

Mortarboard

This is a 3-ft.-sq. sheet of ½-in. marine-grade plywood nailed to a pair of 2 x 2's or 2 x 4's.

Brushes

Story pole

Improvise a story pole with a length of 1 x 2 equal to the planned height of the wall. Mark the height of each course of bricks (including mortar joints) on the pole.

Hawk

To construct a hawk, screw a 6-in. length of old broom handle or 1½-in. dowel to the center of a 1-ft.-sq. sheet of ½-in. marine-grade plywood.

Combination raker-jointer

Convex jointer

V-jointer

The bricklayer's language

Bat: A segment of a brick that has been cut across its width. A half brick is called a *half bat.*

Bed joint: The horizontal layer of mortar between *courses* of a brick or concrete block wall.

Bond: 1. The adhesion of mortar to masonry units (mortar bond); 2. the interlocking of masonry units by means of overlapping bricks or metal ties to form a structural whole (structural bond); 3. the pattern made by bricks arranged in a fixed sequence (pattern bond).

Butter: (v.) To trowel mortar onto the end and/or side of a brick or block before placing the unit in position.

Closure: 1. A whole or cut brick used to complete a *course;* 2. a supplementary or short length of brick used at corners of a wall to maintain the bond pattern.

Course: A horizontal row of masonry units in a wall.

Header: A brick laid flat on its broad surface with its short end facing out.

Head joint: The vertical layer of mortar between adjacent bricks or blocks in a wall.

Lead: A stepped-back end or corner of a masonry wall that is built up first to establish alignment.

Point: (v.) To trowel mortar into joints after bricks are laid. *Tuck-pointing,* or *repointing,* is the process of repairing joints by chiseling out crumbling mortar and adding fresh mortar.

Rowlock header: A brick laid on its narrow side with its short end facing out.

Rowlock stretcher: A brick laid on its narrow side with its broad surface facing out.

Sailor: A brick that stands upright with its broad surface facing out.

Soldier: A brick that stands upright with its narrow side facing out.

Stretcher: A brick laid flat on its broad surface with its narrow side facing out.

Throw: (v.) To cast an even line of mortar from a trowel.

Wythe: A vertical tier of bricks in a wall. A single-wythe wall is one brick thick; a double-wythe wall is two bricks thick.

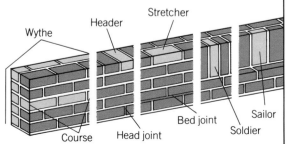

Wythe · Header · Stretcher · Course · Head joint · Bed joint · Soldier · Sailor

Many of the tools required for concrete work (p.147) are also used for bricklaying: a 4-foot spirit level; a 50-foot steel tape; two or more buckets and a square-ended shovel, for measuring and mixing mortar ingredients; and a sturdy contractor's wheelbarrow, for mixing and hauling mortar. Of the specialty bricklaying tools, most are inexpensive; some you can make yourself:

Mason's line and line pins or *blocks,* to keep the courses in a masonry wall straight and true. *Bricklayer's hammer,* to cut and trim bricks. *Brick chisel,* used with a small sledgehammer to cut

bricks. Soft- and hard-bristled *brushes,* to clean masonry surfaces. *Mortar box* and *hoe,* for mixing mortar. *Brick trowel,* to apply and spread mortar. *Pointing trowel,* to finish and repair mortar joints. *Jointers,* to shape mortar joints. *Mortarboard,* to hold a reserve of mortar. *Hawk,* to hold small amounts of mortar to be scooped up with a trowel. *Builder's square,* to check that corners are true right angles. *Story pole,* a measuring stick used to check that each course of bricks in a wall is the right height (a *brick mason's spacing rule* is used for the same purpose).

Mixing and handling mortar

To make large quantities of mortar, rent a power mortar mixer, similar to the type used for concrete (p.150). Mix small batches by hand in a mortar pan or contractor's wheelbarrow. The procedure is similar to that for mixing concrete: use separate buckets or shovels to measure out each of the dry ingredients in the desired proportions (pp.162–163), place them in the pan or wheelbarrow, and mix thoroughly with a square-ended shovel or a mortar hoe. If you're making a portland cement–lime mortar, mix the cement and sand first; then add the hydrated lime and mix again.

Once the dry ingredients have been thoroughly blended, make a depression in the center of the mixture and pour in a little water from a hose or bucket. With the hoe, pull dry ingredients from the edge of the depression into the water and mix. Keep mixing in water a little at a time until the mortar has a smooth, workable, "buttery" consistency. To test the mix, make a furrow across its surface with the hoe; if the furrow holds its shape and the mortar slides readily from the hoe, the consistency is right. Let the mortar stand for about 5 minutes; then mix it again before using it.

Use fresh cement products (see p.147 for storage and safety directions); mix only as much mortar as you can use in 1½ hours. After that the mortar becomes unworkable and should be discarded. If the mortar starts to dry out as you work, retemper it by adding a little water and mixing thoroughly. Do this only once; if the batch dries out again, throw it away. Don't retemper colored mortar.

Handling a trowel properly is the key to laying bricks correctly and quickly. If you are laying bricks for the first time, practice your troweling skills by throwing lines of mortar on a 2 x 4, which is about the same width as a brick, until you get the knack.

When the mortar is ready, transfer two shovelfuls onto a mortarboard set up next to the work site. Holding the trowel with your thumb on top of the base of the handle and your other fingers wrapped around it in a relaxed way, load the trowel and throw the mortar as illustrated at right.

1. Cut a slice of mortar from the mound on the mortarboard, using a sawing motion of the trowel. With the back of the trowel blade, shape the mortar into a "sausage" about the length and width of the blade.

2. Load the trowel by sweeping it under the mortar slice from behind with a smooth forward motion. As you lift the trowel, snap your wrist down slightly to bond the mortar to the trowel blade.

3. To throw a mortar line, set trowel tip, face up, where line is to begin. As you pull trowel toward you, turn blade 180°. The mortar should roll off in an even line, one brick wide, 16 in. long, and 1 in. thick.

4. Furrow the mortar gently by running trowel tip, face down, along center of line. The purpose of this is to spread the mortar so that it will be evenly distributed when the brick is pressed into it.

 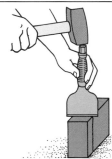

5. To butter a brick before laying it, hold it upright and tilted at a slight angle. Pick up a small amount of mortar on the trowel and swipe it onto the end of the brick. Squash mortar down against all four edges.

6. Shove brick in place, its buttered end pressed against adjoining brick. Continue pressing until head and bed joints are the right thickness. Trim excess mortar with trowel edge; use excess to butter next brick.

Cutting bricks

Professional masons often cut bricks with a few taps of a bricklayer's hammer. The rest of us, however, are better advised to use a brick chisel and a small sledgehammer. To cut bricks with a circular saw, see p.60. Always wear saftey goggles when cutting bricks.

Pencil cutting line around brick. Place brick on sand or earth, then score along line by gently tapping brick chisel with a small sledgehammer.

Place chisel on scored line, with its handle tilted slightly toward waste end of brick. Strike chisel hard with hammer. The brick should part neatly in two.

Masonry/How to lay bricks

The garden wall shown on these two pages in various stages of construction is among the easiest of bricklaying projects: a low, freestanding, single-wythe (one-brick-thick) wall, with all bricks laid end-to-end in the pattern called *running bond*. (For more on brick bond patterns, see pp. 168–169.) The basic bricklaying skills demonstrated here can also be applied to the more complex single- and multi-wythe structures on pages 170–172.

Footings. A brick wall must rest on a concrete footing (p. 156) that extends below the frost line. As a general rule, the footing should be as thick vertically as the width of the wall it supports and twice as wide. Footing requirements may vary, however, depending on the wall's dimensions and on local soil and weather conditions. Check with your building department to make sure that the proposed wall conforms to the building code (p. 193). Make sure, too, that the ground on which you plan to build the wall is well drained and free of the root systems of large trees. If the wall will be near a property line, consult your neighbors. Plan the job so that you won't have to work in temperatures below 40° F; in cold weather bricklaying is best left to professionals.

Let the footing cure for several days before building the wall. Have all tools and materials (pp. 162–164) near the job site, and place piles of bricks at convenient intervals along the footing.

The dry run. Mark the ends and front face of the wall on the footing (step 1, at right); then lay the first course of bricks without using mortar (step 2). This dry run allows you to foresee any layout problems and to estimate (and precut) the number of partial bricks required. With the running bond, you should need only one half bat at each end of every other course. Widen the space between bricks slightly to minimize cut bricks.

Preparing the bricks. If a brick is too dry, it will absorb moisture from the mortar it's laid in, weakening the bond. To test for moisture, take a sample brick and with a grease pencil draw a circle the size of a quarter on the face to be mortared. Drop 20 drops of water from a medicine dropper within the circle. If water is still visible after 90 seconds, lay the bricks without wetting. If the water has been absorbed, hose the bricks until you can see water running off them; then wait 15 minutes to let surface water evaporate. (Don't lay bricks dripping wet.) By the time you have mixed the mortar, the bricks should be ready to use.

Laying the wall. When you're satisfied with the dry run, remove the bricks and lay the first course in mortar (steps 3 to 6). Build up the leads, or ends, of the wall five courses high (steps 7 and 8); then fill in between leads (step 9), using a mason's line to keep each course level, plumb, and aligned. Check the accuracy of your work periodically with the story pole and level. If a brick is out of alignment, tap it gently into position with the end of the trowel handle.

As you work, scrape off any excess mortar with the edge of the trowel blade (step 11); tool the joints when they are thumbprint hard (step 12). Let the mortar cure for about a week before scrubbing the wall with masonry cleaner (p. 186).

1. Measuring in from the edges of the footing so that the wall will be centered on it, mark the front corners of the wall on the footing with a grease pencil or the scratch of a nail. Snap a chalk line between the two points to serve as a guideline when laying the first course of bricks.

2. Lay the first course without mortar along the chalk line. Align bricks end to end, allowing a ⅜-in. space between bricks for mortar (use the tip of your little finger to space the bricks). If there's a small gap at the end of the wall, insert a cut brick in the center or widen all joints slightly.

7. Make sure first course is level and aligned. Throw a mortar line 2½ bricks long at one end of first course; furrow mortar with tip of trowel blade. Start second course with a half brick in order to stagger the joints; then lay two full bricks. Use story pole to check thickness of bed joints.

8. Instead of completing second course, build up lead, or end, of wall five courses high, making each course a half brick shorter than the one below it and furrowing the mortar between courses. Level and plumb each course in the lead as it is laid; do frequent story-pole checks.

3. When you've adjusted the dry run, mark spaces between bricks on footing, then remove bricks. Starting at one end of wall, throw a mortar line 1 in. thick and 1½ bricks long along chalk line. (Use troweling method described on page 165, but don't furrow mortar for first course.)

4. Lay first brick on mortar bed, pressing it down until mortar is about ⅜ in. thick. (Top of brick should be even with first line on story pole.) Level brick across its length and width, using trowel handle to tap brick into place. Set level vertically against brick face to check for plumb (step 8).

5. Lay, level, and plumb a brick at other end of wall; then run a mason's line between the bricks. To hold the line, tie it around two loose bricks set on top of the mortared end bricks. The line should be taut, flush with top edges of end bricks, and about ¹⁄₁₆ in. in front of them.

6. Working from both ends toward the center and using the line as a guide, finish first course, buttering one end of each brick before laying it (p.165). If necessary, cut last, or closure, brick to fit. Butter both ends of closure and ends of adjacent bricks; then slide closure in place.

9. Build lead on other end of wall. Stretch a line between leads so that it's flush with top edges of second course. To hold the line, drive pins into mortar joints (as shown here), or hook line blocks to second-course end bricks (step 3, p.165.) Working in from leads, complete second course.

10. Continue filling in between leads, using line, level, and story pole as guides. In addition to checking for level and plumb, use level as a straightedge to keep bricks aligned. If a badly placed brick can't be tapped into alignment, remove brick and mortar and place them again.

11. With practice, you'll be able to throw mortar lines long enough to accommodate three to four bricks at a time. As you work, use trowel blade to scrape off mortar that oozes from joints. When using line pins, remove them as each course is finished and fill holes with mortar right away.

12. Periodically press your thumb into mortar joints. If a thumbprint remains, the joint is ready to be compressed and shaped. Using a jointer or a metal rod, finish the head joints first, then the bed joints. For more on finishing mortar joints, see p.168.

Whether *struck* (finished with a trowel) or *tooled* (shaped and compressed with a special jointing tool), neat, well-finished mortar joints not only give a wall a professional look, they help ensure its structural integrity and moisture resistance. You can shape mortar joints in various ways to create different decorative effects, but the main purpose of jointing is to compress the mortar in order to make a strong bond and seal out water.

Seven of the most popular joint shapes—some more watertight than others—are illustrated at right. *Flush, weathered,* and *struck joints* are formed with a trowel blade. For *concave, V-,* and *raked joints,* you can buy a tool designed specifically for the joint (p. 164) or improvise a tool using a bent piece of ¾-inch metal rod or a piece of wood.

Start jointing (vertical, or head, joints first) when the mortar is thumbprint hard—neither soft enough to smear nor so hard that it is difficult to shape. As you build up the wall, test the mortar often with your thumb (see step 12, p. 167); this is especially important in hot, dry weather, when mortar hardens faster. If you wait too long to tool the joints, the mortar may turn black when it comes in contact with a metal jointing tool.

After finishing the joints, scrape off *tags* (bits of excess mortar) with the edge of a trowel blade. When the joints have hardened a little more, remove remaining tags by sweeping the wall with a soft-bristled brush. Let the wall cure for about a week before washing off mortar stains with a mild solution of muriatic acid or other masonry cleaner (p. 186).

Point vertical (head) joints first,

then the horizontal (bed) joints.

Flush joint. Made by cutting off excess mortar with trowel blade so that joint is flush with wall face. Because mortar isn't compacted, this joint is neither strong nor weathertight.

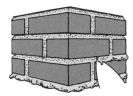
Weathered joint. The most waterproof of the troweled joints. Made by running trowel tip against bottom of upper course at a 30° angle so that joint slopes in from bottom to top.

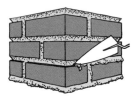
Struck joint. Opposite of weathered joint. Tooled from above so that joint slopes in from top to bottom. Tends to collect water. Should not be exposed to heavy rain or freezing weather.

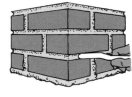
Concave joint. A well-compacted, waterproof joint made by dragging a convex jointer or a bent metal rod along joints. One of the most commonly used mortar joints.

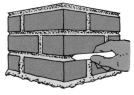
V-joint. Similar to the concave joint in strength and water resistance. Formed with a V-jointer or the corner of a board.

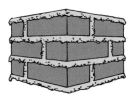
Raked joint. Made by removing mortar to a depth of ¼ to ½ in. with a joint raker or a flat-ended stick. Because a raked joint can collect water, it should not be used on exterior walls.

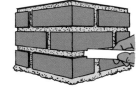
Extruded joint. A rustic joint made by letting mortar ooze from between bricks without tooling. Since mortar isn't compacted, joint is weak and should not be exposed to severe weather.

The pattern in which bricks are arranged in a wall serves both decorative and structural purposes. In most of the traditional bond patterns illustrated here, the head, or vertical, joints are staggered from course to course. In addition to producing interesting patterns, staggering the head joints helps distribute the wall's load along its entire length.

Running and *stack bonds* are single-wythe (one-brick-thick) patterns, with all bricks laid as stretchers (except at ends and corners) and no bonding headers to tie wythes together; double thicknesses are linked with metal ties (p. 172) staggered at regular intervals along the wall. In the *common, English,* and *English garden wall bonds,* header courses alternating with stretcher courses create the structural bond between wythes. In *Flemish bond,* headers and stretchers alternate in the same course. *Clipped headers* (half bricks) may be used to simulate a double-wythe pattern in a single-wythe wall.

Check with your local building department to make sure that your chosen bond is structurally suitable for the type and location of your planned wall.

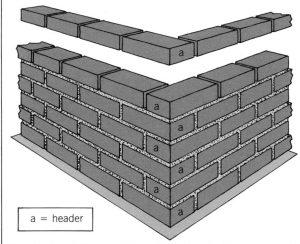
a = header

Running bond. Simplest of the traditional bond patterns; commonly used in low single-wythe garden walls and in brick veneer. Except at corners, all bricks are laid as stretchers. To stagger head joints, every other course in a straight wall begins and ends with a half bat. Corners are formed by alternating stretchers and headers (a).

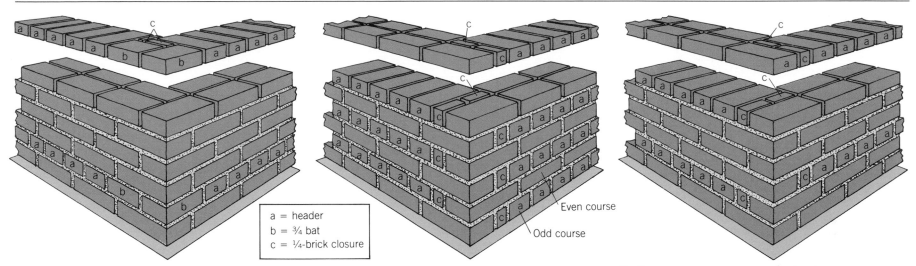

a = header
b = ¾ bat
c = ¼-brick closure

Common, or American, bond. In this double-wythe variation of running bond, every fifth, sixth, or seventh course is a header course, tying the two wythes together. In header courses, each leg of a corner starts with a ¾ bat (b); ¼-brick closures (c) are used to fill corner. (For more on building double-wythe walls with corners, see p.170.)

English bond. Made up of alternating stretcher and header courses. In a wall with a corner, header courses are odd-numbered in one leg, even in the other. Headers (a) are centered on stretchers, vertical joints in all stretcher courses align, and ¼-brick closures (c), placed one brick in from corners, stagger header courses.

English garden wall bond. A variation of the English bond, in which three courses of stretchers alternate with one header course. As in English bond, header courses are odd-numbered in one leg of the wall, even in the other. Headers are centered on stretchers, and ¼-brick closures (c) are needed to stagger joints in header courses.

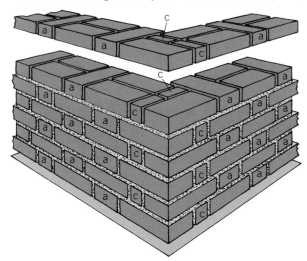

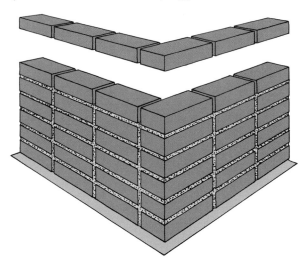

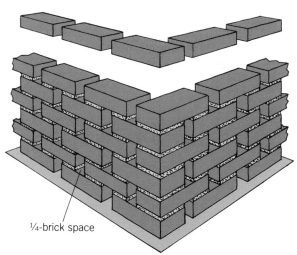

¼-brick space

Flemish bond. Consists of identical courses in which pairs of stretchers laid side by side alternate with single headers. Headers in alternate courses are centered over intermediate stretchers. Quarter-brick closures (c), placed one brick in from corners, are used in alternate courses to stagger joints.

Stack bond. (Also called *block* or *jack-on-jack bond*.) In this one-wythe pattern consisting of all stretchers, each brick is stacked directly on top of the one below it, without staggering the joints. Because all vertical joints align, the bond is inherently weak; it is used mainly for veneering (p.172).

Open, or honeycomb, bond. A decorative variation of the running bond, in which bricks are laid as stretchers with a ¼-brick space between them. For extra stability, space on either side of corner bricks is slightly reduced. Makes an attractive screening wall for garden or patio.

Masonry / Solid brick walls

One-wythe wall. A freestanding straight wall more than 2½ feet high should be at least two bricks thick. An exception is the *serpentine wall,* whose S-curves supply enough lateral strength to build a one-wythe (one-brick-thick) wall up to 8 feet tall. The curves' radius must not exceed twice the wall's height. The wall's depth (the distance between two parallel lines touching the outermost points of the curves) should be at least half its height.

In *pier-and-panel walls,* one-wythe panels up to 8 feet tall are built between reinforced piers 8 to 16 feet apart. The piers rest on 18- to 24-inch-diameter footings placed below the frost line. Reinforced panels can be laid on solid ground. Walls without reinforcement need continuous footings.

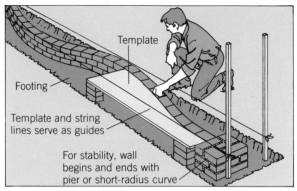

In building a serpentine wall, a plywood template serves as a guide for laying out the wall and building up the courses. The template should span two half arcs from center point to center point.

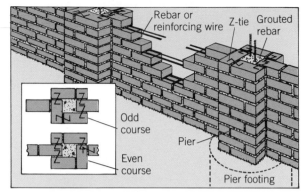

In a pier-and-panel wall, rebars set in footing extend into piers, which are filled with grout (p.163) as wall rises. Bond pattern is staggered so that panels tie into piers from a different side in each course.

A double-wythe wall with corners. The single-wythe walls described above require careful engineering. In comparison, building a double-wythe wall with corners is fairly simple. The wall at right is in the common, or American, bond, but the same techniques can be adapted to other patterns (p.168).

The *collar joint* (the vertical joint between wythes) must be mortared. If you lay both wythes at the same time, butter the inner side of each backup brick. But if the bond pattern permits, lay the front wythe first. Then, using a steel trowel (p.147), apply a ½-inch mortar coat in small sections to the wall's inner face. Press backup bricks against the mortar.

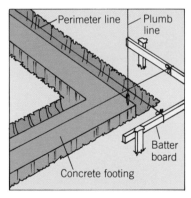

1. Dig footing trench as shown on page 156. (Use 3:4:5 triangulation method to create right angles; set up batter boards at ends and corners of wall.) Place footing, then reattach perimeter lines to batter boards. Use a plumb line to mark corners and ends of wall on footing. Snap chalk lines between marks.

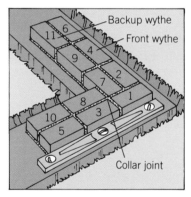

2. Lay first course dry, with backup wythe ½ in. behind front one. Adjust collar joints so that headers (step 3) will fit exactly across two wythes. Set first course of lead (stepped-back corner) in mortar in order shown. Butter ends and sides of backup bricks to create a solid mortar layer between wythes.

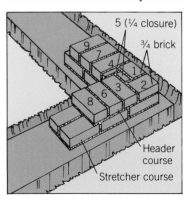

3. Use level and story pole to level, align, and plumb first course of lead. With a builder's square, check that corner is 90°. Start laying header course in order shown, using ¾ bricks at corner and ¼ closures to fill in. Shove each header into place, its buttered side pressed against adjoining brick.

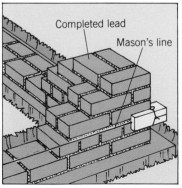

4. Complete the lead with three stretcher courses (headers and stretchers alternate at corners). Build leads at remaining corners and ends of wall. Fill in between leads, using mason's line as guide. For a taller wall, build leads on top of completed section, with every fifth or sixth course a header course.

5. The simplest way to cap a wall is with a course of headers laid on edge (rowlocks). Starting flush with one edge of a corner, lay rowlock course dry. Cut closure bricks as needed; insert them three or four bricks from ends. Lay rowlocks in mortar, buttering each succeeding brick on its broad face.

170

Building a brick barbecue

When planning a backyard barbecue, first consider the site and its prevailing summer breezes. Locate the barbecue downwind from your and your close neighbors' homes. Position it so that the wind will blow smoke away from the cook and the dining area. Consult your local building and fire departments before undertaking such a project.

Barbecue grills, fire grates, and ash trays are available at home centers and hardware stores. Buy these items first because they will determine the barbecue's dimensions.

If you have a sound concrete-slab patio, you can use part of it as the base for a barbecue. Otherwise build a new slab, following the directions for a basic walkway slab on pages 152–153. Make the slab 6 inches thick and at least 2 inches larger all around than the barbecue. Place the slab over a 6-inch gravel layer; reinforce it with 6-inch-square wire mesh (p. 157).

Built of SW-grade bricks (firebricks aren't needed), the barbecue at right is a three-wythe wall with corners, rising 13 courses high. The outermost wythe is in running bond; the inner wythes, in stack bond (pp. 168–169). Headers in every other course link the inner wythes, but the main structural bond is created by Z-shaped metal ties set in mortar between alternating courses and staggered vertically.

The grill, fire grate, and ash tray are supported by 7-inch lengths of ⅜-inch rebar embedded in the mortar joints between courses 7 and 8 (for the ash tray), 9 and 10 (for the fire grate), and 12 and 13 (for the grill). Cap the barbecue with a course of solid (uncored) bricks, as shown, or with a flagstone countertop cut to size (p. 181) and mortared in position.

A brick barbecue constructed without mortar

A mortarless barbecue is easy to build but requires a completely stable and level base. A concrete slab is best.

Standard SW-grade bricks are used to build the firebox and the adjacent optional work surface. The bricks are laid in a simple pattern consisting of alternating pairs of headers and stretchers. The inner bricks of the fourth and seventh courses project slightly into the firebox to support the grills.

Grill

4. Top course consists of an inner row of stretchers and an outer row of headers. If desired, attach brackets and a cutting board to the side of the barbecue, following directions on page 86 for drilling into masonry.

3. Before placing inner wythe of eighth course, set eight 7-in. lengths of rebar (four to a side) in bed joint, so that rods project 4 in. into firebox. Install rebars the same way above the 9th and 12th courses.

Z-tie

1. With a chalk line, outline barbecue on base slab. Lay first two courses without mortar, allowing for ½-in. mortar joints. Remove dry-run bricks. Spread a ½-in. mortar bed within the outline. Lay first course of bricks.

2. Build up corner leads three or four courses at a time, using a builder's square to make sure the corners are true right angles. Fill in between leads. Check your work often with story pole and level. Set Z-ties in mortar between every other course, staggering them vertically as shown.

Masonry / Brick veneer

In addition to solid brick walls (pp. 170–171), there are two other basic types of masonry walls. *Cavity walls* consist of two wythes of masonry units separated by a continuous 2- to 4½-inch air space but joined by noncorrodible corrugated metal wall ties. The front wythe may be face brick; the back one, either brick or concrete block.

A *brick veneer wall* is a single non-bearing wythe of bricks applied over an existing structure and anchored to it with metal wall ties so that a 1-inch space exists between the veneer and the backup. Although veneer walls are not structural, they must be solidly supported (see step 1, below). If the existing foundation footing is not wide enough to accommodate the veneer, the footing may have to be enlarged or steel angles bolted to the foundation. Such below-grade structural jobs are best left to professionals.

The air spaces in cavity and ve-neer constructions act as barriers to water seepage. Water that penetrates the outer wall and reaches the air space is channeled out by means of flashing and weep holes at the wall's base (step 2). In cavity walls the air spaces also provide insulation (and room for adding more).

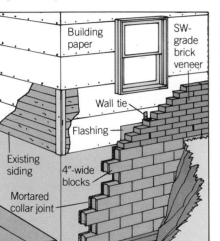

1. Veneer walls are built on existing footings, on footing extensions, or on steel angles bolted to the foundation 1 ft. below grade. Building paper covers existing siding. Below grade, veneer consists of 4-in.-wide concrete blocks mortared to foundation. Above grade, brick veneer and backup are separated by a 1-in. space but linked by wall ties every 32 in. horizontally, every 16 in. vertically, with rows offset.

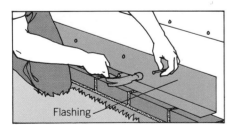

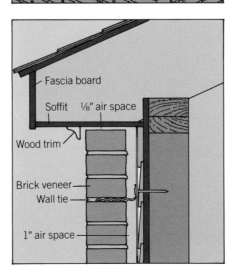

2. Flashing and weep holes drain water from wall. Flashing made of polyethylene, sheet metal, bituminous membrane, or a combination of these materials is installed at wall's base, one course above grade. In the next course, which is laid on mortar spread over bottom of flashing, weep holes are created every 2 ft. by omitting mortar from head joints or by setting rope wicks or plastic tubes in mortar.

3. Six-in. wall ties anchor veneer to backup. (Ties are bent in half. One leg is nailed to wall stud; the other is set in mortar between courses.) Window- and doorframe extensions may be needed to fit veneer. Tilted rowlocks are placed beneath each sill; steel lintels support bricks above windows and doors. Flashing and weep holes are required above wall openings and below sills.

4. As veneer wall goes up, air space behind it must be kept free of mortar or debris that could form moisture bridges. A space of at least ⅛ in. should separate top of veneer and soffit (underside of eaves). This gap is concealed by either fascia board or wood trim. If veneer does not fit behind fascia, eaves must be extended.

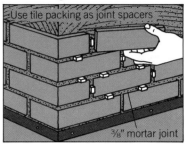

Veneering an interior wall

Applying a veneer of standard bricks to an interior wall often involves major structural work. An alternative is to cover the wall with ½-inch-thick brick tiles set in special brick adhesive mortar. The tiles are usually sold in packages containing enough straight and corner pieces to cover about 4 square feet of wall. The mortar, sold ready-mixed in gallon tubs (enough for 10 to 15 square feet of wall), is applied with a ¼-inch notched trowel.

Make sure the wall is clean, dry, and sound. Read package directions carefully. In general, work away from outside corners. To stagger the courses, alternate long and short ends of corner tiles. Smooth joints with a jointer.

A mortarless brick walkway

Whether set in mortar or laid on sand without mortar, bricks make an attractive and durable walkway or patio. For mortarless installation, use SW-grade paving bricks 4 inches wide, 8 inches long, and 1⅝ to 2¼ inches thick. (You'll need about 475 of these units to pave 100 square feet). Pavers can be laid in many different patterns, some of which are illustrated below. Because unmortared pavers tend to shift, a firm restraint is needed at the walk's perimeter. Four edging options are outlined on this page.

For proper drainage, slope the walk about ¼ inch per foot (p. 152). The most economical base for a mortarless brick walk is 2 inches of sand covered with roofing felt. (The felt prevents grass from growing between the bricks.) But where subsurface drainage is a problem, lay the bricks on a base consisting of 4 inches of gravel topped by a 1-inch layer of stone screenings (very fine gravel); cover with roofing felt.

Herringbone

Basket weave

Running bond

Ladder weave

Edgings

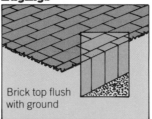
Brick-in-earth borders are easiest to install. Here, a row of *sailors* (bricks standing on end, side by side) is set in a narrow trench.

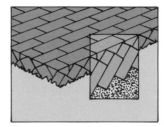
Tilted sailors, set in earth at a 45° angle, create a sawtooth edging. Support brick bases with packed earth; make sure tops are level.

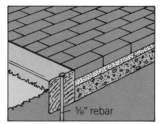
Landscaping ties make neat borders. Anchor each tie with 3-ft. lengths of rebar driven into holes drilled near ends and at center.

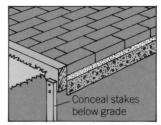
Redwood or pressure-treated 2 x 4's supported by stakes, as in concrete forms (pp. 152–153), can also serve as edging.

Pavers
Redwood 2 x 4
Pressure-treated stake
Roofing felt   Gravel   Stone screenings

1. Outline walk with stakes and strings (see step 1, p. 152). Lay at least part of walk in a dry run to work out problems with your chosen pattern. Remove bricks. Dig paving bed to required depth (brick thickness plus 2 in. for sand base; brick thickness plus 5 in. for a gravel base). Dig edging trench; install edging.

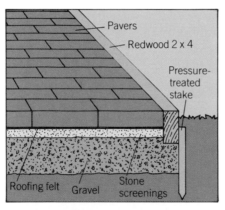
Notched screed

2. For a sand base, fill excavation with 2 in. of sand. Level with 2 x 4 screed cut to walk width and notched at ends to paver thickness. Moisten sand; compact it with a tamper (p. 153). Add new sand; spray and screed again. For a gravel base, place and screed 4 in. of gravel, then 1 in. of stone screenings.

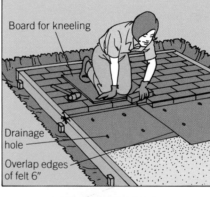
Board for kneeling
Drainage hole
Overlap edges of felt 6"

3. Cover base with 15-lb. roofing felt. For drainage, cut holes in felt with a knife blade. Starting at one corner of walk, lay bricks in chosen pattern. Place bricks firmly on felt, pressing them tightly against one another. Use a 2 x 4 or run a string across walk to keep the joints aligned. Level bricks by tapping lightly with a rubber mallet.

4. Fill gaps at edges with cut bricks (p. 165). When paving is done, adjust brick heights. Spread a layer of dry sand on bricks; sweep sand into joints. Repeat sanding at 2-day intervals until joints are filled and the bricks are stabilized. (You can also lay the bricks in dry mortar, as described on pages 184–185.)

173

Repointing joints. Even well-made mortar joints can suffer damage over time, especially when they are exposed to severe weather. Cracked or crumbling joints are not only unsightly, they also allow moisture to penetrate the wall, where it can freeze, causing even more extensive damage. Inspect exterior masonry every few years—before cold weather makes masonry work impractical—and repair damaged joints as soon as possible.

The process of fixing mortar joints, called *repointing* (or *tuck-pointing*),

involves chiseling out damaged mortar and replacing it with fresh mortar. You will need a small sledgehammer and a cape chisel (or a tuck-pointer's plugging chisel) to remove the old mortar; a joint filler and/or a pointing trowel to work mortar into the joints; and a joint finishing tool. If the damaged area is high up a wall, rent scaffolding (p.383).

New mortar should match the old as closely as possible in composition, color, and joint profile. This is especially important when repointing very

old or historic masonry, whose mortar may differ significantly in strength and flexibility from modern mortars. In this case, contact a preservation agency for the name of a mortar analyst. When repairing newer masonry whose mortar composition is unknown, use an all-purpose Type N mortar (pp.162–163).

To check the color match, mix a small batch of mortar, repoint an inconspicuous area of the wall, and then let the mortar dry (it will lighten in the process). If necessary, add a coloring agent to a new batch and test again.

Efflorescence

Efflorescence is the white powdery substance that sometimes forms on masonry and concrete surfaces. It occurs when internal moisture dissolves soluble salts present in concrete or mortar. The salt solution migrates to the surface, where the water evaporates, leaving behind deposits of crystallized salts.

The moisture in fresh mortar makes new structures especially prone to efflorescence. Masonry walls that are left uncovered and then exposed to rain during construction may also develop the condition. "New building bloom" is more unattractive than harmful and usually disappears on its own through normal weathering. Persistent efflorescence, however, may indicate a leak in the wall's flashing (p.172), a poorly sealed window opening or door jamb, or other drainage problems. Before the efflorescence can be treated, the source of excess moisture must be identified and corrected.

Brush off efflorescence with a stiff-bristled brush or wash it off with water. To eliminate other stains from masonry and concrete surfaces, see p.186.

1. Using a small sledgehammer and cape chisel (shown) or plugging chisel, remove mortar to a depth of at least 1 in. Hold chisel at a sharp angle; try not to chip bricks. Rake joints clean; leave a flat surface at back of cut.
CAUTION: Wear safety goggles when chiseling and cleaning out joints.

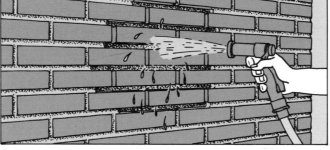

2. Brush joints with a stiff-bristled brush, or use compressed air to blow away loose material. Gently flush cleaned joints with fine spray from a garden hose. To prevent absorption of moisture from new mortar, joints should be damp (but not saturated) when filled.

3. Mix mortar (p.165) so that it's a little stiffer than bricklaying mortar. Spread a ½-in. layer on a hawk. Using back of pointing trowel (left), pick up a small mortar "sausage" and pack it into joint. (Fill vertical joints first, then horizontals.) Or slide mortar from hawk into joint with a joint filler (right).

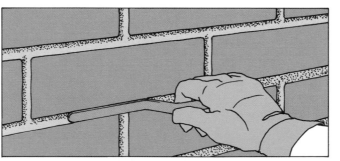

4. Fill deep joints in successive layers, and allow each layer to stiffen somewhat before applying the next one. When joints are completely filled, wait until they are thumbprint hard; then use a jointing tool to compress and shape them in the style of surrounding joints.

Bricklaying tools 164
Mixing and handling mortar 165
Finishing mortar joints 168

Damaged brickwork. Like defective joints, cracked or crumbling bricks weaken a wall by letting in moisture. Replace such bricks as soon as possible (see below). If the damage is in a stack-bond wall or in a critical load-bearing area such as above or below a window or doorway, consult a mason.

When restoring large sections of a wall, work from top to bottom, removing bricks individually by chiseling out the mortar between them. Build up the new section as if laying a new wall (pp. 166–167).

Remove mortar around damaged brick (step 1, facing page); wear safety goggles. Chip brick with chisel until it can be removed. Chisel out remaining mortar; brush and dampen cavity.

Butter base of cavity. Butter top and ends of a damp replacement brick. Place brick on hawk; press it into cavity. Add or trim off mortar as needed. Tool joints when thumbprint hard.

Replacing pavers. A loose, broken, sunken, or raised brick in a patio or walk can be hazardous. Bricks laid in sand (p. 173) are likelier to shift than mortared bricks but are easier to fix. Remove an out-of-level sand-laid brick with a pry bar; take out surrounding bricks by hand. Cut through building paper, if any. Remove or add sand as needed; tamp it down well. When the bed is level, reinstall bricks, replacing any damaged ones. Sweep fresh sand into joints. To replace loose or broken pavers set in mortar, see below.

1. Chip off mortar around bad brick with brick chisel (shown) or cape chisel. If necessary, break up the brick with chisel.

2. Remove brick with pry bar. Chip out crumbling mortar from cavity. Brush away debris. Dampen cavity and new brick.

3. Mortar base and sides of the cavity. Press brick in place. Level it by tapping with trowel handle. Trim excess mortar.

Grouting cracked walls

A long vertical crack in a concrete or brick wall may result from the normal structural settlement of a new building. When the building has settled, the crack will stabilize and can be filled. But such cracks—especially if they open again after being filled—can indicate a serious movement of the earth beneath the structure or a flaw in the foundation. When a large, persistent crack appears in a wall, call in an engineer or builder to determine and correct the underlying cause.

To repair a long vertical crack in a concrete wall, use a grout mix consisting of 1 part portland cement and 2 parts masonry sand, combined with enough water for a paintlike consistency. (Make the grout thin enough so that it flows easily through a funnel.)

To prepare the crack for grouting, chisel out loose concrete and debris, brush it with a stiff-bristled brush, and dampen it. Starting at the bottom and working up in sections no longer than 3 feet, cover the crack with wide waterproof adhesive tape. Pour grout into the taped section, using a funnel to direct the grout into the crack's center. Wait at least 4 hours for the grout to set before moving up to the next section. (To repair cracks in horizontal slabs, see p. 159; to seal cracks in basement walls, see pp. 338–340.)

In a masonry wall, a crack that follows the mortar joints can be repaired by tuck-pointing the joints (see facing page). But if the crack splits bricks as well as mortar, it is more difficult to repair. You can grout it as described above or simply caulk it. Either way, the repair will be visible.

1. Clean and dampen crack. Cover the bottom 3 ft. of the crack with heavy-duty adhesive tape. Insert a funnel into the top of the taped section; pour in grout.

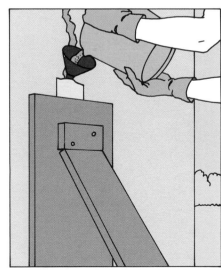

2. If tape adheres poorly, brace a board over it as shown. Let grout set for 4 hr. Remove board and tape. Move up the wall in sections, filling no more than 3 ft. at a time.

Masonry / Installing glass blocks

Bricks and mortar 162
Mixing and handling mortar 165
Finishing mortar joints 168

Made of two sections of pressed glass fused together with a partial vacuum between them, glass blocks transmit light while maintaining privacy, enhancing security, and providing thermal and acoustical insulation. They are often used in basement and bathroom windows, shower walls, and room dividers.

Clear, reflective, or patterned to permit varying degrees of light transmission, standard blocks are 3⅛ or 3⅞ inches thick. They come in 6-, 8-, and 12-inch squares and 4- x 8- and 6- x 8-inch rectangles (face dimensions are nominal, allowing for ¼-inch mortar joints). Hexagonal units are used to turn cor-

ners. End blocks may be used to finish the top or a side of interior walls and partitions.

Unlike bricks, glass blocks don't absorb moisture from the mortar they're set in. Because this slows the mortar's setting time, glass blocks tend to squeeze out wet mortar from between underlying courses. One solution is to install special plastic spacers between the blocks. When the mortar has set, twist off the ends of the spacers and fill the holes with mortar.

Glass block structures are not load-bearing. Glass block walls should be mortared to a concrete base and supported structurally on both sides or on the

top and one side. Although the shower wall shown below would normally require a floor-to-ceiling post along the entrance, extra reinforcement (step 7), securely bonded trim, and a sink top anchored to the wall (not shown) provide enough support. Panels larger than 25 square feet require expansion strips at tops and sides and a coat of asphalt emulsion on the sill, or bottom, plate. Before starting a glass block project, consult a building inspector.

A good mortar mix for glass block is 1 part white portland cement, 1 to 2 parts lime, and 4 to 6 parts sand. Make the mortar drier than for bricklaying.

1. Mark the height of each course of blocks along a plumb line on wall. Include ¼-in. spaces for mortar joints.

2. Lay trial row of blocks along concrete base, allowing ¼ in. between blocks for joints. Mark joint locations.

3. With a brick trowel, spread a ¾-in. layer of mortar evenly along base. Do not furrow the mortar.

4. Butter one end of each block with mortar, and place it against the previously laid block.

Glass block panels

Glass blocks come in preassembled panels that can be slipped into window openings and mortared in place. First remove window casings; then measure opening's width and height (from sill to rim joists or header). Give dimensions to glass block dealer.

To install panel, nail 2 x 4 stop block to header. Set two wedges on sill; slip panel into opening (have helper support it from inside). Tap wedges to center and level panel. Leave ¼-in. gap at top. Check for plumb. Pack sides and bottom with mortar; slope mortar at bottom away from panel for drainage. Let mortar set; remove stop block and wedges. Fill holes with mortar. Caulk gap at top, inside and out.

5. Align and adjust blocks with board, level, and trowel handle. Check each course for level, plumb, and alignment.

6. Embed special panel anchors in mortar between every other course. Screw end of anchor to wall stud.

7. Set reinforcing wire in unanchored mortar beds. Glass block dealers sell anchors, reinforcement, and spacers.

8. When joints are thumbprint hard, finish them with a jointer. Before mortar sets, gently wipe blocks with cloth.

Concrete blocks

Heavier than bricks and more utilitarian than either bricks or stones, concrete blocks are hard to beat in terms of price, versatility, and speed. Usually only one wythe thick, block walls are cheaper and faster to build than brick walls. Hollow-core blocks can be filled with insulation or reinforced (p. 179). If appearance is a factor, use decorative blocks, or you can veneer a plain block wall with stone or brick. Among the many uses of concrete blocks are foundations, exterior and interior walls, retaining walls, and garden screens.

Types of blocks. Standard blocks are precision molded from a mixture containing portland cement and gravel or crushed-stone aggregate. Lightweight blocks contain such aggregates as pumice or expanded shale, slate, clay, or slag. They're easier to handle than standard blocks, but slightly costlier.

Blocks are available in many sizes and shapes, in several decorative styles and finishes, and either solid, hollow, or with preformed insulating inserts. The most commonly used block is the hollow-core *stretcher* measuring 8 inches wide, 8 inches high, and 16 inches long (these dimensions are nominal, allowing for ⅜-inch mortar joints between blocks). Standard stretchers weigh about 40 pounds each; lightweight versions, as little as 25 pounds. Stretcher units usually have flanged ends and two or three hollow cores separated by partitions that taper from top to bottom, making it easier to grip the block. (The partitions are called *webs;* the cores, *cells;* the sides of the blocks, *face shells.*)

Corner blocks resemble stretchers except that one or both of their ends are flush. To establish a running bond pattern (p. 168) in a wall without corners, 8-inch cubes called *half* blocks are set at the ends of every other course. (Most block walls are laid in running bond.) *Partition* blocks, 4 or 6 inches wide and flush at both ends, are used as backing for stone or brick veneer as well as in partition walls. Specially shaped units are available to form control joints (p. 178), sills, jambs, and lintels.

Decorative blocks. *Split* blocks are cut apart to produce a stonelike texture on the exposed sur-

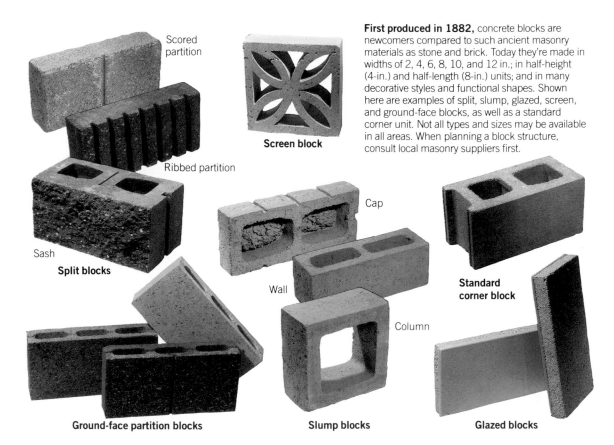

Scored partition

Screen block

Ribbed partition

Sash

Split blocks

Ground-face partition blocks

Cap

Wall

Column

Standard corner block

Slump blocks

Glazed blocks

First produced in 1882, concrete blocks are newcomers compared to such ancient masonry materials as stone and brick. Today they're made in widths of 2, 4, 6, 8, 10, and 12 in.; in half-height (4-in.) and half-length (8-in.) units; and in many decorative styles and functional shapes. Shown here are examples of split, slump, glazed, screen, and ground-face blocks, as well as a standard corner unit. Not all types and sizes may be available in all areas. When planning a block structure, consult local masonry suppliers first.

face. *Slump* blocks resemble adobe. The exposed surfaces of *architectural* blocks are ribbed, fluted, or otherwise patterned. *Screen,* or *grille,* blocks make attractive room dividers and garden screens (p. 179). *Ground-face* blocks are ground smooth to resemble terrazzo flooring.

Estimating block quantities. To calculate the number of standard-size blocks (8 x 8 x 16 inches) needed for a wall, use this formula:

Height of wall in feet × 1½ = number of courses (A). Length of wall in feet × ¾ = number of blocks per course (B). A × B = total number of blocks.

To reduce the need for cutting blocks, plan your project so that all dimensions are multiples of half- and full-size blocks. If there's an opening in a wall, calculate the number of blocks that would fit in it; then to allow for waste, subtract only half this number from your total. For every 100 square feet of solid wall, figure on 112½ standard-size blocks and 8½ cubic feet of mortar. Your masonry supplier can help you determine the number of corner, half, and special-shape units your project requires.

Have blocks delivered as close to the work site as possible. Store them on a dry platform (p. 163), and cover them with plastic sheeting. Unlike bricks, concrete blocks must be dry when laid in a wall.

Masonry/Building with concrete blocks

Whether for foundations or walls, the technique of laying concrete blocks is similar to brickwork. Check local building codes (p.193) before starting a concrete block project.

Block walls must rest on concrete footings that extend below the frost line. Snap a chalk line on the footing to mark the wall's front; then lay the first course of blocks without mortar, leaving ⅜-inch spaces between blocks for mortar joints. After adjusting the dry run and marking the joint spaces on the footing, remove the blocks and begin laying the first course on a full bed of mortar (step 1, at right). (Above the first course, mortar for the bed joints is usually applied only to the face shells, or outer edges, of the blocks.) Lay blocks with the thicker edges of their face shells up to provide a larger area for the mortar bed. Mix mortar as for bricks (p.165), but make it stiffer.

Build up leads first; then lay blocks between them, using a mason's line as a guide for each course (steps 3 and 4). Trim off excess mortar and tool the joints with a convex or V-jointer (p.168) as you proceed. Check your work often with story pole and level. To adjust a block, tap it lightly with the trowel handle while the mortar is still plastic.

To control cracking caused by temperature stresses and shrinkage, concrete block walls require continuous vertical control joints at 40-foot intervals and at wall openings and junctions. Control joints may not be needed in most residential projects, but they are essential in long stretches of wall. There are several ways of forming control joints in walls; one of the most common is illustrated in step 5.

1. Place and furrow a 1-in.-thick, 3-unit-long mortar bed on footing. Press first corner block into mortar to form ⅜-in. joint with footing. Align block with chalk line; level it in both directions.

2. Stand several blocks on end and butter their projecting flanges. Pick up a block by the thick end of its webs, lift buttered end slightly, and shove it against adjacent block.

3. Build up the leads, alternating stretcher and header corner units to create running bond pattern. Use level and story pole frequently to check for level, plumb, and alignment.

4. Use a mason's line stretched between leads as a guide for completing each course. To lay closure block, butter edges of opening as well as flanges on both ends of block. Set block in place.

5. Specially notched half- and full-length blocks are used to create continuous vertical control joints. Rubber joint material fits into the groove created by the control-joint blocks.

6. Intersecting walls can be connected with steel tie bars placed across joint between walls under every sixth course, or (as shown) with metal lath under every other course.

Foundation top must be solid to support floor joists. One way to build a solid course is to embed metal lath in bed joint under top course. Lay the course; fill cores with concrete or mortar.

Sill plates needn't rest on a solid course. To tie plates to blocks, embed 18-in.-long ½-in.-diameter anchor bolts in mortared cores of top two courses. To hold mortar, place lath under cores to be filled.

Cap a concrete block garden wall with solid or solid-top blocks. Mortar the cap blocks in place; make sure the vertical joints between blocks are completely filled.

Footings and foundations 156–158
Mixing and handling mortar 165
How to lay bricks 166–167

Reinforcing block walls

Overlap lengths of ½-in. *horizontal* or *vertical rebar* by about 15 in.; tie them together with 8-gauge iron wire

For extra horizontal reinforcement, embed girder-type *joint reinforcement* in bed joints under every second course

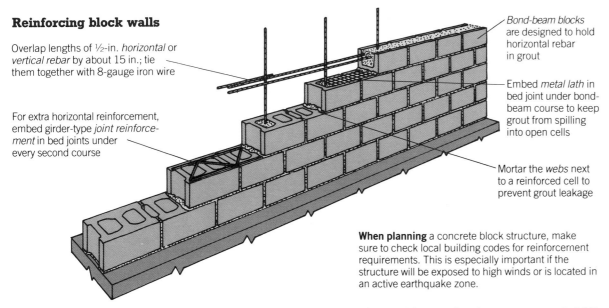

Bond-beam blocks are designed to hold horizontal rebar in grout

Embed *metal lath* in bed joint under bond-beam course to keep grout from spilling into open cells

Mortar the *webs* next to a reinforced cell to prevent grout leakage

When planning a concrete block structure, make sure to check local building codes for reinforcement requirements. This is especially important if the structure will be exposed to high winds or is located in an active earthquake zone.

In a situation requiring extra strength, a block wall can be reinforced both vertically and horizontally. Vertical reinforcing rods (rebars) embedded in the wall's footing extend up through hollow-core blocks. As the wall rises, the cells containing rebars are filled with a portland cement grout (p.163).

Special blocks called *bond-beam blocks* are shaped to hold rebars horizontally in grout. A course of reinforced bond-beam blocks at the top of any concrete block wall greatly enhances its strength.

Finishing concrete block walls

After a block wall has cured (allow at least 3 days), it can be can faced with brick or stone veneer (pp.172, 182), painted (p.367), or coated with stucco—a thick, creamy mix of cement, lime, sand, and water (p.412).

Stucco is usually applied in three coats, but for new masonry two are enough. After dampening the wall, use a steel trowel (p.147) to coat it with a ⅜-inch stucco layer. When this *scratch coat* has partially hardened, score it with a comblike tool called a scarifier. Keep the scratch coat damp for 2 days; then apply a ¼-inch-thick finish coat.

To moistureproof new basement walls, coat their outer surfaces with a ½-inch layer of plaster (a 1:2½ cement-sand mix, applied in two coats like stucco). At the footing, trowel the plaster into a cove shape. Dampproof and, if needed, waterproof the cured walls (p.158); provide for drainage (p.340).

Mortarless construction. Applied to both sides of a dry-stacked block wall, fiberglass-reinforced plaster creates a stronger bond than mortar joints. Mortarless construction requires careful workmanship and is best used in small projects. Reinforced plaster may not be sold or accepted everywhere; consult your building department and masonry suppliers.

Screen block walls

Because they're usually laid in stack bond (p.169), an inherently weak pattern, screen block walls require especially careful planning and workmanship.

For vertical support, build piers into the wall at intervals no greater than 10 feet. The piers are made of hollow-core blocks with vertical channels on one or both sides to hold the screen blocks. To reinforce the piers, stack the blocks around a rebar embedded in the footing; grout their cores. The footing should be twice as wide as the piers; make sure it extends below the frost line. Start by building the piers high enough to accommodate two courses of screen blocks; then lay the blocks in mortar between pairs of piers. For taller walls, embed joint reinforcement (above) under every second course.

Butter vertical edge of block

⅜" mortar joint

1. Lay first course dry. Snap chalk lines on footing to mark position of screen. Mortar pier blocks in place, making sure their channels align with chalk lines. Working in from pairs of piers, lay first two courses in mortar, making sure vertical joints align exactly.

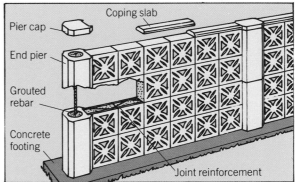

Coping slab

Pier cap

End pier

Grouted rebar

Concrete footing

Joint reinforcement

2. If screen is to be more than two courses high, place joint reinforcement in bed joints under every second course. (Overlap wire by length of a block.) Build wall to a maximum height of 6 ft. Top it off with pier cap and coping slabs laid on mortar bed.

The most ancient of building materials, stone is also one of the most durable, attractive, and satisfying to work with. On the negative side, stonemasonry involves hard work and can be expensive, unless you live in an area where stones are abundant.

Types of stone. Although the two terms are often used synonymously, *stone* is the building material obtained from *rock* found in nature. Granite, limestone, sandstone, marble, and slate are the stones most often used in masonry. Hard, durable, and costly, *granite* is primarily a building stone, while the more easily worked *limestones* and *sandstones* are used for both building and veneering. (All three types of stone are suitable for the stone wall projects on pages 181–183.) *Marble* is an ornamental stone prized for its elegance and ability to take a high polish. *Slate* splits easily into thin slabs for roofing shingles and paving (flagstones).

All stones can be divided into two broad categories. *Fieldstones* are loose pieces of rock that have separated naturally from underlying bedrock and are found scattered on the ground in fields or alongside rivers and creeks.

Blasted or cut from bedrock, *quarried stone* has freshly exposed sharp-edged surfaces that contrast with the weathered look of fieldstone. The cheapest grade of quarried stone is *rubble*—uncut, unsized stone left over from the quarrying process. *Semidressed stone* is rough-cut into rectangular or square shapes and sorted by size; it usually requires further trimming after purchase. *Flagstones* for paving (pp. 184–185) are made by splitting stones into thin slabs. The costliest grade of quarried stone is *dressed stone,* or *ashlar,* which is carefully squared, trimmed, and sized to the buyer's specifications.

The term *ashlar* also refers to the type of construction in which stones are laid in regular horizontal courses. In *rubble masonry,* untrimmed or rough-cut stones are laid in a random pattern without courses.

Obtaining stones. In rocky areas, you may be able to find all the stones you need free for the hauling, either on your own property or in nearby fields. Remember to ask for permission before removing stones from private property. Make sure your source is accessible to a trailer or pickup truck, and be careful not to overload the vehicle. Deposit the stones as close as possible to your building site.

Look for stones with a solid base, a flat top, and one or more straight, flat sides. For a wall with corners, you'll need a supply of stones with two flat sides that meet at a right angle. Your project will go faster if you use larger stones, but you will soon tire if they are too heavy. Try to select pieces that weigh less than 30 pounds. When lifting heavy stones, bend your knees, keep your back straight, and let your legs do most of the work.

If you can't get stones for free, buy them from a local stone yard or quarry. Visit several suppliers and compare inventories and prices. Ask to check the stones before delivery to make sure that most are the right size and shape for your project.

Estimating quantities. Flagstones for paving are sold by the square foot. To determine the square footage of a walk or patio, see p. 148; add an extra 10 percent for waste. Building stones are sold by the ton or by the cubic yard. If you figure a wall's cubic volume (multiply height by length by width in feet; then divide by 27 to convert to cubic yards), your supplier will be able to determine how much stone you need. If you are using cut stones, buy 10 percent extra for waste. Because a volume of rubble dumped into a truck can be a third or more air, buy at least 25 percent more than the wall's estimated volume.

Four types of stone walls

A rustic dry wall is built of fieldstones laid without mortar in a random pattern determined by the shapes of individual pieces.

This retaining wall, constructed of fieldstones laid in mortar without regular coursing, is a good example of wet-wall construction (p.182).

Quarried rubble, including some massive pieces, was used to build this mortared and uncoursed freestanding wall.

A variety of textures and shades enhance the appeal of this coursed wall, made of semi-dressed quarry stones set in mortar.

Building a dry stone wall

A stone wall usually consists of two wythes (parallel tiers) of larger stones, with smaller stones serving as filler between the wythes. To tie the structure together, *bonding stones*—long, flat stones spanning the wall's full width—are set at regular intervals in the wall.

A dry, or mortarless, stone wall is held together by friction and gravity alone. To keep such a wall from collapsing, the weight of each stone must press straight down on the stones below it. Position each piece so that it rests securely on a firm, flat bed and overlaps two or more stones in the underlying course. The resulting pattern, with staggered vertical joints, roughly resembles the running bond pattern in brickwork (p. 168). For greater stability, the ends and faces of the wall are *battered* (sloped toward the center) about 1 inch per foot of height.

A low dry wall can be built in a flat, shallow earth trench. For walls higher than 3 feet, you may have to dig below the frost line—check your local building code. (Unless you're a practiced stonemason, it's best to limit the height to 3 feet.) Make the width of the base two-thirds the wall's height.

You can trim a stone with a stonemason's hammer, but to split one you will need a stone chisel and a small sledgehammer. Wear leather gloves when handling stones; use safety goggles when cutting them. Try to observe a stonemason cutting stones before attempting to do it yourself.

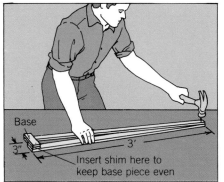

1. To check the wall's batter (slope), make a *batter gauge* by nailing three 1 x 2's to form a 90° triangle. Its height should equal the wall's height; its base, the required batter (1 in. per ft. of height).

2. Outline wall with stakes and string. For a wall up to 3 ft. tall, dig a level 6-in.-deep trench. Set bonding stones at both ends of trench and every 4 ft. between. Using the heaviest stones, lay first course.

3. Make first course as level as possible. Place each stone with its flattest side up, its next-best side facing out. Dig deeper if needed to seat a stone more securely. Fill center with small stones.

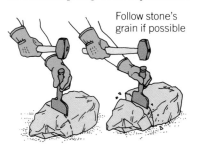

To cut fieldstone, mark cutting line with grease pencil. Place stone on sand or earth; use chisel and sledgehammer to score along line. Place chisel on scored line; strike hard with hammer.

4. Using string line and batter gauge as guides, lay second course so that it's set in slightly from the first. Slope large stones toward center. Stagger vertical joints; place bonding stones every 4 ft.

5. Build up wall course by course, choosing stones that fit snugly and make a fairly even bed for next course. Use small stones as needed to shim up larger ones and to fill chinks.

6. Save the broadest, flattest stones for capstones (wall's top course). Most capstones should span the width of the wall. To prevent frost damage, set the top course in mortar (p.182).

To cut flagstone, mark and score cutting line on both sides. Place stone on a 2 x 4, with scored line 1 in. beyond edge of board. Knock off waste end by tapping it with a small sledgehammer.

Masonry / Mortared stone walls

Unlike dry stone walls, which are flexible and move with the earth, mortared walls are rigid. To prevent cracking caused by ground heave in winter, a mortared wall needs a concrete footing—preferably reinforced (p.158)—whose base rests on gravel or compacted soil below the frost line. The footing for a stone wall is usually at least 6 inches thick and 6 inches wider than the wall's base; check local building codes for exact specifications.

The techniques for dry-laying stone walls (p.181) also apply to mortared stone walls. Place the largest, heaviest stones at the base; the broadest and flattest pieces at the top; and rubble in the center of the wall. Lay each stone so that its top surface slopes toward the wall's center, not out or to one side. Stagger the vertical joints by laying one stone over two or two over one. Install bonding stones at regular intervals in each course.

Mortared walls can be built with straight sides or with a slight batter (inward slope) of ½ inch per foot of height. They can also be less massive than dry walls. A mortared wall 3 feet high, for example, can be 18 inches wide, as opposed to 24 inches for a dry wall. (You may need a permit to build a wall higher than 3 feet; consult your local building department.)

A standard mortar mix for stone masonry is 1 part portland cement to 3 or 4 parts sand; to increase the mortar's workability, some masons add ½ part fireclay (p.162) instead of the usual hydrated lime, which can stain stones. The mortar should be thicker than for brickwork; the stones must be clean and dry before they're set in mortar.

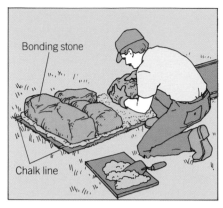

Bonding stone

Chalk line

2 x 4 brace

Wedge

1. Snap chalk lines on footing to mark wall faces. Lay first course dry, with bonding stones at both ends and every 4 ft. between. Starting at one end, remove stones; spread a 2-in.-thick mortar bed on footing. Set stones in mortar. Use pointing trowel to pack mortar into vertical joints. Fill center of wall with rubble and mortar.

3. To keep a heavy stone from squeezing mortar out of its bed joint, insert wooden wedges in joint. When mortar sets, remove wedges; fill holes with mortar. Use a 2 x 4 to brace large, irregularly shaped stones until mortar sets. Add no more than 2 ft. a day to wall's height; otherwise, stones' weight may force mortar out of underlying joints.

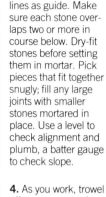

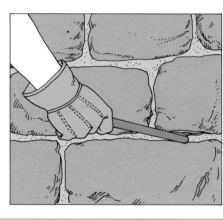

2. Build up wall in courses, using string lines as guide. Make sure each stone overlaps two or more in course below. Dry-fit stones before setting them in mortar. Pick pieces that fit together snugly; fill any large joints with smaller stones mortared in place. Use a level to check alignment and plumb, a batter gauge to check slope.

4. As you work, trowel off excess mortar from joints; clean stone faces with wet sponge. When mortar joints are thumbprint hard (in about 30 min.), rake them with a stick to a depth of up to 1½ in.; or point them as for brickwork (p.168). Use stiff-bristled brush to smooth joints and remove mortar particles from stones.

Stone veneer

An easier, less expensive way to duplicate the look of a stone wall is to face a reinforced concrete block wall (pp.177–179) with a veneer of natural stone or of lighter, cheaper (but quite realistic) synthetic stone. Supported by the footing of the wall it covers, the veneer is set in mortar, with larger pieces at the bottom and vertical joints staggered. Wall ties (p.172), spaced 2 feet apart horizontally and offset from course to course, reinforce the bond between veneer and wall.

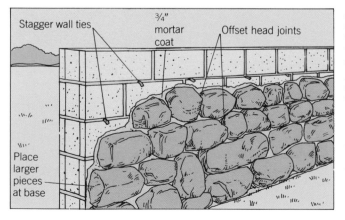

Stagger wall ties

¾" mortar coat

Offset head joints

Place larger pieces at base

Attach wall ties to existing block wall with masonry fasteners (pp.86–87); or insert ties in bed joints between courses as a new wall is being built. Using a steel trowel (p.147), apply ¾-in. mortar coat to wall; set veneer pieces in mortar, bending wall ties into mortar joints between stones.

Stone retaining walls

Built to hold back the earth on sloping land, retaining walls are used to control erosion and create level terraces. Because such walls must be extra-strong to withstand the pressure of earth and water behind them, their construction is usually strictly regulated by local building codes. Be sure to obtain all necessary permits before undertaking such a project.

Retaining walls can be built of concrete, concrete block, brick, pressure-treated landscaping ties, or stone (dry or mortared). The simplest type of retaining wall is made of stones set in earth rather than mortar, a technique that dates back to Roman times.

The first step in building an earth-and-stone retaining wall is to excavate the slope to form an L-shaped terrace whose vertical leg tilts back slightly into the hillside. At the excavation's base, dig a flat trench 6 inches deep and 2½ feet wide (for a 3-foot-high wall). Lay the first course as for a free-standing dry wall (p. 181), but leave a 6-inch space between the wall and the hillside. After you've laid the first course, fill this space with gravel for drainage, pack soil into the joints between the wall stones, and cover the stones with a compacted layer of soil.

As you build up the wall, stagger the vertical joints, bed each course in a layer of soil, and fill the space behind the wall with gravel. Inset each course to create a batter, or slope, of 2 inches per foot of height. For a decorative look, cap the wall with a layer of sod and insert plants in the joints.

A mortared stone retaining wall (right) must rest on a concrete footing below the frost line. Building techniques are the same as for a freestanding wall (see facing page), except that the front face of the retaining wall must be battered 1 inch per foot of height.

Whether built of stone, concrete, or brick, a retaining wall requires good drainage. Without it, water pressure can build up behind the wall and eventually topple it. When excavating the site for a retaining wall of mortared stone, leave a foot of space behind the wall for a fill of drain rock and gravel.

To allow underground water to seep through the wall, space weep holes at 2-foot intervals along its base. Create the weep holes by placing ¾-inch plastic pipes in the mortar bed between the first and second above-grade courses. Make sure the pipes extend all the way through the wall and slope down from back to front.

Begin backfilling after the wall has cured for 48 hours. Install 4-inch perforated drainpipe behind the wall, about 6 inches below grade. Embed the pipe in at least a foot of drain rock, cover the rock with filter fabric, and continue backfilling with coarse gravel topped with about 15 inches of topsoil.

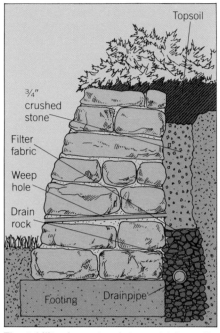

The stability of a mortared stone retaining wall depends on good drainage.

Raising and moving large stones

Two 2 x 4's, worked in opposition, serve as levers to dislodge boulders. After loosening stone with pick and shovel, pry it with one 2 x 4, then with the other, until you can use one of the levers as a ramp to get stone out of hole.

Move large stones short distances with a logging chain hooked to a vehicle or winch. After attaching chain, flip rock over. Chain's upward pull keeps rock from digging into earth. Exercise caution when moving large stones.

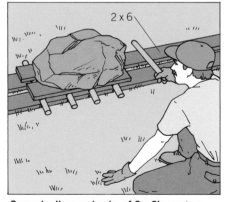

Several rollers and pairs of 2 x 6's create a temporary moving roadway for transporting a large stone over limited distances. Lay stone on a pair of 2 x 6's over rollers. Pick rollers up from rear and lay them in front of advancing stone.

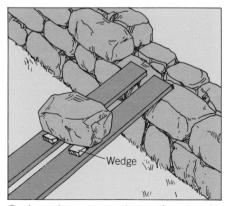

To place a large stone at the top of a wall under construction, roll it up an improvised ramp. Use long boards to create a gradual slope. Place wooden wedges under stone to keep it from rolling back.

Masonry/Patio construction

When choosing materials for a patio, consider the style of your house. A tile or brick patio may suit a formal house, whereas flagstones or adobe blocks have a more informal look. The 24- x 24- x 2-inch flagstones in the patio shown here complement a wide variety of contemporary styles. Precast concrete slabs or patio blocks are the least expensive paving units; ceramic tiles, the costliest.

A patio is only as durable as its base. The simplest, most flexible base consists of sand alone or sand over gravel (p.173). Sand-bedded paving units, however, are vulnerable to frost heave and may require adjustment each spring. Laying the pavers in wet mortar over a concrete slab provides the greatest durability but is costly and time-consuming. A third option, described here, combines the convenience of sand bedding with some of the permanence of wet-mortaring. In the dry-mortar method, paving units are laid on a base consisting of 3 to 4 inches of gravel topped by a 3-inch layer of dry-mix mortar (five bags of portland cement per cubic yard of masonry sand). Joints between pavers are filled with more dry mix; then the surface is wetted to set the mortar.

Planning a patio. Sketch a plan on graph paper; allow for ½-inch joints between paving units. For a border of plants between house and patio, allow

Paving materials

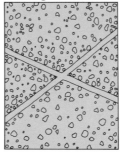

Aggregrate panels consist of ⅜- to ¾-in. pebbles embedded in concrete. They are available in 18- × 18- × 1½-in. units at garden and home centers. The panels can be laid on a base of sand or mortar.

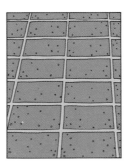

Adobe blocks laid in sand make attractive and durable patios in arid regions such as the southwestern United States but are likely to crumble in colder, wetter climates.

Ceramic tiles lend a formal air. They come in a range of colors and textures, but their cost is high. Being light and thin, ceramic tiles are best set in mortar over a concrete slab.

Irregularly shaped flagstones cost less than rectangular ones shown on facing page, but are more difficult to lay and may be less strong. Set them in wet mortar over a concrete slab. To cut flagstones, see p.181.

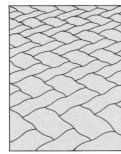

Interlocking concrete pavers, typically measuring 4 × 8 × 2⅜ in., make attractive and durable patios. Like brick pavers (p.173), interlocking concrete pavers are set in sand, but they are less likely to shift out of alignment.

Patio blocks are lightweight concrete paving slabs. They typically measure 8 × 15 × 2 in. and come in pastel colors. Lay them on sand; sweep sand into joints between blocks. Don't use for driveways or heavily trafficked walks.

Walkways 152–153
Bricks and mortar 162–163
Working with stone 180–181

at least 18 inches. For a tree within or near the patio, leave an unpaved surface around it equal to 1 foot for each foot of trunk diameter when full grown.

To ensure proper drainage, slope the patio away from the house. To do this on a flat site, outline the patio with mason's line tied to stakes, hang a line level (p.47) on the strings, and adjust level (p.47) on the strings, and adjust

the strings until they're level. Then lower the strings on the outer stakes by ¼ inch per foot of width. Thus the outer edge of a 12-foot patio would be 3 inches lower than the edge near the house. If your patio site slopes sharply away from the house, you may have to add fill and a retaining wall (p.183).

Ordering materials. Look in the

Yellow Pages for suppliers of stone, brick, and masonry materials; let the supplier figure the number of paving units required. In general, it takes 475 4- x 8-inch brick or concrete pavers or 25 24- x 24-inch flagstones to pave 100 square feet. To figure the square footage of your patio and the cubic volume of gravel, sand, or dry mix you will

need, see the formulas on page 148.

Before delivery, clear space near the work site where materials can be unloaded. If a truck can be driven to the site, ask the driver to dump the gravel into the excavated base. If sand and gravel must be dumped on the lawn, protect it with plastic sheets. Be sure to enlist a helper for this project.

Laying a flagstone patio in dry mortar

1. After outlining the patio area, make sure that it's parallel with the house; check corners with a framing square. Hang a line level on strings and make all strings level. Then lower strings on outer stakes to slope the patio (see text).

2. Dig out patio area to a depth of 8 in. (3 in. for gravel, 3 in. for mortar, 2 in. for pavers). Loosen hard soil with a pick before shoveling it into a wheelbarrow for removal. (When pushing wheelbarrow over string, have helper hold down string with his foot.)

3. Shovel in a layer of gravel 3 in. deep. Spread the gravel evenly with a rake. Make sure the depth is accurate by measuring it in several places — the surface of the gravel should be 5 in. below grade.

4. Mix 1 part portland cement to 5½ parts masonry sand. If your wheelbarrow has a 3-cu.-ft. capacity, fill it with sand and blend in half a bag of cement. Spread a 3-in. layer of dry mix over the gravel; level it with the rake.

5. Move the heavy flagstones into position by "walking" them along the ground, advancing first one corner, then the other. Align a stone's edges with the strings and drop the stone into position on the dry mix.

6. Lay a 2 x 4 across each stone; place a level on the 2 x 4 to check that the stone is level. To firm and level a stone, lay a 1 x 1 on it and tap the wood (never the stone) with a small sledgehammer. Pack dry mix under edges of stone.

7. When you have laid one row of stones, drive stakes at each end of the row and stretch a string between the stakes so that it touches the tops of the flagstones. Check that all the stones are even with one another.

8. Use a brick trowel (p.164) to fill joints with dry mix. Press mix into place with a joint filler (shown; see also p.174). After all joints have been filled, sweep off excess mortar to keep it from staining stones. Gently hose down patio to set the mortar.

Concrete and masonry surfaces generally require little maintenance. New structures may develop efflorescence, a powdery deposit that is usually easy to brush or wash off (p.174). Mortar smears on brick or concrete block surfaces can be removed with a weak muriatic acid wash, described below.

The safest, least abrasive way to clean older structures is by scrubbing with water and a stiff-bristled fiber brush. If water is not enough, add a mild household detergent to it. Don't use steel brushes, which may leave scratch marks and cause rust stains.

A heavy accumulation of dirt may require more aggressive cleaning methods, such as steam cleaning, high-pressure water blasting, or sandblasting—treatments best left to qualified cleaning contractors.

A variety of chemical products are available for removing dirt and specific stains from concrete and masonry. Chemical cleaners are applied in liquid form with a brush or sprayer; in some cases (see below) the cleaning agents are mixed with inert absorbent materials such as whiting, talc, clay, or fuller's earth and applied as a poultice to the stain.

▶ **CAUTION**: Concrete and masonry cleaning products can be corrosive and highly toxic; handle them with great care. Follow package directions. Wear rubber gloves and safety goggles. Provide adequate ventilation when working indoors. Always test a cleaner on an inconspicuous part of the surface to be cleaned. Saturate the surface with water before and after applying a chemical cleaner. Protect windows, doors, and trim from contact with the cleaner. Do not use acid cleaners on stones or on black, gray, brown, tan, or light-colored bricks.

Removing stains from concrete and block

● **Bitumens (asphalt, tar, or pitch):** Scrape off bitumen (applying dry ice to molten tar makes it easier to remove). Scrub stain with household scouring powder and water. Rinse with water. If stain has penetrated deeply, apply a poultice made by mixing talc or whiting with kerosene or benzene. Let poultice stand until it dries; then brush it off with stiff-bristled brush. Scrub with scouring powder; rinse well.

● **Chewing gum:** Scrape off gum. Apply a poultice made of denatured alcohol mixed with talc or whiting. When paste has dried, brush it off with a stiff-bristled brush. Scrub with scouring powder; rinse.

● **Copper or bronze:** Mix 1 part ammonium chloride (sal ammoniac) with 4 parts talc or whiting; add enough household ammonia to make a smooth paste. Apply poultice to stain; let stand until dry. Brush off and repeat if necessary. Scrub and rinse with water.

● **Graffiti:** Apply commercial spray-paint remover following manufacturer's directions.

● **Iron rust:** Brush stain with a solution of 1 lb. oxalic acid crystals per gal. of water. Let stand for 3 hr.; scrub and rinse with water.

● **Mildew:** Using a soft brush, apply a solution of 1 oz. laundry detergent, 3 oz. trisodium phosphate (TSP), 1 qt. chlorine bleach, and 3 qt. water. Rinse with water.

● **Mortar smears:** Same treatment as for brick.

● **Oil and grease:** Scrape off excess oil or grease. Scrub soiled area with scouring powder or masonry detergent. Rinse well with water. If stain persists, apply a commercial degreaser or emulsifying agent (available at masonry and automotive supply dealers).

● **Paint (wet):** Soak up wet paint with soft cloth or paper towels; try not to spread the stain as you blot up the paint. Scrub the stain with scouring powder and water. Wait 3 days, then treat as you would a dry paint stain (below).

● **Paint (dry):** Scrape off as much hardened paint as possible. Apply a commercial paint remover, following manufacturer's directions. Scrub off any residue with scouring powder and water. If the color has penetrated the surface, try removing it with a weak solution of muriatic acid (see *Mortar smears,* below).

● **Smoke:** Scrub stain with commercial scouring powder and rinse with water. Cover persistent stains with a poultice made of talc or whiting mixed with laundry bleach.

Removing stains from brick surfaces

● **Bitumens:** Same treatment as for concrete.

● **Brown stain:** Occurs when bricks containing manganese dioxide coloring agents are washed with an acid solution. To remove stain, soak surface with water; then brush on a solution of 2 parts peracetic acid (or 1 part acetic acid and 1 part hydrogen peroxide) in 6 parts water. When reaction has ended, flush surface with water.
CAUTION: This solution is dangerous. Mix and handle carefully. Wear protective clothing and goggles; provide adequate ventilation.

Instead of acid cleaners, use cleaners specially formulated for bricks containing manganese; follow package directions.

● **Copper or bronze:** Same treatment as for concrete.

● **Graffiti:** Same treatment as for concrete.

● **Green stain:** Vanadium salts used in the manufacture of certain bricks can cause a yellow or green efflorescence—usually after bricks have been washed with an acid solution. To remove stain, soak surface with water. Brush on a solution of ½ lb. sodium hydroxide per qt. of water. Let stand for 2 or 3 days; rinse well with water.
CAUTION: Sodium hydroxide, a component of household drain cleaners, is caustic and toxic; mix and handle it carefully.

Masonry suppliers sell cleaning compounds formulated to remove green stain; use according to manufacturer's directions.

● **Iron rust:** Same treatment as for concrete.

● **Mortar smears:** To reduce the need for later cleaning, tool joints carefully when they're thumbprint hard and brush bricks as soon as mortar has dried. After a brick structure has cured for about a week, remove large mortar particles with a nonmetallic scraper. To wash off smears, prepare a 10% solution of hydrochloric (muriatic) acid by adding 1 part acid to 9 parts clean water. Mix the solution in a nonmetallic container; add the acid to the water, *never* the other way around. Saturate the area to be cleaned with water before brushing on the acid solution. Let stand 5 to 10 min., then rinse thoroughly with water. In addition to muriatic acid, masonry suppliers sell a variety of brick cleaning compounds.

● **Moss:** Apply commercial weed killer according to package directions. For residual stains, use treatment recommended for removing *Mildew* from concrete (see above).

● **Oil and grease:** Same treatment as for concrete.

● **Paint:** Same treatment as for concrete.

● **Smoke:** Same treatment as for concrete.

Cleaning stone

● **Granite:** Wash with a mild laundry detergent. Rinse with water. Wipe surface dry; polish with a piece of chamois.

● **Limestone and sandstone:** Scrub with a stiff-bristled fiber brush and water. Don't use detergent on these stones.

● **Slate:** Wash with a mild laundry detergent. Rinse, then polish with pumice powder on a dampened felt pad.

● **Synthetic stone:** If washing with a mild laundry detergent fails to clean synthetic stone, scrub it with medium-fine pumice powder; rinse with plenty of water.

● **Marble:** Wipe off dirt with a damp sponge; buff dry. To remove stubborn dirt, apply dry borax with a damp cloth; rinse with warm water and buff dry. To remove grease or oil stains, apply a poultice made of talc or whiting mixed to a paste with acetone (nail polish remover). Let paste stand overnight; then sponge it off and buff marble. To remove food stains, use a poultice made of hydrogen peroxide and a few drops of household ammonia mixed with talc or whiting.

Chapter nine

Your house
Structures, and planning improvements

Contents

In a way, a house resembles the human body. Look at it, and what you see is the "skin," but not what's under the skin. Like the body, a house has a skeleton that supports it—the framing. The framing is covered with flooring, siding, and wallboard, plaster, or paneling, but beneath this skin is a network of plumbing and electrical lines, and insulation to keep out cold and heat.

Before making repairs that go more than skin deep, you will need to know what's inside your house's walls, beneath its floors, above its ceilings, and under its roof. This chapter is specially designed to help you find out. It also contains some general advice on how to go about planning and financing major repairs or improvements to your home, and how to select and deal with contractors. The chapter concludes with a few hints on making your home meet your special needs as you grow older or if someone in your family is handicapped.

Platform framing

A house with platform framing, the most common of all the types of wood framing, is like a stack of lidless boxes topped with a roof. During construction, the walls—studs, sills, and plates—can be nailed together on the subfloor and raised into place.

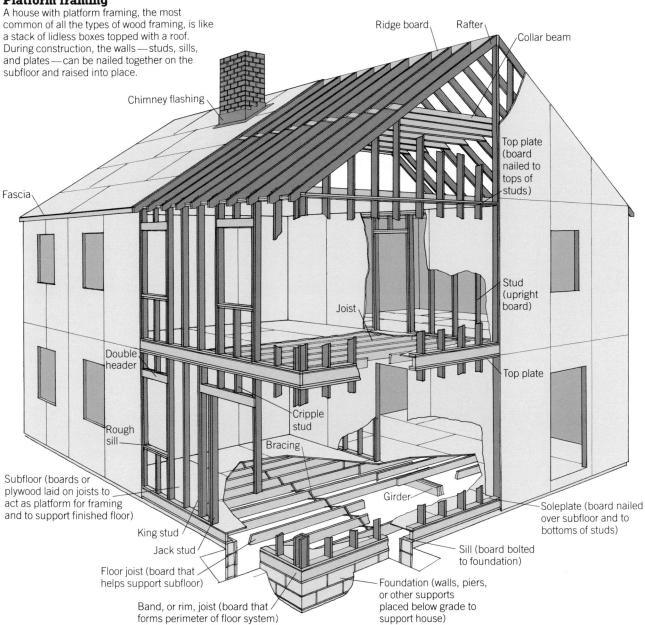

Ridge board

Rafter

Collar beam

Chimney flashing

Top plate (board nailed to tops of studs)

Fascia

Stud (upright board)

Joist

Double header

Top plate

Rough sill

Cripple stud

Bracing

Subfloor (boards or plywood laid on joists to act as platform for framing and to support finished floor)

Girder

Soleplate (board nailed over subfloor and to bottoms of studs)

King stud

Jack stud

Sill (board bolted to foundation)

Floor joist (board that helps support subfloor)

Band, or rim, joist (board that forms perimeter of floor system)

Foundation (walls, piers, or other supports placed below grade to support house)

If you are planning to make major repairs or improvements to your house, you need to have some idea of how it is constructed. Even though you may not be making any structural changes, you will need to know what to expect if you cut into a wall—whether you're putting in a door or window or simply installing an electrical box.

Houses have various styles of framing—the hidden structure, or skeleton, that supports the walls and roof. Most houses have framing made of softwood lumber, but some are framed with steel. In houses with walls of solid brick, stone, concrete block, or adobe, there is generally no underlying framing, but there may be reinforcement.

The dimensions of the framing material are governed by building codes. If you are replacing or adding framing members to your house, be sure to check your local codes (p.193).

Platform framing. In this most common type of framing, the subfloor of the first story extends to the outside edges of the foundation and forms a platform upon which the walls of the house rest. The framing consists mainly of 2 x 4's, 2 x 6's, and wider boards that are used as studs, joists, and plates, as shown in the illustration at left.

Balloon framing. Many houses built between the 1830's and the 1940's have balloon framing. In this system, the walls are nailed to studs (generally 2 x 4's) that extend the entire height of the frame, from the sill to the roof plate, even when there is more than one story. Wood fire-stops of the same thickness and width as the studs should be present at each floor level, at the midpoints between the floors, and between the outer ends of the joists. These keep the vertical and horizontal spaces from acting as flues in the event of fire. Balloon framing is rarely used in new houses because of the high cost and general unavailability of the long lumber needed for the studs.

Post-and-beam framing. An even older type of framing, post-and-beam is enjoying a revival because of the expansive spaces it creates. Horizontal wood beams, which support the subfloors and roof of the house, are connected to upright wood posts with mortise-and-tenon joints (pp. 104–105) or some other strong joint.

The beams are generally 6 inches wide and 10 inches deep. Posts that support the subfloors are usually 8 inches thick; those that hold up the roof, 6 inches thick. The posts are set 6, 7, or 8 feet apart, in contrast to other wood-framing techniques in which studs are set 16 or 24 inches apart.

Other types of framing. Like a post-and-beam structure, a steel frame, with its members welded or bolted together, is strong enough to allow large, open spaces. It is also ideal for supporting a heavy wall system, such as poured concrete.

Concrete block and stone houses have no frames, although concrete blocks may be reinforced with steel bars. In the southwestern United States, houses without frames are constructed of adobe blocks (sun-dried mud bricks). A house may also be built with double brick walls or single brick walls backed with tiles or concrete blocks. A brick-veneer house has standard wood framing behind a single layer of bricks.

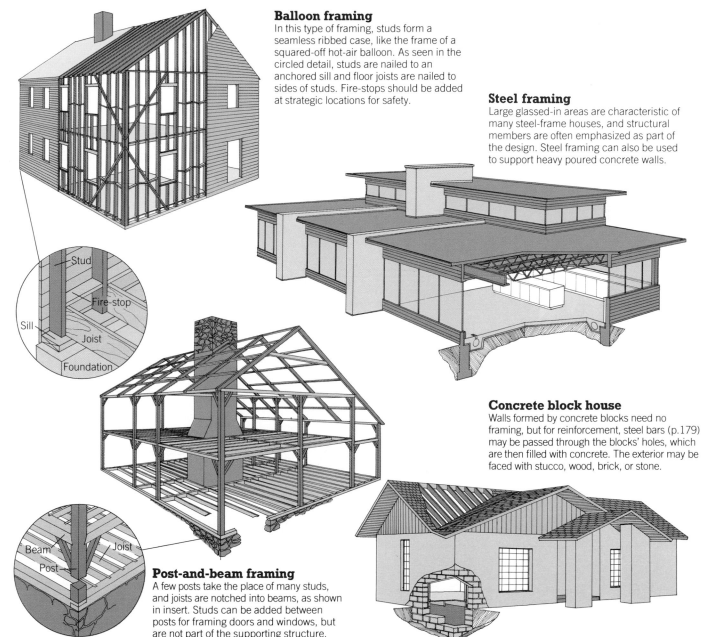

Balloon framing
In this type of framing, studs form a seamless ribbed case, like the frame of a squared-off hot-air balloon. As seen in the circled detail, studs are nailed to an anchored sill and floor joists are nailed to sides of studs. Fire-stops should be added at strategic locations for safety.

Steel framing
Large glassed-in areas are characteristic of many steel-frame houses, and structural members are often emphasized as part of the design. Steel framing can also be used to support heavy poured concrete walls.

Concrete block house
Walls formed by concrete blocks need no framing, but for reinforcement, steel bars (p.179) may be passed through the blocks' holes, which are then filled with concrete. The exterior may be faced with stucco, wood, brick, or stone.

Post-and-beam framing
A few posts take the place of many studs, and joists are notched into beams, as shown in insert. Studs can be added between posts for framing doors and windows, but are not part of the supporting structure.

What you see when you look at a finished wall is merely its covering, which may be in the form of wood, vinyl, or aluminum siding, shingles or shakes, or brick, stone, or stucco. Behind the covering may be hidden layers of wood sheathing, building paper, or other materials.

Most houses (especially newer ones) also have insulation in their outside walls. The insulation may be attached to the studs or held in place by friction, or it may have been blown or sprayed into the empty spaces inside the walls after the house was built.

Superinsulated houses. Some houses are built with more than the usual amount of insulation, making them less costly to heat and air-condition. Structurally, this type of house may differ from the standard, for it is designed to create a tighter envelope to keep heat inside during the winter and outside during the summer. A common design not only uses fiberglass insulation between the studs but adds panels of rigid foam insulation to the outsides of the studs, extending down to the exterior of the foundation. In other systems, entire walls are factory-made and installed on the site intact. Channels for electrical wires and plumbing pipes are precut into the panels.

Generally, a vapor retarder—a type of plastic sheeting that both eliminates drafts and keeps moisture from damaging the structure—is applied to the interior side of the wall under the wallboard. If you live in a superinsulated, you should never cut into the insulation or you may seriously damage the vapor retarder and defeat its purpose. Because the construction methods used in superinsulated houses provide such an efficient seal, some type of ventilating system (p.463) is often added to eliminate excessive moisture and such pollutants as cooking gas and cigarette smoke.

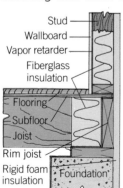

Cedar shakes and other wood shingles

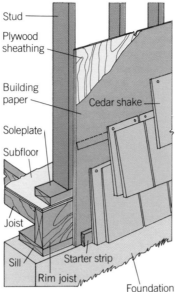

Almost any kind of wood shingles—or even asphalt shingles—can be used on exterior walls. Shakes (shingle-like coverings made by splitting wood along the grain rather than sawing it) are also common. Sheathing consisting of sheets of plywood or manufactured wood or 1-in.-thick boards is nailed to the studs. Building paper or house-wrap and sometimes furring strips are tacked to the sheathing. The shingles are nailed to the strips or sheathing in overlapping courses, or rows. Each course may be single or double.

Vinyl, aluminum, and wood siding

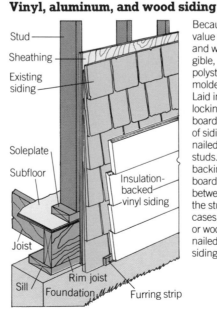

Because the insulating value of vinyl, aluminum, and wood siding is negligible, it often comes with polystyrene insulation molded to its underside. Laid in courses of interlocking or overlapping boards or strips, this type of siding is generally nailed directly to the studs. If there is no backing, insulating board may be placed between the siding and the studs. In some cases, aluminum, vinyl, or wood siding may be nailed down over existing siding, as shown here.

Brick veneer

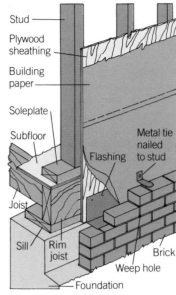

A single wall of brick (about 4 in. thick) may be used as facing on a wood-frame house. It is applied over sheathing and a thick layer of building paper. The brick sits on a recess in the foundation wall 1 in. from the sheathing, allowing moisture that gets inside the walls to run down the inside face of the brick and to drain through weep holes near the base of the wall. The brick veneer is attached to the sheathing with metal ties, spaced about 24 in. apart along the mortar joint every four or five courses. Flashing is used at the sill level.

Stucco

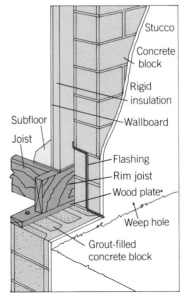

A mixture of portland cement, lime, and sand, stucco is applied over concrete block in two or three coats. Rigid insulation is inserted between blocks and wallboard on interior of wall. Near base of wall, flashing is installed between insulation and blocks, and passed between layers of blocks to exterior. Weep holes along this passage allow condensing moisture to drain out. On wood frames, sheathing is nailed to studs and covered with building paper and metal lath. Three coats of stucco are applied over lath.

Interior construction

The interior walls of a house are generally covered with paneling, wallboard, or plaster and lath, with openings left for electrical boxes, heating vents, and gas and water pipes. Wires and pipes also pass through holes in the framing. There may be insulation in the exterior walls and in walls that connect with an unheated space, such as a garage.

Wallboard or paneling is nailed to the studs or, on a masonry wall, to furring strips that are attached to the masonry to provide air gaps. These gaps prevent moisture drawn in by capillary attraction from damaging the wall.

Plaster is applied over lath. It may be gypsum lath (plaster between thick layers of porous paper), a meshlike metal or wire lath, or wood lath (parallel slats with spaces between them).

Ceilings and floors. Wallboard or plaster and lath also cover the ceilings. The ceiling just below the attic may be backed with insulation and a vapor retarder. Plywood or diagonally laid boards are nailed to the joists to form the subfloor. The finished flooring is applied over the subfloor.

Load-bearing walls. Because joists are not long enough to run the full width of a house, most houses have a central steel or wood *girder*. Butted or overlapping floor joists are laid across the girder and one exterior sill. The exterior walls and the walls above the girder (identifiable by the butting or overlapping joists above them) bear the load of the house and can't be removed or weakened without shifting the weight elsewhere—a job for professionals. The remaining walls are not load-bearing and can be removed without affecting the structure.

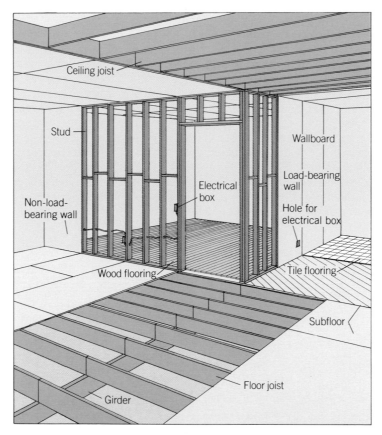

Ceiling joist
Stud
Non-load-bearing wall
Wood flooring
Electrical box
Wallboard
Load-bearing wall
Hole for electrical box
Tile flooring
Subfloor
Floor joist
Girder

What's in your wall? Drill a test hole and discover:

Breakthrough or resistance	Waste material	Building material
Quick breakthrough	White dust	Wallboard or plaster
Delayed breakthrough	White dust, then gray	Thin plaster over wood lath
Delayed or no breakthrough	White dust	Thick plaster
Moderate resistance	Light wood shavings	Wood stud
Heavy resistance	Silver shavings	Metal stud
Very heavy resistance	Gray-brown dust	Concrete or concrete block
Heavy resistance	Red dust	Brick or hollow tiles
Moderate resistance	Gray dust	Mortar

Finding a stud

Whether you are making a repair or simply trying to hang a heavy picture, you may need to locate a stud in your wall. The traditional method is to tap the wall lightly with your knuckles or a hammer wrapped in cloth and listen for a solid rather than a hollow sound. Or look for signs of a nail in the wallboard.

A surer method is to use an electronic stud finder. This handy gadget measures the changes in a wall's density. Simply press a button on the finder and pass the finder over the wall. A light flashes when the tool reaches the edge of a stud (or other framing member) and goes out when it passes over the opposite edge. Mark the edges of the stud on the wall with a pencil; then measure to find its exact center.

Stud finder

Magnetic stud finders detect the nails that fasten wallboard or paneling to the studs, but they may pick up metal-clad cable or galvanized pipes by mistake. As a last resort, drill a small, sharply angled hole in an inconspicuous spot, and push in a piece of coat hanger wire until it hits a solid surface. Locate one stud, and you'll usually find the others 16 or 24 inches apart on center. However, their spacing may be altered for a door or window or at a partition, where the studs are doubled.

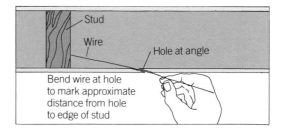

Stud
Wire
Hole at angle
Bend wire at hole to mark approximate distance from hole to edge of stud

Your house/Roof construction

Roof repairs and shingles 384–385
Flashing 390–393

Most house roofs are either flat or peaked. The commonest design is the *gable roof,* consisting of two planes that meet at a central peak and slope down to the building's long walls. The triangular sections on the ends are the gables that give the structure its name. Dormers are often added to gabled roofs to provide ventilation and light. The *hip roof* is similar to the gable roof except that all four sides are sloped. A *flat roof* generally overhangs the outside walls of the house. On many houses, the various types of roofs are combined and variations on the basic styles are used.

Gable roof. Most roofs contain structural elements similar to those in a gable roof. The primary members are the *rafters.* The tops of the rafters are cut diagonally to fit flush against the wide *ridge,* which runs the length of the roof at its peak. The bottoms of the rafters are notched to fit flush on the top plate. Below the ridge, *collar ties* made of 2 x 6's, 1 x 6's, or 1 x 8's span the space between opposing rafters to keep them from spreading.

Sheathing, consisting of plywood panels or of tongue-and-groove boards, is laid over the rafters, and a layer of asphalt-impregnated felt is laid over the sheathing. Shingles or other roofing materials cover the felt. With wood shingles or shakes, both of which need ventilation, rows of narrowly spaced furring strips may be nailed to the rafters over or in

place of solid sheathing. At all joints, metal flashing is added to make the roof watertight.

Flat roof. There are no separate rafters in a flat roof; instead, the ceiling joists of the top story support the roofing. The joists are usually wider than normal, often 2 x 10's or even 2 x 12's. If the roof overhangs the exterior walls of the house on the sides parallel to the run of the joists, *lookout rafters* are used to create the overhangs. They must be tied to a doubled joist, and the distance from the doubled joist to the outside wall is usually twice the overhang. In a flat-roofed post-and-beam house (p.189), heavy beams—or doubled, tripled, or steel-reinforced boards—take the place of the joists.

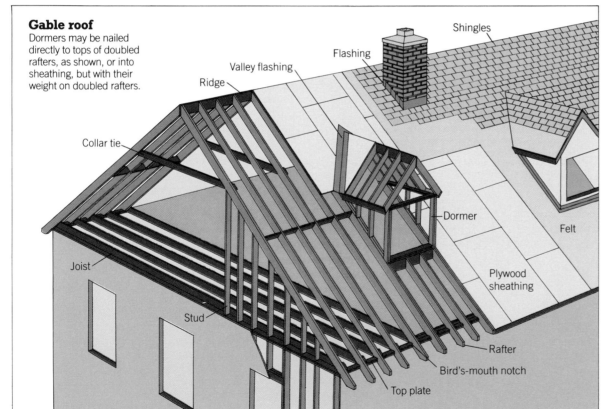

Gable roof
Dormers may be nailed directly to tops of doubled rafters, as shown, or into sheathing, but with their weight on doubled rafters.

Shingles
Flashing
Valley flashing
Ridge
Collar tie
Joist
Stud
Rafter
Bird's-mouth notch
Top plate
Dormer
Felt
Plywood sheathing

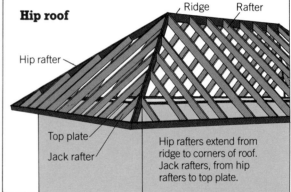

Hip roof
Ridge
Rafter
Hip rafter
Top plate
Jack rafter
Hip rafters extend from ridge to corners of roof. Jack rafters, from hip rafters to top plate.

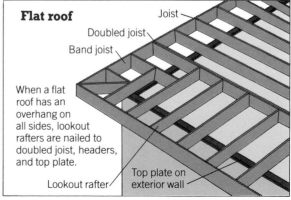

Flat roof
Joist
Doubled joist
Band joist
When a flat roof has an overhang on all sides, lookout rafters are nailed to doubled joist, headers, and top plate.
Lookout rafter
Top plate on exterior wall

Planning projects

A new home seldom needs repairs, but you may be considering improvements ranging from installing smoke detectors to turning an unfinished basement into a family room. In an older house the most pressing needs may be keeping up with repairs and regular maintenance, whether it's fixing a sticking window, replacing a faucet, or repainting dingy walls. In either case you must plan, find out how much it will cost, and decide whether to do it yourself or hire a professional.

Repairs and maintenance. Your first priority should be to repair any defects that may cause more damage, such as replacing a broken windowpane or fixing a leak in the roof. Then move on to other, less pressing, jobs. If you lack do-it-yourself experience, tackle the simpler jobs first; then move on to the more complex tasks as your skills improve.

Whatever the level of your expertise, you will find easy-to-follow directions for most repairs in the following pages. The quickest way to locate the information you need is to check the Table of Contents or Index. Also, watch the cross-references at the tops of the pages. They will refer you to related jobs that are covered elsewhere in the book. Even if a job is too complicated for you to do yourself, you can see what's involved and can thus deal more knowledgeably with professionals and avoid being overcharged.

Ideally, you shouldn't wait for a breakdown to prompt you to take care of your property. By undertaking regular general maintenance on both the interior (p.272) and the exterior (p.382), you can forestall the damage

and frustration that result when one small, unattended problem snowballs.

Modest improvements. Once all the needed repair and maintenance jobs have been taken care of, you'll no doubt consider brightening up the house with a paint job, new carpeting, or more modern faucets. You might even consider jobs that cross into the area of improvements, such as converting a closet into a half bathroom or installing new kitchen cabinets.

In planning major improvements, go through your house from top to bottom, inside and out, making notes on what you would like to change. The master plan that results will probably be too extensive to accomplish all at once, but with your desires spelled out, you can decide which improvements take priority. Do one job at a time at your own pace; give yourself some breathing time between projects; and soon you'll have the satisfaction of a more attractive and comfortable home.

How far to go. Some of the larger-scale improvements not only will make your home more comfortable to live in but may add to its value if you sell it. Such improvements include putting new cabinets, countertops, and ceramic tile in your kitchen and bathrooms; building a deck or patio; adding a skylight; adding a fireplace; or converting your basement or attic into living space. Directions for these projects are given in the following chapters. You may also add to the value of your house (if you don't drive it out of the price range for its neighborhood) by adding one or more rooms. Naturally, your profit will be greater still if you do the work yourself.

Building permits and codes

Even though it's your house, you can't simply jump in and make any repairs and improvements you like with whatever materials strike your fancy. In the interest of community safety—and the protection of neighbors' rights—cities, towns, and counties have laws that place restrictions on both new construction and home improvements.

Zoning ordinances limit the size and shape of your house and how close it can come to a road or neighboring property. They may also keep you from installing a shop or commercial enterprise. For work involving structural changes, indoors or outdoors, you may need a permit. Some jobs, such as working on the house foundation, framing, plumbing, or electrical system, may also have to be checked at various stages by an inspector.

Still other laws impose minimum standards for work done on your house and for the quality and strength of the materials used. In general, each community has three sets of codes, one for general construction work, one for plumbing, and another for electrical work. These codes cover every aspect of the job, down to the type of nails and size of electrical wires.

Most communities adopt one of four comprehensive model codes. But because communities can and do make changes in these model codes, specifications differ from place to place, sometimes within

the same county. Even in a given locality the codes may change every few years to keep up with new materials and standards. Before you plan any work on your house, check with your local building department for details.

When following a code, bear in mind that it gives the *minimum* specifications for safe construction, but not necessarily the most efficient or durable ones. You may want to use better materials than those specified in the codes.

If you fail to get a permit or follow a local code, you may have to tear out the offending work, and you'll be guilty of a misdemeanor and subject to fines for each day you're in violation of the code.

Never assume you won't need a permit. Often a job you'd never expect to require one does. Generally you need a permit to:
- Convert part of your basement into a family room.
- Turn a garage into a guest room.
- Add, wall in, or roof over a patio.
- Run a new electrical circuit.
- Install a new heating system.
- Build a retaining wall more than 4 feet high.
- Put in a barbecue with a chimney that is more than 6 feet high.
- Break through the curb to install a driveway.
- Drill a well.
- Dig a pool deeper than 2 feet.
- Erect an antenna, tower, or flagpole more than 45 feet high.

The first step in estimating the cost of any job is to decide exactly what you want to do and how you want the completed project to look. With this in mind, you can determine the kind of work involved and the tools and materials you will need.

Estimating costs. Make a rough sketch or diagram of the project and fill in the measurements. Based on these measurements, make a list of the materials needed to complete the job, allowing about 10 percent extra for wastage on each item.

If you are framing a wall, for example, use the measurements to estimate the number and sizes of the studs and plates. How many panels of wallboard will you use? How many nails (p.80)? If you are putting in electrical switches and outlets, list those plus wiring, connectors, and other equipment. Include any tools you will need to buy or rent. Then, by determining the number of square feet in the wall (height multiplied by width), estimate the amount of primer and paint required to finish the wall (p.361).

To make sure your list is complete, reread the directions for carrying out all parts of the project. Make sure that you have listed all necessary materials, no matter how insignificant. Then get prices for each item, and add up the costs.

Prices. Shop around for the best prices. Watch advertisements for sales, and check prices at various home centers, lumberyards, hardware stores, building supply stores, and discount outlets. If you are thinking about a future project, make a file of pertinent ads and magazine articles for later reference.

One of the most convenient shopping guides for hardware and decorative materials is a mail-order catalog. Sometimes catalog prices are slightly lower than those of local dealers. For basic building materials, such as lumber, plywood, and wallboard, it is easier to deal with a local building supplier.

Understanding materials. Familiarize yourself with home improvement materials so that when you plan your project, you will be able to deal knowledgeably with suppliers or contractors. Among the best sources of information on new materials are the various home improvement magazines, such as *The Family Handyman.* By writing to their advertisers, you can obtain brochures and pamphlets to help you evaluate the newest building products.

More and more products in the home improvement market are designed for installation by the homeowner. These products help achieve desired effects quickly and inexpensively. For example, prefinished wall panels are far easier and cheaper to install than a wall of individual planks that must be hand-finished. Prehung (factory-framed) doors can save you time and frustration, as well as money.

If you are modernizing a kitchen or bathroom, visit showrooms of suppliers who sell ready-built cabinets, countertops, and sink units. Because such units are mass-produced, they often cost less than building a cabinet from scratch. The money you save could make the difference between doing the job and not being able to afford it.

Financing home improvements. If the improvements you are planning are relatively minor, you may be able to manage them by digging into your savings or stretching the family budget. If they are major, you may have to arrange a loan.

Generally, extensive home improvements are financed through conventional lending institutions: banks, credit unions, and savings and loan associations. You may also be able to borrow against your life insurance policy at a comparatively low rate, but this will reduce the amount the policy will pay by the amount you owe until you repay the loan.

Shop for a loan as you would any other major purchase. Investigate all the types of loans you are eligible for, and decide which best suits your particular circumstances. Consider not only the annual interest rates (which vary from bank to bank), but also the finance charges, the costs of life insurance (if required), the penalties for late payment or default, the amount of each payment, and the total number of payments. Multiply the amount of each payment by the number of payments to determine the full amount you will be paying back.

HUD and VA loans. If the improvements you are making are not extensive but will make your home more livable and useful, you might be able to get a loan backed by the U.S. Department of Housing and Urban Development (HUD). Or if you are a U.S. veteran and bought your house under a GI mortgage, you can probably get a VA loan. Because they are backed by the government, HUD and VA loans generally have lower interest rates, and security is required only for very large loans (the amount varies).

Passbook loans. You can borrow money at a fairly low interest rate by pledging the amount you have in the bank to pay out the loan if you default. It would cost less merely to withdraw the money from the account to finance the work and then pay it back in monthly installments, but doing this requires great discipline and determination.

Personal loans. If your credit is good, you may be able to get a personal loan of a small amount of money on your signature alone. However, it is more likely that you will have to put up some collateral that would be sold to pay off the loan in case of default, and the interest rate is often higher for a personal loan than for a home improvement loan.

Mortgage loans. If the collateral you are offering is the home, consider a second mortgage to get the money for the improvements. For the most part, interest rates on second mortgages are higher than on first mortgages, but lower than on other types of loans. The term for a second mortgage is usually 15 years, and the combined first and second mortgages generally may not exceed 75 percent of your home's appraised value.

A home equity loan is a variation on the second mortgage in that a lien is placed on the property, which means that if you default on payment you risk foreclosure and the loss of your home. Typically home equity loans have adjustable rates and work as revolving lines of credit, allowing you to draw money only as you need it over a period of 5 to 10 years.

Finally, you might be able to refinance your first mortgage into one new higher loan amount. Be aware, however, that most mortgage transactions involve new closing costs as well as a reappraisal of your home.

Working with contractors

Although you will probably elect to do most of your own home repairs and small-scale improvements, you may need some outside help if you are planning a major project. Before deciding whether or not to do a job yourself, plan exactly what you want done and plot out the steps involved in doing it. Consider both your skills in doing the work—with the help of this manual—and the time it would take you to complete the job. For example, you may feel competent enough to remodel your kitchen, but if you can work only on weekends, the project may take months to complete. Can you make do without your full cooking facilities for that long?

If you decide not to do the work yourself, estimate how many professional workers you may need to hire. To install a new sink, for example, you might need not only a plumber but also a carpenter to build a counter for it and other workers to patch and paint the wall where it was cut for the pipes. You may decide to save money by hiring only the plumber and doing the rest of the work yourself, or you might hire the workers to complete the whole job.

If you must deal with a number of workers, consider hiring a general contractor, especially if the job is sizable. A competent contractor has a thorough knowledge of the building process and is experienced at hiring, handling, and scheduling various workers, or subcontractors. In addition, because of his professional contacts, he can usually get materials and labor at lower costs than you, and so make a profit without charging you any more than you would pay if you acted as your own contractor.

Selecting a contractor. Choose a contractor carefully. Get as many recommendations as you can from friends who have had remodeling work done, and try to see the work the recommended contractors were responsible for. Using the questions listed in the boxed feature at right, pick the most desirable two or three candidates from your list. Meet with each of them, and submit written specifications for your project that clearly delineate the work you want done, the materials you want used, and the standards of workmanship you expect. Ask for written bids.

Study the bids carefully. If there are large price differences, discuss them with the contractors to find out why. Don't automatically take the lowest bid; that contractor may cut corners to bring down the price.

The written contract. Have a lawyer look over the contract before you sign it, and be sure that it clearly spells out everything you expect from the contractor, including warranties on his work and a statement of who will be responsible if the completed work does not comply with government standards. Assume nothing, and never rely on oral promises—they are unenforceable.

Be sure that the contract includes the exact nature and extent of the work to be done and the materials to be used—including quality, quantity, weight, color, size, and brand name, where applicable. The contract should also include the starting date, the estimated finishing date, and everything you expect the contractor to take care of, from obtaining the building permits to cleaning up. For your own protection, have a clause included that protects you from liens (claims) on your property by subcontractors in the event that the contractor fails to pay them.

Carefully check the financial terms of the contract. You should not be called upon to make a down payment of more than one-third the total contract price. Generally the outstanding amount should be paid at specified intervals, but you should not have to pay for work before it is finished. Arrange to hold back a percentage of the contract price (often 10 percent) until the job has been completed and inspected.

Final considerations. As the work progresses, keep a close eye on what is being done. Try not to make changes in the plans. This is often expensive. For example, if you ask the contractor to add a trash compactor to your kitchen, he may agree without telling you that it will require running new wiring—you may end up paying triple the amount you expected. If you do make a change in the plans, find out how much it will cost and get it in writing.

Don't make the final payment until the work is completed to your satisfaction. If an inspection is required by law, withhold payment until it is made.

How to hire a contractor

If you decide you need a contractor to handle a home improvement project, you will want someone who will finish the work promptly, with expertise, and without creating any legal headaches that may arise from having him and his workers in your house. Getting the right contractor is a matter of asking the right questions. Here are the basic ones:

- Is the contractor properly licensed?
- Does the contractor have a street address or just a post office box number, which may make it hard for you to find him if needed?
- How long has he been in business? (Statistics show that the majority of new contractors go out of business within 3 years.)
- Does the Better Business Bureau have a record of complaints against him?
- Will the contractor give you the names and addresses of satisfied customers?
- Can you talk to the contractor, and does he listen to what you say?
- Will the contractor show you copies of his insurance policies, including workers' compensation and liability insurance?
- Is the contractor familiar with local building regulations and codes, and will he obtain any necessary permits and give you copies?
- Will the contractor guarantee all materials and workmanship?
- Will the contractor request your written approval before making changes or substitutions in materials and workmanship?
- Will he arrange for cleanup and removal of debris from the premises, both on a daily basis and after the job is completed?
- If he is late in completing the work, will the contractor pay a penalty? (Most contractors will agree to this only for large projects and generally only if you offer them a bonus for early completion.)

Your house/Meeting special needs

Make your home easier to live in for everyone—from the hale and healthy to the elderly or physically handicapped. If you make equipment easy to operate and household items accessible without climbing or reaching, your home will immediately become more comfortable. Should you become ill or less agile, or if you have visitors who are in any way handicapped, you will be prepared.

Here are some suggestions: Replace any round doorknobs in your house with lever handles, or add clamp-on lever adapters (p.438); they are easier to open whether you have arthritis or your hands are merely full. Make lights more visible with illuminated switches, or put in timers or light-sensitive switches that turn lights on or off when the daylight ends or returns. Install programmable thermostats (p.474) that will turn the heat up or down at preset hours.

Firm footing. Make walking around the house easier by using cushion-backed carpet (p.319) with a dense, level-loop pile—the shorter the loop, the better. Glue it directly to the floor. Avoid throw rugs or low tables that are easy to trip over. Keep thresholds to a maximum of ¼ inch high.

Mark the edges of wooden stairs with textured tape. The tape's abrasive surface keeps the foot from slipping and signals the edge of the step. On both sides of stairs, install handrails that curve outward after the last step. The railings provide support, and the outward curve signals that the last step is underfoot. If you are putting in new stairs, make the risers low enough to negotiate easily.

Wheelchair living. In the event that a wheelchair must be used in your home, it will require ample space for maneuvering. Avoid clutter wherever the chair might be wheeled. If the house entrance isn't at street level, build a ramp that rises no more than 1 inch for every 12 inches of its length, and preferably 1 inch for every 20 inches. Also, be sure that all light switches, faucets, and other essential equipment are low enough to be reached easily while seated. Doorways may have to be widened, and thresholds should be eliminated.

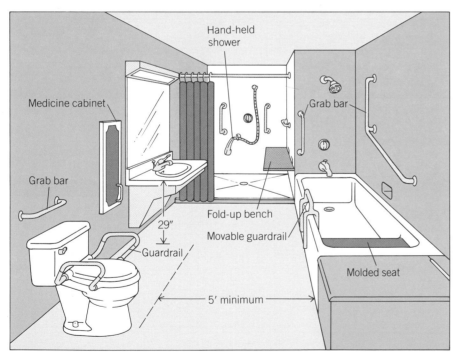

In bathroom, install tub with molded seat or stall shower with hinged bench that folds against wall. Put in single-lever faucets (p.211) and a hand-held shower head (p.212) that can also be fixed in wall bracket for regular showering. Screw grab bars into walls where needed, anchoring them into studs. Leave enough room next to toilet to fit a wheelchair, in case one is ever needed. Put medicine cabinet on wall beside sink and low enough to reach easily, but keep it locked when children are around. Finally, lay nonslip rubber flooring.

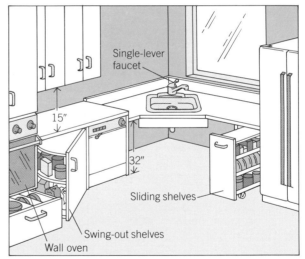

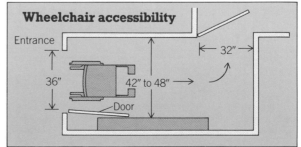

Wheelchair accessibility

In kitchen, lower the upper cabinets from standard 18 in. to 15 in. above countertops. To allow someone to sit at kitchen counter or sink, lower a 30-in.-wide section from the standard 36 in. to 32 in., and leave empty space beneath it to accommodate a chair. (Sink must not be more than 6½ in. deep.) In remaining lower cabinets, use sliding or swing-out compartments for easy access. Put in a wall oven and a side-by-side refrigerator and freezer. Use single-lever faucets, and install an adapter under the sink to automatically mix hot and cold water to a preset temperature. A built-in jar and bottle-top opener will help dislodge tight caps.

To accommodate a wheelchair, hallways should be at least 42 (preferably 48) in. wide. If there is furniture in hall, its depth should be deducted from measurement. Interior doorways should be at least 32 in. wide, and entrance doors, 36 in. wide. Offset hinges are available that swing a door out of its frame to one side, to increase the size of the opening (p.435).

Contents

Plumbing
Repairs and installations

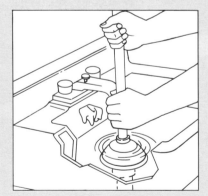 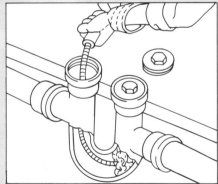 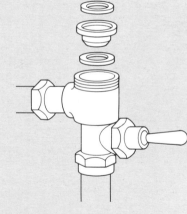

There's much you can do to keep the plumbing in your home functioning well, as this chapter shows. Beginning with an overall description of a home plumbing system, the chapter goes on to describe the basics of repair and maintenance, showing how to deal with everything from a leaky faucet to an overflowing toilet. Next comes a section on pipes and fittings. Instruc-

tions are included for cutting and joining all the various types of pipes you're likely to encounter.

The chapter concludes with a section on installing new lines and fixtures, such as a sink, a replacement toilet, and a whirlpool bath. Even though you may decide to hire a plumber for such jobs, by learning what's involved you'll be able to deal more knowledgeably with a professional.

197

Plumbing/Home systems

House plumbing consists of a *water supply system* and a *drain-waste-vent*—or *DWV*—*system*.

Water supply system. Water usually enters the house through a main service pipe, which is often metered. The water is under pressure to ensure adequate flow. Parallel supply lines, one leading out of the water heater, carry hot and cold water to fixtures and appliances. Vertical pipes, called *risers,* carry water between floors. The horizontal supply pipes have a slight downward pitch toward one or more drain valves. Air chambers (p.214) create cushions for the pressure-driven water to push against when a faucet or appliance is turned off.

Shutoff valves at the water heater, boiler, individual fixtures, and sometimes risers control the water flow. The main shutoff, whether indoors or outdoors, is generally near where the service line enters the house; it may be on the meter. On a private system, it will be near where the line leaves the storage tank.

DWV system. A separate set of drainpipes carries used water and waste out of the house into a municipal sewage system, septic tank, or cesspool. *Waste pipes* carry off used water; *soil pipes* carry discharge from the toilets. Because gravity is used to carry off waste, the slope of these pipes is carefully calculated, usually at a pitch of ¼ inch per foot. Clean-out plugs are generally placed in each horizontal section of drain for removing blockages.

At each fixture the drainpipe contains a curved (generally U-shaped) trap, a pipe that "traps" water in its curve. The water in the trap creates a block that keeps foul air from escaping into the house through the open drain. Toilets have built-in traps.

A plumbing system must be vented to let sewer gases escape, to equalize air pressure in the system so that waste and water can flow freely, and to prevent water from backing up from one fixture into another. *Vent pipes* include a central soil stack that runs from the main house drain up through the roof, where it vents into the open air. Individual vent pipes may run from a fixture up through the roof and into the open air, or *revent pipes* may run from a fixture to a main vent.

Water supply system

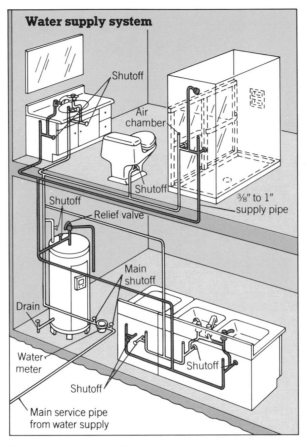

DWV system

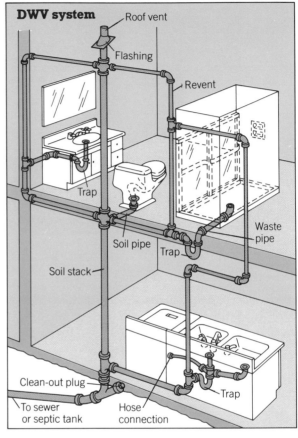

Emergency shutoff valves

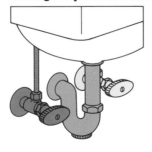

Sinks. Separate valves control hot and cold water.

Toilets. Valve at rear controls flow of water into tank.

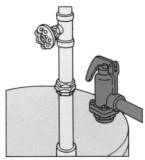

Water heater. Valve at top shuts off water to unit.

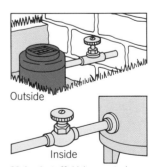

Main shutoff. Valve controls water supply entering house.

Water supply

Sources of water

Municipal water systems supply water to homes in urban and some suburban communities, but many homes have private systems. The most common private system is a well with a pump to provide the necessary water pressure—generally between 40 and 60 psi (pounds per square inch).

Most water supplies need to be treated for impurities. Rain, as it falls through the atmosphere, picks up minute particles of dust and dirt and absorbs carbon dioxide. In reservoirs, cisterns, lakes, rivers, springs, and wells, water collects bacteria, dirt, minerals, and chemical compounds caused by reactions with soil and rock. Most impurities are removed at the local water-treatment plant before the water reaches your house; more can be removed after it enters your house and before reaching your tap (pp.224–225).

Deep well

Shallow well

Deep well

Water table

Lake, river, reservoir

Spring

Aquifer (recharge area)

Upper confining bed

Consolidated rock

Water-bearing rock

Lower confining bed

Ground water occurs in subterranean rock layers.

Cross-connections

A cross-connection occurs when water that should go into the DWV system gets into the supply system, where it pollutes the drinking water. To keep the two systems safely separate, watch out for these cross-connections.

A frequent offender is a faucet in a bathtub or sink that is submerged if the basin fills up. Dirty water in the basin can then siphon into the faucet—even if it is closed—if there is a vacuum in the water supply.

Such a vacuum can be caused by a heavy water draw elsewhere in the house or by a pressure drop from a hydrant being opened nearby. A spray hose attached to a faucet and left lying in a sink can also cause a cross-connection.

Some older toilets have cross-connected water inlets. Check under the tank lid that the inlet valve is above the high-water line. If it isn't, replace the valve with an anti-siphon relacement valve (p.207).

Have a plumbing leak?

The plumbing problem you are most likely to run into is a leak of one sort or another. When something in your house springs a leak, find a quick solution with this handy index.

Leak in:	See page:	Leak in:	See page:
Bathtubs at rim	232–233	Sink strainers	203
Faucets	209–212	Soldered joints	220
Pipes	11, 215	Stoppers	213
Shower stalls	234	Toilets	206–208

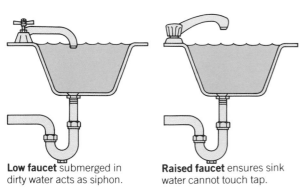

Low faucet submerged in dirty water acts as siphon.

Raised faucet ensures sink water cannot touch tap.

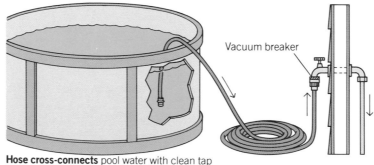

Hose cross-connects pool water with clean tap water. Add vacuum breaker to faucet to correct.

Vacuum breaker

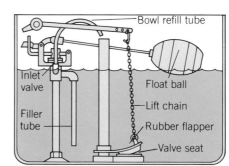

Bowl refill tube

Inlet valve

Filler tube

Float ball

Lift chain

Rubber flapper

Valve seat

Toilet inlet valve should be above the high-water mark.

Plumbing/Private wells

Because of the danger of contamination, wells that provide drinking water should be at least 100 feet deep. Consequently, if you are planning a new well, have it drilled by a well contractor. A drilled well is far more likely to tap into a safe water supply than a dug well or a driven well (one made by driving a wide pipe into the ground).

Drilling a well. The exact depth of the well depends upon local codes (p.193) and the depth of the water-bearing rock layer (p.199). A well must penetrate deep enough below the water table to ensure a dependable water supply even in dry weather. Codes may also set a minimum distance from a potential source of contamination, such as a septic system.

If you need a new well, shop carefully for a trustworthy contractor who knows the geology of your area; drilling is customarily billed on a per-foot basis with you, not the contractor, paying for each foot.

From well to house. Once a well is drilled, a pump is installed. The pump sends water through the well lines to a pressure tank in the house. The tank, in turn, feeds the water supply lines.

There are two basic types of pumps in use today. A submersible pump, like the one shown at right, is lowered into the well casing and pushes the water up into the pressure tank; it can be used for wells of any depth. A jet pump is connected at the surface and sucks the water up to the surface and into the tank; it is best for shallow wells and generally cannot be used in a well deeper than 120 feet.

In a standard pressure tank, the incoming water pushes the air into the upper third of the tank, where it forms a springlike cushion. When air pressure reaches a preset level—usually between 50 and 60 pounds per square inch (psi)—the spring action of the compressed air triggers a pressure switch, which shuts off the pump. As water is drawn from the tank, pressure diminishes. When it reaches a preset level—30 to 40 psi—the switch turns the pump on again. The tank should be large enough to provide at least 9 gallons of drawdown (the amount of water used between the time the pump shuts off and turns on again.)

Small pressure tanks with permanently sealed-in air cushions are also available. Instead of relying on direct air pressure, the *air-cell tank* contains an elastic diaphragm that separates the air cushion from the water. For greater capacity two or more tanks can be installed in a single system.

Fixing a waterlogged tank. If the tank loses too much air pressure it becomes "waterlogged," causing the pump to switch on and off frequently. To rectify this problem, shut off power to the pump and attach a hose to the drain valve at the bottom of the tank. Open the valve and keep it open until there is no more pressure in the tank. Then open a faucet in the house and drain all water out of the tank. Once the tank is empty, turn off the faucet, close the drain valve on the tank, remove the hose, and turn the pump back on.

Periodically inspect the outside of the tank. If a leak develops, it will usually appear first as an oozing rusty blemish. Tank plugs are available, but plugging is only a temporary measure. Replace the tank as soon as possible.

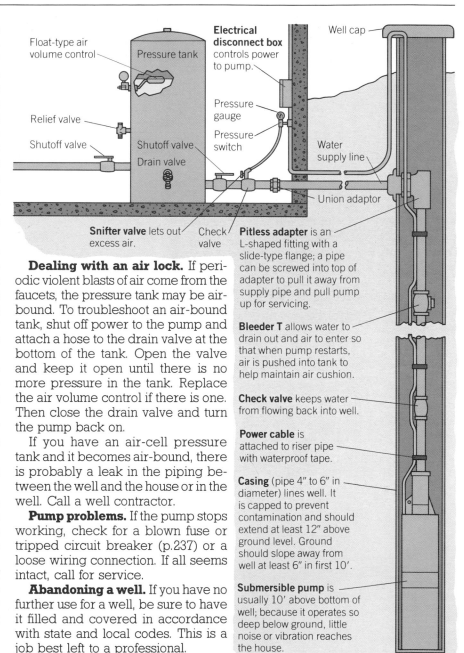

Float-type air volume control

Relief valve

Shutoff valve

Pressure tank

Electrical disconnect box controls power to pump.

Pressure gauge

Pressure switch

Shutoff valve

Drain valve

Well cap

Water supply line

Union adaptor

Snifter valve lets out excess air.

Check valve

Pitless adapter is an L-shaped fitting with a slide-type flange; a pipe can be screwed into top of adapter to pull it away from supply pipe and pull pump up for servicing.

Bleeder T allows water to drain out and air to enter so that when pump restarts, air is pushed into tank to help maintain air cushion.

Check valve keeps water from flowing back into well.

Power cable is attached to riser pipe with waterproof tape.

Casing (pipe 4″ to 6″ in diameter) lines well. It is capped to prevent contamination and should extend at least 12″ above ground level. Ground should slope away from well at least 6″ in first 10′.

Submersible pump is usually 10′ above bottom of well; because it operates so deep below ground, little noise or vibration reaches the house.

Dealing with an air lock. If periodic violent blasts of air come from the faucets, the pressure tank may be air-bound. To troubleshoot an air-bound tank, shut off power to the pump and attach a hose to the drain valve at the bottom of the tank. Open the valve and keep it open until there is no more pressure in the tank. Replace the air volume control if there is one. Then close the drain valve and turn the pump back on.

If you have an air-cell pressure tank and it becomes air-bound, there is probably a leak in the piping between the well and the house or in the well. Call a well contractor.

Pump problems. If the pump stops working, check for a blown fuse or tripped circuit breaker (p.237) or a loose wiring connection. If all seems intact, call for service.

Abandoning a well. If you have no further use for a well, be sure to have it filled and covered in accordance with state and local codes. This is a job best left to a professional.

Septic systems

Because of the amount of digging necessary, you will probably not want to build your own sewage disposal system, but in order to maintain it properly, you should know how it operates. In a typical private septic system, waste is piped out of the house into a watertight holding tank, or septic tank, where anaerobic bacteria (bacteria that grow in the absence of air) break the waste down into solids (sludge), liquid (effluent), and scum. The sludge settles to the bottom of the tank, the scum rises to the top, and the effluent flows into a distribution box, which channels it through nonwaterproof or perforated pipes to different parts of a drainage field of loose gravel.

Location and size. The septic system must be located a safe distance from both house and well, and it must be large enough to do its job efficiently. The exact location and minimum size are dictated by local codes. Generally the tank's size is based on the number of bedrooms in the house. The extent of the drainage field is further determined by the character of the soil. Before building a septic system, a contractor digs holes in various parts of the property to conduct percolation tests—to see how fast the soil absorbs water.

Inspection and cleaning. The tank should be inspected and pumped out every 2 or 3 years, depending on the size of the system and the number of people in the household. The proportions of sludge, effluent, and scum must be carefully balanced for the tank to function properly. If particles of sediment get into the effluent and flow out into the drainage field, a health hazard results. Pumping removes the sludge and part of the scum to restore the proper balance. Consult with your contractor on how often you should have your tank inspected. Failure to keep the tank clean can cause serious problems.

To facilitate cleaning and inspection, locate and mark the plumbing and outlet covers of your system. If you don't know where they are, refer to your plot plan or check with your local building department. Sketch a map of your yard, showing the sewage line, septic tank, and drainage field.

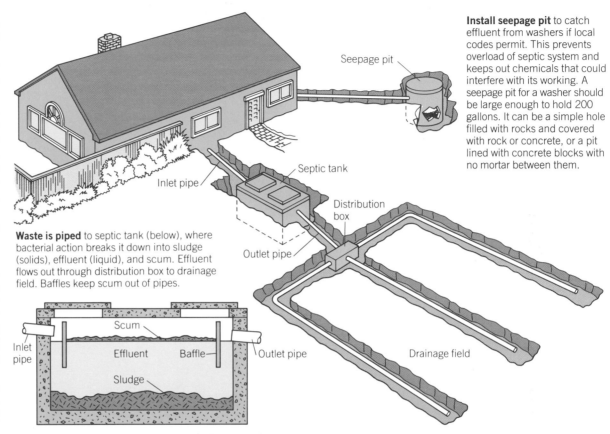

Install seepage pit to catch effluent from washers if local codes permit. This prevents overload of septic system and keeps out chemicals that could interfere with its working. A seepage pit for a washer should be large enough to hold 200 gallons. It can be a simple hole filled with rocks and covered with rock or concrete, or a pit lined with concrete blocks with no mortar between them.

Seepage pit

Septic tank

Inlet pipe

Distribution box

Outlet pipe

Drainage field

Waste is piped to septic tank (below), where bacterial action breaks it down into sludge (solids), effluent (liquid), and scum. Effluent flows out through distribution box to drainage field. Baffles keep scum out of pipes.

Inlet pipe

Scum

Effluent

Baffle

Outlet pipe

Sludge

Septic system maintenance

- Have your tank cleaned every 2 or 3 years.
- Stagger baths and wash loads to avoid overloading the system during any one period.
- Don't pour paint thinner, pesticides, photographic chemicals, or motor oil into drains or toilets.
- Never dispose of grease, fat, coffee grounds, paper towels, or facial tissues in sinks or toilets.
- Use only white nonfluffy toilet tissue; dyes are harmful to bacteria needed for decomposition.
- Be sparing in your use of chemical drain cleaners, toilet bowl cleaners, and bleach.

- Use a garbage disposer sparingly or not at all.
- Direct the runoff from roof gutters and downspouts away from the drainage field.
- Don't drive or park over the drainage field.
- Call for service if smelly water rises from the drainage field or if water backs up out of drains.
- Don't use commercial tank treatments; they can liquefy sludge, which can then flow into the drainage field and clog its lines. To hasten decomposition, every 6 months mix ½ pound of brewer's yeast in warm water and flush it down a toilet.

Plumbing/Tools

If you work around your house, you probably already have many of the tools needed for plumbing work. Among the general-purpose tools you will need are hammers, chisels, screwdrivers, pliers, a hacksaw, soldering tools, and various wrenches. You can buy specialized tools as required, or merely rent them for a particular job.

Wrenches. In addition to the wrenches you probably have in your tool kit, several specialized wrenches may be needed for plumbing. Chief among them is the *pipe wrench,* an adjustable wrench with serrated jaws. You will need two of them—one for holding a pipe or fitting and the other for turning the connecting piece. If you grip a polished surface, such as chrome pipe, with a pipe wrench, tape the tool's jaws or wrap corrugated cardboard or rags around the surface. This prevents damage from the wrench's teeth. Don't use a pipe wrench on thin pipe; it might crush it.

Spud wrenches are used for turning large flat-sided nuts, such as the locknuts on a sink drain. Get an adjustable one. *Socket wrenches,* which fit over nuts or valves, may be needed to turn the valves of

faucet stems. Instead of jaws, *chain wrenches* and *strap wrenches* have lengths of chain or fabric that loop around a pipe to hold it. Use them on large-diameter pipes and hard-to-reach connections. (A strap wrench won't damage a polished finish.) A *basin wrench* is a long-handled tool with an adjustable jaw at a right angle to the handle. You'll need it for hard-to-reach connections beneath a sink.

If you are fixing a leaky faucet, you may need an *Allen wrench* of the appropriate size to insert into the opening of the faucet's valve seat to loosen and remove it. If the valve seat cannot be removed, get a *valve-seat dresser,* or *grinder,* for smoothing rough spots on the valve seat.

Cutting and flaring tools. You can cut most small pipe with a hacksaw; the blade should have 24 or 32 teeth per inch. Special *pipe cutters* are available for copper, steel, or plastic pipe. You will need a *reamer* for removing burrs from the freshly cut pipe—either a hand-held tool or a bit for your drill. If you are working with brass or steel pipe, you may require a set of *dies* and a *diestock*—a wrench for holding dies—to cut threads (p.222).

Flaring tools are used to widen the ends of flexible metal or plastic pipe before joining with a flare fitting. You can get individual flaring tools (one for each size pipe) or a more sophisticated mechanical tool that will flare all sizes (pp.218 and 221).

Drain-clearing tools. A *plunger* is essential for clearing clogs. Get one with a funnel-type cup. The flexible tube extension, necessary for plunging a toilet, can be folded inward to fit over a drain.

If the plunger fails to clear a clog, you'll need an *auger.* A trap-and-drain auger, or snake, is a long flexible tube with a spiral hook at one end and a locking handle at the other. Power-driven snakes are available for clearing main drains. The shorter closet auger, used for toilets, has a crank handle.

Putty, tape, and packing. In addition to tools, you will need pipe joint compound, a paste applied to pipe threads to prevent leaks and make disassembly easier. Sometimes pipe tape is wrapped around the threads in place of the compound. Plumber's putty seals joints between sinks or tubs and their drains or faucets. You may also need a supply of stringlike packing, called wicking, to repair faucets.

Basic plumbing tools

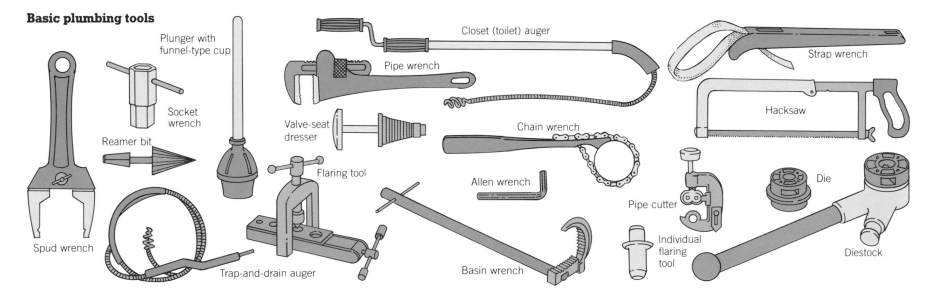

Plunger with funnel-type cup · Closet (toilet) auger · Strap wrench · Pipe wrench · Socket wrench · Reamer bit · Valve-seat dresser · Chain wrench · Hacksaw · Flaring tool · Allen wrench · Die · Pipe cutter · Spud wrench · Trap-and-drain auger · Basin wrench · Individual flaring tool · Diestock

Sink and bathtub drains

If a drain becomes clogged, bail out any excess water. Remove the sink stopper (p.213) and clean it of debris. Then try the remedies shown at right; if one doesn't work, proceed to the next. Try to avoid the use of chemical drain cleaners; they are corrosive to pipes and dangerous to people. If you do use them, exercise extreme caution (p.13).

Fixing a leak. Occasionally a leak develops in the U-shaped trap under a sink. In that case, try tightening the coupling nuts that hold the trap in place, but tape the jaws of the wrench you use to keep them from scratching the chrome finish. If the leak persists, the washers inside may need replacing. Remove the trap, as shown in step 4 at right, and take off the old washers. If the pipe threads are corroded, clean them with a wire brush and coat them liberally with joint compound; then put in new washers and reassemble. If the cleanout plug in the trap is leaking, treat it in the same way.

Occasionally a leak results from a break in the seal between the strainer and the sink. To fix it, remove the strainer as shown below and clean it. Replace the gasket, if there is one, or apply a ¼-inch rope of plumber's putty around the underside of the strainer's lip. Replace the strainer.

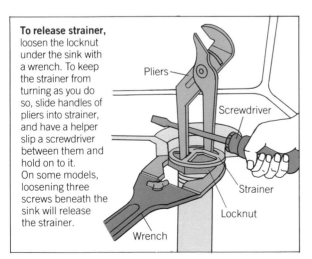

To release strainer, loosen the locknut under the sink with a wrench. To keep the strainer from turning as you do so, slide handles of pliers into strainer, and have a helper slip a screwdriver between them and hold on to it. On some models, loosening three screws beneath the sink will release the strainer.

Pliers
Screwdriver
Strainer
Locknut
Wrench

Unclogging sink drains

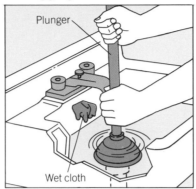

Plunger
Wet cloth

1. Remove stopper or strainer, and block the overflow opening with wet cloth to create a vacuum. Position plunger over drain, and cover cup with water. Tilt cup to release trapped air. Plunge forcefully up and down 10 times; remove the plunger abruptly. Repeat several times.

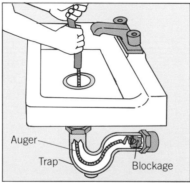

Auger
Trap
Blockage

3. If the problem persists, feed auger through drain hole, cranking the tool's handle clockwise, until it hits clog— an area of mushy resistance. (Area of hard resistance is a bend in pipe.) Work auger back and forth to break up the clog, then flush drain with hot water.

Unclogging tub drains

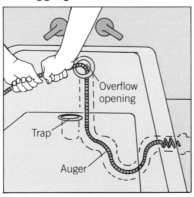

Overflow opening
Trap
Auger

Remove overflow plate and stopper assembly (p.213), and feed an auger through the overflow opening. Work head of auger down into trap below floor, and break up blockage as in step 3 above.

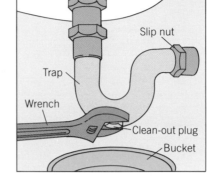

Slip nut
Trap
Wrench
Clean-out plug
Bucket

2. If drain is still plugged, place a bucket under trap, unscrew clean-out plug, and let the water drain out. (If trap has no clean-out plug, remove the entire trap, as in step 4.) Probe inside trap and pipe with bent wire to free clog. Screw plug back in (or reconnect trap).

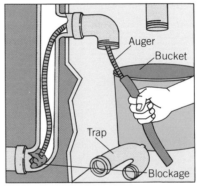

Auger
Bucket
Trap
Blockage

4. If drain is still clogged, place a bucket beneath trap to catch water. Holding trap in place, use a wrench with taped jaws to unscrew slip nuts. Remove trap, drain it, and clean it; replace washers if worn. Feed auger into pipe in wall and break up blockage. Reassemble trap.

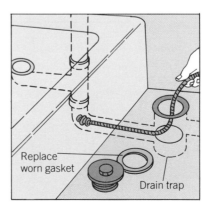

Replace worn gasket
Drain trap

In older homes, bathtubs may have a cylindrical drum trap on floor near tub, as shown here. On other bathtubs, access to drainpipe is through a nearby trapdoor. Unclog both types with auger as you would any drain.

Bail the excess water from a clogged toilet, and use a plunger with its cup extended. Don't flush, or you'll have a flood. And don't use chemical cleaners; they are corrosive to pipes and harmful to people, and cannot penetrate the trap enough to be effective. If you put them into a stopped-up toilet, you will be left with a bowl full of dangerous chemicals.

If the plunger doesn't work after several tries, attempt to snag the obstruction with a hook made

Cut here

out of a wire coat hanger, or cover your hand with a plastic garbage bag and pull it out manually.

Using an auger. If the toilet is still clogged, try a closet auger. Its sharp bend makes it easier to get started and helps protect the bowl's finish. If you don't have a closet auger, you can try using a trap-and-drain auger. If you have difficulty making it go into the trap (and you probably will), cover your arm with a plastic bag and push it in by hand.

Blockage in the drain system. Toilets and other fixtures may back up or run slowly because of a blockage in one of the drainpipes of the main DWV system rather than in the fixture. To locate the blockage, remember that waste flows downward; therefore, the obstruction will be below the lowest stopped-up fixture and above the highest working fixture. If fixtures on the top floor are clogged but those on the lower floor are not, the upper stack is blocked. If all fixtures are blocked, the main drain is probably clogged. If fixtures drain sluggishly and smell bad, the stack vent may be blocked.

To locate a clog in a drainpipe, partially loosen the cleanout plug nearest the affected fixtures; if water drips out, the clog is between that cleanout and the sewer. If not, check the next plug up the line (away from the sewer). Generally there are cleanouts wherever a branch makes a sharp turn,

but some older houses have only a single main cleanout, located near the bottom of the soil stack.

If the problem persists, try the house trap, if you have one. You will probably find its two cleanout plugs at floor level near where the main drain leaves the house. Spread papers to soak up the overflow. Make sure that no one runs water or flushes a toilet. If no water seeps out when you open the plug nearest the outside sewage line, the clog is in the trap or in the main drain between the trap and the main cleanout. If water does seep out, the clog is probably between the trap and the sewer; call a plumber.

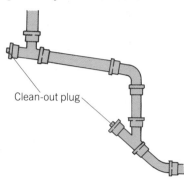

Clean-out plug

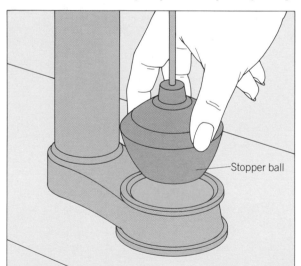

If toilet appears clogged, don't flush. Remove tank cover, and raise stopper ball with hand to release a little water from tank into bowl. If water level in tank doesn't drop, or water level in bowl rises, push stopper down again to stop flow. Bail out excess water.

Stopper ball

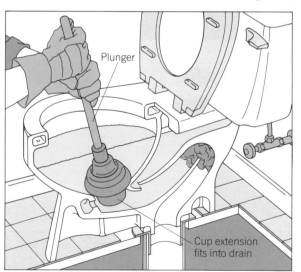

Plunger

Cup extension fits into drain

Place plunger snugly over trap, and make sure there is enough water to cover its rim. Stand directly over handle for maximum force; rapidly pump up and down 10 times; then abruptly pull plunger out of bowl. Vacuum action should loosen blockage.

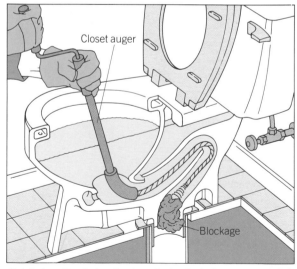

Closet auger

Blockage

Rotate handle of closet auger slowly clockwise as you push in toward clog. If it becomes hard to turn, back out a little until it turns freely, then crank it again. When its head cuts into the clog, move auger back and forth until all solid material is broken up.

Clearing the main drain

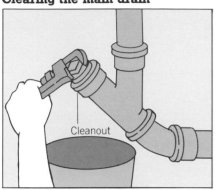

Cleanout

1. Place bucket under cleanout; use a pipe wrench to partially loosen plug by turning it counter-clockwise. Loosen plug just enough to let fluid in pipe run out into the bucket. When bucket is full, tighten plug, empty bucket. Repeat until completely drained.

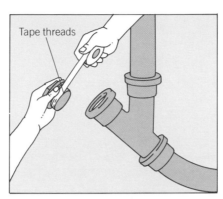

Tape threads

3. Before replacing the plug, clean the threads with a stiff brush, and wrap them with pipe tape or coat them with pipe joint compound. After replacing plug, flush all toilets twice to wash out remaining debris. If you have failed to find the clog, you may be able to reach it from the trap in the main drain (if the trap is accessible).

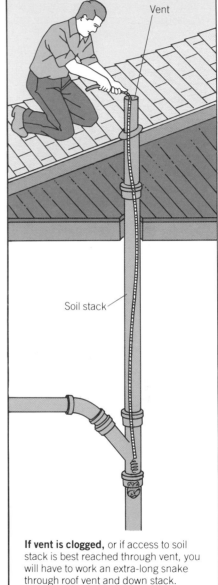

Vent

Soil stack

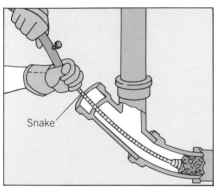

Snake

2. Remove plug and use a trap-and-drain auger (snake) that is ¼ in. in diameter and 25 to 100 ft. long. Feed snake slowly into pipe until you feel soft resistance of the clog. Vigorously work snake back and forth while turning it to break up clog. Withdraw auger, clean it, and repeat until you're sure drain is clear.

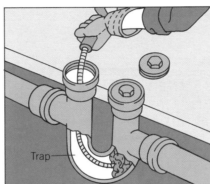

Trap

4. Locate the trap and open the plug nearer the outside sewer line. Probe trap with snake and break up clog. If you don't find one, open other plug and probe the main drain between trap and main cleanout. Clean trap and plugs with wire brush; wrap threads with pipe tape or coat them with pipe joint compound; recap.

If tree root is blocking waste line, rent a power auger with root-cutting bit. Insert cable into pipe, turn on motor, and feed in cable without forcing. When auger bit reaches root, hose water into pipe to flush away debris, and work cable slowly back and forth to cut into root and clear away blockage. Then withdraw auger, clean threads, and reinstall cleanout plug.

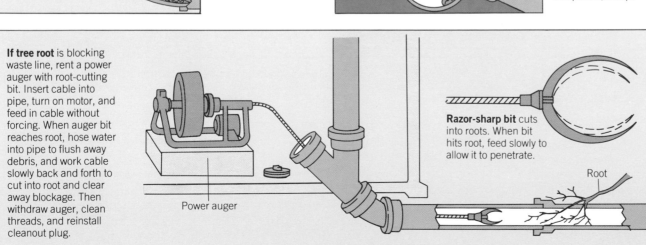

Power auger

Razor-sharp bit cuts into roots. When bit hits root, feed slowly to allow it to penetrate.

Root

If vent is clogged, or if access to soil stack is best reached through vent, you will have to work an extra-long snake through roof vent and down stack. Unless you're experienced, leave this job to a professional.

Plumbing/Toilet tank problems

Most toilet tanks work in much the same way. The flush handle tips up the lift arm, raising the tank ball from its valve seat. The discharge pipe is then open, and water flows from the tank into the bowl. When the tank is nearly empty, the tank ball falls back into the valve seat, cutting off the flow.

The float falls with the water level, opening the ballcock valve just as the discharge pipe is closed. This allows water to enter through the tank filler tube, and additional water flows in through the bowl refill tube and the overflow tube. The float rises as the tank refills. When the float reaches a preset level, the tank is filled and the float arm closes the ballcock valve, shutting off the water.

Maintenance and repair. Although the water in a toilet tank is clean, mineral deposits collect in it, and the metal parts may rust. Scrubbing with steel wool or sandpaper removes these impurities.

If you have a problem with your toilet tank, consult the troubleshooting chart on this page, and try the remedies in the order given. When you need a replacement part, search for the manufacturer's name and the model number incised inside the lid of the tank and buy a compatible part, or bring the old one with you and try to match it.

Leaking or sweating toilets. If your toilet tank or bowl develops a leak, check all pipes and connections. If a pipe is corroded or the tank or bowl itself is cracked, replace it. If the leak appears near a joint, clean away any corrosion, replace any gaskets or washers, and tighten the connection—but not too much, or you may crack the porcelain.

When cold water enters a toilet and meets the warm air of the bathroom, the tank or bowl may sweat. To reduce sweating, empty the tank, dry it thoroughly, and line it with ½-inch polystyrene or foam rubber. Use a kit or cut your own liners to fit the tank walls and floor. Glue the liners in place with silicone cement, and let the adhesive dry thoroughly (at least 24 hours) before refilling the tank. Another remedy for sweating is to have a plumber add a tempering valve to partially heat the water before it enters the tank, but this can be a big job.

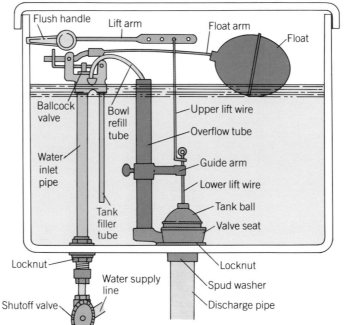

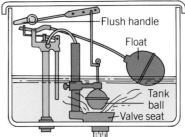

Depressing flush handle pulls tank ball from valve seat, letting water flow to bowl.

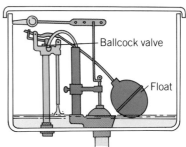

Sinking float opens ballcock valve and lets in outside water to refill tank.

Troubleshooting a toilet

Problem	Solution
Water runs continuously	Adjust lift wires or chain so that tank ball drops straight into valve seat. Clean tank ball and valve seat. If overflow tube is corroded, unscrew, discard, and screw in new one.
Water spills into overflow tube	Bend float arm down a little.
Water runs after flushing	Bend float arm upward or replace if corroded. Scour valve seat or replace (p.208) if corroded.
Whistling sounds	Put new washers in ballcock valve plunger. Replace ballcock assembly with floating-cup ballcock.
Splashing sounds	Reposition refill tube to eject directly into overflow tube. Put new washers in ballcock valve plunger.
Tank flushes partially	Shorten lift wires or chain to make tank ball rise higher. Raise guide arm ½ in. on overflow tube. Bend float arm upward to raise water level.
Tank sweats	Insulate tank by lining with sheets of polystyrene or foam rubber. Have plumber install a tempering valve to heat water in tank.
Tank leaks	Tighten connections to the water supply line. Replace spud washer at discharge pipe. Install a new tank (p.228).
Toilet leaks at base	Tighten nuts beneath bolt caps on base of bowl. Disconnect toilet from floor and replace seal under bowl (p.228).

Easy, low-cost improvements

When piece-by-piece repairs prove ineffective, replace the ballcock valve or the tank ball mechanism. Both are available in kits. If you have a cross-connection (p.199), get a toilet tank repair kit with an anti-siphon feature.

To install either device, first turn off the water to the toilet—the shutoff valve is usually under the tank. Flush the toilet to drain it, and sponge up any remaining water. Remove the old device; then dry the tank thoroughly. Hook up the replacement mechanism according to the manufacturer's instructions. Then turn on the water again.

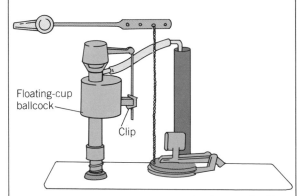

Floating-cup ballcock allows you to raise the water level in the tank by pinching its clip and moving it up. Plastic and stainless steel parts resist rust.

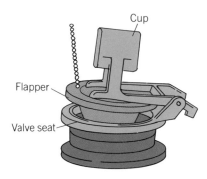

Hinged flapper sits more securely in valve seat and does not jiggle out of place as easily as tank ball. Self-timing cup controls duration of flush.

Solving toilet problems

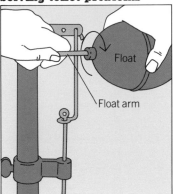

1. Check water level in tank; it should be about ½ in. below top of overflow pipe. If it is lower, the float may not rise high enough to shut off the ballcock valve. Unscrew float by turning it counter-clockwise on float arm. Shake it for possible water inside. If water has leaked into it or if it feels mushy, replace it.

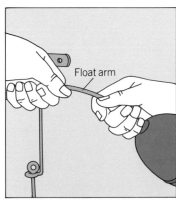

2. If float is sound, reposition float arm. To make water rise higher in tank, bend float arm slightly upward from center. (To lower water level, bend the arm downward.) If the arm won't bend under hand pressure, grip it with pliers on either side of center. Flush toilet. If water level is still low, bend arm a bit more.

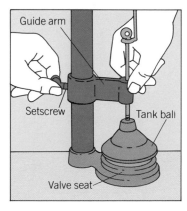

3. Check alignment of tank ball. Shut off water to tank, lift off cover, and flush toilet. Watch as tank ball drops. If it doesn't fall straight into the valve seat, loosen setscrew on guide arm, then reposition arm so that tank ball is poised directly above valve seat. Tighten setscrew, refill tank, and flush toilet to test it.

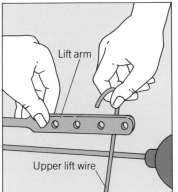

4. If tank ball still won't seat right, empty tank, move upper lift wire to different hole in lift arm, and straighten or bend wires slightly to make tank ball drop straight into valve seat. If the tank ball is held by a chain, try moving chain to another hole on the guide arm. Lengthen chain slightly if it is taut when tank ball is seated.

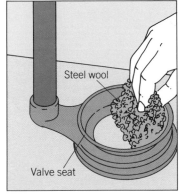

5. If water escapes when tank ball seats properly, there may be a buildup of mineral deposits on tank ball and valve seat. With the tank dry, unscrew tank ball and wash it with warm water and detergent. Gently scour rim of valve seat with fine steel wool. Replace tank ball, turn on water, and test-flush.

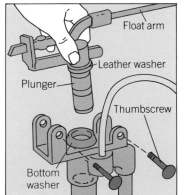

6. If float and arm are OK but water still trickles in, replace washers on plunger in ballcock valve. With water off, remove pins or thumbscrews holding float arm. Pull up plunger. Pry off leather washer, and pull off or unscrew the bottom washer. Scrape the grooves clean and install new washers.

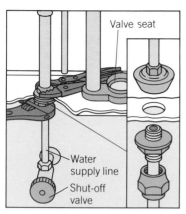

Valve seat

Water supply line

Shut-off valve

1. Turn off water supply to toilet and flush the toilet. Remove the lid and sponge up excess water. Loosen the setscrew; remove stopper assembly (p.206). Disconnect the water supply line, using an adjustable wrench to unscrew the nut beneath the tank at water inlet pipe. At the same time, hold hex nut inside tank with locking pliers.

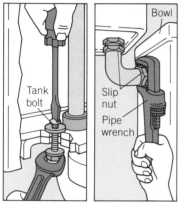

Bowl

Tank bolt

Slip nut

Pipe wrench

2. If tank is mounted on bowl, remove the tank bolts with a screwdriver and an open-end wrench. Lift the tank off the bowl, and lay it on its back. (To avoid scratches, lay it on an old towel.) For a wall-mounted tank, use a large pipe wrench to remove slip nuts at both ends of 90° pipe between the tank and bowl.

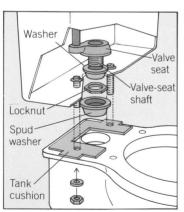

Washer

Valve seat

Valve-seat shaft

Locknut

Spud washer

Tank cushion

3. Unscrew locknut from the valve-seat shaft and pull valve seat into the tank. Place new valve-seat assembly in tank; make sure parts are in proper order. Reattach tank to bowl (tighten nuts alternately to keep tank aligned) and reconnect water supply line; or reattach 90° pipe to tank and bowl. Replace stopper assembly and turn on water supply.

Instead of a tank to store water, a flushometer toilet, also called a pressure-flush-valve toilet, contains a valve and a control stop that regulates water pressure and the length of the flush. Although this toilet saves water, it requires a large-diameter water supply pipe—1 to 1½ inches—and it is noisier than a tank toilet. A flushometer toilet will have one of two types of valves: diaphragm or piston. The piston valve is better for hard-water areas.

In both types a screw in the control stop can be adjusted to vary the amount of water released for each flush. Sometimes the screw is hidden under a decorative cover. Turn the screw clockwise to decrease the flow, counterclockwise to increase it.

Insufficient flushing when the screw is fully open usually suggests the need for valve repairs. If the flushing cycle continues longer than usual or the water flow does not stop, a clogged bypass channel is generally the cause. Clear it with a fine wire. Replacement parts are available in kits at plumbing supply stores. Look for the manufacturer's name on an old part before buying a new one, or take the old one with you to the store.

Repairing the handle

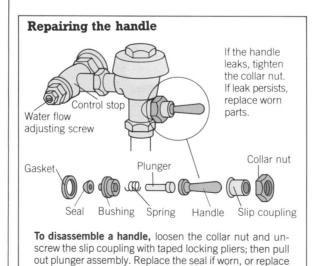

Control stop

Water flow adjusting screw

If the handle leaks, tighten the collar nut. If leak persists, replace worn parts.

Gasket

Plunger

Collar nut

Seal   Bushing   Spring   Handle   Slip coupling

To disassemble a handle, loosen the collar nut and unscrew the slip coupling with taped locking pliers; then pull out plunger assembly. Replace the seal if worn, or replace the entire plunger unit. Clean parts before reassembling.

Diaphragm valve   **Piston valve**

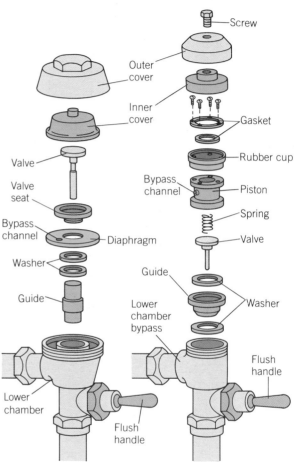

Screw

Outer cover

Inner cover

Gasket

Rubber cup

Bypass channel

Piston

Spring

Valve

Guide

Washer

Flush handle

Valve

Valve seat

Bypass channel

Diaphragm

Washer

Guide

Lower chamber bypass

Lower chamber

Flush handle

To replace a diaphragm valve, turn off water supply and unscrew outer cover with a taped pipe wrench. Take off the inner cover; then remove diaphragm assembly. Replace the diaphragm, valve seat, and worn parts inside guide. To get into guide, hold it with a pipe wrench. Unscrew valve seat with another wrench or pliers. Replace parts; reassemble.

In a piston valve, replace the rubber cup separately or, to avoid replacing worn valve at a later time, replace entire valve assembly. After turning off water supply, unscrew nut to take off outer cover; then unscrew the inner cover. Pull out the piston assembly. To replace cup, remove screws joining cup and piston. Replace parts and reassemble.

Compression faucets

There are several types of compression faucets, but all work in a similar way: When you turn the handle to shut off the water, the stem moves down and an attached washer prevents water from flowing through the valve seat. Packing around the faucet stem keeps water from flowing out of the stem.

This faucet can leak for three reasons: the washer at the valve seat has eroded, the valve seat itself is damaged, or the packing is worn. If the spout drips, a worn washer or valve seat is at fault. If you're not sure which handle is causing the problem, turn off one of the water supply valves; if the drip stops, the problem is with the handle it supplies. Feel around the valve seat; rough spots call for replacing. If you can't get the seat out, reface it with a valve-seat dresser. Worn packing is usually the culprit if a handle leaks; sometimes the stem needs replacing.

Your faucet's construction may vary from the one shown, but the repair steps will be similar. Washer shapes are different; some screw into the stem assembly, others snap in. Some faucets use a self-forming packing material; others use O-rings. Some stem assemblies are in a removable sleeve; its valve seat can be replaced easily if worn.

Before taking apart a faucet, shut off both water supply valves and open both handles to drain the faucet. Close the stopper to keep small parts from falling down the drain, and line the sink with an old towel. Line up parts as you remove them; reassemble them in reverse order. Coat interior parts with a heatproof, waterproof grease before reassembly.

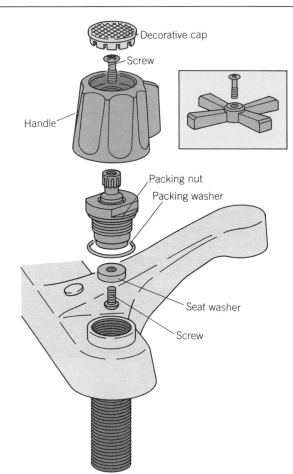

Decorative cap
Screw
Handle
Packing nut
Packing washer
Seat washer
Screw

1. Using a screwdriver, pry off the decorative cap and remove screw that secures faucet handle to stem. Pull the handle from the stem.

2. Remove packing nut with adjustable wrench, turning counterclockwise. Gently pull up stem assembly, or turn it counterclockwise by hand.

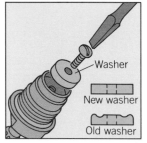
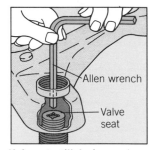

Washer
New washer
Old washer

Allen wrench
Valve seat

Replacing worn washer. If the new washer doesn't fit, reverse the old one for a temporary fix. Always use a brass screw to install a washer.

If faucet still leaks, replace valve seat. Use Allen wrench to unscrew (counterclockwise), and remove seat. Grease new seat with pipe joint compound.

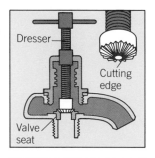
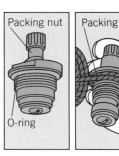

Dresser
Cutting edge
Valve seat

Packing nut
Packing
O-ring

To reface a seat, use valve-seat dresser. Screw tool into faucet until cutter is flush against seat. Turn handle back and forth a few times. Flush out grindings.

To stop handle leaks, tighten packing nut. If it still leaks, remove old packing (or O-ring). Refill nut, adding 1½ times the packing; nut will compact it.

Freezeproof faucets

Some faucets for outdoor use are designed so that they won't freeze. The handle, spout, and packing are outside the house, but the valve seat and washer are inside. The stem is tilted to let water drain out of valve. Repairs are same as for compression faucet, but redressing seat requires a long-handled tool; it may be easier to replace unit than to find the tool.

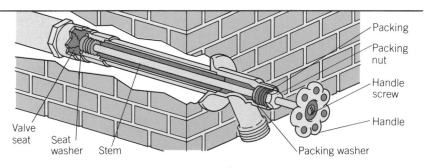

Valve seat
Seat washer
Stem
Packing
Packing nut
Handle screw
Handle
Packing washer

Plumbing/Washerless faucets

Ball faucet

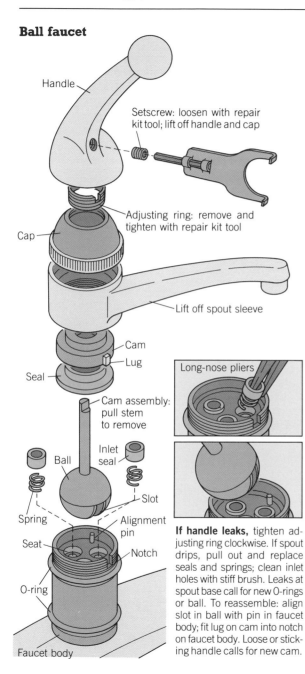

Handle

Setscrew: loosen with repair kit tool; lift off handle and cap

Adjusting ring: remove and tighten with repair kit tool

Cap

Lift off spout sleeve

Cam

Lug

Seal

Cam assembly: pull stem to remove

Inlet seal

Ball

Slot

Spring

Alignment pin

Seat

Notch

O-ring

Faucet body

Long-nose pliers

If handle leaks, tighten adjusting ring clockwise. If spout drips, pull out and replace seals and springs; clean inlet holes with stiff brush. Leaks at spout base call for new O-rings or ball. To reassemble: align slot in ball with pin in faucet body; fit lug on cam into notch on faucet body. Loose or sticking handle calls for new cam.

Parts inside different style faucets may vary, but their function is the same. When you move the handle, one part shifts, opening a channel through which water flows. There are four types of mechanisms—ball, ceramic disc, cartridge, and tipping valve. Some have two handles; others one. In some you pull the handle up to turn on water. In one-handle faucets, the knob or lever also controls temperature.

If a faucet drips or leaks, an O-ring or another part, such as a cartridge or valve seat, may need replacing. If the water flow is restricted, try cleaning the aerator in the spout's tip. Reassemble it carefully; a reversed part will block it.

Before making a repair, turn off the sink's water supply and open the faucet so that water drains out. Plug the drain so parts can't fall down it, and line the sink with a towel to protect against damage from dropped tools. The hardest task may be finding the screw that releases the handle; sometimes it's under a decorative cap or hidden beneath the handle.

Ceramic disc faucet

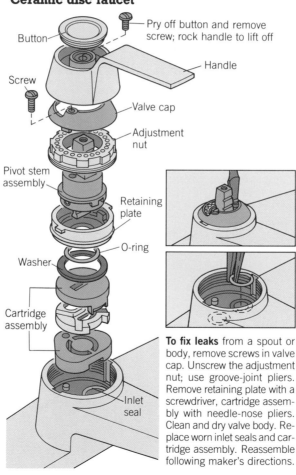

Button

Pry off button and remove screw; rock handle to lift off

Handle

Screw

Valve cap

Adjustment nut

Pivot stem assembly

Retaining plate

O-ring

Washer

Cartridge assembly

Inlet seal

To fix leaks from a spout or body, remove screws in valve cap. Unscrew the adjustment nut; use groove-joint pliers. Remove retaining plate with a screwdriver, cartridge assembly with needle-nose pliers. Clean and dry valve body. Replace worn inlet seals and cartridge assembly. Reassemble following maker's directions.

Cartridge faucet

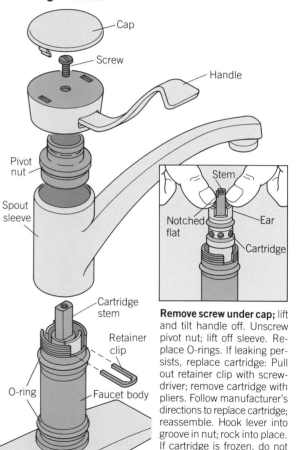

Cap

Screw

Handle

Pivot nut

Spout sleeve

Stem

Notched flat

Ear

Cartridge

Cartridge stem

Retainer clip

O-ring

Faucet body

Remove screw under cap; lift and tilt handle off. Unscrew pivot nut; lift off sleeve. Replace O-rings. If leaking persists, replace cartridge: Pull out retainer clip with screwdriver; remove cartridge with pliers. Follow manufacturer's directions to replace cartridge; reassemble. Hook lever into groove in nut; rock into place. If cartridge is frozen, do not force; replace faucet.

As you disassemble parts, line them up in sequence to make reassembly easy. Replacement parts, as well as kits, are readily available in hardware and plumbing supply stores. Make sure new parts match; each make differs slightly. Parts for tipping valves, which are no longer made, are hard to find; you may have to replace the faucet.

Some faucets have a spray attachment. If the water flows slowly, a tangled hose may be the culprit—try untangling it. Or a clogged aerator or diverter valve, which switches the water between faucet spout and sprayer, may be responsible. To disassemble the aerator, look for a retaining screw beneath a cover.

You can clear a blocked hose by running water through it with the spray head removed. Water will run through the hose rather than to the spout.

Leaking spray head. To stop leaks from the base of a spray head, unscrew it from its coupling. Detach the coupling from the hose by prying off the retaining snap ring; replace the washer.

Repairing a tipping valve

With tape-wrapped wrench unscrew spout ring; pry up body. For leak at spout base, replace O-ring. If spout drips, replace valve seat. Unscrew strainer plugs and remove parts. Clean strainers. Replace old screw on wobbly handle, or tighten adjusting screw a quarter turn. Reassemble.

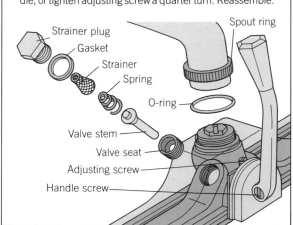

- Strainer plug
- Gasket
- Strainer
- Spring
- O-ring
- Valve stem
- Valve seat
- Adjusting screw
- Handle screw
- Spout ring

Aerator and diverter

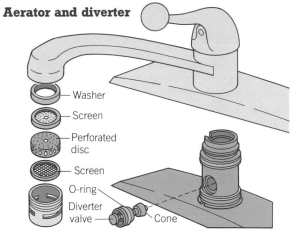

- Washer
- Screen
- Perforated disc
- Screen
- O-ring
- Diverter valve
- Cone

Slow water flow. Unscrew aerator; soak parts in vinegar and clean them; reassemble in correct order. If flow is still slow, remove spout sleeve (p.210). Pull diverter from side of body; or unscrew it partially and pull it from top of body with pliers. Clean parts; if cone is loose, replace diverter. Reassemble. Remove aerator; flush water lines.

Spray attachment

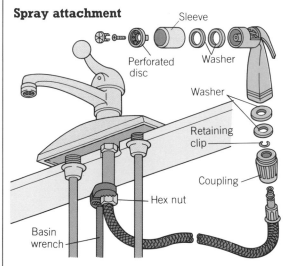

- Sleeve
- Perforated disc
- Washer
- Washer
- Retaining clip
- Coupling
- Hex nut
- Basin wrench

To replace worn spray hose, unscrew it from its hose attachment with pliers or a basin wrench; buy a new hose, preferably made of nylon-reinforced vinyl and of same diameter. In case new hose does not match spout attachment, take the hex nut to plumbing supply store to match with correct adapter.

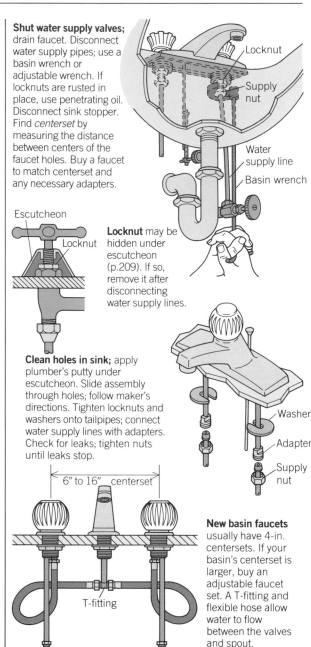

Shut water supply valves; drain faucet. Disconnect water supply pipes; use a basin wrench or adjustable wrench. If locknuts are rusted in place, use penetrating oil. Disconnect sink stopper. Find *centerset* by measuring the distance between centers of the faucet holes. Buy a faucet to match centerset and any necessary adapters.

- Locknut
- Supply nut
- Water supply line
- Basin wrench
- Escutcheon
- Locknut

Locknut may be hidden under escutcheon (p.209). If so, remove it after disconnecting water supply lines.

Clean holes in sink; apply plumber's putty under escutcheon. Slide assembly through holes; follow maker's directions. Tighten locknuts and washers onto tailpipes; connect water supply lines with adapters. Check for leaks; tighten nuts until leaks stop.

- Washer
- Adapter
- Supply nut

6" to 16"   centerset

T-fitting

New basin faucets usually have 4-in. centersets. If your basin's centerset is larger, buy an adjustable faucet set. A T-fitting and flexible hose allow water to flow between the valves and spout.

The operating parts inside a tub faucet are similar to those in a sink faucet, and the repairs of each type are the same. In some tub faucets, parts are recessed behind the tile; break the tile and re- move the bonnet nut to reach them. A diverter valve may also need repairing or replacing. If the tub faucet lacks a separate shutoff valve, turn off the water supply to the entire house or to one floor.

Washerless tub faucet

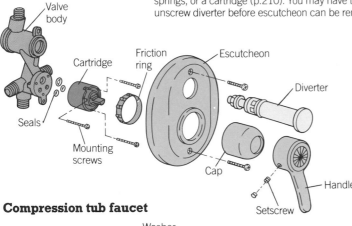

A leaking washerless faucet needs its internal parts cleaned or replaced. They may include O-rings, springs, or a cartridge (p.210). You may have to unscrew diverter before escutcheon can be removed.

Compression tub faucet

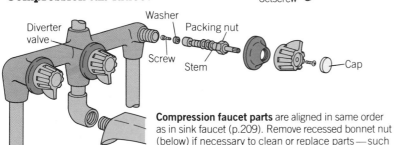

Compression faucet parts are aligned in same order as in sink faucet (p.209). Remove recessed bonnet nut (below) if necessary to clean or replace parts—such as a washer or O-ring—or to try refacing valve seat.

Removing a bonnet nut

To reach a recessed bonnet nut, you'll have to chip away surrounding ceramic tile with a hammer and cold chisel. Remove enough material so that you can slip a deep socket wrench over the nut; turn the wrench counterclockwise to loosen the nut. Repair wall with sealant or tile (p.315).

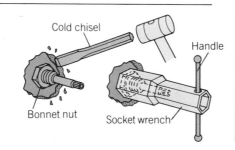

Shower heads

Clean a shower head by soaking it in vinegar to remove mineral deposits; unblock clogged holes with a tooth- pick. Stop a leak by tightening all con- nections. To install a new hand-held shower, remove the old shower head with an adjustable wrench. Screw shower hose onto the shower arm.

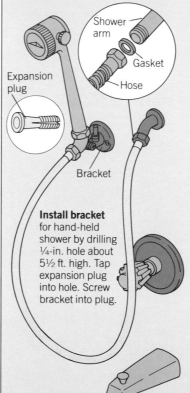

Install bracket for hand-held shower by drilling ¼-in. hole about 5½ ft. high. Tap expansion plug into hole. Screw bracket into plug.

Tub–shower diverter

A diverter valve switches water from tub spout to shower head. One type is built into the spout and has a knob that, when pulled up, raises a gate and diverts water to the shower head. This valve cannot be repaired; once dam- aged, the entire spout must be replaced. A diverter valve separate from a tub spout works like a compression fau- cet—turning a handle clockwise moves a stem into the valve seat, and water is diverted into the shower head. A counterclockwise turn reopens the passage to the spout.

If tub faucet drips when you shower, take apart valve by same steps as for a compression faucet (p. 209). Replace worn washers, O- rings, and packing. If hollow housing is worn and water flow still isn't diverted, replace diverter valve.

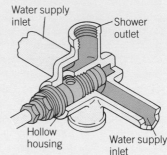

To replace a valve, insert a hammer or wrench handle into the tub spout; turn counterclockwise to unscrew the spout. Replace with a new spout of equal length. If unavailable, buy a nipple to attach the new spout. Screw in by hand.

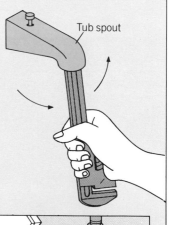

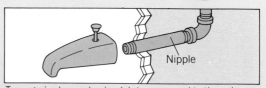

To seal nipple, apply pipe joint compound to threads.

Fixing sink and tub pop-up stoppers

Most bathroom sinks and tubs have a pop-up drain stopper. Although adjustments to them are simple, they may require several tries to get it just right.

In bathroom sinks, a knob on the faucet body controls a three-part linkage: a vertical lift rod; a vertical flat rod pierced with holes, called a *clevis;* and a horizontal rod that pivots up and down on a plastic ball inside the drain, raising and lowering the stopper. Usually the stopper can be lifted straight out of the drain or comes out after a twist. One type of stopper is secured by a pivot rod that threads through a loop at the base of the stopper; remove the rod first.

If water seeps through the drain when the stopper is closed, remove the stopper. Clean the drain of any hair and debris—a bottle brush may help. Look on the stopper for a rubber seal (a heavier model won't have one), and replace the seal if it's damaged. If water still seeps through, the stopper isn't seated properly; adjust the linkage mechanism.

First adjust the lift rod under the sink. Although this adjustment is simple, working in the confined space may be awkward, and you may need a flashlight. The lift rod runs from the pull control on top of the faucet body down through the basin. If you cannot loosen the setscrew with your fingers or tape-wrapped pliers, apply penetrating oil to the threads and let it sit for half an hour. If tightening the lift rod has made the stopper slightly difficult to operate, then adjust the pivot rod.

If water leaks near the retaining nut after you release water from the basin, the pivot ball assembly will need repairs. Replace worn parts.

Tub pop-up stopper

To stop a leak, pull stopper out of drain; a rocker arm will follow. Clean the stopper, rocker arm, and flange. Replace O-ring if it is worn. To adjust a stopper, unscrew tub's overflow plate and pull out the entire linkage assembly (it may have a spring or plunger). Clean with a stiff brush; soak in vinegar to remove mineral deposits. Loosen adjusting nuts on striker rod by the middle link. If tub won't hold water, slide middle link up the rod slightly. If water drains too slowly, lower the middle link. Replace worn parts before reassembling.

Pop-up stoppers

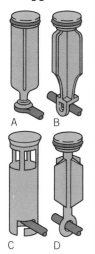

Stoppers A and B lift out. Twist C a quarter turn counterclockwise; lift out. To remove D, loosen retaining nut; pull rod from stopper.

Sink pop-up assembly

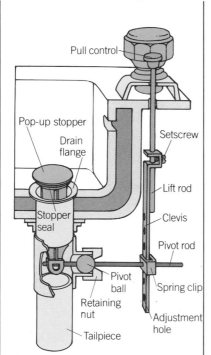

Setting lift rod

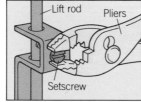

Loosen the setscrew with fingers or tape-wrapped pliers. Pull the knob up and push the stopper down; retighten screw.

Setting pivot rod

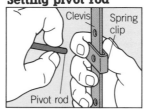

Squeeze spring clip and slide rod free of clevis. Move rod and clip into next hole up. Try stopper again; repeat if necessary.

Pivot ball leaks

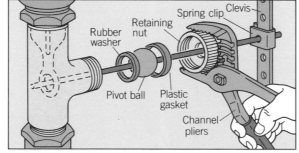

Tighten retaining nut. If leak persists, unscrew nut and replace washers or gaskets. Clean ball; if badly scratched, replace it.

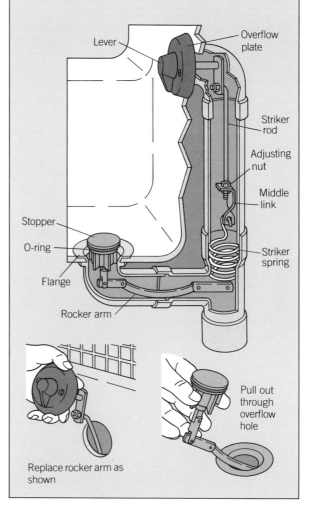

Replace rocker arm as shown

Water hammer and whistling

When you close a faucet or an appliance shuts off, you may hear a banging noise known as water hammer. Water moving under pressure has suddenly been stopped by the closing of a valve; the pressure forces the pipe to shake and may damage the valve. If your house is not equipped with water-hammer arresters, or air chambers, install one for each affected fixture. Air inside the chamber cushions the water pressure and stops water hammer.

There are several types of water-hammer arresters: a capped pipe twice the diameter of the supply pipe and up to 2 feet in length; a coil of flexible copper tubing, which can be installed without cutting into the wall; and an almost-round model that has a ring around its center. The first two types sometimes fill with water. If that happens, turn off the main water supply and open all the faucets. When they have drained, close the faucets and turn on the main water supply. Inside the ball model is a diaphragm; it may tear and the unit need replacing.

A pressure-reducing valve can stop water hammer by lowering water pressure to the house; but it may reduce water flow, affecting upper-floor fixtures. The valve can also correct a whistling sound, which may indicate high water pressure. (If you have a water pump, check its pressure first.) Whistling may also mean water flow is restricted. Make sure all valves in the supply lines are fully open.

Other plumbing noises

Loose pipes may bang as water is turned off. Check the pipe clamps or hangers and resecure them, or add more fasteners if necessary. If a pipe bangs as it passes through a stud or sill, enlarge the hole.

A pipe should be able to slide slightly on its

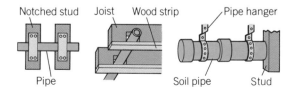

Notched stud   Joist   Wood strip   Pipe hanger

Pipe   Soil pipe   Stud

Water-hammer arresters

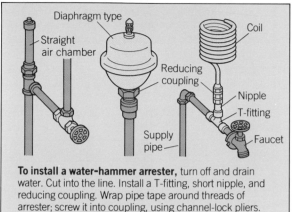

Diaphragm type   Coil

Straight air chamber

Reducing coupling

Nipple

T-fitting

Supply pipe   Faucet

To install a water-hammer arrester, turn off and drain water. Cut into the line. Install a T-fitting, short nipple, and reducing coupling. Wrap pipe tape around threads of arrester; screw it into coupling, using channel-lock pliers.

Pressure-reducing valve

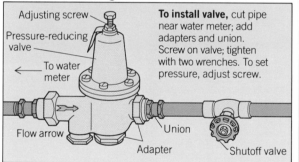

Adjusting screw

Pressure-reducing valve

To water meter

Flow arrow

Union

Adapter   Shutoff valve

To install valve, cut pipe near water meter; add adapters and union. Screw on valve; tighten with two wrenches. To set pressure, adjust screw.

hangers. When you turn on the hot water, a cold pipe expands. A clinking or ticking sound means the pipe is too tightly anchored. Listen to locate the sound; then search along the pipe to find the tight place. Loosen the support, and add a piece of rubber or felt between the pipe and the support.

Running water sounds may come from an open faucet, a leaking toilet (p.206), a furnace humidifier connected to the cold-water line, or an automatic water softener when it backflushes. Drainage system noises may be from faulty venting, a plugged vent, or incorrect drainpipe size (p.216).

Before cold weather strikes, you should protect pipes in unheated areas from freezing. Temporary measures include letting a faucet run slightly (running water freezes more slowly than still water); aiming an electric heater, heat lamp, or 100-watt bulb at exposed pipes; keeping doors open between heated and unheated rooms; and wrapping pipes with newspaper tied with string.

Insulation won't prevent freezing during a long cold spell, but it will for a short term. It will also reduce heat loss from hot-water pipes and condensation on cold-water pipes. Insulation can be bought preformed to fit pipes or in strips to wrap pipes and fittings. Electric heat tape wrapped around pipes will prevent freezing as long as the power is on.

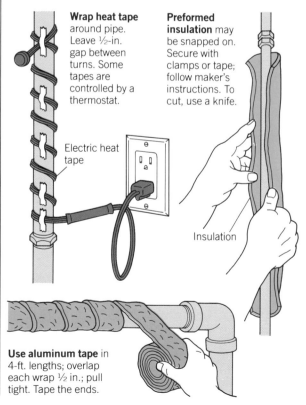

Wrap heat tape around pipe. Leave ½-in. gap between turns. Some tapes are controlled by a thermostat.

Preformed insulation may be snapped on. Secure with clamps or tape; follow maker's instructions. To cut, use a knife.

Electric heat tape

Insulation

Use aluminum tape in 4-ft. lengths; overlap each wrap ½ in.; pull tight. Tape the ends.

Frozen and leaking pipes

Thawing frozen pipes is a slow, time-consuming, but necessary process. Water expands as it freezes; so frozen pipes or joints may burst or leak. Check for bursts, and repair before defrosting the pipe. Thaw exposed pipes gradually with a hair dryer, propane torch (p.11), or other heat source. For a pipe behind a wall, clamp a heat lamp to a chair (p.11), or let water run if the pipe isn't completely blocked. The warmer running water will help melt frozen water.

Repairing leaking or burst pipes. Turn off water to the damaged section of pipe, then open a faucet. For a small leak in a waste pipe, force a toothpick into the hole and break off the end (water swells the wood, plugging the hole). Be sure the surface is bone dry; then seal with electrical tape. Wrap the tape tightly, overlapping each turn by at least half its width and using at least three layers. If a joint leaks, tighten its unions or resolder the joint (pp.217–223).

If you cut out a section of pipe, support its ends with temporary hangers or wire. Sawing may loosen joints; the pipe may sag and pull away from the wall.

Thawing frozen pipes

Before starting to thaw a frozen pipe, close the shutoff valve to the pipe or close the main water valve. Open a faucet to allow melting ice to run out and let steam pressure escape when the pipe is heated — this is especially important if you use a propane torch. Be sure to work from the open faucet toward the frozen area. As the ice melts, check for leaks and repair any you find. **CAUTION:** Never use a propane torch on plastic pipe.

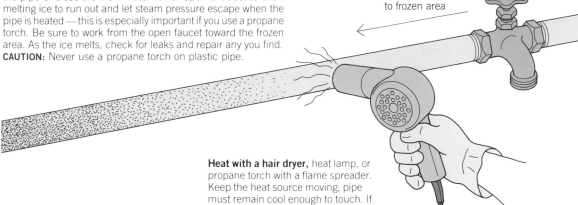

Work from faucet to frozen area

Heat with a hair dryer, heat lamp, or propane torch with a flame spreader. Keep the heat source moving; pipe must remain cool enough to touch. If water inside boils, pipe might burst.

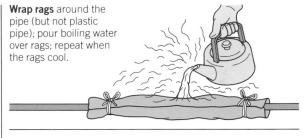

Wrap rags around the pipe (but not plastic pipe); pour boiling water over rags; repeat when the rags cool.

Wrap grounded wetproof heating pad, electric blanket, or heat tape around the frozen pipe.

Fixing a burst pipe

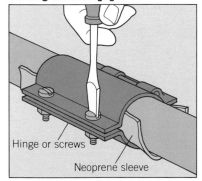

Hinge or screws

Neoprene sleeve

Apply a pipe clamp over rubber or neoprene pad. Clamp should extend 1 in. past leak. Screw tight.

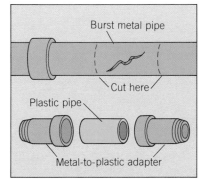

Burst metal pipe

Cut here

Plastic pipe

Metal-to-plastic adapter

Cut out damaged pipe, and replace it with plastic pipe of same diameter. Use metal-to-plastic adapters (p.216).

EPOXY PUTTY

Use epoxy for leaking joint in a waste pipe; follow maker's directions. Don't use epoxy on a pressurized water supply pipe.

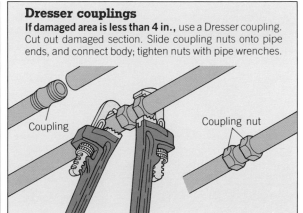

Dresser couplings

If damaged area is less than 4 in., use a Dresser coupling. Cut out damaged section. Slide coupling nuts onto pipe ends, and connect body; tighten nuts with pipe wrenches.

Coupling

Coupling nut

Plumbing/Pipes and pipe fittings

The type and size of pipe you can use in your home is regulated by plumbing codes. Before choosing any pipe—or indeed before undertaking any major plumbing job—check your local codes (p.193). You should also find out whether you need a permit. Some local ordinances require a licensed plumber to perform or to inspect certain work.

Generally water supply pipes may be plastic, copper, galvanized steel, or brass. DWV (drain-waste-vent) pipes may be cast iron, copper, plastic, or steel. Polyethylene tubing is used for outdoor cold-water applications but seldom inside a house.

Fittings. Sections of pipe are joined by fittings. A large variety of fittings are available for connecting pipes of different types or diameters, for making curves with rigid pipe, or for joining sections of pipe in straight runs or branches. If you can't find a single fitting to make a particular connection, try a combination of two or more.

Most fittings are available in two ways, standard and flush-wall. Standard fittings are used for water supply pipes. Flush-wall fittings are needed for drainage pipes—they have smooth inside joints that offer no obstruction to the flow of waste.

Measuring pipe. Pipes are always referred to by the measurement of their inside diameter (i.d.). However, the nominal size of a pipe sometimes bears little relation to its actual size. A pipe that is nominally ¼ inch may actually be slightly larger or smaller than that. If you are buying pipe to connect to an existing line, take a fitting or a piece of the pipe with you. If you can't, measure the pipe's actual inside diameter as shown below; then refer to a conversion chart at your plumbing supply outlet. If you are adding a supply line, use the pipe size specified by the fixture manufacturer.

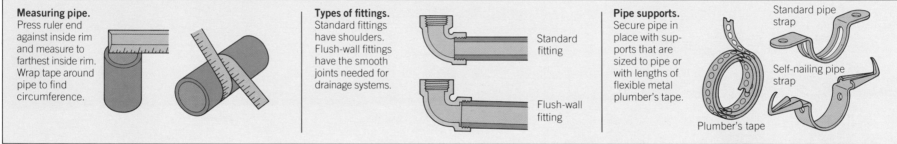

Measuring pipe. Press ruler end against inside rim and measure to farthest inside rim. Wrap tape around pipe to find circumference.

Types of fittings. Standard fittings have shoulders. Flush-wall fittings have the smooth joints needed for drainage systems.

Standard fitting

Flush-wall fitting

Pipe supports. Secure pipe in place with supports that are sized to pipe or with lengths of flexible metal plumber's tape.

Standard pipe strap

Self-nailing pipe strap

Plumber's tape

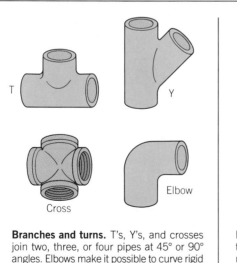

T

Y

Cross

Elbow

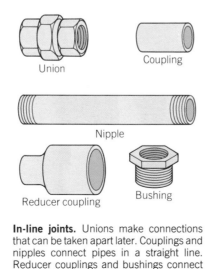

Union

Coupling

Nipple

Reducer coupling

Bushing

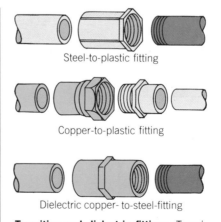

Steel-to-plastic fitting

Copper-to-plastic fitting

Dielectric copper- to-steel-fitting

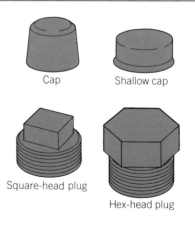

Cap

Shallow cap

Square-head plug

Hex-head plug

Branches and turns. T's, Y's, and crosses join two, three, or four pipes at 45° or 90° angles. Elbows make it possible to curve rigid pipe. Reducer T's, Y's, and elbows connect pipes of different diameters.

In-line joints. Unions make connections that can be taken apart later. Couplings and nipples connect pipes in a straight line. Reducer couplings and bushings connect pipes, or pipes and fittings, of different sizes.

Transition and dielectric fittings. Transition fittings join plastic and metal pipes. Various dielectric couplings connect pipes of different metals and also prevent electro-chemical reactions that cause corrosion.

Caps and plugs. Caps fit over the ends of pipes to seal them; plugs are screwed into the ends of pipes or fittings. Drainpipe cleanouts are often fitted with plugs to give access for clearing blockages.

Rigid plastic pipe

Because it is less expensive, lighter, easier to work with, and more durable than metal pipe, rigid plastic pipe is widely used in house plumbing. It meets all of the national plumbing codes and is fully approved by the federal government. However, some municipalities may still prohibit its use; so check your local plumbing codes.

Types. There are three types of rigid plastic pipe. CPVC (chlorinated polyvinyl chloride), suitable for hot- and cold-water supply lines, is sold in 10- or 20-foot lengths with inside diameters of ½ or ¾ inch. It is rated for pressure up to 100 psi (pounds per square inch). Use pipe with the pressure rating prescribed by local code. Because plastic pipe is less able than metal to withstand a sudden pressure change, be sure to install water-hammer arresters (p. 214).

PVC (polyvinyl chloride), used mainly for drain lines, is particularly resistant to chemicals. It comes in 10- and 20-foot lengths in a variety of diameters.

ABS (acrylonitrile butadiene styrene) is used only for drain lines. It is sold in 10- and 20-foot lengths in different diameters for stacks and main drains.

Making connections. Plastic pipe is joined by chemical welding—by applying a solvent cement that dissolves the surface of the pipe and its fitting so that they bond together. Each chemical variety of pipe requires its own solvent cement, and CPVC and PVC must be cleaned with a primer before being cemented. Follow the pipe manufacturer's recommendations, work in a well-ventilated area, and refrain from smoking or lighting a match. Solvent cement is highly flammable.

You can join rigid plastic pipe to metal pipe with transition fittings (facing page). However, you should not use different types of plastic pipes in the same system, as this can result in leaks.

1. Cut pipe to length in miter box, using hacksaw with blade that has 24 or 32 teeth per in. Or use plastic-pipe cutter and proceed as you would for copper pipe (p. 220).

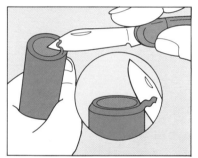

2. Smooth inside of cut with knife or fine file, and outside with fine (120-grit) sandpaper. Bevel outside edge to keep it from forcing solvent cement out of fitting.

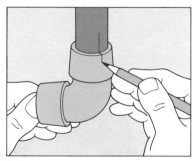

3. Insert pipe into fitting, and adjust fitting to correct position. Mark both pipe and fitting so that they can be quickly positioned once solvent cement is applied.

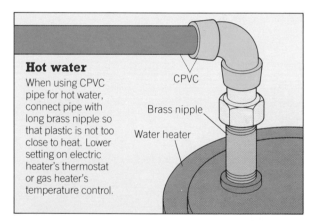

Hot water

When using CPVC pipe for hot water, connect pipe with long brass nipple so that plastic is not too close to heat. Lower setting on electric heater's thermostat or gas heater's temperature control.

CPVC

Brass nipple

Water heater

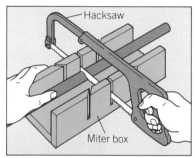

4. Liberally coat mating surfaces of pipe and fitting with solvent cement. (If you are working with CPVC or PVC pipe, first apply primer; wait 15 sec.; then apply cement.)

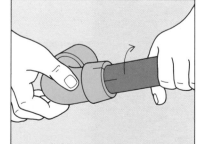

5. Push pipe fully into fitting at a quarter turn off final position. Twist fitting to spread solvent cement and align marks. Work quickly; cement sets in 60 sec.

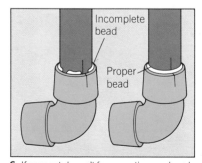

Incomplete bead

Proper bead

6. If cement doesn't form continuous bead, separate pieces and reapply. Hold together 30 sec.; wait 3 min. before starting next joint, 12 hr. before running water.

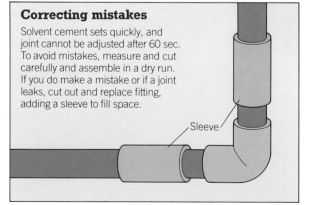

Correcting mistakes

Solvent cement sets quickly, and joint cannot be adjusted after 60 sec. To avoid mistakes, measure and cut carefully and assemble in a dry run. If you do make a mistake or if a joint leaks, cut out and replace fitting, adding a sleeve to fill space.

Sleeve

Plumbing/Flexible plastic tubing

Flexible plastic tubing is particularly useful when plumbing in hard-to-reach places where visibility and space are limited. Because of its long lengths and flexibility, few fittings are required, making it easy and inexpensive to work with and presenting minimum resistance to water flow.

Types. PB (polybutylene) tubing, suitable for hot- and cold-water supply lines, is able to withstand pressure up to 100 psi (pounds per square inch) and temperatures up to 180°F. It is available in 25- and 100-foot coils, and in inside diameters of ½, ⅜, and ¾ inch. If you use it for hot water, replace the pressure-temperature relief valve on your water heater to match the pipe's rating.

PE (polyethylene) is used only for transporting cold water, such as from a well or to an underground sprinkler system. It is sold in 100-foot coils in diameters of ½, ¾, and 1 inch with pressure ratings up to 100 psi and 125 psi. A utility grade, which is not suited for high pressure or drinking water, is also available.

Fittings. Flexible plastic tubing can be joined with nonthreaded nipple fittings, which are simply pushed on and clamped, or with "instant" one-step connectors, which are a bit more expensive. The compression and flare fittings used with copper pipe can also be used with plastic tubing; they are especially convenient for connecting it to faucets and other fixtures.

Repairing or replacing a sprinkler head

The small water holes in the spray heads of a sprinkler system may become clogged with dirt or mineral deposits. If this happens, it's an easy matter to clean the head. Little else can go wrong, but when it does, it's generally easier to replace the head than to attempt to repair it. When buying a new sprinkler head, take the old one with you to the hardware or plumbing supply store to be sure that the threads of the new head match those of the old.

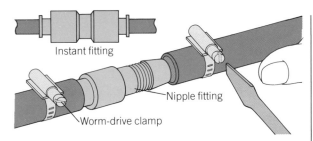

Instant and nipple fittings. Cut tubing ends square for both types. Push tubing into instant fitting until it locks in place. For nipple fittings, slip stainless steel worm-drive clamps over tubing ends; force tubing over fitting; screw clamps tight. To separate, loosen clamps, pour hot water over tubing to soften; pull off by hand.

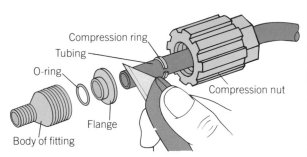

Compression fittings. Cut end of tubing, making certain that the cut is perfectly square, so that it will seat properly in fitting. Slide compression nut over cut end of tubing; then slip on compression ring, flange, and O-ring. Hand-screw the compression nut onto threaded body of fitting; tighten connection with two wrenches.

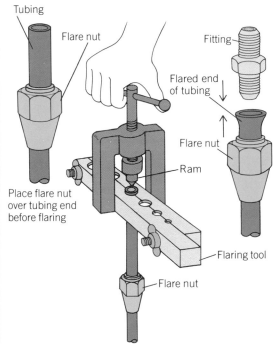

Flare fittings. Soak squared ends of tubing in warm water to soften plastic. Slip flare nut over tubing, and clamp end of tubing in opening it best fits in flaring tool. Screw in ram. Remove tubing from flaring tool, push fitting into flared end of tubing, and screw flare nut to fitting. Use two wrenches to tighten. (See also p.221.)

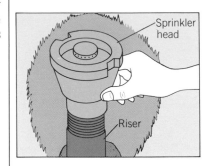

Use trowel to dig out enough dirt from around sprinkler head to grasp it. Unscrew the head; its riser may come out as well. If dirt falls into the pipe hole, turn on water for a few seconds to flush out dirt, or suck it out with a wet-dry vacuum (p.76).

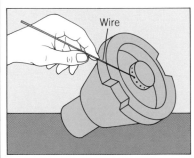

Clear clogged holes of sprinkler head with length of stiff wire. If the problem persists, replace the head. If riser came out with head, clean its threads and install cleaned or new head on it. Grasp head and screw riser back into underground pipe.

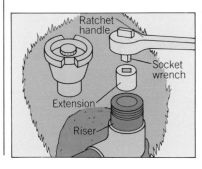

To raise head that has sunk into ground, replace riser with one long enough to bring head to its proper height. If the riser is difficult to unscrew, force extension for a ½-in. socket wrench into riser, attach ratchet handle, and unscrew riser.

Moving a sprinkler head

If you change the layout of your garden by moving flower beds or bushes, or if you build a new deck or patio that covers part of your old lawn, the placement of the sprinkler heads may need changing. Moving a sprinkler head to a new location needn't require digging up the entire lawn. Simply use a narrow extension pipe of ½-inch flexible plastic tubing, and carefully cut and lift the sod only in the immediate area.

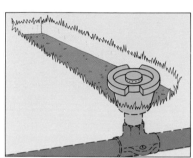

1. Carefully cut and fold back the sod between the old and new locations. Dig a narrow trench about 4 in. deep along the cleared space; dig out enough dirt around the sprinkler head to free it. Then remove the sprinkler head and its riser.

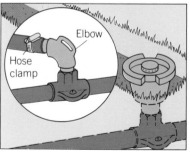

Elbow

Hose clamp

2. Screw an elbow fitting into exposed underground tubing. If necessary, remove more dirt to reach it. Push end of extension tubing over elbow, and secure it with a hose clamp. Run extension tubing to new location, and cut it to fit.

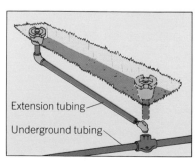

Extension tubing

Underground tubing

3. Install another elbow on tubing end. Screw the riser, with its sprinkler head attached, into elbow. If head is too high, dig out more dirt from underneath elbow; if it's too low, use a longer riser. Fill in the trench and re-lay the sod.

Installing a sump pump

If your basement floods often or its floor is below the level of the sewer line, you may need to install a sump pit to collect the water and a sump pump to suck it out of the pit. When water in the pit reaches a certain depth, a float-operated switch turns the pump on; after enough water is pumped out, bringing the level back down, the switch turns the pump off. You can use either a pedestal pump (shown below) or a submersible one. Submersible pumps tend to develop switch problems. On pedestal pumps the float can be adjusted. If you are going away for a length of time, you can adjust the float to switch the pump on and off at a lower than usual level of water.

The sump pit—available at lumberyards—is a cylinder of galvanized corrugated metal or plastic about 18 inches in diameter. To install one, break through the floor and dig a hole 2 feet deep and wide enough to accept the pit. Cover the bottom of the hole with 2 to 3 inches of gravel, fit in the pit, install a pump according to the manufacturer's instructions, and cover the pit.

Use 1¼-inch plastic pipe to carry water from the pump to a drain. To prevent backflow, install a 1¼-inch plastic check valve. Plug the power cord into an outlet at least 4 feet above the floor and protected by a ground fault interrupter (p.240).

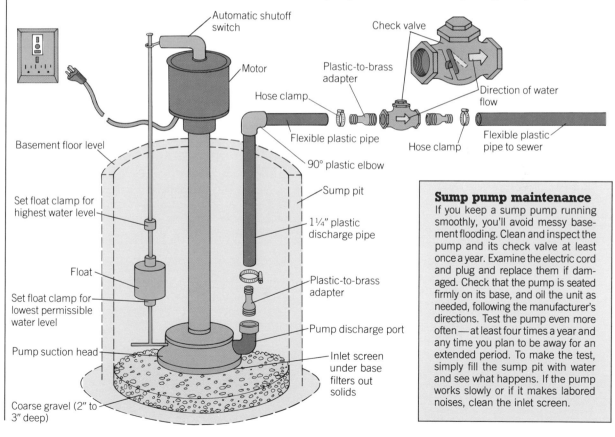

Automatic shutoff switch

Check valve

Motor

Plastic-to-brass adapter

Hose clamp

Direction of water flow

Flexible plastic pipe

Basement floor level

Hose clamp

Flexible plastic pipe to sewer

90° plastic elbow

Set float clamp for highest water level

Sump pit

1¼" plastic discharge pipe

Float

Set float clamp for lowest permissible water level

Plastic-to-brass adapter

Pump discharge port

Pump suction head

Inlet screen under base filters out solids

Coarse gravel (2" to 3" deep)

Sump pump maintenance

If you keep a sump pump running smoothly, you'll avoid messy basement flooding. Clean and inspect the pump and its check valve at least once a year. Examine the electric cord and plug and replace them if damaged. Check that the pump is seated firmly on its base, and oil the unit as needed, following the manufacturer's directions. Test the pump even more often—at least four times a year and any time you plan to be away for an extended period. To make the test, simply fill the sump pit with water and see what happens. If the pump works slowly or if it makes labored noises, clean the inlet screen.

Plumbing/Rigid copper pipe

There are many advantages to doing plumbing jobs with rigid copper pipe. It is light and durable, resists mineral deposits, can be used with either mechanical or soldered connectors, and is convenient to work with, add to, and repair. But it is also costly.

Copper pipe is available in 10- and 20-foot lengths and in three weights. K, the heaviest of the three, is used primarily for underground lines outdoors. L, a medium-weight pipe, is the best for indoor plumbing. M, the lightest, is also generally adequate for indoor plumbing, local codes permitting.

A soldering process called sweating is used to join rigid copper pipe. Sweat-soldered joints are stronger and less likely to leak than mechanical connections; use non-acidic paste flux (p.134) and solid-core wire solder. For water supply pipes, use silver solder or some other lead-free solder (the U.S. Environmental Protection Agency has banned the use of lead solder in water supply systems). A propane canister torch is sufficient for heating a joint to be sweat soldered.

Make sure the surfaces to be soldered are clean and dry so that the solder can flow evenly and adhere securely. Even the grease from a fingerprint can create a problem. If a trickle of water persists in flowing through a leaky valve, tightly pack the pipe end with small pieces of soft bread to absorb the trickle. Once the joint has been soldered, remove the aerator from the nearest faucet and turn on the water; the bread will disintegrate and flow out.

When soldering a joint near a previously soldered one, wrap a damp rag around the first joint to keep its solder from melting. If you are soldering a fitting that takes more than one piece of pipe, sweat all the pieces at once. You can fix a leaking joint by heating it to melt the solder, pulling it apart, and resoldering.

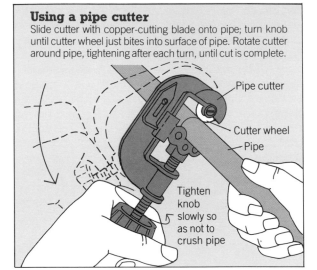

Using a pipe cutter
Slide cutter with copper-cutting blade onto pipe; turn knob until cutter wheel just bites into surface of pipe. Rotate cutter around pipe, tightening after each turn, until cut is complete.

Pipe cutter
Cutter wheel
Pipe
Tighten knob slowly so as not to crush pipe

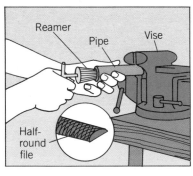

Sweat soldering.
1. Cut pipe as shown above, or use a miter box and a hacksaw with a 24- or 32-teeth-per-in. blade (p.224). Remove burrs with a reamer or a half-round file. Check mating surfaces; dents and flat spots cause leaks.

Reamer
Pipe
Vise
Half-round file

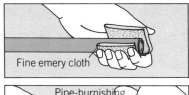

Fine emery cloth

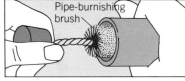

Pipe-burnishing brush

2. Burnish inside of fitting and outside of pipe end with a fine emery cloth or a special brush. Clean only to shine; too much abrasion can enlarge joint gap and make joint leak. Make sure pipe is fully supported. Don't touch the clean surfaces.

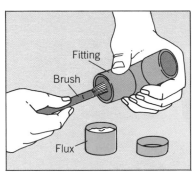

Fitting
Brush
Flux

3. Brush a light coating of flux over the pipe end and inside rim of fitting. *Note:* If pipe is connected, turn off water and open a faucet before starting work, or when pipe is heated, air pressure may build up and push solder out of joint.

4. Assemble joint, pushing pipe into fitting until pipe butts fitting's inside shoulder. Twist pipe or fitting back and forth to distribute flux; then adjust position of fitting. Shield any nearby surfaces with fireproof sheets to protect from flame.

Shoulder
Flux

Touch solder to pipe to check heat
Torch

5. Light torch and move flame first over thicker metal of fitting, then over pipe, circling the pipe and fitting to heat all the metal uniformly. When it is hot enough to heat metal (solder touched to the metal will melt), remove heat.

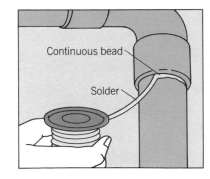

Continuous bead
Solder

6. Touch solder to point where pipe enters fitting (flux will pull solder into joint). Pull solder around the pipe to form a continuous bead along rim of fitting; leave no gaps, or joint will leak. Let metal cool before moving, or solder will crack.

Flexible copper tubing

Because it can be bent, reducing the need for fittings and allowing gentle curves, flexible copper tubing is convenient to install and offers less resistance to water flow than rigid pipe. However, because it doesn't present as neat an appearance in long runs as rigid pipe with its straight lines and precise right angles, it is used mostly where it won't show. Perhaps the most convenient use of flexible copper tubing is in plumbing remodeling jobs because it can be snaked in behind walls, above ceilings, and through small openings.

There are two common weights. Type L, of medium weight, is suitable for household plumbing. Type K, a heavier tubing, is reserved mainly for underground lines. Both are available in coils that run 15, 30, 60, or 100 feet in length.

Bending. You can bend tubing by hand over your knee or around a homemade form (p. 138) or inside a special bending spring that fits the tubing snugly. To avoid kinks, fill the tubing with sand before bending and wash it out after. Try to avoid sharp bends; they restrict not only the amount of

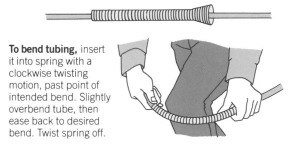

To bend tubing, insert it into spring with a clockwise twisting motion, past point of intended bend. Slightly overbend tube, then ease back to desired bend. Twist spring off.

water the tubing can handle but the rate of its flow as well. If you must have a 90° turn, make the bend as wide and gradual as you can to avoid kinking.

Joining. Flexible copper tubing can be joined with flare fittings or compression fittings, or it can be sweat soldered. A well-soldered joint is stronger and more durable than one made with a fitting, but fittings are easier to work with and can be disassembled at any time with a pair of wrenches.

Before using a fitting, cut the ends of the tubing square; then clean off any burrs, and proceed as shown below. Flare joints can leak unless carefully made; even a small dent in the end of the tubing can create a problem. You can use either a small individual flaring tool (it will have to match the diameter of the tubing you are working with) or a die-type mechanical flaring tool, which will accept any of a number of different size tubings.

If you prefer to sweat solder your flexible tubing, handle, measure, cut, and solder it the same as you would rigid copper pipe (facing page).

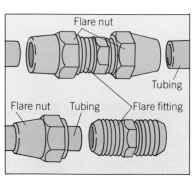

Flare fittings.
1. Cut tubing 2 in. longer than needed, so that if finished joint leaks, you can cut off end and reflare the tubing without making it too short. Clean off burrs with file or emery cloth. Slide flare nut from fitting over end of tubing.

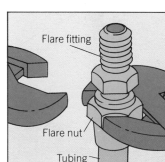

3. If you're using a mechanical die-type flaring tool, clamp tubing in appropriate die so that end protrudes ⅜ in. past face of die. Tighten the wing nuts and screw in tool's ram, tightening it until point enters tubing and flares it.

2. If you are using an individual flaring tool (specific to one diameter only), clamp the tubing securely with its end protruding. Using a hammer, carefully tap flaring tool into the end of the tubing until the tubing is flared.

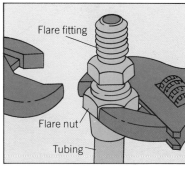

4. Remove tubing from tool and push fitting into flared end of the tubing. Screw flare nut to fitting, using two wrenches to tighten joint—one to hold nonthreaded part of fitting and one to turn nut. If joint leaks, cut off flared end and start over.

Compression fittings
Slide compression nut over tubing; slip on compression ring. Insert tubing into fitting. Screw compression nut onto fitting; tighten with two wrenches to lock ring onto tubing.

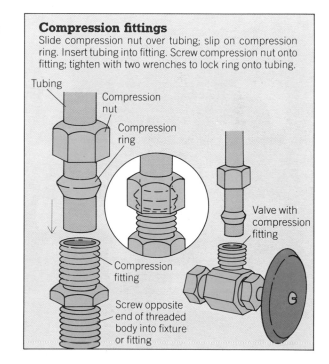

Plumbing/Brass and steel pipe

Because they can withstand tremendous pressure, brass and galvanized steel pipe are suited for use in water supply systems. Both come in the same sizes and use the same fittings. In diameters larger than ½ inch, there are three wall thicknesses: standard, extra-heavy, and double extra-heavy.

Galvanized steel pipe is coated inside and out with zinc to prevent corrosion, but the uncoated threads may rust and the rough interior can collect mineral deposits and become clogged with scale.

Brass pipe lasts longer than steel, but it is expensive. If you wish to patch a section of brass pipe with galvanized steel, make all connections with dielectric fittings to prevent corrosion caused by electrochemical reactions between the metals.

Joining. Brass and steel pipes are easily joined with threaded fittings. You can usually buy lengths of prethreaded pipe or have your supplier thread the pipe for you. If not, cut the pipe squarely, smooth its ends, clamp it in a vise, and form the threads with a die (thread cutter) and diestock (die holder), as shown at right. Before joining threaded pipe, brush the threads with joint compound or wrap them with tape (facing page) to make them watertight.

Unions. A length of pipe installed with threaded fittings cannot be unscrewed as one piece, since loosening it at one end will tighten the fitting at the other end. The solution is to cut the pipe and install a union. You should also install unions when running new pipe, so that repairs can easily be made later.

Threading pipe

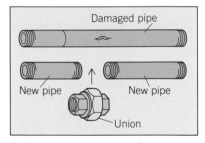

Lock die into diestock and slide it over pipe end. Pressing into pipe, turn stock clockwise until die bites into pipe. Add cutting oil to oil port in stock, and continue without applying pressure. If stock binds, back off a quarter turn, brush away metal chips, and add more oil.

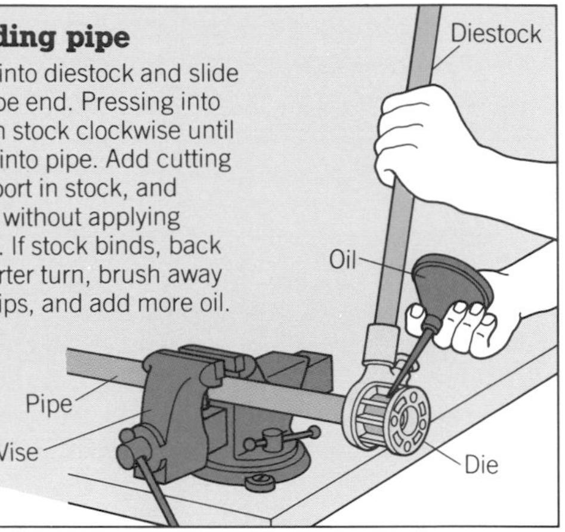

Determining pipe lengths

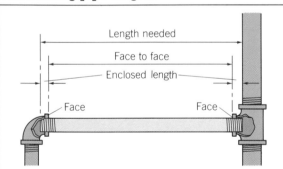

To determine the length of pipe needed to complete a connection, measure the distance from the face of one fitting to the face of the other. To this measurement add enclosed length of pipe that will enter fittings at both ends.

| Pipe size (inches) | Enclosed length (inches) | |
	Standard fittings	Drainage fittings
½	½	(none)
¾	½	(none)
1	⅝	⅝
1¼	⅝	⅝
1½	⅝	⅝
2	¾	⅞
3	(none)	1
4	(none)	(none)

Replacing a leaky pipe

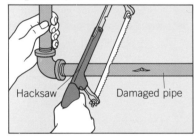

1. Turn off water supply. Cut through damaged section with a hacksaw. On a long pipe run, support pipe to minimize vibration and avoid breaking seals on other joints on line.

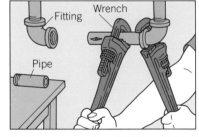

2. Unscrew pipe from fittings, using two pipe wrenches—one to hold fitting, the other to turn pipe. Again, work carefully to keep from breaking seals on other joints.

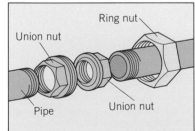

3. Buy or cut two lengths of pipe which, when assembled with a union, match the length of the damaged pipe. Thread replacement pipe (see above), if needed.

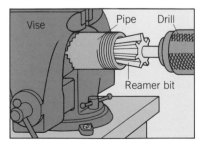

4. Use reamer or half-round file to clean burrs from inside of pipe, and file outside of pipe smooth. Brush threads with joint compound or apply tape (facing page).

5. Screw union nut onto one pipe end. Slip ring nut over other pipe end, and screw on other union nut. Tighten both union nuts with two wrenches.

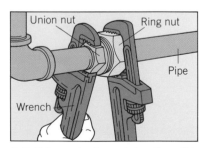

6. Butt faces of union nuts together, slide ring nut to center of union, and screw it onto the exposed threads of the union nuts. Tighten with two wrenches.

Cast-iron pipe

Sealing and joining pipe

Brush joint compound evenly over pipe ends, using just enough to fill the threads. This protective layer will lubricate, seal, and rustproof joints, and make them easy to disassemble. Don't coat inside of fitting.

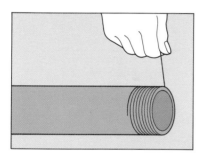

As extra security against leaks, wind threadlike wicking carefully into threads of pipe before you apply compound. Use it especially when reassembling old joints.

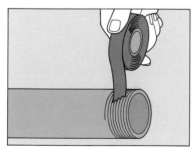

Pipe tape is a handy substitute for joint compound. Wind the tape tightly around the threads, circling the pipe clockwise 1½ times. The tape should be wound tight enough to make the pipe threads show through.

Insert pipe into fitting and begin screwing the two together by hand. Tighten with two pipe wrenches until only three threads remain outside of fitting. Tightening more may strip the threads or crack the fittings.

Because of its durability and low cost, cast iron has long been the material of choice for drain, waste, and vent (DWV) pipe. Cast-iron pipe and fittings come in two weights—*service weight* and a thicker-walled *heavy weight*. Service weight is easier to handle, but some local plumbing codes do not permit its use. Both weights can be cut with a hacksaw and cold chisel or, more easily, with a DWV pipe cutter, which can be bought or rented. Cast-iron pipe is available in diameters of 1½, 2, 3, and 4 inches and in lengths of 5 and, less commonly, 10 feet.

An older type of pipe, called *hub,* or *bell and spigot,* is joined with molten lead—a job that should always be left to a professional. However,

Hubless fitting   Hub fitting

Spigot   Bell

hubless, or *no-hub,* pipe is somewhat easier to work with: it is joined with neoprene sleeves and stainless steel shields that clamp on and are easily removed. You can patch either type of cast-iron pipe with either hubless cast-iron pipe or plastic pipe, provided that local codes allow you to do so.

Because of its weight, cast-iron pipe must be fully supported. Using pipe strap or the clamps shown below, support horizontal runs of hubless pipe at every joint and at 4-foot intervals between joints. Add supports for vertical runs at every floor.

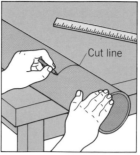
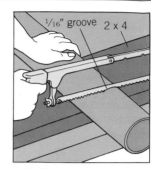

Cutting: 1. Use chalk or crayon to mark a cut line around entire circumference of pipe. Elevate part to be cut on board.

2. Holding pipe firmly in place, use a hacksaw to cut a groove ¹⁄₁₆ in. deep along the cut line. Turn pipe as you do so.

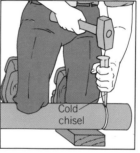

3. Insert blade of cold chisel in groove. Rotate pipe slowly and tap chisel with hammer until pipe breaks off.

To use DWV pipe cutter, wrap chain around pipe, turn knob to push cutter into pipe, and work handle back and forth.

Hubless joint

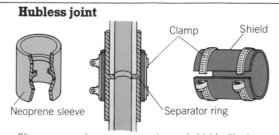

Slip neoprene sleeve over one pipe and shield with clamps over other. Push other pipe into sleeve; butt them against separator ring. Slide shield over sleeve; tighten clamps.

Pipe supports

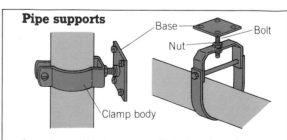

Screw base of horizontal or vertical pipe clamp into overhead joist or wall stud. Slip clamp body over pipe and attach clamp to its base with bolt and nut.

Plumbing / Home water treatment

The most common water problem faced by home-owners in the United States is "hard" water—the kind that refuses to lather, leaves rings around the bathtub, turns white clothes gray in the wash, and most destructively, clogs appliances and plumbing lines with mineral deposits. Calcium and magnesium are most often responsible for hard water.

A simple antidote is the "ion-exchange" water softener. As water passes through a resin in the softener's tank, calcium and magnesium are exchanged for sodium. When the sodium in the resin is depleted, it is recharged by backflushing with a brine solution. You can rent a water softener from a water treatment company, or you can buy and install a self-maintaining model yourself.

Softening water saves the plumbing, but it creates an elevated sodium content. This is unhealthy for someone on a sodium-restricted diet. A compromise: Treat only the hot-water lines or install a separate tap for drinking and cooking water.

Not all problems with water impurities are as clear-cut as hard water. There are three categories of contaminants: organics (mostly synthetic chemicals), inorganics (such as mercury, arsenic, fluoride, nitrate, silver, and lead), and microorganisms (bacteria, protozoa, and viruses).

Most of the inorganics are easily detected and removed from public water supplies and home wells. A troublesome inorganic is lead, which can leach out of lead pipes or the plumbing solder used in homes built in the mid-1980's.

Many microorganisms are kept under control by chlorination and filtration in public water systems. Well owners should test for microorganisms once a year and, if necessary, install a chlorine feeder.

The organics—pesticides and industrial wastes, for example—are often toxic to humans. If there is excessive use of these chemicals in your area, you should have your water tested. Testing for organics is expensive, so be specific. One group of organic compounds, trihalomethanes (THM's), causes concern because they are suspected carcinogens and they are by-products of chlorination.

Water problems and their remedies

Symptom	Cause	Solution
Soap scum makes rings on bathtubs and sinks. White deposits build up in faucets, shower heads, and electric coffee pots. Soaps and detergents don't lather well; clean clothes look gray.	Magnesium and calcium compounds. "Hard" water.	Install an ion-exchange water softener on hot-water pipes or whole system. Clean clogged pipes, water heater, washing machine, and other affected equipment.
Rust forms around drains in sinks, bathtubs, and laundry tubs. Clothes have rust stains after washing. Water has a reddish tinge to it. Rust-colored slime in toilet tank.	Iron compounds or bacterial iron.	Install an ion-exchange water softener for low levels of iron. If problem persists, install an oxidizing filter or a chlorination feeder and an activated carbon filter.
Water has a "rotten egg" smell. Washed silverware tarnishes. Water looks black.	Hydrogen sulfide.	Install an oxidizing filter. If problem persists, install a chlorination feeder system, a particle filter, and an activated carbon filter. Replace badly corroded pipes and appliances or fixtures.
Rust or green stains around drains. Corroded metal pipes.	Acid water (low pH).	Install a neutralizing particle filter. If problem persists, install a continuous feeder with an alkaline solution. Check pipes for corrosion.
Water has unpleasant taste and a slight yellow or brownish color.	Algae or other organic matter suspended in the water.	Install a particle filter. For more serious problem, install a continuous chemical feeder with a chlorine solution. Last, add an activated carbon filter.
Water looks cloudy or dirty.	Suspended particles of silt, mud, or sand.	Install a particle filter first. Then use an activated carbon filter to remove color caused by organisms.
Illnesses in the family such as dysentery, diarrhea, or hepatitis.	Disease-producing bacteria or viruses in the water.	Test for coliform bacteria first. These nonpathogenic organisms indicate potential contamination from human or animal waste, which can then be tracked down. You must identify the contaminant before a water quality expert can recommend treatment.

Before you buy any treatment equipment, have your water tested; then consult with a water quality expert. You may suspect other contaminants because of a particular industry in your area or the high incidence of a disease. A local health department, an environmental conservation office, or the Cooperative Extension Service can recommend a lab that is properly certified to test drinking water.

Most home water treatment equipment deals with a limited number of impurities. Some units are used in conjunction with others. A point-of-entry (POE) installation treats the entire water supply of a house. Point-of-use (POU) installations can be under the kitchen sink, on a countertop, or on a faucet.

Types of home water purifiers. The simplest water treatment devices are *particle filters*, which use different media (synthetic granules or sand, for example) to strain out large particles. Attached both POE and POU, they are good for sifting out heavy sediment, but they are not effective against many inorganics and organics.

Oxidizing filters employ manganese-coated media to remove pollutants such as iron and hydrogen sulfide. Often used with softeners, they are installed POE. They require periodic maintenance.

Activated carbon filters, installed POE or POU, adsorb a variety of undesirable chemical compounds, including THM's. The U.S. Environmental Protection Agency recommends their use only on microbiologically safe water (they can promote bacterial growth). How often filters need replacing depends on how much water goes through and how many contaminants are trapped.

Reverse osmosis filters, also called membrane filters, are semipermeable; water molecules pass through while iron molecules and large organics are stopped. The EPA recommends them for microbiologically safe water only. Units are installed POU, but still waste gallons of water a day. The membrane must be replaced periodically.

Distillers purify water through boiling, evaporation, and condensation. They remove bacteria and inorganics effectively, but they are expensive to operate and must be cleaned of salts frequently.

Feeder systems, mainly for private wells, add disinfectants or neutralizing chemicals to the water supply at a preset rate. Feeders are complex and require professional installation and servicing.

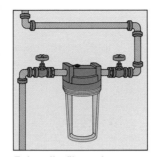

To install a filter unit or a water softener in a vertical pipe, first shut off the water. Cut out a 4-in. section of pipe and install a loop as shown. Position the filter on the lower part of the loop. Some units have built-in shut-off valves; check instructions before installing your own.

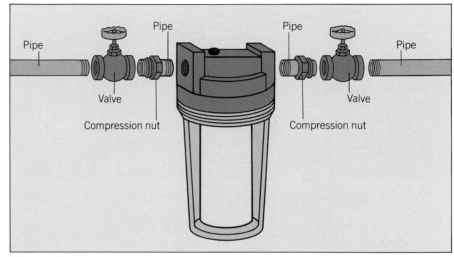

Filters and softeners must be installed horizontally; the drawing shows how the parts line up.

How to save water

Changing habits can, over the course of a year, save more water than investing in water-saving appliances. Taking a 3-minute shower, for example, uses less water than taking a bath (9 gallons versus 36 gallons). Brushing your teeth or shaving with the tap running wastes at least 5 gallons of water; washing dishes under an open faucet, 30 gallons.

Wait until you have a full load before running the dishwasher or the washing machine. A dishwasher uses up to 16 gallons of water per cycle; a washing machine may use as much as 60 gallons.

Some inexpensive hardware saves water. A faucet flow controller cuts the stream of water by as much as 4 gallons a minute with minimum loss of spray force. A shower flow control insert (right) reduces usage to 3 gallons a minute.

Many new appliances have water-saving features: shallow-trap toilets use less water per flush, dishwashers have low-water cycles, and clothes washers have water level controls. Single-control shower valves let you preset the water temperature, saving the water wasted while you make hot and cold adjustments with two separate valves.

The bottom line on saving water, however, is plumbing maintenance. A dripping faucet or a running toilet can drain impressive amounts of water in a week or a month; make prompt repairs.

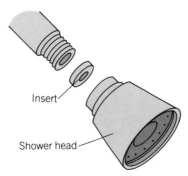

Insert

Shower head

A shower flow control insert can be a simple, inexpensive ring like this. There are other similar designs that also reduce the flow of water from 5–8 gal. per min. to 3 gal. per min. Or you can buy shower heads with built-in flow control. All save water as well as the energy to heat it.

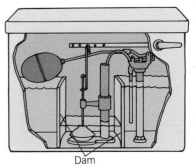

Dam

Toilet dams shrink the water-holding capacity of a toilet tank, thus saving up to 2 gal. of water per flush. A 1-qt. or ½-gal. plastic bottle is just as effective in displacing water. Fill with water so it doesn't float, recap, and put in tank. Don't use bricks; they will disintegrate.

Plumbing/Running new lines (roughing in)

Adding plumbing for a new bathroom or kitchen, or even running lines for a new shower, requires the installation of water supply and DWV pipes in the walls, floors, and ceilings to the point where connections can be made to the fixtures. This work of *roughing in* requires skill and experience. The basic information given here will help you to plan new plumbing, but you should probably leave the actual work of roughing in to a professional. In fact, most plumbing and building codes require that it be either done or inspected by a licensed plumber.

Planning. When planning extensive additions, check that your water pressure, water heater, and septic system (if you have one) can handle the increased demand. Then map out your present system, including the supply lines, vents, house drain, branch drains, and accessible cleanouts. Also note the types and sizes of the pipes. Using this map,

you will be able to see where you can tie in to supply and drain lines and whether or not the existing drains and vents are adequate for your plans. The illustration below shows the roughing in for a typical one-story house.

Before running lines for a new fixture, mark the walls where the water supply and waste lines must be located. Many fixtures come with templates for this purpose. If not, position the fixture with its outlet pipes and trap loosely in place. Then plan the routing of the waste pipe, sloping it 1 inch for every 4 feet of run to ensure good drainage. Use a chalk line and level to mark the positions of the lines.

Connecting new pipes to existing water supply and waste lines may require the removal (and later restoration) of sections of the wall, ceiling, or floor and subfloor. On the first floor, it may be possible to gain access from the basement and to hang the pipes

with plumber's tape. In an unfinished attic, pipes can be run across the tops of the floor joists if the attic is heated. Otherwise, it is better to run them parallel to rather than cutting through studs and joists. If lines must pass through the structural framing members, the rules given at the bottom of the facing page should be observed.

Clearance must also be considered when running lines. Copper DWV pipes up to 3 inches in diameter can fit into a standard wall framed with 2 x 4's if they run vertically, and not through the studs. Plastic and cast-iron pipe can be run only through 2 x 6 walls; if run through 2 x 4 walls, which have a clearance of only 3½ inches, they may cause the wallboard to bulge. Threaded pipes require additional clearance to allow for tightening. Insulation must also be taken into account when estimating space allowances.

DWV and supply lines for a one-story house (schematic)

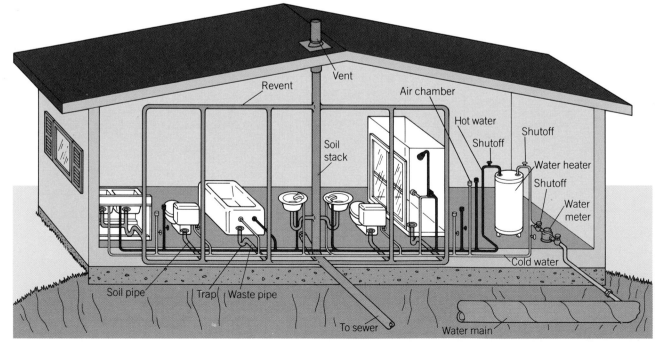

Plan piping layouts to take the most direct route; avoid obstacles wherever possible. The supply pipes can usually be routed parallel to DWV, but without slope. Where possible, install new fixtures back-to-back with existing fixtures tied in to the soil stack. If your house has two or more stories, you can arrange them piggyback style, with the new fixtures on the floor above or below existing ones, but you might have to add separate vent pipes for the lower fixtures. Often a new sink, tub, or shower can be tied directly in to an existing branch drain; this is the simplest and most cost-efficient approach, but local codes may require a toilet to have its own DWV pipe or to drain into a branch line that is at least 3 in. in diameter.

The distance between the trap of a fixture and its vent pipe is strictly regulated; check your local code. Use T- or Y-fittings to connect new pipe runs to existing lines. Hook up vents for new toilets, sinks, and tubs to the main stack or other existing vent pipes. Check your local codes for the required method of venting and the maximum distance a fixture can be from its vent pipe. There are generally no restrictions on how far a fixture can be from the main supply lines.

If the new plumbing is far from existing plumbing, run a secondary vent pipe through the roof and a new branch drain to the soil stack or to the main house drain through an existing cleanout. If you have a basement, you can extend the new lines from there.

When a wall doesn't have enough room to accept pipe, you can build out the wall with 1 x 1's, 2 x 2's, or 2 x 4's and resurface it. Do this over the entire height of the wall or only the lower portion where the pipes are run, creating a ledge above the pipes.

Supporting the pipes. Pipe runs must be correctly supported or they will vibrate and eventually joints may open, causing leaks. Galvanized pipe should be supported every 10 feet; plastic pipe, every 4 to 6 feet. Copper pipe should be supported every 6 feet with either copper clamps and screws or plastic or wood braces—any metal other than copper will set up a corrosive reaction. Copper or plastic pipe running close behind a wall should be covered with a metal strip to protect against fasteners put through the wall for pictures or shelves.

Installing DWV lines. When the new pipes are run, the DWV assembly should be completed first.

If a toilet is being installed, the closet bend (the curved drainage pipe that connects the toilet floor flange to the soil stack) is installed first and connected with a T to the soil stack. The soil stack and any other vertical vent pipes are run with branch fittings in place to receive the branch drains and vents. Codes may require that the vent size be increased to 3 or more inches just below the roof with a vent increaser. Flashing is also installed (p.391).

Working out from the stack, the branch waste and revent lines are then installed. Accessible cleanouts should be placed in every horizontal drain run, maintaining the minimum distance between them required by code. Finally, all fixture drains and waste lines should be brought out of the walls and capped until the fixtures are about to be installed.

Running supply lines. Hot- and cold-water lines are run side by side, spaced 6 to 8 inches apart to keep the hot water from warming the cold and vice versa. The existing hot- and cold-water mains are extended, and reducing T's are installed for the branches. Then the branch and fixture runs are installed. At the point of entry into a room, each pipe is fitted with a T and a *stubout* that passes through the wall, reaching at least 4 inches into the room. The top of the T requires a water-hammer arrester (p.214).

Testing connections. Once all the pipes have been connected, test the connections. Install rubber plugs (you can rent them) on the closet bend and sewer line. Turn on the water and look for leaks in the water supply lines. Look again several hours later. Run water from a garden hose into the main soil stack until it is full. Wait 20 minutes, and then look for leaks in the DWV lines. If there are none, you can remove the plugs and close the wall, ceiling, or floor; your plumbing system is leak-free.

Running pipe through framing members

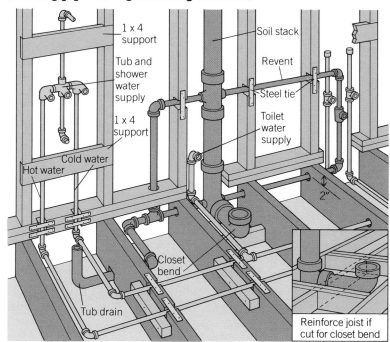

1 x 4 support
Soil stack
Tub and shower water supply
Revent
Steel tie
1 x 4 support
Toilet water supply
Cold water
Hot water
2"
Closet bend
Tub drain
Reinforce joist if cut for closet bend

To run lines inside walls, under floors, or above ceilings, you must drill holes in framing members or even, when unavoidable, notch them. When doing so, observe these rules to avoid weakening structural members.

Holes. Center a hole in a joist so that it is at least 2 in. from top or bottom edge and its diameter is no more than one-third of joist depth. Holes in studs can cover 40 percent of stud width in a load-bearing wall (p.191) or 60 percent in other walls or in doubled studs.

Notches. In joists, cut notches only near ends, never in center third. Notch no more than one-quarter of joist depth; then insert pipe and nail a steel tie across notch and a 2 x 2 on each side of joist to support pipe. Never notch a stud more than two-thirds of its depth. Don't notch lower half of stud deeper than one-third without adding a steel tie. In a nonbearing wall, you can notch upper half of stud to half its depth if it is flanked by at least two unnotched studs.

Closet bend. If toilet closet bend is parallel to the joists, install a brace between the two joists and immediately under the pipe. Use shims to fill any gap between pipe and brace. If a section of joist must be cut out, reinforce cut joist at each end with screwed-in double headers (inset) and add supporting brace under pipe.

Supporting pipes

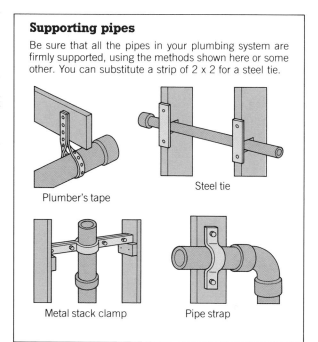

Be sure that all the pipes in your plumbing system are firmly supported, using the methods shown here or some other. You can substitute a strip of 2 x 2 for a steel tie.

Plumber's tape
Steel tie
Metal stack clamp
Pipe strap

Plumbing/Replacing a toilet

Before buying a new toilet, measure the rough-in of the old one—the distance from the wall behind the toilet to the center of the two closet bolts that secure the bowl to the floor. If the bowl has four bolts, measure to the rear bolts. The rough-in of the new toilet can be shorter than the old one, but not longer.

Check local plumbing codes before buying any type of toilet. Choose a model with its flush-valve assembly already installed. Look for a low-water-consumption toilet—one that flushes effectively but uses less than 2 gallons of water per flush, compared to an average of over 5 gallons for a standard toilet.

Buy a pair of closet bolts and a wax gasket; they are not usually provided with the toilet. There are two types of closet bolts. The strongest type has wood-screw threads on one end and machine-screw threads on the other; these are the type to use if the floor under the flange is wood. The other type has a flat head that slides into a slot in the flange. Select the bolts that will fit your flange. Also buy plaster of Paris to seal the toilet base, and plumber's putty to bond the caps to the bolts; both are found at plumbing supply or hardware stores.

Handle a new toilet with care—if dropped, it may chip or crack. You may need an extra pair of hands to help lift and move the toilet.

If you find a cracked flange when you remove the old toilet, call a plumber to install a new flange. If the flange is too low—it should be ¼ inch above the floor—you'll probably need a new flange too. However, if the old toilet didn't leak at the base of the bowl, you can try installing a special wax gasket with a plastic sleeve that fits into the flange. This may solve the problem without replacing the flange.

If the old water supply line doesn't reach the new toilet, replace it with flexible tubing. If you already have flexible tubing and it's kinked, worn, or corroded, replace it with new tubing (p.218). Install a shutoff valve (pp.230–231) if there isn't one already.

If you want to put a toilet in your basement, you'll have to install a macerator pump into a pit in the floor. This is a difficult task; it's best to call in a professional plumber.

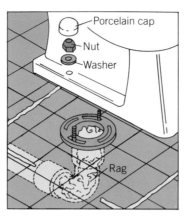
Porcelain cap
Nut
Washer
Rag

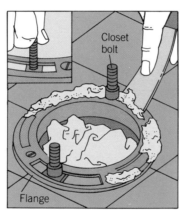
Closet bolt
Flange

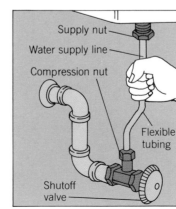
Wax gasket
Horn

1. Turn off the water supply; flush twice. Sponge out remaining water in tank and bowl. Disconnect the water supply line and detach the tank (p.208). To remove bowl, pry off or unscrew caps; remove nuts and washers. Rock bowl to break floor seal; lift it straight up. Catch remaining water in pail. Plug closet bend with rag to keep debris out, sewer gas in.

2. Scrape old wax gasket and plumber's putty from flange and floor. Unscrew old bolts; or twist bolts a quarter turn, then remove them from large end of slots. Dip new bolts in plumber's putty and insert into flange. If flange has slots, carefully align bolts with center of flange opening and parallel to wall.

3. Turn new bowl upside down on a box or crate covered with old towels. (You may need a helper to do this.) Gently press the new wax gasket over the bowl's horn—the discharge opening on the underside of the bowl. The gasket provides a waterproof seal. Remove the rag from the closet bend.

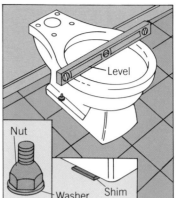
Level
Nut
Washer
Shim

Supply nut
Water supply line
Compression nut
Flexible tubing
Shutoff valve

4. Turn bowl upright; lower it onto bolts. Press down, twisting bowl slightly until it no longer rocks. With carpenter's level, check across bowl; level with thin metal shims if needed. For two-piece toilet, attach tank (p.208). Adjust bowl to align tank with wall. Set washers and nuts on closet bolts. To avoid cracking bowl, tighten nuts alternately.

5. Pour water into bowl; check for leaks. Check the caps' fit on the bolts; if bolts are too long, cut them with a hacksaw. Fill the caps with plumber's putty; press them onto bolts. Seal base of the bowl with plaster of Paris; use your finger to apply it. Plaster of Paris dries fast—work quickly. Wipe away excess plaster with a damp cloth.

6. Reconnect water supply line. Replace it with flexible plastic tubing if necessary. Use pipe tape or pipe joint cement on threads, and tighten the nuts snugly. Turn on water and check for leaks around the new connections. Install the toilet seat following maker's directions. Fit cover onto the tank.

Replacing a bathroom sink

A bathroom sink, often called a lavatory, can be set into a vanity in the same way a kitchen sink is set into a cabinet (pp.230–231), or it can be attached to the wall with a variety of supporting brackets.

If you're replacing an old wall-hung sink, check the old sink's bracket. Because a sink and bracket must match, if possible buy a new sink with the same type of bracket as the old one. For additional support, install a pair of adjustable legs. They are available in several styles.

Sinks are made of porcelain-coated cast iron,

vitreous china, or synthetic marble. To avoid chips and scratches, handle a sink carefully. When you purchase the sink, also buy a faucet. Make sure the centersets match (p.211).

If you're installing a sink in a new location, first follow the instructions for running new pipe lines (pp.226–227). You will then be able to follow the steps below to install the sink. Be sure to install shutoff valves (pp.230–231) on the supply pipes to avoid having to turn off the main water supply when making future repairs. If there are no shutoff valves

on the old sink, this is a good time to add them.

To remove an old bathroom sink set on a pedestal, first turn off the water supply. Open both faucets to drain the water, and then disconnect the supply lines and drainpipe. Dismount the basin from the pedestal by removing the bolts. Loosen the plaster of Paris at the pedestal's base by rocking the pedestal back and forth. If this doesn't work, wrap the pedestal in an old towel and, wearing goggles, use a hammer and cold chisel to dislodge it. Use a scouring pad or sandpaper to remove any plaster still stuck to the floor.

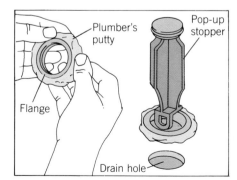

1. Shut off water supply to sink; drain faucet. Disconnect the water supply pipes; use a basin wrench (p.211) to remove the nuts. Remove trap, using a taped pipe wrench at its joints.

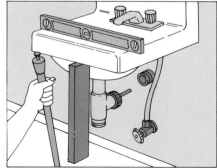

2. Remove anchor screws, if any, under apron of sink. Lift sink off bracket. Remove bracket and patch wall, or clean bracket for reuse. If you're reusing faucet, take it out (p.211) and clean it.

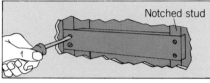
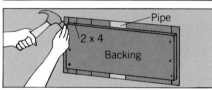

3. For wallboard (with or without tiles), install 2 x 4 backing 31 in. above floor. Cut hole in wall; notch studs; screw 2 x 4 to studs. If pipes block board, use 1 x 6. For plaster wall, fasten with toggle bolts.

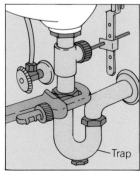

4. To install bracket, measure, mark, and level placement of bolts or screws. (Drill pilot holes into backing.) Screw bracket in. Bracket may be like the one in step 2 or one of those above.

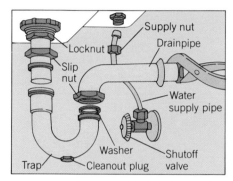

5. Install the faucet (p.211) without connecting the water supply lines, and install the drainpipe assembly following manufacturer's directions. Hang or bolt the sink to the wall.

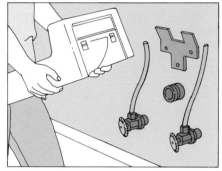

6. To add leg supports, brace sink with a 2 x 4. Attach each leg by placing it into a hole or in a corner under the sink's rim. Use level to make sure sink is even; tighten adjusting part of legs.

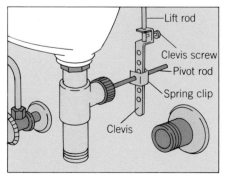

7. To connect stopper assembly, slide lift rod into hole in faucet. Under sink, attach clevis to lift rod with the clevis screw. Pinch the spring clip and slide pivot rod into a clevis hole.

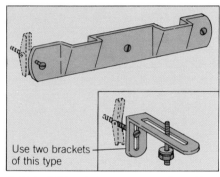

8. Connect water supply lines to faucet tailpipes using a basin or adjustable wrench; add shutoff valves if there are none. Use a pipe wrench to connect trap to drain tailpiece and to drainpipe.

Plumbing / Replacing a kitchen sink

Home plumbing systems 198–199
Replacing a faucet 211
Working with pipes 216–223, 226–227

Most kitchen sinks and many bathroom sinks are mounted in decks, or cabinets. If you are replacing a deck-mounted sink, but not the deck, be sure to get a new sink that will fit into the same opening or a larger opening. You can enlarge an opening that is too small by following the directions in step 2, but if you buy a sink requiring a smaller opening, you will have to replace the deck or at least put a new top on it.

All deck-mounted sinks are installed in the same way, whether double or single, kitchen or bathroom. The main difference is that with a double sink, two drains must be connected to the trap instead of one. A T-fitting is used for this purpose. To include a garbage disposer, as shown below, install it in place of one of the two drain flanges (facing page).

A slight change in the position of the new plumb-ing can be accommodated by flexible water supply connectors and by plastic trap-and-drain kits. Connectors, which may be plain copper, chrome-plated copper, or flexible plastic, come in a range of lengths. Join the connectors to your shutoff valves with compression or flare fittings (pp. 218 and 221). If you don't have shutoff valves, now's the time to add them. You can buy kits that include the valves, flexible tubing, fittings, and instructions.

Before installing the new sink, assemble the sink flange, drain, and faucet plus supply connectors—this is easier than having to reach under the sink once it is in place. If you are reusing the same fau-cet, disconnect it from the old sink and clean its base of old putty. If you are installing a garbage disposer on one side of the sink, do not install a flange and drain on that side.

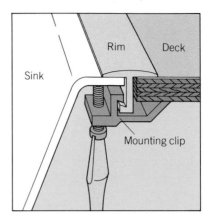

1. Shut off water to the sink, and open faucets to drain them. Disconnect supply pipes and traps, and unscrew any mounting clips under sink. Run putty knife between sink rim and deck to loosen. Pull out sink while helper pushes from below. Clean deck of old putty.

Rim Deck
Sink
Mounting clip

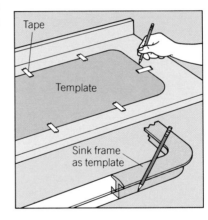

2. Use template that comes with new sink, or bottom edge of sink frame, to mark cutout on deck. Or turn sink upside down, trace around its rim, and draw parallel line ⅜ in. inside traced line. Cut opening, using saber saw (p. 57) with its faceplate taped to protect deck. Test-fit sink in opening.

Tape
Template
Sink frame as template

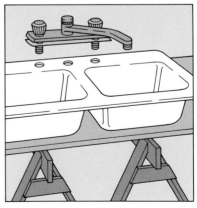

3. Before installing sink, assemble the faucets and apply plumber's putty to underside of bases. Insert faucets in sink, align them, and press them down firmly. Attach washers and nuts under sink. Install flexible connectors to hot- and cold-water tailpieces, letting their ends hang free.

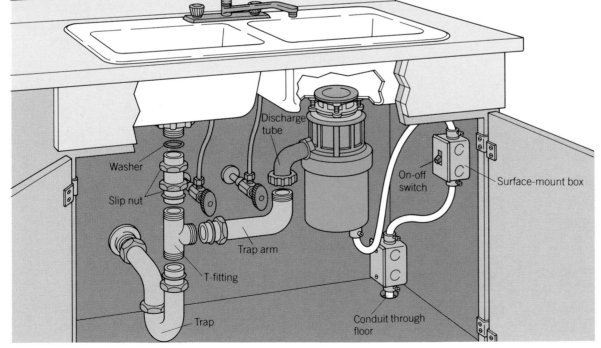

Washer
Slip nut
Discharge tube
On-off switch
Surface-mount box
Trap arm
T-fitting
Trap
Conduit through floor

230

Installing a garbage disposer

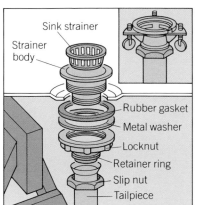

Sink strainer
Strainer body
Rubber gasket
Metal washer
Locknut
Retainer ring
Slip nut
Tailpiece

4. Apply plumber's putty around drain hole rim and press drain into hole. From below, slip on all other parts, following maker's directions. Tighten with a wrench, keeping strainer from turning by inserting handles of pliers and a screwdriver (p.203), or tighten screws or wing nuts (inset).

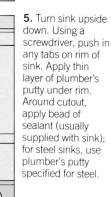

Sink
Mounting clip
Tab

5. Turn sink upside down. Using a screwdriver, push in any tabs on rim of sink. Apply thin layer of plumber's putty under rim. Around cutout, apply bead of sealant (usually supplied with sink); for steel sinks, use plumber's putty specified for steel.

Shutoff valve
Stubout

6. Lower sink into position, align, and press down until putty squeezes out. Engage mounting clips, tightening each a little at a time. Connect traps and drainpipes. If no shutoff valves exist, install them at stubouts for both hot- and cold-water supply pipes. Connect tubing from faucets to shutoffs.

To install a garbage disposer, you need a sink with a full-size drain opening, and a separate electric circuit with a conveniently located on-off switch. If the electrical work is already in place, make sure it conforms to local codes (p.238). If it is not in place, call in an electrician; working with a combination of electricity and plumbing is dangerous unless you are experienced. If you are removing an old disposer, first unplug the unit, or turn off the electricity (p.237) and disconnect the wiring.

Preparation. Remove the sink's basket strainer (p.203) and scour all putty from around the drain hole. If you have a two-compartment sink, remove the waste connector that joins the two drains to the trap. Then follow the step-by-step directions that come with your disposer. Some units simply plug in, but many must be wired as shown in step 3.

Most disposers have a fitting that allows you to tie in your dishwasher's drain line. If you want to make this connection, pry out the knockout plug by inserting a screwdriver tip into the disposer's dishwasher drain hole. Once the disposer is installed, slip the dishwasher drain hose over the fitting and secure it with a hose clamp.

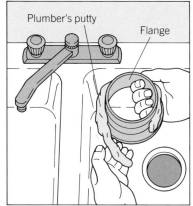

Plumber's putty
Flange

1. Separate the disposer's sink flange and its mounting assembly: the flange fits over the drain hole; the mounting assembly under it. Roll plumber's putty between your hands to form a snake, and run it around rim of disposer flange. Seat flange in the drain hole and press it down evenly and firmly.

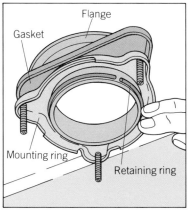

Flange
Gasket
Mounting ring
Retaining ring

2. From below, slip gasket over bottom of flange, followed by backup ring, if any, and mounting ring with its screws. While holding flange in place, snap retaining ring over ridge on mounting ring. Tighten screws on mounting ring until nearly all putty squeezes out from between sink and flange. Trim putty and clean sink.

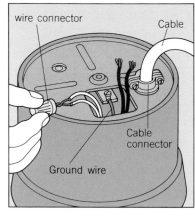

wire connector
Cable
Cable connector
Ground wire

3. With power off, remove cover plate from bottom of disposer, push cable from on-off switch into cable hole, and tighten connector screws. Pull out wires from cable and unit; connect white wires to white wires and black to black. Fasten the switch's ground wire to disposer's ground screw. Replace cover plate.

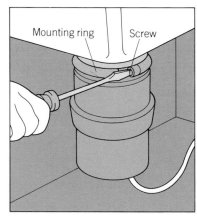

Mounting ring
Screw

4. Fit unit over sink flange and connect, following maker's directions. For type shown, hold unit with mounting lugs under screws of mounting assembly; turn the mounting ring until the unit is engaged; tighten mounting lugs with screwdriver. (Other models are attached with bolts.) Connect pipes as shown on facing page.

Plumbing/Installing a bathtub

Cast-iron or steel tubs, both porcelain-enameled, look and wear much the same, but cast-iron tubs are extremely heavy and hard to handle. Fiberglass tubs are lightweight and can be used with wall surrounds—convenient for covering walls in poor condition. Most wall surrounds are made up of three or more panels and either come with the tub or can be bought separately. One-piece units consisting of the tub and its surround are also available, but they are too large to be brought in through a door; they can be installed only in a new bathroom before the walls are added.

When buying a bathtub, be sure it will fit the available space. If you must alter the size of the tub enclosure, do so at the end opposite the drain to avoid moving pipes. To make the enclosure smaller, frame the wall out the required distance. You can slightly enlarge the enclosure by cutting into the wall, but only if it is not a load-bearing wall (p.191). If existing pipes don't align with the inlet and outlet holes on the new tub, reroute them.

To take out an old tub, turn off the water supply; remove the overflow plate, strainer (p.231), faucets, spout, shower head, and diverter valve. Wearing

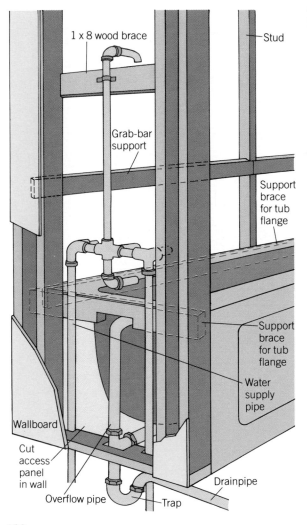

1 x 8 wood brace — Stud — Grab-bar support — Support brace for tub flange — Support brace for tub flange — Water supply pipe — Wallboard — Cut access panel in wall — Overflow pipe — Trap — Drainpipe

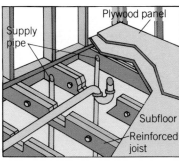

Plywood panel — Supply pipe — Subfloor — Reinforced joist

1. If tub is heavy or if pipes cut through the floor joists, double the joists, fastening them together with machine bolts. Then install subfloor with holes cut for pipes. For extra support, cut plywood size of tub, bore holes for pipes, and nail to subfloor.

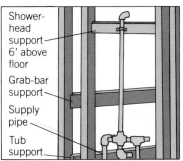

Shower-head support 6' above floor — Grab-bar support — Supply pipe — Tub support

2. Build or alter size of enclosure, adding an access panel for pipes, if possible. Nail 2 x 4's to studs to support tub edge. Notch studs and nail in 2 x 4's to support the shower head and grab bars. Run supply pipes if not already in place.

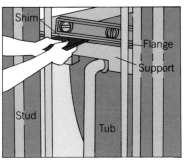

Shim — Flange — Support — Stud — Tub

3. Slide tub into place, resting rim on 2 x 4 supports. Level tub by toenailing or gluing wood shingles to enclosure to act as shims. Screw tub flange to 2 x 4's. To anchor fiberglass tub, push thin slurry of sand and cement under base with stick.

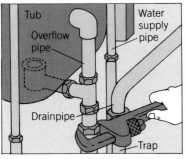

Tub — Water supply pipe — Overflow pipe — Drainpipe — Trap

4. Connect the water supply pipes; then connect the drain and overflow pipes to the inlet side of the trap to keep sewer gases from escaping into the bathroom. Turn on water; check drain and supply pipes for leaks.

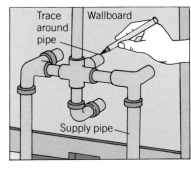

Trace around pipe — Wallboard — Supply pipe

5. Nail cement-base backer board (a water-proof wallboard) to studs, covering walls without faucets first. Position final panel and trace around pipes on back. Cut holes from back with hole saw; then nail panel into place.

Surround panel

6. Cover wallboard with tiles or tub surround; cut holes in final panel of tub surround as you did in wallboard, but first cover front of panel with masking tape to prevent chipping. Attach tub spout, faucets, shower head.

Home plumbing systems 198–199
Faucets and shower heads 211–212
Working with pipes 216–223, 226–227

gloves and protective goggles, use a pry bar to pry off any old wall surround or to remove the tiles for several inches above the tub. Cut away the wallboard from around the top of the old tub and disconnect all pipes. Remove any screws or nails in the flange along the upper rim of the tub. Get help to pull the tub away from the walls and position the new one.

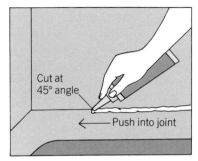

7. Caulk joints with silicone sealant. Cut tube spout at 45° angle far enough back to produce caulk bead to fill joint. Clean and dry area; move tube forward, squeezing to force even bead into joint. Let dry overnight. (Use same process to fix leak at tub rim.)

Cut at 45° angle
Push into joint

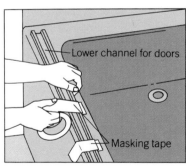

8. To install enclosure doors, follow maker's instructions. Use a hacksaw to cut the bottom channel to fit length of tub. Apply thick bead of silicone sealant to underside of channel and hold it firmly in position with masking tape until sealant sets.

Lower channel for doors
Masking tape

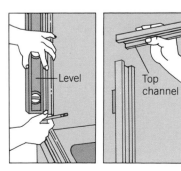

9. Plumb the side channels with level. Mark screw holes; drill with masonry bit into stud. Attach side channels with 2-in. wood screws. Cut top channel to size; fit in place. Install doors by hooking rollers into upper channel tracks.

Level
Top channel

Fiberglass shower stall

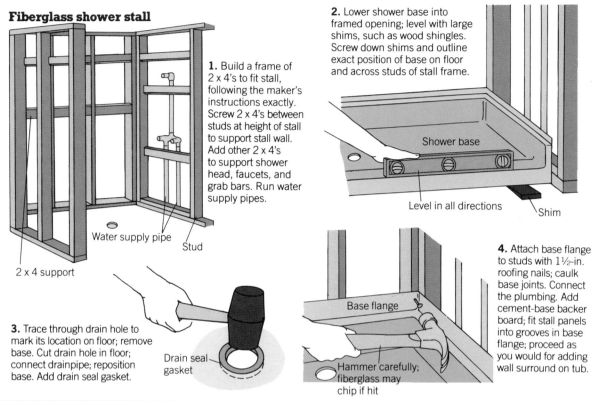

1. Build a frame of 2 x 4's to fit stall, following the maker's instructions exactly. Screw 2 x 4's between studs at height of stall to support stall wall. Add other 2 x 4's to support shower head, faucets, and grab bars. Run water supply pipes.

Water supply pipe
Stud
2 x 4 support

3. Trace through drain hole to mark its location on floor; remove base. Cut drain hole in floor; connect drainpipe; reposition base. Add drain seal gasket.

Drain seal gasket

2. Lower shower base into framed opening; level with large shims, such as wood shingles. Screw down shims and outline exact position of base on floor and across studs of stall frame.

Shower base
Level in all directions
Shim

4. Attach base flange to studs with 1½-in. roofing nails; caulk base joints. Connect the plumbing. Add cement-base backer board; fit stall panels into grooves in base flange; proceed as you would for adding wall surround on tub.

Base flange
Hammer carefully; fiberglass may chip if hit

Installing a whirlpool bath

A whirlpool bath is a tub with four or more jets, factory-installed pipes, and a pump to circulate water at pressure through the jets. Supply and waste pipe connections are the same as those on a standard tub, but you must build an access panel in the surrounding framing to reach the pump for servicing. (The pump is usually at the end opposite the drain). Follow the manufacturer's instructions to install the tub; then have an electrician wire and ground the pump.

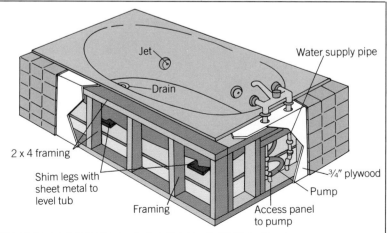

Jet
Drain
Water supply pipe
2 x 4 framing
Shim legs with sheet metal to level tub
Framing
¾" plywood
Pump
Access panel to pump

Plumbing/Replacing a tiled shower floor

Although most of the water from a shower runs off the tiles into the drain, some of it seeps through the grout between the tiles and through the porous mortar bed under the tiles of the shower floor. A waterproof pan placed under the floor catches this water, but in time the pan may corrode, creating leaks in the shower floor that can damage the structure below. Most older pans are made of lead or tar-covered asphalt, but they can be replaced by sheets of chlorinated polyethylene (CPE) membrane—available at most plumbing supply stores.

To install a new pan, you must dig out and replace the entire shower floor—a big, messy job that involves working with cement, tile, and cement-base backer board (a waterproof wallboard). Before you tackle it, make sure the problem really is a leaky pan and not a damaged pipe or loose fitting. Make this simple test: Remove the strainer from the drain, plug the drain securely, then run about 2 inches of water into the shower. Let the water stand for 2 hours and check its level. If some of it has leaked out, the pan is defective. If not, the problem is elsewhere.

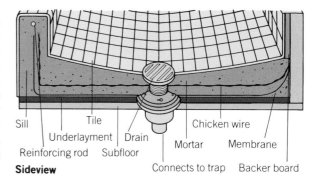

Sill · Tile · Chicken wire · Underlayment · Drain · Mortar · Membrane · Reinforcing rod · Subfloor · Connects to trap · Backer board

Sideview

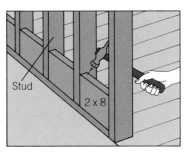

1. Remove lower part of shower wall down to studs. Wearing gloves and protective goggles, use chisel to break up and remove floor tiles and mortar. Replace subfloor if damp or rotted. Nail 2 x 8's between stud bases as backing for membrane.

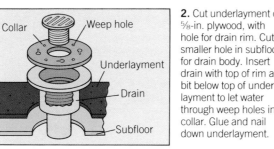

2. Cut underlayment of ⅝-in. plywood, with hole for drain rim. Cut smaller hole in subfloor for drain body. Insert drain with top of rim a bit below top of underlayment to let water through weep holes in collar. Glue and nail down underlayment.

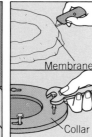

3. Cut membrane to cover floor, plus a 2-in. overlap at walls, 8-in. at entrance. Position the membrane and staple it to 2 x 8 backing. Feel for drain and cut hole in the membrane to free it. Bolt drain collar into place; screw in riser.

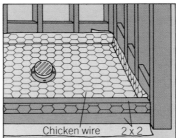

4. Cut chicken wire to size of membrane. Temporarily nail 2 x 2 across shower floor, 1½ in. in from the entrance. Then stretch the mesh over floor and 2 x 2; staple it to 2 x 8 backing. Add a second 2 x 2 over first. Cut drain hole in wire.

5. Mix mortar (p.165) to consistency of wet sand; pour over floor. Smooth mortar to make it flush with top 2 x 2 at perimeter, but sloping down to drain. Let set 12 hr. Remove 2 x 2's from entrance; fold membrane and wire straight up at entrance.

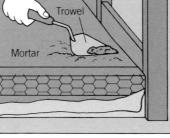

6. Trim membrane and wire 1 in. above mortar; staple it to wall framing at front. Near entrance, drill holes in framing; insert ⅜-in. steel rod (rebar). Cut two pieces of plywood 5 in. wide and long enough to bridge entrance less double thickness of wallboard.

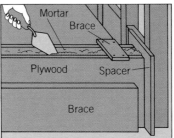

7. Across entrance, toenail plywood to subfloor, brace with scrap wood. Place wallboard-thick spacers between studs and ends of form. Mix mortar of mudlike consistency (a bit wetter than before) and fill form; tap form to pack it tightly.

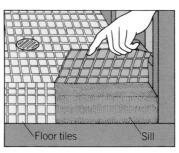

8. Let the mortar set at least 24 hr.; then remove the form and braces. Apply floor tiles (p.315), fitting them carefully around drain. Let tile adhesive set at least 24 hr.; then fill all the joints with grout.

9. Cover shower walls with cement-base backer board, securing it with galvanized nails. Add wall tiles (p.314) or some other type of waterproof wallcovering. *Note:* Waterproof walls should extend at least 6 ft. above shower floor.

Chapter eleven

Electricity
Home wiring basics, installation, and repairs

Contents

Working with electricity is neither difficult nor dangerous—as long as you understand this powerful force and treat it with respect. In the following pages, electrical safety rules are presented in clear, understandable terms. You'll learn how your system works and how to assess it, upgrade it, add to it, and make repairs. You'll also be able to tell whether a wiring job is within your reach or best left to a licensed electrician. If you decide not to undertake a task yourself, you can use this section to plan improvements and deal more knowledgeably with professionals.

If you're a beginner, read the first half of the chapter carefully before attempting any electrical projects; pay special attention to the safety precautions on page 243. In the second half you'll find information to help you improve your home's lighting and enhance its safety and security.

Think of electricity as a stream of negatively charged particles, called *electrons,* flowing through a conductor, much as water flows through a pipe. (A *conductor* is a material, such as copper, whose resistance to electrical flow—measured in *ohms*—is low; an *insulator,* such as rubber or plastic, offers high resistance.) The rate of electrical flow, or *current,* is measured in *amperes (amps).* One ampere is equal to 6.28 billion billion electrons passing a given point per second.

The electrical pressure that causes current to flow through a conductor is measured in *volts.* Light fixtures and small appliances operate on 120 volts; electric ranges and other heavy-duty appliances require 240 volts.

The amount of power delivered by a current under pressure to a lamp or appliance is measured in *watts.* To determine wattage, multiply amperes (current) times volts (pressure). For example, ½ amp of current at 120 volts will power a 60-watt bulb. A thousand watts equals a *kilowatt.* A kilowatt used for an hour is a *kilowatt-hour (kwh),* which is the unit utilities use to measure and bill you for electricity.

Simple circuitry. To do its job, elec-

tricity must flow in a closed loop, or *circuit,* from a power source to a power user, such as a light bulb, and back to the source. If the circuit is interrupted, say by an open switch, the flow stops.

In a typical household lighting circuit (p.238), current flows at 120 volts from a *hot bus bar* in the house's *main service panel* through a *hot (live) wire* (usually color-coded black) to a light bulb, which transforms current and voltage into heat and light. From the light fixture, a *neutral wire* (usually color-coded white) carries current at zero volts back to the panel's *ground/ neutral bus bar,* which is *grounded,* or connected to the earth. In the event of a circuit malfunction, a *grounding wire* (bare copper or color-coded green), running with the hot and neutral wires, provides a safe path to earth for abnormal current flow (p.240).

How power reaches your home. The electricity generated by a power plant and delivered to your home by your local utility is called *alternating current (AC)* because it flows alternately, first in one direction, then in the opposite, completing 60 cycles every second. (Batteries produce *DC,* or *direct current.*) From the power plant,

current travels over high-voltage transmission lines to substations, where *transformers* reduce the voltage for distribution to local lines. Neighborhood transformers lower voltage to 120 and 240 volts for home delivery.

Most homes built after World War II have three-wire electrical service, in which a neutral wire and two 120-volt hot wires provide 100 to 200 or more amps at both 120 and 240 volts. Older homes may still have two-wire service, in which one neutral and one hot wire deliver 30 to 60 amps at 120 volts only.

Electrical service may be routed to a home through overhead wires running from the nearest utility pole to the *service entrance head* located high on one side of the house. Here the utility's wires are spliced to the *service entrance wires,* which are usually encased in metal or plastic tubing, called *conduit,* or combined in a *service entrance cable* (p.244). From the service head, the wires pass through a meter, which records your electricity use, and into the main service panel, where current is split and distributed through branch circuits throughout the house. Alternatively, electrical service may be routed underground to a home.

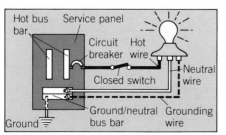

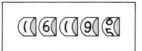

An electric circuit is a continuous path from power source to power-using appliance and back to source. With switch open, no power flows.

How to read an electric meter. Odometer-style meters (left) are easy to read. Old-style meters (right) have four or five dials, each numbered 0 to 9, with numbers arranged alternately clockwise and counterclockwise. Begin at far left dial. If pointer is between two num-

bers, record the lower one; if it's exactly on a number, check next dial to right. If pointer on next dial has passed 0, record the number indicated by first pointer. If next pointer has not reached 0, record next lower number on first dial. Both meters shown here read 16,195 kwh.

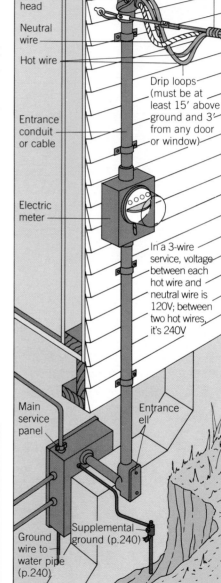

Raintight service entrance head

Neutral wire

Hot wire

Entrance conduit or cable

Electric meter

To utility pole

Drip loops (must be at least 15' above ground and 3' from any door or window)

In a 3-wire service, voltage between each hot wire and neutral wire is 120V; between two hot wires, it's 240V

Main service panel

Entrance ell

Ground wire to water pipe (p.240)

Supplemental ground (p.240)

Circuit breakers and fuses

Distributing power throughout the home 238
Circuit mapping 239
Tools, testing, and safety 242–243

Branch circuits are designed to carry only a certain amperage—typically 15 or 20 amps. If a circuit draws more amperage than it can handle, the wires overheat and may cause a fire. To prevent this, each circuit is protected at the service panel by an *over-current protection device*—in newer systems, usually a circuit breaker; in older ones, a fuse. The device's amperage rating matches that of its circuit. When a circuit draws excess current, the circuit breaker switches off or the metal strip inside the fuse melts and breaks, stopping current flow.

Two common causes of circuit failure are *overloads*—too many lights or appliances operating on the circuit—and *short circuits,* involving either the circuit wires or a lamp or appliance connected to them. A short occurs when a worn hot wire touches a worn neutral (or another hot) wire, creating a short-cut for a large, out-of-control current surge. Before resetting a breaker or replacing a fuse, make sure you identify and correct the source of the problem.

▶ **CAUTION:** Before working at a service panel or doing any other electrical work, read the safety precautions on page 243; follow them carefully.

A heavily used circuit that fails when you turn on a high-wattage appliance is probably overloaded. Try moving some appliances to a less crowded circuit. *Never* attempt to remedy an overload by replacing a blown fuse with one of a higher amperage rating.

If the circuit fails again right after you reset the breaker or replace the fuse, check for a short circuit. Turn off the main disconnect; unplug all lamps and appliances from the circuit. Look for damaged plugs or cords—a common cause of shorts; repair or replace them (p.257). With lamps and appliances still unplugged, reset the breaker or replace the fuse; turn on the main power. If the circuit fails right away, the short is in the house wiring. Call an electrician. If the circuit fails only when you turn on a lamp or appliance, the short is in the device; repair or replace it.

Unlike circuit breakers, plug fuses give a visual clue to the cause of a circuit failure. An overload breaks the fuse's metal strip but leaves its glass window clear; a short usually discolors the window.

Shutting off the main power supply

 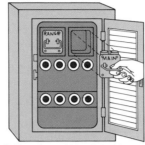 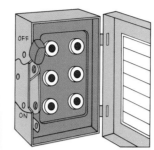

1. Circuit breaker panel   2. Fuse box with pullout blocks   3. Fuse box with lever switch

A circuit breaker panel (1) usually has one or more large main breakers at top. Flip them to *Off* to cut power to the panel. (Trip all breakers if there is no main disconnect.) In fuse box (2), the main cartridge fuses may be mounted on pullout blocks. To cut power, remove main pullouts. If box has lever disconnect (3), switch it to *Off*. To cut power to one circuit, find its breaker or fuse (p.239); trip breaker or remove fuse.

Circuit breakers

Single-pole circuit breaker protects 120-volt lighting and appliance circuits.

Double circuit breaker serves 240-volt appliances, such as an electric range or dryer.

To reset a tripped breaker flip toggle to *On* setting. In some models, you must flip toggle to full *Off* or *Reset* position before returning it to *On*.

A worn breaker may shut off persistently or have a deformed case. To replace it, turn off main power. Remove panel cover. Use voltage tester (p.243) to make sure power is off. Depending on brand of breaker, pull or snap it out of its panel slot; disconnect its wire(s). Replace with one of same brand and amperage. **CAUTION:** Jobs inside service panel require extreme care. They are usually best left to a licensed electrician.

Plug, or Edison-base, fuses and circuit breakers

Standard plug fuse comes in 15-, 20-, 25-, and 30-amp sizes.

Time-lag fuse allows a brief overload caused, for example, by a starting motor.

S-fuse and permanent fuse-box adapter prevent use of wrong size fuse. Only one size fuse fits adapter.

Screw-in breaker replaces standard fuse. When breaker trips, button pops out. Push to reset.

Replacing a plug fuse. Follow precautions on page 243. Keep flashlight and spare fuses near fuse box. Standing on dry surface and using only one hand (keep other hand by your side or in a pocket), turn off main power, grasp blown fuse by its glass rim, and turn it counterclockwise. Replace blown fuse with one of same amperage rating.

Cartridge fuses

  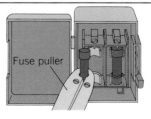

Fuse puller

Ferrule-type cartridge fuses, rated up to 60 amps, usually serve large-appliance circuits.

Knife-blade cartridge fuses, rated up to 600 amps, protect main power circuits.

Replacing a cartridge fuse. If fuse is mounted in a pullout block, remove block and pull out fuse. If it's secured to power source by fuse clips, turn off lever disconnect; use fuse puller to remove and replace fuse. Identify blown fuse with continuity tester (p.243).

The main service panel. After passing through the electric meter and into the house, a modern three-wire (120/240-volt, 100- to 200-amp) electrical service enters the main service panel as shown below. The two hot service wires (usually black), each delivering 120 volts, attach to the terminals of the main disconnect. Two metal strips, called *hot bus bars,* issuing from the main disconnect, receive current and distribute it to branch circuits through circuit breakers or fuses mounted on one or both hot buses. (A 120-volt circuit draws power from one hot bus; a 240-volt circuit, from both.) The neutral service wire (generally white) attaches to the *ground/neutral bus bar,* which is linked to earth by the ground wire. Some panels have separate neutral and ground bus bars.

Branch circuits carry electricity from the service panel to receptacles, switches, and light fixtures. A 120-volt circuit consists of a black insulated hot wire, a white insulated neutral wire, and in a well-wired system, a bare copper or green insulated grounding wire. The hot wire attaches to the lug screw of a single-pole circuit breaker or to the power takeoff terminal next to a fuse. The neutral and grounding wires are connected to the ground/neutral bus bar. (Because neutral and grounding wires must form a continuous path to ground, they are never connected to circuit breakers, fuses, or switches.) A 240-volt circuit has two insulated hot wires, usually one black and one red, which attach to a double-pole circuit breaker or to the terminals of a cartridge fuse pullout block.

There are three types of branch circuits. *Lighting circuits* are 120-volt, 15- or 20-amp general-purpose circuits that power all the light fixtures in a house as well as receptacles for lamps, television sets, vacuum cleaners, and small appliances in all rooms except the kitchen, laundry, and workshop. The National Electric Code (below) calls for one 15-amp circuit for every 600 square feet of finished (or potentially usable) floor space. (Such a circuit can handle 1,800 watts: 15 amps × 120 volts = 1,800 watts.) A 20-amp lighting circuit for every 500 square feet of floor space is preferable (and may be required by some codes).

Small-appliance circuits are 120-volt, 20-amp circuits (with a wire capacity of 2,400 watts) that power receptacles for small appliances and power

tools in the kitchen, laundry, and workshop. The NEC calls for two small-appliance circuits in the kitchen (one or both of which may extend into a pantry or dining room) and a separate 20-amp circuit for the laundry. Another 20-amp circuit for workshop tools is advisable. Small-appliance circuits cannot be used to power light fixtures or permanent appliances.

Individual appliance circuits are 20- to 50-amp circuits, each dedicated to a single major appliance, such as a water heater, electric range, or clothes dryer. Such circuits supply 120 volts, 240 volts, or, as in the case of a range, a combination of both voltages. Because personal computers are sensitive to voltage irregularities and microwave ovens tend to create them, both items should also be on dedicated circuits.

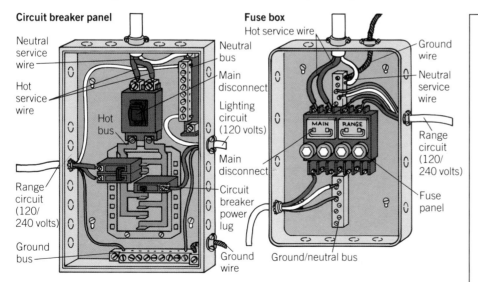

Circuit breaker panel

Neutral service wire
Hot service wire
Hot bus
Range circuit (120/240 volts)
Ground bus

Fuse box

Hot service wire
Neutral bus
Main disconnect
Lighting circuit (120 volts)
Main disconnect
Circuit breaker power lug
Ground wire
Ground wire
Neutral service wire
Range circuit (120/240 volts)
Fuse panel
MAIN   RANGE
Ground/neutral bus

In most homes a circuit breaker panel (left) distributes power. Older homes may have either a single fuse box (right) or a main panel at the service entrance wired to one or more subpanels (p.241). Fuse boxes and breaker panels vary in design. Yours may differ from those shown here.

Codes, permits, and standards
The National Electric Code (NEC) is a set of rules for safe electrical installation. Local codes are based on the NEC but tend to be stricter. Before installing new wiring or adding to existing wiring, contact your local building inspector for up-to-date code information.

Except for simple repairs, such as replacing a receptacle (p.246), you may need a permit from the local building department (p.193) whenever you alter or add to wiring. You may have to submit a written description and a rough sketch of your plans and, in some areas, take a simple electrical proficiency test. You will also have to schedule

inspections as work progresses.

Some local codes require that all wiring be done by a licensed electrician. Others permit you to install new circuits up to the service entrance panel, as long as a licensed electrician inspects your work and completes the hookup. This is a safe practice even when not required by code.

UL listing. When buying electrical devices or parts, look for the Underwriters Laboratories (Und. Lab. or UL) listing mark stamped on the product. This certifies that the item has been tested by UL—a not-for-profit testing firm—and meets its safety standards.

Circuit mapping

The first step in assessing your electrical system is to determine whether you have a two-wire (120-volt) or a three-wire (240-volt) service. To do this, check the number of wires entering the service head or read the voltage listed on the meter. Next, look for the system's service rating (the maximum number of amps it can handle), usually stamped on the main disconnect. The minimum NEC requirement for new homes is 100 amps. A higher rating is better; older homes may still be operating on 60 or even 30 amps.

Before doing any electrical work, make a map of all existing circuits:
1. Assign a number to each circuit breaker or fuse in the service panel.
2. Draw a floor plan of your home. Use a full sheet of paper for each floor.
3. Label each room. Using the codes at right, record the location of all receptacles, switches, and lights. Make sure all receptacles are working.
4. Turn off the first circuit at the service panel by removing its fuse or tripping its breaker. Walk through the house, flipping on lights and testing receptacles with a voltage tester (p.243) or a lamp that you know works. Check both outlets of duplex receptacles. Do not forget garage, attic, and outdoor lights and receptacles. If a light doesn't work or a receptacle fails to light the tester, it's part of the turned-off circuit.
5. On the map, write "1" next to each dead receptacle, switch, or light. Write a description of the first circuit on an adhesive label; stick it on the inside of the service panel door.
6. Turn the first circuit back on. Map remaining circuits in the same way. On the map, color-code each circuit.

Electrical symbols

⊖ Duplex receptacle
⊜ Range outlet
⊜ Dryer outlet
⊜ Water heater outlet

S Switch
○ Light fixture
⟋ Switch wiring
H Permanent baseboard heat

A typical circuit map

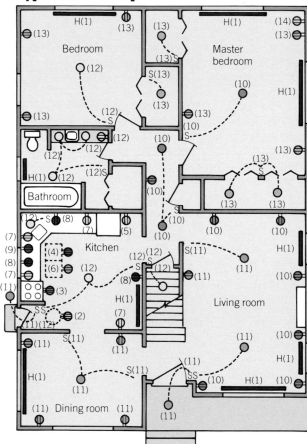

A 15-amp lighting circuit should serve no more than 10 receptacles and fixtures; a 20-amp lighting circuit, no more than 13. A small-appliance circuit should power only 6 receptacles. An appliance rated at 1,000 watts or more (p.241) requires its own circuit. Lighting circuits should be distributed so that if one fails, an entire room or floor isn't left dark.

Main service panel

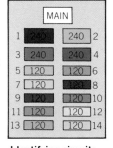

1. Permanent baseboard heat
2. Water heater
3. Kitchen range
4. Dryer
5. Refrigerator
6. Washer
7. Small kitchen appliances
8. Small kitchen appliances
9. Dishwasher
10. Living room, hall, master bedroom
11. Living room, dining room, outside lights
12. Bedroom, bathroom, kitchen, basement
13. Bedrooms and closets
14. Computer

Identifying circuits. Numbered labels affixed to the main service panel identify the numbered circuits on the floor plan shown at left.

Receptacles on one small kitchen appliance circuit (7) alternate with those on the other (8) so that running several appliances at once won't cause overload.

Tools, testing, and safety 242–243
Wires and cables 244
Receptacles 247

Electricity / Grounding an electrical system

Circuit breakers or fuses are a home's first line of defense against electrical accidents. Equally important is the grounding system, which normally doesn't carry current but in an emergency provides a safe path to earth for abnormal current flow.

The basic principles of grounding are simple: electricity always seeks the path of least resistance to a point of zero voltage (the earth), and it flows more readily through copper wire than through most other materials, including your body. Suppose the hot wire to a wall switch comes loose and touches the metal switch box. Without proper grounding, the box is now charged. If you touch its cover plate, you complete the path to earth and receive a shock.

In a grounded system, a bare or green insulated copper *grounding wire* screwed to the box carries fault current safely to the service panel's *ground/neutral bus bar*. From there, current flows through the *main ground wire* to a *grounding electrode* in the earth, usually a cold-water pipe (see below).

Grounding receptacles. The NEC requires that in new homes an uninterrupted grounding connection link all receptacles and metal boxes to the ground/neutral bus; the receptacles must be the three-slot type, which extends grounding protection to tools or appliances with three-prong plugs. Replace two-slot with three-slot receptacles, but only if they can be grounded within the box. The means of grounding can be a grounding wire or the continuous metal sheathing of an armored cable or metal conduit system (p.244). To check the availability of grounding, cut power to a receptacle (p.237); remove its cover plate. Pull out the receptacle and look for bare or green insulated wires in the box or for armored cable connectors (p.245) attached to it. (The grounding connection provided by armored cable alone is unreliable; a separate bonding strip should supplement it.) Use a voltage tester to test a box for ground before installing a grounding receptacle.

If your home is served by ungrounded nonmetallic cable, you can't convert to three-slot devices without upgrading the system.

Ground-fault interrupters

A *ground fault* occurs when a loose hot wire comes into contact with, say, a metal switch box or the metal housing of a grounded power tool. Unlike the large surge of current produced by a *short circuit* (p.237), the misdirected current in a ground fault may not be enough to shut down a circuit, but it can give you a bad shock. If you're standing in water, the shock can be fatal.

Portable GFI

To guard against the dangerous combination of electricity and water, substitute ground-fault interrupters (GFI's) for standard receptacles in bathrooms, kitchens, garages, workshops, and outdoor areas. A GFI monitors the current flowing through a circuit's hot and neutral wires. In normal operation, the current is the same in both wires. But even a slight imbalance, indicating a ground fault, causes the GFI to cut power to the protected receptacle(s) in a fraction of a second. To restore power, press the GFI's *Reset* button.

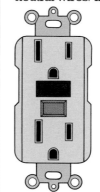

GFI receptacle

A *portable GFI* plugs into a three-slot receptacle, protecting that receptacle only. A *GFI receptacle* replaces a standard one; depending on how it's wired (p.247), it can protect all receptacles farther along on the same circuit. A *GFI breaker* protects an entire circuit at the service panel.

Test GFI's monthly: pressing the *Test* button should cut power to the receptacle or circuit; pressing the *Reset* button should restore it. Replace a GFI if it fails the test.

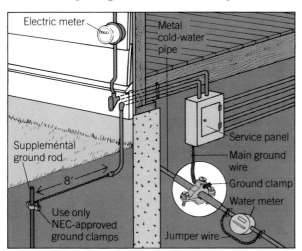

Electric meter — Metal cold-water pipe — Supplemental ground rod — 8' — Use only NEC-approved ground clamps — Jumper wire — Service panel — Main ground wire — Ground clamp — Water meter

The service panel is usually grounded to an underground cold-water pipe with jumper wire clamped to either side of water meter. Because of growing use of plastic pipes, NEC calls for one or more supplemental electrodes, such as an 8-ft.-long, ½-in. copper rod driven into soil. Metal well casing (p.200) also makes a good grounding electrode. Check local codes for grounding requirements.

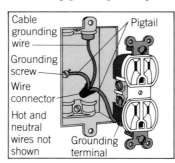

Cable grounding wire — Grounding screw — Wire connector — Hot and neutral wires not shown — Pigtail — Grounding terminal

In a grounded metal receptacle box, wire connector links cable grounding wire(s) with two short wires, or pigtails — one to box, the other to receptacle. In armored cable systems without a separate grounding wire, a pigtail links the receptacle directly to the box.

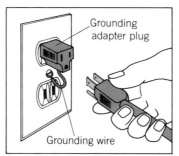

Grounding adapter plug — Grounding wire

Grounding adapter plug lets you use three-prong plug in two-slot receptacle, but only if voltage tester shows that cover-plate screw is grounded. If it is, loosen screw; slip connector at end of adapter's grounding wire under screw. Tighten screw. Plug in adapter; test it for ground (p.243).

Assessing and upgrading your electrical service

If your home has two-wire (120-volt) electrical service (p.236), consult your local utility about converting to three-wire (120/240-volt) service. If you have three-wire service but its capacity is under 100 amps, consult your utility and an electrician about upgrading the system and installing a higher-rated service panel. If the grounding system is faulty or nonexistent, your home is unsafe; call an electrician.

Aluminum wire. Homes built before the mid-1970's may have aluminum wiring, now known to be a fire hazard. If you don't know what type of wiring you have, look for exposed cables in the basement or attic, or check the wires inside a receptacle box (facing page); aluminum wire sheathing will be marked AL or ALUMINUM. If in doubt, call an electrician.

If your wiring is aluminum, use only receptacles and switches marked CO/ALR. Replace any receptacles and switches that are unmarked or marked CU or CU CLAD ONLY.

Estimating power requirements. Even with a three-wire, 100-amp service, your home may be underpowered or inadequately wired. Telltale signs are circuit breakers or fuses that trip or blow often, a light that flickers or a TV image that shrinks when an appliance is turned on, appliances that don't operate at full power, or the need for too many extension cords. (The last symptom may simply indicate an insufficient number of receptacles; the NEC recommends at least one for every 12 feet of wall space in a room.) To calculate amperage needs, use a circuit map, the wattage chart below, and this formula:
1. Add the wattage of (a) lighting circuits (figure 3 watts per square foot of living space); (b) small-appliance circuits (1,500 watts each); and (c) major appliances, except heating and cooling systems (check chart or appliance nameplate for wattage).
2. Suppose the total for a 2,000-square-foot home is 31,000 watts. Subtract 10,000 watts; multiply the result by .40 (31,000 − 10,000 × .40 = 8,400 watts).
3. To this figure, add 10,000 watts plus the heating or cooling system wattage, whichever is higher; in this example, add 5,000 watts for central air conditioning (8,400 + 10,000 + 5,000 = 23,400 total watts).
4. To convert to amps, divide total watts by 240 volts (23,400 watts ÷ 240 volts = 97.5 amps). A 100-amp service would just meet this home's needs. Any addition to the house or the purchase of a major appliance would require upgrading the service to at least 125 amps, preferably to 150 or 200 amps.

Improving the wiring system. As long as you don't exceed the capacity of your service panel, you can add new receptacles and fixtures, by either extending an existing circuit or installing a new one. Before extending a circuit, check your circuit map to make sure the additional receptacles or fixtures will not overtax the circuit. To install a new circuit, there must be space for it at the service panel. If there isn't, consult an electrician about combining underused circuits, substituting half-size for full-size breakers, or connecting a subpanel to the main panel. When adding a circuit, run the cables yourself (pp.250–251), codes permitting, but have an electrician inspect the work and make the final hookup at the panel(s).

Typical wattage ratings*

Appliance	Watts	Appliance	Watts	Appliance	Watts
Air conditioner, central	5,000	Freezer, frost-free	500	Range, oven only	4,000–8,000
Air conditioner, room	800–1,800	Freezer, standard	400	Range, cooktop only	4,000–5,000
Blender	300	Furnace fan	500	Refrigerator, frost-free	615
Broiler, countertop	1,140	Garbage disposer	400–900	Refrigerator, standard	325
Clothes dryer	4,856	Hair dryer	600	Saw, circular	1,200
Coffee maker	1,200	Heater, baseboard	1,600	Sewing machine	75
Computer	300	Heater, portable	1,322	Stereo	300
Dishwasher	1,200	Heating pad	65	Television, color (solid state)	145
Drill, portable	360	Hot plate, two-burner	1,650		
Electric blanket	200	Iron	1,100	Toaster	1,146
Fan, portable	171	Microwave oven	1,450	Vacuum cleaner	720–1,300
Fan, window	200	Mixer	127	Washing machine	512
Food processor	200	Radio, clock	71	Water heater	2,000–5,000

*The wattage figures listed here are averages. Your appliance wattages may vary. For an exact figure, check the appliance nameplate. If the rating is given in amps, multiply amperage by voltage (either 120V or 240V) to obtain wattage.

Surge protectors

Computers, microwave ovens, VCR's, and solid-state televisions are standard equipment in many homes. Though more efficient than the older generation of home equipment, these electronic devices are also more sensitive to power surges—sudden sharp changes in circuit voltage.

Surges usually occur when the power company switches from one utility to another, when lightning strikes near a power line, or when electric motors are switched on or off. Even static electricity can cause a surge. Surges damage transistors in solid-state audiovisual equipment; result in data loss, faulty output, or total circuit failure in computers; and cause a microwave oven to lose its preset timings.

A *surge protector* is a receptacle designed to sense high voltage surges and absorb them before any device plugged into it is damaged. A simple way to safeguard costly equipment, surge protectors are available as plug-in adapters, permanent receptacles, or multi-outlet strips (above).

Electricity / Tools, testing, and safety

For most minor electrical repairs, you'll need a hammer, screwdrivers (standard, cabinet, and Phillips tip), long-nose and slip-joint pliers, a keyhole saw, a hacksaw, a utility knife, a steel measuring tape, and an electric drill with spade and masonry bits (p.52). A screwdriver tip that holds a screw, an offset screwdriver, and a nut driver (p.30) make it easier to work in tight areas.

With some additional electrician's tools, you can handle more complex jobs. A *cable stripper* slices through the sheathing on nonmetallic cable; a *wire stripper* removes the insulation from the wires. A *multipurpose tool* will measure, strip, and cut wire; crimp wire connectors; and cut and thread machine screws. This tool is made in different designs with different functions; buy one that suits your needs best. *Diagonal cutting pliers* will cut No. 6 or smaller wires. *Lineman's pliers* have a wire cutter near the pivot and serrated jaws that hold and twist wires. They're also useful in removing knockouts from electrical boxes (p.245).

To remove and insert a cartridge fuse, you'll need a *fuse puller.* To bend thin-wall or rigid conduit (p.260), buy or rent a *conduit* or *tubing bender* (p.138). *Fish tape,* a tool for running cable behind walls (pp.250–251) or through conduit, is made of flattened steel wire and sold in several lengths. For most jobs you'll need two tapes.

Other supplies. To connect wires, keep a stock of several sizes of screw-on and crimp-on wire terminals and connectors along with waterproof electrical tape.

Electrician's tools

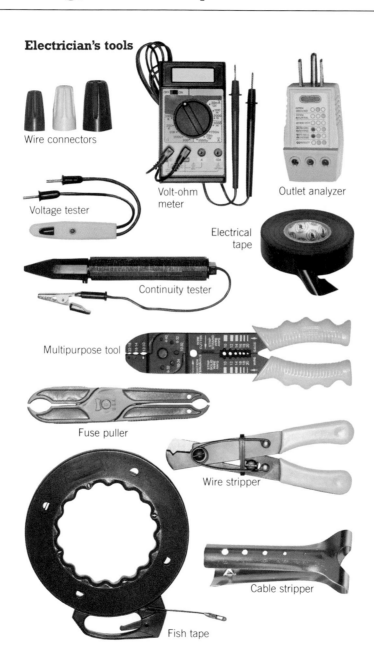

Wire connectors

Voltage tester

Volt-ohm meter

Outlet analyzer

Electrical tape

Continuity tester

Multipurpose tool

Fuse puller

Wire stripper

Cable stripper

Fish tape

Testing

An electrician's basic diagnostic tool is a *continuity tester,* a battery-powered device with a light bulb, probe, and alligator clip. When the clip and probe complete a circuit, the bulb lights. Use this tester—with the power off—to detect shorts and other wiring flaws in sockets, switches, and appliance and extension cords (p.259), and to see if a fuse is good.

Equipped with a bulb and two probes—but not a power source—the *120/240 voltage,* or *neon-light, tester* lights up when voltage is present. Use it to find the incoming hot wire when more than one black wire is in a box and to check for proper grounding.

If you work inside a service panel (not recommended for novices), it is essential to check for current leakage after turning off power to the panel (p.237). Remove the panel cover. Touch one voltage tester probe to the ground/neutral bus (p.238), the other to an open space first on one, then on the other hot bus. If the tester lights, call an electrician.

▶ **CAUTION:** Always use a voltage tester to make sure that any switch, receptacle, circuit, or appliance you are going to work on is really dead.

Polarity. When plugged into a receptacle, an *outlet analyzer* indicates an open grounding, hot, and neutral wire; and in a polarized receptacle, wrong-way polarity. A polarized receptacle has one long and one short slot. A polarized plug, with one prong wider than the other, fits the receptacle only one way. Polarized receptacles must be wired with the neutral wire connected to the long slot and the hot wire to the short slot. If the wires are reversed and a polarized appliance is plugged in, you may get a shock. If the analyzer warns of wrong-way polarity, turn off the power and rewire the receptacle (p.247). If you find that the outlet is properly wired, the problem is elsewhere in the circuit; call an electrician.

A *volt-ohm meter,* or *multitester,* tests for continuity, power, and grounding and measures voltages and resistance. Some testers have digital readouts, others a needle that sweeps across a dial. Choose one that measures 250 volts AC, and with RX1, RX10, and RX100 settings to test resistance.

Testing for continuity

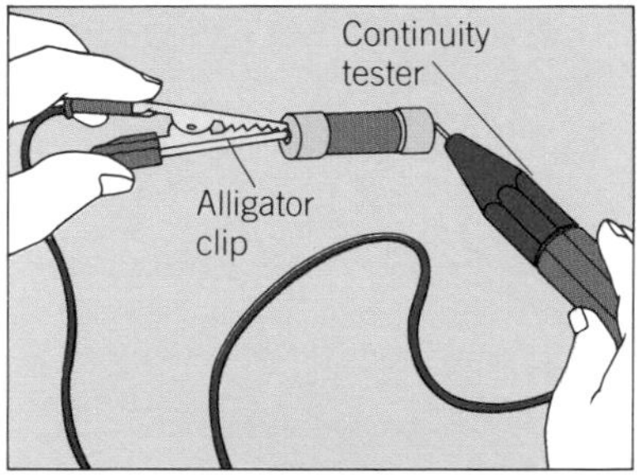

Fuses. To see if a cartridge fuse is good, touch one end with the alligator clip of a continuity tester, the other end with the probe. For a plug-type fuse, place clip on contact at base of fuse, the probe on the metal threads. If fuse is good, the tester bulb will light up.

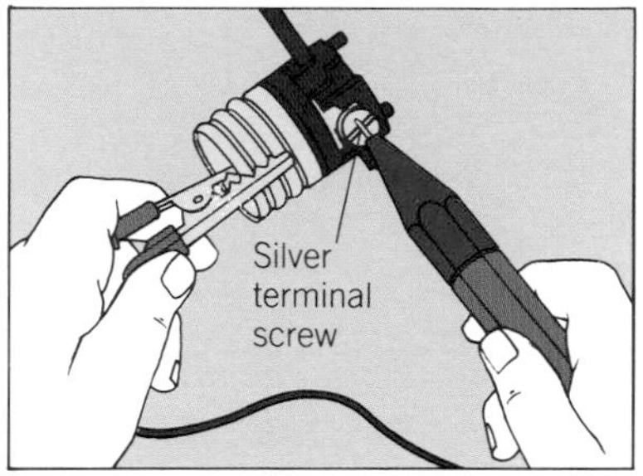

Lamp socket. If lamp doesn't light a good bulb, unplug it; remove socket (p.259) and test it. Clamp clip to metal screw shell; touch probe to silver terminal screw. Repeat test for brass screw and center terminal. If socket is good, tester will light. (In this case, lamp switch may be faulty; see test below.) If tester doesn't light, replace socket.

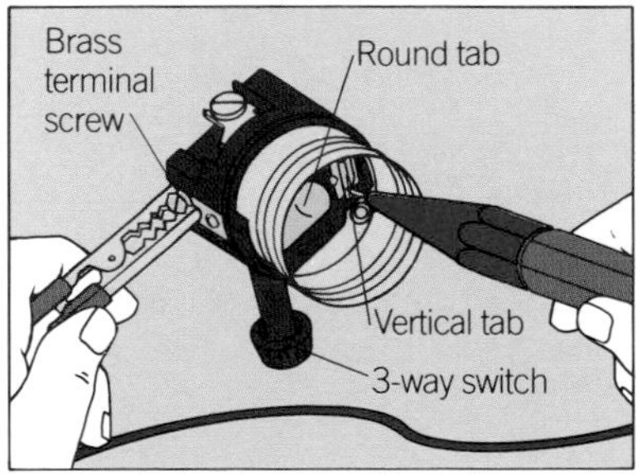

Lamp switch. Attach clip to brass terminal screw. *Three-way switch:* Turn switch to first *On;* touch probe to vertical tab. With switch at second *On,* touch probe to round tab. With switch at third *On,* touch probe to both tabs. Tester should light at all settings. *One-way switch:* tester should light with switch at *On* and probe at round tab.

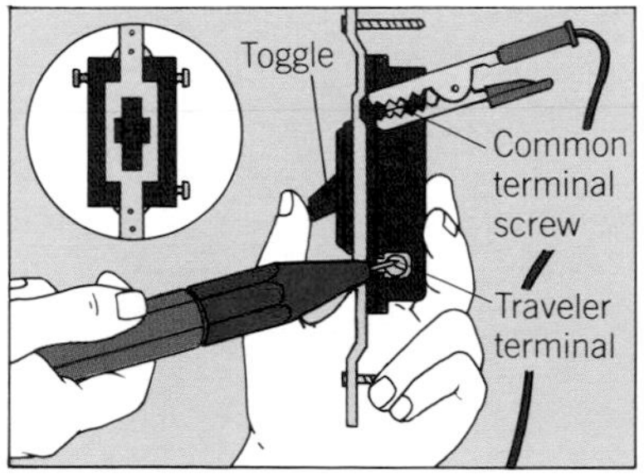

Single-pole wall switch: Cut power; disconnect switch. Set clip on one terminal, probe on other. Tester should light with switch at *On. Three-way switch:* Set probe on a traveler terminal, clip on common terminal. Tester should light with toggle up or down. Set probe on second traveler terminal. Tester should light with toggle in other position.

Using a voltage tester

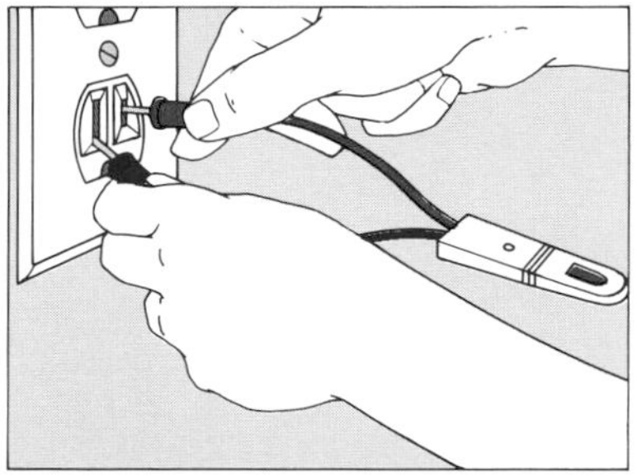

Check that power is off in a receptacle before working on it. Turn off power; insert probes into slots. If bulb doesn't light, power is off. Test both sockets of a duplex receptacle. Then remove cover plate, and touch probes to bare ends of each pair of black and white wires attached to receptacle. Tester should not light.

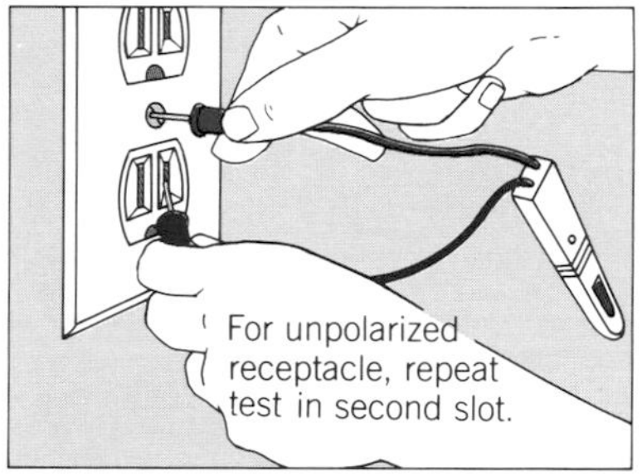

Check for grounding in a receptacle with power on. Put one probe in short (hot) slot; touch second probe to bare metal cover plate or plate screw. Or insert second probe in grounding slot, if any. If tester glows weakly or not at all, receptacle isn't well grounded. With power off, remove cover plate; look for loose grounding connection.

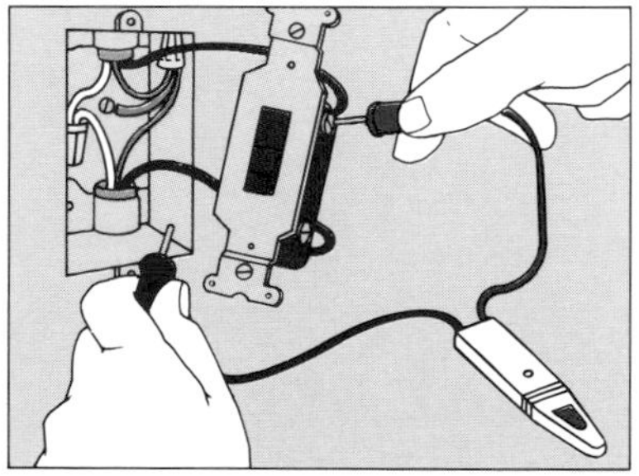

To test for power at a switch, turn off power to circuit; remove cover plate. Place one probe on metal box or, if box is nonmetallic, on bare grounding wire. Touch each switch terminal with second probe. If tester lights, power is on; go back to service panel and turn off correct circuit.

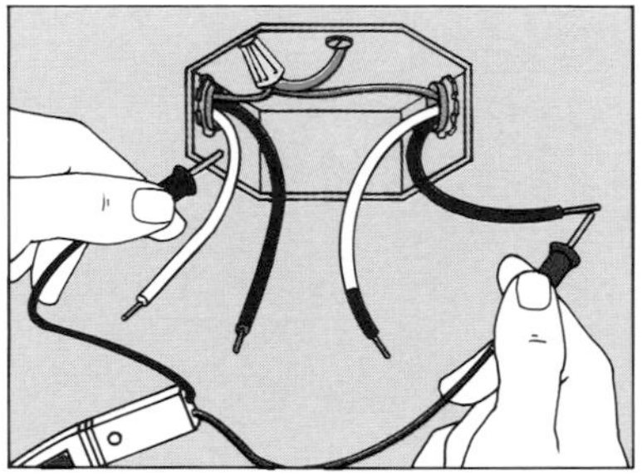

To find incoming hot wire in a box, cut power to circuit. Remove switch, receptacle (p.247), or fixture from box (p.254). Bend loose wires away from each other and box. Restore power. Carefully touch a probe to metal box (or to grounding wire if box is plastic); touch second probe to each black wire. Tester should light at hot wire.

Safety precautions

- Always turn off power to a circuit before working on it (p.237). Place a sign at the service panel to warn others not to turn on the circuit that you're working on.
- Never stand on a wet or damp floor when working with electricity. If necessary, cover the floor with rubber mats or dry boards.
- Once you've turned off a circuit breaker or pulled a fuse, check with a voltage tester that the power actually *is* off.
- When testing a fixture or removing a fuse, keep one hand behind your back, if possible, to avoid making a complete circuit of your body.
- Before touching any wire, use a voltage tester to make sure it isn't live.
- When working on electrical wiring or appliances, never touch plumbing pipes or fixtures or gas pipes; this can cause a shock.
- Never replace a fuse with one of higher amperage.
- Check your work with a voltage tester or outlet analyzer to make sure that it's properly wired and grounded.
- Use rubber- or plastic-handled tools.
- Near overhead wires, don't climb on an aluminum or wet wood ladder.
- Wear heavy rubber gloves if you are working on or in a service box.
- Before working on an appliance, unplug it. Even when unplugged, a television set can give a shock; don't open its back.
- To protect small children, install safety covers in unused receptacles.
- When unplugging a lamp or an appliance, pull the plug—not the wire.
- When using electrical appliances, such as a hair dryer, never touch grounded gas or plumbing fixtures, such as a faucet.
- An extension cord is intended only for temporary use—don't leave it plugged in. Don't run one under a rug or where it may be stepped on or tripped over.

Distributing power throughout the home 238
Grounding an electrical system 240
Connecting wires 247

Electricity/Wires and cables

The most common conductor of electricity is copper wire, usually sheathed with an insulating material and available in a wide range of sizes, each designated by an American Wire Gauge (AWG) number (the higher the number, the smaller the wire). A wire's size determines its *ampacity* (the amount of current it can carry): the greater a wire's diameter, the higher its ampacity.

Most house wiring is Type TW—thermoplastic insulated, weather-resistant—or Type THW, which is both heat- and weather-resistant. The insulation color usually indicates a wire's function, but not always—use a voltage tester to check (p.243). In most cases, the hot wire is black (if a circuit includes a second hot wire, it may be red or blue). The neutral wire is white. The grounding wire may be green, green and yellow striped, or bare copper. Except for the smaller gauges, a wire's type and AWG number are stamped on its insulation. No. 8 and larger wires are stranded, rather than solid, for greater flexibility. No. 12 (20-amp) wire has largely replaced No. 14 (15-amp) as the standard residential wire.

Individual circuit wires may be run through metal or plastic pipes called *conduit* (p.260). More often, circuit wires are combined in cable, either nonmetallic-sheathed cable (commonly known by the trademark Romex) or steel armored cable (known by the trademark BX). Nonmetallic-sheathed cable is available in several types (far right).

Wire gauges, ampacities, and uses

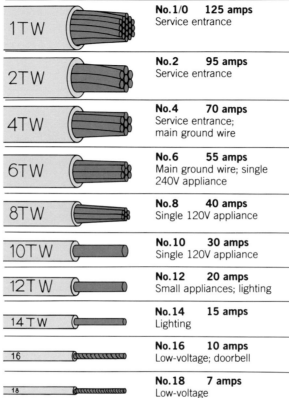

No.1/0   125 amps
Service entrance

No.2   95 amps
Service entrance

No.4   70 amps
Service entrance; main ground wire

No.6   55 amps
Main ground wire; single 240V appliance

No.8   40 amps
Single 120V appliance

No.10   30 amps
Single 120V appliance

No.12   20 amps
Small appliances; lighting

No.14   15 amps
Lighting

No.16   10 amps
Low-voltage; doorbell

No.18   7 amps
Low-voltage

Types of cable

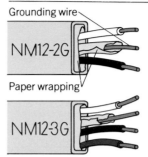

Grounding wire

Paper wrapping

NM (nonmetallic-sheathed) cable is standard house cable, usable only in dry locations. Two-wire cable contains two conductors (hot and neutral), plus grounding wire, all wrapped in paper and sheathed in plastic. Three-wire cable has two hot wires, a neutral, and a grounding wire. Indicated on cable sheathing are cable type, wire size, number of conductors, and presence of grounding wire (G).

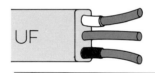

Wires in NMC cable are encased in solid plastic, with no paper overwrap or fibrous fill. NMC cable can be used in damp or corrosive locations but not underground.

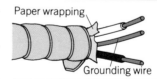

Waterproof UF (underground feeder) cable can be buried in earth. Service entrance cable (not shown) brings electrical service into a house, overhead or underground (p.236).

Paper wrapping

Grounding wire

Armored cable is usable only in dry indoor locations. A grounding wire (shown) or a metal bonding strip (facing page) supplements armor's limited grounding capability.

Removing cable sheathing

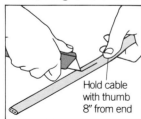

Lay cable end on flat surface. Cut shallow lengthwise groove down middle of cable with utility knife. Slit sheathing along groove; don't cut wire insulation.

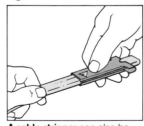

A cable stripper can also be used to slit sheathing. Slip tool over cable; squeeze handles so blade pierces sheathing. Pull stripper off cable end.

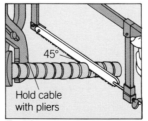

Peel back slit sheathing; remove overwrap or filler. Without damaging wire insulation, cut off loose sheathing with utility knife or cutting pliers.

Hold cable with pliers

To strip armored cable, place hacksaw blade 6 in. from cable end; saw through top of armor (don't cut wires). Twist off loose armor; remove paper wrapping.

Stripping wire insulation

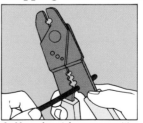

1. Use wire stripper or multi-purpose tool to remove 1 in. of insulation from end of wire. Place wire in right size hole and press handles together.

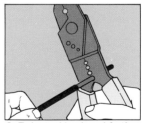

2. Twist tool back and forth until the insulation is cut through and you can slide it easily off the wire.

Electrical boxes and accessories

Wherever electrical wires are joined together or connected to the terminals of a switch, receptacle, or fixture, they must be enclosed in an electrical box. Made of galvanized steel or thermoplastic and available in many sizes and designs, electrical boxes isolate wire connections from flammable building materials. The number of wires you can bring into a box depends on its size; see chart below.

Switches and receptacles are generally housed in rectangular or square boxes; lighting fixtures, in octagonal or round boxes. Usually square or octagonal, a *junction box* houses only wire or cable connections (no devices).

Boxes must be covered yet accessible. A junction box requires a solid cover plate; other boxes are sealed by the fixtures mounted in them or by switch or receptacle cover plates.

Number of conductors per box*

Box size	Wire gauge			
	No.14	No.12	No.10	No.8
Octagonal boxes				
4" (side) x 1½"	7	6	6	5
4" (side) x 2⅛"	10	9	8	7
Square boxes				
4" (side) x 1¼"	9	8	7	6
4" (side) x 1½"	10	9	8	7
4" (side) x 2⅛"	15	13	12	10
Switch boxes				
3" x 2" x 2¼"	5	4	4	3
3" x 2" x 2½"	6	5	5	4
3" x 2" x 2¾"	7	6	5	4

*Each of the following counts as one conductor: a switch or receptacle; an insulated hot or neutral wire entering box; all grounding wires in box; all cable clamps.

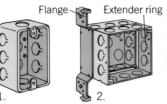 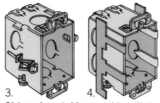 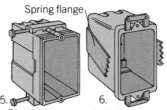 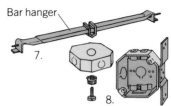

Metal "handy" box (1) is widely used to house switches and duplex receptacles. Rounded edges make it suitable for surface wiring. Flange of square box (2) is nailed to stud; extender ring doubles box capacity.

Old-work metal boxes with adjustable ears and side clamps (3) or brackets (4) are mounted in existing walls. Metal switch boxes with removable sides (not shown) can be ganged together.

Plastic boxes, used with NM cable, needn't be grounded. Check codes for restrictions on plastic box use. New-work box (5) is nailed to exposed stud. Spring flanges secure old-work box (6) to existing wall.

A ceiling box can be mounted between joists with an adjustable bar hanger (7). Flanged box (8) is nailed to side of joist.

Connecting NM cable to box

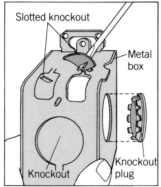 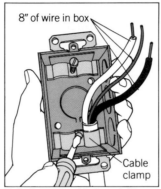 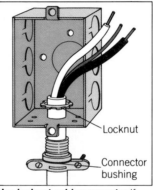 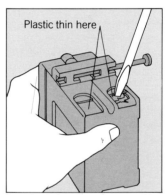

Knockouts are removable discs on metal box through which cable is fed. Pry out slotted knockout with screwdriver, or rap on knockout with plier handle and twist off. Seal unused opening with knockout plug.

To install NM cable in metal box with built-in clamp connector, loosen clamp screw; insert cable through knockout closest to clamp. Slip cable under clamp. Tighten clamp screw.

Use locknut cable connector if metal box lacks built-in clamp. Slip connector bushing over cable; tighten bushing screws. Insert wires and bushing into box. Screw locknut tightly onto bushing.

In a plastic box, knockouts are thin sections of box walls. To open, press down hard with screwdriver. If cable is stapled to stud within 8 in. of box, it may not have to be clamped to box; check local codes.

Connecting armored cable to boxes

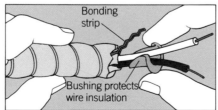 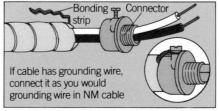 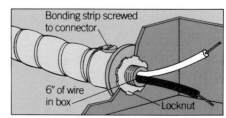

1. Only metal boxes can be used with armored cable. After stripping cable (facing page), insert fiber or plastic bushing against cut end of armor.

2. Bend bonding strip back against armor. Slide armored cable connector over armor. Attach bonding strip to connector screw. Tighten screw.

3. Feed cable wires and connector into box through knockout. Tightly secure connector to box with locknut.

Electricity / Switches

A wall switch or receptacle (facing page) is connected to the circuit wires inside an electrical box by a screw or by push-in terminals on the side or back of the device. Receptacles are wired to the hot and neutral sides of a circuit. Because the current must flow uninterrupted through the neutral wire, switches are wired to a circuit's hot side only.

The most common type of wall switch, the *single-pole switch* controls a receptacle or fixture from one location. It has two brass-colored terminal screws and/or push-in terminals; its toggle is marked *On* and *Off.* Used in pairs to control a fixture from two locations, a *3-way switch* has two brass-colored *traveler* terminals for the wires between switches and a dark *common* terminal, which connects to the incoming hot wire or to the fixture. (A push-in common terminal is marked COM or COMMON.) A 3-way switch's toggle has no *On/Off* markings.

A switch may wear out, or you may want a quieter model or one with a grounding screw or other feature. The new switch should be the same type (single-pole, 3-way, etc.) and have the same amp and voltage ratings as the old; make sure the ratings are adequate for the appliance or light being switched.

How to read a switch

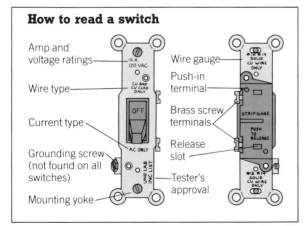

Amp and voltage ratings

Wire type

Current type

Grounding screw (not found on all switches)

Mounting yoke

Wire gauge

Push-in terminal

Brass screw terminals

Release slot

Tester's approval

Stamped on a switch or receptacle are amp and voltage ratings, UL listing mark, and type of wire and current compatible with it. Push-in terminals, viewed by some electricians as unreliable, take only copper wire. Devices used with aluminum wires must be marked CO-ALR.

Replacing a single-pole switch

CAUTION: Before removing switch or receptacle cover, shut off power to the device's circuit (p.237).

Remove cover-plate screws and plate; loosen switch's mounting screws. Without touching wires, gently pull out switch. Use voltage tester to make sure circuit is off (p.243). Loosen screw terminals; disconnect wires from old switch. If you're replacing a switch because you think it's defective, test it with continuity tester (p.243). Position new switch so that it's off when toggle is down; connect hot wires to it. If new switch has grounding screw, run a pigtail (facing page) from switch to grounding screw in box; in armored cable system, run pigtail to metal box (p.240). Tighten screw terminals; tuck wires and switch into box. Screw switch to box, cover plate to switch. Restore power; test switch.

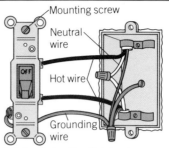

Mounting screw

Neutral wire

Hot wire

Grounding wire

Middle-of-circuit switch has two black wires attached to its brass terminals. Neutral wires bypass switch.

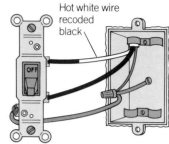

Hot white wire recoded black

In a switch loop circuit (p.252), white wire attached to switch is hot and should be blackened at both ends with paint or electrician's tape.

Replacing a 3-way switch

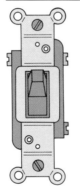

When one of a pair of 3-way switches fails, you must first locate the faulty one. Cut power to circuit; pull first switch out of box (see above). Check that circuit is dead with voltage tester. Mark wire attached to common terminal with tape. Remove wires from switch; test it with a continuity tester. If switch is good, reconnect it and check second switch. To connect a switch, attach taped wire to switch's common terminal, remaining hot wires to traveler terminals. Ground switch as described above and install in box.

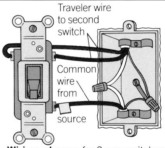

Traveler wire to second switch

Common wire from source

Wiring schemes for 3-way switches vary. Here, two-wire cable from source powers first switch.

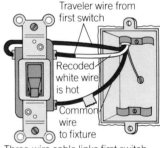

Traveler wire from first switch

Recoded white wire is hot

Common wire to fixture

Three-wire cable links first switch to fixture and to second switch. For more on wiring 3- and 4-way switches, see p.253.

4-way and other switches

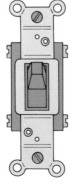

Used with two 3-way switches to control a light from three places, *4-way switch* (left) has four brass screws and an unmarked toggle. *Double-pole switch* for 240V appliances has four brass screws and an *On/Off* toggle. Some switches have toggle that glows when switch is off or pilot light that shines when switch is on. *Locking switch* requires a key to operate. With *time-delay switch,* light stays on about 45 sec. after switch is turned off. *Time-clock switch* turns light on and off at preset intervals. *Dimmer switch* (right) adjusts light intensity.

Installing a dimmer switch

Single-pole dimmer

Dimmer leads

Control knob

Circuit hot wires

Wire connector

Dimmers—for incandescent fixtures only—come in single-pole and 3-way models. Knob-controlled dimmers usually handle 600 watts; toggle dimmers, 300 watts. Fixture wattage must not exceed dimmer capacity. **Single-pole dimmer:** Cut power to old switch; remove it (see above). Attach dimmer leads to hot wires with wire connectors. Mount dimmer; attach cover plate and knob. **Three-way dimmer:** Attach black dimmer lead to common wire, red leads to traveler wires. Install only one dimmer in a 3-way circuit.

Tools, testing, and safety 242–243
Wires and cables 244
Boxes and accessories 245

Receptacles

Connecting wires

Wire connections must be tight. Use a wire connector just big enough for the size and number of wires being joined. To splice solid or stranded wires, see below. To join stranded to solid wire, strip 1 inch of insulation from the stranded wire, ½ inch from the solid. Hold the ends parallel; wrap the stranded wire clockwise around the solid. Screw on a connector.

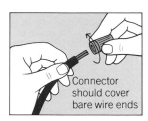

To splice wires, strip ¾ in. of insulation from wire ends. Hold ends parallel (or twist together with long-nose pliers if connector package so specifies). Screw on connector clockwise until tight.

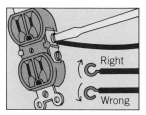

To attach wire to screw terminal, strip ¾ in. of insulation off wire end. With long-nose pliers, bend wire into loop. Loosen screw. Hook wire clockwise around screw shaft. Tighten screw.

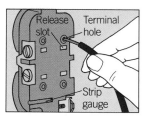

Strip gauge on devices with push-in terminals shows how much insulation to remove. Feed wire into terminal up to insulation. To remove wire, shut off power, push screwdriver into release slot.

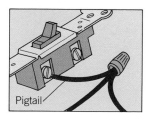

A pigtail is a short wire linking two or more circuit wires to one terminal. (Never connect two wires directly to one terminal.) Join wires and pigtail with connector. Attach pigtail's other end to terminal.

A 120-volt, 15- or 20-amp duplex receptacle consists of two sockets, each accommodating a standard 120-volt plug. In new installations, three-slot grounded receptacles are required; they're recommended for rewiring work. Most new receptacles are polarized (p.242). Receptacles, like switches, have screw terminals and/or push-in terminals. A duplex receptacle has two silver-colored screws, to which neutral wires attach; two brass-colored screws, to which hot wires attach; and a green grounding screw. (Neutral push-in terminals are marked WHITE.) Break-off tabs between the sockets allow you to "split" a receptacle electrically (p.252). The same data is stamped on a receptacle as

120/240-volt, 30-amp grounded receptacle for clothes dryer

on a switch (facing page). When replacing a receptacle, make sure the new device's ampere and voltage ratings match those of the old and don't exceed the breaker or wire capacity. Replace an ungrounded receptacle with a grounded one, but only if the circuit is grounded (p.240).

Large appliances require 240- or 120/240-volt receptacles rated 30 amps or more. A receptacle's ampere and voltage ratings determine its slot design, which matches only one type of appliance plug.

Replacing a receptacle

A defective receptacle won't hold a plug properly or may cause circuit failure whenever you plug in an appliance. To replace, turn off power to circuit (p.237); use voltage tester to make sure circuit is dead (p.243). Remove cover-plate screws and plate; loosen receptacle's mounting screws. Pull out receptacle; disconnect wires. If old receptacle was split (p.252), remove same break-off tab on new one. Connect wires to new receptacle: black wire(s) to brass screw(s), white to silver screw(s), grounding pigtail to green screw. Remount receptacle and restore power. Test new device with voltage tester.

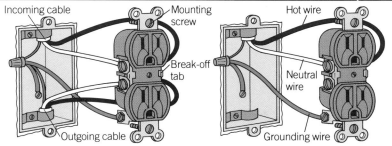

Middle-of-circuit receptacle is wired to incoming and outgoing cables.

Wiring for end-of-circuit receptacle. (Some codes require that neutral or all wires be joined to receptacle with pigtail.)

Installing a GFI receptacle

Receptacle safety features include self-closing covers and locking devices that keep a plug from being pulled out by accident. Ground-fault interrupters (p.240) are required wherever moisture increases risk of shock. Before wiring a GFI receptacle, read package directions; test that power is off to receptacle you're replacing (p.243). GFI receptacles have screw terminals or wire leads. Attach incoming cable wires to screws or leads marked LINE; outgoing wires to screws or leads marked LOAD (black wires to brass screws or black leads, white wires to silver screws or white leads). To identify incoming hot wire, see p.243.

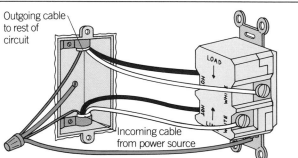

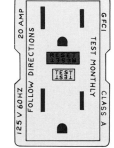

Wiring for middle-of-circuit GFI receptacle. If GFI is at end of circuit, attach cable wires to LINE leads (or screws); cap the unused LOAD leads with wire connectors.

To install new outlets (the term, as used here, refers to junction boxes, switches, and fixtures, not just receptacles), first determine the types you want and where you want them. Depending on the capacity and layout of your wiring, run a new circuit from the service panel or extend an existing circuit. Before adding a circuit, calculate your present power usage (p. 241) to make sure the new circuit won't overtax the system; also check the service panel to see if there is space for a new breaker or fuse. (To make room in a full panel, see p. 241.)

Extend a circuit only if it's grounded (p. 240) and not already operating at or near capacity (p. 239). If an extension is possible, pick an accessible outlet to serve as its power source. The simplest source is a junction box in which wires from the new and existing cables are joined; other options are illustrated at right. The power source must always be "hot" (don't use an end-of-circuit switch or fixture or a switch-controlled receptacle); its box must have an unused knockout and be big enough to house the new wires (p. 245).

▶ **CAUTION:** Cut power to an outlet before working on it (p. 237). Use a voltage tester to make sure it's dead (p. 243).

To calculate cable needs, plan the shortest route from power source to new outlet(s); measure it (pp. 250–251). Add a foot for each splice, plus 20 percent for errors. The size and type of the new wires should match that of the existing wiring. No. 12 (20-amp) wire can be used in 15- or 20-amp circuits; No. 14 (15-amp) wire in 15-amp circuits only. Check codes (p. 238) before starting work; get a permit if needed.

Tapping into an existing circuit

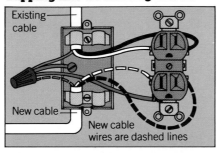

Existing cable
New cable
New cable wires are dashed lines

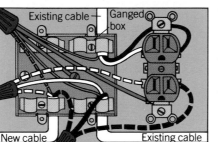

Existing cable — Ganged box
New cable — Existing cable

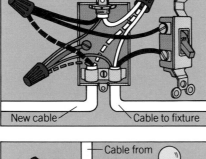

Cable from source
New cable — Cable to fixture

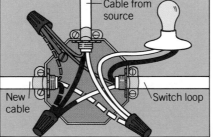

Cable from source
New cable — Switch loop

● Hot wire   ○ Neutral wire   ●● Grounding wire

End-of-circuit receptacle is a good place to start a circuit extension, as long as receptacle isn't switch-controlled. With power off, pull receptacle from box. Run new cable into box (p. 245). Connect new cable's black wire to receptacle's unused brass screw, white wire to unused silver screw. Splice new to existing grounding wires in box.

Middle-of-circuit receptacle has wires from two cables connected to it. Adding a third may require enlarging box with an extender or ganging two boxes. Cut power to receptacle; disconnect a pair of black and white wires. Run new cable into box. Use pigtails (p. 247) to attach new and disconnected black wires to brass screw, white wires to silver screw. Splice all grounding wires.

To tie into a switch, cut power to it; check wiring to make sure switch is in middle of circuit (p. 246). If it is, restore power; carefully identify incoming hot wire with voltage tester (p. 243). Cut power; disconnect hot wire. Run new cable into box. Pigtail new and incoming black wires to switch terminal. Splice new white and grounding wires to existing white and grounding wires.

Tap only middle-of-circuit fixtures connected to two cables. Cut power to fixture; remove it (p. 254). Restore power; use voltage tester to find incoming hot wire (p. 243). Shut power off; join black wires from new and incoming cables to switch loop's hot white wire (recoded black; see p. 246). Join white wires from new and incoming cables and fixture. Splice all grounding wires.

The type of electrical box and mounting hardware you'll need depends on whether they'll be set in wallboard, wood, or plaster. When routing cable, first cut holes for the boxes. Mount wall boxes at the same height from the floor as existing boxes (usually 4 feet for switches, 12 to 18 inches for receptacles).

When you have decided where you want a box, locate studs or joists that might obstruct it (p. 191). To check for pipes and other obstacles, drill a test hole into the wall. Bend an 8-inch length of stiff wire to a 90° angle, insert it in the hole, and turn it full circle. If you hit anything, repeat the test a few inches away until you find a clear area.

In wallboard and wood walls

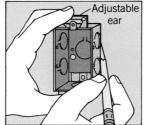

Adjustable ear

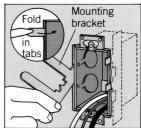

Fold in tabs
Mounting bracket

Separate mounting brackets are often used to mount boxes in wallboard. Trace box outline on wall (left), omitting adjustable ears. Cut along outline with wallboard knife. Run cable into box. Adjust ears so box front is flush with wall. Hold box in wall; slip brackets between box sides and wall (right). With long-nose pliers, pull bracket tabs forward; fold tightly against side of box.

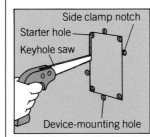

Side clamp notch
Starter hole
Keyhole saw
Device-mounting hole

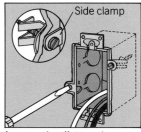

Side clamp

To install a box with side clamps in a wood wall, trace box outline on wall; include notches for clamps but omit adjustable ears. Drill ⅜-in. starter and device-mounting holes. Cut along outline with keyhole saw. Run cable into box. Adjust ears so box is flush with wall. Mount box; tighten clamp screws until ears are drawn against wall.

Installing ceiling boxes

Tools, testing, and safety 242–243
Electrical boxes and accessories 245
Connecting wires 247

In plaster-and-lath walls

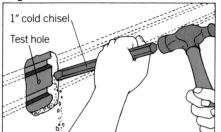

1. Chisel off enough plaster around test hole to expose full width of a lath. Center box with adjustable ears over lath. Trace box outline on wall (omit ears). Apply masking tape around outline; score outline with utility knife.

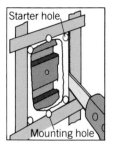
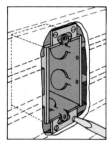

2. Drill ⅜-in. starter and device-mounting holes. Cut along outline with keyhole saw. Remove tape. Chip off enough plaster for ears to fit against lath. Run cable into box. Adjust ears so box is flush with wall. Anchor box to lath with wood screws.

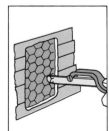

If plaster is backed by metal lath, use box without ears. Cover box site with tape. Trace box outline on tape. Score outline with utility knife. Chisel off plaster from lath. Cut lath with mini-hacksaw. Mount box with brackets (facing page).

From an unfinished attic

1. After locating joists (p.191), mark fixture site and drill ⅛-in. hole from below. Check for obstructions (facing page). If area is clear, use 18-in.-long bit to drill up into attic floor. In attic, find board with hole; cut section between joists with keyhole saw.

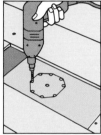
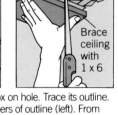

2. From attic, center box on hole. Trace its outline. Drill ¾-in. holes at corners of outline (left). From below, cut opening in wallboard ceiling by sawing from hole to hole with keyhole saw (right). For plaster-and-lath ceiling, tape outline before cutting.

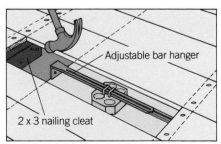

3. Screw box to hanger. Snip tabs from ends of hanger with cutting pliers. Fit hanger between joists so box is directly over hole, its lip flush with ceiling. Run cable to box. Screw hanger to joists. Nail cleats to joists, floorboard to cleats.

From below

In wallboard. 1. Locate joists adjacent to fixture site (p.191); check for obstructions (facing page). Cut 8-in. square opening at site. Insert steel tape; measure distance from corner of opening to side of joist. Add ¾ in. and mark this distance on ceiling.

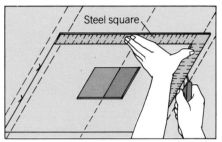

2. Measure to joist centerline from each corner of opening. Use steel square to mark centerlines on ceiling; connect lines to form 16- or 24-in. square. Score and cut out square with utility knife and wallboard saw. Trim opening; pull nails from joists.

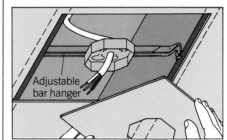

3. Cut wallboard patch ⅛ in. smaller than hole. Outline box on patch; cut out opening. Mount box so it's centered on opening. Run cable to box. Screw patch to joists with drywall screws; seal edges with joint compound and tape (p.279).

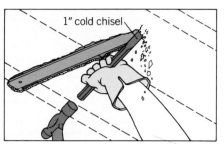

In plaster and lath. 1. Chip hole in ceiling with hammer and chisel to expose width of one lath. Chisel along length of lath until you see a nail, indicating a joist crossing. Repeat in opposite direction until you come to another joist.

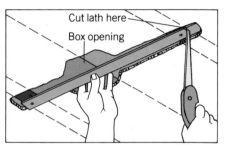

2. Trace box outline at center of channel. Drill ⅜-in. holes at corners. Tape outline edges. Cut out opening with keyhole saw. As you cut, brace ceiling with piece of 1 x 6. Cut exposed lath at outside edges of joists with keyhole saw. Pull out lath nails.

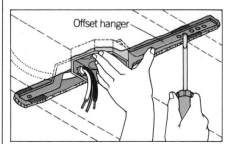

3. Attach box to offset hanger. Hold box in opening; mark hanger screw holes on both joists. (Lengthen channel if necessary.) Drill pilot holes in joists. Run cable into box. Screw hanger to joists. Patch channel with patching plaster (p.280).

Electricity / Running cable

House construction 188–191
Tools, testing, and safety 242–243
Wires and cables 244

In new construction

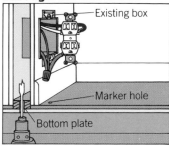
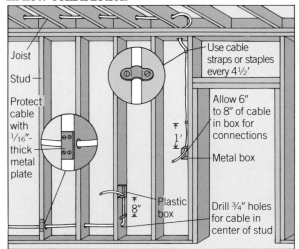

Joist

Stud

Protect cable with 1/16"-thick metal plate

Use cable straps or staples every 4½'

Allow 6" to 8" of cable in box for connections

1'

Metal box

Plastic box

8"

Drill ¾" holes for cable in center of stud

Staple NM cable to sides of studs and joists, or run cable through holes drilled in centers of studs and joists. If hole is less than 1¼ in. from edge of framing member, nail metal plate to edge. Staple cable to stud within 8 in. of plastic box, 1 ft. of metal box.

In an existing house

Except for surface wiring (facing page), the least disruptive route for new cable in an existing house is across an unfinished basement or attic. To "fish" cable when there's no access from above or below, you may have to cut holes in walls, ceilings, or floors in addition to the openings for electrical boxes.

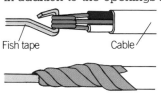

Fish tape   Cable

Hook cable wires over end of fish tape. Wrap with electrician's tape.

▶ **CAUTION:** Turn off power to an outlet before you do any work on it (p.237); use a voltage tester to make sure the power is off (p.243).

Running cable in a finished house can be difficult. Enlist a helper. You'll need one or two fish tapes—flat wires with hooked ends used to pull, or "fish," cable through the spaces between studs or joists. Fish tapes are sold in coils of 25 to 100 feet, with or without reels; or you can make your own out of galvanized steel wire.

Through the basement

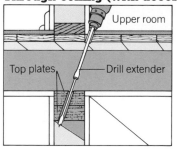

Existing box

Marker hole

Bottom plate

1. Cut power to outlet you're tapping; pull it out of box. Remove knockout from bottom of box. Drill 1/16-in. or 1/8-in. hole through floor next to baseboard below outlet. Insert wire in hole. Find wire in basement. About 2 in. over from wire, bore up through bottom plate with ¾-in. spade bit.

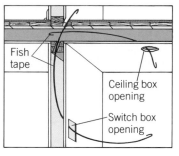

Fish tape

Fish tape

2. Have your helper feed fish tape through box knockout into wall cavity. From basement, feed second fish tape through hole in bottom plate. Maneuver your tape behind wall until it snags tape from box.

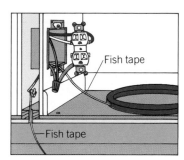

Fish tape

Cable

3. Pull tapes into basement; unhook them. Strip 8 in. of insulation from cable end; hook cable wires to fish tape from box. Feed cable up from basement as helper pulls fish tape and cable through box knockout. Have helper unhook cable and clamp it to box.

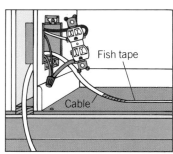

New box

Cable   Joist

4. Cut opening for new box. Run cable to it through holes in joists, or staple or strap cable to side of a joist. Repeat steps 1 to 3 to fish cable to new box. Mount box; connect cable to both outlets. (To fish cable from an unfinished attic, drill through top plates rather than bottom one.)

Through ceiling (with access from above)

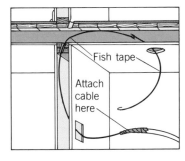

Upper room

Top plates   Drill extender

1. To run cable from ceiling fixture to wall switch, with access from room above, remove baseboard in upper room. Using ¾-in. spade bit and 18-in. drill extender, bore diagonally through upper floor and top plates of wall below.

Fish tape

Ceiling box opening

Switch box opening

2. Feed a 12-ft. fish tape hooked at both ends from upper floor through hole in top plate. Have helper pull tape out through switch box opening. Feed another tape through ceiling box opening. Maneuver both tapes in ceiling cavity until they hook.

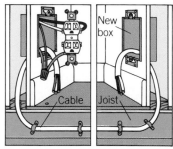

Fish tape

Attach cable here

3. Pull tape through ceiling box opening until the second tape emerges. While you hold second tape, have helper hook cable to other end of tape at switch box. Pull tape and cable through ceiling box opening.

Existing outlet

Chisel groove in plaster

New outlet

Fish tape

Staple cable to lath

Behind baseboard. Pry off baseboard between new and old outlets (p.293). In plaster, drill holes below boxes; chisel groove between holes. Fish cable between boxes; staple it to exposed lath. In wallboard, cut off bottom 2 in. of wall with utility knife. Notch studs. Fish cable through notches. Cover notches with 1/16-in. metal plates. Replace baseboard.

Electrical boxes and accessories 245
Branch circuits; mounting boxes 248–249
Repairing damaged wallboard 278–279

Through ceiling (without access from above)

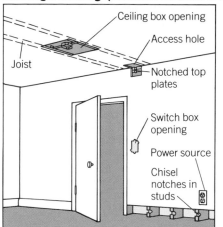

Ceiling box opening
Access hole
Joist
Notched top plates
Switch box opening
Power source
Chisel notches in studs

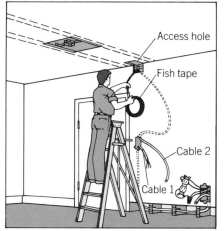

Access hole
Fish tape
Cable 2
Cable 1

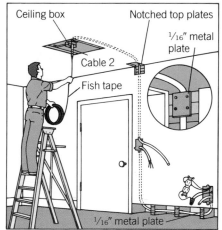

Ceiling box
Notched top plates
$^1/_{16}$" metal plate
Cable 2
Fish tape
$^1/_{16}$" metal plate

1. Cut holes for ceiling and switch boxes. Mount ceiling box (p.249). Cut 4-in.-wide access hole at junction of wall and ceiling in line with ceiling box. Chisel a vertical notch in top plates. Remove baseboard; cut opening for cable (facing page).

2. Feed fish tape from switch opening to floor; pull cable 1 up to opening. Run other end of cable through notched studs to power source. (Cover notches with metal plates.) Feed tape from access hole to switch opening. Pull cable 2 to access hole.

3. Run fish tape from ceiling box to access hole. Have helper attach cable 2 to tape; pull cable out through ceiling box. Inset cable in notched top plates; cover notch with metal plate. Replace baseboard. Patch ceiling opening and access hole.

Around a door

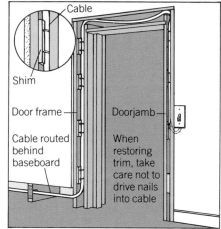

Cable
Shim
Door frame
Doorjamb
Cable routed behind baseboard
When restoring trim, take care not to drive nails into cable

Carefully pry off door trim. Run cable around doorway between frame and jamb (p.434). Shims inserted between frame and jamb to align door may obstruct cable; notch them if needed. Carefully staple cable to shims or frame.

Surface wiring

If you cannot (or don't want to) run cable behind walls and ceilings, an easier—if conspicuous—alternative is surface wiring, in which wires travel through channels, or raceways, that are attached to walls and ceilings. With a one-piece metal raceway, you still have to fish wires; two-piece metal or plastic channels have snap-on covers that eliminate the need for fishing. Check your local code for restrictions on raceway use.

Surface wiring systems come with instructions; follow them carefully. In general, this is the procedure:
1. Select an existing receptacle to power the circuit extension.
2. Plan and mark on walls and ceilings the path of the extension and the location of outlets.

3. Determine how many raceways and the number and type of boxes and accessories you'll need.
4. With the power off, remove the existing receptacle from its box. Screw the base of an outlet extension box to the existing wall box. Install the bases of all new wall and ceiling boxes.
5. Cut channels to size with a hacksaw. Attach one-piece channels with mounting clips every 2½ feet; screw bases of two-piece channels to wall.
6. Fish wiring through one-piece raceway. Use wire holders to secure wiring in the base of two-piece channels.
7. Wire and mount all new outlets.
8. Rewire and mount the existing receptacle in the outlet extension box.
9. Snap on channel covers and/or elbow and connection covers.

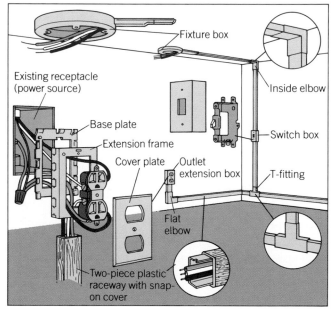

Fixture box
Existing receptacle (power source)
Inside elbow
Base plate
Extension frame
Switch box
Cover plate
Outlet extension box
T-fitting
Flat elbow
Two-piece plastic raceway with snap-on cover

A surface wiring system consists of raceways fastened to walls and ceilings with mounting screws or clips. Outlet extension box enables you to tie the circuit extension into an existing receptacle. You'll also need outlet and fixture boxes equipped with base plates; elbows and T-fittings; connection covers; and wire holders (for two-piece channels).

Another way to add receptacles is with pre-wired multi-outlet strips (not shown) attached to walls with mounting clips. Strips are plugged into grounded receptacles or are permanently wired. (Local codes may restrict use of plug-in strips.)

Electricity / Wiring variations

Illustrated here are nine of the many possible combinations of switches, fixtures, and receptacles. Even if a circuit you want to wire differs from those shown, these basic diagrams can help you plan a variation to suit your needs.

▶ **CAUTION:** Always turn off power to a circuit you are working on (p.237), and use a voltage tester to make sure the circuit is dead (p.243).

In figure 1, power passes through a single-pole switch controlling an end-of-circuit fixture. Figures 2 and 3 illustrate the wiring variation known as a *switch loop*. Wiring for middle- and end-of-circuit receptacles is shown in figure 4; for a split receptacle, in figure 5. On the facing page are schematics for 3- and 4-way switches, which control a fixture from two and three locations respectively.

Neutral wires are coded white; grounding wires are bare copper. The hot wire in two-wire cable is black; the second hot wire in three-wire cable is red. A white wire whose ends have been blackened with paint or tape is hot.

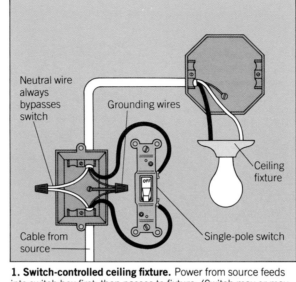

1. Switch-controlled ceiling fixture. Power from source feeds into switch box first, then passes to fixture. (Switch may or may not have grounding terminal.)

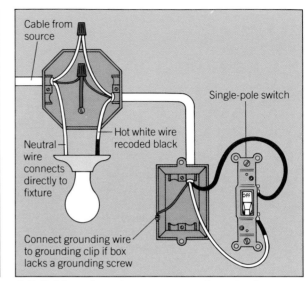

2. Switch loop. Power from source enters fixture box first. Hot wire is routed to controlling switch. White wire from switch is recoded black to show that it's hot.

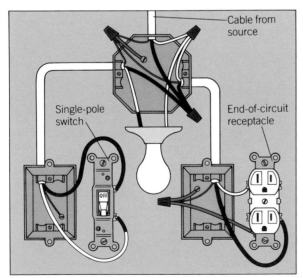

3. Switch loop with added receptacle. In this variation, switch loop controls fixture only, not end-of-circuit receptacle.

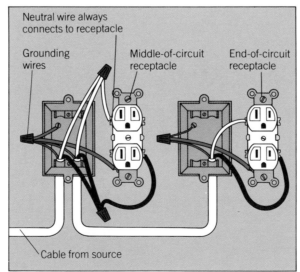

4. Receptacles wired in tandem. Power passes through one (or more) middle-of-circuit receptacles to end-of-circuit receptacle. (All receptacles should be grounded.)

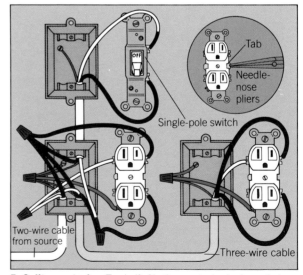

5. Split receptacles. Top half of both receptacles is always hot; bottom half is switch-controlled. Three-wire cable links receptacles. To split receptacle, break off tab between hot (brass) terminals.

Wires and cables 244
Switches and receptacles 246–247
Installing ceiling fixtures 254

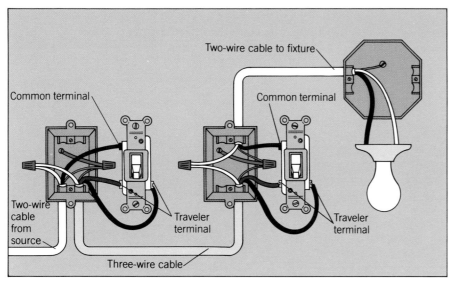

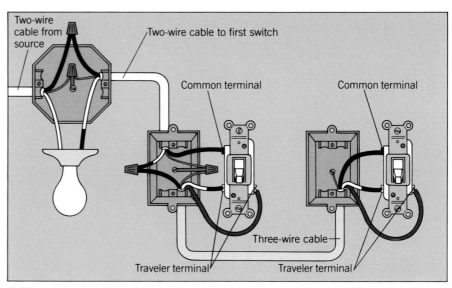

6. Three-way switches (fixture after switches). Cable hot wire attaches to first switch's common (dark-colored) terminal. The two hot wires of a three-wire cable attach to pair of brass-colored traveler terminals on each switch. Fixture hot wire connects to common terminal of second switch.

7. Three-way switches (fixture before switches). Power cable enters fixture box first. Incoming hot wire is routed to first switch's common terminal. Red and recoded white wires of three-wire cable link traveler terminals of both switches. Black wire hooked to common terminal of second switch leads back to fixture.

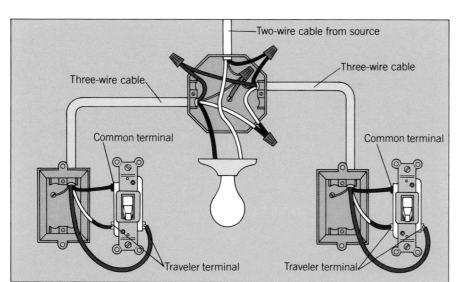

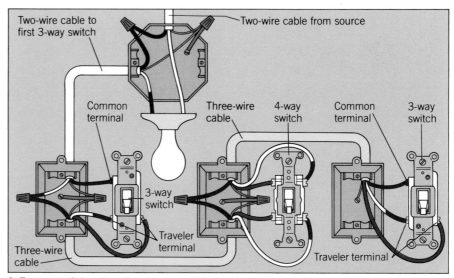

8. Three-way switches (fixture between switches). Power cable enters fixture box first. Incoming hot wire is routed to first switch's common terminal. Two lengths of three-wire cable, joined at fixture box, link switches to each other and to fixture.

9. Four-way switch and two 3-ways control a light from three places. In this case, incoming hot wire is routed through fixture box to common terminal of first 3-way switch. Three-wire cable connects both 3-way switches to 4-way switch. Black wire from common terminal of second 3-way switch leads back to fixture.

Electricity / Ceiling fixtures

Wiring most ceiling fixtures is simply a matter of joining the fixture wires to the circuit wires—black to black and white to white—with wire connectors (p.247). The hardware used to mount ceiling fixtures varies, depending on their size and design. A strap-mounted fixture (see below) attaches to a mounting strap, which is either screwed to the ceiling box mounting tabs or fastened with a locknut to the threaded central stud found in some boxes. A center-mounted fixture attaches to the threaded stud rather than to a mounting strap. The stud usually has to be lengthened with a reducing nut and a nipple. When mounting a chandelier, an adapter called a hickey is used to connect the nipple to the ceiling box stud. If the box doesn't have a central stud, fasten a nipple to a mounting strap and screw the strap to the box.

▶ **CAUTION:** Before working on a ceiling fixture, cut power to it at the service panel (p.237). Just turning off the wall switch is not enough. Once you've exposed the wire connections, use a voltage tester to make sure the power is off (p.243). Stand on a sturdy ladder. Never let the fixture hang from its wires. Have a helper hold it, or suspend a lightweight fixture from the ceiling box with a bent coat hanger.

Replacing an existing fixture. With the power off, loosen the setscrews or cap nut holding the glass diffuser to the fixture. Remove the diffuser. Loosen the setscrews or center nut holding the fixture to the ceiling box. Lower the fixture to expose the mounting hardware and wiring. (If the fixture you're removing is a chandelier, loosen the collar or setscrews at the bottom of the canopy; lower the canopy.) With the fixture securely supported, remove the mounting strap and/or nipple. Disconnect the fixture wires; take down the fixture.

To install a new fixture, screw the mounting hardware to the ceiling box. Have a helper hold the fixture near the box while you connect the wires. Screw the fixture to the mounting hardware. Push up a chandelier's canopy; secure it in place. Screw in the light bulbs; mount the diffuser, if any.

Recessed ceiling fixtures

To save installation time, recessed fixtures often come prewired and grounded to their own junction boxes. (House cable runs directly from the power source to the built-in box containing the fixture wires.) Insulation must be kept at least 3 in. from recessed fixtures. However, on some models (not shown), the housing is UL listed for direct contact with insulation.

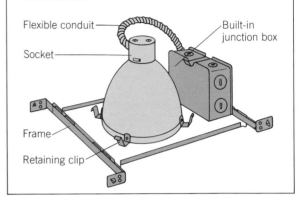

Flexible conduit · Socket · Frame · Retaining clip · Built-in junction box

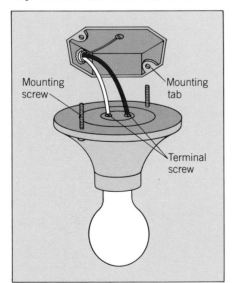

Single-bulb porcelain fixture is screwed directly to mounting tabs in the ceiling box. Such fixtures usually have terminal screws.

Mounting screw · Mounting tab · Terminal screw

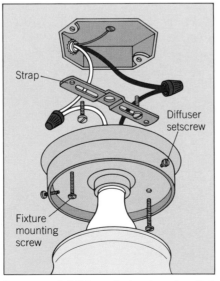

Strap-mounted fixture attaches to a strap that you screw to tabs in ceiling box (shown) or fasten to a threaded stud in center of box.

Strap · Diffuser setscrew · Fixture mounting screw

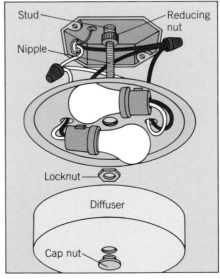

Center-mounted fixture is connected to a nipple fastened to box stud with a reducing nut, which is threaded differently at either end.

Stud · Reducing nut · Nipple · Locknut · Diffuser · Cap nut

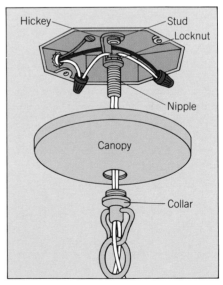

Chandelier wires are fed through a nipple and a hickey. Fixtures weighing over 50 lb. must be secured to joist or cross brace (facing page).

Hickey · Stud · Locknut · Nipple · Canopy · Collar

254

Boxes and accessories 245
Switches and receptacles 246–247
Wiring variations 252–253

Ceiling fans

A ceiling fan can make your home more comfortable all year long: in summer, the normal counterclockwise rotation of the blades circulates cooling breezes; operated in reverse in winter, the fan forces rising warm air down from the ceiling. Most fans feature two or more speeds and a reversing motor for summer or winter use; the motor can be controlled by a wall switch or a built-in pull chain. A light fixture often comes with the fan or can be attached to it. The fan's blades should be at least 1 foot below the ceiling, 7 feet above the floor, and 2 feet from the nearest wall.

If you're installing a ceiling fan in place of a light fixture, the fan connects to the existing wires in the ceiling box. If you're mounting a ceiling fan where there was no fixture, and thus no electrical box, you'll have to mount a new box and run a new circuit or extend a circuit to it (pp.248–251). You can also power the fan with a surface wiring system (p.251) or with a swag kit—an extension cord threaded through a decorative chain that runs from the fan across the ceiling and down the wall to a receptacle; the chain hangs from swag hooks that screw into the ceiling.

▶ **CAUTION:** Before replacing an existing fixture with a ceiling fan, cut off power to the fixture's circuit at the circuit breaker panel or fuse box (p.237). Carefully remove the fixture (facing page) without touching any wires; use a voltage tester to make sure that the power is off (p.243).

Assembly and mounting methods for fan models will vary; follow package directions carefully.

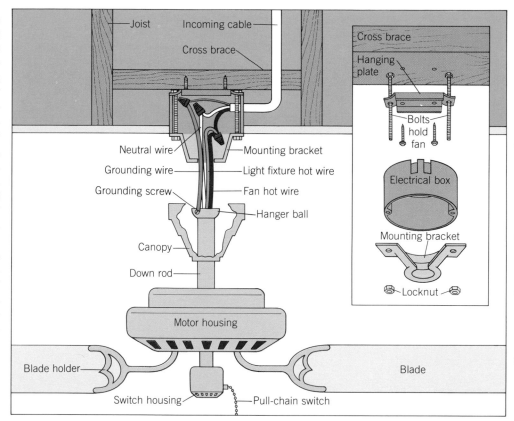

- **Ball-and-bracket mounting assembly** shown here is found on many ceiling fans. NEC prohibits hanging fans from mounting tabs of standard electrical box. Use a box that meets NEC specifications for ceiling fans (inset); screw it securely to a ceiling joist or to a wood cross brace or metal hanger mounted between joists.

- With box well anchored, screw mounting bracket in place. Insert down rod through canopy; run fan wires up through down rod. Secure down rod to motor assembly. Lift fan motor into position. Insert hanger ball in mounting bracket.

- Connect cable wires to fan wires: black to black, white to white, grounding wire to mounting bracket or to grounding screw on down rod.

- Fan equipped for a light fixture will have another hot wire, usually blue. Connect blue wire to cable and fan black wires. (Fan and light will both be controlled by pull chains.)

- Slide canopy up against ceiling; tighten canopy setscrews. Attach blades to motor. To avoid wobble, make sure blades are level and balanced (see package directions).

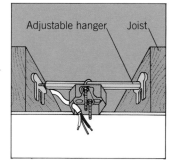

If you don't have access to ceiling from above, adjustable hangers can be installed from below through 4½-in. hole in ceiling (p.249).

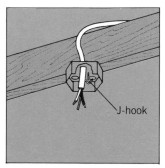

Some fans hang from a J-hook that passes through a hole in the ceiling box and screws directly into a joist or wood cross brace.

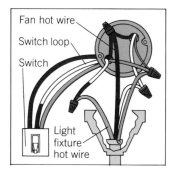

In this hookup, power to the fan's light fixture is routed through a wall switch. The fan itself is controlled by a pull chain.

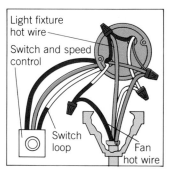

Wall switch and speed control operate fan; pull chain controls light. In another hookup (not shown), wall switches control both fan and light.

A fluorescent bulb generates about 4 times as much light per watt as an incandescent. Once used only in kitchens or workplaces because of their harsh light, today's fluorescents produce light in a wide range of whites and colors. Bulbs come in many shapes and sizes with socket pins to fit fluorescent fixtures or screw-type bases to replace incandescent bulbs.

The ordinary fluorescent fixture consists of a ballast and a bulb in a metal channel. The *bulb* is an airtight glass tube with cathodes at the ends. It holds argon gas and mercury vapor, and is coated with phosphor inside. The *ballast* is a transformer that boosts 120-volt house current to the 300-plus volts needed to light the bulb, then reduces voltage to keep it lit. (This surge makes the bulb burn out faster if turned on and off frequently.) When the switch goes on, power flows between the cathodes, heating the gases and phosphor so they glow, or "fluoresce."

Older fixtures (and many small modern ones) have a separate starter to preheat the gases. Also available is an instant-start style preferred by industrial users for its low maintenance; but bulb life is only about 9,000 hours. Most homes have rapid-start fixtures; these bulbs may last 20,000 hours.

Fluorescent problems are rare and usually easy to fix (facing page). A starter is inexpensive to replace, but a ballast costs so much that when one fails, it's often more economical to buy a new fixture.

The light output of fluorescent bulbs decreases with time. Replace an old or burned-out bulb with a new one of the same type (double-pin or single-pin), length, and wattage. Double-pin rapid-start and starter-type bulbs are interchangeable; instant-start bulbs have single pins. If a fixture has no bulb, check the ballast to find the right size.

Dispose of old bulbs carefully. The gases and phosphor aren't poisonous, but the bulb may implode if broken, sending glass fragments flying. Never throw a bulb into a fire or an incinerator.

Fluorescent bulbs give off less light at temperatures below 50°F. Install a cold-rated ballast in an unheated garage or basement.

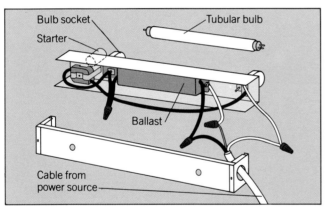

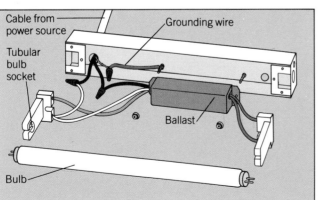

Starter-type fixtures are called preheat fixtures because they have two circuits—one to give bulb the initial energy surge needed to heat and light its gases, one to supply continued current. This two-step process takes 15 to 20 sec. The starter is wired to the sockets that hold the bulbs. Then the sockets are wired to the ballast, which is wired to the house current.

Rapid-start fixture lights in 2 or 3 sec. The ballast, which is relatively large and heavy—nearly 4 lb. in a standard two-bulb fixture—contains the starter. It also controls both the power boost and the continuous lighting. The ballast is wired to both sockets and to house current.

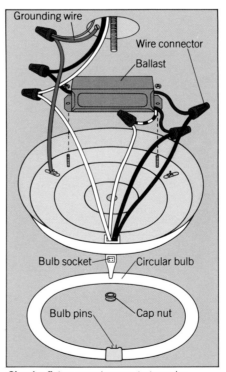

Circular fixture may have a starter or be rapid-start. Pins at one side of the circle fit into a socket wired to the ballast and to house current. Brackets hold other sides.

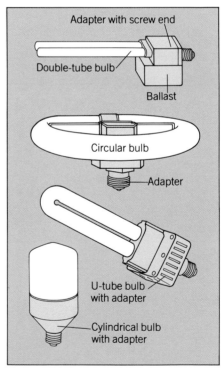

Compact bulbs that screw into incandescent sockets vary from double tubes and a circle with separate adapters to U-shaped and cylindrical bulbs with adapters in the bases.

Troubleshooting checklist

CAUTION: Before repairing a fluorescent fixture, turn off the power at the service panel (p.237).

Problem	Solution
Bulb won't light	**1.** Check plug or wall switch; look for blown fuse or tripped breaker at service panel (p.237). **2.** Clean pins; reseat bulb. **3.** For rapid-start fixture, replace bulb. For starter-type fixture, reseat starter; if bulb still fails, replace starter before replacing bulb. **4.** As a last resort, replace ballast.
Light swirls or flickers inside bulb	**1.** Leave new bulb lighted for several hours to stabilize it. **2.** Cold temperature may cause a flicker that will stop when bulb warms. **3.** Replace an old bulb. **4.** Replace starter, if any. **5.** Replace ballast. **6.** Orange flashes indicate cathode failure. Replace bulb before it overheats ballast.
Light blinks on and off	**1.** Blinking means an old bulb is dying; replace it. **2.** Reseat a new bulb in its socket. **3.** Examine bulb pins. If bent, straighten them with long-nose pliers. Sand pins lightly. **4.** Straighten socket contacts with pliers; sand lightly. Remove residue with toothbrush before replacing bulb. **5.** Remove bulb and cover plate to expose wiring; check voltage and grounding with a voltage tester. Tighten wiring connections. **6.** Replace starter. **7.** Replace ballast.
Bulb burns out too fast	**1.** Bulb has been turned on and off too often. Replace it; leave light on for longer periods. **2.** Reseat and, if necessary, replace starter, if any. **3.** Tighten wiring connections. **4.** Replace ballast.
Ends of bulb are discolored	**1.** Gray rings at tube ends are normal. If new bulb has black rings, replace starter; if bulb is old, replace it. **2.** Make sure wiring connections are tight. **3.** If only one side of a bulb discolors, take it out, turn it over, and reinstall it. **4.** If bulb is new and one end darkens, turn it in its socket—end for end. **5.** Check plug, switch, and service panel.
Fixture hums constantly	**1.** Some noise is inevitable. If a ballast also emits a sharp smell, it's defective; replace at once. **2.** If noise is the only trouble, tighten ballast connections. **3.** Replace fixture with an A-rated model—the quietest kind.

Principles of lighting

Lamps and light fixtures give a room the welcoming glow that spells home. They can dramatize or soften colors, create a festive or soothing mood, call attention to objects you want to show off, and provide safe work areas and snug places to read.

Residential lights fall into three categories: *general, accent,* and *task.* General lighting—usually from one or more ceiling or wall fixtures—radiates throughout a room as sunlight does. Accent and task lights focus on individual areas and may come from movable lamps, fixed fluorescents, track lights, or recessed spotlights.

Single-use areas, such as a hall or laundry, can be lit by one set of fixtures and one level of light. Rooms with multiple uses call for several kinds of fixtures and light levels (see below).

The rule of thumb for general lighting in living and sleeping areas is to have 1 watt of incandescent light for each square foot. Double the watts for a kitchen or workshop. With fluorescent bulbs, the minimum drops to about ⅓ watt per square foot in living rooms, ¾ watt in kitchens. Reflector bulbs save energy too. A 50-watt "R" bulb is as bright as a 100-watt "A" bulb. ("A" is the code for ordinary incandescent bulbs.)

Accent lights are usually spotlights, either in recessed fixtures or on tracks. Install them 12 to 24 inches from the wall they are lighting; aim the bulb at a 30° angle from the vertical so it does not shine in anyone's eyes. (The bigger the bulb, the broader its beam.)

Movable and built-in task lights should produce 150 to 225 watts incandescent, 22 to 32 watts fluorescent. Set desk and sewing lights 15 inches above the work surface; the lights over kitchen counters may be as high as 24 inches.

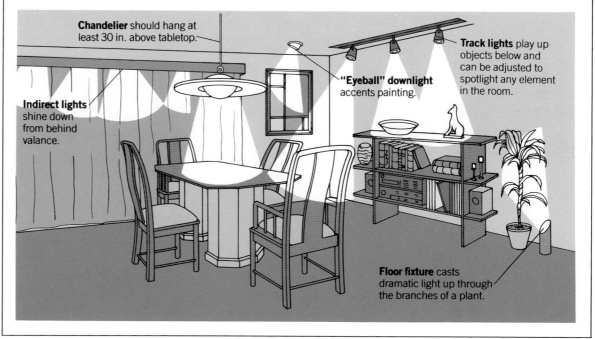

Chandelier should hang at least 30 in. above tabletop.

Track lights play up objects below and can be adjusted to spotlight any element in the room.

"Eyeball" downlight accents painting.

Indirect lights shine down from behind valance.

Floor fixture casts dramatic light up through the branches of a plant.

Electricity / Track lighting

Mounting and wiring methods may vary; follow manufacturer's directions

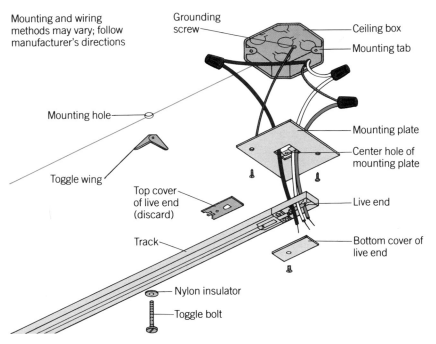

Grounding screw

Ceiling box

Mounting tab

Mounting hole

Toggle wing

Mounting plate

Center hole of mounting plate

Top cover of live end (discard)

Track

Live end

Bottom cover of live end

Nylon insulator

Toggle bolt

Fixtures

Spotlight

Flashlight

Baffle light

Globe light

Wall washer

Pin light

Adaptable to most lighting situations, track lights come in 2-, 4-, or 8-foot lengths and are joined with fittings to form L-shapes, U-shapes, V-shapes, or crosses. You can mount tracks flush to the ceiling or use clips to adjust them to uneven surfaces. They can be recessed or suspended below the ceiling.

The lamps, which snap or clip onto the track, can be moved and angled as you like. Incandescent lamps come in shapes ranging from cylinders to globes. Some systems accept bright low-voltage tungsten-halogen bulbs. Special adapters let you hang pendant fluorescent lamps from the tracks.

You can install a track wherever there's a ceiling outlet, or you can run a cable from a wall outlet. Because the tracks weigh so little, they can be hung with toggle bolts. (Some tracks, instead of being permanently wired, merely plug into a receptacle.)

The tracks are prewired; you just connect them to house current with wire pigtails (p.247). A mounting plate or canopy covers the connection. Usually connections are made at one end of the track (the live end), but styles differ; some systems let you bring in power anywhere along the track.

Installing track lighting

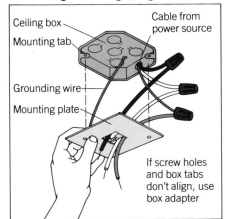

Ceiling box

Mounting tab

Grounding wire

Mounting plate

Cable from power source

If screw holes and box tabs don't align, use box adapter

With power off, attach 6-in. pigtails to black, white, and grounding wires in ceiling box. Attach copper wire from mounting plate to box; feed pigtails through plate. Screw plate to ceiling box.

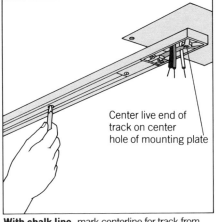

Center live end of track on center hole of mounting plate

With chalk line, mark centerline for track from center of mounting plate. Hold track in place; mark holes for toggle bolts. Drill holes. Remove both covers from track's live end. Discard top cover.

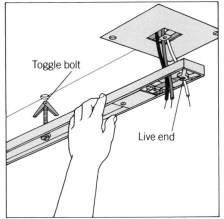

Toggle bolt

Live end

Slide nylon insulators over toggle bolts. Push bolts through track; thread toggle wings onto bolts. Insert (but don't tighten) bolts in ceiling holes. Run pigtails through openings in live end.

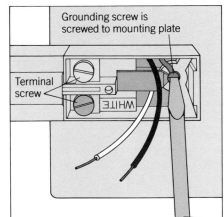

Grounding screw is screwed to mounting plate

Terminal screw

WHITE

Connect pigtails to terminals in live end—black to brass, white to silver, grounding to green. Screw grounding screw to center hole of mounting plate. Replace bottom cover. Tighten toggle bolts.

Lamp and cord repairs

If a lamp flickers or won't light, try a working bulb in the socket; if it fails to light properly, inspect the plug and cord. If a plug's prongs are bent or corroded, or if its insulating disc is missing, the plug is unsafe; replace it.

Replace a cord whose sheathing is frayed or cracked or exposes wires. A cord that's been yanked out of an outlet often may be damaged only near the plug. In this case, unplug the cord, cut off its damaged section, and put a new plug on the trimmed end.

To test a lamp's switch and socket, unplug it and use a continuity tester as shown on page 243. The switch usually is part of the socket; replace the whole unit if the switch fails.

Lamp cords are flat or round; plugs must match. Traditionally a cord's hot and neutral wires (the latter is usually

Underwriters knot

ridged) are split, stripped partway, tied into an Underwriters knot, and attached to terminal screws in the plug. Newer plugs snap or clamp onto the cord's end, which needn't be stripped.

Which terminals the neutral and hot wires attach to doesn't matter except where outlets and plugs are polarized (p.242). Replace old polarized plugs with new ones.

The cords of power tools, large appliances, and computers may contain a third, grounding, wire. If you must temporarily use an extension cord with such appliances and tools (with some you can't), make sure it's a three-wire cord, and plug it into a grounded outlet (p.240).

Wiring plugs

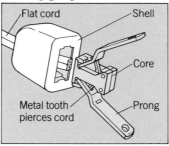

Flat cord — Shell
Core
Metal tooth pierces cord — Prong

Clamp-style flat-cord plug. Pinch prongs to free plug core. With prongs spread open, feed blunt-cut cord through hole in shell into top of core. For polarized plug, insert cord so that its ridged neutral side connects to wide prong. Squeeze prongs together. Slide core into shell.

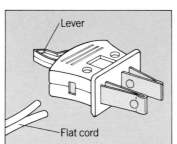

Lever

Flat cord

Snap-on flat-cord plug holds blunt-cut wires slit apart about ¼ in. Lift the lever at top or side of the plug. Insert cord into hole in plug; close the lever.

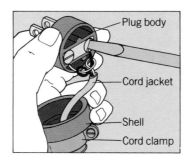

Plug body
Cord jacket
Shell
Cord clamp

Two-prong round-cord plug. Pry out plug body with screwdriver. Feed cord into shell. Remove 1¼ in. of cord jacket, ¾ in. of wire insulation. Tie wires into Underwriters knot. Twist bare wire ends clockwise and connect to plug screws. Snap plug body into shell; tighten cord clamp.

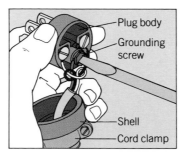

Plug body
Grounding screw
Shell
Cord clamp

Three-prong round-cord plug. Pry out body from shell with screwdriver. Feed cord into shell. Strip cord and wires (see above). Tie black and white wires into Underwriters knot. Hook white wire to silver screw, black to brass, grounding to green. Snap plug body into shell. Tighten clamp.

Rewiring lamps

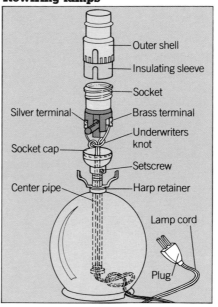

Outer shell
Insulating sleeve
Socket
Silver terminal — Brass terminal
Underwriters knot
Socket cap
Setscrew
Center pipe — Harp retainer
Lamp cord
Plug

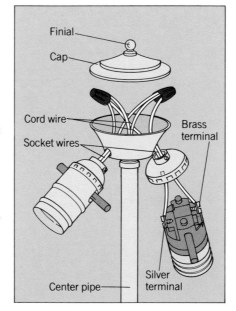

Finial
Cap
Cord wire
Socket wires
Brass terminal
Silver terminal
Center pipe

One-socket lamp: 1. Unplug lamp. **2.** Pry off base cover (usually felt). **3.** At base undo nut holding threaded center pipe. **4.** Pull pipe partway out top. **5.** Unscrew socket; pull off its shell and insulating sleeve. **6.** Unscrew socket terminal screws; lift off socket. **7.** Cut off old plug; splice end of new cord to old cord to guide it up pipe; discard old cord. **8.** Split top 2 in. of new cord. Strip ½ in. of insulation off wire ends; form wire ends into loops. **9.** Screw in new socket. **10.** Tie Underwriters knot. **11.** Hook each loop around a terminal screw—hot wire to brass, ridged neutral wire to silver; tighten terminal screws. **12.** Slip on insulating sleeve and outer shell. **13.** Tighten nut at base. **14.** Add a new plug (see left). **15.** Reassemble lamp.

Two-socket lamp: 1. Unplug lamp. **2.** Unscrew finial and cap where sockets meet. **3.** Remove outer shells and sleeves of both sockets; undo terminal screws; lift off sockets. **4.** With long-nose pliers pull out wires connecting sockets to cord wire in center tube. **5.** Remove wire connectors or tape. **6.** Cut off old plug. **7.** Pry off base cover. **8.** Undo nut holding pipe at base. **9.** Splice new cord to old cord; pull it through pipe from base; discard old cord. **10.** Divide top 4 in. of cord and strip ½ in. **11.** Twist new cord's neutral wire to neutral wires from both sockets with wire connector; twist hot wires together. **12.** Fold wires into lamp; return cap and finial. **13.** Slip on insulating sleeves and outer shells. **14.** Bolt pipe. **15.** Add new plug. **16.** Reassemble lamp.

Bending metal tubing 138
Tools, testing, and safety 242–243
Wires and cables 244

Electricity/Outdoor wiring

By bringing power outdoors, you can extend the usable hours of your backyard or patio, do away with awkward extension cords, and enhance your home's security. Basic wiring techniques are the same indoors and out, but because receptacles, switches, and fixtures will be exposed to the elements, they must be housed in weatherproof boxes. Outdoor receptacles must also be protected by a ground-fault interrupter (p.240). Usually buried underground, outdoor wiring can be either individual Type TW wires encased in metal or plastic conduit or Type UF (underground feeder) cable.

Some electrical codes permit direct burial of UF cable in a trench at least 1 foot deep. Others require that conduit protect all underground wiring (individual wires as well as cable). Most codes require that above-ground outdoor wiring run through conduit.

Plastic (PVC) conduit is easy to cut (with a hacksaw) and join (with conduit glue), but it must be buried 18 inches deep. Rigid metal conduit is joined with threaded couplings. It's harder to cut than plastic and bending it takes some effort (p.138), but it requires only a 6-inch-deep trench. The use of thinwall metal conduit underground may be prohibited by code.

Before starting an outdoor wiring project, check building and electrical codes and obtain needed permits. Determine where and how to run power from inside to outside the house: you can tap an existing circuit (as long as it's not already operating near capacity) or, if you plan extensive outdoor wiring, run a new circuit from the service panel (consult an electrician in this case). Next, map out an efficient route for the outdoor circuit (p.239). When planning outdoor lighting, be aware of glare and its effects on neighbors and passersby. Use shielded fixtures placed well out of sight lines.

▶ **CAUTION:** Before working on a circuit, turn off power to it at the service panel (p.237); use a voltage tester to make sure power is off (p.243).

A convenient way to bring power outside is to run cable between back-to-back boxes on opposite sides of an exterior wall (right). To extend power to a freestanding outdoor outlet, see the facing page.

Weatherproof boxes and fittings

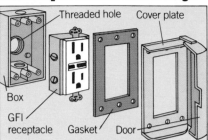

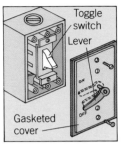

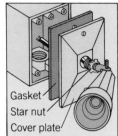

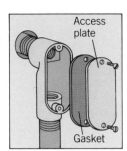

Outdoor box for GFI receptacle has spring-loaded door, threaded holes for conduit, and a gasket to seal gap between cover plate and box.

Outdoor switch box has external lever that flips toggle of standard switch.

Outdoor fixture requires bulbs made of glass that won't shatter when wet.

LB fitting routes wiring through house wall into the ground.

Installing an outdoor wall receptacle

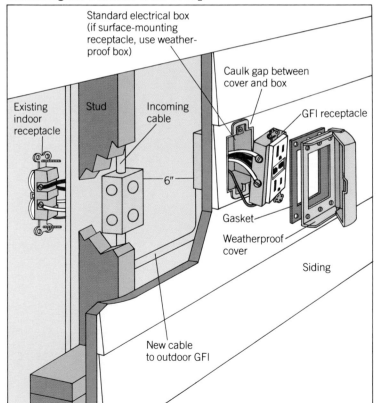

- **Locate an existing receptacle** on inside of exterior wall, near desired site of new outdoor GFI receptacle. Find studs on either side of existing receptacle (p.191).

- Cut power to receptacle at service panel. Remove cover; use voltage tester to make sure power is off. Disconnect receptacle; remove a knockout from bottom or rear of box.

- Using a reference point accessible from both sides of wall, measure position of indoor receptacle; mark it on wall's exterior. Also mark stud locations. Mark another point between studs, 6 in. from existing receptacle. Center new box on last mark; trace box outline on wall. At corners, drill ⅜-in. holes through siding; cut outline with reciprocating saw.

- If wall is masonry, use masonry bit to drill several holes within outline; knock out excess masonry with cold chisel and hammer.

- Feed cable from indoor box to opening for outdoor box (push aside any insulation). Run cable through cable connector into new box. Screw new box to siding, or mortar it in place if wall is masonry (p.162).

- Connect new and existing cable wires to indoor receptacle (p.248); attach new cable wires to outdoor GFI receptacle (p.247). Remount indoor receptacle. Screw GFI receptacle to new box; screw weatherproof cover to receptacle.

Installing a freestanding outdoor outlet

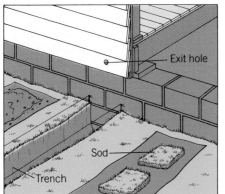

Find an available circuit to tap into, preferably in basement or attic. If in basement, locate the exit hole in header joist at least 3 in. from floor joists, flooring, and sill plate (pp.188–189). Drill ¼-in. test hole through wall to check location; enlarge hole with a ½-in. spade bit. Outside, below exit hole and centered on it, lay out a trench at least 6 in. wide. Cut sod 3 in. deep, remove, and lay on plastic sheets. Dig trench to depth required by code. Cut power; run cable to exit hole.

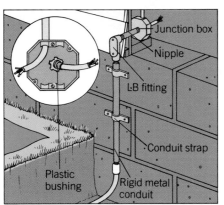

Remove knockout from back of a junction box; mount box over exit hole. Screw top of LB fitting to a nipple long enough to span wall. Cut length of conduit long enough to extend 4 in. into trench; screw to bottom of fitting. From outside, push nipple into hole. From inside, secure nipple to box with star nut. Fit plastic bushing onto nipple and conduit ends. Strap conduit to wall. Remove back plate from LB fitting; feed UF cable up through conduit and fitting into box.

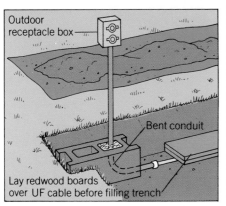

If code permits, run cable in trench to receptacle site (if not, encase cable in conduit). At site, widen trench to hold concrete block. Bend length of conduit into L-shape, its base 1 ft. long, its upright leg extending 18 in. above ground. Run cable through conduit. Set base of L in trench; lower block over upright leg. Fill block cavity around conduit with dry-mix concrete (p.149). Attach outdoor box to conduit; install receptacle. With power still off, splice UF cable to house wiring at junction box. Fill trench.

Wiring a clock-timer

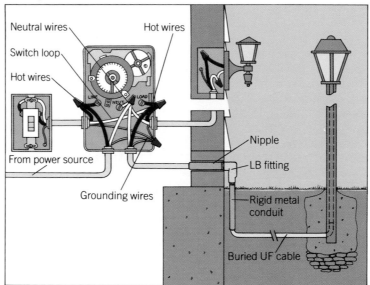

Indoor clock-timer turns outdoor lights on and off at preset times. Optional manual switch overrides timer. Mount clock in junction box near exit hole for outdoor circuit. Surface-mount a switch box nearby. With power off, extend a house circuit to junction box. Run cable between junction and switch boxes; bring outdoor circuit cable(s) into junction box. Connect incoming hot wire and black switch wire to clock terminal marked *Line;* connect outgoing hot wire(s) and white switch wire (recoded black) to *Load* terminal. Attach neutral wires to *Neutral* terminal. Splice grounding wires as shown. Wire and mount manual switch.

Mounting a soffit light

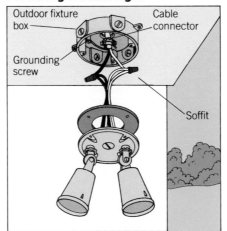

Drill hole in soffit for cable. With power off, run switch-controlled circuit extension to soffit. Secure cable to outdoor fixture box with cable connector. Screw box to soffit. Connect hot and neutral cable wires to fixture wires, grounding wire to grounding screw in box. Mount fixture in box.

Tapping an existing outdoor fixture

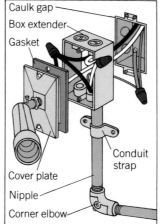

Cut power to fixture and disconnect it. Screw nipple (short length of conduit) to corner elbow; screw nipple to conduit hole in bottom of box extender. Attach extender to fixture box; clamp nipple to wall. Run cable through elbow into extender. Run other end of cable through conduit to other wall-mounted devices or to trench. Connect new cable to house and fixture wires; replace fixture.

261

Electricity / Low-voltage outdoor lights

Among the advantages of low-voltage over 120-volt outdoor lighting systems are lower installation cost, flexibility (components are easy to move around), and reduced energy consumption (low-voltage fixtures use 7- to 35-watt bulbs; solar-powered systems use no electricity). A typical low-voltage kit consists of 4 to 14 or more fixtures, low-voltage cable, and a weatherproof transformer that plugs into a standard 120-volt receptacle and reduces household current to a safe 12 volts. (If you buy components separately, make sure the total wattage doesn't exceed the transformer's capacity.) The cable can be buried in a 2- or 3-inch-deep trench or laid on the ground and covered with mulch. However, if the cable will run where it might be damaged by mowing or digging, bury it at least 1 foot deep.

Low-voltage fixtures generally consist of a lamp head and a fixed or detachable ground stake. They are available in such styles as floodlights, globes, and the tier lights shown here. Transformers come with manual controls, automatic timers, and/or photoelectric eyes that turn the lights on at dusk and off at dawn. Provided a transformer is within reach of a grounded receptacle, it can be mounted outdoors or in, but one equipped with a photoelectric eye must be mounted outdoors.

Before installing low-voltage lights, spend time planning the layout. Follow kit directions carefully.

Flood- and accent lights add a dramatic touch to a garden path.

1. Most low-voltage fixtures are easy to wire. Simply place cable over contacts in cable channel at base of fixture head. Press cable down firmly to hold it in place.

2. Slide the closed ground stake over the cable channel. Pressure of stake causes fixture's electrical contacts to pierce cable. Spread open the legs of ground stake.

3. Press cable together at fixture base and fold into one leg of ground stake. Line up the cable with notches on both sides of stake. Snap the legs together to close the stake.

4. To install fixture, dig a hole about 8 in. deep. (If you drive stake into the ground without a hole, you may damage light or stake.) Insert stake in hole; fill with dirt.

5. Cover cable with mulch or bury it in a shallow trench. If there's any possibility that cable may be damaged by a lawn mower or garden tool, bury it 1 ft. deep.

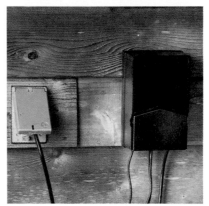

6. Mount transformer and photoelectric eye, if any, near grounded receptacle. If transformer isn't prewired, connect cable to low-voltage terminals on transformer; plug in power cord. Set timer and adjust sensitivity of photoelectric eye.

Doorbells and chimes

A doorbell (or chime) system consists of the sounding device, a front- and (optional) rear-door button, and a transformer, which lowers 120-volt current to the 6 to 24 volts required by most systems; 18- or 20-gauge bell wire links the components. The transformer must be wired to a house circuit in a junction box, often in the basement or near the service panel; make sure the transformer won't be controlled by a switch anywhere on the circuit (p.239). To install a system, pick a site for the sounding device (usually on a wall at least 6 feet above floor level); then find a junction box on which to mount the transformer.

▶ **CAUTION:** Before installing the transformer, at the service panel turn off power to the circuit you're tapping into (p.237). Remove the junction box cover; use a voltage tester to make sure power is off (p.243).

To estimate how much wire you'll need, measure the distances between components; add another 15 feet for connections and route turns. Follow package directions for installing the system (see below for the basic procedure). Although bell wires can be exposed, where possible fish them behind finished surfaces (pp.250–251).

If you're replacing a doorbell, check the old transformer to make sure it provides enough voltage for the system. If it doesn't, replace the transformer. Before repairing a doorbell (right), check the service panel for a tripped breaker or blown fuse (p.237).

Troubleshooting and repair

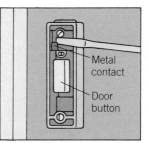

1. If doorbell won't ring, remove button cover and clean contacts with sandpaper; pry them up with screwdriver. If this fails, loosen mounting screws; pull out button. Disconnect wires and touch ends together. If bell rings, button is faulty; replace it.

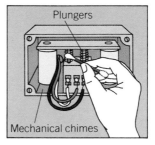

2. Doorbells or chimes often don't work because their clappers or plungers are dirty. Use a cotton swab dipped in alcohol to clean gong and clapper (doorbell) or plungers (mechanical chime unit). Do not clean electronic chimes.

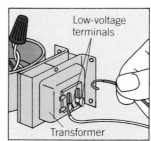

3. Tighten loose wires at bell or transformer. Wrap frayed wires with electrician's tape. To repair breaks, strip ends; join with wire connectors. **CAUTION:** Grasp low-voltage wiring by its insulation. Turn off power when working at the transformer.

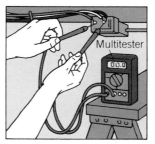

4. To test transformer, restore power to its circuit. Set a multitester to ACV scale and turn dial to 50-volt range. Touch multitester probes to transformer's low-voltage terminals. If tester registers no voltage, transformer is defective; replace it.

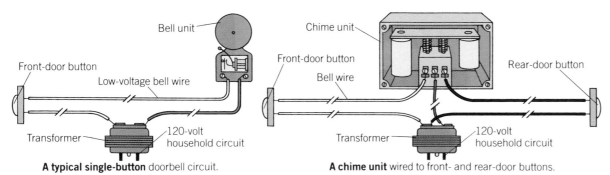

A typical single-button doorbell circuit.

A chime unit wired to front- and rear-door buttons.

Installing a doorbell or chimes

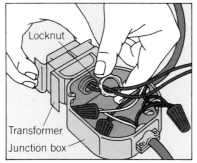

1. With power off, remove a knockout from junction box; insert transformer wires. Using wire connectors, join one transformer wire to a black cable wire, the other to a white cable wire. Fasten transformer to box with locknut.

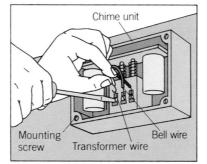

2. Drill holes for door button wires and mounting screws at doorknob height, 4½ in. from door edge. After running bell wires, connect one wire from transformer and one from sounding device to button's terminal screws.

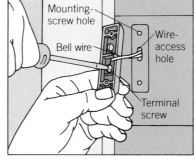

3. Drill wire-access and mounting-screw holes for chimes (shown here) or bell. Mount chime unit; connect wires from transformer and door button(s) to correct terminals on chime unit (usually marked by manufacturer).

Electricity / Home security systems

By installing an alarm system yourself, you'll cut costs considerably. Before buying one from a hardware or electronics store, consider how much security your home really needs, and take into account that a well-lighted exterior may be enough to deter a burglar.

Use the following information to decide what kind of system will be best for your home. The burglar alarm may be a simple one that needs only a screwdriver for installation. Or you may choose a more complicated hard-wired system that re-quires such tasks as fishing wires behind walls (pp.250–251). Whatever the system, it should include installation instructions; follow them carefully.

Security systems can be hard-wired or wireless. A *hard-wired system* runs on low-voltage electricity. A master control panel containing a transformer is wired to an electric circuit; switches and sensors are connected to the panel. A good one operates on a *normally closed (NC) circuit.* When the circuit is broken—for example, when a burglar cuts a wire—an alarm sounds. Because you activate, deactivate, or override the system whenever you leave or arrive, place remote-control pads near all doors to the house and an additional pad in the master bedroom. Both keyed and digital units are available.

A *wireless system* consists of isolated sensors or contact switches that operate independently of other devices and contain their own alarms. Units are battery powered or plug into a receptacle or operate on a normally closed circuit. They may

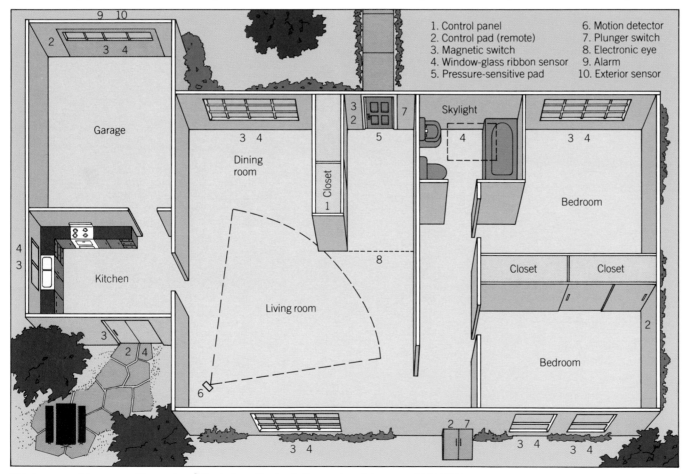

1. Control panel
2. Control pad (remote)
3. Magnetic switch
4. Window-glass ribbon sensor
5. Pressure-sensitive pad
6. Motion detector
7. Plunger switch
8. Electronic eye
9. Alarm
10. Exterior sensor

This home combines several types of security devices. The key to the numbers is in upper right corner.

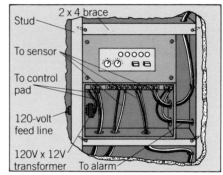

Place control panel of a hard-wired system in a hidden spot, usually between studs; connect components according to the manufacturer's instructions. Panel's test lights and buttons will indicate if it is functioning properly.

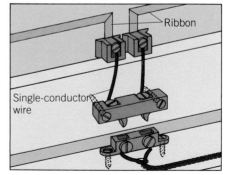

Window ribbon sensor will trigger alarm when glass is broken. Glue ribbon around the glass perimeter carefully so ribbon doesn't tear; join each end to a takeoff connector that is wired to the central control panel.

transmit to a control box by radio frequency.

Perimeter protection. Various types of sensors will detect disturbances at entry points—doors and windows specifically. A *magnetic switch* comes in two parts: one is set in a door or window frame, the other attached to the door or the window sash. When an intruder opens the window or door, contact is broken and the alarm sounds. For extra window protection, add a screen with a built-in alarm. A *plunger switch* has a push button that pops out when

a door or window is opened, setting off an alarm. To outwit an intruder who decides to smash the glass in a window, attach ribbon sensors to the glass or set glass-breakage sound detectors within each room.

Additional security. In case an intruder bypasses a perimeter system, add interior and exterior motion or heat sensors, available in both wired and wireless models. Their sensing mechanisms are either infrared beams (electronic eyes), ultrasonic sound waves, or passive infrared beams; the latter

detect body heat. The most fail-safe models combine two types of sensors; both must be triggered before the alarm will sound, thus reducing false alarms. Another type of sensor, a pressure-activated device, is placed under carpeting in doorways and on stairs.

You'll also have a choice of alarms: A silent alarm automatically dials a police station or security company, often for a monthly fee, whereas on-site alarms may take the form of piercing sirens and flashing lights. A system may have both types of alarms.

Position control pads near all entrance doors. To allow time to exit home, adjust the pad to delay alarm by 30 sec. The code to operate a digital control pad can be changed if necessary.

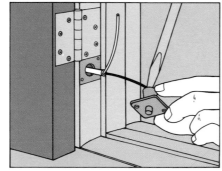

Recess a plunger switch in hinge side of doorjamb by feeding low-voltage wires through jamb. Alarm is triggered when door opens. (Low-voltage wires are not designated hot or neutral. Wires in 2-wire cable may be red and white or black and white.)

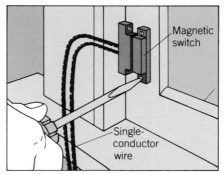

Magnetic switch keeps alarm circuit closed with window closed. When window is opened, circuit opens, triggering alarm. You can connect a series of switches with single-conductor wire, which may be red, white, or black.

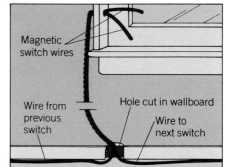

Hide low-voltage wire running around the perimeter of a home behind baseboards and door and window trim. Remove trim (p.293); fish wire behind wallboard. Secure wires to wall with staples or tape; replace trim.

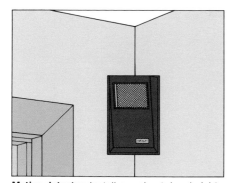

Motion detector. Install one about door height; aim it across room. Battery-operated model allows you to adjust signal range and to set alarm for immediate or delayed response. Some models may be triggered by pets.

An electronic eye should be inconspicuous; install one across a main walkway or hall. Most have two parts: a sender and a receiver. An intruder walking through will interrupt the beam, tripping the alarm.

On-site alarm. Place the unit high up and beyond reach, such as at a gable peak. Run the wiring through the attic to keep an intruder from cutting it easily.

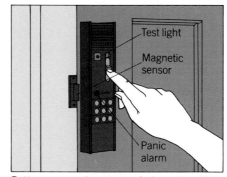

Battery-operated contact switches with self-contained alarms are available for doors and windows; also use them on medicine cabinets and utility closets to sound alarm if child opens door. Settings allow instant or delayed alarm.

Electricity / Telephone wiring

Whether replacing an old telephone or adding a new extension, you'll find telephone wiring is easier than other electrical work. For one thing, you'll be working with low-voltage current (p.262); for another, *modular* connections make installation a snap. With this system, small plastic clips on the ends of wires plug into special jacks. If your telephone wiring is pre-1974, you can convert it to a modular system: adapters are available to convert old jacks to modular ones, switch old telephones to fit modular jacks, turn one line into two to five lines, and extend the length of a line without splicing it.

Each telephone system has a demarcation point where the telephone company's responsibility ends and yours begins; never work on the telephone company's side. The demarcation point may be at *a network interface,* located where the wire enters the house. In an older system, it may start at a *protector* mounted near the main breaker or fuse panel; call your local telephone company before working on it.

Adding an extension. Determine the best route to the new phone location. If you're starting at an outside protector, staple the cable under a lap of siding, drill through the wall at the jack location,

and cover the interior hole with a jack so that no wiring shows; caulk around the outside hole. Inside, fish wiring behind walls and along floor joists, hide it in channels, run it under carpet (only near a baseboard), staple it to the baseboard with insulated staples, or rout a groove on the inside of the baseboard and tuck the cable in it. Jacks can be flush-mounted in a concealed box or surface-mounted. ▶ **CAUTION:** Do not install jacks in damp areas. To avoid shocks from incoming calls, keep the handset off one extension phone while you are working. If you wear a pacemaker, never work on telephone wiring.

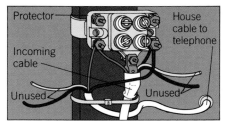

Cable installed by telephone company may have six or more color-coded wires. Check protector to see which color wires are in use. When adding an extension, use same-color wires.

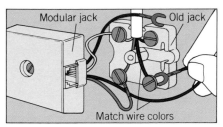

To connect new phone to old jack, convert jack. Remove cover. At terminals cut wires to old phone; leave house cable wires alone. Attach modular jack's spade connectors or caps to terminals.

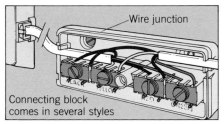

To add two or three extensions, install a wire junction at connecting block or jack for existing line. To connect wires, follow maker's directions. To add up to five extensions, install another wire junction.

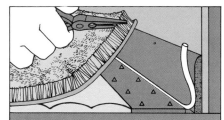

To hide cable under carpet, using long-nose pliers, pull carpet from tackless strip. Lay cable in space between strip and baseboard; use putty knife to press carpet back down in place.

Installing a flush-mounted wall jack

1. Cut hole in wall for a concealed box. Check fit of box; then remove it. Drop a weighted string into hole.

2. Drill ¼-in. hole above baseboard; or remove baseboard to hide hole. Using a bent coat hanger, catch string.

3. Bend stripped ends of cable around string; then tie string to cable and wrap with electrician's tape.

4. Pull the cable through box opening and through the box itself. Install box in the opening.

5. Screw wall jack to box. Attach wires; cover. Fill hole with spackling compound; paint. Or replace baseboard.

Telephone repairs

Systematically checking the parts of a telephone system will isolate a problem. There may be a wiring flaw: bare wires touching each other, a snapped wire, or a bare wire touching a grounded object. Or the disturbance may be in one of the telephones.

Start by disconnecting any accessories, such as speakers and answering machines; plug a telephone directly into the jack. If it works, the problem is one of the accessories. If not, plug the telephone into a neighbor's jack. If it works, your house wiring is at fault.

Next, with a working telephone, try placing calls from each extension or jack in your home. Disconnect all other extension phones; "disposable" phones can fault other phones. This may isolate a faulty jack or line.

Telephone body. Switch handset cords from one phone to another; try both phones to find a damaged cord. If you have an older standard rotary telephone or a push-button model with a 500 or 2500 number, its parts are repairable. An electronic phone can't be fixed; return it or replace it. If you take a phone apart, always unplug it first; an incoming call can deliver a shock. To detach the cover, remove two screws from the bottom of the body.

Problems in a phone can result from loose screws, spade connectors, or springs, or from dirty contacts. If you find wires secured to terminal screws, tighten them to reestablish firm contact. For spade clips, press down on each one to make sure it's secure. If it's loose, pull it free, clean both contact surfaces with emery cloth, and press it back in place. If you find switch-hook springs unhooked, reconnect them. To correct a problem in the handset, unscrew the ear- and mouthpieces. Replace the transmitter or receiver in the handset with one from another phone; or use fine (120-grit) sandpaper to clean the contacts in the transmitter or the terminals in the receiver.

Problem	Possible cause	Solution
No dial tone	Handset cord or line cord defective	Replace cord
	Modular plugs on handset cord or line cord defective	Repair or replace. Check wall outlets for loose connections.
	Switch hook defective	1. Unstick buttons from cradle 2. Replace broken spring 3. Clean contacts
	Receiver defective	Replace
Dial tone stays on	Rotary dial defective	Clean contacts
Dials wrong numbers	Rotary dial defective	1. Remove dial, sand contacts 2. Spring weak, replace dial
Dial tone, but phone doesn't ring	Bell clapper jammed	Adjust clapper or case
	Switch hook defective	Clean contacts
Rings, but low volume	Bell clapper jammed	Adjust clapper or case
Other party can't hear	Handset cord to transmitter defective, or transmitter defective	Replace cord or transmitter
You can't hear	Handset cord or receiver defective	Replace cord or receiver
	Switch hook or rotary dial defective	Clean contacts
Called party hears distortion	Loose handset or line cord connections	Check connectors. Replace or repair cord.
	Transmitter defective	Replace transmitter

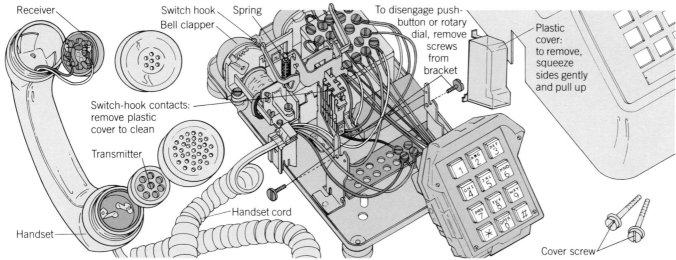

Receiver · Switch hook · Spring · Bell clapper · To disengage push-button or rotary dial, remove screws from bracket · Plastic cover: to remove, squeeze sides gently and pull up · Switch-hook contacts: remove plastic cover to clean · Transmitter · Handset cord · Handset · Cover screw

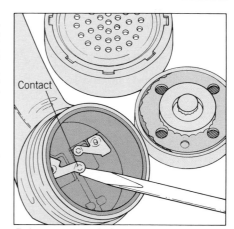

Contact

To improve transmission, unscrew mouthpiece; remove transmitter. Sand any dirt on contacts or transmitter; bend contacts upward slightly.

Codes and permits 193
Grounding 240
Ladders and safety 383

Electricity/Television antennas

Improve television reception by installing an antenna. Separate antennas are needed to pick up VHF and UHF telecasts, but a combination antenna will pick up both and FM radio transmissions as well.

Antennas are rated by *mileage range* and *gain* for one television set. Mileage range is the distance a signal can be pulled in. Gain refers to the antenna's ability to increase the signal's strength.

The antenna you buy will depend on where you live. In a city, competing signals distort high-gain reception; it's best to buy a highly directional moderate-gain antenna. In a suburban area where signals are fewer and weaker, select a moderately directional high-gain antenna. In rural areas signals are even weaker; add an amplifier.

Mount an antenna on the side of the house or on the roof ridge. Never strap it to a chimney; wind shaking the antenna can damage the masonry. A 10-foot mast is tall enough, unless you live in a valley or far from transmitting signals. If the mast rises more than 10 feet above its top mounting bracket, secure it with guy wires. For a mast taller than 20 feet, contact a professional, who may suggest an antenna tower.

Run a lead-in wire between the antenna and the television set by the shortest possible route; use flat or shielded 300-ohm twin wire or 75-ohm coaxial cable. Install standoffs to keep the wire away from electrical wires, gutters, pipes, and other metal objects—and to prevent it from rubbing against siding or roof shingles. Leave enough wire to form a drip loop before the cable enters the house; this stops water from running down the wire and into the wall.

▶ **CAUTION:** If the antenna or a ladder touches a power line, you could get a lethal shock. Position the antenna so that the distance between it and any power line is at least twice the maximum length of the antenna plus the mast assembly. Install the antenna on a calm day.

Coaxial cable

Shielded 300-ohm twin wire

Flat 300-ohm twin wire

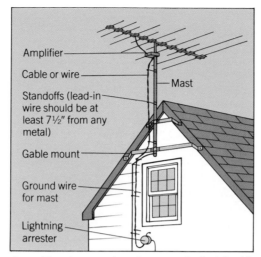

Amplifier
Cable or wire
Mast
Standoffs (lead-in wire should be at least 7½" from any metal)
Gable mount
Ground wire for mast
Lightning arrester

Assemble antenna and mast on ground; attach lead-in wire before mounting. Install two rows of standoffs on wall every 1½ to 2 ft.; seal with silicone caulk. Attach mounting bracket; insert mast into it. Keeping nearby tall trees trimmed may improve reception.

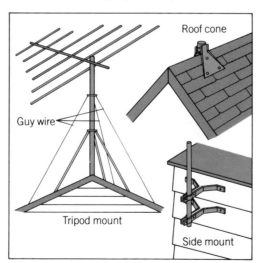

Roof cone
Guy wire
Tripod mount
Side mount

Types of mounts include roof cone for peaked roofs, tripod mount for peaked or flat roofs, and side mount for end of house. To attach guy wires, have a helper hold antenna while you install wires. Anchor wires to roof with screw eyes; seal screw eyes with roofing compound.

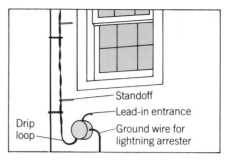

Standoff
Lead-in entrance
Drip loop
Ground wire for lightning arrester

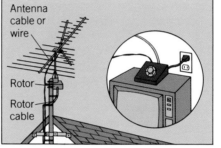

Antenna cable or wire
Rotor
Rotor cable

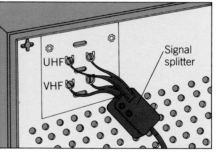

UHF
VHF
Signal splitter

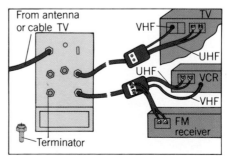

From antenna or cable TV
VHF
UHF
UHF
VHF
TV
VCR
FM receiver
Terminator

Drill hole into wall for lead-in wire. Run wire through row of standoffs and hole; form drip loop. Install lightning arrester, following maker's directions. Clamp No. 10 AWG copper wire to mast; run it through other row of standoffs and attach to cold-water pipe or grounding rod.

A rotor that will electronically turn the antenna to programmed positions picks up signals coming from several directions and may eliminate ghost images. A separate cable attached to rotor enables you to turn the antenna from control box inside house.

Connect lead-in wire to television set or signal splitter, which divides antenna signal into VHF, UHF, and FM. If signal is going to a single location—for example, entertainment center—position the signal splitter near television.

To operate several television sets and accessories from various points in house, install signal splitter at a central location (basement or attic); it "splits" signals to be sent to different locations. Plug unused outlet with terminator to prevent interference.

Lightning protection

Satellite dishes

No matter how remote your home is, a satellite dish antenna and receiver can pull in signals from far away and close to home. Once 12- or 15-foot dishes were needed to capture the faint signals of first-generation satellites, but now dishes measure only 6 to 8 feet in diameter or less.

When selecting a dish, consider the number of signals you wish to receive (you should get a minimum of 18 signals), the quality of the signals, and the dish's compatability with your television.

A satellite dish must be positioned with a clear view of the southern sky—unobstructed by trees, high-tension wires, or microwave towers. Although a system can be set up by the homeowner, most are professionally installed and tuned. Tuning is an exacting procedure, and each manufacturer's equipment requires a slightly different approach. It's easier and safer to install a satellite dish on the ground. To support the dish against strong winds, make sure it's set in a good concrete foundation. Roof and tower installations should be done only by a professional.

In addition to facing south, the dish's *azimuth,* or compass point, is set on the most westerly satellite; then the angle of the dish is adjusted upward to capture the southerly arc of various satellite signals. Fine tuning is done by adjusting the dish's *actuating arm.* Once tuned, the actuating arm will automatically swing the dish to the appropriate satellite when you change channels on your receiver.

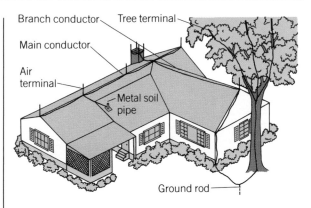

Changes in building materials, such as plastic pipes replacing metal pipes, may require safeguarding your home with a lightning protection system—especially if you live in an area with frequent or severe thunderstorms. Have a professional install the system following standards set by the Underwriters Laboratories.

Air terminals—small metal rods—are placed 20 feet apart (or 25 feet for rods over 2 feet tall) along high points on the roof. *Conductors,* braided copper or aluminum cables, connect the terminals to each other. Metal objects on the house—such as vent pipes, gutters, aluminum siding, and air conditioners—and plumbing, electrical, and telephone systems are connected to the main conductor or to branch conductors. If a tree within 10 feet of the building rises higher than the building, protect it with special tree terminals. At least two copper *ground rods* are driven into the ground at opposite corners of the house. These carry the electrical charge into the ground, dispersing it harmlessly.

Inspect the system annually. Check for loose or damaged air terminals and ground rods, and make sure the conductors are securely clamped and that all their connections are good.

Protecting appliances. To guard electrical appliances from lightning strikes to power lines far away, every home should have a *surge protector* installed by a professional at the service panel, or use surge protectors designed for receptacles (p.241).

When siting antenna tower, consider wind's force and direction during storms. The tower should be anchored to a concrete base, supported with at least three steel-cable guy wires anchored to roof and to ground, and if near house, secured to roof fascia as well. It should be grounded according to local code requirements.

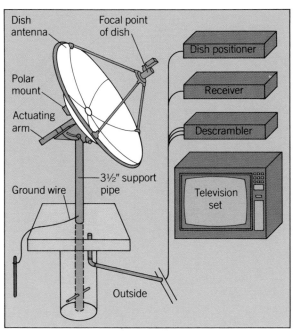

A residential satellite system consists of a dish antenna, motorized steering mechanism, dish positioner, receiver, and descrambler. In many systems a single control incorporates a receiver, positioner, and descrambler in one unit, called an IRD.

Responsible for saving thousands of lives, smoke detectors belong in every house. In new homes, many local codes now require a hard-wired 120-volt system installed at the time of construction. Some local codes also require battery-operated units as a backup. In existing homes, battery-operated units give adequate protection when the detectors and batteries are properly tested and maintained. (Dirt can set off a false alarm.)

Smoke detectors work in two basic ways. An *ionization* unit emits a small amount of radiation that's detected by a sensor. Smoke blocks the radiation from reaching the sensor, tripping the alarm. A *photoelectric* unit is triggered when smoke breaks a beam of light. The ionization unit responds to quick-burning fires from paper, wood, and fat; a photoelectric model—less

susceptible to false alarms from kitchen fumes—responds to slow-burning fires from mattresses and upholstery. One type of smoke detector combines both of these methods, forming a superior detection system. A heat detector, sensitive to changes in temperature, is useful in kitchens, furnace rooms, and laundry rooms.

Smoke detectors come with a variety of features. Some battery-operated models have a built-in light to illuminate your escape route. Another plugs into a receptacle—but first make sure the receptacle isn't on a circuit operated by a switch. A safety device prevents it from being unplugged. Some models have a monitor light to indicate that the battery is working; others can be tested by shining a flashlight on a sensor; yet another gives off warning beeps when the battery is low.

Effective placement of smoke detectors

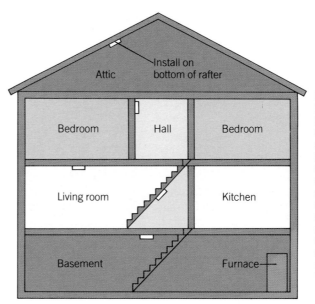

Attic — Install on bottom of rafter

Bedroom | Hall | Bedroom

Living room — Kitchen

Basement — Furnace

Each floor, including the basement, should have at least one smoke detector—one at top of each stairwell and one in any hallway leading to bedrooms. Keep smoke detectors away from drafts at vents, windows, and doors. Avoid dead-air spaces in corners and at ends of hallways. Center smoke detector on a ceiling, keeping it at least 4 in. from any wall. Locate a wall-mounted unit 4 to 12 in. below ceiling.

Battery-operated smoke detector

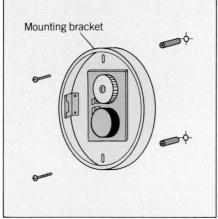

Mounting bracket

1. To install mounting bracket, hold bracket to the wall or ceiling and mark screw locations with a pencil. Drill holes for screw anchors (p.85). Insert anchors; screw bracket to wall.

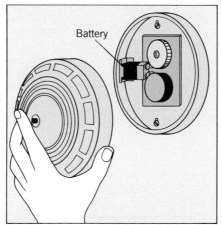

Battery

2. After installing the battery, place the smoke detector's cover over the bracket and snap or twist it in place. Test the battery every month; replace it once a year on specific date, such as Halloween or Independence Day.

Wiring detector to house circuit

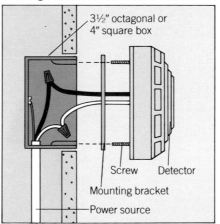

3½" octagonal or 4" square box

Screw | Detector

Mounting bracket

Power source

To install a 120-volt smoke detector, extend a circuit to ceiling or wall (pp.248–249). Join the incoming black wire to the smoke detector's black lead, the incoming white wire to the white lead, and the grounding wire to the box.

Testing and maintenance

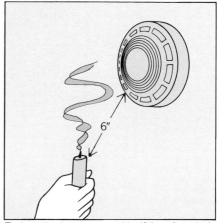

6"

Test smoke detectors monthly. If there is no test button, hold lit candle 6 in. below detector. If alarm doesn't sound, blow out candle; let smoke drift into detector. If it still doesn't sound, check power source. To clean, vacuum detector yearly.

Chapter twelve

Interiors
Repairs and improvements

Brighten your surroundings and your spirits by giving the inside of your home a face-lift. In this chapter you'll learn how to redecorate your walls, ceilings, and floors—and to repair damage, fix squeaks, and replace broken parts. (Painting and wallpapering are covered in another chapter, beginning on page 349.) If you're running out of storage space, install new cabinets and shelves or even add a closet. And if your family is growing, consider converting your attic or basement into living space. Guidance for all of these projects is given in the following pages. The chapter ends with advice on dealing with mildew, rot, insect and animal pests, and hazardous materials.

Contents

Keeping a house in good working order is a top-priority concern for all homeowners. It contributes to your comfort and enjoyment, and it's vital to maintaining the value of your property.

"A stitch in time saves nine" holds especially true in preventive house maintenance. Conducting an investigation of your house's systems at appropriate times of the year can save you money as well as inconvenience.

A periodic checkup needn't be an arduous task. It may add up to just a few hours a year. You can probably take care of most minor repairs yourself. Unless you are adept and experienced, let professionals do such major jobs as reroofing and running new electrical circuits. Have your septic tank professionally inspected and pumped out every 2 to 3 years, depending on its size and use.

An ideal time to make checks is when a system is not in use. In the spring a house often shows signs of wear from severe winter weather. At this time check the exterior (p.382); also check your dehumidifier and cooling system (have its refrigerant level increased if need be). Anytime between late summer and fall, have your heating system and humidifier checked, cleaned, and serviced.

If any part of a system seems unduly worn, a replacement may be better than a repair. When in doubt, contact an expert—such as a professionally trained, qualified house inspector.

When fall comes around, clean the filter of your cooling system and vacuum its accessible parts. While you're at it, check your dehumidifier for dirt buildup. This is also a good time to inspect for insects and animals that may have taken up residence in unsuspected parts of your house. Your local humane society or your state conservation department will provide information on how to safely remove such invaders as squirrels and raccoons or will tell you how to get help.

Some of the items in the checklist are seasonal—to be done in spring or fall. Others can be done any time of year. "As required" items may need doing only every 2 or 3 years or as often as is necessary.

Heating and cooling systems	Spring	Fall	Annually	As required
Have oil-fired burner checked and tuned professionally.			●	
Have gas pilot safety device of gas-fired burner checked.				●
Change or clean forced warm-air furnace filter.				●
Check belt on blower of warm-air system; deflection should not be more than ½ in.			●	
Check ducts of warm-air system for leaks or worn duct tape.				●
Bleed air from hot-water radiators.				●
Vacuum exterior of furnace or boiler.			●	●
Have chimney flue inspected yearly and swept when necessary.			●	
Have central cooling system checked professionally.	●			
Clean or change air conditioner filters.				●
Clean and service humidifier.	●			
Clean dehumidifier; service if needed.				●

Plumbing system	Spring	Fall	Annually	As required
Check for leaks: faucets, valves, outdoor faucets, toilets, sink, drainpipes.			●	
Drain sediment from water heater (draw out 1 gal.).			●	
Check water heater gauge; should be set at 140° F (120° F if dishwasher has own heating element).			●	
Have pressure and temperature relief valve on water heater checked by a plumber.		●		

Electrical system	Spring	Fall	Annually	As required
Inspect all cords and plugs for wear.	●	●	●	
Have electrician check fuse or breaker box if blowouts are frequent.				
Check light switches, wall outlets, and ceiling fixtures for loose parts and malfunctioning.				
Trip main switch to prevent corrosion buildup.			●	
Check ground fault interrupters.				

Interior surfaces	Spring	Fall	Annually	As required
Check for cracks in walls.				
Have dark stains and bulges on ceilings and walls, and peeling paint, checked by a professionally trained, qualified house inspector.	●			
Check sealant around tubs, showers, and tile floors.				
Clean dingy tile grouting.	●	●		

Foundations and basement	Spring	Fall	Annually	As required
Have beams checked for termites and powder post beetles.				
Check for dampness, leaks, and cracks.				

Floors	Spring	Fall	Annually	As required
Check tiles and plastic surfaces for cracks and damage.				
Check wooden floors for wear.				

Wallboard

Also known as drywall, gypsum board, or plasterboard, wallboard is commonly used to construct walls and ceilings. It can also serve as an underlayment for ceramic tiles. Wallboard is composed of compressed gypsum (calcium sulfate dihydrate) covered on both sides and side edges with kraft paper. (Some kinds have an aluminum foil backing that acts as a vapor retarder for exterior walls.) Wallboard is fire-resistant and, when installed in dual layers, can help soundproof, too.

Wallboard is fairly easy to hang (install), but if you're new at it, have some friends help you move the heavy panels. Panel thicknesses range from ¼ to ⅝ inch; ½ inch is used in most residential work. Common width is 4 feet; length, 8 feet up to 16 feet.

Wallboard types. *Standard*, which is the most widely used type, has tapered long edges and

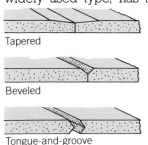

Tapered

Beveled

Tongue-and-groove

blunt short ends; it has a smooth face (which you can paint or wallpaper) and a rough one. *Water-resistant*, which has tapered edges, is used as a base for installing either ceramic or plastic tiles; it is used in kitchens, laundry rooms, and bathrooms. (Within bathtub areas or shower stalls, use *cement-base backer board* under ceramic tile.)

Predecorated, which requires no finishing, comes in a variety of decorator colors, textures, and patterns. Its top surface may be printed, coated, or have a vinyl covering—all of which are easy to clean. Wallboard *sheathing*, which has tongue-and-groove edges, is used under exterior siding, masonry veneer, stucco, and shingles. It provides protection against water and wind and gives support to framing. Wallboard sheathing as well as water-resistant wallboard will sag if applied to ceilings; instead use standard wallboard on kitchen, bathroom, or laundry-room ceilings and coat with alkyd primer (p.361) to make it water-resistant.

Installation. Wallboard must be carefully measured, cut, and fastened to wood or metal studs or joists. The joints of abutting panels are finished with joint compound and tape (pp.276–277).

Tools and materials. For measuring, marking, and cutting, use a wallboard T-square (4 feet) or straightedge, a utility knife, and a wallboard saw. For nailing, use a bell-face hammer; for fastening with screws, a cordless screwdriver is convenient. Use 1⅜- or 1⅝-inch ringed nails or 1¼- or 1⅞-inch Type W screws, depending on panel thickness. One pound of nails or ½ pound of screws will secure 200 square feet of wallboard; use 5 pounds of nails or 2½ pounds of screws for 1,000 square feet. When installing a ceiling, brace each panel with a T-bar support.

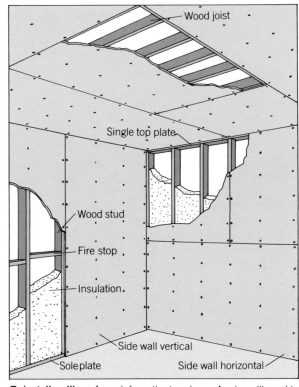

Wood joist

Single top plate

Wood stud

Fire stop

Insulation

Side wall vertical

Sole plate

Side wall horizontal

To install wallboard, work from the top down. Apply wallboard to the ceiling, then to the top half of the walls; cover the bottom half last. This method reduces damage to panels during installation and results in snugger ceiling-wall joints.

Estimating materials needed

Wallboard area	Ready-mix joint compound	Joint tape
100–200 sq. ft.	1 gal.	120 ft.
300–400 sq. ft.	2 gal.	180 ft.
500–600 sq. ft.	3 gal.	250 ft.
700–800 sq. ft.	4 gal.	310 ft.
900–1,000 sq. ft.	5 gal.	500 ft.

Wallboard nails and screws

Ringed nail. A threaded nail that holds wallboard securely.

Cement-coated nail. Its coating gives this threadless nail good holding ability.

Cooler nail. Widely used on the West Coast for wallboard installation.

Type W (wood) screw. For fastening wallboard to wooden studs.

Type G (gypsum) screw. For fastening one sheet of wallboard to another.

Type S (steel) screw. For fastening wallboard to metal studs.

Wallboard is relatively easy to prepare for installation; if you make a mistake in measuring or cutting, it generally can be corrected. And the material is cheap. Handle wallboard with care to avoid damaging its kraft paper covering. If moisture seeps through, the gypsum core will crumble.

Storage. Stack wallboard panels flat or rest them on edge in a cool, well-ventilated area. If you have many, make several small stacks; the weight of one tall stack could cause the floor joists to collapse.

Estimating needs. Measure the wall surfaces, total their square feet, and add 15 percent to allow for miscuts. Include standard-size doors and windows (use these cutouts as scrap), but subtract the measurements of picture windows and large doorways. Measure the floor to determine the ceiling's size. Divide the total by 32 (the number of square feet in a 4 x 8-foot panel) to get the number of panels needed. Or draw a plan on graph paper with each square representing 1 square foot.

If your ceiling is 8 feet 1 inch or lower, plan to install wall panels horizontally. When you know how many panels you'll need, consult the estimation chart (p.273) to calculate the required quantity of joint compound and joint tape.

▶ **CAUTION:** Wear safety goggles and a spray-paint respirator when cutting wallboard. Gypsum particles can irritate eyes and respiratory tract.

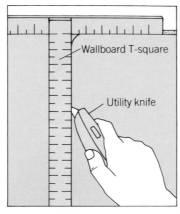
Wallboard T-square
Utility knife

To cut wallboard, place a 4-foot wallboard T-square or a straightedge against the marked line on the panel. Steady the T-square with your hand and foot; then carefully draw a utility knife along this line, cutting through the wallboard's face paper.

To break the panel, position yourself behind it, and hold its top edge firmly with a hand on either side of the incision. Raise your knee and place it against the back of the scored line. Tap your knee against this area as you bend the panel toward you. Bend until the core breaks.

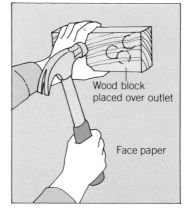
Wood block placed over outlet
Face paper

To make a cutout (here for an electrical outlet), position panel as if installed. Hammer lightly on wood block placed over outlet area to make impression. Or trace a template of outlet on panel. (Make interior door cutouts after installing panel, if jambs aren't more than ½ in. beyond studs. Otherwise measure and cut before installing.)

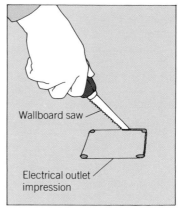
Wallboard saw
Electrical outlet impression

Saw from a corner, starting at one of the four drilled ¼-in. corner holes, with a keyhole saw or a wallboard saw; follow the lines of the outlet impression. If necessary, smooth rough edges with medium (80-grit) open-coat sandpaper or with a rasp.

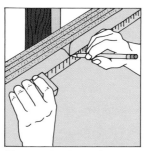

Measure the size desired on the face of the panel. Mark dimensions near the top and bottom edges (or side edges for a vertical cut).

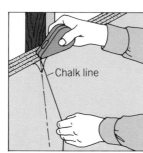
Chalk line

Anchor a chalk line (p.46) to the bottom edge mark, unreel it, and hold it taut against top marked edge; then snap it.

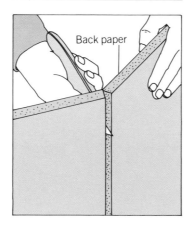
Back paper

Slice the back paper with your utility knife, cutting upward or downward along the break in the panel. Free the panel from the scrap end. If the cut edge is ragged, smooth it with medium (80-grit) open-coat sandpaper.

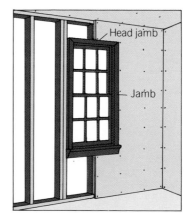
Head jamb
Jamb

On windows and doors position panel seams near midpoint of head jamb to avoid their alignment with head jamb corners. Recut adjoining panels if necessary. Wallboard cracks can occur as head jamb expands or contracts. If full panel can surround window (facing page), all the better.

Installing wallboard

The best way to "hang" wallboard is to begin with the ceiling and work your way down. Get several friends to help with the heavy lifting. A T-bar support will help hold a ceiling panel in place while you work on it. Make your own support: Nail a 2-foot section of a 1 x 4 across the end of a 2 x 4 that is an inch or so longer than the ceiling-to-floor distance.

Install the first ceiling panel in a corner so that its length is perpendicular to the joists and its tapered edge is positioned on the center line of a joist, where another tapered edge will abut it. Stagger butt-end joints if possible; avoid running them in a line.

On walls higher than 8 feet 1 inch or 4 feet wide or less, install wall panels vertically; nail the long edges to studs. Work from the upper part of the wall downward. Match tapered end to tapered end and butt end to butt end. Before hanging wallboard on masonry or on uneven plaster, install furring strips (p.283).

Fastening. Attach panels to studs with wallboard screws, adhesive and ringed nails, or just the nails. Screws hold the best, and you can undo them to recut a panel; kraft paper gets torn when you try to remove nails.

You may want to use your head while doing a ceiling (a foam-rubber pad under your hard hat will help ease the burden); it makes an excellent support while you fasten a panel.

Before nailing panels, apply wallboard adhesive to the studs. Protect outside corner edges with metal corner beads (p.276). Add door, baseboard, and ceiling moldings (p.99).

Wallboard adhesive

Apply wallboard adhesive to studs before nailing up wallboard; it increases holding power. At about 48 in. from the ceiling, drive two large nails halfway into studs so you can rest an upper wall panel in snug position while nailing it fast. Using a bell-face hammer, drive nails at 8-in. intervals, ⅜ in. from edges of panel and door's jambs. Drive the nails flush with the panel; then without breaking paper, dimple surface with final blow (insert) to bring the panel tight against stud.

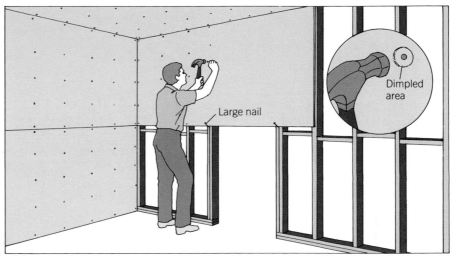
Large nail

Dimpled area

T-bar support

Position one end of the first panel in a corner of the ceiling while a helper assists by propping up the opposite end with a T-bar support ("dead man").

Using a cordless screwdriver, drive wallboard screws into panel at 12-in. intervals, ⅜ in. from edge, to fasten it to joists. Stagger butt-end joints if possible. Screwdriver's magnetic tip will prevent screws from falling.

Framed opening, top

Framed opening, side

Cut out unfinished doorway, using a wallboard saw. Work upward, sawing along framed opening's side. When saw meets opening's top, turn the blade and saw horizontally, holding bottom of panel to steady it.

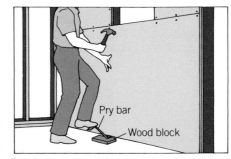
Pry bar

Wood block

Rest lower wall panel on a pry bar; step on pry bar to raise panel until it is butted against the panel above it. Hold panel in place as you fasten it to the studs. Cut out rest of doorway or window outline, sawing along side jambs first.

Interiors / Wallboard joints and corners

The secret to finishing wall and corner joints successfully is to work patiently. The drying time between each of the three applications of joint compound is 24 hours. Professionals may take up to 3 days to complete the task.

It's easy to finish tapered joints because of the gutter formed when two tapered edges abut. Butt-end joints, however, lack this advantage, and so you must apply compound thinly to avoid buildup over the crack.

Tools and materials. For finishing, purchase three wallboard knives (4-, 6-, and 10-inch blades), all-purpose ready-mix joint compound ("mud"), and wallboard tape (see estimation chart, p.273). In addition, you'll need to have a mud pan or a hawk, a 10-inch hand trowel, a paint roller, fine (150-grit) closed-coat sandpaper (or, for wet-sanding, a small-celled polyurethane sanding sponge), and several pails of water for rinsing tools.

Preparations. Stir the compound with a stick until it has soft-butter consistency. Add water if needed. Pour a quart of compound into a mud pan. To prevent lumping, cover compound in the container with 1 inch of water and reseal. Make a wallboard-tape holder from a bent wire coat hanger; hook it to your belt. Protect floors with plastic sheeting. Work from top to bottom: Treat ceiling joints first.

▶ **CAUTION:** When sanding, wear goggles and a spray-paint respirator. Make sure the area is well ventilated.

Corners. Protect outside corners and door jambs with metal corner beads before you finish them. Install J-beads (metal J-shaped casings) at recessed windows for finished edges.

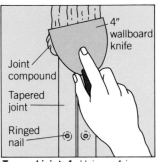

Tapered joint. 1. Using a 4-in. wallboard knife, spread joint compound generously into gutter of adjoining tapered edges. Press wallboard tape into compound, submerging it slightly.

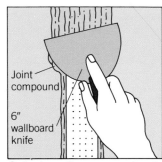

2. Hold knife at a 45° angle and run it over tape to expel bubbles and force excess over gutter edges. Wipe with damp sponge; then thinly coat with compound. Let dry completely (24 hr.).

3. Apply another compound coat with 6-in. wallboard knife; feather compound into surface, extending 2 in. beyond first coat. Let dry entirely (24 hr.). Apply final coat with 10-in. knife.

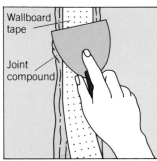

4. Sand dried compound lightly with fine (150-grit) closed-coat sandpaper until smooth; avoid scratching wallboard paper. Or wet-sand, rubbing lightly with dampened sanding sponge.

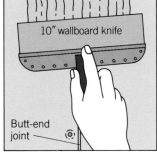

Butt-end joint. With 10-in. wallboard knife, spread thin coat of compound over joint. Feather excess beyond edges. Tape and proceed as for tapered edges, but apply coats in very thin layers.

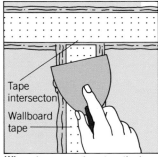

Where tapes meet, cut vertical joint tape so that it just meets tape of horizontal joint. At intersection tapes should not overlap; crossing one over another forms a bump.

Nail dimples

Spread compound over nail dimples until almost filled. Let dry completely (24 hr.). Repeat until flush with wallboard (two or three applications may be needed). Sand as in step 4.

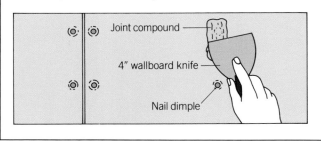

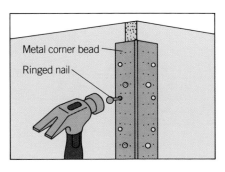

Fasten corner bead at 5-in. intervals with ringed nails or with wallboard screws. Drive fasteners through smaller holes of corner bead (larger holes are meant for compound), through wallboard, and into the stud.

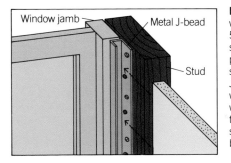

Fasten J-bead with wallboard screws at 5-in. intervals. Drive screws through smaller preformed holes into stud, with seat of J-bead flush with window jamb. Slide wallboard into J-bead, then drive wallboard screws through wallboard into studs.

1. Inside corners. Apply joint compound generously to inside corner with 6-in. wallboard knife, making sure that crack is completely filled. Feather excess on each side of crack.

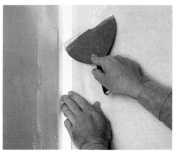

2. Press vertically creased wallboard tape into compound-treated corner with wallboard knife. Feather excess compound at edges. Let dry completely (24 hr.).

3. Apply thin second coat of compound, one side at a time. (Avoid compound buildup on wallboard; this could result in hairline cracks.) Feather edges and let dry completely (24 hr.). Apply third coat; let dry 24 hr.; then sand lightly.

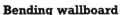

10" wallboard knife

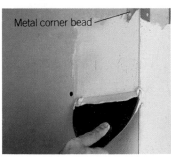

Metal corner bead

Cover corner beads with joint compound, using 6-in. wallboard knife. Feather edges and let dry thoroughly (24 hr.). Treat with two more coats of compound as you would a joint (facing page), but do not use tape.

Finishing and texturing wallboard

To check that finished joints are smooth and even with the wallboard surface, press your cheek against a panel about 1 foot from a finished joint; direct a flashlight beam along the panel in line with your view. Lightly wet-sand bumps in compound with a damp sanding sponge; rinse and wring out the sponge often. Before wallpapering, apply latex wallboard primer. Let dry fully (several hours).

Before painting, apply skim coat of thinned joint compound with a 10-inch hand trowel; smooth it. It should have the consistency of soft ice cream; thin with water if needed. Protect against splatter: Wear painter's overalls, a cap, and goggles; cover floor and windows with plastic sheeting. When the skim coat is dry (24 hours), coat with latex wallboard primer. Paint when fully dry (several hours).

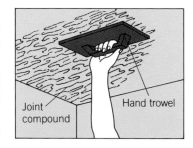

Joint compound — Hand trowel

Texturing ceilings. For a brocade-like finish, lightly press hand trowel loaded with compound onto the ceiling. Flatten peaks with trowel. Begin at a corner and work toward center; do 3 sq. ft. at a time. Blend section borders. Let dry for 48 hr.

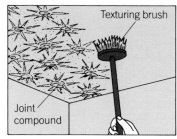

Texturing brush

Joint compound

Jab texturing brush into wet compound that has been rollered onto ceiling. The stiff bristles will make a distinct pattern. Slightly overlap the marks as you progress. (Practice this technique or others on scrap before doing the job.) Let dry for 48 hr.

Bending wallboard

There are several ways to bend wallboard so that it will conform to a curved wall. Quarter-inch wallboard is thin enough to withstand bending without any preparation. To bend a thicker panel, however, you must either wet it to make it flexible or else cut beveled kerfs in the area to be bent.

The wetting is crucial: If the panel is too moist, it will be difficult to transport and may even fall apart; if it's not wet enough, it will break when you bend it. Trim and make cutouts; with a mister, spray 5½ cups of water on a 4- x 8-foot panel (½ inch thick or thicker). Carefully fasten the moistened wallboard to studs with ringed nails; hammer blows must not tear the kraft paper when dimpling. Let the installed wallboard dry completely (24 hours); then finish it with joint compound.

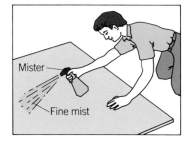

Mister

Fine mist

Using a mister, spray side of panel to be compressed. Stack it between flat, dry panels; let sit for a couple of hours. Transport each panel on a dry panel. Tilt, position against studs, remove dry panel, and fasten (p.275).

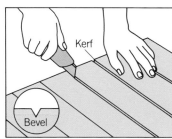

Kerf

Bevel

Cut beveled kerfs 3 in. apart along measured lines running full length of panel area to be compressed. Support with a plywood panel. Make kerfs ⅛ in. wide and no deeper than ¼ in. for a 4-ft. radius. Transport and install as described above.

Interiors/Repairing damaged wallboard

Wallboard is easily marred and damaged but, fortunately, easy to repair. Leftovers from your project—ready-mix joint compound, wallboard tape, scrap wallboard, wallboard screws or ringed nails—make good repair materials. (Scrape unused joint compound into a plastic bag, then tightly knot the bag and seal in a smaller can; storage time this way is 2 years.)

If you run out of scrap wallboard, try looking for some around a building that's undergoing renovation; salvage only scrap that is whole and clean. If you've run out of wallboard supplies altogether, consider buying one of the several kinds of wallboard patching kits that are on the market. Choose one that's suitable for the job; follow the instructions on the package to the letter. You can buy a wall-board patching kit at most hardware stores and home centers; some lumberyards may stock them as well.

Damage. It's easy to accidentally mar wallboard panels while installing them; they are heavy and somewhat unwieldy, especially if you are doing the job by yourself. Dents, gashes, and broken corners can easily occur at this stage of installation. It may take a number of years for other kinds of damage to become apparent. When a doorknob bangs frequently into a wall, for instance, a dent or a hole will eventually appear. And as your house shifts and resettles over time, it may even stress the walls to the extent that cracks appear.

If the wallboard was not flush to the studs or joists when it was fastened, its ringed nails may in time pop from the wood, breaking the wallboard's paper surface. This may also occur if the studs or joists were unseasoned and have shrunk, or as a result of moisture changes in the wood.

Tools. You will need a metal rule for measuring the damaged section of wallboard and the matching patch; a utility knife for cutting scrap to size and for paring rough edges of holes; three wallboard knives (4, 6, and 10 inches) for applying joint compound; and fine (150-grit) closed-coat sandpaper to smooth dried compound or a small-celled polyurethane sponge to wet-sand it.

Allow each compound application to harden thoroughly (24 hours). Coat with wallboard primer and let dry completely (several hours) before painting or wallpapering.

Dent or surface scratch

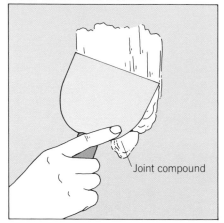

1. Using a 6-in. wallboard knife, fill the sanded dent with joint compound. Let dry thoroughly (24 hr.). Compound shrinks while drying; apply a second coat, then lightly wipe it with a damp sponge to level it with surrounding wallboard. Let dry completely (24 hr.).

Popped nails

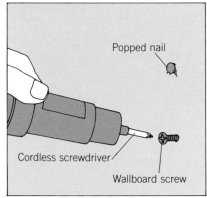

1. Measure and mark a distance of 2 in. below or above popped nail. At this point drive wallboard screw or ringed nail through panel into the stud or joist.

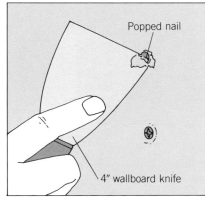

2. Scrape loose paper and crumbled compound from area around popped nail with 4-in. wallboard knife, taking care not to damage sound areas of panel.

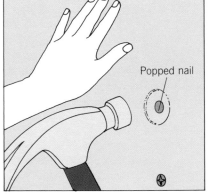

3. Drive popped nail ¹⁄₃₂ in. below surface with a hammer. Smooth with fine (150-grit) closed-coat sandpaper. Give nail and screw areas three coats of compound (let each dry 24 hr.). Wet-sand until smooth.

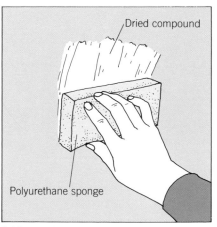

2. Wet-sand with a wet (but well wrung out) small-celled polyurethane sponge. Rub dried compound lightly until smooth; rinse and wring out sponge often. Or sand lightly with fine (150-grit) closed-coat sandpaper until surface is smooth and even; take care not to mar surrounding paper.

Small hole

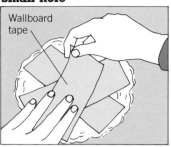

Wallboard tape

1. Apply thin coat of compound around hole; then cover with tape, crisscrossing it over hole. Press tape ends into the compound. (If using mesh tape, crisscross it directly over hole without applying compound.)

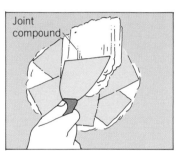

Joint compound

2. Coat tape with compound, using 6-in. wallboard knife to smooth it. Feather edges of patch and let dry 24 hr. If patch cracks, apply another coat of compound and let dry 24 hr. Sand or wet-sand as described on facing page.

Fist-size hole

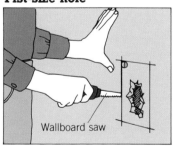

Wallboard saw

1. Cut out a rectangle around hole with wallboard saw. Apply a special glue—wallboard adhesive—to ends of a 1 x 2 that's 4 in. wider than hole. Insert 1 x 2 horizontally, hold it in place, and fasten it to wallboard with wallboard screws.

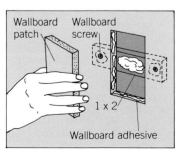

Wallboard patch   Wallboard screw

1 x 2

Wallboard adhesive

2. Glue patch (⅛ in. smaller than hole) to 1 x 2 with wallboard adhesive. Coat seams of patch with compound. Seal with wallboard tape. Coat with compound, feather, and let dry (24 hr.). Wet-sand as described on facing page.

Large gash

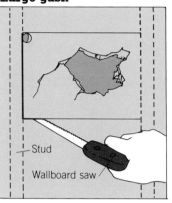

Stud

Wallboard saw

1. Locate studs either side of gash (p.191). Mark a rectangular section around damaged area, reaching from stud to stud. Cut it out with wallboard saw. From scrap, cut wallboard patch that's ⅛ in. smaller than the cutout.

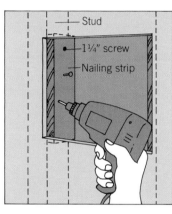

Stud

1¼" screw

Nailing strip

2. Cut 1 x 3 nailing strips ½ in. longer than exposed area of studs, and position them on inner sides of studs so that they extend ¼ in. above and below edges of hole. Drill pilot holes. Fasten nailing strips to stud edges with 1¼-in. screws.

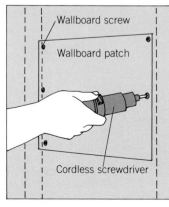

Wallboard screw

Wallboard patch

Cordless screwdriver

3. Screw patch to nailing strips, making sure screws don't collide with those in strips. Fill seams with joint compound, using 10-in. wallboard knife. Seal seams with wallboard tape. Coat tape with compound, feathering excess into surrounding surface. Let dry 24 hr.; then lightly sand or wet-sand as described on facing page.

Removing wallboard

If damage is so severe that you must replace entire panels of wallboard, first empty the room of all furnishings; remove hanging objects in adjoining rooms (the vibrations may knock them down); tape doors closed; cover the floor with plastic sheeting. Remove wall trim with a flat bar (p.293).

▶ **CAUTION:** Turn off water and electricity (p.10) in case you accidentally break pipes or cut wiring while tearing down wallboard. Wear safety goggles, a spray-paint respirator, work gloves, work shoes, and a hard hat.

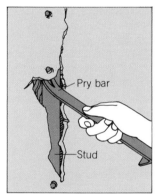

Pry bar

Stud

Locate studs (p.191). Chip joint compound from wallboard seams at studs with a cold chisel and hammer. With pry bar (p.22), pry fasteners and, if possible, remove wallboard panel by panel. Save whole pieces for scrap.

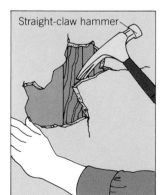

Straight-claw hammer

If you can't remove the wallboard panel by prying at seams, break up wallboard sections with a straight-claw hammer or flat bar. Spray the air frequently with a mister to reduce flying dust.

A gypsum plaster–perlite mixture and ready-mix joint compound (p.276) are the only materials you need for plaster repairs. Both are cheap and available at most hardware stores and at some lumberyards. Ask for the *regular* formulation of perlited plaster. Have someone help load the 50-pound bag into your car, or have it delivered.

Plaster is applied to a lath—material fastened to studs or joists. The lath may be wooden strips (in pre-1930 houses), gypsum lath (wallboardlike), or metal (in commercial buildings).

Most plaster repairs require two or three applications, depending on the hole size; for the final layer, use joint compound. Perlited plaster sets in about 2 to 4 hours; it is finish-ready in 24 hours. For extensive repair, call a professional plasterer.

The plaster in the mixture you buy is mainly pulverized gypsum rock. Perlite, a pulverized volcanic glass, makes the mixture light. When you add water, the mixture assumes the texture of soft ice cream; when totally dry, it's rock-hard.

Prior to plastering, fix any leaks or other causes of excess moisture (pp.199 and 384); give the damaged area several weeks to dry thoroughly. Before repairing large areas, ready the room (p.279). For plaster to set properly, the room temperature must be kept within the 55°F–70°F range for 24 hours before plastering and until the plaster has set.

Tools. Have ready a plastic tub, three wallboard knives (4, 6, and 10 inches), a utility knife, a rectangular trowel, a hawk (p.164), fine (150-grit) closed-coat sandpaper, cold and wood chisels, a ball peen hammer, a mallet, an electric drill, and a small-cell polyurethane sponge. Rinse tools often.

Mixing. From the instructions on the bag, calculate the plaster–water ratio for the amount you need. Pour the plaster into fresh water in a plastic tub; swirl with your rubber-gloved hand to mix it. Large holes need a thicker consistency of plaster. Mix enough plaster for about an hour's work.

▶ **CAUTION:** Wear safety goggles, a long-sleeved shirt, and cotton work gloves. When breaking a plaster wall, wear a sanding respirator as well.

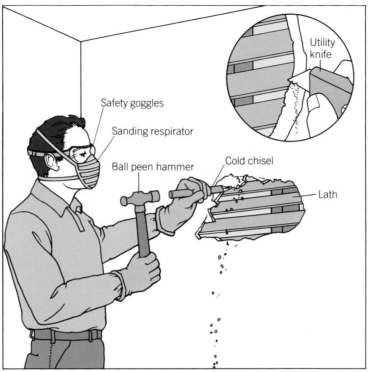

Safety goggles

Sanding respirator

Ball peen hammer

Cold chisel

Utility knife

Lath

Large holes. 1. Chip away damaged plaster with a cold chisel and a ball peen hammer, being careful not to damage the lath underneath. Undercut the hole's inside edge with a utility knife.

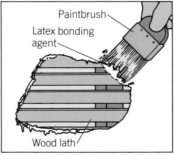

Paintbrush

Latex bonding agent

Wood lath

2. Brush latex bonding agent on exposed lath and edge of plaster hole to make it less absorbent. Or dampen the area well with a mister.

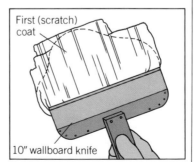

First (scratch) coat

10″ wallboard knife

3. With a 10-in. wallboard knife, apply plaster about ⅜ in. thick. As it begins to set, cross-scratch it so that the next coat will adhere well.

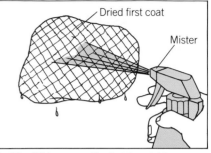

Dried first coat

Mister

4. After 24 hr., spray the first (scratch) coat with a mister. Apply second (brown) coat about ⅜ in. thick. Cross-scratch as in step 3. Let it rest overnight.

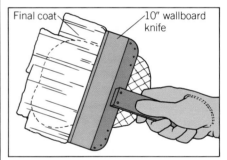

Final coat

10″ wallboard knife

5. Apply joint compound over second coat. Feather excess compound, blending it in with wall. Let dry completely (24 hr.). Wet-sand (p.278) until smooth.

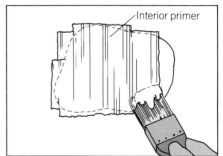

Interior primer

6. Finish by painting with a coat of interior primer. After it has dried thoroughly (several hours), it will be ready for painting or for hanging wallcovering.

Repairing cracks

Cracks and small holes are easy to repair; usually they need just one application of plaster. Alternatively, they can be repaired with a strip of fiberglass-mesh tape, then finished with joint compound (p.278). Cracks may be caused by a shifting foundation, atmospheric conditions, or poor construction. The crack will recur if the cause is not remedied.

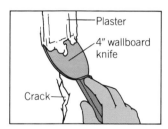

1. Using a 4-in. wallboard knife, apply plaster to a crack that has been trimmed, undercut, and sprayed with a mister. Allow it to dry thoroughly (24 hr.).

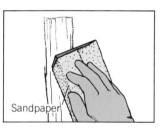

2. Sand smooth with fine (150-grit) closed-coat sandpaper. Paint with interior primer. Let dry thoroughly before painting or wallpapering.

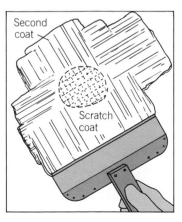

Tennis-ball-size holes. With a 10-in. wallboard knife, feather a coat of joint compound over scratch-coated hole. Begin at center of patch and work outward, going 1 ft. or so beyond edge of patch. Let dry 24 hr. Wet-sand, rubbing compound lightly with a dampened sanding sponge. Paint with interior primer. Let dry completely (several hours) before applying paint or wallcovering.

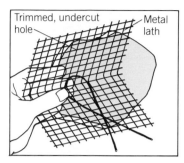

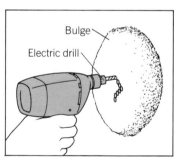

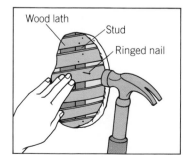

Damaged lath. 1. With wood chisel and mallet, cut away damaged wood lath. (Cut gypsum lath with wallboard saw.) Holding wire looped at lath's center, insert metal lath. When it's properly positioned, pull wire toward you until lath is flush against back side of plaster.

2. Twist wire around dowel to secure metal lath. Apply scratch coat; then cross-scratch as it begins to set. Let dry 24 hr. Remove dowel and snip wire with wire cutters. Apply joint compound, and feather excess. Let dry 24 hr. Wet-sand before painting or papering.

Bulging area. 1. Drill connecting holes in bulge with an electric drill and a worn 3/8-in. bit to make a 1-in.-wide hole. If plaster and wood lath have come loose from stud, carefully chip plaster away from lath with cold chisel and ball peen hammer.

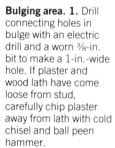

2. Push lath against stud and fasten with ringed nails. Brush latex bonding agent on hole. Fill with scratch and second coats of plaster; finish with joint compound (facing page). Let dry for 24 hr. Wet-sand until smooth, and then prime.

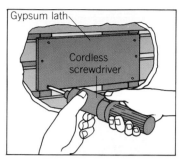

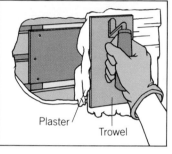

Hole without lath.
1. With a wallboard saw, cut gypsum lath (or 3/8-in.-thick wallboard) to size of area without lath. Use a power screwdriver to fasten corners of gyspum lath patch to studs with wallboard screws.

2. Apply plaster to patch with trowel, filling in recess. Let dry 24 hr.; then apply thin coat of joint compound with 10-in. wallboard knife, feathering excess beyond patch edges. Let dry overnight. Wet-sand until smooth. Prime before painting or papering.

Covering old plaster with wallboard. Find studs (p.191) and mark their locations. Position wallboard edges over studs; drive 2¼-in. wallboard screws through wallboard and plaster. Treat joints, prime, and texture as described on pages 275–277.

Interiors / Wall paneling

Although the term *paneling* commonly brings to mind wood or wood veneer covering the walls of a family room or library, in fact paneling, whether in wood planks or sheets, can improve the appearance of any room. When backed by wallboard (p.273), thick planks help absorb sound.

Planks are solid wood; sheet paneling can have a wood surface or a synthetic surface resembling anything from bathroom tiles to living room wallpaper to—of course—wood. Wall paneling will last longer than paint or wallpaper; choose a pattern that you'll enjoy for many years.

When planks with a penetrating oil finish become dirty, wash them with an oil soap, let dry, then oil anew. Clean varnished and shellacked planks or sheet paneling with a damp cloth (use a mild detergent for stubborn dirt). Repairs are infrequent and fairly easy to make (p.288).

Paneling types. Planks can be either softwood or hardwood and are graded accordingly (p.94). They are as handsome as they are expensive. Plywood surfaced with top-quality veneer is an alternative; it has the real-wood look of planks and it's cheaper. Sheet paneling, backed by a substrate of plywood, particleboard, or hardboard (p.98), costs considerably less. Sheet paneling with a simulated wood, tile, or marble surface, called tileboard, is cheaper yet. Cheapest of all is predecorated wallboard. Its advantage over other types of paneling is that its printed-paper surface can be wallpapered or painted when you tire of it.

Installation patterns. You can install planks or wood-grained paneling vertically, horizontally, diagonally, or in a herringbone pattern. Paneling one wall may be enough to dramatically accent a room.

▶ **CAUTION:** An entirely paneled room can be fire-hazardous, unless the paneling has been installed directly on wallboard or plaster walls. Air spaces between studs and furring strips (facing page) encourage airflow; this helps the flames of a concealed fire to spread quickly. Avoid lacquer finishes; their fumes are volatile. Install a smoke detector on the ceiling of your paneled room.

Substrate	Face	Thickness	Cutting*	Fastening
Wallboard	Simulated wood grains; decorative patterns; decorative vinyl	¼″, ⅜″, ½″, ⅝″, or ¾″	Utility knife	Adhesive and color-matched paneling nails
Particleboard	Simulated wood grains; decorative patterns	5/32″ or ¼″	Hand or power saw with fine-tooth blade	Adhesive and color-matched paneling nails
Hardboard	Simulated wood grains and masonry; decorative patterns; decorative vinyl	⅛″ or ¼″	Hand or power saw with fine-tooth blade	Adhesive and color-matched paneling nails; or just the nails
Tileboard (hardboard)	Simulated tile and marble	Usually ¼″	Hand or power saw with fine-tooth blade	Adhesive and color-matched paneling nails
Plywood	Simulated wood grains; decorative patterns; decorative vinyl	5/32″, 3/16″, or ⅛″	Utility knife; hand or power saw with fine-tooth blade	Adhesive and color-matched paneling nails; or just the nails

*When cutting with utility knife, handsaw, or table saw, panel should be face up. When cutting with circular saw or saber saw, panel should be face down.

Calculating panel needs

On graph paper draw a scale model of the room you plan to sheet-panel. Let each square represent 1 sq. ft. For patterned paneling, make your starting point a conspicuous corner or feature as you would for wallcovering (p.377). Measure the height of the walls; then sketch them on the plan, flopping them out from the floor so that they look like the dropped sides of a box.

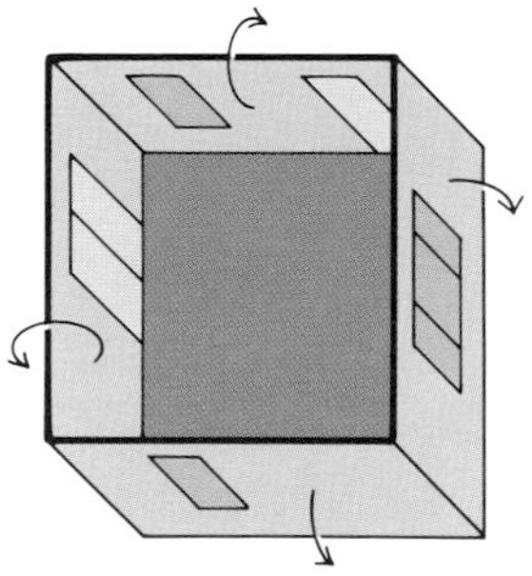

Sheets of wall paneling usually measure 4 x 8 ft. Measure the room's perimeter (here, 76 ft.); round out a fractional total to the next highest number. Divide by 4 (a panel's width), and you get 19—the number of panels you will need for four walls of a room with an 8-foot ceiling. If your ceilings are higher than 8 ft., you will have to special-order 4- x 10- or 4- x 12-ft. panels through a lumberyard or home center. These may not be readily available, and they will be expensive. Or you can install 4- x 8-ft. panels, leaving a gap between floor and paneling to be covered by baseboard molding. Where possible, use window cutouts above doors or above and below windows. Store leftovers for repairs (p.288).

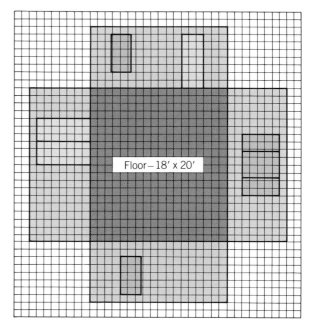

Floor—18′ x 20′

Preparation for paneling

Using a carpenter's level as a straight-edge, check the wall surfaces that you intend to panel. If they are not plumb, install 1 x 2 furring strips and insert shimming wedges where necessary to provide a level surface for paneling. If the walls are straight and even, strip them of wallpaper (p.376); scrape off loose and flaking paint. Repair all dents, gouges, and holes in the wallboard (pp.278–279) or plaster (pp.280–281).

Planks or sheet paneling can be fastened to a clean, level surface or to furring strips or framing with panel adhesive and paneling nails or with just paneling nails. Begin by marking on the wall the location of all studs (p.191), including those around doors and windows.

Molding. Remove trim and baseboards (p.293). Pry window and door trim joints forward with wedge, crowbar, and pry bar until released. If wood starts splitting, cut nails under trim with a hacksaw. Code-mark the backs of reusable molding with their locations; then store. When replacing, you'll have to shorten the length of the molding by the thickness of the paneling on each adjacent wall.

Electrical fixtures. At the circuit or fuse box, turn off the power to all circuits in the room (p.237). Unscrew and remove the faceplates from wall switches and outlets. To accommodate the new distance from the original surface to the paneling surface, you may want to equip electrical boxes with box extenders—adjustable collar-like frames that match the outlet and switch boxes (p.285); they are available at most hardware stores.

Furring strips

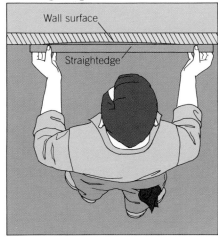

1. Position a straightedge horizontally at several places along wall. If you observe gaps between straightedge and wall, cut furring strips the wall's width from 1 x 2's, locate studs, and install strips with nails driven into studs.

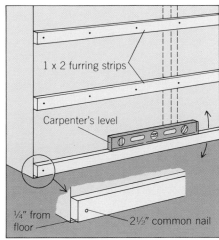

2. Position first furring strip ¼ in. from floor; fasten one end with 2½-in. common nail. Have a helper hold carpenter's level on strip's top edge; raise or lower free end until level's bubble is centered. Nail end; nail strip to intervening studs.

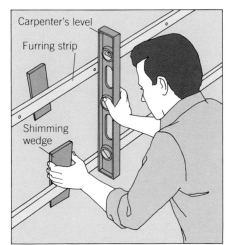

3. Bridge horizontal strips with level to check if they are plumb. Where out of plumb, insert a shimming wedge under strip and adjust it until level's bubble is centered. Planks can be installed on this framework.

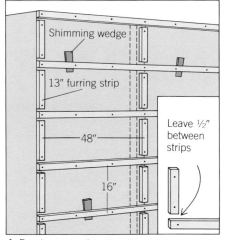

4. For sheet paneling, install a network of 13-in. 1 x 2's to fit vertically between (but not touching) horizontal strips. The vertical strips should be 48 in. apart from center to center, nailed at both ends into studs.

Framing

If you rent and your lease prohibits nailing into walls, make a frame of 2 x 2's for mounting panels. Fasten it in place with a pressure device known as a furniture leveler. A similar frame, made of 2 x 4's, can serve as a room divider.

Measuring. For the top and bottom, mark two 2 x 2's to equal the wall's width. For the vertical members' length, subtract 3 in. from the wall's height; then saw all lengths. Align the top and bottom and mark them at 16-in. intervals for placement of the vertical members.

Fastening. Position vertical members between top and bottom; using 2½-in. common nails, fasten them through top and bottom. Make sure that the frame is square (p.47). Drill ⁵⁄₁₆-in. holes through top at 4-ft. intervals. With a hammer, tap pronged nuts (p.84) into holes. Screw large furniture levelers into pronged nuts. Erect the frame and position it; adjust levelers to secure the frame to ceiling and floor. If the frame is not plumb, adjust levelers further.

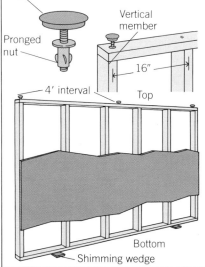

Before installing sheet paneling, let it acclimatize in the room for 2 days: Lean each piece on its long edge against a wall or stack them, inserting four wood blocks between panels, one at each corner.

Grain pattern or color depth may vary slightly or dramatically, particularly if the panels are from different shipments. Rearrange the panels to make differences less noticeable. Number the backs of the panels and their corresponding wall positions to avoid confusion during installation.

Tools and materials. Make sure you have ready a tape measure, a carpenter's level, a pencil compass, a power or hand saw with a fine-tooth blade, a drill and a keyhole saw (for cutouts), a utility knife, a hammer, a pry bar, a nail set, a rubber mallet, paneling adhesive (an 11-ounce tube is enough to glue three panels to a wall), color-matched paneling nails (1-inch if the panels go over furring strips, 1⅝-inch if directly on walls), a color-matched putty stick (to cover sunken plain paneling nails), white chalk, and a felt-tip pen color-matched to the panel grooves, if any.

Removing molding. Your work will look more professional if you remove the moldings beforehand. Using a pry bar and a wedge, carefully pry molding from around doors, windows, and at ceiling and floor (pp.283, 293). If you plan to reuse them, code-mark molding sections on the back for location identification, then store them in bundled groups. The paneling's design may, however, call for an entirely different style or color of molding.

Locating studs. Mark stud locations (p.191) at the wall's base. Although studs are usually spaced at intervals of 16 or 24 inches on center, this spacing is often modified to accommodate a window or door frame or a partition in an adjoining room. If you are installing panels over furring strips, place vertical furring strips over studs every 4 feet and over any studs where spacing is modified; then bridge the intervals with panels cut to fit. If installing panels directly to a wall, be sure that each panel—whether full-size or a cut-to-fit strip—will

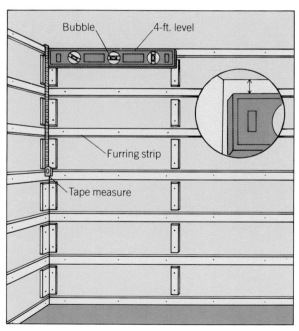

1. Measuring. The easy way: Cut panels to an average of floor-to-ceiling height (less ½ in.); bridge any gaps with molding. For a closer fit: Position a level flush to ceiling. Center bubble, and measure any gap between ceiling and either end of level. If gap shows at level's left end, mark it on panel's right-hand edge; draw line to opposite corner. Cut panel bottom to fit (less ½ in.).

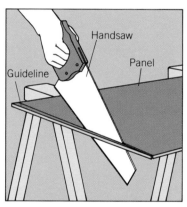

2. Cutting. Place the panel, face up, on two sawhorses or on a worktable. Using a handsaw, carefully cut panel following gap guideline, if any. If cutting with a circular or saber saw, mark and cut with back of panel up.

3. Mounting panel. Apply adhesive to furring strips. Position a panel, and insert ¼-in. shims under panel's bottom edge. Place level against vertical edge; check for plumb; adjust with more shims if needed. Drive four paneling nails partway through panel top at equal intervals.

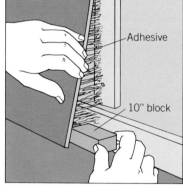

4. Pull panel bottom about 10 in. away from wall; insert wood blocks at each corner. In 10 min., when the exposed adhesive has become tacky, remove blocks. With a rubber mallet pound the panel over furring strips. Nail edges and grooves (if any) to furring strips at 6-in. intervals.

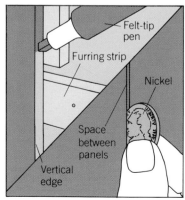

5. Color panel edge with felt-tip pen that matches color of panel grooves. Then color edge of next panel and install it, leaving space of a nickel's thickness between panels to allow for expansion caused by moisture.

have its long edges centered over the studs.

Corners. When you reach a corner and have to cut a panel to fit, use the remaining piece to butt-join the corner—unless doing so interferes with the panel edge–stud relationship. If it does, cut the next panel so that one edge meets the corner and the other centers on a stud; then continue. Butt-joined corners are usually finished with molding.

Measuring and cutting. All ceiling-high panels should be ½ inch less than the floor-to-ceiling measurement, to allow for expansion. Saw ¼-inch paneling face up with a hand or table saw. You can score the face of thin (⁵⁄₃₂-inch) paneling with a utility knife; then flex the cut section until it snaps. Before applying glue, test-fit a panel; also check that it will be plumb. When fastening to furring strips, apply adhesive to strips; then nail with 1-inch paneling nails. When fastening to a wall, run a bead of paneling adhesive near the edges of the panel's back; then crisscross the midsection. Use 1⅝-inch panel-

ing nails at 12-inch intervals to fasten panel grooves to intermediate studs, and at 6-inch intervals to fasten edges. Finish the room with stained or finished baseboard and ceiling moldings.

Curves. Thin paneling (⁵⁄₃₂ inch or less) with a plywood or hardboard substrate and a real wood face ply can be bent to conform to a gradually curving wall surface, such as a circular staircase wall. Don't choose paneling with a grooved surface; it could easily break at a groove. Before making your final choice, test a panel by bending it against the curved surface without forcing it. If it cracks or resists, choose a thinner panel. Have a helper hold the panel in place while you install it.

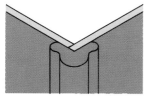
Corner-guard molding

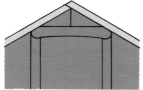
Inside corner molding

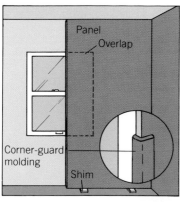

Untrimmed opening. Hold the panel, supported by shims, with its free edge overlapping window or door. Transfer measurements to panel face; saw out required opening. Install panel. Cover edge with corner-guard molding.

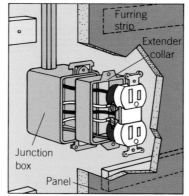

Box extender. Turn off power (p.237), remove faceplate, and unscrew switch or receptacle. Slide extender over box and adjust it to reach panel face. Using longer screws, refasten receptacle or switch. Replace the faceplate.

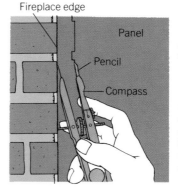

Irregular edge. Cut panel ½ in. wider than wall space. Tack panel, overlapping adjacent panel, so that edge to be cut abuts the irregular edge (here a fireplace). Open compass to ½ in. Scribe contour onto panel. Cut with a coping or saber saw.

Trimmed opening. Measure 4 ft. from last panel to window trim. Measure overlap; then measure from ceiling to trim's top edge and from floor to its bottom edge. Transfer measurements to panel. For electrical outlets, measure and transfer the same way. Drill corner holes; cut with keyhole or saber saw.

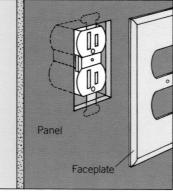

Outlet in thin panels glued to wall. Turn off power (p.237), remove face-plate, and chalk receptacle edge. Position panel as if installed; strike with rubber mallet over outlet to transfer chalk to panel's back. Drill hole on outline; cut with keyhole saw. Install panel; screw faceplate to outlet.

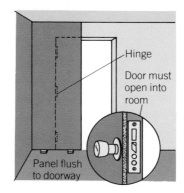

Paneling a door. Remove door from hinges. Place panel over opening as if installed. Mark opening on panel's back; position and mark next panel. Cut, and glue cutouts to door with paneling adhesive. Sand edges with fine (120-grit) closed-coat paper. Rehang door.

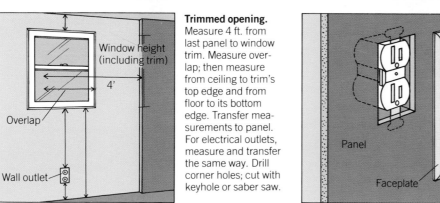

Paneling planks of solid wood—usually pine or oak—come in lengths of 8 to 16 feet, widths of 3 3/16 to 12 inches, and thicknesses of 5/16, 3/8, and 3/4 inch. Some planks are prefinished. Tongue-and-groove planks (shown here) are widely used; their joints create a V-shaped channel. Other types are ship-lap (edges overlap) and straight-edge, the latter installed with or without battens over the seams.

Estimating. How many planks you will need de-pends on the installation pattern (p.282) and the planks' width. Ask the lumberyard or home center to calculate exactly from your wall measurements.

Storing. Stack planks, their ends interspersed with wood blocks, or lean them singly against the room's walls. Give them 2 weeks to acclimatize.

Installation. In northern climates, cover the interior side of exterior walls with a vapor retarder of polyethylene sheeting; seal plank surfaces and edges with a water-resistant compound. If you apply stain and finish, make certain that they are compatible with the compound. If the walls are uneven, install horizontal furring strips (p.283). Extend the doorjamb or window-jamb depth with 1-inch wood strips equal to the combined thickness of a plank and a furring strip. Add extenders (p.285) to electric boxes. Install the planks up to the jamb extensions; then trim the extensions with casing molding.

Installing planks vertically

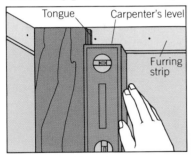

1. Position first plank in a corner, groove edge abutting adjacent wall and tongue edge facing right. Position carpenter's level against tongue edge to check for plumb. Adjust furring strip with shims if needed.

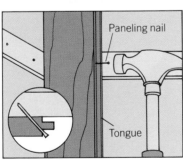

2. Drive paneling nail diagonally through tongue's base and into each furring strip. If planks are wider than 6 in., also face-nail into furring strips with color-matched nails placed one-third of plank's width away from groove edge.

3. Drive next groove onto tongue of installed plank with a mallet and a piece of plank scrap. Lightly tap the scrap until the planks fit snugly. Nail to furring strips as described above.

Corners

Inside corners. Cut tongue from last plank or cut plank to required width. Plane right rear edge to slight angle. Position next-to-last and last planks, tongue meeting groove. Push both until they interlock. Flatten and face-nail planks into furring.

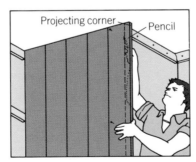

Outside corners. 1. Position and tack last plank. Mark overlap on plank's back side. Unfasten plank and cut off excess with hand or circular saw; then face-nail.

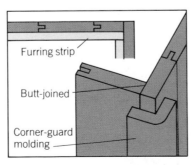

2. Cut groove edge from plank to be installed around corner; mount so that plank overlaps edge of previous plank. Cover with corner-guard molding.

Uneven ceiling

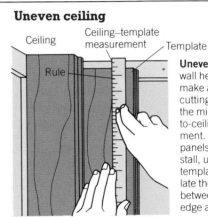

Uneven ceiling. If wall height varies, make a template by cutting a plank to the minimum floor-to-ceiling measurement. Cut and fit panels as you install, using the template to calculate the difference between its top edge and ceiling.

Finishing. Cut 1-in. wood strips (width should equal combined thickness of furring strip plus plank) to lengths of doorjambs or window jambs. Fasten to jambs with paneling adhesive and finishing nails set at 1-ft. intervals. Install planks flush to extensions. Bridge them with casing molding.

Wainscoting   Repairing planks

Planks or paneling covering a wall's lower part is called wainscoting. On an even wall surface you can fasten wainscoting directly with paneling adhesive—but first remove any wallcovering (p.376). Install wallboard (p.275) over bumpy or damaged walls; if badly out of plumb, install furring strips (p.283). Buy $^5/_{16}$-inch-thick planks. In northern climates prepare the exterior walls and the planks as described on the facing page. In warm, humid climates you need only to seal the planks.

1. Snap chalk line on wall at chosen wainscoting height, usually 30 to 36 in. Apply vertical zigzags of paneling adhesive, one for each of three planks. Install planks in the order shown on facing page.

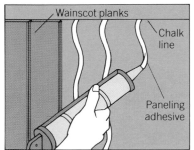

2. Locate studs (p.191) and mark near bottom of planks. Position primed, finished baseboard molding flush to wainscoting and to floor. Nail through to studs, using color-matched paneling nails.

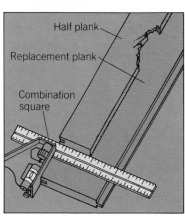

3. Position primed, finished wainscot cap or corner-guard molding snugly over plank tops and flush to wall. Using color-matched paneling nails, fasten at 1-ft. intervals to planks. (Predrill holes in hardwood molding.)

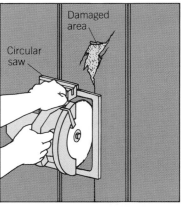

1. Remove the baseboard (p.293). Draw a line extending entire length of plank, bisecting damaged area. Adjust a cordless saw blade to plank's thickness; to be safe start with $^5/_{16}$ in. Cut plank along entire length of line; wear safety goggles. **CAUTION:** Turn off power to all house circuits before cutting (p.237).

2. Insert flat end of pry bar into damaged area; slide bar under sawn edge of plank half, and begin prying it loose from the adjacent plank. Insert pry bar under tongue-edge half and groove edge of adjacent panel; pry both up partway to release tongue from groove.

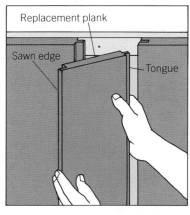

3. Position sawn plank half on top of replacement plank, bottoms and grooves aligned. Using a combination square, mark the proper length on the replacement plank and draw a line across. Cut to length with hand or circular saw.

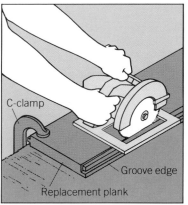

4. Using a C-clamp, secure replacement plank, face down, to work table. Mark groove bottom on both ends of plank; connect with line running length of panel. Adjust blade of circular saw to width of groove edge. Cut it off, leaving other groove edge intact.

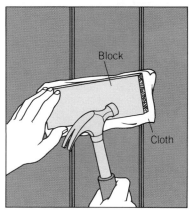

5. Insert replacement plank obliquely in gap so that you can easily slip its tongue into groove of adjacent panel. Push the plank flush to furring strips, with its remaining groove edge resting on the tongue of the next plank.

6. Lightly hammer cloth-buffered block on replacement plank, moving the block from place to place, to ensure a snug fit. Drive a color-matched paneling nail through plank's top and another through bottom, fastening them to furring strips.

Interiors/Panel repairs

Securing a loose panel

1. Position padded wood block on fastened panel near edge of loose panel. Insert pry bar's flat end under loose or bowed panel and pry area partly open, using block for leverage. Work carefully, prying up edge along entire loose section.

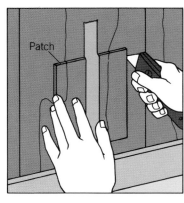

2. Keep pried area of panel wedged with wood scrap. Apply paneling adhesive in a generous bead on exposed substrate (furring strips, plaster, or wallboard). Keep area wedged open until adhesive is tacky (10 min.). Remove wedge; press panel against substrate.

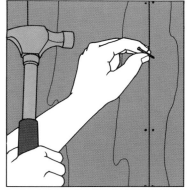

3. Hammer padded block on panel over glued area. Drive color-matched paneling nails into panel along glued edge at 5-in. intervals. Or use brads; then, with a nail set, sink them below panel surface. Fill holes with color-matched wood putty.

Patching a panel

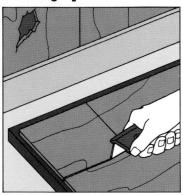

1. Choose panel scrap that matches damaged area's grain (and grooves, if any). Place it face up on scrap wood. With utility knife, cut out a patch that is slightly larger than hole; bear down harder and cut deeper with each successive stroke.

2. Center patch over damaged area, lining up any grooves with those in the panel. Using a strip of masking tape, fix patch to panel. With a sharp utility knife, score patch's outline on panel's surface. Untape patch.

3. Cut the panel carefully, following the outline of the patch. Cut deeper with each stroke. Pry damaged area loose with putty knife. If panel is glued to wall, add pressure to surrounding area while prying to avoid damage to sound part of panel.

4. If panel is glued to furring strips, make a framed support for patch. Cut four 1 x 3 strips to frame the perimeter of the hole. Glue strips with paneling adhesive to hole—half under panel, half exposed. Allow adhesive to dry—4 hr., or follow manufacturer's instructions.

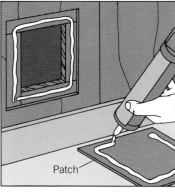

5. Apply paneling adhesive to back of patch, drawing a continuous bead near edges. Also apply adhesive to exposed surfaces of 1 x 3's. Allow glue to become tacky (10 min.) before placing patch.

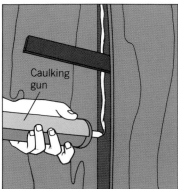

6. Carefully fix patch to 1 x 3 frame, aligning grain and grooves (if any). Drive paneling nails at 3-in. intervals around patch's edge. Sink nails with nail set; fill holes with color-matched wood putty. Or use paneling nails of the same color.

Ceiling tiles

Wood- or mineral-fiber ceiling tiles will conceal a damaged ceiling and help reduce noise. If the original ceiling is level and in good condition, the tiles can be glued in place. If not, install furring strips (shimming as needed to create a level surface), and staple the tiles to the strips.

Let the materials acclimatize in the room for at least 24 hours. For installing furring strips, have ready 1 x 3's, 8d nails (or 2½-inch wallboard screws), 1⅛-inch wallboard nails, a hammer (or a power screwdriver), a staple gun, and 9/16-inch staples, a utility knife, a chalk line, a level or straightedge, and a tape measure. The adhesive method requires cutting and measuring tools, a wide putty knife, and the adhesive recommended by the manufacturer. Always wear safety goggles, a dust mask, gloves, and long sleeves. Don't scratch an itch. When done, wash your work clothes thoroughly and shower well.

▶ **CAUTION:** Never tile a ceiling in which heating coils are imbedded.

Plan installation on graph paper; then check measurements against ceiling. Test corners for squareness; the one closest to 90° is the starting corner. Locate joists as you would studs (p.191). Measure ceiling in several places (it may be wider at one end). To calculate border width, add 12 in. to any leftover inches, then divide by 2. For example, a ceiling 10 ft. 6 in. long needs 9-in. borders (6 + 12 = 18 ÷ 2 = 9). Using original measurements, find the ceiling's true center. Mark border guidelines and adjust centerlines so that they fall at a seam. If tiles are flanged, shift centerlines an additional ½ in. away from starting corner. Snap chalk lines at this position. Recheck measurements before tiling.

					Border guide
1	4	5	9		
2	6	8	13		Furring strips perpendicular to joists
3	7	12		Strip	
10	11		Joist	90°	Centerline

1. Center first furring strip over centerline at right angle to joists. Screw or nail strip to joists. Work from center out, using spacer.

2. At border-tile distance from each wall, snap chalk lines along ceiling's length and width. These lines *must* parallel centerlines.

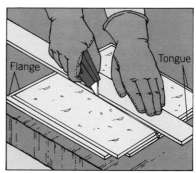

3. Cut border tiles to size, face up, using utility knife and straightedge. Leave long flanges intact. Cut off corner tile's tongue.

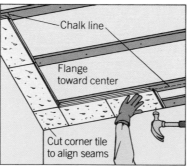

4. Line up border-tile flanges with chalk lines. Nail blunt ends; staple flanges. Install tiles in sequence shown at left.

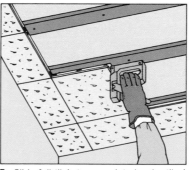

5. Slide full tile's tongues into border tiles' grooves. It should be snug but not forced. Staple through flange into furring strip.

Adhesive method. Prime tile's back with light coat of glue. Put golf-ball-size dabs of glue 2½ in. from edges. Press in place.

Replacing a damaged tile

1. Cut close to edges of damaged tile with utility knife; pry out remains of tile with putty knife. Scrape debris from furring strips, or old adhesive from base.

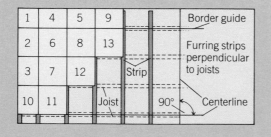

2. With utility knife, trim replacement tile to fit. If you are using adhesive, put four dabs on tile's back 2 to 2½ in. from edges.

3. Set tile in place. If gluing, press until level with other tiles. If over furring strips, drive 4d finishing nail into each corner of tile. Sink heads with nailset; fill with putty.

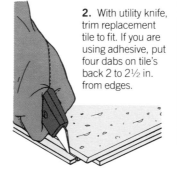

Ceiling panels offer the same advantages as tiles, but are "dropped" into an interlocking metal grid suspended from an existing ceiling or from the exposed joists of an unfinished one. Usually ½ to ¾ inch thick, the 2- x 2- or 2- x 4-foot panels come in wood fiber, mineral fiber, and fiberglass, and in many colors and patterns. They are easily removed for access to wiring, pipes, and ductwork.

Materials. The grid consists of 8- or 12-foot-long T-shaped main runners spanning the length of the room, perpendicular to the joists; 2- or 4-foot-long T-shaped crosspieces that snap into slots in the runners; and 10-foot-long wall angles. To calculate the number of panels needed, divide 4 square feet (for 2- x 2-foot panels) or 8 square feet (for 2- x 4-foot panels) into the ceiling's area (length × width); add 5 percent for error. You'll also need screw eyes and 18-gauge hanger wire (to hang the run-

ners), string, 6d nails, and metal snips (to cut grids).

Preparation. Let the panels acclimatize to the room for a day. Find the wall studs (p.191); mark their locations with a pencil at the height of the new ceiling (allow 3 inches between new and old ceilings; 6 inches if recessed fixtures are planned). If the joists aren't exposed, locate them also, and mark their locations with chalk lines. Draw the ceiling to scale on graph paper; lay out the grid on the plan (below).

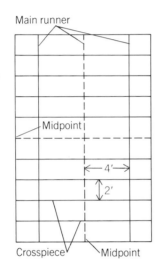

On ceiling plan, draw two lines linking midpoints of opposite walls. Begin plotting grid with main runner on longer midpoint line. Space other runners at 2- or 4-foot intervals, depending on panel size and on how you want to orient rectangular panels. Cut-to-fit border panels on opposite sides of room should be same size and as large as possible (preferably at least 24 in. for 4-ft. dimension; at least 12 in. for 2-ft. dimension.) If plan doesn't work, try again with a row of panels centered on midpoint line. Plot position of crosspieces in same way.

Main runner

Midpoint

←—4'—→

2'

Crosspiece   Midpoint

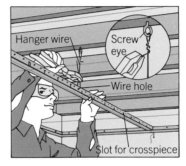

Guide string
Chalk line for main runners
Wall angle
Use framing square to make sure strings cross at 90° angle.

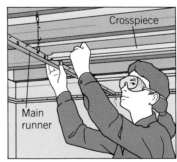

Hanger wire   Screw eye
Wire hole
Slot for crosspiece

4. Insert screw eyes into joists along chalk lines (usually one every fourth joist; check grid package directions). Run 1 ft. of hanger wire through each eye; wrap end around itself (insert). Run free wire end through round runner hole. Use strings as guides to adjust runner height. Wrap wire end.

Crosspiece
Main runner

5. If room is longer than 12 ft., cut additional runner sections to fit; snap interlocking runner ends together. (Make sure slots for crosspieces coincide with string crossings.) Using strings as guides, snap crosspieces into runner slots. Trim border crosspieces to fit.

Chalk line

1. Snap chalk line on walls all around room at desired height for new ceiling. Check line with carpenter's level to make sure it's level.

Wall angle   Chalk line

2. Place base of wall angles at chalk line. Nail them to studs. Cut adjoining pieces with snips so they meet at stud. Butt inside corners; miter outside ones.

3. Mark position of main runners by snapping chalk lines across ceiling or joists, perpendicular to joists. Stretch strings across room at ceiling height to mark locations of runners and crosspieces. (Tie strings to nails; wedge nails under wall angles.) Snip runners so that slots for crosspieces coincide with string crossings.

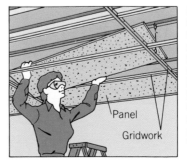

Panel
Gridwork

6. With grid in place, check for level; adjust wires if needed. Remove strings. Cut border panels to fit (p.289). Install border and full-size panels by rows. Tilt panel, insert through grid, straighten, and drop onto flanged edges of grid. If desired, add molding (p.99) where tiles meet walls.

Installing recessed lighting

Electrical tools, testing, and safety 242-243
Adding or extending a branch circuit 248-249
Wiring variations 252-253

A suspended ceiling makes it easy to install lighting fixtures wherever needed. By substituting translucent panels for standard ones, light from a fixture above the ceiling softly illuminates the room below. The panels are available in several styles, including "egg crate," whose small square openings diffuse light and allow ventilation. Plan the location of translucent panels when you lay out the ceiling grid.

Panel-size fluorescent fixtures (sold in kits with mounting equipment) are installed over the main runners of a suspended ceiling grid. Incandescent fixtures measuring 12 x 12 inches are often used in place of a tile in a tile ceiling (p.289); the fixture is attached to the furring strips that support the tiles. Such fixtures can also be set in 12-inch-square holes cut into the panels of a suspended ceiling. Some models come with outriggers—metal supports that carry the fixture's weight to the ceiling grid. If a fixture doesn't have outriggers, fasten it to 1 x 2 furring strips that extend to the gridwork.

▶ **CAUTION:** Make sure that the fixture you buy for a wood-fiber panel ceiling is safe; heat from an inappropriate fixture could cause a fire. UL-listed fixtures are marked "Suitable for surface mounting on low-density cellulose fiberboard." When you buy bulbs, make sure the wattage doesn't exceed the fixture manufacturer's recommendation.

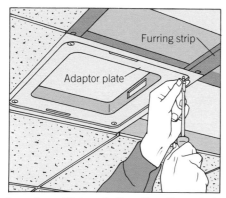

Incandescent fixture. 1. For a tile ceiling, select a fixture measuring 12 x 12 in.—the same size as a tile. Screw fixture's adapter plate to the furring strips that support the tiles.

2. Install fixture junction box and socket on adapter plate. With power off (p.237), run a switch-controlled circuit extension from nearby electrical box to fixture. Connect cable to fixture (p.254).

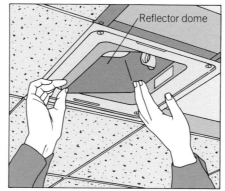

3. Fit hole of reflector dome over socket; then snap dome into place. (Dome's polished surface serves to amplify light.) With a soft cloth, wipe dome's surface free of fingerprints.

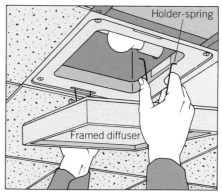

4. Screw in a light bulb. Slip holder springs of framed diffuser into slots in adapter plate. Once in place, fixture frame will project several inches below ceiling.

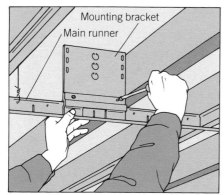

Fluorescent fixture. 1. To install fixture over a suspended ceiling, position mounting brackets on midpoint of upright leg of opposing main runners. Screw bracket sections together.

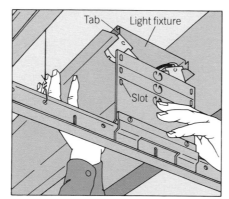

2. Attach fixture to mounting brackets by sliding the two tabs at each end of fixture through matching slots of opposing brackets.

3. Shut off power (p.237). Run a switch-controlled circuit extension to fixture. Wire the fixture and install fluorescent tubes (pp.256–257). Install reflector panels over fixture top.

4. Remove panel next to fixture space. Through this space, slide translucent panel into place below fixture. Replace adjoining panel.

Correctly installed baseboards and moldings hide gaps caused by settling, seams, and flaws. Well-chosen trim sets a style for your room.

Moldings may be of carved wood or shaped polystyrene. To calculate how much to buy, measure the room's perimeter and round all figures upward (see diagram). Buy in long lengths to avoid splicing and to reduce waste. If wood trim will be given a natural finish (pp. 118–124), try to match the grain patterns. Whenever possible, use the

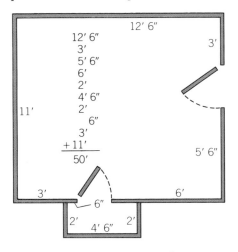

same piece to wrap around corners so that the grain pattern continues through the joint. If you must splice, select pieces with similar grain and color. Scarf the joint (p. 111) so that the splice will be less noticeable.

Molding is tricky to fit and join. Practice on scrap until you get the feel of it. Begin installations by fitting the outside miters (p. 109). Then fit the inside corners and cope the joints (right). Last, if the trim will abut a door frame, cut butt joints (p. 100) where they meet.

From ceiling to floor, different kinds of trim are used for crown molding, picture rail, chair rail, wainscoting, baseboard, and shoe molding. You can re-create the classic elegance of a Federal room or the sleek geometry of Art Deco by combining appropriate molding profiles (p.99). Baseboards (below) are attached with finishing nails driven into the wall studs and soleplate. Decorative and practical, baseboards cover gaps between the floor and the walls.

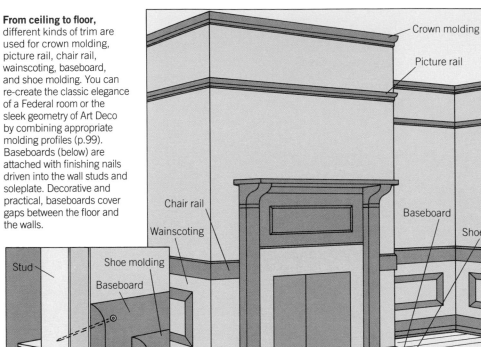

Crown molding
Picture rail
Chair rail
Wainscoting
Baseboard
Shoe molding
Stud
Shoe molding
Baseboard
Soleplate

Crown molding
Crown molding
Base cap
Cove molding
S4S

Crown molding, or *cornice,* was traditionally built up of several different pieces to form a single intricate profile, then cut to fit around the room. It often required an extra nailing plate for adequate support (*above*). The advent of plastics has simplified this process. Preformed and lightweight, polystyrene moldings are easy to cut and install and can be painted. Some systems come with formed corner blocks, eliminating the need for miter cuts. Fill seams with paintable caulk.

Coping a joint
When moldings meet at an inside corner, cut one piece so that it overlaps the adjacent piece and its profile follows the contours of the latter. This is known as *coping the joint.* A coped joint resists separating better than a mitered joint and, because the pieces overlap, irregularities are concealed. Always miter outside corners.

1. With a sharp pencil, carefully trace the molding's contours onto the face of the overlapping piece.

2. Clamp molding securely. Trim waste with coping saw (p.26). A saber saw (p.57) is faster but less flexible.

3. Test-fit coped edge against identical scrap. With file or fine-tooth rasp, adjust shape and undercut (bevel) back.

Installing a baseboard

1. Cut baseboard to approximate lengths and place them in position around the room. Plan the cutting so that splices will fall in inconspicuous areas. If the floor is very uneven, hold baseboard in place and trace floor's contour onto baseboard with a compass (p.49). Trim with saber saw.

2. Fit outside corners first, marking miters carefully. Lines drawn on the floor to extend the lines of the wall will help you align cut. To ensure accuracy, clamp baseboard in a steel miter box and make the cut with a backsaw (p.25).

3. Attach baseboard with pairs of 6d finishing nails. Drive top nail into a wall stud, bottom nail into the soleplate (facing page). If you find working this close to the floor awkward, predrill the nail holes with a bit slightly smaller than the nails. Countersink nailheads with a nail set (p.23).

4. On an inside corner, one piece is cut square to butt flush against the wall. Cope the adjacent piece (facing page) to follow contours of first piece. Refine and undercut coped joint with a four-in-hand rasp (p.43) for a gapless fit.

5. At doorways, mark cut with opposite coped end tightly in place. Make the baseboard slightly (1/16 in.) longer to allow for any fitting and adjustment.

6. Bow baseboard slightly between door frame and adjacent wall, and release. Slightly oversize board forces coped joint tight against adjacent piece. Nail in place. Mark and cut shoe molding following same procedure. Secure molding with brads long enough to anchor in soleplate.

Removing baseboards

If you want to install an electrical outlet, locate wall studs, or replace a damaged baseboard, you may have to remove the baseboard in a way that preserves it for reinstallation or for use as a template.

A baseboard may have three elements: a shoe molding, the main board, and a shaped top strip. Each can be removed by prying, but if they were pieced to cover a long expanse, the joints may be in different places.

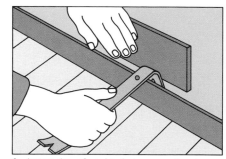

1. Insert claw of pry bar between wall and baseboard. With scrap pad behind bar, pry gently outward, using wall stud for support.

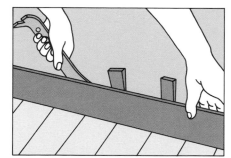

2. Continue prying, inserting wedges as you are able to, until baseboard is loose enough to pull away from wall.

3. Mark replacement baseboard, using old one as a template. Cut to length, scarfing joint (p.111) for an invisible seam. Nail in place.

293

If any part of your house is customized, it will be the staircase. Usually the last structure installed, a staircase is built (or adjusted, if bought ready-made) to fit the finished space. At its simplest, a staircase is composed of two *stringers* that support horizontal *treads* and vertical *risers*. Together, a tread and a riser make a *step*. Although this structure has many variations, there are two basic methods of construction: In an *open-stringer* staircase the upper edge of each stringer is cut in a sawtooth pattern. The treads and risers rest on the tops and against the edges of the "teeth." In a *closed-stringer* staircase the top and bottom edges of the stringers are straight and parallel. Grooves are cut into the stringers' faces, and the treads and risers are inserted into them.

A staircase may have one open and one closed stringer: The steps may be fixed to a closed stringer on the wall side and on the other side rest on the edges of an open stringer. If the staircase is very wide, one or more strong boards called *carriages* may run beneath the steps to support the treads.

If one side of a staircase is open, repairs can be made from either above or below the steps. If both sides are closed, and repairs have to be done from underneath the stairs, you will need to break through—and replace—the sheathing or remove and replace enough steps to allow access to the structure. If your house is old, the staircase may have been modified by repairs. Proceed cautiously when dismantling steps; they might not be installed identically. Fortunately, structural repairs are rarely needed; eliminating squeaks is more common.

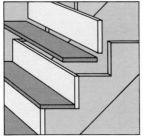

Open-stringer staircase.

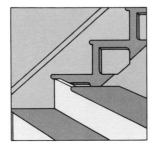

Closed-stringer staircase.

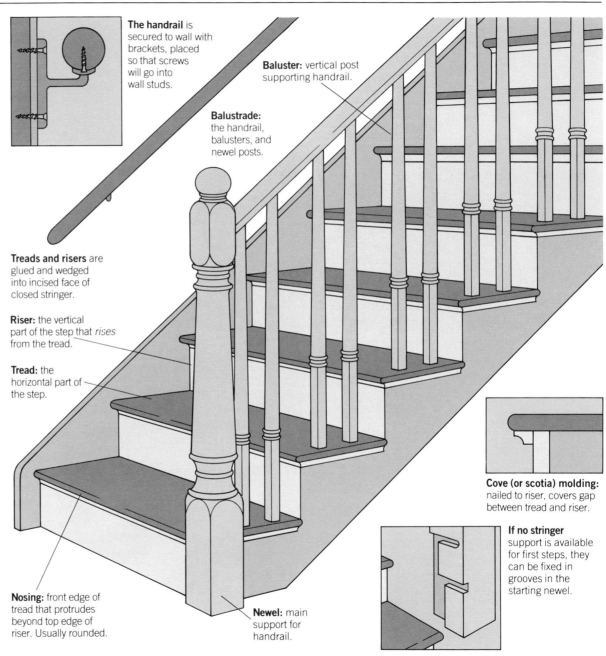

The handrail is secured to wall with brackets, placed so that screws will go into wall studs.

Baluster: vertical post supporting handrail.

Balustrade: the handrail, balusters, and newel posts.

Treads and risers are glued and wedged into incised face of closed stringer.

Riser: the vertical part of the step that *rises* from the tread.

Tread: the horizontal part of the step.

Cove (or scotia) molding: nailed to riser, covers gap between tread and riser.

If no stringer support is available for first steps, they can be fixed in grooves in the starting newel.

Nosing: front edge of tread that protrudes beyond top edge of riser. Usually rounded.

Newel: main support for handrail.

Eliminating squeaks

Most squeaks are caused by loosened parts rubbing together. Isolate the source of the noise by walking on the offending stair. The easiest parts to tighten are the treads, risers, stringers, and moldings. Structural elements, including the nails and glue that hold the staircase together and the wedges that fill the joint between the tread and the riser, should be checked and tightened or, if necessary, replaced. Precut wedges can be purchased at a lumberyard.

Wedges can easily be made from scrap wood (p.105) or leftover wood siding and shingles.

A dry lubricant such as powdered graphite can silence or considerably muffle some squeaks. It won't, however, afford a permanent cure. Once you have determined the source of the noise, apply one of the techniques detailed below to eliminate it. If the repair can be made on the underside of the staircase, it will also be invisible.

Tightening loose balusters

Sometimes the settling of the house causes a staircase to sag or twist, loosening the balusters. This can easily be repaired with glue and wedges. Schedule this project for late evening when the staircase won't be used, so that the glue can set overnight.

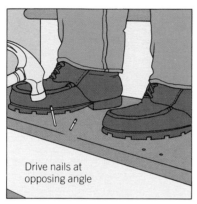

Locate squeak by having someone walk on tread. If the squeak comes from front edge of tread, drive finishing nails through tread into riser. Sink nailheads with nail set.

Drive nails at opposing angle

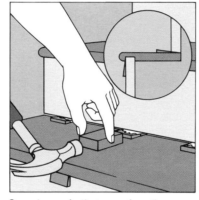

Correct squeaks that come from the rear of a tread by inserting thin glue-coated wood wedges between tread and riser. (Wedge will parallel step's joints.)

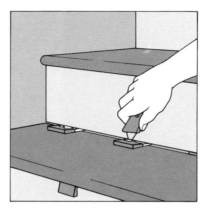

Trim wedges with a sharp utility knife so that they are flush with riser. Install quarter round or ½-in. cove molding to conceal resulting gap.

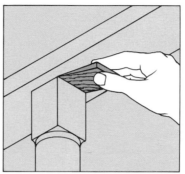

1. Cut a strip of wood with the grain running the length of the strip. Make it slightly thicker than the widest gap between the top of a baluster and the handrail. Cut the strip into shims, and sand or plane them to form wedges.

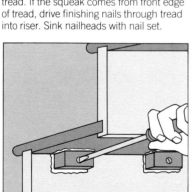

Glue and screw wooden blocks under step to silence squeaks that come from the front of a tread and the top of riser.

Metal shelf brackets fastened to underside of tread and back of riser will halt general creaking.

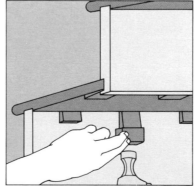

Tighten existing wedges to stabilize treads and risers. Install additional ones if extra support is needed.

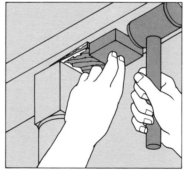

2. Coat wedge with glue and insert it at the top of a baluster. Tap it into position, using a mallet and a block of scrap wood. When glue is dry, trim wedge flush with baluster.

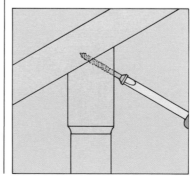

Another method is to drill a countersunk hole (p.53) at an angle through the baluster and into the handrail. Drive a screw through the hole, drawing the rail and baluster together.

Interiors/Repairing a balustrade

A balustrade is a series of vertical posts (*balusters*) that support a handrail. Baluster bottoms are shaped into dowels or dovetails to seat securely in the treads. If the balusters are to be set in the stringer, their square bottoms are cut to match the stringer's slope; thin wooden strips (*fillets*) are nailed between the balusters to secure them.

The first post in the balustrade is the *newel post*. Larger than the balusters, the newel is structural as well as decorative: it anchors the balustrade.

Despite the variety of pieces in a balustrade, it is a simple—and usually stable—structure. The most common problem is loose or broken balusters. A loose baluster can be repaired by driving a wedge between it and the tread or handrail. Replace any broken ones. Balusters can be bought at home centers or lumberyards.

Tightening wobbly newel posts

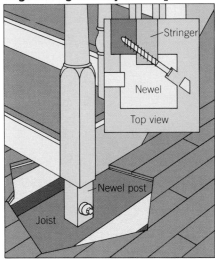

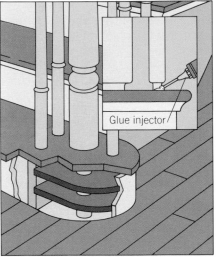

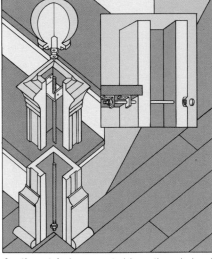

Some newels have a dowel or plank that pierces the floor and is bolted to a joist. To repair, tighten bolt. If still shaky, drill hole through base of newel into stringer, install lag screw. Cap hole with dowel.

To tighten newel set in bullnose tread, pry newel and balusters up slightly, inject glue around bases, then replace. For added strength, drive finishing nails on an angle through balusters into tread.

Another style is supported by a threaded rod. The rod may be upright in the newel's center or may pass through the base and under the first tread. To tighten the newel, tighten the rod.

Replacing balusters

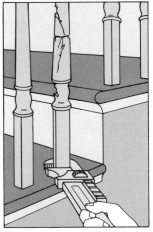

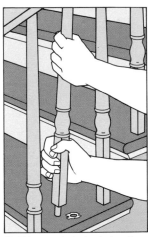

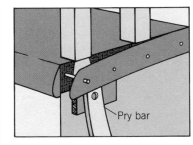

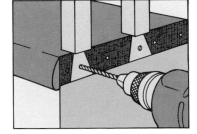

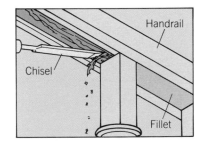

1. To remove a doweled baluster, saw it in half. Twist sharply with pipe wrench to break glue bond. Or saw flush, then bore out waste.

2. Trim new baluster to length. Put glue in tread hole. Insert top into handrail, then scoot bottom across tread and pop into hole.

1. To remove a dovetailed baluster: Carefully pry off end trim. Avoid cracking the trim so that you can reuse it after new baluster has been installed. Saw baluster flush with tread. Chisel waste from socket.

2. Cut new baluster to length. Put top in handrail, bottom in tread's socket. Tap into place with block and hammer. Drill pilot hole through dovetail into tread. Drive nail. Replace trim, and sink the nailheads (p.23).

1. On a closed staircase, baluster is *filleted* into handrail and stringer. To replace baluster, chisel out fillet behind the baluster. Tap baluster loose from nails and take it out. Clean old glue from the groove.

2. Mark angles on new baluster with T-bevel (or copy from old one). Cut to fit. Set baluster against the existing fillet; toenail in place. Cut new fillet. Glue and nail it to handrail behind the new baluster.

Replacing treads and risers

When replacing a worn or damaged tread, try to remove it without altering the shape too much. Sometimes you can simply turn the tread over. If it is too battered, use the old tread as a template for cutting a new one. Treads with precut nosings can be bought at lumberyards.

The steps may separate from the stringer as your house settles. If the gap is less than ½ inch, drive wedges between the wall and the stringer. Trim the wedges flush with the stringer and cover them with molding. If the gap is greater than ½ inch, get professional advice before attempting a repair. Don't try wedging; you could split the stringer. You may simply need to install wider steps. On the other hand, a structural problem not directly related to the staircase may be causing the gap.

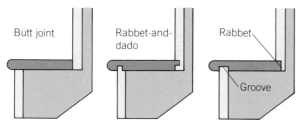

Butt joint   Rabbet-and-dado   Rabbet   Groove

Steps can be assembled with a variety of joints.

Replacing a tread

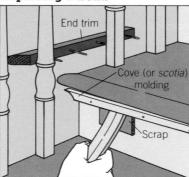

End trim

Cove (or *scotia*) molding

Scrap

1. With small pry bar, carefully remove end trim and cove molding from beneath nosing. Place thin piece of scrap wood under pry bar to avoid marring the riser.

2. Remove balusters (facing page). Pry up old tread until nail-heads protrude. Remove nails with claw hammer. If tread is jointed to riser, you may need to saw through joint to release tread.

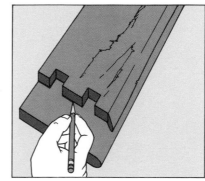

3. Trace outline of old tread onto new, and cut it. Make cutouts for the balusters, if needed. If bottom of old tread is in good condition, try reinstalling it upside down rather than replacing it.

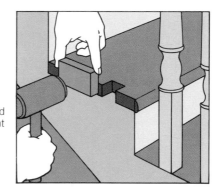

4. Tap new tread into place with a block and hammer or mallet. Test-fit balusters and end trim. If necessary, shave balusters with rasp. Replace balusters, end trim, and cove molding.

Replacing a riser

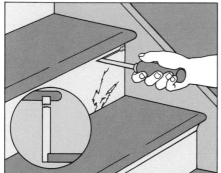

1. Remove end trim, balusters, and molding (see step 1, above). To separate a jointed riser from tread, drill overlapping holes below upper tread, insert keyhole saw, and cut. Pull tread out.

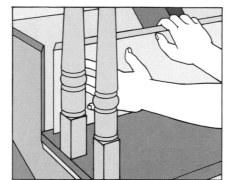

2. Cut new riser. Position it against stringers. If riser edge is mitered against an open stringer, check that joint aligns. Rasp or plane as needed for smooth fit.

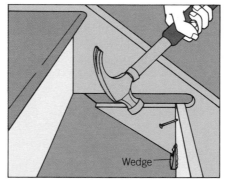

Wedge

3. On the side with closed stringer, first glue in a wedge, then the riser. (Buy ready-made stair wedges when you get other repair materials.) Drive nails at an angle through riser into stringer.

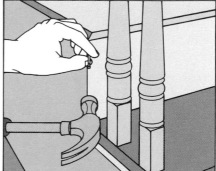

4. Glue and nail the mitered joint on the outer corner. Wipe off excess glue, and sink nails below the surface with a nail set (p.23). Replace tread, balusters, end trim, and molding.

In a closed-stringer staircase, the steps are inserted into grooves cut into the side supports (the *stringers*). Wedges in the stringer grooves beneath and behind the treads and risers provide additional support. With this arrangement, you need to get under the staircase to make repairs effectively. There are two ways to do this: You can either remove one or more steps and come in from the top, or if you have access to the bottom, you can break through the surfacing material to expose the underpinning.

The bottom of a staircase may be surfaced with lath and plaster, hardboard, or wallboard. Remove just enough to allow you to do the repair—a strip equal to the height of the damaged step plus an inch or two should be enough. If the covering is wallboard or hardboard, drill four corner holes and cut out a small panel. Use a cold chisel to remove plaster; repair the plaster with a wallboard panel. If you are replacing steps, buy ready-made treads and wedges at a lumberyard.

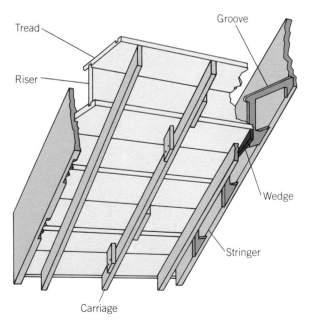

Tread

Groove

Riser

Wedge

Stringer

Carriage

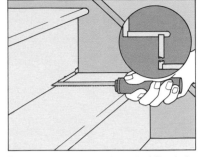

1. If treads and risers have been wedged into stringer, chip out the wedges with a wood chisel and mallet. Work carefully; avoid gouging the stringer.

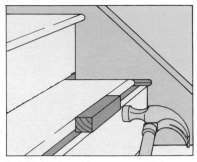

2. To remove a jointed tread, drill a hole through the riser. Insert a keyhole saw and cut the joint completely across the step. If tread is not jointed, remove nails or screws.

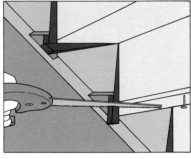

3. With block and hammer or mallet, carefully tap the loosened tread back under the trimmed riser. Pull tread free from underneath the stairs.

4. Use old tread as a template, or measure from groove to groove and cut new tread to that length. If working from below, slide tread into position. If above, skip to step 8.

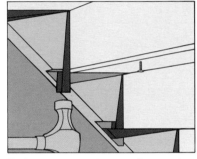

5. Coat a wedge with glue. From underneath the stairs, drive it up behind the riser with a hammer. If wedge doesn't seat tightly, use a thicker one or add a shim.

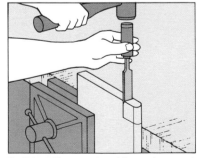

6. Chisel or saw off any part of the wedge that projects below the tread. Repeat steps 5 and 6, adding wedge below tread. Trim wedge flush with edge of stringer.

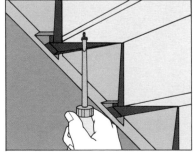

7. For additional support, fasten tread to riser with screws. Drill pilot holes through tread up into riser. Position them evenly along length of tread, 6 to 8 in. apart.

8. If installing new tread from above, cut notch in nosing. The notch should be as deep as the riser is thick so that the tread will fit under riser. Keep the cut-off piece.

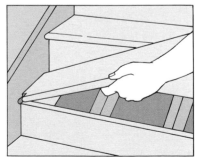

9. Slide notched end of tread into the stringer. Pull tread forward to clear riser, and drop into position. Slide tread under riser, restore notch, and nail in place.

Wood floors

Handsome and resilient, wood is an excellent flooring material. It is available either solid or laminated, in strips, planks, or tiles. Wood flooring is generally cut from hardwood, with oak the most common species. Solid strip flooring (up to 3¼ inches wide) and tiles have precut tongue-and-groove joints. Solid plank flooring, which is sometimes available in softwood, ranges to about 9 inches. Most types can be bought either prefinished or unfinished.

Laminated wood flooring comes in two forms: ⅛-inch-thick hardwood veneered to a solid pine

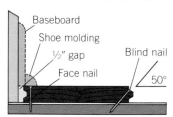

Baseboard
Shoe molding
½" gap
Face nail
Blind nail
50°

core or several thin hardwood strips glued together (similar to plywood). As with solid wood flooring, laminates are available in a variety of designs and finishes and as strips or tiles. Laminated floors are installed with adhesive and can be laid over any type of subfloor (including clean, dry concrete).

Types of flooring

Material	Forms	Advantages	Disadvantages	See pp.
Wood	Solid, laminate	Easy care, resilient	Not water-resistant	300–307
Vinyl	Sheet, tile	Inexpensive, easy to install	Subject to tearing, wear, damage	308–311
Ceramic	Glazed, unglazed	Easy care, very durable	Non-resilient; grout discolors	312–315

Installing an underlayment

Any floor needs a stable, sturdy, clean, flat base to support its weight. (It is preferable that the floor also be level but essential only for ceramic tile.) A floor's base is often composed of two layers: a *subfloor* of planks or plywood installed over the joists and an *underlayment* of plywood or hardboard above it. The subfloor may run parallel to, perpendicular to, or diagonally across the joists. If the subfloor is free of defects and at least ¾ inch thick, you need only nail down any loose or squeaky areas and clean it before laying the final flooring.

An underlayment should be added if the subfloor isn't thick enough or smooth enough for the final floor. A good underlayment helps prevent squeaks

and cracked finishes on wood floors and uneven wear on vinyl floors. For most wood and vinyl floors, a base of ⅛- to ¼-inch-thick plywood is adequate. Ceramic and other heavy tiles need a thicker base to support their weight and to prevent flexing (which can cause the tiles or the joints to crack). For these floors a combined subfloor and underlayment thickness of at least 1⅛ inches is recommended. Cement board is the best underlayment for ceramics (pp.312–313). Hardboard and plywood aren't sufficiently rigid or moisture-resistant.

If the new floor is higher than the adjoining one, add a threshold or molding to finish the edge. Trim the door so that it swings freely over the new floor.

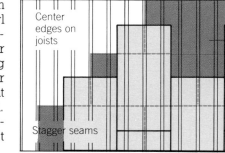

Center edges on joists

Stagger seams

Floor joists

Subfloor

Under-layment

1. Lay subfloor over joists, covering entire area. Stagger seams. Leave a ¹⁄₃₂-in. expansion gap around each 4 x 8 panel; ½-in. at wall. Fasten with panel adhesive and 8d coated box nails. Install underlayment perpendicular to subfloor, using same procedure.

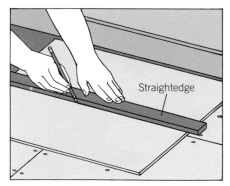

2. To fit border piece, place it atop previously installed panel, then push it to within ½ in. of wall. Place straightedge on top panel, align it with edge of lower panel, and mark cutting line.

Straightedge

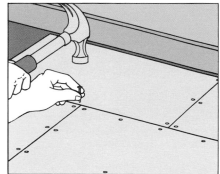

3. Cut off overlap and test-fit, remembering to stagger seams. Apply adhesive to subfloor and fasten with 8d nails. Drive nailheads just below surface. Repeat until border is complete.

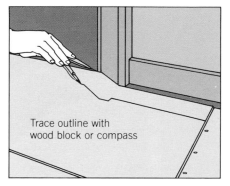

Trace outline with wood block or compass

4. To fit underlayment around door trim or other protrusion, transcribe rough outline onto plywood (Final floor will be cut to fit trim shapes exactly.) Cut with saber saw or coping saw.

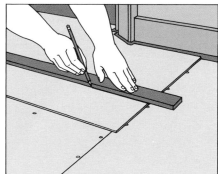

5. Place panel in position against trim; then pull it back ½ in. from wall for expansion gap. Draw line where panels overlap, and cut. Apply adhesive and secure with nails.

Interiors/Solid wood floors

Proper handling of solid wood flooring in the interval between delivery and installation is essential. Wood is susceptible to damage if stored in damp conditions. Put the flooring in a well-ventilated area and protect it from moisture. In dry weather, let the floor-ing acclimate to the room for at least 4 days so that residual dampness can evaporate. If it's humid, wait for drier weather before installing the flooring. Moisture absorbed from the air makes the wood swell: If the boards are installed while damp, they will shrink as the water evaporates, leaving gaps between them. (*Note:* Some boards will be distorted, even with conscientious attention to storage.)

The flooring should parallel the room's long dimension. Allow an expansion gap around the

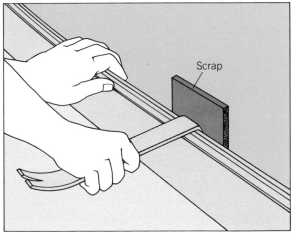

1. Remove shoe molding and baseboard with pry bar. Avoid damage by prying against scrap pad. Preserve these materials for reinstallation.

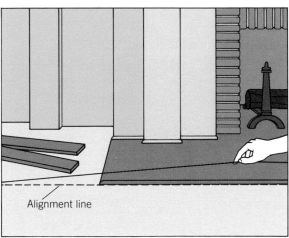

2. Begin installation by fitting irregular areas, such as door frames or hearth. When fitting around a hearth, snap a chalk line to extend straight lines and ensure alignment.

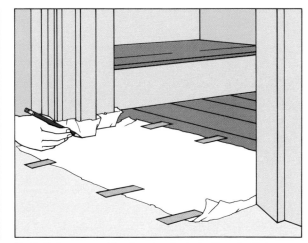

3. To fit doorway, cut flooring close to desired length. Make paper template of trim outline (or use contour gauge, p.49). Transcribe shape onto boards; cut with saber saw or coping saw.

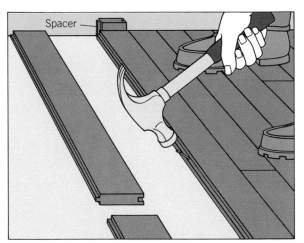

7. Blind-nail subsequent courses through tongue at 45° angle into subflooring (see p. 299). Drive nails every 10 to 12 in. for strip flooring, every 6 to 8 in. for plank flooring.

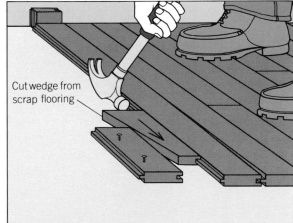

8. Force warped board into position by driving wedge between it and a piece of scrap nailed to subfloor. Slightly warped boards can be positioned by levering against scrap block with pry bar.

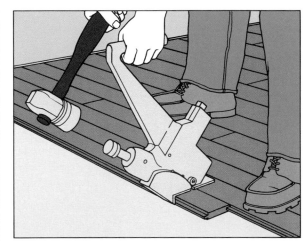

9. If using a power nailer: each mallet blow pulls floorboards together and drives nail at correct angle. Load nails in tool according to manufacturer's instructions.

room's perimeter equal to the wood's thickness; it will be hidden under the baseboard. Do a trial layout to determine the best arrangement of the floorboards. Scatter end-to-end joints evenly over the floor, avoiding clusters of short boards.

Cover the underlayment (p.299) with 15-pound asphalt-saturated felt. Overlap the felt 3 inches at the seams. Start installing the boards where they are hard to fit, such as around a door, and work toward the areas where they will just drop into place.

Rent a power nailer—which comes with appropriate nails—to speed installation. If you prefer to use a hand hammer, use 7d screw-type nails to reduce splitting. Set the heads flush with the tongue to let the groove slide easily into place.

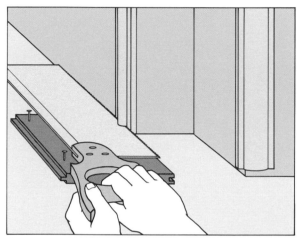

4. Another method of fitting in doorway is to cut trim so that flooring will slip underneath it. Rest blade of backsaw on piece of scrap flooring and cut through molding.

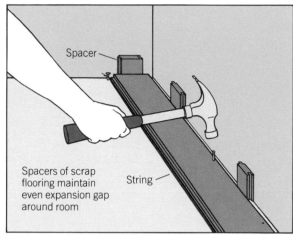

5. Snap chalk line (p.46) or stretch string across room to align first course of floorboards. Place straightest board with groove toward wall. Nail through face close to wall; work from middle to each end.

6. Use hammer to drive each subsequent course tight against previous course. Protect tongue by hammering against piece of scrap flooring.

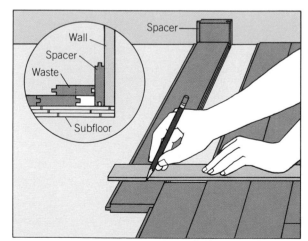

10. To fit floorboard at course's end, overlap final piece to mark length; then trim it to fit. If the final space is too narrow to accommodate board, rip board lengthwise (tongue side is waste).

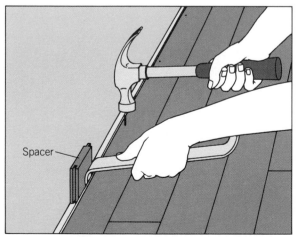

11. Because last course can't be blind-nailed, pull it tight with pry bar and nail through face close to edge near wall. Drive nailheads flush. Replace baseboard and molding.

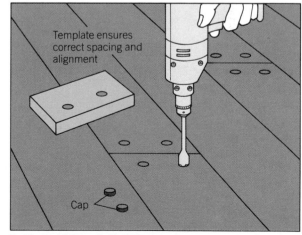

End-to-end joints of plank floors are glued to plywood subfloor with construction adhesive. For antique pegged look, drill holes with spade bit and insert caps cut from dowels.

Interiors / Laminated floors

Baseboards and moldings 292–293
Wood floors 299
Solid wood floors 300–301

This flooring material, made of thin layers of wood glued together and shaped into tongue-and-groove panels, may be applied directly to any level subfloor. Installation is a simple matter: spread the adhesive recommended by the manufacturer and press the panels into it. For best results when gluing a laminated floor over an existing solid wood floor, orient the new panels at 45° or 90° to the seams of the old floor.

Begin the installation with the areas that are the most difficult to fit. Lay out and cut any irregular pieces, such as for a hearth or doorway (p.300). Saw long pieces into random lengths so that the end-to-end joints don't fall next to one another.

1. Fit irregular areas (p.300), then set guideline. Pressing trowel's notched edge against floor, spread adhesive to line. (Notches regulate adhesive depth, so that it won't ooze at joints.)

2. Lay flooring in long runs, staggering the end joints. Install boards with a light sliding motion. Push grooves tightly over tongues. Leave ½-in. expansion gap around room perimeter.

3. Press flooring into adhesive either with rented 100-lb. roller, by leaning hard on a rolling pin, or by walking over entire surface. Put heavy objects on any spots that don't adhere.

Installing a floating floor

These laminated panels are installed (*floated*) over a ⅛-inch-thick high-density foam underlayment. Glue is applied to the tongue-and-groove joints between panels, and no nails are required. The foam, which comes with the flooring, absorbs small irregularities in the subfloor. It also provides some insulation, making it ideal for installing over concrete. In this case, put a 6-mil polyethylene vapor retarder under the foam (facing page).

Fit the flooring following the steps on pages 300–301. The finished floor will expand and contract as the temperature and humidity change. Leave a ½-inch gap around the edge of the room to accommodate this movement. Cover the gap with molding. Stagger the end joints, as described above.

1. Allow materials to come to room temperature. Unroll underlayment. With utility knife, trim to fit snugly against walls and around doorways. Seal seams with duct tape (p.90).

2. Mark off expansion gap between flooring panel and wall with spacers made from scrap flooring placed every 18 in. Install first panel with groove facing wall.

3. Work in room-length runs whenever possible. Glue each panel to previous one with yellow carpenter's glue. Drizzle a thin bead of glue onto bottom surface only of groove.

4. With hammer or mallet, tap tongue and groove tightly together along entire seam. Hammer against a piece of scrap flooring to avoid marring the tongue.

Wood floor over concrete

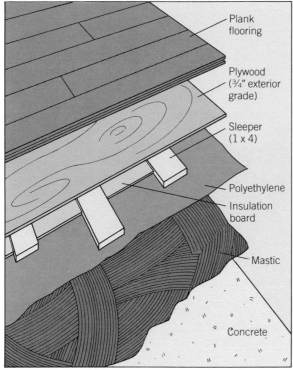

Diagram shows sequence of materials installed over slab.

Plank flooring

Plywood (¾" exterior grade)

Sleeper (1 x 4)

Polyethylene

Insulation board

Mastic

Concrete

Before you begin installing a wood floor, test the concrete for dryness by taping an 18-inch-square piece of polyethylene film to the slab. Test several places on the floor. If, after 24 to 48 hours, there is no moisture under the film, the slab is sufficiently dry.

Solid wood flooring and laminated panels each have specific support requirements. Strips need dry random-length 1 x 4's (*sleepers*). Planks need sleepers and an underlayment of ¾-inch-thick exterior-grade plywood. Laminates can go directly on the concrete or over an underlayment.

Fill cracks and pits with cement-base self-leveling compound before laying the flooring. Prepare the old floor according to directions; then mix and pour compound over the entire surface. (Although called self-leveling, most will need some screeding.) Fast-setting compounds set in 24 hours; delayed-set compounds need up to 2 weeks.

1. Level concrete with cement-base self-leveling compound. When thoroughly dry, spread asphalt mastic over entire surface with fine-tooth trowel. Let dry about 2 hr.

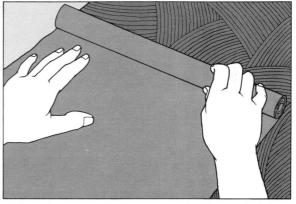

2. To make a vapor retarder, press sheets of 6-mil polyethylene into mastic. Overlap edges 4 to 6 in. and seal with contractor's sheathing tape. Puncture bubbles with pin to release trapped air.

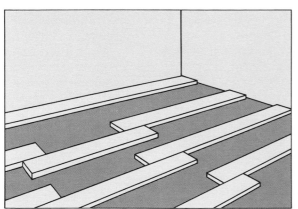

3. Cut sleepers 18 to 48 in. long; longer ones will twist, causing sags in floor. Place sleepers so that centers of boards are 12 in. apart, and lap ends at least 4 in. Secure with masonry nails.

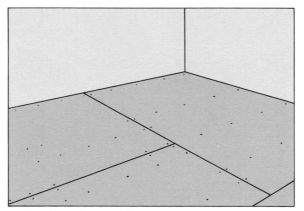

4. Rigid insulation board (extruded polystyrene) can be placed between sleepers for added insulation and moisture protection. Nail plywood underlayment (p.299) to sleepers.

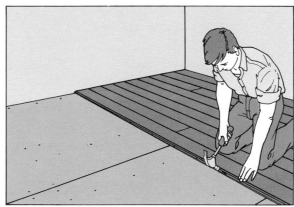

5. Install flooring over underlayment as directed in relevant pages of this book, or follow the flooring manufacturer's recommendations.

If a floorboard has a large split or an irreparable flaw, you will have to replace the damaged section with new flooring. The new piece should be the same type of wood as the rest of the floor and should blend with the surrounding boards' grain pattern and color as closely as possible. If you bring the new board from a damp area—such as a basement—let it dry for a week or two before installing it. Otherwise, it will shrink and leave an unsightly gap. In any case it's a good idea to let the replacement board acclimatize overnight in the room before installing it.

You can save yourself the work of replacing a split floorboard by repairing the damage as soon as it becomes visible. The longer you wait, the worse it will get and the harder it will be to conceal. When you repair or replace a floorboard, cover the nailheads with wood putty. Putty comes in wood tones and can be tinted with Japan colors (p.119). It won't absorb stain once it's dry, so tint it before applying it.

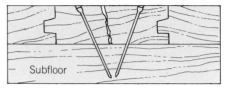

To repair a small split in a floorboard, drill angled pilot holes every 1–2 in. along both sides of split and just past its ends. Drive nails; sink heads. Fill holes and the split with wood putty.

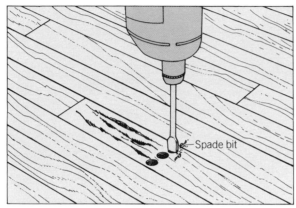

1. To replace a damaged floorboard, bore several large holes across it with a spade bit. Avoid drilling through subfloor. If flooring rests directly on joists, drill over joist for support.

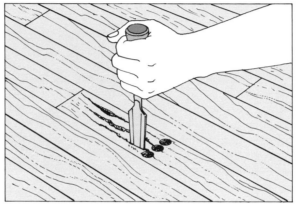

2. Split board down the middle with a wide butt chisel, or chisel along board's edge to cut tongue. Remove damaged section with pry bar. Square off ragged edges of holes.

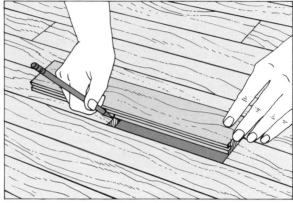

3. Measure opening carefully and cut replacement board slightly ($1/32$ in.) longer. Test new piece against opening before installing it. Plane or rasp board's end for a snug fit.

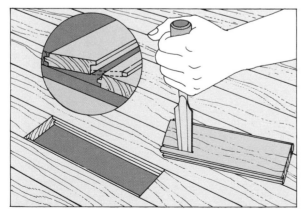

4. Turn replacement board over. If necessary, chisel off lower groove edge so that the new board can drop into place over tongue of adjoining board.

5. Coat both sides of new joint with yellow carpenter's glue. Insert new board; pound it flush with adjoining boards with a mallet and wood block.

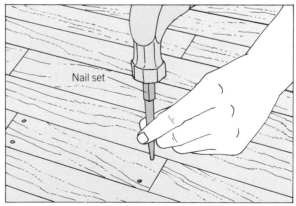

6. Drill pilot holes for finishing nails at each end of board and along the sides; make holes slightly smaller than nail size. Sink nailheads (p.23). Stain and finish to blend with other floorboards.

Eliminating squeaks and sags

The first step in stifling a squeak is to pinpoint its origin. A floor generally consists of three layers: the joists, the subfloor, and the floor. Squeaks occur where the layers separate and rub together when you walk on them.

A sprinkling of powdered graphite or talcum powder between the floorboards may silence a squeak temporarily. For a permanent cure you will need to tighten the parts that are rubbing. If the main floor is squeaking and you have access to the joists from the basement, you may be able to solve the problem by repairing or adding bridging (1 x 4 lumber or preformed steel), support blocks, or shims. If the floor has buckled, you can draw it and the subfloor back together with wood screws.

When the flooring is inaccessible from below, you must make repairs from its finished side. If the floor is warped, secure the high points of the curve by driving nails or screws through the floorboards and 1½ inches into the joists. Cover the fasteners' heads with color-matched wood putty.

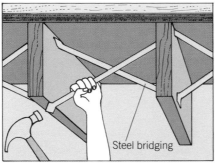

Install steel bridging by hammering pronged end into one joist, L-shaped end into adjacent one. Set bridging at opposing angles to form X's.

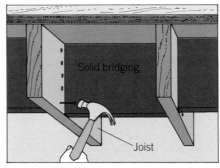

Make solid bridging from lumber of the same dimensions as joists. Place it a maximum of 6 ft. apart; stagger pieces to permit end nailing.

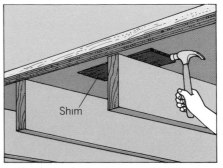

Tap lightly glued shims between joist and subfloor under squeak. Be sure wedging doesn't raise floorboards.

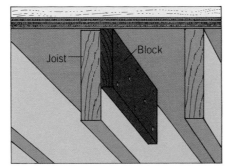

If joist has warped, push 2 x 6 block against subfloor; nail it to joist. If necessary, gently lift floor with house jack so that block is set properly.

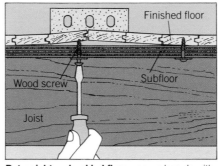

Put weight on buckled floor; secure boards with wood screw that penetrates halfway into flooring. Drill pilot hole; put washer under screwhead.

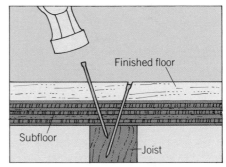

To repair floor from above, drill angled pilot holes. Drive galvanized finishing nails into subfloor and, if possible, joist. Sink and fill nailheads.

Raising a sagging floor

One of the most serious problems a homeowner can face is a sagging floor. A sag affects every floor above it and causes sticking doors and windows, cracked ceilings and walls, and roof leaks. The instructions below will correct a light sag or prevent a deep one from worsening. Always discuss your strategy with a contractor or home inspection engineer (p.195) before attempting any repair.

Place two jack posts or short house jacks on a heavy wooden beam. Short house jacks need 4 x 4 extension posts to reach the joists. Put a 4 x 8 beam atop the posts.

Raise the support beam *gradually.* Turn the handles just until you feel resistance; then stop. Wait 24 hours, then give each handle another quarter turn. Repeat the turning and waiting until the floor is level.
▶ **CAUTION:** Do not exceed the rate of one quarter turn every 24 hours.

Check with the local building department to determine how to fix the floor in place once it is level. Some codes allow the jack posts to be left in place, but you might have to weld the screw or encase it in concrete so that it is fixed in position. Other codes require the installation of a lally column (a steel tube filled with concrete) on a concrete footing (p.156) at each end of the support beam.

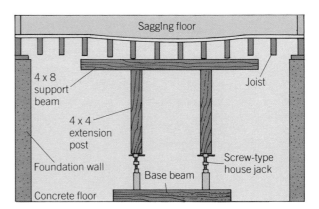

A good finish protects a wood floor from dirt, abrasion, and moisture. Floor finishes come in two basic formulas: *surface finishes* (polyurethane, varnish), which build a hard film on top of the wood, and *penetrating sealers,* which sink into the wood and harden between its fibers. Follow the manufacturer's safety and application recommendations exactly.

All finishes except lacquer will darken the wood; some finishes come in colors, and stain can be applied before the finish to create a specific color. Always test the whole sequence on an inconspicuous area or on scrap flooring to determine the final result.

Sand the entire floor (facing page) before applying finish. Floor sanders can be rented. Although the ones shown below are fairly common, models vary. Have the rental agent demonstrate proper technique. Be certain that you can safely operate the machine before leaving the store. Three grits of sandpaper are usually provided for both the sander and the edger. Start with the coarsest grit and sand the entire floor. Sand again with the medium grit and then the fine.

Type of finish	Appearance	Durability	Application	Comments
Polyurethane **Oil-base** **Water-base** **Swedish** **(2-part,** **water-base)**	Available in various degrees of luster from matte to glossy. Somewhat plastic looking. **Oil-base** and **water-base** will darken or yellow wood. **Swedish** dries clear.	Excellent. Well suited for kitchens and baths. Resists water, alcohol, and abrasion. If chipped or gouged, extremely difficult to spot-repair.	Easy—follow directions for product you buy. If applying over old finish, scuff it with fine sandpaper. **Oil-base** dries slowly. **Water-base** dries more quickly, needs more coats to build to same thickness as oil-base. Never scuff with steel wool if using water-base; the filaments left behind rust and speckle the finish.	Most common surface finish. Stain (p.119), bleach (p.118), or pickle (next page) before finishing. For best results, use products from the same manufacturer. **Swedish** requires professional application if used on unfinished wood. Damp-mop; do not wax.
Varnish	Available in a range of lusters from matte to glossy.	Very good, although slightly softer than polyurethane. High-gloss formula more durable than matte formula.	Easy; dries moderately fast. Use tack cloth before applying finish. Keep room dust-free.	May darken with age. Poor-quality varnish becomes brittle. Small flaws can be repaired with touch-up spray. Damp-mop floor; wax optional.
Penetrating sealer	Natural-looking sheen, not glossy. Enhances beauty of wood grain; may darken with age. Available in various wood colors.	Good protection, especially when waxed, but less durable than polyurethane or varnish.	Extremely easy; takes a long time to dry completely. Brush or wipe on liberal amount; let stand for time recommended by manufacturer; wipe off with clean lint-free rags.	Easy to spot-repair with additional applications of finish or with commercial refurbisher (often called *deglosser*). Wax annually; buff to remove scuffs.

Preparing a floor sander

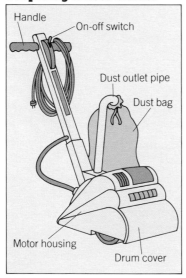

Handle · On-off switch · Dust outlet pipe · Dust bag · Motor housing · Drum cover

Upright floor sander

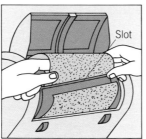

Slot

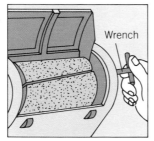

Wrench

1. To add paper, unplug sander. Lift drum by depressing lever, and open cover. Loosen drum with a wrench. Wrap new paper tightly around drum, and tuck ends into slot. (Some models hold paper with a screw-down bar.)

2. Tighten drum with wrench, closing slot. (If using screw-down bar, make sure screwheads are fully down.) Plug in; turn on. Stand clear and check that paper is tracking evenly. If necessary, turn off power, unplug sander, and adjust.

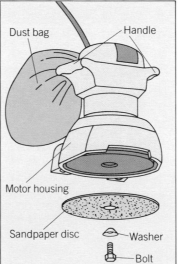

Dust bag · Handle · Motor housing · Sandpaper disc · Washer · Bolt

Edger

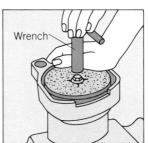

Wrench

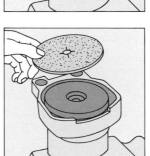

1. Edgers, also called disc sanders, are used to sand close to base-boards or in small areas, such as stairs. To install or change sanding disc, unplug machine and turn it upside down. Remove bolt and washer with wrench.

2. Center new sanding disc on sander's base. Replace bolt and washer, and secure tightly with wrench. Paper grits used in disc sander should follow same progression — coarse, then medium, then fine — as in the upright sander.

Refinishing wood floors

Sand parquet with successively finer grits and in directions as shown. **Sand strips** along the grain. Overlap cuts to avoid ridges.

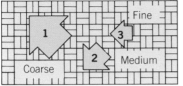

If an existing finish is severely damaged and the flooring is at least ¼ inch thick, you can sand and refinish the floor. Prepare for sanding by removing all furniture, taking off shoe moldings, and covering vents. Seal doorways and windows with plastic sheets. Inspect the floor: set nailheads ⅛ inch below the surface, fill holes with wood putty, repair cracks, and secure loose boards (p.304). For safety, wear goggles, a dust mask, and ear protection. To avoid marring the floor, wear clean rubber-soled shoes.
▶ **CAUTION:** Sanding dust, finishes, and finish fumes are flammable. Extinguish pilot lights; do not smoke.

Sanding

Lift drum off the floor. Turn on power and lower drum until it contacts floor. Sand with the grain, maintaining a slow, even pace. If you need to stop, tilt drum off floor. Keep sander in constant motion and overlap cuts to avoid gouging and ridges.

Edger sands where drum can't reach: close to baseboards and door frames, in closets, on stair treads. Hold both handles firmly. Keep disc flat on floor to avoid gouging. Sand with identical succession of paper grades as for main part of floor.

A sandpaper block (p.50) or a paint scraper (p.356) will clean even the tightest areas—in corners, under radiators—where neither power sander can reach. Remove swirls from the edger with the sanding block, working with the grain.

Finishing

After sanding, vacuum floor and walls. Wipe down moldings, window-sills, and door frames so that dust won't fall off later and mar the finish. Let dust settle overnight, then vacuum again, using brush attachment. Wipe floor with tack cloth (p.118).

Brush polyurethane across grain, then along it. For varnish, use wide brush or foam roller. Apply penetrating sealer with lint-free cloth; let stand 15 min., then wipe off. With all types, work in small sections, overlapping strokes before previous section is dry.

Scuff polyurethane or varnish between coats with window screening or very fine sandpaper mounted on electric buffer. Vacuum before applying next coat. If wax is desired, let final coat dry at least 24 hr., then apply two coats of paste wax.

A pickled finish

Pickling changes color and accentu-ates grain. Floor must be clean, dry, and free of old finish. To make solution, thin paint 30 to 40 per-cent with appropriate thinner. Test on hid-den area. Then brush on, working from farthest wall to door wall.

Let solution stand 20–60 min. The longer it's left on, the more opaque the finish. (Latex paint dries faster; work in smaller sections.) Wearing rubber gloves, scrub solution off with rags, wiping in grain direction. Continue procedure until floor is done.

When paint has dried completely (oil-base paint may take a week), sand carefully with pad sander and fine paper. Sand just to smooth surface, leaving paint in the wood's grain. Seal with three coats of nonyellowing water-base polyurethane.

Interiors/Installing sheet flooring

Unlike true linoleum, which is made from linseed oil, sheet flooring is laminated vinyl, available in 6-foot and 12-foot widths. Take a sketch of the room with all measurements—length, width, sizes and locations of cabinets and doors—to the store. The retailer will help you figure out how much to get to avoid seaming, or to match the pattern if seams are unavoidable.

There are three ways to install vinyl: loose-lay, full-bed adhesion, or perimeter adhesion. Loose-lay is the easiest. It requires only the strength to move the flooring into position and a sharp utility knife for trimming. Full-bed adhesion requires some special equipment. A perimeter adhesion installation is a specialized job for a particular type of flooring and is best left to a professional.

Vinyl can go over any clean, flat, and sound base. Install an underlayment only if the base floor is uneven or damaged. Acclimatize the flooring to the room for at least 24 hours. Empty the room; remove any shoe moldings. Unroll the vinyl, and trim it to within 3 inches on all sides to allow for final fitting. Overlap vinyl at seams and shift to match the pattern. When aligned in its final position, place buckets of water on it so that it doesn't shift as you work. Trim to final size, following the room's contours.

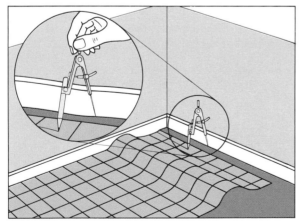

To transcribe an uneven wall line, orient flooring pattern so that it looks straight, then pull it 1 in. from wall. Span gap with compass; run point along wall, pencil point on vinyl.

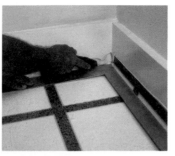

Begin fitting at longest, straightest wall. Make successively deeper cuts to inside corner until vinyl lies flat. Press vinyl between wall and floor with straightedge; trim along wall with sharp utility knife. Leave ⅛-in. expansion gap between walls and vinyl.

At outside corners, cut alignment will change as the flooring settles. For greatest precision, trim just a little at a time, keeping the cut as straight as possible. Take care that the weight of the flooring doesn't cause tearing.

Fit flooring to doorway by cutting a flap that overlaps the threshold, then making several vertical cuts that follow the molding's contours. Make small horizontal cuts to remove the flaps.

Fitting around fixtures requires a template. Put a sheet of paper on each side of the fixture, and scribe the shape with a compass. Tape template to vinyl, and cut out shape. Slit vinyl from edge to cutout, then press in place around fixture. Trim as needed with sharp utility knife.

Flat metal strips protect edges at doorways and secure seams. Fasten with screws or nails driven into floor, not through vinyl. If there is no threshold, trim vinyl to centerline of bottom of closed door. If no door, trim to edge of adjoining floor.

For invisible seam, overlap flooring at least ½ in., being certain to match pattern. Weight down securely, then fit to room. Lay straightedge along center of seam overlap and cut through both layers. Fasten from below with seam tape or adhesive.

Full-bed adhesion.
1. Fit flooring as described for loose-lay installation. Fold one half of vinyl back on itself. With toothed trowel, spread adhesive evenly on floor. Work from corners into center. Gently unfold vinyl into adhesive, taking care to position it properly.

2. Push 100-lb. linoleum roller over glued vinyl to force out trapped air bubbles. If you can't rent a roller, lean heavily on a rolling pin or slide your stocking feet over the entire surface. Work from center out to edges; then glue and roll other half of floor.

Choosing floor tile

Tile comes in an astonishing array of colors, patterns, and finishes; and in many sizes, shapes, and materials (see chart below). When selecting tile, remember that the more texture and variation a tile has, the better it will disguise seams, scratches, irregularities in the base floor, and dirt. For easy maintenance, avoid solid colors such as black or white; for better safety, avoid slick finishes.

To determine how many tiles to buy, sketch the room on graph paper and note down all measurements. Include cabinets or other protrusions; then subtract their individual areas from the total floor area. Divide large or oddly shaped rooms into smaller shapes—for example, two rectangles or a square and a triangle—and combine their total area. Take the sketch with you when you go to buy the tile, and let the retailer check your calculations. Always buy a little more than you think you'll need—some tiles may be chipped or scratched, or the color may be slightly off. Keep any leftover tiles for repairs.

Wood and vinyl tiles are commonly available in 12-inch and 9-inch sizes; ceramic tiles come in a wider range of sizes. If buying 12-inch tiles, the total floor area (in square feet) equals the total number of tiles needed for a one-color or parquet floor. The chart at right gives the number of 9-inch tiles needed for a variety of common room sizes. Similar charts are available where you buy tile to help you calculate the number of odd-size tiles.

If tiles of two colors are to be laid in a checkerboard pattern or in alternate rows, halve the total amount and buy equal quantities of each color. Use graph paper to plot out complex patterns. Let the paper's squares stand for the tiles, shade in the colors, then count up the number needed of each.

Room length in feet

Room width in feet	6	7	8	9	10	11	12	13	14	15
6	71	83	95	107	118	130	142	152	165	176
7	83	97	110	125	138	152	165	179	193	206
8	95	110	126	142	158	173	189	205	220	236
9	107	125	142	160	178	195	213	230	248	266
10	118	138	158	178	196	216	236	256	275	294
11	130	152	173	195	216	238	259	281	303	324
12	142	165	189	213	236	259	283	306	330	353

There are two formulas for calculating how many 9-in. tiles to buy. Find the room's area (length x width) in square feet; multiply the area by 144, then divide that number by 81. Or simply multiply the area by 1.78. The chart shows some totals, plus a 10-percent damage allowance, for average-size rooms.

Type of tiles	Appearance	Durability	Maintenance	Adhesive	Comments
Wood block Parquet	Laminated or solid; many patterns, species, and thicknesses	Durable; seal with polyurethane if installed near water	Dry dust-mop; vacuum regularly to prevent dirt from being ground in	Wood floor mastic	Warm underfoot; some laminates can be installed directly on concrete
Vinyl	Many patterns, colors, textures; some simulate stone, wood, and other natural materials	Water-resistant; resists grease and household chemicals	Regular mopping and waxing; special formulas designed for no-wax floors	Multipurpose floor tile adhesive, or self-stick	Resilient; extremely easy to install
Cork	Natural-looking; available in colors and patterns	Fragile, may chip; some have protective vinyl overlay	Seal untreated cork with polyurethane; damp-mop treated cork	Multipurpose floor tile adhesive	Resilient, insulative, warm underfoot
Ceramic, glazed	Many patterns, colors, sizes, shapes, including mosaics; tile of uniform size so that grout joints can be neat and regular	Extremely durable, water-resistant	Very easy, wash with mild detergent; no sealer or wax	Ceramic floor tile adhesive or tile-setting mortar	Hard and cold underfoot; non-resilient; noisy to walk on; slippery when wet
Ceramic, unglazed (quarry tile)	Many shapes and sizes; tiles in same batch may vary in size, requiring irregular grout joints	Extremely durable, water-resistant	Wash with mild detergent; reseal periodically with commercial sealer for porous surfaces; don't wax—surface will become slippery	Ceramic floor tile adhesive or tile-setting mortar	Hard and cold underfoot; non-resilient; noisy to walk on; chips easily; irregular size makes fitting more difficult
Brick and clay pavers	Available in a number of earth tones; clay pavers look like brick but are only ¼ in. thick	Extremely durable	Seal with sealer formulated for porous floors	Tile-setting mortar	Hard and cold underfoot; non-resilient
Slate and flagstone	Smooth to coarse surface textures; shapes may be irregular	Scratches easily; coat with slate sealer	Mop; reseal as necessary	Tile-setting mortar	Hard and cold underfoot; non-resilient; may be expensive; irregular shapes need careful fitting

Interiors/Installing a tile floor

The techniques shown here are for wood or vinyl tile. Ceramic tile has additional requirements. Read and follow the manufacturer's recommendations for the material you select.

Let the tiles acclimatize to the room for at least 24 hours. If you are installing wood tiles, follow the humidity restrictions for solid wood flooring. Empty the room; remove shoe moldings and baseboards (p.293). Trim the door casings (p.301) to fit the height of the new floor; also trim the door so that it will swing freely. If necessary, install an underlayment (p.299).

▶ **CAUTION:** Wear a sanding respirator when removing old flooring. Old vinyl may contain asbestos; have it tested and, if necessary, professionally removed (p.348).

1. Tile needs a smooth, flat, clean base. Install underlayment over old tile, if possible, or remove tile. To remove tile, warm with hair dryer or clothes iron set on moderate heat. Pry up with wide putty knife. Scrape old adhesive from floor.

2. Snap lines from centers of opposite walls. Some jobs need lines to cross at visual center, not true center. For diagonal installation, snap lines from corner to corner. In any configuration, intersecting lines must meet at 90°.

3. To establish even borders around room, lay dry runs of tile along snapped lines. Adjust center until borders are at least half a tile wide. Recheck with square; snap new guidelines. If installing wood tile, allow a ½-in. expansion gap at wall.

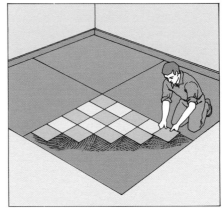

4. Work in quadrants. Spread adhesive to recommended thickness. Install tiles from center out in reverse pyramid, aligning them with chalk lines. To keep adhesive from oozing up, drop tiles gently into place; avoid sliding them.

5. Cut border tiles after full-size tiles are installed. To mark, place tile to be cut upside down on fixed tile in last row. Place second tile on top, against wall. Mark first tile, and cut with sharp utility knife.

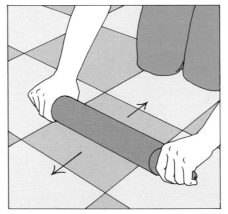

6. Transcribe odd or curved shapes onto tile with a compass (p.49) or make a cardboard template. Door casings can be trimmed so that tile will slip under (p.301). To fit freestanding fixtures, see p.308.

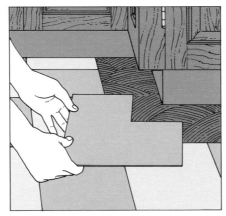

7. With rolling pin or rented 100-lb. roller, force out any air bubbles and press tile into adhesive. Roll both along length of room and across its width. Allow adhesive to set for the amount of time prescribed on label before walking on floor.

For wood tile, fit tongue into groove and drop—don't slide—tile into place. Fit the groove of scrap flooring over tongue and tap each tile to ensure snug fit against adjacent tile. Scrap flooring protects wood from hammer marks.

Repairing resilient flooring

Flattening a curled tile

1. Cover tile with aluminum foil. With clothes iron set at moderate heat, warm tile to make it pliable. Lift curled corner with putty knife. Scrape old adhesive from floor and raised corner.

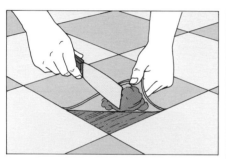

2. Dab fresh adhesive on underside of tile. Avoid overgluing. Wipe up any excess with the solvent recommended by the manufacturer (usually mineral spirits).

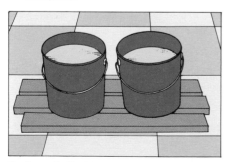

3. Press tile firmly back into place. Clean glue seeps with solvent. Weight tile down until adhesive sets—buckets of water will do. Scrap wood under buckets distributes pressure evenly.

Replacing a tile

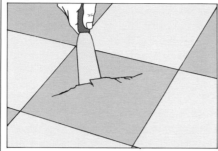

1. Cover damaged tile with foil, warm with iron, and pry up with putty knife. To avoid marring edges of surrounding tiles, cut into center of tile with utility knife, then pry from center outward.

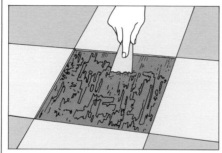

2. Remove old adhesive from the floor with a scraper or putty knife. Test-fit the new tile in the opening. If it's too big, trim it with a knife. Keep checking the fit to avoid overtrimming.

3. Use iron over foil to make tile flexible, apply adhesive, and drop into place. Clean off any seepage with recommended solvent. Put weights on tile as shown at left until adhesive is dry.

Repairing scratches and blisters

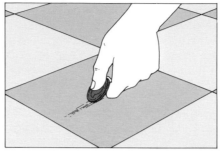

A slight scratch may be removed by rubbing along its length with the rim of a coin. Or rub lightly with a little paste wax on soft cloth; remove excess wax from surrounding area.

Fill small holes with putty made from epoxy and acrylic paint. Follow manufacturer's instructions for mixing epoxy. Mask hole with tape; fill with putty. Allow to air dry.

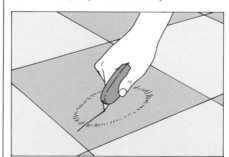

Slit blister with utility knife ½ in. past ends. Cover with foil; warm with iron. Pack in adhesive with putty knife. Press tile flat, clean off seeps, and weight down until adhesive dries.

Patching sheet vinyl

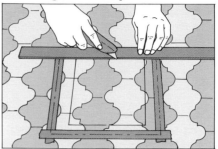

1. Cut patch larger than damaged area. Align pattern, and tape patch in position over damage. Cut through both patch and old floor with utility knife, using straightedge as guide.

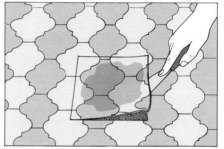

2. Remove patch and original flooring. You may need to pry up old flooring with putty knife. If necessary, cover with foil and warm with iron. Completely clean old adhesive from subfloor.

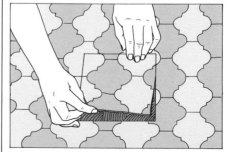

3. Test-fit patch. If necessary, trim with sharp knife or sandpaper. Apply adhesive, and press patch into place. Clean away glue seeps; weight down until adhesive dries.

Interiors / Ceramic tile

When selecting tile, consider its composition as well as its color and shape. Ceramic tile is classified by its porosity. *Nonvitreous tile* is highly porous, *semivitreous* is moderately porous, and *vitreous* is least porous. Choose vitreous tile for areas where splashing is likely. Tile is also rated for use on floors or walls. Some are dual-purpose; ask your retailer about the recommended use for the tile you select. Match tile size to room size—small tiles in a small room, big tiles in a spacious one.

For best results, install ceramic tile over concrete, a fresh or cured mortar bed, or cement board. Similar to wallboard, cement board has a mortar core and is covered with reinforcing fiberglass mesh. It is available in 4- x 8-foot and 3- x 5-foot panels.

Precautions. Be certain the subfloor is strong and stiff enough to support tile—some installations can weigh over 8 pounds per square foot. Never set tile directly on wood. Wood, including plywood, expands and contracts, causing cracks. If you have a wood subfloor, install a waterproofing membrane. It will help to protect the installation by absorbing some of this movement.

Laying tile over vinyl poses many problems. Vinyl has a slick surface that resists adhesives. It may be cushion-backed or loose-laid, which allows too much flexion, or it may contain asbestos. Generally it is best to cover vinyl with an underlayment recommended by the tile manufacturer. If the vinyl is so severely damaged that it must be taken up, hire a reputable asbestos abater to test and, if necessary, remove it.

Preparation. Whatever the underlying substance, it must be flat, clean, and free of dust, debris, wax, and grease. Even tiny bumps and dips can cause cracked tiles or grout. A floor must be level as well as flat so that the adhesive bed's thickness is

Squaring a room

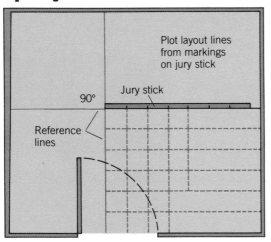

Plot layout lines from markings on jury stick

90°

Jury stick

Reference lines

1. To speed layout, make a *jury stick* from a straight piece of wood 6 to 8 ft. long. Mark entire length of stick into spaces that are equal to average tile size plus grout width.

2. Establish reference lines by snapping chalk line from centers of opposite walls or center of a focal point (doorway, window, fireplace). These lines must intersect at 90°.

3. With jury stick, measure from center to wall and set border width. Borders should be equal at opposite walls and at least a half-tile's width deep. If necessary, shift reference lines so that they will fall in the center of a grout line.

4. Plot layout lines from reference lines. Align jury stick with one reference line, mark off grout lines, then repeat at another point on line. Connect marks by snapping chalk lines. Work in 3- x 3-ft. areas. Add lines as needed.

Pattern layouts

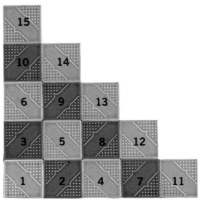

Jack-on-jack pattern is easy to install. Start with a perfectly square corner and install tiles in diagonal rows.

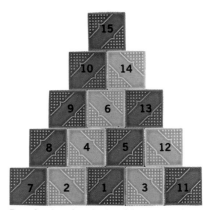

Running bond, or broken joint, pattern is more exacting than jack-on-jack. Divide room into manageable areas for best results.

Trim tile

Well-chosen trim tile gives a professional look and makes cleaning easier. Not all manufacturers produce a complete line of trim, and some don't make any. If you can't get trim that matches the main tiles, try a complementary color. Align trim's grout lines with those of the main field.

Countertop edge trim seats securely over a right-angled edge.

Bullnose and radius bullnose trim come in a wide array of variations. They give a smooth finish to the top edge of tiles, wrap corners, or form baseboards. Because of its deep arc, radius bullnose tile (bottom left) can be installed over existing tile.

Cove trim has a concave edge suitable for baseboards. Like bullnose trim, it comes in shapes to finish corners and edges. The pieces in the bottom row at left wrap outside corners. Inside corner pieces can be bought, or conventional tile (top row) can be mitered to fit.

Installing an underlayment 299
Choosing floor tile 309
Installing a tile floor 310

constant. If an underlayment is necessary, cement board is the best choice.

Waterproofing. Vitreous ceramic tile is often used where there is a great deal of water. But if water leaks under the tiles, serious structural damage can occur. To prevent this, install an impervious membrane—for example, a trowel-applied membrane or chlorinated polyethylene (CPE)—before applying the tile adhesive and tile. For extra water resistance, you can mix a latex or acrylic additive into the adhesive and grout instead of water, but first check with your tile supplier; the additives may allow the grout to embed in the tile's glaze, causing discoloration. Check the installation periodically for damage and promptly repair or replace damaged or missing tile, grout, and caulk (p.315).

Adhesives. There are two kinds of adhesives: *thinset adhesive* and *organic mastic*. Thinsets are powdered cement-base products that you mix with either water, a latex or acrylic additive, or epoxy. They resist heat and water and are the most versatile. Mastics come premixed in a solvent or latex base. Not as strong or flexible as thinsets, they may deteriorate if exposed to heat or water. Read the label to be sure that you select an appropriate adhesive, and follow the instructions carefully.

For tile to look its best, the room's elements should be square, level, and plumb. This is rarely the case. You will need to taper border tiles to accommodate out-of-square walls or a sloping floor (facing page). The principles of planning a pattern and installing tile are explained on page 310. When setting ceramic tile, snap a set of intersecting *reference lines* to establish an accurate 90° angle and a grid of *layout lines* to align each row of tile. If installing odd-sized tiles, align their centers, not their edges.

Tools for cutting tile

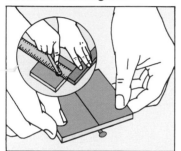 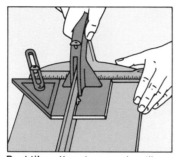 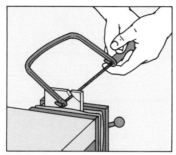  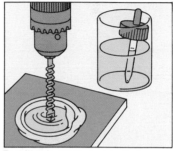

Run glass cutter against straightedge, scoring glazed surface. Put score mark over nail; press down. Place cut edges where they will be hidden.

Rent tile cutter where you buy tile. Align tile on floor of cutter; then pull scoring wheel across tile. Depress cutting lever with steady pressure.

Rod blade on coping saw cuts curves in soft tile. Sandwich tile between scrap wood and secure in vise. Smooth edge with tile rubbing stone.

Tile nippers also cut curves. Mark outline with pencil, then nibble out small pieces with nippers. Smooth edge with 80-grit carbide sandpaper.

To drill hole, lightly punch starting mark in glaze. Surround mark with a ring of plumber's putty; fill ring with water. Drill gently with carbide bit.

Grout and caulk

A powder made from sand and cement, tile grout is mixed with either water or, to increase durability, an additive. Traditionally white, grout is also available in colors, but these may be inconsistent if the grout isn't mixed well or if it dries unevenly. For best results, follow the label's instructions.

Let the tile adhesive set for the recommended amount of time before grouting. Don't let the grout dry on the tile; remove the last traces of haze by scrubbing the tiles with clean cheesecloth.

Apply caulk wherever the tile meets another material. Grout and caulk must cure before they will withstand water; check the label for the recommended amount of time.

1. Pack grout into joints with rubber-bottom float. Wipe several times on both diagonals. To remove excess, scrape float across tile parallel to joints.

2. Clean grout from tiles by wiping with damp sponge on opposite diagonals. With finger in damp sponge, press joints lightly. Rinse and wring sponge for each pass.

Caulking. Push bead of flexible caulk into space between tub and wall and around edges of installation. Smooth with damp sponge or lightly soaped finger.

Interiors / Tiling a wall

Tile can go over almost any clean, flat, stable surface that will support its weight. If you have doubts about the surface, or are tiling an area where splashing will occur, install ½-inch cement board. Easy to work with and highly water-resistant, cement board doesn't shift in response to atmospheric changes.

When tiling a room, do the walls before the floor. Plan the installation on paper first. Then plot the reference lines and layout grid (pp.310, 312). Where walls are out of plumb and fixtures, such as a tub, are not level, you will need to cut the border tiles to accommodate the wall's actual dimensions.

The installation procedure (below) is identical for pregrouted tile sheets and for individual tiles—just think of the sheet as a tile. After setting each square yard of tile, level the surface with a rubber mallet and a tile beater or a scrap of 2 x 4 wrapped in newspaper or cloth (facing page).

1. Cut cement board with carbide blade in circular saw. Face board's smooth side out if setting tile with mastic; textured side out for thinset adhesive. Secure with galvanized dry-wall screws at 6-in. intervals; set heads flush.

2. Tape all seams and the joint where cement board abuts original wall, using the fiberglass tape recommended by manufacturer. Don't apply joint compound to these seams; they will be covered with adhesive. (If using mastic, fill joints with thinset adhesive.)

3. Establish reference and layout lines (p.312). Draw enough layout lines to work accurately in 3- x 3-ft. areas. Check that lines are level, plumb, and intersect at 90°. Any error in the first row will multiply as rows are added.

4. Spread adhesive with smooth edge of square-notched trowel; then comb with notched edge to form ridges. (Check adhesive directions for recommended notch size.) Spread adhesive up to, but not over, reference lines for first tile.

5. Press first tile or tile sheet precisely into place. (It affects the placement of all other tiles.) Use spacer to keep grout lines uniform. With level, check that each course is straight. Maintain alignment of grout lines through corner.

6. Center soap dish in a two-tile space. Cut tile to fit on both sides, allowing same-size grout lines. To fit tile around pipe (not shown), either drill hole with water-cooled carbide bit or hole saw (p.313), or cut tile in half and nibble out shape with tile nippers.

Decorative accents

Whether tiling a floor or a wall, choose accents thoughtfully and plan their arrangement carefully. You will be living with them for a long time. If you have trouble visualizing how the tile will look, try taping same-size blocks of construction paper or sketches or photocopies of the tile to the wall. Move these around until you have a pleasing arrangement; then plot the final installation on graph paper.

Random or widely spaced accent tiles should be balanced throughout the installation. Leave spaces and set them last.

Strip accent with uncut tiles above it is easy to install on partially tiled wall. Decorative tile enlivens jack-on-jack pattern.

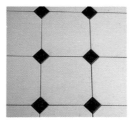

Square tile with clipped corners inset with smaller tile allows a second color and diagonal effect without laying tiles diagonally.

Lay hexagonal floor tiles with edges, not points, parallel to longest walls. A rectangular border completes the design.

Border tile looks best if walls and floor are close to square and plumb. Irregularities are emphasized by the straight lines of the tiles.

Tiling a floor

Although the planning and installation procedures are similar for all kinds of tile (pp.310, 312–313), doing a floor with ceramic tile has specific requirements. The surface beneath the tile must be flat, level, and absolutely rigid.

A slanting floor will have an uneven adhesive bed, and any give in the floor will crack the tiles and grout.

In rooms where water is present, a moisture barrier—trowel-applied membrane or chlorinated polyethyl-ene (CPE)—and an underlayment of cement board are essential.

When tiling an entire room, align the grout lines of all the elements—floor, walls, ceiling, and trim—for the best effect.

Replacing damaged tile

Whatever its location, the technique for replacing ceramic tile is the same (below). Wear gloves and safety goggles for protection from tile shards.

To repair grout, clean out the joint with a chisel or grout saw, and vacuum any dust. Dampen joint, then apply fresh grout (p.313).

In small areas, trace layout grid directly from tile. Loose-lay two rows of tile out from long wall or large fixture. Allow grout space. Mark tile ends, then draw parallel lines across floor with straightedge.

To complete grid, loose-lay tiles along one line. Mark top and bottom dimensions of tile on floor. Extend lines with straightedge. With steel square, check that lines intersect at exactly 90°.

Spread thinset adhesive with smooth edge of notched trowel; then comb with notched edge. Keep adhesive clear of one set of intersecting lines. Work in quadrants, and work toward door.

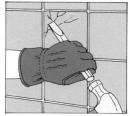

1. Remove grout from joints with a chisel or grout saw. Chip out cracked tile with hammer and cold chisel. Scrape out old adhesive.

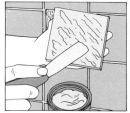

2. Vacuum debris out of space. With putty knife, apply adhesive to wall and to back of new tile. Keep adhesive ¼ in. shy of tile edges.

Align first tile precisely against 90° intersection in grid. Drop tile into place, and press it gently into adhesive. Avoid sliding. If adhesive oozes up between tiles, clean it away immediately.

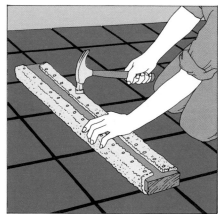

Make tile beater by padding 2 x 4 with carpet or layers of newspaper covered with cloth. Tap beater with hammer or mallet to level tiles' surface. Let adhesive set before applying grout.

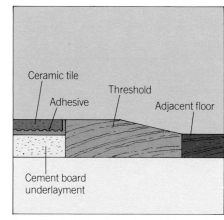

Ceramic tile

Adhesive

Threshold

Adjacent floor

Cement board underlayment

If new floor is higher than adjacent floor, replace original threshold with a shaped one. Precut marble thresholds can be bought; wooden ones can be shaped with a bench plane or a belt sander.

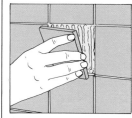

3. Center tile in space and press it into place. Set surface flush by gently pressing on tile. Remove excess adhesive. Secure with masking tape.

4. When adhesive has set, dampen joints; then apply grout, forcing it into seam with wet finger. Before grout hardens, remove excess.

Besides being decorative, carpet insulates against the cold, helps to absorb sound, and cushions the floor. When making a selection, consider the look, feel, and durability of the carpet.

Several types of fibers are used in making carpet. *Wool* is a natural fiber with a softness lacking in synthetic fibers. Wool retains its shape after being crushed, a characteristic known as resiliency. Because the supply of wool is limited, wool carpeting is expensive. *Nylon* wears longer than other synthetics and is resilient and stain-resistant. Nylon carpets come in *generations,* the latest one having more beneficial characteristics—such as stain resistance—and being more expensive. *Polyester* is made in bright, clear colors and has a soft feel, but it lacks the resilience of wool. *Olefin,* or polypropylene, is a strong fiber highly resistant to water, but it is available in a limited color selection. Olefin may be used for outdoor carpeting and in high-traffic areas.

Most carpets are tufted, a method of construction that produces carpets in large quantities. Woven carpets, such as Axminster and Wilton, require more time to make. The carpet's construction helps determine its pile and appearance.

Carpets are available with different piles (see below). Check the pile's density by bending a corner of the carpet. The less backing you see through the yarns, the denser the pile—and the more durable the carpet. The *face weight* of a carpet is the weight of a square yard of its face fiber. However, pile density is more important to the carpet's durability. Examine the *twist* of the pile by comparing different carpet samples. The tighter the twist, the longer the carpet will retain its original appearance. If the yarn has been *heat-set,* the twist is built in. To check the direction of the pile, brush the fibers. If you go against the pile, it will be more difficult than brushing with the lay of the pile.

Padding. All carpets, except cushion-backed carpet (p.319), should be laid over padding. It increases the life of a carpet, prevents the carpet from slipping, increases insulation, acts as a sound barrier, and cushions the carpet. Padding comes in a variety of widths; make sure that its seams don't fall under the carpet's seams. *Hair* or *felt* padding wears well and gives firm support, but it may stretch and is not mildew-resistant. *Rubberized felt* padding has the same good qualities of felt padding, but because of its rubber backing, it won't stretch. *Sponge rubber* padding is resistant to mildew. A flat sponge padding is best for heavy-traffic areas. *Urethane foam* padding can be used in all types of traffic areas, and it is also mildew-resistant. When you squeeze this padding, it should retain at least half its thickness.

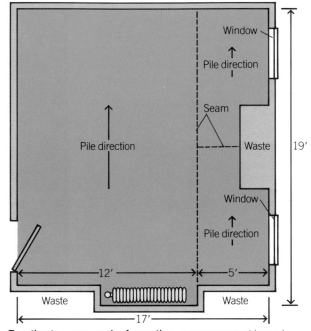

To estimate square yards of carpeting, measure room at longest and widest points (include doorways and alcoves); add 3 in. to each dimension; multiply width by length; divide by 9. Carpet comes 12 and 15 ft. wide. If possible, avoid seams; or place them in low-traffic areas. Lay with pile in same direction; match patterns. To avoid fading, face pile away from windows. For additional smaller sections, order extra length of carpet and divide its width.

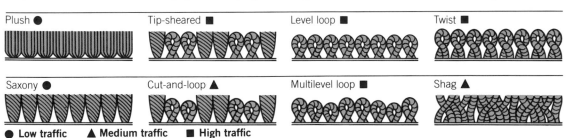

Types of pile
Yarn is stitched in loops to form a *loop* pile; a *cut* pile is made by cutting the loops. If some loops are not cut, it becomes a *cut-and-loop* pile. Varying the height of the fibers creates different patterns.

Plush ● Tip-sheared ■ Level loop ■ Twist ■

Saxony ● Cut-and-loop ▲ Multilevel loop ■ Shag ▲

● **Low traffic** ▲ **Medium traffic** ■ **High traffic**

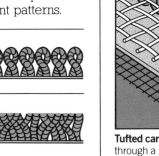

Tufted carpet is produced by up to 2,000 needles stitching yarn through a primary backing. The tufts are then set with a latex rubber and attached to a secondary backing.

Primary backing
Latex binding
Secondary backing

Laying standard carpet

Prepare the floors before laying the carpet. Hammer nails flush and remove tacks in wood floors. Nail down loose boards; plane down ridges of warped boards. Fill cracks between boards with strips of wood or with wood putty. If floors are warped or cracked beyond repair, cover with plywood (pp.95–97) or hardboard (p.98). Treat ridged or cracked stone or concrete floors with a floor-leveling compound to reduce carpet wear.

Use tackless strips to secure a carpet to the floor. Tackless strips are wooden battens with pins projecting at a 60° angle. The strips come with pins up to ¼ inch in height, and they are sold in 4-ft. lengths.

To fit carpet over tackless strips, rent both a knee kicker and a power stretcher from a rental agency or carpet dealer. For a seam, rent a heat-bond iron. To cut the seam, use a row cutter or a utility knife. Trim edges with a utility knife.

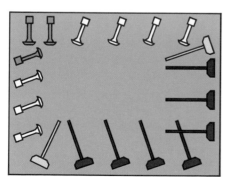

To lay carpeting for large room, use both knee kicker and power stretcher. With knee kicker, move carpet at corner (blue). Use a power stretcher at adjacent corners (green). Move carpet with knee kicker along walls adjacent to first corner (yellow). Use power stretcher along two remaining walls (red).

Nail tackless strips to the floor, end to end and ¼ in. from baseboard. Face pins toward the wall. Remove shoe molding first.

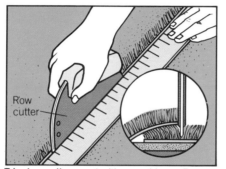

Trim loop-pile carpet with yarn side up. For seams, overlap carpet edges by 1 in. Cut along straightedge with utility knife or row cutter.

Row cutter

Press knee kicker into carpet. Push knee against pad, and hook carpeting over pins. For large rooms, use power stretcher (see left).

Lay down the padding and attach it to floor every 6 to 12 in. with a staple gun. Use utility knife to trim padding along tackless strips.

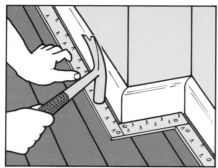

To join a seam, place hot-melt tape under edges of carpet. Move 250° F heat-bond iron slowly along tape. Press carpet into tape; weight down.

Seams should butt

Trim excess carpeting with utility knife; leave ¾-in. overlap. With putty knife, tuck overlap into space between wall and strip.

Trim cut-pile carpet with backing side up. Mark measurements by snapping a chalk line; cut with a utility knife along a straightedge.

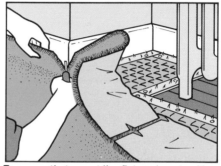

To ensure that carpet lies flat, make cuts with utility knife at inside and outside corners and around obstacles.

Finish edge at door with a metal threshold bar. This type folds over; hammer against wood block. If door no longer swings open, plane it (p.437).

317

Interiors / Carpeting a staircase

A staircase can be covered with fitted carpet, best laid by a professional, or with a runner, which is easier and less costly to lay.

Runners come in standard widths of 27 and 36 inches; they are sold by the running yard. To estimate the number of running yards you'll need, measure in inches the depth of one tread and the height of one riser; add the two together plus an additional 2 inches; multiply by the number of steps. Add 18 inches to the total; then divide the result by 36. For a winding staircase, measure each tread separately at its widest point.

To estimate padding, add the depth of a tread, half the height of a riser, plus 2 inches; multiply by the number of steps. The padding should be 2 inches narrower than the runner. Cut padding for each step long enough to cover the tread and half of the riser. To prevent the padding from showing in an open staircase, clip its bottom corners.

Buy durable carpet and padding. Because a staircase is heavily trafficked, the carpet will wear quickly—especially at the tread's nosing. Tuck under the extra 18 inches at the bottom of the staircase. When the carpet wears, you can unfasten and shift the runner a few inches; then reattach.

Fastening. The runner can be tacked down every 3 inches with tacks, but it will be more difficult to shift when it wears. You can nail two tackless strips cut to the length of the padding to each step. Or you can place double-faced carpet tape at the angle between riser and tread and on the nosing.

Before laying the carpet, clear the staircase of old tacks and nails; remove any molding. Paint or refinish exposed wood, if needed. Mark each tread with a pencil for carpet and padding placement. To decrease wear, lay the carpet with the pile facing toward the bottom step. If you use carpet that has unfinished sides, score the backing with an awl 1¼ inches from each edge; fold the carpet under.

Straight staircase

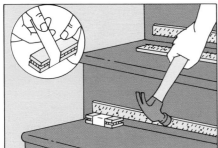

To make spacer, tape two blocks of tackless strip together, pins facing in. Set tackless strip on two spacers; nail it to riser, pins pointing down. Nail a strip to tread ½ in. from riser, pins facing riser.

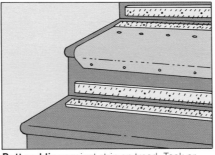

Butt padding against strip on tread. Tack or staple padding to tread and riser every 4 in. along top and bottom edges. Repeat procedures on all steps, but don't pad bottom step.

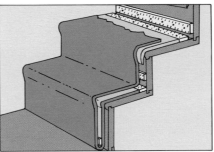

Position runner, pile face down, on bottom tread; butt it against strip, and tack. Roll runner over nosing onto landing. Nail a strip across runner at bottom of riser. Pull runner up and over tread.

Wear safety goggles

Push runner into tread strips with knee kicker (p.317). Press runner into angle and onto riser strips, using a stair tool and hammer. At top riser, fold end under at nosing; tack every 4 in.

Winding staircase

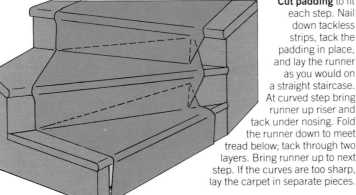

Cut padding to fit each step. Nail down tackless strips, tack the padding in place, and lay the runner as you would on a straight staircase. At curved step bring runner up riser and tack under nosing. Fold the runner down to meet tread below; tack through two layers. Bring runner up to next step. If the curves are too sharp, lay the carpet in separate pieces.

Patching carpet

Cut out damaged carpet area with a utility knife held against a straightedge. Using the old piece as a guide, cut out a new piece of carpet.

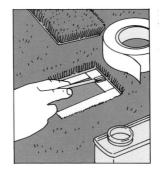

Slide double-faced carpet tape partway under carpet; apply seam cement to carpet edges. Set in new carpet piece; make sure pile and patterns match. Weight down carpet until the cement sets.

Cushion-backed carpet

Replacing damaged floorboards 304
Basement dampness 338

Laying cushion-backed carpet wall-to-wall is simpler than laying standard carpet. The ¼- to ⅝-inch backing eliminates the need to install separate padding. The carpeting comes in many styles, such as berber and cut pile, and in a wide range of colors. It is made with different fibers, may have a dense pile, and is usually stain-resistant.

The carpet is laid down with an all-purpose white latex adhesive or with double-faced carpet tape. The adhesive is hard to remove, but it holds the carpet in place better, reducing wear. Double-faced carpet tape (below) is easier to remove, but it won't hold the carpet in place as securely.

To lay the carpet, you'll need a linoleum knife, straightedge, hammer, and carpet knife. For the adhesive method, add a notched trowel. For seams, buy a seam adhesive recommended by the carpet dealer; spread it along the primary backing (the center layer between the pile and the padding) at the seam edges. To estimate how much carpet is required, see page 316.

Before laying the carpet, remove the shoe molding around the floor's edge; vacuum and wash the floor. Fill in any holes or cracks; secure loose boards or tiles (p.311). If the flooring is concrete, make sure it is dry; damp concrete will decay some carpet backings. Replace the shoe molding after you've laid the carpet.

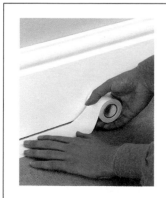

Double-faced tape. Set 2-in. tape around room's edges; leave top paper in place. In heavy-traffic area, set tape 1 ft. apart diagonally across room. Rough-fit carpet; fold it back. Remove paper from tape; press carpet down and trim. To make a seam, set 5-in. tape halfway under carpet; spread carpet edge with adhesive. Join pieces.

1. Rough-fit the carpet, leaving 3 in. excess all around. Cut it on back side with a carpet knife. For a seam, snap a chalk line on the floor. Trim seam edges, using straightedge as a guide. Spread adhesive on floor (step 3), extending 3 ft. to each side of chalk line. Set one carpet piece in place; spread seam adhesive along its edge. Butt second piece against the first.

2. To expose floor for adhesive, fold two corners of carpet back toward the middle of room; then fold point of carpet toward opposite end. This will uncover half of the floor. After first half of carpet is adhered to floor, repeat step with second half.

3. Spread a layer of all-purpose white latex adhesive evenly over the exposed floor, using a ³⁄₃₂-in. notched trowel. Then let the adhesive set until it is tacky, about 10–15 min., before continuing with the next step.

4. Unfold the carpet in reverse of the order in which it was folded. Lay each section gradually and slowly to avoid bumps. Working from the center out, smooth out bumps by shuffling your feet along the carpet as it is laid. Repeat steps 2, 3, and 4 until all sections are adhered to the floor.

5. To remove air bubbles, push on the carpet with a piece of 2 x 4 held at a 45° angle. Move from one end of the room to the other. If carpet has a seam, start on one side of the seam and work away from it toward the wall. Then work on the other side.

6. Finish edges at the walls, first creasing the carpet with the back edge of a linoleum knife. Then cut off excess with a carpet knife. Carpet should be flush with the wall. At a doorway, finish with a metal threshold bar (p.317). Replace the shoe molding.

Interiors / Window shades

Roller window shades come in an array of colors and patterns. Used to insulate, to block light, or for privacy, the shade's cloth may be vinyl or a woven fabric, and it may be translucent or opaque. Shades are sold by the width, measured from the tip of the spear to the tip of the pin—usually 37 to 120 inches. Longer rollers are all steel, but most rollers are wooden.

The roller is hollowed at one end to hold a long spring controlled by a ratchet. The shade is held in position by a pawl that latches into the tooth of the ratchet. When you lower the shade, the pawl is freed. The more you lower the shade, the more the spring tension increases. When you raise the shade, the spring uncoils and the shade wraps around the roller.

If the shade doesn't roll up fully, increase the spring tension by pulling it down halfway; take the roller off its brackets and reroll the shade by hand. If the shade winds up too rapidly, release tension by taking down the roller and partially unrolling the shade. If the ratchet fails to hold the shade in place, oil the pawl sparingly.

A shade is hung by inserting the spear and pin into brackets mounted inside the window recess or on the window frame. Depending on where the brackets are mounted, the shade may roll down behind the roller or in front of it (right). The brackets must be level for the shade to roll up evenly.

To make a shade narrower, remove the cloth, pull off the metal cap at the pin end, and pull out the pin. Saw the roller to size; trim the cloth, align it parallel to the roller, and reattach it. Fit on the cap, and hammer in the pin.

Anatomy of a roller shade

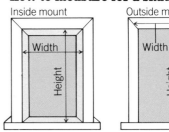

Outside mounting bracket for pin

Pin

Inside mounting brackets

Spring

Ratchet tooth

Pawl   Spear

Outside mounting bracket for spear

Conventional roll

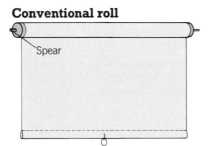

Spear

When you set the spear bracket at the left of the window and the pin bracket at the right, the cloth unwinds behind the roller—hugging the glass and slightly reducing heat loss.

Reverse roll

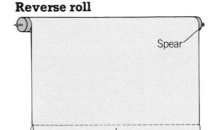

Spear

When the pin is at the left of window and spear is at the right, cloth unwinds in front of the roller and hides it. But the shade loses insulating value.

How to measure for a shade

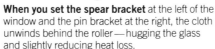

Inside mount   Outside mount

Width   Width

Height   Height

For inside mount, measure width between side jambs and height from top jamb to sill.
For outside mount, measure across top and down to sill; add 3 in. to each measurement.

Making a decorative shade

Any tightly woven fabric becomes a shade cloth when ironed to a muslin lining with fusible web (sold at sewing supply stores). Follow maker's directions to bond the web to fabric.

Using an old shade as a pattern, add 1 inch to the width of the materials for trimming and 2 inches to the length for a slat casing. Assemble the layers with decorative fabric face down and lining face up; overlap web strips between the two.

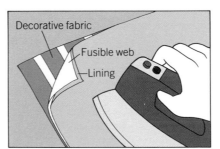

Decorative fabric

Fusible web

Lining

Iron fabric, fusible web, and lining in 18-in. sections. Turn the fabric over; press the other side. Trim ½ in. from each side; seal the edges with white glue or zigzag stitching.

Sew a slat casing; place slat from old shade inside it. Pencil a guideline across roller's length. Align squared fabric, right side up, with line; staple it to roller. Attach a shade pull.

Blinds and pulley shades

Venetian, mini, and micro blinds

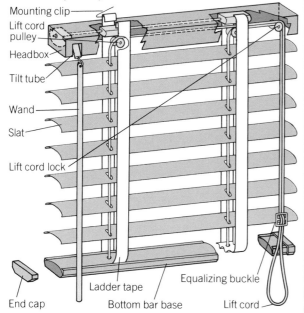

Mounting clip
Lift cord pulley
Headbox
Tilt tube
Wand
Slat
Lift cord lock
End cap
Ladder tape
Bottom bar base
Equalizing buckle
Lift cord

Balloon and pleated shades

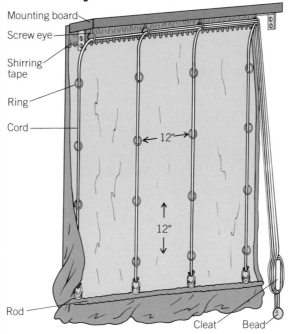

Mounting board
Screw eye
Shirring tape
Ring
Cord
12"
12"
Rod
Cleat   Bead

Pulley shades

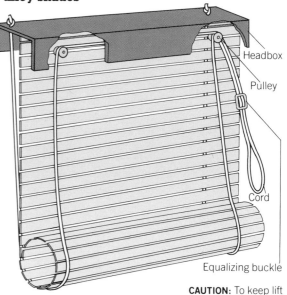

Headbox
Pulley
Cord
Equalizing buckle

CAUTION: To keep lift cords out of children's reach, use a cleat, paper clamp, or clothes pin, or tie cord to itself.

The same types of gears and pulleys inside a headbox operate venetian blinds, mini blinds, and micro blinds. A ladder tape or string at the sides (and sometimes in the center) of the blind supports the slats. When the lift cord is pulled, it raises or lowers the slats. To lock the cord in place, pull it to one side. A cord or wand turns a tilt tube to angle the slats.

To replace worn ladder tapes and lift cord, lay the blind on a table. Expose the bottom ends of the tapes and cord by removing the end caps and sliding out the bottom bar base. Unknot and remove the cord from the slats. Tape the new cord to one end of the old cord; pull it through the pulleys and the lock. Leave a loop to adjust the blind. To replace the ladder tapes, attach the top ends of new tapes to the tilt tube; then slide the slats back into the tapes. Pull the cords through the holes in the slats, running through alternate sides of the tape rungs. Adjust the equalizing buckle so the slats raise evenly.

Select your own fabric to make a balloon window shade (above) or a horizontally pleated shade. Both shades are lifted and lowered by hidden rings and cords; both are hung from a mounting board.

To make either shade, line the fabric and seam the sides. (For a balloon shade, add 3 inches to its width for each scallop; 1 foot to length). At the fabric's bottom edge stitch in a rod casing. Sew rows of rings the length and width of the material 12 inches apart. (Sew shirring tape along the top of a balloon shade). Staple the fabric to the mounting board. Feed cords into the rings; knot each cord to a bottom ring. (To let the shade "balloon" out, knot three rings together.) Slide the rod into its casing. Attach screw eyes to the board; mount the board on the window frame. Thread the cords through the screw eyes; the cords are held in a bead and fastened to a cleat. Or attach the cords to a roller (from a shade) below the mounting board; the cords will wrap around the roller.

The pulley shade rolls up in a cylinder on its bottom rod. Some versions of the shade—woven wood and tortoise-finish bamboo are examples—feature a headbox and add a lock similar to that on a venetian blind. On matchstick or wood slat shades, the pulley-and-cord mechanism may be exposed, or it may be covered with a matching flap valance.

Pulley shades are operated by a single length of cord. To install a new cord, unroll the shade and remove the old cord. Knot the new cord to one end of the top support. Bring the cord down behind the shade, underneath it, and up its front; feed the cord through the pulley at that side, then across the shade and over the pulley on the other side. Leave enough cord to form a loop to adjust the shade; then bring the cord back over the pulley, down the front and up the back of the shade, and tie it to the support. Feed the loop through the equalizing buckle and adjust it so that the shade rolls up evenly.

Interiors / Traverse rods

Draperies hung from a traverse rod can be drawn back by day to reveal a view and let in air and sun, and they can be closed at night for privacy.

For draperies that part at the center, called two-way draw, a cord travels from an *overlap master slide* along a channel in the rod, over a pulley at one end, and back through the channel to an *underlap master slide.* It then continues to the other end of the rod and another pulley before returning to the first slide. A one-way draw to right or left works on a single master slide; you can order a rod that draws in one direction, or you can convert a two-way draw rod to draw one way or a one-way draw rod to draw in the other direction.

Because a traverse rod telescopes, you can adjust its length. Hang it from end brackets set inside a window, against the frame, or on the wall above it. Add intermediate supports for rods that are more than 48 inches long.

With a conventional rod, set drapery hooks low enough so that the draperies will hide the rod. Conceal the ends of the rod by hooking the draperies into two holes in each end bracket. With decorative rods, of course, set hooks to display them, and leave the ends bare.

If a cord breaks or pulls loose, restring it as diagrammed below. Be sure to use the correct kind of cord; it's available where rods are sold.

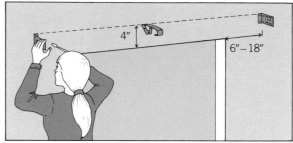

To mount traverse rod at a window that lacks a molding, position the top of the brackets 4 in. above the window and 6 to 18 in. beyond each side. For hollow wallboard or solid plaster walls, use toggle bolts (p.85), molly bolts, or screw anchors (p.87).

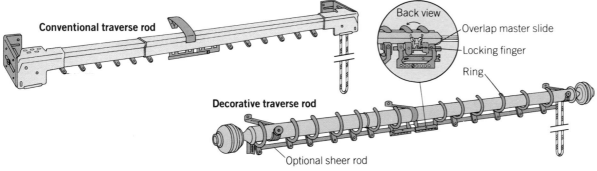

Conventional traverse rod

Back view
Overlap master slide
Locking finger
Ring

Decorative traverse rod

Optional sheer rod

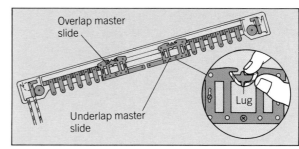

Overlap master slide
Underlap master slide
Lug

Before hanging rod, place it face down on floor and extend it to the required length. Pull cord to draw overlap master slide left. Move underlap master slide right. Pull cord at the openings in underlap master slide; hook it under the lug.

How a traverse rod works

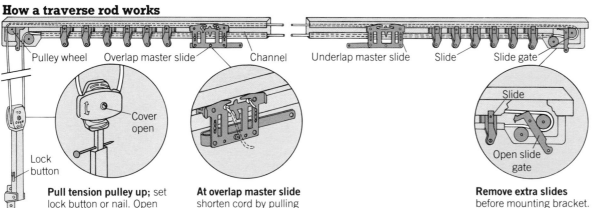

Pulley wheel   Overlap master slide   Channel   Underlap master slide   Slide   Slide gate

Cover open

Lock button

Slide
Open slide gate

Pull tension pulley up; set lock button or nail. Open cover; slip cord in. Knot cord (right); reset pulley.

At overlap master slide shorten cord by pulling knot nearest pulley. When cord is taut, reknot it.

Remove extra slides before mounting bracket. Push slide gate open; slip slides out.

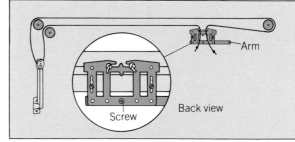

Arm

Screw   Back view

Converting a two-way draw to a left-to-right draw. Pull rod apart at middle; unhook and discard underlap master slide. Remove screw from overlap master slide's arm (if slide isn't a solid piece); reverse arm and reattach screw. Slip off overlap slide; transfer slides to left. Replace overlap slide, rejoin sections, and pull cord taut to right. For a right-to-left draw, reverse directions; for decorative rod, move one ring to right of locking finger.

Vertical blinds

Drawn across windows like traverse draperies, vertical blinds look like venetian blinds set on end—instead of horizontal slats, they have vertical *vanes.* The vanes rotate 180° to give maximum control of light and privacy. They can be drawn apart at the center, or they can be drawn to the left or right. The vanes can be opaque or translucent and are made of fabric, aluminum, or vinyl. They are usually about 4 inches wide.

The blinds are mounted inside a window recess, on the wall, or from the ceiling in front of the window. Their mounting brackets are concealed by the headrail under them, which in turn encloses a track. Carriers, which slide along the track when a cord is pulled, support vanes from hangers. Some vanes are held straight at the bottom by weights.

To hang vertical blinds completely inside a window, the window recess must be at least 4½ inches deep. If you don't mind the vanes protruding beyond the frame, the recess can be 3½ inches deep and still hold the brackets and headrail. The alternative is to mount the brackets on the wall. Add at least 1½ inches to the desired length of the blinds to allow the headrail and bracket to clear the top of the window molding. The back edge of the vanes must be at least 1 inch from the wall, and may be up to 2½ inches away from it.

How a vertical blind works

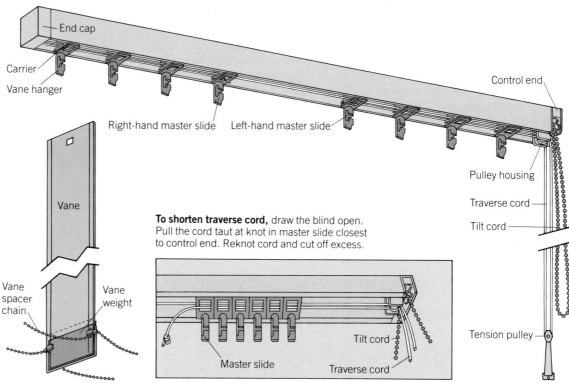

To shorten traverse cord, draw the blind open. Pull the cord taut at knot in master slide closest to control end. Reknot cord and cut off excess.

Installing fabric vanes

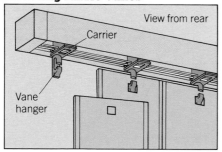

With the front of the vane facing you, slide the vane hanger onto a carrier. If a vane is crooked, twist its top until the carrier clicks into place.

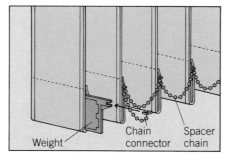

Slip a weight into the pocket of each vane. Clip a spacer chain to each weight; allow for vane width plus slack between them. Cut off extra chain, using scissors.

Installing vinyl or aluminum vanes

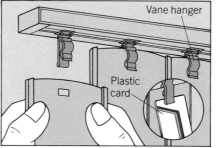

While holding vane facing you, turn vane hanger's short leg forward. Push vane up between hanger legs until it snaps in place. (To free a vane with a hook, slip a plastic card between the vane and the hanger's long leg.)

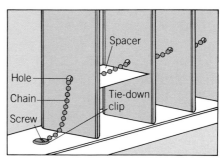

Thread chain through holes at the bottom of the vanes; use spacer to determine chain length. Trim excess chain 1 in. beyond last vane; attach it to a tie-down clip.

For most houses, heat lost through windows represents 15 to 35 percent of the heating bill. In the summer, air-conditioned air can be diminished by outdoor heat. Some of this can be corrected by insulating windows—but if window frames and sashes are not properly caulked and weatherstripped, you'll lose the effectiveness of the insulation.

Shades, blinds, and draperies that are white, light-colored, or metallic on the outside will reflect sunlight, keeping out heat; dark colors will absorb it. For the best control of heat and air flow, seal the edges of coverings to window frames or install shutters (facing page). Storm windows (p.432) or thermal glass (p.426) will also help control heat loss; so will inexpensive plastic films (facing page) sold in kits to use either indoors or outdoors.

To rate the effectiveness of your window covering options, check the R-value chart below. The R refers to a material's *resistance* to heat transfer; the higher its R-value, the better the material insulates the window.

R-values for conventional window treatments

Window device	Unsealed/ partial seal	Sealed with 1" to 4" air space
Blind, mini, venetian, or vertical	R-.12 to R-.2	Difficult to seal
Draperies, lined	R-.2	R-.35
Draperies or curtains, unlined	R-.2	Difficult to seal
Film, heat-shrink or molding strip		R-.3
Shade, balloon	R-.3	Difficult to seal
Shade, quilted		R-2.5 to R-5.5
Shade, roller, inside mount	R-.38	R-.66
Shade, woven wood	R-.3 to R-.5	Difficult to seal
Shutters, solid	R-2 to R-7	R-3 to R-9
Window, single-glazed	R-.9 to R-1	
Window, double-glazed	R-1.8 to R-2	
Window, storm	R-.9	R-1.8

To estimate how well your window's components insulate, add their R-values as listed above. A single-glazed window with a storm window outside and a roller shade plus draperies inside has a potential R-value of 2 to 4. If the shade reflects heat, add another .80 to the R-value.

Effects of insulation

Winter

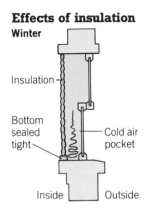

Insulation

Bottom sealed tight

Cold air pocket

Inside — Outside

Summer (most climates)

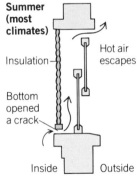

Insulation

Hot air escapes

Bottom opened a crack

Inside — Outside

Summer (hot, humid climates)

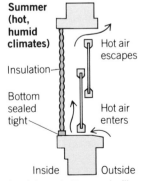

Insulation

Hot air escapes

Bottom sealed tight

Hot air enters

Inside — Outside

In winter, a bottom seal will keep cold air out. In summer, let rising hot air escape from lowered top sash while insulation retains cool room air.

A quilted shade

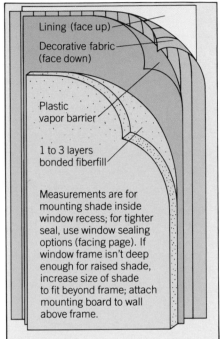

Lining (face up)

Decorative fabric (face down)

Plastic vapor barrier

1 to 3 layers bonded fiberfill

Measurements are for mounting shade inside window recess; for tighter seal, use window sealing options (facing page). If window frame isn't deep enough for raised shade, increase size of shade to fit beyond frame; attach mounting board to wall above frame.

Cut materials to size of window, but add 3 in. to width and 4 in. to length of decorative fabric, 1 in. to width and 4 in. to length of plastic and lining. Layer materials; pin edges together. Sew ½-in. side seams, and then ½-in. bottom seam.

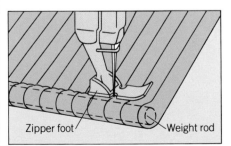

Zipper foot — Weight rod

Turn fabric right side out. If using magnetic tape (facing page), add it beforehand; if a weight rod, slide it between layers to bottom of shade. Stitch above rod, using zipper foot. Turn under top edge ½ in.; topstitch ½-in. top and side seams.

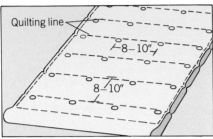

Quilting line

8–10"

8–10"

To make channels for quilt effect, topstitch shade horizontally every 8 to 10 in. For ring locations, mark 8 to 10 in. apart vertically along quilting lines. There must be at least three rows of rings. Sew rings through all layers of shade.

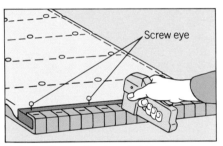

Screw eye

Cut a 1 x 2 mounting board ¼ in. narrower than shade. Fold top 4 in. of shade over board; staple shade to back of board. Put screw eyes in board over each column of rings; attach a pulley to end of board.

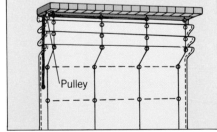

Pulley

Tie a cord to each bottom ring; thread it up column of rings, and through screw eyes and pulley. (Attach magnetic strips to window stops.) Knot cords; pull shade up. Attach board inside window recess with screws or bolts.

Window sealing options

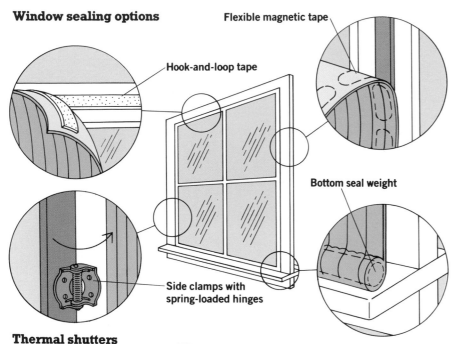

Flexible magnetic tape

Hook-and-loop tape

Bottom seal weight

Side clamps with spring-loaded hinges

Thermal shutters

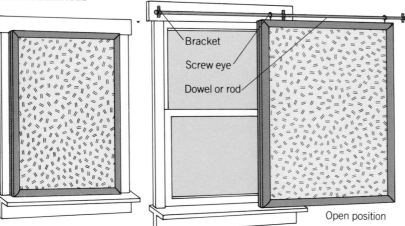

Bracket

Screw eye

Dowel or rod

Open position

Shutter with spring-loaded hinges (above) has a 5.5 R-value. Fabric stretched taut on back and front of a 1 x 2 frame covers 1 in. of fiberfill. Molding hides fabric's edges.

Gliding shutter with a 4.0 R-value is a 1 x 2 frame faced with hardboard—painted or covered by a poster or wallpaper—that encloses a 1-in.-thick sheet of fiberglass board insulation. Molding trims its edges. Screw eyes at the top slide on a dowel or curtain rod held by brackets.

Heat-shrink film: indoors

Bracket

Wipe dust and grease from window trim with denatured alcohol. Cut double-faced tape with a utility knife. With paper side toward you, press strips to face or outside edges of trim. Put tape on underside of sill, if any.

Cut the film 2 in. larger than the taped area. Remove the paper from the tape across the top of the window. Stretch the film over it, and press it flat. Uncover the side and sill tapes, pull the film down, and press into place.

Set a hair dryer to a high temperature. Move it slowly back and forth across window, holding dryer about ¼ in. from film. The heat will shrink the film, removing all creases and wrinkles. Cut off excess film with the utility knife.

Molding-strip film: outdoors

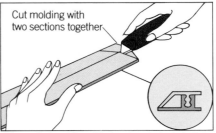

Cut molding with two sections together

Clean window trim with denatured alcohol. Cut molding from a kit to required lengths. Miter corners at 45° angles; use shears, utility knife, or backsaw. For bottom strip on sill, cut 90° angle.

Peel paper from the backs of the molding channels; set them in place. Cut film about 4 in. oversize; tape it above the window. Holding top molding-strip insert over film at top center of window, snap it into molding channel (below).

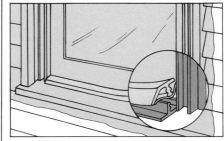

Install the bottom insert, then the sides, always working from center toward the edges. Trim excess film from the edges with a utility knife. Leave film year-round (air-conditioning costs are cut) or store during summer.

Interiors / Adding a closet

Measuring and marking 46–47
Wallboard 274–277
Hanging a door 444–445

When framing closet, reinforce corner with doubled studs. Spacer blocks between studs provide nailing surface for fastening wallboard. *Rough opening* shown here is framed with doubled studs to accommodate a wide decorative *trim* (molding that surrounds the finished opening). With narrower trim, use a single stud. After the frame is enclosed with wallboard, line the rough opening with special lumber, called *jamb stock,* to support doors.

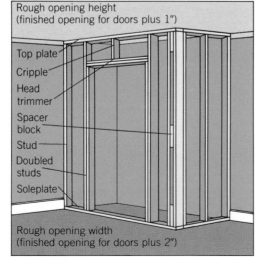

Rough opening height (finished opening for doors plus 1")

Top plate
Cripple
Head trimmer
Spacer block
Stud
Doubled studs
Soleplate

Rough opening width (finished opening for doors plus 2")

Allow several weekends for this project. The framing goes fairly fast, but the wallboard takes time. And installing a door properly—even a prehung unit—can take longer than you think.

Planning. If you choose a corner for the closet, you'll need to build only two walls. The closet interior should be at least 24 inches deep and, for a bedroom, 48 inches wide. The exterior dimensions will be 4½ inches larger because of the thickness of the framing and wallboard. It's helpful to sketch the door wall's framing on graph paper.

Locate the wall studs (p.191); find the floor joists in the same way. It's best to anchor the end studs of the closet walls to the wall studs and the plates to the joists with nails or screws. If the framing members don't align, you can glue the closet to the walls and ceiling with construction mastic. First, scrape the wallpaper or paint from the wall (p.376); then apply the mastic in a bead to the framing members that abut the walls and ceiling. Position the frame so that it is square, level, and plumb; then use shims to push it tightly against the walls and ceiling for a good bond.

Buy the doors beforehand. Door options include plain or prehung hinged doors and gliding, accordion, or bifold doors. Each style comes with installation instructions that tell you what size to make the opening.

Tools and materials. You'll need a hammer, screwdriver, and pry bar; a crosscut or circular saw, wallboard saw, and utility knife. For accurate measurements use a steel tape measure, chalk line, level, framing square, and plumb bob. Cut the studs, top plate, and soleplate from 2 x 4's, the

Framing the walls

Framing square

1. With steel tape, chalk line, and framing square, measure and mark closet's outline on floor. Transfer corners to ceiling with plumb bob. Draw outline on ceiling, guidelines on walls. Measure for top plate and soleplate separately; they may differ. Cut plates. Remove baseboard (p.293) from interior closet area (save for exterior, if desired).

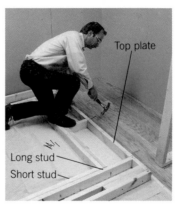

Top plate
Long stud
Short stud

2. Align soleplate and top plate; mark long studs' positions with X; short studs with T. Space studs (except at door and corner) 16 in. on center. Nail long studs through plates. Frame door opening with short studs. Nail first head trimmer in place on short studs. Center a 2 x 4 cripple stud on second trimmer, set in place, and secure with nails through long studs.

Frame
Chalk line

3. Tilt each frame into place; align with chalk lines. Nail corner studs together. Check that framework is plumb; shim bottom so that it's tight against ceiling. Screw frame to wall studs, ceiling joists, and floor at 2-ft. intervals; or glue it with construction mastic. Saw threshold section from soleplate. Run wires for lighting if desired. Install wallboard.

cleats from 1 x 4's, and any shelves or partitions from ¾-inch plywood. To sheathe the framing and finish the closet you'll need wallboard and some special lumber—4⅝-inch-wide doorjamb stock with rabbeted side jambs, trim and doorstop molding, a closet rod and holders, and shims. Be sure to get the right hardware for the door. Assemble the framing with 16d nails; attach the sheathing with 3-inch wallboard screws.

Measuring and cutting. The long studs are 3½ inches shorter than the room's height (the thickness of the top plate and soleplate plus ½ inch clearance to raise the frame). Cut the short studs that line the rough opening 1½ inches shorter than the height recommended by the door's manufacturer (to accommodate the soleplate).

Alternative closet interior. Multiple shelves (p.328) and double rods make for efficient use of space. Divide area with plywood partitions screwed to shelf (p.97) and anchored with glue blocks or quarter round molding.

Installing the jamb

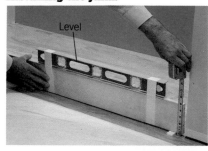

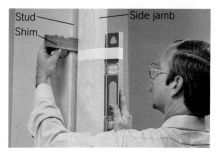

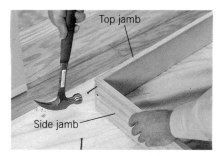

1. Check across the threshold with a level; if the floor isn't level, measure side jambs individually. Cut bottom of side jambs to accommodate the door. For bifold doors (shown here), the jambs must be tall enough to allow the doors to pivot and clear the track.

2. Tape level to edge of jamb stock. Using jamb as straightedge, hold it against stud to check plumb. If out of plumb, correct by inserting shims from both sides of jamb (creates flat surface) as needed. Fasten shims to studs with 8d finishing nails. Untape level.

3. Cut top jamb to length. Nail top jamb to side jambs with 8d finishing nails. Raise the jambs into place within rough opening; nail side jamb to shims on studs.

4. The threshold's measurement should equal span of top jamb; shim as needed. Center a shim between head trimmer and top jamb. Check for level; fasten jamb, shim, and trimmer with 8d nails.

Doors and rods

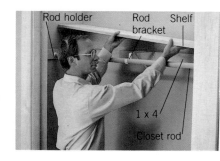

1. Following the manufacturer's instructions, screw bifold-door track and pivots to top jamb. Hang doors; then attach remaining door fixtures as instructions direct.

2. If needed, tap shims to further align side and top jambs to rough opening. (It's all right if shims split.) Using utility knife, score protruding shim ends and break them off. Nail doorstop molding to side jambs to hide door hinges. Install trim.

3. Using level, draw line on closet back and side walls 66 in. above floor. Position a 1 x 4 cleat above line; nail to studs. For double rods, mount the top one 76 to 84 in. above floor, bottom one 36 to 42 in.

4. Screw purchased closet-rod holders to 1 x 4's on end walls. Measure, cut, and fit rod and plywood shelf. Use combination shelf-and-rod brackets screwed to studs for additional support.

Interiors/Shelving

Shelf supports

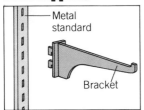

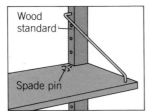

Metal brackets hook into rear standards. For heavy loads, get three-hook bracket.

Wood standards. Metal rods support shelf from above; spade pins support from below.

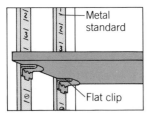

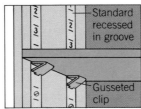

Side-mounted metal standards may be screwed to surface or set in grooves.

Gusseted clips can hold heavier loads than the flat clips at left.

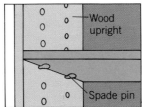

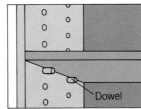

Spade pins are inserted in holes drilled in uprights. (Method shown at far right).

Hardwood dowels ⅜ in. in diameter, cut to 1-in. lengths, are sturdier than pins.

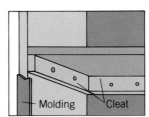

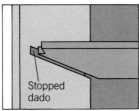

Wood cleats cut from 1 x 2's provide extra support at rear, preventing sagging.

Stopped dado (p.102) gives shelf added rigidity and is not visible from front.

When choosing a shelving system, consider what you want to store, organize, or display; its weight and quantity; and how much that quantity might increase. Shelves can be mounted on a wall or in a cabinet in a variety of ways and can be fixed or adjustable. Generally, vertical support is provided by metal or wood *standards*, and horizontal support comes from *brackets, clips, dowels,* or *pins.* Sometimes a wood *cleat* can be installed to support the shelf on two or three sides.

Spacing. The load that a shelf can carry depends on the spacing of its supports, the type of brackets you use, and the strength of the shelf itself. For light objects, such as clothing or stemware, use 1-inch-thick softwood or ¾-inch plywood, supported by rear standards screwed into every other stud. When planning, make sure that the shelf's overhang at each end will not exceed 12 inches.

For moderately heavy loads, such as books, use the same lumber as for light loads but install standards at each stud. Very heavy loads, or moderate loads on standards set more than 16 inches apart, call for thicker shelves. Glue two sheets of ¾-inch plywood together, cut the shelf (with an overhang of less than 8 inches), and reinforce the long edges with 1 x 2's. If you are mounting shelves on a material other than wood or wallboard, see pp. 80–86 for the correct fasteners.

Planning. Keep frequently used items on shelves that are higher than knee level and no more than 10 inches above your head. Put lighter, less used items on high shelves, heavier objects on low shelves.

Mounting standards

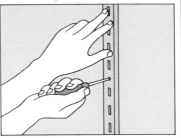

1. Position standard over wall stud. Using awl, mark through standard's middle screw hole. Drill pilot hole. Screw standard partway, enough so that it's secure.

2. Place level flush against standard. Adjust standard until bubble is centered. Mark and drill other pilot holes. Insert screws; then tighten the first screw.

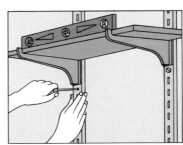

3. Hook brackets into same-numbered slots of both standards. Position second standard. Place shelf on brackets and level on shelf. Move standard to center bubble; then install.

Shelves in a cabinet

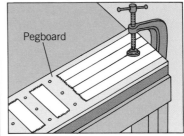

1. Tape alternate rows of holes in scrap pegboard to make a template. Before assembly, clamp template to front edge of cabinet side.

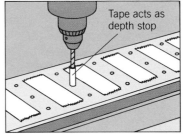

2. Drill ⅜-in.-deep holes through center of untaped rows. (Use stop or tape to gauge depth.) Shift template to back edge of cabinet side; repeat. Make holes in opposite side the same way.

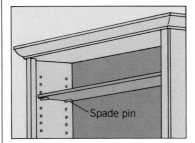

3. Assemble and fasten cabinet components (p.113). Insert spade pins or dowels in corresponding holes of uprights. Install shelf.

Kitchen cabinets

Plastic laminates 140–141
Finding a stud 191

Drab or worn cabinet exteriors can be renewed with natural wood finish (p.121), paint, or new facings that adhere to the old. But if insufficient or damaged cabinets call for new ones, shop around at kitchen and bath centers to find out what's available and to get professional advice. Take along floor and wall plans mapped out on graph paper. Before buying, recheck your measurements. If possible, have the dealer or manufacturer's representative take the final measurements.

Widths of base cabinets vary from 9 to 60 inches, increasing in increments of 3 inches. They measure 24 inches from back to front and 34½ inches high. A countertop adds 1½ inches. (Order these two items at the same time.) Wall cabinets are generally 12 inches from back to front, and 30, 33, or 36 inches high. Taller models eliminate open space above the cabinets but must be ordered specifically.

Wall cabinet widths run from 12 to 60 inches; a wide cabinet is cheaper and more useful than several small ones. Special-use cabinets are 24 inches deep and up to 84 inches high; widths vary.

Draw the floor plan on graph paper, showing the floor's dimensions and any fixed utilities such as a sink; then draw in the base cabinets' depth and widths. Make a separate sketch of the wall plan; include the locations of studs, windows, and doors. On this sketch, plan the size and number of cabinets you need. Allow 18 inches between top of the countertop and the bottom of the wall cabinets.

Tools and materials. You'll need a hammer, a keyhole saw, a drill, a screwdriver, a level, a tape measure, several C-clamps, flathead wood screws, 1¾- and 2½-inch roundhead screws, shims (tapered cedar shingles), molding, 2 x 4's and plywood triangles for braces, and a sturdy stepladder.

Preparation. Empty the kitchen and remove the old cabinets. Clean and prime the walls (p.356). Mark the studs' centers (p.191) with floor-to-ceiling lines. With a level and tape measure, find the highest spot on the floor where the base cabinets will rest. If the difference between the lowest and highest points is less than ½ inch, you can shim the cabinets at the low levels. However, if it is more than ½ inch, you should have the floor leveled by a contractor. Following your wall plan, draw horizontal guidelines to mark the bottom and top of the base and wall cabinets. These lines must be level. If the walls are damaged or out of plumb, install horizontal furring strips (p.283) where the cabinets' mounting rails will be fastened.

Gaps between the cabinets and the walls will be bridged with molding (p.99); gaps between cabinets will be covered with strips that match their fronts.

The L-shaped kitchen

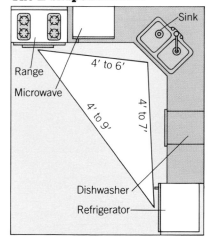

Sink, range, and refrigerator locations should form a triangle with enough counter space between appliances for food preparation, serving, stacking, and cleaning up. On the other hand, the triangle's legs should be short enough to minimize walking. Never place a heat-making appliance—range or dishwasher—next to the refrigerator.

The U-shaped kitchen

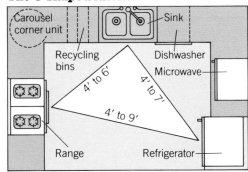

The galley kitchen

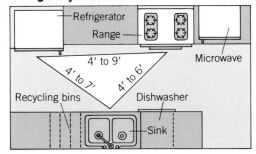

Wall plan for cabinets and studs

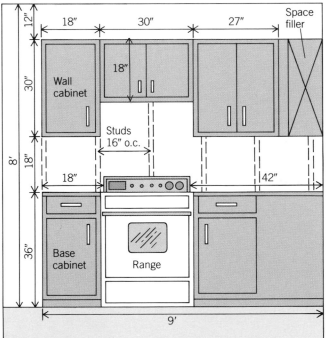

When planning cabinets, start at a corner and plot their dimensions according to the sizes detailed above. (Mark hinge positions and track the doors' arcs on the floor plan to be sure that they will swing freely.) If you're working from a catalog, label each piece with its model number. Adjustable shelves inside the cabinets are more efficient than fixed shelving. When finished, note how many and what size filler strips, if any, you need. Take this sketch with you when you go to place your order.

Interiors/Installing ready-made cabinets

Mounting wall cabinets

1. Make a brace tall enough to support a wall cabinet at the proper height. Set brace in position, and if necessary, put shims under it to raise it to the exact level. Lift first cabinet onto brace. Make sure it is level and that its top edge is even with guideline marked for cabinet's top. If you need to adjust brace's height, remove the cabinet first.

2. Drill pilot holes in cabinet's top mounting rail, going into studs near each side. Drive a 2½-in. roundhead screw just deep enough into each hole to secure cabinet. Use a level to check that the cabinet's front is plumb. Shim the back, if necessary, placing shims at studs. Fasten bottom mounting rail as you did the top.

Once you have located the studs and marked the cabinets' positions on the walls (p.329), installing them is straightforward. While mounting, check that the cabinets are level and plumb; if they aren't, the doors and drawers won't function properly. Floors are seldom level or walls plumb; to align the cabinets accurately, wedge shims behind and under them.

Preparation. Remove all drawers, doors, and loose shelves. Label each part and its corresponding location

with masking tape for speedy identification when you put them back.

If you're starting with an empty room, install the wall cabinets first. (This way the base cabinets won't be in the way of the ladder.) Begin in or near a corner. Support the cabinets with a T-bar (p.275), or a brace made from 2 x 4's and plywood triangles (right). Ask a helper to steady the cabinets while you fasten them. Test the wall's composition (p.191), and use appropriate fasteners. (p.86).

3. Move brace; put next cabinet atop it. Adjust for level; clamp stiles. Counterbore holes in stiles; fasten with flathead wood screws that penetrate at least halfway into second stile. Drill the mounting strip; adjust for level and plumb; then fasten to studs. Repeat with remaining cabinets. Check that all are level and plumb; tighten mounting screws.

Installing base cabinets

1. Position first cabinet according to plan. Drive shims under and behind cabinet to bring it level, plumb, and even with guideline on wall. Shims placed behind cabinet must be located at studs. To avoid marring floor, drive shims by hammering against a wood block. Cabinet levelers (p.116) can be used on base cabinets.

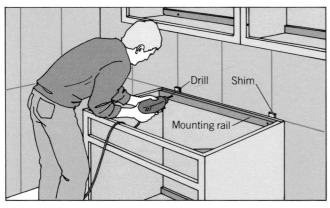

2. Near each end of mounting rail, drill a pilot hole through rail (and shim, if any) into stud. Drive 2½-in. roundhead screws just deep enough to secure cabinet. Test again for level and plumb. Adjust shims if necessary.

3. Level next cabinet with shims so that it lines up with first cabinet and with wall markings. Clamp cabinets' stiles together. Counterbore holes in stiles; fasten with wood screws that penetrate at least halfway into second stile. Attach to wall as for first cabinet. Repeat with remaining cabinets.

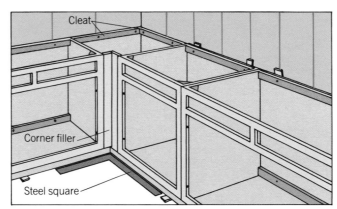

4. At corner, fasten 1 x 3 cleats to walls to support counter. Cover gaps between cabinets, in corners, or between cabinets and wall with filler strips. Cut strips to fit; attach them to stiles with wood screws.

5. Recheck all units for level and plumb; if necessary, adjust shims. Tighten all screws. Using a keyhole saw with its handle reversed, cut partway through shims; then break them off. Cover gap with quarter-round molding (p.99) or vinyl cove base. Cover screwheads in stiles with dowels colored to blend with the cabinet's finish.

6. To attach counter, drill hole at an angle through cabinets' wood corner braces with adjustable pilot-hole bit. With a helper, set counter in place, snug against wall. With same bit, drill through brace holes partway into counter. Secure it to braces with 1¾-in. roundhead screws.

Interiors/Finishing an attic

Decide how you will use the converted attic. Consult a builder or architect while developing your plans. He or she can tell you whether your plan is feasible, your budget is reasonable, and what permits, inspections, and variances you will need. Reading the relevant sections (right) will help you decide what you can do yourself and what to leave to a professional. You will save time, money, and aggravation by realistically allocating the tasks.

▶ **CAUTION:** If your attic is crisscrossed with roof supports (p.402), you have a webbed or truss system and you *cannot make any changes at all.*

Assessing the space. Building codes specify minimum floor area and ceiling height requirements for different rooms. Generally, 50 percent of the finished floor must have a ceiling height of 7½ feet.

Have a professional check the house's foundation and utility systems. A finished attic adds a story to the house: the structure must be able to support the extra load. (Some codes require strengthening the walls of the lower stories.) If you want to add a bathroom, you must be able to hook new plumbing into the existing system. (If you are on a septic system, adding a bedroom, even without adding a bathroom, may also mean having to increase the size of the tank and drainage fields.) Check also that your heating system is sufficient for the additional space.

Planning construction. The floor joists must support the increased load. Strengthen them as needed by repairing, doubling, or adding joists. Again, building codes have prescribed minimums to use as a guide. You may need to install or enhance a permanent staircase—folding attic stairs are inadequate for daily use. Plan a second exit for emergencies.

When choosing the kinds of windows you want and where you want them, keep in mind that they may serve as emergency exits. Provide for insulation and ventilation to maintain comfortable temperatures and to avoid condensation that can damage the roof. Install an auxiliary circuit breaker box, if needed, and new circuits. Be generous with electrical outlets. You may want extra wiring or outlets

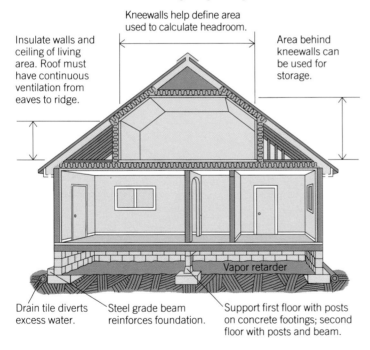

Kneewalls help define area used to calculate headroom.

Insulate walls and ceiling of living area. Roof must have continuous ventilation from eaves to ridge.

Area behind kneewalls can be used for storage.

Drain tile diverts excess water.

Steel grade beam reinforces foundation.

Vapor retarder

Support first floor with posts on concrete footings; second floor with posts and beam.

Finishing an attic is a complicated project that affects the house from foundation to roof. In houses built after 1970, the exterior walls' framing, lower floors, and foundation may need bolstering to support the increased load. Older houses tend to be overbuilt and may not need any shoring up. A building inspector, contractor, or architect can tell you whether reinforcing is needed, what materials to use, and where to put them.

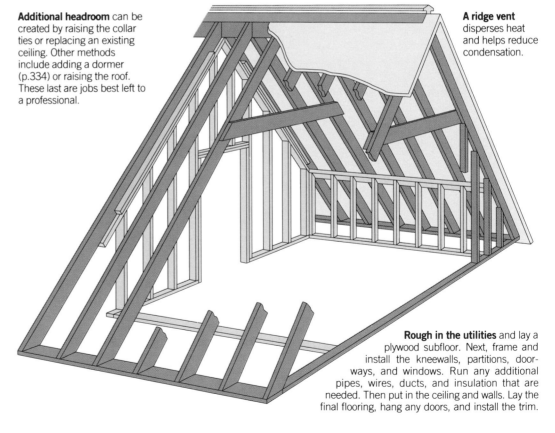

Additional headroom can be created by raising the collar ties or replacing an existing ceiling. Other methods include adding a dormer (p.334) or raising the roof. These last are jobs best left to a professional.

A ridge vent disperses heat and helps reduce condensation.

Rough in the utilities and lay a plywood subfloor. Next, frame and install the kneewalls, partitions, doorways, and windows. Run any additional pipes, wires, ducts, and insulation that are needed. Then put in the ceiling and walls. Lay the final flooring, hang any doors, and install the trim.

for media equipment, air conditioners, or a computer. Install smoke detectors (p.270). When shopping for fixtures and furniture, measure them—and your staircases and door frames—to be sure that you can get them into the attic.

Building sequence. Begin with the floor: Run any pipes, wires, ducts, and insulation. Lay a subfloor if there's no floor in the attic. Run the utilities in the walls and ceiling. Install a vapor retarder between the insulation and the finish material in the ceiling and walls. Schedule inspections as you go; for example, the wiring must be inspected before it is enclosed by the floor, walls, or ceiling. For finishing, work from the ceiling down.

Installing kneewalls and partitions

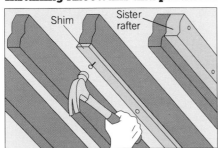

1. Rafter edges must form a level plane for top plate of kneewall. Test by holding a level or straightedge across edges. Raise low spots with shims or by doubling the rafter.

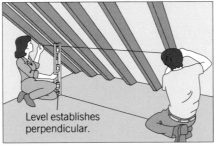

2. Snap a chalk line across floor and rafters to establish position of kneewall. Measure distance between end rafters. Cut two 2 x 4's to this length (for kneewall's top plate and soleplate).

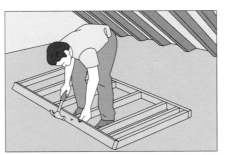

3. Cut 2 x 4's for kneewall's studs. Transcribe rafter angle onto one stud; use it as a template to bevel remaining studs. Nail studs to plates, 16 or 24 in. apart. (Studs needn't align with rafters.)

4. Set kneewall in position. Check plumb with a level; shim as needed. Nail wall to floor and rafters. Top plate of partition wall (next step) must align over the space between kneewall's end studs.

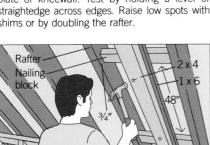

5. For top plate of partition, nail 2 x 4 blocks between rafters ¾ in. in from rafters' edges, and 48-in. apart. Nail 1 x 6 to blocks, parallel to rafters. Center a 2 x 4 on the 1 x 6; fasten with nails.

6. Align 2 x 4 soleplate directly below top plate, and nail it to floor. Mark stud positions at 16-in. intervals along soleplate. Transfer measurements to top plate with level and straightedge.

7. Set tallest 2 x 4 on its mark. With level, check that it is truly vertical. Mark and cut top bevel. Install stud by toenailing it to both plates. Repeat procedure for remaining studs.

8. Install shortest stud on final mark; don't double corner stud. Finish walls and ceiling with wallboard (1 x 6 in top plate and doubled studs at end of kneewall provide nailing surfaces in corners).

Planning and building a shed dormer require a high level of skill and experience. Consult with a reputable contractor or architect before beginning. If you have the slightest doubt about your ability, give all or part of the job to a professional. For example, a contractor can do the framing and exterior sheathing; then you can finish the interior.

A dormer must provide sufficient headroom in the attic, complement the architectural style of the house, and support the roof. It must be waterproofed and properly insulated and ventilated (pp.456–462) to avoid damage from moisture.

Be sure to obtain the proper permits (p.193), equipment, and supplies. You will be cutting a large hole in the roof; have an adequate supply of tarps or plastic on hand in case it rains. Erect a brace to support the roof during construction.

The pictures on the facing page show the major steps involved in adding a shed dormer. Other styles have different construction requirements. The pro-

cedure shown will have to be adapted to meet your specific needs, but it can guide your construction or form a sound reference for a consultation with a contractor.

▶ **CAUTION:** If your roof is supported by webbed trusses (p.402), you cannot make any changes to the structure. Even adding a floor can increase the stress on the trusses enough to cause roof collapse.

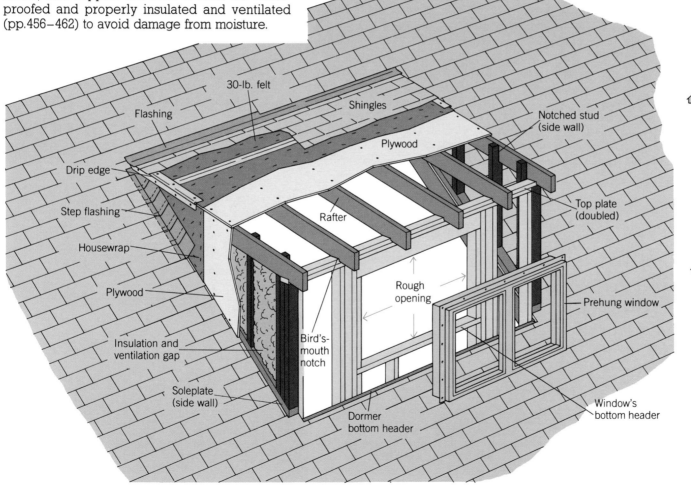

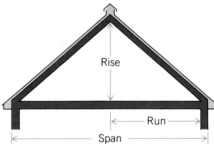

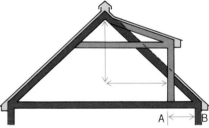

Changing the roof's shape affects the integrity of the remaining structure. Since the ceiling joists will be floor joists, they may need strengthening. The span AB also influences whether the joists need shoring up. A safe AB span is determined by the relationship of the joists' size, the span of the dormer's rafters, and its width.

The roof's span is part of the calculation for the pitch of the dormer's roof. Pitch determines what materials you can use on a roof (p.388). Although used interchangeably, slope and pitch are actually two different things. Slope is the ratio of the rise to the run, whereas pitch is the ratio of the rise to the span.

1. If there is no floor in the attic, install a subfloor (p.299) before doing anything else. Mark dormer's outline on ceiling, following plan drawings. Measure across ridge board (A), then down rafter (B and C). Count across rafters, and mark other side.

2. Drive a nail, or drill a hole, through each corner to mark the dormer's dimensions on the roof. Use nails that are long enough to penetrate the roof's layers and protrude on the exterior. If drilling, use a bit large enough to make a conspicuous hole.

3. Build a brace from 2 x 4's to prop up the roof. Install brace 8 in. outside top of intended dormer opening, and toenail it securely. If AB span (see detail, facing page) is longer than 4 ft., support lower rafters with another brace.

4. Frame front wall from 2 x 4's (or 2 x 6's, if more insulation is desired). Top plate should extend 3½ in. (5½ in.) beyond end studs to catch side wall studs and end rafters. Frame rough opening for window.

5. Working outside on roof, snap chalk lines to outline dormer opening. With a carbide blade in a circular saw, carefully cut out roof. Set blade depth to penetrate sheathing, but not deep enough to sever rafters. Install toeboards (p.383) for safety.

6. From inside, knock roofing off in sections, using a 2 x 4 as a ram. Rough-cut the rafters. Use a level (or plumb bob) to establish final cutting line on first rafter. Transcribe cutting line onto other rafters with a T-bevel.

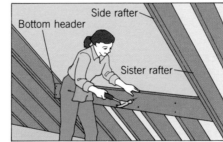

7. Nail a same-size *sister* rafter to each side rafter. Install a double header at the top, a single one at the bottom. Headers must be one size larger than rafters. (If rafters are 2 x 4, headers are 2 x 6.) Remove braces when headers are in place.

8. Set front wall into position; it must be parallel to top header. Check that it is square, level, and plumb, and remains so during nailing. Drive 16d nails through wall's soleplate into floor joists. Secure wall to rafters with 8d or 10d nails.

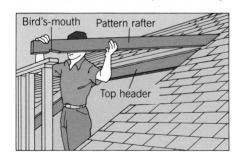

9. To make pattern rafter, cut rafter end to match roof's pitch; then mark and cut bird's-mouth notch at front wall's top plate. Check that rafter fits at opposite end, and use it as a template for remaining rafters. Nail rafters to top header and roof.

10. Install soleplate on doubled side rafters; then frame side wall with 2 x 4's. Mark each stud by holding it against rafters. Notch studs at top to support rafters. Base of notch and bottom of stud will be beveled to match rafter angle.

11. Sheathe finished frame with exterior-grade plywood; then cover dormer with housewrap or 30-lb. felt. Do the roof first, then the sides, then the front. Install flashing (pp.390—391) wherever dormer meets original roof.

12. Install window in front wall as directed on page 427 or by manufacturer. Interior work can begin while exterior work —adding roofing, trim, and siding to match or complement house —is being completed.

Interiors / Adding a sunspace

Footings and foundations 156
Switches and receptacles 246
Running cable 250–251

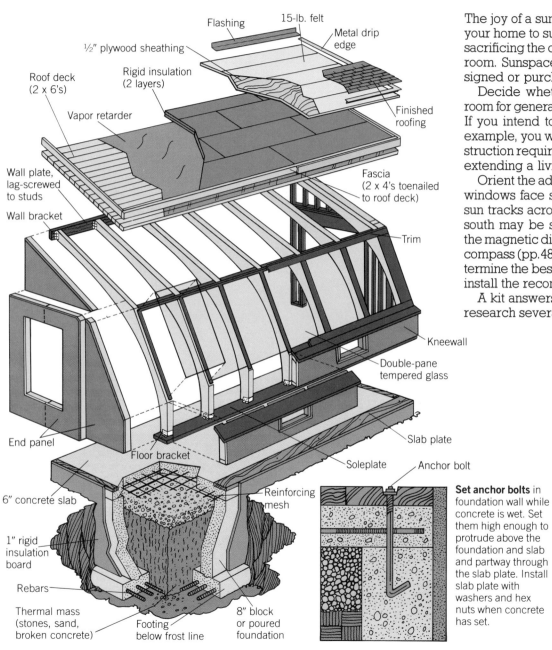

Flashing

15-lb. felt

Metal drip edge

½" plywood sheathing

Roof deck (2 x 6's)

Rigid insulation (2 layers)

Vapor retarder

Finished roofing

Wall plate, lag-screwed to studs

Fascia (2 x 4's toenailed to roof deck)

Wall bracket

Trim

Kneewall

Double-pane tempered glass

End panel

Floor bracket

Slab plate

6" concrete slab

Soleplate

Anchor bolt

Reinforcing mesh

1" rigid insulation board

Rebars

Thermal mass (stones, sand, broken concrete)

Footing below frost line

8" block or poured foundation

Set anchor bolts in foundation wall while concrete is wet. Set them high enough to protrude above the foundation and slab and partway through the slab plate. Install slab plate with washers and hex nuts when concrete has set.

The joy of a sunspace is that it opens your home to sunlight and air without sacrificing the comfort of an enclosed room. Sunspaces can be custom designed or purchased as a kit.

Decide whether you will use the room for general or specific purposes. If you intend to install a hot tub, for example, you will have different construction requirements than if you are extending a living room or kitchen.

Orient the addition so that the main windows face south. Watch how the sun tracks across your house—solar south may be slightly different from the magnetic direction indicated by a compass (pp. 488–489). Once you determine the best location for the room, install the recommended foundation.

A kit answers some problems, but research several before buying. Kits vary widely in their degree of prefabrication, completeness, clarity of instruction, and terms of warranty. If you intend to erect the room yourself, be certain the warranty covers a nonprofessional installation. Upon delivery, check that all pieces are present.

Even with a kit, a sunspace is a complex project. And because lumber is not perfect, no kit is perfect. Each part must be tested for squareness, level, and plumb; and adjusted if needed.

A sunspace may be framed with laminated arches (shown), wood posts and beams, or steel beams. Each style requires specific tools and techniques, which will differ from those shown here. Be honest about what you can do yourself. If you subcontract the difficult parts of the job, you'll still save money and probably get better results.

Whether building from plans or from a kit, check to see if your contract or warranty covers weatherproofing and breakage during installation. The huge glass panes can be hard to seal—and are expensive to replace.

1. Snap chalk line across wall to guide placement of wall plate. Check that line is level; then temporarily nail the plate to house. Plate position may need adjusting when floor plate and arches are set. Brackets spaced across wall plate will support arches.

2. Fasten soleplate to slab plate with lag screws. (Slab plate is installed when concrete is poured.) Brackets on soleplate and wall plate must align exactly. Track placement with a plumb bob, long spirit level, square, and snapped chalk lines.

3. Set arches in end brackets first. Place center arch next; then work from center out to each end. Nail arches to floor plate brackets; then adjust wall plate so that arches are plumb along their entire length. Attach the wall plate to house wall with lag screws. Nail arches to wall plate brackets.

4. Set front kneewall panels into place and secure. (All parts should be cut, drilled, and marked for identification.) After kneewall panels are in place, install the windowsill, then the precut window brackets.

5. The side wall is composed of three prefabricated panels. Plumb the panels by dropping a plumb bob from outside edge of arch. Nail side wall panels to arches, and drive lag screws through soleplate into slab plate. Leave rough opening for window as indicated by manufacturer. (Window is installed last.)

6. Nail roof boards to arches; trim their edges. Toenail 2 x 4's around roof's perimeter to frame insulation. Staple a 6-mil polyethylene vapor retarder to roof deck. Install two layers of rigid insulation over roof boards, staggering seams. Sheathe with ½-in. plywood. Cover plywood with felt paper; flash house wall joint. Install metal drip edges, and fascia boards.

7. Carefully lift glass into place to check fit; then remove it. Load cartridge of silicone caulk into caulking gun. Lay a wide bead of caulk on wood where glass will rest. Replace glass. Caulk seam above glass; then smooth bead with a wet finger. Cover caulk and window edges with trim.

8. Lift prefabricated roof panels into position abutting top plate. Align carefully over arches, and fasten with galvanized roofing nails. If plans include skylight, leave rough opening indicated by manufacturer. Roof will be finished with materials appropriate to its pitch (pp.334, 388) and compatible with house's style.

9. Set prehung window (p.427) into rough opening left in side wall. Plumb window in opening, shimming as needed. Nail or screw window to sheathing. After all windows are installed, apply siding. Complete the interior: Run any cables; install electrical outlets and fixtures; finish walls; lay desired flooring; hang prehung door (p.444) in connecting wall.

Even if there are no visible puddles from leaky cracks, moisture may still be seeping through the concrete walls and floor of the basement. This migration of water through concrete, masonry, and wood is called *capillary attraction*. Most houses are constructed loosely enough to naturally vent this moisture, but when cracks are closed up to conserve energy, the moisture is trapped inside. The result is high indoor humidity; the consequences can be peeling paint, mold and mildew, and excessive condensation on windows, leading to wood rot. Use the chart at right to help solve your dampness problem. To distinguish between condensation and seepage, perform the test illustrated below.

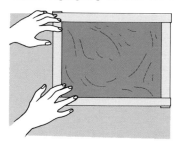

Condensation test. Dry spot on floor or wall with hair dryer; tape 12-in. square of heavy plastic or foil to spot. Check in 2 days. Seepage will cause underside of plastic or foil to be wet; condensation will form on opposite side.

Waterproofing paints. Interior waterproofing paints are available to help reduce dampness, but they offer little or no protection from serious water problems, and on hollow-block walls they may even compound the problem. Always treat leakage problems before using waterproofing paints.

There are three basic types of waterproofing paints: epoxy, powder, and ready-mix. Epoxy is expensive and also must be carefully mixed; powder must be mixed with water and applied quickly. Epoxies generally work best, followed by powders and ready-mix paints with cement bases.

Before application, fix any cracks and holes (facing page) and remove any whitish powder, or efflorescence (p.174), or the paint won't adhere. Wear rubber gloves and goggles; if the ventilation is poor, wear a respirator. Follow the directions on the label—you may have to pretreat the walls with muriatic acid (p.186) or add a top coat of another product.

Troubleshooting a damp or wet basement

Problem	Cause	Solutions (Try one at a time.)
Condensation	Warm humid air meets a cool surface.	Increase ventilation; close windows in hot humid weather, open them on cool dry days; use a dehumidifier (p.498); vent clothes dryer (p.342); insulate sweating pipes (p.214).
Leaks	Water pushes through cracks or holes, or through mortar between concrete blocks or between walls and floor.	Fill all cracks, holes, and joints between walls and floor (facing page), unless they contain a working drain; treat as for seepage; as a last resort, add a sump pump (p.219).
Seepage	Inadequate or faulty gutters; improper grading; poor drainage; high water table.	Repair or add gutters and downspouts; install splash blocks (p.399) or, better, connect downspout with storm sewer; regrade (p.340); cover exterior wall with water-repelling material and install drainpipes (p.340).

Causes of leaks in a basement

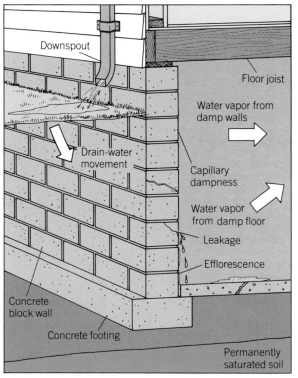

When soil is saturated around basement, water pushes through cracks or penetrates concrete by means of capillary attraction.

Cures for a damp basement

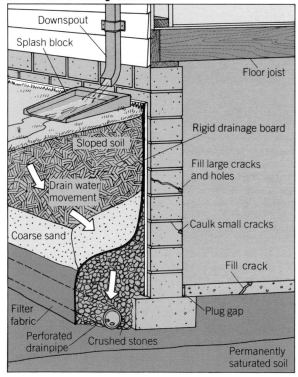

Roof runoff is another source of water problems; diverting it can be a simple matter of adding splash blocks or, at worst, regrading.

Repairing foundation leaks

Water may enter a basement through cracks or holes in the wall, mortar joints between concrete blocks, or the floor. Unless the foundation is absolutely watertight, moisture can also be forced up through the joints between the concrete slab and the walls. Large quantities of water coming through these joints may signal a problem with groundwater and the need for installing drainage pipes around the perimeter of the house (p.340).

Leaky walls and floor. Repair all cracks and holes in the foundation or basement floor as soon as possible. Any water caught in them will expand if it freezes, enlarging the crack. If a crack reopens after it has been repaired, you may have a serious structural problem; consult an engineer.

Fill cracks with hydraulic cement, available at hardware stores. Hydraulic cement hardens in just a few minutes, even under water, and because it expands as it dries, it bonds tightly with the existing concrete. Mix the cement with cold water as the label directs—it should be the consistency of soft modeling clay.

Two-part epoxy is a more permanent sealant, but it is more expensive and harder to work with. Epoxy may also be injected, but this is work best left to a professional.

Other leaks. Seams around window and door frames may also let in water; caulk these with silicone or polyurethane sealant. Also caulk where outdoor structures, such as steps or decks, meet concrete walls, and around anything that projects through the walls, such as a dryer vent (p.342).

Vapor retarder

In new houses, building codes require a vapor retarder of 4- or 6-mil polyethylene film (a plastic sheet) laid over several inches of crushed stone or gravel under a concrete floor. If your house is old and has a thin concrete floor over dirt, consider adding a vapor retarder and pouring a 2-inch-thick concrete floor over it.

Laying a vapor retarder over the exposed soil of a crawl space will help keep moisture from entering the house and damaging its wooden understructure. If you can't dig a trench as shown below, use pea gravel or bricks to anchor the plastic.

Crawl spaces are often fitted with vents in opposite walls, but if there is a vapor retarder and no soil gas (radon) problem, venting may be unnecessary. Follow local codes and construction practices.

1. Wearing goggles to protect your eyes, enlarge crack, hole, or joint with mason's or ball peen hammer and cold chisel. Make the opening larger inside than at surface to lock cement in place. In block walls, don't go deeper than ¾ in., or you may break through to hollow core.

Mason's hammer
Cold chisel

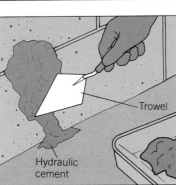

3. Fill crack with hydraulic cement to within ½ in. of surface. After it hardens, apply second coat to fill crack completely. If water is flowing through the crack, press cement in with a trowel and hold trowel in place for 3 to 5 min., until cement hardens.

Trowel
Hydraulic cement

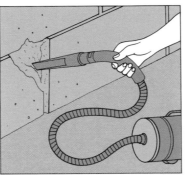

2. Remove debris with a stiff brush, then vacuum. Right before applying fresh cement, moisten the crack slightly with a sponge or spray it with a mister.

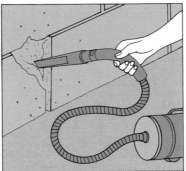

To fill a hole, form cement into a cone about 4 in. long; shape its base about 1 in. larger than diameter of hole. Force cone, point first, into hole and press in place for 3 to 5 min., until cement hardens. Then trowel the surface smooth.

Shape cement into cone

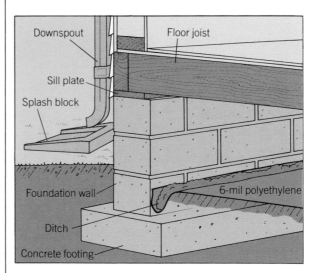

Downspout
Floor joist
Sill plate
Splash block
Foundation wall
6-mil polyethylene
Ditch
Concrete footing

To install vapor retarder in dry crawl space, dig a 2-in.-deep ditch around perimeter of space. Lay sheets of 6-mil polyethylene film over ground, overlapping them at least 2 ft. and extending their edges into ditch. Return excavated soil to ditch to hold down plastic. If crawl space gets wet and you cannot solve problem, extend plastic across soil and up walls to above grade level, without digging ditch. Hold plastic in place by fastening furring strips along its top edge with masonry nails, or run plastic up wall and nail it to sill plate.

Interiors / Basement waterproofing

Most basement moisture problems result from poor grading of the ground around the foundation. Water standing near the walls saturates the soil, and moisture moves through any available opening. Often the remedy is proper channeling of roof runoff. Make sure gutters and downspouts are clean and in good repair; if the house has no gutters and the roof overhang is less than 2 feet, consider installing them (pp.398–399). Install splash blocks under the shoes of the the downspouts, making sure that the ground beneath them slopes away from the house.

Proper grading. Poorly graded soil or improperly pitched walks, patios, stoops, and driveways can funnel surface water to the foundation walls, where it will eventually leak or seep through. If possible, have the land graded so that it slopes down and away from the house. Ideally, the soil should slope 2 inches per foot for the first 3 or 4 feet, and then 1 inch per foot for another few feet, for a total of at least 6 feet. Repave or repair walks, driveways, or patio surfaces to lead water away from the house.

Shrubs and flowers shade the ground and restrict air movement so that dampness builds up in the soil. Move shrubs and flowers 4 to 6 feet out from the foundation walls (from the road they will still appear to be next to the house); plant grass or some other dense ground cover between the house and the borders.

If the ground slopes toward the house, dig a gentle depression, called a swale, at least 6 feet out, and regrade the ground between it and the house to divert water away from the foundation walls and into the swale. Fill the swale with crushed stones, cover it with topsoil, and seed it with grass. If surface runoff is severe, install a drain in the swale.

Waterproofing the foundation. As a last resort, you may need to have the ground around the house excavated to the foundation footings, drainpipes installed to lead the water away from the foundation, and a water-repelling system added to the foundation walls. The water-repelling system may consist of an exterior waterproofing compound shielded by pieces of rigid drainage board and a filter fabric to keep soil from clogging the system. (The filter fabric may be attached to the drainage board or sold separately.) You can follow the procedure shown at right for a shallow foundation; order the materials through a building supply center if they are not in stock. But if you have a full basement, you'll need to hire a contractor with a backhoe. In any case, always consult a contractor before choosing a waterproofing system.

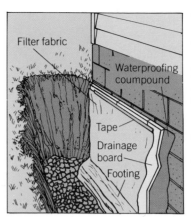

To drain foundation:
1. Dig trench to base of footings, and shovel in 2 in. of egg-size crushed stones. Paint foundation walls and footings with exterior waterproofing compound. Attach rigid drainage boards to walls with spots of adhesive. Tape filter fabric to board, if it is not already attached. Drape loose bottom of fabric on footing.

Filter fabric / Waterproofing coumpound / Tape / Drainage board / Footing

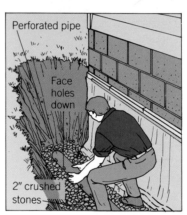

2. Install lengths of perforated plastic drainage pipe (4-in. diameter) along bottom of trench on top of stones with holes facing down. Run the pipes at least 10 ft. out from house to open air, or connect them to a storm sewer or seepage pit (p.201) if codes permit.

Perforated pipe / Face holes down / 2" crushed stones

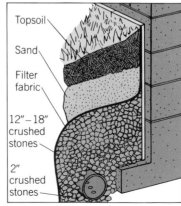

3. Shovel 12 to 18 in. of crushed stones over drainpipes; then cover the stones with loose bottoms of the filter fabric. Add a layer of sand, fill rest of trench with soil, sloping surface away from house, and seed it with grass.

Topsoil / Sand / Filter fabric / 12"–18" crushed stones / 2" crushed stones

Deflecting water

If ground slopes toward house, causing water to collect near wall, dig a swale—a shallow trench with gently sloping sides—at least 6 ft. from house.

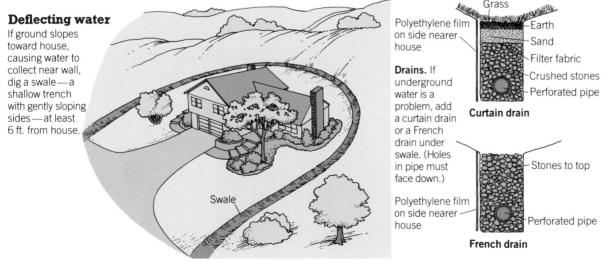

Swale

Drains. If underground water is a problem, add a curtain drain or a French drain under swale. (Holes in pipe must face down.)

Grass / Polyethylene film on side nearer house / Earth / Sand / Filter fabric / Crushed stones / Perforated pipe

Curtain drain

Stones to top / Polyethylene film on side nearer house / Perforated pipe

French drain

Remodeling a basement

Planning projects 193
Wallboard and paneling 273–288
Adding a wall 343

Before beginning construction, talk to your building inspector about permits and building codes (p.193). Some municipalities require a permit even for adding wall paneling. Most codes specify a minimum ceiling height of 7½ feet in a finished basement. If part of the space will be used as a bedroom, an exterior door or window may be required by law. If you have a private septic system (p.201), be sure it is large enough to pass the code requirement for the total number of bedrooms in the house. Stairs leading to a finished basement must also meet standards.

Floors. Carpet, ceramic tile, vinyl, and some wood floors (p.302) all may be laid directly over concrete, provided it is in good condition. Resurface damaged concrete or cover it with a wood subfloor (p.303), if doing so won't interfere with the code requirement for ceiling height. If the basement has a history of dampness, however, do whatever is necessary to solve the problem (pp.338–340); avoid using wood or any other perishable materials.

Perimeter walls. In warm climates, concrete walls are often just painted (p.367). In cold climates, insulate the walls (p.342) from the ceiling to 2 feet below grade. Install ½-inch-thick wallboard over the insulation, or glue paneling with a sufficient fire rating directly to rigid insulation board.

▶ **CAUTION:** Do not insulate basement walls more than 2 feet below grade unless you are sure that the basement has a working perimeter drain, the soil around the foundation is coarse, and the ground slopes away from the house; otherwise water may seep down, freeze, and crack the foundation.

Ceilings. If there is adequate headroom, conceal ducts and pipes with a suspended ceiling hung from the joists (p.290). If you are adding walls to divide the basement into separate rooms, install the suspended ceilings after the walls are framed.

Where there is not enough headroom to add a dropped ceiling, paint or box in exposed pipes and ducts (p.342), or reroute them between the ceiling joists, and nail wallboard to the joists. Another way of covering a basement ceiling is to nail furring strips to the joists and staple ceiling tiles (p.289) to the strips.

Plumbing. If you are thinking of adding a new bathroom or laundry room in the basement and no plumbing hookups exist, consult a plumber before going too far with your plans. If the basement lies below the main drain, installing plumbing will be complicated and expensive and you may want to reconsider. You must also follow local codes.

Electrical requirements. Run new electrical circuits (p.248) to the basement to meet your power needs, including lights, air conditioning, and stationary power tools (if you're adding a workshop). Also plan wiring for telephones (p.266) and cable television. Consult an electrician to be sure that the wiring meets all safety requirements. Codes may require that an electrician approve the work or even do it.

Heating. If the furnace and ducts do not generate adequate heat, consider installing electric baseboard heat. You can also try tapping into a duct to install a new register, but this is seldom successful. If you have a hot-water system, you may be able to extend the pipes, but first consult a plumber or a boiler serviceperson.

Building permits and codes 193
Wallboard and wall paneling 273–288
Insulation 457–459

Interiors/Finishing basement walls

Before covering a concrete or concrete block wall, pinpoint and eliminate any source of dampness (pp.338–340). If you decide to insulate the basement walls, see the preceding page. There are two ways to proceed: One is to glue 1-inch-thick foam insulation to the wall, nail furring strips over it, and glue rigid foam panels between the furring strips. Attach the furring strips to the walls every 16 inches on center if you will be covering them with thin paneling or every 24 inches if you will be installing ½-inch wallboard. Fasten the strips with a bead of construction adhesive and masonry nails (p.86). On concrete block walls, nail into the joints between the blocks. If the walls aren't plumb, shim the furring strips with shingles.

The alternative method is to install a frame of 2 x 3's 1 inch from the wall, stuff strips of fiberglass insulation into the 1-inch space, wedge fiberglass batts between the 2 x 3's, and cover everything with 6-mil polyethylene film. This is almost like framing a non-load-bearing wall (facing page), and it will reduce the size of the open space by a few inches, but it serves to cover any irregularities in the masonry wall. In either case, cover the insulation with paneling or wallboard that meets fire code standards.
▶ **CAUTION:** When working with insulation, wear long sleeves, gloves, and a full face mask.

Insulating basement walls

Fasten 1-in.-thick foam panels to wall with ¼-in. beads of foam-panel adhesive; nail furring strips over panels. Glue ¾-in.-thick foam panels between furring strips.

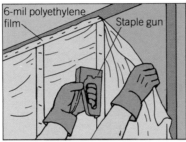

Cover the insulated wall with sheets of 6-mil polyethylene film to form a vapor retarder. Staple the film to the furring strips, pulling it tight across the insulation.

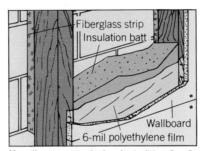

If walls are out of plumb, build a 2 x 3 frame backed with 1-in.-thick fiberglass strips to insulation level (see p.341). Place fiberglass batts between 2 x 3's; add film.

Hiding ducts, beams, columns, and pipes

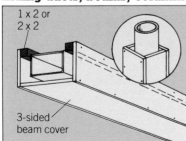

Cover beams, columns, and ducts that are less than 11 in. deep with three or four boards. Attach cover to ceiling with 1 x 2's or 2 x 2's. Stain and finish cover or paint it.

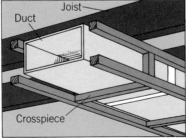

To box in large duct, build frame of 2 x 2's to cover sides of duct. Nail frames to overhead joists, and crosspieces to bottoms of frames. Mount wallboard on frames.

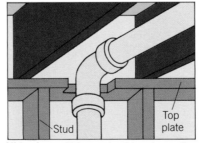

Hide pipes within non-load-bearing walls (p.191) or between ceiling joists. Pass pipes through holes or notches in top and bottom plates (p.227).

Installing a clothes dryer vent

Clothes dryers must be vented to discharge moisture and lint outdoors. Supplies with instructions are available in kits. In a basement, locate the vent in the band, or rim, joist above the foundation wall. Eliminate bends as much as possible. If the vent must pass through a window, remove the windowpane and replace it with metal, plywood, or thick acrylic.

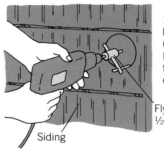

1. From outside, cut hole with a fly cutter (p.56) or hole saw. Follow kit instructions for hole diameter and caulking directions.

2. Push vent pipe into hole and screw vent to wall. (Vent may have louvers, a hood, or a trapdoor.)

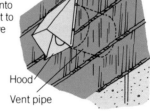

3. Slip back plate over part of vent pipe that protrudes through the inside wall, and push it tight against wall.

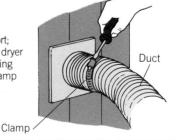

4. Clamp duct to dryer's exhaust port; stretch it between dryer and vent, minimizing bends. Tighten clamp near end of pipe.

Framing a partition

To divide a basement into smaller rooms, you'll need a non-load-bearing partition wall (p. 191). You can construct the frame on the basement floor and raise it into place. A partition wall consists of upright studs (generally 2 x 4's) nailed between horizontal plates. To make it easier to position the frame and to nail on baseboard later, double the soleplates: nail the lower plate to the floor; then construct the wall's framework and slide it into place on top of the nailed-down plate.

Next, nail the frame to the ceiling joists and the studs or the foundation wall. If the ceiling and existing walls are already covered with wallboard, you can nail through the wallboard, but be sure the nails enter the underlying framing members.

In most walls the studs are spaced 16 inches apart on center to provide adequate nailing for wallboard, but walls that are to be covered with ½-inch wallboard can have studs spaced 24 inches on center.

If the wall needs a door, buy a prehung door and construct a rough opening to the measurements given by the door manufacturer. These openings consist of two jack studs to frame the doorway, a head trimmer to bridge the top of the jack studs, and—if the wall is high enough—cripple studs, which run from the head trimmer to the top plate.

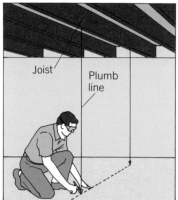

1. Mark location of wall on ceiling joists. Transfer lines to floor by dropping a plumb bob from ceiling at each end, marking points on floor and snapping a chalk line through them. Cut top plate and soleplates, and fasten the lower soleplate along line on floor with concrete nails. Wear safety goggles while working with concrete nails.

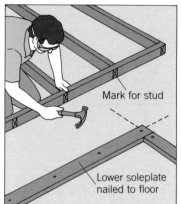

2. Lay remaining plates side by side, and draw lines across them to locate studs, using a square as guide. Cut studs long enough to reach from floor to ceiling minus thickness of top plate and both soleplates and minus another ¼ in. to allow you to raise frame. Cut framing for any door openings. Fasten all framing pieces together with 16d nails.

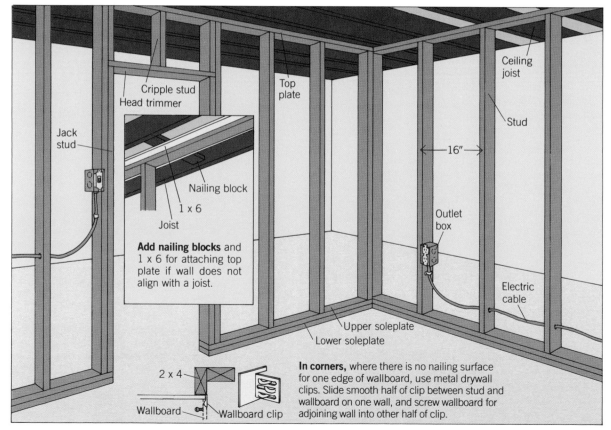

Cripple stud
Head trimmer
Top plate
Ceiling joist
Jack stud
Stud
Nailing block
1 x 6
Joist
16"
Outlet box
Electric cable
Add nailing blocks and 1 x 6 for attaching top plate if wall does not align with a joist.
Upper soleplate
Lower soleplate
2 x 4
Wallboard
Wallboard clip
In corners, where there is no nailing surface for one edge of wallboard, use metal drywall clips. Slide smooth half of clip between stud and wallboard on one wall, and screw wallboard for adjoining wall into other half of clip.

Joist
Plumb line
Mark for stud
Lower soleplate nailed to floor

3. With a helper, lift frame and slide it into place over lower soleplate. Nail top plate to ceiling joists and end studs to connecting walls. Fill any gaps by pushing wood shims between soleplates. Nail upper soleplate to lower. Run plumbing lines (pp. 226–227), install electrical boxes (pp. 248–249), and add wallboard (p. 275).

Mildew

A black fungus that sometimes appears as a white, red, or green powder, mildew grows on most surfaces and spreads rampantly in dark unventilated places. Although it's unlikely to cause major damage to the structure of a house, mildew is unsightly and emits an unpleasant musty odor. Its spores can also cause allergic reactions in susceptible people.

Mildew is prevalent in humid summer weather. You're likely to discover it wherever air cannot move easily: in basements, bathrooms, crowded closets, and closed cabinets. Because building materials hold a lot of moisture, mildew can thrive during the first year after a new home is built.

Fighting mildew. Start attacking this fungus by decreasing dampness and increasing air circulation. In closets, replace wooden shelving with wire racks and install louvered doors. Empty and air out the closet; then clean it with chlorine bleach and water. Or dry the air inside by burning a 60-watt light bulb for 24 to 48 hours. If mildew reappears, leave the bulb on constantly. To prevent fire, keep the bulb at least 18 inches away from stored items.

In the basement, correct any moisture problems, and if necessary, run a dehumidifier (p.498). Cover the floor with vinyl flooring instead of carpeting. In bathrooms and the laundry area, install exhaust fans and repair any plumbing leaks.

To keep mildew from growing on exterior siding, trim back shrubbery to let air circulate and the sun dry the siding. (This may also clear up interior mildew caused by dampness inside the exterior walls.) Prevent condensation in attics by installing combination soffit and ridge vents.

Paint. Before repainting, clean mildew off the surface (see chart)—otherwise the mildew will eat through the new paint. Mix a mildewcide additive, available at paint supply stores, into the primer and the paint. Or select a paint with zinc oxide pigment. Oil paint resists fungal attack better than latex; among latexes, acrylic is the most resistant. Coating unfinished wood with a water-repellent preservative containing a fungicide will deter mildew.

Type of surface	Mildew removal method	Comments
Ceramic tile, vinyl, and grout	Commercial mildew remover, or 1 qt. chlorine bleach mixed in 1 gal. water.	For commercial product, follow directions on label. Wear rubber gloves. Open windows when using either cleanser.
Clothing, household fabrics	Soap or detergent and water. For remaining stains, lemon juice and salt, or 2 tbs. bleach to 1 qt. warm water.	Rinse material well; dry in sun. If stains remain, dampen with lemon juice solution; dry in sun. Or use bleach solution; wait 5–15 min.; rinse with water. Don't use bleach on noncolorfast fabrics, silk, or wool; check label.
Exterior siding and trim (unpainted)	Mix 1 qt. chlorine bleach with 3 qt. water.	Before cleaning, cover shrubbery and ground with plastic sheet. Never mix ammonia with bleach. After cleaning, coat with wood preservative or paint with mildewcide.
Leather	Mix 1 c. denatured or rubbing alcohol with 1 c. water.	Wipe on with cloth; let air-dry. If still mildewed, wash with sudsy mild soap, saddle soap, or detergent. Let air-dry.
Painted surfaces	Add 1 qt. chlorine bleach to 3 qt. water. Stir in ⅓ c. powdered laundry detergent.	Keep surface wet until stains are removed; wait 2 min., then rinse with water. Never mix bleach with ammonia. Repaint with paint containing mildewcide. Wear gloves; open windows.
Wallpaper	No cure.	Fungus feeds on wallpaper glue. Rewallpaper after cleaning; mix borax into paste. Or paint wall with paint containing mildewcide.
Wood, plastic laminate, metal, plaster	Add 1 c. chlorine bleach to 1 gal. water; or make a vinegar and borax solution—add as much borax as will dissolve in vinegar.	Because water raises grain in wood and bleach can stain plastic laminate, vinegar-borax mixture is preferable. Never mix bleach with ammonia. Wear gloves; open windows.

Wood-decaying fungi

One attacker of untreated wood, *wet rot* occurs in wood repeatedly exposed to water, such as window frames soaked by rain. The rotted area is dark and spongy, and the fungus is visible in brown veinlike strands. First the paint peels away; eventually the wood splits. So-called *dry rot,* characterized by white strands that turn into woollike sheets, thrives in damp unventilated areas such as basements, crawl spaces, and under stairs. It spreads rapidly; infested timbers become brittle and cracked. To check for damage, probe the wood with an awl.

To treat rot, eliminate the source of moisture and, for dry rot, improve ventilation. If the rot is minor, scrape down to good wood, apply a wood preservative, and refinish. For deeper damage, dig out the decay, soak the cavity with a wood preservative, and fill it with an epoxy wood filler. To repair structural damage, let the wood dry out. Attach a 2 x 8 sister joist—or wood as wide and thick as the original piece—to the damaged wood. The sister joist must be longer than the damaged area.

Replace porch post while supporting roof with jack post. Remove old post and install new one, centering it over a support pier under the floor. Or, after removing the post, cut out the damaged wood and replace it with new wood, using a lengthening joint (p.111). Replace exterior rotted wood with pressure-treated wood. But before replacing post, check the concrete footing (pp.156–157).

Wood-boring insects

Termites have straight bodies and antennae. Worker, left, is wingless and gray-white; soldier, not shown, has enlarged jaw. Winged reproductive termite, center, is dark and has equal-size fore and hind wings. Winged carpenter ant, right, has narrow waist, shorter hind wings, and elbowed antennae.

Subterranean termites, the most common species, can be found nationwide; they feed on wood, causing structural damage to a house. They nest underground, but when searching for food—cellulose in wood—they travel through shelter tubes built above ground. They can invade a building through improperly sealed joints, through untreated wood that touches the soil, through cracks as small as 1/32 inch in concrete or masonry, through holes in termite shields, and through the hollow core of a cement block.

To discourage termites, keep shrubbery away from foundation air vents, don't let water from sprinklers hit the house, and don't raise the soil grade at the house foundation. Use pressure-treated lumber to make repairs wherever wood contacts the soil or concrete. To control termites, call in a state-certified pest-control operator. Some operators use nonchemical controls such as nematodes, a natural predator, electrical probes for dry-wood termites, and sand barriers. These methods may be effective in certain situations but are basically unproven.

Carpenter ants differ from termites in having narrow waists and from other ants in having a *pedicel,* the stem by the ant's abdomen, with only one *node,* not two. They tunnel in moist or damaged wood to nest. Coarse sawdust is one sign of an infestation.

To help keep carpenter ants out of your home, caulk exterior cracks (p.411), weatherstrip windows and doors (pp.452–454), eliminate moisture problems, trim tree branches that touch the house, keep woodpiles away from the house, unclog gutters, and replace decayed wood.

To get rid of carpenter ants, kill the reproductive ants in the nest; dust boric acid powder into it with a squeeze bottle. If the nest area is inaccessible, drill holes around it and apply boric acid powder or an insecticide containing chlorpyrifos, diazinon, Baygon, or malathion. On the West Coast, satellite colonies—ones that form away from the queen—develop quickly, even in sound wood, and require professional extermination.

Powder-post beetles lay eggs in cracks in wood. Larvae tunnel into the wood, mature, and surface through small holes. Signs of infestation are exit holes

Powder-post beetle

and fine sawdust. For minor damage, dry out the wood; ventilate the area. Refinish surfaces after the beetles exit. If the wood can be probed easily with an awl, damage is severe—replace the wood. The insecticide chlorpyrifos can control the insects. Or remove the wood finish (p.117) if necessary; wet the area with deodorized kerosene. Don't smoke or use near flames or pilot lights. Refinish the wood to stop new infestations. You may have to call a professional.

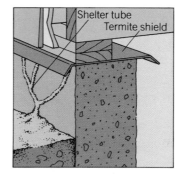
Shelter tube
Termite shield

Metal termite shield is installed at foundation during construction. Shield causes termites to build shelter tubes in open instead of behind foundation coverings, such as masonry veneer or rigid foam insulation. Inspect for shelter tubes outside and in crawl space regularly.

Termite checklist

Use the following suggestions as a guide to determine if you have termites, or hire a professional.

- Inspect house when the soil temperature is between 50° F and 55° F. In the South, check year-round.
- Tap on suspect timbers; a hollow sound may indicate a termite infestation.
- Probe suspicious areas with an awl. If the awl penetrates easily, there could be structural damage.
- Because termites swarm to create new colonies, look for large numbers of flying insects or discarded wings in basement, crawl space, and near foundation in spring months.
- Look for shelter tubes on outside foundation and basement walls. Seal cracked brick veneer or stucco over a foundation. Check openings where pipes enter house.
- Inspect crawl spaces and any other area with a dirt floor.

- Inspect wood trellises, fences, and planter boxes that are close to the house, as well as any lumber or wood structure that is near the ground. Remove piles of lumber or firewood and any tree stumps near the house.
- Check any type of roof shingles for structural integrity, as well as eaves, roof overhangs, and fascia boards.
- Check siding for signs of buckling and peeling, and for stains. These may indicate termite infestation.
- Inside the house, check foundation walls for tunnels, especially at cracks and joints between floor and walls. Scrutinize joint where a garage slab meets the wall. Check near pipes going through floors, and around any leaks. Also check near water- or space-heating units.
- Inspect windowsills, thresholds, and wood stairs and their stringers (p.294). Watch for blistered or peeling paint on any wood structure that is close to the ground.

Carpenter bees

Similar in appearance to bumblebees, carpenter bees nest in tunnels in exterior wood, often behind a roof's fascia or in other wood trim; they prefer unfinished, rough-surfaced wood. After dark in spring or early summer, spray insecticide, such as diazinon or Sevin, into hole. Plug opening with caulking compound or dowel. Apply a finish to wood.

To prevent insects from entering your home, make sure window and door screens fit and are undamaged. Seal openings, such as where utilities enter, with caulking compound. Because food and water attract insects, clean well in corners, in cabinets, and around pipes and plumbing fixtures; store food in sealed containers; keep trash outside in closed containers; and clean clothing before storing it.

Once insects enter the house, eradicate them with a surface spray, space spray, or powder insecticide. Apply a surface or a residual spray with a spray gun, a pressurized can, or a brush to places where insects breed and travel. Residual sprays leave a fine film that continues to kill insects weeks after application. A space spray is dispensed from a spray can or aerosol bomb and kills insects on contact. Dust an insecticide powder, which usually has a residual effect, in breeding and feeding areas.

▶ **CAUTION:** Before using an insecticide, read the precautions on the label; use it only as directed. Do not let it drift onto food, eating and cooking utensils, or food preparation surfaces. Be careful not to inhale it or get it on your skin or in your eyes. Wash hands and face with soap and water after using any insecticide. Don't smoke when handling pesticides. Never spray near an open flame or a furnace. Do not touch surfaces where residual sprays have been used. After you spray, leave the room, keep it closed, and stay out for the length of time stated on the label—then ventilate the room. Do not hang a chemically treated strip in rooms where people or pets will be present for long periods, particularly infants or sick or elderly people; don't use where food is prepared or served. Store insecticides in a cool, dry place out of reach of children and pets—never near food. If an insecticide gets in someone's mouth or is swallowed, call a poison control center or doctor immediately. Label should list antidote.

Insect	Habitat	Control measures
Ants	Live in colonies; attracted to sweet and greasy food. To find colony, follow foraging path from food supply to nest.	Spray residual spray containing propoxur, diazinon, or chlorpyrifos across path to nest. Apply around windowsills, baseboards, table legs, and under sinks. If nest is outdoors, apply dust or granular carbaryl or diazinon. For carpenter ants, see p.345.
Carpet beetles / Clothes moths	Both beetles and moths lay eggs in rugs, furs, and fabric containing wool or other animal fibers. When eggs hatch, the larvae feed on these materials.	Apply nonstaining residual spray along edges of carpets, behind radiators, and in clothes closets. Remove clothing from the closets first so that interiors can be thoroughly sprayed. Store moth-free and freshly cleaned clothing in sealed containers with moth crystals. Vacuum rugs, carpets, upholstery, and slipcovers frequently. Dispose of vacuum cleaner sweepings from these infested materials immediately.
Cockroaches	Hide in warm, dark, humid places. Yellowish brown to black in color; ¼ to 3 in. long. Nocturnal, hide by day. Eat glue, starch, food, and garbage.	Use residual sprays in cracks and crevices; if it's not effective, use one with different active ingredient, or dust with boric acid power. For severe infestations, apply a residual spray and space spray; then place bait traps along baseboards. Professional help may be necessary.
Flour and grain beetles	Small brown beetles, usually found in or near containers of flour, meal, and other grain products, pet food, and birdseed.	Dispose of infested food; scrub shelves, cupboards, and other storage areas. Store grain products, pet foods, and birdseed in tightly sealed containers. For extreme infestation, remove foods; spray or brush pyrethrins or diazinon in corners of storage area.
Houseflies	Breed in decaying organic matter and garbage. May breed in grass caught in lawn mower. Spread germs of many diseases harmful to man and beast.	Screen all windows and doors. Kill flies in house with fly swatter or space spray. Seal garbage in containers outdoors. Keep yard free of garbage and animal droppings.
Silverfish	Live in cool, damp places. Eat starch, protein, sugar, and fabrics that have been sized. Active after dark.	Use a residual spray or dust that contains propoxur, chlorpyrifos, or diazinon. After spraying, dust or blow silica aerogel or boric acid powder into wall voids through small openings or where pipes and other utilities pass.
Spiders (not true insects)	Except for black widow and brown recluse, most spiders found on United States mainland are harmless, even beneficial. Spin webs in crevices and corners.	Control insects on which spiders feed. Remove webs with extension tool of vacuum cleaner. Use residual spray of propoxur, diazinon, or chlorpyrifos in protected crevices and corners.
Wasps	Stinging insects; family includes hornets and yellow jackets. Often build nest on or near occupied dwellings or in ground; prey on other insects.	Wait for frost to kill wasps; then remove nest. Or use wasp and hornet spray containing carbaryl, propoxur, resmethrin, or malathion. Apply to outdoor nests after dark on cool evening. If wasps are getting indoors, seal off openings into room.

Unwelcome animals

The best way to keep creatures out of the home is to deny them entrance. Bats can fit through ¼- x 1½-inch cracks. Seal holes and cracks with caulking compound, or cover with sheet metal or ¼-inch hardware cloth. Also cover ventilation and chimney openings with the cloth; keep them unclogged.

If you deny the intruder food and water, it may leave. Mend leaks; store food in metal and glass containers; place garbage in tightly sealed metal cans.

Signs of infestation include gnawing marks on doors, windows, electrical wires, and packaged goods. Look for droppings around food and in hidden corners. Listen for scurrying noises when turning lights on. Dust flour along baseboards where rodents travel and in protected areas where they hide; check for tracks later.

Traps. Several types of traps will catch animals. All must be properly set and placed in the right location to work. Spring-loaded *snap traps* and *glue traps* catch mice and rats. A snap trap will usually kill a rodent right away. *Live traps* catch an animal without harming it (though the trapped animal may hurt itself trying to escape); you must then release it elsewhere. State laws govern which animals can be trapped and relocated; check with your local conservation or environmental protection agency.

Poisons kill mice and rats, but if one dies behind a wall, your home may acquire an odious smell. If a rodent goes outside before dying, it may poison a pet or wild animal that eats it. Multiple-dose anticoagulant poisons pose less risk to children and pets. Before using any poison, check with a Cooperative Extension Service agent.

▶ **CAUTION:** When handling an animal or releasing it from a live trap, take care; when cornered, it may bite. Wear gloves to guard against rabies. Keep poisons away from children, and use only as directed on makers' labels. Dispose of poisons carefully (p.348).

Capturing mice, rats, and bats

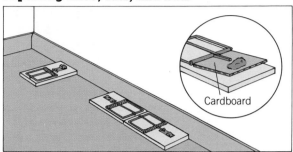

Set snap traps for mice and rats 6 ft. apart. Place bait side against baseboard or, as shown, with two traps butted against each other, bait sides apart. To increase sensitivity of trigger, attach a 2-in. piece of cardboard to trigger; then bait and set trap.

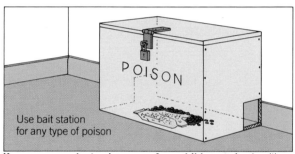

Keep mouse and rat poison away from children and pets with a bait station. Make a box with a hinged lid; cut 2½-in.-wide openings on opposite sides of box. Set box by baseboard; place bait inside. Or you can nail an 18-in.-long board to wall over bait.

To remove lone bat roosting on wall in daytime, place empty coffee can over bat; gently slide cardboard between can and wall. Release bat outdoors. At night close entries to rest of house, turn on lights in room with bat, open window or door, and wait for it to leave.

Animal	Characteristics	Control measures
Bats	Nocturnal; colonies sometimes roost in attics. Eat insects. Carriers of rabies.	To find entries, watch for bats at dusk; seal openings before May or after July. To let bat out but not in, install ½-in. polypropylene bird netting over opening from outside; attach it 6 in. above and 2 ft. to each side; use duct tape or staples. Allow 2 ft. to hang below loosely.
Mice and rats	Mice build nests between walls or in holes. Rats will gnaw through wood.	Bait snap or live traps with peanut butter, bacon, or gumdrops. Before handling traps for rats, scrub hands; leave traps unset but baited for 3 days. Check with your local county or state health department or Cooperative Extension Service before purchasing a poison. Some poisons kill in one dose; others require several doses.
Raccoons	Enter attic through openings in eaves. Carriers of rabies.	Check local laws on animal trapping. Bait live traps with fish or fish-flavored cat food, bread soaked in honey, marshmallows, or peanut butter. Raccoons often avoid traps. Be patient and keep trying. If unsuccessful, call your local SPCA.
Skunks	Sometimes make their home under porches, buildings, and mobile homes. Carriers of rabies.	First, determine when skunk leaves den by sprinkling flour in front of entrance in daytime; look for tracks after dark when animal should be out foraging. Check for young that may be in den; if den is empty, board up entry.
Squirrels	Enter attic through chimney opening. Gnaw on electrical wires. Carriers of rabies.	Check local laws on animal trapping and transporting. Bait live trap with corn, nut meats, peanuts, peanut butter, sunflower seeds, or rolled oats. Peanut butter is a favorite. Release animal 5 or more miles away in a wooded area.

347

The presence of potentially harmful chemicals in your home may be more common than you realize.

Asbestos. Banned in most new products, asbestos was onced use in pipe, duct, and wall insulation, spackling and wallboard joint compounds, textured paints and ceiling materials, fuse boxes, floor and ceiling tiles, shingles, and siding. Asbestos fibers become a health risk only when they're released into the air; undisturbed, they pose no risk. To avoid airborne fibers, do not sweep, dust, sand, or vacuum asbestos-containing materials. If you're not sure a material contains asbestos, consult a professional or the Consumer Product Safety Commission. In most cases, leave asbestos material alone; if it's flaking or crumbling and must be removed, call an asbestos abatement contractor or the local health department.

Lead can be found, especially in an older home, in lead-base paint, lead pipes, and lead solder. If lead-base paint is in good condition, you need not take any action. But if the paint is peeling or cracked, cover it with wallpaper or a building material such as paneling. Never sand or burn lead-base paint, and don't paint over it. If an object can be removed from the premises, send it out for chemical stripping of the paint; if it cannot be removed, call in a professional. If you must work with lead pipes, ventilate the area well, wear protective gear (p.354), and avoid making dust. Do not heat the pipe—this will produce harmful vapors. Lead requires special disposal; take it to a recycling center or to a hazardous waste collection site.

Formaldehdye. Emissions from this chemical, found in many household materials, can produce headaches, nausea, dizziness, vomiting, and coughing. The most significant source in a home is furniture made of manufactured wood (p.98). To detect emissions, buy a *dosimeter* from an industrial health and safety supply company. Usually the emissions will decrease with time. To further reduce them, seal the product with polyurethane varnish (p.121) or a layer of plastic laminate (pp.140–141), increase ventilation, and maintain moderate temperature and humidity with air conditioners and dehumidifiers. If someone in your home is sensitive to formaldehyde, avoid products containing it.

Radon—a radioactive gas that occurs in soil, water, and natural gas—enters a house through a basement, crawl space, or slab-on-grade floor. Contact your state's radiation protection office for information on radon detection kits and on how to remove radon from your home. Reduce radon levels by sealing cracks in basement walls and floors (p.339) and installing a simple subslab, crawl space, or basement ventilation system. In some cases, more intricate techniques may be needed. Mechanical ventilation may also reduce levels of other indoor air pollutants, such as formaldehyde and nitrogen dioxide.

Other household substances must be disposed of according to your state's regulations. Reduce the amount of these substances in your home by buying only what you need; if possible, choose alternatives that are known to be less toxic. Keep abreast of information on the disposal of hazardous materials. Follow disposal directions on package labels. Instead of throwing away leftovers such as oil paint or insecticide, give them to someone who'll use them up.

Key to disposal instructions

H **Household refuse.** Throw out with garbage going to sanitary landfill or incinerator. Rinse containers with water before disposal. Dispose of aerosol cans only in landfills.

W **Wrap refuse** in newspaper and plastic; add to household refuse.

D **For small amount,** dilute with plenty of water and pour down drain or toilet, but not if you have a septic system. If getting rid of large quantities, recycle or dispose of during a hazardous waste collection day.

S **Solidify.** If necessary, add an absorbent material (cat litter, sand, charcoal, sawdust). When dry, wrap twice in plastic; then place with household trash.

E **Let evaporate** away from children and pets. Double-wrap in plastic; then add to household refuse.

R **Take to** special recycling center or send back to manufacturer.

C **Do not discard waste.** Save it for special collection day or consult your local Cooperative Extension Service, environmental conservation department, or health department for instructions.

Item	Disposal instructions						
Color key	H	W	D	S	E	R	C
Aerosol can (empty)	H						
Antifreeze			D¹			R	
Battery, car						R	
Battery, D-cell or smaller		W				R¹	
Cleaner, abrasive, powder	H						
Cleaner, drain (lye)			D				
Cleaner, mildewcide		W					C¹
Degreasing chemicals							C
Diesel fuel						R	
Fiberglassing material**							C
Flea collar							C
Fluorescent lamp ballast*							C
Gasoline					E		C¹
Glue, solvent-base					E		C¹
Glue, water-base					E		
Insecticide, garden							C
Insecticide, roach/ant killer							C
Kerosene						R	
Mineral spirits/turpentine**					E		C¹
Mothballs (or flakes)							C
Oil, light lubricating/motor						R	
Oven cleaner (lye)			D				
Paintbrush cleaner, phosphate			D				
Paintbrush cleaner, solvent							C
Paint, latex				S	E¹		
Paint, oil (alkyd)							C
Paint remover or thinner					E		C¹
Paint, rust-inhibiting							C
Paint/varnish stripper (lye)			D				
Polish, furniture (solvent-base)							C
Rat/mouse poison, arsenic							C
Rat/mouse poison, warfarin		W					
Rust remover (phosphoric acid)			D				
Smoke detector, ionization						R	
Spot remover (solvent)					E		C¹
Varnish							C
Weed killer							C
Wood preservative or stain							C

Note: For more than one method, the one marked ¹ is preferable.
* Pre-1978 or without a label saying it contains no PCBs.
** After solidifying or evaporating, store for collection day.

Chapter thirteen

Painting and wallpapering
Redecorating like a pro

Contents

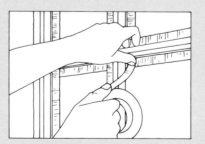

Few do-it-yourself projects give as much immediate pleasure as painting and wallpapering. A fresh coat of paint on a house's exterior makes it look brighter and more inviting. If you pick the colors knowledgeably, new paint also will show off your home's best architectural features and hide its faults. Inside, a different color paint or a new wallcovering quickly rejuvenates a room.

Neither painting nor wallpapering is difficult. The secret lies in using the right tools, carefully preparing all the surfaces, and following the application techniques described here.

Round sash and trim brush

1" varnish or enamel brush

Varnish touch-up brush

1½" trim brush

Angled sash and trim brush

4" interior-exterior wall brush

Paintbrushes come in as many sizes and shapes as there are painting jobs to do. For covering large flat surfaces like clapboard siding there are hefty 6-inch brushes. For interior walls a lighter 4-inch brush might be just as efficient and less tiring. Trim and woodwork take narrower brushes.

Painters differ on the best shape for such delicate work as the wooden mullions between windowpanes. Some like an angled brush that releases paint just at its tip. Others swear by a round sash brush. When precision counts, a brush with a chiseled edge (below) gives the greatest control.

Buying tips. The best brushes are full and thick. Each bristle will be "flagged" on the tip—looking like human hair with split ends—to hold more paint. The bristles should feel springy, not stiff, when you press them against your palm, and they should fan out evenly. Bristles should be firmly glued on either side of a divider that is no more than a third of their width and held by a band (the ferrule) fastened with nails. Handles should be sturdy and comfortable to hold.

Synthetic bristles—nylon, polyester, or a blend of both—are economical and work well with all kinds of paints. Natural bristles, like the oil-base paints they are designed to apply, have lost popularity. They absorb water and get soggy if they are used with water-base products.

Chiseling, shown here in profile, is accomplished by tapering each bristle and staggering the lengths of individual bristles. The narrowed tip of a chiseled brush applies paint to a surface. The result is crisp, clean edging and a minimum number of bristle marks in the paint finish.

To clean a paintbrush, soak it first in the appropriate solvent—water for water-base paints, paint thinner or mineral spirits for oil-base ones. Drill a hole in the brush so you can suspend the bristles in liquid without their touching bottom and getting crimped.

Work the bristles between your fingers all the way to the ferrule to loosen and dislodge remaining paint. Wear rubber gloves if you are working in any solvent other than water.

Rinse in solvent several times, then spin or shake out the excess liquid (in a cardboard box if you want to contain the spray). Use a metal brush comb as shown to dislodge any tenacious paint particles and to straighten out the inner bristles. Hang the brush up to dry.

Fold in order

For long-term storage, wrap the dry brush in heavy paper as shown, or in foil, to keep it dust-free. Hang a wrapped brush or lay it flat, but never rest it upright on its bristles. That ruins the tips.

Pads

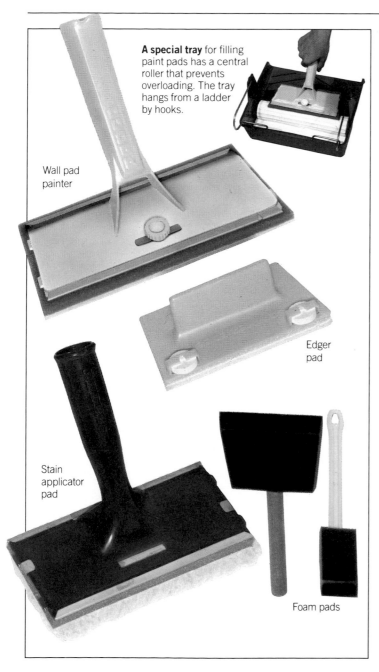

A special tray for filling paint pads has a central roller that prevents overloading. The tray hangs from a ladder by hooks.

Wall pad painter

Edger pad

Stain applicator pad

Foam pads

There is hardly a painting chore that has not had a special paint pad designed to address its particular needs. Pads are made not only in a variety of shapes and sizes, but also in a mix of materials and holding devices. There are edging pads with adjustable wheels that let you cut a straight line as you paint next to the ceiling. There are triangular paint pads that do corners, and narrow rectangular ones for window trim. There are even paint pads that fit under the overlap on shingles and shakes.

Paint pads come in a wide choice of naps—from ⅜-inch synthetics for painting flat surfaces to thick mohair for applying smooth stains without brush marks and even deeper-piled synthetics for one-coat coverage of rough stucco walls.

Not everyone is comfortable with paint pads. For many painters who use brushes with confidence and satisfaction, paint pads seem to match neither the control offered by brushes nor the speed associated with rollers. Others, however, find paint pads efficient to use and easy to care for. Many people, for example, treat inexpensive foam pads as throwaways.

Paint glove
The mitt at right has a paint-holding nap for quick coverage of staircase balusters, railings, gutters, or pipes. Wearing the glove, a painter dips it into paint, then clasps thumb and forefinger together around the object and moves the glove down the length until the surface is coated with paint.

To clean a paint pad, first blot out as much paint as possible on thick layers of newspaper. Then remove the pad from its holder.

Wash the pad in water if you were using water-base paint, or in paint thinner or mineral spirits if you were using oil-base paint. Wear rubber gloves in mineral spirits or paint thinner.

Do a final wash in detergent or soap and water. Detergents containing ammonia are particularly effective on oil paints. Rinse the pad thoroughly under running water.

Blot or squeeze out all the excess water on old towels or newspapers, and leave the pad standing on edge to dry. Wrap the dry pad in heavy brown paper, foil, or plastic to keep it clean.

Spatter shield

Extension pole

For large flat surfaces no painting tool matches a roller for ease, speed, and solid coverage. Originally designed for painting interior walls, rollers with specialized sleeves or attachments simplify other indoor and many outdoor painting jobs as well. A roller firmly screwed onto an extension pole or broom handle lets you tackle ceilings without a ladder and do floors without bending down.

Frame design. A traditional roller frame, shown below, has a spring-type mechanism called a cage to hold the pile cover, or sleeve, that applies paint. A well-designed cage will hold the sleeve securely without needing a wing nut and, at the same time, will permit you to slide the sleeve off and on easily. A cage should spin smoothly on nylon bearings. The handle and frame should feel sturdy in your hand.

Alternative designs are a splatter-shield frame (left), which helps contain flying paint—useful when you are working on a ceiling—and a yoke frame (below), which its advocates believe applies the pressure more evenly across the roller surface.

Roller frames come in many sizes

to hold special-purpose sleeves, from the V-shaped doughnut for painting inside corners to short 3-inch rollers for doing trim.

Roller sleeves. The best covers have a uniform, fluffy, lint-free pile and a tough water-resistant center. Cheap roller covers hold less paint, splatter more, and tend to mat.

The smoother the surface you want to paint—and the smoother the desired finish—the shorter the pile you need. A glossy enamel on a flat wall requires a sleek nap of ¼ inch or less. General-purpose sleeves for flat finish paints have ⅜-inch naps.

A roller with a cover pile as deep as ½ inch can quickly work paint into the hollows of rough stucco. A longer nap—¾ inch—makes roller coverage of concrete floors, brick walls, and chain link fences fast and easy.

Sleeves also come in different fibers. Lamb's wool is best for applying oil-base paints; Dynel works well with water-base paints. Acetate and polyester can be successfully used with either. Mohair covers give the smooth, textureless finish that high-gloss enamels and varnishes need.

Loading a roller

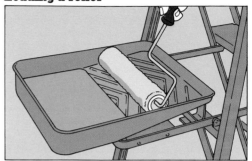

Immerse the roller in paint at the deep end of the roller tray. Then rotate roller back and forth over the ribs on the tray's shallow end until the sleeve is evenly coated with paint, but not dripping when you lift it up.

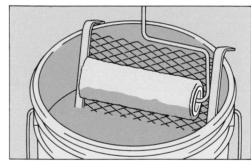

To distribute paint evenly, professional painters work a freshly loaded roller up and down against a portable metal grid, shown here in a 5-gal. paint bucket. Such grids are also used in roller trays with disposable liners.

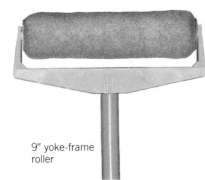

9″ yoke-frame roller

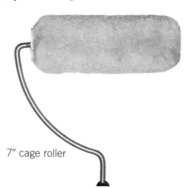

7″ cage roller

3″ trim roller

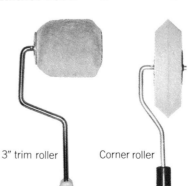

Corner roller

Types of rollers. The red roller (far left) has a spatter shield and an extension pole for painting ceilings and floors. Next are two surface rollers, the first a 9-in. yoke-frame roller and the second a 7-in. cage type. Two trim rollers follow, a 3-in. cage model for flat woodwork and narrow wall spaces, and a V-shaped design for corners.

Power painters

Care of rollers

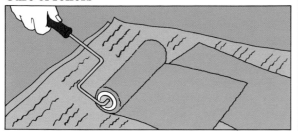

To clean a roller, first press out excess paint on newspaper. When the sleeve is as free of paint as you can get it, slide it from the frame. Don't clean rollers for short breaks. You can safely wrap a working sleeve in a tightly closed plastic bag for several hours.

Use the appropriate solvent to work out the remaining paint with your fingers. For water-base paints, it will be water. For oil-base paints, use mineral spirits or paint thinner and wear rubber gloves. Finish with a detergent-and-water wash; then rinse.

Squeeze out excess water with your hands, checking that all signs of paint are gone. Dried residue will ruin the sleeve.

Spin the sleeve dry with a spinning device from the hardware store. Wrap the dry sleeve in foil and store it on end.

For a big job, roller painting can be speeded with an appliance that automatically feeds paint from a central source to its specially designed roller by way of a long hose. A button on the roller handle lets you adjust the flow.

The advantages: You don't have to keep reloading the roller from a tray or bucket every few minutes. When you are working from a ladder, you are saved the inconvenience of moving both the ladder and your paint supply each time.

Models powered by electricity, a hand pump, or a CO_2 cartridge all perform essentially the same tasks. They come with brush and pad attachments as well as roller frames with a variety of sleeves in different naps.

The drawbacks: Cleaning these appliances, particularly the hoses, is time-consuming. So is maintenance. They waste ample amounts of paint.

Their best use is for exterior housepainting with big areas to cover and lots of ladder work.

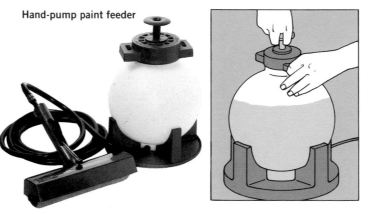

Hand-pump paint feeder

The paint feeder (left) has a hand pump. Working the lever up and down 20 times (box) keeps a gallon of paint flowing quietly to its roller. The electric model (below, left) is more powerful, but it is noisy when it pumps. Its extras include an extension rod, a pad, and a faucet adapter for cleaning. To use this power painter (below), load a 1-gal. paint can into the base and plug it in. The hose gives you a painting range of 18 ft.

Electric paint feeder

Roller

Faucet adapter

Pad

Extension rod

Paint siphon

353

Speed alone could justify the extra masking that spray-painting requires. However, spraying has another advantage over brush or roller painting: it covers intricate shapes—louvered shutters, trellises, and fencing, for example—far more evenly than hours of handwork with a brush, roller, or pad. And spraying does it in minutes.

For big jobs—walls, ceilings, and house exteriors—two kinds of sprayers are available. One uses compressed air to atomize paint and project it onto a surface (p.77). The other, an airless sprayer, pumps liquid paint through a spray-gun tip at extremely high pressure to create a denser, more directed mist of paint for covering a surface.

The airless sprayer (below) is simpler to use and works faster than a compressed-air sprayer, but an airless spray gun must be used with great respect. Paint is forced through the tip of an airless spray gun at pressures up to 3,000 pounds per square inch and at speeds as high as 200 miles per hour.

▶ **CAUTION:** Such powerful propulsion can inject paint through your skin and into your body, causing serious injury that requires immediate attention in a hospital emergency room. Not all doctors know how to handle these injuries. Without prompt and proper treatment, you could face the prospect of losing a limb by amputation—or worse. When using an airless paint sprayer, at all times follow these safety rules:

• Never point a spray gun at yourself or at any other person.

• Keep children and pets well away when you are spray-painting.

• Unplug airless equipment before unclogging a spray tip or before any other disassembly or maintenance procedure.

• Never leave an airless sprayer—plugged in or not—lying about unattended.

Safety gear

Protective glasses, masks, and respirators belong in a toolbox as much as pliers do. Safety goggles guard your eyes against flying particles and liquids—but not against fumes. Wear goggles while sawing, drilling, sanding, wire-brushing, planing, or spray-painting. (They won't fog up if they have ventilation holes.)

Inexpensive disposable masks—fitted with a metal nosepiece—give you relief from nuisance odors, dusts, and mists. Those labeled "sanding respirator" provide more protection than ones called "latex paint mask."

For working with toxic substances—such as lacquers or urea formaldehyde—you can buy a special disposable respirator or invest in a dual-cartridge respirator with disposable filters. Read labels for appropriate filters.

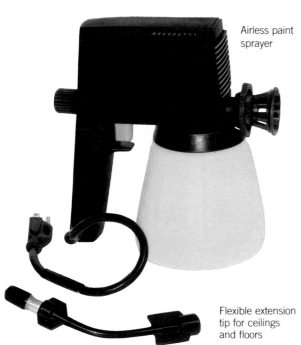

Airless paint sprayer

Flexible extension tip for ceilings and floors

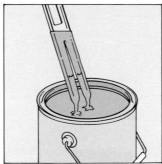

A viscosity test stick helps to gauge whether paint has been thinned enough for a sprayer. Paint must drain from a notch to a particular point on the stick in a predetermined number of seconds to be viable. Most paints need at least 10 percent dilution for spraying.

Straining paint through several layers of nylon stocking material or cheesecloth will prevent lumps and debris from clogging the spray tip.

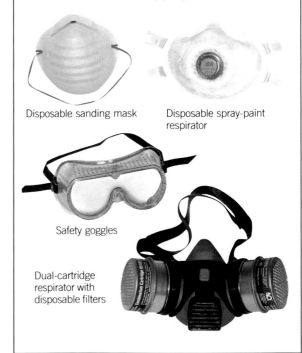

Disposable sanding mask

Disposable spray-paint respirator

Safety goggles

Dual-cartridge respirator with disposable filters

Preparation for spray-painting. Any surface that you do not want coated must be masked before you begin to paint. Although an airless sprayer can be controlled more readily than an air compression sprayer, they both create a mist of paint that can drift onto any nearby surface. Outdoors, for example, you need to shield shrubbery and cover your car or put it in the garage. Indoors, carry out all the customary preparations (pp.356–357), and in addition, mask all windowpanes with newspaper held with masking tape.

Getting started. Set up your spray equipment according to the manufacturer's directions. (If you rent a sprayer, be sure to get instructions with it.) First you should flush the unit with a solvent—water for latex paint or mineral spirits for alkyd—and then start pumping paint either through a suction tube and hose in a paint can or from the paint holder attached to the nozzle. Check that the spray tip you pick is the right one for the type of coating you are using. Thin stains, for example, take the smallest spray tip openings; heavy latex paints, the largest.

If you've never used a sprayer before, first load it with water and spray against an outside wall or a piece of scrap plywood. Without making a mess, you can practice using the controls until you are comfortable with them.

The specific painting techniques shown at right apply to both kinds of power spray equipment—and to individual cans of spray paint. These small cans are expensive and wasteful for big jobs, but they are a great convenience for many small ones. Priming a newly patched area of wall or ceiling, for example, is quick and easy with a spray can.

Cleaning up. Follow manufacturer's instructions for your particular sprayer. Essentially, you pump excess paint out of the hose first. Then, using the appropriate solvent—mineral spirits for alkyd paint and water for latex paint—you flush out the sprayer. Clean individual components by soaking them in the applicable solvent. When the sprayer is reassembled, you should lubricate metal parts with household oil for rust protection.

Spraying techniques. Hold a spray painter 10 to 12 inches from the surface to be painted, and keep it upright. Try a sample spray to check the pattern. The ideal spray pattern is wide, finely atomized, and even throughout. Three variables determine that pattern: the viscosity of the paint, the size of the spray tip, and the pressure control.

Because it is the easiest variable to adjust, experiment first with turning the pressure control knob. If changing the pressure doesn't help, check the tip and the thickness of the paint. Too small a spray tip for thick paint causes heavy spatters in the middle of the spray and lighter coverage at the edges. Using too large a tip with thin paint produces a coarse spray. The design will be widely spattered and the coverage poor.

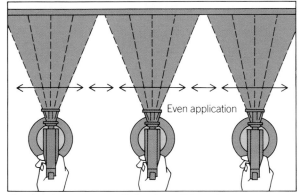

Keeping the sprayer parallel to the wall is the key to even spray-paint application. As you move along, flex your wrist to maintain the same 12-in. distance from the surface you are painting. This will result in an even, consistent spray pattern.

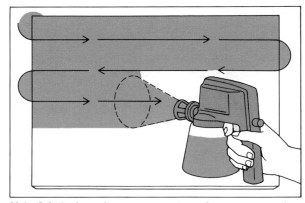

Make 3-ft. horizontal sweeps across the surface you are spraying, overlapping each strip of paint by about 1 in. Go slightly beyond the edges of the area before starting the return pass. The secret to good spraying is thin, even coats.

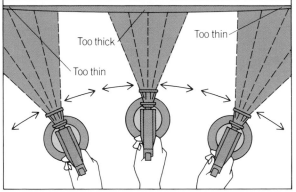

Arcing the sprayer as you swing your arm creates an unsatisfactory pattern, with thin spots at the edges and too much paint in the middle. To overcome the temptation to swing your arm, move your whole body parallel to the surface.

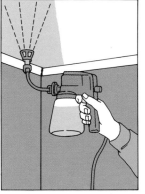

A flexible extension tip points the spray up so that you can make easy sweeps on ceilings or undersides of shelves.

For floors, bend the extension tip down. Simply tilting a sprayer with a normal tip creates an uneven pattern.

The key to a good-looking and long-lasting paint job is painstaking preparation. The scraping tools shown below testify to the number of different surfaces that may need stripping before they can be repaired, sanded down, scrubbed, and primed for a fresh coat of paint.

The triangular shave hook, or molding scraper, digs accumulated paint and dirt out of the crevices in decorative woodwork. Similar tools with different heads scrape paint off curved wood molding. The razor scraper uses standard blades and takes paint off glass. The 6-inch flexible wall scraper, or wallboard taping knife, removes wallpaper and softened paint from flat surfaces. It is also used to level off applications of plaster compound. The

flexible putty knife is equally versatile, but for smaller jobs. The hook scraper, which you draw toward you, takes paint off flat wood surfaces like windowsills and door frames.

Before starting a redecorating project, step back and look at each room you are planning to paint as if you were seeing it for the first time. You may notice flaws you have learned to overlook but now have a chance to remedy.

A room ready for painting is shown on the facing page. The agenda for proper preparation:

Check for big problems. A sagging ceiling, for example, may be evidence of a roof leak or a seeping radiator on the floor above. Track down the cause of wall or ceiling damage and clear that up

before you repair the wallboard or plaster.

Clear the walls. Take down pictures and curtains to look for cracks, holes, and peeling paint on walls and ceiling. Check the woodwork for loose paint, nicks, popped nails, and separations at corners or at wall junctures (p.359). If there is wallpaper, you'll probably want to strip it (p.376), whether you are painting or repapering.

Assemble your materials. For masking you'll need plastic drop cloths, newspaper, masking tape, plastic bags; for access, ladders and boards for scaffolding. For repairs, have on hand spackling compound, wood filler, a heat gun or chemical paint remover, sander and sandpaper, tack cloth, vacuum cleaner, and a spray can of primer. For

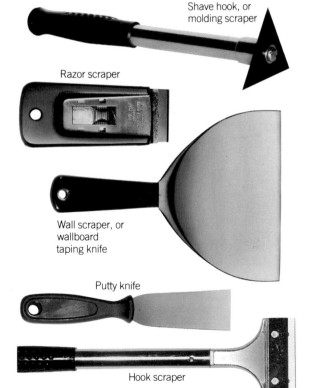

Shave hook, or molding scraper

Razor scraper

Wall scraper, or wallboard taping knife

Putty knife

Hook scraper

Repairing an area of flaking paint

1. Scrape off all the loose paint in the area with a blunt flexible scraper, being careful not to gouge the wall. What paint is left must stick tightly to the surface, or your repair will not last.

2. Apply spackling compound to the edges of the patch area with a putty knife or wall scraper. Your aim is to taper the compound to eliminate the difference in thickness between the paint layer and the wall and return the area to a smooth, unbroken surface.

3. Level the patch with a broad scraper or another tool large enough to give an overall flush finish that fills in the paint edges without making any ripples elsewhere. Let the compound dry thoroughly.

4. Use a sanding block, first with medium-grit sandpaper, then with fine-grit sandpaper, to complete the smoothing process. Wear safety goggles and a sanding respirator or a mask for this job.

cleaning you'll want detergent, bleach, bucket, and sponge; for safety, goggles and respirators.

Remove furniture and rugs. The more space you have to work in, the easier patching and painting will be. What furniture stays should be clustered in the middle of the room and covered with drop cloths. A rope tied around the bottom of the pile will keep the cloths in place.

Dismantle hardware. Remove knobs, latches, and locks on doors and wood window frames. Take down curtain rods and brackets. Remove picture hooks. Turn off electricity to the room (p.237); then unscrew plates from electrical switches and outlets. If there is a ceiling lighting fixture, either disconnect it and take it down or loosen its plate and enclose it—plate and all—in a large plastic bag secured at the top with tape.

Finish masking. Wall sconces, standing radiators, and thermostats need to be protected. Cover the entire floor (or carpeting) with plastic drop cloths, but ring the outer edges of the room with several layers of newspaper taped below the baseboards. Make a path of newspapers from the door into the center of the room. Newspaper absorbs wet paint and allows it to dry; plastic doesn't. Paint on a plastic cloth stays wet, and if you step on it, you are likely to track it into other rooms.

Make repairs. Fix walls, ceilings, and woodwork with the techniques described here and on the next two pages as well as in the sections on wallboard repair (p.278), plaster repair (p.280), and removing baseboards (p.293). Prime patched areas to ensure uniform paint coverage.

Wash down all surfaces to be painted. Use a heavy-duty detergent such as trisodium phosphate (TSP) or a nonphosphate equivalent, bought at a paint supply store. Even fingerprints can keep paint from bonding properly. Clean any damp or mildewed areas with a 1:3 household bleach and water solution. Rinse, and let the area dry completely before painting. Glossy surfaces may also need sanding or an application of commercial deglosser for new paint to adhere properly.

Mask windowpanes with tape, as shown, or with liquid glass coating—up to ⅛ in. from the muntins. An unbroken film of paint adhering to the panes protects the muntins from harmful condensation.

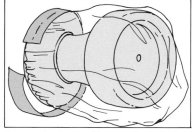

Cover a doorknob with a small plastic bag held by tape if the escutcheon's edge is flat enough to hold the tape securely where it meets the door. This trick saves removing the doorknob and all its hardware.

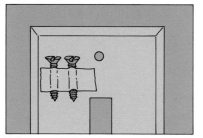

To keep track of small pieces of hardware, tape them to the object with which they are used. The screws shown above, for example, are safely attached to the switchplate they normally hold in place.

Painting/Woodwork preparation

Wood trim—if it is in good shape—needs little more than scrubbing with a strong detergent like trisodium phosphate or its nonphosphate equivalent before you can repaint it. Very glossy paint also may need to be sanded or treated with a deglosser so that the new coat of paint will adhere. However, once paint on wood begins to craze (crack) or peel badly, it's better to remove it than to try to repair large patches. Taking off old paint is a tedious and messy job, but it creates a clean base for a durable new coat.

You can remove old paint with a heat gun (below) or with a chemical stripper (right). Nontoxic strippers work slowly—they soften old paint in hours rather than minutes—but they save exposure to caustic substances and fumes.

Bare wood—even though it has been previously painted—needs to be sanded smooth, wiped free of dust with a commercial tack cloth (or a cotton rag soaked in paint thinner), and sealed with a primer before it is repainted. (Preparation and finishing techniques for natural, stained, or varnished woodwork are discussed on pages 117–124.)

Removing paint with chemical stripper

Brush paste-type paint stripper onto woodwork. A nontoxic stripper may not require gloves (read the label), but always wear safety goggles to protect your eyes from splashes.

Test if paint is soft with a putty knife (there will be no blisters or wrinkles if you use nontoxic stripper). For two or more paint layers, you may have to scrape once, reapply stripper, and scrape again.

Scrape off softened paint with a putty knife, a wall scraper, or for intricate molding, a dampened sponge and a shaving hook that can dig paint sludge out of nooks and crevices.

Final sanding comes after all the paint has been cleaned off according to the manufacturer's instructions. A wedge of folded sandpaper will reach recesses in the wood.

Removing paint with a heat gun

Hold the heat gun about 1 in. from the paint. To prevent scorching the wood, keep the gun moving constantly. Work it back and forth over one small area—about 6 in. square—at a time.

The paint will soften and begin to blister as shown within seconds. Guns can reach temperatures as high as 1200° F; so you must wear heavy work gloves for protection.

Scrape off softened paint, holding a putty knife in one hand while moving the gun over flat surfaces with the other. For complicated moldings, set gun in its stand while you scrape.

Sand bare wood with the grain, using a fine (150-grit) paper. (First all the paint sludge must be removed with steel wool.) Power sanding saves time on flat surfaces.

Repairing nicks and dents

Scrape away loose paint around the damaged area with a putty knife or wall scraper. Be sure all the paint you leave adheres tightly, or it will flake later.

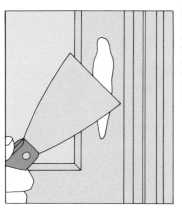

Fill in the hole with plastic wood filler or spackling compound; then level the patch with a wallboard taping knife, and leave it to dry thoroughly before you begin sanding it.

Sand the patch with fine (150-grit) paper until its surface is even and smooth. The repaired area is now ready for priming with a primer compatible with the final coat of paint.

Fixing separated joints

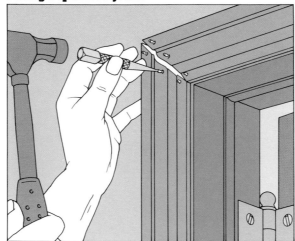

Joints in door frames or window frames can pull apart as the wood shrinks. Small separations aren't serious and can be camouflaged with spackling compound or wood filler. First check for popped nails. Countersink them with a hammer and nail set as shown; then fill the holes.

Treating knots

 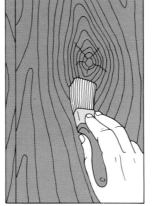

Wood knots can bleed through paint to stain the finish, or they may ooze resin that hardens into lumps under the paint. Use a razor scraper to remove resin deposits (left). Clean the area with paint thinner or mineral spirits. Seal knots (right) with shellac or a special primer designed for this purpose.

To fill joint openings in a stepped or decorative frame, use a flexible putty knife to apply the compound. Shape the compound to match the pattern of the molding. If the opening is deep, you may need to apply two layers of compound. Sand the dried patch carefully to conform to the shape of the molding.

Preparing and painting old radiators

Cast-iron radiators give off more heat when painted with standard interior paint rather than metallic paint. Many old radiators are decorative and can be painted to show off the design. First, radiators must be stripped of old paint and rust. Use a metal scraper or the wire brush attachment on an electric drill. Prime with a rust inhibitor. The hard-to-reach fins can be spray-painted.

Painting/Safe working platforms indoors

Most interior walls and ceilings can be reached easily with a stepladder. Opened out on a level floor with its spreader braces and its bucket shelf locked into place, a stepladder makes a stable work station. Whether you are hanging paper or painting, if you stand below the top two steps and refrain from reaching too far to left or right, you'll be reasonably safe.

▶ **CAUTION:** Never set up a ladder in front of a closed, unlocked door. Either open the door so that people can see the ladder, or lock it so that no one can inadvertently barge through and knock into the ladder.

For working on large ceilings or high walls, scaffolding becomes more efficient than a ladder. A

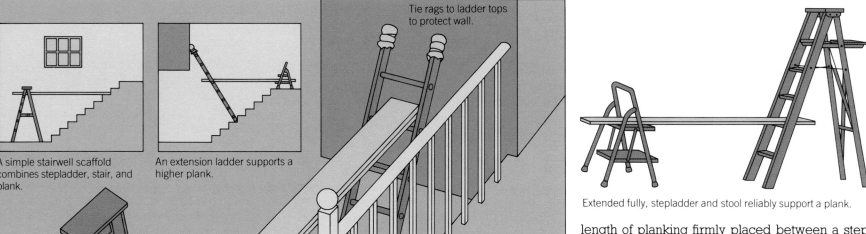

Tie rags to ladder tops to protect wall.

A simple stairwell scaffold combines stepladder, stair, and plank.

An extension ladder supports a higher plank.

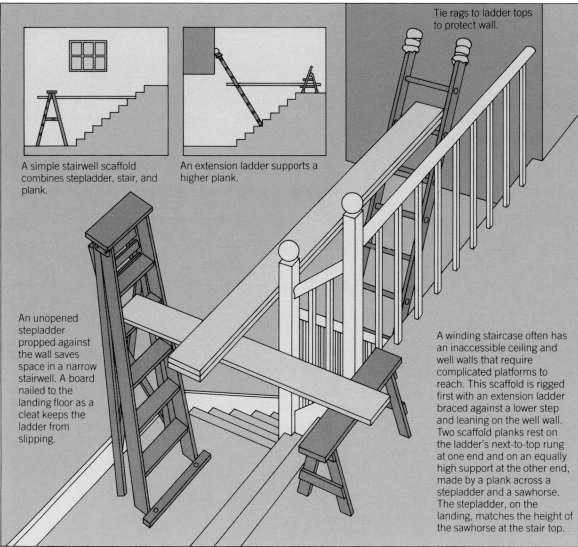

Extended fully, stepladder and stool reliably support a plank.

An unopened stepladder propped against the wall saves space in a narrow stairwell. A board nailed to the landing floor as a cleat keeps the ladder from slipping.

A winding staircase often has an inaccessible ceiling and well walls that require complicated platforms to reach. This scaffold is rigged first with an extension ladder braced against a lower step and leaning on the well wall. Two scaffold planks rest on the ladder's next-to-top rung at one end and on an equally high support at the other end, made by a plank across a stepladder and a sawhorse. The stepladder, on the landing, matches the height of the sawhorse at the stair top.

length of planking firmly placed between a step stool and a stepladder gives you safer lateral range than a ladder alone, and it doesn't have to be moved as frequently.

You can buy scaffold boards (1 foot wide x 2 inches thick x 8 feet or longer) at lumberyards, or you can rent them from a paint store or home center. These sturdy planks rest safely on sawhorses, ladders, steps, and landings or on a combination of supports if a few rules are followed: The board should extend at least 1 foot beyond each of its freestanding supports. If the span between supports is 5 feet or more, put a second board on top of the first for added strength. For spans longer than 10 feet, rig an additional support in the middle. Use C-clamps to hold planks firmly in place.

Reaching the ceiling and upper walls of a stairwell usually requires more elaborate scaffolding. An improvised combination of extension ladder, stepladder, sawhorses, and planks—with a few cleat boards nailed down for safety—can make the most remote surfaces accessible.

Buying paint for interior use

The chemistry of modern paints makes it possible to coat and protect almost any surface with a specially formulated paint. You must, in fact, be very specific in discussing your paint needs with your dealer. The nature of the surface you plan to paint, what it has been coated with before, and the kind of wear it will get—all are important factors.

Don't economize on paint quality. Buying a manufacturer's premium line is worth the investment. Application will be easier and the paint job will last longer. To save money, buy a primer or undercoat—which costs less—instead of priming with a finish paint. Also, watch for sales. Check labels for compatibility of primer and paint.

To estimate the number of gallons of paint you need, compute the square footage of the area you plan to paint and divide by the manufacturer's estimated coverage per gallon. Paint feeders (p.353) and sprayers (pp.354–355) will require more.

Latex-base paint. Easy to apply, quick drying, nontoxic when inhaled, and requiring only soap and water for cleanup, latex paints come in high gloss, semigloss, eggshell (satin or low luster), and flat finishes. There are also formulas to meet special needs, such as latex floor enamels, textured paints for less-than-perfect walls and ceilings, and epoxies for waterproofing cellar walls. Because they are water-thinned, latex paints cause rust on unprimed metal; coat it first with a rust-inhibiting metal primer. Latex primers don't seal out moisture as well as oil-base ones. Freezing ruins stored latex paint; it will separate and give off a foul odor.

Solvent-thinned paint. Now made with synthetic resins called alkyds instead of linseed and other oils, these paints, particularly in a glossy finish, give a smoother, richer, more scrubbable coating than latex. Alkyd paints dry more quickly than oil paints and have less odor, but they do pose environmental problems. Provide good ventilation and wear a respirator during application. Alkyd paints, their solvents, and solvent-soaked rags are toxic and combustible; follow local hazardous waste disposal regulations (p.348).

Interior paint choices. Surfaces inside a house that you may wish to paint are listed below. Paint and other coating choices are spelled out across the top of the chart. Pick a surface and follow its column across the chart. Each colored square suggests a suitable covering. To identify the product, follow the column above the colored square to the top of the chart.

Surface	Latex primer	Alkyd primer	Aluminum paint	Rust-inhibiting metal primer	Zinc-dust primer	Cement paint	Waterproofing paint	Block filler	Masonry sealer	Gloss enamel (latex) •	Gloss enamel (alkyd) •	Semigloss enamel (latex) •	Semigloss enamel (alkyd) •	Flat paint (latex)	Flat paint (alkyd)	Textured paint (latex)	Acrylic enamel (latex) •	Floor enamel (latex) •	Floor enamel (alkyd) •	Epoxy paint
New plaster	■	■					■		■	■	■	■	■	■	■					
Previously painted plaster										■	■	■	■	■	■	■				
New wallboard (drywall)	■									■	■	■	■	■	■	■				
Previously painted wallboard										■	■	■	■	■	■	■				
Uncoated wallpaper	■													■						
Vinyl wallcovering														■						
Wood paneling*	■	■											■	■						
Acrylic-finish paneling												■								
New plywood or particleboard	■	■												■			■			
Previously painted plywood														■						
New wood floor *	■																1	1	1	
Previously finished wood floor *																	■	■	■	
New wood trim *	■	■								■	■	■	■	■						
Previously finished wood trim *										■	■	■	■	■						
Vinyl-clad trim	■																			
Acoustical tile														2						
New masonry		■				■	■		■								■			■
Previously treated masonry																	■		■	■
New brick	■																			
Steel (cabinets, window frames, radiator covers)				■																
Aluminum (door and window frames)			■																	
Galvanized metal (heating ducts)					■	■														
Cast iron (radiators)				■																

● A black dot indicates the paint is formulated for several surfaces and materials; look for the appropriate choice.

1 Use a thinned finish coat as a primer (following manufacturer's directions).
2 Apply a thin coat to avoid damaging the tiles' acoustical properties.
* For natural finishes, see chart, p.123; to paint over natural finishes, see *Woodwork preparation*, pp.358–359.

Painting / How to use color

Knowing the principles of color lets you change the look and feeling of a room for the price of a few gallons of paint and a free weekend.

Color can transform a room. Pale shades open it up and give it a sense of spaciousness. Because colors with a lot of white in them reflect light, they brighten dark hallways and rooms with a northern exposure, which get the least sunlight. White ceilings seem higher because the color makes them appear to recede.

Dark colors make a room cozy and intimate. They are often used in quiet places like studies and dens. Dark colors can also disguise architectural faults like uneven walls, and they hide signs of wear in heavy-use areas.

Blues, violets, greens, and grays in any number of tints and shades give a cool, serene feeling to a room. Intense cool colors are refreshing, while subdued cool hues have a tranquil effect. Reds, oranges, and yellows warm a room. Intense warm colors create excitement; subtler hues, sociability.

Pure colors like those you see in the chart (right) are neither diluted by white pigment nor darkened with black pigment. This makes them vibrant, energetic, and, in too great a quantity, a little tiring. Expanses of bright, intense color belong in active spaces like recreation rooms. Bright accents, however, can add excitement to soft color schemes.

A color wheel helps you see the relationships between colors. Red, yellow, and blue are primary colors. Orange, green, and violet are considered secondary colors: each is created by combining two primary colors. Tertiary colors are a mixture of a primary and a secondary color.

Harmonious color schemes can be diagramed on the color wheel. Colors that are opposite each other—blue and orange, for example—are complementary colors and good decorating partners. For three-color harmony, use colors equidistant from each other on the wheel (triad scheme), or pick a base color and the two colors on either side of its complement (split complementary scheme).

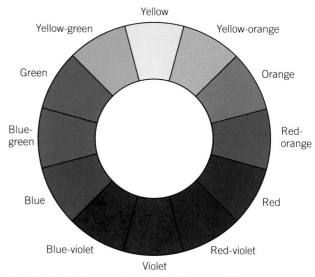

A color wheel shows the interrelationships of the 12 basic colors. Color schemes based on the wheel—even in lighter or darker values—maintain color balance.

Related colors, like the greens and blues in the dining room (left), make for visual harmony. Next to each other on the color wheel, related colors work well together. However, to add interest, a contrasting, or complementary, accent of pink in the wallpaper border makes a nice touch.

A monochromatic scheme based on earthy terra-cotta colors unifies the disparate elements in the kitchen (left) and gives the odd-shaped room a wholeness. The deep tone of the floor tiles is echoed in an even richer value on the countertops and backsplashes. The curtains and eating area ceiling are lighter gradations that blend well with the warm beiges of cabinets, walls, ceiling, and chair.

Special paint effects

Interesting finishes can be created on painted walls with a technique called glazing. A glaze is a thin coat of paint (either transparent or opaque) in a different color applied over a base coat to soften its effect. Glaze can be applied with sponges or rags to make a pattern. Or it can be rolled on conventionally and then be partially blotted off with special brushes or rags to form a design.

Glazes can be bought, or you can make your own (start with a 4:1 water-paint ratio for latex paints and a 3:1 solvent-paint ratio for alkyds). The only rule in glazing is always to use latex glazes with latex paints and alkyd glazes with alkyd paints. Latex glazes are cloudy and dry quickly; you can apply several layers of color in a short time. Alkyd glazes are shinier and allow more drying time to work in. Before tackling a wall, experiment with colors, techniques, and designs on a piece of hardboard.

Sponging. 1. An easy technique that works well with either latex or alkyd paint, sponging adds glaze to a base coat in a subtle mottled pattern. Start by applying the chosen base color (blue in this case) with a roller or pad. Let it dry completely.

2. Using a sponge you have practiced with, apply glaze in a second color (pink here). Dab it on with firm strokes. Work in 3-ft. squares. When the sponge gets too soggy with paint to make a clean pattern, set it aside and use a fresh one. (Clean up used sponges later.)

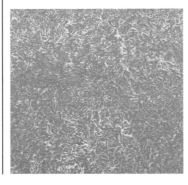

3. Apply an optional second color glaze (yellow here) when the first glaze is dry. Use fresh, clean sponges. You might want to vary the application pattern of the second glaze to add interest. Try, for example, smaller or larger patches of glaze or use another type of sponge—synthetic or natural.

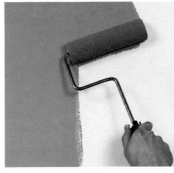

Stippling. 1. In this technique, you get an effect by removing glaze in a pattern. It works best with alkyd paint, which dries more slowly, giving you extra time to work. Apply a coat of alkyd glaze (blue paint in picture) over a thoroughly dried alkyd base coat (cream) with roller or pad.

2. With the glaze still tacky, press a coarse brush against it in quick, firm jabs which will reveal the base color and give the wall a textured look. Stippling is easiest when two people work: one glazes while the other follows with the stippling tool.

3. Stippling tends to soften colors and is particularly effective when deep glaze shades are used over a white or light base (blue over cream here). You can buy a professional stippling brush, which creates a freckled pattern, in art supply stores; or use a softer brush to get a mottled finish.

Rag-rolling. 1. This technique works best with alkyd paint and glaze. Start with a base coat (cream here) and let it dry completely. Have plenty of rags (old cotton sheets are good) cut up and ready for use before applying the glaze (rose in picure).

2. With folded, rolled, or crumpled strips of cloth, blot off part of the glaze in an irregular pattern that will look consistent over a whole wall. Before you start, work out a technique on boards. Reroll rags or pick up fresh ones often. A partner will make the rag-rolling go much faster.

3. Cotton rags were used for this particular pattern of rag-rolling. Other fabrics will create different textures and patterns. Sharply contrasting colors, like burgundy over tan, will give a more dramatic effect than the rose over cream shown here.

Painting / Ceilings and walls

The time-tested sequence for painting rooms efficiently and neatly is to work from top to bottom. Start with the ceiling. Paint the walls next; then the windows, doors, and other woodwork, finishing with the baseboards.

You'll need a combination of paint applicators. If you use the proper size brush, roller, or pad for each part of the job, the work will go faster.

Mixing paint. Paint separates when it sits, so you must mix it thoroughly before you use it. Let your paint dealer mix it on a machine if you will be painting right away. If you have had the paint for a while, turn the can upside down and let it sit for 24 hours before you open it.

To mix a full can manually, first pour about a third of the liquid into another container; stir the remainder with a wooden paddle until it is well mixed. Then gradually stir the reserved liquid back into the can. You can also buy a special propeller-like metal attachment for your power drill to mix paint.

Pour paint from a large can into a smaller container or roller tray, and reclose the can. This keeps your supply from drying out, picking up stray grit, or spilling.

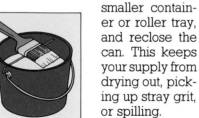

For breaks improvise a rest for your brush: suspend a coat hanger wire between holes you punch on either side of the paint bucket (above). If a brush sits in the paint container, it will absorb too much paint and its bristles will crimp.

To "cut in" with a brush, paint a 2-in. strip around all the edge areas that a roller cannot easily reach. Hold a trim brush as you would a pencil. Dip the bristles a third of their length into paint; gently press out excess paint against the side—not the rim—of the bucket. Apply paint to the wall in smooth, overlapping strokes.

A pad edger has rollers—often adjustable—along the side to keep the paint a uniform distance from a corner or a door or window frame. To load a pad, dip it no deeper than its pile into flat tray of paint, or run it back and forth across the roller of a pad tray (p.351). Cutting in can be done very quickly with a pad.

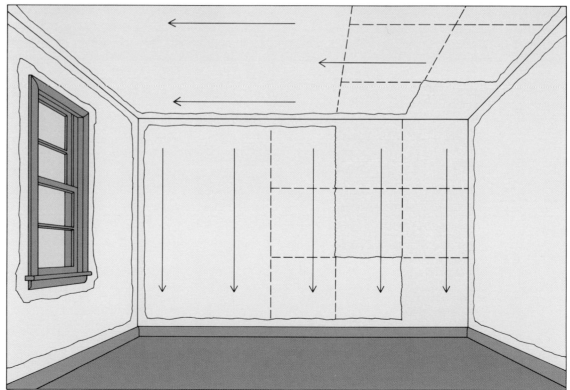

Plan of attack. Paint a ceiling across its width, rather than its length, as shown by the arrows. After cutting in, start working from a corner in 3-ft. squares. When the ceiling is low, using a roller on an extension pole is less tiring than standing on a scaffold and using a standard roller. Paint walls in 3-ft. square sections starting at the ceiling line and moving down to the baseboard, then returning to the top to paint the next 3-ft. strip.

Minimizing the mess. Clean up spills with a damp rag as you go along. Moisten it with water for latex paints and with paint thinner for alkyds.

To keep paint from collecting in an open can rim and slopping over the side, punch holes in the groove with a hammer and a small nail. Paint will drain back into the can and not over the edge.

Clean the rim of old paint cans before you open them. Lift out and discard any hardened skin that may have formed. Strain the paint through a nylon stocking to remove any accumulated lumps or dirt.

When you are finished, consolidate the leftover paint. Wipe off the paint can, cover the top with plastic to prevent splashes, and hammer the lid on securely. Label and date the can.

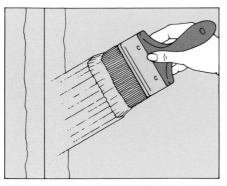
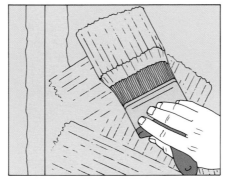
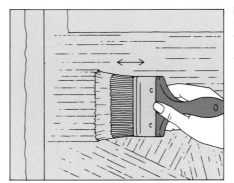

Basic brush technique for flat surfaces is to paint first in short strokes in many different directions over a small area of about 2 sq. ft. (far left and center left); then level the paint with a back-and-forth horizontal motion before reloading the brush (left). Start your next section about 2 ft. below the first and work back into the wet paint to minimize brush marks. Hold the 3- or 4-in.- wide brush used for large areas with your thumb on one side and all four fingers on the other. If your hand gets tired, switch to a tennis grip (hold the brush as if shaking hands with it).

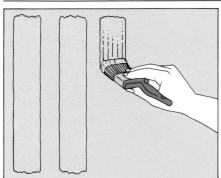

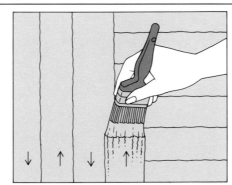

Applying high-gloss enamel requires a different technique. Start with three vertical stripes about 2 ft. long and not quite a brush width apart (far left). Before reloading the brush, work it horizontally across the stripes, filling the gaps and smoothing out the paint (center left). Now, with the brush almost dry, brush lightly over the section again with vertical strokes (left). Begin the next section below the first one and repeat the procedure, taking care to blend the areas so that no joint shows.

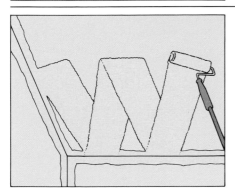
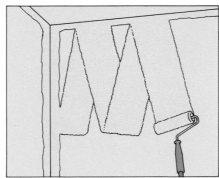
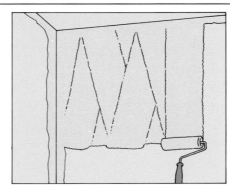

Roller technique for ceilings and walls is similar. You can work in 3-ft. squares, which is about the coverage of a single roller-load of paint. The first stroke made with a freshly loaded roller should be away from you. Then you need to distribute the thickest part of the paint evenly over the square. On a ceiling this makes a "W" pattern (far left); on a wall it becomes an "M" (center left). To avoid roller marks, make these patterns without lifting the roller. To fill in, work the roller back and forth without lifting it off the surface (left). Repeat the procedure on the next square.

Painting/Windows, doors, and woodwork

Interior trim—especially doorjambs, windowsills, and baseboards—takes a beating in everyday use. This woodwork is usually painted with semigloss or high-gloss paint. Either withstands frequent scrubbings. Most trim also benefits from a primer, or undercoat. New wood and wood that has been stripped of old paint *must* have a primer. (On new or stripped trim you'll also need a *sealer* under the primer to prevent knothole resins from oozing or stains from bleeding through the paint.)

Both wood- and steel-frame casement windows (windows that open out like French doors) need a primer: steel ones, a rust-inhibiting metal primer; wood ones, a water-resistant primer. (Because the muntins and sashes get outdoor exposure, some painters put exterior paint on both sides of casement windows.) Aluminum windows, which don't have to be painted, can be protected from dirt and pitting with a metal primer and paint or with a clear polyurethane finish.

The rule of thumb for painting trim is to work horizontally first, then vertically, and to proceed from the inside toward the outside. In painting a casement window, for example, most professionals follow this order: horizontal muntins, vertical muntins, sash top rail and bottom rail, sash stiles (sides), and last the window frame, starting with the top. The rule, which is not absolute, bends here because it is customary to paint the sides of the frame next and finish with the windowsill and the apron beneath it.

Double-hung windows are more time-consuming to paint because it is difficult to get at some of the surfaces. However, following the sequence of steps outlined below at left will guide you through the process with a minimum of false starts.

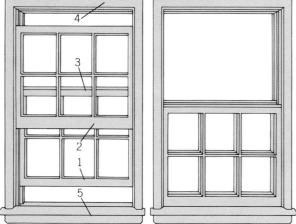

Open double-hung windows for painting, with the inner (lower) sash raised and the outer (upper) sash lowered until their positions are almost reversed. Paint the lower half of the outer sash first (1), then the entire inner sash (2). Return the sashes to normal position, but ajar. Paint the rest of the outer sash (3), the frame (4), and the sill (5).

Paint window jambs after the the window itself has dried. Work the sashes up and down a few times to keep them from sticking. Then push both sashes down as far as they will go. Paint the upper jamb and let it dry. (Don't paint metal channels.) Push the sashes up and paint the lower jamb. Lubricate the dry channels with silicone spray.

On a paneled door, start by painting the two top panels, and proceed in top-to-bottom order (1, 2, 3). Next paint the horizontal sections (4), again working from top to bottom, and end with the vertical sections (5). Paint the door edge last (facing page). On new doors, paint both top and bottom edges.

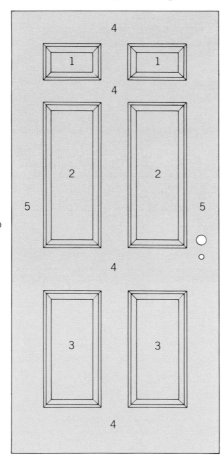

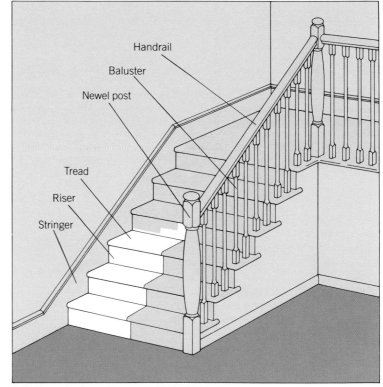

Painting order for stairs starts with the balusters, newel post, and handrail in turn. Then, beginning at the top and working down one step at a time, paint the treads, risers, and stringer on one side of the stairs, leaving the other half open for traffic. When the paint is dry, start again at the top and work on the other half of each step. Alternatively, paint every other step, so users can step over the wet ones.

Practical approaches. The room you paint in must be above 40° F and well ventilated, particularly if you are using alkyd (oil-base) paint. In humid or rainy weather latex paint dries better than alkyd, but neither adheres well in cold temperatures.

Take down louvered doors and indoor shutters; you can spray-paint them (pp.354–355) outdoors or in a garage in a fraction of the time it takes to coat them with a brush. (However, you will need a brush to smooth out paint in the corners, where it collects and tends to drip.)

Paint windows early in the day, so they will dry enough to handle before you have to close them.

To paint built-in cabinets or bookcases, work from the inside out and from top to bottom. (Remove drawers and paint their fronts separately.) Paint back walls first, then side walls, shelves (bottoms, tops, edges), and finally doors.

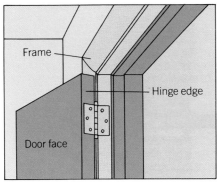

Door color. Door faces and frames should match when door is closed. Paint hinge edge same color as adjacent visible door face (blue above); latch edge matches side of door (not visible above) opening into the room (beige).

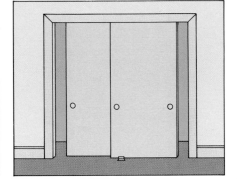

Gliding closet doors. Slide doors open as shown and paint the outer one and the exposed half of the inner one. Reverse positions of doors; finish inner door. For back sides, repeat the process inside closet. Paint edges last.

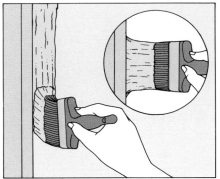

Beading. To make a straight edge, press a chiseled brush flat against surface until beads of paint show at the tip (insert). In a single, steady motion, spread these beads along the line you want to make.

Baseboard. Use a plastic or metal paint guard from a store (cardboard gets too soggy) to protect the floor or carpet. This is easier and faster than masking with tape, but you must wipe paint off the guard often.

Painting concrete

To hold paint, a seasoned concrete surface must be sound and clean. Repair cracks or chips (p.159) first. Remove stains (p.186) and then scrub (right). Smooth concrete needs etching. Use a 10:1 water–muriatic acid wash (p.186) and rinse immediately.

Before you paint new concrete, neutralize its alkalis with a solution of 3 percent phosphoric acid and 2 percent zinc chloride. Don't rinse. Use acrylic masonry paint.

Unprimed concrete block walls will drink up paint: prime them with a latex block filler or—on still-damp new walls—portland cement paint.

Scrub concrete steps with hot water and trisodium phosphate or other heavy-duty cleaner. Use a stiff brush; rinse thoroughly; allow to dry. Vacuum before painting.

First coat of paint should be worked in with a brush to ensure filling cracks and crevices. Let this coat dry completely—24 hr. is safest—before applying a second one.

Paint a concrete floor with a medium- or long-nap roller on a pole. Working in 3-ft. squares, make your way from a far corner toward the door, where you can exit.

Painting / Problems

A well-prepared and properly applied paint job should last, under normal circumstances, up to 7 years. When paint begins to deteriorate sooner, there is often a preventable reason. Studying specific paint problems around your home, such as those shown below, will help you diagnose the cause and avoid future paint failure.

Most paint problems show up outdoors because exterior surfaces are subject to more moisture and to greater extremes in temperature than interior ones. However, moisture seeping in behind the paint—a common cause of flaking, for example—also can happen indoors. So can problems caused by incompatible primer and paint, poor surface preparation, or inferior paint.

Alligatoring, or checking. Paint has many reptilian-looking interconnected cracks. The outer coat has not adhered properly to the paint beneath. It could have been applied to an incompatible paint, a badly prepared surface, or a not-yet-dry first coat. Or too many layers of paint may have built up over time. *Solution:* Strip down to raw wood and reapply primer and paint.

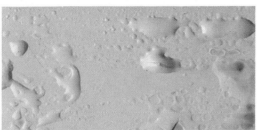

Blistering. Bubbles form under paint. Open a blister. (1) If it reveals raw wood, moisture has worked its way under the paint. *Solution:* Check for sources of water such as leaky gutters, missing caulk, or winter ice dams and fix before repainting. (2) If opened blister reveals paint, the temperature was too high when the top coat was applied. *Solution:* Sand and repaint.

Chalking. Most exterior paints are formulated so that the surface gradually breaks down into a powdery chalk that takes dirt and grime with it when rain washes it away. This feature keeps the paint looking clean. Chalking surfaces, however, will not hold new paint. *Solution:* Scrub a chalking surface with detergent and rinse well before repainting.

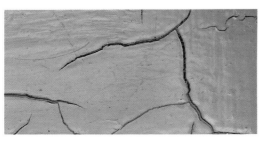

Cracking and scaling. Fissures open in the paint, allowing in moisture, which lifts off the paint. Usually caused by aging paint that has lost its elasticity and can't change with temperature and humidity changes, it may also result from moisture seepage or air pollution. *Solution:* Fix moisture problem, strip the surface, and repaint. Wash newly painted areas periodically.

Flaking and peeling. Paint simply doesn't stick. The surface might have been dirty. It might have had too many layers of paint already. Or the wrong type of paint may have been used. On masonry, flaking can be caused by alkali leaching into paint. *Solution:* Strip to the surface, clean carefully (for cleaning masonry, see p.186), and reapply appropriate coating.

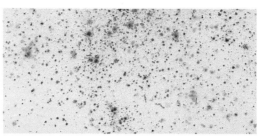

Mildew. Paint appears dirty or sooty, but cleans up quickly with a bleach solution. Usually found in shady, protected areas that don't get enough sun or air to prevent growth of the fungus. *Solution:* Scrape down area, scrub with 3:1 water—chlorine bleach mixture or a commercial fungicide; let dry thoroughly. Prime with a mildew-resistant coating; repaint.

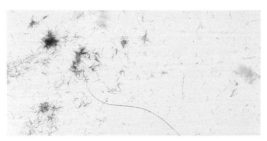

Tackiness. Paint remains sticky to the touch (and collects lint and dust particles) long after it should have dried. Sometimes caused by painting over a coat that is not dry or by applying alkyds in damp weather, more often this problem is caused by poor-quality paint. *Solution:* Strip the paint with a heat gun or chemical remover, and repaint with a better grade of paint.

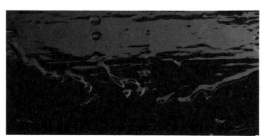

Wrinkling, running, and sagging. The paint puckers, drips, or lumps. Often the result of applying too thick a coat or of poor painting technique, it can also be caused by painting over an under-coat that is not yet dry. *Solution:* Strip the surface and repaint. Use a thinner paint and brush it out thoroughly as you apply it (p.373). Let paint dry completely between coats.

Exterior preparation

Ladder safety 383
Caulking 411
Weatherstripping 452–454

Painting the outside of your house is an important investment in maintenance. A good paint job protects wood siding and trim from water damage and rot while it guards metal gutters, downspouts, and railings from rust and corrosion. And in preparing for a paint job, all the seams and joints in the outer shell of the house are inspected and recaulked.

A checklist for examining your house and planning preparation work for painting is shown below.

You could discover that the structure is in fine repair and the paint is still sound. All your house may need to look fresh is a good scrubbing with detergent and rinsing with a hose.

If you find otherwise, organize a plan for the job, which must be tackled in good weather. Be sure you have ladders and scaffolding to reach all areas of the house (p.383). Clip back tree limbs and bushes that will get in the way. Remove shutters,

light fixtures, and hardware, but leave storm windows in place to keep sanding dust from blowing inside. Clean and repair gutters and downspouts (pp.396–397). Repairs to siding (pp.406–410) and to masonry (pp.174–175) come next; then scraping, sanding (p.371), and caulking (p.411). With the sanding done, remove the storm windows and reglaze where needed. Finally, scrub the whole exterior with heavy-duty detergent, rinse, and allow to dry.

Gutters and downspouts. Check for leaks and clogs; make repairs. Flaking paint should be wire-brushed off metal outsides to make a smooth surface. Apply appropriate metal primer and repaint.

Wood siding. Make needed surface repairs and recaulk joints. Countersink bleeding nails; coat with metal primer; fill holes with putty. Scrape and sand smooth. Prime raw wood. Apply two coats of paint.

Windows. Sand down wood, or wire-brush metal frames; replace missing putty (p.421). Apply appropriate primer (rust-inhibiting for metal) and paint.

Stone. Stone is never painted, but its mortar should be checked for leaks and repointed as needed.

Soffits. Strip smooth with a wire brush and a sander. Check for mildew and treat if necessary (facing page). Prime and apply one or two coats of new paint.

Brick chimneys. Check brick joints (p.174) and flashing (p.392), and make repairs. Brick need not be painted, but it can be. Brush it down to remove dirt and loose particles, and use appropriate paint (p.370).

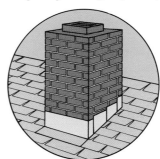

Wrought-iron trim. Sand down rust spots to bare metal with a wire-brush attachment on an electric drill. Apply a rust-inhibiting primer, then two coats of enamel. Use a paint mitt (p.351) or a spray gun to save time.

Wood shutters. Remove from house and mark location on each. Scrub, sand smooth, and either spray-paint (and touch up with a brush) or brush-paint only. Work on shutters in garage or workshop when weather stops exterior painting.

Doors. Check weatherstripping; replace if necessary. Remove brass hardware and polish it; coat with acrylic lacquer to retard oxidation. Scrape down flaking paint, repair cracks or holes with wood putty, and sand smooth. Apply primer to raw wood areas. Follow with two coats of paint.

Light fixtures. Polish brass and spray with water-proof clear lacquer. Black iron needs sanding, rust-inhibiting primer, and high-gloss paint.

Fascia boards. Often behind gutters, they need sanding down to sound paint. Seal any knots. Check for mildew and treat (facing page), prime raw wood, and repaint with one or two finish coats.

Screens and storm windows. Remove outside wood-frame types to paint in the garage. Aluminum storms and screens don't need painting, but take them out to have better access for painting wooden window frames.

Painting/Buying paint for exterior use

House siding is usually protected with flat paint, and trim with glossy enamel. Wood shingles and shakes can be either painted like siding or stained and protected with a clear finish for a natural look. The chart at right shows types of coatings suitable for the various exterior surfaces of your house.

Ask your paint dealer about additives. Houses that are heavily shaded, for example, often have mildew problems. You can have a fungus-inhibiting additive mixed into the paint you choose.

Many exterior paints are designed to be self-cleaning: they gradually "chalk," or give off a powdery white substance that rain washes away along with the dirt and grime that cling to it. This process keeps paint looking fresh. However, such paints are a poor choice for areas above red brick walls or dark siding, which the chalk will stain.

Exterior latex paints are easy to apply (although they show brush marks), dry quickly, and clean up with water. Other advantages: They resist the alkali found in concrete and masonry that disintegrate alkyd paints; they are permeable to moisture, so they blister less and allow dampness to escape.

Exterior alkyds and oil-base stains take longer to dry and require hazardous solvents for cleanup. Alkyd trim enamel, however, has a hard waterproof finish that many professionals still prefer.

How much paint to buy. For siding, multiply the average height of your house (from foundation to eaves) by the perimeter (measured with a ball of string). Divide this number by 500 (a gallon of paint's average coverage in square feet) to get the number of gallons of paint you need for each coat. A new house requires a primer and two finish coats. An older house in good condition may need only one coat of new paint.

Spray-painting (pp.354–355) spreads the equivalent of two coats of paint in one application, so buy enough for two coats. Power painters (p.353) save time but waste paint. Buy generously if you use one.

A rule of thumb for trim paint is to buy 1 gallon for every 6 you buy for siding. The average house of six to eight rooms takes a gallon of trim paint.

Exterior coating choices. Surfaces outside a house that you may want to protect are listed below. Paint and other coating possibilities are spelled out across the top of the chart. Pick a surface and follow its column across the chart. Each colored square suggests a suitable covering. To identify the product, follow from the colored square to the top of the chart.

Surface	Exterior latex house paint	Exterior alkyd house paint	Exterior latex enamel	Exterior alkyd enamel	Exterior acrylic enamel	Exterior latex stain	Exterior alkyd stain	Exterior oil stain	Epoxy paint	Spar varnish	Water-repellent preservatives	Latex porch and floor paint	Alkyd porch and floor paint	Portland cement paint	Masonry block filler	Aluminum paint
Raw wood (siding, shakes, shingles, porches, and trim)	●	●	●	●	●	▒	▒	▒		▒	▒	●	●			
Painted wood (siding, shakes, shingles, porches, and trim)	▒	▒	▒	▒	▒							▒	▒			
Hardboard siding	●	●	●	●	●											
Stained wood (siding, shakes, shingles, and trim)						▒	▒	▒		▒	▒					
Redwood siding	▒	▒				▒	▒	▒			▒					
Aluminum siding	▒	▒	▒	▒	▒											▒
New concrete or concrete block	●	●							●			●	●	▒	▒	
Previously treated concrete or concrete block	▒	▒										▒	▒			
Brick	●	●												▒	▒	
Stucco	●	●												▒	▒	
Asbestos-cement shingles or board*	●													▒	▒	
Asphalt fiberglass-base shingles	●															
Ceramic tile or glass			▒	▒	▒											
Steel (gutters, downspouts, window frames)	●	●	●	●	●											▒
Wrought iron			●	●	●											▒
Galvanized metal (gutters, downspouts)	●	●	●	●	●											▒
Aluminum (windows, doors)	●	●	●	●	●											▒
Copper or bronze										▒						

A black dot indicates that a primer is recommended under the finish coat.

* Old asbestos-cement shingles and board can be safely painted: Wash them down with detergent and chlorine bleach, using a brush attachment for a hose (facing page) to keep fiber particles from becoming airborne. A masonry block filler, available at paint stores, and an exterior latex finish coat will seal in the harmful fibers.

Preparing the exterior

If an exterior paint job is to look good and to last, all loose paint must be removed and the edges of sound paint feathered smooth before you start. If your house was last painted before 1972, have the paint tested for lead (p.348). Lead paint must be removed by hazardous materials specialists.

To take paint off wood siding, some painters swear by a 7-inch disc sander. They use 16-grit sandpaper to get to bare wood and then follow up with 60-grit paper to smooth over any gouges or cuts. Other approaches are shown below.

No method is effortless. A certain amount of handwork—scraping, washing, and sanding—is required even when you use chemical strippers. Strippers are expensive; save them for trim.

Professional pressure washer delivers up to 2,000 lb. per sq. in. of water power to remove loose paint from siding or shingles. It minimizes scraping chores and then cleans when detergent is added. Rent it or buy attachment for your air compressor (p.77).

Wire brush attachment for an electric drill speeds stripping of metal surfaces like aluminum gutters and downspouts and wrought-iron railings. Wear goggles and gloves to protect yourself from flying paint chips and grit.

Shortcuts for cleaning surfaces

Hose brush attachment with an extension pole speeds washing painted surfaces. Mix solution of TSP (or another heavy-duty detergent), chlorine bleach, and water. Rinse. Without this treatment grease, dirt, and pollution will keep new paint from adhering.

A garden sprayer also can be used in exterior paint preparation. It is ideal for treating mildew-infected areas with a 3:1 water–chlorine bleach solution (no detergent), which kills the fungus. Don't rinse the area, but allow it to dry before painting. If mildew is not completely eradicated, it will reappear under new paint.

A hook scraper shaves paint off wood with sharp replaceable blades. Practice gives you a feel for how it works. Applying too much pressure, particularly across the grain, gouges the wood instead of removing just the paint.

An electric heat gun is safer to use (p.358) than a blowtorch, which painters once favored for removing paint. High temperature softens paint, making it easy to scrape off with a putty knife. Always wear protective gloves, goggles, and mask.

371

A bright color scheme with high contrasts makes a house look large and sunny. The yellow siding and cream trim play off against the brown of the roof. The one accent, dark green shutters, calls attention to windows and doors, while relating the house to its foundation shrubbery.

A subtler color mix gives the same house a different look. A deep gray unifies two kinds of siding and the garage door with the roof, while a lighter gray highlights the shutters, and white brightens the window trim. A deep red door—the only accent—completes a handsome color scheme.

Paint protects the exterior of a house; color makes it attractive and inviting. An effective color scheme can draw attention to a building's best architectural features and minimize its defects.

Although there are no absolute rules for picking house colors, some guidelines are helpful. Start with the colors you can't change: the roof, brick facing, a stone foundation or chimney, a flagstone walkway to the front door. Look for paint shades that match or harmonize with these colors.

Then consider the immediate neighborhood. You may want your house to be distinctive, but not out of character with the rest of the street. One architectural style may lend itself better to some colors than to others. A Spanish-style stucco, for example, almost demands light pastels, whereas a New England farmhouse can take deeper, richer colors. Landscaping may be significant as well: A house heavily shaded by trees will disappear if you paint its main body in dark colors, which absorb light. Dark colors look best when the house dominates its setting and gets plenty of sunshine.

The basic components of a house color scheme are body color, trim color, and accent color. If you live in a Victorian house with a number of interesting architectural details, you might even consider four colors—adding a second, contrasting trim color to call attention to intricate moldings or ornate brackets that might be missed otherwise.

Body color. This is the dominant color that can most change the look of a house. A light body color makes a small house appear larger. A dark body color can bring a big, rambling house into proportion. Whatever the color, painting an odd-shaped porch or an ugly garage door the same shade as the body of the house will visually integrate the awkward features into a more harmonious whole.

Pick the body color first. It should either contrast with the roof color or—to make an integrated whole of a smaller house—be a variation of it. A light to medium shade is the safest choice, particularly if your house has large expanses of siding. (Dark colors always look darker on the house than they do on a paint sample.)

Body color is also affected by sunlight. It is worth the extra money to buy a trial quart of paint, paint a section of your house, and observe how the color looks at different times of day before making a final commitment to the color.

Trim color. This usually is applied to fascias, soffits, cornice moldings, window frames and sashes, door frames, and porch railings. (For a practical reason—to minimize the effects of dirt and footprints—porch floors are usually painted a neutral color different from the rest of the trim.)

White or off-white soffits reflect light onto the areas below. (To downplay a part of a house that is flawed, paint soffits with the body paint color.) White windows seem bigger and brighter.

Accent color. A contrasting color that highlights special features of the house, an accent is most effective when it is used sparingly. Often only the front door is painted with the accent color. A warm, intense accent color like deep red can make the entrance of a house an inviting focal point. It is also common to paint shutters the accent color. The front door can then be given the same color, or it can be highlighted with a second accent color.

Testing color schemes. If you want to change the color scheme of your house, try out different combinations on paper before investing in paint. Take a photograph of the house (preferably black and white) and have it blown up to an 8- x 10-inch size. Make black-and-white copies on a copying machine. Then try out different color combinations with colored marking pens. The shades may not be exact, but they will show the effects of using various colors on different elements of the house.

Exterior application

Plot exterior painting so that you finish each unbroken section of siding in a single session. This way you will avoid obvious paint "seams" in walls.

Exterior painting is fair-weather work. The day must be dry, particularly if you are using alkyd paint, which won't adhere to moist surfaces. Latex paint can be applied to slightly damp surfaces, but not to wet ones or cold ones. The temperature must be between 50° F and 90° F for either type of paint to go on properly. On hot days, avoid working in direct sun. Paint the west side of the house during the morning and the east side in the afternoon.

Mask elements carefully. Nothing makes a paint job look less professional than spatters on a lower roof or on hardware. Buy or rent canvas drop cloths (less slippery than plastic) to cover the surfaces below where you are working. Protect outdoor meters, air conditioners, faucets, and mailboxes with sheets of plastic held in place with masking tape. Before covering shrubbery with drop cloths, tie back any bushes that may get in your way.

Place ladders and scaffolding carefully (p.383), and make sure you have either a sturdy platform or a reliable hook to hold your paint can or tray.

Start painting at the top of walls and work down. Siding gets painted first, then trim and windows. Doors and porch railings come next, and finally thresholds, porch floors, and steps. Shutters and fixtures that you have taken down to paint can be done at any time.

Brush technique.
1. To paint lap siding (clapboard), apply paint to the underside of the board first. Avoid paint runs down the brush's handle by pressing out excess paint against the inside of the paint can when you load the brush. Use a steady stroke along the bottom edge of each board. Periodically check for skips from the ground below. Spread out runs or drips as you go.

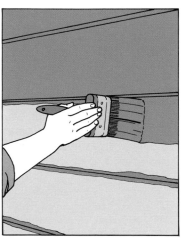

2. Apply paint to siding in short strokes across each board (up and down on vertical boards). Spread out the paint with smooth, even strokes. Press the bristles against cracks and rough surfaces to force paint in. Feather off the edges of each section to avoid seam lines between work areas.

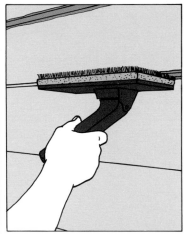

Paint pad. 1. Applying paint to lap siding with a paint pad works equally well. Load one side of the pad and paint bottom edges of siding boards with long strokes. Check for skipped places and runs as you go, filling in gaps and smoothing out paint drips along broad side of board.

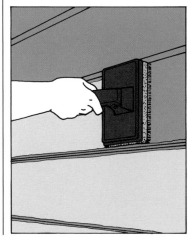

2. Pull a paint pad slowly but firmly along the length of each siding board (pull pad down vertical siding). If the pad is narrower than the boards, carefully over-lap strokes so that you won't create a distinct line in the middle of the siding board.

Special shingle pads, made specifically for painting (or staining) striated shakes and shingles, are fast and easy to use. The edge of the pad drives paint under laps; the pad's pile pushes paint into grooves. Start at the top of a shingle and move the pad down with the grain.

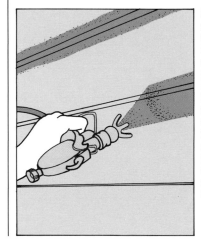

Spray-painting of lap siding or shingles is a two-step job. First, hold gun horizontally as shown, and spray up and under the bottom edge of each board or shingle to force paint into all the crevices. Then return the spray nozzle to its upright position and paint the surface of each lap in a series of even, parallel strokes (pp.354–355).

373

Hanging wallcoverings takes some special equipment, plus a few standard tools such as a stepladder. You must have a *pasting table* (minimum 6 x 3 feet) whether you apply paste or not. You'll need the surface for measuring, cutting and trimming, and for folding, or "booking," your strips. You can rent a table from a wallpaper store or improvise with plywood on sawhorses.

If you have chosen prepasted paper, you will need a *water tray* for activating the glue. For other wallcoverings you will need a *paste brush* and *bucket* for applying the proper adhesive (some people prefer a paint roller and tray).

A *plumb bob* and *chalk*—or a level and a pencil, if you prefer—help you align the paper vertically even if the walls are not perfect. A *straightedge* or a *metal ruler* measures and also acts as a guide for trimming selvages. Used with the *razor blade trimming knife*, a *wallboard taping knife* ensures clean cuts at baseboard and ceiling. You'll need plenty of fresh razor blades; changing after every cut makes finer edges. Good sharp *shears* are used to cut the wallpaper off the roll.

Smoothing brushes work out air bubbles. Those with long, soft bristles are best for delicate flocked or embossed papers; short bristles, for standard papers and vinyls. A *seam roller* reinforces adhesion where strips abut. A *bucket* and *sponge* are for cleaning up excess paste as you go.

How much paper to buy? Measure the perimeter of the room (2 x length plus 2 x width). Multiply this number by the height of the walls. This is your square footage. For a ceiling, multiply length by width. For a border, measure just the perimeter. Take these figures—with a count of windows and doors in the room—to your dealer.

Most, but not all, wallcoverings are sold in double or triple rolls. Single rolls contain 36 square feet, which average 30 usable square feet after trimming waste and matching patterns. Papers with large repeats won't give you as much. For safety, order more than you need so that all rolls will be from the same dye lot (color variations among lots can be significant). Return the extra, or use it as drawer liner or gift wrap; save some for repairs.

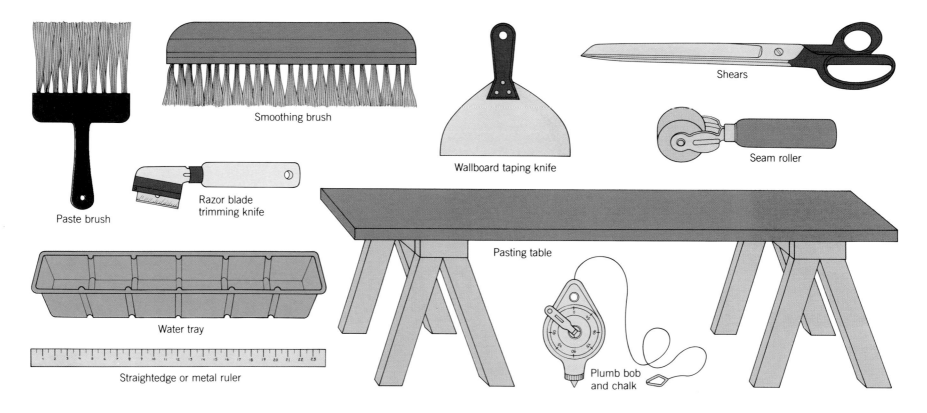

Smoothing brush

Shears

Wallboard taping knife

Seam roller

Paste brush

Razor blade trimming knife

Pasting table

Water tray

Plumb bob and chalk

Straightedge or metal ruler

Types of wallcoverings

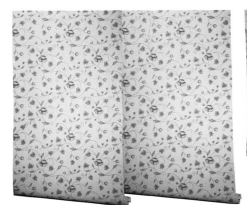

A straight match, or set match, pattern aligns easily across strips.

A drop pattern requires extra paper to make a match at the top of two strips.

A random pattern—stripes, for example—doesn't need to be matched.

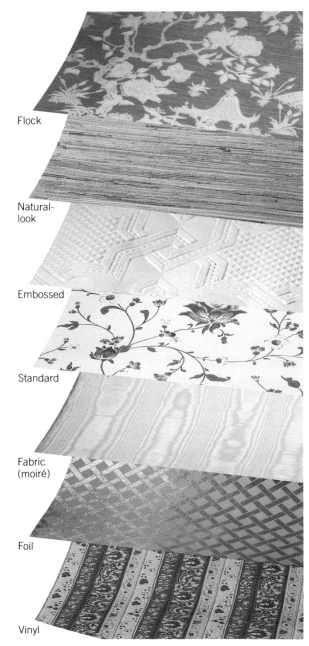

Flock

Natural-look

Embossed

Standard

Fabric (moiré)

Foil

Vinyl

Standard papers: Printed wallpapers are usually the least expensive wallcovering and are easy to hang, particularly the prepasted ones. Papers, however, will tear if they are not handled carefully, and uncoated papers are hard to clean. Vinyl-coated paper is tougher: It can be wiped off (but not scrubbed) with soap and water and it doesn't rip as easily. Hand-screened or hand-printed papers are often distinctive, but costly; they may need edge trimming, and their inks may run if they get wet.

Vinyls: Vinyl is bonded to a paper or cloth backing in sturdy, scrubbable wallcoverings. They hold their colors through sun exposure and washings, making them ideal for kitchens, playrooms, bathrooms, hallways, and children's rooms. Prepasted vinyls are the easiest to hang, but pasting these walloverings is not hard. Use the recommended adhesive with a mildew retardant because the outer layer is impervious to moisture and nonbreathable. Vinyl also requires special vinyl-to-vinyl glue for overlaps, such as around corners.

Foils and metallics: These sleek, shiny papers add drama and reflected light to powder rooms, alcoves, and windowless kitchens. (They create glare in sunny areas.) Foils show every fault in a wall, so lining paper (p.376) is recommended for less-than-perfect surfaces.

Flocks: Modern versions of traditional patterns with velveteen-like raised designs are now made of synthetic fibers. Flocks come with paper, vinyl, or foil backings. Washable flocks are easy to handle; the others are tricky to hang and clean.

Natural-look coverings: Made now of synthetics as well as natural materials, grass cloth, hemp, burlap, and even cork are bonded to a paper backing. Moisture makes these wallcoverings separate; they dry faster if they are hung over lining. Some are unevenly dyed; reverse every other strip top-for-bottom to keep color shadings consistent.

Embossed coverings: Made of paper or plastic, these coverings with raised designs can hide minor imperfections in walls. Some require painting. Seam rollers and stiff smoothing brushes tend to crush them; use a soft brush or cloth pad instead. They are often heavier than other wallcoverings.

Fabrics: Applied directly to a prepasted wall, damask, suede, and other fabrics can give a room distinction. Because fabric stretches, it is hard to hang. Use clear, nonstaining cellulose paste.

Borders: Printed paper or vinyl borders come in rolls that may be prepasted or not. Borders can coordinate with other wallcoverings—to separate two patterns or to finish off an edge—or they can be used alone as decorative trim.

Textured and embossed wallpapers hide minor flaws in walls or ceilings, but many wallcoverings—the foils are an example—highlight imperfections. For satisfying and lasting results, prepare the surfaces you plan to paper as carefully as those you are about to paint (pp.356–357).

One solution for less than perfect walls and ceilings is to put up a lining paper—an economical, unpatterned paper—to cover faults. Lining paper will create a smooth surface. It also absorbs excess paste moisture from water-sensitive coverings like grass cloth or foil and keeps their backings from

separating. Lining paper is easy to hang. Often applied horizontally, it doesn't need matching. Seams needn't abut completely; some paperhangers leave a ⅛-inch gap.

Surfaces that are to be papered must be sealed; otherwise they will draw water from the paste and weaken the adhesion. Sealing also prevents corrosive elements in the wall from leaching to the surface and staining the paper.

Alkyd sealer is usually recommended because vinyls and foils don't adhere well to latex coatings. An alternative sealer is wallpaper sizing, a glue

designed to be a base for wallcoverings. You apply it with a roller just like paint.

Normally it's best not to apply new wallcovering over an old one. Risk it only if the old paper still adheres tightly. First, however, reglue loose edges and seal the surface with sizing or alkyd undercoat.

There are several ways to take off old wallcoverings (see below). Cloth-backed vinyls simply peel off. Other coverings take more effort.

Paint the ceiling and trim *before* you paper a room. It is easier to wipe paste off fresh paint than to remove paint splatters from new paper.

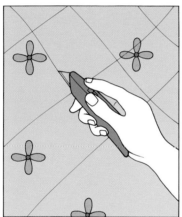

Scoring old wallpaper with a utility knife or razor blade before applying a chemical remover or steam speeds the softening of the paste. Because vinyls and foils are impervious, they must be scored or neither agent will get to the paste to break its hold.

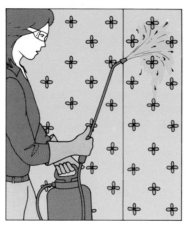

Chemical wallpaper remover can be applied with a sponge, but it is easier and faster to use a garden sprayer. Mix remover according to the manufacturer's directions, and wear protective goggles and gloves if they are suggested. Chemical remover disintegrates the paste.

An electric steamer can be rented from a home center or hardware store. You fill the steamer's tank with water; it is then heated electrically. The steam is pumped by way of a hose into a perforated plate, which you hold against the wallcovering until the adhesive is softened.

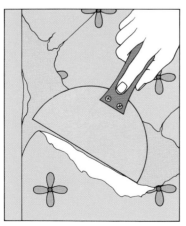

Scrape wallcovering from wall with a taping knife or wall scraper as soon as the glue is loosened by chemicals or steam. Be careful not to gouge the surface. When working with a steamer, you can remove only small sections at a time before more steam is needed.

Peelable coverings (also called strippable) should come off easily when you pry up a corner and pull. Afterward, use warm water to soften the paste residue; scrape off the excess with a wide taping knife or wall scraper.

Remove old adhesive by washing down walls with a heavy-duty detergent such as trisodium phosphate (TSP) or, in restricted areas, its nonphospate equivalent. Rinse and allow walls to dry thoroughly before applying new paper.

Planning your approach

Successful wallpapering takes time, patience, and careful planning. Some necessary exercises before you start:

1. Check your paper. Be sure that all the rolls have the same run number. If they don't, return them and re-order. Open and inspect each roll for defects. This is particularly important for expensive papers that represent a sizable investment. Reorder if you must replace a bad roll.

2. Find the starting point. Where you should begin varies with the design of the room and the pattern of the paper (see below). Mark with a ruler and pencil exactly where each strip will go. This lets you anticipate problems and work out solutions ahead.

3. Set up the room. Clear out as much furniture as you can, and stack the rest in the middle of the floor. Put drop cloths or newspaper around the periphery of the room and under your pasting table.

4. Organize your tools. Set up the stepladder at your starting point. If you will be pasting at the large table, use another table for your tools or wear a carpenter's apron to hold them. Buy several dozen razor blades for your trimming knife and provide a safe place for discards.

5. Study the paper pattern. Hold it up to the ceiling line. Check where the pattern's repeat looks best. If the ceiling-wall juncture is uneven, for example, don't use a horizontal band as your starting point at the top.

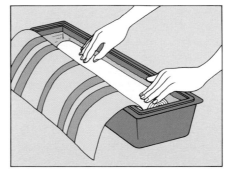

To soak prepasted paper, roll up a cut strip with the pattern side in, and place it in a two-thirds-filled water tray. You may need to put a weight like a rock inside the roll to keep it submerged.

Apply prepasted paper directly from the water tray to the wall if the instructions say so. Place the stepladder sideways in front of the tray and draw the paper up as you climb.

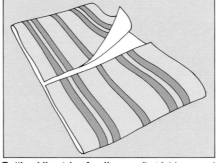

To "book" a strip of wallpaper, first fold one end to the middle, then the other, keeping the pasted sides together and the folds uncreased. Booking makes wallpaper pliable and easier to handle.

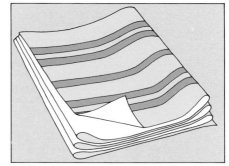

Ceiling strips, because they are often longer, are booked accordian-fashion as shown here. Pasted sides touch only pasted sides. The compact fold allows easy hoisting and holding.

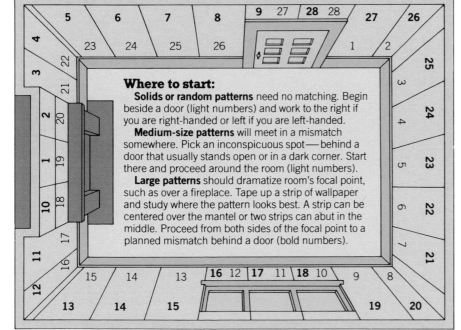

Where to start:

Solids or random patterns need no matching. Begin beside a door (light numbers) and work to the right if you are right-handed or left if you are left-handed.

Medium-size patterns will meet in a mismatch somewhere. Pick an inconspicuous spot—behind a door that usually stands open or in a dark corner. Start there and proceed around the room (light numbers).

Large patterns should dramatize room's focal point, such as over a fireplace. Tape up a strip of wallpaper and study where the pattern looks best. A strip can be centered over the mantel or two strips can abut in the middle. Proceed from both sides of the focal point to a planned mismatch behind a door (bold numbers).

A tidy way to paste

Cut a strip of wallcovering to size and place it pattern side down on the pasting table. Mentally divide it into quadrants. Position the first quadrant (1) so its outside edges hang over the table by ¼ in. Apply the paste. Slide the strip across so quadrant 2 overhangs the table. Paste it. Book the pasted quadrants. Paste quadrants 3 and 4 in the same way. Book them. Paste never touches the table and the paper stays clean.

Wallpapering/Basic procedures

No house has perfectly vertical walls. If wallcoverings are to look natural, they must be hung against a plumb line. You can make a plumb line with a weighted plumb bob on a chalked string (below). Or you can find true vertical with a level, and mark it with a pencil against the level or a straightedge.

Your first plumb line will be a guide for aligning the first strip of wallcovering you put up. Draw it a strip's width from your starting point. Each time you turn a corner, create a new plumb line to get a fresh alignment. Corners are never perfectly square and usually require a little fudging.

Cut strips of wallcovering 4 inches longer than the wall measurement, providing 2-inch allowances at the top and the bottom. With a drop match pattern (p.375), you'll save time and paper by cutting alternately from two different rolls—one for each part of the drop pattern.

If you are working with an untrimmed wallpaper, remove the selvage: Put each strip of paper on the pasting table. Using a straightedge as a guide, make the cuts with a razor blade trimming knife.

Follow manufacturers' recommendations for the proper paste to use and how long to "book" (p.377). Not all prepasted papers are alike. Some need booking, whereas others go straight from the water tray onto the wall.

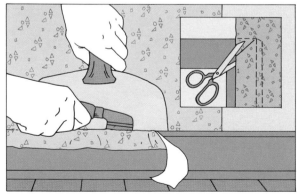

To make a plumb line, tack a cord you have rubbed with chalk to the top of a wall. Attach a plumb bob (or other small weight) to the loose end. Holding the bob where it falls naturally, pull the cord back. Let go. The cord will chalk a plumb line as it hits the wall.

Align the first strip by the plumb line, not by a doorway or corner. Leaving 2 in. excess at the ceiling, press the top of the strip in place. Then unfold and align the rest. Stand back and look. The paste allows time for making adjustments.

Smooth out air bubbles with a smoothing brush or a clean paint roller. Work from the middle outward to either side in the pattern shown. Use firm strokes to ensure a good bond. For wrinkles, lift the strip and press it into place again.

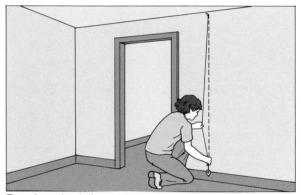

Trim to fit, using a broad taping knife as a guide. Cut with a fresh razor blade. Over the doorway (inset), clip the paper across the door frame corner as shown to allow a tight fit on either side. Trim around the door frame with razor and taping knife.

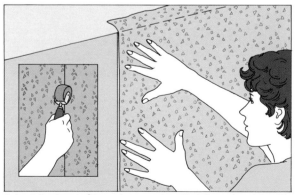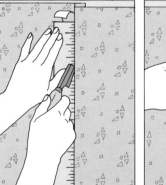

Join strips by abutting edges so close that they almost buckle. (They will shrink back as the glue dries.) Push the new strip gently into place with both hands. Pulling an edge will stretch it. Roll and seal the seam after 10 to 15 min.

A double-cut seam (good at corners) starts with an overlap. Use a straightedge as a guide to slice through both layers of paper. Remove the cut strip on top, then open the seam to peel off the cut strip below. Press cut edges together. Later, roll the seam.

Special situations

Every room offers its own particular challenges to the wallpaper hanger. Most can be handled with patience, common sense, and a few tricks that have more than one application.

If wallcovering strips overlap just beyond an inside corner, for example, they can hide the corner's irregularities and reestablish a plumb line for covering the rest of the wall. The same technique minimizes faults at outside corners.

Covering a switchplate is essentially no different from covering an outlet cover. The steps for papering a recessed window and a slanting wall also would apply to any niche or alcove. Dealing with an arched doorway prepares you to handle other curves you might encounter as you paper.

Covering a switchplate

  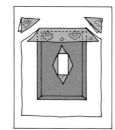 

Cut an X over the switch; then trim around the switch box. Loosely mount the plate. Fold a piece of paper over top of plate, matching it to the pattern on the wall. Clip the corners and switch hole; then fold and glue or tape paper around plate.

Recessed windows

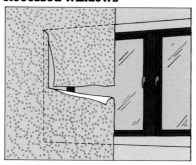 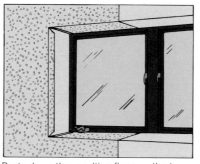 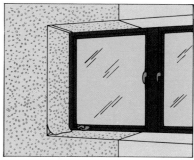

Hang a strip of wallcovering over the recessed window. Cut through the middle to 1 in. from the edge of the recess. Cut up and down to corners as shown.

Paste down the resulting flaps on the top and bottom of the recess, and trim the edges at the window frame. Paste the 1-in. vertical flap around the corner.

Cut a strip of wallcovering to fit the side of the recess. Paste it down, overlapping the corner piece. Use special glue for vinyl paper to adhere to vinyl.

Turning corners

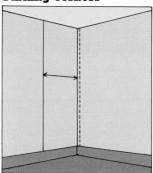

Nearing a corner, measure the distance from the edge of the last strip to the corner in several places. Add ½ in. to the largest number and cut a strip of wallcovering to that width, saving the second section. Hang first section around the corner, pressing it into the angle.

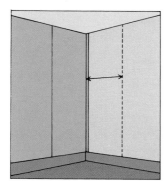

Draw a plumb line at a distance from the corner equal to the width of the second section of the cut wallcovering strip. Align this section with the plumb, and let it overlap the first section as it will. (For overlapped vinyl, use special adhesive or it won't stick properly.)

Arches

Paper across an arch as though it were a solid wall. Then trim paper around the curve 2 in. from its edge. Make "teeth" as shown; paste them under. Cut a strip of wallcovering a fraction under the width of the inside of the arch. Paste it into place over the teeth. To keep a pattern right side up, apply separate strips to either side of arch.

Slanted walls

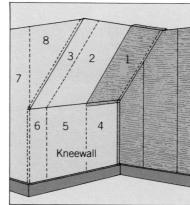

Finish adjacent wall with ½-in. corner overlap. Draw new plumb lines. Paper slanted wall first (1, 2, 3), making ¼-in. overlap to the kneewall. Next step is to paper kneewall (4, 5, 6); then paper first full strip around corner (7). Fill in triangle last (8). Hang it as if it were a full strip; then trim to fit.

Wallpapering/Covering a ceiling

If you want to have wallcovering on the ceiling, you should apply it *before* you paper or paint the walls. Choose a random pattern without a right-side-up (flowers growing up a wall and across a ceiling will be upside down from the far perspective).

Plan to work across the width of the room, so that the strips of wallcovering will be shorter and less awkward to handle. Start by a window (right), and proceed across the room. The last strip, which may be an odd size, should be farthest from the brightest light.

Just like a wall, a

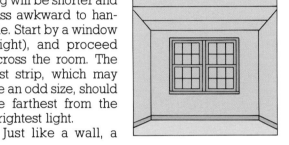

ceiling needs to be cleaned, patched, sanded, and sealed before it is papered. If you have an elaborate overhead light fixture like a chandelier, take it down. First turn off power to the circuit (p.237) and test that it is off (p.243). Simple fixtures (below right) are easy to paper around. Protect the floor from paste with drop cloths. Put together a sturdy platform high enough so that you can comfortably reach overhead to work on the paper.

If you are papering the walls as well as the ceiling of a room, leave a ½-inch overlap at the ends of each ceiling strip. If not, crease the paper in the angle between wall and ceiling; cut off the excess with a trimming knife against a straightedge.

A clean paint roller on an extension pole makes a good smoothing tool. It rests your arms to work from the floor instead of the platform.

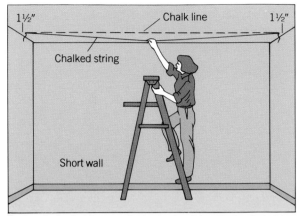

Tack a chalked string parallel to short wall for aligning first strip. Put tacks 1½ in. from each long wall and a strip's width minus ½ in. (for overlap) from the short wall. Snap string to mark line.

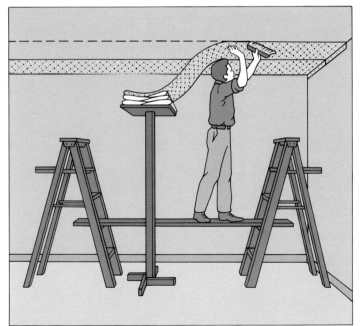

Working solo to paper a ceiling, you'll need a sturdy high-rise holder for the booked strips of wallpaper. This one is improvised from 1 x 3's and scrap plywood. A strip of soggy pasted paper the width of a room is too heavy to hold with one hand while you try to work with the other hand.

Working in tandem to paper a ceiling is easier. While one person aligns the beginning of a strip and starts to press it to the ceiling, the other holds the booked remainder directly behind and ready to be smoothed. To strengthen a platform for two, place a second plank on top of the first one.

Fitting trimly around light fixtures

As you near a light fixture, hold the strip over it. Mark where the center of the fixture will fall. Use scissors to pierce the wallpaper at that point. Working out from the center point, cut a circle of wedges almost to the edge of the fixture. Slip the strip of wallpaper over the light and continue smoothing it into place across the ceiling. Make a neat edge around the fixture with a razor blade trimming knife.

Contents

Exteriors
Repairs, replacements, and improvements

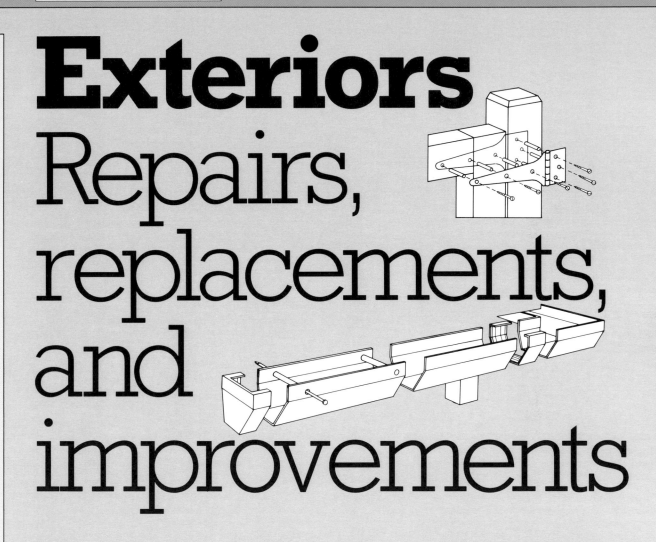

To be a real haven, your home must be watertight and weatherproof. This chapter begins with a regular schedule of inspection and maintenance that will keep it so. It shows you how to repair roofs, gutters, and siding, and tells you how to be a smart consumer when you contract for more complex work. (A separate chapter covers repairing and upgrading windows and doors.)

Not all exterior projects are strictly upkeep. Installing a skylight, for example, is a wonderful way to brighten a dark room. And putting up a new fence—whether it's for privacy or to keep the dog in bounds—will give you more useful outdoor living space.

All the elements play a part in deteriorating the exterior of a house—especially water. Once water penetrates, it can cause a variety of problems ranging from roof leaks to cracks in masonry. You can, however, prevent or alleviate the severity of the toll that nature takes by periodically inspecting your property for signs of damage. In most cases, it's best to begin in the spring.

First view your roof with binoculars; climb onto it only if signs of deterioration warrant closer inspection, if it is dry, and if the roof is not too steep. Use a safely positioned ladder (facing page). Check possible sources of leaks, especially after a heavy storm—damaged flashing, curled or missing shingles, loose mortar in chimney joints. On a flat roof, remove debris and check flashing for damage and the roofing surface for cracks and breaks. Make repairs promptly. If you can't locate a leak's source, ask a professional roofer to investigate.

An ice dam—a buildup of ice and snow at the roof's edge—can cause gutters to sag and water to creep under the shingles. Take steps to prevent future ice dam formation (p.399) before you make any gutter repairs (pp.396–397). Debris-filled gutters can also cause leaks; clean them out regularly in the spring after trees have bloomed and again in the fall after the last leaves have dropped.

Check the foundation of your house at least once a year. Have a professional look at ever-widening cracks as well as any bulges in a foundation wall. If puddles collect near the foundation or the basement has a moisture problem, consider the remedies shown on pages 338–340. Have a qualified contractor repair serious leakage. If you find signs of termites near foundation walls (p.345) or even suspect their presence, call an exterminator. Termite invasions are not always obvious; the pests can get into wood through the hollow core of blocks, through the joints and bolt holes in metal termite shields, and through cracks in concrete.

Let the checklist at right serve as a guide to regular maintenance and as an early warning system to alert you to problems before they become a crisis.

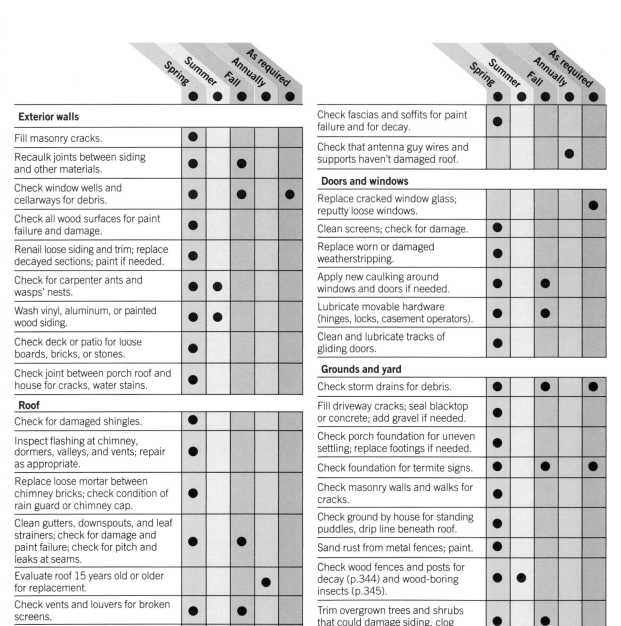

Exterior walls	Spring	Summer	Fall	Annually	As required
Fill masonry cracks.	●				
Recaulk joints between siding and other materials.	●		●		
Check window wells and cellarways for debris.	●		●		●
Check all wood surfaces for paint failure and damage.	●				
Renail loose siding and trim; replace decayed sections; paint if needed.	●				
Check for carpenter ants and wasps' nests.	●	●			
Wash vinyl, aluminum, or painted wood siding.	●	●			
Check deck or patio for loose boards, bricks, or stones.	●				
Check joint between porch roof and house for cracks, water stains.	●				

Roof	Spring	Summer	Fall	Annually	As required
Check for damaged shingles.	●				
Inspect flashing at chimney, dormers, valleys, and vents; repair as appropriate.	●				
Replace loose mortar between chimney bricks; check condition of rain guard or chimney cap.	●				
Clean gutters, downspouts, and leaf strainers; check for damage and paint failure; check for pitch and leaks at seams.	●		●		
Evaluate roof 15 years old or older for replacement.				●	
Check vents and louvers for broken screens.	●		●		
Check for birds' nests.			●		

	Spring	Summer	Fall	Annually	As required
Check fascias and soffits for paint failure and for decay.	●				
Check that antenna guy wires and supports haven't damaged roof.				●	

Doors and windows	Spring	Summer	Fall	Annually	As required
Replace cracked window glass; reputty loose windows.					●
Clean screens; check for damage.	●				
Replace worn or damaged weatherstripping.	●				
Apply new caulking around windows and doors if needed.	●		●		
Lubricate movable hardware (hinges, locks, casement operators).	●		●		
Clean and lubricate tracks of gliding doors.	●				

Grounds and yard	Spring	Summer	Fall	Annually	As required
Check storm drains for debris.	●		●		●
Fill driveway cracks; seal blacktop or concrete; add gravel if needed.	●				
Check porch foundation for uneven settling; replace footings if needed.	●				
Check foundation for termite signs.	●		●		●
Check masonry walls and walks for cracks.	●				
Check ground by house for standing puddles, drip line beneath roof.	●				
Sand rust from metal fences; paint.	●				
Check wood fences and posts for decay (p.344) and wood-boring insects (p.345).	●	●			
Trim overgrown trees and shrubs that could damage siding, clog gutters, or harbor pests.	●		●		

Ladders and safety

You need at least two kinds of ladders in your home: a stepladder for heights up to 10 feet and an extension ladder for heights up to 28 feet. The former should have grooved treads, nonslip safety shoes, and angled metal braces on the lowest tread. An extension ladder should have a reinforced bottom rung, pivoting safety shoes, and a mechanism that locks the two sections together firmly. (An articulating ladder can be made to serve as both by bending it—it has six hinged joints—into the desired form.) Ladders are available in wood, aluminum, or fiberglass—the last being the costliest but safest.

Ratings. Buy a ladder that's rated Type I (heavy duty—each rung is capable of supporting 250 pounds) or Type II (medium duty—225 pounds per rung); they're sturdier and safer than Type III (light duty—200 pounds per rung). Or for 300-pound support, buy Industrial IA.

Ladder check. Before you buy a ladder, inspect it for cracks, knots, dents, and other defects. Stand on the lowest tread, grip the side rails, and shake it. If it wobbles, choose another.

If you're doing extensive repairs or painting siding, rent scaffolding. Be sure to equip the scaffold with guardrails and toeboards of 2 x 4's. Make the guardrails at least 42 inches high, and fasten toeboards to all platform edges to prevent objects from falling.

▶**CAUTION:** A metal or wet wood ladder that touches a power line can give a lethal shock. When moving a ladder, avoid overhead wires; when on an aluminum ladder, use grounded double-insulated power tools only.

Extension ladder. 1. To raise, stand ladder near wall and lift top end, rung by rung, to desired length, 3 ft. above working level.

2. Distance between wall and ladder's feet should be at least one-quarter the ladder's working height (rung where you'll stand).

Face the ladder and hold side rails when climbing up or down. Haul tools up after you are set, or carry them on a belt.

Climb onto a roof only after placing a ladder so that it extends 3 ft. above roof's edge. Never climb onto a roof from gable end.

When working on a ladder make sure your hips stay within the side rails. Don't lean out beyond this range.

Ladder accessories

Wood truss block makes wood stepladder treads sturdier. If the ladder becomes wobbly, tighten nuts of reinforcing rod while holding truss in place.

Attach a stabilizer to side rails following the manufacturer's directions. "Arms" keep ladder 10 to 15 in. away from wall to let you work on a window.

On a steep roof, anchor the ladder in place with ladder braces (also called ladder hooks); you can buy them at a building supply store.

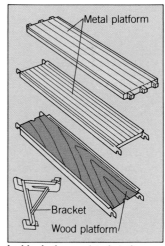

Ladder jacks consist of platforms (made of metal or wood) and brackets that attach to ladder rungs. A jack creates a scaffold with two ladders as support.

The first clue that there is a breach in your roofing system will be signs of moisture inside the house. You may notice a slightly discolored spot on a wall, a loose piece of wallcovering, peeling paint on a ceiling, or a damp smell along a hallway.

Serious detective work is sometimes needed to trace that first evidence of water seepage to its source on the roof. Water driven by wind into a chimney crack or underneath a damaged shingle will frequently take a circuitous route through a house (right). Unfortunately, detected or undetected, a leak will cause damage all the way down the building's interior spaces.

It is easier to find a roof leak if your attic ceiling is unfinished. On a rainy day, you can check the underside of the roof with a flashlight; you may see where water is leaking through. (A strong beam will pick up signs of moisture on rafters.) Mark the spot (see emergency measures, far right) so you can assess and fix the damage on the outside when the weather clears; see pp.385–389 for repairs to specific roofing materials. Minimize the effects of a leak with a well-placed bucket during a storm.

If you see no water, check the insulation between the joists for dampness and discoloration. Using safety precautions for handling fiberglass (p.458), pull it out, batt by batt, to look for stains and feel for wet spots. (Put back dry sections as you go.)

Tracing the origins of a leak when your attic has a finished ceiling is more difficult. There is one rule: however convoluted the route, water eventually runs down. If there is a leak on the first floor, for example, try to find signs of dampness in the rooms above it. Check plumbing pipes and radiators that could be causing the problem. When you've exhausted all the indoor possibilities, you'll have to examine the vulnerable parts of the roof that might pertain (list at right). You can do that only when the weather clears and the roof has dried.

▶ **CAUTION:** Never climb onto a wet roof. You risk not only hurting yourself but further damaging the roof as well. (Some roofing warranties, in fact, become invalidated if you walk on the roof.)

How water can travel

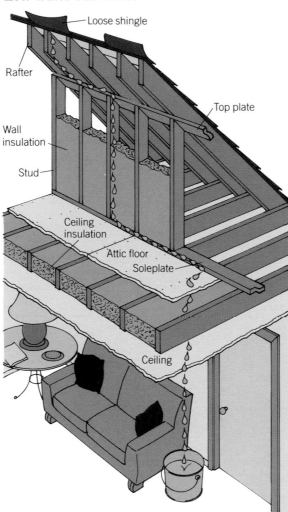

A leak's journey starts with a point of entry—in this case a damaged roof shingle—and proceeds on an unpredictable course determined by whatever channels the water. Here the water follows a rafter, then a top plate, from which it seeps through a section of attic wall insulation until it reaches the soleplate, which directs it to a joint in the floor. The water runs into the insulation below and finds its way through a seam in the vapor retarder to a ceiling. There it is discovered—yards wide of its original source.

Emergency measures

Damage control during a storm can be as simple as this bucket and string rig. The string, attached to the ceiling at the source of water, acts as a wick to guide the water to the bucket.

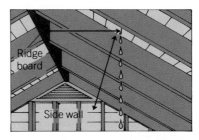

Mark an attic leak site inside instead of puncturing the roof with a nail. If you measure from leak to ridge board and leak to side wall, on the roof the leak will be those distances from ridge and rake edge.

A sheet-metal patch, cut to size, can be positioned under a damaged shingle to make a quick repair. Use a hammer and wood block to tap the patch into place. For other temporary repairs, see p.11.

Roof areas most likely to give way

- Flashing (pp.390–393)
- Joints between roof and siding
- Deteriorated flat roof coverings (p.388)
- Damaged or missing shingles, tiles, or slates on sloped roofs
- Damaged chimney masonry (p.400)
- Roof drainage systems (pp.396–399)
- Vent pipes (p.391)
- Skylights (pp.402–405)
- Valleys (p.391)
- Hips and ridges
- Dormers
- Ventilation units
- Areas where ice dams form (p.399)
- Exposed nails
- Open seams in roofing materials
- Missing window or door drip caps (p.391)

Asphalt shingles

Asphalt shingles—the most often used roofing material in North America—are made of a mat base (either fiberglass or a mixture of wood and paper) impregnated with asphalt and finished on one side with embedded ceramic or mineral granules. These granules give the shingles color (they come in many shades) and sun protection.

Fiberglass-mat shingles are more expensive but also more durable, more fire-resistant, and less hefty. (Mineral-fiber shingles, once made of asbes-

tos, are more like slates than asphalt shingles. They are rigid and heavy. Asbestos shingles should be repaired only by a qualified contractor.)

Properly maintained, an asphalt shingle roof will last 15 to 20 years. It can be reshingled once if the framing or trusses can take the added weight of a second layer and snow in the area doesn't add an extra burden. Normal wear and tear takes a toll. Sun can blister and curl shingles, dry them out, and make them brittle enough to crack in cold weather.

Strong winds can loosen and blow the mineral granules off shingles and, by lifting edges, loosen them and the nails that hold them. Ice dams (p.399) can work water up under shingles, and falling debris can tear or break them.

Asphalt shingle repairs (below) are not hard. Follow ladder safety rules and work only in mild weather—never in rain or high winds. If you must step onto the roof, wear soft-soled shoes for grip (and to minimize damage to shingles).

Repairing a shingle

A partially lifted or curling shingle can be glued down with a dab of roofing cement under the corner. Do this work in warm weather when shingles are supple enough to bend without cracking.

A torn shingle can be salvaged by first applying roofing cement under both sides of the tear and then pressing down firmly to seal the adhesive. For added security, also nail the tear (below).

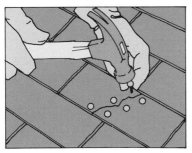

Reinforce a repair by hammering roofing nails around all the open edges. Cover the nailheads with roofing cement to prevent leakage through the nail hole.

Replacing a shingle

To remove shingle that's damaged, gently lift shingles above it and take out the nails with a pry bar. Being careful not to crack the good shingles in the process, pull out the fractured pieces.

Slip a new shingle underneath the raised shingles above. Using a pry bar, nail down new shingle (below). Finish by dabbing roofing cement under all affected shingles and pressing them down.

Hammering on pry bar saves shingles above from excessive bending, which might crack them. Position the top of the bar over a nail-head and hammer on the bar several inches below—free of the upper shingle.

Fixing ridge and hip shingles

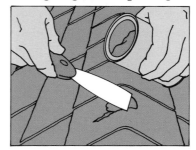

Ridge shingle cracks can be fixed with an application of roofing cement if the cracks are less than ½ in. long. Pinhead-size holes can be patched the same way.

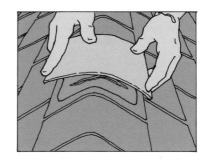

Large ridge shingle flaws should be repaired with an asphalt shingle patch, cut to overlap the damaged area by 3 in. on all sides and gently bent to fit. Cement patch into place, and nail down its corners (below).

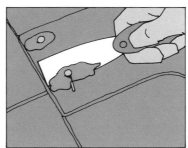

To prevent leakage, dab areas to be nailed with roofing cement before you finish driving in the nail. Afterward, cover the nailhead with cement as well.

Slate, a natural stone, is quarried in blocks, split into thin layers, and trimmed to size for roofing. Tough, long-lasting (from 50 years for Pennsylvania black slate to 200 years for Vermont sea-green slate), waterproof, and fireproof, slate's only fault is its weight. Framing for a slate roof must support 900 pounds per roofing square (100 square feet); asphalt shingles average 300 pounds per square.

Falling debris can crack or dislodge slates. Slate nails may wear out (a serious situation on an old roof). Replacing a cracked slate is safer than repairing it. However, work that can't be done from an extension ladder calls for a professional; slate roofs are steep, slippery, and easily damaged by people walking on them.

Roofers have traditional tools for working on slate (right), but you can use a hacksaw blade, a nail set, and a hammer. The blade will cut the nails holding a damaged slate. The nail set and hammer will cut a slate to size and punch new nail holes.

Classic tools

Slate hammer also cuts and makes holes.

A slate ripper, or rip iron, pulls hidden nails.

Replacing a slate

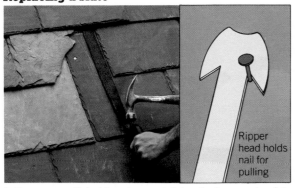

Ripper head holds nail for pulling

1. To remove nails holding damaged slate, slip ripper under slate above. When you hook a nail (there are two per slate), hammer down on ripper's knee. The nail will pop right out.

3. Position new slate so that it aligns with other slates in its course. Drive galvanized steel nails through nail holes (copper nailheads are too big to fit between old slates). Nail set keeps gap open.

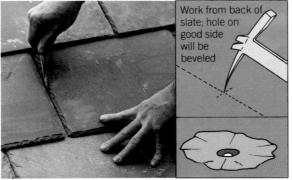

Work from back of slate; hole on good side will be beveled

2. Slip new slate into place, and mark gap between two slates above it with a nail set. Make two nail holes along this line on back side of new slate, either with a slate hammer or with a nail set.

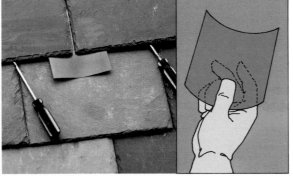

4. A copper bib protects the new nail holes and nails from water. Slightly raise two shingles above new shingle with two old screwdrivers while you slip bib into place. Its curve holds it snug.

Cutting slate

Use a nail set and hammer to punch a close series of holes along the marked line where you want a cut to be made. Work on back of slate.

A soft slate will separate without further work (left). You may need to tap a tougher slate against the edge of a table to make the break.

Rough edges can be smoothed with hammer taps along the finished cut. Support the slate against a table as you work.

The cutting edge of a slate hammer makes accurate, clean cuts, either straight or curved. Steady the slate against a table.

Wood shingles and shakes

The most common roofing-grade wood shingles and shakes (No. 1 Blue Label) come from the heartwood of western red cedar. Others are made from white cedar and spruce. Wood for roofing must have strength, a fine grain, and a low contraction and expansion rate. It should also shed water well. Wood shingle roofs that are treated with a preservative every 3 to 5 years may last up to 30 years; shake roofs that are properly maintained can serve for 50 or more years.

Wood shingles have two smooth sides because both are sawn. Shakes, traditionally split with a froe and a mallet, are rough on both sides. Hand-split shakes are sawn in two and have one smooth side.

Both kinds of wood roofs have similar problems: cracked, splintered, or curled individual shingles or shakes caused by wetting and drying. Falling branches and people walking on the roof will often break curled shakes and shingles.

Temporary repairs are simple. If both sections of a cracked shingle or shake are intact, slip a metal patch underneath to keep water out. A cupped or curled shingle or shake can be nailed down for a short-term solution, but it may swell and crack. Damaged shingles and shakes are best fixed by replacing them, as shown below.

1. Remove old shingle, using a chisel and wooden mallet to split it into pieces that you can then pull out. Hold upper shingles up with wedges of wood. Take care not to damage the good shingles in courses above and below.

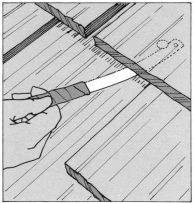

2. Cut nails that held old shingle by inserting hacksaw blade (the end you hold wrapped in tape) or a mini-hacksaw under shingle that covers them. New shingle should be cut to fit with ⅛-in. gap on each side to allow for swelling.

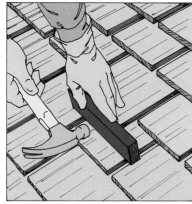

3. Tap new shingle into place with a hammer and wood block. It should align at its butt edge with the other shingles in its course.

4. Nail down as shown in space between shingles on upper course. Use aluminum or galvanized roofing nails. Waterproof the nailheads by inserting metal bib from below (facing page).

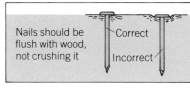

Nails should be flush with wood, not crushing it — Correct / Incorrect

Maintaining a clay tile roof

Strong and durable, tile roofs last 50 to 100 years, but falling branches and people walking on them can crack or break individual tiles, which are brittle. Clay tiles come in many shapes from flat to half-round. Most designs have interlocking pieces, making them difficult to replace. You should call in a professional to make permanent repairs. Broken tiles that you can reach from a ladder can be made temporarily watertight by slipping a piece of metal underneath. Tile ridges and hips, set in mortar, must periodically be rebedded (below). If you can reach the area from a ladder, you can do the work yourself. Otherwise, hire a roofer who specializes in clay tiles.

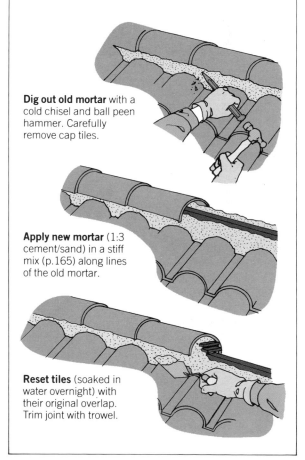

Dig out old mortar with a cold chisel and ball peen hammer. Carefully remove cap tiles.

Apply new mortar (1:3 cement/sand) in a stiff mix (p. 165) along lines of the old mortar.

Reset tiles (soaked in water overnight) with their original overlap. Trim joint with trowel.

Because it can't shed rain and snow like a sloped roof, a flat roof must be more waterproof. In fact, the slope or pitch of a roof determines the kind of roofing material to use. *Slope* is described in inches of vertical rise per foot of horizontal run. A gently sloped roof rising 4 inches for every 12 inches of house it covers is said to have a 4 in 12 slope. *Pitch* is expressed as a fraction—the ratio of rise to the total span of the roof (p.334). (Slate and tile roofs must have a minimum 4 in 12 slope or a pitch of 1:6; usually such roofs are steeper.)

Any roof that has a 2 in 12 slope or less requires built-up, soldered metal, or either asphalt or synthetic rubber roll roofing. Synthetic rubber roofing, once seen only on commercial buildings, is replacing built-up roofing in residential use. Roofers who do both commercial and residential work often will install it on homes. It is lightweight, long-lasting, and easy to repair with rubber patches. The more traditional built-up roof alternates layers of adhesive and roofing felt—at least three layers and sometimes as many as five. On hot-process built-up roofs hot tar is the adhesive; on cold-process roofs, asphalt cement. Either must be installed with appropriate flashing by a professional.

Sun is hard on built-up roofing, which explains the protective layer of gravel or mineral-surfaced asphalt roll roofing often placed on top. Ultraviolet rays oxidize and shrink the adhesive. Heat bakes out the oils and makes the surface brittle. Walking on a built-up roof breaks it down even further.

Inspect a flat roof often. An isolated blister in asphalt roll roofing or on a built-up roof is no cause for alarm. Leave it undisturbed. A group of blisters is worrisome. If asphalt roll roofing is badly blistered and cracked, consider doing the reroofing yourself (below). Call in a professional to look at a built-up roof with blisters or other signs of extensive damage like cracks and tears. You can extend the life of a flat roof with a coating of reflective asphalt aluminum paint; it lubricates the membrane and reseals the surface against water.

Patching a worn spot on asphalt roofing

Brush the area clean. Cut out the damaged section with a utility knife. Use this piece as a pattern to cut a patch of asphalt roll roofing to fit.

Apply roofing cement to the exposed area. Use a putty knife to work adhesive under all the cut edges; then coat the center section generously.

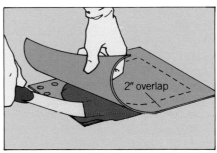

Apply patch. Use two or more layers of patches and roofing cement if the first doesn't lie flush with rest of roof. Nail patch around edges.

Cut a cover patch to overlap repair by 2 in. on each side. Apply roofing cement and lay down patch, making sure all its edges are sealed.

Installing asphalt roll roofing

To get double coverage (and a longer life for the roof), pick roofing with a 17-in. mineral surface exposure and a 19-in. selvage. Remove old roofing, repair deck, and install new drip edges at eaves and rake. Cut roof-wide strips off the roll; stack them at the high end of roof to uncurl. Work in warm (45° F) weather; you want asphalt to be flexible. Finish the roof with appropriate flashing where it joins house (pp.390–391).

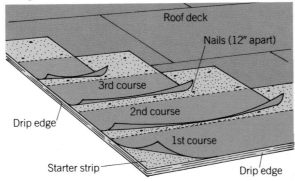

Roof deck

Nails (12″ apart)

3rd course

2nd course

Drip edge

1st course

Starter strip

Drip edge

Nail starter strip of selvage (cut from roll) with rows of nails spaced 1½ in., 8 in., and 14½ in. from edge. Like other courses, selvage should overhang eaves and rake by ½ in.

Apply first course over starter strip. Nail its selvage as you did starter strip. Fold back first course and apply roofing cement as shown. Unfold and press into cement with clean broom.

Metal roof maintenance

Many different metals are used for roofing. Copper, with its aged green patina, is prominent in older cities. The so-called tin roof used so often on farm buildings in the past is today more likely to be corrugated galvanized steel or aluminum, but it looks much the same. Other metal roofs are not so recognizable. Terne (steel coated with an alloy of lead and tin) is usually painted. Some modern aluminum roofing is die-stamped to look like wood shingles, and steel roofing panels resemble clay tiles.

Properly installed metal roofs are durable. Copper roofs, which require professional installation but little maintenance, can last 50 years or more; aluminum shingles and thick (26-gauge) galvanized steel roofing panels—seamed, ribbed, or corrugated—can last as long if they are put up correctly and well maintained.

However, metal roofs are subject to corrosion, particularly if different metals touch each other. A galvanized steel panel laid over copper flashing, for example, invites a corrosive chemical reaction when it rains unless the surfaces are coated with a bituminous paint. For the same reason, it is important to use nails or screws of the same metal as the roofing panels.

Painted steel or terne roofs must be repainted and touched up to prevent rust. Pinhole leaks in metal roofs can be fixed with a coating of roofing cement or an asphalt-base sealant. Larger holes or tears can be mended by soldering on a patch of the same metal. Steel and terne should be soldered with a noncorrosive resin flux; copper, with an acid flux. If your roof is steep, let a roofer do it.

Aluminum roofing need not be painted, but it often is for aesthetic reasons. Because the metal can't be soldered, aluminum roofing panels are joined by interlocking edges and attached to the deck by screws with prefitted washers that can hold tight against wind and changing temperatures. (Nails loosen under these conditions.) Always screw metal roofing at the top of a rib, not in a valley. A screw should compress the washer without bending the rib.

Soldering a patch

1. Clean damaged area thoroughly. Cut a patch of the same metal at least 2 in. larger than hole. Snip corners and fold edges under ½ in. Sand turned edges to a shine and position over hole. Coat edges of patch and roof surface with flux.

2. Position patch and hold it in place with bricks or stones. With an electric soldering iron, heat solder at edge of patch until solder flows into the joint. Work the solder around the patch until all sides are sealed.

Patching aluminum

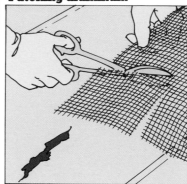

1. Cut two fiberglass patches large enough to cover damaged area. With a wire brush, clean the area thoroughly; then coat it with roofing cement.

2. Apply a fiberglass patch over the fresh roofing cement. Using a flexible putty knife, cover the patch with more roofing cement. Add a second fiberglass patch. Finish the repair with a final coat of roofing cement.

Coating a pitted roof

Renew a metal roof that has developed pinholes or deep pitting with an application of an asphalt-base liquid sealant. Start at the high end of the roof and work coating into joints with a stiff push broom as you go. Return to the ladder and finish from it. Coatings don't permanently fix a roof; they buy you an extra year or so of service.

The key to waterproofing the exterior shell of a house is flashing. Wherever there is a joint—between sections of a roof, around a chimney or roof vent, where roof and siding meet—special care must be taken to keep water out. Joints are vulnerable because the two sides, particularly if they are made of different materials, may expand and contract at different rates. They also may pull apart as a house settles. Flashing must be flexible enough to accommodate these changes, watertight enough to shed rain and snow, and sturdy enough to direct streams of water away from points of entry.

Flashing materials. Copper, galvanized steel, and aluminum are the most common. Neoprene collars are used for flashing around vents. Older houses may have lead or terneplate (a lead-tin alloy on steel) flashing, which should be professionally removed (p.348).

You can purchase metal flashing in sheets or rolls, which you cut with metal snips and shape over a board, or in preformed units designed for drip edges, window and door drip caps, step flashing, or valley flashing (diagram right). You can also order custom-made flashing for difficult joints. Copper flashing—often used on slate or tile roofs—is the most expensive but lasts the longest. Galvanized steel, even if it's prepainted, is inexpensive but needs periodic repainting to prevent rusting. Aluminum flashing, at the middle in price and in durability, comes unfinished (weathering to dull gray) or prepainted in a variety of colors.

Repairs. Water can work its way through pinsize holes in flashing. Holes signal a weakening of the metal. Use roofing cement as a stopgap. Hire a professional to replace the flashing. Holes in copper or steel caused by accidents (not wear) can be fixed with a soldered patch (p.389).

Leaks at the juncture of shingles and valley flashing can be prevented by applying new waterproof membranes made of rubberized asphalt and polyethylene. Self-bonding and self-sealing, they keep a tight seal along the sides of valley flashing, but you must remove shingles to put down a membrane.

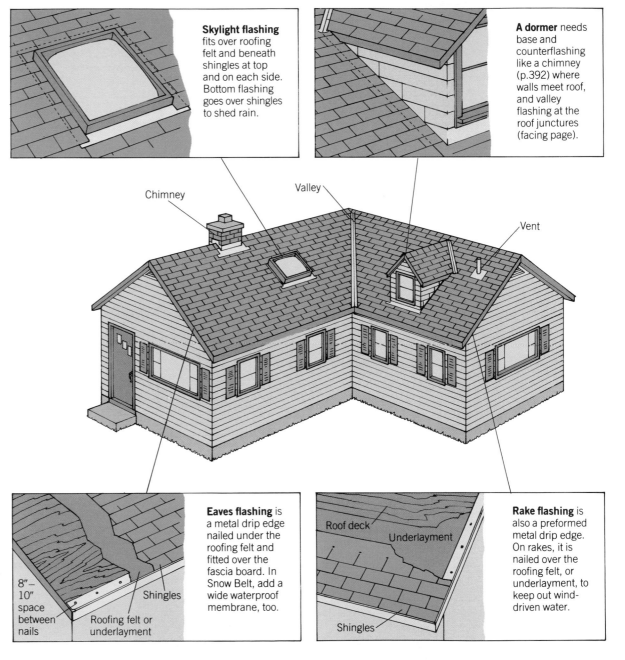

Skylight flashing fits over roofing felt and beneath shingles at top and on each side. Bottom flashing goes over shingles to shed rain.

A dormer needs base and counterflashing like a chimney (p.392) where walls meet roof, and valley flashing at the roof junctures (facing page).

Chimney

Valley

Vent

Eaves flashing is a metal drip edge nailed under the roofing felt and fitted over the fascia board. In Snow Belt, add a wide waterproof membrane, too.

8"–10" space between nails

Shingles

Roofing felt or underlayment

Rake flashing is also a preformed metal drip edge. On rakes, it is nailed over the roofing felt, or underlayment, to keep out wind-driven water.

Roof deck

Underlayment

Shingles

Replacing vent flashing

1. Carefully remove shingles on either side of vent with a pry bar. Use a putty knife to scrape out any old adhesive there and under the shingle above vent. (Bend shingles gently so they won't crack.) Pull out old flashing.

2. Slip the new flashing unit over the vent. The neck of the neoprene sleeve should fit vent pipe tightly. Lift shingle above vent and slide top of new flashing underneath. Nail flashing at top and sides where holes will be covered by shingles.

3. Replace the shingles over sides of the new flashing (shingles must cover nailheads). The bottom edge of flashing should lie over the shingles below it, where it will shed, not trap, water.

Valley flashing options

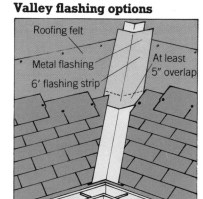

Roofing felt
Metal flashing
6' flashing strip
At least 5" overlap

An open valley is lined with metal that is nailed or clipped under the roof's shingles, slates, or tiles. The roof material must be trimmed so that nothing interferes with the flow of water down the valley, which usually channels water into a gutter.

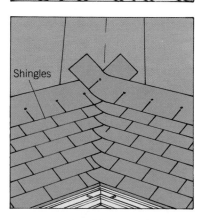

Shingles

A closed valley is used with asphalt shingles to make a seamless roof. Roll roofing, metal, or membrane is laid in the valley first. In a woven valley, shingles form a single continuous pattern. In another closed valley type, the shingles are mitered where they meet.

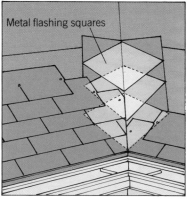

Metal flashing squares

To repair flashing beneath a closed valley, squares of metal are pushed up the valley from below. If square pieces are bent slightly, they bypass nails and glide all the way to the valley's top, waterproofing the entire joint.

Drip cap flashing

Shingles
Housewrap
Drip cap flashing
Interior wall
Drip cap

Windows and doors create vulnerable joints. Drip cap flashing, nailed under the housewrap and over the top trim of a door or window, prevents water being blown, or drawn up, under siding.

W-flashing

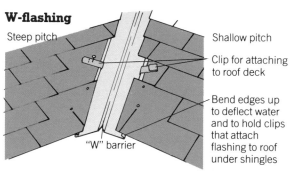

Steep pitch
Shallow pitch
Clip for attaching to roof deck
Bend edges up to deflect water and to hold clips that attach flashing to roof under shingles
"W" barrier

W-flashing is used in valleys between roofs with different pitches. An upward fold in the center keeps water from steeper side from sloshing up under shingles on less sloped side.

Z-flashing

Preformed seam flashing waterproofs horizontal joints in exterior panel siding, such as plywood or hardboard. If they are not flashed, such seams can act like wicks to draw up water. Leave a gap (⅛ in.) between bottom of panel and flashing to let water escape.

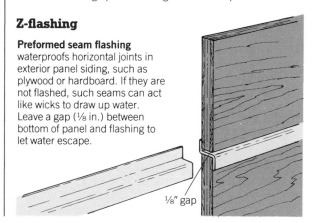

⅛" gap

Cutting metal 128
Shaping sheet metal 136–137
Ladders and safety 383

Exteriors/Chimney flashing

A chimney, whether it abuts an outside wall or rises from inside the house, is built on its own foundation. The whole structure moves and settles independently, causing the joints between chimney and roof to shift too. Flashing for these joints must absorb movement and still shed water.

Both problems are solved with two-part flashing (right). First a base flashing is attached to the roof and bent up the sides of the chimney. Then the joints are counterflashed with a second layer of flashing, which is attached to the chimney and allowed to overlap, or "cap," the base flashing. Because the two sets of flashing are not attached to each other, they can move freely—one with the chimney and the other with the house. The overlap of the counter- or cap flashing keeps out water.

If chimney flashing is installed correctly, it won't require roofing cement, which would eventually dry out and crack, allowing leaks. Counterflashing may require new mortar now and then, but barring accidents, good flashing should last 30 years. Then, instead of patching it, you should replace it. If your roof is slate or tile, which shouldn't be walked on, or if it is high and steep, hire a roofer.

Chimneys can be flashed with copper, aluminum, or galvanized steel. (Lead flashing, common once, is still used by roofers, but it is hazardous to work with.) Most pieces of chimney flashing must be custom-cut to fit properly. You can, however, buy preformed step flashing. Sheets or rolls of flashing material are available from roofing supply stores. Patterns for the different components of chimney flashing are shown on the facing page.

Using a cricket. A chimney that emerges from the roof a foot or more below the ridge top presents a special waterproofing problem. The up-roof joint of chimney and roof creates a V-shaped pocket that may collect debris and water. Constant dampness will corrode the flashing and cause a leak. To prevent pooling in this cavity, a small A-frame structure called a *cricket* is installed behind the chimney. Waterproofed with flashing, a cricket directs rain and snow away from the joint.

Base flashing. Installation starts at the bottom of the chimney. A down-roof piece (the apron) goes *over* the shingles and up the front of the chimney. Side tabs wrap around corners. Step flashing (right) covers the sides of the chimney, with tabs wrapping at the corners. The final up-roof piece, if there is no cricket (facing page), goes *under* shingles and up the chimney.

Step flashing is the most reliable base flashing for the sides of a chimney. A series of overlapping metal rectangles, bent 90°, interlace with the shingle courses abutting the chimney. End pieces wrap corners (below). Each piece of metal is nailed to the deck under a shingle.

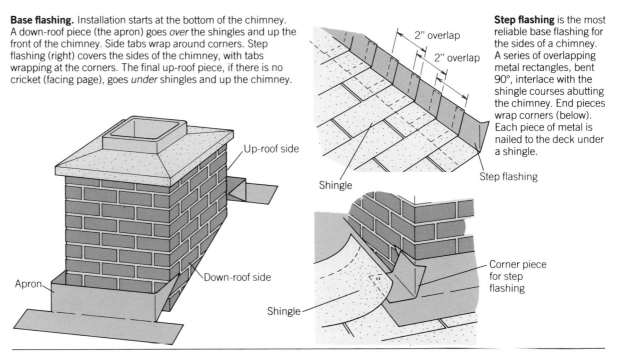

Up-roof side

Shingle

Apron

Down-roof side

2" overlap

2" overlap

Step flashing

Corner piece for step flashing

Shingle

Counterflashing is bent 90° near the top to form a 1-in. lip that's inserted in the chimney's mortar joints, where it is secured with fresh mortar or polyurethane caulk. Counterflashing overlaps base flashing by at least 4 in. Side counterflashing is a series of overlapping strips inserted in succeeding courses of the brick.

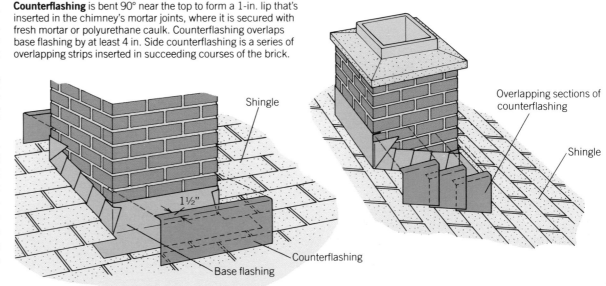

Shingle

1½"

Counterflashing

Base flashing

Overlapping sections of counterflashing

Shingle

Replacing damaged chimney flashing

Finishing mortar joints 168
Asphalt shingles 385

1. Chip out old mortar with a cape chisel and a small sledgehammer. Wear safety goggles. Remove old flashing. Clear a 1½-in. deep groove in mortar where new flashing can be installed.

2. Lift shingles along the sides and up-roof joint of chimney to locate nails that hold the flashing. Work when temperature is 50° F or warmer so that the shingles are pliable.

3. Unnail old base flashing with a pry bar, taking care not to rip the roofing paper beneath it. New flashing also will be nailed to the sheathing, but not in the same holes.

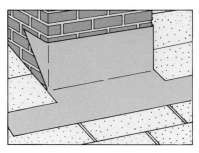

4. Install new base flashing, starting with the down-roof piece. Nail ends of apron under side shingles. Stepflash the sides next (facing page). End by nailing up-roof piece (or cricket flashing) to deck.

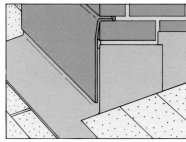

5. Insert counterflashing into mortar joints, the down-chimney piece first. Next, wrap side pieces over the down-chimney piece. Finally, wrap the up-chimney piece over the sides.

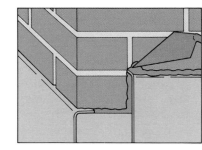

6. Seal the counterflashing with fresh mortar (p.168). Press shingles along sides and up-roof joint of chimney back into place. They will cover the nails securing flashing to roof deck.

Flashing patterns

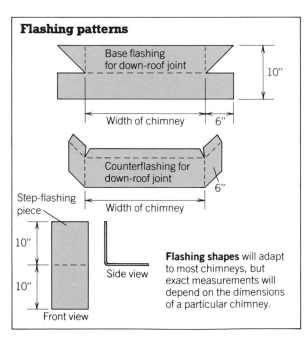

Base flashing for down-roof joint

10"

Width of chimney | 6"

Counterflashing for down-roof joint

6"

Width of chimney

Step-flashing piece

10"

10"

Side view

Front view

Flashing shapes will adapt to most chimneys, but exact measurements will depend on the dimensions of a particular chimney.

Chimney crickets. Braced by 2 x 4 boards nailed to the deck, a cricket, or chimney saddle, is often as high as half the chimney's width. Its triangular roof pieces are cut from plywood and match the slope of the roof. Cricket flashing (pattern right) is cut from a sheet of metal; its pieces can be soldered together if it is copper. The flanges along the sides are nailed to the roof deck; shingles are then laid over them. The flanges at the cricket's juncture with the chimney go up the back of the chimney and are covered with counterflashing (right). Small crickets may be made of soldered heavy-gauge metal that needs no flashing.

Plywood triangle

Chimney

Cricket counterflashing pattern

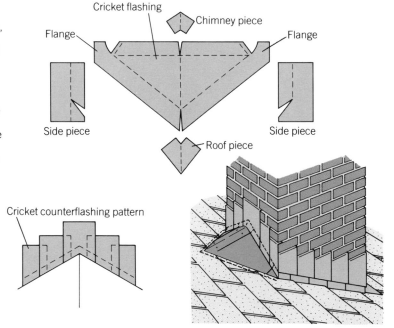

Cricket flashing

Chimney piece

Flange

Flange

Side piece

Side piece

Roof piece

An asphalt or fiberglass shingle roof usually can be reshingled once. This gives the benefit of a new roof (15 to 20 years of wear) without the added work and expense of removing and disposing of the old shingles. In heavy snow areas, reshingling may be impractical: the weight of two sets of shingles plus snow may be too much for the framing or trusses to support. Get an expert's opinion.

To prepare a roof for reshingling, remove the old ridge shingles. Nail down loose, curling, or torn shingles, and replace missing shingles, to make a smooth surface for the new roof. Install new drip edges over the old shingles on eaves and rakes.

Plan to reflash valleys, dormers, and chimneys.

Standard three-tab asphalt or fiberglass shingles come in bundles of 27; three bundles make up a *square,* the basic roofing unit, which covers 100 square feet. To estimate how much roofing you need, calculate the square footage of the roof and divide by 100. This will give you the number of squares of shingles. Each 5 feet of ridge or hip requires four shingles, and the starter course along each eave requires an extra shingle for each 3 feet of run. Roofers usually add 10 to 20 percent to the original estimate for these extras. You will need aluminum or galvanized roofing nails that are long

enough to penetrate through new and old shingles and ¾ inch into the roof deck. Count on buying about 2 pounds of nails per square of shingles. Staple guns are not recommended for reshingling; the staples would have to penetrate too many layers.

Reshingling with asphalt or fiberglass shingles must be done when the temperature is warm enough (50° F or higher) to keep the shingles pliable. Follow ladder safety rules, wear soft-soled shoes for grip (and to protect the roof), and carry your tools in an apron or a belt holder. If it rains, keep stored bundles of shingles dry under a tarp. Don't work in the rain; wet shingles are slippery.

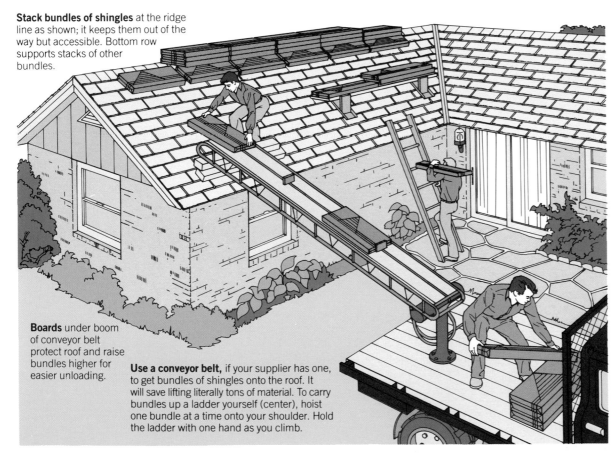

Stack bundles of shingles at the ridge line as shown; it keeps them out of the way but accessible. Bottom row supports stacks of other bundles.

Boards under boom of conveyor belt protect roof and raise bundles higher for easier unloading.

Use a conveyor belt, if your supplier has one, to get bundles of shingles onto the roof. It will save lifting literally tons of material. To carry bundles up a ladder yourself (center), hoist one bundle at a time onto your shoulder. Hold the ladder with one hand as you climb.

Rooftop scaffolds

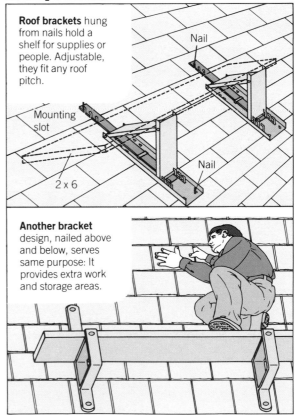

Roof brackets hung from nails hold a shelf for supplies or people. Adjustable, they fit any roof pitch.

Nail

Mounting slot

2 x 6

Nail

Another bracket design, nailed above and below, serves same purpose: It provides extra work and storage areas.

Nailing shingles

Standard three-tab shingle takes four nails. Proper nail position is shown below.

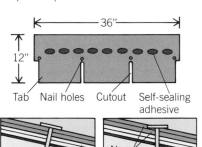

Tab Nail holes Cutout Self-sealing adhesive

Correct Old shingles New shingles Wrong

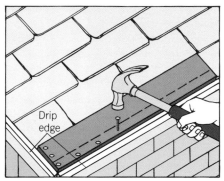

For starter course, remove tabs; trim shingles with metal snips to cover exposure of old shingles (usually 5 in.) plus new drip edges. Cut 6 in. from end, so old seams will be covered. Nail at eaves.

Drip edge

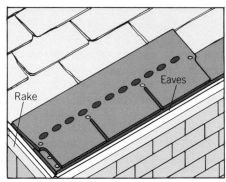

First-course shingles are trimmed 1 in. at top. They should abut bottom of old third course and match overhangs of starter course at rakes and eaves. Nail course down from rake to rake.

Rake Eaves

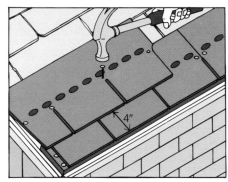

Second-course shingles are used full width and abut at top with old fourth course, leaving a 4-in. exposure on first course. Trim 6 in. from left end of first shingle to keep tab pattern consistent.

4"

How pattern continues

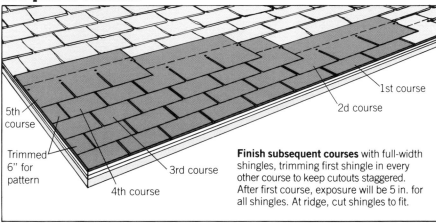

1st course
2d course
5th course
Trimmed 6" for pattern
3rd course
4th course

Finish subsequent courses with full-width shingles, trimming first shingle in every other course to keep cutouts staggered. After first course, exposure will be 5 in. for all shingles. At ridge, cut shingles to fit.

Shingling at a valley

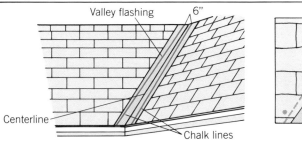

Valley flashing 6"
Centerline
Chalk lines

Flashing
Chalk line
Nail

Mark valley flashing with chalk lines on either side of centerline. Start lines 6 in. apart at ridge, but angle them out (1 in. per every 8 ft.) toward eaves. Finish each course of shingles to cover chalk lines.

Shingles next to flashing must be nailed directly to roof deck, not through flashing, which needs room to expand and contract. After installing shingles, trim them along chalk lines with metal snips.

Shingling the ridge

Ridge shingles are created, three at a time, by cutting a standard shingle along dotted lines in pattern (right). Each ridge shingle is gently bent, mineral surface out, along centerline (below) to conform to the angle of the ridge.

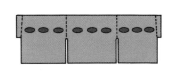

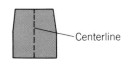

Centerline

Ridge shingle Shingle courses
Rake
Center shingle

Start shingling at ends, aligning ridge shingles with courses at rakes. Work back to middle.

Cap the ridge with a rectangular piece of shingle at the center to secure final overlap.

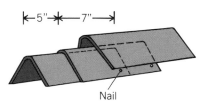

5" 7"
Nail

Nail ridge shingles as shown; overlapping shingles cover nail holes. Nail center shingle at four corners; seal nails with roofing cement.

Exteriors / Maintaining gutters and downspouts

Gutters and downspouts direct rain and snowmelt away from the foundation of a house. They should connect to an underground drain that leads to an appropriate spillout or a community storm drain, or to a concrete splash block, which disperses the runoff down the natural grade of the property.

Dry wells are a problematic alternative. They gradually clog up, and in periods of heavy rain, even new dry wells can back up because they can't handle the sudden high volume of water.

Gutters that leak or overflow or downspouts and drainage pipes that become clogged may cause water to collect near the house and seep through foundation walls into the basement. This is why gutter screens and leaf strainers don't always work. They keep debris out of the gutter, but because leaves cling to the screening or to the leaf strainer, they also keep water out of the drainage system. There is no substitute for cleaning out your gutter system regularly in the spring and the fall.

Other upkeep depends on the gutter material. Copper and vinyl are the most carefree. Wood needs treatment with a water-repellent preservative every 2 years. Aluminum joints tend to leak and must be recaulked periodically. Galvanized steel requires regular painting to prevent rust.

Cleaning and inspecting

To remove debris, start at downspout end and work toward upper end. Use trowel if leaves are wet and matted. For metal gutters, which may have sharp edges, wear heavy gloves. On the outside of the gutter, mark with chalk any loose fittings and areas of rust, corrosion, or chipped paint, so that you can find them easily to fix later.

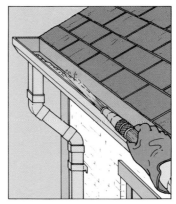

Flush gutter with a hose from the upper end to finish cleaning it out and to check for leaks and stoppages. If water flows but puddles form in the gutter, mark the areas. The gutter sags at that spot; realign the hangers (facing page). If water doesn't flow at all, there is a blockage in the downspout or the drain. Check gutter joints for seepage.

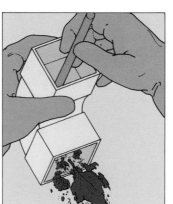

Unclog an elbow by dismantling it, if you can, and poking out debris with a stick. (Use a hose or a plumber's snake on soldered systems that you can't take apart.) If water still doesn't flow, the blockage is in the vertical downspout pipe or in the underground drainage pipes (facing page).

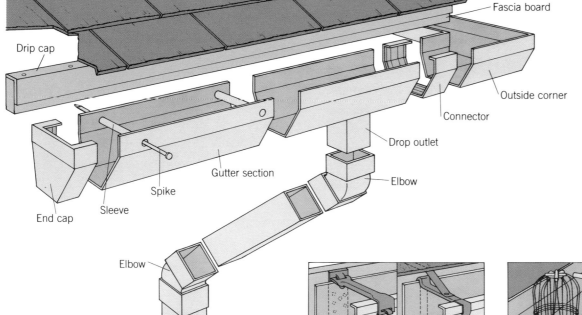

Drip cap · Shingles · Fascia board · Outside corner · Connector · Drop outlet · Gutter section · Elbow · Spike · Sleeve · End cap · Elbow · Downspout bracket · Downspout

Alternative hangers are a bracket (left), attached to the fascia board, or a strap (right), nailed to roof under shingle.

Leaf strainer set in drop outlet may prevent clogs.

Basement dampness 338–339
Ladders and safety 383
Installing new gutters and downspouts 398–399

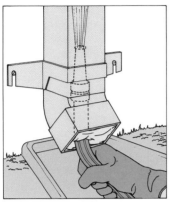

Unblock a downspout with a hose inserted from bottom. Stuff the opening around the hose with rags so that all the water's force goes to blasting out whatever is stopping up the pipe (it could be a tennis ball). Have a partner watch at top of the downspout (but not leaning over it) and tell you when the debris has been dislodged.

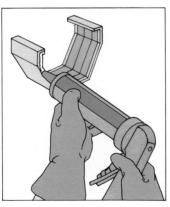

Underground blockage should be considered if water won't flow and the drainage system feeds into an underground dry well. The drainpipe elbow may be the site of a stoppage, or the dry well may be too clogged to disperse water as it once did. Either situation requires digging to check out.

Leaks at joints where connectors are used are common. To reseal a joint, take it apart and clean all the pieces. Allow them to dry completely. Apply a gutter seal or a 1-part polyurethane caulk to the connectors; then slip the gutter pieces back into place.

Patching metal gutters

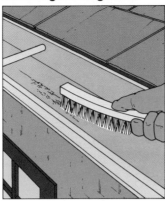

1. Scrape area with a wire brush or abrasive pad. Remove all rust on steel gutters, or it will continue to eat away at the metal under the patch. Wipe the scraped surface clean with paint thinner and allow it to dry thoroughly.

2. Use a putty knife to coat cleaned area with a ⅛-in. layer of 1-part polyurethane caulk or gutter seal (available at hardware stores and home centers). Cut a patch of fiberglass or metal to cover damaged area plus a 2-in. margin on all sides.

3. Smooth the patch in the adhesive, using a dry wadded cloth. Blind-rivet a metal patch at both ends. Caulk that oozes out around the patch can be spread to seal the edges. Coat top of patch with adhesive. A few patches buy you time; a lot of rust or many holes indicate that gutters need replacing.

Realigning a gutter

1. Mark a level line under a gutter run: Drive a nail into the fascia at the low end of the run (remove gutter first). Stretch string to a nail at the high end of the run. Use a level to adjust that nail until string is level. Starting at the low end, make marks for realigning gutter. For water to drain, the distance from level line must increase ¼ in. every 4 ft.

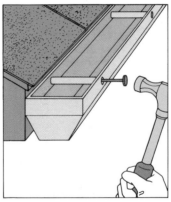

2. Correct gutter's pitch by adjusting placement of hangers along the run to conform to the new measurements made in step 1. Pull spikes out with locking-grip pliers. Remove gutter. Fill holes with epoxy wood putty; sand and paint. Drive spikes through fascia into rafter or truss ends at correct height.

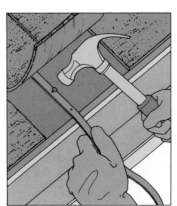

3. Straps and brackets require two different techniques. Reset straps as shown on a warm day when asphalt shingles are pliable enough to lift. (Slates, tiles, or wood shingles will have to be removed.) To reposition brackets, take down gutter. Unscrew each bracket. Fill old holes in fascia with wood putty; sand and paint. Rescrew brackets at new height.

You can choose from a variety of materials when you decide to buy a new roof drainage system:

Copper is expensive and must be soldered by a professional, but it is strong, durable, corrosion-resistant, and nearly maintenance-free. It weathers green unless you coat it with a clear sealant.

Aluminum is moderately priced and corrosion-resistant. It comes unfinished or factory painted. A drawback is that unless they are riveted (preferably by a professional), aluminum joints will leak. The metal expands and contracts too much for sealants to hold permanently. Also, aluminum is lightweight and it dents easily; bracing a ladder against an aluminum gutter will distort the gutter.

Vinyl is tough, maintenance-free, and moderately priced. Vinyl gutters and downspouts are easy to put up (joints snap together without a sealant) and thus are the best choice for homeowner installation (this and facing page). Vinyl systems come in white or brown, and can be painted on the outside (interiors will absorb too much heat if not left white). Dents in vinyl pop back out.

Steel—galvanized or with an enamel finish—is strong and inexpensive, but subject to corrosion. Use a rust-inhibiting primer before painting. When painting new galvanized steel, wash it first with a 50-50 solution of white vinegar and water.

Wood gutters are usually part of a house's architectural design. They are expensive and prone to rot unless meticulously maintained (pp.396–397).

Calculating needs. Make a sketch of the roof. Write down the measurements for the runs of gutter, and calculate the number of downspouts (one for every 35 feet of gutter run), drop outlets, corner pieces, and end caps you need. Gutters come in 10-foot sections, so for a 26-foot run you would need three full sections (cut the third one to get the 6-foot piece). For each joint between pieces you need a connector, and for every 30 inches of gutter run, a hanger (spike and ferrule, bracket, or roof strap, depending on the system and the style of your house). Downspouts should be strapped in place every 6 feet. Each downspout requires two elbows to bridge the soffit and—unless it leads into a drainpipe—a third elbow and a splash block.

Gutters come in two standard widths: 4 inches and 5 inches. Generally, the narrower width will serve up to 750 square feet of roof. However, a house set under trees benefits from wider gutters because they clog less quickly.

1. Remove old gutter system; repair fascia. Install new drip edge (p.390) if needed. Snap a level chalk line across top of fascia (blue line). Mark slope (p.397) from high end of run to drop outlet site (red line). Attach brackets along slope every 30 in.

Level line
Gutter slope line

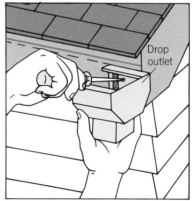

2. Screw on drop outlets, end caps attached, level with marked slope line. Drop outlet should extend 1 in. past corner of house. Runs of 35 ft. or more should slope from high point at middle of run to drop outlets at each end.

Drop outlet

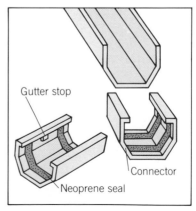

3. Connect gutter pieces on ground before you install them, using special connectors that have their own gasketlike seals. They require no caulk or other adhesive, but allow gutter to expand and contract without breaking watertight seal.

Gutter stop
Connector
Neoprene seal

Installation techniques for vinyl gutters

Snow line

Ideal gutter placement allows snow to slide off roof without interruption, while rain is caught and diverted from house.

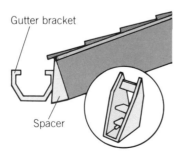

Gutter bracket
Spacer

On slanted fascia board or on rafter end, use a triangular spacer to position each gutter bracket at the correct angle.

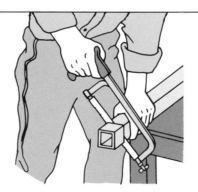

To cut vinyl gutter or pipe, use a hacksaw with a fine-tooth blade. Remove any burrs around cut with fine sandpaper.

Preventing ice dams

4. Mount gutter run on its brackets, starting at high end and finishing at drop outlet, where gutter snaps into place. Mounting gutter is easier with two people, one at each end; if you are working alone, support one end in a loop of string hung from a bracket.

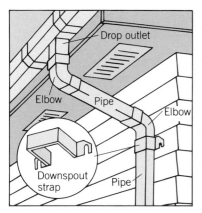

5. Use two elbows and, if necessary, a length of pipe to bring downspout from drop outlet to house wall. Chalk a plumb line to align lower portion of pipe correctly. Use screws or masonry fasteners (pp.86–87) to attach straps or brackets to siding every 6 ft.

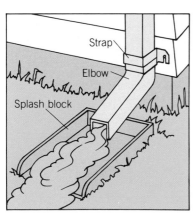

6. Finish drain with an elbow and a piece of pipe leading into a concrete splash block if there is no drainage system connection there. A splash block diverts water away from the house foundation and prevents soil erosion under downspout.

Ice dams, backups of ice under snow at the eaves of a roof, are most easily recognized by festoons of icicles hanging from the gutters after the first big snow. Ice dams are formed when escaping attic heat melts snow at the ridge or peak of the roof. The meltwater seeps down the roof under the snow and refreezes at the eaves, which are colder. Insulated by a blanket of snow, the ice then prevents subsequent melt-off from draining into the gutters; instead, the meltwater backs up under the shingles and works its way into the house.

A metal or synthetic rubber shield under the shingles along the eaves will avert damage from ice dam leaks. Electric heat tapes, which may prevent icicles from forming in gutters, don't prevent ice dams; they push them farther up the roof.

The cure for an ice dam is a cold roof, which allows snow to melt slowly and evenly and runoff to drain safely into gutters. Only a combination of ventilation (feeding cold air into the attic through the soffits) and adequate insulation (keeping heat out of the attic) can create a cold roof.

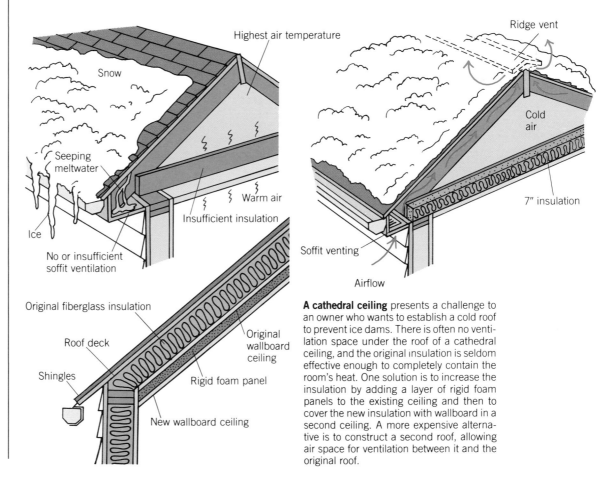

A cathedral ceiling presents a challenge to an owner who wants to establish a cold roof to prevent ice dams. There is often no ventilation space under the roof of a cathedral ceiling, and the original insulation is seldom effective enough to completely contain the room's heat. One solution is to increase the insulation by adding a layer of rigid foam panels to the existing ceiling and then to cover the new insulation with wallboard in a second ceiling. A more expensive alternative is to construct a second roof, allowing air space for ventilation between it and the original roof.

Exteriors / Chimney repairs

Ladders and safety 383
Improving fireplace efficiency 483
Zero-clearance fireplaces 484–485

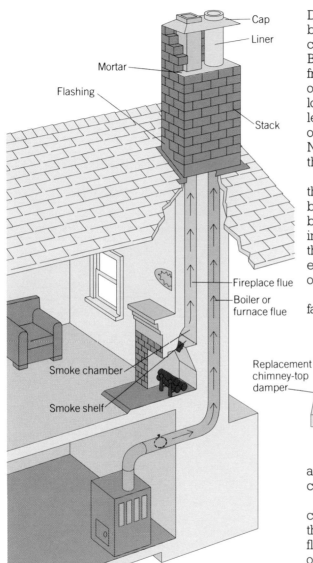

A chimney consists of a *stack,* or column of bricks, stones, or concrete blocks, and one or more hollow *flues* that carry smoke out of the house. There should be a separate flue for each fireplace, stove, boiler, or furnace. Chimney interiors are protected with *flue liners.* A sloped concrete *cap* at the top of the stack sheds water.

Defects in masonry chimneys are often neglected because they cannot easily be seen. Such neglect can be dangerous; inspect your chimney carefully. Because it's best not to walk on a roof, examine it from the ground through binoculars. Look for loose or missing bricks, serious cracks, a damaged cap, or loose or deteriorated flashing. If the chimney stack is leaning, call a chimney expert; repairing this serious fault is beyond the scope of the homeowner. Never attach an antenna to a chimney; it will loosen the bricks and mortar in time.

Brickwork. If the mortar between the bricks of the chimney is crumbling, repoint as you would any brick structure, and if you find a few loose or missing bricks, replace them (pp.174–175). Before proceeding with any chimney repairs, close the damper to the fireplace to confine any soot that may be loosened while you work. If the chimney has more than one flue, close the dampers to all of them.

Damper. If your damper rusts or is damaged by a falling brick, you will need to replace it. However, damper housings are mortared into place, and replacing them requires ripping out the brickwork just above the fireplace. To avoid this messy job, simply lift the old damper from its housing and remove it; then install a chimney-top damper, controlled by a cable hanging down the chimney.

Flue liners. At least once a year, examine the chimney wherever it is visible as it passes through the house and attic. Either have a helper shine a flashlight up the flue while you check for light leaks, or build a smoky fire by burning wet wood or damp shredded newspaper and cover the chimney with a heavy wet cloth; smoke will leak through any cracks. Don't build a fire until you have the lining replaced.

Chimneys can be relined with poured concrete or steel. A rigid steel liner is inserted into a straight chimney and surrounded by a blanket of insulation. In a chimney with bends, a flexible corrugated stainless steel liner is inserted and a mixture of cement, water, and insulating material is poured around it.

Concrete liners are poured in two ways. In one method, a long balloon, or bladder, is inserted into the chimney and inflated. Concrete is then poured around the balloon to form the liner; when the concrete is dry, the balloon is deflated and removed. In the other method, a bell, or buoy, is lowered into the chimney and is electrically vibrated and slowly raised as the concrete is being poured.

Flashing. If you see water stains near the chimney, check the flashing on the roof. If it is loose, rake out the joint it was embedded in, reinsert the edge of the flashing, and remortar or caulk the joint. If the flashing has deteriorated, replace it (pp.392–393).

Chimney tops. Trees overhanging a chimney may create a canopy effect, causing your fireplace to smoke intermittently; they can also catch fire. Clip the branches back at least 10 feet from the chimney top. It is also a good idea to have a spark arrester or weather cap (facing page) to keep live embers in and water, snow, and small animals out of the chimney. If your chimney has a wire mesh guard, clean it from time to time to keep it from clogging.

If the chimney cap has cracks or holes, repair them with fresh mortar to keep water from running into the chimney. If the cap is badly cracked and the mortar is pulling away from the bricks, replace the cap. Begin by removing the old cap with a bricklayer's chisel and a 2½-pound hammer. Be sure to protect your eyes by wearing goggles. Put the pieces you remove into a bucket and lower it to the ground with a rope; don't let the pieces bounce down off the roof. Clear away all loose material, dampen the top course of bricks, and form a new cap with several thick layers of concrete mix, sloping them so that water will run off the outside of the chimney.

▶ **CAUTION:** Before doing any work on a chimney, read pp.383–393 on ladders and roof repairs. If you have any doubts whatsoever about working on a roof, call in a chimney expert.

Chimney cleaning

Chimney accessories

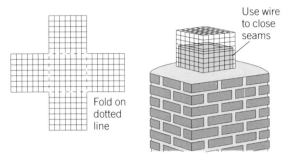

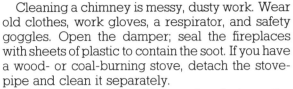

Use wire to close seams

Fold on dotted line

Simple spark arrester keeps live embers from blowing out and causing fires. Buy one or make your own by cutting incinerator wire, folding it into an open box, and wiring its sides together.

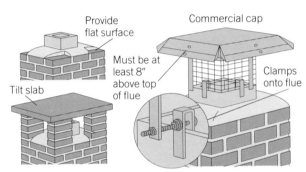

Provide flat surface

Commercial cap

Must be at least 8" above top of flue

Clamps onto flue

Tilt slab

Weather cap can be constructed by leveling four corners of chimney cap, adding columns of brick, and topping them with a stone or concrete slab. Or you can buy a guard that clamps onto chimney top.

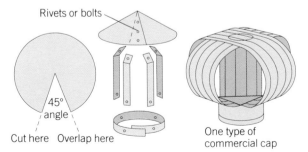

Rivets or bolts

45° angle

Cut here   Overlap here

One type of commercial cap

Prevent downdrafts with homemade cone-shaped guard. Cut out sheet-metal top, collar, and straps; bolt or rivet together; wedge into place over flue top. Various commercial guards are also available.

If a chimney is not cleaned regularly, unburned gases and tars from the smoke condense on the chimney's surface and can cause fires—a common and serious problem. Depending on how much a fireplace or stove is used, what is burned in it, and how hot the fire is, a chimney may need cleaning from one to three times a year. A chimney sweep may use a sophisticated video scanner to inspect a chimney. But you can shine a flashlight up the flue and inspect it yourself; if you find ¼ inch or more of crusty, flaky, or powdery residue, sweep the chimney as shown below. If the deposits are gummy, tarry, or hard and glazed, call in a professional.

Cleaning a chimney is messy, dusty work. Wear old clothes, work gloves, a respirator, and safety goggles. Open the damper; seal the fireplaces with sheets of plastic to contain the soot. If you have a wood- or coal-burning stove, detach the stovepipe and clean it separately.

After sweeping the chimney, brush down the smoke chamber—the space between the damper and the flue—and the smoke shelf, or you'll create a fire hazard. After all the dust has settled, remove it with a heavy-duty vacuum cleaner, such as a wet-dry vacuum (p.76). Don't risk using your household vacuum; the fine dust may damage it.

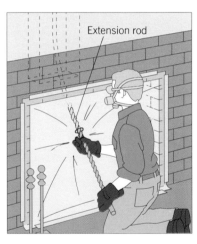

Extension rod

To work up: Fit flexible rod into brush to serve as handle (see below). Tape plastic sheet over fireplace, but before completing taping, cut a hole in middle of plastic and pass end of rod through it, leaving brush in fireplace. Work brush up and down flue, adding sections of rod as you go higher. When finished, vacuum away soot.

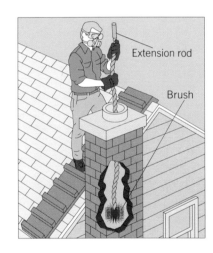

Extension rod

Brush

To work down: Seal fireplaces and other openings inside house with plastic. On roof, attach section of flexible rod to brush and push brush into flue, working it vigorously up and down. Add section of rod to end of first, and work your way down flue. Continue until you reach bottom. Remove plastic covers and vacuum away soot.

Chimney brushes and handles

Use a brush with stiff wire bristles (or one with synthetic bristles for the pipe of a coal stove). To calculate brush size, measure length and width (or diameter) of inside of flue and choose a brush as close to that size as possible. Attach interconnecting flexible fiberglass rods for brush handle.

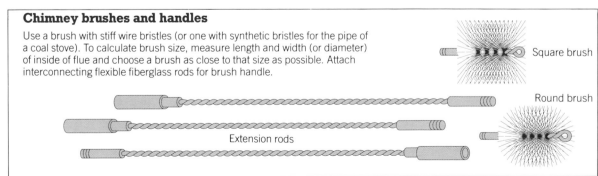

Square brush

Round brush

Extension rods

Exteriors / Installing a skylight

House framing 188–192
Ladders and safety 383

You can install a skylight in any room in a one-story house or on the top floor of a multistory house. Ideally, position it on a north-facing part of the roof to keep out direct sunlight, or fit it with blinds or a shade. Be sure to get any needed permits and follow local building codes (p.193). If the ceiling is horizontal, construct a shaft with straight or sloping walls leading to the roof.

In a cathedral ceiling, you need only frame the skylight by running headers between the rafters, but first move any electrical wires running across the path of the window; they are often found in special channels between the planking and the roofing. Also, check the roof construction before proceeding; the visible beams of a cathedral ceiling may be purely decorative, with the rafters between ceiling and roof.

Selecting a skylight. In the summer, a skylight can let in heat. In the winter, warm moist indoor air can create excessive condensation when it hits a cold windowpane. Consequently, skylight panes are often treated to reduce the amount of heat they transmit. Their resistance to heat transfer is given as the R-value. The higher the R-value, the more insulating the material.

Get a skylight with a gutter or some other system for draining condensation, especially if it is to be installed in a bathroom or kitchen. Also, make sure that the unit can be opened to let out moist air or to create a cooling updraft.

Installation. Before installing a skylight, you must cut and frame openings in the roof and ceiling. Once the skylight is in place, build the connecting shaft. Directions for the framing and for building a sloping shaft are given here.

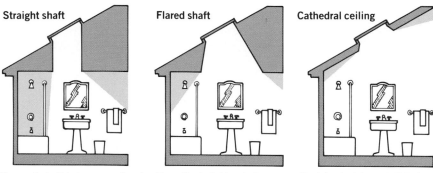

Straight shaft   Flared shaft   Cathedral ceiling

Shape of shaft between roof and ceiling affects light entering room. Straight shaft funnels light into narrow beam; flared shaft spreads light. Skylight in cathedral ceiling lets in the most light.

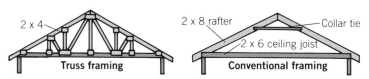

2 x 4   Truss framing

2 x 8 rafter   Collar tie   2 x 6 ceiling joist   Conventional framing

Rafters can be cut for placement of large skylight. But in some houses, trusses are used in place of rafters. Never cut a truss; you will weaken roof structure. Instead, install a skylight that bridges truss.

Ceiling framing

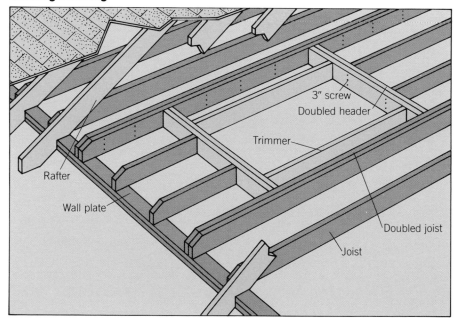

3" screw
Doubled header
Trimmer
Rafter
Wall plate
Doubled joist
Joist

1. Draw outline for opening on ceiling, making it any size you wish but at least as large as skylight. Drive long nail into each corner to identify area from above. Wearing gloves, goggles, and a dual-cartridge respirator (p.354), go into attic and remove all insulation from area marked by nails.

4. Mark any joists that cross opening 3 in. back from the opening on each side. Cut through the joists at these marks, holding the joists to keep them from falling. Start the cut with a power saw, but finish with a handsaw. Remove the cut-out sections.

2. Reroute any electrical wires, plumbing lines, and heating pipes or ducts in the area. Return to room, remove nails from ceiling, and drill holes at nail holes. Use a keyhole or wallboard saw to cut along cut lines made on ceiling, and carefully remove wallboard from cutout.

3. Following the drawing on the facing page, double the joists on each side of the opening. Fasten the new joists to their mates with 3-in. drywall screws placed every 16 in. (If you nail the joists together, the hammering may jar the finished ceiling and damage it.)

5. Cut four headers from same size lumber as joists, making them long enough to stretch between pairs of doubled joists. With 3-in. screws, fasten one header to ends of cut joists on each side of opening. Secure ends of headers by screwing into them through doubled joists.

6. Screw remaining headers to first ones to double them. Then cut trimmers from same size lumber to form long sides of frame. Mark position of each trimmer on doubled headers and carefully position trimmer. Fasten it into place by screwing into its ends through doubled headers.

Roof framing

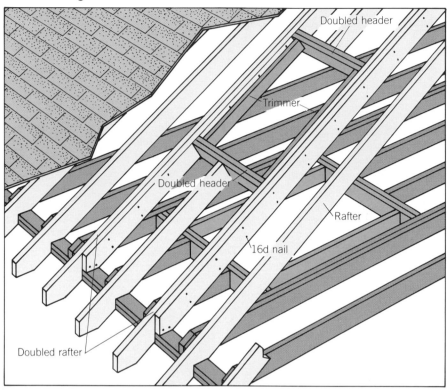

A rough opening for the skylight must be cut into the roof and framed. Following the directions on the next page, mark the location of the opening on the underside of the roof sheathing in the attic, centering it over the opening in the ceiling. Double the flanking rafters, as you did the joists on either side of the ceiling opening. Then cut the opening, and cut and install the framing members shown in the drawing above. If you will have trouble getting the long rafters into the attic, you might reverse the order of work: Cut the opening first; then bring the new rafters in through the roof.

Once the roof opening has been framed, set and flash the skylight. Each manufacturer uses a different installation system, so follow the directions that come with your unit. Generally, however, installation procedures include three basic steps: loosening or removing the surrounding shingles, assembling and fastening the frame of the skylight to the framing around the roof opening, and installing flashing.

(continued)

403

Exteriors / Installing a skylight (continued)

1. Measure and mark center point on headers at both ends of opening in ceiling. Go into attic and suspend a plumb bob from underside of roof sheathing to marks just made on headers; mark these points on sheathing and draw a straight line between them for centering skylight.

2. Using centerline drawn in previous step, draw outline of roof opening on sheathing, squaring lines off on rafters. Use dimensions given in installation instructions provided by skylight manufacturer, or measure skylight's outer dimensions and add 1 in. to each.

3. Double the rafters on each side of the roof opening, fastening them together with 16d nails spaced 16 in. apart. Drive 8d nails into sheathing and through roofing at each corner of drawing. Carefully climb on roof, and snap chalk lines between these nails to outline opening.

4. Fit power saw with a carbide-tip blade, and set blade depth to just clear sheathing. Cut along lines through shingles and sheathing, being careful not to damage rafters. Remove shingles and sheathing. Then saw through and remove sections of rafters that cross the opening.

5. Cut four headers from same size lumber as rafters. Working in attic, nail first ones into place across ends of cut rafters. Toenail ends of headers into doubled rafters. Nail other two headers to first ones, doubling them. From 2 x 4's, cut two trimmers to fit length of opening; nail them into place.

6. Return to the roof and loosen the shingles within 6 to 12 in. around the opening by prying out the roofing nails with a flat pry bar. Remove shingles where necessary. Work carefully so that you won't damage the shingles—you will have to replace them later.

7. Assemble skylight and fasten it to roof sheathing and trimmers according to manufacturer's directions. In model shown here, skylight frame is screwed down through metal braces. As you work, keep checking that top and bottom of skylight are level and corners square with roof frame.

8. Install flashing in strict accordance with manufacturer's instructions. Generally you begin by installing one piece of step flashing (p.392) under each shingle, starting at bottom and working up. You will then probably have to add cover flashing or a waterproof frame over the step flashing.

Shaft framing

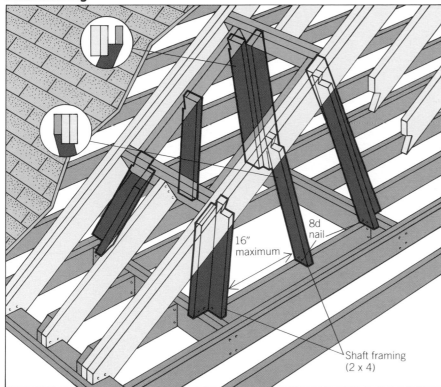

16" maximum

8d nail

Shaft framing (2 x 4)

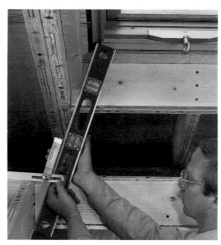

1. Measure and cut 2 x 4's to form framing for shaft walls, and notch pieces where needed, as shown in drawing at left. The pieces must stretch from the framing members of the roof opening to those of the ceiling opening. Measure the angles for the ends of the framing pieces with a T-bevel.

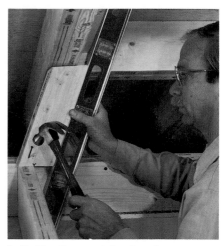

2. Position the corner framing pieces one at a time, using a straightedge to align them exactly. Fasten them into place by toenailing them with 8d nails into the headers, trimmers, joists, and rafters surrounding the roof and ceiling openings, as shown in the drawing at left.

With the skylight in place, the next step is to construct a shaft connecting it to the ceiling opening below. If the distance between the roof and the ceiling is fairly small, simply fill the space with panels of ⅝-inch plywood, nailing them to the rafters and ceiling joists.

A deep shaft must be fitted with a number of framing members cut from 2 x 4's, as shown. To help you measure and mark the angles for the ends of these pieces, use a T-bevel (p.48). Install the framing members; then insulate the spaces between them and add

a vapor retarder (p.458).

Cover either type of shaft—deep or shallow—with wallboard. Then tape the joints and smooth the finishing compound carefully—the bright light that pours through the shaft will show every flaw. Add a bead of caulk to the seam between the skylight and the wallboard, and paint the shaft.

An attractive alternative to using wallboard is to cover the shaft with tongue-and-groove boards. Mask gaps at the edges with molding, and finish with stain or polyurethane varnish.

3. If the shaft opening is more than 16 in. long, cut additional framing members from 2 x 4's to act as studs in the walls of the shaft. Nail the studs into place as you did the corner pieces. They will serve as nailing surfaces for the wallboard that lines the inside of the shaft.

4. Install fiberglass insulation between studs, wearing a respirator to keep from inhaling harmful particles. Staple sheets of 4- or 6-mil polyethylene film over the insulation to act as a vapor retarder. Finally, attach wallboard or paneling to shaft walls and add an appropriate finish.

Siding—the outside shell that gives a house its characteristic look—works with the sheathing and building paper or housewrap beneath it to weatherproof exterior walls. Whether siding is made of shingles, laps, or panels, it needs to be maintained carefully to do its job. The chart below spells out upkeep requirements for different kinds of siding.

Cleaning. Most siding benefits from twice-a-year scrubbings. (It is safe to wash asbestos-cement shingles—if they are intact. Crumbling asbestos shingles, however, are hazardous; hire an abatement contractor to seal them or remove them.) For simply getting rid of dirt, use a mixture of 1 cup of nonabrasive household detergent to 1 gallon of warm water. Apply with a brush—a long-handled rotating car-wash brush (p.371) is good. Then rinse with clear water (use a hose with the nozzle set to a medium spray). Natural-finish wood siding such as cedar shingles or redwood laps may need an annual mildew treatment in addition to cleaning. Apply a 1:3 solution of fresh chlorine bleach and warm water with a soft-bristle brush. Wear rubber gloves, a dust mask, and safety goggles. Protect adjacent plants and the ground under them with plastic drop cloths. Do not rinse (more water encourages fungi).

Stain removal. Some discolorations take special attention. Red tannin, for example, streaks natural wood, and unputtied nails will rust. To remove these stains, mix 1 pound oxalic acid with hot water in a gallon glass container to make a paste. Apply it to the stains with an old brush. Let the paste dry; then remove the residue by dry-brushing. Repeat the process if necessary.

▶ **CAUTION:** Oxalic acid is toxic. Use goggles, a spray-paint respirator, and rubber gloves when handling it, and wear long sleeves and long pants.

Countersink any exposed or rusty nails and fill the depressions with wood putty to prevent the stains from recurring.

Types		Cost	Ease of installation	Life span	Fire resistance	Maintenance and finish
Wood shingles and shakes		Moderately expensive	Moderately difficult	30 yr. or more	Poor	Treat with preservative in humid climates. Wash as needed; scrub with bleach solution to control any mildew. Stain or apply sealant every 5 yr. (optional). Replace missing or damaged shingles or shakes.
Wood lap boards		Expensive	Moderately difficult	30 yr. or more	Poor	Wash as needed. Paint, stain, or apply clear sealant (optional). Repaint every 7 yr. Restain or reseal every 3 to 5 yr. Repair or replace damaged boards (p.410).
Board and batten		Moderately expensive	Easy	30 yr. or more	Poor	Wash as needed. Paint, stain, or apply clear sealant (optional). Repaint every 7 yr. Restain or reseal every 3 to 5 yr. Repair or replace damaged boards.
Hardboard and plywood panels		Inexpensive to moderately expensive	Easy	20 yr. or more	Poor	Wash as needed. Paint unfinished panels every 7 yr. or stain every 3 to 5 yr. Repair or replace damaged panels.
Aluminum		Moderately expensive	Easy to moderately difficult	40 yr. or more	Good	Wash as needed. Repair dents and repaint. Replace or patch damaged areas. After 15 yr., chalking may occur. Remove it by scrubbing with detergent and water and then rinsing. Coat with clear metal sealer, or repaint.
Vinyl		Inexpensive	Easy to moderately difficult	40 yr. or more	Good (it won't burn, but may melt near intense heat)	Wash as needed; rinse with clear water. Replace damaged areas (p.408).
Mineral-fiber shingles		Inexpensive	Moderately difficult	40 yr. or more	Good	Wash as needed; to remove chalking in later years, scrub with detergent and water and rinse with clear water. Replace missing or damaged shingles.

Replacing shingles and shakes

Single course

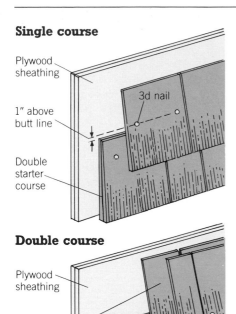

Plywood sheathing

1" above butt line

3d nail

Double starter course

Double course

Plywood sheathing

Under-course shingles

5d nail

Outer-course shingles

Wood shingles and shakes are usually made of red or white cedar. Shingles, which are sawn, appear smooth and uniform; shakes, made by splitting wood, are thicker and coarser in texture. Shingles come in standard lengths of 16, 18, and 24 inches and measure about ¼ inch at the butt, or thick, end. Shakes are either 18 or 24 inches long and range from ½ to ¾ inch at the butt. Both are available in four grades: grade 1 is best for roofs and siding. The lesser grades can be used for the underlayer in double-course shingling (left).

Installation. Shingles and shakes are installed in single or double overlapping rows (courses). Single-course installation exposes no more than half the length of each piece. In double coursing an inner layer of shingles covers the wall, so more of the outer shingles can be exposed.

Shingles and shakes are usually set side by side with a ¼- to ⅛-inch gap between to allow for swelling. In single-course application they are fastened with 3d rust-resistant shingle nails about ½ inch from each edge and 1 inch above the butt line that will be formed by the shingles above. Double-course shingles and shakes are fastened with long 5d or 6d galvanized nails, which are left exposed. Driven 2 inches above the butt line, the nails penetrate the upper portion of the course below.

1. Remove the damaged shingle or shake by splitting it in several places along the grain with a wood chisel and mallet. Pull out all the pieces.

2. To remove old nails under course above, slip a hacksaw blade under shingle and cut off nailhead. Pull out exposed nails with claw hammer.

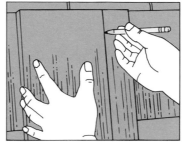

3. Measure and cut replacement shingle to align with rest of course. Use a saw, or score several times with a utility knife and break.

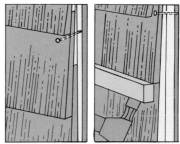

4. To hide nails under upper course, align new shingle ½ in. below its course. Angle nails as shown. They straighten as you tap shingle into place.

Mineral-fiber shingles

Made of portland cement reinforced these days with fiberglass, this sturdy, almost slatelike type of shingle used to be made with asbestos. Unfortunately, you can't tell what fiber a shingle contains just by looking. The presence of asbestos, however, becomes a problem only if the shingles are cracking or crumbling or if you need to remove them. Then you must have a sample tested in a lab; if the shingles are found to contain asbestos, you should call in an asbestos abatement contractor (p.348). Even working with fiberglass shingles requires some safety measures: wear safety goggles, gloves, and a spray-paint respirator.

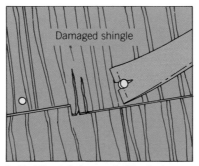

Damaged shingle

1. To take out damaged shingle, loosen nailheads, which are exposed, with pry bar and lift out nails. Free of nails, the old shingle should slip right out.

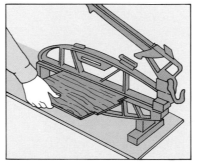

2. Cut new shingles to size with a rented shingle breaker if you have more than a few to do. It's faster and causes less dust than repeated scoring and breaking.

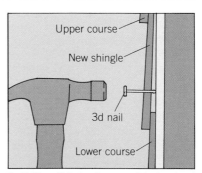

Upper course

New shingle

3d nail

Lower course

3. Drill nail holes in new shingle about 2 in. from butt. Install shingle by sliding it beneath course above and over course below. Fasten with galvanized 3d nails.

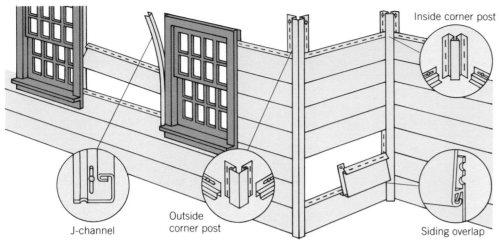
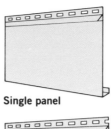
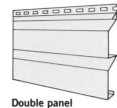
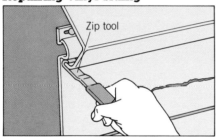
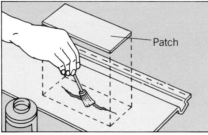
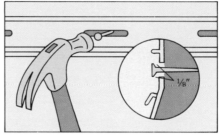
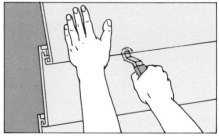

Inside corner post

Single panel

Double panel

J-channel

Outside corner post

Siding overlap

Vinyl and aluminum siding have much in common: both are durable, easy to install, and nearly maintenance-free. Both are also resistant to insects, moisture, and fire. Aluminum siding comes in more colors—especially darker ones—than vinyl. In fact, vinyl colors tend to fade within a few years, and — unlike aluminum—vinyl cannot be repainted. Hot sun may make vinyl sag somewhat; cold weather makes it brittle and subject to breaking or cracking on impact. Abrupt changes in temperature cause aluminum siding to expand or contract noisily if it doesn't have an insulating backing. Aluminum siding also scratches and dents easily. Because aluminum is a conductor of electricity, aluminum siding should, as some building codes require,

Repairing vinyl siding

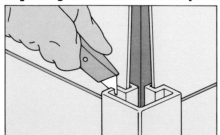
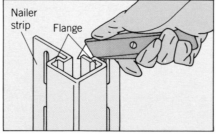

Zip tool

Patch

⅛"

1. To remove a section, insert zip tool beneath bottom edge of overlapping section. Pull down, sliding tool horizontally. Remove nails with pry bar.

2. Prepare rear side of cracked area with PVC cleaner. Glue scrap siding, finished side down, to prepared surface with PVC cement.

3. To refasten siding, drive nails horizontally in center of prepunched nailing slots. Leave a ⅛-in. gap between nailhead and vinyl (inset).

4. To relock overlapping siding, pull its bottom edge downward with zip tool; with hand, press edge over ridge on upper edge of siding below.

Repairing an aluminum or vinyl corner section

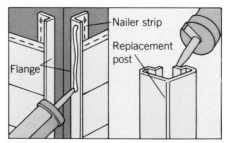

Nailer strip   Flange

Nailer strip

Replacement post

Flange

Flange

Blind rivet

1. Remove damaged corner post by first scoring its sides with a sharp utility knife. To free post from flanges, bend it back and forth with pliers.

2. Remove nailer strips from replacement post, using scoring and bending technique described in step 1. Leave flanges attached to post.

3. Apply caulking compound to flanges of nailing strips still fastened to the house and to flanges on replacement post.

4. Attach replacement post by installing blind rivets through both pairs of flanges. Use a long-nosed riveter as shown on page 133.

be grounded (p.269) for lightning protection.

Replacing siding. If your house has wood or mineral-fiber siding in reasonably good condition, you can simply install new aluminum or vinyl siding over it. If the old siding is in bad shape, you have two choices. You can strip it (a tedious job that presents an often expensive disposal problem) and attach new siding to the wall sheathing beneath, or you can install furring strips over the old siding to hold new siding. If stripping reveals rigid foam sheathing, you'll need furring strips anyway. An air space between rigid foam sheathing and siding prevents a buildup of heat in summer that could buckle vinyl or aluminum siding.

▶ **CAUTION:** If you must remove asbestos siding,

hire a qualified contractor (p.348). It is safe, however, to simply cover it with new siding.

To put up furring strips, nail 1 x 3's horizontally at the top and bottom of each wall; bridge these with vertical furring strips over each stud (p.283); nail additional strips around all door and window frames.

The installation process for vinyl and aluminum siding is similar. The ends of horizontal sections are enclosed in J-channels or corner posts fastened to the walls. The siding is fastened section by section directly to wall sheathing or to furring strips with large-head aluminum siding nails. The top and bottom edges of each section overlap and interlock.

Repairs. A damaged section of vinyl siding can be removed, repaired, and replaced without mar-

ring other sections. Pry the damaged panel from the wall with a zip tool (bought from a siding supplier, who should show you how to use it), patch the crack or hole, and reinstall the section (facing page). For large problems, remove the damaged siding and replace it with a new section.

Because aluminum siding is difficult to remove without denting or creasing, damaged areas are usually cut out and the hole is covered with a new section of siding (below).

When fitting replacement siding sections—vinyl or aluminum—against a corner post or J-channel, allow a gap of ¼ inch (or ⅛ inch on a hot day) between the ends of sections and the post or channel so the siding can expand in high temperatures.

Dents in aluminum siding

1. To repair a large dent, begin by drilling one or more ⅛-in. holes in or along the deepest part of the depression. (For small dents, start at step 3.)

2. Install sheet-metal screws with flat washers into holes. Then use pliers to pull on the screws, raising the dented metal. Save a paint chip.

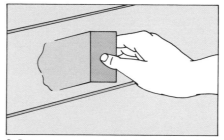

3. Remove screws and apply two-part auto-body filler to remaining depressions. Before it hardens, level filler with the surrounding surface.

4. Sand hardened filler and apply metal primer. Finish with two coats of aluminum siding paint (matched to the color of the saved paint chip).

Replacing a section of aluminum siding

1. Remove damaged area by cutting it out with metal snips (p.128). Leave upper portion of old siding (where it is attached) intact.

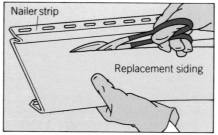

2. Cut replacement piece of siding, allowing for a 3-in. overlap at each end of hole. Trim away the nailer strip along patch's upper edge.

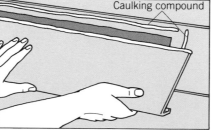

3. Apply caulking compound around the cutout edges. Fit the patch in place, with its trimmed edge beneath the old siding.

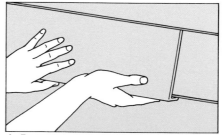

4. Fasten top of replacement section to upper portion of old siding with roofing cement. Lock bottom edge into section below it.

Exteriors/Repairing wood lap siding

Finding a stud 191
Termite control 345
Painting exteriors 368–373

Overlapped wood siding ranges from traditional clapboard (3 to 4 inches wide) to modern 12-inch boards. Lap siding can be cut straight (top and bottom edges are the same width) or beveled (thicker at the butt end than at the upper edge). If beveled siding is made by slicing a milled board lengthwise on a diagonal, it will have a smooth side (usually painted when it is exposed) and a rough side (usually stained when it faces out).

Wood lap siding has a long life if it is properly maintained (p.406). Flatten warped boards, for example, with rust-resistant screws long enough to reach into the sheathing or studs beneath. Scrape out areas of dry rot and coat them with a dry-rot inhibitor; then fill with wood putty (tinted for stained boards). Promptly repair small cracks and holes (p.359). Mend split boards (below left), but replace badly damaged ones (below).

Repairing a split

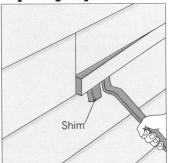

1. Remove any nails holding siding board in place near the split. Pry out bottom section of damaged board with a pry bar to expose edge of split. Insert a shim (wedge) to hold the split section out.

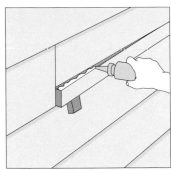

2. Apply waterproof glue as far along the exposed edge of the split as you can. When the glue becomes tacky, remove the wedge and push the section back into place. Use a wet cloth to wipe up any excess glue.

3. Nail both upper and lower sections into place through sheathing (or at nearest stud if there is no sheathing beneath) to reinforce the glue. Drive rust-resistant nails flush on a stained board; countersink nails and fill holes with wood putty on a painted board. Sand and repaint.

Replacing a damaged section of lap siding

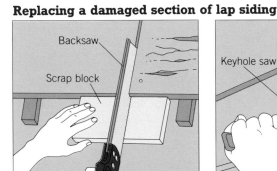

1. To remove bad piece, plan to make cuts at centers of studs on either side of damage. Drive shims under board to hold it out. Set scrap block flush against butt edge where you start cutting with backsaw.

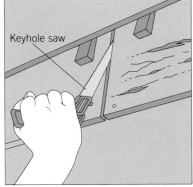

2. Finish cut with a keyhole saw held as shown. To get access to covered part of damaged board, move shims; wedge them under course above. Repeat these two steps to make the second cut.

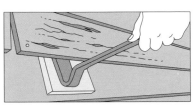

3. To remove exposed nails, put scrap block under pry bar and lift piece under nail (top). Put pry-bar blade next to nailhead and hammer it to pop up nail. Remove nail, then damaged piece.

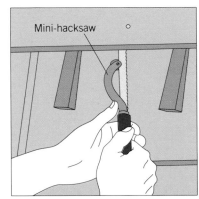

4. To remove recessed nails, wedge shims under damaged board to gain access to nail shafts. Slip a mini-hacksaw under board and cut nails flush with board beneath. Remove damaged piece.

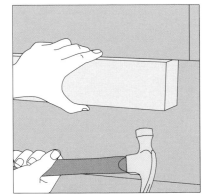

5. Cut a replacement board to fit. Coat sawn edges with wood preservative. Tap into place with hammer and scrap block. Nail down the boards on either side of each seam (four nails). Caulk seams.

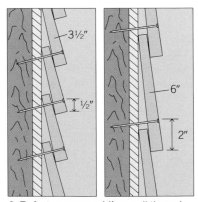

6. To fasten narrow siding, nail through two courses (left), penetrating the bottom of the upper board and the top of the lower one. Nail wide laps, which expand more, through only one course (right).

Caulking

Exterior wood stains and preservatives

Any exposed wood—shingles, shakes, siding, or decks—must be protected from the sun's ultraviolet rays (which attack wood cell molecules and turn them gray), from water (which causes the wood to swell), and from insect and fungal damage (which can destroy wood). Paint is one option. Stains, preservatives, and water repellents are other choices for new or previously stained wood. (Painted wood must be stripped first.) Even pressure-treated wood needs protection from UV rays and water. Most stains and preservatives can be applied with a brush, a roller, a pad, or a spray gun. Read the label. Expect to reapply every 2 to 5 years. Surface preparation is minimal, but two coats are usually called for.

Semitransparent penetrating stains contain enough pigment to block UV rays but still allow the wood grain to show through. They also contain wood preservatives or water repellents or both. Because they penetrate the wood rather than forming a surface film, these stains don't peel. They suit rough-cut wood.

Opaque stains, like paint, block UV rays but cover the natural wood grain and color. Most effective on smooth wood surfaces, they form a surface film that may later peel.

Water-repellent preservatives combine a water repellent (wax or silicone), a fungicide, and often an insecticide in a clear base.

Bleaching oils, designed to speed up the natural graying of wood, contain a gray pigment to block UV rays. When the wood attains the desired color, you must apply a water-repellent preservative to protect it.

Restoratives contain caustics such as oxalic acid or sodium hydroxide that bleach out the gray in weathered wood and bring the wood back to its original color. Wear protective clothing and goggles when applying them.

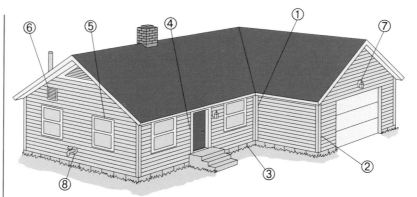

Where to caulk

1. Along seams at inside corner moldings. **2.** Along seams at outside corner moldings. **3.** Along joints where siding meets foundation. **4.** Along joints between door frame and siding. **5.** Along joints between window frames and siding. **6.** Around vents from dryer, bathroom, and kitchen. **7.** Around through-wall holes made for outdoor electrical outlets or lights. **8.** Around through-wall plumbing pipes (gas and water, for example).

Caulking compound seals the seams of a house's exterior shell to keep out water, cold or hot air, and pests. Don't buy cheap caulk for outdoor use. Pay a little more for a 1-part polyurethane mixture (available at hardware or building supply stores). When properly applied, it will maintain its flexibility and adhesion for as long as 40 years. Various silicone caulks (check the labels) are particularly good on glass; they make an excellent glazing compound. Wear gloves and goggles when you work with these materials. Use mineral spirits for cleanup.

Neat caulking (below) takes a little practice. When recaulking, you must prepare the surfaces carefully or the new caulk will not adhere well. Remove old caulk with a putty knife, scrape or wire-brush both sides of the seam thoroughly, and wipe the surfaces clean with mineral spirits. If the seams are wider than ½ inch, fill them first with backer rod, a foam caulking rope you can buy at building supply stores, and then caulk.

How to apply caulking compound

1. Place tube in caulking gun as shown; pull trigger several times to tighten plunger against tube. For good caulk adhesion, the day (and seam) must be dry and above 45° F.

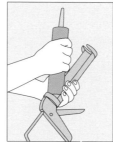

2. Cut end of nozzle at 45° angle. A ⅜-in. opening is right for most jobs. Caulk should seal on two sides only (inset), not at back too. Insert nail in nozzle to pierce inner seal.

3. Place nozzle against seam. Slant gun 45° in direction it will travel. Squeeze trigger gently for even flow. To finish, push nozzle into caulk, then twist it sharply and remove it.

Finishing touches

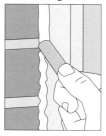

4. To ensure a neat finish and firm contact on either side of a seam, smooth fresh caulk with a frozen-ice stick. Caulking should have a slightly concave shape.

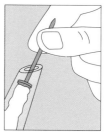

5. To reseal tube, insert nailhead into nozzle, pointed end out. Clean up promptly, following manufacturer's instructions. The unused compound can be saved if kept from freezing.

411

Stucco is a siding material made of portland cement, sand, lime, and water. It is applied in three coats over metal or wood lath; in two over concrete or masonry. The total thickness should be about 1 inch. Apply stucco on an overcast day when the temperature is between 50°F and 85°F.

Buy stucco premixed or mix your own: In a wheelbarrow, blend 1 part masonry cement with 3½ parts sand; gradually add water as you chop and stir with a trowel. The mixture must hold its shape; it should neither crumble nor slump. For the final coat, mix 2½ parts masonry cement and 3½ parts sand. Mix with water until its consistency is that of soft butter. To match the color of the existing stucco, use colored cement in the final coat or add pigment to white cement.

Filling cracks. Open a crack to sound stucco, undercut its edges, and wet it (p. 159). Fill narrow cracks with caulk or premixed stucco repair compound; pack wide cracks with regular stucco. Coat the patch with latex house paint. Before repairing large cracks, have a contractor inspect them and correct any structural problems.

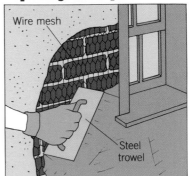

Repairing adobe plaster

Buy fine adobe soil at an adobe yard (they're listed in Yellow Pages in parts of the Southwest). Mix 1 gal. of water-soluble asphalt emulsion with 30 shovelfuls of adobe soil and enough water to make a smooth, stiff mixture. Prepare damaged area as for stucco, but nail wire mesh directly to adobe surface (omit building paper). Apply plaster in three coats like stucco, using same tools. As soon as one layer feels dry, moisten it, then trowel on next coat. Total thickness should be about 1 in. or equal to that of existing plaster.

Large patches 1. Wear safety goggles. Chisel off bad stucco down to base. Cut out damaged lath. Staple asphalt building paper over patch. Nail self-furring wire mesh lath over paper with 1¼-in. roofing nails.

2. Spray patch with mister. With a steel trowel, press stucco into lath to within ¼ in. of surface. If base is concrete or masonry, wire-brush exposed surface and omit first coat (skip to step 4).

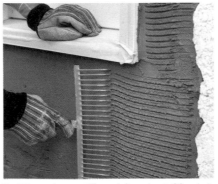

3. When stucco stiffens (after about 30 min.), scratch surface with a rake or a comblike tool called a scarifier (shown) to depth of ⅛ in. Let scratch coat harden overnight. Spray every 4 to 6 hr.

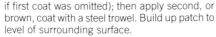

4. Spray hardened scratch coat (or base material if first coat was omitted); then apply second, or brown, coat with a steel trowel. Build up patch to level of surrounding surface.

5. Before it hardens, level new stucco to old with a wooden straightedge; work board upward over patch with sawing motion (left). Smooth and compact patch with sponge trowel (right) or wood float.

6. Cure stucco for 48 hr.; dampen twice a day. Let patch dry for 5 days. Dampen again before applying final coat, ⅛ in. thick, with large brush. (If final coat is colored, match color of old stucco when it's wet.)

7. If desired, texture final coat within 30 min. For a spattered effect, flick stucco from a brush (left); practice on scrap wood. Lightly run a steel trowel over patch to flatten peaks and blend edges (right).

Before building a fence, there are several details to consider. The type of fence you choose will depend on its function. If you want to define the boundary lines of your property, a picket fence may suit your needs, but if the goal is to keep children or a dog in the yard, a chain link fence may be a better choice. A tall closed fence allows total privacy; a tall partly open fence will screen the wind. Both provide some shade for part of the day.

Aesthetics should play a part in your selection. Consider what style of fence will suit your house and the surrounding community, and think about what your neighbors' view will be.

Price will be a factor of course, but if you get along well with your neighbor, he may agree to share the cost of installing a fence and help with its maintenance. Make sure you write down the terms of your agreement. In some states the agreement can be passed on to future property owners.

Property lines. If your neighbor doesn't want to help install a fence, you still have a legal right to put one up on your own property. Check with the local building department; codes may limit fence height or fix a distance that it must be set back from the property line. A survey, attached to your deed, will help determine the boundary lines to your property. (If you can't find your deed, get a copy from the county clerk's office.) If you're still not sure of the property line's exact location, set the fence well within the estimated boundary, or have the boundary staked by a surveyor.

Obstructions. Check with utility companies to make sure there are no electric, gas, or water lines below ground where you plan to dig any fence-post holes. If there are, reposition the post locations. You may also have to build your fence around a tree, leaving room for the tree to grow, or over large rocks. Adjust the bottom of the fence above the rocks, keeping the top rail level.

Fencing around an obstruction

If a tree blocks a fence line within your property, build the fence around the tree; make sure not to damage tree roots when digging holes for the posts.

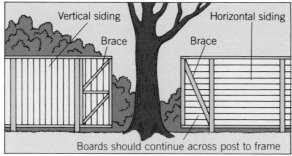

If a tree is on fence line between your property and a neighbor's, leave gap so tree can grow. Attach a framed section no more than 4 ft. wide to post with lag bolts. Brace as shown.

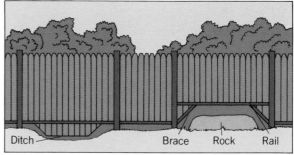

If a large rock blocks fence line, raise bottom rail over it; shorten siding. Add a brace on each side of rock. If a ditch is in fence line, extend siding below rail, leaving space for drainage.

Plotting a fence on a slope

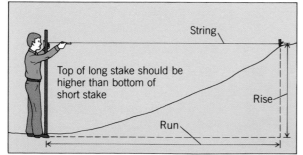

To find rise and run of a slope, drive a short stake at top of slope and long stake at its bottom. Tie a string to the stakes, attach a line level, and adjust string until it's level.

Use rise and run measurements to determine on paper if you prefer to follow slope by keeping rails parallel to it—suitable for post-and-rail fences—or if you prefer a stepped fence (right).

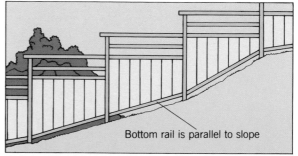

A stepped fence is adjusted to slope. If the slope is uneven, post heights and intervals between posts may differ. Fence panels are cut to fit the slope.

Exteriors/Setting fence posts

Measuring and marking 46–47
Mixing concrete 150
Plotting a fence 413

Posts for mailboxes, bird feeders, and basketball backboards are set in the same way as fence posts. Use pressure-treated 4 x 4 or 6 x 6 lumber for end posts and gate posts; line posts can be 4 x 4's if the fence is under 4 feet tall. To prevent decay, protect each post with a cap—available in several styles—unless they will be covered by a top rail that runs over the posts. Treat cut wood with a preservative.

Set posts no more than 8 feet apart. To determine the number of posts for precut siding panels, divide the fence length by 6 or 8 feet, the usual panel sizes. Allow for a gate; decide whether panels will overlap posts. If 6 or 8 feet doesn't divide evenly into the fence length, cut a panel to fit leftover space. For even sections, divide the length equally; cut the siding to size.

Dig postholes with a *posthole digger;* rent one from a lumberyard. For a fence under 6 feet tall in firm well-drained soil, fill holes with gravel or well-tamped soil. In loose soil or for a fence over 6 feet tall, encase posts in 8- to 12-inch-diameter concrete.

1. To locate posts, drive stakes into ground where the end posts will be. Attach a string to both stakes; keep the string above grass, and make sure it's taut. To position line (intermediate) posts, measure distance with steel tape; drive stakes into ground at proper locations.

2. Dig holes for posts, making them slightly wider than post and increasing the width at bottom. Make them deep enough for at least 20 in. of post's length if post is under 6 ft., or 30 in. of post for a fence 6 ft. tall or higher. Add an extra 6 in. to make room for gravel. In clay soil or for concrete, increase hole's width to 2 to 3 times post's diameter.

3. Shovel 5 to 6 in. of gravel into the bottom of each hole. Or place a large flat rock inside each hole, and then add the gravel. Besides providing drainage, this will prevent decay, especially in posts that are set in concrete collars, where it's important to keep their ends out of the concrete.

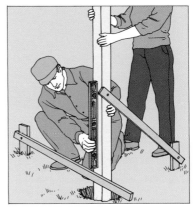

4. To brace end post, drive two stakes into soil at adjacent sides of post. Attach 1 x 2 to each stake with one nail. Set post in hole. Check plumb with level on a face of post; nail brace to post. Plumb adjacent face; nail brace. To check height and plumb of line posts, hang line level on two strings run between end posts at top and bottom.

5. Place 2 to 3 in. of gravel in hole. Shovel 4-in. layers of soil on top; tamp each layer down with 2 x 4. Mold soil, sloping from post down to ground. For concrete, overfill hole; using trowel, slope concrete away from post. Check plumb of post. Let concrete set a week; remove braces. Fill gaps with flexible urethane sealer.

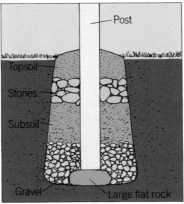

Post
Topsoil
Stones
Subsoil
Gravel
Large flat rock

If frost heaving is a problem and flooding is not, after setting post in bottom layer of gravel, fill hole with subsoil to within 6 in. of top; use a 2 x 4 to tamp it down. Force large stones around post. Fill hole with topsoil; mound it up around post. In sandy soil or in places where water level is high, use concrete instead of soil and rocks.

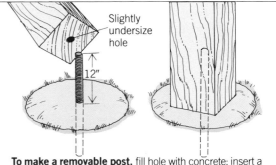

Slightly undersize hole
12"

To make a removable post, fill hole with concrete; insert a 1-in.-diameter bar 1 ft. into concrete before it sets. Drill undersize hole 18 in. deep in base of post; set post on bar.

414

Attaching rails and siding

Finish the fence by adding rails to the posts, and if you like, by adding siding. You can buy these materials precut or prefabricated, or you can cut and make your own. Use pressure-treated wood; follow safety precautions (p.93). Treat fresh cuts and areas that will touch the cuts with a wood preservative. Before assembling the fence, coat the pieces with a water-repellent sealant, stain, or paint.

Lap, butt, rabbet, and mortise-and-tenon joints can be used to attach rails to the posts. Check that they are square, and fasten them securely, using galvanized nails. For a finished look, sink the nails slightly and cover them with wood putty.

A fence supporting heavy siding will need a middle rail. Because boards will eventually shrink and create gaps, you may want to use tongue-and-groove boards or hide the gaps with battens.

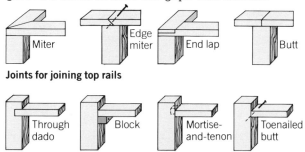

Joints for joining top rails

Miter | Edge miter | End lap | Butt

Joints for joining bottom or middle rails

Through dado | Block | Mortise-and-tenon | Toenailed butt

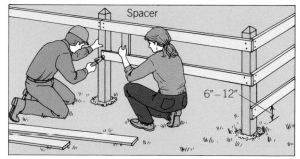

For a post-and-board fence, cut 1 x 4 or 1 x 6 boards to fit between posts—measure from centers of line posts, and add full width of end posts. Attach top row of boards with nails; check with a level. Use spacer to align middle and bottom rows of boards.

Attaching rails for picket fence. For bottom rails, cut 2 x 4's to fit between posts set 6 ft. apart. Toenail (p.81) rails to posts; for extra support attach wood blocks or angle irons. For top rails, trim 2 x 4's to end at centers of posts; nail them to post tops.

For a post-and-rail fence, make through holes in posts and shape rails. After setting end post, place rails in holes. Place line post in hole, and while tilting it, insert other end of rails. Check plumb of line post; tamp down earth. Repeat at next post.

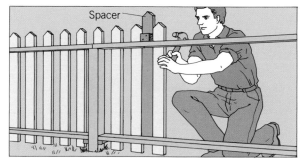

To attach pickets, place first picket along edge of end post with tip 6 in. above rail. Check its plumb; nail it in place. Continue down fence, using one picket as spacer. Attach a block of wood to spacer to hook it over rail. Adjust spacing for fit at end of fence.

Some other fence styles

The vertical-board fence is a simple construction that provides privacy; the harlequin-pattern fence establishes boundaries yet remains friendly to neighbors; and the board-and-board provides wind protection but allows a breeze to pass through. (A solid fence forces wind above it; then wind swoops down a few feet away.)

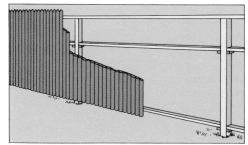

Cedar vertical-board fence; use water-resistant sealer.

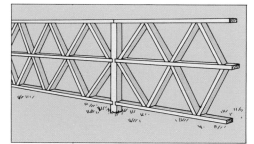

Harlequin-pattern fence using 1 x 2's and 2 x 4's.

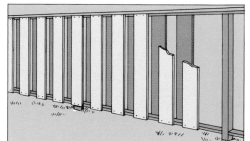

Board-and-board fence: boards on both sides of rails.

415

Nails 80
Bolts and nuts 84
Setting fence posts 414

Exteriors/Fence repairs

Because fences are exposed to the elements of nature, inspect your fence for damage annually in the spring. Check all sections for splits, loose nails, rot (p.344), and termite infestation (p.345). Inspect the posts for decay below and at ground level, along areas where rails are attached to the posts, and at the tops of the posts. If a post has an uncovered flat top, trim it to form an angle to let water

drain off, or add a metal or wood cap or a continuous top rail. Also look for rot where pickets and boards are attached to rails.

If a post has been heaved up by frost, drive it back down into alignment. If it's out of plumb, straighten it and tamp down the earth. If it lacks a concrete collar, you might have to add one (p.414). If the fence is exposed to severe wind, the post

may also have to be secured with guy wires or by driving a 6-foot steel pipe into the ground and strapping the post to it. To reduce wind pressure on a solid fence, remove some of the siding so that it's partially open.

When replacing any part or adding repair pieces, use pressure-treated wood. Remove nails with a nail puller; pry pickets off with a flat pry bar (p.23).

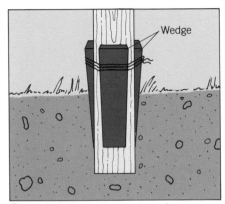

To steady a slightly wobbly decay-free post, drive pressure-treated wood wedges into ground around post; wrap with wire. Or use two-piece metal sleeve; drive it into ground and nail to post.

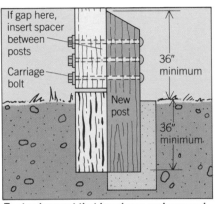

To steady a post that has decay underground, sink a new shorter post next to it in concrete; bolt them together. Saw through old post 2 in. above soil line. Remove decayed wood.

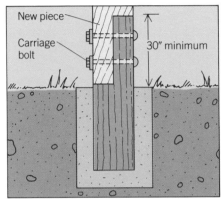

If a 6 x 6 post is rotted above ground, saw top part of post off below damaged area. Make a new section from pressure-treated wood; join it to old post with half-lap joint (p.101) and carriage bolts.

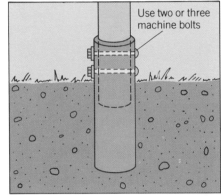

To repair a metal pipe post, cut off damaged section (p.128). Drill aligned holes (p.129) into new piece and anchored post. Insert new pipe into or over old pipe 24 to 30 in.; bolt together.

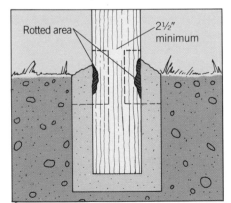

Ground-level rot in post set in concrete. 1. Chisel away decayed wood below soil. (You may have to chisel away concrete too.) Drive three large nails halfway into each side of post.

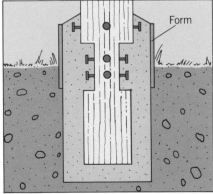

2. Make plywood form to surround old footing; coat its insides with motor oil. Mix concrete (p.150); fill form. Tamp concrete down, then slope it. When concrete has set, remove form.

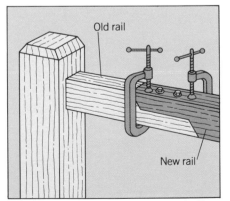

To replace part of a rotted or splintered rail, cut out damaged area. Splice in new piece made from pressure-treated wood. Glue; screw or bolt pieces together. Use C-clamps until glue dries.

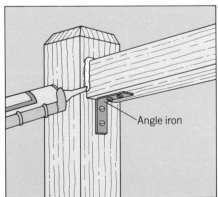

To replace a rail, saw off old one as close to post as possible; cut a new piece to exact length required. Join it to posts with angle irons at each end; caulk with sealing compound.

Gates

Design a gate to complement or contrast with the fence. Because the opening and closing of gates puts stress on the posts, the posts must be firmly set. When measuring space between posts for the size of the gate, allow room for hinges and latches.

A selection of hinges and latches will allow you to choose between a gate that swings both ways and one that swings in one direction, either in or out. Attach hinges to the gate before setting it in place.

Annual maintenance should include checking the gate's frame for squareness and looking for loose or missing screws and loose or rotted joints. For repairs to posts, see facing page.

To set gate post, use 6 x 6 lumber. Dig hole with posthole digger. Shovel 5 to 6 in. of gravel in bottom of hole, or set large flat rock inside hole. Place post in the hole and brace it (p.414). Overfill hole with concrete, and using a trowel, slope concrete away from post. Let concrete set for a week.

Gate repairs

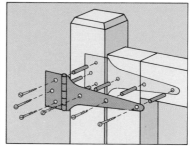

To repair loose hinge, remove any loose screws. Plug the holes with wood dowels, but first dip the dowels in waterproof glue. Drive the screws into the dowels.

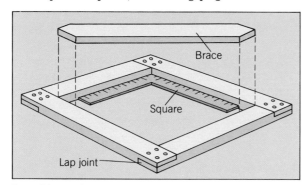

Assemble gate frame face down, driving galvanized nails into lap joints (p.101). Cut brace to butt against rails; run it from bottom hinge corner to upper opposite corner. Make sure frame is square.

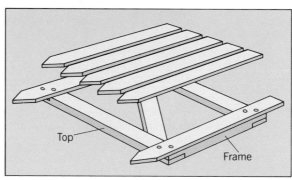

Nail two outer pickets or boards flush with gate frame; make sure they will be level with fence pickets. Space the remaining pickets or boards evenly between them, keeping a level line across top.

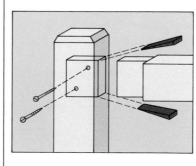

If holes cannot be plugged with wood dowels, try moving the hinges to a new location, or secure the hinges with bolts going through the post.

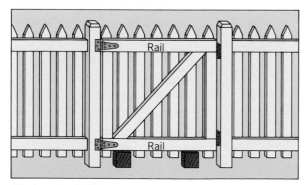

Attach one leaf of hinges to gate rails. Set gate in place; support with wood blocks on sides and at bottom while securing other leaf of hinges to gate post and attaching latch.

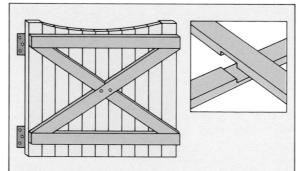

To support a large gate, make a cross brace from 2 x 4 lumber; miter ends to fit frame. Use a half-lap joint (p.101) where the two pieces cross; for support, add glue and screws.

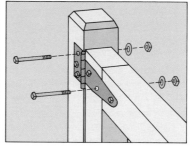

To tighten a mortise-and-tenon joint, dip hardwood wedges into waterproof glue and insert them into the joint; then drive two screws through the joint.

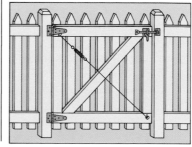

To resquare a sagging gate, brace it with a turnbuckle and wire. Use screw eyes to attach the wire to diagonal corners of gate, the opposite direction of gate's wooden brace.

Exteriors / Installing a chain link fence

Long-lasting and almost maintenance-free, a 300-linear-foot chain link fence can be installed, with a friend's help, in a couple of days: one to set the posts, the other a week later to attach the rails and mesh. Posts, rails, wire mesh, and hardware can be bought from a fence supplier; he might also rent you a posthole digger and a fence stretcher.

Set the posts in concrete no more than 10 feet apart. Dig holes 12 inches wide and 36 inches deep for end (corner and gate) posts. For line posts, dig the holes 8 inches wide and 36 inches deep. Mark the ground line on the post with a crayon before setting it. The end posts should be 2 inches taller than the wire mesh, and line posts should be 2 inches shorter than the wire mesh.

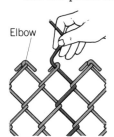

Elbow

To reduce the length of the wire mesh, use pliers to unbend the elbow of one strand at the top and at the bottom of the mesh. Remove the wire by twisting it in a corkscrew motion. To join two pieces of wire mesh, again using pliers and a corkscrew motion, weave a strand (removed from the end of the mesh) between the two sections. (You may have to remove a strand from one section to match the weave of the two pieces.)

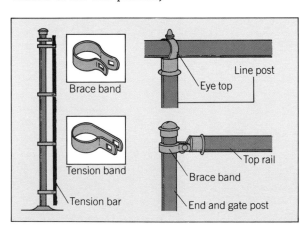

Brace band
Tension band
Tension bar
Line post
Eye top
Top rail
Brace band
End and gate post

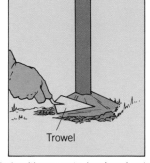

Trowel

1. Dig hole and set post in it. Fill hole with concrete, leaving about 1 in. of concrete above ground. Using a level, check plumb of post. Brace post with guy wires, and slope concrete (p.414).

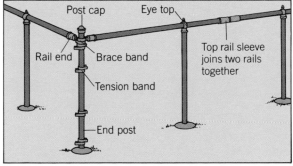

Post cap
Eye top
Rail end
Brace band
Tension band
Top rail sleeve joins two rails together
End post

3. Slide tension bands and brace bands onto end posts; add post caps. Add eye tops to line posts. Slip rail through eye tops; cut to fit with hacksaw; add rail ends. Bolt rail to brace bands.

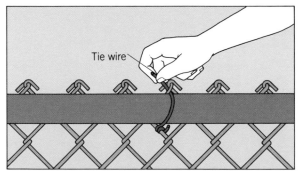

Tie wire

5. Tension of mesh is correct when it is taut but gives slightly if pushed. Remove extra mesh. Insert tension bar; bolt to tension bands. Tie mesh to top rail every 24 in., to line posts every 12 in.

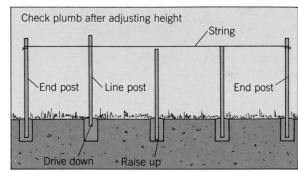

Check plumb after adjusting height
String
End post
Line post
End post
Drive down
Raise up

2. Before concrete sets, check height of line posts. Stretch a string between two end posts 4 in. below top. If line post is below string, raise post; if above string, drive post down. Let concrete set a week.

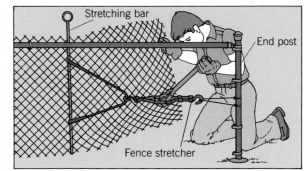

Stretching bar
End post
Fence stretcher

4. Slip tension bar into first row of mesh; bolt bar to tension bands. Wire mesh loosely to rail. Set a stretching bar 3 ft. from other end of mesh. Attach stretcher to bar and end post. Stretch mesh.

6. To set gate, install bottom post hinge with pin pointing up and top post hinge with pin pointing down. Position gate with top aligned with top of fence. Adjust hinges; set gate latch.

418

Contents

Windows and doors
Repairs and improvements

Much is demanded of your home's windows and doors—they must keep heated or cooled air in; admit light and air but not weather; and function effortlessly despite battering by sun, wind, rain, snow, and use.

The repair and maintenance steps in this chapter will help you keep these moving parts working reliably. You will also learn about the various options for improving energy efficiency, increasing security, and reducing maintenance.

Windows/Types and terms

There are two basic types of windows: operable and fixed. An operable window has a sash that slides in channels or turns on hinges. A fixed window can't be opened.

The most common operable style is the *double-hung* window. It has two sashes that slide vertically in parallel tracks. If only one sash moves, it is a single-hung window. In a *gliding* window (p.430), the sashes move horizontally. *Casement* windows (p.428) are side-mounted on hinges.

Other operable windows are *jalousies, awnings,* and *hoppers.* Jalousies are a series of glass louvers governed by pivots. The pivots are linked so that some or all of the louvers open simultaneously. An awning window is top-hinged so that the sash swings out and up; a hopper is bottom-hinged—the sash swings in and down.

Fixed windows can take any shape imaginable: squares and rectangles; circles, half-circles, and ovals; hexagons, triangles, even parallelograms. Use them alone or in combination as picture windows or architectural enhancement.

The parts of a window. The names of the pieces that make up a window are derived from the structure of a double-hung window and are standard no matter what type of window you have. The *framing* is the structural support in the wall. The *jambs, inner* and *blind stops,* and *parting strip* (or parting *bead*) finish the interior of the opening and guide the sashes' movement. The exterior *sill* is tilted so that rain runs off. The inner sill, or *stool,* and the *apron* finish the bottom of the window. The molding that covers the framing is the *trim* or *casing.* When talking to professionals, use these terms rather than the imprecise "window frame."

Regardless of whether it is glass or plastic, the material in the sashes is the *glazing.* The glass is cut into *panes;* small panes are sometimes called *lights.* Windows may be *single-, double-,* or *triple-glazed.* This indicates the number of layers of glazing. Although initially more expensive, multiple layers cost less in the long run because they are more energy-efficient.

The double-hung window

In this style the sashes move up and down in channels created by the strips and stops. The upper sash is on the outside and slides down behind the lower, or inside, sash, which slides up. The sashes are regulated by weights and pulleys (p.422), or a spring balance (p.423), or friction (p.423). Weights and springs are concealed behind the side jambs; friction channels are attached to the jambs.

Whatever the style, a window is a self-contained unit complete with one or more sashes, its framing members, and—if it moves—the channels and mechanisms needed to operate it. The diagrams at right detail the structure of a double-hung window, which fits a framed opening as any other style of window might. In fact, if you take away the trim, nails, and shims that secure the unit, you can pull it out and slide in another of identical size and similar or different style (p.427).

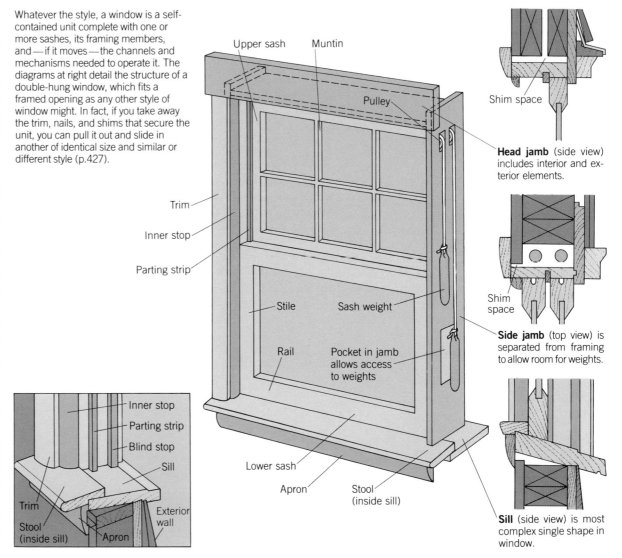

Upper sash — Muntin

Pulley

Trim

Inner stop

Parting strip

Stile — Sash weight

Rail — Pocket in jamb allows access to weights

Lower sash

Apron — Stool (inside sill)

Inner stop
Parting strip
Blind stop
Sill
Trim
Stool (inside sill) — Apron — Exterior wall

Shim space

Head jamb (side view) includes interior and exterior elements.

Shim space

Side jamb (top view) is separated from framing to allow room for weights.

Sill (side view) is most complex single shape in window.

Repairing a double-hung window

Reglazing a wood sash

Whether you use glass or plastic (p.426), replacing a broken pane in a single-glazed window is simple. (For double- or triple-glazed windows, get a new sash from a building supplier or the manufacturer.)

The new pane should be as thick as the original and ⅛ inch smaller than the opening. Instructions for cutting glass are on page 431; for cutting acrylic sheets, on page 143. A glazier, hardware store, or home center will cut a pane to your specifications.

Often a window's muntins are rabbeted to hold the glass. If they're not, apply compound to the interior, but don't add glazier's points.

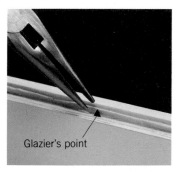

Glazier's point

1. Wearing heavy gloves, remove broken pane. Pull out old glazier's points with needle-nose pliers. (Glazier's points come in two styles: diamond, shown here, or push type, step 4.)

2. Scrape out old compound with a chisel or putty knife. Sand the sash. Paint the raw wood with sealer or primer so that it won't absorb oil from the fresh glazing compound. Measure the opening for the pane, and deduct ⅛ in. from both dimensions. Cut the pane (p.431).

Glazing compound

3. Rub a lump of glazing compound between your palms to make a ⅛-in.-thick rope. Working outside, press this rope around the opening. Set the new pane against the compound, and press firmly, flattening the rope. The excess compound should squeeze out around the glass's edges.

4. Install glazier's points every 4 to 6 in. on the muntins. Be sure the points are snug against the pane. Use an old screwdriver or stiff-bladed putty knife to push them into the wood.

5. Make a slightly thicker rope (about ⅜ in.) of compound. Press this rope over the glazier's points and against the pane.

6. Hold putty knife at an angle and draw it across compound to form a smooth bead. Scrape away any excess that oozed onto the interior pane. When compound has cured (check label for curing time), paint it to match the window, overlapping the glazing about ¹⁄₁₆ in. to seal against moisture.

Freeing a balky sash

The most common causes of a stuck sash are paint-bound edges, accumulated dirt, and warped or swollen wood. Sometimes an excess of weatherstripping holds the sashes shut and must be trimmed. And a broken cord or chain will make a sash uncooperative until repaired (p.422). If the wood has swollen from humidity, wait for drier weather before doing any repairs. Widening the channels or planing the sashes' edges may leave the sashes loose and rattling when the humidity drops.

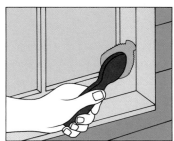

1. Break paint seal by gently driving a paint zipper (shown) or the blade of a stiff putty knife into the long joints between sashes, strips, and stops.

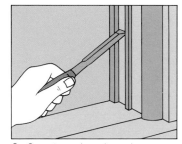

2. Operate each sash, and scrape or chisel off paint globs or hardened dirt from the channels at both sides. Sand and lubricate channels (far right).

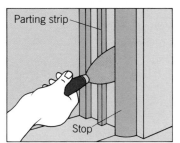

Parting strip

Stop

To widen the channel, remove the stop by carefully prying it off the jamb. Then reinstall it slightly farther away from the parting strip.

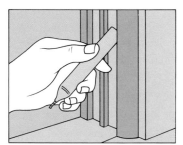

Lubricate channels by rubbing with hard soap, paraffin, or wax; or coat them lightly with petroleum jelly; or mist with silicone. Remove excess.

Each side of each sash in a traditional double-hung window is counter-weighted to balance the sash's movement. A length of cord or flat-link chain is secured to each weight, threaded over a pulley set in the jamb, and attached to the sash. The weights are hidden behind the side jambs. Newer windows may have spring lifts or friction sash channels (facing page).

If a sash won't stay open (or closed), one or both cords may be broken or stuck. Check the pulleys first. If the cord is out of the groove, work it back into place with a screwdriver.

If the cord or chain is broken, you can either replace it or install new friction sash channels (facing page). Cord (for lightweight windows) and chain (for heavier ones) are available at hardware stores and home centers. If you buy chain, get stainless or plated steel, or bronze; these metals resist rust. Cotton cord with a nylon core is almost as long-lasting as chain; size 7 or 8 will fit most pulleys.

Cords stretch and chains wear at the same rate. Replace both cords even if only one breaks. Get two pieces, each about three-quarters the height of the whole window. Adjust the length when you attach them.

Friction sash channels. Made of vinyl or aluminum, these channels are sold in kits. They eliminate the need for sash weights. If you install channels, be sure to fill the weight pocket with insulation.

Spring-lift sashes. Although contained in channels or tubes, the spring's tension can be adjusted if it becomes loose or tight. If one needs replacing, buy an identical model.

Removing sashes

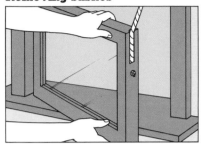

1. Carefully pry off inside stops (p.420), and keep them for reinstallation. Lift lower sash out and rest it on stool. Near the top on each side of the sash there is a slot where the cord or chain is secured.

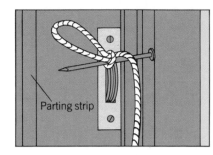

Parting strip

2. Untie cord's knot (or unscrew chain). Ease cord up to pulley. Tie cord around a nail to keep it from falling behind jamb. Repeat on other side. To remove top sash, pry off parting strips; free cords. (Reverse steps to replace sashes.)

Replacing sash cord with chain

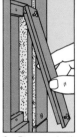

1. Remove both sashes. Open the sash-weight pockets, and take out all four sash weights. Untie (or cut) and discard cords.

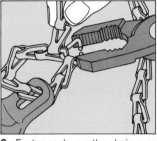

2. For top sash, run the chain over rear pulleys, behind jambs, and out pockets. Attach chains to weights by threading wire through loops.

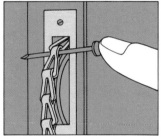

3. Pull on chain, raising the weight close to the pulley. Put nail through chain to hold in place. Set sash on stool and thread chain through slot.

4. Snip off any excess chain; then screw end to sash. Replace sash. Reinstall parting strips. Repeat for lower sash. Replace stops.

Replacing cord in vinyl windows

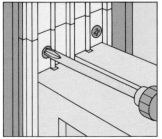

1. Lower top sash completely. Remove screws from upper half of left jamb liner. Raise both sashes. Remove screws from lower half of liner.

2. Carefully pry up the bottom of the jamb liner, and slip it out. Lower bottom sash. Swing out its left side to expose slot where cord is attached.

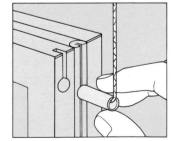

3. Unhook the left sash cord. Ease the cord up to the head jamb. Release the right cord, and remove the sash. Repeat to remove top sash.

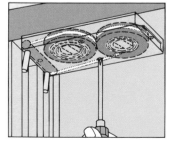

4. Unscrew head jamb liner; take out old balance; put in new. Attach cords to sashes. Restore head jamb, sashes, cords, and left jamb liner.

Installing friction sash channels

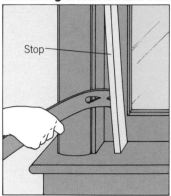 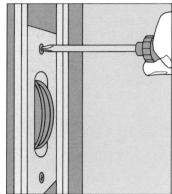   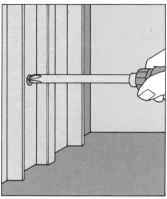

1. Carefully pry off and save the stops. Lift out the lower sash; remove weights and cords through sash pockets (or cut cords and let weights fall inside the jambs). Pry off and discard side parting strips; leave top parting strip in place on head jamb. Free the upper sash the same way.

2. Remove the pulleys. Wearing gloves, goggles, a respirator, and long sleeves, stuff as much fiberglass insulation as you can through the weight pockets. Fill top with loose granular insulation, such as perlite, through pulley holes. If sash guides are metal, pull them out with pliers.

3. Chisel ½ in. off both ends of top parting strip. If new channels are too tall, mark a cutting line along the bottom following the sill's slant, and cut off excess with tin snips (p.128). Squeeze the sides of the new side parting strip, and cut it with a fine-tooth hacksaw.

4. Scrape, sand, and prime the side jambs. Put sashes in channels so that the lower sash will be on the interior. Tape sashes and channels together. Grasp sashes at top and bottom. Feed the bottom of the assembly out the window. Put the top in position inside the jambs; then swing the bottom in.

5. Lubricate sashes with wax or silicone spray, then operate them. If they bind, remove them and plane or trim their edges. (Always prime and paint exposed raw wood.) If sashes are loose, add shims behind the channels. Screw channels to jambs; reattach the stops with finishing nails.

Adjusting spring-lift sashes

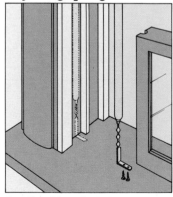 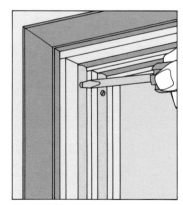 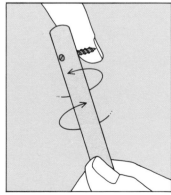 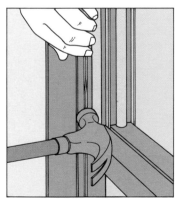 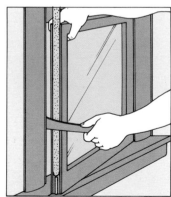

An adjustable spring balance is a spiral rod that's attached to a spring encased in a tube. The tube is screwed to the the top of the side jamb, and the rod is fastened to the sash's bottom.

If sashes don't stay closed or are hard to open, you need to adjust the spring's tension. The screw that holds the tube to the side jamb also governs the spring's tension. Hold the tube in place and loosen the screw until it is free of the jamb. Don't let the screw come out of the tube.

If lower sash creeps up, spring's tension is too tight. To loosen it, grasp screw and carefully unwind spring for two or three turns counterclockwise. If sash is hard to move, tension is too loose. Keeping a finger on the screw, grasp tube and wind it clockwise. Reattach the tube to the jamb.

Broken spring. 1. Remove the inner stops from the side jambs. If stops are wood, pry them off carefully and keep them for reinstallation. If they are aluminum strips, gently bend them away from the sash with finger pressure and light hammering.

2. Remove the tube's top screw. Insert a pry bar between the sash and the jamb; carefully pull the sash free. Remove the spiral rod by unscrewing the bracket holding it to the sash's bottom. Install replacement unit the same way. Refit sash and adjust spring tension.

Shaping sheet metal 136–137
Mildew 344
Lead-base paint 348

Windows/Sill repairs and drip cap

Over the years, both good weather and bad can damage wood sills. Because the sill is horizontal, it is prone to damage from rain, snow, ice, and the sun's ultraviolet rays. Damp-dry and freeze-thaw cycles turn minor flaws in the paint into cracks, which allow fungus to invade the wood.

Warning signs of rot are mildew stains and peeling or checked paint. Tap a suspect sill with a hammer. If it feels spongy or sounds hollow, probe with an ice pick or awl to determine how deep the rot goes. If it is superficial, you can sand or scrape down to sound wood. If the damage is deeper, repair the sill with an exterior-grade epoxy patching compound, or sheathe it with fiberglass or metal.

When rot is widespread, replace the sill. Lumberyards and home centers sell windowsill stock of different thicknesses by the board foot (p.94).

After repairing or replacing a sill, sand, prime, and paint it to ensure its long life. Installing a drip cap keeps water from seeping inside the wall by preventing capillary attraction.

Filling rotted wood

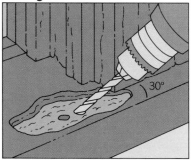

1. Scrape away rot; let sill dry out. (This can take a month; cover sill in bad weather.) When wood is dry, drill a honeycomb pattern of 3/16-in. holes into, but not through, the damaged area. Angling drill makes a more secure base for consolidant.

2. Wearing rubber gloves and using a disposable brush or squeeze bottle, saturate damaged area with epoxy consolidant. Allow to dry. (Follow label directions for drying time.)

3. Mix filler with hardener. Apply it with gloved fingers or putty knife. Overfill slightly to allow for sanding. Filler hardens quickly—don't mix more than you need, and work rapidly. When dry, sand, prime, and paint sill.

Replacing a sill

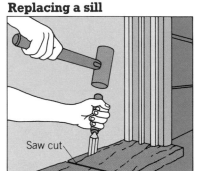

Saw cut

1. Raise the sash; remove the stool and apron. Saw rotted sill in thirds. (Avoid damaging the siding.) Pry out the pieces. If they won't come out, split the sill into smaller pieces with a chisel, keeping the sill as intact as possible. Remove any nails.

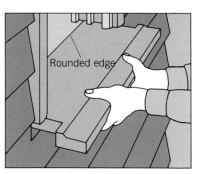

Rounded edge

2. Using the old sill as a guide, cut new sill from stock of the same thickness. Sand the new sill, rounding the edges slightly. (This makes it easier to install.) Seal sill and exposed surfaces with wood preservative. When dry, slide sill into position.

3. Fasten sill to trim with galvanized finishing nails. Sink nailheads, and fill holes with wood putty. Fill gaps wherever sill meets trim with paintable exterior caulk (p.411). Seal, prime, and paint (or varnish) sill. Reinstall apron and stool.

Installing a drip cap

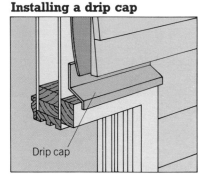

Drip cap

A preformed drip cap can be either aluminum or plastic. Both materials come in white and brown to blend with trim or siding. To install, cut slightly wider than window; pry up or remove siding; slip cap into place; then restore siding. Caulk the cut ends.

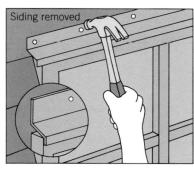

Siding removed

For a better fit.
1. Rebend a preformed aluminum cap, or make one from sheet aluminum (pp.128, 136). Be sure that the cap slopes away from the house. Remove the siding, and fasten cap to wall with galvanized nails.

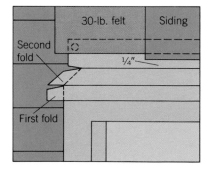

30-lb. felt   Siding

Second fold

First fold

1/4"

2. Clip overhang at each bend with tin snips. Fold edges in so that wind can't blow water under cap. Install housewrap or 30-lb. felt to cover nailheads. Reattach siding, leaving a 1/4-in. gap as shown to prevent water from seeping under the siding.

Installing trim

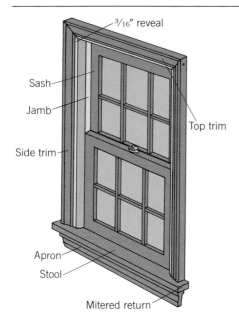

³/₁₆" reveal

Sash

Jamb

Top trim

Side trim

Apron

Stool

Mitered return

Before beginning, check the jamb corners with a square to be sure that they are 90°. If they're not square, you'll have to adjust the miters to fit. Allow the same width *reveal* (a thin strip of the jamb) on all sides, since slight variations will stand out. And until everything fits, drive finishing nails only partway so that they can be removed easily. Finally, after driving and setting the nails, tap in the corner nail to align and tighten the miter.

A stool gives a traditional look and a wider ledge. You can buy stool stock already milled to fit over the sill, although you may have to saw or plane it a little for a close fit. Or you can omit the stool if you prefer a simpler look. Just add a fourth piece of trim beneath the window.

Mitering a return

A *return* hides end grain. It is a short piece of lumber that wraps a corner and heads back (returns) to the wall. To match grain through the corner, cut the apron from the stock's middle (allow at least 6 in. excess at each end). Then cut the returns from the scrap. Edge-miter the apron's ends and the scraps so that they will form a 90° angle when joined.

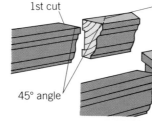

1st cut

2nd cut

3rd cut

45° angle

Brad

1. Glue mitered scraps to their respective apron ends. Secure with masking tape.

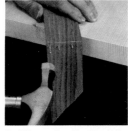

2. When glue is dry, reinforce joints with 1-in. brads. Predrill holes to avoid splits.

3. Remove excess with backsaw. The apron and returns look like a single piece.

1. Measure and cut stool. It should be long enough to extend 1½ in. past the window trim, and notched to seat against the side jambs. Cut from the middle of the stock; keep the scrap to cut returns. Center stool against jambs, and mark notches.

2. Subtract ¹/₁₆ in. from depth of notch. (This provides clearance so that the sash can open and close freely.) Cut out notch with saber saw.

3. Level and fasten stool to windowsill with 6d finishing nails; predrill holes in hardwood. Prop stool from below if necessary to maintain level during nailing.

4. Measure for top trim, adding ⅜ in. for the reveals. Cut side pieces longer by 1 in.; miter corners. Measure side pieces for final cut by reversing ends: rest mitered end on stool; mark length on square end and cut. Predrill corner nail holes.

5. Install the top trim, then the sides. Be sure that the top piece is level. Drive nails partway; check that the miter fits properly; then sink nails.

6. Cut apron so that its corner will align with the exterior edge of the side trim. Add mitered returns to apron (far left). Predrill holes, and nail apron to wall with 6d finishing nails. Support the apron with a block from the floor, and nail down through the stool with 4d nails.

Windows/Upgrading and energy efficiency

The main reason to upgrade windows is to increase their energy efficiency. But upgrading also can free you from the annual ritual of putting up and taking down storms and screens.

Heat loss is greatest where the glazing meets the sash and where the sash meets the jambs. The simplest way to combat this is to caulk the exterior, weatherstrip the interior, have heat-reflecting film applied to the glass, and use insulating window treatments. More permanent solutions are replacing single-glazed sashes with double- or triple-glazed ones, and installing either a *replacement* or a *prehung* window.

A prehung window comes complete with its jambs. Choose this if you want to change the size and shape of the original opening or if you are cutting a new opening. A replacement window consists of sashes and a pair of jamb liners that fit inside the original jambs. Professional installation may be included in the cost of prehung or replacement windows. A simpler (and usually cheaper) alternative is to find a hardware store or home center that will build a double-glazed sash to fit the existing jambs. You may need new friction sash channels in which to mount the new sashes (pp.422–423).

The sash material, the glazing, and the seal between them all affect the window's performance. The best insulation comes from multiple glazing layered with dense gas, low-E film, nonconducting seals, and an insulation-filled fiberglass frame. With the array of combinations available, you can tailor your selections to suit your needs precisely.

Framing material	Good insulator	Poor insulator	Rotproof	Rot-prone	Low maintenance	High maintenance	Heavy	Lightweight	Low cost	High cost	Comments
All wood	•			•		•	•		•		Expands and contracts with humidity changes; subject to water damage and insect attack; needs regular painting.
Vinyl-clad wood	•			•	•		•			•	Wood subject to water and insect damage; vinyl brittle in extreme cold and soft in extreme heat.
Aluminum-clad wood	•		•		•		•			•	Wood subject to water and insect damage; aluminum corrodes in salt air.
All aluminum		•	•		•			•	•		Anodized or baked-on finish outlasts mill finish; dents easily; expands and contracts with temperature changes; corrodes in salt air.
Thermal-break aluminum	•		•		•			•	•		Anodized or baked-on finish outlasts mill finish; dents easily; expands and contracts with temperature changes; corrodes in salt air.
All vinyl	•		•		•		•		•		Becomes brittle in extreme cold; expands and softens in extreme heat.
Fiberglass	•		•		•			•		•	Withstands heat, cold, moisture; can be painted.
Steel		•	•			•	•			•	Must be coated to resist rust; needs regular painting.

Single, double, and triple glazing refers to the number of layers of glass or plastic that are in the sash. Double- and triple-glazed windows have either air or a dense gas mixture between the layers to inhibit heat flow. The gas mixture, usually argon- or krypton-base, is a better insulator.

Low-emissivity glass (often called *low-E*) and film-insulated glass deflect heat, allow light in, and reflect ultraviolet rays that fade fabrics and finishes.

R-value is a measure of a material's resistance to heat flow. The higher the number, the greater the resistance.

Glazing	R-value	Thickness	Comments
Triple-layer glass	3–3.5	1″–1½″	Very heavy. May need extra framing, professional installation.
Film-insulated glass	4–6	¾″–1″	Heavy. Transparent polyester film suspended between layers lets light in; keeps heat out in summer, in during winter.
Double-layer glass with low-E film	2–6	¾″–1″	Heavy, transparent. Metallic coating reflects heat: In cold climates, install with coating on outside layer facing indoors; in hot climates, on inside layer facing outdoors.
Double-layer glass	2	¾″–1″	Heavy; also comes bronze-tinted, reflective. May need professional installation to maintain warranty.
Tempered glass	1	⅛″–¼″	Resistance to impact-shattering is 5 times greater than that of ordinary glass. Must be cut by a glazier.
Single-layer glass	1	⅛″–¼″	Comes clear, tinted, patterned, textured, embedded with wire, reflective. Easy to cut and install (p.430).
Acrylic	1	⅛″–¼″	Lightweight, shatterproof, can be cut with a saw. Weather- and stain-resistant.
Polycarbonate	1	⅛″–¼″	Lightweight, shatter-resistant, can be cut with a saw. Comes white or bronze-tinted; dulls with age; scratches easily.

Installing a prehung window

This job is easier if the new unit is the same size as the old. If it isn't, you'll need to enlarge or reduce the opening, then reframe it. This demands some carpentry skill—and if the exterior wall is brick or stone, the services of a mason. If you do change the size of your windows, get a larger size. It's easier to cut the walls back than to extend them and have to match the exterior and interior wall finishes.

Prehung windows include the sashes, the sill, the head and side jambs, and the exterior trim; some also have a drip cap. They come in an array of stock sizes, styles, and finishes. To order a window, you need three measurements: the *outside dimensions,* the *rough opening* (r.o.), and the *wall's thickness.* Measure carefully. Make a sketch of the opening, and indicate exactly where you measured. Take this with you when you go shopping. Check that the warranty will apply in a do-it-yourself installation.

Installing a window is painstaking but not especially difficult. However, the unit is unwieldy; have someone help you with it. Before beginning, read the installation instructions completely to be sure you have everything you need to finish the job.

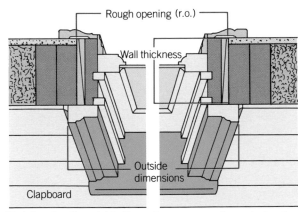

To determine the outside dimensions, measure from edge to edge of the exterior trim. (If the exterior is brick, measure just the size of the opening.) The wall's thickness is the side jamb's width excluding the trim's thickness. The rough opening is defined by the framing. Pry off the interior trim and measure from inside edge to inside edge.

1. Strip off old trim and remove all window components to expose framing. Measure the new window, and adjust the opening as needed. Check that the window is square (see step 3); add or adjust braces. Gently pry up siding and slip housewrap or 30-lb. felt under edges around the perimeter of the opening. Check that the sill plate is level, and add shims if it is not.

2. If window does not have a drip cap, install one (p.424). Lift the window into place. Using 1¾-in. galvanized roofing nails, nail one top corner. Check that the sill is level, add or adjust shims until it is, then drive nails partway into shims. Nail opposite top corner. Don't sink nails completely; you may have to move them as you fit the window.

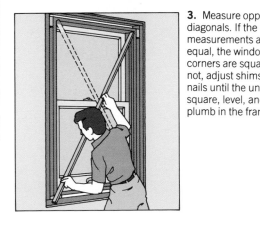

3. Measure opposite diagonals. If the measurements are equal, the window's corners are square. If not, adjust shims and nails until the unit is square, level, and plumb in the framing.

4. Insert paired shims along the sides at the window's bottom, middle, and top. To pair the shims, insert one shim's blunt end into the gap, then slide in the narrow end of the other. Fasten with finishing nails. Check that the window remains square, level, and plumb throughout this procedure. Operate the sashes to be sure they move easily.

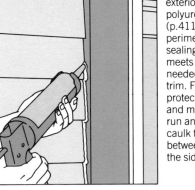

5. Run a bead of exterior-grade polyurethane caulk (p.411) around the perimeter of the window, sealing the gap where it meets the sheathing. If needed, attach exterior trim. For additional protection against air and moisture seepage, run another bead of caulk to seal any gaps between the trim and the siding.

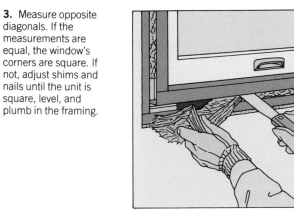

6. From the interior, fill gaps with fiberglass insulation. Don't overfill the gaps or fill with expanding foam: either may distort the frame. Attach interior trim. **CAUTION:** Read and follow manfacturer's instructions exactly when working with insulating materials. Protect yourself by wearing gloves, goggles, a respirator, and long sleeves.

427

Windows/Casements

Whether the sash in a casement window is wood, metal, or a vinyl-clad material, it is attached to the frame with side-mounted hinges and secured by a latch handle. The sash, operated by a crank or slide, swings out. Each element of these windows that slides, rotates, or rubs against another part benefits from annual cleaning and lubrication. Silicone is a good all-purpose lubricant. A penetrating lubricant, light machine oil, automobile grease, or petroleum jelly can be used on metal parts. Paraffin is helpful where wood rubs against wood.

If a sash won't open fully, odds are that the arm or the slot in which it moves is clogged with debris—dirt, rust, grease, or paint. Clean wood with a scraper and sandpaper; wash vinyl with a mild detergent; scrub metal parts with a stiff-bristled brush. Then mist the parts with silicone. If the crank sticks, unscrew it; then clean and lubricate its gears. If an arm is bent, remove it and try straightening it with pliers or judicious blows from a mallet. If it can't be straightened, replace it. Parts are available at home centers, lumberyards, and window supply stores.

To guard against general rattling, tighten all visible hinge and handle screws and bolts. Snug the window with weatherstripping (p.453). If a window fails to latch closed tightly, shim the catch. Unscrew the catch, and use it as a template to cut a shim from cardboard, thin wood, metal, or plastic. Poke or drill holes in the shim to accommodate the screws. Place the shim against the jamb and reinstall the catch.

Hardware

Casement windows are held closed with a latch; two common styles are shown at right. Older casements are operated by means of a sliding rod (below); newer ones, by a crank-driven gear (far right). There are two styles of rod. If either style sticks, tighten any loose screws, clean the passage the rod slides in, and lubricate the rod with silicone.

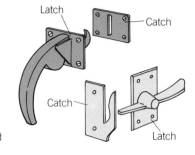

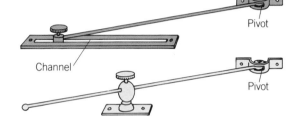

Channel • Pivot • Pivot

Replacing glass

Glass is held in metal sashes by spring clips, and in wood by glazier's points (p.421). To replace a broken pane, remove shards carefully. Pull old clips from compound with pliers. Scrape, sand, and repaint the sash channel. When paint is dry, form glazing compound into a thin rope and lay it in the channel. To form a tight seal, press new pane firmly against compound so that it oozes slightly from between the glass and the channel. Insert clips.

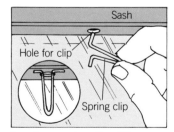

Sash • Hole for clip • Spring clip

Insert new spring clips. Clips come in two styles. One fits into holes in the sash channel (above); the other hooks under a lip (right).

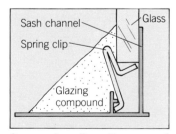

Sash channel • Glass • Spring clip • Glazing compound

Cover spring clips with a rope of glazing compound. Draw a putty knife over the compound on both sides of the pane to form bevel.

Fixing a crank handle

1. To remove gear assembly and hinge arm, open the window partway. Unscrew the bolts that hold the crank mechanism to the frame. (You may also need to loosen a setscrew on the handle.)

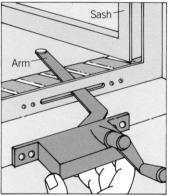

Sash • Arm

2. The arm slides in a track on the bottom of the sash. Holding the sash steady, slide the arm to the left or right until it is free of its track; then pull the mechanism away from the window. In some cases, you may need to unscrew the arm or the gear assembly from hinged fittings.

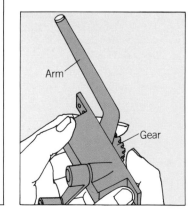

Arm • Gear

3. Inspect the crank handle, arm, and gear assembly for broken or worn parts. Check that the gears mesh properly. Clean the mechanism with kerosene; lubricate it with lightweight machine oil. If the arm is bent and cannot be straightened, or if the gears do not mesh, replace the mechanism.

4. Use a stiff-bristled brush to scrub accumulated dirt, hardened grease, paint, or other debris from track, frame, and under sash. Sand, prime, and paint sash as needed.

Track

5. Thoroughly lubricate track on the bottom of the sash with automobile grease or petroleum jelly. Apply it with gloved fingers; wipe off any excess with clean lint-free rags or paper towels.

6. Reassemble the mechanism and handle, and reattach them to the window. Lubricate the crank handle and hinges with a light coat of silicone, penetrating lubricant, or light machine oil. Open and close the window several times to distribute the lubricant.

Awnings and hoppers

An awning window is essentially a casement with its hinges on the top rather than at the side. It opens by means of a scissors-type linkage called *arms* operated by a crank (or *roto-handle*). Most awning windows may be tilted flat for washing from the inside. Detachable hinges permit removal of the sash for maintenance or repair. Hoppers open from the top and are held closed by a latch.

Hoppers open in. They are hinged at the bottom and pulled open (or pushed closed) at the top. The size of the opening is restricted by the hardware: a hinge, chain, or bar.

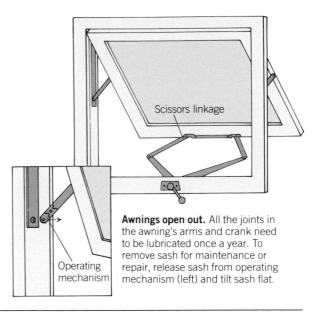

Scissors linkage

Operating mechanism

Awnings open out. All the joints in the awning's arms and crank need to be lubricated once a year. To remove sash for maintenance or repair, release sash from operating mechanism (left) and tilt sash flat.

Jalousies

Because of their poor energy performance, jalousies are rarely the primary windows in a home. However, since these louvered windows allow maximum ventilation, they can be a good choice for an enclosed porch. A screen (or storm window) can be easily installed on the inside.

The windows are opened and closed by a system of pivots and levers driven by a crank handle. If the window becomes difficult to operate, lubricate the moving parts. The operating system has a fixed and an active side. If the system is damaged, you'll need to replace the entire active side.

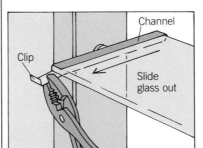

Channel

Clip

Slide glass out

To replace a glass louver: 1. Open the window until the louvers are horizontal. With pliers, gently press back the clips just enough to release the glass.

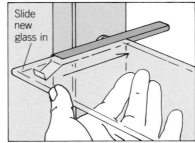

Slide new glass in

2. Slide the new glass into the channels. Bend the ends of the clip holders into their original shape. This holds the glass firmly in place.

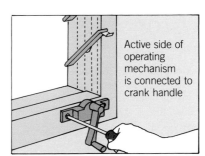

Active side of operating mechanism is connected to crank handle

To replace pivot mechanism, remove all louvers. Unscrew the active side unit from the jamb. Install the new unit. Use a level to align channels with those in the fixed side.

A typical gliding window consists of one stationary sash and one that moves horizontally. In some styles (usually wood windows), the sash rides on an upper track. But in most gliding windows the sash slides in the bottom track and is stabilized by the upper channel. This channel is deeper than the bottom track so that the sash can be removed (far right).

The simplest glide mechanism is a groove in the sash's bottom that fits over a ridge in the track. Older windows often have wooden tracks; newer ones have metal or vinyl tracks, and some also have nylon glides or rollers that the sash rides on.

Whatever its composition or construction, the track is a dust-catcher. Keep it clean with regular vacuuming and an occasional scrubbing. For hardened dirt in a vinyl track, scrub with a toothbrush and household detergent. Use fine steel wool or an abrasive sponge on metal or wood. Keep the track and the upper channel lubricated with silicone.

Aluminum sashes can become spotted with oxidation deposits (similar to rust). These are easily removed by washing with a mild abrasive cleaner or with fine steel wool and detergent. A light coat of automobile paste wax will help prevent oxidation in the future.

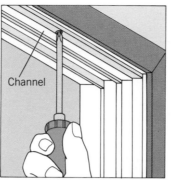

Channel

Removing sashes.
1. Close and lock the movable sash. With a Phillips screwdriver, tighten the screws in the channel over the sash just enough to pull the channel upward. (Other types may simply lift out, as in the next step.)

Channel

Sash

2. Always remove the movable sash first. Unlock the sash and slide it to the center of the window. Grasp its sides, and lift it straight up into the channel. Swing the bottom out toward you; then pull the sash down and out of the channel.

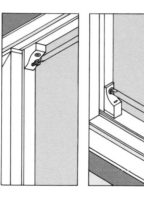

3. To remove fixed sash, unscrew the corner brackets at the top and bottom of the sash. Put the brackets and screws in a safe place.

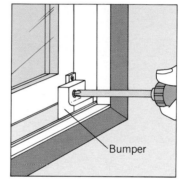

Bumper

4. Unscrew the bumper from the track. Slide the fixed sash to the center of the opening. Lift it into the upper channel; tilt it away from you, toward the outdoors; and remove it. To replace the sashes, reverse the steps.

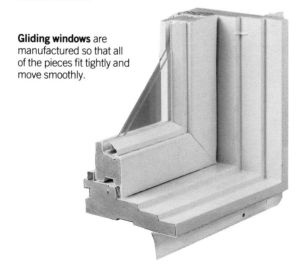

Gliding windows are manufactured so that all of the pieces fit tightly and move smoothly.

Hardware

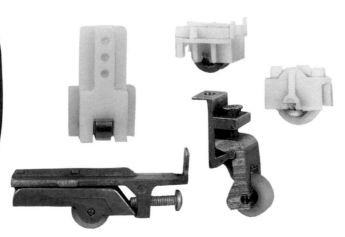

The latch is attached to the upright (or *stile*) of the movable sash. Replace a broken latch rather than trying to repair it.

Rollers are designed to support a particular window and move freely in the track. There are hundreds of styles; some common ones are shown at left. If you need to replace a roller, get one from the window's manufacturer. If you can't, take it to a window supply store and get as close a match as possible.

New pane in a metal sash   Screen repairs

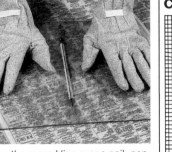

To cut glass, place it on a firm surface well padded with newspaper. With a glass cutter, score a line once alongside a nonskid straightedge.

Place the scored line over a nail, pencil, or thin dowel. Press down firmly. (Or grasp glass on both sides of the line, and sharply snap it apart.)

Gasket and mastic. 1. Remove sash. Pry gasket out of sash; then pull out the glass shards with pliers. Wear gloves when handling glass.

2. With a putty knife, apply mastic to new pane's edges. Press glued edges gently against sash. Reinstall gaskets. Return the sash to the window.

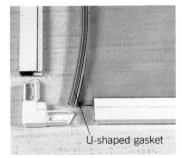

U-shaped gaskets. 1. Remove sash; unscrew the corners to release one side of the sash. Take side piece off, and pull shards out of the gasket.

2. Fit the gasket around the new pane; then slide it into the three-sided sash. Reattach the side piece. Return the sash to the window.

Closing and patching holes

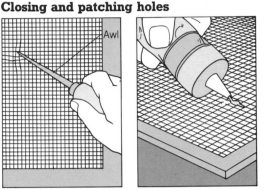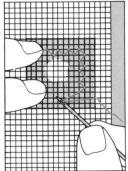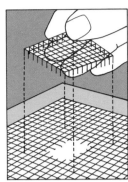

A tiny hole can often be fixed by reshaping mesh with an awl, a toothpick, or a straightened paper clip.

Close a small hole with waterproof glue. Use sparingly. Wipe away drips before the glue hardens.

Repair large hole in plastic or fiberglass by sewing a patch over the hole. Pull "threads" from screening of the same material.

For hole in metal mesh, pull cross threads from patch's edges. Bend wires; push them through mesh around hole. Crimp ends.

Replacing a metal-frame screen

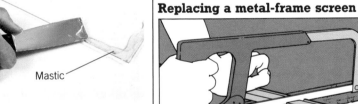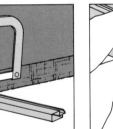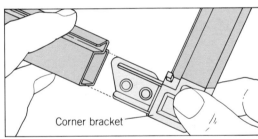

1. With a hacksaw, cut framing pieces to length, leaving ends square. Remember to subtract the length of the two corner brackets (see right) from measurements.

2. To assemble frame, push corner brackets into framing pieces. If sawing pinched the framing pieces closed, pry them open with an old screwdriver.

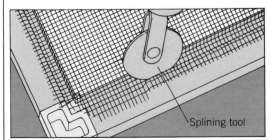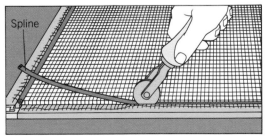

3. Cut screening ½ in. larger than frame all around; trim corners diagonally. Push screening into groove with the convex roller of a splining tool or a stiff-bladed putty knife.

4. Cut spline to length with a utility knife. With concave roller of splining tool, force the spline and screening into groove. Use short, firm strokes. Cut off excess screening.

Windows/Storms and screens

Storm windows come in two basic styles. An *add-on storm* is suspended from hooks and held closed with a gate hook and eye. These are exchanged for screens in warm seasons.

A *combination storm* is screwed to the exterior trim. Its sashes and screen slide in tracks and can be raised or lowered to suit the season. Maintain and repair this kind of window the same way you would a gliding window (p.430).

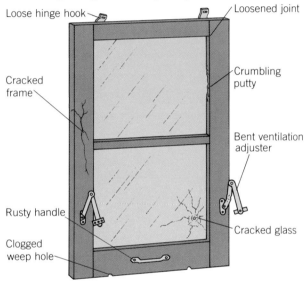

Loose hinge hook — Loosened joint

Cracked frame

Crumbling putty

Bent ventilation adjuster

Rusty handle

Cracked glass

Clogged weep hole

Inspect and repair add-on storms before installing them.

Inside window sweats if storm window leaks cold air. Storm sweats if warm air escapes around inside window's edges. Weatherstrip leaky edges. Weep holes let condensation run out.

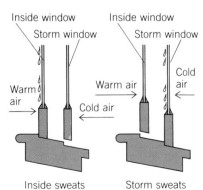

Inside window
Storm window

Warm air
Cold air

Inside sweats

Inside window
Storm window

Warm air
Cold air

Storm sweats

Repairing a wood-frame screen

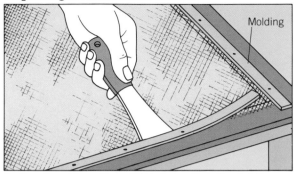

Molding

1. Pry off molding with a stiff-bladed putty knife. Cut the new screening 1 in. larger than the opening in all directions.

3. Staple or tack screening to one end of frame. Draw screening taut; fasten opposite end.

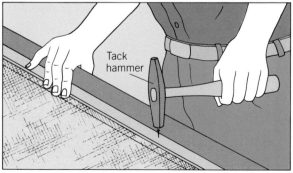

Tack hammer

5. Attach molding with wire brads. (Use old molding if it is sound.) Sink brad heads; fill holes. Prime, and paint as needed.

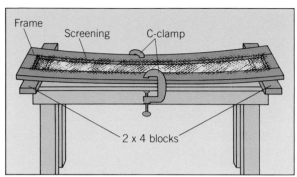

Frame
Screening
C-clamp

2 x 4 blocks

2. Bow the frame by placing 2 x 4 blocks under each end and clamping center to work surface.

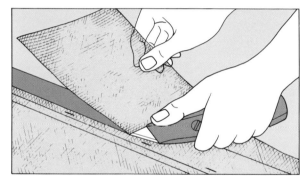

4. Remove clamps. Fasten screening to sides. (If using fiberglass, fold all edges under to form a hem.) Trim excess with utility knife.

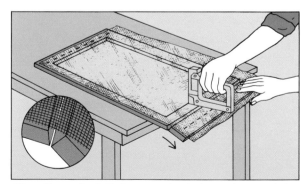

Alternative method. Fasten screening to frame at one end, to a board at other end. Push on board to pull screening taut.

Window locks

To delay—and thus deter—thieves, install locks on your windows. Don't rely on the clamshell (or butterfly) latch often found on double-hung windows. It's not really a lock—its purpose is to draw the sashes together to reduce drafts and rattling.

You can improvise a lock by drilling a hole through the interior sash and partway into the exterior sash, then inserting a bolt, dowel, or large nail into the hole. Use a peg that is slightly narrower than the hole so you can remove it easily when you want to open the window. The ready-made locks shown below are variations on this idea. If possible, get keyed locks from a single manufacturer so that one key will fit them all. To ensure your family's safety, keep a key near each window, hidden from outside view, so that the window can be opened quickly in an emergency.

If the local fire code permits it, additional security can be had by replacing single glazing with polycarbonate or wire-embedded glass. More drastic measures include installing shutters, a grille, or a gate.

Locks for double-hung windows

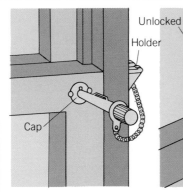
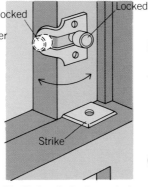

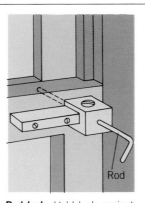
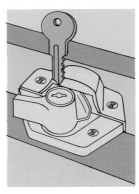
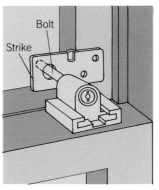

Locking pin. Install one on each side of sash. Drill recommended size hole through top corner of lower sash into bottom of upper sash. Mount cap and pin holder. Pin fits through cap and into hole.

Ventilating lock. Screw lock to the side of top sash 1 in. or more above the meeting rail. Screw strike plate to top rail of lower sash directly below lock. Use one or more on each side to regulate window opening.

Security bolt. Drill bolt hole through top of lower sash, partway into bottom of upper sash. Counterbore (p.83) the hole to accommodate the washer. Insert washer and bolt. Tighten with a nut driver.

Rod lock. Hold lock against top rail of lower sash, and use it as a template to mark the holes. Drill rod's hole through lower sash and partway into top sash, screw holes partway through lower sash.

Key turnbuckle. Remove clamshell latch. Mount new lock with one-way screws. If new screws align with existing screw holes, fill holes with wood putty or wood matchsticks; then redrill.

Key bolt. Retract bolt and mount lock at top corner of lower sash. Throw bolt and align strike. Screw strike to side rail of top sash. For ventilation, mount a second strike 2 or 3 in. higher.

Security for gliding windows

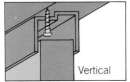

Screw stop. A screw installed vertically in top channel prevents sash from being lifted out (top). A horizontal screw (bottom) keeps sash from sliding.

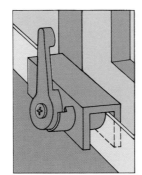

Track stop. Rotate the handle counterclockwise to loosen bolt. Slip the stop over the window track. Turn the handle clockwise to tighten the bolt.

Key track stop. A slot at the lock's back fits over the track. Lock can be used whether window is open or shut. Turn the key to anchor the lock.

Casement lock

One-way screw can't be removed

Key latch. Open the old latch and unscrew it. Fit the new one to the frame and mount it with one-way screws. (When buying lock, you must specify whether it is for the right or left side of the sash.)

Doors/Basic structure

Doors come in three basic types—solid wood, solid-core, or hollow-core—all of which may be bought prehung (hinged in their jambs). The solid core may be wood, steel, or an insulative foam; a "hollow" core is often a cardboard or fiber mesh. Either kind of core can be covered with wood veneer or fiberglass, but a steel skin needs a solid core. Hollow-core doors are lighter and cheaper than the solid-cores, but less durable and less fire resistant. Use them between rooms and for closets or bathrooms.

Entry doors must be solid wood or solid-core. For the best insulation and least maintenance, choose a steel- or fiberglass-covered foam-core door. Steel must be painted—and scratches repainted—to prevent rust.

If you want a wood entry door, look for one that has a laminated core encased in an aluminum-foil moisture barrier. Wood expands and contracts in response to weather changes; the laminated core helps prevent warping. Other wood doors must be refinished (pp.117–123) every few years to prevent warping.

A fire door must have a solid core.

The National Fire Protection Association's Life Safety Code details how many you need and where to place them for the best protection.

Doors come in standard widths, beginning at 2 feet and increasing by 2-inch increments up to 3 feet. Nonstandard sizes can be ordered. For easiest installation, buy a prehung door and have it bored for the lockset.

Parts of a doorway

A door is encased in the *side jambs, head jamb,* and *sill.* The jambs are nailed to the *framing;* then the hinges are installed and the door is hung.

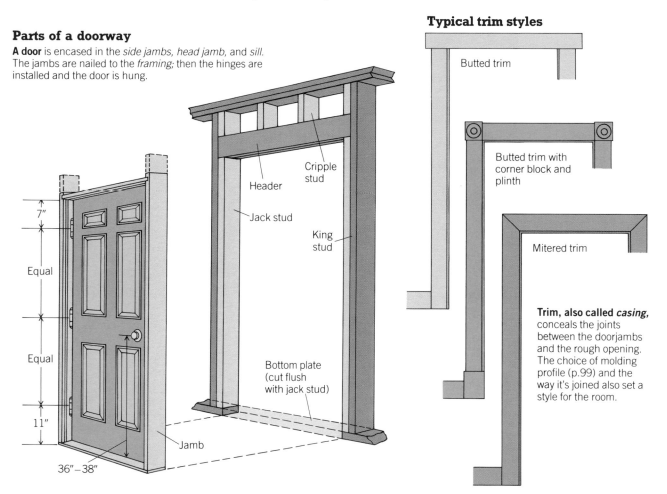

Typical trim styles

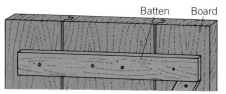

Butted trim

Butted trim with corner block and plinth

Mitered trim

Trim, also called *casing,* conceals the joints between the doorjambs and the rough opening. The choice of molding profile (p.99) and the way it's joined also set a style for the room.

Door types

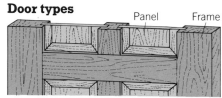

Panel   Frame

Solid wood frame-and-panel doors are sturdy, have a traditional look, and require upkeep.

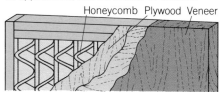

Batten   Board

Solid wood board-and-batten doors have a rustic appearance; can be interior or exterior.

Honeycomb Plywood Veneer

In hollow-core doors, wood veneer is glued to plywood over a cardboard honeycomb.

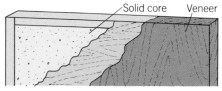

Solid core   Veneer

Solid-core doors consist of veneer over a steel, foam, or particleboard center.

Hinges

Hinges come in an array of sizes, shapes, metals, and finishes. Choose hinges that relate to the door's width, thickness, and composition. They must support the weight, yet swing easily.

Most hinges can be installed in only one orientation and are specified as *right-* or *left-handed.* The hinges' location and handedness determine the door's swing. To find the swing, stand outside the door. If it opens into the room, it has a "normal swing;" if it opens out, it has a "reverse swing." To avoid error when you buy hinges, take along a sketch of the desired result.

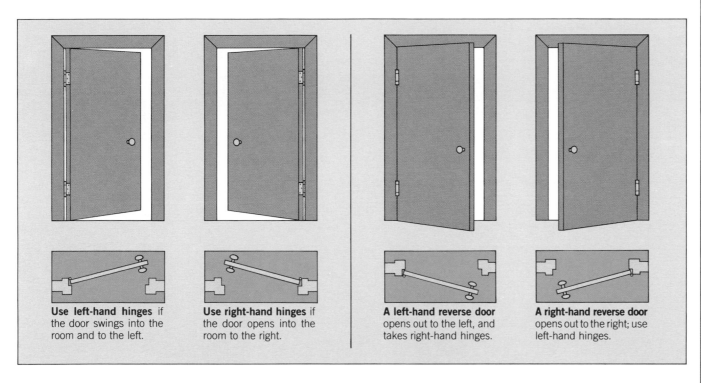

Use left-hand hinges if the door swings into the room and to the left.

Use right-hand hinges if the door opens into the room to the right.

A left-hand reverse door opens out to the left, and takes right-hand hinges.

A right-hand reverse door opens out to the right; use left-hand hinges.

Types of hinges

A hinge is named for its pivoting mechanism. The flat part with the screw holes is the *leaf,* and the size is the length of the edge parallel to the pivot. For a door 32 in. wide and up to 1⅜ in. thick, use 3½-in. hinges. A heavier door needs heftier, or more, hinges.

Butt hinge has a fixed pin; it can be used on right- or left-hand door.

Loose-pin hinge permits removal of door without removal of hinges —just pull out the pin.

Ball-bearing hinge has permanent lubrication. Use on heavy doors.

Slip-joint hinge can be lifted apart without dismantling leaves or pin.

Swing-clear hinge swings door out of doorway, allowing wheelchair access.

Bumpers and holders

Rubber-tipped bumpers prevent doorknobs from marring walls. Holders keep doors ajar or fully open. Some common styles are shown below.

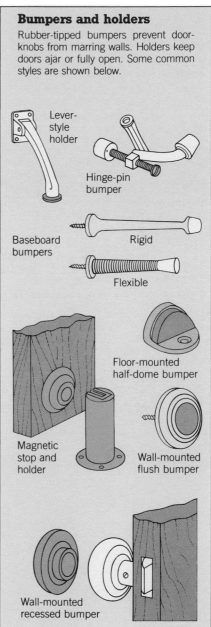

Lever-style holder

Hinge-pin bumper

Baseboard bumpers

Rigid

Flexible

Floor-mounted half-dome bumper

Magnetic stop and holder

Wall-mounted flush bumper

Wall-mounted recessed bumper

Door problems may come from the door itself or from the hinges, latch, or jambs. Hinge-related repairs are the easiest to make, so check them first. Often the screws have worked loose or are turning in their holes without gripping. Latch problems (facing page) usually result when the plate and the bolt are misaligned.

A badly deformed door should be replaced; minor warping may be overcome by adding a third hinge. If the house's settling has pushed the jambs out of square, a wood door can be planed or trimmed to fit the new shape; doors of other materials may need to be replaced. Strip paint from the door's edges if it causes binding.

Troubleshooting doors

Problem	Solution
Door rubs at top or bottom corner	Tighten or shim hinges.
Door springs open	Adjust hinge or hinges.
Door sticks in humid weather	Wood under paint swells, makes door tight. Lightly sand door edges and jambs; if necessary sand down to bare wood, prime, and repaint with one coat of finish. If severe, you may have to strip the paint and plane the door.
Door continually sticks along one or more edges	House may have settled, pulling jamb out of square and plumb, or door may have warped. Remove door; plane as needed.
Door won't clear new carpet or flooring	Saw door bottom.
Latch bolt won't engage strike plate	Shim out strike plate, reposition strike plate on jamb, or adjust doorstop.
Door rattles	Adjust strike plate; add weatherstripping.

Checking hinges

With the door closed, slip a piece of thin cardboard between the jambs and the door—the door is binding wherever the cardboard doesn't move freely. A door that won't shut may need a hinge adjustment to change the angle of the door as it hits the strike plate.

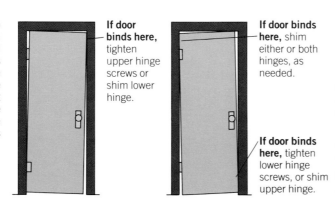

If door binds here, tighten upper hinge screws or shim lower hinge.

If door binds here, tighten lower hinge screws, or shim upper hinge.

If door binds here, shim either or both hinges, as needed.

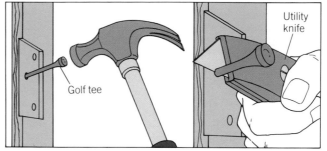

Golf tee

Utility knife

Plug enlarged screw hole with glue-coated wooden golf tee or matchstick, dowel, or toothpicks. When glue is dry, trim plug flush. Drill pilot hole; insert screw. For a slightly enlarged hole, drill pilot hole through jamb; drive 1½-in. screw into stud behind jamb.

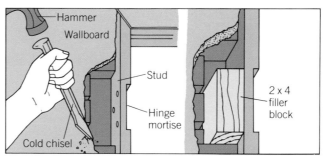

Hammer

Wallboard

Stud

Hinge mortise

Cold chisel

2 x 4 filler block

If above fails, install a block behind the jamb. Pry off molding. Cut out a 10-in.-long section of the wall. Cut block from scrap 2 x 4; then glue it to stud behind hinge mortise. Drill new pilot holes through jamb and into block. Install hinge leaf with 1½-in. screws.

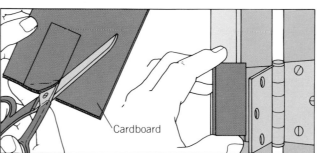

Cardboard

Shim out a hinge that has been mortised too deeply into the jamb. Remove hinge leaf; cut a thin piece of cardboard the same size as the leaf. Reinstall leaf with shim behind it, driving screws tight. Test the door. If mortise is still too deep, add another shim.

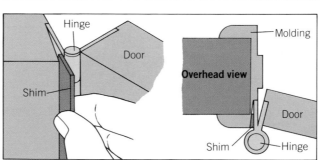

Hinge

Door

Shim

Molding

Overhead view

Door

Shim

Hinge

If the door springs open, the top hinge may be mortised too deeply, the mortise may not be flat and plumb, or the hinges may not align. Shim half width of leaf with cardboard, level the mortise surface, or reset bottom hinge leaf to align with top one.

Removing and planing a door

When removing a door, pull the pin from the bottom hinge first. When re-installing it, seat the top pin first. Because it's easier to reset hinges than to refit locks, always plane the door's hinge side rather than the lock side. Strip paint from the door's edge before planing. Check the door's fit often, so that you don't remove too much wood. Finish the planed edge with a clear wood sealer (pp. 120, 123) to keep the door from absorbing moisture.

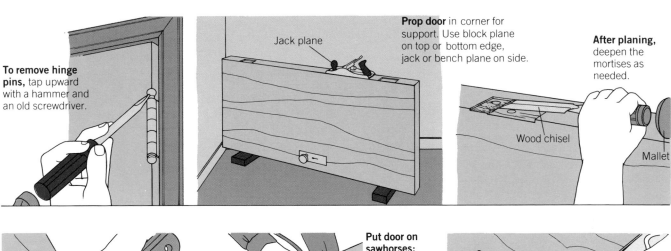

To remove hinge pins, tap upward with a hammer and an old screwdriver.

Jack plane

Prop door in corner for support. Use block plane on top or bottom edge, jack or bench plane on side.

After planing, deepen the mortises as needed.

Wood chisel

Mallet

Sawing a door bottom

The most common reason to trim a door is to create 3/16- to 1/4-inch clearance above new flooring or carpeting. To avoid marring the door's finish when sawing, cover a circular saw's base with masking tape. Depending on the amount trimmed, sawing the bottom of a hollow-core door may expose a cavity; fill it with the cut-off portion of the door. Before rehanging it, seal the door's bottom with clear wood sealer.

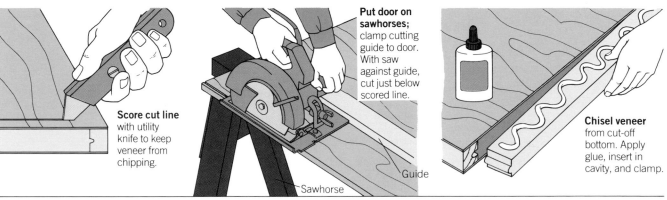

Score cut line with utility knife to keep veneer from chipping.

Put door on sawhorses; clamp cutting guide to door. With saw against guide, cut just below scored line.

Guide

Sawhorse

Chisel veneer from cut-off bottom. Apply glue, insert in cavity, and clamp.

Doors that won't latch

If a door doesn't latch properly, it may be hitting the stop before the latch bolt engages the strike plate. To correct this, move the strike plate by unscrewing it, plugging the screw holes with wood matchsticks or thin dowels, and redrilling the holes. Correct any misalignments between the latch bolt and strike plate. Minor misalignment can sometimes be fixed by enlarging the strike plate's opening with a file.

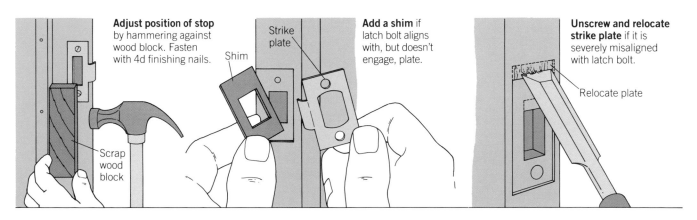

Adjust position of stop by hammering against wood block. Fasten with 4d finishing nails.

Scrap wood block

Strike plate

Shim

Add a shim if latch bolt aligns with, but doesn't engage, plate.

Unscrew and relocate strike plate if it is severely misaligned with latch bolt.

Relocate plate

Whether you're installing a doorknob or a lock, the procedure is the same. A *lockset* includes the trim, the knobs (or lever handles), and a latch bolt assembly. A *spring latch* can be pried with a knife or credit card; a *deadlocking latch* is similar to the spring latch but a piece projects in front of the latch, stopping the latch from being pushed back. A *deadbolt* can be moved only with a key or a thumb turn.

Installed by boring holes into the face and edge of a door, a *cylindrical lock* may operate with a key in the outside knob, a thumb turn or button in the inside one. If an inexpensive lock is damaged, replace it.

A *mortise lock* (p.441), housed in a mortise chiseled into the door edge, is usually found in an older home. Installation of a mortise lock should be left to a professional, but you can repair or replace a damaged lock yourself. Mortise locks vary in size; repair plates will hide a different-size replacement lock.

In an *interconnected lock* (facing page), a latch bolt and a deadbolt are combined in one lockset—both retract by turning the inside knob, allowing a fast exit during a fire or other emergency.

Because these locks are penetrable to a burglar, strengthen the lock and door following the reinforcing measures described on page 441. Adding an auxiliary lock—a *rim lock* or a *deadbolt* (p.440)—is also recommended to increase security. Both types are relatively inexpensive and easy to install.

Problem	Cause	Solution
Frozen lock (key won't enter cylinder)	Accumulated moisture has formed ice in lock	Scrape ice from cylinder opening. Heat key with match. Insert warmed key in cylinder as far as it can go. Remove key and repeat until full penetration is possible. Turn key gently and carefully to free tumblers.
Binding key (key won't turn)	Cylinder may have turned so that cam can't throw bolt	Loosen setscrew; turn cylinder to correct position. If using duplicate key, check against original—it may be a poor copy. If lock has been picked or a wrong key has been used, tumblers may be damaged. Replace cylinder.
Key broken in lock	Key inserted improperly or incompletely before turning; forcing an incorrect key or ill-fitting replacement key	Remove broken part with pliers, thin stiff wire, or coping saw blade. If this doesn't work, remove cylinder from lock, hold it face down, and tap to dislodge broken part. Or push out broken part by poking thin stiff wire from opposite side.
Stuck bolt (key turns but bolt doesn't move)	Bolt misaligned with strike plate	Tighten or shim door hinges (pp.436–437); change location of strike plate or enlarge its opening. If bolt is paint-bound, scrape off all dried paint and lubricate bolt.
Key turns freely but does not operate locking mechanism	Tailpiece of cam is loose or broken	Have repaired by a locksmith or replace lock.
Key doesn't insert smoothly	Keyway and tumbler area dirty	Scrape key's teeth across pencil lead (graphite), or puff powdered graphite into keyway; turn key in lock several times to work the graphite into the mechanism. Spray with penetrating lubricant, but do not oil.
	Foreign object in keyway	Carefully remove as for broken key.
Lock sticks or is slow in responding	Lock interior is dirty and gummy	Remove lock and clean as for key that doesn't insert smoothly.

Handicap handles

These handles allow handicapped people to open doors easily. They also permit people with full hands to open doors with their elbows. The lever handle adapter fits over standard doorknobs.

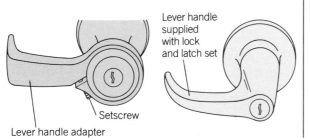

Lever handle supplied with lock and latch set

Setscrew

Lever handle adapter

Privacy lock

A type of cylindrical lock, the privacy lock is normally used on interior doors for bedrooms and bathrooms. It has a button or thumb turn on the inside knob, which locks the door so it can't be opened from outside. If the door is accidentally locked from within, unlock it by pushing a narrow rod or a nail into the hole in the outside knob. To install, follow directions for cylindrical lock (facing page).

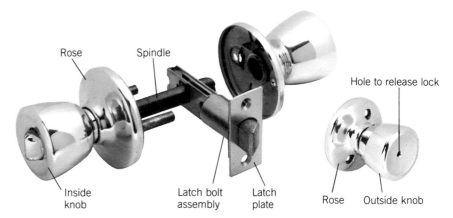

Rose Spindle Hole to release lock

Inside knob Latch bolt assembly Latch plate Rose Outside knob

Installing a cylindrical lock

If the screws provided for the strike plate are shorter than 3 inches, replace them with 3-inch-long screws.

Because the door can splinter as you bore a hole for the cylinder, stop boring when the tip of the hole saw breaks through the door surface; continue from the other side.

In some models, the cylinder can be replaced if damaged. For key-in-knob models, follow directions (right) to remove the knobs.

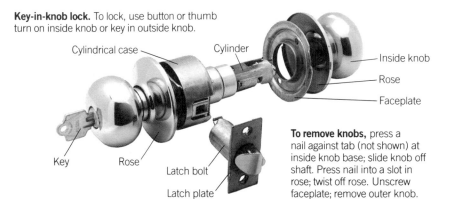

Key-in-knob lock. To lock, use button or thumb turn on inside knob or key in outside knob.

Cylindrical case
Cylinder
Inside knob
Rose
Faceplate
Key
Rose
Latch bolt
Latch plate

To remove knobs, press a nail against tab (not shown) at inside knob base; slide knob off shaft. Press nail into a slot in rose; twist off rose. Unscrew faceplate; remove outer knob.

Interconnected lockset

Available in two styles, one type has two locks that operate from the outside with the same key; the other type has an upper lock and a spring-loaded latch and requires two keys. Inside, the locks or lock and latch operate from a single knob.

Because the presence of two bolts (or a bolt and a latch) requires two recesses that are chiseled with precise accuracy, an interconnected lockset is best installed by a professional.

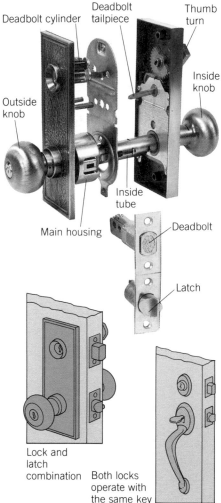

Deadbolt cylinder
Deadbolt tailpiece
Thumb turn
Inside knob
Outside knob
Inside tube
Main housing
Deadbolt
Latch

Lock and latch combination
Both locks operate with the same key

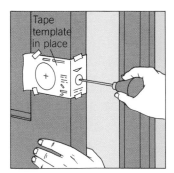

With template and awl, mark center of hole for cylinder on door face, center of hole for bolt on door edge.

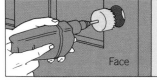

Bore hole for cylinder in door face with hole saw (top). For latch bolt, bore in door edge with spade bit.

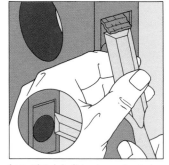

Insert latch bolt in door edge hole. Position latch plate; trace it; remove it and bolt. Chisel mortise for plate.

Reinsert latch bolt in door edge hole. Screw latch plate securely to the door edge.

Attach exterior knob and cylinder to latch assembly with door open; follow manufacturer's directions.

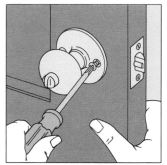

Insert rose and interior knob, aligning the screw guides and stems. Screw in place securely.

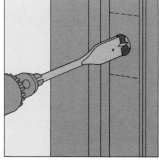

Mark position for strike recess on jamb; align it with latch bolt. Bore ½-in.-deep hole with spade bit.

Hold strike plate on jamb; trace it. Chisel hole for bolt. Chisel jamb until plate fits flush; fasten with screws.

Doors / Auxiliary locks

Offering a neat appearance, the deadbolt is an auxiliary lock that will increase security. As reliable as the deadbolt but easier to install, the rim lock has a bulky appearance. Home insurance rates may be lowered by installing either lock.

Buy a deadbolt lock with a bolt that will extend an inch from the door's edge. Deadbolts have one or two cylinders; a two-cylinder model unlocks with a key both inside and out. In a door with glass panels, it prevents a burglar from reaching through a broken pane to unlock the door. But because it inhibits fast emergency exits, the lock is restricted by code. (You can replace the glass with polycarbonate plastic.)

Foam-core steel doors are difficult to drill; if you have one, call in a professional to install a lock.

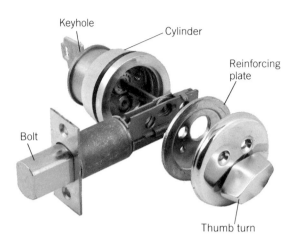

Keyhole — Cylinder — Reinforcing plate — Bolt — Thumb turn

Installing a rim lock

Mount a rim lock on the inside of the door near its edge, 6 inches above the knob. A vertical bolt slides into eyes on a strike plate installed along the jamb. If a strike mortise is cut too deep, shim the strike. Replace the kit's screws with 3-inch-long screws.

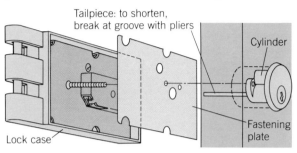

Tailpiece: to shorten, break at groove with pliers — Cylinder — Lock case — Fastening plate

Bore hole for cylinder; insert cylinder from outside. Screw on fastening plate. Bolt lock case to door following manufacturer's directions.

Installing a deadbolt

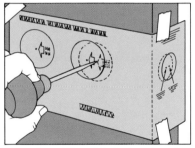

To mark position of lock, tape template 6 in. above knob. With awl, mark centers of lock and bolt holes on door.

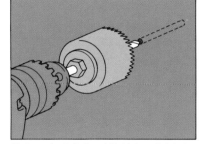

To bore lock hole, drill ⅛-in. pilot hole. Then drill halfway through with hole saw; finish hole from opposite side.

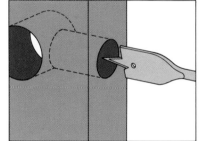

Wedge door in open position. Using spade bit, drill a bolt hole in door edge. Continue until bit drills into lock hole.

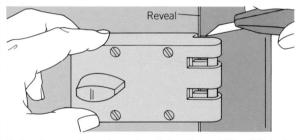

Reveal

Swing door gently against edge of door frame. With utility knife, score lines where lock case touches reveal. Open door.

Slide bolt into hole; position plate, outline it, and remove. Chisel mortise for plate. Replace bolt and plate; screw in place.

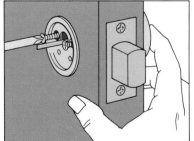

Install cylinder assembly with bolt in locked position; follow maker's directions. Using key, test bolt for smooth operation.

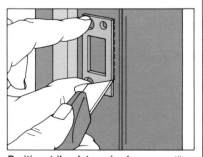

Position strike plate on jamb; score outline with utility knife. Chisel bolt hole; chisel jamb until plate fits flush; fasten with 3-in. screws.

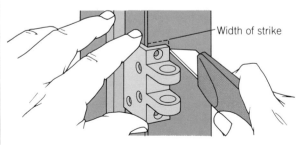

Width of strike

Holding strike between lines, score a vertical line strike's width away from edge. Chisel scored area. Hold strike in mortise; score strike's other side; chisel mortise. Screw in strike.

Mortise lock

Containing a latch bolt for interior doors or both a latch bolt and a deadbolt for exterior doors, a mortise lock is installed in a recess cut in the door's edge. The door must be a minimum of 1⅜ inches thick. Because it's difficult to cut a deep mortise in wood where there's little room for mistakes, mortise locks are rarely installed. If you already have one on your door, consider securing it with a reinforcing plate—the mortise can weaken the door. For added security, add an auxiliary lock (facing page).

With the purchase of a conversion kit, a mortise lock can be replaced with a cylindrical lock with considerable ease. These kits come with instructions, templates, and oversize metal escutcheons (faceplates) to cover the old holes in the door.

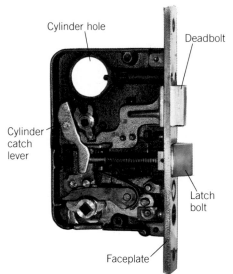

Cylinder hole

Deadbolt

Cylinder catch lever

Latch bolt

Faceplate

Converting a mortise lock

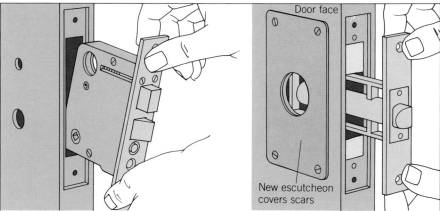

Door face

New escutcheon covers scars

Remove knobs and hardware; slide lock out of mortise in door edge. Mark position for lockset hole, using template. Drill hole halfway with hole saw; finish from opposite side. Insert new latch assembly; enlarge mortise with chisel or build it up with epoxy wood filler as necessary. Mount new strike plate in jamb, enlarging mortise if needed. Install escutcheon on door face. Attach lockset assembly. Test latch mechanism for smooth operation.

Additional security measures

A *swing bar guard* will let you open a door a few inches to view callers before admitting them. Easy to install, it's much stronger than a door chain (not shown). A *peephole* installed at eye level allows you to view the visitor without opening the door.

A wide U-shaped piece of steel, a *door-reinforcing plate* (not shown), fits over the door edge and around the knob and cylinder. It protects the door against abuse, such as kicks and hammer blows. Professional installation is usually required; some models can accommodate a variety of locksets and door thicknesses.

For a door that swings outward, adding a nail in each hinge (far right) makes it difficult to remove them. Work on one hinge at a time.

Installing viewing apparatus

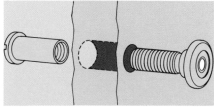

For peephole, cut hole. Insert viewer; screw on ring. If door has thin center panel, place it by door's edge.

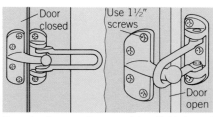

Door closed

Use 1½" screws

Door open

For swing bar guard, screw plate with U-shaped arm to door frame, the other plate at door's edge.

Reinforced strike

To replace weak strike plate, remove old strike; enlarge mortise for new strike box and plate.

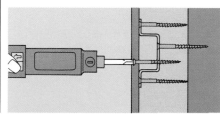

Insert strike box; drill pilot holes for screws. Attach plate and box with 3-in.-long screws.

Protecting lock and hinge

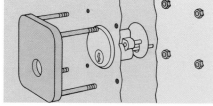

Cylinder guard covers all of lock except for key slot. Install with nuts on inside.

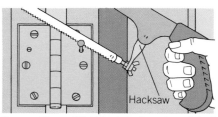

Hacksaw

Remove hinge; drill ¼-in. hole through each leaf; replace it. Drive nail halfway into hole; saw off head.

These doors come in two quite different types: *bypass* and *patio* doors. Bypass doors are lightweight movable panels suspended on a track with multiple channels so that they can slide past each other. They are often used for closets because they allow access to the full width of the space. Patio doors, usually made of glass in wood, metal, or vinyl frames, have one fixed and one or two sliding panels. The movable panels rest on rollers that travel in a bottom track.

Maintenance. With either style, keep the tracks clean and lubricated. Patio door tracks need more upkeep: vacuum out loose dirt, scrub out compacted dirt with a toothbrush. Use a silicone lubricant to keep the door moving freely. Don't use grease or oil—they attract and hold dirt.

Repairs. If bypass doors become balky, check the roller brackets (far right). Problems arise if their adjustment screws work loose, allowing the doors to slip out of alignment. Check that the brackets are properly positioned and the screws are tight.

Problems with patio doors usually stem from the tracks. Inspect them for burrs, bends, or other deformities, and repair or replace them as needed. (Parts are often manufacturer-specific. If you can't get parts from the manufacturer, or don't know who made your door, check with a hardware store. Take the old part with you and get as close a match as possible.)

Removal. Most gliding doors can be lifted straight up out of the track, but some have openings that the wheels slide through. Always have someone help you lift and move a patio door.

Top track keeps gliding door parallel to stationary one.

Bottom track of patio door is shaped into channels to guide door and screen.

Adjust height of rollers with screwdriver in hole in door's edge or face.

Bypass door hardware

Roller brackets keep the door level and maintain uniform clearance between the bottom of the door and the floor. There are dozens of styles of hanging brackets—some with one wheel, others with two. (A double-wheel bracket will support a slightly heavier door than will a single-wheel one.) All are designed so that you can adjust the height of the door easily without taking it down. To adjust door, loosen screws and slide them up or down in slot.

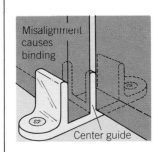

Misalignment causes binding

Center guide

To work smoothly, bypass doors must be plumb (check with a level) and properly positioned in the bottom guide. If the doors bind in the guide, unscrew it and reposition it, making sure that the doors remain plumb.

Patio door track repair

For minor bends, cut a block of wood to fit tightly in the track, and insert it. With the wood as a backing, flatten the sides with light quick hammer blows. A more serious deformity will require replacement. Some tracks can be replaced with a kit (available from a window and door hardware specialist); others will have to be replaced by a professional installer. At the same time, replace worn rollers.

Block

Track

Opening a doorway

Determine that the wall is non-load-bearing (p.191). Outline the doorway. Before cutting it, find out if heating ducts, pipes, or electrical cables run behind the proposed opening. If they do, reroute them or relocate the doorway. Buy the door before creating the rough opening. A prehung door (p.445) eliminates the need to frame each jamb within the rough opening. A door blank (p.444) requires more precise framing and installation.

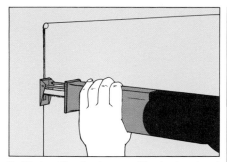

1. Mark outline for doorway. Wearing head and eye protection, cut away plaster and lath with reciprocating saw (p.62). Cut wallboard with keyhole or wallboard saw. Don't cut studs.

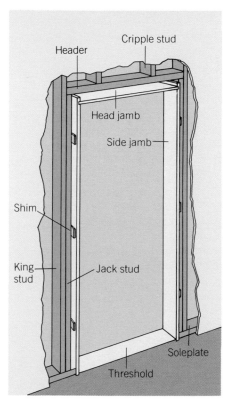

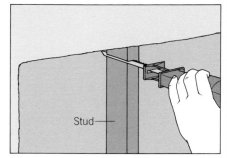

2. To create cripple studs, mark wall studs to length with square; cut with a reciprocating saw. Remove stud stubs below the cut by hammering or yanking them sideways. Install king studs, if needed.

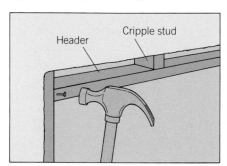

If using a door blank, cut opening 5 in. wider and 2½ in. higher than door. If using a prehung, follow manufacturer's instructions.

3. Nail a jack stud on each side of opening to support header and provide nailing base. Level and install 2 x 4 to form header. Cut through and remove soleplate. Install door.

Closing an interior doorway

Buy new stud lumber that is close to the same size as the existing studs—usually 2 x 4's or 2 x 6's. Cover the opening with wallboard, even if the wall is plaster; shim it so that it is flush with the existing wall. Add a baseboard and moldings (p.99) that match the existing trim. Paint or wallpaper the entire wall. (If closing an exterior doorway, pack the cavity with insulation, add a vapor retarder, and finish both sides to blend with the walls.)

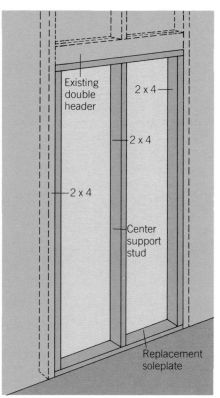

Remove the door and its jambs, threshold, and trim. (Wear safety gear during demolition.) Install a soleplate and studs as shown above and at right.

1. Remove the door. Pry off trim from jamb side, so as not to damage wall. Next, take out threshold. If necessary cut it in thirds and remove in pieces (p.454).

2. Pull side jambs toward each other at the bottom. This should provide enough leverage to free the head jamb, allowing all three jambs to come out as a unit. If not, pry each out separately.

3. Cut studs one by one, or assemble a frame to fit in the opening (see left). Check that studs' edges are even with existing wall studs, and nail in place. Sheathe with wallboard (pp.273–277).

Doors/Hanging a door

If you need to replace a door and its jambs are in good shape, you can buy a new door, or *door blank,* from a home center. Standard door blanks are 6 feet 8 inches tall and 30, 32, or 36 inches wide. Other sizes can be ordered. Measure the original door and get a same-size blank. The old door's dimensions may be a bit smaller than the blank—doors are cut to fit the opening. If the jambs are in bad shape—or if you're not deft with hand tools—a prehung unit (facing page) is a better choice.

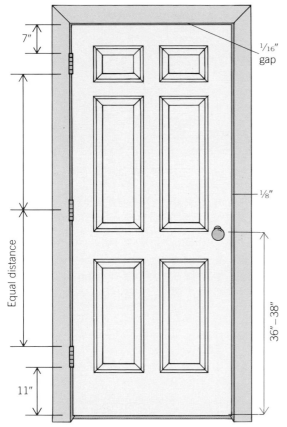

A properly hung door swings freely without noise or binding, closes securely, and doesn't rattle. To achieve this, the door is trimmed to allow specific clearances around its perimeter. Have the knob and latch holes of a new door bored when you buy it.

Gap

1. Determine how out-of-square the jambs are by setting a framing square in the corner formed by the hinge jamb and the top jamb. Measure gap between top jamb and far end of square's long leg. If the corner is square, skip to step 3.

2. Measuring from door's top edge, mark gap on knob side of door. Place a straightedge along line from hinge-side corner to gap mark. Score line deeply with utility knife. Set saw blade just outside line, position and clamp a straight-edge to guide cut, and trim door.

3. Measure height of hinge jamb; then subtract 9/16 in. for clearance. Measure down both sides of door, marking height near bottom edge. Score line and cut door as in step 2. To prevent chipping, bevel all cut edges with medium sand-paper or a file.

4. Hold door against the hinge jamb, and prop it in the opening with wedges. (Have a helper drive some in from the other side.) Shim it from the bottom until its top edge is 1/16 in. from the top jamb. (A quarter is a handy 1/16-in. spacer.)

Quarter

5. Transcribe locations of hinges and their length from hinge jamb onto door edge. Scribe carefully with a utility knife or a very sharp pencil. Precision is essential—even a 1/32-in. error will keep the hinge from fitting properly.

6. Measure how much of the hinge leaf is mortised into the hinge jamb. Transfer this dimension to door edge. Align a hinge leaf with the length and width marks on the door; deeply score its outline with utility knife.

Installing a prehung door

7. Carefully chisel out the mortise for the hinge leaf. Work from the center out to each end, paring thin shavings until the mortise is flat and as deep as the hinge is thick.

8. Set hinge leaf in mortise. Punch guide holes off-center: slightly away from the hinge pin. Drill pilot holes and drive screws, tightening one completely but leaving the others loose.

9. Hang door; tighten screws. Close door and check gaps. Adjust gap on hinge side with shims (p.436). Plane edges for an exact fit. Paint or varnish door, including edges. When dry, install knob or lockset.

Because a prehung door comes hinged in its jambs, you're relieved of the painstaking task of fitting the hinges. Installing an interior door is a straightforward matter of stripping the opening, dropping the door into position, shimming it plumb, and nailing it. If you're installing an exterior door (below), pay careful attention to the manufacturer's instructions so that you get a weathertight seal around it. To expose the rough opening, remove the trim and pry off the old jambs and sill.

1. Apply a bead of polyurethane caulk to the rough sill before beginning. Center door unit in rough opening, with threshold resting on rough sill.

2. Using a carpenter's level, check that hinge side is plumb. Insert shims to hold the door steady. Tack it in position by driving galvanized 16d finishing nails through exterior door trim into jack stud.

3. From both sides of door, tap solid wood shims directly behind each hinge, into the space between the hinge jamb and the jack stud. Take care that the shims don't push the door out of plumb.

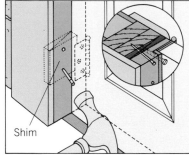

4. Working on the outside, drive two finishing nails through the hinge jamb into the jack stud at each hinge. (Nails pass through shims inserted in step 3.)

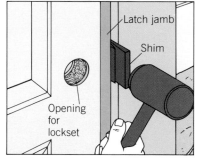

5. Weatherstrip the lock jamb (p.454), if necessary. Adjust jamb to obtain a tight seal between door and weatherstrip. Shim behind strike plate as shown, and at top and bottom of jamb.

6. Adjust shims inserted in previous step to provide 3/32 in. clearance between door and lock jamb. Nail through lock jamb and shims into jack stud. Finally, drive long screws through empty holes in hinges.

Doors/Storm, screen, and shower doors

Storm doors may be made of wood, aluminum, or vinyl. Wood doors, or doors with a wood or foam core, are the most energy-efficient; vinyl and aluminum resist warping.

A combination door has interchangeable glass and screen panels and allows a smoother transition between seasons than do individual storm and screen doors. If you have a combination door, be sure to switch from glass to screen in the early spring. Heat trapped between the storm and entry doors can build to the point of melting the weather-stripping or warping the door.

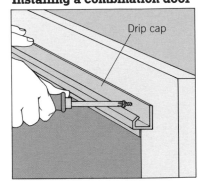

A prehung storm door has mounting flanges (left) that speed accurate installation. Before buying a door, get the *inside dimensions* of the opening (below). Measure from side jamb to side jamb in two places and from sill to head jamb in two places. Use the smaller measurement in each case. Note also which side of the door will be hinged.

Latch-side mounting flange

Door sweep

Hinge-side mounting flange

Head jamb

Width

Height

Height

Width

Sill

Installing a combination door

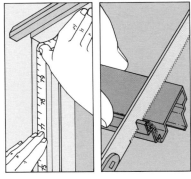

Drip cap

1. Follow the manufacturer's installation instructions to establish the height of the drip cap. Attach cap to top of door opening with one screw.

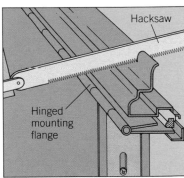

Hacksaw

Hinged mounting flange

2. Trim hinged mounting flange to length with a hacksaw. To determine length, measure from below drip cap to sill, and subtract ⅛ in. (or amount specified in instructions) for clearance.

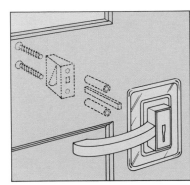

Drip cap

3. Run a bead of caulk down hinged mounting flange. On hinge jamb, align top outside edge of flange with end of drip cap; drive in top flange screw. With a level, check that door is plumb; shim if needed, and install remaining screws.

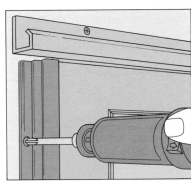

4. Remove drip cap, caulk along its back, and reinstall it. Measure latch jamb from below drip cap to sill, and hacksaw the latch mounting flange to length. Take care not to dislodge weatherstripping.

5. Apply caulk to back of the latch mounting flange, and screw it in place. Check that gap between the flange and the door's edge is even from top to bottom. (Manufacturer's instructions will detail size of the gap.)

6. Install door sweep, handle, automatic closer, and any other hardware following manufacturer's instructions. Turn tensioning screw on door closer to adjust speed at which door closes.

A variety of hardware (below) is available for storm and screen doors. Hinges, latches, catches, and closers are designed to answer the problems of fit and regulating the door's operation.

A wooden screen door is installed the same way that an interior door is hung (pp. 444–445). Re-screen the door or repair tears in the screening the same way you would for a window (p. 431).

Shower doors require little maintenance other than cleaning the tracks. It's wise to replace glass panels with acrylic—take the door off its hinges and lay it on a flat surface to work on it.

Storm- and screen-door hardware

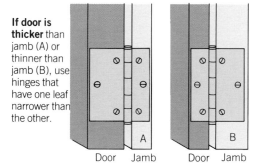

If door is thicker than jamb (A) or thinner than jamb (B), use hinges that have one leaf narrower than the other.

Door Jamb   Door Jamb
A   B

Bolt

Arm

Wall bracket

Screw adjusts speed

Door bracket

Hydraulic door closer hangs on bracket attached to door and jamb.

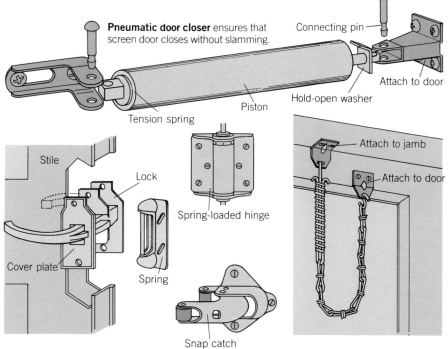

Pneumatic door closer ensures that screen door closes without slamming.

Tension spring   Piston

Connecting pin

Hold-open washer

Attach to door

Stile

Lock

Cover plate

Spring

A strong latch keeps door from whipping open in wind.

Spring-loaded hinge

Snap catch

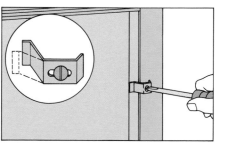

Attach to jamb

Attach to door

Chain retainer regulates how wide a door can open.

Replacing storm-door glass

1. Loosen screws in clips and carefully take out broken glass and surrounding frame. Wear heavy gloves and long sleeves for safety.

2. Measure opening, subtracting 1/32 in. per ft. in both directions for expansion. Replace glass with acrylic; have it cut to size when you buy it.

3. Set acrylic in opening; tighten the clips. (Except for combination door, you don't need a frame.) If needed, bend clips against plastic.

Replacing shower-door glass

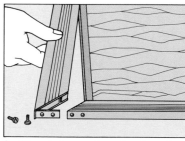

1. Take door off hinge and unscrew its corners. With an old screwdriver driven by light hammer blows, gently push frame away from glass.

2. Wearing gloves for safety, peel gasket from glass. Clean gasket and frame. Cut 1/8-in. clear acrylic (p. 143) slightly smaller than opening.

3. Fit gasket around acrylic. Press frame over gasket on all sides. Replace all screws at corners and rehang the door.

Doors/Roll-up garage doors

Sectional garage doors have more moving parts than any other door in the house; for that reason they require more maintenance to function well. They should slide up smoothly with the first tug on the handle and descend gently after a single pull.

To keep a roll-up garage door working well, you should oil the roller bearings, pulleys, lock mechanism, and cables every 6 months. Wipe the tracks clean and spray them with silicone or a penetrating lubricant—grease or oil will collect grit. Rub candle wax along the inside edges of the doorstop (the trim in front of the door) to prevent door sections from chafing as they go up and down.

Check each track's alignment once a year. The bottom sections should be plumb. Hold a level against the track; if the bubble isn't centered, adjust the track brackets as shown below.

Loose hinges or loose brackets can cause misalignment of a garage door; tighten them once a year. If lag screw holes are stripped, consider converting to carriage bolts. Using the existing hole, drill through the door. Insert a bolt from outside and secure it with a washer and a nut inside. Check the fit of the lock bars in the slots of the strike plates (adjustable brackets make fixes simple). Bent or broken rollers should be replaced (home centers and hardware stores stock them). Put in a new cable before a frayed one gives way.

When an extension spring breaks, it is easy to replace it (facing page). Torsion springs, used for

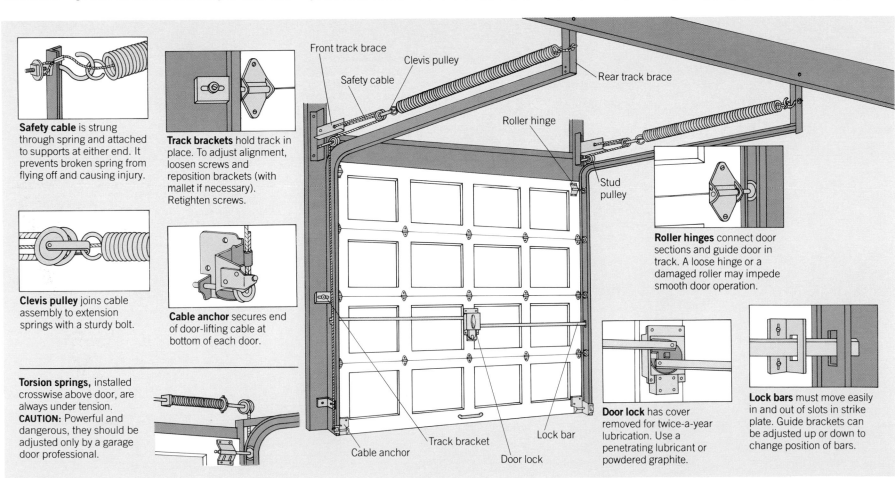

Safety cable is strung through spring and attached to supports at either end. It prevents broken spring from flying off and causing injury.

Track brackets hold track in place. To adjust alignment, loosen screws and reposition brackets (with mallet if necessary). Retighten screws.

Clevis pulley joins cable assembly to extension springs with a sturdy bolt.

Cable anchor secures end of door-lifting cable at bottom of each door.

Torsion springs, installed crosswise above door, are always under tension. **CAUTION:** Powerful and dangerous, they should be adjusted only by a garage door professional.

Front track brace

Clevis pulley

Safety cable

Rear track brace

Roller hinge

Stud pulley

Roller hinges connect door sections and guide door in track. A loose hinge or a damaged roller may impede smooth door operation.

Door lock has cover removed for twice-a-year lubrication. Use a penetrating lubricant or powdered graphite.

Lock bars must move easily in and out of slots in strike plate. Guide brackets can be adjusted up or down to change position of bars.

Track bracket

Cable anchor

Door lock

Lock bar

heavy doors, require a professional garage door installer to make repairs or adjustments.

Springs lose tension over time. To adjust the tension on a pair of extension springs, lock the door open (right). Move the top end of each spring's cable to a fastener closer to the spring for less tension or farther away from it for more tension. A properly adjusted garage door should stay positioned at any point between 8 inches above the ground and 8 inches below the fully open position.

Roll-up door repairs

Problem	Solution
Sluggish operation	Lubricate rollers, hinges, and pulleys with lightweight machine oil twice a year. Don't oil tracks (oil collects dirt); wipe tracks clean and spray with silicone or penetrating lubricant.
Rollers don't roll smoothly	Inspect rollers: If damaged, replace. If clogged with grease and grit, remove and clean in a solvent like mineral spirits and reinstall. If rollers are OK, check the alignment of the tracks with a level. Adjust brackets until vertical parts of tracks are plumb. Straighten or replace any bent track. Tighten screws on loose hinges.
Frayed cable	Replace cable while door is locked open (right). Cables must be of equal length if door is to move smoothly.
Door flies open too fast	Loosen tension by repositioning the hook ends of each cable closer to the springs on the cable anchors.
Door is hard to open	Tighten tension by repositioning the hook ends of each cable farther away from the springs on the cable anchors. Equalize tension on springs. Check that tracks are not too far apart.
Door lock sticks	Lubricate latch mechanism with powdered graphite. Check fit of lock bars into slots on strike plate; adjust brackets up or down until they support lock bar in correct position.

Replacing extension springs and cable

1. Secure door open by locking pliers onto the track right below a roller. Unplug your power garage door opener if you have one. Replace both springs even if only one is broken. Uneven tension will cause unnecessary wear and tear on door mechanism.

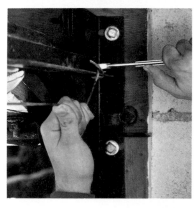

2. Remove safety cable holding old spring. Loosen nut and bolt (or other device) that secure old cable to front track brace. Hold on to the cable so that other hardware doesn't start to swing.

3. Lower spring to vertical position. Remove cable from clevis pulley, and unhook old spring from track brace. Unbolt clevis pulley to free old spring. Attach new spring first to pulley, then to track brace. Put safety cable back in place.

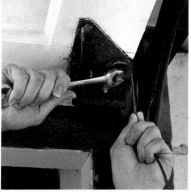

4. Remove end of old cable from anchor at bottom of door. Old doors may have a nut and washer; new ones will have a cable loop stud to make adjustments easier. Attach new cable to anchor. Pull out old cable; measure new cable against it for length.

5. Run new cable up side of door and over the top of the stud pulley. Feed it around clevis pulley as shown. Make sure flat side of pulley remains vertical as you stretch cable back toward front track brace.

6. Secure cable to bracket (an S-hook is used here). Clevis pulley should be even with horizontal track section. Repeat process on other side of door. Then work door and adjust cables to get a smooth operation. Rub cables with an oily rag to prevent rust.

Being able to open your garage door by a battery-operated transmitter as you approach in a car is a convenience, especially in bad weather. If you install the opener yourself (about a 3-hour job for two people), it won't be an extravagance.

Automatic garage door openers have either a chain drive, a plastic strap drive, or a screw drive. All can open even the heaviest double door with a ¼- or ⅓-horsepower motor—if the door is properly balanced and maintained. Larger motors are not

necessary if a garage door's springs are still lively and the tracks are plumb.

Most garage doors, even one-piece flip-up models, can be operated by an automatic opener. Units that you install yourself usually require a minimum of 1½ to 3 inches of clearance between the rafters of the garage and the highest point of the door's arc on its way up. If the door extends above its opening when it is closed, you may be able to trim the top section to make room. Otherwise, consult a dealer.

Additional features. Autoreverse circuitry is standard: the opener reverses itself in 2 seconds or less if the door is blocked by an object higher than 1 inch off the ground. So are automatic lights (they go on when the opener is activated and stay on for up to 5 minutes) and a manual release for opening the door when the power goes out. Most models include a remote control transmitter and a wall button; you can order other electronic controls (some even activate other lights in the house).

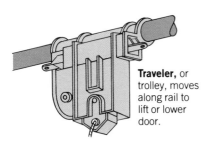

Traveler, or trolley, moves along rail to lift or lower door.

Header bracket secures rail above door.

Idler assembly holds pulley that guides chain drive.

Before you start . . .

There are several considerations to be addressed before installing an opener:

● **Power supply.** You'll need a standard 120V grounded (3-prong) receptacle within reach of the opener's power unit cord (usually 3 to 6 ft.).

● **Old locks.** You must deactivate or remove the garage door bar lock. (The opener provides its own security with the transmitter and/or a separate key.) You can burn out an opener's motor very quickly by asking it to strain against an old bar lock inadvertently placed in lock position.

● **Reinforcement.** If your door is lightweight fiberglass or aluminum, you'll need to strengthen the top section with metal bars.

● **Safety.** Remove any rope handles; they could become caught in door mechanism and strain the motor. (The opener will have its own manual control for power outages.) Locate push-button switches where convenient but out of young children's reach. Replace safety cable as shown on page 448.

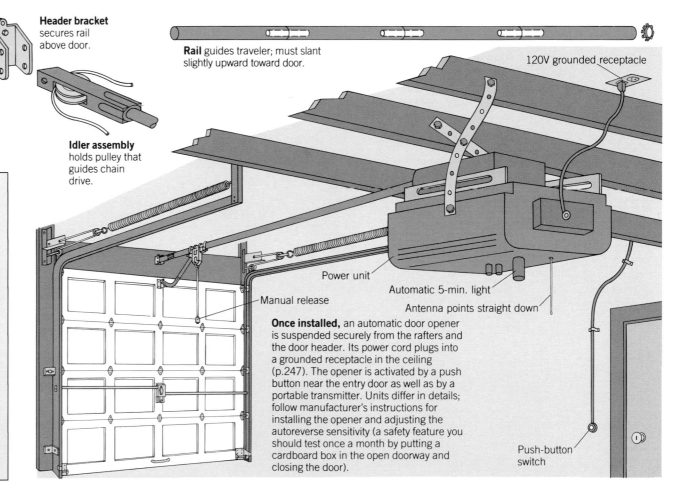

Rail guides traveler; must slant slightly upward toward door.

120V grounded receptacle

Power unit

Manual release

Automatic 5-min. light

Antenna points straight down

Push-button switch

Once installed, an automatic door opener is suspended securely from the rafters and the door header. Its power cord plugs into a grounded receptacle in the ceiling (p.247). The opener is activated by a push button near the entry door as well as by a portable transmitter. Units differ in details; follow manufacturer's instructions for installing the opener and adjusting the autoreverse sensitivity (a safety feature you should test once a month by putting a cardboard box in the open doorway and closing the door).

Electrical tools, testing, and safety 242–243
Adding or extending a circuit 248–249
Running cable 250–251

Assembling the parts

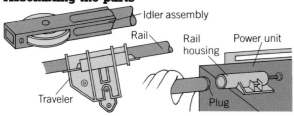

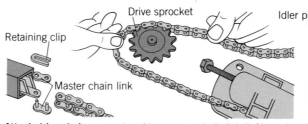

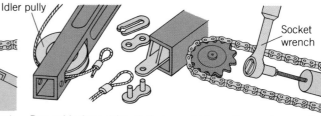

Join rail sections: place plug button in one end and that end into the power unit housing (right). Slip the traveler, or trolley, onto other end of rail and attach idler assembly to that end (left).

Attach drive chain to traveler with a master chain link (left); push retaining clip with old screwdriver until clip locks into place. Extend chain to power unit; pass it around drive sprocket (right).

Run cable from drive chain around idler pulley, and secure to traveler with another master chain link and retaining clip. Adjust chain tension (it should sag ½ in.) by turning screw on power unit.

Installing the unit

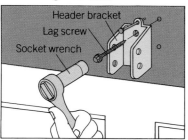

1. Center header bracket on wall above door (bottom edge 2 in. above high point of door's arc). Fasten the bracket to wall with two lag screws.

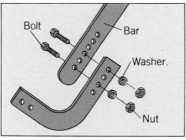

4. Attach straight steel bar to bottom of traveler. Bolt this bar to L-shaped arm that raises and lowers door. A choice of mounting holes allows adjustments for distance to door.

7. Unscrew pushbutton cap; attach wires (stripped of ¼ in. of insulation) as shown. Mount switch inside garage. Attach other ends of wires to power unit terminals (below).

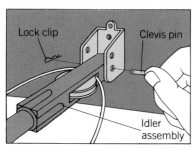

2. Place power unit on stepladder so that it is level with header bracket while you fasten idler assembly to header bracket with clevis pin. Secure pin with lock clip through hole in its end.

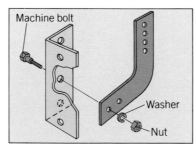

5. Attach door bracket to other end of arm piece with machine bolt that permits arm piece to move freely as the door is raised and lowered.

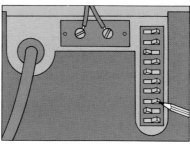

8. Find rocker switches in power unit. To create a transmission code to activate your opener, use a sharpened pencil to set switches in a random off-on pattern.

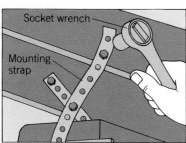

3. Bolt the metal mounting straps or brackets (whichever provided) to power unit. Fasten their other ends to beams or ceiling joists with lag screws.

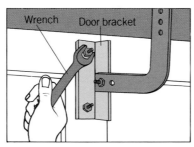

6. Hold bracket on door and mark for bolt holes. Drill holes from inside; insert carriage bolts from outside; tighten nuts from inside.

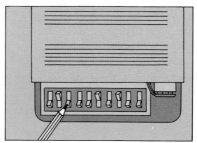

9. Open the transmitter and find rocker switches there. Set switches to the identical off-on pattern you used in power unit. Door will respond to signal from your preset transmitter exclusively.

Weatherstripping/Windows

Windows need an airtight seal to prevent heat loss in winter and air-conditioning loss in summer. New windows usually have built-in weatherstripping, and fixed sashes can simply be caulked. But older windows that are opened and closed often need an extra barrier to seal air leaks between sashes or around their edges.

Weatherstripping is no substitute for storm windows; in cold climates you will need both. If you have exterior storm units, for example, you must seal the interior windows to prevent condensation from forming on the inside of the storm window. Weatherstripping can't compensate for a warped window or one that is badly out of plumb; consider replacing such damaged windows (p.427).

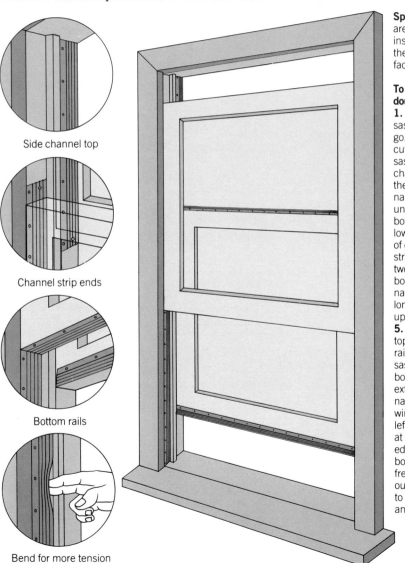

Side channel top

Channel strip ends

Bottom rails

Bend for more tension

Spring metal strips are applied from inside the house with the nailing flanges facing toward you.

At top rail

To weatherstrip a double-hung window: **1.** Raise the lower sash as far as it will go. Nail metal strips, cut 1 in. longer than sash, to both side channels. **2.** While the lower sash is up, nail a strip across the underside of its bottom rail. **3.** Close lower sash. Nail top of each 1-in. channel strip extension with two nails. **4.** With both sashes down, nail strips (cut 1 in. longer than sash) to upper side channels. **5.** Nail metal strip to top of upper sash rail. **6.** Raise upper sash and nail down bottoms of 1-in. extensions with two nails each. **7.** Set window as shown at left. Nail strip, flange at top, to the inside edge of upper sash's bottom rail. **8.** Bend free side of all strips out with your fingers to increase tension and make tighter fit.

Where sashes meet

At bottom rail

Tubular gaskets are nailed to double-hung windows from the outside: **1.** Nail a strip, cut to fit, to top rail of the upper sash so that the gasket presses tightly against the window trim. **2.** Apply a strip to the bottom rail of the lower sash (the gasket will face down). **3.** Side strips are usually nailed along the window's stiles. However, if sashes are loose, applying gasket to parting strip may give a better seal. **4.** To seal joint between sashes, apply strip under the bottom rail of the upper sash.

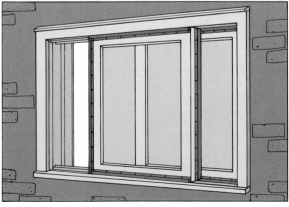

A gliding window is sealed the same way as a double-hung window, with either spring metal strips or tubular gaskets. In your mind's eye turn it 90°, and you will see that it is actually just a double-hung window turned on its side. If one sash is stationary, caulk it and weatherstrip the other sash.

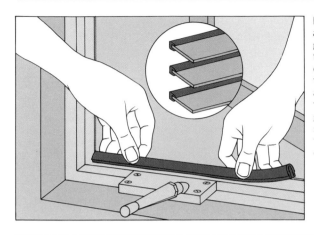

Metal casement windows are easily sealed with special gaskets designed to slip over the metal window frames. Miter corners with scissors for a neat fit, and use an appropriate adhesive (p.88). As it closes, the window compresses the gasket, creating a tight fit. A similar gasket is available for the upper edge of each pane of glass in a jalousie window (inset).

Wood casement windows can be inconspicuously sealed with spring metal strips applied in the sash channels. The nailing flange faces outward, the free side of the strip inward. For a casement window to close properly, tubular gaskets must be applied inside to window stops, not sashes, making the windows somewhat unsightly.

Types of weatherstripping

Tubular gasket

Tubular gaskets are made of vinyl or rubber, with or without a foam filling. They are durable and effective even when gaps around window or door are uneven. Applied from outside, tubular gaskets take sub-zero temperatures well.

Spring metal strip

Made of bronze, stainless steel, or aluminum, these long-lasting strips fit unobtrusively in window or door channels and use tension to create a seal. They may make a tight-fitting door or window hard to open.

V-strip

V-strips, made of metal or vinyl, also use tension to create a tight seal. They are installed in window and door channels. Vinyl strips often come with adhesive backing. However, metal V-strips, applied with nails, last longer.

Adhesive-backed foam

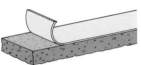

Adhesive-backed foam provides an inexpensive quick fix for a filtration problem. Very easy to apply, the foam may lose its resiliency and effectiveness during a single season.

Foam-edged wood strip

Foam-edged wood lasts longer (and costs more) than plain adhesive-backed foam. Self-sticking, it is easy to install on even surfaces but wears out in several seasons.

Grooved gasket

Grooved gaskets, made of various plastics, fit metal casement windows or jalousie windows. Compression makes them effective, and they last 10 years or more.

Astragal

Astragal weatherstripping, vinyl or aluminum, is used on double doors (French doors). A T-shaped type consists of a single piece that attaches to the less-used door. Another design interlocks two separate strips, one for each door.

Magnetic

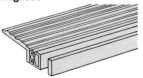

Magnetic seal for gliding doors works like the seal on a refrigerator door. One part, attached to door trim, holds a magnet and a gasket. Other part, attached to door, is metal. The magnet holds door against gasket in a tight seal.

Door sweep

A door sweep consists of a rigid flange, screwed or glued to door bottom, and a flexible flap that seals against the threshold. Made of various materials, some new sweeps lift automatically to clear the rug as you open door.

Door shoe

A door shoe is a metal frame with a vinyl gasket under it; shoe slides onto bottom of door. Screwed into place, it is caulked to keep door bottom dry. Gasket makes seal with threshold. Door may need trimming for shoe to fit.

Threshold gasket

Threshold gasket features a vinyl insert in the center of an aluminum replacement threshold. Vinyl presses against bottom of door when door is closed, making a seal. To replace worn vinyl insert, slide new one into channel.

Garage door gasket

Garage door gasket, made of weather-resistant rubber, is nailed to bottom of overhead door. Flanges spread on impact and seal opening, whether it is even or not.

Weatherstripping/Doors

Because they are opened often, doors are a major source of air leakage. When closed, they should seal tightly—even down to the mail slot (you can buy letter-box flaps and even keyhole covers). Don't weatherstrip a badly hung door until you adjust the hinges (p. 436). To apply weatherstripping, tack each piece at the top and bottom, and test how well the door closes or compresses the strip before continuing to install it. And remember to treat the doors leading to unheated parts of the house.

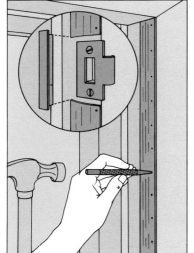
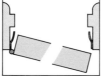

Spring metal strips (and V-strips) are nailed with the free edge facing out (above). Cut strips with metal snips. Nail across top first, then down sides. Use a nail set to avoid making dents in the strips. Leave gap at strike plate; cut a short piece (inset) to nail onto stop.

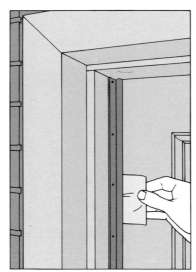
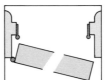

Tubular gasket strips are applied to face of door stops. To make a good seal, gasket should be slightly compressed when door is shut. Test seal as you proceed (a piece of paper should barely slide between door and edge of tube). Start at top and work down each side.

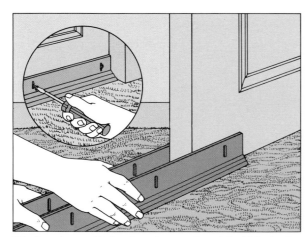

Slip door shoe, cut to length, onto open door. Adjust it to door's thickness by sliding pieces into correct groove. Close door. Drill pilot holes and start screws through slots (inset); adjust so that fit is tight but door opens easily. Tighten screws. Caulk edges.

To install garage door sweep, first repair and paint bottom of door if needed. Disengage automatic opener. Prop door open with a 2 x 4 and cut sweep to fit. Nail or screw the sweep to bottom of door with shorter flap facing the interior.

Installing a weathertight threshold

A new threshold with a gasket insert will fill a gap at the bottom of a door. An adjustable model (screws raise or lower its height) compensates for an uneven door and saves having to plane the door for a good fit.

Door stop

Remove the old threshold, or saddle, with a pry bar. If it won't lift easily, use a backsaw to cut it at each end. Center piece will then lift right up. (Protect carpet or floor with cardboard held in place with masking tape.)

Tap out end pieces with mallet and chisel. Cut the new threshold to width with a hacksaw. If it is higher than old one, trim door stops to fit. Clean sill under old threshold with mineral spirits.

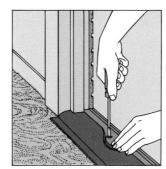

Position threshold with the gasket flap facing outdoors. Lift flap and insert the installation screws. Close door to test threshold height. Remove gasket to reach adjustment screws. Tighten or loosen screws until door has close but easy fit.

Chapter sixteen

Home climate
Heating, cooling, insulation, and humidity control

Contents

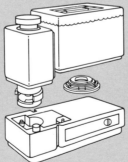

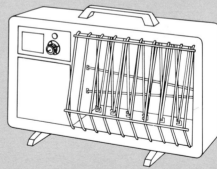

You can keep your home comfortable summer and winter by making sure it is well insulated and ventilated and by maintaining and balancing its heating and cooling systems. This chapter shows how to keep your home cozy and safe and at the same time save money. Beginning with a discussion of insulation and ventilation, it goes on to describe the various heating systems most commonly found in private homes, with suggestions on adjusting, maintaining, troubleshooting, and improving them. There follows a similar section on cooling your home in the summer. The chapter concludes with ways of controlling humidity and air quality the year around.

The severity of the local climate has a lot to do with how comfortable your home is, but a number of other factors also play essential roles. A well-insulated, fairly airtight structure is the first prerequisite. Properly sized and well-maintained heating, cooling, and ventilation systems are close seconds.

Comfort audit. If your home is less comfortable than you would like it, do a thorough assessment of the structure. Your local utility company may provide a free or low-cost energy audit (some utilities even use heat-sensitive infrared video scanners, which show how a home is losing heat). If this service is not available, do your own audit by moving through your home and searching out all drafts, cold (or hot) surfaces, improper humidity, and stale air.

Drafts are caused by indoor air that loses its heat to windows and exterior walls; the colder and taller the surfaces, the faster the drafts move. When you sit near cold surfaces, you radiate heat to them; the colder the surface, the faster you radiate and the more uncomfortable you feel. Sitting beneath an uninsulated hot ceiling in July has the opposite effect; even if the air is cool, the ceiling will radiate heat and cause discomfort.

Remedies. Insulating your house and adding weatherstripping (pp.452–454) and storm windows (p.432) or double-glazed sashes (pp.426–427) help warm or cool interior surfaces and cut down on drafts. If a home is too dry in winter and too humid in summer, the culprit may be excessive air leakage. Cutting down on leaks by caulking openings (p.411) and taping ducts (p.466) may increase wintertime indoor humidity sufficiently to eliminate the need for humidifiers. Finally, controlling ventilation generally improves indoor comfort.

▶**CAUTION:** If your home has combustion appliances—hot-water heaters, fireplaces, or heating systems fired by gas, oil, wood, or propane—they must be provided with adequate air for safe use. While most fairly airtight homes have sufficient air for this purpose, some do not. If you make your house more airtight, it may be necessary to pipe air directly to the room in which the appliance is located.

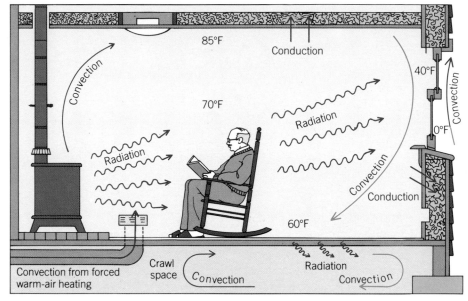

Heat travels through solid materials—such as wallboard, insulation, or siding—by *conduction;* if you put your hand against a cold window, you will feel heat being conducted out of your hand. Heat moves through air or liquids by a mixing action called *convection;* for example, warm air rises from a stove while cool air drifts down the inside of a cold single-pane window. Warm room air also escapes through leaks in a ceiling by natural convection. Heat from warm objects—such as the sun or a stove—travels by *radiation* to any nearby object that is cooler.

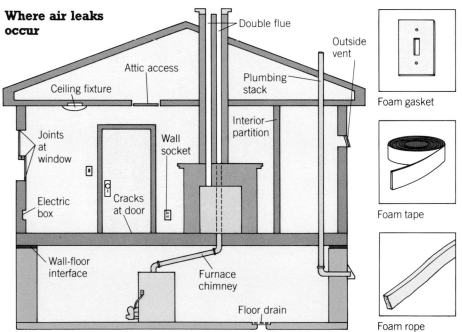

Where air leaks occur

Double flue · Outside vent · Attic access · Plumbing stack · Ceiling fixture · Interior partition · Joints at window · Wall socket · Electric box · Cracks at door · Wall-floor interface · Furnace chimney · Floor drain

Foam gasket

Foam tape

Foam rope

To locate air leaks, wait for a cold, windy day or close all but one window, seal a box fan in remaining window, and turn it on to pull air out of house. Then pass a thread or thin strip of tissue near all penetrations of house interior and look for a waver. To stop air leaks, fit thin foam gaskets behind covers on electrical outlets and switches; line attic hatch with adhesive-backed foam tape; and use foam rope or a can of expanding foam to plug leaks around plumbing or other penetrations in walls, ceilings, and floors. Also, force caulk into small cracks in basement walls and slabs, around trim, and into joints between chimney and wall. In addition, apply aluminized tape around joints in duct runs (p.466).

Insulation basics

The capacity of an insulating material to resist heat flow is called its R-value. The higher the R-value, the better the insulator. Insulation usually comes in the form of batts in thicknesses ranging from 2½ to 12 inches; in 2- or 4- x 8-foot sheets of rigid foam that are ½ to 4 inches thick; or as loose-fill, which comes in bags.

The priorities for adding insulation are generally (1) the ceilings below unheated spaces, (2) uninsulated ductwork in attics or crawl spaces, (3) exterior walls, and (4) under floors or against foundation walls. The amount of insulation you should add to a finished house depends on the local climate and utility costs, but the chart below gives general recommendations of the U.S. Department of Energy. Adding insulation makes your home more comfortable, increases its resale value, and lets you downsize heating and cooling equipment when it comes time for replacement.

Recommended R-values for added insulation

	Ceiling below a ventilated attic		Floor over cold space	Outside wall	Dry crawl-space wall
	Electric heat	Gas, oil, or heat pump	All fuel types	All fuel types	All fuel types
1	30	19	None	11–13	11
2	30	30	None	11–13	19
3	38	30	19	11–13	19
4	38	38	19	11–13	19
5	49	38	19	11–13	19
6	49	49	19	11–13	19

Insulation costs and performance

The chart below is designed to help you pick the best insulation for the job at the lowest cost. A scale of 1 to 10 indicates cost range, 10 being the highest cost; actual prices are not given because of fluctuations in the market. Even the cost comparisons given may change, and they may vary a bit from one market to the next. CFC's (chlorofluorocarbons), once widely used in the manufacture of insulation, have been found to be harmful to the ozone layer when released into the atmosphere. Most manufacturers eliminated their use in the early 1990's, but a few companies may still use them in rigid foam insulation. Check before you buy.

Type of material	R-value and thickness	Relative cost per R-value	R-value per inch	Best uses	Advantages	Disadvantages
Fiberglass batts	R-11 (3½") R-13 (3⅝") R-19 (6") R-30 (9") R-38 (13")	2.0 2.1 1.9 1.9 1.9	R-3.0– R-3.8	Walls, floors, attics, and cathedral ceilings	Easy to install; both noncorrosive and nonflammable; stable R-value; makers stand behind their products	Susceptible to gaps during installation; does not resist air leakage
Loose-fill wool or fiberglass	R-30 (14")	1.1	R-2.2– R-4.0	Flat or shallow ceilings	Better coverage than batts over trusses and ceiling joists	Low R-value per inch
Loose-fill cellulose	R-30 (9")	1.0	R-2.8– R-3.7	Flat or shallow ceilings	Better coverage than batts over trusses and ceiling joists; suppresses air leakage into attics; can be blown into walls	Messy to install; some small manufacturers lack good quality control
Extruded polystyrene rigid foam	R-3 (½") R-5 (1") R-10 (2")	8.1 8.0 8.0	R-5.2	Walls and foundations	Highest compressive strength; performs well below grade	Relatively high cost per R-value; may contain CFC's
Expanded polysterene rigid foam	R-2 (½") R-4 (1") R-8 (2")	5.3 5.3 5.3	R-3.8– R-4.3	Over walls, in foam-core panels	Lowest-cost foam; does not contain CFC's	Not recommended for below grade
Polyurethane rigid foam	R-3 (½") R-6 (1")	9.6 8.3	R-5.7– R-7.2	Over walls, in foam-core panels	High R-value per inch for tight spaces	R-value drops in time; high cost per R-value; may contain CFC's
Phenolic rigid foam	R-8 (1")	8.3	R-8.3	Over walls, roof decks	Best fire-resistant properties of all foams; stable R-value	High cost per R-value; may contain CFC's
Reflective bubble-pack insulation	R-value varies with use, not thickness	4.0–10.0	R-6– R-15 (needs air space)	Crawl spaces in cold climates; heating ducts	Blocks loss of downward radiant heat; acts as air-vapor barrier if joints are taped	Expensive, and performance not as well documented as other insulations
Radiant barrier	No R-value; equivalent to an R-11 when added above existing R-11 insulation in hot climates			Staple to rafters	In hot climates, often saves more energy than increased attic insulation	Not proven for use in cold climates

Home climate/Installing insulation

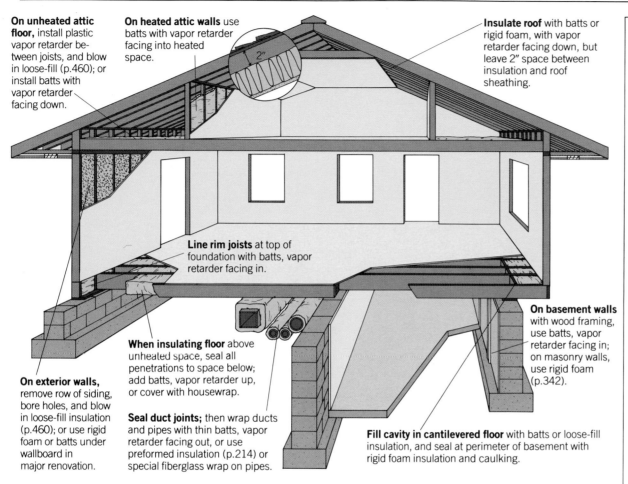

On unheated attic floor, install plastic vapor retarder between joists, and blow in loose-fill (p.460); or install batts with vapor retarder facing down.

On heated attic walls use batts with vapor retarder facing into heated space.

2"

Insulate roof with batts or rigid foam, with vapor retarder facing down, but leave 2" space between insulation and roof sheathing.

Line rim joists at top of foundation with batts, vapor retarder facing in.

On exterior walls, remove row of siding, bore holes, and blow in loose-fill insulation (p.460); or use rigid foam or batts under wallboard in major renovation.

When insulating floor above unheated space, seal all penetrations to space below; add batts, vapor retarder up, or cover with housewrap.

Seal duct joints; then wrap ducts and pipes with thin batts, vapor retarder facing out, or use preformed insulation (p.214) or special fiberglass wrap on pipes.

Fill cavity in cantilevered floor with batts or loose-fill insulation, and seal at perimeter of basement with rigid foam insulation and caulking.

On basement walls with wood framing, use batts, vapor retarder facing in; on masonry walls, use rigid foam (p.342).

Fiberglass insulation generally comes as loose-fill or in 8-foot-long batts that have been cut from large rolls, or blankets. Batts may have a facing of paper or aluminum foil, which serves as a vapor retarder, or they may be unfaced. They are generally 14½ or 22½ inches wide. For irregularly sized cavities, cut the batts about ¾ inch wider than the space; compress them with a straight board and use a serrated knife. Split batts by hand to fit on both sides of electrical wiring. Where the insulation must cross electrical boxes or other obstructions, notch it to fit the space without being compressed; permanently compressing a batt reduces energy savings. Also avoid gaps; they sharply reduce the insulation's effectiveness.

▶ **CAUTION:** Fiberglass particles can be harmful. When handling fiberglass insulation, wear sturdy, loose, long-sleeved clothing, gloves, goggles, a hat, and a dual-cartridge respirator (p.354). If particles do get on your skin, don't scratch; shower as soon as possible. In attics, light your workspace and lay planks or plywood across the joists for support. Finally, cover any flammable facing on batts with wallboard.

Vapor retarders

The best way to reduce the passage of water vapor into an insulated space is to seal all penetrations (p.457). A second way is to use a vapor retarder on the warm side of the insulation. Suitable vapor retarders include 4- to 6-mil polyethylene film, special low-permeation paints, and the facing on fiberglass batts, rigid foam, or bubble-pack insulation.

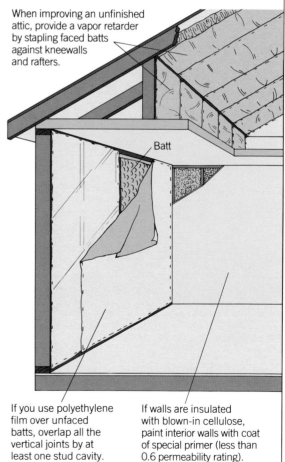

When improving an unfinished attic, provide a vapor retarder by stapling faced batts against kneewalls and rafters.

Batt

If you use polyethylene film over unfaced batts, overlap all the vertical joints by at least one stud cavity.

If walls are insulated with blown-in cellulose, paint interior walls with coat of special primer (less than 0.6 permeability rating).

Batts in the attic

In unheated attic, install faced batts with facing down. Starting above outside wall plates, roll batts toward center, using a yardstick to push batts into tight spaces. Leave area above eave vents clear. **CAUTION:** To prevent fire hazard, keep insulation 3 in. away from recessed light fixtures (unless marked "I.C.") and metal flues.

To install faced batts in ceiling of heated attic, work from top down, stapling paper flanges of batt facing to front edges (not sides) of rafters. Butt batts together at joints. At ridge beam, cut batts at angle to keep insulation flush. Don't use too much insulation; leave a 2-in. gap between insulation and roof sheathing.

Radiant barriers

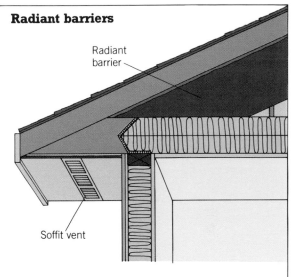

In Deep South and other hot, sunny areas, a layer of shiny foil beneath shingles helps deflect heat from roof and keep attic cooler. To add a radiant barrier to house, staple 4-ft.-wide fiber-reinforced radiant barrier material to bottom edges of rafters, shiny side facing down.

Crawl-space insulation

In floors above unheated spaces, cover with housewrap or push batts between joists with facing up against subfloor. To hold batts in place, staple string to bottom edges of joists in zigzag pattern across batts. Or cut segments of clothes hanger wire slightly longer than width of cavity, and jam them across spaces, bowing them upward.

For unvented crawl-space walls, fit pieces of batt against band joist between floor joists. Then cut batts 1 to 2 ft. longer than crawl-space wall, and nail them to sill with long furring strips. Fold excess out onto ground. On walls that run parallel to joists, shove batts up until tops touch floor; then nail with furring strips directly to band joist.

In humid climates, you can use 4-ft.-wide bubble-pack insulation to insulate floor above vented crawl space and provide vapor and air barrier at same time. First, along perimeter, push pieces of batt flush between floor joists and against band joist. Then staple bubble pack to bottoms of joists and to sill. Seal joints with aluminized tape.

Cellulose—paper treated with a fire retardant—is the usual loose-fill chosen by do-it-yourselfers. It is sold at lumberyards, which generally will lend or rent a blowing machine, consisting of a hopper for holding the insulation, a blower motor, and a hose at least 70 feet long. When blown into walls at the proper density, cellulose can reduce a home's air leakage by 20 to 33 percent. Make sure the product you buy has been inspected (the bags should be stamped UL and NAHB/NRC).

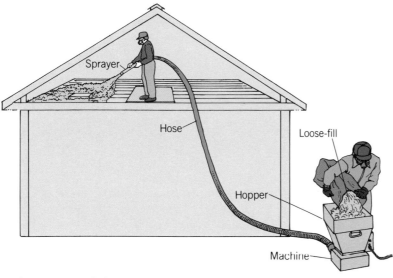

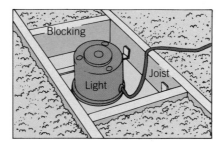

In an attic, you can blow loose-fill over any existing insulation. Have helper pour loose-fill into machine hopper while you guide hose sprayer in attic. Cover tops of exterior walls with insulation, but keep soffit vents open, blocking them with foam baffles (facing page). For fire protection, nail wood blocking between joists to keep insulation 3 in. or more from recessed ceiling light—unless light is rated "I.C." Stop now and then to clear air. When finished, insulate and weatherstrip attic hatch.

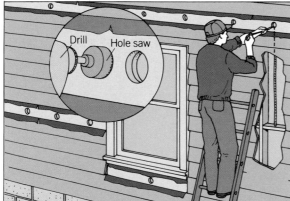

Blowing into house wall: 1. Shut off electrical power along wall. Remove layer of siding (pp.407–410). Drill 2- to 3-in. holes between studs (every 16 or 24 in.) in exposed sheathing. Push a steel tape measure up and down inside the wall cavity to locate blocking. Remove siding and drill holes below any blocking.

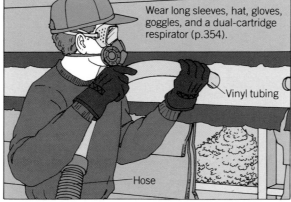

Wear long sleeves, hat, gloves, goggles, and a dual-cartridge respirator (p.354).

2. Tape 5 ft. of 1¼-in. flexible vinyl tubing to blower's hose. Starting at bottom of cavity and moving upward, blow in insulation 1 ft. at a time. A 30-lb. bag should fill three 16-in.-wide cavities in 2 to 4 min. Don't overfill cavity, or you may loosen wallboard inside. Once filled, stuff fiberglass from a batt into holes; replace siding.

Ventilation helps dissipate unwanted attic moisture during the winter and hot air in the summer. Because warm air rises, vents are placed in the soffits or low on the rooftop to let in fresh air, and along the ridge of the roof or in the gables to let the warm air escape. The drawings at right show a few common arrangements. Although gable vents work well and are easy to add, a continuous ridge vent is more effective; add one if you are reroofing.

Ventilation is especially needed in unused attics where insulation has been increased to keep heat from leaking out of the rooms below in winter. Because little heat comes in from below, attic temperatures drop sharply. The moisture in what little house air does leak into the attic condenses on surrounding cold surfaces, staining the interior and leading to localized structural rot.

Codes generally require a ventilation area equal to at least one three-hundredth of the attic floor area, split evenly between low soffit vents and high ridge vents. But consider your climate: the milder the climate, the more effective ventilation is at keeping your attic dry in the winter and cool in the summer.

Fan-driven vents are often used in attics, but they create noise and tend to fail prematurely. Even more important, they are generally no more effective than properly installed nonmechanical vents. But they should not be confused with whole-house fans (pp.492–493), which can be used quite effectively to help cool your home in the summer. However, if you install a whole-house fan, you may have to increase the amount of attic ventilation, as the fan will exhaust much more air than a moisture ventilation system.

House construction 188–190
Finding a stud 191
Ladders and safety 383

Soffit vents

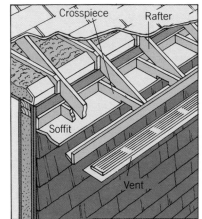

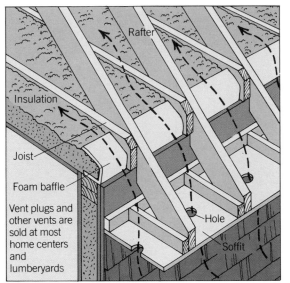

Soffit vent plug

Vent plugs: Drill hole slightly smaller than plug between each pair of rafters. Install special foam baffles between ceiling joists to keep insulation from covering vents and to prevent cold air from moving under insulation (particularly batts). Push vent plugs into place.

Continuous vent: Cut opening in thin soffit material to accept vent. Screw vent into crosspieces that hold soffit. Or install shorter rectangular vents in same way, positioning one between each pair of rafter ends.

Gable vents

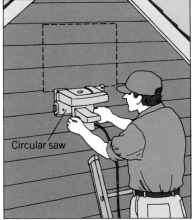

1. Mark house siding to position vent opening, which should be ¼ in. larger than vent dimensions (excluding flanges). Following marks, cut opening through siding and sheathing. Cut siding far enough back from edges of hole to accept vent flanges and trim.

2. In attic, cut any obstructing stud 1½ in. above and below opening. Frame opening with wood blocking. From outside, push vent into hole until flanges fit flat against the sheathing. Nail through flanges and sheathing into blocking. Cover flanges with trim. Caulk between trim and siding.

For a triangular vent, measure outside to be sure vent will fit below gable trim. In attic, mark position of vent opening on wall and drill holes through wall to indicate where to cut on outside without cutting into rafters. Proceed as for installing rectangular vents.

Continuous ridge vent

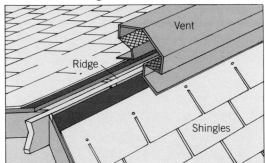

Cut a 2-in.-wide gap along peak. Snap chalk lines to mark cut lines on both sides of ridge. Use knife to cut through shingles and felt. Cut through sheathing with circular saw set to proper depth. *Do not cut into rafters.* Caulk bottom of vent and nail it into place with gasketed roofing nails.

Roof vent

1. From attic, drive nail through roof to mark center of vent. On roof, find nail; around it cut away shingles and then sheathing in shape of vent opening but a bit larger. In attic, nail supports between rafters at upper and lower edges of opening.

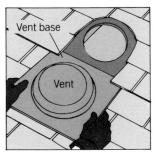

2. On roof, pry up enough roofing nails above opening to allow vent base to slide under roofing and protect opening. Coat underside of edges of base with roofing cement, slide vent into position, and fasten it down with galvanized gasketed roofing nails.

A bathroom exhaust fan lets you directly expel moisture that would otherwise lead to condensation, peeling paint, mold, mildew, or even structural damage. Because it eliminates the need for adding long ducts, the ideal location for a bathroom fan is high on an outside wall close to the shower and as far as practical from the entry door. A second option is to mount it in the ceiling with 3- or 4-inch diameter ductwork leading to the outside. For best results install a wall-mounted control with a 30-minute timer near the door. If the room gets excessively damp, add a humidistat to turn the fan on or off as the humidity of the room rises or falls.

Vented kitchen range hoods with fans can exhaust smoke, grease, heat, undesirable odors and combustion products, and moisture generated by cooking. Hoods without vents filter grease out of the air but recirculate the same air back into the room, and are less effective. Choose a hood that is as wide as the cooking surface and has a variable-speed fan. Install it up to 24 inches above the top of the range.

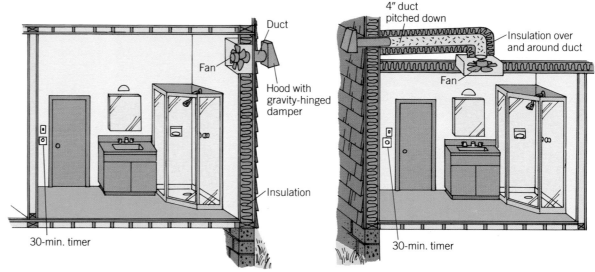

Install exhaust fan in outside wall, if practical, and run short duct from fan to outside. Cap duct with hood with gravity-hinged damper to close vent when fan is off. Don't use louvers; they impede airflow.

If wall installation is impractical, install fan that accepts 4-in. round duct in ceiling. Run duct from fan, sloping downward, across attic to outside; seal any joints. Wrap with insulation to reduce condensation.

Installing a typical exhaust fan in an outside wall

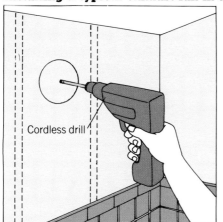

1. Mark position of vent on wall between studs. With electric power off, drill hole at center of mark all the way through outside wall; avoid pipes and electric wires. Cut opening in wallboard large enough to accept vent duct but smaller than fan mounting plate. Cut opening in outside wall.

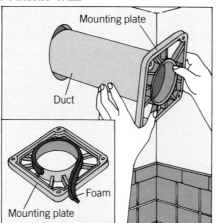

2. Line ridge on rear of fan mounting plate and inside perimeter of plate with adhesive-backed foam (inset). Push duct over it. Slide duct into opening so that mounting plate fits snugly against wall. Outside, mark duct where it exits wall; remove and trim duct at mark with hacksaw.

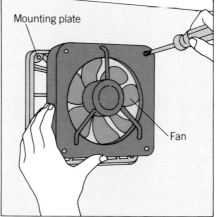

3. Return duct to opening and mark position of mounting holes. Drill pilot holes for screws; then feed electric cable through mounting plate (p.250). Screw mounting plate to wall. Make electrical connections following manufacturer's instructions. Attach fan assembly to mounting plate.

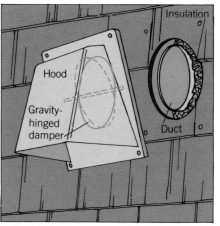

4. On outside of house, use old screwdriver to stuff fiberglass insulation between end of duct and edges of hole in wall, or use spray foam insulation. Screw hood with gravity-hinged damper over duct. Have helper turn fan on and off; check damper. Caulk between hood and house siding.

Heat recovery ventilator

Tightly built homes can experience problems with lingering odors and high humidity, resulting in damaging condensation during cold snaps. Generally these problems can be solved with the ordinary ventilation described in the preceding three pages. But if you live in a moderately cold climate with high utility rates and the conventional means of ventilation don't solve your problem, your home may be a candidate for a heat recovery ventilator (HRV).

Compared to opening a window, an HRV—also called an air-to-air heat exchanger—provides continually controlled ventilation and somewhat better comfort. Heat from stale exhaust air is used to temper the incoming air so that fresh air enters your home closer to room temperature than to the outside temperature. During the winter, an HRV will usually supply a very low flow of fresh air between 40° F and 60° F; exact temperatures depend on the outdoor temperature, the rate at which the air flows through the unit, and the machine's efficiency.

Most HRV's are designed to ventilate the entire home. Typically, four to eight supply and return ducts run through the basement, crawl space, or attic where the HRV itself is also installed. Adding a whole-house ventilator can be expensive and should be done by a professional.

It is also possible to install a small plug-in HRV on an exterior wall or in a window. Such units ventilate only a single room, like a window-mounted air conditioner, but they cost less than whole-house systems and are easy to install. Some models include multiple filters that clean the air as well. For the most effective air mixing, install a wall-mounted unit high on an outside wall but at least 1 foot from the ceiling or the nearest wall. Keep it away from thermostats and seating areas, in a spot where some fan noise and cool air movement won't be a bother.

▶ **CAUTION:** Don't install an HRV where the outside ducts will be near a garage or driveway; if you do, the fan may draw car exhaust fumes into the house. Also, an HRV is not meant to replace a kitchen range hood; it will clog with grease. Instead, install a vented range hood with a fan in addition to an HRV.

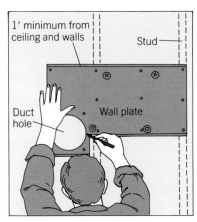

1. Locate two studs, and hold HRV wall plate (or template) against wall, with screw holes over studs and the duct opening away from them. Trace outline of duct opening on wall. With electric power off, drill hole at center of outline all the way through the outside wall, avoiding pipes and electric wires.

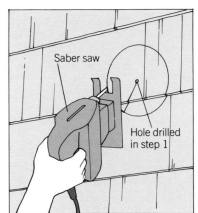

2. Cut duct opening in wallboard (or cut and frame opening for entire unit, if maker so instructs); remove insulation. Go outside and cut duct opening in house siding and sheathing, using drilled hole to locate position. Return inside and screw wall plate (if any) into place on wall.

3. Test-fit duct and mark where it exits wall on outside. Remove duct from wall and hacksaw it at mark. Slide duct back into place from inside, and screw its flange to wall plate. Go back outside and caulk between duct and wall. Then screw weather hood into place over duct.

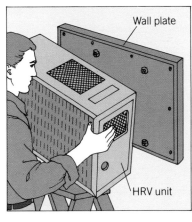

4. Return indoors and hang the HRV on its wall plate following the manufacturer's instructions. Install any filters, and plug unit into a nearby electrical outlet. *Note:* Check the manufacturer's instructions; unit may need a dedicated circuit or 220V current.

How a heat recovery ventilator works

In an HRV, one fan exhausts stale indoor air while another draws in fresh outside air. Both airstreams pass separately through a core of many thin metal or plastic surfaces. As it passes through the core, exhaust air from house transmits its heat through core walls to cooler air from outside. Drain carries away condensate. In whole-house HRV, heater can be added to supply duct to further warm incoming air during severely cold weather.

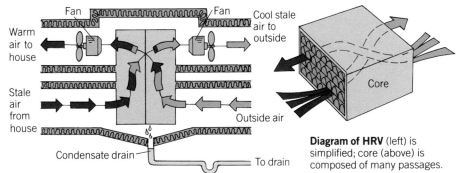

Diagram of HRV (left) is simplified; core (above) is composed of many passages.

Home climate/Heating systems

In general terms, a heating system converts fuel (gas or oil) or energy (electricity or the sun's rays) into heat, which it then distributes throughout the house. The function of all heating systems is to maintain comfortable wintertime temperatures. Yet from one system to the next, the delivery method, means of heat generation, and fuel that generates the heat vary.

The most common whole-house heat delivery systems are warm air, hot water, steam, and fluid-based radiant heat. In each of these, air or a liquid is heated in a furnace or boiler and sent to the various parts of the house through ducts, pipes, or tubes. The heated air in a warm-air system is blown into the rooms through ducts and registers. In other systems, steam or a liquid heats radiators or convectors, or the floors, ceilings, or walls of the house; these in turn give off their heat to the rooms. The furnace of a warm-air system and the boiler in the other systems house a burner that can be fueled by gas, oil, propane, butane, electricity, or even wood or coal, depending upon their availability and the local preference.

Other systems heat the home entirely by electricity, as in electrical radiant heat and baseboard convectors. Heat pumps extract heat from outside air and "pump" it indoors. Solar panels, fireplaces, wood-burning stoves, and electric and gas space heaters are also found in homes, but generally they provide auxiliary heat, supplementing a whole-house system.

One or more thermostats control a whole-house system. A thermostat regulates the temperature of the surrounding space and the time of heat delivery, but not the rate of delivery. In the following pages, thermostats and burners are treated separately from the major heating systems.

Zoned systems. For heating (and cooling) purposes, a house may be divided into zones, each with its own thermostat. Instead of sending heat to all the rooms in a house, a zoned system heats individual rooms or groups of rooms separately. For example, bedrooms, which need heat at different times than other rooms, are often placed in a different zone. Zoned heating provides slightly improved performance and control; the more you set back heating devices in unoccupied rooms, the more you will save on energy.

Effect of humidity. Wintertime comfort is more than a matter of delivering properly warmed air. Comfort is also affected by the temperature of surrounding surfaces, the speed of indoor air movement, and the indoor humidity. (Air at a given temperature feels warmer if the humidity is high.) A home with air leaks may suffer from low indoor humidity; sealing the leaks (p.456) or installing a humidifier (p.499) will raise the humidity level.

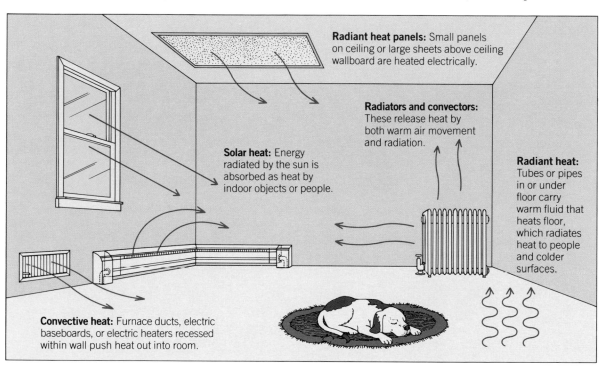

Radiant heat panels: Small panels on ceiling or large sheets above ceiling wallboard are heated electrically.

Radiators and convectors: These release heat by both warm air movement and radiation.

Solar heat: Energy radiated by the sun is absorbed as heat by indoor objects or people.

Radiant heat: Tubes or pipes in or under floor carry warm fluid that heats floor, which radiates heat to people and colder surfaces.

Convective heat: Furnace ducts, electric baseboards, or electric heaters recessed within wall push heat out into room.

Common heating systems

System	Heat delivered by	Most common fuels	Means of distribution
Warm air	Forced convection (blower)	Natural gas, fuel oil, propane, butane, or electricity	Ductwork from furnace; electric heaters recessed in wall
Hot water	Convection, or convection and radiation	Natural gas, fuel oil, propane, butane, or electricity	Pipes and convectors or radiators
Steam	Convection, or convection and radiation	Natural gas, fuel oil, or electricity	Pipes and radiators
Radiant heat	Radiation, or radiation and convection	Gas, oil, propane, or butane for floor systems; electricity for ceiling systems and exposed panels; wood and coal for stoves	Pipes or tubes in or under floors, wiring within plaster or above wallboard, panels mounted on ceilings or walls, firebox and flue pipe for stoves

Warm-air heating systems

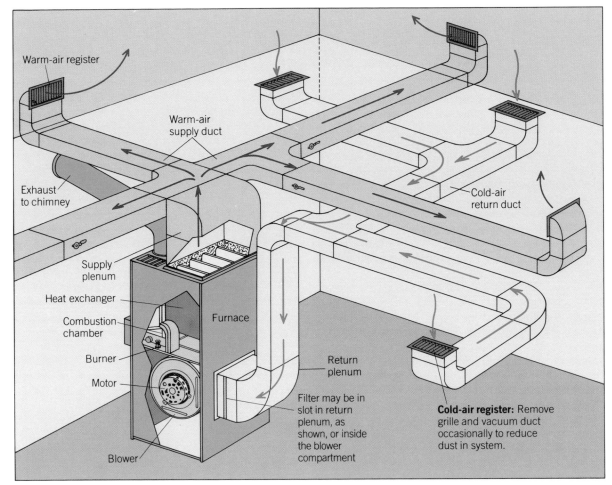

Warm-air register

Warm-air supply duct

Exhaust to chimney

Cold-air return duct

Supply plenum

Heat exchanger

Combustion chamber

Furnace

Burner

Motor

Return plenum

Filter may be in slot in return plenum, as shown, or inside the blower compartment

Blower

Cold-air register: Remove grille and vacuum duct occasionally to reduce dust in system.

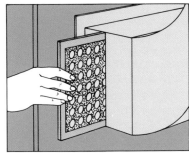

Clean filter monthly, or replace it with one of same size, but turn off power to furnace first. Or install a washable filter that whistles when clogged; clean it monthly. Clogged filter wears blower motor and reduces efficiency by cutting airflow.

Clean the blower once a year. Turn off power and open the blower compartment. Clean fan blades with a bottle brush, and vacuum the housing. Oil the blower or not, following instructions in owner's manual.

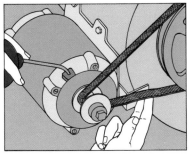

Check fan belt, if any, once a year, with power off. If frayed or stiff, replace it. Press lightly on belt; it should deflect ½ to ¾ in. If not, tighten or loosen by turning adjustment bolt. If motor is not factory-lubricated, add 3 to 6 drops SAE 10W30 oil.

Because it is easy to maintain and readily combines with whole-house air conditioning, humidification, and air cleaning, warm air is often used for heating homes. Have a warm-air system serviced by a heating contractor once a year, and take the simple maintenance steps outlined (above right) to keep it working smoothly all winter.

A warm-air system contains five elements: a furnace to heat the air, a distribution network of ducts, registers on walls or floors, an exhaust flue, and a thermostat. The furnace contains a burner, a combustion chamber, and a heat exchanger; the latter is a chamber that keeps the house air separate from the harmful gases generated by combustion. A motor—either belt-driven or direct-drive—powers a blower, which circulates house air through the heat exchanger and into the supply plenum (the main duct leading from the furnace). From there, smaller ducts carry warm air to the individual rooms, where it enters through adjustable registers.

Cool air from the rooms is pulled back to the furnace through return ducts; just before reentering the furnace's blower (in the return plenum or in the blower compartment itself), the return air is filtered to keep the blower clean. Combustion gases emanating from the burner exit through the exhaust flue.

A few old furnaces still use *gravity circulation,* which relies on the natural convection created by the buoyancy of hot air and the fact that cold air falls. These systems have larger ducts and no blower.

On the average, homes with ductwork leak 25 percent more air and require as much as 25 to 40 percent more heating and cooling energy than homes without ductwork. This is due to the fact that an air-moving system creates pressure differences within the house as well as in the ductwork itself. In addition to normal leaks, the pressurization draws outside air into crawl-space ducts, forces air out through cracks in the house shell and in the supply ducts, or pulls outside air in through cracks in the house shell and in the return ducts.

To get a warm-air system to work efficiently, make sure that the house shell and all the ducts that pass through unheated spaces are properly sealed. Also be sure that there are enough return ducts for your system; if all return air comes from one location or if the house has two stories and no return duct from upstairs, add another return duct. You can distinguish between supply and return ducts by touch when the furnace is on: supply ducts feel warm; return ducts, cool.

Adusting the blower switch. Ignition of the burner starts a new cycle, but useful heat is delivered only when the blower operates. You

Fan *On*
Fan *Off*
Limit pointer

Blower switch

can save on your heating bill by setting the fan to come on earlier in the cycle and to run longer after the burner shuts off. Take the cover off the blower switch on the side of the furnace, and shift the lowest of the three set points (fan off) down slightly; lower the middle set point (fan on) by exactly the same amount; then run the furnace through a test cycle.

Adjusting the blower speed. Increasing the speed of a furnace's blower may boost heat distribution, or it may worsen the problem; try it and see. You can adjust a belt-driven model as shown below, but adjusting a direct-drive model may require a wiring change, which should be left to a heating contractor.

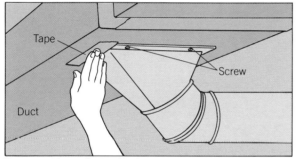

Tape
Screw
Duct

Reconnect loose ducts with sheet-metal screws. Clean dust and grease from joints with a cloth soaked in nonflammable cleaning fluid. Wrap joints with pressure-sensitive aluminized tape, pressing out any air bubbles (they prevent tape from adhering properly).

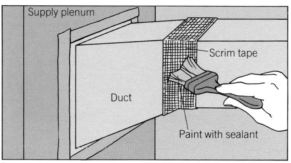

Supply plenum
Scrim tape
Duct
Paint with sealant

For more permanent sealing, especially where ducts exit the supply plenum, wrap the joint with 3-in.-wide fiberglass scrim tape and then paint over the mesh with a water-base duct sealant (available at air-conditioning supply outlets).

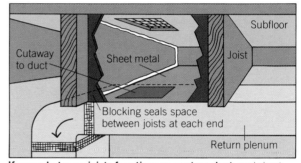

Subfloor
Cutaway to duct
Sheet metal
Joist
Blocking seals space between joists at each end
Return plenum

If space between joists functions as a return duct, seal sheet metal to joists with nonshrinking caulk, such as siliconized acrylic. Also seal floor joists to subfloor, and check blocking at end of cavity for tight fit. Clean off and tape over joints in return plenum.

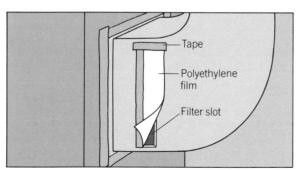

Tape
Polyethylene film
Filter slot

Tape piece of polyethylene film along top and one edge of furnace's filter slot (generally a 1- x 20-in. opening in return duct), but leave other side and bottom free of tape to allow access to filter. When blower runs, suction will pull film in to seal slot.

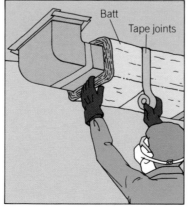

Batt
Tape joints

Insulate ducts in unheated spaces by wrapping them with spiral R-8 or R-11 batts or with 4-ft. lengths of bubble-pack insulation. Seal all the joints with aluminized tape. **CAUTION:** Do not remove any paperlike asbestos coating that might be on ducts. If you see any, call in a professional to deal with it.

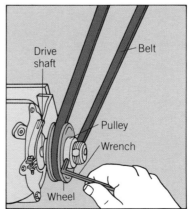

Drive shaft
Belt
Pulley
Wrench
Wheel

Increase blower speed of a belt-driven furnace motor by replacing pulley wheel on drive shaft with a wheel one size larger. Turn off power and loosen hex-head setscrew on outer part of pulley; remove old wheel and slide on new one; tighten setscrew. Replace belt, if needed. Adjust belt tension as shown on preceding page.

Balancing heat distribution

To provide even heating, adjust the supply registers or the dampers in the ducts so that each room receives sufficient heat relative to its size and exposure. Also make sure that the amount of air that the fan supplies is equal to the amount of room air returned to the furnace. To achieve this balance, leave open the door to any room that has a supply duct but no return duct, or cut a 1-inch gap between the carpet and the bottom of the door (p.437). Without this air passage, some of the heated air blown into the room will be forced out through cracks in the walls and around windows, or less air will be able to enter.

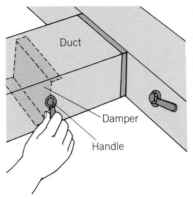

Balancing is by trial and error. To start, open dampers on the ducts leading to chilly areas, reduce airflow to overheated rooms. Dampers are usually found where ducts branch. Turning damper handle parallel to duct allows full airflow; shifting it to perpendicular closes duct. If distant rooms still lack heat, have a booster fan installed in duct.

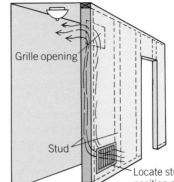

Add grille to room with two supplies and no return (undercutting door 1 in. won't let enough air out of room). Cut opening for grille in wall that separates room from hallway. Cut another opening in hallway wall in same cavity, but high up to allow air to flow freely but dampen sound transmission. Screw grilles in place over openings.

Installing a humidifier

If your home is too dry in winter, increase humidity by cutting down on air leaks or by installing a humidifier in your heating system. A humidifier diverts some of the air returning to the furnace, humidifies it as it passes through a water-soaked evaporator, and mixes it with the warm-air supply. A duct-mounted *humidistat* turns the humidifier on and off as needed. Set it lower in very cold weather to avoid causing condensation.

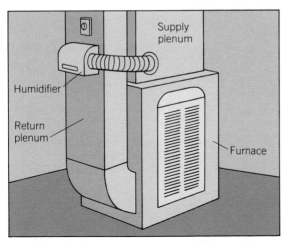

Humidifier on return plenum moistens air for supply ducts.

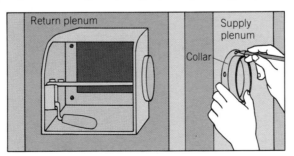

1. Tape supplied template (cutting guide) to return plenum next to furnace. Because humidifier tray will hold water, level template carefully. Drill starter hole with large bit, and use tin snips to cut rectangular opening in plenum, following template.

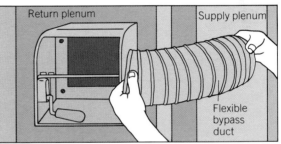

2. Drill starter holes for screws, and attach humidifier over opening in plenum with self-tapping metal screws. Stretch flexible bypass duct out sufficiently to mark connecting location on supply plenum; minimize bends in duct.

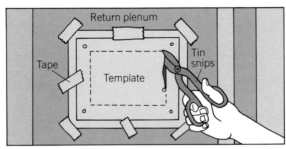

3. Holding duct collar in place on supply plenum, mark for mounting holes and circular opening. Drill holes; cut out opening; attach duct collar to plenum with self-tapping screws. Screw bypass duct to plenum collar and to collar on humidifier.

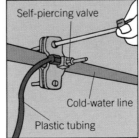

4. Attach connector assembly to cold-water pipe, as directed. Run plastic tubing between valve and humidifier pan.

5. Attach humidistat to return plenum; run low-voltage wiring from it to humidifier. Plug cord into outlet.

Home climate / Hot-water heating systems

In a hot-water, or *hydronic,* heating system, water is heated in a gas, oil, or electric boiler and circulated through pipes to convectors in the rooms. In some older systems, instead of convectors there are radiators that look like steam radiators. As the water passes through the metal convectors, it heats them; they, in turn, give off their heat to the room. A number of different piping arrangements are used in hot-water systems, as illustrated below.

A pump called a *circulator* drives the water through the pipes and convectors whenever the room thermostat calls for heat. It's usually positioned near the boiler in the return line, where the water is coolest. A *flow-control valve* keeps the water from flowing when the pump is not operating, and so keeps the system from overheating the convectors.

Because water expands when it is heated, an airtight expansion tank is installed near the boiler to take in the excess. As water enters the tank, the air inside is compressed, making it possible for the volume of the water to increase without building up much pressure in the system. Without room for expansion, pressure could build up rapidly, breaking a pipe or a boiler casting. If the expansion tank fills up, the excess water escapes through the safety relief valve on top of the boiler. Older types of tanks (facing page) must be drained when they get too full of water; newer *diaphragm tanks* have an elastic divider separating the air from the water, and should be drained only by a boiler serviceperson or plumber.

Gravity systems. Some older systems have no circulators, but rely on the principle that water expands when heated and so becomes lighter as its weight is extended over a greater space. Because the heated water is lighter, it rises through the pipes and is replaced by the cooler, heavier water, which is pulled down through the return pipes by gravity.

Improving efficiency. To reduce heat loss, insulate any pipes that run through crawl spaces or other unheated areas (p.214). To help balance the heat delivered to various rooms, you can partly close the shutoff valve on individual convectors or

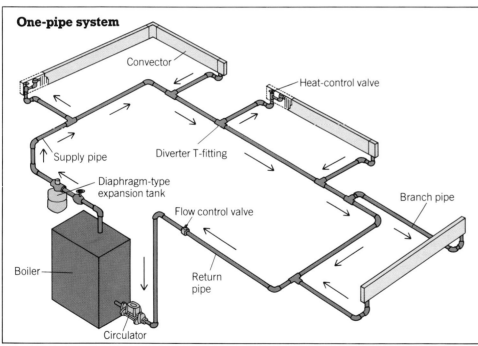

One-pipe system

Convector · Heat-control valve · Supply pipe · Diverter T-fitting · Diaphragm-type expansion tank · Flow control valve · Branch pipe · Boiler · Return pipe · Circulator

In single-pipe system, supply pipe carries hot water from boiler, past each convector, and back to boiler. Short branch pipes take the water from the supply pipe to the individual convectors and back again. When the heat-control valve on the inlet side of a convector is open, a special T-fitting diverts part of the water from the main line into the branch line feeding that convector. If an individual convector is shut off, the hot water does not stop flowing, but simply bypasses the shut-down convector and proceeds along the main pipe to the next convector. The single-pipe system is widely used in small and medium-size houses.

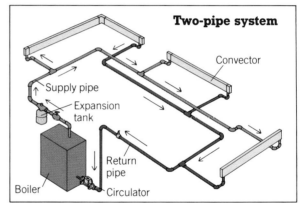

Two-pipe system

Supply pipe · Expansion tank · Convector · Return pipe · Boiler · Circulator

Best for large houses, this system uses one pipe to carry hot water to the convectors and another to return the water to the boiler. Because it flows through a separate pipe, the cooler return water doesn't pass through the other convectors, and so the supply water remains hotter as it travels to the far ends of the system.

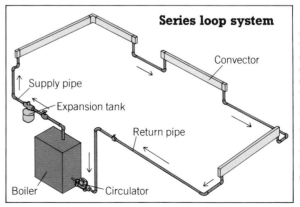

Series loop system

Supply pipe · Expansion tank · Convector · Return pipe · Boiler · Circulator

In this simplest of the hot-water systems, one pipe runs from the boiler, through each convector (in one end and out the other), and back to the boiler in an uninterrupted loop. You cannot turn off one convector in the loop without shutting them all off, but a system may have two or more loops.

radiators, allowing less hot water to enter. Or you can install separate thermostatic valves on the convectors, but these can be expensive.

Maintenance. Twice a year, oil the circulator pump and motor if they are not permanently lubricated. Before doing any repair work on a boiler, shut off the power to it; wait until the system cools;

then, if required for the job, drain the boiler as you would when replacing a radiator (p.470).

When water is heated for the first time in a long while or just after the boiler has been refilled, it releases air, which gets trapped in the convectors and keeps the hot water out. To get rid of the trapped air, vent the convectors (p.470).

Zoned heating

To save energy, a hot-water system can be divided into zones of one or more rooms with different amounts of heat sent to each zone. This lets you make occupied rooms warm and cozy while keeping the other rooms cooler. Any number of zones is possible. Typically, a two-zone system groups living areas, kitchen, and bathrooms in one zone and bedrooms in another.

Zone valve

Zones are created by running branch lines off the main supply pipe to each desired zone, and adding a thermostatic zone valve in each branch line to turn the hot-water supply on or off. One boiler and one circulator—or two in large houses—are used with multiple zone valves. Alternatively, a separate circulator can be used for each zone, eliminating zone valves.

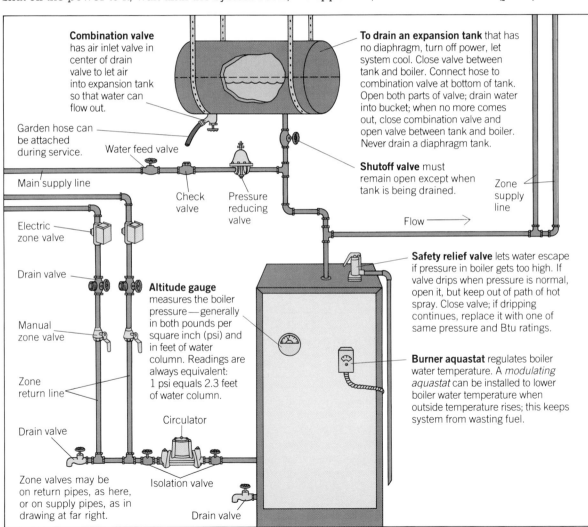

Combination valve has air inlet valve in center of drain valve to let air into expansion tank so that water can flow out.

Garden hose can be attached during service.

Water feed valve

Main supply line

Check valve

Pressure reducing valve

Electric zone valve

Drain valve

Manual zone valve

Altitude gauge measures the boiler pressure—generally in both pounds per square inch (psi) and in feet of water column. Readings are always equivalent: 1 psi equals 2.3 feet of water column.

Zone return line

Drain valve

Circulator

Zone valves may be on return pipes, as here, or on supply pipes, as in drawing at far right.

Isolation valve

Drain valve

To drain an expansion tank that has no diaphragm, turn off power, let system cool. Close valve between tank and boiler. Connect hose to combination valve at bottom of tank. Open both parts of valve; drain water into bucket; when no more comes out, close combination valve and open valve between tank and boiler. Never drain a diaphragm tank.

Shutoff valve must remain open except when tank is being drained.

Zone supply line

Flow

Safety relief valve lets water escape if pressure in boiler gets too high. If valve drips when pressure is normal, open it, but keep out of path of hot spray. Close valve; if dripping continues, replace it with one of same pressure and Btu ratings.

Burner aquastat regulates boiler water temperature. A *modulating aquastat* can be installed to lower boiler water temperature when outside temperature rises; this keeps system from wasting fuel.

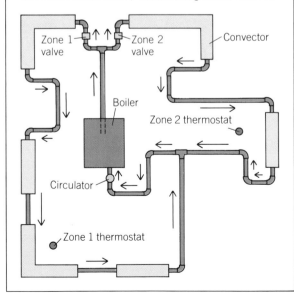

Zone 1 valve

Zone 2 valve

Convector

Boiler

Zone 2 thermostat

Circulator

Zone 1 thermostat

Metal convectors and radiators give up part of their warmth by radiation, but most of the heat comes from convection—when air contacts the hot metal, it rises and is replaced with cooler air. Generally found only in older hot-water systems, radiators are made of cast-iron tubing. Convectors, much lighter in weight, are either grilled cabinets or long, low baseboards. Inside they contain thin-wall copper or steel tubing surrounded by metal fins that increase the heated area. You can replace one or more radiators with convectors as shown at right, but use dielectric fittings (p.216) to connect pipes of different metals.

Vent all the convectors or radiators in the system after refilling the boiler or turning the system back on for the first time in a long while. The vent valves on a radiator are near the top at the end opposite the inlet valve. On convectors, the valve is usually hidden by the cover.

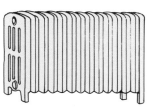

Cast-iron radiator

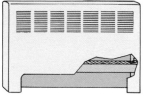

Upright convector

Never place anything on or in front of a convector or radiator; it could obstruct the airflow. If you paint a convector or radiator, use standard paint; metallic paint will reduce heat transfer by as much as 25 percent. Dust also cuts down on efficiency; vacuum the convectors and radiators regularly. Also, straighten bent convector fins with needle-nose pliers, and be sure that the convector covers are not bent or misaligned.

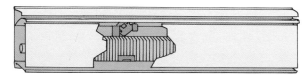

Baseboard convector is low-lying, but still should not be blocked.

Venting a system

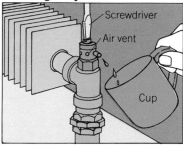

Screwdriver

Air vent

Cup

Trapped air can keep hot water out of a convector or radiator. To vent it, open the air vent and keep it open until water spurts out. Catch the water in a cup, but be careful—it will be hot. Start with convector at lowest level if more than one is cool.

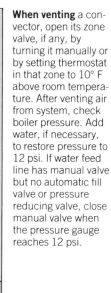

Motorized zone valve

Drain valve

Manual zone valve

When venting a convector, open its zone valve, if any, by turning it manually or by setting thermostat in that zone to 10° F above room temperature. After venting air from system, check boiler pressure. Add water, if necessary, to restore pressure to 12 psi. If water feed line has manual valve but no automatic fill valve or pressure reducing valve, close manual valve when the pressure gauge reaches 12 psi.

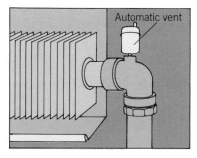

Automatic vent

Automatic vent valve slowly releases air from convector as system fills with water. Vent should be kept clean. If it drips water, replace it.

Replacing a radiator with a convector

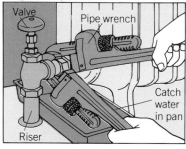

Valve

Pipe wrench

Catch water in pan

Riser

1. Turn off system; close water feed valve; open radiator valves; let system cool. Attach hose to boiler drain valve; open radiator vent; drain out water. Loosen connections with pipe wrenches (or with propane torch for soldered joints). Pull out radiator.

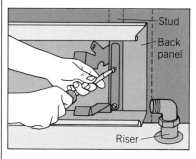

Stud

Back panel

Riser

2. Position baseboard convector so that its connectors align with riser pipes and the convector's back panel can be screwed directly into studs. Mark position for back panel (including screw holes); drill pilot holes in wall; screw back panel into place.

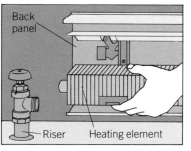

Back panel

Riser   Heating element

3. Install the finned heating element on the back panel. Clean threads on risers that will be connected to unit, using wire brush; wipe with clean rag and wrap with pipe tape (p.223). If riser is too far away, add needed extensions and fittings.

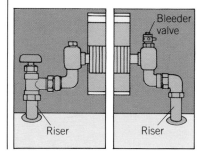

Bleeder valve

Riser   Riser

4. Make plumbing connections, using reducing bushings or dielectric fittings, if needed (p.216). Open inlet valve and attach convector cover. Turn on water and flush out boiler. Turn off boiler drain valve and fill boiler. Turn system on. Vent system a bit later.

Radiant heat

In radiant systems, a large surface is heated by water pipes or by electric film or cables. Thermostats control the delivery of heat. Quiet and even, radiant heat cuts down on cold spots and drafts.

Hydronic systems. In pre-1970 radiant systems, hot water mixed with antifreeze circulates through metal piping embedded in concrete floors or plaster walls or ceilings. In newer systems, fluid may be pumped through durable plastic tubing. You may have to change the fluid in all these systems to maintain its corrosion resistance. If the piping fails due to a shifting slab, have a portion of the slab jackhammered and leveled, or abandon the system and install new hot-water convectors (p.470).

Electric radiant heat. Heat can also be sent through wiring above, within, or on the ceiling. To reduce high energy bills, increase insulation in the ceilings, basement, and crawl space (pp.457–460). If a radiant system above a ceiling fails, consider replacing it with surface-mounted panels rather than tearing out the ceiling for repairs.

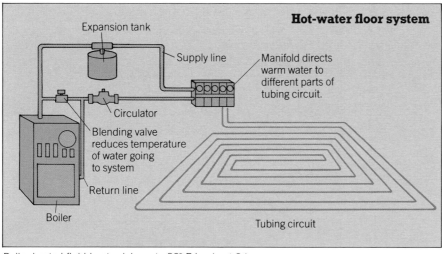

Hot-water floor system

Expansion tank · Supply line · Manifold directs warm water to different parts of tubing circuit. · Circulator · Blending valve reduces temperature of water going to system · Return line · Boiler · Tubing circuit

Boiler-heated fluid heats slab up to 86° F in about 3 hr.

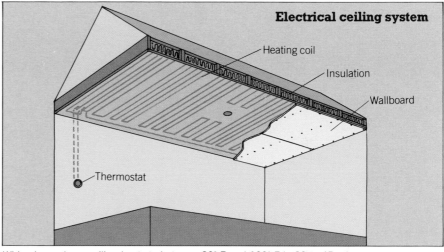

Electrical ceiling system

Heating coil · Insulation · Wallboard · Thermostat

Wiring in or above ceiling heats to between 90° F and 100° F in 30 to 45 min.

Radiant heating panels and film

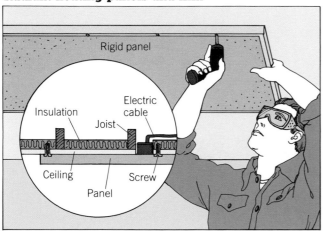

Rigid panel · Insulation · Electric cable · Joist · Ceiling · Screw · Panel

Rigid panels of 1-in. fiberglass, 2 ft. wide and 2 to 8 ft. long, contain a heating element that is charged by either 120 or 240V. To install, run feed wire to the wall thermostat, then up to junction box attached to ceiling joist. Connect panel wiring to junction box; then screw panel frame to ceiling. Or mount panels flush with surface of ceiling.
CAUTION: Before working on electric wiring, turn off power to circuit (p.237); check that it's off (p.243).

Metal foil or conductive strips of graphite ink embedded in tough plastic film can also provide electric radiant heat. Simply staple the film to bottoms of exposed ceiling joists, make electrical connections following manufacturer's directions, and cover ceiling with wallboard. Or install panels made of gypsum embedded with electric wires by sliding them between ceiling joists, making electrical connections, then adding wallboard to ceiling.

In a steam system, water is heated in a boiler until it vaporizes and rises through pipes to radiators or convectors. When the steam hits the cooler radiator surfaces, it condenses and the water runs back to the boiler.

A steam system may be *one-pipe* or *two-pipe*. In a two-pipe system, the steam flows through one set of pipes and the condensate returns through another. In a one-pipe system (below), the steam and water travel through the same pipe in opposite directions.

Safety controls. When water is heated to steam, pressure builds up in the boiler. To operate the boiler to suit current weather conditions, the boiler has a pressure control. Check the pressure gauge just after the boiler switches off. If it is far above the pressure setting, have the control replaced immediately. Boilers also have a pressure safety valve that will open before an unsafe pressure level is reached.

If the water in the boiler falls below a safe level, the low-water cutoff turns off the burner. The water level should be midway in the glass gauge when the boiler is not operating.

Venting. Quick-release air vents let air escape from the main steam lines and individual radiators. As the steam advances, pressure forces the air out of the vents. As the steam reaches the vent, its heat causes an alcohol solution inside the vent's *float* to expand and push against the base of the float; this causes the base to flex and push the body of the float up, closing the escape hole. Change a vent that spits or drips water, leaks steam, or fails to open.

Maintenance. Radiators require a free flow of air to work efficiently. Don't block them with furniture, and cover them only with special vented covers. Vacuum the radiators often.

Have the system checked by a service person annually, and follow the steps described on the facing page. If the system operates poorly, call a professional. Malfunctions can be difficult to pinpoint without special equipment.

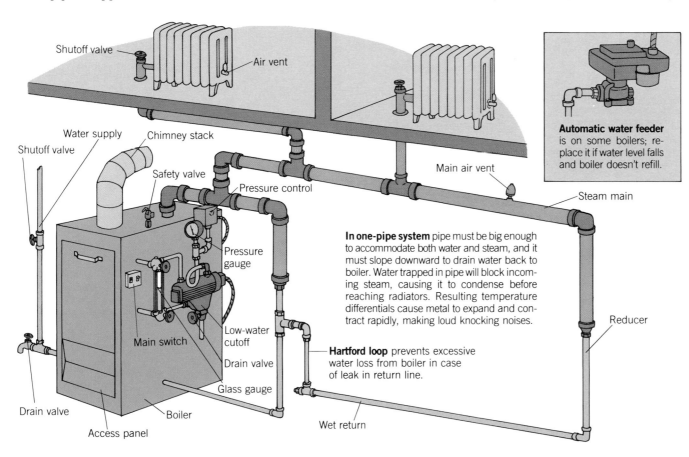

Shutoff valve

Air vent

Water supply

Chimney stack

Shutoff valve

Safety valve

Pressure control

Main air vent

Automatic water feeder is on some boilers; replace it if water level falls and boiler doesn't refill.

Steam trap
On some two-pipe steam systems, each radiator is fitted with a steam trap (instead of an air vent). The trap holds steam inside the radiator until it gives up all its heat. If return pipes feel very hot or if steam comes out of main air vent in great quantities, one or more traps may be defective; have them checked. If a trap leaks, steam will pass directly into return pipe and be wasted; replace leaky trap.

Steam main

Pressure gauge

Low-water cutoff

Main switch

Drain valve

Glass gauge

Drain valve

Boiler

Access panel

In one-pipe system pipe must be big enough to accommodate both water and steam, and it must slope downward to drain water back to boiler. Water trapped in pipe will block incoming steam, causing it to condense before reaching radiators. Resulting temperature differentials cause metal to expand and contract rapidly, making loud knocking noises.

Hartford loop prevents excessive water loss from boiler in case of leak in return line.

Wet return

Reducer

Supply pipe

Trap

Return pipe

Maintaining a steam heating system

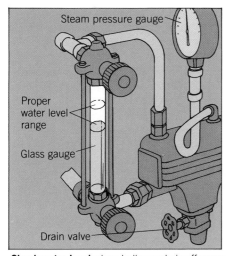

Check water level when boiler cycle is off every 10 to 14 days in cold weather (less often if you have automatic water feed). If water level is less than halfway up glass gauge, open water supply valve until water reaches proper level.

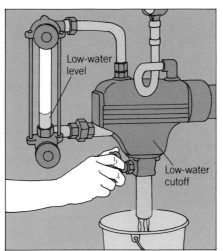

Flush low-water cutoff once a month in heating season to prevent buildup of sediment. Turn down thermostat, put bucket under pipe, open valve, and let water run until it's clear. Be careful; water will be hot. Close valve; refill boiler to proper level.

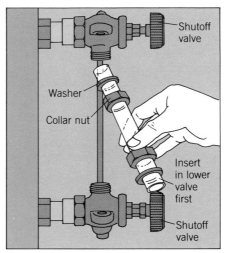

If glass gauge is dirty, turn off boiler main switch; let boiler cool. Shut off valves above and below gauge; loosen nuts; lift glass up and out, and clean it. Slide clean (or new) glass into place, tighten connections, turn valves on, and turn boiler on.

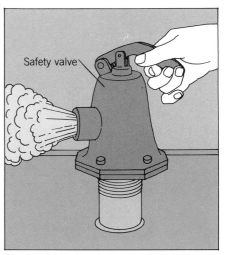

Check safety valve once a year. With boiler running, pull up lever or handle and allow small amount of steam to escape. Watch that valve reseats properly and does not leak steam. If it sticks or appears clogged, shut off power and have valve replaced.

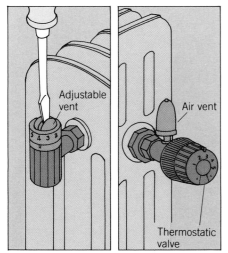

Check air vents on radiators for clogging by listening for hissing sound and checking radiator for heat. If valve is adjustable, open fully when checking. Replace clogged vent with one of same size. If room overheats, add thermostatic valve to radiator.

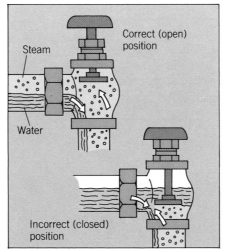

Prevent knocking in one-pipe system by opening or closing radiator valves fully, never partway. Because steam enters radiator and water leaves through same valve, a half-closed valve mixes water and steam together, causing knocking at valve.

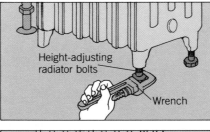
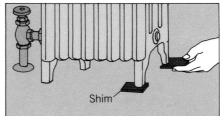

To stop knocking in one-pipe radiator, tip end opposite pipe a bit higher to keep water from collecting at bottom and blocking incoming steam. If radiator has height-adjusting bolts in legs, simply loosen them; otherwise slide shims under legs.

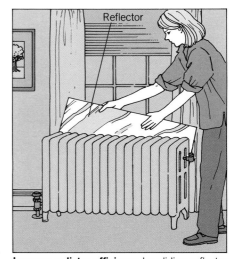

Increase radiator efficiency by sliding reflector between it and outside wall to reflect heat back into room and keep it from being lost to outside wall. You can buy insulated reflectors or make them with corrugated cardboard and aluminum foil.

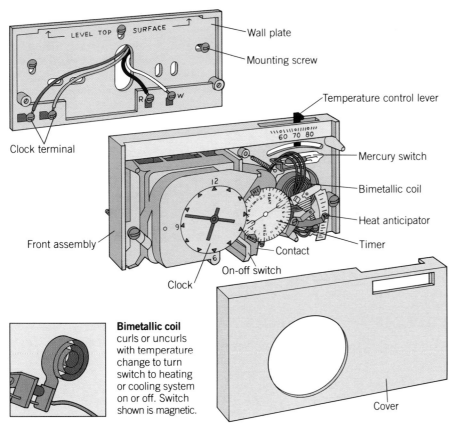

Wall plate

Mounting screw

Clock terminal

Front assembly

Temperature control lever

Mercury switch

Bimetallic coil

Heat anticipator

Timer

Contact

On-off switch

Clock

Cover

Bimetallic coil curls or uncurls with temperature change to turn switch to heating or cooling system on or off. Switch shown is magnetic.

A thermostat is a heat-sensitive switch that controls the flow of electricity to a heating or cooling system. It turns the system on or off as the room temperature varies from preset levels.

What makes a thermostat work is a bimetallic coil—a sandwich of two metal strips that contract or expand at different rates as they become cool or warm. Because the strips are bonded together, the coil flexes to allow both metals to contract or expand; the flexing movement trips a switch that turns the heating or cooling system on or off. The switch may be magnetic or, more often, a sealed tube of mercury; when the coil tips the tube, the mercury flows over electric wires, completing the circuit and turning the system on.

Most thermostats for heating systems also contain a heat anticipator. This device heats the bimetal coil so that it switches the boiler or furnace off a bit early, letting the heat already traveling through the system bring the room temperature to the desired level.

Types of thermostats. Thermostats working on low-voltage current can control a heating system, cooling system, a fan, or a mixture of these. Most thermostats for electric baseboards are line (120V) voltage.

A thermostat may simply turn on the heat or air conditioning when the temperature reaches a set level, or it may adjust the system to let the house get cooler (or warmer) at night or when no one is home, thereby saving fuel. Older set-back thermostats let you make these adjustments by sticking plastic-headed pins into position around a clock. Other models let you program a variety of times and temperatures using a keypad; if you buy one, be sure it has an override feature so that you won't have to reprogram the unit if your schedule changes temporarily.

Placement. The thermostat must be mounted where the temperature of the surrounding air is average for the entire space being heated or cooled—generally on an inside wall away from drafts. Never place a thermostat near a lamp, fireplace, portable heater, or an appliance that gives off heat.

Troubleshooting a thermostat

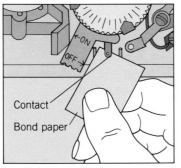

Contact

Bond paper

If thermostat doesn't work, check settings and look for burnt fuse or tripped circuit breaker. If OK, remove cover; tighten connections; make sure unit is level. Turn to lowest setting to close metal contacts; pass piece of heavy paper between contacts to clean them.

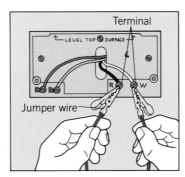

Terminal

Jumper wire

To test thermostat, run jumper wire across terminals and turn on power; if heat switches on, thermostat is defective; replace it. (To make your own jumper wire, strip ½ in. of insulation from each end of 5-in. length of insulated wire, but hold only insulated part.)

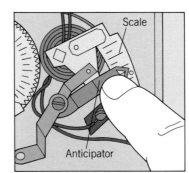

Scale

Anticipator

Adjust anticipator to correct wide swings of temperature. Remove cover. If heat starts and stops too often, nudge anticipator a tiny distance toward higher setting; if it starts and stops too seldom, toward lower setting. Wait a few hours to see if adjustment was enough.

Replacing a thermostat

You can replace an old thermostat with a simpler or a more complex model, as long as the new thermostat is compatible with your system and uses the same current (house current for electric baseboards, low voltage for most others). Always turn off the power before working on a thermostat, even if it operates on low voltage. Although there's little risk of shock from a low-voltage unit, it is wise to be safe.

You will have to connect two wires to the terminals in the thermostat, and possibly a third (ground) wire. If the thermostat has a clock, there will be two additional wires, plus two more if the thermostat controls both heating and air conditioning. If the old thermostat had no clock and the new one does, you'll have to run new wiring.

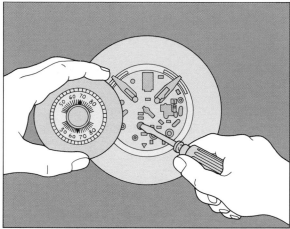

1. Turn off power at boiler, furnace, or air conditioner and at service panel. Pry cover off old thermostat, unscrew front assembly, and disconnect its wires, labeling them with old terminal designations.

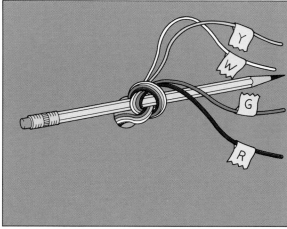

2. Loosely gather all the labeled wires together and tie them in a slipknot around a pencil or a stick to keep them from slipping through the hole in the wall and getting lost.

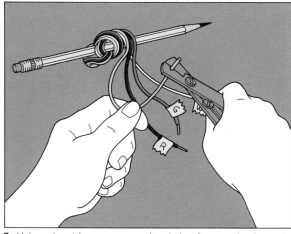

3. Using wire strippers, remove insulation from each wire up to ⅜ in. from end. Clean off any corrosion from bare wire ends with fine sandpaper or steel wool.

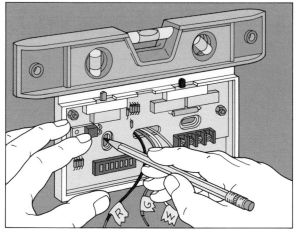

4. Slip wires through wall plate of new thermostat. Position wall plate, level it, and mark mounting hole positions. Remove wall plate, drill holes for screws, and screw wall plate into place.

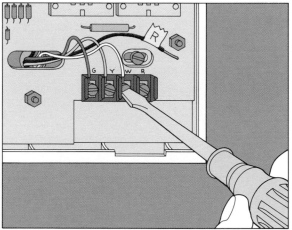

5. Connect wires, following labels and instructions provided by manufacturer of new thermostat. Push excess length of wire back through wall plate and into hole in wall.

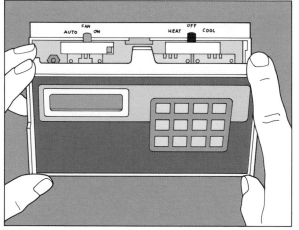

6. Attach front assembly of new thermostat to wall plate, and install proper size batteries if any are needed. Snap cover onto thermostat, turn the power back on, and program thermostat.

A gas burner burns natural gas or LP (liquified petroleum) gas to heat water or air in a boiler or a furnace. When the thermostat calls for heat, it signals the burner control to open a valve, sending gas into the ports in the burners, where it mixes with air and is ignited by a pilot light or electronic ignition. Burning gas heats the heat exchanger (the chamber containing air or water); combustion gases escape through a vent pipe. A draft diverter hood on the vent pipe (or built into the outlet of a furnace) controls draft and stops air currents from backing down and blowing out the pilot light. An automatic vent damper may close to prevent heat loss after the flame goes out, but many utilities don't permit this—it can fail to open. A thermocouple causes the gas to be shut off if the pilot light goes out.

Energy efficiency. If you add to your house's insulation, its heating needs will be reduced and the burner may be too large for the house. You may be able to have the burner's orifice size reduced up to 20 percent. If you convert an oil burner to a gas burner, make sure it's a power burner—it uses less gas. To allow an efficient flow of gases, keep the burners and air shutters free of dust and dirt.

Maintenance. Annually, before winter, have a heating contractor or the utility company inspect the burner. They have instruments to test combustion efficiency, to properly adjust the air and gas supply, and to clean the fuel passages and vent pipe.

To clean the burner, turn off its main gas valve and the electric power. Remove a panel to the combustion chamber. Slide the burners out; they may have to be unbolted or twisted and lifted out. If the pilot and thermocouple are attached to a burner, remove them. Clean debris and rust from the burners and combustion chamber with a stiff brush; vacuum them, and the air shutters, using a crevice tool. Unplug ports and spuds carefully with a toothpick.

▶ **CAUTION:** Make sure the burner has an adequate air supply (p. 456). Don't relight the pilot light or make any repairs if there's a strong gas odor. Close the main valve; call the gas company from a neighbor's house. Don't operate any electrical switches.

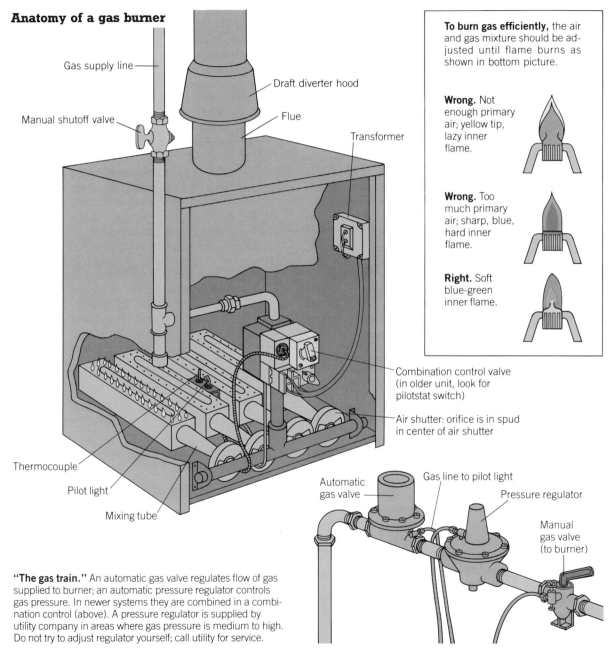

Anatomy of a gas burner

Gas supply line

Draft diverter hood

Manual shutoff valve

Flue

Transformer

Combination control valve (in older unit, look for pilotstat switch)

Air shutter: orifice is in spud in center of air shutter

Thermocouple

Pilot light

Mixing tube

To burn gas efficiently, the air and gas mixture should be adjusted until flame burns as shown in bottom picture.

Wrong. Not enough primary air; yellow tip, lazy inner flame.

Wrong. Too much primary air; sharp, blue, hard inner flame.

Right. Soft blue-green inner flame.

Automatic gas valve

Gas line to pilot light

Pressure regulator

Manual gas valve (to burner)

"The gas train." An automatic gas valve regulates flow of gas supplied to burner; an automatic pressure regulator controls gas pressure. In newer systems they are combined in a combination control (above). A pressure regulator is supplied by utility company in areas where gas pressure is medium to high. Do not try to adjust regulator yourself; call utility for service.

Relighting a pilot

For combination control (far right), remove outer access panel. Turn gas knob and main electric switch to *Off;* air out burner 5 min. Turn thermostat to lowest setting; remove burner access panel. Turn main gas knob to *Pilot* position; while depressing gas knob for 1 min., light pilot (near right). Replace burner access panel; turn gas knob to *On;* turn main electric switch to *On;* adjust room thermostat to desired setting; replace outer access panel.

For older burner (below), follow same procedures but instead of gas knob, turn manual gas valve and pilot gas valve to *Off.* After airing burner 5 min., turn pilot gas valve to *On;* press in red button on pilotstat switch for 1 min. while lighting pilot. **For either procedure,** if pilot doesn't light, wait 5 min.; then repeat steps. If it still doesn't light, replace thermocouple (center right) or call gas company.

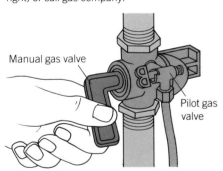

Manual gas valve

Pilot gas valve

Cleaning the pilot orifice

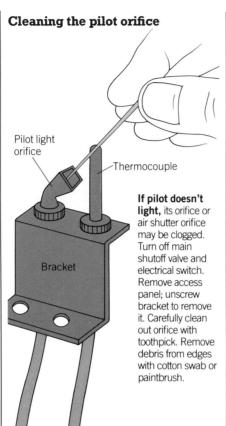

Pilot light orifice

Thermocouple

Bracket

If pilot doesn't light, its orifice or air shutter orifice may be clogged. Turn off main shutoff valve and electrical switch. Remove access panel; unscrew bracket to remove it. Carefully clean out orifice with toothpick. Remove debris from edges with cotton swab or paintbrush.

Replacing a thermocouple

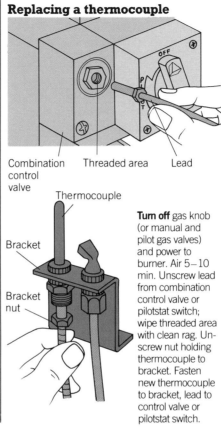

Combination control valve

Threaded area

Lead

Thermocouple

Bracket

Bracket nut

Turn off gas knob (or manual and pilot gas valves) and power to burner. Air 5–10 min. Unscrew lead from combination control valve or pilotstat switch; wipe threaded area with clean rag. Unscrew nut holding thermocouple to bracket. Fasten new thermocouple to bracket, lead to control valve or pilotstat switch.

Adjusting the flame

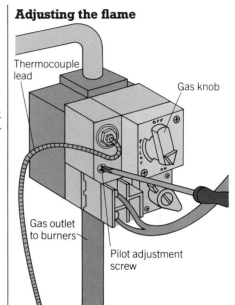

Thermocouple lead

Gas knob

Gas outlet to burners

Pilot adjustment screw

If pilot light is too low, thermocouple will cut off gas supply. On some models a pilot adjustment screw on the control unit regulates pilot flame. Remove screw cap; turn screw counterclockwise to raise flame, clockwise to lower it. Models vary; check manufacturer's directions.

Troubleshooting a gas burner

Problem	Cause	Solution
Burner will not go on.	Burner isn't receiving power.	Check for a turned-off switch, a tripped circuit breaker, or a blown fuse.
	Gas supply is cut off.	Turn on manual gas valve. When valve is open, the handle is parallel to the pipe.
Pilot will not light.	Pilot orifice or air shutter is clogged.	Clean orifice with toothpick.
	Thermocouple is defective.	Replace thermocouple (see above).
Pilot will not stay lighted.	Pilot flame is too low.	Adjust pilot adjustment screw.
	Thermocouple is defective.	Replace thermocouple (see above).

Problem	Cause	Solution
Pilot light has small blue flame.	Pilot orifice is clogged.	Clean orifice with toothpick.
	LP gas pressure is low.	Call gas supplier.
Flames in burners are yellow, weak.	Too little primary air.	Have air and gas mixture adjusted to burn with soft blue-green inner flame.
	Ports, vents, and chamber are dirty.	Clean ports with toothpick; remove debris from vents and chamber with stiff brush and vacuum.
Flames in burners are noisy, violent.	Too much primary air.	Adjust primary air.
	Dirty orifices.	Clean out orifices.

Although several types of burners exist for the combustion of oil, the gun-type high-pressure oil burner is the most common. When a thermostat calls for heat, a pump in the burner housing sends oil under high pressure to the nozzle, where it is sprayed in a fine mist, mixed with air from a blower, and ignited by an electric spark. The ignition system contains a transformer, which changes the house current into a high-voltage spark that jumps across electrodes by the path of the oil spray.

After the gases heat the heat exchanger (which contains air or water), they flow through the stack into a separate flue in the chimney. A draft regulator mounted on the stack controls the velocity of this flow, called *draft*.

Controls. In addition to room thermostats, oil burners have a primary-control relay connected to one of two types of sensors—one that detects heat in the stack or one that senses light from the flame at the end of the burner. The primary relay shuts off the burner if the oil spray doesn't ignite. (Without this relay, the pump would continue to send oil into the combustion chamber, causing a dangerous buildup of oil.) If the burner shuts off, you can try to restart it by pressing the reset button on the primary control; do this only once. If it starts but shuts down again, call for professional service.

Maintenance. Before each heating season, have your burner and other related parts (such as the boiler or furnace) checked, cleaned, and adjusted by your service person. Consider taking out a service contract.

In addition to annual professional service, keep the area around the burner clean. Dust can prevent the blower from working; dirt can cause the burner to fail. Periodically vacuum the openings that admit air to the burner's blower with a crevice tool. Do not sweep dirt under the burner.

Increasing efficiency. If the boiler or furnace has an observation window, look at the flame in the combustion chamber; it should be bright yellow, and it should produce no smoke. If the flame is dark orange or sooty, or if you can see smoke exiting from the chimney outside, have your service person adjust the burner.

In some cases, the burner installed in a home was incorrectly sized, creating more heat than needed. Adding insulation to your house reduces its heating needs, making an oversized burner less efficient. One remedy is to have the burner nozzle replaced with one that has a smaller opening. (Tightening the house may also decrease oxygen for combustion, p. 456.)

If a burner doesn't run at 75 percent efficiency or better after a tune-up and a nozzle replacement, it's a candidate for replacement. Replacing the old burner with a flame-retention model, although expensive initially, will pay for itself within a few years.

Underground oil tank. Excessive water in the tank or filter may indicate water entering the fill pipe or a vent. The tank can eventually corrode; if it does, oil may leak into the groundwater, and water and sediment may get into the burner. If this happens, the old tank should be replaced or emptied and filled with sand, and a new tank installed. If the burner seems to use more oil than normal, the tank may have a leak.

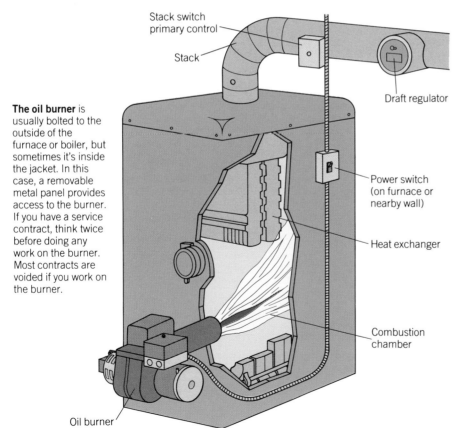

Stack switch primary control

Stack

Draft regulator

The oil burner is usually bolted to the outside of the furnace or boiler, but sometimes it's inside the jacket. In this case, a removable metal panel provides access to the burner. If you have a service contract, think twice before doing any work on the burner. Most contracts are voided if you work on the burner.

Power switch (on furnace or nearby wall)

Heat exchanger

Combustion chamber

Oil burner

Maintaining your oil burner

Oil cup

If the motor has oil cups (to lubricate the motor), place a few drops of high-grade machine oil in each cup midway through the heating season (about 3 mo. after it starts). Some motors have sealed bearings that require no added lubrication. Look for the oil cups on both ends of the motor. Don't add too much oil—2 or 3 drops are enough.

Servicing and troubleshooting

The following procedures should be included in most service contracts.

With the burner running, it is observed for obvious problems. The quality of the ignition, the flame color, and the intensity of the flame are checked. A combustion efficiency test is analyzed and recorded.

The oil tank, oil lines, and valves are inspected.

The heat exchanger, stack, and chimney base are cleaned with brushes, vacuumed, and checked for cracks and other damage. The combustion chamber is also inspected.

All furnace or boiler parts unrelated to the burner are inspected.

The oil filter is replaced. The retainer bowl is cleaned; its contents is inspected for water and sediment.

The gasket is replaced if necessary.

With the electrode-nozzle assembly removed, the tubing, electrodes, and the end cone are thoroughly cleaned. The nozzle is checked for correct specifications and replaced.

Transformer bushings and springs are checked; the cad cell or stack relay switch is tested and cleaned.

The fuel pump gasket is replaced, and its strainer cleaned.

Wiring is inspected for fraying.

The fuel pump is given a pressure test and adjusted to the manufacturer's specification.

The burner is restarted. A second combustion efficiency test is performed and compared to the first test; air is adjusted if necessary. The draft damper is checked and adjusted.

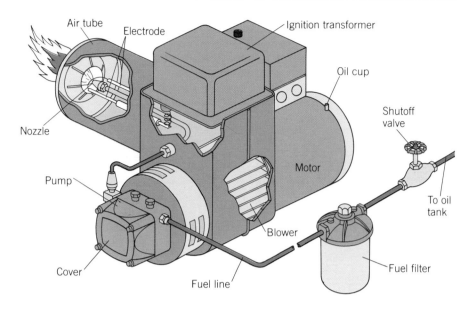

Labels: Air tube, Electrode, Ignition transformer, Oil cup, Shutoff valve, Nozzle, Motor, To oil tank, Pump, Blower, Fuel filter, Cover, Fuel line

Servicing procedures

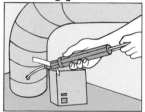 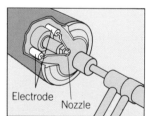  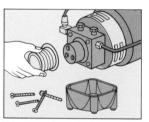  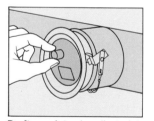

A smoke tester is inserted in the stack to check the combustion gases.

The nozzle should be replaced every year to maintain correct oil atomization.

Labels: Electrode, Nozzle

The oil filter is changed, its bowl inspected for sediment and water.

Pump strainer is cleaned, or replaced if damaged; the gasket is replaced.

Blower vanes are cleaned after transformer is swung to side with power off.

Draft regulator is adjusted to maintain proper draft while burner is running.

When the burner malfunctions

If your oil burner fails to start, try the steps below before calling for service.

- Check the emergency switch. There may be two of these, one on the furnace and another on a nearby wall or at the head of the stairs.
- Check your house electrical panel for a blown fuse or tripped circuit breaker. If a fuse blows or a breaker goes off right after you replace or reset it, call for service.
- Check your oil supply (p. 14). Although the oil shouldn't drop below a quarter tank, 2 in. of oil in the tank should permit the burner to run. (Don't trust the fuel level gauge; it may be faulty.)
- Make certain that the thermostat is set higher than the room temperature.

- If the thermostat has a *Day/Night* switch, make sure it is set correctly. If it is, remove the thermostat cover and check for dirt or corrosion on the thermostat contact points; pass a piece of stiff paper or a crisp dollar bill between the contact points to clean them.
- Try pushing reset button on primary control. Push it only once, or you may overfill the combustion chamber. If the burner starts but immediately stops again, call for service.
- If burner sputters or goes off, there may be dirt in the oil filter or air in the fuel lines. Call for service.
- If the furnace or boiler operates but produces little heat, the trouble is in the heat distribution system rather than the oil burner. See pp. 465–473.

Electric boilers

In compact electric boilers, water is heated by fast-acting electric elements immersed in the water. This process takes place inside a small cast-iron shell within the boiler cabinet. As with gas and oil boilers, a small pump circulates the heated water to pipes, convectors, or radiant-heat tubing. Heat delivery is controlled by thermostats in individual rooms or zones.

Electric boilers are expensive to operate. When faced with a major repair, consider replacing your electric boiler with a gas- or oil-fired one rather than repairing it unless your local electric rates are significantly below the national average. High-efficiency boilers fueled by either gas or oil are relatively compact. Get one that can be vented through a side wall.

Electric furnaces

Although similar in some ways to gas- and oil-fired furnaces, an electric warm-air furnace does not have a burner, heat exchanger, or exhaust flue. Instead, a blower forces air past two to five heavy-duty electric heating coils within the furnace cabinet. Ductwork identical to that used for gas or oil furnaces distributes the heat. To prevent a current overload, the electric coils heat on a rotating basis. Routine maintenance of an electric furnace involves cleaning filters and caring for the blower motor (p.465). You may also have to change an internal fuse occasionally (first turn off power to the unit).

The generation of heat by the coils is 100 percent efficient, but electric furnaces are usually the most expensive sources of home heating, and they can suffer from the same ductwork problems as other furnaces (pp.466–467). If your electric furnace requires a major repair, consider replacing it with a high-efficiency gas- or oil-fired furnace that vents out an outside wall. Or if you live in a moderate climate, install a heat pump (pp.490–491) to provide both heating and cooling, but make sure that the existing ductwork is adequate; heat pumps typically require larger ducts than furnaces.

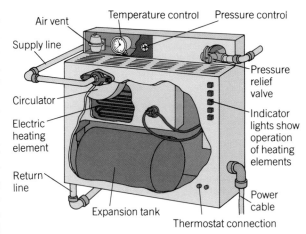

Fast-acting electric boilers are small enough to mount on a wall.

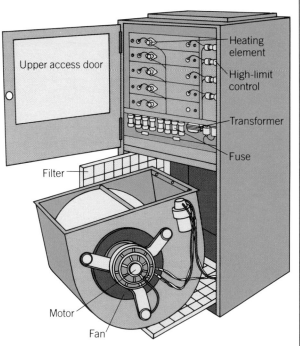

Coils in electric furnace give off concentrated heat, much like an iron.

Electric convectors

Because the heat can be controlled by individual room thermostats, electric convectors are less wasteful than an electric furnace. Wall-mounted baseboard convectors contain resistance elements that heat to a high temperature when current passes through them; air passing over the elements warms and rises, drawing cooler air from floor level and leading to natural air circulation within the room. Recessed convectors rely on small blowers to circulate heated air. Although they cost more than baseboard units and generate some fan noise, recessed convectors do not interfere as much with furniture placement. Keep convectors clean with a vacuum extension tool; otherwise their efficiency will be lowered.

Metal fins in baseboard convectors increase area of heat exchange.

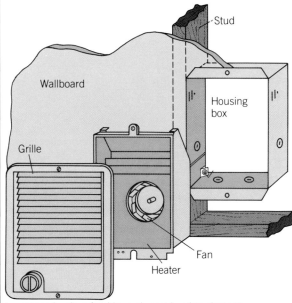

In recessed unit, a fan blows air past heating elements.

Troubleshooting electric heaters

Problem	Possible cause	Solution
No heat.	Thermostat is set too low.	Move thermostat setting up until heat goes on.
	Draperies or furniture is blocking airflow through heater.	Remove the obstruction.
	Circuit breaker is off or fuse has blown.	Switch circuit breaker on; replace blown fuse.
	Circuit breaker switches off or fuse blows again.	Check for a short circuit in heater wiring.
	Thermostat is defective.	Turn off circuit breaker to heater circuit, or pull fuse. Run jumper wire (p.474) across thermostat terminals. Turn on power. If heater operates, replace thermostat with similar model.
	Resistance wire in heating element is defective.	Turn off circuit breaker to heater circuit, and check wire with continuity tester (pp.242–243); replace element with one of same voltage rating.
	Wiring connections inside heater are loose.	Turn off circuit breaker or pull fuse to heater circuit; check and tighten all connections.
	House wiring is defective.	Have electrician check wiring.
Heater cycles on and off frequently.	Draperies, furniture, or debris is blocking airflow.	Remove the obstruction.
Heater will not shut off.	Heat loss from room is greater than heater capacity.	Close doors and windows. Add weatherstripping and caulking to doors and windows. Provide additional insulation or additional heaters.
	Thermostat is defective.	Rotate thermostat knob to lowest setting. If heater continues to run, replace thermostat.
Heater emits smoke or odors.	Dust, dirt, and lint have accumulated inside.	Vacuum heater with extension tool. Repeat every 6 mo.
Fan doesn't operate (in fan-driven heater).	Jammed blades.	Turn off power to heater. Remove cover or grille; look for and remove obstruction.
	Wires are not connected to fan motor.	Turn off power to heater. Connect fan motor wires.
	Fan motor is defective.	Use volt-ohm meter (pp.242–243) to see if power is reaching motor. If it is, replace motor; if not, check wiring, switch, and circuit breaker or fuse.
Fan blades turn, but no heat.	Resistance wire in heating element is defective.	Turn off circuit breaker to heater circuit, or check wire with continuity tester (pp.242–243); replace element with one of same voltage rating.
	Wiring connections inside heater are loose.	Turn off circuit breaker or pull fuse to heater circuit; check and tighten all connections.

CAUTION: Before making any repair, unplug heater or turn off power to heater.

Portable electric heaters

In a centrally heated home you can save money by setting the thermostat at 60° F or less and running portable heaters in the one or two rooms you are occupying at the time. Use any of the heaters shown here, but be sure to get a model that will shut off automatically in case the unit tips over, and never use an extension cord. Don't place a heater near flammable materials or water; keep it far from the central heating thermostat because the thermostat may stay satisfied and not turn on the heat for other rooms.

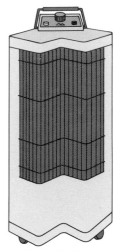

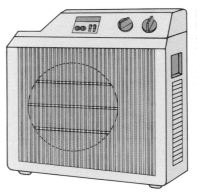

Fan convection heater has electric coils, much like toaster elements, that heat to a high temperature. A small fan blows room air across the coils and circulates heat within the room. Generally these inexpensive heaters will warm a room quickly.

In a liquid-filled heater, electric elements heat water or oil, in which they are immersed. Heat delivery is a bit slower than other heaters, but temperature is even. Buy one with a grille to protect from burns.

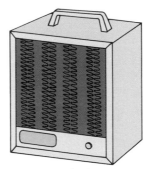

Ceramic convection heater uses fan to pull room air past ceramic heating element. Lower element temperature makes it safer than fan convection heaters, but grille may heat enough to cause burns.

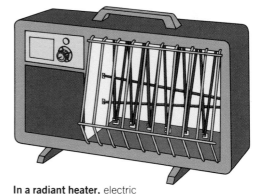

In a radiant heater, electric elements are placed in front of a reflective metal surface and behind a safety grille. Heat from elements radiates straight out, warming person in front of it rather than room. Some models use fans to help push heat out.

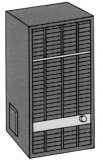

Vented gas heater

For a new addition to a house or for a recently finished attic or garage room, it is often more economical to buy and install a space heater than to connect the unheated area to the existing heating system. A space heater also helps save money another way: it lets you warm a limited living area on a chilly evening without turning on the whole heating system.

A vented gas space heater, which may cost twice as much as an electric space heater initially, can pay for itself over time because the fuel (natural gas or propane) is cheaper. A vented gas heater is safer than an unvented model because it has an outside source of oxygen through the fresh air intake and it vents exhaust gases to the outside. Unvented gas heaters—even those with depletion sensors that cut off the unit when oxygen is low—can pollute indoor air. Some states outlaw these heaters in residential buildings.

Unvented gas heaters have another problem: they produce a damaging amount of condensation. An unvented 15,000-Btu-an-hour gas heater may generate as much as a pint of water vapor an hour. A vented gas heater exhausts moisture outdoors.

A direct-vent gas heater has both the fresh air intake and the exhaust in a double-wall pipe that goes directly through an outside wall (below, left). Other vented gas heaters, such as the catalytic combuster and the fireplace insert shown below, exhaust gases through flexible metal or plastic flues that are narrow enough to be routed through interior wall spaces to a roof outlet. This allows the heaters to be mounted on inside walls.

Capacities for vented gas heaters range from 5,000 Btu an hour (direct-vent units) up to 90,000 Btu (largest catalytic combuster). In a moderate climate, a vented gas heater can warm as much as 1,500 square feet of space with average insulation.

Safe heating with kerosene
Kerosene heaters, with a reputation as fire hazards and interior air pollutors, have been banned in many areas. New direct-vent equipment (often fed by exterior fuel tanks) makes this efficient and inexpensive fuel safer to use; unvented kerosene heaters are still dangerous.

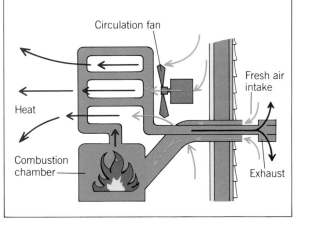

Direct-vent heater

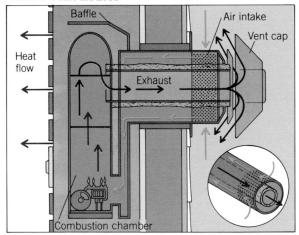

Located on an outside wall, the direct-vent gas heater has a vent within a vent instead of a flue. Air is drawn in through the outer vent (or ring) to the combustion chamber, where it provides oxygen for burning the gas. Exhaust flows around a baffle and then out the center ring through a windproof vent cap to the outdoors.

Vented catalytic heater

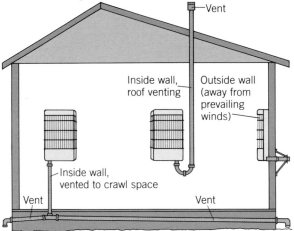

A superefficient catalytic heater burns gas with flameless combustion at 90-percent efficiency. The catalyst, usually platinum, causes a heat-producing chemical reaction with oxygen and gas. A small fan sends exhaust outdoors through a pipe, which can be routed several ways (some heaters also require a water drain).

Gas fireplace

A live flame rising from ceramic logs gives the look of a wood fire without the bother. A gas fireplace can be installed as a fireplace insert (vented up the flue as shown), as a freestanding unit with vent pipe through the roof, or against an exterior wall with direct venting to the outside.

Making a fireplace more efficient

The ideal fireplace is built in the middle of the house, has its own fresh air intake, and has a fan to circulate heat through vents in several adjacent rooms. It has glass doors and a tight-fitting damper with several settings. A crackling fire in such a fireplace is not only a cheerful sight on a chilly evening but also a genuine source of supplemental heat.

However, most fireplaces fall short of this model: they get a minus efficiency rating because, without their own supply of air, they actually rob a house of warmed air by drawing it up the flue.

Furthermore, wood fires in old fireplaces pollute the air (some communities ban wood fires on days when the air is bad), and they pose a fire hazard: inefficient burning of wood creates flammable creosote, which builds up in the flue, ready to ignite and feed a chimney fire.

Fireplace upgrade. If you use your fireplace infrequently, the important consideration is preventing heat loss when it is not in use. Check the tightness of the damper (p.400). Add glass doors (right) to minimize the amount of warm air lost as a fire dies down. To increase heat in the room during an occasional fire, buy a tubular grate with a blower (right).

If you use your fireplace more than just occasionally, consider an insert. A well-designed fireplace insert for burning gas (facing page) or wood (right) will give you the charm of a flame with as much as 80 percent heat efficiency. A good insert also provides a thermostatically controlled, cleaner-burning fire with either fuel.

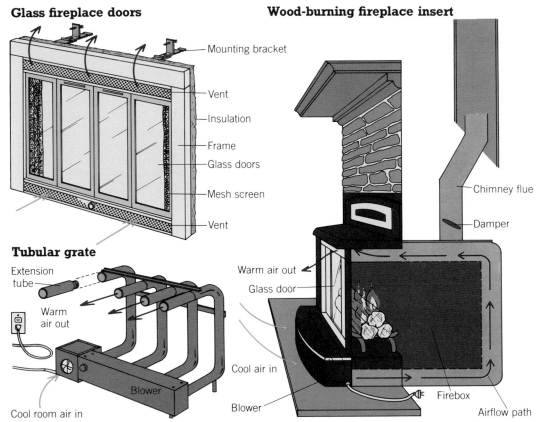

Glass fireplace doors

Mounting bracket
Vent
Insulation
Frame
Glass doors
Mesh screen
Vent

Tubular grate

Extension tube
Warm air out
Blower
Cool room air in

Wood-burning fireplace insert

Chimney flue
Damper
Warm air out
Glass door
Cool air in
Blower
Firebox
Airflow path

Glass fireplace doors cut volume of heated room air sucked up flue. An insulated frame fits around opening to hold doors, which can be removed for cleaning. Vents at top and bottom open and close for draft control. Metal mesh screen can be pulled across to check sparks when doors are open.

Tubular grate, if it has extension tubes and a blower, can help circulate more fire heat. Cool room air enters tubes at fan intake, is warmed by fire, and exits at top, where it is blown back into the room.

A wood-burning fireplace insert is, in effect, a wood-burning stove small enough to fit within an existing masonry fireplace. The best models incorporate catalytic combusters and secondary combustion chambers to maximize heat and burn off pollutants. Fans circulate heat through vents above glass viewing door.

Fireplace safety

- Check the flue regularly for creosote buildup, and have the chimney checked and cleaned annually.
- Keep an approved fire extinguisher within easy reach of the fireplace, and install smoke detectors.
- Always open the damper and look up the flue before lighting a fire (if you can't see all the way, there may be an obstruction); don't close the damper until the fire is completely out.
- Never use gasoline or charcoal lighter fluid to start a fire; it could cause an explosion.
- Burn only wood cut for fuel in the fireplace. Treated lumber, pine branches, leaves, trash, and plastics either contain harmful chemicals or flare up too fast.
- Never use more than one artificial log at a time (they can explode if stacked on each other or if they are added to a natural wood fire).
- Keep flammable items (furniture, rugs, pillows) at least 3 feet away from the fireplace, and dispose of fireplace ashes in a metal container.
- If you suspect a chimney fire, close the damper if you can safely reach its handle, get everyone out of the house, call the fire department, and hose down the roof.

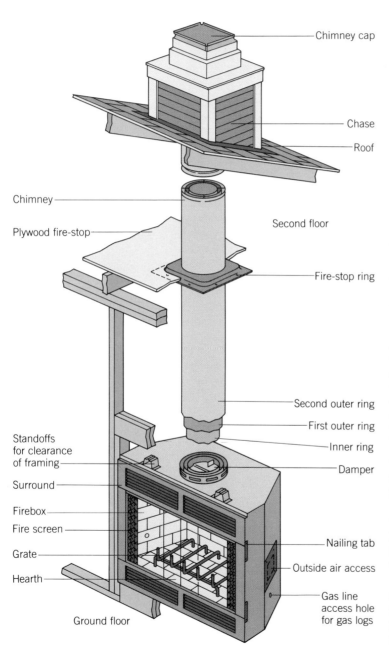

Chimney cap

Chase

Roof

Chimney

Second floor

Plywood fire-stop

Fire-stop ring

Second outer ring

First outer ring

Inner ring

Damper

Standoffs for clearance of framing

Surround

Firebox

Fire screen

Grate

Hearth

Nailing tab

Outside air access

Gas line access hole for gas logs

Ground floor

The charm and appeal of a fireplace is almost universal. Real estate dealers claim that a fireplace is one home improvement that almost always pays off (an average 130 percent return on investment).

However, having a mason build a traditional fireplace in your house is expensive, starting with a concrete foundation that begins below the frost line and ending with a tile-lined chimney that reaches from the firebox to well above the roof.

Much more economical and practical is to install a factory-made fireplace system designed to fit safely within normal house framing. Consisting of a metal cabinet attached to a multi-walled metal chimney, such a fireplace is said to have "zero clearance" construction: burnable materials can safely touch the standoffs (5/16 inch to 2 inches at most) built into the fireplace. The unit can be placed almost anywhere in the house because its chimney doesn't require a masonry casing and can accommodate a few turns in its path to the roof.

Design choices. Zero-clearance fireplaces come in many configurations besides the in-wall model. A see-through version serves as a divider between two rooms; another design has glass viewing doors on three sides; and there is even a glass rectangle that makes an island of fire in a room. If you like traditional fireplaces, there are factory-made units with brick-lined fireboxes that can be faced with brick or stone to imitate masonry construction.

▶ **CAUTION:** Before buying a fireplace, check with your local building department about codes and fire regulations. You may need to have the finished fireplace inspected before you use it.

Go to a store that specializes in fireplaces and wood stoves, where you are likely to get more knowledgeable advice than in a home center. Such stores will also provide professional installation if you wish.

Features to look for. Zero-clearance fireplaces come with many heat-enhancing options: fresh air intake and glass doors (some building codes now require both), vents, adjustable damper, circulating blower. All add to a fireplace's efficiency.

1. Build framing for the fireplace: outside the wall as shown, or remove wallboard (p.279) and frame within the wall. Clearances for combustible framing lumber range from 5/16 in. to 2 in. (check manufacturer's instructions).

6. Nail metal fire-stop ring to underside of plywood fire-stop to fill any gaps around chimney. (Fire-stops are required by building codes.) Then brace chimney to nearest studs with metal straps (not visible here).

2. Position firebox on plywood platform (a concrete-like hearth is built into firebox base). Check that firebox is level (use shims if necessary), and measure clearances on either side and at standoffs on top.

3. Secure firebox by nailing its tabs to framing on each side. Attach air hose (if included) to side of firebox. The flexible aluminum piping leads to an outside wall, where you install a fresh air intake through the wall.

4. Plan a chimney path to the roof between joists at each floor level (use a chimney elbow if necessary). Build a plywood fire-stop at each floor; then cut a hole in it for the chimney to go through (shown here from second floor level).

5. Attach first section of chimney to top of firebox, securing inner ring, then outer rings. Second section must be lowered through fire-stop hole from second floor and fitted into a metal fire-stop ring before it is attached.

7. Install plywood fire-stop between second floor and attic as shown, and again cut a hole for the chimney to go through. Attach fire-stop ring and insert chimney sections. Build chimney to bottom of outside chimney chase.

8. Lower final section of chimney through the chimney chase from the roof, and attach it securely, ring by ring, to attic sections. If roof is steep or chimney chase is inaccessible, hire a professional for this step.

9. Install chimney cap on top of chimney from the roof (second chimney cap here is for heating system flue). Chimney chase is finished with wood siding, permissible with zero-clearance chimney construction.

10. Required noncombustible hearth (marble here) and glass doors complete the fireplace. How the framing is covered (wallboard, wood mantel, and wood trim here) is a question of taste, not safety.

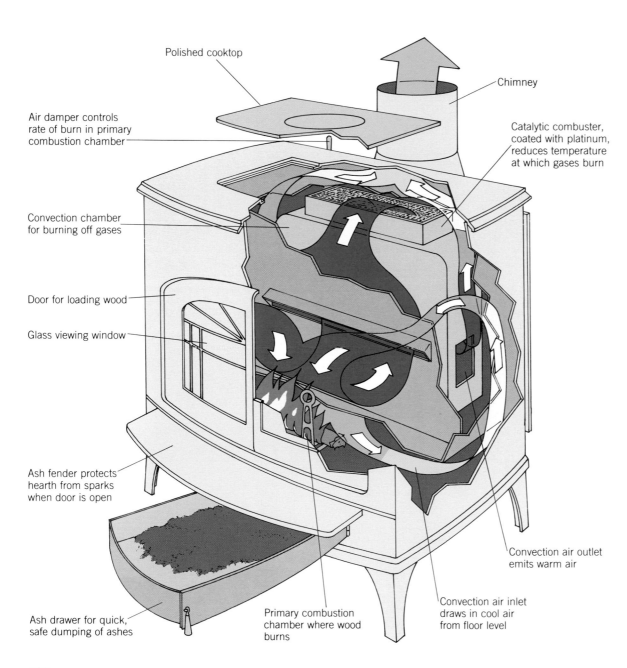

Polished cooktop

Chimney

Air damper controls rate of burn in primary combustion chamber

Catalytic combuster, coated with platinum, reduces temperature at which gases burn

Convection chamber for burning off gases

Door for loading wood

Glass viewing window

Ash fender protects hearth from sparks when door is open

Convection air outlet emits warm air

Ash drawer for quick, safe dumping of ashes

Primary combustion chamber where wood burns

Convection air inlet draws in cool air from floor level

The energy crisis of the 1970's revived interest in wood stoves—and precipitated a new crisis in the many communities where wood stoves came back into use. Burning wood in traditional wood stoves, it turned out, was not only inefficient for warming houses but also created air pollution.

To keep the air clean, first individual communities, then states, began to regulate wood stoves. Finally the U.S. Environmental Protection Agency stepped in and set national standards for new stoves that lowered allowable emissions from a typical 30 to 40 grams of particulates an hour to 4.1 for catalytic stoves and 7.5 for noncatalytic stoves.

The result is a whole new generation of wood stoves that are far safer, more efficient, and cleaner burning than their predecessors. Some of the new stoves have insulated secondary combustion chambers where heat builds up enough to ignite the unburned gases that normally escape up the chimney (and pollute the air). Other new stoves have catalytic combustors, which reduce the temperature at which the gases will ignite, allowing them to burn off with the wood and, as a bonus, to generate 50 percent more heat. The most efficient new wood stoves (higher than 80 percent ratings) combine both technologies. Burning off the gases emitted by burning wood also dramatically cuts creosote buildup in the chimney, diminishing the threat of chimney fires.

Picking a stove. Go to a store that specializes in stoves and fireplaces. To compare different stoves, use the Oregon efficiency ratings and the EPA emissions ratings. For size and heating capacity, follow manufacturers' recommendations. A stove with a thermostatically activated damper control can heat a surprisingly large space with a minimum amount of restoking. (Such stoves can burn unattended for as long as 8 hours.) Wood stoves can be vented through fireplace flues or through their own chimneys; however, stoves require floor protectors and minimum clearances to combustible walls or wall shields. Check local building codes and fire regulations before installing a stove.

Coal stoves

In some areas, hard anthracite coal is a cheap, readily available fuel. In that case, a coal stove is more economical than a wood stove. (Soft bituminous and lignite coals aren't suitable fuel for stoves because they give off volatile gases.)

Coal stoves are neither regulated nor rated by the EPA. Anthracite coal burns cleanly and contains no creosote or particulate pollutants. It does, however, create fly ash, a nonflammable deposit that can seriously plug up a chimney, particularly around elbows or joints. Chimneys that serve coal stoves must be inspected at least as regularly as fireplace or wood-stove chimneys.

Some coal contains more metal impurities than others; in mass these create "clinkers," a hard residue that clogs the grate and smothers the fire. To protect yourself from buying an inferior grade, go to a reputable dealer and test a bag or two of coal before ordering a full season's supply.

Although a coal fire is trickier to get started than a wood fire, it can burn much hotter for much longer without attention. Coal needs a lot of air to burn; thus a coal stove has a grate for holding the fuel and an air intake beneath the grate, so that air is drawn continuously up through the whole bed of coals. Once the fire is going well, its rate of burn can be regulated with the damper.

The grate of a coal stove has outside handles that allow it to be shaken periodically to knock ashes off the burning coals into an ash drawer below. If the ash is not shaken down, it could put out the fire.

To build a fire, lay kindling over crumpled paper. Add a mix of split wood: softwood (pine or spruce) for quick ignition and hardwood (maple or ash) for long burning. Open damper and light paper. When fire burns well, add logs.

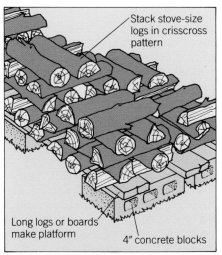

Stack stove-size logs in crisscross pattern

Long logs or boards make platform

4" concrete blocks

To store and season wood, stack it outside as shown so that air can circulate around it. Green wood needs at least 6 mo. to lose its high water content. Seasoned wood burns cleaner and gives off more heat than green wood.

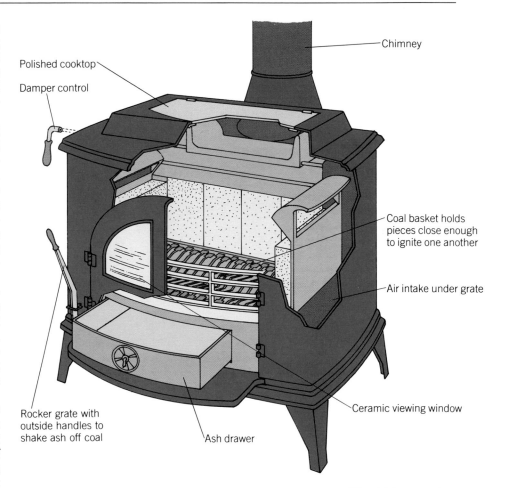

Chimney

Polished cooktop

Damper control

Coal basket holds pieces close enough to ignite one another

Air intake under grate

Rocker grate with outside handles to shake ash off coal

Ash drawer

Ceramic viewing window

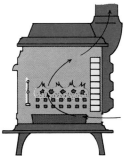

A coal fire starts with a paper and kindling base, just like a wood fire. But don't add any coal until there's a bed of hot wood coals. For the first round, put in a single layer of coal (more would smother fire).

Add more coal only when the first layer glows red and is ready to ignite more coal. Now fill the basket, and keep damper open until added coal begins to burn. Shake ashes off coal two or three times a day.

Passive solar features are building elements that collect and store solar energy to provide indoor comfort and reduce heating bills. Unlike active systems, in which boxlike heat collectors are isolated on roofs and generally involve pumps or fans, passive systems are integral parts of the building itself. The concept is simple and was first used several thousand years ago.

Any passive solar system incorporates four basic features: (1) south-facing glass to admit solar energy; (2) heat-storage materials, such as brick and concrete; (3) a means of distributing the heat (radiation or convection, occasionally boosted by a small blower that moves the heat from a sunspace to a north-side room); and (4) some type of control to prevent summer overheating—properly designed overhangs, for example, are very effective above south-facing windows.

In most climates, solar features are very cost-effective when installed in new homes or additions. However, adding them to an existing home may be expensive compared to the savings achieved. You will have to decide whether or not the other benefits—such as more views, better light, more space, or improved comfort—outweigh the cost.

When passive solar heat makes sense. Before deciding whether or not to add solar heating elements to your home, answer the following questions. If the answer to all of them is yes, your home is a good candidate for a passive solar retrofit.

• Does your home have good access to the sun? One of its walls must face within 30 degrees of south; the closer it is to facing due south, the easier it will be to block out unwanted summertime solar gain. The solar wall should be mostly unshaded between the hours of 10 A.M. and 2 P.M in December. Your state energy office should be able to help you locate a site selector tool that can show the extent of your wintertime solar access.

• Does your home presently underutilize its solar potential? To answer this question, add up the area of all the glass on the south-facing walls. It should amount to at least 4 to 5 percent of the total floor area of the house (for example, 40 square feet of glass per 1,000 square feet of floor space). If it does not, the solar potential is underutilized.

• Do you live in a climate that is cold and sunny during the winter? For an assessment of your region's solar potential, contact the state energy office.

• Is your home well insulated? It makes little sense to add relatively expensive solar features without taking all cost-effective steps to tighten and insulate a home (p.457).

• Are your fuel costs higher than the national average? Your energy office and utility company can provide this information too.

Choosing a system. The appropriateness of a particular passive solar system depends on several factors. If the walls of the house are solid masonry—either concrete block or brick—your best choice is a sunspace. If you live in an arid climate, consider mass-storage (Trombe) walls. If the walls are frame, your best choice is to add south-facing windows, air collectors, or a sunspace. If your front porch faces south, one of the most cost-effective techniques is to convert it to a sunspace. If you have a room with a concrete floor (such as a converted garage) or a walk-out basement that faces south, consider adding south-facing windows.

If you decide that passive solar heating is appropriate, consult a solar designer or experienced builder before attempting any of the measures suggested—particularly before adding a sunspace.

A wall facing within 15 degrees of south receives less than half as much summer sun as a roof or a wall facing east or west.

Plant deciduous trees to shade east and west windows.

Summer sun

Overhangs or awnings above south windows block out high summer sun.

Winter sun

South-side windows collect the most heat from the low winter sun.

Buildings and trees must not block low winter sun from south wall.

Adding glass. If you add glass to a south wall, distribute it evenly for more comfort. If the glazing is heavily concentrated in one area—such as in a sunspace—isolate that area from the home with glass doors to provide protection from extreme temperatures in both summer and winter.

Low-emissivity, or low-E, glazing (p.426) cuts down on heat loss around the clock and even in bad weather. Use it for windows and sunspaces. Patio-door replacement glass is a cost-effective choice for mass-storage walls and air collectors. Shop for low-iron glass; it transmits the most solar energy.

Normally you need no extra heat-storage materials unless your south-facing glass area is more than 8 percent of your home's floor area. Generally the more glass you have, the more heat-storage material you need. However, a sunspace can be built for high or low amounts of heat storage, depending on whether it is to be used as a plant-growing or a heat-producing space.

Sunspace

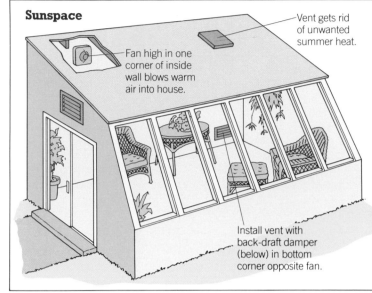

Vent gets rid of unwanted summer heat.

Fan high in one corner of inside wall blows warm air into house.

Install vent with back-draft damper (below) in bottom corner opposite fan.

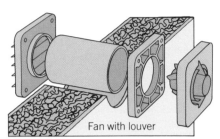

Fan with louver

Install fan to move warm air into adjacent rooms when no one is home to open connecting doors or windows. Automate fan with a 4° F cooling thermostat (for example, one that turns on at 85° F and off at 81° F). Fan should move 3 to 9 cu. ft. of air per min. per sq. ft. of south-facing glass, or more if sunspace has little heat-storage material. Duct warm air directly to a north-side room.

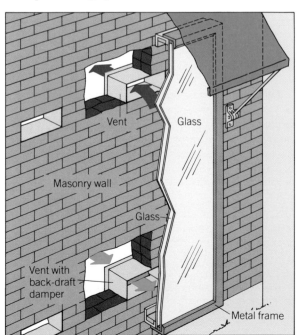

Vent

Glass

Masonry wall

Glass

Vent with back-draft damper

Metal frame

Mass-storage (Trombe) wall.
If you live in an arid climate, convert a solid, uninsulated masonry wall into a heat-storage unit by covering it with double glazing held 1 to 4 in. from surface. Masonry will absorb sun's energy and conduct heat through to living space 8 to 12 hr. later; indoor surfaces reach peak temperature between 6 and 10 P.M., depending on wall thickness. Because air space between wall and glazing can exceed 150° F, use durable metal framing and glass rather than wood framing and plastic. To nearly double efficiency, cut high and low vents in wall to pull warm air indoors during winter. Install a back-draft damper (see right) in lower vent to prevent reverse flow of cold night air. Seal frame carefully to wall to prevent air leaks. Shade wall or vent it to outdoors in summer months.

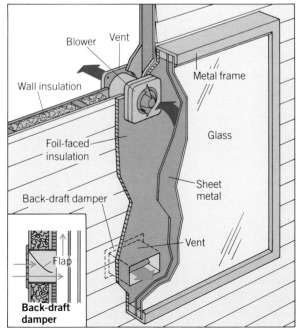

Blower   Vent

Metal frame

Wall insulation

Foil-faced insulation

Glass

Sheet metal

Back-draft damper

Vent

Flap

Back-draft damper

Air collector. If you have a frame house, add a collector consisting of a single layer of glazing, a frame, an absorber surface, a layer of foil-faced insulation, two wall vents, and a thermostat-controlled blower that moves 3 cu. ft. of air per min. per sq. ft. of collector area. For absorber, use sheet metal painted black or brick veneer (no insulation required). When sun heats absorber plate, warming air to 90° F, blower forces air indoors through top vent and draws cool indoor air out bottom vent. To prevent cold air from flowing into room at night, install a back-draft damper in lower vent. (Buy one, or cover screen with sheet of plastic and tape in place across top.) Seal collector carefully; leaks may cut performance in half. Collector temperatures can exceed 200° F; use metal frame and glass for safety and durability.

Home climate/Heat pumps

A heat pump is a mechanical refrigerant system—much like an air conditioner or refrigerator—that can both heat and cool your home. Most heat pumps are *split systems,* with an outdoor coil, an indoor coil, and a compressor. During the winter, the system extracts low-grade heat from outdoors and transfers it indoors. During the summer the heat pump is reversed, absorbing unwanted heat from indoors and sending it outdoors. A thermostat, ducts, and blowers control and distribute the warm and cool air.

While it is hard to imagine squeezing any useful heat energy from 30° F wintertime air, a refrigerant at -20° F will indeed be warmed when circulated through the outdoor coil that is 50 degrees warmer. During this process, however, the compressor and fans consume energy. The ratio of the amount of heat delivered to the amount of energy consumed is called the COP (the Coefficient of Performance). Depending on the outdoor temperature, the COP of a good heat pump in the heating season ranges from 1.0 to 3.0—that is, from 1 to 3 Btu's of heat delivered per Btu of electricity consumed; it is slightly higher during the cooling season. Equivalent rating systems used for heat pumps are the Heating Season Performance Factor (HSPF) and the Season Energy Efficiency Ratio (SEER); these use the watt as a unit of measure and are simply 3.4 times the size of the COP because there are 3.4 Btu's per watt.

Supplementary heat. As outdoor temperatures fall, the heating capacity of a heat pump declines. To compensate, supplementary electric heating elements switch on at the *crossover point*—the point at which an air-source heat pump does not have enough heating capacity to satisfy the needs of the home. With most heat pump thermostats, it's inefficient to lower the temperature setting at night; it may increase reliance on supplementary heating.

Maintenance. Have a heat pump serviced annually by a qualified contractor. In addition, routinely vacuum the indoor coil, change the blower filter, and wash the outdoor coil with a hose. You may also have to lubricate the fan motor or adjust the blower and drive belt; check the owner's manual.

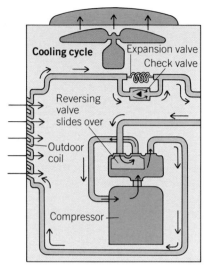

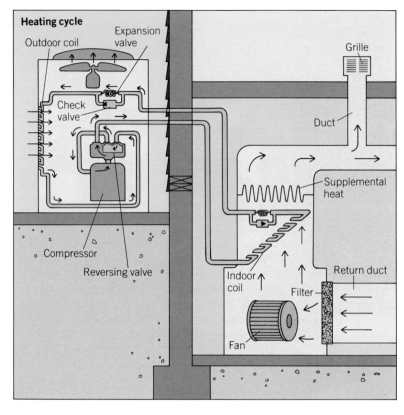

In heating cycle (left), a refrigerant passes through outdoor coil as a gas, drawing some heat from air. The gas moves to compressor, where high pressure raises its temperature. It then moves to indoor coil, where it releases heat and condenses into a liquid. An expansion valve allows the liquid to move from high pressure to low, which lowers its temperature, and vaporizes it again. The cycle then repeats. To provide cooling (above), a valve reverses system.

Troubleshooting problems	Possible solutions
Frost on outdoor coil in winter and on indoor coil in summer; irregular defrosting patterns	Buildup is normal function of humidity, temperature, and coil design. Keep condenser clean; clean the coils; replace the filter—more airflow reduces length of defrost cycle. If problem persists, check owner's manual to locate and clean the airflow sensing tube.
Refrigerant leaking red dye	Call repairman. If unattended, can lead to compressor failure.
Odors when heat pump kicks on	Check that the drip pan, which catches condensate from indoor unit, is draining.
Heat inadequate in very cold weather	Unit may be undersize. Shut off vents in unused rooms. Consider adding duct boosters or auxiliary heaters. Supplementary heating coil may be broken; have it replaced.
Frequent on-off cycling	Check thermostat; could be broken or have improperly set anticipator.
Cold air from register blowing onto frequently used seating places	Adjust diffusers to direct air away from seating; seal any ductwork in attic or crawl space; have in-line electric supplementary heater installed in problem duct.

Ground- and water-coupled systems.
Most heat pumps extract heat from the air, but some use heat from the ground or from water for heating or cooling. In a ground-coupled heat pump, fluid is circulated through plastic pipes that are buried in the ground. In a water-based system, the pipes may be submerged in a lake or stream, but more often well water is brought to the heat pump and then either discharged or reinjected into another well, as groundwater temperatures vary less than lake and stream water.

Advantages. Heat pumps that rely on ground and water temperatures are more efficient than air systems because ground and water temperatures don't go to the extremes of air temperatures. Also, because no outdoor condensing unit is required, ground-source heat pumps don't need defrosting in the winter and should last longer. However, they are more expensive to install.

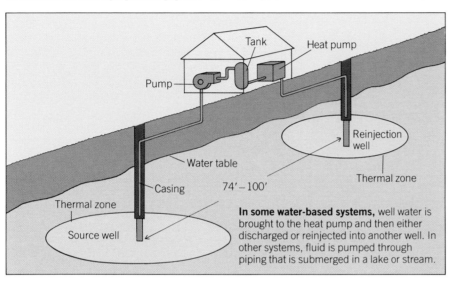

In some water-based systems, well water is brought to the heat pump and then either discharged or reinjected into another well. In other systems, fluid is pumped through piping that is submerged in a lake or stream.

Tank

Heat pump

Pump

Water table

Reinjection well

Casing

Thermal zone

74'–100'

Thermal zone

Source well

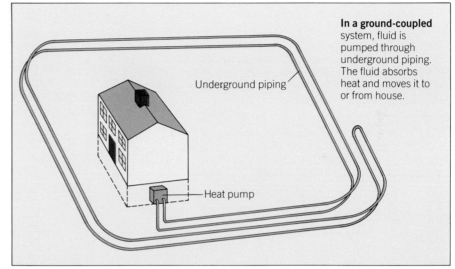

In a ground-coupled system, fluid is pumped through underground piping. The fluid absorbs heat and moves it to or from house.

Underground piping

Heat pump

The air screen

To greatly improve efficiency in summer (especially in warm, humid climates), shade the outdoor condensing coil with air screen to make it possible for cooling coil to dissipate heat faster. In the winter, remove the shading to better capture the sun's warming rays.

Hot-water supply

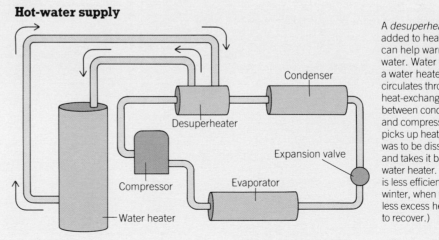

Condenser

Desuperheater

Expansion valve

Compressor

Evaporator

Water heater

A *desuperheater* added to heat pump can help warm tap water. Water from a water heater circulates through a heat-exchanger coil between condenser and compressor, picks up heat that was to be dissipated, and takes it back to water heater. (System is less efficient in winter, when there is less excess heat to recover.)

Home climate/Cooling your home

Tight construction keeps out hot summer air as well as keeping in warm winter air. In the summer, don't rely on air conditioning alone to make your home comfortable. Take the steps shown below to keep the heat out. About 25 percent of the summer heat that gets into a house comes through the windows; another 25 percent seeps through cracks; and 20 percent enters through walls and ceilings. Most of the rest is generated inside by cooking, bathing, and heat-producing lights and appliances.

Installing a whole-house fan

In areas where nights are cool and dry, a whole-house fan can cool a house at a fraction of the cost of air conditioning. Usually centrally located in the attic, a whole-house fan pulls hot indoor air into the attic and exhausts it through vents. Cool night air is drawn through selectively opened doors and windows.

A fan should change the air in the house every 2 minutes. To get the right size, calculate the volume of all rooms to be cooled: multiply height × width × length of each room and add the totals; divide the total by 2 to obtain the *design airflow rate* in cubic feet per minute (CFM). Select a fan that provides the design airflow rate at $\frac{1}{10}$ inch static pressure, a measurement that represents the amount of push or pull produced by a fan. Check that the attic vents (pp.460–461) have at least 1 square foot of free area for every 750 CFM of airflow; add more if there isn't.

Always open at least one exterior door or window before operating a whole-house fan. For best results, open windows and doors of rooms that are in use. Most whole-house fans have 12-hour timers and speed control switches; some have thermostats too. In the winter, cover the fan opening with an insulated panel.

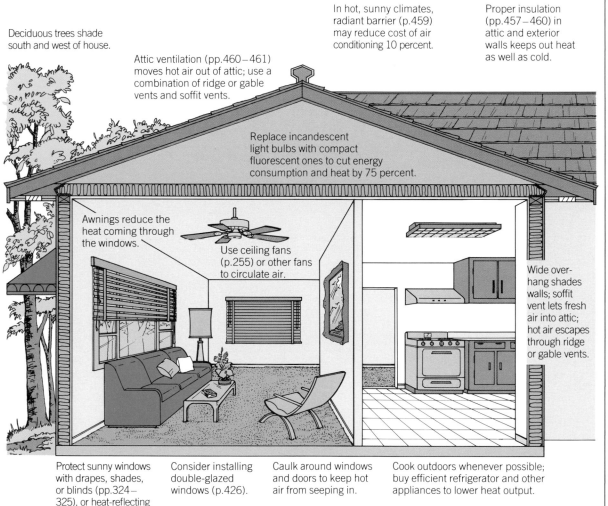

Deciduous trees shade south and west of house.

In hot, sunny climates, radiant barrier (p.459) may reduce cost of air conditioning 10 percent.

Proper insulation (pp.457–460) in attic and exterior walls keeps out heat as well as cold.

Attic ventilation (pp.460–461) moves hot air out of attic; use a combination of ridge or gable vents and soffit vents.

Replace incandescent light bulbs with compact fluorescent ones to cut energy consumption and heat by 75 percent.

Awnings reduce the heat coming through the windows.

Use ceiling fans (p.255) or other fans to circulate air.

Wide overhang shades walls; soffit vent lets fresh air into attic; hot air escapes through ridge or gable vents.

Protect sunny windows with drapes, shades, or blinds (pp.324–325), or heat-reflecting film (pp.426–427).

Consider installing double-glazed windows (p.426).

Caulk around windows and doors to keep hot air from seeping in.

Cook outdoors whenever possible; buy efficient refrigerator and other appliances to lower heat output.

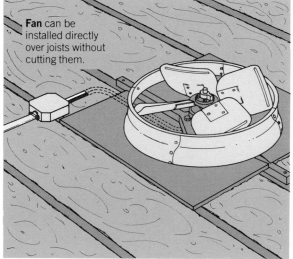

Fan can be installed directly over joists without cutting them.

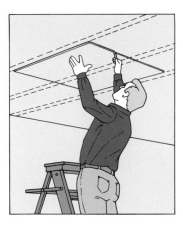

1. Select fan location; ideally, it should be over a central hallway. In the attic check that there are no electric wires, pipes, or other obstructions above fan location, and make sure there is at least 20 in. clearance between joists and roof. Use template supplied by manufacturer to mark cutout on ceiling.

2. Wearing long sleeves, gloves, goggles, and a respirator, go to attic and remove insulation above area to be cut. Return below. Wearing goggles, cut ceiling opening along lines drawn earlier, being careful not to cut into ceiling joists. Use a wallboard saw or a circular saw with its blade depth set to equal the thickness of the wallboard. Carefully remove wallboard you have cut.

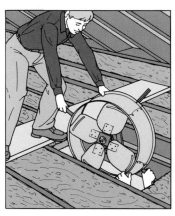

3. If fan is unassembled, assemble it according to the manufacturer's directions. Lift the assembled fan through the hole in the ceiling and rest it on the joists.

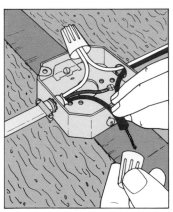

4. Turn off electric power at service panel (p.237), and use voltage tester to make sure power is off (p.243). Install junction box on joist and run fan cable to box, stapling wire to joist along the way. Following manufacturer's instructions and local codes (p.193), connect wires to the 120V house wiring inside junction box and run control wire down through wall. Install fan controls in hallway below.

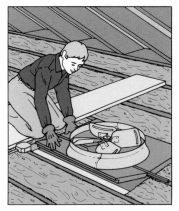

5. Lower fan into position over opening and fasten fan to joists with the screws provided. Using hacksaw, cut notches in fan shield to fit over joists; then install the shield and screw it into place against joists. If the fan is accessible to people or animals, also install a screened cage or other guard as safety measure.

6. Paint louvered shutter to match ceiling, if you wish. From hallway below, position louvered shutter over ceiling opening and screw it into place. Handle shutter carefully; its louvers contain aluminum blades and springs to hold blades closed when fan isn't operating.

Choosing an air conditioner

Air conditioners cool, dehumidify, and filter the air. They can be bought to condition a single room (pp.494–495) or the whole house (pp.496–497).

Energy ratings. The energy used by air conditioners is measured in British thermal units (Btu's): 1 Btu is the amount of energy it takes to heat 1 pound of water by 1 degree F. You can also think of a Btu as approximately the amount of energy released by completely burning a kitchen match. Air conditioners are sold by the ton, an industrial term that represents the amount of energy it takes to melt 1 ton of ice in a day, which is equivalent to 12,000 Btu's per hour. For example, a 3-ton air conditioner has a capacity of 3 × 12,000, or a total of 36,000 Btu's per hour.

An air conditioner's capacity is the sum of two factors: sensible heat and latent heat. Sensible heat is the energy that is removed from air to cool it. Latent heat is the energy that is removed from water vapor to condense it. In humid climates latent heat requirements are higher—as much as 30 percent of the total load.

Sizing. Accurate sizing is critical. An undersize unit does not maintain comfort during the hottest days. An oversize unit wastes energy and cycles on and off excessively, causing inefficient operation and a shortened life for the equipment. In addition, an oversize unit does not dehumidify properly, leaving the air feeling cold and clammy.

Most air-conditioning loads vary from 1½ to 1⅔ tons per 1,000 square feet of living space, but you can't rely on this rule of thumb. Ask the dealer to do the sizing calculations; or if you are buying a room air conditioner, make your own calculation and check it against one of the dealer's charts.

Air-conditioning loads are calculated by measuring the area of exterior windows, walls, and ceilings, and multiplying each by a factor that quantifies heat gain. The calculation must also take into account the local climate, the number of south-facing windows, the desired indoor temperature, and the heat generated by people, lights, and appliances. (For more information on sizing a central system, see page 497.)

The components of a room air conditioner are contained in a compact box that can be mounted in a window or through a wall. Individual units are usually less expensive to install in an existing home than a central system. Because a room air conditioner cools only the room in use, it may also be more energy-efficient. A small to medium-size unit can be installed by a homeowner.

Every air conditioner contains two *coils,* which are composed of panels of aluminum fins and loops of copper tubing. A compressor circulates refrigerant through both of the coils. One fan draws room air across the *evaporator coil,* where the air is cooled and dehumidified. Another fan blows outdoor air over the *condenser coil,* where the heat absorbed from the indoor air is ejected. A barrier with a door separates indoor air from outdoor air. To permit ventilating the room with outside air, the door may be opened.

Room air conditioners are labeled with an Energy Efficiency Ratio (EER), calculated by dividing the capacity of the unit, in Btu's per hour, by the number of watts of electrical energy needed to run it. Select room units with an EER of 9 or higher.

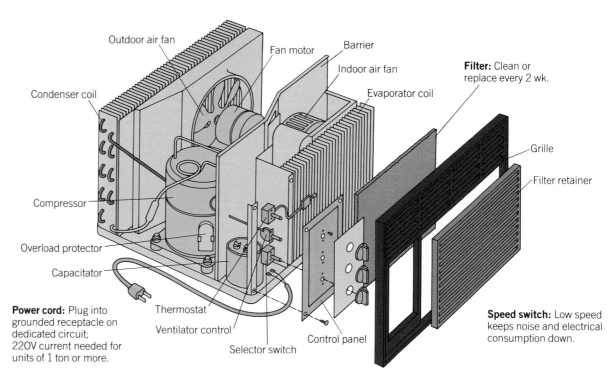

Outdoor air fan

Fan motor

Barrier

Indoor air fan

Filter: Clean or replace every 2 wk.

Condenser coil

Evaporator coil

Grille

Filter retainer

Compressor

Overload protector

Capacitator

Power cord: Plug into grounded receptacle on dedicated circuit; 220V current needed for units of 1 ton or more.

Thermostat

Ventilator control

Selector switch

Control panel

Speed switch: Low speed keeps noise and electrical consumption down.

Window installation

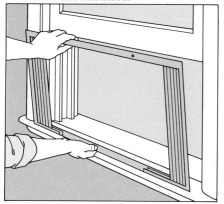

1. Easiest to install is a unit that comes with window mounting kit. Expandable curtain assembly fills gap between the air conditioner and window opening. Screw it to window frame.

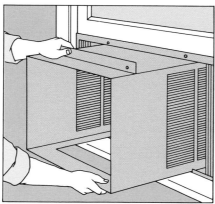

2. Remove air conditioner from casing. Slide casing into window opening and screw into sill and sash. Casing must be tilted slightly (about ¼ in.) to outdoors to drain condensate when operating.

3. If casing extends more than 1 ft. beyond outside sill, it needs exterior bracing to support it. Fasten bracing to wall with noncorroding screws. Adjust pitch with leveling screw.

Leveling screw

4. Slide air conditioner into casing. Room unit may weigh as much as 300 lb.; get help when lifting. Seal around casing with foam rubber, and seal between upper and lower sashes if necessary.

Wall installation

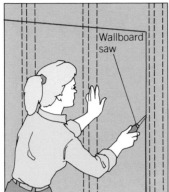

1. Select a location for room unit, avoiding walls exposed to direct sunlight and making sure airflow won't be obstructed. Because cold air sinks, mounting high on wall is preferable. Strip away wall covering to expose three or four studs, depending on width of unit. Use a wallboard saw to cut wallboard or a chisel to chip away plaster. Remove insulation; move any pipes or electric wires from area.

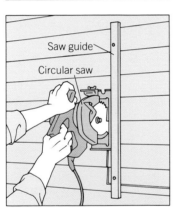

2. To mark corners of cutout on exterior wall, drill holes from inside, using bit long enough to penetrate both sheathing and siding. Using holes as guides, mark outline of cutout on house siding ¼ in. higher and wider than the air conditioner casing. Nail a straightedge to the wall as a guide, and saw through sheathing and siding.

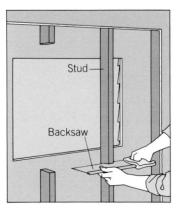

3. From inside, use a backsaw to cut back studs above and below opening to make room for the header, sill, and jamb that will be built to frame air conditioner and support structural load. To estimate length of cutback, add height of unit, thickness of two 1 × 4's, and width of two 2 × 4's (or of two 2 × 6's if the house is framed with 2 × 6's).

4. Nail together a header and a sill of two 2 × 4's or of three 2 × 6's to match house framing. Both must meet local code requirements (p.193) and span the space between the uncut studs on both sides of rough opening. Insert ½-in. spacers between pieces to make sill and header same thickness as house studs.

5. Nail header and sill into studs, and add a vertical 2 × 4 or 2 × 6 on each side. Assemble a rectangular jamb with 1 × 4 or 1 × 6 jamb stock (p.327). The inside dimensions of finished jamb should be same as those of outside wall cutout. Depth of jamb should equal depth of studs plus thickness of interior wall finish. Slip jamb into rough opening and fasten with finishing nails.

6. Remove the air conditioner from its casing. Slide casing into wall opening and screw casing into jamb. If unit extends more than 1 ft. beyond sill, metal support bracing (facing page) may be supplied by manufacturer. If so, fasten it to unit and to outside wall according to manufacturer's directions.

7. Water that condenses on the evaporator coil drips from the back of an operating room air conditioner. To ensure proper drainage, pitch the casing toward the exterior slightly (about ¼ in.). To set the pitch, use the adjusting screw on the support bracing, if any, or add shims indoors between bottom of casing and jamb; check with a ¼-in. block and a level.

8. Slide air conditioner into casing. The weight of room units ranges from 50 to 300 lb., so get someone to help you. Always lift an air conditioner from the base pan on the bottom; never pull or lift from plastic parts. Take care not to damage the aluminum coil fins or the electrical wiring. Add front panel, if separate.

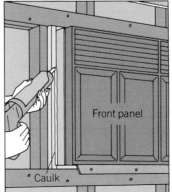

9. Caulk around the casing and frame, both inside and outside. Use backer rods for gaps larger than ½ in. Restore the interior wall with wallboard or plaster. Nail trim around unit on the interior wall; match the existing door and window trim, if you like.

A central air-conditioning system circulates cool air throughout the house with a network of ducts. Typically, these same ducts are used for heating in the winter. An outside condenser unit contains a compressor, condenser coil, and fan. Indoors, an evaporator coil is installed on the supply duct of the warm-air furnace. Refrigerant tubes connect the evaporator coil to the outdoor condenser unit.

When the thermostat calls for cooling, the compressor switches on and circulates refrigerant through both coils. The furnace blower forces indoor air through the evaporator coil, where it is cooled, dehumidified, and then circulated throughout the house. Heat taken from the indoor airstream is transferred to the condenser coil, and then to the outdoor air.

Cost-effectiveness. When adding a cooling system to a home that already has warm-air heating, central air conditioning is often less expensive than equipping every room with an air conditioner. However, if your home has some other type of heating system, you will have to add ductwork. Sometimes ducts can be installed economically in a crawl space or a basement. But where walls and ceilings must be opened, the cost of ducts may be so high that installing individual room units turns out to be the less expensive alternative.

Room air conditioners can actually be more energy-efficient because you can operate them only in rooms in use, cooling each one to the temperature you want. But a central air-conditioning system is quieter because the noisiest component, the compressor, is located outside. And unlike room units, central systems do not protrude through walls or windows.

Determining system size. Central air conditioners usually range from 1¼ to 1⅔ tons for every 1,000 square feet of living area. Hot humid climates require larger units, whereas cool dry climates may utilize smaller ones. Accurate sizing is critical. An oversize unit will cycle excessively, causing inefficient operation, shortened compressor life, and inadequate dehumidification. Ask your air-conditioner dealer to do the sizing calculations.

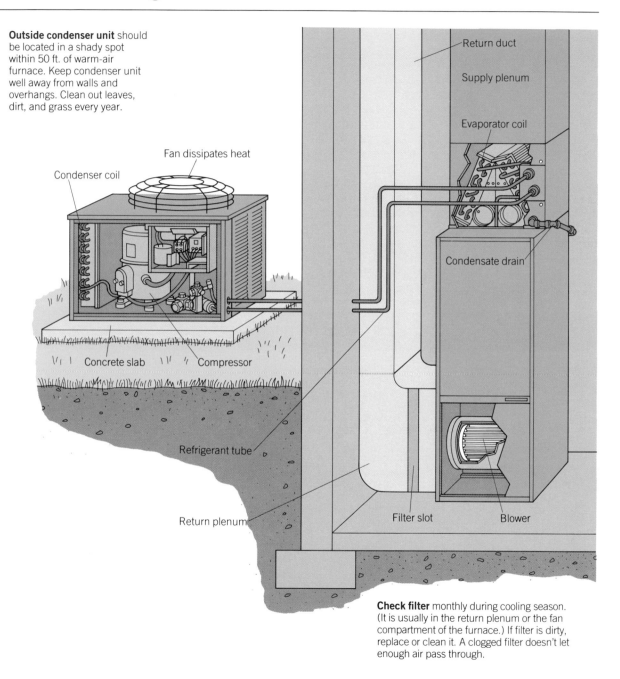

Outside condenser unit should be located in a shady spot within 50 ft. of warm-air furnace. Keep condenser unit well away from walls and overhangs. Clean out leaves, dirt, and grass every year.

Fan dissipates heat

Condenser coil

Concrete slab   Compressor

Refrigerant tube

Return plenum

Return duct

Supply plenum

Evaporator coil

Condensate drain

Filter slot   Blower

Check filter monthly during cooling season. (It is usually in the return plenum or the fan compartment of the furnace.) If filter is dirty, replace or clean it. A clogged filter doesn't let enough air pass through.

Selecting the most economical unit

Central air conditioners are labeled with a SEER (Seasonal Energy Efficiency Ratio) number. The higher the SEER number, the more efficient the unit. Although 10.0 is suitable for most locations in the United States, you may want to check if a unit with a higher efficiency rating is worth the added expense. You can do this by comparing the unit's price plus installation costs with the money you can save in energy costs. Start by getting bids for installing a central air conditioner from at least two contractors; in addition to prices, ask the contractors what size units they propose to install and their SEER numbers. Then use the following formula to calculate the annual operating cost for each unit:

$$\frac{Capacity}{SEER} \times \frac{Cooling\ load\ hours}{1,000} \times Electric\ rate$$

Capacity is the nominal number of Btu's of energy the unit extracts from the indoor air. To get the ca-pacity of a unit, multiply the air conditioner's tonnage by 12,000. *Cooling load hours* are indicated on the map below. You may need to check with your local utility to get the *electric rate* in dollars per kilowatt hour ($/kwh). And so, if you want to find the annual operating cost for a 10.0 SEER, 3-ton air conditioner in a location with 1,400 annual cooling hours and a .08 $/kwh electric rate, calculate it as follows:

$$\frac{36,000\ Btu's}{10.0} \times \frac{1,400\ hours}{1,000} \times .08\ \$/kwh = \$403.20$$

When comparing two units, divide the difference in purchase price by the difference in annual operating costs to get the payback period. This tells you how many years it will take for the energy savings to add up to the additional cost for the higher-priced, more efficient unit. Generally a payback period of 3 to 8 years, or less, is considered a worthwhile investment.

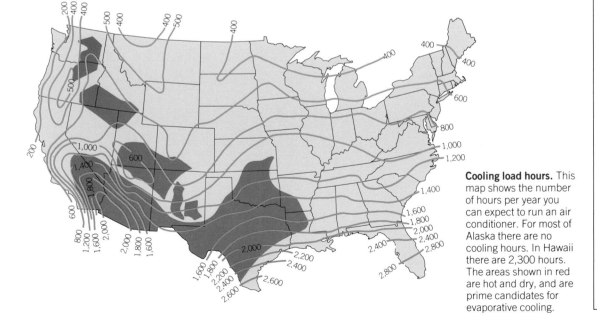

Cooling load hours. This map shows the number of hours per year you can expect to run an air conditioner. For most of Alaska there are no cooling hours. In Hawaii there are 2,300 hours. The areas shown in red are hot and dry, and are prime candidates for evaporative cooling.

Cooling in a hot dry climate

If you live in the American Southwest or some other dry area, consider air-conditioning your home with an evaporative cooler. These coolers use the natural process of water evaporation to cool indoor air. They contain a blower, fibrous pads, a small pump, and a water reservoir. When the unit is operating, the pump draws water from the reservoir and distributes it through small-diameter plastic tubes to the pads to keep them saturated. The blower draws outside air through the dampened pads to cool it, and then forces the cooled air into the house through grilles in a wall or ceiling. The cool, fresh incoming air pushes the warm, stale indoor air out of the house through the windows, which should be

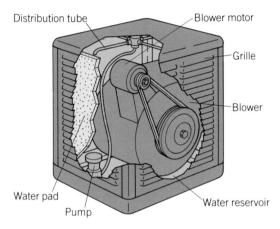

left open in the rooms to be cooled to allow for a free flow of air throughout the system.

An evaporative cooling unit can be mounted on the roof, flush in a gable wall, or on a concrete slab next to the house. Window units are also available.

A typical evaporative cooler has two small electric motors (for the pump and the blower) with a total of ½ to ¾ horsepower. A comparable refrigerant-charged central air-conditioning unit contains three motors with a total of 3½ horsepower, and consumes 4 to 5 times as much energy.

Maintenance. At least twice during the cooling season, check the pads of an evaporative cooler for mineral deposits or dust buildup, and replace them when necessary. In the winter, drain the reservoir and insulate the evaporative cooler to reduce heat loss. One easy way is to fill a plastic trash bag with insulation (p.457) and stuff it behind the grille the cooled air comes through.

Home climate/Controlling humidity room by room

Dehumidifiers

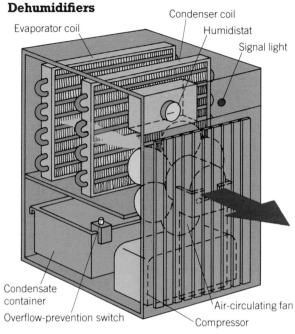

Evaporator coil
Condenser coil
Humidistat
Signal light
Condensate container
Overflow-prevention switch
Air-circulating fan
Compressor

If your house lacks central air conditioning (which dehumidifies the whole house in hot weather) or a heating system with a humidifier (for adding moisture to the air when outdoor temperatures are cold), you can still maintain control over the humidity in your home with portable plug-in appliances.

Dehumidifiers

Like an air conditioner, a dehumidifier (left) has a refrigeration system to cool room air and a fan to move air over a cold evaporator coil that collects moisture. However, a dehumidifier also has a warm condenser coil that reheats the air before circulating it back into the room. Condensate is directed to a container that you empty by hand or to a drain, either right below the unit or reached via a hose. A dehumidifier should have a humidistat that automatically turns off the unit when the air reaches a preset dryness level and an overflow-prevention switch that turns the unit off when the condensate container is full and switches on a warning light.

Dehumidifiers are particularly useful in remov-

ing dampness from below-grade basement rooms, where there is no need to also cool the air. But dehumidifiers can handle only moisture created by condensation, not wetness from water seepage. For a dehumidifier to work well, you must keep the space enclosed by shutting windows and doors.

Buying guide. Large-capacity dehumidifiers are the most efficient. They can remove 40 to 50 pints of moisture a day from a room when the temperature is 80° F and the relative humidity is 60 percent (an arbitrary standard created by the Association of Home Appliance Manufacturers for comparing one model to another). When the temperature is higher than 80° F and the humidity is lower than 60 percent, a big machine will remove slightly fewer pints of moisture per day, but far more than a small-capacity dehumidifier. When temperatures drop below 65° F, the coils in many small dehumidifiers ice up. Large units handle low temperatures better.

Maintenance. A yearly vacuuming of the coils and oiling of the fan (after unplugging the unit and allowing hot components to cool) are the only

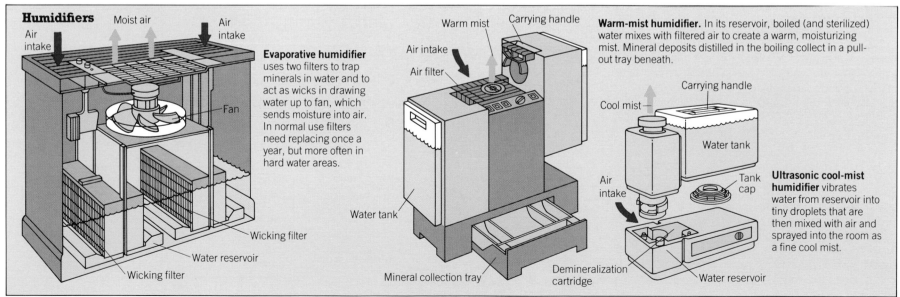

Humidifiers
Moist air
Air intake
Air intake
Fan
Wicking filter
Water reservoir
Wicking filter

Evaporative humidifier uses two filters to trap minerals in water and to act as wicks in drawing water up to fan, which sends moisture into air. In normal use filters need replacing once a year, but more often in hard water areas.

Warm mist
Carrying handle
Air intake
Air filter
Water tank
Mineral collection tray
Demineralization cartridge

Warm-mist humidifier. In its reservoir, boiled (and sterilized) water mixes with filtered air to create a warm, moisturizing mist. Mineral deposits distilled in the boiling collect in a pull-out tray beneath.

Carrying handle
Cool mist
Water tank
Air intake
Tank cap
Water reservoir

Ultrasonic cool-mist humidifier vibrates water from reservoir into tiny droplets that are then mixed with air and sprayed into the room as a fine cool mist.

chores required if the dehumidifier empties into a drain. If you use the condensate container, you should scrub it frequently to eliminate mold and bacteria. Put several tablespoons of fresh chlorine bleach in the container after you empty it, to keep the condensate from nurturing organisms.

Humidifiers

Adding moisture to dry heated air in winter can ease dry throats and reduce static electricity and shrinking of wood furniture. Unfortunately, the process can also spew white mineral dust, molds, and bacteria into the air if you are not meticulous in following the manufacturer's directions for using your humidifier. There are three basic types of room humidifiers: evaporative, ultrasonic cool-mist, and warm-mist units.

Evaporative. Old evaporative units, in which room air is blown over a rotating belt of dampened sponge, are difficult to clean. The sponge tends to collect minerals, molds, and bacteria, which are then released into the air. New models use treated filters as wicks to bring cleaner water to the fan for dispersal. The disposable filters trap minerals and discourage bacteria but must be replaced.

Ultrasonic cool-mist. High-frequency vibration breaks water into droplets that are impelled into the air as a mist in this type. When demineralized or distilled water is used (making the unit more expensive to run), mineral deposits in the mist are kept to a minimum. (Many units now come with a demineralization cartridge.) However, to reduce bacteria and molds, you should scrub the water reservoir every time you refill it.

Warm-mist. These units are designed to solve some humidifier maintenance problems. Before being dispersed, the reservoir water is heated to a boil. This distills out minerals and kills bacteria and molds. The heated water is then combined with filtered air to create a warm, but not scalding, mist. Unlike old-fashioned steam vaporizers, which could cause bad burns, these warm-mist units are not dangerously hot to the touch.

As houses have become better sealed for climate control, concern about indoor air quality has grown. In a "tight" house, for example, it takes several hours for the air to change completely (in a loosely weatherstripped house it takes less than an hour).

Common indoor pollutants—dust, pollen, bacteria, viruses, spores, mite pellets, animal dander, and tobacco smoke—not only irritate people but also clog such equipment as audiovisual players, computers, and heating and cooling systems.

An electronic air cleaner offers relief by a process called electronic precipitation. A pre-filter first screens out large particles; then in the electronic unit, small particles are electrically charged and collected on a plate that acts as a magnet. This plate and the pre-filter *must* be cleaned monthly; run them through a dishwasher cycle or scrub them in a tub. Electronic air cleaners produce ozone, a respiratory irritant, that is also produced by hair dryers and power tools. High airflow dilutes the ozone and good maintenance minimizes it.

An electronic cleaner installed in the return-air duct of a warm-air heating or central air conditioning system will extend the life and efficiency of the equipment. For houses with other kinds of heating or cooling systems, there are room-size models.

Some indoor pollutants are still best removed by ventilation. To clear out smoke, unpleasant odors, or noxious gases, open a window or a skylight, or turn on the kitchen or bathroom exhaust fan.

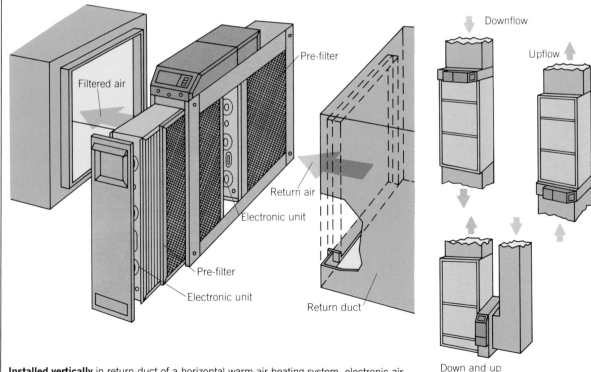

Installed vertically in return duct of a horizontal warm-air heating system, electronic air cleaner replaces filter. It can also be mounted horizontally with up or down airflow (right).

To keep the air inside a well-insulated and well-sealed house healthy—particularly for people who suffer from respiratory allergies—a central vacuum system can be helpful. Many common allergens, such as dust, pollen, molds, and mite pellets, aren't trapped by the filter in a regular vacuum cleaner. In fact, they are blown back out by the exhaust action of the vacuum and stay suspended in the air for several hours.

A central vacuum system solves this problem by sucking dirt and debris into a single receptacle located away from the house's main living spaces, in the garage or the basement. Dust-size particles are vented outdoors (but not onto walks or patios).

Besides cutting down on dust, central vacuums offer an easy, convenient, and quiet way to clean. Suction is activated when you plug a vacuum hose into a wall outlet; disengaging the hose turns off the motor. Outlets are placed at strategic spots around the house so that all areas can be reached with the hose. Usually about 30 feet long, the hose has attachments for different cleaning chores.

Choose a motor size to match the cleaning power you want, not the size of your house. Vacuum motor power is expressed as water lift (suction power) and cubic feet of airflow per minute.

PVC pipes lead from the wall outlets to the vacuum power unit and the canister. In a new house, these pipes are laid after the wiring and plumbing but before the wallboard is installed. However, putting a central vacuum system into an existing house is not difficult. The main pipe runs between joists or through the attic; branch pipes run between studs or through closets. An installation usually takes a service person one day. Using a kit and doing it yourself may take a little longer.

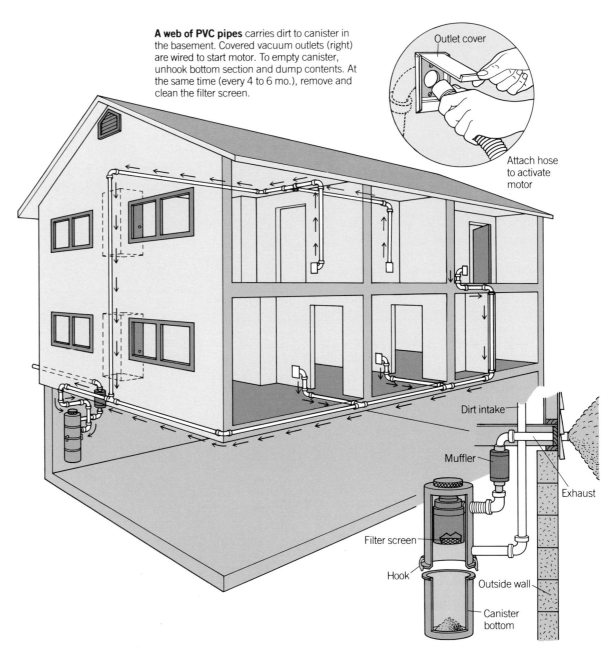

A web of PVC pipes carries dirt to canister in the basement. Covered vacuum outlets (right) are wired to start motor. To empty canister, unhook bottom section and dump contents. At the same time (every 4 to 6 mo.), remove and clean the filter screen.

Outlet cover

Attach hose to activate motor

Dirt intake

Muffler

Exhaust

Filter screen

Hook

Outside wall

Canister bottom

Furniture
Repairs and restoration

Contents

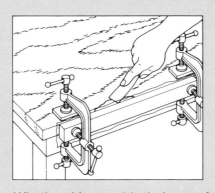 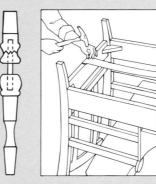 

Whether it's an old chair you found at a flea market, a dresser you bought at a garage sale or secondhand shop, or your own dining room table that has suffered from years of use, turning a drab, dilapidated piece of furniture into an attractive and functional beauty can give you a great feeling of accomplishment.

In this chapter you will find techniques for restoring a finished surface to its original condition (or to one that will look almost new), for repairing cracks and breaks, and for straightening warped wood. Also covered are methods for reupholstering a chair, recaning a seat, refurbishing wickerwork, and removing stains from carpets, draperies, and upholstery.

The techniques described here are suitable for the care and repair of ordinary furniture. If a cherished antique needs repair, or if you can't identify the finish, it's best to take the piece to a professional restorer.

Damage to furniture and other finished wood items falls into three categories: surface damage, damage that penetrates the finish, and damage that penetrates the wood. To avoid making minor damage worse, begin with the gentlest repair method that could cure the problem. Take fine furniture to a professional restorer.

To revive old finished surfaces that are merely dull or sticky, wipe with furniture cleaner and a soft cloth. If the furniture cleaner is ineffective, wipe the surface with mineral spirits. Then apply a mixture of lemon extract and mineral oil—10 drops to 1 quart—to replenish the natural oils removed by the cleaner. One or two thin coats of paste wax will protect the repaired finish.

Stains. Remove light-colored stains, such as white rings left by moisture, by rubbing the surface with a fine abrasive. Start with a cloth dabbed in toothpaste or in silver polish containing whiting. If that is ineffective, try sprinkling table salt on the stain and gently rubbing with a cloth dipped in mineral oil. The coarsest abrasive to try is rottenstone, rubbed with a cloth dampened with mineral oil. Removing dark stains usually requires refinishing.

To remove light scratches, cloudiness, or alligatoring in shellac, lacquer, and some varnishes, try reamalgamation—wipe the finish with the appropriate solvent; it will dissolve a thin layer of the finish and then evaporate, permitting the finish to reharden. Use denatured alcohol as a solvent for shellac; lacquer thinner for lacquer; and either one or a combination of the two for varnish. If you aren't sure of the finish type, experiment on an inconspicuous area to determine which solvent or combination softens it.

For other finishes, and to repair deep scratches, use stain to tint the blemish. Then fill the damaged area with paste wax or spray it with a clear, hard finish such as acrylic or polyurethane.

Repair damaged wood with a filler. Plastic wood dough is adequate for coarse repairs. Use latex wood filler or water-base putty for delicate repairs. Fill small blemishes in stained wood with a matching furniture-wax stick.

To reamalgamate finish, clean area. Dissolve finish with suitable solvent, using paintbrush; let dry. To darken, apply equal parts of denatured alcohol and shellac mixture; let dry between coats. Rub with paste wax.

For a large area, using gauze or cheesecloth, gently rub solvent on damaged area until finish dissolves. Let dry overnight. Rub with paste wax.

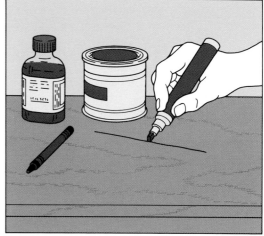

Disguise a deep but fine scratch by coloring the area carefully with wood stain—use a toothpick—or with a crayon or felt-tip pen. Scratches passing through differently colored areas may require several stains. Wipe excess stain from surrounding wood immediately. After stain has dried, cover repair with paste wax.

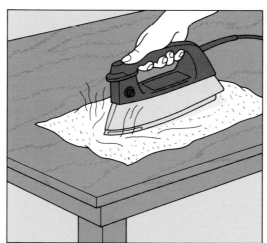

To remove a shallow dent, prick the finish with a pin in several places in deepest part of dent. Dampen the dent with water; then cover it with a damp towel. Press the tip of a hot iron on the towel over dent for a few seconds. Check the results; repeat if necessary. Refinish repaired area or entire surface after wood has dried.

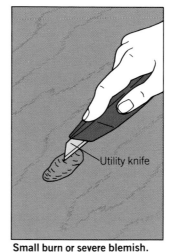

Small burn or severe blemish.
1. Scrape damaged area clean. Hold a colored furniture-wax stick over blemish; touch its end with a hot palette knife (next step). Apply several layers.

Utility knife

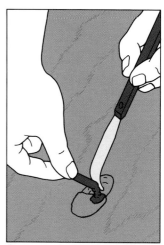

2. Allow melted wax to overfill area slightly. After wax cools, level it by scraping with a utility knife; hold blade perpendicular to surface. Protect repair by spraying it with clear, hard compatible finish.

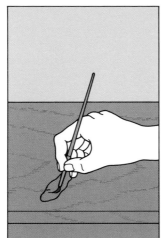

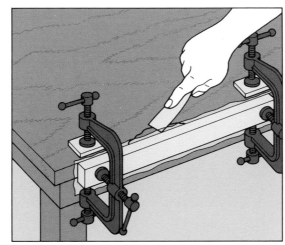

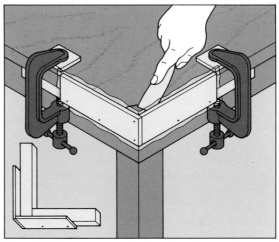

Repairing a gouge. 1. Scrape the depression clean; fill it with a tinted latex-base wood filler or water-base putty. Wipe away any excess filler from the surrounding surface promptly.

2. After filler hardens, sand it smooth. Hide repair by painting on wood grain using artist's oil colors and a delicate brush. When dry, spray repair with compatible finish or refinish entire surface (p.117).

To restore a nicked edge, clamp board along edge to act as form, with plastic wrap between. Fill nicks with tinted latex-base wood filler or water-base putty. If nicks are deeper than ¼ in., apply filler in layers; allow each one to dry. Remove form, sand surface smooth, and disguise repair by painting on grain. Refinish repaired area or entire surface.

For a nicked corner, make an L-shaped mold: squared pieces of wood form base; two thin boards nailed to base form sides. Clamp form to corner with plastic wrap between. Fill missing area with latex-base wood filler, plastic wood dough, or water-base putty in ¼-in. layers; let dry between layers. When filler has dried, remove form; sand. Paint on wood grain; refinish.

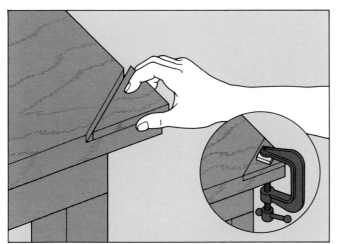

To rebuild a broken corner, patch it with a precisely cut piece of similar material. Use a router, sharp block plane, or chisel to create a smooth bed for the patch. Be sure corner is square where horizontal and vertical surfaces meet. Test-fit patch before applying glue. To prevent marring surface, place scrap blocks under clamp jaws. Refinish.

Patching solid wood

To repair a large damaged area in solid wood, patch it with a piece of wood that matches. Make the patch first—irregularly shaped pieces are the least conspicuous—and place it over the damaged area. Trace around the patch with a knife; then rout or chisel out a cavity to the shape and thickness of the patch. Fasten the patch with wood glue. Sand or plane the surface smooth, and refinish.

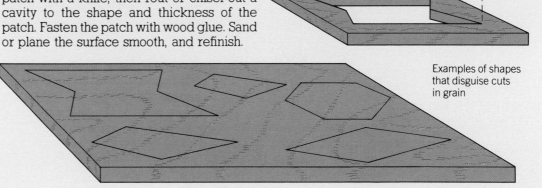

Examples of shapes that disguise cuts in grain

Furniture / Veneer restoration

A thin layer of decorative wood, veneer is glued over a core of sturdier, less valuable solid wood, plywood, or manufactured wood paneling. Because veneer is thin and brittle, minor damage can easily become worse if not repaired promptly. Take fine veneered furniture to a professional restorer.

Most older veneer is glued to the core with hide glue, which softens and loosens with moisture or heat. (The adhesives used with newer veneer are less likely to loosen.) Controlled moisture and heat are used to soften the glue and make the veneer more pliable for repairs. If scraping the old glue out proves difficult, soften it by injecting hot water from a dropper or glue injector under the loose veneer.

Loose veneer. First warm it with a clothes iron on low heat placed over a damp towel; then weight it down for 12 hours. If this doesn't work, replace the old glue. When repairing veneer, use liquid hide glue or yellow glue. Any other type can cause new damage because it may react to changes in humidity differently than the surrounding glue. To prevent glue from sticking to a clamping device, lay wax paper or plastic wrap between the repair area and the clamp. Wipe away excess glue with a damp rag or a sponge, and allow 12 hours for the glue to set.

For veneer patches, buy a piece that closely matches the original in color and grain from a woodworking supply house or a craft store.

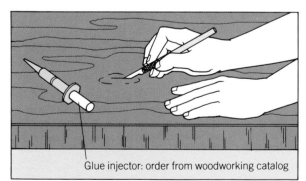

To flatten a blister, slit it with a hobby knife along wood grain. Using a glue injector, apply glue beneath veneer. Press repair flat, wipe away excess glue, and weight or clamp for 12 hr.

Glue injector: order from woodworking catalog

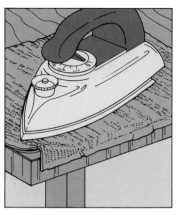

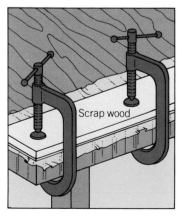

Regluing lifted veneer.
1. Make the veneer pliable by placing a slightly damp towel over the damaged area and, using a clothes iron set on low, applying heat for 5 to 10 sec. Check surface for scorching; repeat if necessary. Moisture may damage shellacked surface. If veneer is already pliable, go on to next step.

2. Scrape away as much old glue as possible, using a razor blade. With a paintbrush, apply a thin coat of fresh glue to core and to underside of veneer. Press veneer flat. For a large area of damage, roll the surface with a rolling pin to distribute glue thoroughly.

3. Wipe away excess glue with damp cloth. Place wax paper over the repair and the surrounding area. Clamp or weight repair for 12 hr. If you are using clamps, place scrap wood under their jaws to distribute pressure.

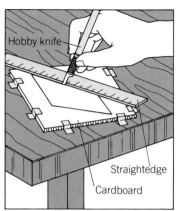

Hobby knife

Straightedge

Cardboard

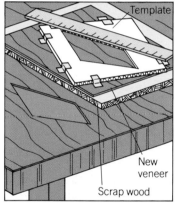

Template

New veneer

Scrap wood

Patching veneer.
1. Tape thin cardboard over damaged area. Using a hobby knife, cut through cardboard and veneer. Follow grain of wood as much as possible; avoid cutting straight across the grain. To simplify trimming edges of a large area, cut out diamond or other similar shape; use a straightedge as a cutting guide. Save cardboard for template.

2. To protect surface, place new veneer on scrap wood. Tape template onto new veneer, matching grain of patch to grain of old veneer as closely as possible. Cut patch from new veneer; use straightedge along template edges as a guide for hobby knife.

3. Remove all traces of old glue. Apply a thin coating of new glue to damaged area and to entire underside of the patch; then swiftly press the patch into place before it can swell. Wipe away excess glue with a damp cloth. Place wax paper over patch and surrounding area. Clamp or weight the patch for 12 hr. If using clamp, place scrap wood under jaws.

Moisture-related repairs

Wood warps when its surfaces absorb unequal amounts of moisture or when it is subjected for a long time to heavy loads without adequate reinforcement. Unfortunately, straightening warped wood is often tricky and sometimes impossible. To avoid this problem when building or repairing a wood object, select wood without defects (p.92) and always finish it on all surfaces. Take fine furniture that has warped to a professional.

Wide tabletops and drop leaves that have been sealed and finished on one side but not on the other are especially vulnerable to warping. This is because the finished side is usually impervious to humidity changes while the unfinished side is exposed. If warping seems to be seasonal, wait until the table flattens—usually during winter when indoor air is least humid. Then carefully seal the underside with varnish or polyurethane, or better yet, refinish the entire piece. To prevent further warping, fasten wooden cleats across the underside.

To flatten an individual board, it often helps to soak the concave side with wet rags for approximately 24 hours. If possible, dry the convex side simultaneously by illuminating it with a heat lamp. Then sandwich the board between pairs of homemade wooden clamps fastened together with bolts or C-clamps, leaving them in place for 2 to 4 weeks. Repeat if necessary; then sand the wood and coat it with a sealer. Alternatively, place the board with its soaked side down on a flat surface, and weight it with concrete blocks for several weeks. A warped board must be securely braced soon after straightening; otherwise it may warp again.

Cabinet doors may stick because of warping or because of loose or misaligned hinges. Check that the cabinet is level. Then try tightening the hinges (p.436) or realigning them, or try installing shims. Plane a door only as a last resort. If it has a latch that is easily removed, plane the latch edge. If the hinges are easier to remove, plane the hinge edge.

To prevent shelves from warping, reinforce them with wood blocks, a wood strip attached along the rear edge, or supports available at hardware stores.

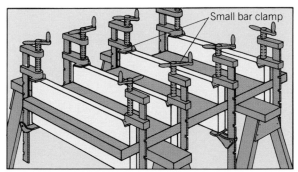

To correct a warp, wet concave side. Then clamp board or tabletop between pairs of 2 x 4's placed on edge at 10-in. intervals. If warp is severe, tighten clamps gradually to prevent cracks.

Small bar clamp

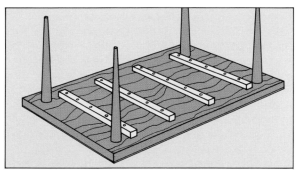

To keep tabletop or board from warping again, fasten cleats made from 2 x 2's or larger lumber to its underside with screws and glue. The cleats should be perpendicular to the wood grain.

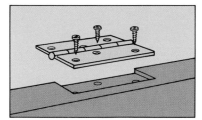

Sticking cabinet door. 1. Remove the hinges carefully; slide them out sideways to avoid chipping mortises.

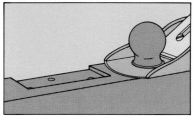

2. Use razor-sharp plane to remove thin shavings from hinge side of door edge. Check fit of door after every stroke or two.

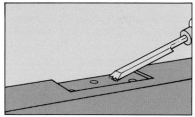

3. Deepen mortises with a chisel to compensate for planing, keeping recessed surface flat. Refasten hinges.

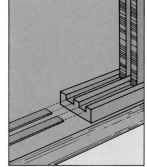

Sliding cabinet doors. If a door is tight, widen the channel by sanding; use medium-grit sandpaper folded over a scrap of wood slightly thinner than the channel. If the channel is too large, shim its edges or base with a strip of weatherstripping (p.453) cut to fit and glued in place. Weatherstripping will also reduce the friction of the door against the base of channel.

Reinforcing weak shelves

Install blocks or braces at shelf ends and along rear edge. To prevent bow in shelf up to 1 ft. wide, glue 1 x 2 wood strip along rear edge. Add braces for support if necessary. To flatten a bow, reinstall shelf upside down.

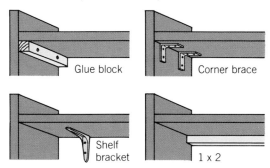

Glue block

Corner brace

Shelf bracket

1 x 2

Furniture/Fixing drawers

Drawers can jam or stick for several reasons. Humidity may swell the wood, causing parts to rub. This is usually a temporary problem that disappears during dry seasons. Other causes are wear, neglect, and overfilling.

To diagnose a sticking drawer, remove it and its contents. On a drawer with wooden runners, look for shiny spots on the sliding parts. Also look for signs of uneven wear—especially on the bottoms of runners—and for looseness, breakage, or missing screws or nails. Lubricating, sanding, or planing parts that fit too tightly will often remedy sticking. But before removing any wood, be sure the condition isn't temporary, caused by humidity.

If the sliding mechanism is plastic or metal, check the alignment of the parts and look for signs of looseness, breakage, or missing fasteners. Also inspect any rollers; if they don't operate smoothly, clean with ammonia. If they are damaged, replace them.

Sometimes drawers may stick because their joints are loose or no longer square. To remedy this, disassemble the drawer carefully and reglue it. Make sure you remove all old nails and glue blocks before reassembly.

If a drawer jams because it is too full, remove the drawer below it, press upward on the bottom of the stuck drawer, and slide the drawer forward; avoid overfilling the drawer in the future. If the bottom bulges downward because it's warped, turn the bottom upside down or replace it with a new one—you may have to disassemble and rebuild the drawer.

If a drawer slides too far back into the cabinet, install new drawer stops.

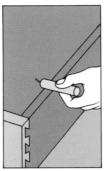 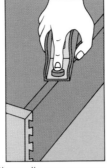

Rub sticking runner with candle wax, or spray with silicone lubricant. If it still sticks, lightly plane runner's bottom and exterior side; rewax runner.

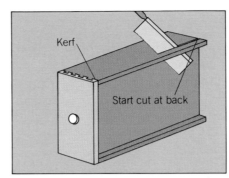

Damaged runner. 1. Remove runner with a fine-tooth panel or dovetail saw; first cut kerf at front. Plane or sand sawn area flush with drawer bottom.

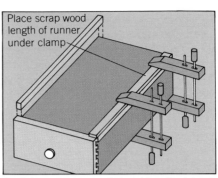

2. Cut new runners of straight-grained hardwood. Glue them to drawer with yellow glue; nail with finishing nails. Clamp along entire length.

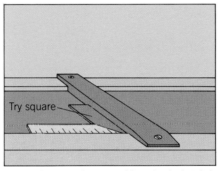

To repair loose drawer guide, check that it is perpendicular to the drawer's front. Tighten the screws or replace them.

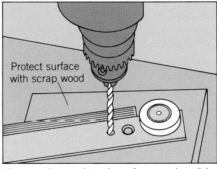

If screws in metal track are loose and can't be tightened, try larger screws. If that doesn't work, remove track and drill new holes in it.

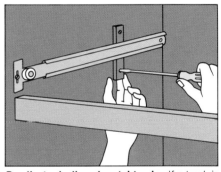

Readjust misaligned metal tracks. If a track is bowed, install a filler block to keep the track parallel to the drawer side.

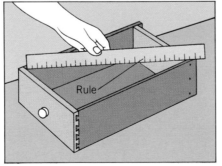

Drawer joints. 1. To check for squareness, measure diagonally from inside corner to inside corner; then measure other diagonal. They should be equal.

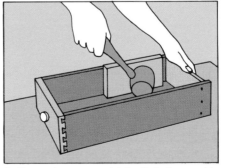

2. To repair unsquare joints, first disassemble drawer by carefully knocking it apart. Use a rubber mallet or a hammer and wood block near joint.

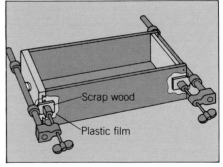

3. Reglue drawer pieces, using bar clamps. Check joints with a rule during and after clamping. Adjust clamps until measurements are equal.

Loose joints and breaks in wood

Repairing loosened joints or broken pieces of furniture requires knowledge of woodworking and adhesives. Ingenuity and special tools may be needed as well. Although most furniture can be restored at home, take fine furniture to a professional.

You can repair a loose joint by regluing it. First scrape away the old glue from all surfaces with a cabinet scraper; then sand off any remaining glue with a coarse- to medium-grit abrasive paper.

To disassemble a piece of furniture, carefully use a mallet against a block of wood, but don't force a tightly glued joint apart or you may break the wood. Try dissolving the glue by injecting a mixture of 1 part distilled white vinegar and 1 part hot water into the joint with a glue injector; do this a few times over 2 or 3 hours. If glue doesn't respond to this mixture, try lacquer thinner or acetone. Once the joint is apart, allow the wood to dry overnight before continuing.

If disassembling and cleaning a loose joint is impractical and strength is secondary, inject glue into the joint. Or you can apply a product that, when injected, causes the wood to swell, tightening the joint.

Broken parts can sometimes be repaired by gluing alone, but if little surface area exists for glue to bond or if the area of the break is subject to heavy use, bracing may also be needed. External bracing in the form of glue blocks, metal braces, or wood splints is the easiest to rig. Internal bracing, which usually consists of dowels (p.108), is more difficult but the finished repair is less noticeable.

Tightening joints

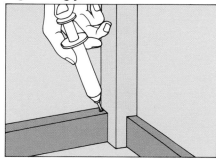

To tighten a loose joint without disassembling it, drill a small hole into the joint at a seam; inject glue, using a glue injector.

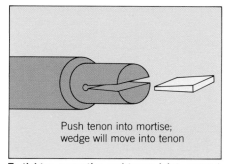

To tighten a mortise-and-tenon joint, expand tenon. Drill small hole (to deter splitting); then saw a slot into it. Insert a thin wedge partway.

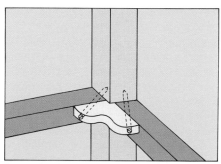

Support block strengthens leg joint. Attach wood block with glue and screws. Or substitute a metal brace (p.112).

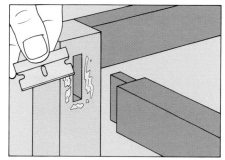

Regluing joint. 1. Disassemble the pieces, and scrape away as much of the old glue as possible, using sharp knife or single-edge razor blade.

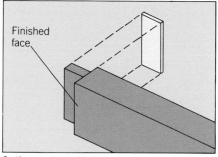

2. If tenon is undersize, glue thin wood shim to side opposite finished face. Before gluing, check fit in mortise. If misaligned, shim both sides.

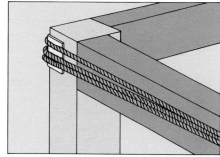

3. Apply glue, and clamp joint until dry. Use pipe clamp or rope; to prevent marring, place scrap wood under clamp jaw, cardboard under rope.

Repairing breaks

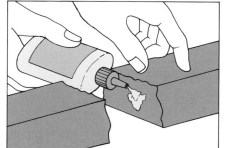

Nonsupporting element. 1. Apply glue to both broken pieces. Press together; wipe off excess glue with damp cloth; cover with wax paper.

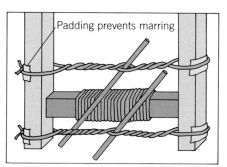

2. Clamp until glue dries. If you don't have clamps, wind rope around repair. Use additional rope with rod to make tourniquet.

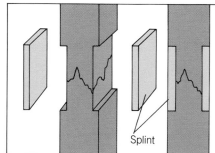

To strengthen a repair, reglue break; when dry, chisel or rout recesses and fill with ¼-in. splints. If piece can be shortened, make a lap joint (p.101).

Over a period of time, the joints and parts of a wood chair can begin to weaken or break. Temperature and humidity changes, simple day-to-day use, refinishing with a paint-stripping product—all of these can cause a joint to loosen. Because a weak joint can lead to a break, make repairs at the first sign of trouble.

Before you begin pulling legs, rungs, or spindles apart, locate the specific problem area. Often a minor trouble spot can be easily fixed. To tighten a loose joint, first try using a liquid wood sweller. Or you can inject yellow glue into the joint with a glue injector—available from woodworking catalogs. Tighten an enlarged socket by inserting toothpicks or matchsticks into it while the glue is still wet. Seat the joint firmly, and clamp it until the glue dries.

If the joint is still loose after the glue has dried, more extensive repairs will be required. You'll have to dismantle the chair and reglue it. Work slowly and carefully; don't force a tight joint apart. For correct reassembly, as you remove a piece, label it and its corresponding part with a letter or number on masking tape. Wipe away any excess glue immediately with a damp cloth. This will save scraping it off later, and it will allow any future stain to penetrate properly.

Cracks and breaks. For a small crack, inject yellow glue into the damaged area and clamp it securely until the glue dries. In some cases you can create a clamp by tightly wrapping masking tape around the glued repair. For a severe break, insert a dowel into the piece to give extra support.

Repairing a broken leg

When a turned leg breaks near its top, apply yellow glue to both pieces of the break; clamp them together until the glue dries. Saw the leg just below the break. Locate the center of the lower piece; insert a brad. Cut off the brad head (p.108). Align the two pieces; push them together. Remove the brad; at both marks drill holes large enough to hold a ⅜-in.-diameter dowel that is at least 3 in. long. (If there's room in the leg, you can insert a wider dowel.) Test-fit the dowel by inserting it into both pieces. Apply a light coat of glue to the dowel, including its end grain, and to the holes. Assemble the leg; clamp it until the glue dries.

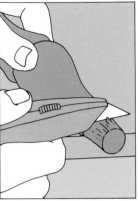

2. Scrape away old glue from the dowel ends with a utility knife or chisel. Sand lightly.

3. Sand socket sides with sandpaper wrapped around dowel. Remove glue from socket bottom with a chisel.

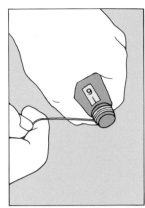

4. Test-assemble the joint. If a piece fits loosely, apply glue to its end and wrap cotton thread around it tightly.

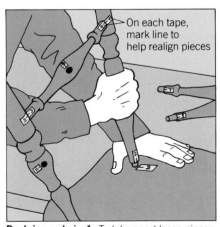

Regluing a chair. **1.** To take apart loose pieces, carefully rock or twist them. Lightly tap any stubborn ones with a rubber mallet or hammer on a block; or use vinegar solution (p.507).

On each tape, mark line to help realign pieces

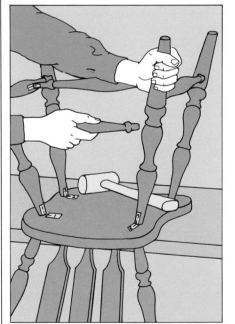

5. Apply a thin layer of glue to dowel ends and sockets. Tap in place with a mallet. Wipe away any excess glue with a damp cloth.

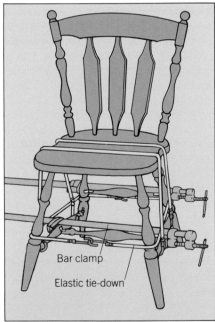

6. With chair on level surface, clamp joints with bar clamps, band clamps, elastic tie-downs, or a combination. Check joints' alignment; let glue dry completely before removing clamps.

Bar clamp

Elastic tie-down

Mending a loose or broken rung

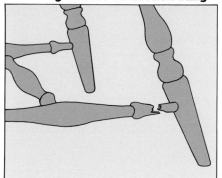

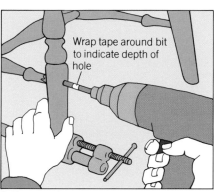

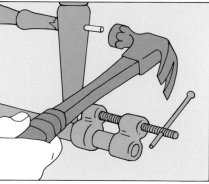

1. A loose or broken rung will put pressure on joints and other pieces, causing additional structural damage. Repair it as soon as possible.

2. For a broken rung, glue pieces together; then clamp them back into sockets with a bar clamp or elastic tie-downs (this also applies for a loose rung). Wipe off any excess glue.

3. To strengthen a weakened joint, drill a hole through the leg and into the end of the rung. Test-fit a ¼-in.-diameter dowel that is at least 2 in. long; make sure it reaches beyond crack.

4. Apply glue to dowel and inside the hole; tap it into hole just slightly below surface of the leg. (You may have to use a nailset.) Allow glue to dry; cover dowel hole with matching wood putty.

Revitalizing outdoor chairs

Regular use and exposure to weather can cause wear and tear on the best of outdoor furniture. Although the manufacturer of an expensive piece may be willing to recondition it, giving a chair a face-lift is easy enough to do yourself.

Whether it's wood or aluminum, refurbish the frame after stripping a chair of its old cover. For the wood frame of a director's chair, repair any loose joints, and refinish or paint the frame if you like. Clean an unpainted aluminum frame with soapy scouring pads, followed by a coat of car wax. If the frame is enameled, clean it with an unabrasive household cleaner.

When you remove the old polypropylene webbing from aluminum chairs, pay close attention to how the webbing is attached. Save the screws or C-shaped clips.

Polypropylene and vinyl tubular webbing can be purchased as kits at home centers or hardware stores.

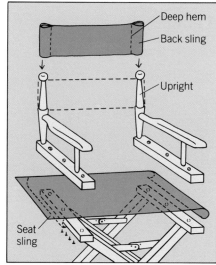

Director's chair. Remove old slings; use them as patterns. Hem the edges of the fabric to prevent unraveling. For the back sling, sew deep hems on two edges and slip them over uprights. Attach the seat sling by tacking it along the underside of the seat frame. Reassemble frame; make sure screws are tight.

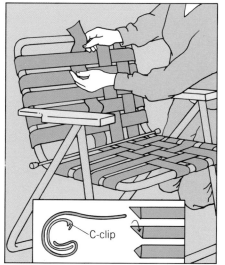

Polypropylene webbing. Cut a strap; fold over one corner, then other, to form a triangle. Make a hole with an awl or punch; push screw through it, and attach to frame. (Or fasten strap with C-clip.) Pulling strap tight, repeat at other end. Continue, attaching all straps in same manner. Weave vertical straps between horizontal ones.

Tubular vinyl webbing. Locate starting hole at corner of frame. Fold over end of webbing 1 in.; push screw through it and attach to frame. Tautly wrap webbing around chair, each row touching the previous one, until last attachment point is reached; fasten as at starting hole. Repeat for chair seat.

509

Furniture/Reupholstery basics

Traditional coil-spring upholstery

- Jute webbing supports springs
- Cambric dust cover
- Decorative fabric
- Glazed cotton
- Muslin lining
- Rubberized hair padding
- Edge roll
- 10- to 12-oz. burlap covers springs
- Coil spring
- Nylon or six-ply spring twine

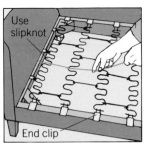

Use slipknot

End clip

Zigzag springs. To realign, tack twine to rails; knot it to springs. Refasten any loose end clips.

To reinforce weak webbing, tack new strips over old. Leave old ones in place.

Webbing replacement

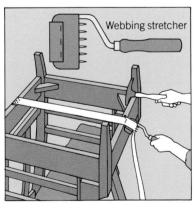

Tack hammer

1. Remove webbing. Center one end of new piece on rear seat rail; fold under 1 in. Fasten webbing to rail with five tacks in a zigzag fashion; start at middle of webbing, tack corners, then midpoints.

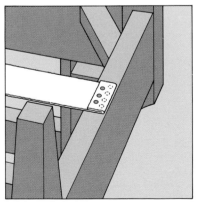

Webbing stretcher

2. Unroll webbing across seat frame; grasp it in webbing stretcher teeth. Hold stretcher against front rail at a 45° angle; bring handle down until it's on same plane as chair rail.

3. Anchor webbing with four evenly spaced tacks. Remove stretcher. Cut strip, leaving 1½ in. excess. Fold it over; tack down with three tacks. Attach other back-to-front strips; interweave and attach side strips.

Under the fabric covering, upholstery takes different forms. *Spring seats* and backs have webbing tacked to the frame. Coil springs are stitched to the webbing; padding cushions the coils. In some spring seats, *zigzag springs* replace both the webbing and the coils. In a *padded seat* or back, solid wood or webbing is topped with foam padding.

The fabric cover usually needs replacing first. Choose a fabric that is tightly woven and heavier than drapery fabric—it will last longer. Stretch a sample piece in both directions; it should spring back into shape quickly.

An old upholstered chair or sofa may be padded with horsehair. If it is salvageable, hand-wash the horsehair in soapy water and rinse well; comb it out as it dries. If the horsehair isn't reusable, replace it with Algerian fiber, cotton, or curled hair.

Disasssembly. Remove as few of the upholstery layers as possible. Repairs for a spring seat or back may involve only retying a coil spring or supporting worn webbing with new webbing. A cover may be replaced several times before the rest of the upholstery will need replacement.

Slit the seams and remove the fabric pieces; use the pieces as patterns for cutting new ones (with the nap smoothed down on vertical sections, to the front on horizontal ones). To aid in reassembly, as you dismantle the upholstery, write down, sketch, or photograph the position of each piece of material, its layered sequence, and how it was attached.

Baste-tacking. To check for correct placement of the fabric, drive tacks in halfway. First center the material and secure it with a tack in the middle of each rail; continue from the middle to each corner. Once it is correctly positioned, do the final tacking.

Upholstery tools include a tack hammer, upholstery shears, webbing stretcher, and tack lifter. You can buy these, along with webbing, needles, twines, and tacks, from an upholstery supply outlet.

Padded seats. Buy polyurethane foam padding with a density of 1.8 to 4 pounds per cubic foot. For a fixed seat, buy 1½- to 2-inch-thick foam sheeting; a removable seat requires 1 to 1½ inches.

Four-way hand-tied springs

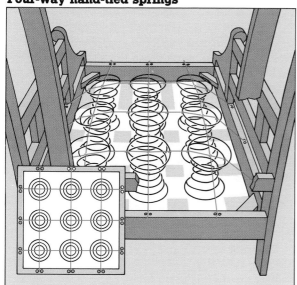

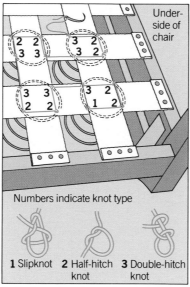

Numbers indicate knot type

1 Slipknot **2** Half-hitch knot **3** Double-hitch knot

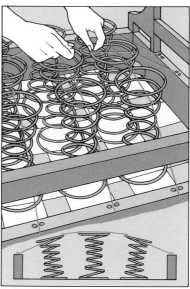

Where webbing strips cross, anchor spring's bottom coil with heavy button twine tied in four equally spaced knots. Hold each spring in place with a heavy spring twine crossing it lengthwise and crosswise. Knot lengths of twine to spring and to each other wherever they intersect. (Follow steps at right.)

1. Center spring where strips cross. Pull twine through webbing, over bottom coil, and back through webbing. Make a slipknot; then make two half-hitch knots followed by a double-hitch knot.

2. Wrap twine on two tacks set partway in back rail; hammer down. With twine taut, knot spring's second top coil, then top coil. For other springs in row, knot top coils; treat front spring same as back. Tack twine end.

3. Continue by tying rows front to back, then side to side; knot twines to each other wherever they meet. Pull twine just enough to shape seat with flat or rounded contour. Tack burlap over tied-down springs.

Reupholstering a fixed padded seat

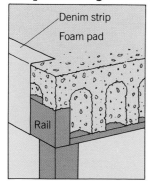

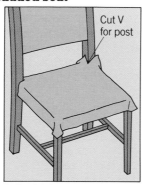

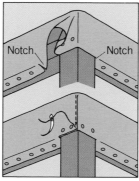

1. Cut foam slightly larger than old pad and to fit frame. Glue denim strips to foam's top edges and sides with white glue; let dry. Tack ends under rails.

2. Cut fabric so that it will have 1 in. to turn under seat. Cut V's for posts; leave enough fabric to turn under for smooth edges.

3. With edges turned under, tack centers of front, back, and sides of fabric under rails; then tack to corners. Cut notches at front corners; sew at fold; tack.

Reupholstering a removable padded seat

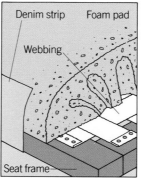

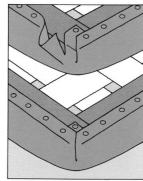

1. Cut foam ½ in. larger than seat all around. For curved edges, glue strips to foam with white glue; let dry. Pull strips taut and tack under frame.

2. With edges turned under, tack fabric to frame; work from centers to 2 in. from corners. Notch fabric corners, cutting out excess.

3. At each corner, pull notched point of fabric over frame, and tack it down. Then tack fabric at both sides, folding it, if necessary, to fit smoothly.

Furniture/Recaning a chair

The bark of a rattan palm, cane is a resilient material if properly maintained. To clean it, scrub with a mixture of 1 tablespoon salt in 1 quart hot water; use a cloth or soft brush. Wipe it with a clean cloth; dry with a hair dryer. To shrink overstretched cane, place the seat in warm water for a few minutes, and let dry.

There are two types of caning: woven and spline. A chair with holes around the seat frame is woven by hand; one with a groove around the frame is fitted with prewoven cane and a spline.

Handwoven seat. Cane comes in hanks; most chair seats require 250 feet. *Binder,* a wider strand that borders the weaving, comes with the cane. Buy cane from a caning supplier or crafts store; check the Yellow Pages. You'll also need scissors, pegs or golf tees, and an awl.

For a new chair, use a ³⁄₁₆-inch bit to drill holes every ⅝ inch (see chart) around the seat. Before reweaving an old seat, clean the holes with an awl. Separate the cane strands; remove imperfect ones to use as binder fastening. Coil each strand; soak a

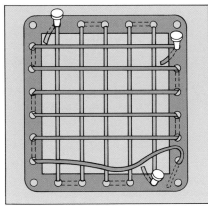

Handwoven seat. 1. Insert cane end into corner hole; leave 4 in. under chair, and peg. Weave cane from back to front; then weave strands from side to side on top of back-to-front strands.

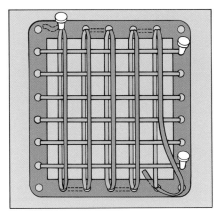

2. Weave second series of back-to-front rows over side-to-side strands; lay strands consistently to left or right of first back-to-front rows. Wet underside with warm damp towel.

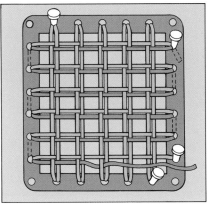

3. Weave second series of side-to-side rows. Pass strands under first series of back-to-front strands (step 1) and over second series of back-to-front strands (step 2).

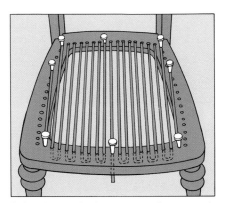

Splayed seat. 1. Start back-to-front strands from center holes (count in from each corner hole). To keep weave parallel, skip holes at back corners; weave separate strands at sides.

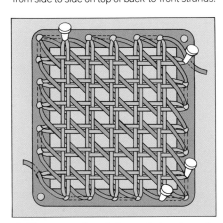

4. Weave a series of diagonal strands under back-to-front strands, over side-to-side strands. To make room in holes, push other strands aside with awl. Dampen cane with warm damp towel.

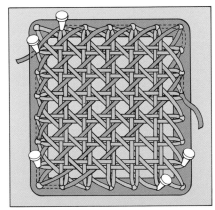

5. Weave a second series of diagonal strands at right angle to the first. Pass the strands over the back-to-front strands and under the side-to-side strands.

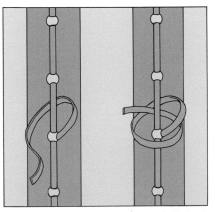

6. Dampen loose ends; tie them off. To knot, pass end under and then over adjacent weave. Bring end under weave and through loop; pull tight. Trim to 1 in. Attach binder (facing page).

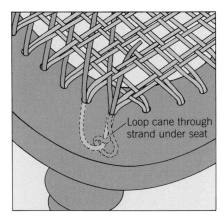

Loop cane through strand under seat

2. Diagonal rows don't always align with holes. To keep pattern, bring cane up through hole it entered, or skip hole and fill it on return weave.

few at a time in warm water for 15 minutes. As you remove one coil, replace it with another. Weave with the cane's shiny side up; keep the tension uniform but slightly loose. Pegs hold loose ends in place.

Spline cane seat. Buy prewoven cane webbing 2 inches larger than the seat. To find the spline size, measure the width of the groove; allow for the web-bing thickness. The spline should be a few inches longer than the length of the groove. Make sure you also have white glue, a utility knife, a mallet, and a wooden wedge—half a clothespin will do.

To finish either type of caning, singe any frayed cane with a moving match while it is still wet. When the cane is dry, seal both sides with polyurethane.

Size of hole	Space between holes	Width of cane
⅛ in.	⅜ in.	Superfine
³⁄₁₆ in.	½ in.	Fine fine
³⁄₁₆ in.	⅝ in.	Fine
¼ in.	¾ in.	Medium
⁵⁄₁₆ in.	⅞ in.	Common

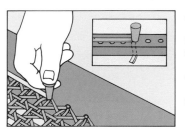

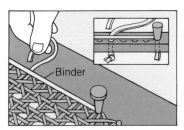

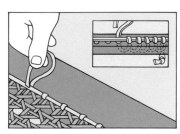

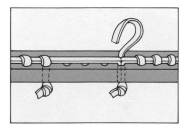

Attaching binder. 1. Push awl through holes to make room for stitching. Peg end of binder into the back center hole. Hold binder taut while stitching in place.

2. Knot a length of cane. Bring it up through fourth hole from peg. Bring it up over the binder; then bring it down through the same hole on other side of binder.

3. Bring the cane under seat to the next hole. Repeat stitching around seat, wrapping the cane around the binder until you reach the peg.

4. Remove the peg; thread loose end of binder through hole and knot it to other end. Stitch past hole until all the holes have cane stitching. Tie off, and trim the end. Singe off frayed edges of cane; seal with polyurethane.

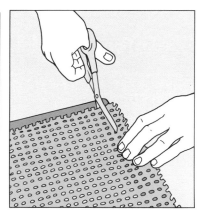

Spline cane seat. 1. Cut webbing to size; allow an extra ½ in. on all four sides. Soak webbing for 10 min. in warm water. Cut spline to size; let it soak in warm water.

4. Moving from center outward, push cane into groove. To maintain uniform tension, work a little at a time on opposite sides. Trim off protruding edges with utility knife.

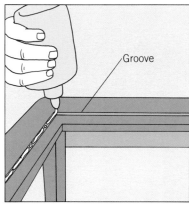

2. Squeeze a generous amount of white glue into the groove. Position the webbing, glossy side up, over seat. Be sure pattern is correctly aligned.

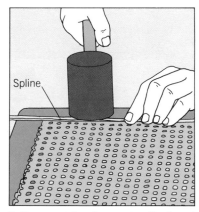

5. Remove spline from water. Starting at middle of one side, press narrow edge of spline into groove. With a mallet, tap it level with seat's surface.

3. At center point on each side, force an inch or two of webbing into groove with wood wedge. Keep it square to seat. Start on one side, do opposite side, then front and back.

6. Work around seat and back to starting point. Mark end with pencil; cut off excess spline. Push end into place and tap down with mallet. Singe off frayed ends; seal.

Furniture/Wicker and rattan maintenance

The technique of weaving with strands or poles of cane, fiber rush, Oriental sea grass, rattan, reed, or willow is called wickerwork. Repairs to wicker involve reattaching loose pieces and replacing broken strands.

To find matching material, look in the Yellow Pages under *Rattan.* If you don't know what type was used in a chair, ask an expert. To make them pliable, soak all materials (except fiber rush) in warm water up to 30 minutes; but because this can cause swelling, first try using them dry. For tools you'll need a hammer, wire cutters, and needle-nose pliers. You'll also need ½-inch brads and yellow glue.

Rattan. *Poles* come in bundles, and *wide binder,* the wrapping material, in hanks. To make them pliable, soak them for 15 to 20 minutes in warm water. Bend a pole by applying water, heat, and pressure; clamp thick poles until they dry. Strengthen a joint with screws; then wrap it with wide binder.

Refinishing. Rattan, reed, and willow in good condition can be stripped if left to a professional who specializes in wicker. Once stripped, let the wicker dry completely; apply a stain or varnish, or paint. Be sure the finish you pick is compatible with the wicker material. Painting is best done outdoors with oil-base gloss enamel spray paint, but first apply a primer. Clean the wicker thoroughly beforehand.

Maintenance. To clean, use a soft brush—or a toothbrush in hard-to-reach areas—and warm soapy water. Twice a year wet the wicker to restore its moisture. Rinse it with a hose or give it a shower on a breezy day when you can dry the wicker in the shade.

Repairing wicker

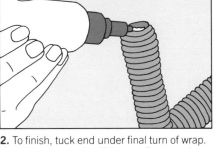

Unraveled wrap. 1. Cut off the old piece, and tack down its end. Near old end, tuck and tack down end of a new presoaked piece. Wind new wrap tightly and evenly around frame.

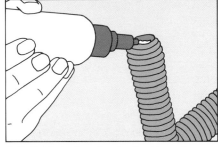

2. To finish, tuck end under final turn of wrap. Tack it in place, snip off the end flush, and apply glue around edge of wrap.

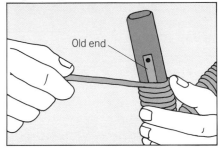

Reweaving a strand. 1. Using wire cutters, snip out the damaged material from furniture's underside, letting spokes support cut ends. Cut new piece 1 in. longer than old piece.

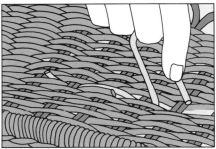

2. Starting at furniture's underside, weave in the new wicker, following the pattern. Pull the wicker tight as you work. Snip ends; tuck against spokes.

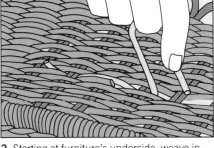

Replacing a spoke. 1. Snip off a damaged or broken spoke at its top and bottom, a few strands into the horizontal weave.

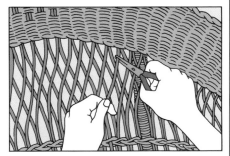

2. Using needle-nose pliers, push new spoke into place, following original pattern. First try weaving with a dry piece; if that doesn't work, use a soaked piece. Apply yellow glue to all ends.

Joining rattan

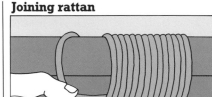

To join parallel poles, insert cane into a predrilled hole, apply glue to poles, and wrap cane tightly over glued area. Tuck cane end under wrapping, pull it tight, and cut.

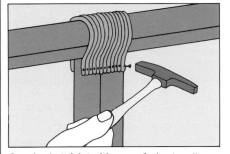

Covering butt joint with cane. 1. Apply yellow glue to joint. Place cane strips, butted together, along joint; nail each end in place with a brad.

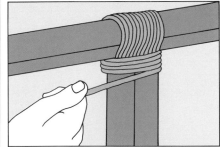

2. To cover brads, apply yellow glue along bottom ends of cane strips. Wrap with a length of cane until ends are completely covered.

Removing stains from furnishings

Whenever you buy a household item such as a sofa, carpet, or draperies, keep a record of its fabric contents. If a stain occurs, you'll be one step closer to removing it. If you don't know the fiber content of a stained fabric, try applying a gentle detergent in a hidden area; if it doesn't harm the fabric, try it on the stain. If it doesn't work, move on to a stronger removal method until you find one that does work.

Always carefully check labels on any cleaning agents. Pretest all stain removers, including ammonia, bleach, and vinegar, by applying several drops to a hidden area; blot it gently with a white absorbent cloth. If color transfers to the cloth, or if a color change occurs, do not use the remover.

Try to remove a stain as soon as possible. If you can, place a white absorbent cloth under the area. Remove moisture from the stain by blotting it up with a white absorbent cloth. If the stain was created by a solid substance, first lift it off with a dull-edged utensil such as a spatula or knife, and scrape it away.

When removing stains, don't overwet the fabric; use solutions, detergents, and solvents in small quantities. Working from the outside of the stain in, blot the stain with a white absorbent cloth; change it as it becomes soiled. Do not rub; it can cause the stain to spread. Try each suggested technique in the order given until the stain has disappeared. After you've removed it, blot up as much moisture as possible.

To soften a hardened stain, dampen it with a few drops of a cleaning agent. Then dampen an absorbent cloth with the same agent; press the cloth against the stain for 30 minutes or longer. Reposition the cloth when it picks up any stain. Add more cleaning agent as necessary to keep the cloth damp.

▶ **CAUTION:** Use stain removers in a well-ventilated room far away from electric or gas appliances, open flames, and cigarettes. Never mix chlorine bleach with ammonia; the combination may produce toxic gases. Always wear rubber gloves when working with enzyme products. Never use ammonia, heavy-duty detergent, or chlorine bleach on wool. Remove bleach from fabric completely. If you spill a stain remover on fabric or skin, wash it off immediately.

Major stains

Dyes
Beets, bluing, carrots, cherries, grass, green vegetables, soft drinks containing food dye, tempera paint

After blotting, consult a professional upholstery or carpet cleaner. Treat dye in an unpatterned cotton drapery like a protein stain.

Oils
Bacon fat, butter, face cream, grease, hair lotion, hand lotion, lard, margarine, mayonnaise, colorless salad dressing, suntan lotion

Sponge with dry-cleaning solvent. With absorbent cloth, apply dry spotter or paint-oil-and-grease remover. Keep stain moist with spotter or remover; blot occasionally with clean absorbent cloth. Dab with dry-cleaning solvent. Repeat (except for initial sponging) until no more stain comes out. Blot and air-dry. With medicine dropper, apply several drops of detergent solution and then a few drops of ammonia. Work into stain. Continue until no more stain comes out. Dab with water. Blot and dry.*

Proteins
Baby formula, blood, dairy products, egg, feces, gelatin, mucus, pudding, school paste, urine, vomit

Blot stain. Apply absorbent cloth moistened with enzyme product. If fabric is strong, tamp with bowl of spoon. Dab stain with water, then ammonia solution, and water again. Blot. Dab area with vinegar solution, then water. Blot and dry.*

Tannins
Alcoholic beverages, berries, coffee, fruit juices, preserves, jellies, soft drinks without dye, tea, tomato juice, washable ink

Sponge with water. With absorbent cloth, apply detergent solution and a few drops of white vinegar. Cover with cloth moistened with detergent and white vinegar. If fabric is strong, tamp with spoon. Dab with water. Blot and dry.*

Combination stains (oil and dye; wax and dye)
Group A: Ballpoint pen ink, barbecue sauce, candle wax, carbon paper, carbon typewriter ribbon, crayon, felt-tip pen ink, floor wax, furniture polish, gravy, hair spray, makeup, pine resin, salad dressing containing food dye, shoe polish, tar, tomato sauce

Spray or sponge with dry-cleaning solvent. Blot to remove excess dye. Use solvent until no more stain comes out. Then sponge with detergent solution. Dab with water. Blot and dry.* If stain remains, apply bleach solution, if safe for fabric, with medicine dropper. Dab with water until all bleach is out. Blot and dry.*

Group B: Chocolate, cocoa, ketchup

Sponge with dry-cleaning solvent. After fabric dries, follow directions for tannins (above), but don't sponge stain with water first.

Other stains

Chewing gum
Apply dry-cleaning solvent with cloth. Peel off excess gum. Cover stain with cloth moistened with solvent; change it often. Dab with solvent. Blot and air-dry.

Coffee or tea with cream or milk
Sponge or spray with dry-cleaning solvent. Apply warm water and vinegar. To remove traces, use an oxygen bleach, if safe for fabric. Dab with water until all bleach is out. Blot and dry.*

Lead pencil
Use art-gum eraser to lift off excess, but avoid hard rubbing. Dab with dry-cleaning solvent. Blot and air-dry.

Mustard
If stain has dried, brush off excess. Sponge on dry-cleaning solvent, then detergent solution with a few drops of vinegar added. Apply hydrogen peroxide with medicine dropper. Dab with water. Blot and dry.*

Paint, alkyd (oil-base)
If paint has dried, removal may be impossible. Treat while wet by dabbing with paint thinner. Blot and air-dry.

Paint, latex (water-base)
If paint has dried, removal may be impossible. Treat while wet by dabbing with warm water. Blot and dry.*

Stain removal solutions

Ammonia solution
1 tbsp. ammonia in ½ c. water, or add ammonia to detergent solution

Bleach solution
1 tsp. chlorine bleach in 1 tbsp. water

Detergent solution
1 tsp. mild liquid detergent in 1 cup water

Dry spotter
1 part coconut oil or mineral oil to 8 parts dry-cleaning solvent

White vinegar solution
2 tbsp. vinegar in 1 c. water, or add vinegar to detergent solution

Supplies to keep on hand
White cloths, neutral-color sponges, household ammonia (without added color, fragrance, or suds), 3% hydrogen peroxide, chlorine bleach, oxygen bleach, heavy-duty liquid laundry detergent, mild liquid detergent, dry-cleaning solvent, paint-oil-and-grease remover

*With hair dryer set on low, hold the dryer 12 in. from the fabric and move it constantly.

Metric conversion

The United States is the only industrial nation still using the English system of weights and measures. Most countries use a version of the metric system, the International System of Units. The basic units of the metric system are the *gram* for weight, the *liter* for volume, and the *meter* for length. Other units are related to these units by multiples and divisions of 10. For example, the *kilogram* is 1,000 grams, and the *centimeter* is $\frac{1}{100}$, or .01, of a meter.

As more industries change to the metric system to stay competitive in the world market, it will become necessary to learn how to convert to this system. Soda bottles, wine, and aspirin are already sold in metric units. In the future, drill bits, screws, and bolts may be based on this system. Once you know the metric system, it becomes much easier to calculate the amount of materials required for a job. Instead of 12 inches to a foot, 3 feet to a yard, and 1,760 yards to a mile, you'll find 1,000 millimeters in 100 centimeters or 1 meter. Tables to convert from one system to the other appear at right. The linear conversion table provides already calculated equivalents for some common measurements.

Fahrenheit and Celsius. The two systems for measuring temperature are Fahrenheit and Celsius (or centigrade). To change from degrees Fahrenheit, used in the United States, to degrees Celsius, subtract 32, then multiply by $\frac{5}{9}$. For example, 68° F − 32 = 36; 36 × $\frac{5}{9}$ = 20° C. To convert degrees Celsius to degrees Fahrenheit, multiply the degrees by $\frac{9}{5}$, then add 32 to that figure. For example: 20° C × $\frac{9}{5}$ = 36; 36 + 32 = 68° F.

	1/64	1/32	1/25	1/16	1/8	1/4	3/8	2/5	1/2	5/8	3/4	7/8	1	2	3	4	5	6	7	8	9	10	11	12	36	39.4
Inches (in.)	1/64	1/32	1/25	1/16	1/8	1/4	3/8	2/5	1/2	5/8	3/4	7/8	1	2	3	4	5	6	7	8	9	10	11	12	36	39.4
Feet (ft.)																								1	3	3¼†
Yards (yd.)																									1	1½†
Millimeters* (mm.)	0.40	0.79	1	1.59	3.18	6.35	9.53	10	12.7	15.9	19.1	22.2	25.4	50.8	76.2	101.6	127	152	178	203	229	254	279	305	914	1,000
Centimeters* (cm.)							0.95	1	1.27	1.59	1.91	2.22	2.54	5.08	7.62	10.16	12.7	15.2	17.8	20.3	22.9	25.4	27.9	30.5	91.4	100
Meters* (m.)																								.30	.91	1.00

To find the metric equivalent of quantities not in this table, add together the appropriate entries. For example, to convert 2⅝ inches to centimeters, add the figure given for the centimeter equivalent of 2 inches, 5.08, and the equivalent of ⅝ inch, 1.59, to obtain 6.67 centimeters.

* Metric values are rounded off.
† Approximate fractions.

Conversion factors

To change:	Into:	Multiply by:
English system to metric system		
Inches	Millimeters	25.4
Inches	Centimeters	2.54
Feet	Meters	0.305
Yards	Meters	0.914
Miles	Kilometers	1.609
Square inches	Square centimeters	6.45
Square feet	Square meters	0.093
Square yards	Square meters	0.836
Cubic inches	Cubic centimeters	16.4
Cubic feet	Cubic meters	0.0283
Cubic yards	Cubic meters	0.765
Pints	Liters	0.473
Quarts	Liters	0.946
Gallons	Liters	3.78
Ounces	Grams	28.4
Pounds	Kilograms	0.454
Tons	Metric tons	0.907

To change	Into:	Multiply by:
Metric system to English system		
Millimeters	Inches	0.039
Centimeters	Inches	0.394
Meters	Feet	3.28
Meters	Yards	1.09
Kilometers	Miles	0.621
Square centimeters	Square inches	0.155
Square meters	Square feet	10.8
Square meters	Square yards	1.2
Cubic centimeters	Cubic inches	0.061
Cubic meters	Cubic feet	35.3
Cubic meters	Cubic yards	1.31
Liters	Pints	2.11
Liters	Quarts	1.06
Liters	Gallons	0.264
Grams	Ounces	0.035
Kilograms	Pounds	2.2
Metric tons	Tons	1.1

Index

523

Credits

Photos on pages 70 (top and left center) by Black & Decker, Inc.

Photo on page 368 (right top) by Virginia Wells Blaker

Photo on page 174 by Brick Institute of America

Photo on page 72 (left) by Robert Bosch Power Tool Corporation

Photos on pages 180 and 356 (repair) by Kenneth Chaya

Photos on pages 130 (taps), 131 (above), 133 (right) by Ernest Coppolino

Photos on pages 56, 61, 63, 64, 66, 70 (bottom), 72 (right), 73 (right), 74 by Delta International Machinery Corp.

Photos on pages 176, 262, 266, 277, 292, 293, 302, 314, 315, 319, 326, 327, 330, 362 (left), 363 (left, right), 402, 403, 404, 405, 412, 425, 444, 445, 449 by *The Family Handyman*

Photo on page 180 (left) by Sally French

Photos on pages 165, 166, 167, 178, 308 by Gene and Katie Hamilton

Photos on pages 76 and 77 by Merle Henkenius

Photos on pages 18, 22, 24, 26, 27, 28, 29, 30, 32, 34, 35, 36, 38, 40, 41, 46, 47, 48, 52, 55, 57, 58, 62, 68, 117, 118, 119, 120, 121, 122, 124, 127, 128, 130 (wrenches), 131 (below), 133 (left), 162, 177, 237, 242, 307, 312, 350, 351, 352, 353, 354, 356 (tools, left), 358, 363 (center), 368 (left center bottom, left bottom, right center bottom), 375, 386, 430, 431, 435, 438, 439, 440, 441, 484, 485 by Morris Karol

Photo on page 368 (left top) by James McInnis

Photos on page 185 by Joel Musler

Photo on page 184 by Steven Napolitano

Photo on page 362 (right) by National Kitchen and Bath Association

Photo on page 70 (right center) by Porter-Cable

Photos on page 146 by Portland Cement Association

Photos on pages 319 (left corner), 368 (left center top, right center top, right bottom) © The Reader's Digest Association Limited, London

Photo on page 73 (left) by Ryobi America Corporation

Photo on page 78 by Shopsmith, Inc.

Photo on page 337 by Solar Additions Inc.

Grolier Book Clubs, Inc. HOME AND WORKSHOP GUIDE TO SHARPENING by Harry Walton. Copyright © 1967 by Harry Walton. Used by permission.

The Taunton Press, Inc. PROVEN SHOP TIPS edited and drawn by Jim Richey. Copyright © 1985 by The Taunton Press, Inc. Used by permission.